PUBLIC PAPERS OF THE PRESIDENTS

OF THE UNITED STATES

PUBLIC PAPERS OF THE PRESIDENTS

OF THE UNITED STATES

John F. Kennedy

Containing the Public Messages, Speeches, and

Statements of the President

JANUARY 20 TO DECEMBER 31, 1961

1961

UNITED STATES GOVERNMENT PRINTING OFFICE

WASHINGTON : 1962

PUBLISHED BY THE
OFFICE OF THE FEDERAL REGISTER
NATIONAL ARCHIVES AND RECORDS SERVICE
GENERAL SERVICES ADMINISTRATION

FOREWORD

IN RECENT YEARS our Presidents—in a happy reversion to the historical consciousness of the early Republic—have acknowledged a responsibility not only to make history but to record it. In 1938 President Franklin D. Roosevelt began the systematic publication, year by year, of his Public Papers and Addresses. The Roosevelt volumes were issued under private auspices; but in 1957 the National Historical Publications Commission made the wise recommendation that the documentary publication of presidential papers become a public obligation.

The General Services Administration has now published the papers and addresses of President Eisenhower. Within a few years it will complete the documentary record of the Truman years. We shall then have a comprehensive record of the Presidency for more than thirty years. This, I trust, will be continuously enlarged by the contribution of future Presidents, as well as by the comprehensive collection and publication of the papers of past Presidents. I am especially pleased that during this Administration the volumes will appear as soon as possible after the end of each calendar year.

These pages contain the full and exact texts of my speeches, messages, press conferences and statements of the year 1961. (For the presidential campaign of 1960 the student is referred to the valuable volumes compiled by the Committee on Commerce of the United States Senate and published in 1961.) This volume makes no pretense at revealing new information, or at providing new interpretations, or at setting forth a complete historical panorama. But it will, I hope, convey the enormous range of problems which confronted the American government and people in the first year of the seventh decade of the 20th century—the eighteenth of our national existence under the Constitution. And I believe that it will suggest the manner in which our people in this year began to come to a new and sober realization of our common perils and opportunities.

A review of these months discloses, in my judgment, fresh beginnings and new momentum. The nation has commenced the work of laying the foundations for forward movement at home and in the world. We shall only be able to discover in later volumes how well the undertakings and prospects outlined in this book have been fulfilled. This volume, therefore, belongs most properly to the men and women whose hard work, generous counsel and patriotic service gave the year 1961 its significance and hope.

PREFACE

IN THIS VOLUME are gathered most of the public messages and statements of the President of the United States that were released by the White House during the period January 20–December 31, 1961. Similar volumes covering the administration of President Eisenhower and the first year of President Truman are also available. Volumes covering the period January 1, 1946–January 20, 1953, and the year 1962 are under preparation.

This series was begun in 1957 in response to a recommendation of the National Historical Publications Commission (44 U.S.C. 393). An extensive compilation of the messages and papers of the Presidents, covering the period 1789 to 1897, was assembled by James D. Richardson and published under congressional authority between 1896 and 1899. Since that time various private compilations were issued, but there was no uniform, systematic publication comparable to the *Congressional Record* or the *United States Supreme Court Reports*. Many Presidential papers could be found only in mimeographed White House releases or as reported in the press. The National Historical Publications Commission therefore recommended the establishment of an official series in which Presidential writings and utterances of a public nature could be made promptly available.

The Commission's recommendation was incorporated in regulations of the Administrative Committee of the Federal Register issued under section 6 of the Federal Register Act (44 U.S.C. 306). The Committee's regulations, establishing the series and providing for the coverage of prior years, are reprinted at page 845 as "Appendix D."

Preface

The text of this book is based on Presidential materials issued during 1961 as White House releases and on transcripts of news conferences. Original source materials, where available, have been used to protect against errors in transcription. A list of White House releases from which final selections were made is published at page 821 as "Appendix A."

Addresses and speeches have been printed as actually delivered. In a few instances the White House issued advance releases, based on the prepared text of addresses or remarks, which differ from the text as actually delivered. Such releases have been appropriately noted. In Item 499, the note includes quotations from the prepared text because of substantial differences as delivered.

Proclamations, Executive orders, and similar documents required by law to be published in the *Federal Register* and *Code of Federal Regulations* are not repeated. Instead, they are listed by number and subject under the heading "Appendix B" at page 839.

The President is required by statute to transmit numerous reports to Congress. Those transmitted during the period covered by this volume are listed at page 844 as "Appendix C."

The items published in this volume are presented in chronological order, rather than being grouped in classes. Most needs for a classified arrangement are met by the subject index. For example, a reader interested in veto messages will find them listed in the index under the heading "veto messages."

The dates shown at the end of item headings are White House release dates. In instances where the date of the document differs from the release date that fact is shown in brackets immediately following the heading. Other editorial devices, such as text notes, footnotes, and cross references, have been held to a minimum.

Remarks or addresses were delivered in Washington, D.C., unless otherwise indicated. Similarly, statements, messages, and letters were issued from the White House in Washington unless otherwise indicated.

The planning and publication of this series is under the direction of David C. Eberhart of the Office of the Federal Register. The editor of the present volume was Warren R. Reid, assisted by Mildred B. Berry. Frederick L. Holborn, Special Assistant in the White House Office, provided aid and counsel in the selection and annotation of the materials. Frank H. Mortimer of the Government Printing Office developed the typography and design.

WAYNE C. GROVER
Archivist of the United States

BERNARD L. BOUTIN
Administrator of General Services
April 23, 1962

CONTENTS

CONTENTS

LIST OF ITEMS

List of Items

List of Items

List of Items

List of Items

List of Items

List of Items

List of Items

List of Items

List of Items

List of Items

List of Items

List of Items

List of Items

List of Items

List of Items

List of Items

xxxv

List of Items

List of Items

List of Items

List of Items

List of Items

List of Items

List of Items

List of Items

List of Items

List of Items

List of Items

List of Items

List of Items

List of Items

John F. Kennedy

1961

1 Inaugural Address.
January 20, 1961

[Delivered in person at the Capitol]

Vice President Johnson, Mr. Speaker, Mr. Chief Justice, President Eisenhower, Vice President Nixon, President Truman, Reverend Clergy, fellow citizens:

We observe today not a victory of party but a celebration of freedom—symbolizing an end as well as a beginning—signifying renewal as well as change. For I have sworn before you and Almighty God the same solemn oath our forebears prescribed nearly a century and three quarters ago.

The world is very different now. For man holds in his mortal hands the power to abolish all forms of human poverty and all forms of human life. And yet the same revolutionary beliefs for which our forebears fought are still at issue around the globe—the belief that the rights of man come not from the generosity of the state but from the hand of God.

We dare not forget today that we are the heirs of that first revolution. Let the word go forth from this time and place, to friend and foe alike, that the torch has been passed to a new generation of Americans—born in this century, tempered by war, disciplined by a hard and bitter peace, proud of our ancient heritage—and unwilling to witness or permit the slow undoing of those human rights to which this nation has always been committed, and to which we are committed today at home and around the world.

Let every nation know, whether it wishes us well or ill, that we shall pay any price, bear any burden, meet any hardship, support any friend, oppose any foe to assure the survival and the success of liberty.

This much we pledge—and more.

To those old allies whose cultural and spiritual origins we share, we pledge the loyalty of faithful friends. United, there is little we cannot do in a host of cooperative ventures. Divided, there is little we can do—for we dare not meet a powerful challenge at odds and split asunder.

To those new states whom we welcome to the ranks of the free, we pledge our word that one form of colonial control shall not have passed away merely to be replaced by a far more iron tyranny. We shall not always expect to find them supporting our view. But we shall always hope to find them strongly supporting their own freedom—and to remember that, in the past, those who foolishly sought power by riding the back of the tiger ended up inside.

To those peoples in the huts and villages of half the globe struggling to break the bonds of mass misery, we pledge our best efforts to help them help themselves, for whatever period is required—not because the communists may be doing it, not because we seek their votes, but because it is right. If a free society cannot help the many who are poor, it cannot save the few who are rich.

To our sister republics south of our border, we offer a special pledge—to convert our good words into good deeds—in a new alliance for progress—to assist free men and free governments in casting off the chains of poverty. But this peaceful revolution of hope cannot become the prey of hostile powers. Let all our neighbors know that we shall join with them to oppose aggression or subversion anywhere in the Americas. And let every other power know that this Hemisphere intends to remain the master of its own house.

To that world assembly of sovereign states, the United Nations, our last best hope in an age where the instruments of war have far outpaced the instruments of peace, we renew our pledge of support—to prevent it from becoming merely a forum for invective—to strengthen its shield of the new and the weak—and to enlarge the area in which its writ may run.

Finally, to those nations who would make themselves our adversary, we offer not a pledge but a request: that both sides begin anew the quest for peace, before the dark powers of destruction unleashed by science engulf all humanity in planned or accidental self-destruction.

We dare not tempt them with weakness. For only when our arms are sufficient beyond doubt can we be certain beyond doubt that they will never be employed.

But neither can two great and powerful groups of nations take comfort from our present course—both sides overburdened by the cost of modern weapons, both rightly alarmed by the steady spread of the deadly atom, yet both racing to alter that uncertain balance of terror that stays the hand of mankind's final war.

So let us begin anew—remembering on both sides that civility is not a sign of weakness, and sincerity is always subject to proof. Let us never negotiate out of fear. But let us never fear to negotiate.

Let both sides explore what problems unite us instead of belaboring those problems which divide us.

Let both sides, for the first time, formulate serious and precise proposals for the inspection and control of arms—and bring the absolute power to destroy other nations under the absolute control of all nations.

Let both sides seek to invoke the wonders of science instead of its terrors. Together let us explore the stars, conquer the deserts, eradicate disease, tap the ocean depths and encourage the arts and commerce.

Let both sides unite to heed in all corners of the earth the command of Isaiah—to "undo the heavy burdens . . . (and) let the oppressed go free."

And if a beach-head of cooperation may push back the jungle of suspicion, let both sides join in creating a new endeavor, not a new balance of power, but a new world of law, where the strong are just and the weak secure and the peace preserved.

All this will not be finished in the first one hundred days. Nor will it be finished in the first one thousand days, nor in the life of this Administration, nor even perhaps in our lifetime on this planet. But let us begin.

In your hands, my fellow citizens, more than mine, will rest the final success or failure of our course. Since this country was founded, each generation of Americans has been summoned to give testimony to its national loyalty. The graves of young Americans who answered the call to service surround the globe.

Now the trumpet summons us again—not as a call to bear arms, though arms we need—not as a call to battle, though embattled we are—but a call to bear the burden of a long twilight struggle, year in and year out, "rejoicing in hope, patient in tribulation"—a struggle against the common enemies of man: tyranny, poverty, disease and war itself.

Can we forge against these enemies a grand and global alliance, North and South, East and West, that can assure a more fruitful life for all mankind? Will you join in that historic effort?

In the long history of the world, only a few generations have been granted the role of defending freedom in its hour of maximum danger. I do not shrink from this responsibility—I welcome it. I do not believe that any of us would exchange places with any other people or any other generation. The energy, the faith, the devotion which we bring to this endeavor will light our country and all who serve it—and the glow from that fire can truly light the world.

And so, my fellow Americans: ask not what your country can do for you—ask what you can do for your country.

My fellow citizens of the world: ask not what America will do for you, but what together we can do for the freedom of man.

Finally, whether you are citizens of America or citizens of the world, ask of us here the same high standards of strength and sacrifice which we ask of you. With a good conscience our only sure reward, with history the final judge of our deeds, let us go forth to lead the land we love, asking His blessing and His help, but knowing that here on earth God's work must truly be our own.

NOTE: The President spoke at 12:52 p.m. from a platform erected at the east front of the Capitol. Immediately before the address the oath of office was administered by Chief Justice Warren.

The President's opening words "Reverend Clergy" referred to His Eminence Richard Cardinal Cushing, Archbishop of Boston; His Eminence Archbishop Iakovos, head of the Greek Archdiocese of North and South America; the Reverend Dr. John Barclay, pastor of the Central Christian Church, Austin, Tex.; and Rabbi Dr. Nelson Glueck, President of the Hebrew Union College, Cincinnati, Ohio.

2   Exchange of Greetings With Leaders of the Soviet Union. *January* 21, 1961

Nikita Khrushchev,
   Chairman, Council of Ministers, U.S.S.R.
Leonid Brezhnev,
   Chairman, Presidium of the Supreme Soviet, U.S.S.R.

Please accept this expression of my appreciation for your kind message of congratulations on the occasion of my inauguration as President of the United States of America. I welcome your expression of hope for a fundamental improvement in relations between our two countries and in the world situation as a whole; it is a hope which we share. We are ready and anxious to cooperate with all who are prepared to join in genuine dedication to the assurance of a peaceful and a more fruitful life for all mankind. Speaking on behalf of the Government and people of the United States of America, as well as on my own behalf, I can assure you that the efforts of the United States Government will be directed toward this imperative goal.

   Sincerely,

   JOHN F. KENNEDY

NOTE: The message from Mr. Khrushchev and Mr. Brezhnev, dated January 20 and delivered to the White House at 4 p.m. on the same day, follows:

Dear Mr. President:

We congratulate you on the occasion of your inauguration. Availing ourselves of this opportunity we wish to express the hope that by our own joint efforts we shall succeed in achieving a fundamental improvement in relations between our countries and a normalization of the whole international situation. We are convinced that, step by step, it will be possible to remove existing suspicion and distrust and cultivate seeds of friendship and practical cooperation between our peoples. On its side, the Soviet Government is always ready to support any good undertakings in this direction and do everything in its power in order that durable peace may be established in the world, so that all nations may live in friendship and without enmity.

   N. KHRUSHCHEV
   L. BREZHNEV

3 Remarks at a Meeting of the Democratic National Committee. *January* 21, 1961

I WANT to express my appreciation to all of you for your kind welcome, and also to take this occasion to express my great appreciation—and I think the appreciation of us all—to Senator Jackson who assumed the chairmanship of the Democratic Party at the Convention, who was greatly responsible for our success in November and has been an invaluable aid during the transition. Whatever has been done that is useful in the party in the last 5 or 6 months he has played a great part in it. And I feel that the party has served a most useful national purpose—and while Senator Jackson is obligated to serve the people of Washington in the Senate, I know that we can continue to count on him in the days to come for counsel and advice and support. So I hope we will all stand and give a good cheer to Scoop Jackson.

Scoop automatically loses his share of the $4-million debt—we are not going to let him in on it. John Bailey has become the proprietor, along with Mac, of this enterprise. I think we are particularly fortunate to have John Bailey. I heard Governor Lawrence in his seconding speech say the trouble with everything is that they don't know enough of what is going on here in Washington; they ought to get out in the field. I agree with him completely. We have got a man from the field who knows what's wrong here in Washington, and I am delighted that John Bailey is going to take over this job. He is more popular today than he will be any time again in his life. I will feel that he is doing a good job when you all say, "Well, Kennedy is all right, but Bailey is the one who is really making the mistakes." That's the way it was in Connecticut. Ribicoff was never wrong, it was always Bailey's fault. So that is what he is going to do down here.

But I am delighted that he is going to do it. It is a sacrifice for him. But I think we are getting the services of someone who works in the party year in and year out, understands what the party can do, understands what the role of the Chairman is—and I must say that I am delighted to see him assuming the position vacated by Senator Jackson.

Lastly, I want to thank all of you for being with us at the inaugural. The party is not an end in itself—it is a means to an end. And you are the people who, in victory and defeat, have maintained the Democratic Party, maintained its traditions and will continue to do so in the future. I hope the relationship between all of us can continue to be as cordial as possible. I believe in strong political organizations in our country. The Republican Party is strong and vigorous today after the election of 1960. I think we are, also. And when we do that, I think we serve great national purposes.

The party is the means by which programs can be put into action—the means by which people of talent can come to the service of the country. And in this great free society of ours, both of our parties—the Republican and the Democratic Parties—serve the interests of the people. And I am hopeful that the Democratic Party will continue to do so in the days to come. It will be in the interest of us all, and I can assure you that I will cooperate in every way possible to make sure that we do serve the public interest.

You have done so well in the past. We couldn't possibly have won without your help. I look forward to working with you

4

in the future, and I want you to know that here in Washington, we may not know always what is going on as well as you do, but at least we are trying.

Thank you.

NOTE: The President spoke at 1:19 p.m. in the East Room at the Mayflower Hotel in Washington. During his remarks he referred to Henry M. Jackson, U.S. Senator from the State of Washington and retiring chairman of the Democratic National Committee; John M. Bailey, Chairman of the Democratic National Committee and Democratic State Chairman for Massachusetts; Matthew McCloskey, Treasurer of the Democratic National Committee; Governor David L. Lawrence of Pennsylvania; and Abraham A. Ribicoff, Secretary of Health, Education, and Welfare, and former Governor of Connecticut.

4   Remarks at the Swearing-In Ceremonies for the Members of the Cabinet. *January 21, 1961*

I WANT to thank the Chief Justice for his help today and for his good work, and I also want to congratulate and express my appreciation to the members of the Cabinet who have been sworn today.

Quite obviously, whatever success we may achieve will depend in great part upon their dedication and their effort, and the success which they achieve will depend in good part upon the dedication and effort of the hundreds of thousands of men and women of this country who serve our National Government.

As a citizen, I think we are fortunate to have them all. As President of the United States, I find it heartening, and therefore it is a great pleasure for me to welcome them as part of the official family. They are all patriotic men who are devoted to the welfare of this country—and I am confident that they will meet their responsibilities with high distinction.

NOTE: The ceremonies were held in the East Room at the White House.

5   Statement by the President Concerning the Appointment of Frank B. Ellis as Director, Office of Civil and Defense Mobilization. *January 23, 1961*

OCDM as presently constituted is charged with the staff function of mobilization planning and, at the same time, with the operating functions of civilian defense. Both these tasks are of vital importance to our national security. I consider it imperative that they be organized and performed with maximum effectiveness. Accordingly, I am asking Mr. Ellis, as his first order of business, to join with the Director of the Budget in a thoroughgoing review of our nonmilitary defense and mobilization programs. I am asking Mr. Bell to arrange for close consultation on the matter with the Secretary of Defense and other appropriate officials. I await the results of this survey with interest and concern.

NOTE: See also Item 295 and note.

6   Memorandum to Federal Agencies on the Duties of the Director of the Food-for-Peace Program.   *January 24, 1961*

Memorandum for the Heads of Executive Departments and Agencies:

I have today issued an Executive Order relating to the duties of the Director of the Food-for-Peace Program. This Order amends Executive Orders 10893 and 10900, providing for the administration of the mutual security and related functions and of the Agricultural Trade Development and Assistance Act of 1954, as amended, respectively. It provides that the Director of the Food-for-Peace Program shall be responsible for the continuous supervision and coordination of the functions under section 402 of the Mutual Security Act of 1954, as amended, as well as those functions under the Agricultural Trade Development and Assistance Act of 1954 which are delegated by Executive Order 10900. These provisions of law deal with the use of American agricultural commodities in furtherance of the foreign policy of the United States.

The purpose of this memorandum is to describe further the role of the Director of the Food-for-Peace Program, who will be located in the Executive Office of the President.

American agricultural abundance offers a great opportunity for the United States to promote the interests of peace in a significant way and to play an important role in helping to provide a more adequate diet for peoples all around the world. We must make the most vigorous and constructive use possible of this opportunity. We must narrow the gap between abundance here at home and near starvation abroad. Humanity and prudence, alike, counsel a major effort on our part.

Many Government functions and activities relate to the overseas movement of agricultural commodities and products of the United States. It is important that responsibility for coordination of all these efforts be centralized so that they can become more meaningful—a more useful instrument of our foreign policy, and more efficient.

Accordingly, I expect to look to the Food-for-Peace Director, working under my direction and with the Secretaries of State and Agriculture in particular, to exercise affirmative leadership and continuous supervision over the various activities in this field, so that they may be brought into harmonious relationship.

The most immediate task which I have asked the Director to undertake is that of conducting an intensive review of all these activities and considering possible improvements in them. He will communicate to me the results of this review and his recommendations for improvement, including recommendations for such legislative changes as may be necessary. I have asked the Food-for-Peace Director to consider very carefully the intimate relationships between our foreign agricultural activities and other aspects of our foreign assistance program and to develop the necessary programs and policies in coordination with the Mutual Security Coordinator.

I know that in all of his endeavors the Director will have your full support and cooperation.

This memorandum shall be published in the Federal Register.

JOHN F. KENNEDY

NOTE: A White House release of the same date announced that a Food-for-Peace Committee, appointed during the campaign and headed by Murray D.

Lincoln, had submitted a report to the President in response to his instructions to prepare recommendations for implementing his 6-point Food-for-Peace Program, made public on October 31, 1960. The report is summarized in the release which also lists the names of the Committee members.

7 Letter to the President of the Senate and to the Speaker of the House Urging Enactment of a Distressed Area Redevelopment Bill. *January 25, 1961*

Dear Mr. ————:

On December 4, 1960, I appointed a task force on area redevelopment, under the chairmanship of Senator Paul H. Douglas of Illinois, to make recommendations for legislative action to relieve the hardship resulting from chronic unemployment and to propose a program for the development of those areas. The report of that task force unanimously recommended prompt legislative action to provide technical assistance, loans for private projects, loans and grants for public facilities, and training and retraining programs to provide new industry, new jobs and new growth.

I am heartily in accord with these recommendations and I recommend the enactment of legislation containing provisions along these lines. The number of areas of substantial and persistent unemployment is now nearly 100. In addition, there are many places where chronic under-employment is predominant. This condition is not confined to our urban metropolitan centers but is spread across rural communities and represents a serious handicap to our national economic health.

The problems have long been the subject of both private studies and Congressional consideration. Private initiative alone is clearly insufficient to accomplish permanent improvement. Nor is it any longer possible for state and local governments to carry the full burden. I believe there must be a cooperative effort in which the Federal Government joins with private industry and local and state governments in a maximum effort to strengthen and improve the economic climate of the communities affected.

The proposed legislation will involve more than one existing department of Government. All must be drawn into the effort. In my judgment, the department best equipped to supervise and coordinate the program is the Department of Commerce. However, if the Congress should decide that a new agency would be more appropriate I believe such an agency could also carry out the objectives I have outlined.

In view of the high rate of unemployment and the long periods of idleness already sustained by so many persons in the communities the legislation will help, I urge prompt consideration and enactment of an area redevelopment bill.

With every good wish,
Sincerely,

JOHN F. KENNEDY

NOTE: This is the text of identical letters addressed to the Honorable Lyndon B. Johnson, President of the Senate, and to the Honorable Sam Rayburn, Speaker of the House of Representatives.

8 The President's News Conference of
January 25, 1961

THE PRESIDENT. I have several announcements to make first.

[1.] I have a statement about the Geneva negotiations for an atomic test ban. These negotiations, as you know, are scheduled to begin early in February. They are of great importance and we will need more time to prepare a clear American position. So we are consulting with other governments and are asking to have it put off until late March. As you know, Mr. John McCloy is my principal adviser in this field, and he has organized a distinguished panel of experts, headed by Dr. James Fisk of the Bell Laboratories—and Mr. Salinger will have a list of the names at the end of the conference—who are going to study previous positions that we've taken in this field, and also recommend to Mr. McCloy, for my guidance, what our position will be in late March when we hope the tests will resume.

[2.] Secondly, the United States Government has decided to increase substantially its contribution towards relieving the famine in the Congo. This will be done by increasing the supply of cornmeal and dry milk, by adding contributions of rice, and by airlifting a thousand tons of food supplies, seeds, and hospital supplies from a number of African nations to the Congo.

It is the intention of the United States Government to meet fully the emergency requirements of the Congo for rice, corn, dry milk and other foodstuffs in our surplus stocks. Assurances have been received from the United Nations that with the help of this program the flow of supplies will be adequate to relieve the distress. The United States Government will cooperate fully to help the United Nations prevent famine in the Congo.[1]

[3.] Third, I am happy to be able to announce that Capt. Freeman B. Olmstead and Capt. John R. McKone, members of the crew of the United States Air Force RB-47 aircraft who have been detained by Soviet authorities since July 1, 1960, have been released by the Soviet Government and are now en route to the United States.

The United States Government is gratified by this decision of the Soviet Union and considers that this action of the Soviet Government removes a serious obstacle to improvement of Soviet-American relations.

Our deepest sympathy and understanding go to the families of the men of the RB-47 who gave their lives in the service of their country. At the same time, I am sure that all Americans join me in rejoicing with the Olmstead and McKone families. The families, as well as the men, comported themselves in these trying times in a way which is truly in the best traditions of the military services of the United States. Restraint in these conditions is obviously not easy. But they can be assured that they have contributed in large measure to the final achievement of the objective which we all sought—release of the men.

[4.] Q. Mr. President, this RB-47 case was regarded by the Russians as an overflight although we took a different position. In the light of this announcement, what will be your general policy on overflights and on such things as the U-2 case, or the U-2

[1] A White House release, dated January 25, describes more fully the Emergency Food Program for the Congo. The release is printed in the Department of State Bulletin (vol. 44, p. 218).

flights? Do you conceive of circumstances which might warrant resumption of such things as the U–2 flight?

THE PRESIDENT. The Soviet Government is fully aware of United States Government views with respect to the distinction between the question of the United States Air Force RB–47 and the incident which occurred over Soviet territory on May 1, 1960, involving an American U–2 type aircraft. Flights of American aircraft penetrating the air space of the Soviet Union have been suspended since May 1960. I have ordered that they not be resumed.

[5.] Q. Mr. President there have been reports that Mr. Khrushchev might come to the United Nations General Assembly for the resumption of the disarmament debates sometime in March. If this were to happen, would you welcome a visit by him to Washington for a get-acquainted meeting?

THE PRESIDENT. I've not heard officially of any proposal by Mr. Khrushchev to come to the United States. I've merely seen newspaper reports and I feel that it would be more appropriate to wait until we had some indication of whether Mr. Khrushchev was planning to come to the United Nations.

[6.] Q. Mr. President, can you tell us something about what your role was, if you had one, in the release of these fliers? Did this come about as a consequence of some action you took?

THE PRESIDENT. Well, this matter has been under discussion by the American Ambassador and Mr. Khrushchev on one occasion and representatives of the Soviet foreign ministry since this weekend. The fliers were released as of 2 a.m. yesterday morning, but in the plane taking off there was a tire that was blown and therefore the plane did not take off. Our last information is that it took off at 5 o'clock our time this afternoon. It

will fly to Amsterdam and then we expect the fliers to be brought to the United States tomorrow afternoon.

[7.] Q. Mr. President, one of your task forces recommended that you resist any early move toward general disarmament negotiations until a firm and fixed U.S. policy could be worked out. What is your reaction to that report and how much time do you think it might take to get a firm fixed U.S. position?

THE PRESIDENT. Well, Mr. McCloy has responsibility over the area of disarmament as well as nuclear testing. He has, as I've said, set up this committee—advisory committee—on nuclear testing. We expect to also get the American position clearer on general disarmament. There is not the same deadline that we've been facing on the nuclear testing where we were supposed to resume in early February, but I can state that this was a matter which was discussed early this week by the Secretary of Defense and the Secretary of State and Mr. McCloy and we are preparing clarification of American positions on disarmament.

[8.] Q. Mr. President, what more can you tell us about the long conversation that Ambassador Thompson had with Mr. Khrushchev, including whether the tone of that conversation was anywhere near as friendly as that of the messages that Khrushchev has sent you?

THE PRESIDENT. I would say the tone was friendly. And as a result of the conversations, as I've said, the decision was made to release the fliers. But the conversations were conducted in an atmosphere of civility.

Q. Could you give us any indication at all as to what other subjects were taken up in addition to the release of the RB–47 fliers?

THE PRESIDENT. No. I think that I have to stand on my previous statement.

[9.] Q. Does your administration plan to take any steps to solve the problem at Fayette County, Tenn., where tenant farmers have been evicted from their homes because they voted last November and must now live in tents?

THE PRESIDENT. We are—the Congress, of course, enacted legislation which placed very clear responsibility on the executive branch to protect the right of voting. I supported that legislation. I am extremely interested in making sure that every American is given the right to cast his vote without prejudice to his rights as a citizen. And therefore I can state that this administration will pursue the problem of providing that protection with all vigor.

[10.] Q. Sir, would you please tell us how it was possible for you to do by Executive order what Mr. Benson always told us was impossible for him to do without more legislation? I refer to the order expanding the distribution of food to the unemployed and giving them more variety in the diet.

THE PRESIDENT. Well, I would not attempt to comment on Mr. Benson. I don't think there's any question of our rights to issue the Executive order under the authority given to us by the Constitution and by legislative action. I think we're within our rights. It is a judgment as to what is the best use to make of the funds that are available—the funds are quite limited. The diet which is being provided for the people who are unemployed is still inadequate. But nevertheless we have used the funds that are available to the maximum. And I don't think there's any question that we were within our rights.

[11.] Q. Mr. President, could you tell us how and when you learned that these fliers were going to be released?

THE PRESIDENT. I learned as a result of the conversations which Ambassador Thompson had with the Soviet officials and therefore we were informed as to the date that they would be released—the time—yesterday.

[12.] Q. Mr. President, there has been some apprehension about the instantaneous broadcast of Presidential press conferences such as this one, the contention being that an inadvertent statement no longer correctible, as in the old days, could possibly cause some grave consequences. Do you feel there is any risk or could you give us some thought on that subject?

THE PRESIDENT. Well, it was my understanding that the statements made by the, by President Eisenhower, were on the record. There may have been a clarification that could have been issued afterwards but it still would have demonstrated, it still would have been on the record as a clarification, so that I don't think that the interests of our country are—it seems to me they're as well protected under this system as they were under the system followed by President Eisenhower. And this system has the advantage of providing more direct communication.

[13.] Q. On the question at issue would you consider reopening diplomatic relations with Cuba and are you considering such a step now?

THE PRESIDENT. Well, at the—take the last part first—we are not considering such a step at the present time. I may say that the United States is interested, and I think that this administration is extremely interested in movements in Latin America and Central America, or the Caribbean which provide a better life for the people. And if American interests may be damaged by those movements—or revolutions, or whatever term you want to use—we feel that this should be a matter that should be negotiated. What we are of course concerned about is when these movements are seized by external forces and directed not to improving the welfare of the people involved but towards imposing an ideology which is alien to this hemisphere. That is a matter of concern particularly when that intervention takes the form of military support which threatens the security and the peace of the Western Hemisphere.

Now, I'm hopeful that governments will be established throughout all of Latin America and governments which are established will, and I think nearly all of them do, share the same view that we have to provide in this hemisphere a better life for the people involved, that we are interested in that, that we are concerned about it, that American policy will be directed towards that end. But we are also concerned that in the name of that peaceful revolution, when it's seized by aliens for their purposes, it's very difficult for the United States to carry on happy relations with those countries.

So in answer to your question we have no plan at present to resume diplomatic relations with Cuba, because of the factors which are involved in that island.

[14.] Q. You said in the past, sir, that the President should be in the thick of the political battle, and I wondered, sir, if you could tell us what part you're playing in the effort to expand the Rules Committee and whether you feel your domestic program— whether the success of your domestic program in part depends on expanding the Rules Committee?

THE PRESIDENT. Well, the Constitution states that each house shall be the judge of its own rules, and therefore the Speaker of the House, Mr. Rayburn, has been extremely anxious that the House be permitted to settle this matter in its own way.

But it's no secret that—I would strongly believe that the Members of the House should have an opportunity to vote themselves on the programs which we will present. That, I think, is the reason the people selected them to go to the House of Representatives and to the Senate and selected me as President, so that we could present programs and consider programs and vote on programs which are put forward for the benefit of the country.

Now I feel that it would be—I'm hopeful that whatever judgment is made by the Members of the House, that it will permit the Members to vote on these bills. This is a very difficult time in the life of our country. Many controversial measures will be presented which will be in controversy and will be debated. But at the end the majority of the Members of the House, the majority of the Members of the Senate, I hope, will have a chance to exercise their will, and that a small group of men will not attempt to prevent the Members from finally letting their judgments be known.

For example, we have the housing bill which is going to come before the Congress this year. We have an aid-to-education bill. We have legislation which will affect the income of farmers. Shouldn't the Members of the House themselves and not merely the members of the Rules Committee have a chance to vote on those measures? But the responsibility rests with the Members of the House, and I would not attempt in any way to infringe upon that responsibility. I merely give my view as an interested citizen. [*Laughter*]

[15.] Q. Are any plans being made to implement the recommendations in the Voorhees report on the Cuban refugee problem? Secondly, do you plan to appoint somebody to continue Mr. Voorhees' work?

THE PRESIDENT. We are considering the recommendations of Mr. Voorhees and the whole problem of the Cuban refugees, but I don't have any statement to make on it at this time.

[16.] Q. Mr. President, what is the official Government position in regard to the Portuguese-seized ship? Can the Navy board it if and when it makes contact?

THE PRESIDENT. Well, I believe that the location of the ship has been determined, and—[*aside to Mr. Salinger*]—perhaps we could give the location of it—at the present time the instructions are for the Navy to continue its accompaniment of the ship. The *Santa Maria* has been located by Navy P2V aircraft, and the position is approximately 600 miles north of the mouth of the Amazon River. It is headed on a course of 117, a speed of 15 knots, and the exact position at 10 minutes after 4 was 10-35 north, 45-42 west. It will be trailed by aircraft and picked up by the destroyers of our African task force.

Now, there are Americans involved; and their lives are involved. But we have not given any instructions to the Navy to carry out any boarding operations. Though, of course, we are concerned about the lives of the Americans involved. And also we are concerned because the ship belongs to a country with which the United States has friendly relations.

[17.] Q. Mr. President, in consequence of Mr. Khrushchev's apparent indication last weekend of willingness to release the American fliers, have you sent any communication to him through Ambassador Thompson or otherwise?

THE PRESIDENT. Well—have I sent a message since the release of the fliers?

Q. Since his communication to us through Ambassador——

THE PRESIDENT. We have had several exchanges with the Soviet authorities. I do not believe that one has taken place since the release of the prisoners but that's partially

because there has been this delay about their leaving Moscow.

[18.] Q. Mr. President, there is meeting here now a nationwide group of labor, agriculture, and industry which wants to abolish all restraints of the Reciprocal Trade Agreements Act. They say that it robs us of gold, robs American workers of jobs. What is your position on such a proposal?

THE PRESIDENT. Well, I think that their meeting here is well within their rights as citizens of the United States and I think that we should listen to their views. This is a matter of great concern. I do think we should be conscious of the fact, of course, that the balance of trade has been substantially in our favor in the last year. But we are continually concerned about those imports which adversely affect an entire industry, or adversely affect the employment of a substantial number of our citizens. The present laws—peril-point and escape clause—of course, all take those matters into consideration. But I'm glad to have them here; I'm glad to have them express their views. I think the Congress should consider their views carefully, and I hope that in their consideration they will consider the whole problem of trade, and I do think we should realize that the balance of trade has been in our favor and the gold flow would have been substantially worse if we had not had this favorable balance of trade.

[19.] Q. Mr. President, in relation to the gold problem, the outgoing administration has ordered a cutback in the number of American military and civilian dependents stationed abroad in the so-called hard-currency nations. The day before your inaugural the outgoing Defense Secretary advised your incoming Defense Secretary in a manner urging that relief should be sought as soon as possible because of what the outgoing Defense Secretary termed the "adverse affect of the order on the morale of the military." Have you had a chance to make up your mind on that position, sir?

THE PRESIDENT. Mr. McNamara and Mr. Dillon have discussed the effect of this order on military morale, military strength, the rate of reenlistment. It's really a question of determining what alternative steps can be secured which would be less harmful but which would protect the flow of gold. I do expect to make some reference to this matter of gold outflow in the State of the Union Address. I will send within a 2-week period after the State of the Union Address a message to the Congress dealing with the gold outflow and our recommendations for meeting it and we will at that time come to some judgment as to whether a more satisfactory method of protecting our gold could be secured than providing for the return of the families of Americans serving abroad in the military.

I will say that our study so far has convinced us that the dollar must be protected, that the dollar can be protected at its present value, that exchange controls are not essential, but it is a most serious problem and it will be the subject of a message to the Congress.

[20.] Q. Mr. President, the State of New York gave you one of your handsomest majorities in the 1960 election campaign, but now the Democrats of New York are rather bitterly divided over leadership. As the leader of the Democratic Party nationally, are you going to take some steps to try and heal the splits in New York?

THE PRESIDENT. Well the people in New York, the Democratic organizations in New York, who are interested in the success of the Democratic Party, they have to make their judgments as to what kind of a party they want to build there. I have asked Mr. Bailey, the new chairman of the Democratic Party, to lend a helping hand in attempting to alleviate some of the distress. [*Laughter*]

[21.] Q. Sir, do you have any plans for quick Federal aid for the unemployed?

THE PRESIDENT. We are going to send a message to the Congress right after the State of the Union Address on what steps we think the Government could profitably take to provide protection for the unemployed and also to stimulate the economy. On the immediate question, I will discuss that in the State of the Union Address on Monday.

[22.] Q. Mr. President, now that the Soviets have released the RB-47 fliers, will you estimate for us the chances of you meeting with Premier Khrushchev?

THE PRESIDENT. Yes. There is no relationship, nor has there been, in the discussion between the two matters. And therefore I have no—there has been no change in my previous statement that there are no plans at the present time for meeting with Mr. Khrushchev.

[23.] Q. Mr. President, will you tolerate the continued abuse of Executive privilege to suppress information which is needed by Congress? For instance, now that you are President, will you direct the USIA to give the Senate Foreign Relations Committee those prestige polls which you urged the previous administration to make available during the campaign?

THE PRESIDENT. Well, let me say that I would have no objection at all to the polls, or at least the results of the polls, being made available. And I'd be delighted to check in and see what we can do about making it available to the Senate Foreign Relations Committee or the House Foreign Relations Committee, if they would like them.

Q. Mr. President, about the abuses regarding the privilege to suppress all sorts of information. What is your position on that?

THE PRESIDENT. Well, that's a statement, really, not completely a question, in——

Q. Sir, but you yourself agreed——.

THE PRESIDENT. That's why I stated that I thought that it would be well to release these polls and that's why I said I'd be glad to release these polls. Now if other matters come up, we'll have to make a judgment whether it is an abuse or whether it is within the constitutional protections given to the Executive, and I would hope that we can within the limits of national security make available information to the press and to the people, and I do think that it would be helpful to release the polls which we discussed last fall.

Q. Mr. President, Press Secretary Salinger said today, indicated today, there might be a need for a tightening of information on national security. Doesn't the policy of deterrence require that the enemy have knowledge of our strength and the ability to carry them out and wouldn't there be a risk of possible miscalculation by tightening up information?

THE PRESIDENT. Well, I think that the enemy is informed of our strength. I think Mr. Salinger in his statement today at lunch indicated his judgment based on his experience so far, that there had been very ample information given so that the enemy can make a determination as to our strength. I am anxious that we have a maximum flow of information but there quite obviously are some matters which involve the security of the United States, and it's a matter on which the press and the Executive should attempt to reach a responsible decision.

I could not make a prediction about what those matters will be, but I think that all of us here are aware that there are some matters which it would not be well to discuss at particular times so that we just have to wait and try to work together and see if we can provide as much information as we can within the limits of national security. I do not believe that the stamp "National Security" should be put on mistakes of the administration which do not involve the national security, and this administration would welcome any time that any member of the press feels that we are artificially invoking that cover. But I must say that I do not hold the view that all matters and all information which is available to the Executive should be made available at all times, and I don't think any member of the press does. So it's a question of trying to work out a solution to a sensitive matter.

[24.] Q. Mr. President, in the past few days the Secretary of State, Dean Rusk, has issued statements—one with your name on it—to the effect that this country wants a return to quiet private diplomacy. Could you give us some idea of the meaning behind this, Mr. President? Are you trying to suggest to Khrushchev that you'd like to resort to this for the time being without offending him or making him go off the cordial path he's on at the present time?

THE PRESIDENT. Would you—the last part of that——

Q. Are you trying to suggest to Mr. Khrushchev by the tone of these—by what you're saying in these statements—that you don't want a summit meeting now and you'd like to go through private channels, and trying to do this without offending him or getting him off the cordial path he's on now?

THE PRESIDENT. Well, I would just say—without accepting the question completely as a premise—I would say that the Secretary of State is anxious to explore with interested countries what chance we have of lessening world tension which is—in some areas of the world—is quite high tonight.

And therefore there are occasions when traditional exchanges between diplomats and the countries involved are in the national interest. And that, I think, is what Mr. Rusk is directing his attention to. And I'm hopeful that from those more traditional exchanges we can perhaps find greater common ground.

[25.] Q. Sir, do you favor Senator Humphrey's suggestion that we send surplus food to Red China through the U.N. or CARE, or some similar organization?

THE PRESIDENT. Well, I'd say two things: firstly, Red China—the Chinese Communists—are exporting food at the present time, some of it to Africa, some of it going, I think, to Cuba, and therefore that is a factor in their needs for food from abroad.

Secondly, we've had no indication from the Chinese Communists that they would welcome any offer of food. I'm not anxious to offer food if it's regarded merely as a propaganda effort by the United States. If there is a desire for food and a need for food, then the United States would be glad to consider that need, regardless of the source. If people's lives are involved—if there is a desire for food—the United States will consider it carefully. I do say that in this case, however, there are these examples of food being exported during this present time or recent history and, secondly, there has been a rather belligerent attitude expressed towards us in recent days by the Chinese Communists and there is no indication, direct or indirect, private or public, that they would respond favorably to any acts by the United States.

[26.] Q. Mr. President, the task force report on space has been criticized as partisan opinion. There also has been criticism that the report was made without any contact with NASA officials, without any attempt at liaison during the transition period.

And there is concern that no one has so far been named to head the agency. Could you comment on these charges, sir?

THE PRESIDENT. Well, I don't—the task force was free to make the kind of report that in their best judgment the events called for. The task force was made up of men of broad experience in this field. I think it was really a blue-ribbon panel. They presented their views. I don't think anyone is suggesting that their views are necessarily in every case the right views. I am hopeful—we have appointed an acting director—and I'm hopeful that before the week is out we will have a director of NASA.

[27.] Q. Mr. President, you have directed your departmental heads to take a new look at the Eisenhower budget. I wonder—with indications that you may have some partial revisions with this budget—can you now say whether you hope or expect to live within the $80,900 million spending figure which your predecessor laid down?

THE PRESIDENT. I would—that study of the budget is now going on and I couldn't give you an answer yet. We haven't finished our study.

[28.] Q. Mr. President, your Inaugural Address was unusual in that you dealt only with America's position in the world. Why, Mr. President, did you limit yourself to this global theme?

THE PRESIDENT. Well, because the issue of war and peace is involved, and the survival of perhaps the planet, possibly our system. And, therefore, this is a matter of primary concern to the people of the United States and the people of the world.

Secondly, I represent a new administration. I think the views of this administration are quite well known to the American people, and will become better known in the next month. I think that we are new,

15

however, on the world scene, and therefore I felt there would be some use in informing countries around the world of our general view on the questions which face the world and divide the world.

[29.] Q. Mr. President, you have spoken of the situation where there are crises in the world now. One of these crises is Laos. Do you have any hope that a political settlement can be negotiated there?

THE PRESIDENT. Well, as you know, the British Government has presented to the Soviet Union—and to the best of my information an answer has not been received by the British—a proposal to reestablish the International Control Commission. We ought to know shortly whether there's any hope that that commission can be reestablished. As to the general view on Laos, this matter is of great concern to us. The United States is anxious that there be established in Laos a peaceful country—an independent country not dominated by either side but concerned with the life of the people within the country.

We are anxious that that situation come forward. And the United States is using its influence to see if that independent country, peaceful country, uncommitted country, can be established under the present very difficult circumstances.

[30.] Q. Mr. President, in discussing with the Soviet Union the release of the RB-47 fliers, did we also take up with Mr. Khrushchev the fate of Francis Gary Powers, a U-2 pilot, and the 11 fliers who are missing from the C-130 which was shot down inside Armenia in 1958?

THE PRESIDENT. The matter of the 11 fliers was discussed and Mr. Khrushchev—the Russians rather—have stated that their previous public statements on these fliers represent their view on the matter: that the newspaper—magazine story which was written by an Eastern German does not represent the facts. So that that would—on the matter of Mr. Powers, we have not discussed him at this time because he is in a different category than the fliers that were released. One was an overflight and the other was a flight of a different nature.

Q. Did the Russians ask any *quid pro quo* or did we make any concessions to them in exchange for the release of these fliers? If not, how do you account for this remarkable turnabout in their relations with us?

THE PRESIDENT. They did not. The statement which I have made is the statement which the United States Government put forward on this matter, which I read to you earlier in regard to overflights. I would not attempt to make a judgment as to why the Soviet Union chose to release them at this time. I did say in my statement that this had removed a serious obstacle in the way of peaceful relations between the Soviet Union and the United States and I would judge that they desired to remove that serious obstacle.

Q. Mr. President, did they accept a reassurance of no more overflights as an exchange?

THE PRESIDENT. It is a fact that I have ordered that the flights not be resumed, which is a continuation of the order given by President Eisenhower in May of this year.[1]

[31.] Q. Mr. President, your own election has stimulated renewed proposals for electoral reform. Do you have any objection to changing the present method of electing Presidents or do you favor any of the proposals?

THE PRESIDENT. Well, I do have some thoughts on it. One, that in the first place, having been through the experience in '56,

---

[1] See 1960–61 volume, this series, pp. 440–441.

I think it was, of an attempt to substantially change the electoral college, it's my judgment that no such change can secure the necessary support in the House, the Senate, and in the States of the Union. The area where I do think we perhaps could get some improvement would be in providing that the electors would be bound by the results of the State elections. I think that that is a—would be a useful step forward.

The electors—after all, when the people vote they assume that the votes are going to be cast in a way which reflects the judgment of a majority of the people of the State and therefore I think it would be useful to have that automatic and not set up this independent group who could vote for the candidate who carried the State or not, depending on their own personal views. That would be the first thing.

Secondly, I'm hopeful that the Congress would consider the suggestions made, I think, first by President Theodore Roosevelt and later by Senator Richard Neuberger, of having the National Government participate in the financing of national campaigns, because the present system is not satisfactory.

Perhaps it would be useful to go into that in more detail later because I do think it's a most important subject. But I would say for the present that this matter of the electors would be an area where I think we could usefully move.

[32.] Q. Mr. President, on a related subject, without being morbid, have you given any consideration to the problem which President Eisenhower resolved with his Vice President—that is, the problem of the succession in case of injury, illness, or some incapacitation—some agreement with the Vice President such as your predecessor had?

THE PRESIDENT. Yes. Well, I haven't developed that at this present time, though I do think that President Eisenhower's decision was a good one, and I think it would be a good precedent. Nothing's been done on it as yet, but I think it would be a good matter on which we could proceed.

Reporter: Thank you, Mr. President.

NOTE: President Kennedy's first news conference, broadcast over radio and television, was held in the State Department Auditorium at 6 o'clock on Wednesday evening, January 25, 1961.

9   Letter to Secretary Ribicoff Requesting Him To Undertake Direction of Cuban Refugee Activities.   *January 27, 1961*

Dear Mr. Secretary:

I want you to undertake responsibility, effective February 1, for directing the Cuban refugee activities now being conducted by the Executive branch of the Federal government, and to make an on-the-scene investigation of the problem within the next week as my personal representative.

I want you to make concrete my concern and sympathy for those who have been forced from their homes in Cuba, and to assure them that we shall seek to expedite

their voluntary return as soon as conditions there facilitate that. I believe that the present program can best be strengthened by directly bringing to bear your personal leadership and the vast welfare, health, and other skills of your Department. I am anxious that you make use of private services available for the refugees to the greatest extent possible.

Both here at home and abroad, I want to re-emphasize most strongly the tradition of the United States as a humanitarian sanctuary, and the many times it has extended its hand and material help to those who are "exiles for conscience's sake." In the presently troubled world, we cannot be a peacemaker if we are not also the protector of those individuals as well as nations who cast with us their personal liberty and hopes for the future.

Immediate action should be taken to assure no interruption in present services for the refugees. I also want your consideration of the use of surplus U.S. foods if needed for them, and possible utilization of the many qualified physicians and other professionally or technically qualified refugees.

In undertaking the task given here, you should coordinate activities in this field with the Secretaries of State, Defense, Labor, and Agriculture, and with the heads of other relevant agencies. Under previous arrangements, funds have already been made available to meet such immediate expenditure as will be requested by you of the Department of State, Department of Defense, or other appropriate agency whose participation in this program of emergency assistance to Cuban refugees you may find essential.

Sincerely,

JOHN F. KENNEDY

10   Remarks at a Swearing-In Ceremony and Reception for Presidential Appointees.   *January 29, 1961*

Gentlemen, Mr. Justice, Mr. Vice President:

I want to welcome all of you here to this reception. The purpose was to complete the swearing-in of those members of the administration who had not had the oath administered to them, and also, and equally important, was our desire to have a chance to see these names we have been reading about in the paper.

One of the unsatisfactory features of a most satisfactory and interesting job has been the fact that we have had a chance to see—and perhaps that will also be true in the future—comparatively few members of this administration.

All of the positions which are held by the men who are being sworn today, and by those of you in the audience who have been sworn before, are all extremely impor-

tant; and the kind of work that you do is vital to the success of this administration, and vital to the success of our country.

And therefore we want—and the Vice President and I hold this view very strongly—the closest possible working relationship between all members of the administration and the White House; so that I hope that this is the first of many visits you pay here, and I hope that you will also, all of you, feel not only free but also a responsibility to maintain the closest contact with each other and with the Vice President and myself.

Now, if the busiest man in Washington would administer the oath of office.

NOTE: The ceremonies were held in the East Room at the White House.

In the last paragraph the President referred to Chief Justice Warren.

11   Annual Message to the Congress on the State of the Union.
January 30, 1961

[As delivered in person before a joint session]

Mr. Speaker, Mr. Vice President, Members of the Congress:

It is a pleasure to return from whence I came. You are among my oldest friends in Washington—and this House is my oldest home. It was here, more than 14 years ago, that I first took the oath of Federal office. It was here, for 14 years, that I gained both knowledge and inspiration from members of both parties in both Houses—from your wise and generous leaders—and from the pronouncements which I can vividly recall, sitting where you now sit—including the programs of two great Presidents, the undimmed eloquence of Churchill, the soaring idealism of Nehru, the steadfast words of General de Gaulle. To speak from this same historic rostrum is a sobering experience. To be back among so many friends is a happy one.

I am confident that that friendship will continue. Our Constitution wisely assigns both joint and separate roles to each branch of the government; and a President and a Congress who hold each other in mutual respect will neither permit nor attempt any trespass. For my part, I shall withhold from neither the Congress nor the people any fact or report, past, present, or future, which is necessary for an informed judgment of our conduct and hazards. I shall neither shift the burden of executive decisions to the Congress, nor avoid responsibility for the outcome of those decisions.

———

I speak today in an hour of national peril and national opportunity. Before my term has ended, we shall have to test anew whether a nation organized and governed such as ours can endure. The outcome is by no means certain. The answers are by no means clear. All of us together—this Administration, this Congress, this nation—must forge those answers.

But today, were I to offer—after little more than a week in office—detailed legislation to remedy every national ill, the Congress would rightly wonder whether the desire for speed had replaced the duty of responsibility.

My remarks, therefore, will be limited. But they will also be candid. To state the facts frankly is not to despair the future nor indict the past. The prudent heir takes careful inventory of his legacies, and gives a faithful accounting to those whom he owes an obligation of trust. And, while the occasion does not call for another recital of our blessings and assets, we do have no greater asset than the willingness of a free and determined people, through its elected officials, to face all problems frankly and meet all dangers free from panic or fear.

I.

The present state of our economy is disturbing. We take office in the wake of seven months of recession, three and one-half years of slack, seven years of diminished economic growth, and nine years of falling farm income.

Business bankruptcies have reached their highest level since the Great Depression. Since 1951 farm income has been squeezed down by 25 percent. Save for a brief period in 1958, insured unemployment is at the highest peak in our history. Of some five and one-half million Americans who are without jobs, more than one million have been searching for work for more than four months. And during each month some 150,000 workers are exhausting their already meager jobless benefit rights.

Nearly one-eighth of those who are without jobs live almost without hope in nearly one hundred especially depressed and troubled areas. The rest include new school graduates unable to use their talents, farmers forced to give up their part-time jobs which helped balance their family budgets, skilled and unskilled workers laid off in such important industries as metals, machinery, automobiles and apparel.

Our recovery from the 1958 recession, moreover, was anemic and incomplete. Our Gross National Product never regained its full potential. Unemployment never returned to normal levels. Maximum use of our national industrial capacity was never restored.

In short, the American economy is in trouble. The most resourceful industrialized country on earth ranks among the last in the rate of economic growth. Since last spring our economic growth rate has actually receded. Business investment is in a decline. Profits have fallen below predicted levels. Construction is off. A million unsold automobiles are in inventory. Fewer people are working—and the average work week has shrunk well below 40 hours. Yet prices have continued to rise—so that now too many Americans have *less* to spend for items that cost *more* to buy.

Economic prophecy is at best an uncertain art—as demonstrated by the prediction one year ago from this same podium that 1960 would be, and I quote, "the most prosperous year in our history." Nevertheless, forecasts of continued slack and only slightly reduced unemployment through 1961 and

1962 have been made with alarming unanimity—and this Administration does not intend to stand helplessly by.

We cannot afford to waste idle hours and empty plants while awaiting the end of the recession. We must show the world what a free economy can do—to reduce unemployment, to put unused capacity to work, to spur new productivity, and to foster higher economic growth within a range of sound fiscal policies and relative price stability.

I will propose to the Congress within the next 14 days measures to improve unemployment compensation through temporary increases in duration on a self-supporting basis—to provide more food for the families of the unemployed, and to aid their needy children—to redevelop our areas of chronic labor surplus—to expand the services of the U.S. Employment Offices—to stimulate housing and construction—to secure more purchasing power for our lowest paid workers by raising and expanding the minimum wage—to offer tax incentives for sound plant investment—to increase the development of our natural resources—to encourage price stability—and to take other steps aimed at insuring a prompt recovery and paving the way for increased long-range growth. This is not a partisan program concentrating on our weaknesses—it is, I hope, a national program to realize our national strength.

II.

Efficient expansion at home, stimulating the new plant and technology that can make our goods more competitive, is also the key to the international balance of payments problem. Laying aside all alarmist talk and panicky solutions, let us put that knotty problem in its proper perspective.

It is true that, since 1958, the gap between the dollars we spend or invest abroad and the dollars returned to us has substantially widened. This overall deficit in our balance of payments increased by nearly $11 billion in the 3 years—and holders of dollars abroad converted them to gold in such a quantity as to cause a total outflow of nearly $5 billion of gold from our reserve. The 1959 deficit was caused in large part by the failure of our exports to penetrate foreign markets— the result both of restrictions on our goods and our own uncompetitive prices. The 1960 deficit, on the other hand, was more the result of an increase in private capital outflow seeking new opportunity, higher return or speculative advantage abroad.

Meanwhile this country has continued to bear more than its share of the West's military and foreign aid obligations. Under existing policies, another deficit of $2 billion is predicted for 1961—and individuals in those countries whose dollar position once depended on these deficits for improvement now wonder aloud whether our gold reserves will remain sufficient to meet our own obligations.

All this is cause for concern—but it is not cause for panic. For our monetary and financial position remains exceedingly strong. Including our drawing rights in the International Monetary Fund and the gold reserve held as backing for our currency and Federal Reserve deposits, we have some $22 billion in total gold stocks and other international monetary reserves available— and I now pledge that their full strength stands behind the value of the dollar for use if needed.

Moreover, we hold large assets abroad— the total owed this nation far exceeds the claims upon our reserves—and our exports once again substantially exceed our imports.

In short, we need not—and we shall not— take any action to increase the dollar price of gold from $35 an ounce—to impose ex-

change controls—to reduce our anti-recession efforts—to fall back on restrictive trade policies—or to weaken our commitments around the world.

This Administration will not distort the value of the dollar in any fashion. And this is a commitment.

Prudence and good sense do require, however, that new steps be taken to ease the payments deficit and prevent any gold crisis. Our success in world affairs has long depended in part upon foreign confidence in our ability to pay. A series of executive orders, legislative remedies and cooperative efforts with our allies will get underway immediately—aimed at attracting foreign investment and travel to this country—promoting American exports, at stable prices and with more liberal government guarantees and financing—curbing tax and customs loopholes that encourage undue spending of private dollars abroad—and (through OECD, NATO and otherwise) sharing with our allies all efforts to provide for the common defense of the free world and the hopes for growth of the less developed lands. While the current deficit lasts, ways will be found to ease our dollar outlays abroad without placing the full burden on the families of men whom we have asked to serve our Flag overseas.

In short, whatever is required will be done to back up all our efforts abroad, and to make certain that, in the future as in the past, the dollar is as "sound as a dollar."

III.

But more than our exchange of international payments is out of balance. The current Federal budget for fiscal 1961 is almost certain to show a net deficit. The budget already submitted for fiscal 1962 will remain in balance only if the Congress enacts all the revenue measures requested—and only if an earlier and sharper up-turn in the economy than my economic advisers now think likely produces the tax revenues estimated. Nevertheless, a new Administration must of necessity build on the spending and revenue estimates already submitted. Within that framework, barring the development of urgent national defense needs or a worsening of the economy, it is my current intention to advocate a program of expenditures which, including revenues from a stimulation of the economy, will not of and by themselves unbalance the earlier Budget.

However, we will do what must be done. For our national household is cluttered with unfinished and neglected tasks. Our cities are being engulfed in squalor. Twelve long years after Congress declared our goal to be "a decent home and a suitable environment for every American family," we still have 25 million Americans living in substandard homes. A new housing program under a new Housing and Urban Affairs Department will be needed this year.

Our classrooms contain 2 million more children than they can properly have room for, taught by 90,000 teachers not properly qualified to teach. One third of our most promising high school graduates are financially unable to continue the development of their talents. The war babies of the 1940's, who overcrowded our schools in the 1950's, are now descending in 1960 upon our colleges—with two college students for every one, ten years from now—and our colleges are ill prepared. We lack the scientists, the engineers and the teachers our world obligations require. We have neglected oceanography, saline water conversion, and the basic research that lies at the root of all progress. Federal grants for both higher and public school education can no longer be delayed.

Medical research has achieved new won-ders—but these wonders are too often beyond the reach of too many people, owing to a lack of income (particularly among the aged), a lack of hospital beds, a lack of nursing homes and a lack of doctors and dentists. Measures to provide health care for the aged under Social Security, and to increase the supply of both facilities and personnel, must be undertaken this year.

Our supply of clean water is dwindling. Organized and juvenile crimes cost the taxpayers millions of dollars each year, making it essential that we have improved enforcement and new legislative safeguards. The denial of constitutional rights to some of our fellow Americans on account of race—at the ballot box and elsewhere—disturbs the national conscience, and subjects us to the charge of world opinion that our democracy is not equal to the high promise of our heritage. Morality in private business has not been sufficiently spurred by morality in public business. A host of problems and projects in all 50 States, though not possible to include in this Message, deserves—and will receive—the attention of both the Congress and the Executive Branch. On most of these matters, Messages will be sent to the Congress within the next two weeks.

IV.

But all these problems pale when placed beside those which confront us around the world. No man entering upon this office, regardless of his party, regardless of his previous service in Washington, could fail to be staggered upon learning—even in this brief 10 day period—the harsh enormity of the trials through which we must pass in the next four years. Each day the crises multiply. Each day their solution grows more difficult. Each day we draw nearer the hour of maximum danger, as weapons spread and hostile forces grow stronger. I feel I must inform the Congress that our analyses over the last ten days make it clear that—in each of the principal areas of crisis—the tide of events has been running out and time has not been our friend.

In Asia, the relentless pressures of the Chinese Communists menace the security of the entire area—from the borders of India and South Viet Nam to the jungles of Laos, struggling to protect its newly-won independence. We seek in Laos what we seek in all Asia, and, indeed, in all of the world—freedom for the people and independence for the government. And this Nation shall persevere in our pursuit of these objectives.

In Africa, the Congo has been brutally torn by civil strife, political unrest and public disorder. We shall continue to support the heroic efforts of the United Nations to restore peace and order—efforts which are now endangered by mounting tensions, unsolved problems, and decreasing support from many member states.

In Latin America, Communist agents seeking to exploit that region's peaceful revolution of hope have established a base on Cuba, only 90 miles from our shores. Our objection with Cuba is not over the people's drive for a better life. Our objection is to their domination by foreign and domestic tyrannies. Cuban social and economic reform should be encouraged. Questions of economic and trade policy can always be negotiated. But Communist domination in this Hemisphere can never be negotiated.

We are pledged to work with our sister republics to free the Americas of all such foreign domination and all tyranny, working toward the goal of a free hemisphere of free governments, extending from Cape Horn to the Arctic Circle.

In Europe our alliances are unfulfilled and in some disarray. The unity of NATO has been weakened by economic rivalry and partially eroded by national interest. It has not yet fully mobilized its resources nor fully achieved a common outlook. Yet no Atlantic power can meet on its own the mutual problems now facing us in defense, foreign aid, monetary reserves, and a host of other areas; and our close ties with those whose hopes and interests we share are among this Nation's most powerful assets.

Our greatest challenge is still the world that lies beyond the Cold War—but the first great obstacle is still our relations with the Soviet Union and Communist China. We must never be lulled into believing that either power has yielded its ambitions for world domination—ambitions which they forcefully restated only a short time ago. On the contrary, our task is to convince them that aggression and subversion will not be profitable routes to pursue these ends. Open and peaceful competition—for prestige, for markets, for scientific achievement, even for men's minds—is something else again. For if Freedom and Communism were to compete for man's allegiance in a world at peace, I would look to the future with ever increasing confidence.

To meet this array of challenges—to fulfill the role we cannot avoid on the world scene—we must reexamine and revise our whole arsenal of tools: military, economic and political.

One must not overshadow the other. On the Presidential Coat of Arms, the American eagle holds in his right talon the olive branch, while in his left he holds a bundle of arrows. We intend to give equal attention to both.

First, we must strengthen our military tools. We are moving into a period of uncertain risk and great commitment in which both the military and diplomatic possibilities require a Free World force so powerful as to make any aggression clearly futile. Yet in the past, lack of a consistent, coherent military strategy, the absence of basic assumptions about our national requirements and the faulty estimates and duplication arising from inter-service rivalries have all made it difficult to assess accurately how adequate—or inadequate—our defenses really are.

I have, therefore, instructed the Secretary of Defense to reappraise our entire defense strategy—our ability to fulfill our commitments—the effectiveness, vulnerability, and dispersal of our strategic bases, forces and warning systems—the efficiency and economy of our operation and organization—the elimination of obsolete bases and installations—and the adequacy, modernization and mobility of our present conventional and nuclear forces and weapons systems in the light of present and future dangers. I have asked for preliminary conclusions by the end of February—and I then shall recommend whatever legislative, budgetary or executive action is needed in the light of these conclusions.

In the meantime, I have asked the Defense Secretary to initiate immediately three new steps most clearly needed now:

First, I have directed prompt attention to increase our air-lift capacity. Obtaining additional air transport mobility—and obtaining it now—will better assure the ability of our conventional forces to respond, with discrimination and speed, to any problem at any spot on the globe at any moment's notice. In particular it will enable us to meet any deliberate effort to avoid or divert our forces by starting limited wars in widely scattered parts of the globe.

(b) I have directed prompt action to step up our Polaris submarine program. Using unobligated ship-building funds now (to let contracts originally scheduled for the next fiscal year) will build and place on station—

at least nine months earlier than planned—substantially more units of a crucial deterrent—a fleet that will never attack first, but possess sufficient powers of retaliation, concealed beneath the seas, to discourage any aggressor from launching an attack upon our security.

(c) I have directed prompt action to accelerate our entire missile program. Until the Secretary of Defense's reappraisal is completed, the emphasis here will be largely on improved organization and decision-making—on cutting down the wasteful duplications and the time-lag that have handicapped our whole family of missiles. If we are to keep the peace, we need an invulnerable missile force powerful enough to deter any aggressor from even threatening an attack that he would know could not destroy enough of our force to prevent his own destruction. For as I said upon taking the oath of office: "Only when our arms are sufficient beyond doubt can we be certain beyond doubt that they will never be employed."

Secondly, we must improve our economic tools. Our role is essential and unavoidable in the construction of a sound and expanding economy for the entire non-communist world, helping other nations build the strength to meet their own problems, to satisfy their own aspirations—to surmount their own dangers. The problems in achieving this goal are towering and unprecedented—the response must be towering and unprecedented as well, much as Lend-Lease and the Marshall Plan were in earlier years, which brought such fruitful results.

(a) I intend to ask the Congress for authority to establish a new and more effective program for assisting the economic, educational and social development of other countries and continents. That program must stimulate and take more effectively into account the contributions of our allies, and provide central policy direction for all our own programs that now so often overlap, conflict or diffuse our energies and resources. Such a program, compared to past programs, will require

—more flexibility for short run emergencies

—more commitment to long term development

—new attention to education at all levels

—greater emphasis on the recipient nation's role, their effort, their purpose, with greater social justice for their people, broader distribution and participation by their people and more efficient public administration and more efficient tax systems of their own

—and orderly planning for national and regional development instead of a piecemeal approach.

I hope the Senate will take early action approving the Convention establishing the Organization for Economic Cooperation and Development. This will be an important instrument in sharing with our allies this development effort—working toward the time when each nation will contribute in proportion to its ability to pay. For, while we are prepared to assume our full share of these huge burdens, we cannot and must not be expected to bear them alone.

To our sister republics to the south, we have pledged a new alliance for progress— alianza para progreso. Our goal is a free and prosperous Latin America, realizing for all its states and all its citizens a degree of economic and social progress that matches their historic contributions of culture, intellect and liberty. To start this nation's role at this time in that alliance of neighbors, I am recommending the following:

—That the Congress appropriate in full the $500 million fund pledged by the Act of Bogota, to be used not as an instrument

of the Cold War, but as a first step in the sound development of the Americas.

—That a new Inter-Departmental Task Force be established under the leadership of the Department of State, to coordinate at the highest level all policies and programs of concern to the Americas.

—That our delegates to the OAS, working with those of other members, strengthen that body as an instrument to preserve the peace and to prevent foreign domination anywhere in the Hemisphere.

—That, in cooperation with other nations, we launch a new hemispheric attack on illiteracy and inadequate educational opportunities to all levels; and, finally,

—That a Food-for-Peace mission be sent immediately to Latin America to explore ways in which our vast food abundance can be used to help end hunger and malnutrition in certain areas of suffering in our own hemisphere.

This Administration is expanding its Food-for-Peace Program in every possible way. The product of our abundance must be used more effectively to relieve hunger and help economic growth in all corners of the globe. And I have asked the Director of this Program to recommend additional ways in which these surpluses can advance the interests of world peace—including the establishment of world food reserves.

An even more valuable national asset is our reservoir of dedicated men and women— not only on our college campuses but in every age group—who have indicated their desire to contribute their skills, their efforts, and a part of their lives to the fight for world order. We can mobilize this talent through the formation of a National Peace Corps, enlisting the services of all those with the desire and capacity to help foreign lands meet their urgent needs for trained personnel.

25

Finally, while our attention is centered on the development of the noncommunist world, we must never forget our hopes for the ultimate freedom and welfare of the Eastern European peoples. In order to be prepared to help re-establish historic ties of friendship, I am asking the Congress for increased discretion to use economic tools in this area whenever this is found to be clearly in the national interest. This will require amendment of the Mutual Defense Assistance Control Act along the lines I proposed as a member of the Senate, and upon which the Senate voted last summer. Meanwhile, I hope to explore with the Polish government the possibility of using our frozen Polish funds on projects of peace that will demonstrate our abiding friendship for and interest in the people of Poland.

Third, we must sharpen our political and diplomatic tools—the means of cooperation and agreement on which an enforceable world order must ultimately rest.

I have already taken steps to coordinate and expand our disarmament effort—to increase our programs of research and study—and to make arms control a central goal of our national policy under my direction. The deadly arms race, and the huge resources it absorbs, have too long overshadowed all else we must do. We must prevent that arms race from spreading to new nations, to new nuclear powers and to the reaches of outer space. We must make certain that our negotiators are better informed and better prepared—to formulate workable proposals of our own and to make sound judgments about the proposals of others.

I have asked the other governments concerned to agree to a reasonable delay in the talks on a nuclear test ban—and it is our intention to resume negotiations prepared to reach a final agreement with any nation

that is equally willing to agree to an effective and enforceable treaty.

We must increase our support of the United Nations as an instrument to end the Cold War instead of an arena in which to fight it. In recognition of its increasing importance and the doubling of its membership

—we are enlarging and strengthening our own mission to the U.N.

—we shall help insure that it is properly financed.

—we shall work to see that the integrity of the office of the Secretary-General is maintained.

—And I would address a special plea to the smaller nations of the world—to join with us in strengthening this organization, which is far more essential to their security than it is to ours—the only body in the world where no nation need be powerful to be secure, where every nation has an equal voice, and where any nation can exert influence not according to the strength of its armies but according to the strength of its ideas. It deserves the support of all.

Finally, this Administration intends to explore promptly all possible areas of cooperation with the Soviet Union and other nations "to invoke the wonders of science instead of its terrors." Specifically, I now invite all nations—including the Soviet Union—to join with us in developing a weather prediction program, in a new communications satellite program and in preparation for probing the distant planets of Mars and Venus, probes which may someday unlock the deepest secrets of the universe.

Today this country is ahead in the science and technology of space, while the Soviet Union is ahead in the capacity to lift large vehicles into orbit. Both nations would help themselves as well as other nations by removing these endeavors from the bitter and wasteful competition of the Cold War. The United States would be willing to join with the Soviet Union and the scientists of all nations in a greater effort to make the fruits of this new knowledge available to all—and, beyond that, in an effort to extend farm technology to hungry nations—to wipe out disease—to increase the exchanges of scientists and their knowledge—and to make our own laboratories available to technicians of other lands who lack the facilities to pursue their own work. Where nature makes natural allies of us all, we can demonstrate that beneficial relations are possible even with those with whom we most deeply disagree—and this must someday be the basis of world peace and world law.

v.

I have commented on the state of the domestic economy, our balance of payments, our Federal and social budget and the state of the world. I would like to conclude with a few remarks about the state of the Executive branch. We have found it full of honest and useful public servants—but their capacity to act decisively at the exact time action is needed has too often been muffled in the morass of committees, timidities and fictitious theories which have created a growing gap between decision and execution, between planning and reality. In a time of rapidly deteriorating situations at home and abroad, this is bad for the public service and particularly bad for the country; and we mean to make a change.

I have pledged myself and my colleagues in the cabinet to a continuous encouragement of initiative, responsibility and energy in serving the public interest. Let every public servant know, whether his post is high or low, that a man's rank and reputation in this Administration will be determined by the size of the job he does, and not by the size of his staff, his office or his budget. Let it be clear that this Administration recognizes the value of dissent and daring—that we greet healthy controversy as the hallmark of healthy change. Let the public service be a proud and lively career. And let every man and woman who works in any area of our national government, in any branch, at any level, be able to say with pride and with honor in future years: "I served the United States government in that hour of our nation's need."

For only with complete dedication by us all to the national interest can we bring our country through the troubled years that lie ahead. Our problems are critical. The tide is unfavorable. The news will be worse before it is better. And while hoping and working for the best, we should prepare ourselves now for the worst.

We cannot escape our dangers—neither must we let them drive us into panic or narrow isolation. In many areas of the world where the balance of power already rests with our adversaries, the forces of freedom are sharply divided. It is one of the ironies of our time that the techniques of a harsh and repressive system should be able to instill discipline and ardor in its servants—while the blessings of liberty have too often stood for privilege, materialism and a life of ease.

But I have a different view of liberty.

Life in 1961 will not be easy. Wishing it, predicting it, even asking for it, will not make it so. There will be further setbacks before the tide is turned. But turn it we must. The hopes of all mankind rest upon us—not simply upon those of us in this chamber, but upon the peasant in Laos, the fisherman in Nigeria, the exile from Cuba, the spirit that moves every man and Nation who shares our hopes for freedom and the future. And in the final analysis, they rest most of all upon the pride and perseverance of our fellow citizens of the great Republic.

In the words of a great President, whose birthday we honor today, closing his final State of the Union Message sixteen years ago, "We pray that we may be worthy of the unlimited opportunities that God has given us."

12   Message Greeting President Quadros of Brazil on the Occasion of His Inauguration. *January* 31, 1961

[Released January 31, 1961. Dated January 27, 1961]

Dear Mr. President:

On the occasion of Your Excellency's inauguration as Chief Executive of our friendly neighbor and wartime ally, the United States of Brazil, I extend to you my warmest personal congratulations and the most sincere good wishes of the people of the United States of America.

Once in twenty years presidential inaugurations in your country and mine occur within days of each other. This year of 1961 is signalized by that happy coincidence. At this time, each of us assumes challenging duties for which he has been freely chosen by his fellow citizens. To each of us is

entrusted the heavy responsibility of guiding the affairs of a democratic nation founded on Christian ideals and aspiring to common goals of peace and human betterment.

It is my earnest wish, Mr. President, to fortify the spirit of cooperation and mutual esteem which has always marked relations between our countries. In that spirit, let us work together to reinvigorate the alliance of American Republics, recognizing the magnitude of the tasks we face, and confident in the strength of the heritage we share.

Sincerely,

JOHN F. KENNEDY

13   Message to President Kubitschek of Brazil. *January* 31, 1961

[Released January 31, 1961. Dated January 29, 1961]

Dear Mr. President:

I welcome the thoughtful message which you sent to me on the occasion of my inauguration, not only because of the constructive and friendly spirit which motivates your comments, but also because I share Your Excellency's deep concern for the social, political, and economic well-being of the peoples of our hemisphere. One of the cardinal objectives of my administration will be the association of the United States with the peoples of Latin America in a common

effort to improve the lives of our peoples under the reign of liberty.

May I take this opportunity, Mr. President, to extend to you, as you leave the high office in which you have so faithfully served your country, my personal best wishes and those of the people and government of the United States of America, for your continued health and prosperity.

Sincerely,

JOHN F. KENNEDY

14   Interview With Dave Garroway Recorded for the 150th
      Anniversary of the Founding of Massachusetts General Hospital.
      January 31, 1961

THE PRESIDENT. Good morning, Dave.

Mr. Garroway: Good morning, Mr. President. I suppose those scenes of Mass. General look pretty familiar to you? You have been on the board of overseers since 1947, I believe?

THE PRESIDENT. Yes, that's right. I must say that I think the work that Massachusetts General does and other similar hospitals around the country, they perform a great public function. And to think that this hospital is celebrating its 150th anniversary. It was begun the year before the war of 1812, and yet there are two other American hospitals that are even older. When we think of the tremendous progress that has been made in medicine, yet even way back then, fellow citizens were concerned about caring for their neighbors—and the Massachusetts General does more than care for the people of that area. There are over a thousand students studying in various parts of the hospital from all over the world, and the influence of Massachusetts General stretches really around the globe through the work of these graduates.

Mr. Garroway: They have put out, I think, $4 million a year, in this one hospital, into research. Is this enough, I wonder? Are we doing enough generally for research in this country?

THE PRESIDENT. I think we can always do better. My family has been particularly interested in one kind of research, and we now have at the hospital a center for research into the causes of mental retardation of children. This center is going to begin building as soon as the snow is off the ground.

I think this is one area where there has been inadequate research. We are fortunate in this case to have a close connection with Harvard University. Dr. Adams from Harvard University is heading the research center. But I do believe that nearly every American family either has some member of its family or some friend who goes through the very harrowing experience of having a child in the family who suffers from mental retardation—the difficulties that the child has and the difficulty that it causes in the family.

I think that rather than caring for these children, which we are attempting to do, though not always adequately, I think it is most important that we try to examine why they are retarded and what could be done about it—whether through surgery or other treatment we could begin to cure them, not merely care for them.

Mr. Garroway: Will eventually we cure everybody, do you think? Will the health of the Nation approach perfection some day, by care and research?

THE PRESIDENT. No, I suppose we are all—we may stretch out our period on this earth but sooner or later we will all begin to—but at least what I think we are all concerned about is that children have a happy childhood, and a fruitful one; and that adults be permitted to work and that older people find their later years to be easier, free from pain and discomfort; and then I think everybody will await their end, but I think there's an awful lot we can do. And the cooperation between medicine, between private individuals who supported Massachusetts General, and between the National Government in providing funds for research, it is a happy relationship, though one that can always be improved.

Mr. Garroway: Do we recognize the importance—I read your article recently, on the subject of physical fitness in this country—for the young and middle aged too?

THE PRESIDENT. Well, I think it is a serious problem. Our society is quite sophisticated and we are in a very dangerous period in our world history. We have unrelenting foes who are determined to destroy us.

Physical fitness goes with mental fitness. It goes with energy—and I am concerned that recent tests have shown a steady decline in the standards of American fitness as compared with European and people around the world. In reading a recent article on guerrilla warfare, I noticed the great emphasis put on physical fitness.

We are in a dangerous period, and I think that we have to be fit. Now it's harder, because our life is easier—we have cars, buses, and all the rest. I think we ought to concern ourselves with making sure that our children are fit, that they are concerned with being energetic—that they use their young years not merely as spectators but as participants in life.

Mr. Garroway: Will you help us to wake up?

THE PRESIDENT. Well, we are trying. I think that this is a great country, and I think it deserves the best of all of us. I think that physical fitness is a part of our survival, and I am hopeful that we can,

through the White House—but really it's a private decision—but at least from this area we are going to try to do our best to emphasize this.

It's really up to every parent. Do your children go every week and watch a basketball game, or do they do something to make themselves fit? I think we are inclined to think that if we watch a football game or a baseball game, that we have taken part in it. That's not what we want.

Mr. Garroway: Well, you don't usually get into this posture of sitting down very much, I understand. You are more than busy——

THE PRESIDENT. I must say that this hospital is a—I am delighted to have this rather long-distance connection with this hospital. It emphasizes not only what this hospital does, but all the hospitals in your community. They all deserve our support.

And I am delighted to have this chance, through Dave Garroway, to emphasize our great national interest in developing our hospitals, developing research, training doctors, training nurses—and spreading the benefits of modern medicine through this country and around the world.

Mr. Garroway: Thank you, Mr. President.

THE PRESIDENT. Thank you very much, Dave.

NOTE: The interview was video-taped in the broadcast room at the White House on January 28 for use on the television program "Today" on January 31.

During his remarks the President referred to Dr. Raymond Adams, Professor of Neuropathology at the School of Medicine, Harvard University.

15 The President's News Conference of *February 1*, 1961

THE PRESIDENT. I have several announcements to make.

[1.] First is one made at the request

of Mrs. Kennedy. Since the election, the birth of our son, and the inauguration, Mrs. Kennedy and I have received over 100,000 letters and telegrams of congratulations and good wishes. They are now building up in available rooms at the White House. Unfortunately, it's not going to be possible for us to acknowledge and answer as we would like to answer each and every message, and therefore I wish to take this opportunity on behalf of Mrs. Kennedy and myself to thank everyone who has been so kind and generous.

[2.] Secondly, I'm happy to be able to announce that the restrictions recently imposed on travel abroad of dependents of service personnel will be lifted as soon as the necessary detailed arrangements can be made in the Defense Department. Secretary McNamara has been able to work out arrangements for equivalent savings in personnel costs abroad, so that this change does not imply any weakening of our determination to protect the value of the dollar.

This is a matter of great importance. The Chiefs of Staff have been most concerned about the effect of this order on morale and on the rate of enlistment, and therefore we have had to make a balanced judgment as to which actions in which areas would be in the national interest, and after giving this matter careful consideration, it is the judgment of the Defense Department that other savings can be made which will be more satisfactory to us and to the position of the Armed Forces.[1]

[3.] Third, I'm announcing that there are going to be set up five pilot projects for foodstamp distribution, and that these will be in areas of maximum chronic unemployment. All the areas have not yet been de-

termined, but one will be in West Virginia, one in Pennsylvania, one in southern Illinois, and the other in eastern Kentucky, with a fifth yet to be determined.

[4.] Next, the Veterans Administration has been instructed to speed up the payment of the National Insurance dividends. This is a sum of over $250 million, which would be paid out throughout this year. We're going to try to pay it out this winter in order to assist the economy at a critical time.

This, of course—the Veterans Administration fund has very ample reserves, very generous reserves. And I feel that this will be of some benefit.

[5.] Lastly, in order to lower the cost of housing credit and stimulate that sector of the economy, I've directed the Federal Housing Administration to reduce the maximum permissible interest on FHA-insured loans from 5¾ to 5½ percent. Complementary action will be taken by the Federal National Mortgage Association.

In addition, I've asked the Community Facilities Administration to reduce interest rates on new loans to local public bodies for the construction of public facilities, and to broaden their eligibility requirements.

And I've instructed the Housing and Home Finance Agency to hasten those approved projects where a speedup can be effected without waste.

Thank you.

[6.] Q. Mr. President, as you know, Adlai Stevenson said the other day it was his guess that you would be happy to meet with Khrushchev if he should come to this country for the U.N. session. I wonder, was he correct in his guess that you would be happy to meet with Khrushchev?

THE PRESIDENT. As Governor Stevenson—Ambassador Stevenson said, I have not discussed the matter with him. I have no idea whether Mr. Khrushchev is coming to the

---

[1] A White House statement of March 6 summarized proposed means for reduction of overseas expenditures by individual members of the Armed Forces, Department of Defense civilian employees, and their dependents in order to effect savings which would have resulted had the number of dependents in foreign countries been reduced as originally directed.

United States or not. There's been no indication, either publicly or privately, that he is planning a visit to the United States, and therefore I think it would be appropriate to wait in regard to what plans we might have as far as seeing him—it would be more appropriate to wait until we have some idea whether he's going to come or not.

[7.] Mr. President, could you tell us something of the reasoning and the background of the apparent restrictions on the RB–47 fliers in publicly discussing their experiences in Russia? We get the impression from the Pentagon that this blackout on any public interviews or discussions of the two fliers is to be more or less an indefinite thing. Now we are told at the Pentagon that this is in the national interest. First of all, I wonder if you could tell us why it's in the national interest, and second, what personal feelings you have in the matter on the reasoning behind this decision to keep these men quiet.

THE PRESIDENT. Well I'll say that when they've finished their short leave and when they have been debriefed by the Air Force, and the Air Force has had an opportunity to have conversation with them, as far as I'm concerned I'd be glad to have them talk to the press. And therefore I would assume they would be available to the press as soon as that leave is over.

[8.] Q. This may be a corollary question, but your administration has indicated that it expects officers of the military on active duty to support, in their public statements, or at least not to be hostile to the foreign policy of your administration. Does this project itself into other areas? What about the Atomic Energy Commission? What about economists working for the executive branch who may have differences about economic policy?

THE PRESIDENT. I think that the procedure

which we have established is a traditional one. I think that the Eisenhower administration made, according to the accounts that I have seen, over 65 known efforts to make sure that speeches by members of the military were in accordance with the general objectives of American foreign policy.

I think—we're going to continue to do that. If a well-known, high-ranking military figure makes a speech which affects foreign policy or possible military policy, I think that the people and the countries abroad have a right to expect that that speech represents the opinion of the National Government.

Now the speech of Admiral Burke which raised this question—when the speech was drafted Admiral Burke may not have known, nor did any of us, whether these fliers would be released, for example. Therefore, there is some value in coordinating statements made by high-ranking responsible officials of our national—involving national security—coordinating them, and making sure that the State Department, the White House, and Defense are informed about the speeches and that they represent national policy.

That has been the policy followed by President Eisenhower; it is the policy which must be followed by this administration.

Now in the question Mr. Morgan asked, it's not intended that this will serve as a restraint on the ability of people in this administration to speak out, particularly when those speeches do not involve national security. I think the important point here is when they involve national security.

[9.] Q. Do you consider the current business slump serious enough to justify a tax cut?

THE PRESIDENT. I do not at this time. I've stated that we're going to make another judgment on the state of the economy in 2 to

3 months and will then decide what action could be usefully taken. But I have not proposed a tax cut at this time nor do I intend to.

[10.] Q. Mr. President, some critics stated that proposals of added Federal expenditures in your State of the Union Message may force us to "kick the bottom out of the money barrel." Could you give us an idea, sir, of how your proposed increased programs would be furnished and in connection with the previous question could it possibly mean an increase in income taxes?

THE PRESIDENT. Well, I think that we can spell out our proposed proposals in the series of messages that we're going to send in the next 14 days. And as I have said, the proposals that we will make will not of themselves unbalance the budget.

[11.] Q. Mr. President, your State of the Union Message was both praised and criticized. Some of the critics said that you painted the picture in dark colors so that should there be any improvement you would get the credit. Would you want to comment on that, sir?

THE PRESIDENT. Well, I would—I painted the picture as I saw it. I also stated that in my judgment, in some areas involving the national interest the news would be worse before it gets better. And I think that the American people might just as well realize that. So that my statement stands as my view of the problems facing the United States at home and abroad at this time. To the best of my ability, it is an accurate presentation. I'm not a candidate for office for at least 4 years, so that there will be many ups and downs I suppose during that period, so that anybody who thinks that if things get better in the spring that we'll be able to say that they're the result of the administration policy and that's the reason that I painted them unnecessarily dark, misunderstands

completely. They are painted accurately as I understand them to be, and anyone who makes the judgment that it was laid on thick for political reasons, I think is making a serious mistake and I hope would give us the benefit of the doubt of an honest view.

Now, other people may look at the same facts and come to a different conclusion. Obviously they have—before my speech and since my speech. But that represents my view as President.

[12.] Q. Mr. President, in the spirit of your Los Angeles campaign speech, are you prepared to move soon by Executive action in the field of civil rights, and if so, in what fields would you make your first step?

THE PRESIDENT. We have been considering what steps could be taken in the field of expanding civil rights by Executive action, and I'm hopeful that we will shortly conclude that analysis and have some statement to make on it. It's not completed as yet.

[13.] Q. In connection with a couple of previous questions, you have stated several times since your election that the country was in for some substantial sacrifices, or that the year 1961 might be a difficult year to live in, and yet some of the measures you have announced seem to be intended to improve the lot of, let's say, more unfortunate sections of the population. Could you be more explicit on what you mean by sacrifices and the difficulties of living in 1961?

THE PRESIDENT. Well, I would hope that a country as powerful as ours—I said it was the most resourceful industrialized country in the world—would not oppose efforts which we would take to make the life of people who live in these chronic depressed areas—to make it easier. I do not feel that all the burdens of hardship should be placed on them. In addition, I do believe that we are heavily involved in critical areas of the world and I cannot today predict what the results will be of events in those areas of the world. I merely state that the tide has not been running with us, that we are heavily involved—heavily committed—by public statements of the former administration as well as by this administration, and therefore I felt that we should inform the people that there are hazards which lurk around us and which may place heavy burdens on us.

I will whenever I think that sacrifices of a particular nature are required, I will go to the people. At the present time, I merely suggest that the times are difficult.

Now, when we talk about five and a half million people unemployed there are still over 60 million people employed. And I think that may be one of the reasons why there is some feeling that I overstressed the dark instead of the bright in my State of the Union Address. But it is the function, it seems to me, of the President to concern himself with that five and a half million unemployed particularly when so many have been unemployed for such a long period of time.

[14.] Q. Mr. President, some people have interpreted your address to the Congress as indicating that you found conditions very much worse upon taking office than you had anticipated. Is this interpretation correct? And, if so, can you give us some specifics?

THE PRESIDENT. I think the situation is less satisfactory than it was last fall. And I don't—and I'm not convinced as yet that the tide in some of the critical areas in which the United States is involved has turned in our favor.

I think that anyone who reads the daily papers knows of the critical events in Laos, the Communist intervention in that area. I think they're aware of the fact that the situation in the Congo has deteriorated sharply recently, with a steady withdrawal

of troops taking place by United Nations countries.

They're also aware of the steps which have been taken in recent months to increase the iron control of Mr. Castro on Cuba; the shipments of thousands of tons of arms to that country; the expansion of the militia. Those are all factors which affect the security of the United States.

[15.] Q. Mr. President, what proposals might the United States make in regard to the Congo now that you mentioned the situation there is deteriorating because of the pullout of troops?

THE PRESIDENT. Mr. Timberlake is here for consultation in Washington now, Ambassador Brown from Laos is here, General Norstad, who's our NATO commander, is here in Washington, and Ambassador Thompson will be coming back next week, so that we are considering carefully what policies we should follow in all those areas of crisis. Particularly we are considering the matter of the Congo carefully and what useful steps might be taken which would prevent a further deterioration. I do not have anything further to say just at this time.

[16.] Q. Mr. President, do you plan any recommendations on the labor-management relations field in your future messages to Congress since you have not covered this subject in your addresses to date?

THE PRESIDENT. I'd have to wait on that. We have no—it's not within the next 14 days.

[17.] Q. Sir, would you clarify your intentions in the field of unemployment compensation? Do you plan now to propose to Congress the establishment of Federal standards, wider coverage, higher benefits, and for their greater duration?

THE PRESIDENT. Well, the first matter which we will address to the Congress will be the question of emergency payments to those unemployed who've exhausted their benefits.

Later in March, we will send to the Congress—or in April—proposals dealing with a more permanent improvement in unemployment compensation standards, duration, and benefits, because there isn't any doubt that, based on our experience in '58, in our experience this year, the unemployment compensation system has not met the needs of the country satisfactorily.

So we will be sending a second message dealing with the subjects which you discussed in your question.

[18.] Q. In connection, Mr. President, with your statement on the military dependents, is this to be a complete repeal of the existing directive?

THE PRESIDENT. Yes.

[19.] Q. Do you agree with the general assessment that the narrowness of the House vote yesterday on enlarging the Rules Committee means rough going ahead for your legislative program?

THE PRESIDENT. Well, the Speaker was successful yesterday and that does mean that the House will have an opportunity to vote on all these bills.

I do think that the House is closely divided on a good many matters which involve legislative proposals, and perhaps the country may be divided, too, but at least we will have a chance to have a vote. And I consider that the most important thing. If the House then doesn't want to support our proposals then at least I feel that the country has indicated its judgment and not the judgment of only a small number of Representatives.

But I would say that we're going to have a close debate in both the House and the Senate on a good many matters and which has always been true if the matters do any-

thing; if they provide for any action, there is bound to be controversy about them. The only way we can get general agreement is when you confine yourself to general statements.

[20.] Q. Mr. President, will you ask for the same new revenues that Mr. Eisenhower asked for in his Budget Message?

THE PRESIDENT. I will. It is a fact, as I suggested in the State of the Union Address, that some of those proposals are generously estimated. For example, I believe that the President's budget calls for a—was it—$900 million deficit in the Post Office; I think the President's budget called for revenue action by the Congress of $843 million. In view of the fact that the Congress has been reluctant in the past I think we have to consider carefully whether we could expect the Congress to ever vote $843 million new revenue on mail and postage.

But nevertheless, we are going to go ahead in general with perhaps—there may be one or two changes but they'll be relatively minor—we are going ahead with the revenue requests of the previous administration.

Q. Have you thought of any new sources of revenue?

THE PRESIDENT. We will be discussing the sources of revenue for any additional programs we suggest, because we will with every program we send suggest a source of revenue for it.

[21.] Q. Mr. President, your predecessor in office called himself a political moderate—said he believed in a middle-of-the-road approach. What do you call yourself politically and how do you define your political philosophy?

THE PRESIDENT. Well I don't call myself anything except a Democrat who's been elected President of the United States and I hope I am a responsible President. That's my intention.

[22.] Q. Mr. President, are there plans afoot now for Prime Minister Macmillan or President de Gaulle or any of the others to meet with you personally in the next few months?

THE PRESIDENT. I would not be able to answer that because any announcement on proposed visits should be timed with the countries that are involved and we have—we're not able to make that timing at this time.

[23.] Q. Mr. President, in connection with your references to a sound dollar, will you give us your ideas as to whether there is any danger of inflation?

THE PRESIDENT. There has been a steady inflationary rise in—throughout the history of the United States. I'm not able to make any judgment as to what would happen to the cost of living in the next 12 months.

We do have the problem—which is before us—of whether the only way we can prevent any increase in the cost of living is to have five and a half million people unemployed, and have only a limited—and have a substantial percentage of our capacity unused.

The question is whether we can maintain a reasonable balance between increase in purchasing power and the cost of doing business with full employment. That is the basic problem. I'm not satisfied to have the cost of living remain constant only by having the economy restrained.

What I was referring to is that we have no intention—two things: first, we have no intention of devaluing the dollar; secondly, we are concerned with price stability. And in all of the programs that we will put forward we will pay due care to the problem of preventing any stimulation of the economy resulting in an excessive increase in the cost of living.

[24.] Q. Mr. President, your budget—

your State of the Union Message to Congress was taken by some to mean a rather sharp criticism of President Eisenhower's military policy and judgment. Would you care to comment on that?

THE PRESIDENT. We are making an assessment of whether the plans we now have for the defense of the United States are matched by the military strength to implement those plans. That preliminary judgment will be finished by the end of February. It may result in some different budget requests and some different command decisions. But until the Secretary of Defense completes that analysis I would not attempt to make any criticisms or suggest that we are going to have to change the plans made by President Eisenhower.

But I do think that the situation grows more serious. The Chinese Communist strength increases. The intervention by the Communists in these critical areas which I mentioned has grown greater and therefore we have to consider whether in the light of this additional threat the strength we now have, not only our nuclear deterrent but also our capacity for limited war, is sufficient. It's not intended as a criticism of any previous action by any previous administration. It merely is an attempt to meet our own responsibilities at this time.

[25.] Q. Mr. President, when you say that your spending proposals by themselves do not unbalance the budget, can you tell us whether you plan to spend more than Mr. Eisenhower proposed spending in fiscal 1962, and if so, how much more?

THE PRESIDENT. I will send to the Congress when the Budget Bureau has completed its analysis our proposals, but they have not been completed as yet.

[26.] Q. Mr. President, Senator Pastore during hearings held yesterday and today on amending section 315 of the Communications Act, raised the question of whether an incoming presidential candidate would agree to debate a so-called outsider on television. And the present Attorney General in postelection remarks expressed some doubt that one who is already President would agree to debate with one who wants to be President. Could you help us clear the air on this, sir, and tell us whether if you're a candidate in 1964 you would agree to debate?

THE PRESIDENT. I would, yes.

[27.] Q. Mr. President, you described the agricultural problem as one of the most serious in our economy. And yet you didn't speak of it at any length in the State of the Union Message. Could you tell us what your present plans are for a new farm program?

THE PRESIDENT. Well, we are going to send to the Congress within the next 7 days, I believe, legislation on feed grains and we're going to send to the Congress within the month of February legislation on wheat. And we are also—we had, of course, the meeting in New York; we had the meeting organized by the Secretary of Agriculture of various farm groups and we had our task force report yesterday on cotton, feed grains, and wheat and I must say that the Secretary of Agriculture is working overtime.

These two matters—feed grains and wheat—we are going to move ahead right away. The situation in cotton is different.

[28.] Q. Mr. President, will you increase price supports?

THE PRESIDENT. I think we—I'd better wait until the Secretary of Agriculture sends the bill and we will then at that time announce what our decision will be on controls and also on what the dollar value will be of the price supports.

[29.] Q. Mr. President, can you explain

what our policy and purpose is in connection with the Portuguese liner *Santa Maria* and whether it goes beyond the safety of the passengers and whether you've had any notes from the Portuguese Government in connection with this?

THE PRESIDENT. Well, the Portuguese Government and the Ambassador, of course, have expressed their great interest in securing the control of the ship again. We've been concerned about the lives of the American passengers aboard. There are also other passengers aboard. We're concerned about their lives. We're also well aware of the interests of the Portuguese Government in securing control again of the ship and I'm hopeful that all these interests can be protected.

Now we have no information that the Portuguese Government has protested or threatened us with a withdrawal of our air rights in the Azores. I believe the Portuguese Government also has denied that, but they are most concerned about it and they've made their concern known to us.

[30.] Q. Mr. President, have you encountered any one particular problem in being the President that you had not anticipated?

THE PRESIDENT. Well, yes, I've—I think the problem of course is the difficulty in securing the clear response between decisions that we might make here which affect the security of the United States and having them effectively instrumented in the field under varying circumstances. It's easier to sit with a map and talk about what ought to be done than to see it done. But that's perhaps inevitable.

[31.] Q. The Germans are reported to be somewhat unhappy because in your State of the Union Message, in speaking of critical areas, you did not mention Berlin or Germany, and this afternoon when you were talking of critical areas you did not mention Berlin and Germany. Is there any significance to your omission? In other words, last fall you anticipated the possibility of some new crisis in Berlin and Germany in the spring. I'm wondering if there has been some change in the situation that has altered your assessment of it?

THE PRESIDENT. No, my view, and I think the United States Government's view, which is the same as the view expressed by the previous administration, remains constant. And it is very difficult to name every area. There is no change in our view on Berlin.

[32.] Q. Mr. President, there are six Americans who have been convicted to 30 years' imprisonment in Cuba, and there are five Americans who have been jailed for more than 6 years in China. Could you say what efforts the United States might possibly make on behalf—what new efforts the United States might make on behalf of the six in Cuba and the five in Communist China?

THE PRESIDENT. Well, we have asked—the Swiss Minister is representing our interest in regard to this trial. We've asked for complete information and we are going to attempt to, within the limits imposed by the nature of the regime in Cuba, to protect the interest of American citizens who are there.

Now, the previous administration on many occasions brought before the Chinese representative—in fact, there were many conversations in Geneva as well as in Warsaw, on the problem of the Americans who have been detained, some of them way back since 1951. This is a matter of continuing concern. And as long as those men are held, it will be extremely difficult to have any kind of normal relations with the Chinese Communists.

There are other matters which affect those

relations too. But this is certainly a point of the greatest possible concern.

Now, we have asked for a delay in the meetings which take place in Warsaw, between the United States representative and that of the Chinese Communists, from February to March, because they have become merely a matter of form and nothing of substance happened.

But I'm going to make it very clear that we are concerned about those men in China. The Americans who have been detained in Cuba, and all the circumstances around their arrest, that is a matter which the Swiss Minister is continuing to keep us informed.

[33.] Q. Mr. President, does your statement about the Warsaw talks mean that you propose to have some matters of substance taken up there in March when the talks are resumed, and can you tell us in general what sort of matters you would deal with?

THE PRESIDENT. No, it just meant that we had no business to discuss in the February meeting that made the talk at this time worthwhile.

[34.] Q. Mr. President, what sort of reaction have you had from the Latin American countries to the five-point program that you proposed, that you outlined in your State of the Union Message to help the Latin American countries, and could you be a little bit more specific about when you expect your food-for-peace mission to sort of go into action in Latin America?

THE PRESIDENT. Well, the food-for-peace mission will be leaving very—in the next few days. We have announced the appointment of Mr. Berle who's had long experience as head of that interdepartmental task force as an assistant to the Secretary. Mr. Berle headed the task force of ours during—between the election and January 20, and I'm very hopeful that under his leadership, of course with the Secretary and the Assistant Secretary, Mr. Mann, that we will be able to implement our commitments to Latin America.[1]

[35.] Q. You said in your State of the Union Message, sir, that you planned to accelerate the missile program. I wonder within that framework if you could say whether that includes the possibility of providing funds in fiscal 1962 to start production on the Nike-Zeus antimissile missile?

THE PRESIDENT. Well the Nike Zeus—there are, of course, funds which have been spent in research on the general area of antimissile missile—that is a matter which is now being considered by the Department of Defense and also by the President's Science Advisory Committee—as to whether the amount of money which we are devoting, which is considerable. Unfortunately, in all of these weapons systems the amounts of money that become involved get into the hundreds of millions and then billions, so very careful judgments have to be made. And the—as a matter of fact, I discussed that particular matter with Mr. Wiesner yesterday, so I can't give you a more precise answer than to say that we are considering it.

[36.] Q. Mr. President, in your State of the Union Message, you spoke of juvenile delinquency. There is growing concern expressed by parents, clergy, and J. Edgar Hoover about the effect on young people of crime and violence in movies and on the air, and the Senate committee is investigat-

ing this. Is there anything you can do about it, or may you ask for legislation?

THE PRESIDENT. I will have to wait, Mrs. Craig. We—as I said at the time in the State of the Union that we are considering what legislation could be enacted. Now when you get into movies, it's very limited—the amount of influence which the Federal Government can exert is quite limited, as you know—quite properly limited. But at least we are concerned with the general problem.

All the steps we take in urban renewal and housing also affect, of course, the kind of atmosphere, the kind of schools we have, the kind of housing we have, the kind of health conditions we have—all affect the atmosphere in which younger people grow up.

We are very much concerned with that area and we also have—are informed about what the Congress is doing. But this is a matter which goes to the responsibility of the private citizen. The Federal Government cannot protect the standards of young boys or girls—the parents have to do it, in the first place.

We can only play a very supplemental role and a marginal role. So that we can't put that problem on the—Mr. Hoover or on the White House or on the Congress. It rests with the families involved—with the parents involved. But we can do something about the living conditions and the atmosphere in which these children grow up, and we are going to do something about it.

[37.] Q. Mr. President, in your State of the Union Address you said, "I shall withhold from neither the Congress nor the people any fact or report past, present, or future which is necessary for a free and informed judgment of our conduct and hazards." Does this apply, sir, to the

---

[1] A White House release of February 8 announced the departure of George McGovern, Director, Food for Peace, accompanied by Arthur Schlesinger, Jr., for Argentina and Brazil on February 13. The release also stated that another mission headed by James Symington, Deputy Director, Food for Peace, and Stephen Raushenbush, a staff member, would leave at the same time for discussions in most of the Latin American countries.

Gaither report and will you make that available amongst other studies of a critical nature?

THE PRESIDENT. I've been reading the Gaither report. I think there are two matters involved. First, some of its provisions are quite dated and rest on assumptions which are no longer valid. Secondly, some portions of it do involve security information. So that we will make a judgment, I hope, shortly, whether overall it would be possible to release those parts of it which would not adversely affect the security of the United States and which would assist us at our present time.

That is really the question. Does the release of this and the material in it, of a report 3 years old, benefit our security position today and help the people make a judgment on it? And I would have to finish

the study of the Gaither report before we give you an answer on that.

[38.] Q. Mr. President, how soon do you expect to submit to Congress your slate of new ambassadors? I'm thinking of posts like London or Paris.

THE PRESIDENT. We are—have of course informed the countries involved and asked for their agreement, which is customary, and as soon as those agreements come back to us we will send the names to the Senate.

Q. Do you plan to do that singly or in a bloc?

THE PRESIDENT. As quickly as possible and if we can get the agreements back en bloc we'll send them en bloc.

Reporter: Thank you, Mr. President.

NOTE: President Kennedy's second news conference, broadcast over radio and television, was held in the State Department Auditorium at 4 o'clock on Wednesday afternoon, February 1, 1961.

16 Letter to the Secretary of the Navy and Statement by the President on the Launching of the U.S.S. Sam Houston. *February 2, 1961*

[Released February 2, 1961. Dated February 1, 1961]

Dear Secretary Connally:

I deeply regret that I am unable to be present for the launching of the *Sam Houston,* particularly since it honors a man whose courage I have always admired.

Would you please read for me the enclosed statement at the launching ceremony and deliver the plaque which I am sending to your office.

Sincerely,

JOHN F. KENNEDY

STATEMENT BY THE PRESIDENT

This historic occasion has double meaning. It signals our determination to strengthen our military tools—to demon-

strate to the world that our seapower, as are all elements of our national power, is a power for peace—a deterrent to any who would violate this eternal objective of God and man. It also allows us to do honor to a great American.

No Polaris submarine will be more appropriately named, for Sam Houston combined the moral courage to defend principle and the physical courage to defy danger. He was fiercely ambitious yet at the end he sacrificed for principle all that he had ever won or wanted. He was a Southerner, and yet he steadfastly maintained his loyalty to the Union. He was a slaveholder who defended the right of Northern ministers to petition

Congress against slavery; he was a heavy drinker who took the vow of temperance; he was an adopted son of the Cherokee Indians who won his first military honors fighting the Creeks; he was a Governor of Tennessee but a Senator from Texas. He was in turn magnanimous yet vindictive, affectionate yet cruel, eccentric yet self-conscious, faithful yet opportunistic. But Sam Houston's contradictions actually confirm his one basic, consistent quality: indomitable individualism, sometimes spectacular, sometimes crude, sometimes mysterious but always courageous.

The contradictions of Sam Houston are repeated in the paradox of the Polaris submarine. It is at once a devastating instrument of incredible destructive power, but at the same time it is conceived with but one purpose—to preserve the peace.

When Sam Houston left the United States Senate, he said, "I wish no prouder epitaph to mark the board or slab that may lie on my tomb than this: 'He loved his country, he was a patriot; he was devoted to the Union.'"

It is my feeling that it would be far more fitting that these words should be inscribed on board this living memorial than on any slab or tomb. Here they will serve not only as a fitting eulogy to a great American, but as an inspiration to the men who serve in this mighty ship.

I have, therefore, delivered to the Secretary of the Navy a plaque bearing this inscription which I request he have mounted in a suitable place on board.

17   Special Message to the Congress: Program for Economic Recovery and Growth. *February* 2, 1961

To the Congress of the United States:

I. OUR GOALS AND PROBLEMS

America has the human and material resources to meet the demands of national security and the obligations of world leadership while at the same time advancing well-being at home. But our nation has been falling further and further short of its economic capabilities. In the past seven years, our rate of growth has slowed down disturbingly. In the past 3½ years, the gap between what we can produce and what we do produce has threatened to become chronic. And in the past year, our economic problem has been aggravated by recession and by loss of gold. I shall shortly send to the Congress a separate message dealing with our international balance of payments and gold position.

The nation cannot—and will not—be satisfied with economic decline and slack. The United States cannot afford, in this time of national need and world crisis, to dissipate its opportunities for economic growth. We cannot expect to make good in a day or even a year the accumulated deficiencies of several years. But realistic aims for 1961 are to reverse the downtrend in our economy, to narrow the gap of unused potential, to abate the waste and misery of unemployment, and at the same time to maintain reasonable stability of the price level. For 1962 and 1963 our programs must aim at expanding American productive capacity at a rate that shows the world the vigor and vitality of a free economy. These are not merely fond hopes, they are realistic goals. We pledge and ask maximum effort for their attainment.

I am proposing today measures both to alleviate the distress arising from unsatisfactory performance of the economy and to stimulate economic recovery and growth. If economic developments in the first quarter of this year indicate that additional measures are needed, I will promptly propose such measures.

The Present Situation and Outlook.

The potential of the American economy is constantly expanding. The labor force is rising by 1.5 percent per year. Output per man rises annually by 2 percent as a result of new and better plant and equipment, modern technology, and improved human skills. These increases in manpower and productivity provide the base for a potential annual growth of 3.5 percent in the nation's total output. This is not high enough. Our potential growth rate can and should be increased. To do so, we propose to expand the nation's investments in physical and human resources, and in science and technology.

But in recent years the economy has not realized even its present possible growth. From the peak of the business cycle in the second quarter of 1953 to the top of the anemic recovery seven years later, gross national product grew only at an annual rate of 2.5 percent. The failure to use our full capacity is the urgent economic problem of the day.

In 1960, the American economy produced $503 billion of output when it was capable of producing at least $535 billion. In the fourth quarter of 1960, actual output could have been 8 percent higher than it was. More than a million and a half unemployed—over one-third of all unemployed—could have had jobs. Twenty billion dollars more personal income could have been

earned in 1960. Corporate profits could have been $5 billion higher. All this could have been accomplished with readily available manpower, materials and machines—without straining productive capacity and without igniting inflation.

The performance of the economy in 1960 was not only well below its full capacity; it also fell short of the modest levels expected by the previous Administration.

Adjusting all figures to the same statistical basis, the Budget projections last January were based on a 1960 national output of $513 billion. In October, output for the year was still expected to exceed $508 billion, implying a rate of at least $521 billion in the fourth quarter. The actual figure turned out to be $503 billion both for the year as a whole and for the last quarter.

Even when the recession ends and economic activity begins to expand again, the problem of unused potential will remain. Even if we were to achieve the $515 billion output projected for 1961 in connection with last month's Budget Message, the gap between potential and actual output would continue to grow and unemployment would hover between 6 and 7 percent of the labor force throughout the year. Under these circumstances, the expectation of minor improvements in business conditions during the next year provides no basis for complacency, no excuse for inaction. And—speaking out of realism, not pessimism—we cannot rule out the possibility of further deterioration if we fail to act.

An unbalanced economy does not produce a balanced budget. The Treasury's pocketbook suffers when the economy performs poorly. Lower incomes earned by households and corporations are reflected in lower Federal tax receipts. Assistance to unemployed workers and the costs of other measures for alleviation of economic distress are certain to rise as business declines. That is why recession—as our $12.4 billion deficit in the fiscal year 1959 recently reminded us—forces the budget into imbalance. That is why the prospect of surpluses in the Federal budgets for fiscal 1961 and fiscal 1962 is fading away.

General Fiscal Policy and the Budget.

The Federal Budget can and should be made an instrument of prosperity and stability, not a deterrent to recovery. This Administration is pledged to a Federal revenue system that balances the budget over the years of the economic cycle—yielding surpluses for debt retirement in times of high employment that more than offset the deficits which accompany—and indeed help overcome—low levels of economic activity in poor years.

If this economy were operating at full potential, the existing Federal revenue system would yield more than $90 billion in fiscal year 1962, instead of the $82.3 billion now estimated, producing a large budget surplus, and permitting retirement of national debt as well as the further development of Federal programs to meet urgent national needs. Debt retirement at high employment contributes to economic growth by releasing savings for productive investment by private enterprise and State and local governments.

The programs I am now proposing will not by themselves unbalance the budget which was earlier submitted, but are designed to fulfill our responsibility to alleviate distress and speed recovery—both through benefits directly available to needy persons and through desirable fiscal effects on the economy. They will sustain consumer spending and increase aggregate de-

mand now when the economy is slack. Many of these expenditures will automatically cease when high employment and production are restored.

Other measures contained in this message propose necessary uses of national economic capacity and tax revenue for our long-range growth, and are essential even in the absence of a recession. They are proposed because the country needs them, can afford them, and would indeed be poorer without them.

Agriculture.

Recession in agriculture has been chronic since the early Fifties. Falling farm income has been a drag on the industrial economy, while economic slack has restricted the job openings which might have eased the adjustment process in agriculture. The marginal or displaced farmer is most painfully aware of the interdependence of agriculture and industry. Restoration of the economy as a whole to satisfactory and rising levels of performance is an important prerequisite to restoring farm prices and income to their rightful levels. The American farmer should receive for his managerial skills, his labor, and his capital investment returns that are similar to those received for comparable human talents and resources in other types of enterprise. To this end the Administration will recommend further specific measures in a separate message on agriculture to be submitted to the Congress at an early date.

II. MEASURES FOR ECONOMIC RECOVERY

1. *Monetary Policy and Debt Management.*

Both full recovery and economic growth require expansion of expenditures for business plant and equipment, for State and local governmental facilities, and for residential construction. To increase the flow of credit for these purposes, long-term interest rates should decline. However, further declines in short-term interest rates, under present conditions, would lead to a further outflow of funds abroad, adding to the deficit in our balance of payments. That would be particularly unfortunate at the present time, just as falling rates abroad have been narrowing the gap between our rates and those of other leading countries.

In these circumstances, monetary policy and debt management must serve two apparently contradictory objectives: checking declines in the short-term rates that directly affect the balance of payments, and increasing the flow of credit into the capital markets at declining long-term rates of interest to promote domestic recovery. These two objectives can be achieved concurrently, but only with close cooperation among all governmental agencies concerned. As a result of measures already under way, there will be an increasing flow of funds at declining long-term rates to finance productive investment. Measures to strengthen this country's ability to hold and to attract internationally mobile liquid funds will be outlined in my subsequent message on the balance of payments.

The Treasury and the Federal Reserve System already are working together to further the complementary effectiveness of debt management and monetary policy. These tools will be strengthened not only for their present tasks but also for restricting inflationary demands on the economy whenever they recur.

2. *Housing and Community Development.*

During the 1960's, we must have the energy and vision to lay sound foundations for meeting the problems which will result from the steady growth of our urban areas

through the balance of this century. This task calls for new initiative and imagination in a great diversity of fields: in housing construction, in the maintenance and improvement of our vast existing stock of housing, in urban renewal, in the provision of essential community facilities, and many others. It calls for the revitalization of administrative machinery at the Federal, State and local levels. It calls for more comprehensive and more practical planning for urban and metropolitan areas. I shall shortly make specific recommendations to the Congress for action in this whole vital area.

Meanwhile, to make sure that general expansion of long-term credit is effective in stimulating residential construction, we have surveyed the range of administrative actions which can be taken promptly to help lower the cost of housing credit.

A reduction of mortgage interest rates is already overdue. Despite the easing of the general money market in the past year, the cost of mortgage credit still hangs just below its postwar peak. I have been assured that officers of many leading lending institutions share my view that present mortgage yields are unrealistic, and are prepared to cooperate in an effort to make mortgage money available at lower rates.

Consistent with this appraisal of the present situation, I have directed the Federal Housing Administration to reduce the maximum permissible interest rate on FHA-insured loans from 5¾ to 5½ percent. The resources of the Federal National Mortgage Association in the secondary mortgage market will help to give effect to this change in the rate. The FNMA stock subscription requirement applicable to sales of mortgages in the FNMA secondary market will be temporarily cut in half. I shall request the Federal Home Loan Bank Board to cooperate in advancing this effort to reach a more realistic level of mortgage lending rates.

What is good policy here for the private housing sector is also good policy for public construction activity. Under the program by which loans are made to local public bodies for the construction of public facilities, the Community Facilities Administration at my direction is reducing interest rates on new loans. This program will also be broadened to make eligible for loans many communities and certain types of public facility projects which are now excluded.

I have instructed the Housing and Home Finance Agency to hasten the initiation or completion of those approved projects in which a speed-up can be effected without waste. In examining new applications for assistance, HHFA will give priority of attention to projects which are fully planned and ready for construction, and to projects located in areas of chronic unemployment. Under the college housing program, available funds will be committed more rapidly than hitherto planned, and efforts will be made to move forward the starting date for previously approved projects.

The Federal Government will do everything in its ability at all administrative levels to quicken the pace of urban renewal work. Given this assurance, mayors and other local officials can by energetic leadership accelerate projects under way or about to begin. I have today telegraphed the mayors of 297 cities to urge that they review their urban renewal projects to find ways of hastening the completion of these vital civic improvements.

3. *Temporary Unemployment Insurance Extension.*

The number of persons out of work and seeking employment has been rising since the early summer of 1960 and has reached

serious proportions in these rigorous winter months. In January 5.4 million persons were unemployed, more than 1.3 million have been continuously out of work for fifteen weeks or longer, 600,000 for six months or more. In addition, workers involuntarily confined to part-time work numbered 1.7 million, a rise of 200,000 over December.

We have long since decided as a nation that we will not turn our backs upon workers and their families undergoing the hardships of unemployment. Furthermore, we know all too well that the loss of income of the unemployed inevitably depresses consumer spending, threatening to deepen the recession and delay recovery. The flow of wage and salary payments, measured at an annual rate, has fallen by $4 billion from August to December.

Our unemployment insurance system serves to mitigate, in some degree, the hardships of displaced employees and helps to strengthen the economy against the forces of contraction. The total number of persons drawing benefits under that system has risen sharply since the middle of 1960, and in mid-January stood at 3.4 million, 1 million higher than a year ago. Although average benefits amount to only $34 per week, total payments are estimated to have been $430 million in January, compared to $264 million in January a year ago. The number of persons exhausting unemployment benefits has also increased. About 500,000 persons who have exhausted their benefits are still unemployed. During the first six months of 1961, nearly 1½ million more persons will use up their unemployment benefits before finding jobs.

In these urgent circumstances, I shall ask the Congress to enact a temporary program for extending the duration of benefits. Under agreements voluntarily entered into between the states and the Federal Government, additional weeks of benefits would be authorized from Federal funds, during the twelve months following enactment, to persons who have exhausted regular benefits since October 31, 1960, and are still unemployed. These extended benefits would equal one-half—up to a maximum of 13 weeks—of the duration provided by the State. The duration of the benefits would be subject to an over-all maximum, State and Federal, of 39 weeks. Where the State law already provides benefits for longer than 26 weeks, the Federal Government would pay, for the period of the emergency, for all weeks of benefits beyond 26, up to a maximum of 39, thus freeing state funds for much-needed increases in benefit amounts. The amount thus going into increased income and purchasing power will be advanced from general revenues and later repaid in full from increased insurance contributions obtained by raising the taxable payroll maximum per employee from $3,000 to $4,800 annually. This increase will maintain the self-supporting basis of the system and enhance its capacity to meet future emergencies.

Our permanent Federal-State unemployment insurance system, which has become an institution essential to the efficient functioning of our labor markets as well as a strong defense against economic contraction, is in need of permanent reform. As I said in 1958, I believe it would be a tragic mistake to embark on a Federal supplementation program geared to the present emergency without also strengthening the underlying system. A mere stop-gap approach ignores the role our permanent unemployment insurance system was intended to play, and establishes instead a precedent for falling back on temporary remedies whenever the system is really needed. The standards of the system have proven inade-

quate to deal with the recession problem.

This time, we must establish a permanent unemployment compensation system which can do the job it was intended to do. A program of federal legislation designed to revise and strengthen the benefit and financing provisions of the system will therefore be recommended to the Congress by the end of March.

4. *Expansion of United States Employment Service.*

I am directing the Secretary of Labor to take necessary steps to provide better service for unemployment insurance claimants and other job applicants registered with the United States Employment Service. This will require expanded counseling and placement services for workers or job-seekers (a) in depressed areas; (b) in rural areas of chronic underemployment; (c) displaced by automation and technological change in factories and on farms; (d) in upper age brackets; and (e) recent graduates from college and high school.

5. *Aid to Dependent Children of the Unemployed.*

Under the Aid to Dependent Children program, needy children are eligible for assistance if their fathers are deceased, disabled, or family deserters. In logic and humanity, a child should also be eligible for assistance if his father is a needy unemployed worker—for example, a person who has exhausted unemployment benefits and is not receiving adequate local assistance. Too many fathers, unable to support their families, have resorted to real or pretended desertion to qualify their children for help. Many other fathers are prevented by conscience and love of family from taking this route, thereby disqualifying their children under present law.

46

I recommend that the Congress enact an interim amendment to the Aid to Dependent Children program to include the children of the needy unemployed. Temporary action is recommended pending completion of a study of a permanent program to aid needy children and certain other groups now excluded from the Federal-State public assistance programs.

6. *Distressed Area Redevelopment Program.*

The Congress is considering legislation designed to reinforce the efforts of areas of heavy chronic unemployment to improve their economic climate. Although State and local governments, as well as private agencies, have been helpful in many instances, the distressed areas constitute a national problem that is properly the concern of the Federal Government.

The subject has been studied by standing and special committees of the Congress, by individual states, by groups of states, and by private study groups. There is general agreement that we should enact legislation providing the means for loans for private projects, technical assistance, loans and grants for public facilities, and programs for training and retraining workers. I urge that any area development program be flexible enough to benefit urban and rural areas alike and to apply to regions of economic distress which include parts of two or more states.

The immediate subsistence needs of the people of these economically depressed areas must be met, but it is equally important that these areas be enabled to acquire the basic facilities, physical plant, and trained labor force necessary to secure their share of the nation's economic expansion.

I have already advised the Congress of my interest in such legislation by letters sent to the Vice President and the Speaker of the House of Representatives last week. I urge that area redevelopment legislation be enacted without delay.

7. *Distribution of Surplus Food.*

We are committed to expanding the variety and quantity of surplus foods distributed to persons who, in a nation of unparalleled agricultural bounty, lack adequate diets.

(a) The first Executive Order issued in this Administration directed the Secretary of Agriculture to "take immediate steps to expand and improve the government program of distributing surplus food to needy families."

(b) Further, I have instructed the Secretary of Agriculture, consistent with the bill enacted by the Congress last year authorizing establishment of pilot Food-Stamp programs, to proceed as rapidly as possible to establish pilot programs for needy families in localities in West Virginia, Pennsylvania, Eastern Kentucky, Northern Minnesota, Southern Illinois and the Detroit area. It is my hope that this pilot program, while providing additional nutrition to those now in need, will pave the way for substantial improvement in our present method of distributing surplus food.

(c) I have also asked the Secretary of Agriculture to make recommendations to improve and strengthen our school lunch program, to make the best possible nutrition available to every school-child, regardless of the economic condition of his family or local school district.

8. *Improvements in the Old-Age, Survivors, and Disability Insurance Program.*

The current softness of the economy underscores the inadequacy of social security benefits in relation to the needs of many present beneficiaries. The average retired

47

worker's benefit is only $74 a month. A majority of these beneficiaries have no other significant income. The basic principle of our social insurance system is undermined when a substantial number of retired individuals must seek public assistance or else subsist below minimum standards of health and comfort. We must not permit the benefits of retired workers and their families to lag behind rises in living costs; we cannot decently exclude our older population from the general advances in standards of living enjoyed by employed workers.

I recommend that Congress enact five improvements in benefits, to become effective April 1. All are clearly justified in equity and decency. They will increase benefit payments for between four and five million people in the next twelve months. Besides meeting pressing social needs, the additional flow of purchasing power will be a desirable economic stimulus at the present time. Early enactment will serve this end.

The Old-Age, Survivors, and Disability Insurance program is financed on a sound actuarial basis, with insurance contributions adjusted to scheduled benefit payments. The benefit improvements I am proposing can be covered by additions of ¼ of 1 percent each to the employer's and employee's contributions, beginning at the next scheduled increase in contributions on January 1, 1963.

The five proposals are:

(1) Raise the minimum monthly benefit for the retired worker from $33 per month to $43 per month, increasing benefits for more than 2,200,000 people in the first 12 months. We wish it could be raised higher—but surely we cannot continue benefits at such an inconscionably low minimum.

(2) Improve retirement protection by paying actuarially reduced benefits to men beginning at age 62. Present law does not permit a man to become eligible for optional retirement benefits before age 65 although such benefits are available to women at age 62 on an actuarially reduced basis. Provision for paying reduced benefits to men beginning at age 62 would make benefits available to older unemployed workers at comparatively little additional program cost. The plight of the older unemployed man is particularly serious in areas of chronic unemployment. However, the difficulties older workers find in reentering the labor market after losing their jobs or after periods of illness exist in all parts of the country. Frequently, as persons approach age 65 they find it difficult to compete in their accustomed occupations because of physical incapacity which may not however have progressed to the point of total disability. Provision for actuarially reduced benefits at age 62 to men as well as women will provide income for 600,000 people, some of whom would otherwise have to turn to public assistance for support.

(3) Provide Benefits for 170,000 Additional People by Liberalizing the Insured-Status Requirement. At present a person can receive benefits only if before retirement he was employed in jobs covered by the social security program for one out of every three quarters after 1950. The proposal is to reduce the required coverage to one quarter out of every four. This is only fair to our present generation of older people, as it brings their eligibility requirement into line with the one that present law contemplates for future generations, i.e., ten years of coverage out of a working life of about forty years.

(4) Increase the Aged Widow's Benefit from 75% to 85% of her Husband's Benefit Amount, raising benefits for 1,550,000

widows. There is no justification either in equity or in the facts of family consumption for this size gap in the level of widows' benefits.

(5) Broaden disability insurance protection. The social security program should provide disability insurance benefits for insured workers and their families after the workers have been totally disabled for 6 months. Under present law, disability benefits are available only if the disabled worker's condition is expected to result in death or to last for a long and indefinite period. The proposed change provides benefits in the first 12 months for 85,000 people (totally disabled workers and their dependents) many of whom otherwise have to resort to public assistance. Since it would no longer be necessary to determine that the disabled person is unlikely to recover, the change removes an important barrier to rehabilitation. It also speeds up determinations of disability. While the change has these desirable effects, it would in no sense be an innovation. Similar provisions are contained in many private insurance contracts and other disability programs.

9. *Early Payment of Veterans Life Insurance Dividends.*

I have asked the Veterans Administration to advance the payment of the 1961 dividend of $258 million on National Service Life Insurance and U.S. Government Life Insurance policies. This payment would normally be distributed throughout the year. Substantial amounts should begin to reach veterans of World War I and II within the next thirty to sixty days—the period of slump—when they are most needed and will do the most good. If sound insurance practices justify it, as I hope further study will show, an additional dividend will be paid

this year from the substantial funds that have been accumulated.

10. *Minimum Wage Increase and Expanded Coverage.*

I urge the Congress to raise the minimum wage immediately to $1.15 and to $1.25 within two years. This will improve the incomes, level of living, morale, and efficiency of many of our lowest-paid workers, and provide incentives for their more productive utilization. This can actually increase productivity and hold down unit costs, with no adverse affects on our competition in world markets and our balance of payments. More than four-fifths of those commodities affected by either export or import trends are produced by industries which would not be significantly affected by a moderate increase in the minimum wage. The proposed new coverage is basically in retail trade and services, which are not affected by shifts in international trade. Moreover, experience with previous minimum wage increases indicates little effect on prices. In the four years following the 1956 increase in the minimum wage, the index of all wholesale prices increased 6.6 percent, whereas the prices charged for commodities produced in low-wage industries showed negligible change.

Coverage should be extended to several million workers not now covered. This will extend the wage standard throughout significant low-wage sectors of the labor market. It will require the payment of a minimum starting at $1.00 for the workers newly included, and a gradual increase to the general $1.25 minimum.

Together, these two principal changes in the Fair Labor Standards Act will go far to protect our lowest paid workers. The proposed minimum rates have been carefully set at levels which will benefit substantial numbers of underpaid workers, but not so high as to prevent ready adjustment to the new standards.

11. *Accelerating Procurement and Construction.*

(a) I have directed the heads of the Departments and agencies to carry out an immediate review of their procurement and construction plans through the end of the current fiscal year with a view to expediting such procurement and construction wherever possible, giving priority to actions which will have an early effect on unemployment. The steps they are taking will be reported to me by March 1.

(b) I have directed the Cabinet and agency heads to submit by February 17 inventories of (1) going public works projects which can be speeded up quickly, but for which additional appropriations might be needed, (2) needed natural resource conservation and development, light construction, maintenance, repair, and other work which likewise can be speeded up or started quickly, and (3) any additional construction or other projects which could be initiated at an early date.

I have instructed the Director of the Bureau of the Budget, in consultation with the Chairman of the Council of Economic Advisers, to work with the agencies in carrying out these directives. They will assemble and appraise the project inventories with a view to determining which projects may be suitable for early initiation or acceleration as part of the recovery program.

Excellent possibilities include programs to improve the roads, recreational facilities, and forests in the Project Work Inventories of the Forest Service, the National Park Service, and the Bureau of Land Management. A particularly high priority will be assigned to projects located in areas of labor surplus.

(c) I have today instructed the Secretary of Commerce to make available to the States immediately the entire balance of Federal-aid highway funds scheduled for this fiscal year. This acceleration of the availability of $724 million is a first step in speeding up the highway program and getting more projects under construction and more men at work this year.

The Secretary will urge the States to place under contract as soon as possible all those projects which are currently in the final stages of planning.

In addition, I have asked the Secretary of Commerce to recommend to me, as part of the inventory of approved construction projects, called for earlier in this message, means of increasing the flow of Federal highway funds into actual new construction if economic conditions require such action.

12. *Government Procurement in Labor Surplus Areas.*

A principal purpose of the proposed Area Redevelopment Act is to create new jobs in chronic labor surplus areas by bringing in new private industries. It would be anomalous for the Government to urge these locations on private industry while ignoring these areas in the location of its own activities. Agencies of the Federal Government, in locating new facilities or deciding upon the use of existing facilities, are directed to give every reasonable preference to labor surplus areas.

And I have today sent a directive to the Secretary of Defense, the Secretary of Labor, and the General Services Administration requesting prompt steps to improve the machinery by which Federal contracts can be channeled to firms located in labor surplus areas.

III. PROMOTION OF ECONOMIC GROWTH AND
PRICE STABILITY

I have emphasized that the solution to our economic problem requires a program that goes well beyond anti-recession measures, important as these are to the relief of distress and the reversal of economic decline. Equally important are measures for the longer pull to restore our economy to its full potential and to accelerate economic growth. Fortunately, the measures to overcome recession, to take up the slack, and to speed growth all reinforce each other.

Today, most industries have the facilities to produce well above current levels. They lack only customers. As a nation, we lose not only $30 to $40 billion of production per year. We also lose the vital incentives which capacity operation gives for expansion and modernization of plant and equipment. The measures I have proposed to reduce unemployment and stimulate markets will help to restore these incentives for economic growth.

1. *Special Tax Incentives to Investment.*

Expansion and modernization of the nation's productive plant is essential to accelerate economic growth and to improve the international competitive position of American industry. Embodying modern research and technology in new facilities will advance productivity, reduce costs, and market new products. Moreover, an early stimulus to business investment will promote recovery and increase employment.

Among the reforms of the Federal tax system which I expect to propose at a later date is a modification of the income tax laws to provide additional incentives for investment in plant and equipment. To avoid a net revenue loss, I will also recommend measures to remove several unwarranted special tax benefits, and to improve tax compliance and administration. It should be possible to reform the tax system to stimulate economic growth, without reducing revenues and without violating the basic principles of fairness in taxation.

2. *Investment in Human Resources.*

Another fundamental ingredient of a program to accelerate long-run economic growth is vigorous improvement in the quality of the Nation's human resources. Modern machines and advanced technology are not enough, unless they are used by a labor force that is educated, skilled and in good health. This is one important reason why, in the legislative programs that I will submit in the days to come, I will emphasize so strongly programs to raise the productivity of our growing population, by strengthening education, health, research and training activities.

3. *Investment in Natural Resources.*

The economic growth of the United States has been favored by an abundant supply of natural resources of almost every sort. But resource needs and supplies are not static. As our needs mount, as past reserves are depleted, and as technological requirements change, we must constantly develop new supplies if growth is not to be inhibited.

Exhaustion of low-cost domestic mineral deposits is a growing problem which calls for technological advance and new national long-range minerals policy.

Our water resources programs, including flood control, irrigation, navigation, watershed development, water pollution control— and above all, water desalinization—require priority attention. In addition, we need to develop sound and uniform standards for sharing costs between Federal, State, and local governments.

Improvement of our forest resources will

51

require expanded Government credit sources for the development of woodland properties, more research on forest management, additional funds for cooperative forest programs, acceleration of the national forest program, and improvement of grazing resources.

Also essential to economic growth are long-range energy resource development and accelerated programs for economical production of energy from nuclear sources, including nuclear fusion. We must begin now also to plan for regional cooperative pooling of electrical power. Both efficiency and growth goals will be served if we interconnect our hydroelectric and thermal power resource plants.

4. *Productivity and Price Stability.*

Rapid technological change is resulting in serious employment dislocations, which deny us the full stimulus to growth which advancing technology makes possible. Labor and industry have demonstrated cooperative initiative in working out solutions in specific plants and industries. Government action is also necessary, not only to maintain an environment favorable to economic growth, but also to deal with special problems in communities and industries suffering from economic dislocations and to help those who through unemployment are bearing an unfair share of the burden of technological change.

I have dealt with some of these problems elsewhere in this message, in connection with unemployment insurance, aid to depressed areas, and efforts to broaden the services of the United States Employment Service.

Government can help further by encouraging labor and management to find ways to smooth the adjustment to technological change and thus to maintain and re-enforce the favorable attitude toward economic

progress that characterizes American business and labor alike. Accordingly, I shall issue an executive order establishing the President's Advisory Committee on Labor-Management Policy, with members drawn from labor, management, and the public. The Committee is directed to advise the President with respect to actions that may be taken by labor, management, and the public which will promote free and responsible collective bargaining, industrial peace, sound wage policies, sound price policies and stability, a higher standard of living, increased productivity, and America's competitive position in world markets. It will consider national manpower needs and the special benefits and problems created by automation and other technological advances. I look to the Committee to make an important contribution to labor-management relations and an understanding of their importance to the stability of prices and the health of the economy.

The course of the American price level depends in substantial measure on wage and price decisions of labor and management. This dependence grows in importance as the economy moves toward full employment. All of us must now be conscious of the need for policies that enable American goods to compete successfully with foreign goods. We cannot afford unsound wage and price movements which push up costs, weaken our international competitive position, restrict job opportunities, and jeopardize the health of our domestic economy.

Price stability will also be aided by the adoption of a tax incentive plan mentioned earlier, which will encourage a higher rate of business investment in improved plants and equipment.

Price increases for many products and services have occurred because these industries have lagged behind in the march of productivity and technological advance. Indeed, in the present economic situation, a stepping-up of productivity improvement throughout the economy would contribute to the achievement of price stability.

We must not as a nation come to accept the proposition that reasonable price stability can be achieved only by tolerating a slack economy, chronic unemployment, and a creeping rate of growth.

Neither will we seek to buy short-run economic gains by paying the price of excessive increases in the cost of living. Always a cruel tax upon the weak, inflation is now the certain road to a balance of payments crisis and the disruption of the international economy of the Western World.

Inflation has no single cause. There have been times in the postwar period when prices rose sharply in response to a rate of total spending in excess of our capacity to produce. The government will not contribute to this process, and we shall use the powerful tools of fiscal and monetary policy to arrest any such movement if it should threaten in the year ahead. Some price increases, particularly among the consumer services, have been caused by the failure of productive resources to move promptly in response to basic shifts in the pattern of demand. We shall seek means to encourage the movement of manpower and capital into sectors of expanding demand.

CONCLUSION

I have sought in this message to propose a program to restore momentum to the American economy. I have recommended measures designed to set us firmly on the road to full recovery and sustained growth. But if these measures prove to be inadequate to the task, I shall submit further proposals to the Congress within the next 75 days. We will do what needs to be done to fulfill the high promise of the American economy.

JOHN F. KENNEDY

18   Remarks on Greeting Representatives of the Baptist World Alliance at the White House. *February* 2, 1961

I WANT TO EXPRESS my great appreciation for you coming here today and I am most impressed in hearing the litany of places—Japan, Korea, the Congo.

It is a wonderful thing, what you are doing. Some of you will be away for 5 years. You have a great tradition in your denomination of freedom and you can't have religious freedom without political freedom. The people of this country are strongly behind you and any help that we can give should be made known.

As I said in the State of the Union Message—one of the great ironies is that the Communists have been able to secure great devotion to their program and too often our people are identified with a devotion to material things. You are helping to change this.

19 Statement by the President Following a Conference With Secretary Ribicoff on Cuban Refugee Problems. *February 3, 1961*

I HAVE CONFERRED with Secretary Abraham Ribicoff concerning the Secretary's on-the-spot investigation made at my direction on the problems of Cuban refugees in southern Florida.

Secretary Ribicoff paid tribute to the refugees as a proud and resourceful people, whose courage and fortitude in the face of tragic disruption of their lives is magnificent.

At the same time he reported that many of the refugees are now in serious need. They are living in extremely crowded quarters. Their resources have been exhausted or greatly depleted. Health and educational facilities are badly overtaxed.

Secretary Ribicoff praised the exceptional efforts of voluntary welfare agencies, and State and local officials, to cope with the problems which have been created by the influx of refugees from oppression in their homeland. But he emphasized that the increasing number of refugees, and the personal circumstances of many of them, had become more onerous than private and local agencies could any longer bear alone.

The Secretary said that immigration authorities estimated there are already 66,000 Cubans in this country, with at least 32,000 in the Miami area. To meet their minimal needs, the personal resources of many of the refugees have been exhausted and the available resources of voluntary and local authorities badly overstrained.

As a result of the conference this afternoon, I have directed Secretary Ribicoff to take the following actions on behalf of the United States Government:

1. Provide all possible assistance to voluntary relief agencies in providing daily necessities for many of the refugees, for resettling as many of them as possible, and for securing jobs for them.

2. Obtain the assistance of both private and governmental agencies to provide useful employment opportunities for displaced Cubans, consistent with the overall employment situation prevailing in Florida.

3. Provide supplemental funds for the resettlement of refugees in other areas, including transportation and adjustment costs to the new communities and for their eventual return to Miami for repatriation to their homeland as soon as that is again possible.

4. Furnish financial assistance to meet basic maintenance requirements of needy Cuban refugee families in the Miami area as required in communities of resettlement, administered through Federal, State and local channels and based on standards used in the community involved.

5. Provide for essential health services through the financial assistance program supplemented by child health, public health services, and other arrangements as needed.

6. Furnish Federal assistance for local public school operating costs related to the unforeseen impact of Cuban refugee children on local teaching facilities.

7. Initiate needed measures to augment training and educational opportunities for Cuban refugees, including physicians, teachers, and those with other professional backgrounds.

8. Provide financial aid for the care and protection of unaccompanied children—the most defenseless and troubled group among the refugee population.

9. Undertake a surplus food distribution program to be administered by the county welfare department, with surplus foods distributed by public and voluntary agencies to needy refugees.

I hope that these measures will be understood as an immediate expression of the firm desire of the people of the United States to be of tangible assistance to the refugees until such time as better circumstances enable them to return to their permanent homes in health, in confidence, and with unimpaired pride.

I am particularly interested in Secretary Ribicoff's proposal to make effective use of the faculty of the University of Havana, three-fourths of which are reported to be in south Florida at the present time. I have asked Secretary Ribicoff to examine how this community of scholars could be most effectively used to keep alive the cultural and liberal traditions for which this faculty has been justly noted. It represents a great inter-American asset, for their own people,

for this country and for the entire hemisphere. I have asked the Secretary to report by March 1st on how these great intellectual abilities can be most effectively employed.

I also want to commend Secretary Ribicoff for the constructive, humanitarian and immediate program proposed to assist the Cuban refugees. He said that he hoped that it would be considered first and foremost an essential humanitarian act by this country. But he also wanted it to indicate the resolve of this nation to help those in need who stand with the United States for personal freedom and against Communist penetration of the Western Hemisphere.

I have consulted with Budget Director David E. Bell on means for financing these interim measures, which are expected to cost about 4 million dollars through the remainder of this fiscal year.

NOTE: Secretary Ribicoff's report on effective use of the faculty of the University of Havana, in the form of a letter to the President dated March 14, was released by the White House on March 17. See the President's letter of that date, Item 86.

20 Telegram to the Mayors of U.S. Cities Urging Increased Urban Renewal Activity. *February 3, 1961*

[Released February 3, 1961. Dated February 2, 1961]

OUR EFFORTS to improve the employment situation can be helped considerably by increased urban renewal activity. Just as in the case of your city, there are many projects now underway or whose final plans have been approved in many cities that can be speeded up creating additional jobs immediately. I have directed the Housing and Home Finance Agency officials in Washington and in regional offices to eliminate all delay and to cooperate with local authorities in beginning construction of these projects at the earliest possible time and in maintain-

ing steady efforts to complete them. Your city's rebuilding program can be accelerated and at the same time jobs can be provided to help meet our nation's unemployment problem. I urge you to do everything within your ability to eliminate delay and I promise you the full cooperation of the Federal Government to this end.

JOHN F. KENNEDY

NOTE: The White House release of the text of this telegram also lists the names of the 297 mayors to whom it was sent.

21 Exchange of Greetings With Dr. Walter Hallstein, President of the European Economic Community. *February 4, 1961*

[Released February 4, 1961. Dated February 2, 1961]

Dear Dr. Hallstein:

I deeply appreciate the kind expression of good wishes extended on behalf of yourself and the Commission of the European Economic Community.

It is my sincere hope that the years to come will see further steady progress toward the goals envisaged by the Treaty of Rome, an objective to which the United States will continue to lend its steadfast support.

The Government of the United States looks forward to close collaboration with the Commission of the EEC, and to the development of relationships between the European Economic Community and the United States, as well as other countries, which will redound to the benefit of the entire free world.

JOHN F. KENNEDY

[The Honorable Dr. Walter Hallstein, President of the Commission of the European Economic Community, Brussels, Belgium]

NOTE: Dr. Hallstein's message, dated January 20, 1961, follows:

The President
The White House

On occasion of your assumption of office may I on my own behalf and on that of the Commission of the European Economic Community convey our warmest good wishes for the challenging years that lie ahead and for your success in tackling the manifold tasks that face us all. For our part, we look forward to a continuing, ever more fruitful friendship between the United States and the European Community.

WALTER HALLSTEIN

22 Letter to the President of the Senate and to the Speaker of the House Transmitting Bills Extending Unemployment Benefits and Providing Aid to Needy Children. *February 6, 1961*

My dear Mr. ————:

I am transmitting herewith two bills: (1) To establish a temporary program for the payment of additional unemployment compensation to workers who have exhausted their State benefits; and (2) To authorize Federal financial participation for a temporary period in State aid to needy children of unemployed parents. I recommended such legislation on February 2 as a part of this administration's program for economic recovery and growth.

The need for prompt enactment of this legislation is clear.

In January, 5.4 million workers were without jobs. About 3.4 million were receiving unemployment compensation, and about one-half million who had already exhausted their unemployment compensation were still unemployed.

Unemployment compensation provides unemployed workers with necessary purchasing power. When this compensation is exhausted the purchasing power ceases. This has a serious impact not only on the worker and his family, but on the economic health of the entire economy. The costs and effects of mass unemployment arising from a national recession clearly reach across State lines. The problem is national in scope, and the Federal Government has the responsibility for taking action as soon as possible to meet it. That is why I propose this temporary program as a first step. The extension of the unemployment compensation program will permit 3 million workers to receive benefits totalling about $950 million.

There is also a pressing need for improving our public assistance. Pending completion of a study of a permanent program in this area, we should take action to help the States provide assistance to children whose need results from the unemployment of their parents. In some cases, the unemployment benefits of these parents have been exhausted; in others, such benefits are not payable or are not sufficient to meet the needs of the large family. Therefore, as part of a national temporary program dealing with the problems of the unemployed, some assistance for the children of needy unemployed workers should be provided.

The enclosed letters from the Secretary of Labor and the Secretary of Health, Education, and Welfare describe the legislation in more detail.

Sincerely,

JOHN F. KENNEDY

NOTE: This is the text of identical letters addressed to the Honorable Lyndon B. Johnson, President of the Senate, and to the Honorable Sam Rayburn, Speaker of the House of Representatives.

The Temporary Extended Unemployment Compensation Act of 1961 (Public Law 87-6, 75 Stat. 8) was approved on March 24, 1961 (see Item 93). An amendment to the Social Security Act authorizing Federal financial participation in aid to dependent children of unemployed parents (Public Law 87-31, 75 Stat. 75), was approved on May 8, 1961.

Secretary Goldberg's letter of February 3 and Secretary Ribicoff's letter of February 4, together with the draft bills, were released with the President's letter.

23 Special Message to the Congress on Gold and the Balance of Payments Deficit. *February 6, 1961*

To the Congress of the United States:

The gold outflow of the past three years has dramatically focused world attention on a fundamental change that has been occurring in the economic position of the United States. Our balance of payments—the accounting which shows the result of all of our trade and financial relations with the outside world—has become one of the key factors in our national economic life. Mainly because that balance of payments has been in deficit we have lost gold.

This loss of gold is naturally important to us, but it also concerns the whole free world. For we are the principal banker of the free world and any potential weakness in our dollar spells trouble, not only for us but also for our friends and allies who rely on the dollar to finance a substantial portion of their trade. We must therefore manage our balance of payments in accordance with our responsibilities. This means that the United States must in the decades ahead, much more than at any time in the past, take its balance of payments into account when formulating its economic policies and conducting its economic affairs.

Economic progress at home is still the first requirement for economic strength abroad. Accordingly, the first requirement for restoring balance in our international payments is to take all possible steps to insure the effective performance of our own economic system—to improve our technology, lower our production and marketing costs, and devise new and superior products, under conditions of price stability. The real wealth of a nation resides in its farms and factories and the people who man them. A dynamic economy producing goods competitively priced in world markets will maintain the strength of the dollar.

Thanks to our international reserves we have time, if we use it wisely, in which to strengthen our domestic economy and make it fully competitive with that of other nations. Our situation is one that justifies concern but not panic or alarm.

In my message on February 2, I dealt with the measures for reviving our domestic economy. The steps I now propose will strengthen our dollar position and insure that our gold reserves are employed effectively to facilitate the commerce of the free nations and to protect the stability of their currencies. Because these steps supplement the policies for strengthening our domestic economy, and because we can take them calmly and deliberately, they are not for that reason any less important or less urgent. Those that are within the present authority of the Executive will be the subject of vigorous action. Where action by the Congress is required I urge early consideration and approval.

For the past decade our international transactions have resulted in a deficit—payments that were in excess of receipts—in every year except that of the Suez crisis, 1957. The surplus of our exports over our imports, while substantial, has not been large enough to cover our expenditures for United States military establishments abroad, for capital invested abroad by private American businesses and for government economic assistance and loan programs. All of these outlays are essential. Our military establishments in foreign countries protect the national security. Private investment promotes world economic growth and trade and, through the return of profits to our country, will strengthen our balance of payments in future years. Our economic assistance programs, much the smallest of

these three items in its effect on payments balance, is vital in the continuing struggle against tyranny and oppression, and the poverty on which they feed.

Over the period 1951 to 1957 the deficit in our balance of payments averaged about $1.0 billion annually. These did not result in a net outflow of gold from the United States; foreign monetary authorities, banks and private individuals held these earnings as dollars or claims on dollars. Thus our gold reserves were $22.8 billions at the end of 1950 and $22.9 at the end of 1957. But during these years the dollar holdings by foreign countries increased from $8.4 billion at the end of 1950 to almost $15 billion at the end of 1957.

These earlier deficits in our balance of payments were, in fact, favorable in their world effect. They helped to restore foreign monetary systems by enabling foreign countries to earn the dollars which they needed to rebuild their international reserves. They made it possible for the industralized countries of Western Europe to restore the convertibility of their currencies, thus freeing world trade and payments from exchange control. This was of benefit to the export trade of the United States. However, this growth in foreign dollar holdings placed upon the United States a special responsibility—that of maintaining the dollar as the principal reserve currency of the free world. This required that the dollar be considered by many countries to be as good as gold. It is our responsibility to sustain this confidence.

In 1958 and 1959 the deficit in our balance of payments sharply increased—to $3.5 billion in 1958 and to $3.8 billion in 1959. This came about mainly because of lagging exports and rising imports. There was no significant increase in our outlays for military expenditures, private investment or government economic assistance. However in these years, unlike the period 1951–57, the deficit resulted in large transfers of gold to foreign accounts as well as a further increase in foreign dollar holdings. For the two years together, 1958 and 1959, gold transfers to foreign accounts were $3.0 billion while foreign dollar holdings by foreign countries increased by another $4.3 billion. These gold transfers did not make the underlying balance of payments fundamentally worse. They did reflect a decision by foreigners to take more of their earnings in gold and to hold less in dollars.

Last year, 1960, the surplus of our exports of goods and services over our imports increased from $2.2 billion in 1959 to $5.8 billion. This was caused, principally, by an increase—amounting to more than $3 billion—in our exports. This once more reduced what may be called our basic deficit—it was only about $1.5 billion for the year. However, during 1960 there was a large movement abroad of short-term capital. Favorable interest rates abroad, a high rate of growth and good investment prospects in Europe and some speculative fears concerning the future value of the dollar all played a part. It is estimated that this outward flow of short-term funds was between $2 and $2.5 billion, and this was the crucial factor in raising the over-all deficit to $3.8 billion. Of this, $1.7 billion were transferred in the form of gold and $2.1 billion took the form of increased foreign dollar holdings.

An outward movement of short-term funds such as that which occurred in 1960 should not be considered a part of the basic deficit. Such movements are quickly reversible in response to changes in interest rates and other business factors here and abroad. Moreover, insofar as short-term funds transferred to foreign financial centers consist of U.S.-owned capital, they create United States claims against the recipient country. In the new era of convertible currencies upon which we have entered, we may expect that short-term money will continue to flow back and forth. I have requested the Secretary of State and the Secretary of the Treasury to work for still closer cooperation between the monetary and financial authorities of the industrialized free nations with a view toward avoiding excessive short-term money flows which could be upsetting to the orderly development of international trade and payments.

In sum our basic deficit of $1.5 billions is of manageable proportions. And it is this basic deficit which affects the real strength of our currency. But the time has come to end this deficit. It must be ended by responsible, determined and constructive measures.

There are other factors which lend basic support to our monetary and financial position. Our gold reserve now stands at $17.5 billion. This is more than 1½ times foreign official dollar holdings and more than 90% of all foreign dollar holdings. It is some ⅖ of the gold stock of the entire free world.

Of this $17.5 billion, gold reserves not committed against either currency or deposits account for nearly $6 billion. The remaining $11.5 billion are held under existing regulations as a reserve against Federal Reserve currency and deposits. But these, too, can be freed to sustain the value of the dollar; and I have pledged that the full strength of our total gold stocks and other international reserves stands behind the value of the dollar for use if needed.

In addition, the United States has a quota in the International Monetary Fund of $4.1 billion. This can be drawn upon if necessary and our access to the Fund's resources must be regarded as part of our international reserves.

Finally beyond its liquid international reserves, the government and citizens of the United States hold large assets abroad. Western European countries whose currencies are now strong owe us long-term governmental debts of $2.9 billion. Our private short-term assets abroad now are estimated at $4½ billion. Our long-term private investments in foreign countries—including both plants owned directly by American companies and securities of foreign business and governments owned by Americans—total over $44 billion, exceeding foreign investments in the U.S. economy by some $28 billion. In any reckoning of international assets and liabilities, the United States has a strong solvent position.

In short, powerful resources stand behind the dollar. Our gold and monetary reserves are large; so are the physical and monetary assets we hold throughout the world. And, in the years ahead, if the program I previously outlined is pursued, the dollar will have the added strength of the reviving power of the American economy itself.

Certain firm conclusions follow:

1. The United States official dollar price of gold can and will be maintained at $35 an ounce. Exchange controls over trade and investment will not be invoked. Our national security and economic assistance programs will be carried forward. Those who fear weakness in the dollar will find their fears unfounded. Those who hope for speculative reasons for an increase in the price of gold will find their hopes in vain.

2. We must now gain control of our balance of payments position so that we can achieve over-all equilibrium in our international payments. This means that any sustained future outflow of dollars into the monetary reserves of other countries should come about only as the result of considered judgments as to the appropriate needs for dollar reserves.

3. In seeking over-all equilibrium we must place maximum emphasis on expanding our exports. Our costs and prices must therefore be kept low; and the government must play a more vigorous part in helping to enlarge foreign markets for American goods and services.

4. A return to protectionism is not a solution. Such a course would provoke retaliation; and the balance of trade, which is now substantially in our favor, could be turned against us with disastrous effects to the dollar.

5. The flow of resources from the industrialized countries to the developing countries must be increased. In all that we do to strengthen our balance of payments, we must be especially mindful that the less developed countries remain in a weak financial position. Help from the industrialized countries is more important than ever; we cannot strengthen our balance of payments at the expense of the developing countries without incurring even greater dangers to our national security.

6. The United States must take the lead in harmonizing the financial and economic policies for growth and stability of those industrialized nations of the world whose economic behavior significantly influences the course of the world economy and the trend of international payments.

To carry forward these policies I propose a program for action, which may be divided into two parts. The first part describes those measures which will improve domestic monetary arrangements and strengthen international cooperation in economic and monetary policy. These measures will help us better to meet short-term demands on reserves such as those of recent years. The measures in the second group are designed to correct the persisting basic deficit in our balance of payments.

I. MEASURES TO EASE THE SHORT-TERM DEMAND PROBLEM

1. *Measures to Improve International Monetary Institutions.*

Increasing international monetary reserves will be required to support the ever-growing volume of trade, services and capital movements among the countries of the free world. Until now the free nations have relied upon increased gold production and continued growth in holdings of dollars and pounds sterling. In the future, it may not always be desirable or appropriate to rely entirely on these sources. We must now, in cooperation with other lending countries, begin to consider ways in which international monetary institutions—especially the International Monetary Fund—can be strengthened and more effectively utilized, both in furnishing needed increases in reserves, and in providing the flexibility required to support a healthy and growing world economy. I am therefore directing that studies to this end be initiated promptly by the Secretary of the Treasury.

2. *Use of United States Drawing Rights in the International Monetary Fund.*

The United States has never made use of its drawing rights under the International Monetary Fund to meet deficits in its balance of payments. If and when appropriate, these rights should and will be exercised within the framework of Fund policies. The United States will also support continued efforts in the Fund to facilitate draw-

ings by other members in the currencies of industrialized countries whose payments positions are in surplus and whose reserves are large. This will help to reduce the burden now borne by the dollar.

3. *Special Interest Rates for Dollar Holdings by Foreign Governments and Monetary Authorities.*

(a) The Federal Reserve Act should now be amended to permit the Federal Reserve System to establish separate maxima for rates of interest paid by member banks on time and savings deposits held in this country by foreign governments or monetary authorities (Section 19, paragraph 14). This authority, when exercised, would enable American banks to make a maximum competitive effort to attract and hold dollar balances which might otherwise be converted into gold. At the same time domestic rates, when desirable for reasons of domestic policy, could be held at a lower level. I will shortly send to the Congress a draft of the needed legislation.

(b) I have directed the Secretary of the Treasury to use, whenever it appears desirable, the authority already extended to him by the Second Liberty Bond Act to issue securities, at special rates of interest, for subscription and holding exclusively by foreign governments or monetary authorities. The exercise of this authority could provide an additional inducement to hold foreign official balances in dollars.

(c) As a final means of holding or attracting foreign dollars, the Congress should enact a measure designed to unify the tax treatment accorded the earning assets of foreign central banks. At present, income derived by foreign central banks of issue from bankers acceptances and bank deposits is exempt from tax under section 861 of the

Code. Income from United States Government securities, however, is taxable to foreign central banks in the absence of applicable tax treaty provisions or a special ruling exempting a particular bank from taxation under particular circumstances. Suggested legislation will shortly be forthcoming.

4. *Prohibition on Holding of Gold Abroad by Americans.*

The recent Executive Order forbidding the holding of gold abroad by Americans will be maintained. It was fully justified on grounds of equity. It will also help to prevent speculation in the gold market. I am directing the Secretary of the Treasury to keep me advised on steps being taken for effective enforcement. I place everyone on notice that those few American citizens who are tempted to speculate against the dollar will not profit in this manner.

II. MEASURES TO CORRECT THE BASIC PAY-
MENTS DEFICIT AND ACHIEVE LONGER-TERM
EQUILIBRIUM

1. *Action by the Senate to Approve the Organization for Economic Cooperation and Development.*

I earnestly request early action by the Senate approving United States membership in the Organization for Economic Cooperation and Development. The OECD, in which the industrialized countries of Western Europe, the United States and Canada will be joined, is of vital importance for assisting, on a cooperative basis, the developing countries of the free world. It will also provide a solid framework within which we can carry out intensive and frequent international consultations on the financial and monetary policies which must be pursued in order to achieve and maintain better balance in the international payments position.

2. *Export Promotion.*

The Department of Commerce will provide energetic leadership to American industry in a drive to develop export markets. Firms and industries will be encouraged to step up their efforts to develop exports and given every assistance in doing so. As American industry comes to realize the vital role of export earnings for our foreign policy, I have little doubt of its response.

We will promptly increase our commercial representatives and facilities abroad. This is a joint program of the Departments of Commerce and State which must proceed with drive and conviction in order to produce effective results. The budget which has already gone to Congress requests $1,250,000 for the State Department to add 41 Foreign Service Commercial Attaches overseas, together with 48 experienced foreign nationals and supporting American staff.

The new budget requests will also allow an increase in overseas commercial facilities. The Commerce Department is doubling its Trade Mission program from 11 to 18 per year and will provide more useful information to our overseas posts. I am ordering rapid completion of our two new foreign trade centers at London and Bangkok and have requested the departments to explore whether three more could be added next year in Africa, Latin America and Europe.

3. *Cost and Price Stabilization.*

Our export promotion efforts, no matter how well devised or energetically pursued, will not be effective unless American goods are competitively priced. Our domestic policies—of government, of business and of labor—must be directed to maintaining competitive costs, improving productivity and stabilizing or where possible lowering prices.

Measures to achieve these ends which are important for the domestic economy are even more vital for our international competitive position. I have already stated my intention of creating an Advisory Committee on Labor and Management Policy to encourage productivity gains, advance automation and encourage sound wage policies and price stability.

4. *Export Guarantees and Financing.*

Our Export-Import Bank must play an increasingly important role in our export promotion efforts. Last year the Export-Import Bank announced a widening of the facilities which it offers for extending credit to American exporters. Despite the improvements made, these facilities are not yet adequate, nor are they comparable to those offered by foreign countries, especially those offered to small and medium-sized exporting concerns and those offered for the financing of consumer goods. I am directing the President of the Export-Import Bank, by April 1, to prepare and submit to the Secretary of the Treasury, as Chairman of the National Advisory Council on International Monetary and Financial Problems, a new program under the Export-Import Bank to place our exporters on a basis of full equality with their competitors in other countries. Also, I have asked the Secretary of the Treasury to initiate and submit by the same date a study of methods through which private financial institutions can participate more broadly in providing export credit facilities.

5. *Foreign Travel to the United States.*

Foreign travel to the United States constitutes a large potential market hitherto virtually untapped. American travelers annually spend some $2 billion in foreign countries. Foreign travelers only spend about $1 billion in this country. Economic conditions in many foreign countries have improved to the point where a strong travel promotion effort by this country can be expected to yield significant results. The Department of Commerce, in cooperation with the Departments of State and Treasury, will announce shortly a major new program to encourage foreign travel in the United States along the lines envisaged in S. 3102, introduced by Senator Magnuson at the last session of the Congress. This program will include the establishment of travel offices abroad; new advertising campaigns; action to simplify our visa and entry procedures for temporary visitors; and efforts to relax foreign restrictions on travel to the United States. The program will be energetically administered in the Department of Commerce. I am asking the Secretary of Commerce to report in full on plans and prospects by April 1.

6. *Agricultural Exports.*

Our agricultural industry, which is of unparalleled efficiency, must make its full contribution to our payments balance. I am directing the Secretary of Agriculture to report on all feasible and internationally desirable means of expanding our exports of farm products, and to emphasize the need for export expansion as a primary objective of our new farm programs.

7. *Policy on Economic Assistance.*

Our foreign economic assistance programs are now being administered in such a way as to place primary emphasis on the procurement of American goods. This assistance, accompanied as it is by the export of American products, does not therefore have a significantly adverse effect on our balance of payments. (Not more than 20% of the funds expended for economic grants, development loan assistance, technical assistance and contributions to international organizations, which amounted to $2.6 billion in 1960, is today available for expenditures outside the United States, and we intend to keep an even closer review of these items.) These restrictions will be maintained until reasonable over-all equilibrium has been achieved. Then the United States will discuss with other capital-exporting countries the desirability of instituting common policies for world-wide procurement in the administration of economic development or assistance programs.

8. *Tariffs, Restrictions and Discriminations Against American Exports.*

Quota discriminations against American exports have largely disappeared with the return of currency convertibility. We will press for prompt removal of the few restrictions that still exist, as well as for the maximum liberalization of remaining non-discriminatory quotas in other industrialized countries, which apply mainly to agricultural exports. In the tariff negotiations now going forward under GATT we shall seek the fullest possible measure of tariff reduction by foreign countries to the benefit of our exports.

9. *Promotion of Foreign Investment in the United States.*

We shall press those Western European countries with strong reserve positions to eliminate the restrictions they still maintain limiting the opportunities for their citizens to invest in the United States and other foreign countries. Also, we are initiating, through the Department of Commerce, a new program to bring investment opportunities in the United States to the attention of foreign investors in the industrialized countries.

10. *Abuse of "tax havens." Taxation of American Investment Abroad.*

I shall recommend that the Congress enact legislation to prevent the abuse of foreign "tax havens" by American capital abroad as a means of tax avoidance. In addition, I have asked the Secretary of the Treasury to report by April 1 on whether present tax laws may be stimulating in undue amounts the flow of American capital to the industrial countries abroad through special preferential treatment, and to report further on what remedial action may be required. But we shall not penalize legitimate private investment abroad, which will strengthen our trade and currency in future years.

11. *Foreign Assistance Contribution to the Less Developed Countries and the Common Defense.*

It is indispensable that the industrialized countries of the free world join in undertaking systematic budgetary contributions for economic assistance to the less developed countries and the common defense. These contributions should be fully commensurate with their economic and financial positions. Some countries are fulfilling this responsibility; it is a matter of disappointment that others have not yet undertaken to do so. Such actions are important in the short run to achieve a better balance in international trade and payments. Even more important, they are essential to the continuing and effective discharge of our common responsibilities for free world security, economic growth and stability.

12. *Reduction of Customs Exemption for Returning American Travelers.*

After World War II, as part of our efforts to relieve the dollar shortage which then plagued the world, Congress provided for two additional increases of $300 and $100 in the duty-free allowance for returning travelers, for a total of $500. The primary purpose for this change having vanished, I am recommending legislation to withdraw this stimulus to American spending abroad and return to the historic basic duty-free allowance of $100.

13. *Centralized Review of Dollar Outlays.*

Through the Bureau of the Budget, it has long been our sound financial practice to centralize the review of total spending of the Departments and Agencies of the Government of the United States, including their spending abroad. Under present circumstances, foreign outlays must be examined in a new perspective. Accordingly, I am instructing the Director of the Bureau of the Budget, in consultation with the Secretary of the Treasury, to develop special procedures for analyzing that part of the requests of departments and agencies for spending authority which will involve overseas outlays to insure that our budgetary decisions will be taken with full understanding of their projected impact on the country's balance of payments.

14. *U.S. Military Expenditures Abroad.*

National security expenditures abroad constitute one of the largest items in the outflow of dollars, amounting to about $3.0 billion a year. We must maintain a fully effective military force wherever necessary and for as long as needed. While it is clear that we must exercise maximum prudence in our dollar outlays abroad, it has become clear that the present limitation on dependents was not the best way to accomplish this savings, and that this limitation was seriously hurting morale and recruitment in the armed forces. At the same time, the Secretary of Defense has informed me that equivalent dollar savings could be made through other measures, including limitations on expenditures abroad by military personnel for tourism and the purchase of durable consumer goods. Accordingly I have directed him to rescind the limitation on dependents and instead to put these measures into effect immediately.

I have also asked him to review the possibilities for savings in the logistic support of our forces, including the combined use of facilities with our allies. We shall also, where appropriate, urge the purchase of the newer weapons and weapons systems by those of our allies who are financially capable of doing so. We shall continue the policy inaugurated last November of emphasizing United States procurement for our military forces abroad wherever practicable, even though some increased budgetary cost may be incurred. Since foreign procurement of this nature has amounted to almost $1 billion a year, significant savings in dollar outflow can be expected—and I am asking the Secretary of Defense to report on these and the other savings by no later than April 1st, to see if further steps are needed then.

CONCLUSION

These measures, combined with increasing confidence in the dollar abroad and steady economic growth at home, can cure the basic long-term deficit in our balance of payments and check the outflow of gold. They symbolize a new dimension of this nation's foreign and domestic economic policies—a new area of difficult problems—but they are problems which can be met by forceful and timely legislative and executive action.

JOHN F. KENNEDY

24 Letter to the President of the Senate and to the Speaker of the House Transmitting a Minimum Wage Bill. *February 7, 1961*

[Released February 7, 1961. Dated February 6, 1961]

My dear Mr. ————:

I am transmitting herewith a draft of a bill to extend the coverage of the Fair Labor Standards Act and to increase the minimum wage. This bill provides needed improvements in the Fair Labor Standards Act, and I urge its prompt consideration. It is designed to carry out a recommendation contained in my message on February 2 to the Congress.

The bill would bring within its protection 4³⁄₁₀ million additional workers and would increase the minimum hourly rate of those already protected by the act to $1.25. This will be done by a series of annual adjustments which have been carefully set at levels to which employers can readily adjust.

Our nation can ill afford to tolerate the growth of an under-privileged and underpaid class. Substandard wages lead necessarily to substandard living conditions, hardship and distress. Since the last increase in the minimum wage both living costs and productivity have increased to such an extent that the proposed bill merely reflects an adjustment to keep pace with these factors.

I am also enclosing the letter I received from the Secretary of Labor commenting briefly upon the provisions in the draft bill.

Sincerely,

JOHN F. KENNEDY

NOTE: This is the text of identical letters addressed to the Honorable Lyndon B. Johnson, President of the Senate, and to the Honorable Sam Rayburn, Speaker of the House of Representatives.

The Fair Labor Standards Act amendments (Public Law 87-30, 75 Stat. 65) was approved May 5, 1961 (see Item 169).

The text of Secretary Goldberg's letter of February 6 and the draft bill, released with the President's letter, are published in the Congressional Record (vol. 107, Feb. 7, 1961, p. 1729).

25 The President's News Conference of *February 8, 1961*

THE PRESIDENT. Good morning. I have several brief announcements.

[1.] One, I would like to announce that I have invited the Prime Minister of Canada, the Right Honorable John G. Diefenbaker, to make a brief visit to Washington, on Monday, February 20, for discussion of matters of mutual interest to our two countries. I particularly am glad he is coming. We will hold a luncheon in his honor at the White House. I think it is most important that harmonious relations exist between two old friends, and therefore I am glad to have this chance to visit with the Prime Minister.

[2.] Secondly, I do want to say a word or two about NATO. This is our central and most important defensive alliance, but in the larger sense it is much more. The members of NATO must be leaders also in and out of NATO itself, in such great causes as the integration of Europe and the cooperative development of new nations. We for our part mean to go on as full and energetic partners in NATO, and in particular we wish to maintain our military strength in Europe. Secretary Rusk is making an especially careful study of our policy in this great organization and I am delighted to say that he will have the help not only of Ambassador Finletter, but of an advisory group under the direction of one of the true founders of NATO, a distinguished former Secretary of State, Mr. Dean Acheson.

[3.] Three, with the approval of Secretary Ribicoff, I am directing the Surgeon General to organize and establish within the Public Health Service a Child Health Center, to deal with the special health problems of children. This is a matter of particular interest to me. Some 400,000 babies are born each year with congenital malformations. I don't think as a country, nationally, and as a matter of fact I don't think probably privately we have done enough on research into the causes of mental retardation. And while a good deal of effort is being expended in this country for the care of these children, I do think it is most important that we devote special effort in the coming months and years to research in the causes of it. I am therefore delighted that we are going to proceed ahead with Governor Ribicoff's strong support.

Thank you.

[4.] Q. Mr. President, in the past 24 hours there has arisen a somewhat hard to understand situation concerning the missile gap. An official of your administration, who was identified in some newspapers this morning as Secretary McNamara, has been quoted as saying that the missile gap which was expected and talked about so much did not exist, nor did he see prospects of it. Your press secretary, yesterday afternoon, denied this story. Now, I wonder if you can set the record clear, if you can tell us your version of what Secretary McNamara said, and what your feelings are about the missile gap. Does it exist, and how and where does it exist?

THE PRESIDENT. My only conversation with Mr. McNamara was not at any off-the-record meeting, if such a meeting took place, but was in a conversation which I had with him yesterday afternoon after the reports appeared.

Mr. McNamara stated that no study had been concluded in the Defense Department which would lead to any conclusion at this time as to whether there is a missile gap or not. In addition, I talked this morning to Mr. Hitch, who is the Comptroller of the Defense Department, who has been given the responsibility by the Secretary of Defense to conduct a review of our strategic weapons in the same way that Mr. Nitze is conducting a review of our tactical weapons. Mr. Hitch informed me that no study has been completed on this matter. He hoped to have a preliminary study completed by February 20th, but he did tell me quite specifically that as of today he is not prepared to make a judgment as to our capacity in strategic weapons.

There are many complicated problems involved. We have the realization that the United States will not strike first, and, therefore, we have to consider what will be available to the United States if an attack took place upon us, not only in missiles, but also in the other arms of our arsenal, SAC, the Navy, Polaris, and all the rest.

So I think in answer to your question, the study has not been completed. It has not come, therefore, across my desk. There will be a study of how the budget for fiscal 1961 and 1962 should be changed in view of our strategic position, but that study will not be completed by either Mr. Nitze or Mr. Hitch, or come across Mr. McNamara's desk to be passed to me, for some days.

Q. Well, sir, during the campaign you seemed to feel very strongly that a serious missile gap did exist then. Do you now feel as strongly?

THE PRESIDENT. Well, what I hope to do is to wait until the Defense Department who I have given this responsibility to, Mr. McNamara, and he has passed the responsibility to members of his department—I hope that we will have a clearer answer to that question. Of course, it is my hope that the United States is fully secure. I will be pleased if that is the result. If it isn't, I think it is important that we know about it, and I will say that we will then—I will then take on the responsibility of passing on to the Congress this collective judgment as to our position and what needs to be done.

So that without getting into the discussion of these stories this morning, I do want to say that it is my information that these studies are not complete, and therefore it would be premature to reach a judgment as to whether there is a gap or not a gap.

[5.] Q. Mr. President, could you tell us what you think about the wisdom—the idea of these background news briefings where governmental officials do not identify themselves as distinguished from this type of wide-open news conference?

THE PRESIDENT. Well, they are hazardous in many cases—[*laughter*]—and I think our Mr. McNamara might agree with that now. On the other hand, I will say that they are important, too. I'd hope it would be possible to work out some satisfactory system where reporters who are charged with cov-

ering matters which are particularly complicated, where they would have a chance to discuss with the responsible official on a background basis so that their stories would be more accurate. I believe there have been such conversations in this administration already and they have been, I think, useful. This one, evidently a controversy has arisen from it, but I hope that it will be possible for the responsible officials and the reporters who are particularly concerned with that area, to work out ground rules so that they could be continued.

[6.] Q. Mr. President, in keeping with your statement about NATO, could you tell us how you would look upon a heads of government meeting of the NATO Council in the near future?

THE PRESIDENT. Well, I would not be able to give you a response to that. There is a planned meeting I believe at Oslo, of the foreign ministers, in May. I have seen newspaper reports that it might be turned into a heads of state meeting. But I must say that there has been no judgment reached; I think it is fair to say that the matter is not as yet under consideration.

[7.] Q. Mr. President, you said during one of your recent messages that this Nation was rapidly approaching its hour of maximum danger or peril—I forget the exact words. Some people have suggested that perhaps you were painting the picture blacker than it is for shock purposes. Could you perhaps spell out for us this morning what you have in mind, and whether you really sincerely feel that we are approaching this peril as you said?

THE PRESIDENT. I sincerely believe what I said in my State of the Union Address about our position in the world. I hold this office for the next 4 years, and I believe that the next 4 years will be years in which this country and its capacity to maintain its position and security will be strongly tested. I think that anyone who looks at the globe and looks at the increasing power of the Communist bloc, the belligerency which marks the bloc, particularly the Chinese Communists, I would say would come to the conclusion that we are going to be severely tested in the next 4 years.

[8.] Q. Mr. President, 3 months ago a Federal court in New Orleans ordered two public schools there desegregated. Since then, what is apparently an organized campaign of intimidation has kept most white children out of those schools and effectively frustrated the court order.

During the campaign you spoke of using your moral authority as President in the civil rights field. Can you tell us what you plan to say or do to help the New Orleans families who evidently want to obey the Constitution but are afraid to do so?

THE PRESIDENT. I will—at such time as I think it is most useful and most effective, I will attempt to use the moral authority or position of influence of the Presidency in New Orleans and in other places. I want to make sure that whatever I do or say does have some beneficial effect and, therefore, it is a matter which we are considering.

Q. But you do not have anything to say specifically about New Orleans today or about what has happened there—for example, last week the man who had tried to send his children to school and then in fear left town?

THE PRESIDENT. We are going to—I will comment. As far as New Orleans goes, it is my position that all students should be given the opportunity to attend public schools regardless of their race, and that is in accordance with the Constitution. It is in accordance, in my opinion, with the judgment of the people of the United States. So there is no question about that.

Now specifically, what we could most usefully do in order to provide an implementation of the court decision in New Orleans, that is a matter which we are carefully considering. On the general question, there is no doubt in my view: students should be permitted to attend schools in accordance with court decisions. The broader question of course is, regardless of the court decisions I believe strongly that every American should have an opportunity to have maximum development of his talents, under the most beneficial circumstances, and that is what the Constitution provides. That is what I strongly believe.

On the question specifically of what we can usefully do in New Orleans in order to provide a more harmonious acquiescence with the court decision, I would feel that we could perhaps most usefully wait until we have concluded our analysis of it.

[9.] Q. Mr. President, the Congress has spent a good deal of time investigating regulatory agencies and Executive interference in them. Now, your assistant, Mr. Landis, has suggested that a White House office be set up to oversee these agencies. Do you feel this might lead to the same kind of Executive interference that the Congress has been investigating?

THE PRESIDENT. Mr. Landis recommended such a White House office in his study. I have asked Mr. Landis to come to the White House, not to fill such an office, of course, which is not established, but merely to work with the White House and with the interested members of Congress who are concerned about improving our regulatory procedures.

He is going to stay some months and do that. I conferred yesterday with Congressman Harris, who has a special responsibility as Chairman of the House Committee on Interstate and Foreign Commerce, and we are going to continue to work together to try to speed up the procedures of the regulatory agencies and improve their actions.

Whether we should have such a White House liaison or center is a matter which we are going to consider. The Congress bears special responsibility for these agencies, and, therefore, I think it is probably not likely that major responsibility in this area would be released to the White House, and I am not completely sure it is wise.

[10.] Q. Sir, this question is a bit on the personal side. You have available to you at the Catoctin Mountains in Maryland a very fine weekend retreat that has been used by former Presidents. Sir, do you plan to use it and if so, do you plan to rename it back to Shangri-La? And also I believe you have two Government yachts at your disposal. Do you plan to use them, too, sir?

THE PRESIDENT. I am not going to use the yachts at the present time. [*Laughter*] I don't plan to use Camp David very often. Now, I will keep—I think the name should be kept Camp David. But I doubt if I will go there very often. On the question of the yachts, we will have to wait and see what the situation is. I believe we have the *Barbara Anne,* and I am not familiar with the other yacht.

[11.] Q. Mr. President, there is a report from Australia this morning, quoting an American scientist as saying that we will have a man in space within 6 weeks. I wonder if you have ordered an acceleration of our space program, or if you consider it for psychological or other reasons that we are in a race with the Russians to get a man into space?

THE PRESIDENT. No, in the first place, I don't know anything about that report. We are very concerned that we do not put a man in space in order to gain some addi-

tional prestige and have a man take disproportionate risk, so we are going to be extremely careful in our work and even if we should come in second in putting a man in space, I will still be satisfied if when we finally do put a man in space his chances of survival are as high as I think that they must be.

[12.] Q. Mr. President, it has been rather reliably reported that you and some of your staff members and Cabinet members were quite active on the Hill by phone and otherwise in the recent rules fight. Could you give us your views as to what your activity and that of your Cabinet members and staff members will be in the coming legislative year, as far as getting your program going?

THE PRESIDENT. We have a liaison officer, Mr. O'Brien, and he has Mr. Wilson who is liaison for the House and Mr. Manatos who is liaison for the Senate, and we will attempt to keep close contact between the White House and the House and the Senate in order to give our program the best possible chance that it has to pass. So we will keep very close contact with the Hill, and I hope that they will be harmonious.

[13.] Q. You said in the past that the release of the two fliers recently helped in our relations with the Soviet Union. Would you care to outline for us, sir, any developments you might hope to take place prior to any possible future summit meeting with Mr. Khrushchev?

THE PRESIDENT. Well, I said that it removed a serious obstacle to harmonious relations with the Soviet Union, the release of the fliers. Mr. Thompson arrives back this week, and I am going to meet with Mr. Thompson on several occasions this week— on Saturday morning with Mr. Thompson, Mr. Bohlen, and Mr. Kennan—to help chart our future relations with the Soviet Union.

There are some things that I think could usefully be done, and must be done if our relations are going to continue to be fruitful. We are concerned, as I am sure they are, with the situation in Laos. We are concerned with the situation in the Congo, as I am sure they are, and I am hopeful that we can make our position clear to them, and accomplish some useful result.

[14.] Q. Mr. President, the Mexican Americans are very concerned because you have not named one of them to a high place in your administration. They say that they are the only ethnic group that worked for you nationally, in the "Viva Kennedy" clubs and GI forums, that has not been recognized. I wonder if you plan to give them some recognition?

THE PRESIDENT. Well, we have, I think, Dr. Garcia, from the State of Texas, who I believe has gone with Ambassador Whitney to Jamaica this weekend. We did offer a position of responsibility to an American of Mexican extraction who was unable to accept it, but it was a position of high responsibility.

I quite agree with you that we ought to use what I consider to be a great reservoir of talent, and I think this is particularly true in our relations with Latin America. So I will just say to you that it is a matter of interest and that we will continue to see if we can provide for—if we can associate them with our administration more closely.

[15.] Q. Mr. President, last weekend the Russians launched a 7-ton satellite in orbit which they said was a test of a new rocket. This has led to worldwide speculation that there might have been a man aboard. What do we know about this Russian rocket and about the recent rumored Russian attempts to launch a man into space?

THE PRESIDENT. Well, I have no information about—that there was a man involved. We have no evidence that there was a man in the rocket. We have, of course, some information, a good deal of which has appeared in the press, about the rocket. And it is a large one and it may be part of their experiments leading up to placing a man in space. But at least as of now we have no evidence that there is a man in there. But I am sure that they will continue these experiments leading up to placing one there.

[16.] Q. Mr. President, in your message to Congress on the gold problem, there was one passage in there in which you referred to interest rates on foreign funds which had a sentence that might lead to the presumption that perhaps you had in mind submitting legislation which would give you a little more authority over domestic interest rates in other fields. Is this a reasonable conclusion? Do you have any intention to expand the authority of the Presidency with respect to domestic interest rates?

THE PRESIDENT. No. As you—we have had consultations with the Federal Reserve Board about what action should be taken to provide that the interest rate on short-term securities would not come down while the interest rate—which does affect the gold flow—while the interest rate on long-term securities remains high, which does adversely affect the economy.

But what, of course, we are interested in is to see the short-term rates remain high enough to protect our gold, while the long-term rates be reduced somewhat in order to stimulate the economy. But this is a matter under the control, of course, directly, of the Federal Reserve Board, with the Treasury having, of course, a direct interest in it.

But it is not intended, to answer your question, that we would propose any legislation or any Executive orders which would increase our control directly over long-term rates.

[17.] Q. Mr. President, in regard to NATO, have you looked into the problem or the recommendation of the previous administration that NATO be given its own nuclear weapons, or will this be left up to the Acheson group, and when will that group be expected to report?

THE PRESIDENT. Well, that was one of the matters, of course, which General Norstad briefly discussed. It is a matter now which is being reviewed by Ambassador Finletter with the aid of Mr. Acheson. That is one of the, I would say, central matters of interest to us now, and both of these men will be working on it.

Q. When will that group report to you, approximately?

THE PRESIDENT. I haven't got a time on it, but I think we ought to move with some speed in it.

[18.] Q. Mr. President, the States now can set their own safety and regulatory standards for atomic industrial development within their own borders. Critics of this do-it-yourself provision believe that it increases the danger of nuclear accidents and favor complete Federal control within these areas. Would you give us your views on it?

THE PRESIDENT. Well, I will have to look into it. I am not informed about it.

[19.] Q. Sir, in all the discussions about the gold problem, there keeps coming back West Germany doing more of its share in aiding underdeveloped areas and taking on more commitments in the common defense. Is your administration making representations either through the Treasury Department or through our Ambassador to get the Germans to do more in these fields?

THE PRESIDENT. Yes.

Q. Could you elaborate on it, sir?

THE PRESIDENT. Well, I think that the proposals that have been made, of course, in our opinion do not meet the problem or the opportunity, and I am hopeful that we can work out a more satisfactory arrangement with the West Germans.

Mr. von Brentano is going to be in the United States, the Foreign Minister, in the month of February. I do hope to see him. In addition, we are considering other methods which could put these negotiations on perhaps a more—a higher level.

Q. Just to follow that up, sir, could you spell out what you mean by "higher level"? Are you finding that you are running into problems with them because of their upcoming election?

THE PRESIDENT. Well, they have a good many responsibilities and problems of their own. In addition to whatever they do in relation to us they have other responsibilities to the French and the British. So in fairness, I must say the matter is not wholly easy for the Germans. However, it is a matter of great importance and I therefore think it might be useful to provide that these discussions should take place on a higher level than they have in the past.

[20.] Q. Mr. President, you spoke during the campaign about the need of getting things moving again. I wonder if you could tell us how well you think you have succeeded so far in creating a new mood in Washington?

THE PRESIDENT. As far as the domestic economy or as far as generally?

Q. Putting some urgency into it.

THE PRESIDENT. Well, I think we have talented people in our Washington group who are giving it a great deal of time and attention. And therefore I am hopeful—

though we have been in office only 2½ weeks—I am hopeful that before the snow is off the ground that we will have been able to stimulate action in a variety of areas.

[21.] Q. Mr. President, in your State of the Union Address, you remarked that morality in private business has not been sufficiently spurred by morality in public business. In the light of the economy-sized malpractice revealed by—carried on by some of the American leading corporations, would you care to comment on this situation and the impact of such private business morality or immorality on the community itself?

THE PRESIDENT. Well, having participated in the investigation of improper practices in the labor-management field for 2 or 3 years, and having had a good deal of public attention given to it, I am hopeful that the Department of Justice, the Antitrust Division which was very effectively led in recent months, and other agencies of the Government will concern—and the Congress—will concern itself about the problem of conflicts of interest and monopolistic practices, as well as even more illicit practices conducted in the American business community. And I hope that the business community itself will consider what steps it could take in order to lift this shadow from its shoulders.

Q. Do you feel, sir, that perhaps business might well establish codes of ethical practice such as the trade unions have established?

THE PRESIDENT. Yes. I am hopeful that the unions will live up to these ethical practices which state a very high standard for them; and I think it would be very beneficial if business groups today would consider what they could do to protect themselves from charges of conflicts of interest of the kind that we have recently seen, and also of the effort made by these large electrical com-

panies to defraud the Government. And I must say I would be interested to watch what progress they can make in that area.

[22.] Q. Mr. President, Admiral Burke's speech was originally checked out and cleared of certain things which I believe Mr. Salinger said might have been sources of unnecessary friction with the Soviet Union. Some Republicans in Congress charged that this was appeasement. Could you sketch in for us the rather difficult ground between appeasement and "unnecessary friction"?

THE PRESIDENT. No. All I would say is that I would hope that those who make speeches in the area of national security, Chiefs of Staff and others, and all others, would attempt to have those speeches coordinated with the Department of State and with the White House, so that we can make sure that those speeches represent national policy. I must say it seems to me that Theodore Roosevelt set a very good standard for us all, and one which I hope this administration will follow by speaking softly and maintaining——

[23.] Q. Mr. President, on Monday Mr. Rusk said that the United States was prepared to take cooperative action with the other American Republics to end tyranny, he said, against either the left or the right. Is it contemplated that we shall ask the other American States to join with us in some steps on the Cuban problem?

THE PRESIDENT. The Cuban problem and the problem of tyranny throughout all of Latin America is a matter which is of course of special concern to Mr. Berle and his group—interdepartmental group—and they have not concluded their analysis as yet.

[24.] Q. Mr. President, Castro is reported to have built a new radio station, one of the largest in the hemisphere, which will begin operations within a few months to broadcast pro-Castro propaganda throughout Latin America. Is there anything we can do or plan to do to counter this?

THE PRESIDENT. We are giving the matter of Cuba and its export of its revolution throughout Latin America a matter of high priority. I could not state what actions will be taken yet until Mr. Berle, Mr. Mann, and Mr. Rusk have concluded their deliberations, which are now going ahead very intensively.

[25.] Q. Mr. President, one of your task forces recommended that you be given discretionary power within limits to cut tax rates as a counter-cyclical device. Can you tell us what you think of this idea?

THE PRESIDENT. Well, in 1958 there were two proposals to cut taxes. One was made in March and I believe the other was made in June. I voted against it in March and voted for it in June, because it seemed to be, according to the economists I talked to, to be helpful. As you remember, I don't think it got more than 23 or 24 votes. The recession was serious and we ended up with a $12 billion deficit. Now we are going to take another look at the economy in April and make a judgment at that time whether we can expect an upturn in the spring or in the summer.

I will say that I am not convinced at the present time that Congress would entertain that proposal, and I would not make it at the present time because I do think we should have more experience and more perspective on the state of the economy before making a proposal which is quite far-reaching, and which would cost the Federal budget perhaps $4 or $5 billion, which is a serious matter and which would limit, perhaps, our ability to go ahead with other programs which in the long run may be more useful. If you have a tax cut, it may last 6 months, if the Congress should grant it, and you lose $5 billion, which is put

back into the economy and expended. With $5 billion or $3 billion devoted to education or health or international security, you can produce a longer range result. So that this is a matter which must be considered from various perspectives. In any case, in April we will try to make another judgment on the state of the economy. What I am concerned about is that the economy will move along, using less than capacity, and it is extremely difficult to take steps which will provide quickly for it to operate at full capacity.

What we are concerned about is that with the tremendous increase in automation that it's possible for business profits to remain substantial and yet for employment to lag. The fact that the steel companies were able to maintain rather substantial profits at a time when they are operating at less than 50 percent of capacity does indicate the kind of problem we face with a good many more than 100,000 steel workers out of work.

In answer to your question specifically, we will come back to what further steps could be taken in April, but I do hope that the Congress will act on the proposals we have now made, which involve most especially the unemployment compensation payments and also the distressed area payments, as well as some improvements in social security. If we could move ahead on those we could get a better idea of perhaps what action should be taken in April.

[26.] Q. Mr. President, the fighting in Laos is continuing. The Soviet airlift is now 2 months old. The Soviet answer to the proposal to revive the International Control Commission has been delayed for some weeks. I wonder if you can tell us how long this Government is prepared to wait before it proposes some new action to resolve this continuing crisis.

THE PRESIDENT. There will be a meeting

at the White House this afternoon on the subject of Laos and what new action we should now take. And I am hopeful that some proposal will be forthcoming from that meeting.

[27.] Q. Mr. President, many States are now re-forming their congressional districts as a result of the 1960 census and inevitably this leads to charges of gerrymandering directed at both parties. Can you tell us where you stand on Chairman Celler's bill to control gerrymandering to a certain extent by such devices as making districts be contiguous and control a certain population within a State?

THE PRESIDENT. Well, even if you could pass those proposals you could still have a good deal of gerrymandering. I represented a district which was about 5 to 1 Democratic, which was contiguous, which was geographically associated with an adjoining district, which was marginally Republican. Now it is very difficult for the Congress or for the Federal Government to enforce standards. What should have happened, of course, is probably under some standards is those two districts cut in a different way which would have provided instead of one Republican Congressman with a very marginal majority, while the Democratic Congressman got 5 to 1, it probably would have

ended up with two Democratic Congressmen, which may or may not have been in the public interest. [*Laughter.*]

But I do think it is very difficult for us to try to draw these lines. There isn't any doubt that they are unsatisfactorily drawn, not only for the Congress, which is not the worst offender, but the State legislatures, where we have very—and have had for many years—notorious examples of gerrymandering, but which is a responsibility for the States, not the Federal Government.

In any case, I am not familiar wholly with Congressman Celler's proposal and exactly what his standards will be, but I will look at it.

Q. Mr. President, in that same connection, could you tell us where you stand or do you have a position on increasing the size of the House of Representatives?

THE PRESIDENT. Well, it is 435 Members now, which is a large body. Congressman Chelf and I believe other Congressmen have proposed increasing it, I think to 450. I will discuss that matter with Speaker Rayburn and get his views as well as the leadership of the House on both sides.

Reporter: Thank you, Mr. President.

NOTE: President Kennedy's third news conference was held in the State Department Auditorium at 10 o'clock on Wednesday morning, February 8, 1961.

26   Remarks at the Dedication Breakfast of International Christian Leadership, Inc. *February 9, 1961*

Mr. Chairman, Dr. Graham, Mr. Vice President—gentlemen:

I think it is most appropriate that we should be gathered together for this morning's meeting. This country was founded by men and women who were dedicated or came to be dedicated to two propositions: first, a strong religious conviction, and

secondly a recognition that this conviction could flourish only under a system of freedom.

I think it is appropriate that we pay tribute to this great constitutional principle which is enshrined in the First Amendment of the Constitution: the principle of religious independence, of religious liberty, of religious freedom. But I think it is also important that we pay tribute and acknowledge another great principle, and that is the principle of religious conviction. Religious freedom has no significance unless it is accompanied by conviction. And therefore the Puritans and the Pilgrims of my own section of New England, the Quakers of Pennsylvania, the Catholics of Maryland, the Presbyterians of North Carolina, the Methodists and the Baptists who came later, all shared these two great traditions which, like silver threads, have run through the warp and the woof of American history.

No man who enters upon the office to which I have succeeded can fail to recognize how every President of the United States has placed special reliance upon his faith in God. Every President has taken comfort and courage when told, as we are told today, that the Lord "will be with thee. He will not fail thee nor forsake thee. Fear not—neither be thou dismayed."

While they came from a wide variety of religious backgrounds and held a wide variety of religious beliefs, each of our Presidents in his own way has placed a special trust in God. Those who were strongest intellectually were also strongest spiritually.

Today our Nation is passing through another time of trial. In many ways, our dangers and our problems are far greater—and certainly infinitely more complex. We will need to draw upon the best that this Nation has—often—and draw upon it physically and intellectually and materially.

But we need also to call upon our great reservoir of spiritual resources. We must recognize that human collaboration is not enough, that in times such as these we must reach beyond ourselves if we are to seek ultimate courage and infinite wisdom.

It is an ironic fact that in this nuclear age, when the horizon of human knowledge and human experience has passed far beyond any that any age has ever known, that we turn back at this time to the oldest source of wisdom and strength, to the words of the prophets and the saints, who tell us that faith is more powerful than doubt, that hope is more potent than despair, and that only through the love that is sometimes called charity can we conquer those forces within ourselves and throughout all the world that threaten the very existence of mankind.

Keeping in mind that "when a man's ways please the Lord, he maketh even his enemies to be at peace with him," let us go forth to lead this land that we love, joining in the prayer of General George Washington in 1783, "that God would have you in His holy protection, that He would incline the hearts of the citizens. . . . to entertain a brotherly love and affection one for another . . . and finally that He would most graciously be pleased to dispose us all to do justice, to love mercy, and to demean ourselves with . . . the characteristics of the Divine Author of our blessed religion, without an humble imitation of whose example we can never hope to be a happy nation."

The guiding principle and prayer of this Nation has been, is now, and shall ever be "In God We Trust."

Thank you.

[The President spoke first to the gentlemen in the hotel's main ball room, and then to the ladies in the east room.]

Madam Chairwoman, Dr. Graham, Mr. Vice President:

It seems to me that in the true Christian spirit next year we should all sit down together, and that we should have gentlemen and ladies pray and reason together, and not confine them in different rooms.

But we are glad we came here—the Vice President and I came under the protection of Dr. Graham.

I do want to say that it is a pleasure to be here and to have participated in the breakfast this morning. I had an opportunity in the White House the other day to talk to a group of men and women from the Baptist World Alliance who have been missionaries, some in the Congo, one lady who has been in Bengal, India, since 1926, others who have been in Thailand and Korea.

I do not regard religion as a weapon in the cold war. I regard it as the essence of the differences which separate those on the other side of the Iron Curtain and ourselves.

The whole basis of the struggle is involved in the meeting this morning: our strong belief in religious freedom, our strong conviction, as I attempted to say in my inaugural, that the blessings which come to us come not from the generosity of the state but from the hand of God—and this alternate concept that the state is the master and the people the servants.

This is really the essence of the issue. We cannot have religious freedom without political freedom, and therefore what we really need is not to confuse a system of freedom with one of disinterest, uninterest, cynicism, materialism, but like the ladies and gentlemen whom I talked to the other day, who have been willing to spend their lives under the most difficult of circumstances, in great hardship, in order to carry the message in which they have such great conviction, it seems to me it shows a lesson for us all.

We must match that faith. We must demonstrate in our lives, whatever our responsibility may be, that we care deeply.

I see no reason why the servants of the Communist system should be marked by a discipline and strong conviction in the ultimate success of their cause. I believe that our cause is just, that ultimately it will be successful. But it can only be successful if we demonstrate our strong conviction in it.

Religious freedom and religious conviction are the two hallmarks of American society, and therefore as a strong believer in both, I wanted to say that I deem it an honor to share this evidence of our common belief in these two great principles at this breakfast this morning. What we do this morning, I hope we can do every day.

Thank you.

NOTE: The ninth annual prayer breakfast sponsored by the International Christian Leadership, Inc., a nondenominational group of laymen, was held at the Mayflower Hotel in Washington. William C. Jones of Los Angeles, Calif., a leader in the group, served as host. Frank Carlson, U.S. Senator from Kansas, and Mrs. Olin D. Johnston, wife of U.S. Senator Johnston of South Carolina, acted as chairmen. The evangelist, Dr. Billy Graham, led in prayer.

27 Special Message to the Congress on Health and Hospital Care. *February 9, 1961*

To the Congress of the United States:

The health of our nation is a key to its future—to its economic vitality, to the morale and efficiency of its citizens, to our success in achieving our own goals and demonstrating to others the benefits of a free society.

Ill health and its harsh consequences are not confined to any state or region, to any race, age, or sex or to any occupation or economic level. This is a matter of national concern.

More than twenty-five billion dollars a

year—over 6 percent of our national income—is being spent from public and private funds for health services. Yet there are major deficiencies in the quality and distribution of these services.

The dramatic results of new medicines and new methods—opening the way to a fuller and more useful life—are too often beyond the reach of those who need them most.

Financial inability, absence of community resources, and shortages of trained personnel keep too many people from getting what medical knowledge can obtain for them.

Those among us who are over 65—16 million today in the United States—go to the hospital more often and stay longer than their younger neighbors. Their physical activity is limited by six times as much disability as the rest of the population. Their annual medical bill is twice that of persons under 65—but their annual income is only half as high.

The nation's children—now 40 percent of our population—have urgent needs which must be met. Many still die in infancy. Many are not immunized against diseases which can be prevented, have inadequate diets or unnecessarily endure physical and emotional problems.

These and other problems of health care can and must be met. Only a part of the responsibility rests with the federal government. But its powers and resources make its role essential in four areas for improving health care: social insurance, facilities, personnel and research.

I. HEALTH INSURANCE FOR THE AGED

Twenty-six years ago this nation adopted the principle that every member of the labor force and his family should be insured against the haunting fear of loss of income caused by retirement, death or unemployment. To that we have added insurance against the economic loss caused by disability. But there remains a significant gap that denies to all but those with the highest incomes a full measure of security—the high cost of ill health in old age. One out of five aged couples drawing Social Security benefits must go to the hospital each year. Half of those going to hospitals incur bills in excess of $700 a year. This is over one-third of the total annual income of a typical couple, more than a modest food budget for an entire year. Many simply do not obtain and cannot afford the care they need.

The measure adopted by the Congress last year recognized the problem of those needy aged requiring welfare assistance to meet their medical costs. But now we must meet the needs of those millions who have no wish to receive care at the taxpayers' expense, but who are nevertheless staggered by the drain on their savings—or those of their children—caused by an extended hospital stay.

In our Social Security and Railroad Retirement systems we have the instruments which can spread the cost of health services in old age over the working years—effectively, and in a manner consistent with the dignity of the individual. By using these proved systems to provide health insurance protection, it will be possible for our older people to get the vital hospital services they need without exhausting their resources or turning to public assistance. The self-supporting insurance method of financing the cost of such health services is certainly to be preferred to an expansion of public assistance, and should reduce the number of those needing medical care under the public assistance program. The State and local money thus freed should be further used to help provide services not included in this proposal, and to assist those not covered.

For it should be stressed that this is a very modest proposal cut to meet absolutely essential needs, and with sufficient "deductible" requirements to discourage any malingering or unnecessary overcrowding of our hospitals.

In essence, I am recommending enactment of a health insurance program under the Social Security system that will provide the following benefits:

First, inpatient hospital services up to 90 days in a single spell of illness, for all costs in excess of $10 per day for the first 9 days (with a minimum of $20), and full costs for the remaining 81 days. Because hospital costs place by far the heaviest and most unmanageable burden on older persons, it is these services that should receive major emphasis in any health insurance program.

Second, skilled nursing home services up to 180 days immediately after discharge from a hospital. To provide an incentive for use of these less expensive facilities, an individual could, in short, receive two days of skilled nursing home care in place of one day of hospital care when this satisfies his requirements.

Third, hospital outpatient clinic diagnostic services for all costs in excess of $20. These services, too, will reduce the need for hospital admissions and encourage early diagnosis.

Fourth, community visiting nurse services, and related home health services, for a limited period of time. These will enable many older people to receive proper health care in their own homes.

I propose that these insurance benefits be available to all persons aged 65 and over who are eligible for social security or railroad retirement benefits.

This program would be financed by an increase in social security contributions of one-quarter of one percent each on employers and employees, and by an increase in the maximum earnings base from $4800 a year to $5000 which would amply cover the cost of all insurance benefits provided. The system would be self-supporting and would not place any burden on the general revenues.

This program is not a program of socialized medicine. It is a program of prepayment of health costs with absolute freedom of choice guaranteed. Every person will choose his own doctor and hospital.

No service performed by any physician at either home or office, and no fee he charges for such services, would be involved, covered or affected in any way. There would be no supervision or control over the practice of medicine by any doctor or over the manner in which medical services are provided by any hospital. The program is a sound one and entirely in accordance with the traditional American system of placing responsibility on the employee and the employer, rather than on the general taxpayers, to help finance retirement and health costs.

II. COMMUNITY HEALTH SERVICES AND FACILITIES

The ability to afford adequate health care is to no avail without adequate health facilities. The financial support which will be available under the health insurance program I am recommending will, in itself, stimulate more facilities and services. But our communities need additional help to provide those services where everybody can use them.

A. *Nursing Home Construction Grants.*

There is now a shortage of 500,000 beds in long-term facilities for people who are sick but who do not require the special services of a general hospital. We must move with greater speed in the construction of more skilled nursing homes; particularly if our new program is to encourage recuperation, if impossible at home, in this kind of facility instead of in our overcrowded hospitals. I am submitting to Congress legislation to double the present authorization of $10 million in matching grants for this construction program.

B. *Grants To Improve Nursing-Home and Home-Nursing Services.*

Increasing the number of nursing home beds will not alone remedy the deficiency in care. Good operation, good service, and proper safety are essential. Nor do all the aged sick and chronically ill need to be cared for in hospitals or nursing homes. At some stages in their illness many people can fare better in their own homes if proper care is available. But most communities do not have home health services. Even limited home nursing services are available in less than 1,000 U.S. communities.

I am therefore proposing stimulatory grants to the states, and through them to communities, to improve the quality of services in nursing homes—to develop organized community home-care health services for the aged and chronically ill—to develop health service information and referral centers—to train additional personnel required for out-of-hospital health services—and to assist in meeting the cost of studies and demonstrations of new and improved means of providing out-of-hospital care. An initial annual appropriation of ten million dollars will lay the groundwork for more efficient and better balanced care for the aged and chronically ill.

To insure maximum Federal attention to the rapid development of this program, I propose that the Congress enact legislation enabling the Public Health Service to create a new Bureau of Community Health to pro-

vide the necessary leadership and assistance to states and communities.

C. *Hospital Research and Development.*

Hospitals account for more than 6 billion dollars a year of the nation's gross expenditures. In this modern age, an enterprise of such size and importance requires continuous and substantial research and development as a basis for operations. Specifically, we need more intensive regional and area planning to attain the maximum economical use from these costly structures; and we need more research into how hospital facilities can be built, and how services within hospitals should be organized and administered, in order to provide the best possible medical care with the personnel available. I am therefore recommending that, in place of an arbitrary appropriations ceiling for research in this area, the Congress have the authority to determine each year the amount necessary for these purposes; and that the Surgeon General be authorized to make project grants for the construction of experimental or demonstration hospitals and other medical facilities.

III. INCREASING HEALTH PERSONNEL

Adequate health care requires an adequate supply of well-trained personnel. We do not have that adequate supply today—and shortages are growing.

We must increase sharply the rate of doctor and dentist training merely to keep pace with our growing population—and we need far more if, as part of our international responsibilities, we are to help meet critical medical needs in key areas of the world. But we not only fall short of our goal to help those nations by exporting sufficient numbers of doctors to provide the nucleus for a world health program, we are actually the beneficiaries of more than a thousand physicians a year who come from foreign lands to practice in the United States.

We have now 92 medical and 47 dental schools. These graduate only 7,500 physicians and 3,200 dentists each year. If during the next ten years the capacity of our medical schools is increased 50 percent, and that of our dental schools by 100 percent, the output will still be sufficient only to maintain the present ratio of physicians and dentists to population.

To do this we must have within the next 10 years substantial increases in enrollment in existing schools, plus 20 new medical schools and 20 new dental schools.

But the great deterrent to the establishment and expansion of these schools is lack of funds. Modern medical and dental schools are extraordinarily expensive to build and operate. Teaching hospitals cost even more. A university which establishes a medical and dental school must do so with the expectation of a substantial drain on its financial resources, and most institutions are not able to find such funds.

Moreover, the average cost to the student of four years of medical school is over $10,000—a heavy burden to come on top of the cost of a four-year undergraduate education. Furthermore, once the student obtains his medical degree, he must still look forward to an average of 3 years of hospital experience, at little or no pay, before he can begin his life's work. It is not surprising that 40 percent of all medical students now come from the 12 percent of the families with incomes of $10,000 or more a year. Nor is it surprising, though disturbing, that while college enrollments generally have been soaring, the number of applicants to medical and dental schools has been dropping; and that many of these

schools are having difficulty in securing enough qualified students who are able to afford such an education.

The federal government has made substantial contributions through fellowships and training aid for graduate students in the physical and biological sciences, and for research training in health fields. The result has been a rapidly increasing number of recruits to these fields.

In contrast there has been very little financial assistance of any kind available to medical and dental students. Only one medical student in 10 receives a scholarship from any source, and these average only $500 a year (compared to an average cost of over $2500). In dentistry even less scholarship aid is available.

Decisive federal action is necessary to stimulate and assist in the establishment and expansion of medical and dental schools, and to help more talented but needy students to enter the health professions while bolstering the quality of their training.

I have four recommendations to be combined in a single measure:

(a) I propose an immediate program of planning grants to help our academic institutions plan new facilities for medical and dental schools and to explore ways of improving the whole educational process;

(b) I recommend a ten-year program of matching grants to assist in the construction, expansion, and restoration of medical and dental schools to increase their capacity. This program should make available $25 million in the first year, and $75 million annually thereafter;

(c) I recommend a program of federal scholarships for talented medical and dental students in need of financial assistance. Federal funds would be available for each institution in a total amount equal to $1500 for one-fourth of the newly entering students, to be awarded in individual four-year scholarships by the institution in proportion to the student's need, with no student being eligible for more than $2000 a year.

(d) Finally, I recommend that the schools receive a cost of education grant of $1000 for each federal scholarship, to make certain that this program does not work further financial injury upon our medical and dental schools whose costs per pupil are never met by his tuition and fees. In addition to assisting our schools now operating, this feature would also give some encouragement to institutions now doubtful about the burden of establishing new medical and dental schools.

For nursing, I must add, the need and shortage are also great; but the problems are different and more complex. We intend to develop for nursing, as we have for medicine and dentistry, a formulation of needs and training requirements; and appropriate proposals will be submitted to the Congress when completed.

IV. IMPROVING THE HEALTH OF OUR CHILDREN AND YOUTH

While meeting the health needs of the older groups in our population, we cannot neglect the needs of the young. One-fifth of our children under five have not been immunized against poliomyelitis. Since 1950, our country has slipped from 6th to 10th place among the advanced nations of the world in the saving of infant lives. Each year some 400,000 babies are born with congenital malformations—and untold numbers of others begin life mentally retarded, afflicted by cerebral palsy or suffering from other serious conditions which require prompt and effective care and additional research.

A. I am recommending that there be es-

tablished in the National Institutes of Health a new National Institute of Child Health and Human Development, which will include a Center for Research in Child Health as well as other broad-ranging health research activities not now covered by the specialized work of the existing institutes.

B. I am recommending to the Congress an increase in appropriations for the existing Maternal and Child Health, Crippled Children and Child Welfare programs of the Children's Bureau. By this means, the fruits of our research can move at a faster pace to those who need them most.

C. In order to provide more unified administration and increased effectiveness of federal efforts for physical fitness, I am designating the Secretary of Health, Education, and Welfare as the Chairman of the President's Council on Youth Fitness. I am asking him to mobilize the full resources of his Department and other interested agencies toward encouraging public and private agencies and individuals to improve the physical fitness of our nation's youth; and I am further asking him to report at an early date on the adequacy of existing school health programs and what changes, if any, are needed in the Federal Government's role in the stimulation of such programs.

V. VOCATIONAL REHABILITATION

This administration intends to see that the rehabilitation of disabled Americans and their return to active and useful lives is expanded as rapidly as possible. Our Federal-State program of vocational rehabilitation and the cooperating voluntary agencies must be assisted in providing more nearly adequate facilities and services to reach the thousands of persons who become disabled every year. We need their talents and skills if our economy is to reach a high level of performance. To this end I shall recommend to the Congress an increase in federal matching funds to expand the vocational rehabilitation program.

VI. MEDICAL RESEARCH

The next ten years will require a vast expansion of this nation's present total effort in medical research, if knowledge is to keep pace with human progress. I recommend:

A. Extension and expansion of the present program authorizing matching grants for the construction of research facilities.

B. Removal of the current limitation on the federal payment of indirect costs of medical research projects, which has handicapped many universities and other research institutions.

C. An increase in the funds for medical research requested in the Budget previously submitted.

CONCLUSION

The measures I have recommended recognize and strengthen the indispensable elements in a sound health program—people, knowledge, services, facilities, and the means to pay for them. Taken together, they constitute a necessary foundation upon which to build.

The health of the American people must ever be safeguarded; it must ever be improved. As long as people are stricken by a disease which we have the ability to prevent, as long as people are chained by a disability which can be reversed, as long as needless death takes its toll, then American health will be unfinished business.

It is to the unfinished business in health—which affects every person and home and community in this land—that we must now direct our best efforts.

JOHN F. KENNEDY

---

28   Letter to the President of the Senate and to the Speaker of the House Proposing Creation of Additional Federal Judgeships. *February* 10, 1961

[Released February 10, 1961. Dated February 9, 1961]

Dear Mr. ————:

I have requested the Attorney General to submit to the Congress legislation to create fifty-nine additional Federal judgeships to relieve serious congestion and delays in many Federal Courts. Fifty will be in the District Courts and nine in the Court of Appeals.

Extensive Congressional hearings have been conducted in both the Senate and the House in recent Congresses and testimony received from representatives of the American Bar Association, State and local associa-

tions, the Judicial Conference of the United States and others interested in and affected by the operations of our courts, showing very clearly that the administration of justice in the Federal Court system is unduly delayed. Despite the tremendous increase of court congestion and judicial lag, no new Federal judgeships have been created since February 10, 1954.

I have asked the Attorney General separately to describe to you the essential details of this essential legislation. Prompt and favorable consideration of the measure will be of direct benefit to millions of people throughout the country.

Sincerely,

JOHN F. KENNEDY

NOTE: This is the text of identical letters addressed to the Honorable Lyndon B. Johnson, President of the Senate, and to the Honorable Sam Rayburn, Speaker of the House of Representatives.

For the President's statement upon signing the Omnibus Judgeship Bill, see Item 195.

29   Statement by the President Upon Announcing the Appointment of Consultants on Government Organization and Operations. *February* 10, 1961

I AM PLEASED to announce the names of four men who have agreed to serve as consultants on major issues affecting the structure and operations of government. The men are:

Robert A. Lovett, of New York, former Secretary of Defense and Under Secretary of State.

Richard E. Neustadt of New York, Professor of Government at Columbia University, who served between last fall's election and the Inauguration as my special consultant on organizational matters.

Don K. Price of Cambridge, Massachusetts, Dean of the Graduate School of Public Administration at Harvard University.

Sydney Stein, Jr., of Chicago, a partner in Stein, Roe, and Farnham, investment counsellors, formerly associated with the Bureau of the Budget in the field of government organization and management.

They will be consulted in matters where the disinterested advice of highly qualified and experienced men in private life may help us find effective solutions to problems of government organization and operation. They will not act as a committee nor will they hold regular meetings. Instead, they will be asked for advice as individuals, under flexible and informal arrangements suited to the needs of the problem at hand. Their regular point of contact will be the Budget Director, who will keep them informed of significant developments and emerging issues.

It is my conviction that the structure and operations of government must be continually adapted to constant changes in the requirements for governmental action and the methods of meeting those requirements. The consultants named today are exceptionally well equipped to help us conceive and carry through the necessary adaptations in timely and orderly fashion. I am grateful for their willingness to serve in this important capacity.

In view of these simpler and more flexible arrangements, the Advisory Committee on Government Organization, created in 1953, will no longer be necessary. Accordingly, I am terminating that Committee by Executive Order.

I am also terminating the Advisory Committee on Management Improvement, which was established in 1949 but has not functioned since 1952.

30   Statement by the President Upon Announcing the Appointment of Aubrey J. Wagner as a Member of the Board of Directors, Tennessee Valley Authority.   *February 11, 1961*

I REGARD Mr. Wagner's appointment as a recognition not only of his own career and capacities but of the loyalty and dedication that has uniquely characterized the staff of the Tennessee Valley Authority over the full period of its development.   The ranks of the agency can boast other men and women who like Mr. Wagner have torn loose from their own geographical roots to devote careers to this region that had become an eddy in the mainstream of progress.

The TVA has done a remarkable job but the job is not done.   It has demonstrated in 27 years that it has the imagination and flexibility to grow with its times but it must prove in its second quarter century that it can remain vigorous as it grows old.   The TVA, like every vital branch of the government, must never allow itself to relapse into an attitude of entrenched bureaucracy.

I want to be sure also that we lose no opportunity to share the great experience of the TVA with other nations faced with the gap between resources and resource development.   I want the agency to study ways in which the lessons it has learned in the Tennessee Valley may be exported abroad and applied to our great objective of human enhancement.

Toward these ends I would like a report from the TVA Board by April 15 so that I may know the directions in which the agency proposes to work in the years immediately ahead.

NOTE: A report entitled "TVA Directions—Past and Future" (20 pp., mimeographed) was submitted to the President on April 26, 1961.

31   Remarks at the Swearing In of Robert C. Weaver as Housing and Home Finance Administrator.   *February 11, 1961*

IT IS a great pleasure to welcome Mr. and Mrs. Weaver to the White House, and also it is a great pleasure for me to participate in Mr. Weaver's swearing-in.

The responsibility which he is assuming is one of the most important in the country. Under Mr. Weaver's leadership, it is our hope that housing, shelter, for all Americans can be substantially improved.

Public housing, urban renewal, private housing, all of this represents a basic aspiration of American families to house themselves securely.   There are, according to our latest Census Bureau figures, over 25 mil-lion Americans who live in substandard housing.   It is the ambition of this administration to try to provide decent housing for all American families, and Mr. Weaver's responsibility will be to lead this important national effort.

So I am delighted to have them here. I have the highest confidence in his ability, his energy, his integrity, his loyalty; and I am confident that he will serve as a force in this important field for a better life for all Americans.

So we are glad to see you, Mr. Weaver, and to present you with this certificate.

32 Letter to the President of the Senate and to the Speaker of the House Transmitting Bill To Provide Health Insurance for the Aged. *February* 13, 1961

Dear Mr. ————:

I am transmitting herewith a bill to provide health insurance benefits for the aged, financed through the social insurance system. I believe the need for such insurance is urgent. Every study has demonstrated that the costs of adequate health care for those over 65 are becoming an accelerated problem.

Enactment of the legislation would not relieve its beneficiaries of their entire responsibility for the costs incurred by them for their medical needs, but it would enable them to meet most of their medical care costs without any humiliating means test.

The financing is based upon the sound and proven social security principles.

The enclosed letter from the Secretary of Health, Education, and Welfare describes the proposed legislation in more detail.

Sincerely,

JOHN F. KENNEDY

NOTE: This is the text of identical letters addressed to the Honorable Lyndon B. Johnson, President of the Senate, and to the Honorable Sam Rayburn, Speaker of the House of Representatives.

Secretary Ribicoff's letter of February 10 was released with the President's letter. A summary of the provisions of the draft bill is published in the Congressional Record (vol. 107, Feb. 13, 1961, p. 2014).

33 Address at a Luncheon Meeting of the National Industrial Conference Board. *February* 13, 1961

Mr. White, Dean Sayre, distinguished guests—gentlemen:

I want, first of all, to express my personal thanks to all of you for having come to our city, and for participating in what I hope will be a most useful and helpful proceeding which will benefit this Government and our country.

It has recently been suggested that whether I serve one or two terms in the Presidency, I will find myself at the end of that period at what might be called the awkward age—too old to begin a new career and too young to write my memoirs.

A similar dilemma, it seems to me, is posed by the occasion of a Presidential address to a business group on business conditions less than four weeks after entering the White House—for it is too early to be claiming credit for the new administration and

too late to be blaming the old one. And it would be premature to seek your support in the next election, and inaccurate to express thanks for having had it in the last one.

I feel, nevertheless, that I can claim kinship here, and have that claim allowed. For I am convinced that the real spirit of American business is not represented by those involved in price-fixing, conflict-of-interest, or collusion. The real spirit is in this room—in your recognition of your public responsibilities, your pursuit of the truth, your desire for better industrial relations, better technological progress, and better price stability and economic growth. And because your organization portrays *that* picture of American business, I am delighted and proud to be here with you.

The complaint has often been made in business circles that the Federal Government is a "silent partner" in every corporation—taking roughly half of all of your net earnings without risk to itself. But it should be also realized that this makes business a not always "silent partner" of the Federal Government—that our revenues and thus our success are dependent upon your profits and your success—and that, far from being natural enemies, Government and business are necessary allies.

For example, the 1960 drop in expected corporate profits of some six to seven billion dollars also caused a loss in Federal revenues of over three billion dollars—enough to pay the Federal share of all of our anti-recession, health, and education proposals for the next fiscal year and still have enough left over to start closing what the Democrats in this administration used to call "The Missile Gap."

An equally critical gap separates the tax revenues of a lagging economy from those which are potentially within our grasp: a gap of at least twelve billion dollars. Even after we are able to launch every program necessary for national security and development, this amount of revenue would still leave a substantial surplus—a surplus essential to help defend our economy against inflation—and, equally important, a surplus that, when applied to the Federal debt, would free additional savings for business investment and expansion.

In short, there is no inevitable clash between the public and the private sectors—or between investment and consumption—nor, as I have said, between Government and business. All elements in our national economic growth are interdependent. Each must play its proper role—and that is the hope and the aim of this administration.

If those of you who are in the world of business, and we who are in the world of government, are necessarily partners, what

kind of a partnership is this going to be? Will it be marked by mutual suspicion and recrimination, or by mutual understanding and fruitful collaboration?

On behalf of my associates in the Cabinet, I want to be very precise: we will not discriminate for or against any segment of our society, or any segment of the business community. We are vigorously opposed to corruption and monopoly and human exploitation—but we are not opposed to business.

We know that your success and ours are intertwined—that you have facts and know-how that we need. Whatever past differences may have existed, we seek more than an attitude of truce, more than a treaty— we seek the spirit of a full-fledged alliance.

Today, I would briefly mention three areas of common concern to which that alliance must be devoted in the next few years: economic growth, plant modernization, and price stability.

I.

First: Economic growth has come to resemble the Washington weather—everyone talks about it, no one says precisely what to do about it, and our only satisfaction is that it can't get any worse.

The economic program which I have set before the Congress is essentially a program for recovery—and I do not equate recovery with growth. But it is an essential first step. Only by putting millions of people back to work can we expand purchasing power and markets. Only by higher income and profits can we provide the incentive and the means for increased investment. And only when we are using our plant at near capacity can we expect any solid expansion.

Capacity operation is the key. No matter what other arguments or stimulants are used, the incentives for investing new capital to expand manufacturing plants and equipment are weak as long as manufacturers are operating at less than 80 percent of their capacity. From 1950 to 1958, we put only one-sixth of our total output into capital formation, while Japan, Germany, Italy, the Netherlands, Canada, and Sweden were all investing one-fifth or more of their total output in capital goods. So it is not surprising that each of these and other nations over the past several years have all surpassed us in average annual rate of economic growth.

I think we can do better. Working together, business and Government must do better—putting people back to work, using plants to capacity, and spurring savings and investments with at least a large part of our economic gains—beginning not when our economy is back at the top, but beginning now.

II.

Secondly: New plant investment not only means expansion of capacity—it means modernization as well. Gleaming new factories and headlines about automation have diverted our attention from an aging industrial plant. Obsolescence is slowing down our growth, handicapping our productivity, and worsening our competitive position abroad.

Nothing can reverse our balance of payments deficit if American machinery and equipment cannot produce the newest products of the highest quality in the most efficient manner. The available evidence on the age of our industrial plant is unofficial and fragmentary; but the trend is unmistakable—we are falling behind.

The average age of equipment in American factories today is about 9 years. In a dynamic economy, that average should be falling, as new equipment is put into place. Instead the available evidence suggests that it has been slowly rising.

Private surveys of machine tools used by manufacturers of general industrial equipment found less than half of these tools over 10 years old in 1949, but ⅔ over that age in 1958. Nineteen percent of our machine tools were found to be over 20 years old.

Meanwhile, other countries have been lowering the average age of their fixed capital. The German example is the most spectacular—their proportion of capital equipment and plant under 5 years of age grew from one-sixth of the total in 1948 to two-fifths in 1957.

All of these facts point in one direction: we must start now to provide additional stimulus to the modernization of American industrial plants. Within the next few weeks, I shall propose to the Congress a new tax incentive for businesses to expand their normal investment in plant and equipment.

But modernization and productivity depend upon more than investment in physical resources. Equally essential is investment in human resources. And I think that this is obvious to those of us who have considered the problems of unemployment and depressed areas. There is no doubt that the maximum impact of a reducing economy falls upon those who are at the bottom of the educational ladder. The first people unemployed are those with the least education, the last people to be hired back are those with the least education. So there is a direct connection between increased emphasis on education in this country and also upon increased productivity and technological change.

Without strengthened programs for health, education, and science and research, the new modern plant would only be a hollow shell. Many of these programs are within the province of State and local governments. Full recovery will increase the tax revenues that they so sorely need. But the Federal Government will have to pay its fair share of developing these human resources.

III.

Finally, Government and business must turn their attention to the problem of price stability. Concern over the resumption of inflationary pressures hangs over all our efforts to restore the economy, to stimulate its growth, and to maintain our competitive status abroad. In recent days, complaints have been voiced in some quarters that this administration was not meeting its responsibilities in this area. But the facts are that, whatever one may regard our responsibilities to be, we are almost totally without direct and enforceable powers over the central problem. A free government in a free society has only a limited influence—provided that they are above the minimum—over prices and wages freely set and bargained for by free individuals and free enterprises. And this is as it should be if our economy is to remain free.

Nevertheless, the public interest in major wage and price determinations is substantial. Ways must be found to bring that public interest before the parties concerned in a fair and orderly manner.

For this reason, I have announced my determination to establish a Presidential Advisory Committee on Labor-Management Policy, with members drawn from labor, management and the public. I want this Committee to play a major role in helping promote sound wage and price policies, productivity increases, and a betterment of America's competitive position in world markets. I will look to this Committee to make an important contribution to labor-management relations, and to a wider understanding of their impact on price stability and our economic health. And in this undertaking, I ask and urge the constructive cooperation of this organization and its members.

———

Economic growth, plant modernization, price stability—these are all intangible and elusive goals. But they are all essential to your success, and to the success of our country. Initiative, innovation, hard work, and cooperation will be required, on your part, and on ours.

But I have confidence in our Nation, confidence in our economy, and confidence in your ability to meet your obligations fully. I hope that my associates and I can merit your confidence as well. For I can assure you that we love our country, not for what it was, though it has always been great—not for what it is, though of this we are deeply proud—but for what it some day can and, through the efforts of us all, some day will be.

Thank you.

NOTE: The President spoke at 1:50 p.m. at the Sheraton-Park Hotel in Washington. His opening words "Mr. White, Dean Sayre" referred to Charles M. White, chairman of the National Industrial Conference Board, and the Very Reverend Francis B. Sayre, Jr., Dean of the Washington Cathedral.

34 Message to the Permanent Council of the North Atlantic Treaty Organization. *February* 15, 1961

IN MY Inaugural Address I pledged to the members of this great organization "the loyalty of faithful friends."

In the three weeks since I became President I have been increasingly impressed by the magnitude of the perils which confront the United States and free nations everywhere. But I have also been increasingly convinced that we can face down those perils, if we mobilize the unified strength and will of the nations of the Atlantic Community.

We of the Atlantic Community are the single most effective obstacle between tyranny and its desire to dominate the world. Our historic bonds of friendship have been strengthened by common values and a common goal—the creation of a world where free men can live at peace and in dignity, liberated from the bonds of hunger, poverty and ignorance. If we act together, this goal is within our grasp. If we falter, then freedom itself will be in mortal danger.

Therefore I pledge the United States, and my own unremitting efforts, to the support of the principles which guide our effort, to the basic concept of unity which gives us strength, and to the institutions we have created to give working life to our common intent.

Effective collective defense is the first mission of our great alliance in NATO. Our task here is to convince any aggressor that an attack on the territory of NATO members would be met with swift and punishing resistance. While relying also on the growing strength of all, the United States will continue its full participation in the common defense effort. I am convinced that the maintenance of U.S. military strength in Europe is essential to the security

of the Atlantic Community and the free world as a whole. Strength in Europe, like strength here in the United States, is an essential condition of peace.

But the interests of NATO, and the Atlantic Community as a whole, are not military alone. The dangers to our security and the challenges to our enterprise take many forms—economic, ideological and political. Through its various instruments the Atlantic Community must equip itself to respond with speed and unity of purpose on every front—by improving our processes of consultation—by expanding the area of our cooperation to include common problems of trade and money, and by uniting in the effort to construct a sound, growing economy for the entire non-Communist world.

This last undertaking—the task of economic development—is vital to the preservation of freedom in the turbulent, emerging continents of Asia, Africa and Latin America; it is also a duty which the strong owe to the weak. It is an undertaking unmatched in scope, in difficulty, and in nobility of purpose.

It is an important and heartening fact that the adventure of assisting the underdeveloped areas has captured the imagination and the idealism of the young on both sides of the Atlantic. This undertaking will require the efforts of all of us—and other nations too. In accomplishing all our economic tasks we must work together in a new intimacy in the OECD, and I hope that through the OECD we shall come firmly to grips with this fundamental problem of aid.

Although the technical task here is economic, our ultimate purpose transcends material considerations. The challenge is to create a new partnership between the old nations in the north and the new nations to the south. In the end, we must build that partnership not merely on a common interest in economic growth, but on a common commitment to the principles of political freedom.

The United States, because of its larger resources, is prepared to bear a heavy share of this burden. But I am confident that the nations of Western Europe will wish to commit an equitable proportion of their own growing resources to the common effort of economic development, as well as to the tasks of the common defense. Without that willingness our effort will surely fail. In all our common enterprises we must establish principles, clearly understood by our governments and our peoples, on which burden-sharing can be based.

We shall also continue to support and encourage the movement toward European integration. This movement is a powerful and unifying force which can multiply free Europe's strength and prestige, can assure increased security and progress for European peoples, and can contribute greatly to meeting the goals of the broader Atlantic Community.

The years ahead will be difficult and dangerous for the friends of freedom. There will be setbacks as well as gains. But if we face candidly the agenda that confronts us, our natural differences will fade and assume tolerable proportions. If we summon to the real tasks we face our resources of mind and will and material strength—if we never lose sight of our common goals—then we will have carried forward in our time the old task of our community: to preserve and extend the values of a civilization which has lighted man's way for more than 2500 years.

NOTE: The message to the Permanent Council of the North Atlantic Treaty Organization in Paris was read by Frederick W. Nolting, Deputy U.S. Representative to NATO.

35   The President's News Conference of *February* 15, 1961

THE PRESIDENT. I have several statements to make first, and then I will be glad to submit to questions.

[1.] Ambassador Stevenson in the Security Council today has expressed fully and clearly the attitude of the United States Government towards the attempts to undermine the effectiveness of the United Nations organization. The United States can take care of itself, but the United Nations system exists so that every nation can have the assurance of security. Any attempt to destroy this system is a blow aimed directly at the independence and security of every nation, large and small.

I am also, however, seriously concerned at what appears to be a threat of unilateral intervention in the internal affairs of the Republic of Congo. I find it difficult to believe that any government is really planning to take so dangerous and irresponsible a step. Nevertheless, I feel it important that there should be no misunderstanding of the position of the United States in such an eventuality.

The United States has supported and will continue to support the United Nations presence in the Congo. The United States considers that the only legal authority entitled to speak for the Congo as a whole is a government established under the Chief of State, President Kasavubu, who has been seated in the General Assembly of the United Nations by a majority vote of its members. The broadening of the government under President Kasavubu is a quite legitimate subject of discussion, and such discussions have been going on in Leopoldville and in New York. But the purported recognition of Congolese factions as so-called governments in other parts of that divided country can only confuse and make more difficult the task of securing Congolese independence and unity.

The United Nations offers the best, if not the only possibility for the restoration of conditions of stability and order in the Congo.

The press reports this afternoon that Prime Minister Nehru has stated, and I quote, "If the United Nations goes out of the Congo, it will be a disaster." I strongly agree with this view. Only by the presence of the United Nations in the Congo can peace be kept in Africa.

I would conceive it to be the duty of the United States and, indeed, all members of the United Nations to defend the Charter of the United Nations by opposing any attempt by any government to intervene unilaterally in the Congo.

[2.] Secondly, I have a statement that we have today recognized the Government of El Salvador. It has announced its determination to bring about free and democratic elections in that country, and it seeks solutions for the economic and social difficulties which that country has faced. These objectives are in consonance with our goal of a free and prosperous Latin America. Manifestos of the government and its agencies have indicated a clear determination to improve the standard of living of the people of that country, particularly those engaged in agriculture. We hope to be able to assist El Salvador in reaching these goals under the spirit of the act of Bogotá.

[3.] Thirdly, this country is most concerned about the very serious problem of unemployment which we have faced this winter and the more than five and a half million Americans who want to work and can't find a job.

We are particularly concerned about the more than 600,000 Americans who have exhausted their unemployment compensation checks and who are now on relief. We have sent to the Congress a program which we believe would be of assistance to the country and to them this winter. We do, as you know, provide for an extension of unemployment compensation benefits for those who have exhausted their benefits. We provide aid to unemployed workers. Today under the law a child of a worker who is out of work can only receive necessary assistance if his family splits up. We would correct that situation.

We sent a program up for aid to distressed areas.

We have sent up legislation improving the minimum wage.

We have sent up legislation to the Hill which will provide for an increase in social security benefits, and it will be followed by other programs as time goes on.

We have also provided for Executive action increasing the amount of food available in those areas of the United States where people live on these food packages.

I hope that we can get action on these programs as soon as possible. Today the Ways and Means Committee of the House held hearings on our program to extend unemployment compensation benefits. I am hopeful that we can move forward this winter so that some relief can be given to our fellow Americans.

In order to provide a stimulus to our economy I have provided, with the cooperation of the departments of the Government, for a speedup in programs using funds now available. Over $250 million, as we have said, will be distributed immediately under the GI dividend program. There are $4 billion for tax refunds which are coming due. As soon as those who are available for these refunds can put their applications in, we will attempt to stimulate and improve and quicken distribution of these funds.

We provided under the instructions given through the State of the Union Address for $700 million, committed this month for additional Polaris submarines and airlift capacity. In addition, we are providing through the Post Office a speedup in the programs to build post offices which had been authorized and approved by the Congress previously; but these programs would be developed in a more concentrated period than they would otherwise have been.

For farmers we have provided $75 million additional for loans to speed spring planting costs and also for farm home loans.

For the Federal highway construction program we are going to make $734 million to be available to the States this month. This program of course calls for action by the States and the local bodies. And we are sending, tonight, telegrams to all the State Governors asking if they also can provide for speedup in their programs.

I want to make it clear that we are going to continue to work in cooperation with the Governors and with the Congress, all agencies of the Government, because we want to see the American economy get back on its feet. We want to see these people working again.

In addition, the Small Business Administration plans to increase by 25 percent the criteria for what small businesses there are that are eligible for defense contracts. By increasing this criteria we will make other small businesses eligible who happen to be in areas where there is high unemployment.

I am hopeful that these programs will all be of assistance. Mr. Goldberg's tour showed that in States like Michigan, nearly 350,000 people are out of work; 12 percent of the people in Gary, Ind.—over 200,000 steel workers; and they need our help.

I will be glad to answer any questions.

[4.] Q. Mr. President, regarding the situation in the Congo and the crisis precipitated there by the Soviet Union, could you evaluate the impact on Soviet-American relations and your hopes that they might be improving?

THE PRESIDENT. This statement was carefully drawn and represents the policy of the United States at this time on these matters, and I am going to confine myself, in all questions on the Congo, to the statement that we have made. I think this is the most effective way to deal with it.

Q. Mr. President, in a related field, however, Mr. Khrushchev this afternoon, I think in a message replying to you, said that he welcomed your proposal that you voiced in the State of the Union Message for pooling American-Soviet efforts in space exploration projects. Do you think this sort of pooling and cooperation you envisioned in your State of the Union Message will still be possible under the tense conditions that developed in the U.N. today?

THE PRESIDENT. I hope it will be possible for the relations between the United States and the Soviet Union to develop in such a way that the peace can be protected and that it will be possible for us to use our energies along peaceful and productive and fruitful lines.

The development of space, preventing outer space from being used as a new area of war, of course, is of the greatest possible concern to the people of this country. I am hopeful that it will be possible, if relations between our two countries can be maintained, can be channeled along peaceful lines; I am hopeful that real progress can be made this year. But it is my earnest hope that our relations can remain harmonious and that it will be possible for us to cooperate in peaceful ventures rather than be differing on matters which carry with them such hazards.

[5.] Q. Along this line, sir, could you tell us how you would feel about a meeting at some time in the next few weeks or months with Mr. Khrushchev? Do you think it would be helpful or if it should be delayed?

THE PRESIDENT. There are no plans nor have there been any plans for any meeting with Mr. Khrushchev. As I said earlier, I have not heard whether Mr. Khrushchev is planning to come to the United Nations meeting. There are no other plans for a meeting at this time.

Q. If he did come, sir, would you welcome a visit of Mr. Khrushchev to Washington?

THE PRESIDENT. I would make a judgment as to what could usefully be done once we knew what Mr. Khrushchev's plans were and what—we would make a judgment as to what actions we would take. But I must say I have not heard that Mr. Khrushchev is planning to come to the United Nations at this time.

[6.] Q. Mr. President, you addressed a conference of businessmen here early this week and one of the officials of that conference noticed afterwards with some satisfaction that you hadn't used the word recession. He said he thought this was a good thing because in fact there was no business recession. Was your omission because you

agreed with him or how do you feel about the word and about the economic situation?

THE PRESIDENT. As you know, if you are unemployed and out of a job you think there is a recession. If you are working, perhaps the impact of the economic slowdown doesn't hit you quite as hard. I think we have been in a recession for some months and that we have not recovered fully from the recession of '58, which is a matter, of course, of great concern.

We are concerned because while there was an economic slowdown in '49, and '54, and '58, we now have an economic slowdown only 2 years after the '58 recession. So this compounds our difficulties. I think that—well, to—to put it precisely to things, then I would call this a recession.

[7.] Q. In line, sir, with your statement a moment ago that you hoped that the relations between United States and Russia would improve, Adm. Arleigh Burke is quoted in some newspapers today in an interview in which he makes some rather sharp comments on American and Russian relations and among other things says that the United States Navy would sail into the Black Sea if it so chose. I am asking, sir, is this in line with your administration policy that all high officials should speak with one voice?

THE PRESIDENT. I have been informed—and perhaps Mr. Salinger can correct me—that that interview was given on January 12, which was before the administration took over January 20 and before we gave any indication that we would like all statements dealing with national security to be coordinated. I would say that this makes me happier than ever that such a directive has gone out. [*Laughter*]

[8.] Q. Mr. President, I would like to change the scene here to Cuba, if I may, for a moment. A member of Congress has raised the issue of possible conflict in our trade policy towards Cuba. He points out that under President Eisenhower's order all exports from this country to Cuba were barred. On the other hand, we are now importing considerable quantities of Cuban goods. Specifically this member of Congress pointed out one liquor company has purchased $12 million of Cuban molasses. Also we are importing considerable quantities of Cuban fruit and vegetables. Have you done anything about it or are you looking into this matter or contemplate doing anything about it?

THE PRESIDENT. The molasses has not been purchased as yet. It was intended, as I understand, to be purchased during the next month, and that is a private transaction. There are seventy, I think, or eighty million dollars worth of fruit, tobacco, and so on which are coming in, mostly to Florida. We are now making a study of what would be the most beneficial action we could take in regard to that.

On the molasses there is some question as to under what conditions we could intervene in that transaction, but, of course, it has been my hope that that transaction would not be consummated. I am not convinced that we are totally without resources and we are considering what we could take to consider that particular transaction. Twelve million dollars, I believe, is supposed to be made into gin—and I am not sure that that is in the public interest. [*Laughter*]

[9.] Q. Sir, on the space probe towards Venus made by the Soviets recently, do you think this would point up any space gap between our two countries, and do you see there is any need for a speedup in our efforts in that field?

THE PRESIDENT. The Soviet Union, as I said in the State of the Union, of course, is

ahead of us in boosters and there is an indication they are going to be ahead of us for some time to come. This was, as I said in my statement at the time, this is a scientific achievement that is an impressive one. We have made exceptional gains in space technology, which may not be as dramatic as Sputnik or as a probe to Venus but which in the long run does, at least I think should, give all Americans satisfaction in the efforts that we have made.

Boosters, however, we are behind on and it is a matter of great concern. The Soviet Union made significant breakthrough in this area some years ago. They have continued to maintain their lead, and it explains why they were ahead of us in Sputnik and it explains why they have been able to put larger objects into space. We have to recognize their chances of continuing to do that unless we are able to make a breakthrough before the Saturn booster comes into operation. Unless we are able to make a scientific breakthrough we have to recognize that we are in a position—secondary position on boosters. It is a matter of great concern. We have sufficiently large boosters to protect us militarily, but for the long, heavy exploration into space, which requires large boosters, the Soviet Union has been ahead and it is going to be a major task to surpass them.

[10.] Q. Mr. President, this is a question on the sound dollar. A relative of yours, a Republican relative, Mr. Bayard Auchincloss of Oklahoma City, has started a one-man campaign to regain—to restore the sound dollar. He has said that the public needs to be inspired by some forceful leadership in Washington to lead them in one major phase—and that is: fighting Government waste. Sir, do you propose to spark such leadership from the White House, or do you have other means in mind by which the public can assist you in regaining the sound dollar?

THE PRESIDENT. Well, I don't want to deny kinship. But I—to the best of my knowledge, he is not related to me.

Q. Your step-second cousin. [*Laughter*]

THE PRESIDENT. Well, then he is related to me. But we have not met; I have not heard from him directly. We want to—as a matter of fact, several members of the Congress—I was Chairman of the Subcommittee on Government Reorganization which attempted to put through some of the Hoover Commission recommendations—we are going to continue to work with a smaller staff beginning, of course, from the White House. And I am hopeful that all members of this Government will not consider now that they have been placed in position of responsibility that the test of their good work is the size of their staff. We are going to continue to try and will seek the cooperation of every citizen of this country in making sure that we get value for every dollar that the Government spends.

The Government spends a great deal of money. In fact, I asked, yesterday, Mr. Bell to talk to Senator Douglas and Congressman Hébert, who conducted hearings on waste in the Pentagon and have suggested it might be possible to save more than $1 billion, to meet with them. And we are going to continue to meet with every citizen, whether he is my relative or not—I would be glad to hear from Mr. Auchincloss. It is an important problem. When the Government spends over $80 billion we know we can do a better job in spending that money more wisely. And I would be delighted and I welcome the view of Mr. Auchincloss or any other citizen and all members of this administration to try to maintain a balance between revenue and expenditures.

[11.] Q. Mr. President, in regard to your program to distribute surplus foods to needy people in other countries, 2 weeks ago Dr. Fry, who is head of the World Council of Churches, advocated that this be done through Government channels and not through church or other private agencies. He said that the private agencies just can't insure that the food is going to reach the most needy, which our Government regulations require. Has your administration formulated a policy on this, or do you have a comment on it?

THE PRESIDENT. Well, of course some does go through the governments and then we have relied upon private agencies. I would be very reluctant to abandon private agencies because they have done a first-class job in assisting us to get this food out.

I would be glad to see his comments and see what his suggestions would be. The alternative, of course, would be for us to distribute through the government involved, and we have never felt that that was better than having it done through voluntary groups. But Mr. McGovern is now in Latin America and he is looking at what we can do in that area, in food for peace, and I am sure that he will come back with some proposals on how we can make this distribution more effective.

Q. May I just say, excuse me, sir, Dr. Fry does not suggest clothing and so forth—he still wants that which is contributed voluntarily to be distributed through the church. But just our Government surplus food.

THE PRESIDENT. We will look into that.

[12.] Q. Mr. President, have you determined whether any employee of our State Department was responsible or had any part in advancing the Communist foothold in Cuba, and if so, sir, will you take steps to remove them from office?

THE PRESIDENT. I think that probably miscalculations were made by our country in assessing in Cuba, but I have no evidence that anyone did it out of any other motive but to serve the United States.

[13.] Q. Mr. President, to clarify an earlier answer you made, is it your view that we can proceed in serious negotiations with the Soviet Union in such areas as arms control and nuclear test ban while they continue to agitate the situation in the United Nations and in the Congo? In other words, can we conduct relations with them in compartments?

THE PRESIDENT. I am hopeful that all countries that are members of the United Nations will make a determination to operate in the Congo through the United Nations. I think that that is essential. As I said in my statement, unilateral intervention by one country or a group of countries outside of the United Nations, would endanger the United Nations and endanger peace in Africa. I am hopeful that that will come to be the judgment of all members of the United Nations. And if it does, I think that we will find ourselves with the prospects of peace increased.

[14.] Q. Following up Mr. Kent's question, Mr. President, the Republican Party as a whole seems to also take the view that your administration has overstated the economic recession. I wonder, sir, if you have given any thought to conferring with the Republican leaders in Congress in hopes of getting their support for your program to solve the economic recession, and if you have made available to them all the information that your administration has on the economic situation?

THE PRESIDENT. To answer your second part, we have made available all the information that we have. I have described it. Everyone can look at these figures and come to the conclusion that—their own conclu-

sion. I see no necessity or desirability of minimizing our problems. I think only by facing the problems with precision is it possible to get action.

I want the cooperation of the leadership on both sides and will make every effort that I can to seek the support of Members of the House and Senate on both sides of the aisle. But anyone who looks at the million cars in inventory today, who looks at the figures on unemployment, who looks at the steel capacity operating at about 50 percent of capacity—who looks at the 600,000 Americans who have exhausted their unemployment compensation, who looks at five and a half million Americans who are out of work, who looks at our decline in economic growth since last spring, I would say would come to the same conclusion that I have: that it is necessary for us to take action.

The fact that a judgment was made the last year about what 1960 would be—1960 was not the most prosperous year in our history as had been estimated earlier. We are now—find ourselves obliged to take action this winter. And by calling it a recession or calling it—saying it is not a recession, calling it a plateau—that's no excuse for not taking action. In my opinion it is essential that we move forward this winter because we don't want to find ourselves in the winter and the spring and the summer debating about our problem of whether we are in an economic recession or whether we have an economic decline and finding at the end of the congressional session that no action has been taken, only that all of my statements have had impact, I believe, of a snowflake in the Potomac, which was the description used by a distinguished Member of the Congress. I hope they have more effect than that.

[15.] Q. Mr. President, your task force

97

on distressed areas considers an independent agency with an administrator directly responsible to you the most efficient way of coping with this urgent problem. They are fearful that it might get fragmented if it were made a bureau in the Commerce Department. Do you have any objection to the creation of an independent agency under your authority?

THE PRESIDENT. I believe that it would be most advantageous to have it in the Department of Commerce with all of the resources of the Department of Commerce to supplement its work. That would be my first choice. If the Congress makes a different judgment, however, I would accept that and say that an independent agency would be useful. But I do think that with Governor Hodges, who is committed to the program, with a Cabinet officer to represent their views at Cabinet meetings, and with the broad range of responsibilities which the Department of Commerce has, that this is the best place to put it. But this is a matter on which I would certainly listen to the Congress if they came to a different conclusion.

[16.] Q. Mr. President, if other nations become reluctant to assign troops to the U.N. for police work in the Congo, would you tell us whether we would consider contributing American units?

THE PRESIDENT. Well, we are now hopeful that the policy which the Secretary General has followed, of securing troops for the Congo from Africa and Asia—we are hopeful that that is going to be successful. And until that fails—I don't think we should go under any assumption that he is going to fail, and if he does fail then we will have to make a new judgment. But I am hopeful that those countries which are most involved with maintaining the security and independence of the African countries and peace in Africa, that they will continue to respond

to the Secretary General's appeal for support. And that is also true, of course, of Asian nations who are also concerned, particularly the smaller countries. We hope that they can maintain control of troop movements and not begin to have troops from larger countries with all of the hazards that that might bring.

Q. Mr. President, in view of your remarks about the Congo and other world problems, do you regard the future developments in the Congo as a kind of good faith test for the prospect of improving the international atmosphere as a whole?

THE PRESIDENT. Well, of course, if we fail—if the United Nations fails in the Congo, if we who are members of the United Nations fail, then of course the future usefulness of the United Nations will be impaired. And I think that this would be particularly serious for smaller countries.

As I said in my statement, the United States is not a small country. We can defend ourselves. Countries which I think must rely particularly upon the United Nations are smaller countries. The smallest country in the United Nations has the same vote in the General Assembly as the Soviet Union and the United States. And therefore I would think that they would be reluctant to see the United Nations fragmented, to see its usefulness impaired, to see the authority of the Secretary General, who represents all the members of the United Nations, to see it lessened. So I regard this as a most important test of the future effectiveness of the United Nations.

Q. Mr. President, do you find that the United States as a great power, as you have described, with legitimate interests all around the world, is sometimes hampered in the pursuit of these national interests by its membership in the United Nations? Could you conceive of a situation perhaps in Latin America where we would be hampered in a place where we had a vital interest by United Nations action?

THE PRESIDENT. Well, I suppose it is possible always to conceive of situations, but I will say that the United Nations action in— for example, the fact that they maintained troops in the Gaza Strip for a number of years, I think, has been helpful in maintaining peace in that area. And the Congo has been an extremely difficult assignment and responsibility for the United Nations. But at least we have not had as yet massive unilateral intervention by great powers with all of the risks of war that that might bring, and with all the dangers to the peace that

that might bring, because of the way the United Nations has met its responsibilities. So, I am a strong believer in the United Nations and while it is possible to say that they might interfere with some legitimate interest of ours in the future, I am prepared to say that their actions in the past, at present, and I believe in the future represent the legitimate common interest of all members of the United Nations.

Reporter: Thank you, Mr. President.

THE PRESIDENT. Thank you.

NOTE: President Kennedy's fourth news conference, broadcast over radio and television, was held in the State Department Auditorium at 7 o'clock on Wednesday evening, February 15, 1961.

36 Exchange of Messages With Prime Minister Adams of the West Indies on the Occasion of the Signing of a Mutual Defense Agreement. *February 16, 1961*

[Released February 16, 1961.   Dated February 9, 1961]

Dear Mr. Prime Minister:

I wish to thank you and your cabinet colleagues for your thoughtful message of congratulation upon my inauguration in office. It gives me particular pleasure upon the occasion of the signing of a new agreement providing for our mutual defense to reciprocate your confidence in the endurance and strength of the present friendly relations between our two countries. The United States looks forward to the time when The West Indies will become an independent member of the British Commonwealth of Nations and to the opportunity of welcoming her into the hemispheric community.

Sincerely,

JOHN F. KENNEDY

[His Excellency, Sir Grantley Adams, C.M.G., Q.C., Prime Minister of The West Indies, Port-of-Spain, Trinidad]

NOTE: Prime Minister Adams' letter, dated February 14, 1961, follows:

The President of the United States
White House

Dear Mr. President:

I offer my sincere thanks for the great kindness of your letter sent to me on the occasion of the signing of the Defence Areas Agreement in Port of Spain. The reading of your letter added a note of the highest significance to the Signing Ceremony.

My Government and I warmly reciprocate your expressions of good will which serve to increase our satisfaction in the close and enduring friendship between our two countries, upon which this Agreement and our cooperation in defence and other spheres, are founded.

We are particularly grateful to you, Mr. President for having made it possible for The Honourable John Hay Whitney to be your special representative at the culminating stage of an understanding, to the success of which Mr. Whitney's broad vision and sincerity have made so unique a contribution.

All has gone well and to good purpose. The presence of Mr. Weaver and Dr. Garcia at this time and their wide knowledge and sympathetic approach to human problems in their respective fields, have enabled us to have with them discussions which proved of the highest value to us.

I would also pay tribute to the magnificent efforts, over many months, of United States Officials and Services who produced work of the highest distinction, enabling this Agreement which gives such mutual satisfaction, to be perfected so expeditiously.

Yours sincerely,

GRANTLEY ADAMS

On February 15 the White House released a statement by Ambassador John Hay Whitney, chairman

of the U.S. delegation in the negotiations with the Federation of the West Indies. The text of Ambassador Whitney's statement is published in the Department of State Bulletin (vol. 44, p. 350). Other members of the delegation included George Weaver, Special Assistant to the Secretary of Labor, and Dr. Hector Garcia.

The agreement between the United States and the Federation of the West Indies concerning U.S. defense areas in the Federation entered into force February 10, 1961, the date of signing. It is printed together with related documents in Treaties and Other International Acts Series 4734 (Government Printing Office).

37   Telegram to the Governors of the States Urging Action To Bolster the Economy by Speeding Up Public Works.
February 16, 1961

[Released February 16, 1961.   Dated February 15, 1961]

Dear Governor ————:

I urge prompt consideration of specific action at every level of government in this country to invigorate our economy, including acceleration of State and local projects that are genuinely useful and will provide immediate jobs and business help. I also personally want to emphasize the fact that the Federal Government has released for obligation this month $724 million for the Federal Aid Highway Program and $350

million in appropriations for direct Federal construction and construction grants primarily for hospitals, schools in federally affected areas, and waste treatment facilities. Use of these funds is now largely dependent on State and local action. I will appreciate your cooperation to speed these and other needed public programs to strengthen the economy in your area and throughout the Nation.

JOHN F. KENNEDY

38   Statement by the President on Secretary Rusk's Decision To Attend the SEATO Council of Ministers Meeting in Bangkok.
February 16, 1961

I AM HIGHLY PLEASED that the Secretary of State, despite his crowded calendar, has decided to attend the SEATO Council of Ministers Meeting at Bangkok on March 27.

The Council Meeting will afford the Secretary his first opportunity to meet personally with the Foreign Ministers of the mem-

ber states of this important organization. This meeting will also provide the Secretary with a far-reaching opportunity to participate in and contribute to SEATO's vital work of promoting peace, stability and regional solidarity in the face of the threat now posed to Southeast Asia by the continuing communist pressures. One of the subjects the Secretary expects to discuss with his colleagues in SEATO will be the most effective way to conduct the future business of that Organization.

Details of Mr. Rusk's itinerary as well as the composition of the Delegation will be announced later by the Department of State.

I understand that the Secretary's time is severely limited and that his route to Bangkok will necessarily be as direct as possible.

NOTE: The list of members of the U.S. delegation accompanying Secretary Rusk to the SEATO Council at Bangkok is published in the Department of State Bulletin (vol. 44, p. 550).

39   Letter to the President of the Senate and to the Speaker of the House Transmitting a Special Program for Feed Grains. *February* 16, 1961

Dear Mr. ————:

I am transmitting herewith a bill to provide a special program for feed grains for 1961. I urgently recommend to the Congress the enactment of this emergency program so that it can cover the 1961 crop.

The existing program has failed. It has resulted in the accumulation of a burdensome and dangerous surplus, mainly of commodities for which there is no adequate outlet even under our expanded programs of providing food for those in need. At the same time, it has failed to protect farm income, and it is threatening to drive down the prices farmers receive for hogs, cattle, poultry and eggs, and milk to disastrous levels. If this program is allowed to continue in effect for this year's crop, the stocks in Government hands will reach even more alarming proportions, a virtually unmanageable storage problem will be created, farm income will continue to suffer, and large amounts of Government funds will be needlessly expended. Immediate action is required to prevent further deterioration of this situation. In order to be effective with respect to this year's crops, a new program should be authorized by March 1st.

I believe that any legislation enacted should fit our over-all goal to use our agri-

cultural abundance to meet the needs of our people, and at the same time provide a fair income for those who produce that abundance. We need to shift our production from commodities of which there is an unmanageable surplus to commodities for which there is a need, even as we curtail our production of those surplus commodities. The Secretary of Agriculture already has authority to take steps toward these goals with regard to some commodities, such as milk, soybeans and cottonseed, pork, poultry and eggs. However, new legislation is needed for effective action with respect to corn and other feed grains. The legislation I am now recommending will fill this gap with the authority needed to round out an emergency program for this year in the feed grain sector of our farm economy.

Although this is an emergency program, it is consistent with our long-range objectives and would accomplish the following: (1) a moderate increase in farm income; (2) a saving of several hundred million dollars of Government funds; and (3) a holding down or reduction of surplus stocks to more manageable proportions. This will be done without any material effect upon consumer prices.

The Government now holds 2.7 billion bushels of feed grains. The investment in feed grains stands at the all-time high of nearly $4 billion. The 1961 crop will soon be planted. By this fall, the nation will be confronted once again with a shortage of space in which to store grain. The shortage may amount to the off-farm space required for as much as 200 to 250 million bushels if we fail to take any preventive action now. The storage problem will be further accentuated in 1962.

The legislative proposals submitted herewith (1) would provide that cooperators would receive a support price of $1.20 a bushel for corn for 1961, and would receive supports for other feed grains in relation to those for corn; and (2) would authorize a special agricultural conservation program under which acreage previously planted to feed grains would be diverted from production for 1961. Unlike the present program under which a support price of $1.06 a bushel is paid to all producers without

regard to any limit on production, producers will not be eligible for price supports under this new program unless they cooperate in the special agricultural conservation program.

This emergency program covers only the 1961 crop. I intend to recommend to the Congress other legislation covering both wheat and feed grain crops for subsequent years.

There is attached hereto a letter from the Secretary of Agriculture setting forth the details of the program. It is important that it be accorded the prompt consideration of the Congress.

Sincerely,

JOHN F. KENNEDY

NOTE: This is the text of identical letters addressed to the Honorable Lyndon B. Johnson, President of the Senate, and to the Honorable Sam Rayburn, Speaker of the House of Representatives.

Secretary Freeman's letter, dated February 16, 1961, was also released.

40   Statement by the President Upon Signing Order Establishing the President's Advisory Committee on Labor-Management Policy. *February 16, 1961*

I AM TODAY issuing an Executive Order establishing the President's Advisory Committee on Labor-Management Policy. The Committee is composed of the Secretary of Labor, the Secretary of Commerce and 19 other members from the public, labor and management. The Secretary of Labor and the Secretary of Commerce will alternate as chairman of the Committee for periods of one year, the Secretary of Labor serving during the first year.

The purpose of this Committee is to help our free institutions work better and to encourage sound economic growth and healthy industrial relations. The Commit-

tee will study, advise me, and make recommendations with respect to policies that may be followed by labor, management, government, or the public which will promote free and responsible collective bargaining, industrial peace, sound wage and price policies, higher standards of living and increased productivity. The Committee has been directed to include among the matters to be considered by it: (1) policies designed to ensure that American products are competitive in world markets, and (2) the benefits and problems created by automation and other technological advances.

I deem this a most important Committee.

It will bring to the great problems in the fields of collective bargaining, industrial relations, wage and price policies, and productivity the experience and wisdom of labor, management and public experts in these fields.

It is my hope that the Committee may help restore that sense of common purpose which has strengthened our Nation in times of emergency and generate a climate conducive to cooperation and resolution of differences.

It is my hope that the advice of this Committee will assist the Government, labor, management, and the general public to achieve greater understanding of the problems which beset us in these troubled times and to find solutions consistent with our democratic traditions, our free enterprise economy, and our determination that this country shall move forward to a better life for all its people.

The membership list of the Committee is attached. It is gratifying that I have been able to obtain the participation of such outstanding persons in the Committee's work. I greatly appreciate the willingness of these public-spirited citizens to serve their country in this way. The fact that such highly qualified persons have agreed to be members of this important Committee augurs well for its success.

NOTE: For citation to Executive Order 10918, see Appendix B.

The following list of members was released with the President's statement:

Management: Thomas J. Watson, Jr.; President of International Business Machines (New York); Joseph Block, President of Inland Steel Corporation (Illinois); Henry Ford, II, Chairman of the Board, Ford Motor Company (Michigan); J. Spencer Love, Chairman of the Board, Burlington Industries (North Carolina); John Franklin, President of the United States Lines (New York); Richard S. Reynolds, Jr., President of Reynolds Aluminum (Virginia); Elliot V. Bell, Editor and Publisher of Business Week (New York).

Labor: George Meany, President of the AFL–CIO; Walter Reuther, President of the UAW; David Dubinsky, President of the ILGWU; George M. Harrison, President of the Railway Labor Clerks; Thomas Kennedy, President of the UMW; David J. McDonald, President of United Steelworkers; Joseph D. Keenan, Secretary-Treasurer of the International Electrical Workers.

Public: Ralph McGill, Editor of the Atlanta Constitution (Georgia); David L. Cole, labor arbitrator from Paterson, New Jersey; Dr. George W. Taylor, University of Pennsylvania, Professor of Labor Relations, Wharton School of Business Administration; Clark Kerr, Chancellor of the University of California; Dr. Arthur F. Burns, Chairman of the National Bureau of Economic Research; Secretary of Commerce Luther H. Hodges (ex officio); Secretary of Labor Arthur J. Goldberg (ex officio).

41 Joint Statement Following Discussions With the Foreign Minister of Germany. *February 17, 1961*

THE PRESIDENT of the United States received the Foreign Minister of the Federal Republic of Germany, Dr. Heinrich von Brentano, on February 17, 1961, for a discussion of questions of mutual interest to both countries. Together with his previous conversations with Secretary of State Dean Rusk, the discussion provided an occasion for a first personal exchange of views between Dr. von Brentano and the New United States Administration. The cordial and frank conversations confirmed the friendly and close relations between the Federal Republic and the United States.

There was particular agreement that the North Atlantic Alliance is a necessary basis for the defense of both countries and that all members of the Alliance have a mutual responsibility for its further strengthening. They confirmed the continuing importance of the goal of German reunification based upon the principle of self-determination and of the preservation of the freedom of the people of West Berlin.

Both governments agreed that the persistent imbalance in the international payments situation called for concerted and vigorous action on the part of the free world. Unless and until this imbalance is substantially corrected it will continue to impede the free world's efforts to provide for the common defense and supply the resources needed by the less-developed countries to meet their legitimate aspirations.

Both the United States and the Federal German Republic have recognized this principle in previous discussions. Proceeding from this basis both governments will continue their talks on appropriate measures which can be taken to contribute to this end. In so doing they will act in concert with their common allies.

The President heard with satisfaction that the Federal Government will be prepared to provide the necessary means to carry on its program for the underdeveloped countries in future years.

42 Statement by the President Upon Signing Order Abolishing the Operations Coordinating Board. *February 19, 1961*

I AM TODAY issuing an Executive Order abolishing the Operations Coordinating Board. This Board was used in the last Administration for work which we now plan to do in other ways. This action is part of our program for strengthening the responsibility of the individual departments.

First, we will center responsibility for much of the Board's work in the Secretary of State. He expects to rely particularly on the Assistant Secretaries in charge of regional bureaus, and they in turn will consult closely with other departments and agencies. This will be our ordinary rule for continuing coordination of our work in relation to a country or area.

Second, insofar as the OCB—as a descendant of the old Psychological Strategy Board—was concerned with the impact of our actions on foreign opinion—our "image" abroad—we expect its work to be done in a number of ways: in my own office, in the State Department, under Mr. Murrow

of USIA, and by all who are concerned with the spirit and meaning of our actions in foreign policy. We believe that appropriate coordination can be assured here without extensive formal machinery.

Third, insofar as the OCB served as an instrument for ensuring action at the President's direction, we plan to continue its work by maintaining direct communication with the responsible agencies, so that everyone will know what I have decided, while I in turn keep fully informed of the actions taken to carry out decisions. We of course expect that the policy of the White House will be the policy of the Executive Branch as a whole, and we shall take such steps as are needed to ensure this result.

I expect that the senior officials who served as formal members of OCB will still keep in close and informal touch with each other on problems of common interest. Mr. Bromley Smith, who has been the Executive Officer of the OCB, will continue to work with my Special Assistant, Mr. Mc-George Bundy, in following up on White House decisions in the area of national security. In these varied ways we intend that

the net result shall be a strengthening of the process by which our policies are effectively coordinated and carried out, throughout the Executive Branch.

43   Letter to the President of the Senate and to the Speaker of the House Transmitting Bill To Amend the Social Security Act. *February* 20, 1961

My dear Mr. ————:

I am transmitting herewith a bill to make five needed improvements in the social security program.

They will not only help to meet pressing social needs, but if promptly enacted these improvements will give our economic recovery program needed impetus. They will result in placing increased purchasing power in the hands of almost five million people. These people are among the lowest income groups in the country.

In addition, the legislation will improve the flexibility and effectiveness of our social security program over the long run and make it better able to contribute to the economic strength of the Nation and the welfare and security of our people.

The enclosed letter from the Secretary of Health, Education, and Welfare describes the legislation in more detail.

Sincerely,

JOHN F. KENNEDY

NOTE: This is the text of identical letters addressed to the Honorable Lyndon B. Johnson, President of the Senate, and to the Honorable Sam Rayburn, Speaker of the House of Representatives.

Secretary Ribicoff's letter, also released, recommended the following improvements in the social security program:

1. Increases in the minimum benefits.
2. Retirement benefits for men at age 62.
3. Liberalization of the insured status requirements.
4. Increases in benefits for widows, widowers, or parents.
5. Providing benefits after 6-months total disability even though it is expected the worker will eventually recover.

44   Letter to the Speaker of the House of Representatives Transmitting a Distressed Area Redevelopment Bill. *February* 20, 1961

Dear Mr. Speaker:

On January 25, in letters addressed to you and to the Vice President, I recommended the enactment of legislation to redevelop areas of substantial and persistent unemployment. Enclosed for the consideration of the Congress is a draft of a bill which would carry out this purpose.

This matter has been the subject of long study by both the Federal Government and private interests. The need is urgent. The benefits to the national economy are clear. When enacted, the legislation will help develop long-term job opportunities in those parts of our Nation which are suffering most from unemployment. It will encourage new industry to locate and existing industry to expand in industrial areas and in underdeveloped rural and small urban areas which require a better balance of industry and agriculture.

The basic provisions of the bill are those which:

1. Provide technical assistance to local communities to enable them to plan intelligently their economic development and to explore methods of expansion of their industrial resources;

2. Provide for participating loans to meet the gap created when conventional lending facilities are unavailable to the local industry;

3. Provide for modernized public facili-

ties, such as access roads, industrial water, industrial parks and public utilities, so that industry will be encouraged to locate in these areas;

4. Provide, in cooperation with State, local and private organizations, for the expansion of facilities and opportunities for training and re-training the labor force in new and improved skills.

I believe it is essential that we enact this legislation at the earliest possible date. It will constitute a major effort to revive and redevelop communities which have too long been handicapped.

Sincerely,

JOHN F. KENNEDY

45 Joint Statement Following Discussions With Prime Minister Diefenbaker of Canada. *February 20, 1961*

PRESIDENT KENNEDY and Prime Minister Diefenbaker met today in Washington to discuss informally a wide range of international problems as well as bilateral questions of interest to the two countries. The Secretary of State, Mr. Dean Rusk, and the United States Ambassador-designate to Canada, Mr. Livingston Merchant, assisted in these discussions together with the Secretary of State for External Affairs, Mr. Howard Green, and the Canadian Ambassador to the United States, Mr. Arnold Heeney.

The President and the Prime Minister welcomed this early opportunity for a friendly exchange of views between neighbors, in a tradition consistent with the long and intimate association between the peoples of Canada and the United States.

The President and the Prime Minister reviewed defense and security problems in all their aspects. They reaffirmed their purpose to work together for peace and freedom in the world. They expressed their

readiness to cooperate wholeheartedly with all countries which sincerely seek this objective whatever the differences in approach or outlook. They recognized the central importance of the United Nations, as well as the essential role of direct diplomatic negotiation, in the pursuit of peaceful settlements. They agreed on the need to work steadily toward effective agreements under international control in the field of disarmament.

In reviewing the bilateral problems between the two countries, emphasis was placed upon the various consultative arrangements of a formal and informal character which have been developed between the United States and Canada as a valuable supplement to the traditionally close and friendly relations between the two governments. The President and the Prime Minister noted with satisfaction that joint meetings are about to take place in Canada between members of both houses of the federal legislatures of the two nations.

The President and the Prime Minister re-emphasized the importance of close consultation on economic matters. They announced that the joint United States-Canada Committee on Trade and Economic Affairs will meet in Washington, D.C. on March 13. This joint Committee at Cabinet level has been of great value over the years in furthering understanding between the two governments on questions affecting economic relations of the two countries.

46   Special Message to the Congress on Education. *February 20, 1961*

To the Congress of the United States:

Our progress as a nation can be no swifter than our progress in education. Our requirements for world leadership, our hopes for economic growth, and the demands of citizenship itself in an era such as this all require the maximum development of every young American's capacity.

The human mind is our fundamental resource. A balanced Federal program must go well beyond incentives for investment in plant and equipment. It must include equally determined measures to invest in human beings—both in their basic education and training and in their more advanced preparation for professional work. Without such measures, the Federal Government will not be carrying out its responsibilities for expanding the base of our economic and military strength.

Our progress in education over the last generation has been substantial. We are educating a greater proportion of our youth to a higher degree of competency than any other country on earth. One-fourth of our total population is enrolled in our schools and colleges. This year 26 billion dollars will be spent on education alone.

But the needs of the next generation—the needs of the next decade and the next school year—will not be met at this level of effort. More effort will be required—on the part of students, teachers, schools, colleges and all 50 states—and on the part of the Federal Government.

Education must remain a matter of state and local control, and higher education a matter of individual choice. But education is increasingly expensive. Too many state and local governments lack the resources to assure an adequate education for every child. Too many classrooms are overcrowded. Too many teachers are underpaid. Too many talented individuals cannot afford the benefits of higher education. Too many academic institutions cannot afford the cost of, or find room for, the growing numbers of students seeking admission in the 60's.

Our twin goals must be: a new standard of excellence in education—and the availability of such excellence to all who are willing and able to pursue it.

I. ASSISTANCE TO PUBLIC ELEMENTARY AND SECONDARY SCHOOLS

A successful educational system requires the proper balance, in terms of both quality and quantity, of three elements: students, teachers and facilities. The quality of the students depends in large measure on both the quality and the relative quantity of teachers and facilities.

Throughout the 1960's there will be no lack in the quantity of students. An average net gain of nearly one million pupils a year during the next ten years will over-burden a school system already strained by well over a half-million pupils in curtailed or half-day sessions, a school system financed largely by a property tax incapable of bearing such an increased load in most communities.

But providing the quality and quantity of teachers and facilities to meet this demand will be major problems. Even today, there are some 90,000 teachers who fall short of full certification standards. Tens of thousands of others must attempt to cope with classes of unwieldy size because there are insufficient teachers available.

We cannot obtain more and better teachers—and our children should have the best—unless steps are taken to increase teachers' salaries. At present salary levels, the classroom cannot compete in financial rewards with other professional work that requires similar academic background.

It is equally clear that we do not have enough classrooms. In order to meet current needs and accommodate increasing enrollments, if every child is to have the opportunity of a full-day education in an adequate classroom, a total of 600,000 classrooms must be constructed during the next ten years.

These problems are common to all states. They are particularly severe in those states which lack the financial resources to provide a better education, regardless of their own efforts. Additional difficulties, too often overlooked, are encountered in areas of special educational need, where economic or social circumstances impose special burdens and opportunities on the public school. These areas of special educational need include our depressed areas of chronic unemployment and the slum neighborhoods of our larger cities, where underprivileged children are overcrowded into substandard housing. A recent survey of a very large

elementary school in one of our major cities, for example, found 91% of the children coming to class with poor diets, 87% in need of dental care, 21% in need of visual correction and 19% with speech disorders. In some depressed areas roughly one-third of the children must rely on surplus foods for their basic sustenance. Older pupils in these schools lack proper recreational and job guidance. The proportion of drop-outs, delinquency and classroom disorders in such areas in alarmingly high.

I recommend to the Congress a three-year program of general Federal assistance for public elementary and secondary classroom construction and teachers' salaries.

Based essentially on the bill which passed the Senate last year (S. 8), although beginning at a more modest level of expenditures, this program would assure every state of no less than $15 for every public school student in average daily attendance, with the total amount appropriated (666 million dollars being authorized in the first year, rising to $866 million over a three-year period) distributed according to the equalization formula contained in the last year's Senate bill, and already familiar to the Congress by virtue of its similarity to the formulas contained in the Hill-Burton Hospital Construction and other acts. Ten percent of the funds allocated to each state in the first year, and an equal amount thereafter, is to be used to help meet the unique problems of each state's "areas of special educational need"—depressed areas, slum neighborhoods and others.

This is a modest program with ambitious goals. The sums involved are relatively small when we think in terms of more than 36 million public school children, and the billions of dollars necessary to educate them properly. Nevertheless, a limited beginning now—consistent with our obligations in other areas of responsibility—will encourage all states to expand their facilities to meet the increasing demand and enrich the quality of education offered, and gradually assist our relatively low-income states in the elevation of their educational standards to a national level.

The bill which will follow this message has been carefully drawn to eliminate disproportionately large or small inequities, and to make the maximum use of a limited number of dollars. In accordance with the clear prohibition of the Constitution, no elementary or secondary school funds are allocated for constructing church schools or paying church school teachers' salaries; and thus non-public school children are rightfully not counted in determining the funds each state will receive for its public schools. Each state will be expected to maintain its own effort or contribution; and every state whose effort is below the national average will be expected to increase that proportion of its income which is devoted to public elementary and secondary education.

This investment will pay rich dividends in the years ahead—in increased economic growth, in enlightened citizens, in national excellence. For some 40 years, the Congress has wrestled with this problem and searched for a workable solution. I believe that we now have such a solution; and that this Congress in this year will make a land-mark contribution to American education.

II. CONSTRUCTION OF COLLEGE AND UNIVERSITY FACILITIES

Our colleges and universities represent our ultimate educational resource. In these institutions are produced the leaders and other trained persons whom we need to carry forward our highly developed civiliza-

tion. If the colleges and universities fail to do their job, there is no substitute to fulfill their responsibility. The threat of opposing military and ideological forces in the world lends urgency to their task. But that task would exist in any case.

The burden of increased enrollments—imposed upon our elementary and secondary schools already in the fifties—will fall heavily upon our colleges and universities during the sixties. By the autumn of 1966, an estimated one million more students will be in attendance at institutions of higher learning than enrolled last fall—for a total more than twice as high as the total college enrollment of 1950. Our colleges, already hard-pressed to meet rising enrollments since 1950 during a period of rising costs, will be in critical straits merely to provide the necessary facilities, much less the cost of quality education.

The country as a whole is already spending nearly $1 billion a year on academic and residential facilities for higher education—some 20 percent of the total spent for higher education. Even with increased contributions from state, local and private sources, a gap of $2.9 billion between aggregate needs and expenditures is anticipated by 1965, and a gap of $5.2 billion by 1970.

The national interest requires an educational system on the college level sufficiently financed and equipped to provide every student with adequate physical facilities to meet his instructional, research, and residential needs.

I therefore recommend legislation which will:

(1) Extend the current College Housing Loan Program with a five year $250 million a year program designed to meet the Federal Government's appropriate share of

residential housing for students and faculty. As a start, additional lending authority is necessary to speed action during fiscal 1961 on approvable loan applications already at hand.

(2) Establish a new, though similar, long-term, low-interest rate loan program for academic facilities, authorizing $300 million in loans each year for five years to assist in the construction of classrooms, laboratories, libraries, and related structures—sufficient to enable public and private higher institutions to accommodate the expanding enrollments they anticipate over the next five years; and also to assist in the renovation, rehabilitation, and modernization of such facilities.

III. ASSISTANCE TO COLLEGE AND UNIVERSITY STUDENTS

This nation a century or so ago established as a basic objective the provision of a good elementary and secondary school education to every child, regardless of means. In 1961, patterns of occupation, citizenship and world affairs have so changed that we must set a higher goal. We must assure ourselves that every talented young person who has the ability to pursue a program of higher education will be able to do so if he chooses, regardless of his financial means.

Today private and public scholarship and loan programs established by numerous states, private sources, and the Student Loan Program under the National Defense Education Act are making substantial contributions to the financial needs of many who attend our colleges. But they still fall short of doing the job that must be done. An estimated one-third of our brightest high school graduates are unable to go on to college principally for financial reasons.

While I shall subsequently ask the Congress to amend and expand the Student Loan and other provisions of the National Defense Education Act, it is clear that even with this program many talented but needy students are unable to assume further indebtedness in order to continue their education.

I therefore recommend the establishment of a five-year program with an initial authorization of $26,250,000 of state-administered scholarships for talented and needy young people which will supplement but not supplant those programs of financial assistance to students which are now in operation.

Funds would be allocated to the states during the first year for a total of twenty-five thousand scholarships averaging $700 each, 37,500 scholarships the second year, and 50,000 for each succeeding year thereafter. These scholarships, which would range according to need up to a maximum stipend of $1000, would be open to all young persons, without regard to sex, race, creed, or color, solely on the basis of their ability— as determined on a competitive basis—and their financial need. They would be permitted to attend the college of their choice, and free to select their own program of study. Inasmuch as tuition and fees do not normally cover the institution's actual expenses in educating the student, additional allowances to the college or university attended should accompany each scholarship to enable these institutions to accept the additional students without charging an undue increase in fees or suffering an undue financial loss.

IV. VOCATIONAL EDUCATION

The National Vocational Education Acts, first enacted by the Congress in 1917 and subsequently amended, have provided a program of training for industry, agriculture, and other occupational areas. The basic purpose of our vocational education effort is sound and sufficiently broad to provide a basis for meeting future needs. However, the technological changes which have occurred in all occupations call for a review and re-evaluation of these Acts, with a view toward their modernization.

To that end, I am requesting the Secretary of Health, Education, and Welfare to convene an advisory body drawn from the educational profession, labor-industry, and agriculture as well as the lay public, together with representation from the Departments of Agriculture and Labor, to be charged with the responsibility of reviewing and evaluating the current National Vocational Education Acts, and making recommendations for improving and redirecting the program.

CONCLUSION

These stimulatory measures represent an essential though modest contribution which the Federal Government must make to American education at every level. One-sided aid is not enough. We must give attention to both teachers' salaries and classrooms, both college academic facilities and dormitories, both scholarships and loans, both vocational and general education.

We do not undertake to meet our growing educational problems merely to compare our achievements with those of our adversaries. These measures are justified on their own merits—in times of peace as well as peril, to educate better citizens as well as better scientists and soldiers. The Federal Government's responsibility in this area has been established since the earliest days of the Republic—it is time now to act decisively to fulfill that responsibility for the sixties.

JOHN F. KENNEDY

47   Remarks at the Presentation of the Medal of Freedom to Paul Henri Spaak, Secretary General of NATO. *February* 21, 1961

MAY I SAY, speaking for myself, that one opportunity to present this medal to Mr. Spaak is an extremely pleasant one.

This is the first such occasion that has been provided to me as President of the United States. The idea of the Atlantic Community, of the close association between members of NATO, has been one that has occupied many men's attention in the years since the end of the war. But I don't think that any man has given more than Mr. Spaak.

Liberty is not easy to find. It is a search that takes us on a hard road. But Mr. Spaak has been willing to follow that road,

and I think that all of us who are members of NATO have benefited from this close attention he has given to the search.

We wish him well in whatever he may do in the future, but I think that he will agree that the service that he has provided to all of us who are members of NATO represents a most distinguished and happy occasion in his work.

We value his association. And this presentation before the members of NATO, before the Ambassadors speaking for their country, I think indicates our high regard for you and our gratitude to you for your work.

NOTE: The President presented the award at a ceremony held at 11:20 a.m. in his office at the White House.

Mr. Spaak responded as follows:

"Mr. President, I ask permission to say a few words, but to say them in French, because my English is never very good.

"When I am touched, it is indeed bad. I am very thankful to you. I am very touched and honored by the medal just awarded to me.

"I am leaving NATO, and one of my regrets is not to work with your administration any longer, as I have in the past, because the medal that you have just presented to me is, for me, a sign that that cooperation during these years has been a happy relationship.

"NATO is a great institution, a very useful institution—it can only function at its best if the United States plays a great role in it and shows its interest. And this medal which is given to me—and personally touches me deeply—seems to me to be also a proof of the importance that the United States Government attaches to NATO—and shows its strong desire to continue to participate in the work of the Organization with the same willingness that it has shown in the past.

"I am therefore doubly thankful. For myself, Mr. President, and for NATO, I thank you most sincerely."

Mr. Spaak served as Secretary General of NATO from May 1957 to March 4, 1961.

48 Remarks to the Delegates to the Youth Fitness Conference. *February 21, 1961*

Ladies and Gentlemen, Mr. Secretary:

I want to express my great appreciation at the opportunity to be here with you, and to express my thanks to all of you for having attended this conference.

I asked those members of the Cabinet who felt they were physically fit to come here today, and I am delighted that Mr. Udall and Mr. Robert Kennedy and Governor Ribicoff responded to the challenge.

Some years ago, another President of the United States who was also interested in physical fitness, Mr. Theodore Roosevelt, expressed some ambition that—I think members of the armed services would improve their physical fitness. As there was some question about his, you will recall that he then rode a horse for a hundred miles.

We don't have to prove it in 1961. We take it for granted that the members of the administration are all physically fit and our presence here today is an effort to encourage all of you in your work.

Since the time of the ancient Greeks, we have always felt that there was a close relationship between a strong, vital mind and

physical fitness. It is our hope that using the influence of the National Government that we can expand this strong spirit among American men and women, that they will concern themselves with this phase of their personal development.

We do not want in the United States a nation of spectators. We want a nation of participants in the vigorous life. This is not a matter which can be settled, of course, from Washington. It is really a matter which starts with each individual family. It is my hope that mothers and fathers, stretching across the United States, will be concerned about this phase of their children's development, that the communities will be concerned to make it possible for young boys and girls to participate actively in the physical life, and that men and women who have reached the age of maturity will concern themselves with maintaining their own participation in this phase of national vigor—national life.

I am hopeful that we can develop here today, with your help and suggestions, a program which will inspire our country to be concerned. I don't think we have to read these tests which we have seen so much of during the last 10 years to realize that because of the generosity of nature, because of the way our society is organized, that there has been less emphasis on national vigor, national vitality, physical well-being, than there has been in many other countries of the world.

I want to do better. And I think you want to do better. We want to make sure that as our life becomes more sophisticated, as we become more urbanized, that we don't lose this very valuable facet of our national character: physical vitality, which is tied into qualities of character, which is tied into qualities of intellectual vigor and vitality.

So I think that you are performing a real service in being here. We want your suggestions and ideas. This has to flow two ways, and we want the flow today to come from you to tell us how you think we can use the influence of the National Government—its prestige—in order to increase the emphasis which we can place in every community across the country, in every home, in this most important program.

I am particularly glad that we have here today teachers from over 67 countries who have been teaching in the United States and traveling through it, and who have now come to the National Capital before they return home. I hope they realize how much we learn from them—this is a two-way street, and all of these program which have brought hundreds of teachers in the last 15 to 20 years, which have brought them to all parts of the country; that each of you leaves behind you an understanding of the problems and opportunities of your country, your culture, your civilization, what you believe; and by your looking at us, we see something of ourselves.

This is a program which we benefit from. In many ways, I think, we are the greater beneficiary, and I hope that when you go back to your countries, that you will tell them something of what we are trying to do here. You will tell them, though we may not always realize our high ambitions and our high goals, that nevertheless we are attempting to advance ourselves, and that there is tremendous interest in what is going on in the world around us.

During the fall, I spoke, as many Members of Congress have spoken, about a Peace Corps. I am hopeful that it will be possible to bring that into realization, but what has been most interesting has been the great response of young men and women who desire not merely to serve the United States, but who desire to serve the cause of freedom which is common I think to all countries and to all people.

I hope that when the Peace Corps ultimately is organized, and young men and women go out around the world, that they will place their greatest emphasis on teaching; and secondly, that they will learn themselves far more than they will teach, and that we will therefore have another link which binds us to the world around us.

I want to express my thanks to all of you, whether you come from across the sea or here in the United States. We are all involved in this great effort together. And therefore I wish you well. I express my thanks to all of you. I want you to know that we here in Washington are intimately concerned with the matters in which you are engaged.

Thank you.

NOTE: The President spoke in the Health, Education, and Welfare Auditorium. In his opening words he referred to Secretary Ribicoff who also serves as Chairman of the President's Council on Youth Fitness.

49 Special Message to the Congress on Natural Resources. *February 23, 1961*

To the Congress of the United States:

From the beginning of civilization, every nation's basic wealth and progress has stemmed in large measure from its natural resources. This nation has been, and is now, especially fortunate in the blessings we have inherited. Our entire society rests upon—and is dependent upon—our water, our land, our forests, and our minerals. How we use these resources influences our health, security, economy, and well-being.

But if we fail to chart a proper course of conservation and development—if we fail to use these blessings prudently—we will be in trouble within a short time. In the resource field, predictions of future use have been consistently understated. But even under conservative projections, we face a future of critical shortages and handicaps. By the year 2000, a United States population of 300 million—nearly doubled in 40 years—will need far greater supplies of farm products, timber, water, minerals, fuels, energy, and opportunities for outdoor recreation. Present projections tell us that our water use will double in the next 20 years; that we are harvesting our supply of high-grade timber more rapidly than the development of new growth; that too much of our fertile topsoil is being washed away; that our minerals are being exhausted at increasing rates; and that the Nation's remaining undeveloped areas of great natural beauty are being rapidly pre-empted for other uses.

Wise investment in a resource program today will return vast dividends tomorrow, and failures to act now may be opportunities lost forever. Our country has been generous with us in this regard—and we cannot now ignore her needs for future development.

This is not a matter of concern for only one section of the country. All those who fish and hunt, who build industrial centers, who need electricity to light their homes and lighten their burdens, who require water for home, industrial, and recreational purposes—in short, every citizen in every State of the Union—all have a stake in a sound resources program under the progressive principles of national leadership first forged by Pinchot and Theodore Roosevelt, and backed by the essential cooperation of State and local governments.

This statement is designed to bring together in one message the widely scattered resource policies of the Federal Government. In the past, these policies have overlapped and often conflicted. Funds were wasted on competing efforts. Widely differing standards were applied to measure the Federal contribution to similar projects. Funds and attention devoted to annual appropriations or immediate pressures diverted energies away from long-range planning for national economic growth. Fees and user charges wholly inconsistent with each other, with value received, and with public policy have been imposed at some Federal developments.

To coordinate all of these matters among the various agencies, I will shortly issue one or more Executive Orders or directives:

(1) Redefining these responsibilities within the Executive Office and authorizing a strengthened Council of Economic Advisers to report to the President, the Congress and the public on the status of resource programs in relation to national needs;

(2) Establishing, under the Council of Economic Advisers, a Presidential Advisory Committee on Natural Resources, repre-

senting the Federal agencies concerned in this area and seeking the advice of experts outside of government; and

(3) Instructing the Budget Director, in consultation with the Departments and agencies concerned, to formulate within the next 90 days general principles for the application of fees, permits and other user charges at all types of Federal natural resource projects or areas; and to reevaluate current standards for appraising the feasibility of water resource projects.

In addition, to provide a coordinated framework for our research programs in this area, and to chart the course for the wisest and most efficient use of the research talent and facilities we possess, I shall ask the National Academy of Sciences to undertake a thorough and broadly based study and evaluation of the present state of research underlying the conservation, development, and use of natural resources, how they are formed, replenished and may be substituted for, and giving particular attention to needs for basic research and to projects that will provide a better basis for natural resources planning and policy formulation. Pending the recommendations of the Academy, I have directed my Science Advisor and the Federal Council for Science and Technology to review ongoing Federal research activities in the field of natural resources and to determine ways to strengthen the total government research effort relating to natural resources.

I. WATER RESOURCES

Our Nation has been blessed with a bountiful supply of water; but it is not a blessing we can regard with complacency. We now use over 300 billion gallons of water a day, much of it wastefully. By 1980 we will need 600 billion gallons a day.

Our supply of water is not always consistent with our needs of time and place. Floods one day in one section may be countered in other days or in other sections by the severe water shortages which are now afflicting many Eastern urban areas and particularly critical in the West. Our available water supply must be used to give maximum benefits for all purposes—hydroelectric power, irrigation and reclamation, navigation, recreation, health, home and industry. If all areas of the country are to enjoy a balanced growth, our Federal Reclamation and other water resource programs will have to give increased attention to municipal and industrial water and power supplies as well as irrigation and land redemption; and I am so instructing the Secretary of the Interior, in cooperation with the Secretary of Agriculture and the Secretary of the Army.

1. *Planning and Development.*

A. We reject a "no new starts" policy. Such a policy denied the resource requirements and potential on which our economic growth hinges and took a heavy toll in added costs and even human life and homes by postponing essential flood control projects. I have requested the Director of the Bureau of the Budget, working with appropriate department and agency heads, to schedule a progressive, orderly program of starting new projects to meet accumulated demands, taking into account the availability of funds, and implementing with the agencies concerned, wherever possible, the very excellent and timely report of the bi-partisan Senate Select Committee on National Water Resources issued three weeks ago.

B. This Administration accepts the goal urged by the Senate Select Committee to develop comprehensive river basin plans by 1970, in cooperation with the individual States. I urge the Congress to authorize the establishment of planning commissions for all major river basins where adequate coordinated plans are not already in existence. These commissions, on which will be represented the interested agencies at all levels of government, will be charged with the responsibility of preparing comprehensive basic development plans over the next several years.

C. A major reason for such planning is the ability to identify both the need and the location of future reservoir sites far in advance of construction. This advantage will be dissipated in great measure if the selected sites are not preserved—for uninhibited commercial and residential development in such areas increase ultimate acquisition costs and may result in pressures against the project required. I urge the Congress to enact legislation permitting the reservation of known future reservoir sites by the operating agency whenever such protection is necessary.

D. The full development of the power and other water resource potentials of the Columbia Basin is a vision that must be fulfilled. The Columbia River Joint Development Treaty with Canada is before the Senate for approval. I urge the Senate to approve this Treaty at the earliest possible time, to permit an immediate start on the immense efforts that can be jointly undertaken in power production and river control in that Basin.

E. This Administration is committed to strengthening and speeding up our flood control program as rapidly as our fiscal and technical capabilities permit. Unfortunately, efforts to reduce flood losses by constructing remedial works are being partially offset by rapid industrial and residential development of flood plain lands.

I am asking all Federal agencies concerned to provide data on flood hazards in specified areas to all 50 States, and to assist in their efforts for effective regulation or zoning of the flood plains. In addition, I have instructed the Federal agencies concerned with urban development—including the Housing and Home Finance Agency and the Bureau of Public Roads—to coordinate their activities with the flood control agencies to insure that their programs utilize flood information to advantage.

F. Complementing larger downstream reservoirs in the control of flood waters are the small watershed projects which are an integral part of our soil and water conservation program, along with terracing, strip cropping, grass waterways and other erosion prevention measures. Nearly 300 million of our nation's 460 million acres of farm crop lands still need these basic practices for preserving our water and soil resources. I have asked the Secretary of Agriculture, in cooperation with other interested Federal agencies, to review the basic objectives of our soil conservation and watershed management programs, and to make certain that any Federal assistance is directed toward realizing maximum benefits for the Nation as a whole. In addition, there should be improved coordination of the various Federal and local activities in this field.

2. *Water and Air Pollution Control.*

Pollution of our country's rivers and streams has—as a result of our rapid population and industrial growth and change—reached alarming proportions. To meet all needs—domestic, agricultural, industrial, recreational—we shall have to use and re-use the same water, maintaining quality as well as quantity. In many areas of the country we need new sources of supply—but in all areas we must protect the supplies we have.

Current corrective efforts are not adequate.

This year a national total of $350 million will be spent from all sources on municipal waste treatment works. But $600 million of construction is required annually to keep pace with the growing rate of pollution. Industry is lagging far behind in its treatment of wastes.

For a more effective water pollution control program, I propose the following—

First, I urge enactment of legislation along the general lines of H.R. 4036 and S. 120 extending and increasing Federal financial assistance for the operation of State and interstate water pollution control agencies.

Secondly, I urge that this legislation increase the amount of Federal assistance to municipalities for construction of waste treatment facilities in order to stimulate water pollution construction in those cities with inadequate facilities.

Third, I urge that this legislation strengthen enforcement procedures to abate serious pollution situations of national significance.

Fourth, I propose an intensive and broadened research effort to determine the specific sources of water pollution and their adverse effects upon all water uses; the effects upon the health of people exposed to water pollution; and more effective means of preventing, controlling, or removing the contaminants—including radioactive matter—that now pollute our rivers and streams so that the water may be safely used.

Fifth, I propose the establishment of a special unit within the Public Health Service under the Department of Health, Education, and Welfare, where control measures to prevent and limit pollution of our water will be developed.

Sixth, this same unit should provide new leadership, research and financial and technical assistance for the control of air pollution, a serious hazard to the health of our people that causes an estimated $7.5 billion annually in damage to vegetation, livestock, metals and other materials. We need an effective Federal air pollution control program now. For although the total supply of air is vast, the atmosphere over our growing metropolitan areas—where more than half the people live—has only limited capacity to dilute and disperse the contaminants now being increasingly discharged from homes, factories, vehicles, and many other sources.

3. Saline and Brackish Water Conversion.

No water resources program is of greater long-range importance—for relief not only of our shortages, but for arid nations the world over—than our efforts to find an effective and economical way to convert water from the world's greatest, cheapest natural resources—our oceans—into water fit for consumption in the home and by industry. Such a break-through would end bitter struggles between neighbors, states, and nations—and bring new hope for millions who live out their lives in dire shortage of usable water and all its physical and economical blessings, though living on the edge of a great body of water throughout that parched life-time.

This Administration is currently engaged in redoubled efforts to select the most promising approaches to economic desalinization of ocean and brackish waters, and then focus our energies more intensively on those approaches. At my request, a panel of the President's Science Advisory Committee has been working with the Secretary of the Interior to assure the most vigorous and effective research and development program possible in this field.

I now pledge that, when this know-how is achieved, it will immediately be made available to every nation in the world who wishes it, along with appropriate technical and other assistance for its use. Indeed the United States welcomes now the cooperation of all other nations who wish to join in this effort at present.

I urge the Congress to extend the current saline water conversion research program, and to increase the funds for its continuation to a level commensurate with the effort our current studies will show to be needed—now estimated to be at least twice the level previously requested.

II. ELECTRIC POWER

To keep pace with the growth of our economy and national defense requirements, expansion of this Nation's power facilities will require intensive effort by all segments of our power industry. Through 1980, according to present estimates of the Federal Power Commission, total installed capacity should triple if we are to meet our nation's need for essential economic growth. Sustained heavy expansion by all power suppliers—public, cooperative and private—is clearly needed.

The role of the Federal Government in supplying an important segment of this power is now long established and must continue. We will meet our responsibilities in this field.

—Hydroelectric sites remaining in this country will be utilized and hydroelectric power will be incorporated in all multiple-purpose river projects where optimum economic use of the water justifies such action.

—The Tennessee Valley Authority will continue to use the financing authority granted it by the last Congress to meet the power needs of the area it serves.

—Our efforts to achieve economically competitive nuclear power before the end of this decade in areas where fossil fuel costs are high will be encouraged through basic research, engineering developments, and construction of various prototype and full scale reactors by the Atomic Energy Commission in cooperation with industry.

—In marketing Federal power, this Administration will be guided by the following basic principles which recognize the prior rights of the general public, consumer and taxpayer who have financed the development of these great national assets originally vested in them:

(1) Preference in power sales shall be given public agencies and cooperatives.

(2) Domestic and rural consumers shall have priority over other consumers in the disposal of power.

(3) Power shall be sold at the lowest possible rates consistent with sound business principles.

(4) Power disposal shall be such as to encourage widespread use and to prevent monopolization.

Finally, I have directed the Secretary of the Interior to develop plans for the early interconnection of areas served by that Department's marketing agencies with adequate common carrier transmission lines; to plan for further national cooperative pooling of electric power, both public and private; and to enlarge such pooling as now exists.

III. FORESTS

Our forest lands present the sharpest challenge to our foresight. Trees planted today will not reach the minimum sizes needed for lumber until the year 2000. Most projections of future timber requirements predict a doubling of current consumption within forty years. At present cutting rates, we are using up our old growth timber in

Western stands. Because of the time requirements involved, we must move now to meet anticipated future needs, and improve the productivity of our nearly 500 million acres of commercial forest land.

Unfortunately, the condition of our forest land area is substantially below par: 45 million acres are in need of reforestation; more than 150 million acres require thinnings, release cuttings and other timber stand improvement measures if growth rates are to be increased and quality timber produced; forest protection must be extended to areas now poorly protected. Losses in growth from insects and disease need to be reduced substantially by wider application of known detection and control measures.

(A) I urge the Congress to accelerate forest development on Federal public lands both as a long-term investment measure and as an immediate method of relieving unemployment in distressed areas.

(B) To make additional supplies of merchantable timber available to small businesses, I have directed the Secretaries of Agriculture and the Interior to accelerate the program of building approved access roads to public forests.

(C) A more difficult and unresolved forest situation lies in that half of our forest land held in small private ownerships. These lands, currently far below their productive potential, must be managed to produce a larger share of our future timber needs. Current forest owner assistance programs have proven inadequate. I am therefore directing the Secretary of Agriculture, in cooperation with appropriate Federal and state agencies, to develop a program to help small independent timber owners and processors attain better forest management standards and more efficient production and utilization of forest crops.

IV. PUBLIC LANDS

The Federal Government owns nearly 770 million acres of public land, much of it devoted to a variety of essential uses. But equally important are the vacant, unappropriated and unreserved public domain lands, amounting to some 477 million acres—a vital national reserve that should be devoted to productive use now and maintained for future generations.

Much of this public domain suffers from uncontrolled use and a lack of proper management. More than 100 million acres of our Federal Grazing Districts are producing livestock forage well below their potential. We can no longer afford to sit by while our public domain assets so deteriorate.

I am, therefore, directing the Secretary of the Interior to

(1) accelerate an inventory and evaluation of the nation's public domain holdings to serve as a foundation for improved resource management;

(2) develop a program of balanced usage designed to reconcile the conflicting uses—grazing, forestry, recreation, wildlife, urban development and minerals; and

(3) accelerate the installation of soil conserving and water saving works and practices to reduce erosion and improve forage capacity; and to proceed with the revegetation of range lands on which the forage capacity has been badly depleted or destroyed.

V. OCEAN RESOURCES

The sea around us represents one of our most important but least understood and almost wholly undeveloped areas for extending our resource base. Continental shelves bordering the United States contain roughly 20 percent of our remaining reserves of crude oil and natural gas. The ocean floor contains large and valuable deposits of cobalt, copper, nickel, and manganese. Ocean waters themselves contain a wide variety of dissolved salts and minerals.

Salt (and fresh water) fisheries are among our most important but far from fully developed reservoirs of protein foods. At present levels of use, this country alone will need an additional 3 billion pounds of fish and shellfish annually by 1980, and many other countries with large-scale protein deficiency can be greatly helped by more extensive use of marine foodstuffs. But all this will require increased efforts, under Federal leadership, for rehabilitation of depleted stocks of salmon and sardines in the Pacific, groundfish and oysters in the Atlantic, lake trout and other desirable species in the Great Lakes, and many others through biological research, development of methods for passing fish over dams, and control of pollution.

This Administration intends to give concerted attention to our whole national effort in the basic and applied research of oceanography. Construction of ship and shore facilities for ocean research and survey, the development of new instruments for charting the seas and gathering data, and the training of new scientific manpower will require the coordinated efforts of many Federal agencies. It is my intention to send to the Congress for its information and use in considering the 1962 budget, a national program for oceanography, setting forth the responsibilities and requirements of all participating government agencies.

VI. RECREATION

America's health, morale and culture have long benefited from our National Parks and Forests, and our fish and wildlife opportunities. Yet these facilities and resources are not now adequate to meet the needs of a fast-growing, more mobile population—and the millions of visitor days which are now spent in Federally-owned parks, forests, wildlife refuges and water reservoirs will triple well before the end of this century.

To meet the Federal Government's appropriate share of the responsibility for fulfilling these needs, the following steps are essential:

(A) To protect our remaining wilderness areas, I urge the Congress to enact a wilderness protection bill along the general lines of S. 174.

(B) To improve both the quality and quantity of public recreational opportunities, I urge the Congress to enact legislation leading to the establishment of seashore and shoreline areas such as Cape Cod, Padre Island and Point Reyes for the use and enjoyment of the public. Unnecessary delay in acquiring these shores so vital to an adequate public recreation system results in tremendously increased costs.

(C) For similar reasons, I am instructing the Secretary of the Interior, in cooperation with the Secretary of Agriculture and other appropriate Federal, state and local officials and private leaders to

—formulate a comprehensive Federal recreational lands program;

—conduct a survey to determine where additional national parks, forests and seashore areas should be proposed;

—take steps to insure that land acquired for the construcion of Federally-financed reservoirs is sufficient to permit future development for recreational purposes; and

—establish a long-range program for planning and providing adequate open spaces for recreational facilities in urban areas.

I am also hopeful that consistent and coordinated Federal leadership can expand our fish and wildlife opportunities without the present conflicts of agencies and interests: One department paying to have wetlands drained for agricultural purposes while another is purchasing such lands for wild-life or water fowl refuges—one agency en-couraging chemical pesticides that may harm the song birds and game birds whose pres-ervation is encouraged by another agency—conflicts between private land owners and sportsmen—uncertain responsibility for the watershed and anti-pollution programs that are vital to our fish and wildlife opportunities.

I am directing the Secretary of the Interior to take the lead, with other Federal and State officials, to end these conflicts and develop a long-range wildlife conservation program—and to accelerate the acquisition of upper midwest wetlands through the sale of Federal duck stamps.

CONCLUSION

Problems of immediacy always have the advantage of attracting notice—those that lie in the future fare poorly in the competi-tion for attention and money. It is not a task which should or can be done by the Federal Government alone. Only through the fullest participation and cooperation of State and local governments and private industry can it be done wisely and effectively. We cannot, however, delude ourselves—we must understand our resources problems, and we must face up to them now. The task is large but it will be done.

JOHN F. KENNEDY

50   Statement by the President Following Settlement of the Airway Labor Dispute.   *February 24, 1961*

I AM GLAD to announce that the parties involved in the present airlines dispute, the Flight Engineers International Association and the Airlines Pilots Association, and the following carriers: Pan American World Airways, American Airlines, Trans World Airlines, Eastern Air Lines, National Air-lines, Flying Tiger Lines, have all agreed to the proposal made by the Secretary of Labor on my behalf on Saturday, and that arrangements are now being made for prompt resumption of operations on these airlines.

The men are immediately available to return to work.

I want to thank all of the parties to the dispute for their cooperation in complying with the request. The Secretary will have a separate statement to make concerning Western Airlines.

JOHN F. KENNEDY

NOTE: A similar statement was recorded for the newsreels in the Fish Room at the White House at 4:30 p.m. on February 23, and was released to the press on that date. The earlier release, entitled "Remarks," differs only in its conclusion, which reads as follows:

"I want to thank all of the parties to the dispute for their cooperation in complying with this request, and I am most appreciative to Secretary Goldberg for his efforts in this regard.

"I am hopeful that these planes and these air lines will be back at work immediately—and we hope that if their operation schedules permit, by this evening."

Secretary Goldberg's statement recommended that the list of air carriers involved in the dispute also include Western Airlines.

51 Joint Statement Following Discussions With Prime Minister Menzies of Australia. *February 24, 1961*

PRESIDENT KENNEDY and Prime Minister Menzies met today in Washington to discuss informally a wide range of international problems. The Secretary of State, Mr. Dean Rusk; the Assistant Secretary of State for Far Eastern Affairs, Mr. J. Graham Parsons; and the Australian Ambassador to the United States, Mr. Howard Beale; assisted in these discussions.

Both the President and the Prime Minister welcome this opportunity to reaffirm the traditional partnership between the peoples of Australia and the United States.

In their review of security problems, the President and the Prime Minister reiterated their strong faith in SEATO and ANZUS as bulwarks for the maintenance of peace in the Pacific. They both expressed their willingness to cooperate with all nations to work together for peace and freedom in the world.

They recognized the central importance of the United Nations and the Office of the Secretary General in the pursuit of peaceful settlements and pledge their joint support of the efforts now being made by the Secretary General to bring peace to the Congo. They deplored current attempts to twist the tragic events in the Congo into an attack upon the United Nations itself.

They welcomed the initiative of King Savang Vatthana proposing a course of action to bring peace, stability and neutrality to Laos, expressing the hope that his efforts will bear fruit.

They agreed that efforts must be continued to arrive at an effective agreement under international control in the field of disarmament.

52 Letter to the President of the Senate and to the Speaker of the House Transmitting Bills Implementing the Message on Health and Hospital Care. *February 24, 1961*

Dear Mr.————:

I am transmitting herewith two drafts of legislation to carry out recommendations I made in my message to the Congress on February ninth.

The first bill would, when enacted, increase opportunities for training physicians, dentists and professional public health personnel. These are the keystones of any health program. Yet we are not presently training enough even to keep pace with our growing population. The enclosed proposal will enable us to narrow substantially our current deficit in this area.

The other bill which I am transmitting will help expand and improve community facilities and services for the health care of the aged and other persons. It will make possible a substantial addition to the number of nursing home facilities to care for long-term patients and it will help relieve the shortages of home health care programs.

The enclosed letters from the Secretary of Health, Education, and Welfare describe the two proposals in more detail. I commend this legislation to you.

Sincerely,

JOHN F. KENNEDY

NOTE: This is the text of identical letters addressed to the Honorable Lyndon B. Johnson, President of the Senate, and to the Honorable Sam Rayburn, Speaker of the House of Representatives.

Secretary Ribicoff's letters, dated February 24, 1961, and the draft bills were released with the President's letter.

53   Letter to the Speaker of the House of Representatives Proposing
     a Reduction in the Duty-Free Allowance for Returning
     American Travelers.   *February 24, 1961*

Dear Mr. Speaker:

In my message of February 6, 1961, I said that the United States faces a balance of payments deficit which is a matter of concern to us and to the whole free world. In order to meet our international responsibilities, to properly formulate domestic economic policies, and to efficiently conduct our economic affairs, we must take into account our balance of payments.

I propose that we strengthen our total position and help insure that our gold reserves are employed effectively to facilitate the commerce of the free nations and to protect the stability of their currencies by returning to the historic basic duty-free allowance of $100 allowed returning American travelers.

The $100 tariff exemption dates back to 1897. After World War II, however, foreign countries faced a dollar shortage and, as one measure to ease this shortage, Congress increased the tariff exemption by $300 in 1948 and by $100 in 1949, bringing the total exemption to $500. However, in the light of the existing balance of payments problem, this more liberal customs exemption, designed to encourage American expenditures abroad, is not presently warranted. Accordingly, the customs exemption should be returned to the traditional amount.

The attached draft of legislation would carry out this recommendation by providing for a return to the $100 duty-free allowance for a four-year period. This proposal would meet the existing situation, and the four-year terminal date would provide an appropriate opportunity for a reappraisal of the measure in the light of the balance of payments position in the future. I urge that Congress give favorable consideration to its prompt enactment.

Very truly yours,

JOHN F. KENNEDY

NOTE: On August 10 the President approved an amendment to the Tariff Act of 1930 providing for a reduction in duty-free allowance for returning American travelers (Public Law 87–132, 75 Stat. 335).

The draft bill was released with the President's letter.

54   Letter to the Speaker of the House of Representatives Proposing
     Exemption of Foreign Central Banks From Income Tax on
     Interest on Government Securities.   *February 24, 1961*

Dear Mr. Speaker:

There is attached a draft of proposed legislation to amend the Internal Revenue Code so that foreign central banks would be exempt from tax on interest they derive from holding obligations issued by the United States Government, if such obligations are held in connection with noncommercial activities of the central bank.

This measure is one of various desirable steps, mentioned in my Message to the Congress of February 6, intended to improve this country's ability to defend its gold reserve by offering competitively attractive dollar obligations to foreign central banks. These official "banks of issue" must have unimpaired freedom to purchase gold from the United States, if they prefer to do so, but we should not perpetuate procedures which, in the case of many countries (and particularly the smaller countries) make United States Government securities relatively unattractive as an alternative to holding gold.

The legislation would bring about uniform tax treatment of all foreign central banks, many of which are now exempt from tax, either because they are considered an integral part of their government, or because of tax conventions. If foreign central banks keep their dollar assets in time deposits or bankers' acceptances, they are already exempt from tax by statute. Thus, the bill would make Government obligations as attractive to foreign central banks, from a tax standpoint, as bank deposits and bankers' acceptances.

A memorandum prepared by the Secretary of the Treasury explaining the bill in greater detail is also attached.

It would be appreciated if you would lay the proposed legislation before the House.

Sincerely,

JOHN F. KENNEDY

NOTE: On May 4, 1961, the President approved an amendment to the Internal Revenue Code of 1954 providing for the requested exemption (Public Law 87–29, 75 Stat. 64).

The Secretary of the Treasury's memorandum and the draft bill were released with the President's letter.

55   Message for the Commission on Civil Rights' Third Annual Conference on Schools in Transition.   *February 25, 1961*

[Released February 25, 1961.   Dated February 24, 1961]

Dr. John Hannah, Chairman
Commission on Civil Rights
The Motor House, Williamsburg, Virginia

Please extend to all the participants of your Third Annual Conference on Schools in Transition my best wishes for a constructive session. The two previous conferences which the Commission has sponsored on the problems of school desegregation have been notable contributions to our national need for better understanding of this vital matter.

It is a continuing contribution for you to bring together for an exchange of views the men and women responsible for maintaining our public schools and for carrying through the process of desegregation.

Let me here pay tribute to these educators—principals, officers of school boards, and public school teachers. The Constitutional requirement of desegregation has presented them with many new responsibilities and hard challenges. In New Orleans today, as in many other places represented in your three conferences, these loyal citizens and educators are meeting these responsibilities and challenges with quiet intelligence and true courage. The whole country is in their debt for our public school system must be preserved and improved. Our very survival as a free nation depends upon it. This is no time for schools to close for any reason, and certainly no time for schools to be closed in the name of racial discrimination. If we are to give the leadership the world requires of us, we must be true to the great principles of our Constitution—the very principles which distinguish us from our adversaries in the world.

Let me also pay tribute to the school children and their parents, of both races, who have been on the frontlines of this problem. In accepting the command of the Constitution with dignity they too, are contributing to the education of all Americans.

Cordially,

JOHN F. KENNEDY

56   Remarks Recorded for the Television Program "Robert Frost: American Poet." *February* 26, 1961

THERE IS a story that some years ago an interested mother wrote to a principal of a school, "Don't teach my boy poetry. He is going to run for Congress."

I have never taken the view that the world of politics and the world of poetry are so far apart. I think politicians and poets share at least one thing, and that is that their greatness depends upon the courage with which they face the challenges of life. There are many kinds of courage—bravery under fire, courage to risk reputation and friendship and career for convictions which are deeply held. Perhaps the rarest courage of all—for the skill to pursue it is given to very few men—is the courage to wage a silent battle to illuminate the nature of man and the world in which he lives. This is Robert Frost's courage. Untiring skill and daring which are his in penetrating many of the mysteries which surround our life have brought him a well deserved recognition which has been given to few men in our time.

Robert Frost is often characterized as an American poet—or a New England poet. And he is, of course, all of these things, for the temper of his region and of his Nation has provided a good deal of the meter and the tone in which he has dealt. But he is not a poet bounded by geography. He will live as a poet of the life of man, of the darkness and despair, as well as of the hope—which is, in his case, limited by a certain skepticism—and also for his wit and understanding of man's limitations which lie behind all of man's profoundest statements.

I asked Robert Frost to come and speak at the inauguration not merely because I was desirous of according a recognition to his trade, but also because I felt he had something important to say to those of us who are occupied with the business of Government, that he would remind us that we were dealing with life, the hopes and fears of millions of people, and also to tell us that our own deep convictions must be the ultimate guide to all of our actions.

He has said it well in a poem called "Choose Something Like a Star," in which he speaks of the fairest star in sight and says:

It asks . . . little of us here.
It asks of us a certain height,
So when at times the mob is swayed
To carry praise or blame too far,
We may choose something like a star
To stay our mind on and be staid.

For that insight, Robert Frost—and for all the others carved with such toil from a long life—men everywhere are grateful.

NOTE: The President's words of appreciation were specially taped for broadcast as part of a television tribute to Robert Frost. During the program, broadcast over the Columbia Broadcasting System at 12:30 p.m. on February 26, Mr. Frost read and discussed his work.

57 Remarks at a Meeting With the Board of Foreign Scholarships and the U.S. Advisory Commission on Educational Exchange. *February 27, 1961*

AS OUR OWN HISTORY demonstrates so well, education is in the long run the chief means by which a young nation can develop its economy, its political and social institutions and individual freedom and opportunity. There is no better way of helping the new nations of Latin America, Africa, and Asia in their present pursuit of freedom and better living conditions than by assisting them to develop their human resources through education. Likewise there is no better way to strengthen our bonds of understanding and friendship with older nations than through educational and cultural interchange.

But as recent task force reports have emphasized, this whole field is urgently in need of imaginative policy development, unification, and vigorous direction. These activities are presently scattered among many agencies of the Federal Government. Only by centering responsibility for leadership and direction at an appropriate place in the governmental structure can we hope to achieve the required results. I shall therefore look to the Secretary of State to exercise primary responsibility for policy guidance and program direction by governmental activities in this field.

I am pleased that in carrying these responsibilities the Secretary of State will have the assistance of Philip H. Coombs. His experience in education, government, and philanthropy at home and overseas qualify him well for the position to which he is being appointed.

NOTE: The White House release announcing the meeting stated that the President had appealed to the educational community, private foundations, and voluntary organizations to continue and expand their support and activity in the international educational and cultural fields. The release further stated that the President had emphasized the point that these institutions have an enormously important role to play in U.S. foreign relations and in building a foundation for world peace.

At the meeting, the release noted, Dr. Robert G. Storey, Chairman of the Board of Foreign Scholarships, and Dr. Franklin G. Murphy, Chairman of the Advisory Commission, reported on the work of their respective groups. The release also noted that Senators Fulbright and Mundt had accompanied the group to the White House, as did Assistant Secretary of State Philip H. Coombs, Robert H. Thayer, Special Assistant to the Secretary, and Saxton A. Bradford, Director of the Department's Bureau of Educational and Cultural Affairs.

58 Special Message to the Congress on the Federal Highway Program. *February 28, 1961*

To the Congress of the United States:

Our Federal pay-as-you-go Highway Program is in peril. It is a peril that justifies a special message because of the vital contribution this program makes to our security, our safety and our economic growth. Timely completion of the full program authorized in 1956 is essential to a national defense that will always depend, regardless of new weapon developments, on quick motor transportation of men and material from one site to another.

American lives are also dependent on this program in a more direct sense. Better, more modern highways—with less congestion, fewer dangerous curves and intersections, more careful grades and all the rest—mean greater highway safety. It has been estimated that more fatalities will be suffered in traffic accidents between now and 1975, when the new system is fully operative, than were suffered by American troops in every conflict from the Civil War through Korea. Last year witnessed 38,000 traffic fatalities and 1.4 million personal injuries. But on our new expressways the ratio of accidents and deaths per mile driven is only a fraction of what it is on ordinary roads. The Interstate System when completed, it is estimated, will save at least 4,000 lives a year.

Finally, proceeding with this program at least as fast as originally scheduled is essential to our economy. This is true not only in terms of the stimulus and employment it provides now, in a time of recession, to such vital industries as steel, construction, cement and others. It is also a key to the development of more modern and efficient industrial complexes—turning marginal land or clogged cities into attractive sites for commercial or industrial development—and to lower motor transportation costs generally.

The Bureau of Public Roads estimates that users of the completed Interstate System will save 42,000 years of travel time every year. The elimination of stop-and-go driving will save users 9 billion costly stops and starts every year.

A study, for example, of a 16-mile section of the Schuylkill expressway in the Philadelphia area showed direct savings to motorists of over $18 million per year, enough to pay the entire cost in three years. Even less tangible, but equally important, are the widened horizons a modern highway network affords the individual and the family—greater recreational opportunities, greater freedom of choice in places to live, work and play—and less time and effort spent in getting there.

It has always struck me as ironic that so many of our citizens—so ingenious in quickly devising ways of ending almost every minor irritant—would so readily tolerate every morning and evening the incredible congestion of our antiquated highways that takes a heavy toll in automotive costs and depreciation, to say nothing of human nerves and tempers. By 1975—and the Interstate System is required by Congress to have enough lanes to move safely all the vehicles expected in 1975—there will be an estimated two or three times as many vehicles as use those roads today. Even though some expressways now seem excessively large, an emergency program then will be too late—we must continue to build those highways now at a steady rate sufficient to assure completion on schedule.

As early in the era of the automobile as 1916, Congress recognized the Federal responsibility in this area—to promote the national defense, interstate commerce, farm and resource development and postal service. The pay-as-you-build 41,000 mile program initiated in 1956 was the most notable and far-sighted recognition of this responsibility in history.

But now, as stated at the outset, that program is in trouble. Revised cost estimates submitted to the Congress early in January reported pursuant to law that to complete the Interstate System on schedule (while meeting the needs of the regular ABC and related primary, secondary and urban Federal aid program) would require, over the life of the program, additional authorizations of $11.56 billion—which means additional revenues to the Highway Trust Fund totaling $9.74 billion, or about $900 million more a year through fiscal 1972 to meet the higher level of expenditures on a pay-as-you-go basis.

The engineering and construction resources are readily available to absorb this increase and step up the program. To deny the increase would postpone completion of the system to five years beyond the original target date. Moreover, the 1956 Highway Revenue Act sought to implement its pay-as-you-go intention with Sec. 209(g)—generally known as the Byrd Amendment—which requires the authorized apportionments to each state to be reduced whenever Trust Fund revenues are estimated to be insufficient to cover them in any individual year. It is now clear that, despite the scheduled diversion, even the 1963 authorizations under present law, which should be apportioned to the states in July of this year, will have to be substantially cut-back below currently authorized and desired levels by this provision unless Congress acts to increase revenues.

I am wholly opposed to either stretching out or cutting back our highway program, and urge the Congress not to rely on either solution. Either step would be unwise at a time when our slump-ridden economy needs greater, not less, construction activity. Either step would be unfair to the individual states who have proceeded in good faith, and in reliance on the Treasury's certification of adequate funds, to make plans and expenditures looking to receiving their full apportionment this July. And to postpone the completion of the Interstate System only further postpones the day when our highways will be adequate to meet our defense, economic and general population increase needs.

1. A NEW PLAN TO FINANCE THE HIGHWAY PROGRAM

Under present law, the highway use taxes (by which the Highway Trust Fund has been financed in accordance with the 1956 pay-as-you-go intent) are scheduled—not for an increase to meet the problems described above—but for a decline: a drop in the gasoline, diesel and related fuels tax from 4¢ a gallon to 3¢ a gallon on July 1.

Such a tax reduction at this time—causing a loss of some $600 million a year—would be wholly contrary to the basic premise on which the 1956 Highway Act was agreed to. Cost reappraisals since enactment of the temporary one cent increase in 1959 demonstrates conclusively that it must be continued, if not further increased. Nor can a reduction now be justified on anti-recession grounds. If tax reductions are deemed necessary to reverse the recession or promote long run economic growth, other tax cuts might prove more effective, or have higher priority.

The scheduled reduction in the gas tax, in short, is fiscally unwise. It was vigorously opposed by the previous Administration. It is opposed by this Administration with equal vigor; and I ask the Congress to prevent this gas tax reduction from taking effect on July 1.

Those favoring the reduction, or opposed to any increase, cite two principal alternative sources of revenue:

(A) *Diversion From General Revenues.* Under present law, the revenues from certain excise taxes totalling over $800 million a year are scheduled to be diverted from the General Fund to the Highway Trust Fund for a three-year period beginning July 1.

It is asserted by its advocates that this amount will compensate for the reduction in the gas tax. But we are not better able to pay our bills as a nation by merely shifting money from one pocket to another. I am pledged, barring a worsening economy, to submit to the Congress programs (aside from any new Defense outlays) which of and by themselves will not unbalance the Budget previously submitted. This will not be easily done. There will be no margin to spare. Congress, by diverting $800 million of badly needed funds from the General Fund, will be deliberately unbalancing the Budget and creating an $800 million deficit. This is a decision which, if it is taken at all, should be taken on its merits, in relation to the state of the economy and the budget as a whole, not as an accidental by-product of the highway program.

The total diversion for three years amounts to some $2.5 billion—and the precedents and pressures to make it permanent through 1972 could cost the General Fund (and cost the general taxpayers, including competing forms of transportation) approximately $10 billion.

It is argued that highway use is related to these excise taxes that are to be diverted (portions of the taxes on the sale of automobiles, parts and accessories). But this program was approved in 1956 on the assumption that these revenues (from taxes which had been in effect in war and peace for more than ten years before the Highway Program was enacted) would remain as always in the General Fund, along with similar excise tax revenues (all of which can theoretically be related to some Federal program but cannot be diverted to support such program). To change the intent of the 1956 Act now only creates a Budget deficit that eventually must be met through new taxes on the general population or a Treasury bond-issue—thus departing from the Program's principle of being financed on a pay-as-you-go basis by the user tax sources then agreed upon.

A new argument in favor of this diversion is based upon a Commerce Department cost allocation study stating that 8% of the program's benefits accrue to others than those whose taxes now finance the Trust Fund. The basis of this part of the study is open to serious challenge; but even aside from that, it must be remembered that:

(a) The Federal Highway Trust Fund is not paying for 100% of this system. A normal portion of ten percent is already borne by the States, reflecting the benefits they receive, and which they are free to raise from non-users if they choose. The Commerce Department Study "makes no suggestion as to the source or level of government which should supply the revenues" for the 8%.

(b) The proposed diversion of more than $800 million cannot possibly be justified by the 8% figure—which equals only $250 million.

(c) The Trust Fund already receives nearly $60 million income from non-users: vehicles used off the highways, motor boats, and the like; and at the same time it is not charged with some $140 million worth of other road programs benefiting the highway user but now charged to General Revenues, though their users must pay gas and other taxes into the Trust Fund.

In short, there is no justification for unbalancing the Budget by the scheduled diversion of more than $800 million from the General Fund to the Highway Trust Fund; and, again maintaining the position strongly taken by my predecessor, I ask the Congress to prevent this diversion.

(B) *Federal Highway Bond Issues.* The other method of financing most commonly suggested in place of the pay-as-you-go principle in this program is the issuance of a special highway bond series. This proposal has important disadvantages.

—At the present time, by increasing Government demands on long-term money, special highway bonds would make more difficult the current efforts of the Government to reduce long-term rates to promote economic recovery.

—Not only do special bond issues inevitably cost more than regular public debt issues, but such a step would also cost the program an estimated $6.6 billion additional in interest payments ($6.6 billion that would not build a single road), and keep the Trust Fund in being and its revenues tied up through most of fiscal 1981. It is unrealistic to assume that those revenues will not be needed for new highway needs from 1972–1981. As a spokesman for the previous Administration earlier testified in connection with highway financing: "We ought to pay our own way and leave future revenue sources available to meet future needs."

—Finally, it is clear that Federal Highway bonds are merely a device to avoid the appearance of deficits and evade the pay-as-you-go principle in this program. A special bond issue is not the answer.

Nor is the answer to be found in any other form of Treasury loan—or in charging tolls on roads that ought to be free—or in raising the 10% share of the program now borne by States with no adequate means of paying a higher share. A national program should not be dependent upon the ability and willingness of every State Legislature to increase its contribution.

Our objective is to finance this program on a pay-as-you-go basis from those user taxes so designated in 1956, at rates sufficient to pay the full cost of the program, without charge on general Federal revenues.

In the absence of a finding that the economy needs stimulus beyond the measures proposed in my previous messages, I cannot recommend that Congress suspend the Byrd Amendment and permit apportionments to be made without reference to estimated revenues.

The pay-as-you-go principle, the basic premise of the Act, requires an increase in the revenues from user taxes this year instead of a reduction. Although reduction in these taxes is sought by many State Governments, motor carriers, oil producers and motorists, it is nevertheless clear that a program essential to the nation, and to their own welfare, requires that they cooperate in determining how present sources are to yield the additional revenues needed.

—The previous Administration recommended an increase in the present 4¢ tax on gasoline to 4.5¢ a gallon. This is clearly acceptable, and would have my support. However, I prefer not to raise taxes on the general consumer at this time, and to emphasize instead a fairer allocation of the burden among those who use the highways.

—I propose as a substitute means of obtaining the same revenue:

——*Retaining the present gas tax of 4¢ a gallon;* and

——*Increasing the following taxes:*

Tax	Present	Proposed
Diesel fuel	4¢ a gallon	7¢
Trucks over 26,000 lbs	$1.50 per 1,000 lbs	$5.00
Highway tires	8¢	10¢
Inner tubes	9¢	10¢
Tread rubber	3¢	10¢

Practically all of the increase in revenues (replacing the general ½¢ rise in gas tax) would come from the heavier trucks that use diesel fuel and weigh over 26,000 lbs. when loaded. This is only fair. Indeed, technical experts in the Bureau of Public Roads advise me that even this increase would not charge heavy trucks their fair share of the cost of this program.

Methods of allocating highway costs and benefits among various classes of users have always varied widely. But previous state and Federal studies, as well as those new Commerce Department studies thus far completed, all assign to heavy trucks and tractor-trailer combinations a share of the cost far exceeding that assigned to automobiles and other users. Their size and weight require a thicker surface or structure, a wider pavement and shoulder, more careful grading and more expensive bridges. The 5-axle combination with full trailer was responsible for some 12 times as much of the cost per mile of travel as automobiles traversing the same highways as analyzed by the new study requested by the Congress.

In terms of ton-miles traveled, as expected, the study again showed heavy trucks to be the primary beneficiaries of the system. But even in the study of benefits received, there was a large gain to the trucking industry from these new highways: less gas, oil and depreciation expense, less strain on the driver, fewer accidents, and much shorter distances and travel time over improved and widened surfaces with fewer sharp grades and curves, less congested traffic and fewer stops, intersections and access roads. In this study also, truck combinations benefited many times as much as the average automobile driver.

Still to be completed is the final study on how much more wear and tear, maintenance and construction costs are due to the large trucks. But on the basis of these three and other studies, it is already clear that passenger cars are paying more than their fair share now—and, as stated in that Report (submitted by Secretary Mueller on January 13, now House Doc. 54),—"There is a definite indication in the results of all three allocation studies that the heavier trucks and combinations (particularly the latter) should be paying considerably more, in relations to the payments by the lighter vehicle groups, than they do now."

I urge the Congress to adopt this alternative. If it is rejected, the Congress should be prepared to increase gasoline taxes on all users as recommended by my predecessor. What is essential is that one alternative or another must be adopted to raise the revenues this program needs to go ahead as scheduled without draining general revenues.

II. OTHER TAX AND COST ALLOCATIONS

The Budget and Trust Fund programs of the previous Administration included two long-standing recommendations on which the proposal submitted above is also based, and in which I join:

(1) That the Congress retain aviation fuel tax receipts in the General Fund instead of transferring them to the Highway Trust Fund as is presently done. This is not a highway use tax in any sense—and it is both fair and logical to devote these tax receipts ($22 million for fiscal 1962) to the General Budget which is in need of all available revenues.

(2) That the Congress transfer the financing of forest and public land highways to the Highway Trust Fund. There is no reason why this program, of benefit primarily to users, should not be supported by users in the Trust Fund established for that purpose, instead of imposing an estimated $37.5 million burden on general revenues.

III. INCREASE LEVEL OF ABC APPORTIONMENTS

The financing plan described above and in tables to be submitted to the Congress also provides for a small but significant increase in the authorization of funds for the more traditional highway program—the regular ABC systems of primary, secondary and urban roads. A trunk line network of modern controlled access highways is only as efficient as its connections to home, office, factory and farm. Now fixed at an annual level of $925 million, I recommend that this authorization be increased by $25 million every two years beginning in 1964 until the $1 billion level is reached and maintained.

IV. COORDINATION WITH URBAN DEVELOPMENT

A Federal Highway program of this scope cannot be isolated from other programs for social and civic improvement, particularly our progress in urban renewal and planning. More effective use of both highway and urban renewal funds can result from increased coordination—as Pittsburgh's Golden Triangle so strikingly demonstrates. I am directing the Secretary of Commerce and the Housing and Home Finance Administrator to increase their joint planning at every level, to improve coordination of urban renewal and freeway construction plans in the same area, and to invite the cooperative efforts of State and local highway and housing officials and private experts.

More specific and urgent, however, are the problems of families displaced by new highway construction. As more and more rights-of-way are acquired and construction begins, tens of thousands of families are required to move from their path and find new places to live—more persons displaced, it has been estimated, than are displaced by all our urban renewal and slum clearance programs combined. For many families of modest income, especially those displaced by expressways in congested urban areas, adequate housing is often difficult, if not impossible, to locate at prices or rents which they can afford, or in places reasonably convenient to their jobs. As a result, many are compelled to accept substandard accommodations. Others, by overcrowding otherwise adequate housing, help to create new slums. Those already in substandard housing—crowded into a tenement in the path of a

new expressway, for example—are hard-put to find any housing at all, yet are given no help or priority by existing Federal Housing programs.

To date this serious problem has been largely overlooked. Neither the Federal Government nor the State highway departments have assumed any positive or explicit responsibility for meeting these needs.

In contrast, the Federal urban renewal law, enacted in 1949, requires that every contract for Federal assistance include provisions assuring the availability of decent, safe and sanitary housing at prices they can afford and in suitable locations for all families displaced by urban renewal projects. I urge that the Federal highway law be amended to require similar assurances of help in finding reasonable housing at reasonable costs for all those displaced from their homes by future Federal-aid highway projects.

Such a step will lessen costly resistance to needed highway projects and their proper location. We must not allow needed progress in highways to come at the expense of unnecessary personal hardship to American families.

V. BILLBOARD CONTROL

The Interstate Highway System was intended, among other purposes, to enable more Americans to more easily see more of their country. It is a beautiful country. The System was not intended to provide a large and unreimbursed measure of benefits to the billboard industry, whose structures tend to detract from both the beauty and the safety of the routes they line. Their messages are not, as so often claimed, primarily for the convenience of the motorist whose view they block. Some two-thirds of such advertising is for national products, and is dominated by a handful of large advertisers to whom the Interstate System has provided a great wind-fall.

The Congress took a wise though very modest step in 1958 by authorizing, through Section 122 of the 1958 Act, the control of outdoor advertising within designated limits of the routes of the Interstate System. States electing to comply with the Federal standards promulgated under that section were to receive an incentive payment of an extra one-half of 1 percent of the cost of interstate highway projects within the State.

Unfortunately that provision expires on June 30th of this year, and a variety of pressures has prevented all but one state (Maryland) from taking advantage of this provision. I urge the Congress to extend this billboard control section for four more years; and to increase the incentive bonus from ½ to 1% of a State's allotment. Should this measure still prove to be insufficient, it may be necessary to adopt more direct means of control, or to at least charge the billboard owners for the benefits they are receiving.

VI. THE HIGHWAY PROGRAM AND THE RECESSION

As mentioned in my message of February 2nd to the Congress, I ordered at that time the immediate release of $724 million of Federal highway funds which would not normally have been available to the States until April 1st. This was only a first step toward speeding up the highway program. Its effects are limited in terms of new construction immediately put under way but it permitted a number of States to let contracts in March that would have been held up until April or May.

If economic conditions warrant, additional steps can be taken by Congress and the Executive, including additional authorization for temporary acceleration for which we already have the plans, men and material ready. Particularly useful at that time, in view of the harsh winter's effects on so many streets and highways, would be authorization of Federal funds for road repair in areas of substantial unemployment. But because of the tight condition of the Trust Fund and General Fund, I shall not make recommendations along these lines unless later appraisal of the state of the economy indicates the necessity of such actions.

CONCLUSION

The program outlined here faces up to our responsibilities for meeting the highway needs of the nation, while maintaining the original concept of a highway program financed by highway users. It is a realistic program designed to meet an urgent problem. I urge its prompt and impartial consideration.

JOHN F. KENNEDY

59   Statement by the President Recorded for the Opening of the Red Cross Campaign. *February 28, 1961*

[Broadcast over radio and television at 6 p.m.]

AS PRESIDENT of the United States and in accordance with custom I have designated the month of March as Red Cross Month, and as Honorary Chairman of the Red Cross I do want to ask the support of all of you for this most important drive.

The Red Cross has been chartered by the Congress to serve the people. It has come to the aid of our neighbors when they have been struck by hurricanes. It aids our sons or brothers who may be in the service. It helps through its blood banks hundreds and even thousands of Americans who might otherwise have lost their lives if it had not been for the vigilance and the work of the Red Cross.

The Red Cross belongs to all Americans and I hope that all Americans will participate in supporting it this month. Over two million volunteers will be crossing the coun-

try in search of your support either through the United Fund itself or through the Red Cross drive.

This is a traditional work in which all of us have participated throughout all of our lives. It deserves our support in future months. The responsibilities placed upon it by our Government, by nature, by our hospitals, by our needs are great. I hope that all Americans will participate in supporting this year in March the Red Cross.

60 Memorandum to Federal Agencies on the Red Cross Campaign. *February* 28, 1961

Memorandum for the Heads of Executive Departments and Agencies:

During the month of March, the American National Red Cross conducts its annual campaign for members and funds. This is one of the three campaigns authorized within the Executive Departments and Agencies. However, those local Red Cross chapters that have raised their financial requirements in federated fund campaigns will not make their appeals at this time.

By Act of Congress the Red Cross is required to provide welfare service to members of the armed forces and their families at home and overseas, and to maintain a

program of disaster preparedness and relief. It also offers other vital services in the fields of Blood, Home Nursing, First Aid and Water Safety. It provides opportunities for the young people of America to participate in community services which prepare them for positions of leadership in the future.

The volunteers and the funds that make this great work possible are provided by the American people. I urge all employees of the Federal Government and the members of the armed forces to continue their generous support of the Red Cross.

JOHN F. KENNEDY

61 Statement by the President Upon Signing Order Establishing the Peace Corps. *March* 1, 1961

I HAVE TODAY signed an Executive Order [1] providing for the establishment of a Peace Corps on a temporary pilot basis. I am also sending to Congress a message proposing authorization of a permanent

Peace Corps. This Corps will be a pool of trained American men and women sent overseas by the U.S. Government or through private institutions and organizations to help foreign countries meet their urgent needs for skilled manpower.

---

[1] Executive Order 10924, 26 F.R. 1789.

It is our hope to have 500 or more people in the field by the end of the year.

The initial reactions to the Peace Corps proposal are convincing proof that we have, in this country, an immense reservoir of such men and women—anxious to sacrifice their energies and time and toil to the cause of world peace and human progress.

In establishing our Peace Corps we intend to make full use of the resources and talents of private institutions and groups. Universities, voluntary agencies, labor unions and industry will be asked to share in this effort—contributing diverse sources of energy and imagination—making it clear that the responsibility for peace is the responsibility of our entire society.

We will only send abroad Americans who are wanted by the host country—who have a real job to do—and who are qualified to do that job. Programs will be developed with care, and after full negotiation, in order to make sure that the Peace Corps is wanted and will contribute to the welfare of other people. Our Peace Corps is not designed as an instrument of diplomacy or propaganda or ideological conflict. It is designed to permit our people to exercise more fully their responsibilities in the great common cause of world development.

Life in the Peace Corps will not be easy. There will be no salary and allowances will be at a level sufficient only to maintain health and meet basic needs. Men and women will be expected to work and live alongside the nationals of the country in which they are stationed—doing the same work, eating the same food, talking the same language.

But if the life will not be easy, it will be rich and satisfying. For every young American who participates in the Peace Corps— who works in a foreign land—will know that he or she is sharing in the great common task of bringing to man that decent way of life which is the foundation of freedom and a condition of peace.

62   The President's News Conference of *March* 1, 1961

THE PRESIDENT. I have three or four announcements which I will make.

[1.] We have extended an invitation to the Chancellor, German Chancellor Adenauer, to come to the United States, and he has accepted our invitation, and we are delighted that he is going to be here in Washington on April 12th and April 13th. I am looking forward very much to meeting him and to having an exchange of views.

[2.] Secondly, I am writing to the Congress, to Congressman Vinson and to Senator Russell, a letter recommending that they consider legislation to restore former President Eisenhower to his military rank of General of the Army. President Eisenhower's outstanding military record and his long public service to our country in war and peace, I think, with that long experience it would be an appropriate act by the Congress if they should restore him to his former military rank.

[3.] Third, it is with some satisfaction that I am able to announce that the week ending today is the first week since last July that there has been no net outflow of gold from this country to foreign countries. While we realize that this complete halt is only temporary, I believe it does signify the confidence in the dollar throughout the world is being restored.

[4.] Fourth, our objective now is to help make effective at the retail level the influence of the Federal Reserve on the wholesale supply of money. We intend first to facilitate the flow of mortgage funds into the hands of prospective home buyers. I have requested Mr. Joseph McMurray, Chairman Designate of the Home Loan Bank Board, to meet with leaders in the savings and loan field, and to urge them to reduce mortgage rates so as to expand the flow of money into mortgages. His first such mission will be to California, where mortgage rates have been among the highest. We trust that his efforts here and around the country will mean real gains for home owners, the housing industry, and the economy.

[5.] And lastly, I have today signed an Executive order providing for the establishment of a Peace Corps[1] on a temporary pilot basis. I am also sending to Congress a message proposing authorization of a permanent Peace Corps. This corps will be a pool of trained men and women sent overseas by the United States Government or through private institutions and organizations, to help foreign countries meet their urgent needs for skilled manpower. It is our hope to have between five hundred and a thousand people in the field by the end of this year. We will send Americans abroad who are qualified to do a job. We will send those abroad who are committed to the concept which motivates the Peace Corps. It will not be easy. None of the men and women will be paid a salary. They will live at the same level as the citizens of the country which they are sent to, doing the same work, eating the same food, speaking

the same language. We are going to put particular emphasis on those men and women who have skills in teaching, agriculture, and in health.

I am hopeful it will be a source of satisfaction to Americans and a contribution to world peace.

[6.] Q. Mr. President, you said in your State of the Union Message that you had ordered a reappraisal of our entire defense strategy and that you would ask the Secretary of Defense to give you his conclusions by the end of February. Can you tell us what any of these conclusions are and would they involve any increased reliance on conventional as opposed to nuclear force?

THE PRESIDENT. The Secretary of Defense has passed to me his conclusions, and at the end of, I would say, about 2 weeks I will have finished our study of it, my study of it, with him, and will then send our recommendations to the Congress.

Secondly, in answer to your question, part of his recommendation is to strengthen conventional forces.

[7.] Q. Mr. President, some economists have voiced the opinion that perhaps the recession has reached a rockbottom and that the economy is on an upturn. Would you give us your views about that, and also answer some suggestions in your political opposition that perhaps some of your antirecession legislation may not be needed because of this expected upturn?

THE PRESIDENT. Well, I hope that an upturn does take place, but I must say that I think the Department of Commerce today is going to release some statistics and figures which do not indicate that an upturn is taking place as yet.

I would say there are still a great many hundreds of thousands of Americans who are dependent upon unemployment com-

---

[1] Executive Order 10924, 24 F.R. 1789.

pensation. There are many—several millions of Americans who can't find work. Members of Congress and others with whom I have talked report from various sections of the country that they still face a most serious situation. I think it would be premature to make a judgment that our economy is on the rise and that therefore there's no necessity for action. I don't take that view at all. I think all of these programs are needed.

And I am hopeful that it will be possible— I am hopeful that we will see the economy move up in the spring and summer, but we can make no predictions about it. And there's not sufficient evidence at hand yet by any Government department to indicate an upturn has taken place as of today.

[8.] Q. Mr. President, under the present U.N. troop command in the Congo, the pro-Communist Gizenga Government seems to be gaining ground, expanding its influence there almost daily. Is this Government satisfied with the conduct of that command and, if not, have we made any representations to Secretary Hammarskjold about it?

THE PRESIDENT. Well, the situation is very uncertain in the Congo and it is not possible to wholly accept the premise upon which your question was based.

The United Nations resolution and, therefore, the new mandate given to the Secretary, is really only a week old. I am hopeful that the resolution will be carried out effectively. We are going to continue to concern ourselves, as members of the United Nations, with its successful implementation.

[9.] Q. Mr. President, what is the role of Mr. Sargent Shriver in the Peace Corps, sir?

THE PRESIDENT. He has been working in organizing the Peace Corps.

Q. Will he continue in this—will he head it now that it is set up?

THE PRESIDENT. Well, we are going to make a judgment about who will be the head and what its staff will be in several days. He has been working on a voluntary basis up to this time.

[10.] Q. Mr. President, back in January the Civil Rights Commission recommended that Federal funds be withheld from public colleges and universities that discriminate on grounds of race, religion, or national origin. How do you feel about this?

THE PRESIDENT. Well, it is not part of the—this matter, this recommendation, as you know, is not included in the legislation that we sent to the Congress. As to whether we should by Executive order withhold funds from certain schools, that is a matter which is under consideration. It will be for—as a part of our general overall study of where the Federal Government might usefully place its power and influence to expand civil rights.

We hope in the next few days to have an Executive order forthcoming which will strengthen the employment opportunities, both in and out of the Government, for all Americans, and it will be followed as time goes on with other actions by the Federal Government to expand employment possibilities.

One of the areas which is being considered, of course, is the field of education; another is the field of housing. There are a great many areas where action might be taken. The one that will be taken first will be in the field of employment.

[11.] Q. It has been suggested, Mr. President, that when we give food to hungry people in other countries, we put it into an international pool so they will not know where it comes from. My question is, if our system can produce an overabundance of food, and the Communist system is not able to produce enough sometimes for their own people, why should we not advertise this to the world and label it, "A gift of the American people"?

THE PRESIDENT. Well, I think we should. And Mr. McGovern informed me—one of the matters I discussed with him was this question, and he told me that in his trip through Brazil, that on all the food that he saw being distributed which had originated in the United States there was clearly marked on it, "A gift of the people of the United States," which I was glad to hear.

[12.] Q. Mr. President, there is a great deal of interest abroad in your attitude and feeling toward the Algerian peace talks that are going on now. Would you comment, please, on what progress you feel might be made?

THE PRESIDENT. Well, I would hope that they are fruitful.

[13.] Q. New England would like to know, sir, if your administration is going to take the limits off of the imports of residual fuel oil.

THE PRESIDENT. Well, as you know, the Secretary of the Interior recently provided for an increase in the importation of oil or residual fuel oil, which I hope will be helpful.

Q. Do you think he will take the limits off completely? They say that is not sufficient to help New England.

THE PRESIDENT. Well, we have to consider the needs of the coal industry and the domestic producers, the needs of New England, and we are trying to reach a balance which will protect the public interest.

One matter which has concerned me, of course, has been the sharp increase, 12 percent, in the cost of fuel in the East and

Northeast United States. That increase has seemed excessive and, as you know, several agencies of the Government are now investigating to find out what was the cause of that, what I would consider to be an excessive increase.

But in answer to your question, we are attempting to reach a balance.

[14.] Q. Mr. President, on the nomination of Charles Meriwether, is there anything in this man's background that might embarrass your administration?

THE PRESIDENT. No, I have sent Mr. Meriwether's name up there after reading the FBI report and other records.

[15.] Q. Mr. President, there is a report that Vice President Johnson is setting up a special office across the street from yours. Does this indicate, sir, that you plan to place before him broader, perhaps unprecedented, Executive responsibilities?

THE PRESIDENT. Well, we have already indicated that he is going to have special responsibilities in the field of space. We are going to recommend to the Congress shortly that the space agency be reconstituted, with the Vice President instead of the President as chairman. In addition, he will have responsibilities in the field of employment opportunities. And also he is concerned—as a member for many years of the Armed Services Committee of the Senate as well as Chairman of the Subcommittee on Preparedness, he has been concerned with national security matters generally. And, therefore, it would seem to me appropriate that he would have some offices in the Executive Office Building so that he could meet these responsibilities most effectively.

[16.] Q. Mr. President, what sort of a response have you gotten from ordinary citizens as a result of your appeal a couple of weeks ago for ordinary people to write in about examples of waste in the Government spending that they have noticed, and have you any other examples which you could tell us about besides the $2,000 officers' club—$20,000; excuse me.

THE PRESIDENT. We have received some letters, and their recommendations are being investigated to find out if the facts are as they state them. But we have none to announce as yet. The investigations haven't been completed.

[17.] Q. Mr. President, your roving Ambassador to Africa has been widely criticized for some of the statements he has made, that is, Mr. Williams, including the one of "Africa for Africans," and the like. Do you find any validity in this criticism, and would you consider that his tour of Africa has been a plus for the United States policy?

THE PRESIDENT. Oh, I don't—I think Governor Williams has done very well. I am wholly satisfied with his mission. It's a very difficult one. Africa is not an easy matter to—the problems of Africa are not easy. And there are a good many conflicting forces that are loose in Africa as well as all parts of the world.

The statement "Africa for the Africans" does not seem to me to be a very unreasonable statement. He made it clear that he was talking about all those who felt that they were Africans, whatever their color might be, whatever their race might be. I do not know who else Africa should be for.

[18.] Q. Mr. President, Mr. Sheppard, who is Chairman of the House Appropriations Committee Subcommittee on Military Construction, stated that the Air Force missile base program, any way you look at it, is in a terrible mess, although he conceded there was some slight improvement in recent months. Do you care to comment, or

will this forthcoming report that you mentioned before comment on that?

THE PRESIDENT. Well, there are a great many difficulties. It is an extremely elaborate system to construct. A good many of the cost estimates were underestimated at the time. There are elaborate communications facilities that have to be developed, and it's not been proceeding altogether satisfactorily.

I think the congressional investigation was most helpful. And I think the Department of Defense will benefit from it, and we will attempt to improve the program.

[19.] Q. Mr. President, the Russians seem to have taken the position that Mr. McCloy's remarks the other day about the general and complete disarmament proposal of Mr. Khrushchev was a slogan, in McCloy's words. The Russians seem to take the position from this that your administration has now rejected this Soviet concept of disarmament. Is that a fact, or what is your attitude about that?

THE PRESIDENT. Well, I think Mr. McCloy was pointing out that you have to, in addition to trying to work for disarmament, you also have to work for a mechanism which will permit an orderly settlement of disputes between nations, settlements which under present conditions might be settled by military action, but which in some future date, if the goal of disarmament was achieved, would have to be settled by another means.

Now, I think it would be premature to make any judgments on what progress can be made in the field of disarmament. It is going to be some time before we have completed our study of what the American position will be on disarmament.

We are proceeding immediately ahead, of course, on nuclear testing. But I did not read into Mr. McCloy's statement any broad position, any broad administration policy, because we have not reached that policy on disarmament.

Q. Do you accept, sir, the view that disarmament is really not a legitimate word for what we are trying to do, that really it's arms control that the West, including the United States, is after or should be after?

THE PRESIDENT. Well, we want to proceed with arms control, leading to disarmament. But, of course, this complete disarmament in 4 years is a goal which has been talked about for a great many years.

I am somewhat familiar with the conversations which took place in Geneva under much less strained conditions from '28 to '29, through '33 and '34. It is extremely difficult to reach satisfactory agreements on disarmament. At that time the world was not divided as sharply as it is today, and yet rather limited progress was made. So this is an extremely difficult matter. I think the first area, of course, is in nuclear testing. That, I am hopeful, we can reach an agreement on.

But we also are going to be concerning ourselves with our position on disarmament. And I hope by this summer we will have completed that analysis. What progress can be made will depend upon the good will on both sides and their willingness to accept realistic inspection systems.

[20.] Q. Mr. President, recently documents were made public indicating that the ideological split between Red China and Russia is perhaps greater than many people have thought. Do you feel that this split might be to the benefit of the United States? And to what extent? For example, do you think that this might bring Russia and the United States closer together, over the long run?

THE PRESIDENT. Well, I wouldn't attempt to make a judgment about what our future

relations are going to be. I am hopeful that we can work out a relationship which will permit us to live in peace and maintain our security and the security of those countries with which we are allied. That is our object.

I am hopeful that the Soviet Union will come to that conclusion also. What factors will be in their minds in making their policy, of course, can only be surmised. But we are attempting, and will be attempting in the coming months, to determine whether any effective agreements can be accomplished with the Soviet Union which will permit a relaxation of world tension. And we should know that in some months.

[21.] Q. Mr. President, one of your campaign complaints was that fewer than a hundred people in the whole Federal Government were working in the field of disarmament and planning for negotiations. Can you tell us how many people you have working on that problem now and what progress you are making towards building up what you would regard as an adequate staff to deal with this question?

THE PRESIDENT. We have, of course, the problem, and have had it, of going into the negotiations in late March. There have been voluntary groups, particularly one led by Dr. Fisk, which has been concerning itself with our position in those negotiations. I discussed with Mr. McCloy the setting up of a longer range operation on disarmament and nuclear testing, and we are now considering whether that should be established as a separate agency in the executive branch or in the State Department, with permanent personnel and a budget under a statutory action by the Congress. I am hopeful—Mr. McCloy is considering it, and we hope to be able to make a recommendation to Congress about the long-range buildup of our disarmament activities in some days.

[22.] Q. Mr. President, what significance, if any, do you attach to the fact that the Russians put part of your news conference on their television, and would you welcome more of this?

THE PRESIDENT. I would welcome more of it. And I am glad that they are doing it, and I hope that it can be expanded so that it gives an accurate reflection of the point of view of this country.

[23.] Q. Mr. President, this last weekend, Vice Chancellor Erhard in Germany suggested that West Germany was not necessarily going to continue aid to underdeveloped areas beyond 1 year. Was it your understanding with the Foreign Minister, Herr von Brentano, when he left here, that this would be on a continuing basis?

THE PRESIDENT. It is my understanding that it would be on a continuing basis, and I am sure that that would be the point of view of the German Government. As to how much they will be able to do on a continuing basis, that is a matter which they have to determine and I am sure will be a subject of discussion between the United States and the Germans and other interested countries. But my impression was very precise, that it would be on a continuing basis. But I do not say that the figures which have been reported in the papers as to how much would be provided on a continuing basis, I did not have any understanding that those were the figures that they would finally reach. The idea of continuity was clearly accepted, and the idea of the figures is a matter of course which would be before the Germans and on which of course we will be talking with them.

[24.] Q. Mr. President, Congressman Anfuso has recommended that this country take the initiative and officially invite Soviet space scientists to meet with U.S. scientists to work out plans for cooperation and peaceful exploration of space in line with your own recommendations. Would you comment on this, and could you tell us what plans you may have now to achieve this end?

THE PRESIDENT. We are attempting to improve our exchange program on a reciprocal basis with the Soviet Union—and have been engaged in that activity for some time.

Q. Yes, but have you defined any special areas in which you could cooperate without any harm to our national security?

THE PRESIDENT. When we have been able to work out any successful exchanges or new exchanges, we will announce them. But we are of course concerned that they will be reciprocal, and national security will be protected, and also that it would contribute to some useful purpose. We have, as you know, had recently here in Washington a meeting which had been arranged some months ago on meteorology, in which the Soviet representative was unable to be here, which was a source of regret. There are other proposals we have made for the long-range exploration of space, weather control, and so on, and we are going to continue to attempt to engage the Soviet Union in a common effort in that kind of activity.

[25.] Q. Mr. President, you told an earlier press conference that for every new program you set up, you would suggest a source of revenue. Does that mean, for example, in the case of the education program that you are going to suggest some special way of financing that?

THE PRESIDENT. No, what I said was that for the proposals that we would make, we would have a suggested source of revenue, and by the end of the month, when we send up our completed budgetary recommendations for '61–62, we will also suggest sources of revenue.

Now, in the case of unemployment compensation, aid to dependent children, social security, highways, and medical care for the aged, we did suggest the appropriation.

On the suggestion of the appropriation on agriculture and on education there is no direct tax link to those, but we will have some proposals to make before the end of the month to bring that section of the budget which we have effected in line with the revenues.

I have excluded, of course, from the beginning, what we do in the field of national security.

Q. A sort of an overall balancing out is what you have in mind in the case of education, and not a specific source, but some general program for changing the revenue?

THE PRESIDENT. I think as I have stated, we are going to suggest revenues for any expenditures that we make which do not have by themselves or linked to them a source of revenue as the other programs did.

Q. Have you made any estimate whether there will be a deficit in fiscal year 1962?

THE PRESIDENT. We will send to the Congress, I believe on March 23, our view on what the '62 budget will look like. We have not completed our programs, and we have not completed our analysis of tax revenues at this time.

Q. Mr. President, there is a report that there is a billion and a half deficit in sight. Is that correct?

THE PRESIDENT. I would prefer to wait until we are able to complete our programs because the amount of the budget is tied pretty much to what we recommend. All these programs, with the exception of defense, will be finished by the 20th, and we will then be in a position to—. Of course, the final budget deficit will depend quite a lot on what we do in the field of national

security. And I have not finished making a judgment on how much we should recommend in addition to the present '62 budget.

[26.] Q. Mr. President, the aide memoire which was handed to Dr. von Brentano emphasized the need for burden sharing on defense and foreign aid in the Atlantic Community. Can you speak somewhat more precisely of your ideas on this burden sharing?

THE PRESIDENT. Yes. I hope that all the members of the Atlantic Community will contribute according to their resources for the maintenance of NATO and for the assistance to the newly emerging countries, and that the burden will be commonly assumed, and the OECD discussions, the discussions—the bilateral discussions with the Germans, discussions which are going to take place in March and in April in Europe—I am hopeful will lead to that result.

[27.] Q. Sir, in view of the criticism that has occurred, could you elaborate on why you have not recommended Federal aid to public and—to private and parochial elementary and secondary schools?

THE PRESIDENT. Well, the Constitution clearly prohibits aid to the school, to parochial schools. I don't think there is any doubt of that.

The Everson case, which is probably the most celebrated case, provided only by a 5 to 4 decision was it possible for a local community to provide bus rides to nonpublic school children. But all through the majority and minority statements on that particular question there was a very clear prohibition against aid to the school direct. The Supreme Court made its decision in the Everson case by determining that the aid was to the child, not to the school. Aid to the school is—there isn't any room for debate on that subject. It is prohibited by the Constitution, and the Supreme Court has made that very clear. And therefore there would be no possibility of our recommending it.

Q. But you are free to make the recommendations you have made which will affect private and parochial colleges and universities?

THE PRESIDENT. Well, the aid that we have recommended to colleges is in a different form. We are aiding the student in the same way the GI bill of rights aided the student. The scholarships are given to the students who have particular talents and they can go to the college they want. In that case it is aid to the student, not to the school or college, and, therefore, not to a particular religious group. That is the distinction between them, except in the case of aid to medical schools, and that has been done for a number of years. Because that is a particular kind of technical assistance the constitutional question has not arisen on that matter.

[28.] Q. Mr. President, in regard to Mr. Meriwether, it has been alleged in the press and in Congress that he was campaign manager to former Admiral Crommelin. Now in fairness——

THE PRESIDENT. In 1950.

Q. Yes. In fairness to Mr. Meriwether, can you state whether this is true and whether it entered into your thinking?

THE PRESIDENT. Yes, he was campaign manager; had association with the campaign in 1950. That's correct.

[29.] Q. Regarding your opening remark about the recommendation by the Defense Secretary to increase our conventional arms strength, would you please give us some of your thinking as to the rationale for this shift, if it is a shift, in our defense spending?

THE PRESIDENT. I would not say it is a shift. I would say it's—there are proposals made by the Secretary which talk about a general strengthening of our Armed Forces, including many areas. So I am not sure that the word "shift" is the most descriptive.

[30.] Q. Mr. President, could you say whether any strengthening of our conventional forces will imply or mean a lessening of emphasis on nuclear weapons, or in our capacity to use them in a pinch?

THE PRESIDENT. I have not heard that. We have reached no decision which would indicate that there has been a change in our reliance. When—if we do reach a change in our reliance in new weapons, we will make it very clear. But no such change has been reached at the present time. What we are anxious to do, of course, is to see conventional forces strengthened not only in Western Europe but throughout the world. And that, it seems to me, was the gist of the Secretary's memorandum and his testimony yesterday and his public statements.

Reporter: Thank you, Mr. President.

NOTE: President Kennedy's fifth news conference was held in the State Department Auditorium at 10 o'clock on Wednesday morning, March 1, 1961.

63   Special Message to the Congress on the Peace Corps. *March 1, 1961*

To the Congress of the United States:

I recommend to the Congress the establishment of a permanent Peace Corps—a pool of trained American men and women sent overseas by the U. S. Government or through private organizations and institutions to help foreign countries meet their urgent needs for skilled manpower.

I have today signed an Executive Order establishing a Peace Corps on a temporary pilot basis.

The temporary Peace Corps will be a source of information and experience to aid us in formulating more effective plans for a permanent organization. In addition, by starting the Peace Corps now we will be able to begin training young men and women for overseas duty this summer with the objective of placing them in overseas positions by late fall. This temporary Peace Corps is being established under existing authority in the Mutual Security Act and will be located in the Department of State. Its initial expenses will be paid from appropriations currently available for our foreign aid program.

Throughout the world the people of the newly developing nations are struggling for economic and social progress which reflects their deepest desires. Our own freedom, and the future of freedom around the world, depend, in a very real sense, on their ability to build growing and independent nations where men can live in dignity, liberated from the bonds of hunger, ignorance and poverty.

One of the greatest obstacles to the achievement of this goal is the lack of trained men and women with the skill to teach the young and assist in the operation of development projects—men and women with the capacity to cope with the demands of swiftly evolving economies, and with the dedication to put that capacity to work in the villages, the mountains, the towns and the factories of dozens of struggling nations.

The vast task of economic development urgently requires skilled people to do the work of the society—to help teach in the schools, construct development projects, demonstrate modern methods of sanitation in the villages, and perform a hundred other tasks calling for training and advanced knowledge.

To meet this urgent need for skilled manpower we are proposing the establishment of a Peace Corps—an organization which will recruit and train American volunteers, sending them abroad to work with the people of other nations.

This organization will differ from existing assistance programs in that its members will supplement technical advisers by offering the specific skills needed by developing nations if they are to put technical advice to work. They will help provide the skilled manpower necessary to carry out the development projects planned by the host governments, acting at a working level and serving at great personal sacrifice. There is little doubt that the number of those who wish to serve will be far greater than our capacity to absorb them.

The Peace Corps or some similar approach has been strongly advocated by Senator Humphrey, Representative Reuss and others in the Congress. It has received strong support from universities, voluntary agencies, student groups, labor unions and business and professional organizations.

Last session, the Congress authorized a study of these possibilities. Preliminary reports of this study show that the Peace Corps is feasible, needed, and wanted by many foreign countries.

Most heartening of all, the initial reaction to this proposal has been an enthusiastic response by student groups, professional organizations and private citizens everywhere—a convincing demonstration that we have in this country an immense reservoir of dedicated men and women willing to devote their energies and time and toil to the cause of world peace and human progress.

Among the specific programs to which

Peace Corps members can contribute are: teaching in primary and secondary schools, especially as part of national English language teaching programs; participation in the worldwide program of malaria eradication; instruction and operation of public health and sanitation projects; aiding in village development through school construction and other programs; increasing rural agricultural productivity by assisting local farmers to use modern implements and techniques. The initial emphasis of these programs will be on teaching. Thus the Peace Corps members will be an effective means of implementing the development programs of the host countries—programs which our technical assistance operations have helped to formulate.

The Peace Corps will not be limited to the young, or to college graduates. All Americans who are qualified will be welcome to join this effort. But undoubtedly the Corps will be made up primarily of young people as they complete their formal education.

Because one of the greatest resources of a free society is the strength and diversity of its private organizations and institutions much of the Peace Corps program will be carried out by these groups, financially assisted by the Federal Government.

Peace Corps personnel will be made available to developing nations in the following ways:

1. Through private voluntary agencies carrying on international assistance programs.

2. Through overseas programs of colleges and universities.

3. Through assistance programs of international agencies.

4. Through assistance programs of the United States government.

5. Through new programs which the Peace Corps itself directly administers.

In the majority of cases the Peace Corps will assume the entire responsibility for recruitment, training and the development of overseas projects. In other cases it will make available a pool of trained applicants to private groups who are carrying out projects approved by the Peace Corps.

In the case of Peace Corps programs conducted through voluntary agencies and universities, these private institutions will have the option of using the national recruitment system—the central pool of trained manpower—or developing recruitment systems of their own.

In all cases men and women recruited as a result of Federal assistance will be members of the Peace Corps and enrolled in the central organization. All private recruitment and training programs will adhere to Peace Corps standards as a condition of Federal assistance.

In all instances the men and women of the Peace Corps will go only to those countries where their services and skills are genuinely needed and desired. U.S. Operations Missions, supplemented where necessary by special Peace Corps teams, will consult with leaders in foreign countries in order to determine where Peace Corpsmen are needed, the types of job they can best fill, and the number of people who can be usefully employed. The Peace Corps will not supply personnel for marginal undertakings without a sound economic or social justification. In furnishing assistance through the Peace Corps careful regard will be given to the particular country's developmental priorities.

Membership in the Peace Corps will be open to all Americans, and applications will be available shortly. Where application is made directly to the Peace Corps—the vast majority of cases—they will be carefully screened to make sure that those who are selected can contribute to Peace Corps programs, and have the personal qualities which will enable them to represent the United States abroad with honor and dignity. In those cases where application is made directly to a private group, the same basic standards will be maintained. Each new recruit will receive a training and orientation period varying from six weeks to six months. This training will include courses in the culture and language of the country to which they are being sent and specialized training designed to increase the work skills of recruits. In some cases training will be conducted by participant agencies and universities in approved training programs. Other training programs will be conducted by the Peace Corps staff.

Length of service in the Corps will vary depending on the kind of project and the country, generally ranging from two to three years. Peace Corps members will often serve under conditions of physical hardship, living under primitive conditions among the people of developing nations. For every Peace Corps member service will mean a great financial sacrifice. They will receive no salary. Instead they will be given an allowance which will only be sufficient to meet their basic needs and maintain health. It is essential that Peace Corpsmen and women live simply and unostentatiously among the people they have come to assist. At the conclusion of their tours, members of the Peace Corps will receive a small sum in the form of severance pay based on length of service abroad, to assist them during their first weeks back in the United States. Service with the Peace Corps will not exempt volunteers from Selective Service.

The United States will assume responsibility for supplying medical services to Peace Corps members and ensuring supplies and drugs necessary to good health.

I have asked the temporary Peace Corps to begin plans and make arrangements for pilot programs. A minimum of several hundred volunteers could be selected, trained and at work abroad by the end of this calendar year. It is hoped that within a few years several thousand Peace Corps members will be working in foreign lands.

It is important to remember that this program must, in its early stages, be experimental in nature. This is a new dimension in our overseas program and only the most careful planning and negotiation can ensure its success.

The benefits of the Peace Corps will not be limited to the countries in which it serves. Our own young men and women will be enriched by the experience of living and working in foreign lands. They will have acquired new skills and experience which will aid them in their future careers and add to our own country's supply of trained personnel and teachers. They will return better able to assume the responsibilities of American citizenship and with greater understanding of our global responsibilities.

Although this is an American Peace Corps, the problem of world development is not just an American problem. Let us hope that other nations will mobilize the spirit and energies and skill of their people in some form of Peace Corps—making our own effort only one step in a major international effort to increase the welfare of all men and improve understanding among nations.

JOHN F. KENNEDY

64 Remarks Recorded for a Television Program Marking Twenty-five Years of Publication of Life Magazine. *March 2, 1961*

AS WE HAVE SEEN in the 25 years since *Life* was first printed, communications have changed dramatically. The people of our country, I think, have a greater understanding and a greater awareness of the problems that we now face as a people. There is, however, no question that in the coming months and years this communication and this understanding must constantly be increased. It will constantly be more important.

The United States is playing an increasingly significant role in the world today as the chief defender of freedom in a time of freedom's maximum danger. The entire democratic system which depends for its success upon majority rule, and therefore for majority understanding, depends in a very real sense on information and communication—for our judgment is no better than our information. The great organizations of communication, therefore, in this country, have an obligation and a responsibility unequaled in our national life, and basic to our national future.

Recently, *Life* magazine published a series of articles on our national purpose. I hope in the coming months and years there will be no doubt in the minds of our own people, and in the people around the world, of our national purpose, of our hopes, of our aspirations, of our determination.

We have seen tonight 25 years of tumult and change in the lives of government, science, and of the people. The next 25 years we will see changes even more drastic. The shots will be heard around the world, and in the lives of us all. It will be our responsibility as a people to make sure that 25 years from tonight the great Republic of the United States is still preserved, still secure, still strong, still purposeful.

NOTE: The program for which these remarks were recorded was broadcast on March 2 from 9:30 to 11 p.m.

65 Remarks at the Dedication of the National Wildlife Federation Building. *March 3, 1961*

Secretary of the Interior Udall, Mr. President, members of the National Wildlife Federation, Members of the Congress, ladies and gentlemen:

Twenty-five years ago Franklin Roosevelt—speaking to the first wildlife conference—expressed his desire "to bring together individuals, organizations, and agencies interested in the restoration and conservation of wildlife resources," so that all concerned groups could "work together cooperatively for the common good."

As a result of this speech the National Wildlife Federation was formed—an organization now affiliated in 50 States, with over 2 million members—with a long record of accomplishment in the protection of our natural, national wildlife resources "for the common good."

I believe it is significant that I, as a citizen of Massachusetts, now address a society devoted to a program which received its greatest support from two New Yorkers, Theodore Roosevelt and Franklin Roosevelt, housed in a building provided in part through the generosity of a citizen of my own State of Massachusetts, Louise Ayer Hatheway of Boston. It is significant because it dramatically illustrates that the development of our natural resources is not a Western opportunity or a Western problem, it is a national opportunity not bounded by geography but common to us all in whatever States we may live.

At the inauguration, Robert Frost read a poem which began "the land was ours before we were the land's,"—meaning, in part, that this new land of ours sustained us before we were a nation. And although we are now the land's—a nation of people matched to a continent—we still draw our strength and sustenance in this city and in every other city across our country from the earth.

Throughout our history our soil and water, our forests and minerals, have provided the resources upon which this country grew—and our power ascended. Today, this great gift of material wealth provides the foundation upon which the defense of freedom rests, here and around the world. And our future greatness and our strength depend upon the continued abundant use of our natural resources.

Thus it is our task in our time and in our generation, to hand down undiminished to those who come after us, as was handed down to us by those who went before, the natural wealth and beauty which is ours. To do this will require constant attention and vigilance—sustained vigor and imagination.

No governmental program will be effective—our resources will not be protected—without the concern and help of every private citizen. By mobilizing private effort through this organization you are helping not only to develop the wildlife resources of our country—but you are helping to create the kind of America that is our common goal: an America of open spaces, of fresh water, of green country—a place where wildlife and natural beauty cannot be despoiled—where an increasingly urbanized population can still go to the country, can still turn back the clock of our civilization and find the material and spiritual strength upon which our greatness as a country depends.

More than one hundred years ago, a Senator from the East, speaking with prophecy, as Senators from the East frequently do, said that "to talk about constructing a railroad to the western shores of this continent manifests a spirit of wild adventure which I never expected to hear broached in the Senate of the United States." But that spirit prevailed, just as it has prevailed in your organization—and this country grew—and that railroad went West. Today we once again call upon that "spirit of wild adventure"—and once again act to develop those resources which lie beneath our earth, in our mountains, in our rivers—and lie most of all in our people.

NOTE: The President spoke at 9:30 a.m. His opening words "Mr. President" referred to Claude B. Kelley, President of the National Wildlife Federation.

66 Joint Statement Following Discussion With Prime Minister Holyoake of New Zealand. *March 3, 1961*

PRESIDENT KENNEDY and Prime Minister Holyoake met today in Washington to review matters of mutual interest. The

Secretary of State, Dean Rusk; the Assistant Secretary of State for Far Eastern Affairs, J. Graham Parsons; the Secretary of the Department of External Affairs of the Government of New Zealand, Mr. A. D. McIntosh; and the Chargé d'Affaires of the New Zealand Embassy in Washington, Mr. O. D. L. White, participated in the discussions.

In welcoming this opportunity to establish a personal association at an early stage of their administrations, the President and Prime Minister declared their desire to make even stronger the friendship and confidence which have always characterized relations between their two countries.

The President and the Prime Minister reviewed the progress so far achieved, and the continuing contribution of the United States and New Zealand, in the struggle to raise living standards in the developing areas of the world. They noted with concern the present inadequacy of food distribution throughout the world and the urgent need for action to alleviate mass hunger and malnutrition which now afflict much of mankind. They recognized the importance of insuring that programs of aid in agricultural commodities should not endanger normal trade.

In exchanging views on defense questions, the Prime Minister and the President were in full agreement on the importance and value of SEATO and ANZUS. Both leaders reaffirmed their adherence to the principles of collective security which these treaties make effective. Both stated their determination to cooperate closely in maintaining security in the Pacific. Prime Minister Holyoake informed the President of the review

of defense policy, which New Zealand is presently conducting with the aim of insuring that it will be able to meet its commitments promptly and effectively.

President Kennedy and Prime Minister Holyoake noted with deep concern the hostile and aggressive attitude of the Chinese communist regime and the particular menace it poses to the peace of Asia, Africa, and Latin America.

The Prime Minister and the President examined the crisis in Laos. Mr. Holyoake drew upon the first-hand experience he had been able to gain during his fact-finding tour of Laos last year. Both men welcomed the recent statement of King Savang Vatthana and expressed the hope that ways could be found in the near future to bring to this Asian nation peace, security and neutrality.

The President and the Prime Minister agreed that disarmament confronted the world with one of its most difficult problems. President Kennedy outlined the steps the United States is taking to coordinate and expand its efforts in this field. Both leaders expressed the hope that future deliberations on this subject would have a successful conclusion. They recognized that effective controls must be a central feature of any agreement.

The President of the United States took this occasion to thank the New Zealand Government and people for the excellent support and hospitality they have extended to the United States in its scientific endeavors in Antarctica.

67   Message to the Members of the National 4–H Club. *March 4, 1961*

MY WARM BEST WISHES to each of you as you look forward to National 4–H Club Week, starting March 4. I would com-

mend you especially for your achievements in leadership and citizenship. Through your emphasis on Head, Heart, Hands, and

Health, you are making a valuable contribution to our country's welfare and progress. Your energy, ability, and perseverance—supported by parents, club leaders, and other public-spirited men and women—are a vital force in America's strength and growth.

Now 2-1/3 million strong, you are learning today to put science to work in your homes and on your farms. Tomorrow your training and experience will help you become leaders in your communities, States, and Nation. There you will have a great opportunity to help provide a more fruitful life for peoples at home and abroad, and to help other countries gain for themselves the peace and freedom they strive for.

I am sure we can count on you in 4-H Clubs everywhere to help us face the challenge that lies ahead. I have faith in the future as we plan and prepare for it together.

68 Statement by the President Upon Signing Order Establishing the President's Committee on Equal Employment Opportunity. *March 7*, 1961

I AM TODAY issuing an Executive Order combining the President's Committee on Government Contracts and the President's Committee on Government Employment Policy into a single President's Committee on Equal Employment Opportunity.[1]

Through this vastly strengthened machinery I intend to ensure that Americans of all colors and beliefs will have equal access to employment within the government, and with those who do business with the government.

The implementation of this policy has been hampered by lack of personnel, by inadequate procedures and ineffective enforcement. As a result Americans who are members of minority groups have often been unjustly denied the opportunity to work for the government or for government contractors.

This order provides for centralization of responsibility for these policies under the Vice-President. It requires the Secretary of Labor—with all the resources of the Department of Labor at his command—to supervise

the implementation of equal employment policies. And it grants, in specific terms, sanctions sweeping enough to ensure compliance.

In this order I am also directing a complete study of current government employment practices—an examination of the status of members of minority groups in every department, agency and office of the Federal government. When this survey—the most thorough ever undertaken—is completed we will have an accurate assessment of our present position and a yardstick by which to measure future progress.

I have dedicated my Administration to the cause of equal opportunity in employment by the government or its contractors. The Vice-President, the Secretary of Labor and the other members of this committee share my dedication. I have no doubt that the vigorous enforcement of this order will mean the end of such discrimination.

In this connection I have already directed all Departments to take immediate action to broaden the government employment opportunities for members of minority groups.

---

[1] Executive Order 10925, dated March 6, 1961, 26 F.R. 1977.

69   Letter to the President of the Senate and to the Speaker of the House on a More Flexible Approach to Economic Assistance for Eastern Europe.   *March 7,* 1961

[Released March 7, 1961.   Dated February 21, 1961]

Dear Mr.————:

In the State of the Union address I asked the Congress for increased discretion to use economic tools as an aid in re-establishing our historic ties of friendship with the people of Eastern Europe.

I urge the Congress to take early action on legislation to accomplish this purpose.   Such legislation—along the lines of the amendment to the Mutual Defense Assistance Control Act of 1951 which was passed by the Senate on September 12, 1959—accompanies this letter.

Sincerely,

JOHN F. KENNEDY

NOTE: This is the text of identical letters addressed to the Honorable Lyndon B. Johnson, President of the Senate, and to the Honorable Sam Rayburn, Speaker of the House of Representatives.

The draft bill, released with the President's letter, is published in the Congressional Record (vol. 107, Mar. 7, 1961, p. 3079).

70   Letter to the President of the Senate and to the Speaker of the House on Federal Aid to Colleges and Universities.   *March 7,* 1961

Dear Mr.————:

I am transmitting herewith drafts of two bills designed to carry out recommendations set forth in my message of February 20th to the Congress for assistance to institutions of higher education.   One bill provides for the construction of academic facilities and for undergraduate scholarships.   The other bill provides for housing facilities for the students.

I consider enactment of this legislation vital.   In the years ahead there will be great increases in the number of students seeking matriculation at our colleges and universities.   If our youth are to have an opportunity to develop their intellectual capacities to the fullest, steps must be taken immediately to increase the available facilities for higher education and to relieve both the students and the universities from impossible financial burdens.   This program is designed to do this.

Enclosed are letters from the Secretary of Health, Education, and Welfare and from the Housing and Home Finance Agency Administrator describing the two proposals in more detail.   I consider the need critical and the program urgent.

Sincerely,

JOHN F. KENNEDY

NOTE: This is the text of identical letters addressed to the Honorable Lyndon B. Johnson, President of the Senate, and to the Honorable Sam Rayburn, Speaker of the House of Representatives.

71 The President's News Conference of *March 8, 1961*

THE PRESIDENT. I have several announcements to make.

[1.] First, I want to say a word on behalf of Radio Free Europe, which is now making its annual appeal for support from all of our citizens. For more than 10 years this enterprise has been reaching out to people in Europe—Eastern Europe; truth, devotion to liberty, is its message. For this radio is at work, with listeners numbering in the millions. The competition of ideas in these countries is kept alive. Individual Americans by giving to Radio Free Europe may be sure that they are bringing a beacon of light into countries to which millions of us are tied by kinship, and whose hope for freedom all of us must share.

This is a peaceful concern but a firm one. Radio Free Europe needs and deserves our generous help.

[2.] Secondly, Mrs. Kennedy and I are giving an afternoon reception at the White House next Monday for the Latin American Ambassadors to the United States, the Council of the OAS, as well as members of Congress concerned with Latin American affairs. I will take the opportunity at the close of the reception to make a major statement of some of my views about the problems of the Americas.

[3.] Third, pursuant to my instructions, each Federal department and agency has renewed its procurement and construction plans for the remainder of the current fiscal year, through June 30, 1961, for the purpose of speeding up its contracts and purchases with available funds. The total of obligations for the remainder of the fiscal year is now planned to be $660 million higher than before the directive. If this acceleration proceeds as planned by the agencies, direct Federal purchases of goods and services will be increased in the January–March quarter by an annual rate of about one quarter of a billion dollars, and in the April–June quarter by an annual rate of about three quarters of a billion dollars.

[4.] Next, I wish to announce that the Prime Minister of Sweden, Mr. Erlander, will make an informal visit to the United States for a period of 10 days, beginning March 28. The Prime Minister and I will meet together on the 29th, after which Mr. Erlander will visit other parts of the United States. I am very pleased with the prospect of meeting the Prime Minister, for we Americans have many close ties with Sweden and its people. And I extend a most hearty welcome to him.

[5.] It has been brought to my attention, next, that 5,000 Indian and Eskimo children under the jurisdiction of the Bureau of Indian Affairs of the Department of the Interior are not in school—cannot attend school until facilities are built for them. These children live on the Navajo Reservation in Arizona and New Mexico, in Alaska, and in the Choctaw Reservation in Mississippi. In addition, other thousands are housed in overcrowded and obsolete boarding and day facilities, some hazardous to their health and safety.

I have instructed the Secretary of the Interior, Mr. Udall, to submit to the Congress without delay plans to correct the situation.

[6.] I am announcing the appointment and scheduled departure this evening of a special mission to review the status and effectiveness of the United States economic policies in Bolivia. The chairman of the three-person mission is Dr. Willard Thorpe, and the other two members are Mr. Jack

Corbett and Mr. Seymour J. Rubin. This mission will arrive in La Paz on March 9 and spend approximately 2 weeks before returning to Washington to report their recommendations for a plan of action to be followed by United States agencies in Washington and Bolivia. An adviser to the mission, Mr. Coerr, Deputy Assistant Secretary of State for Inter-American Affairs, has already arrived.

[7.] Finally, I want to say that in response to the first Executive order the number of people receiving surplus food has doubled from 3,500,000 in December to 6,100,000 at the present time. The value of the food being distributed monthly has doubled—$12.80 before the expanded program went into effect, $24.40 in retail value at the present time. In addition, this has doubled the protein value of the direct distribution of food.

[8.] This is the last statement. The Cuban Red Cross, the American Red Cross, and U.S. Navy today combined in a three-way effort to combat a polio breakout in Guantanamo City, Cuba, some 31 miles from the naval base. Early today the Red Cross directorate at the U. S. naval base in southeastern Cuba had a phone call from a male Red Cross nurse in Guantanamo City saying there was an outbreak of polio, with 3 children dead and 10 more stricken.

All available vaccine had been used by the hospitals in Guantanamo City. And aid was needed to give vaccine for at least 100 more children which they were unable to obtain. The Red Cross director at the base got permission from Adm. Edward J. O'Donnell to send all the vaccine which could be spared. She carried and sent enough vaccine for 160 first inoculations to the northeast gate, where she met the Cuban Red Cross ambulance where the transfer was made.

I want to take this opportunity and this incident to emphasize again that our differences of opinion on matters affecting Cuba are not with the Cuban people. Rather, we desire the closet, and harmonious and friendly, and most sympathetic ties with them.

[9.] Q. Mr. President, you told us last month that you expected to have an answer from the Defense Department about this time on whether there is or is not a missile gap. Are you able to say at this time whether there is or is not?

THE PRESIDENT. We are concluding our review of the recommendations which the Defense Department has made for changes in the Defense budget. I am hopeful that this survey can be completed in the next few days, and then we plan to send the results of our study to the Congress. And at that time we will indicate what I believe to be the relative defensive position of the United States and other countries and what needs to be done to improve it.

[10.] Q. I am sure you are aware, sir, of the tremendous mail response that your news conferences on television and radio have produced. There are many Americans who believe that in our manner of questioning or seeking your attention that we are subjecting you to some abuse or a lack of respect. I wonder, sir, in this light, could you tell us generally your feelings about your press conferences to date and your feelings about how they are conducted?

THE PRESIDENT. Well, you subject me to some abuse, but not to any lack of respect. [*Laughter*] I must say that I do know that there are difficulties, and I know that it places burdens on members of the press to have to stand up, particularly when I am not able to recognize them. On the other hand, if it were changed and one member stood up, then perhaps that would not be a satisfactory device. So I think that along with the old saying about "don't take down the fence until you know why it was put up," I would say that we should stay with what we now have.

[11.] Q. Mr. President, the approach to a peaceful settlement in Laos seems to have run into a dead end, with rejection by two of the proposed members of the three-nation neutral commission, and the Soviet Union apparently still insists upon the approach of an ICC [1] action there and an international conference. I wonder if in your review of the situation you have reached any conclusion as to what step the United States should now take to avoid the expansion of the war in Laos?

THE PRESIDENT. Well, the United States had been hopeful that it would be possible to set up some procedures where neutral nations could guarantee the security of Laos and also isolate it from military pressures on both sides. We are going to have to consider what other procedures might be followed to achieve that goal. But this is a matter now of discussion with our friends and with others, and I am hopeful that we can achieve a result which will bring stability to Laos, permit it to maintain its independence, and bring peace to the area, and self-determination. Those are very difficult goals to achieve, given the situation which we found upon assuming our responsibilities. But we are going to continue and are now continuing to take every step that we can to achieve that goal.

[12.] Q. Mr. President, there has been considerable comment that your program up to now has illustrated what the country can do for the people. I think a lot of people have asked me and I am asking you, sir, at what point does your program tell what the people can do for the country?

---

[1] International Control Commission.

THE PRESIDENT. Well, we are trying to do two or three things in the domestic program. We are trying to protect and provide jobs for people—that is, I think, a matter of concern to all Americans. We are committed to that goal, and the programs which we have sent up to the Hill have that object in mind. We are also trying to strengthen our educational system, which needs to be strengthened over the long period in which we are going to be tested. We are trying to provide for more orderly and effective programs of medical care for the elderly. Now, these programs, in my opinion, are in the public interest, and they are being assessed in that regard.

I would say, as I have said from the beginning, that in time I have no doubt that all of us will find ourselves tested in our attempts to maintain the independence of the United States and the independence of those countries to which we are committed. These programs are an attempt to provide for a viable economy, which I think is essential for the security of the United States and for the security of those countries which are dependent upon it. It is also an effort to provide equality of opportunity to the extent that at least we can do so for all Americans because I think it is in the public interest.

[13.] Q. Sir, would you help to clarify the aid to private schools issue? The National Defense Education Act, passed in 1958, provides loans for private elementary and secondary schools for equipment. And existing provisions, as well as your recommendations, allow for construction loans for private colleges. I wonder if you would give us your view on proposals to add to your school bill provisions for loans, as differentiated from grants for private and parochial elementary and secondary schools.

THE PRESIDENT. You have mentioned

three rather different programs, which involve different purposes and different constitutional problems.

The first program was the National Defense Education Act, where loans were provided for nonpublic schools for specific purposes—languages, I believe, and also for science and engineering. Twenty million dollars was provided of which, interestingly enough, only about $1,300,000 has been used for loans. That was the first.

Now the second type of program you discussed—I supported that program. In my opinion it was—there is not evidence as yet that that suggests a serious constitutional problem because it is tied very closely to national defense.

The second program we are talking about is loans to all colleges. And in my opinion—and also, of course, scholarship assistance to the students. That is in a different position, at least to the best of my judgment, from secondary education. Secondary education is compulsory. It is provided for every student, every citizen. Every citizen must attend school. We are providing a program which we have sent to the Congress, of grants for public schools. And, therefore, in my opinion, that is the program which I hope will be passed.

Now, the problem of loans to secondary education does institute serious constitutional problems. I do not think that anyone can read the Everson case without recognizing that the position which the court took, minority and majority, in regard to the use of tax funds for nonpublic schools, raises a serious constitutional question.

I have expressed my view on them. I think the Congress should consider carefully what its view is on them, and what kind of programs it wants to recommend in this area. The Congress, as I say, has recommended grants to private colleges in the past—I used, I think, a week or two ago, I gave that as an example—in the National Defense Education Act it used loans for specific purposes.

Whether across the board loans are constitutional is a question which, in my opinion, raises a serious constitutional question.

I am hopeful that the Congress will enact grants. If the Congress, the Congressmen, wish to address themselves to the problem of loans, which is a separate matter—we are not talking about, in this bill, loans to secondary education—then I am hopeful that it would be considered as a separate matter, that the Congress will consider the constitutional problems and then consider what action it would want to take.

We will be glad to cooperate in every way. But I am hopeful that while that consideration is being given, that we will move ahead with the grant program.

Q. Mr. President, are you suggesting that Congress, if it wants to provide for long-term, low-interest loans for private and parochial schools, ought to have a separate bill?

THE PRESIDENT. I definitely believe that we should not tie the two together. I think that there are sufficient constitutional questions which the members of Congress will have to consider. I believe in view of the fact that this act is directly, in its title and in its purpose, directed to giving grants to public schools, that we should proceed with that bill.

Now, any other matter, I think—seems to me should be taken up as a separate issue if we want to then discuss loans. I have given my view of the constitutional problems involved in across the board loans. As the questioner indicated, there have been some kinds of loans to nonpublic schools which have been supported by the Congress and signed by the President and about which no constitutional problem has yet been raised, and the National Defense Education Act is the best example.

But across the board loans, as this group knows, this matter was not brought up in the last—President Eisenhower sent several messages to the Congress dealing with Federal aid to education. I believe there were one or two times when it was voted upon in the House. I do not recall that there was a great effort made at that time to provide across the board loans to an aid to education bill. The only time, in my knowledge, that it was brought up was about the end of the last session in August, by Senator Morse, and then just in the Senate. But it was not made a matter of great interest at that time, and I am concerned that it should not be made an issue now in such a way that we end up the year with, again, no aid to secondary schools.

Q. Mr. President, you said last week, as I recall it, that there was no room for debate about this matter.

THE PRESIDENT. That's right. There is no room for debate about grants. There is obviously room for debate about loans, because it has been debated. My view, however, is that the matter of loans, to the best of my knowledge and judgment—though this has not been tested by the courts, of course, in the sense that grants have been—but by my reading of the constitutional judgments in the Everson case, my judgment has been that across the board loans are also unconstitutional.

Q. Does that suggest that you would veto a bill that provided for across the board loans, Mr. President?

THE PRESIDENT. I think I made my view very clear. I think it is always a mistake before we even have legislation to talk about what I am going to do. But I think it is very clear about what my view is of grants

and loans across the board to nonpublic schools. Now, colleges are in a different category. Specific programs of grants, even to colleges which are nonpublic, have been supported by the Congress and signed by the President. Loans and even grants to secondary education under some circumstances might be held to be constitutional. But across the board to all nonpublic schools, in my opinion, does raise a serious constitutional question which after reading the cases and giving it a good deal of thought, in my opinion—at least to my judgment would be unconstitutional.

Now, the President has an obligation, and the Congress, to consider this matter very carefully. I am extremely sympathetic to those families who are paying their taxes for public education and also sustaining the rights—sustaining their children in nonpublic schools. They carry a heavy burden. But I have made my position very clear for many months and I have to make my position clear now, at least as long as I am here, on what I believe to be the constitutional problem. And I also point out that this matter was not made an issue in recent years until this time, except in the case of the amendment offered at the end of the last session by Senator Morse which was just offered in the Senate and was not offered in the House of Representatives, to the best of my knowledge.

[14.] Q. Mr. President, you have taken Executive action in the field of civil rights. Do you feel there is a need now for legislation in this area, and if so do you plan to offer any at this session?

THE PRESIDENT. When I believe that we can usefully move ahead in the field of legislation, I will recommend it to the Congress. I do believe that there are a good deal of things we can do now in administering laws previously passed by the Congress, particularly in the area of voting, and also by using the powers which the Constitution gives to the President through Executive orders. When I feel that there is a necessity for a congressional action, with a chance of getting that congressional action, then I will recommend it to the Congress.

[15.] Q. Mr. President, you and the Democratic Party are on record in opposition to the changing of Indian treaties without the consent of the Indians. The Army Engineers are about to build a huge conduit dam on the upper Allegheny River which will flood a third of a western New York Indian reservation in direct violation of a treaty that was signed by George Washington with the Seneca Indians. Have you any inclination at all to halt that project in favor of the so-called Morgan alternate project which would not violate the treaty?

THE PRESIDENT. My recollection is that this matter has been tested in the courts, has it not?

Q. Yes, it has. The Supreme Court has upheld it.

THE PRESIDENT. Well, I'm not—I have no plans to interfere with that action.[1]

[16.] Q. Mr. President, on the assumption that Mr. Thompson has by now caught up with Mr. Khrushchev, I wonder if you could tell us the contents of your message to the Soviet Premier and what thinking was behind this message at this time?

THE PRESIDENT. Well, I would think that it would be more properly a matter that would best be left to Mr. Thompson and Mr. Khrushchev. It is a letter from me and I think it would be discourteous and unwise to reveal such a letter without any indication that it has been received and some response given. As far as the purpose

of the letter, the purpose of the letter was to give, in general, some of my views on the questions which are at issue now around the world, and also to indicate my strong confidence in Ambassador Thompson to speak for me and for our country at this time in any discussions he might have with Mr. Khrushchev.

[17.] Q. Mr. President, back on the subject of education. There has been rising speculation that the openly developing fights over the issues of segregation and religion as they are involved in the legislation may well stop them before they start. How do you assess the possible damage of those issues as pertaining to your legislation on building schools and loans to teachers' salaries, and do you intend to carry the issue more strongly to the public directly?

THE PRESIDENT. This matter, of course, these two, and of course other groups who are opposed to any action in this area, have all contributed to the fact that this matter has been debated for a number of years, passed the Senate at least two or three times, but we have never gotten legislation, so that, obviously, it is going to be a difficult matter to secure the passage of legislation this year. But I do not think that there is anything more important than to have good schools, well-trained competent teachers. When the Massachusetts Bay Colony was established, one of the first acts that were taken was the establishment of a public school. The Northwest Ordinance, the land grant colleges, all indicate the long traditional interest which our Government and people have had in strengthening our education. We are as good in the long-range sense as our schools are and, therefore, I am extremely interested in seeing the country this year place additional emphasis on education—additional support to education.

In one area alone, as I mentioned some

---

[1] The President later reviewed the problems involved in the Kinzua Dam project. See his letter to the President of the Seneca Nation, Item 320.

time ago, those people who were first thrown out of work are at the bottom of the educational ladder. The papers are filled with ads requiring scientists, technicians, engineers, on the west coast and all across the country. People who can't find jobs are people who were not well educated at the beginning. I think everyone should have a maximum chance to develop his talents. I do not believe that that can be done effectively without passage of this bill this year. I am therefore hopeful that however strong the feelings may run—and I am very conscious of them—on all these other matters, that the program of scholarships for college students, of loans to colleges, because we are going to have double the number of children in 1970 that we do today applying for admission to our colleges, and grants to public schools—I am hopeful that that will be passed this year.

[18.] Q. Mr. President, in order to avoid another snafu, as the one that involved the 45 pieces of machinery that were originally scheduled to go to Russia, what instructions have you issued to the Departments of Defense and Commerce regarding export license for American manufacturers to Iron Curtain countries?

THE PRESIDENT. Well, I am hopeful the procedures can be improved. There was a difference of opinion between the Commerce Department and the Defense Department, and there was a difference in emphasis in the Defense Department's position over a period of time, though they did take the view from the beginning that it was not in the national interest.

It has been, I think, quite unfortunate the way it was handled. I am hopeful that in the future we can set up better procedures so that a better judgment can be made.

But I must say that it is extremely diffi-

cult for those who are making the judgment. Caution tells them to send nothing and therefore—on the other hand, we are anxious to permit some degree of trade which does not weaken our security or increase our danger to be carried on with countries. After all, countries in Western Europe are carrying on very intensive trade with the Soviet Union, and some countries with Communist China. So what they cannot get here they get there. So we wish to bring some reason to it. It is a difficult matter. But after this experience, which has been not always satisfactory, Governor Hodges has given this matter close attention with Secretary McNamara to see if we can improve our procedures. This was not the best example of Government in action.

[19.] Q. Mr. President, I have a two-part question on the RB-47 fliers. First, could you tell us now where and when and under what circumstances the fliers were shot down? And, second, are such flights being continued?

THE PRESIDENT. I think the fliers discussed the matter quite fully with the press last Friday.

[20.] Q. Mr. President, in connection with trade, some domestic groups, including labor unions, are turning to economic boycotts as their answer to import competition. I wonder if you could state your position on this approach to international trade difficulties.

THE PRESIDENT. Well, I am hopeful that those boycotts will not spread. It is not the—Congress has set up certain procedures by which those industries that are hard hit can protect themselves—the peril-point, escape clause, the procedures before the Tariff Commission. Congress is going to have an opportunity to consider the whole matter of reciprocal trade, I believe, next year. I recognize that these workers are hard hit. But they are not always able to make a judgment of what the total national need is and also the need—international need. I have seen some cases where boycotts have been suggested where the percentage of imports is fractional compared to the domestic market, 1 or 2 percent. Well, now, if we are not going to follow the procedures set down by the American people acting through their Congress, but instead every group is going to take it into their own hands, then, of course, we are going to have action taken against us in those countries. We sent abroad a good deal of important goods that employ hundreds of thousands and millions of people. And, as I have suggested before, the balance of trade has been in our favor by four or five billion dollars.

Two can play this game; and, therefore, unions in other countries can refuse to unload our goods. Pretty soon we will find ourselves with an exacerbated situation among friendly nations and also which will be harmful to the gold flow.

[21.] Q. Mr. President, could you give us your thinking on the problem of Communist China in view of the latest word from the Warsaw negotiations, that is, that the Chinese will not consider the admittance of the 32 American correspondents and they will not consider the release of the prisoners? I believe there was some hope that if we could exchange correspondents with the Chinese that it might be a step towards more harmonious relations.

THE PRESIDENT. Well, that was our hope and if they are unwilling to do that, of course that hope has been dimmed. They have been, as we know, extremely belligerent towards us, and they have been unfailing in

their attacks upon the United States. But, of course, I think part of that has been because they recognize that the United States is committed to the defense of—committed to maintaining its connections with other countries, committed to its own defense and the defense of freedom.

But they have been extremely harsh in their attacks upon us and I would like to see a lessening of that tension. That is our hope from the beginning. But we are not prepared to surrender in order to get a relaxation of tension.

[22.] Q. Mr. President, during the debate on the Meriwether nomination, Senator Morse raised some questions about whether this nominee had a police record and he said you had sent up to see him one of your legislative aides who had read certain notes from the FBI files. I wonder if you can enlighten us as to what are the facts so far as this——

THE PRESIDENT. I informed the conference and the Senate that I looked over Mr. Meriwether's FBI record before I sent it to the Senate. Mr. Meriwether is now a member of the Export-Import Bank, confirmed by the Senate, by a rather large figure, and I am confident that he will do a good job.

[23.] Q. Mr. President, in regard to the Peace Corps, to do away with the objection of some countries which may not welcome American corpsmen, the suggestion has been made that you propose a United Nations corps of which the American corpsmen would be a part. Do you have a comment on that?

THE PRESIDENT. Well, I think that that could usefully be considered. It is not intended that any member of the American Peace Corps would go to any country where he was not warmly welcome. In addition, as I have said from the beginning, we are putting our major emphasis, at the beginning, on teachers and I am hopeful that those countries which are interested in understanding our country and our traditions will welcome these young men and women. But they will be sent only where they are welcome and I would certainly feel that we should consider with the United Nations how we can bring our programs into harmony.

Reporter: Thank you, Mr. President.

NOTE: President Kennedy's sixth news conference was held in the State Department Auditorium at 3 o'clock on Wednesday afternoon, March 8, 1961.

72   Remarks of Welcome to President Nkrumah of Ghana at the Washington National Airport. *March 8, 1961*

I WANT TO TAKE this opportunity to welcome again to the United States, which he knows so well, the first citizen of Ghana, President Nkrumah.

Yesterday, in his speech at the United Nations, he quoted a common hero, I believe, Thomas Jefferson. Thomas Jefferson also once said, "The disease of liberty is catching."

It has been the object of our guest's life to make sure that that disease of liberty spreads around the globe. He has fought for it in his own country. He fights for it in Africa—he fights for it in the world.

We share the same basic aspiration for the United States as he works for his own country. We share the same basic aspiration for Africa that he wishes for—and for the world.

It is therefore a great honor and a great pleasure for me, as President of the United States, to welcome a distinguished citizen of a friendly country, and also a distinguished citizen of the world, the President of Ghana, President Nkrumah.

NOTE: The President greeted President Nkrumah at 4 p.m. at the Washington National Airport. President Nkrumah responded as follows:

Mr. President:

As this is our first meeting since your assumption of responsibility as President of the United States, may I be permitted to offer you my personal and hearty congratulations and those of the Government and people of Ghana. We all look forward to a period of continued cooperation and understanding between our two countries.

I hope that our meeting today will strengthen our relations and contribute towards the establishment of lasting peace and stability in Africa and in the world.

These are troublous times. They are also times of opportunity for action. Let us, therefore, emphasize and consolidate the very many things that unite us, and from that starting point tackle the problems which confront us in our time. I am sure, Mr. President, that success will crown our efforts.

I thank you and the people of the United States for the warm welcome that has been accorded to me.

73   Remarks on Introducing President Nkrumah to the Press. *March 8, 1961*

I KNOW that all of you gentlemen are anxious to speak to the President, and I will release him immediately.

I do want to say that the communique is going to go out very shortly, as soon as we can get some copies of it, which will be available to you all and which covers the main points which we wanted to mention.

I just want to say, speaking personally, that we have had a most fruitful talk. I think it's most helpful. We have a very high regard for the President. As I said at the airport, it is a great source of pride to us as Americans that he studied here in the United States, that he knows our country well, that he spent over 10 years of his life here. I think he knows the traditions of our country, and I am sure he knows its aspirations—and I am sure that he knows that we wish for him and for his country the best of good fortune and speedy and swift progress towards a constantly improving standard of living, that we mean to do our part in cooperation with his efforts.

In addition, I emphasized to him that we are anxious for peace in Africa so that the people of Africa can develop their resources. We are anxious also to see the people of Africa living in freedom. This has been a long tradition of this country, stretching back to our earliest beginnings. We ourselves are a revolutionary people, and we want to see for other people what we have been able to gain for ourselves.

So we have been honored to have the President here, and we regard him as a strong figure in his own country, and as a strong figure in Africa; and therefore this exchange of views has been most helpful to this administration. And I am sure he realizes how welcome he is, and it was a great pleasure for me to have an opportunity to introduce him to Mrs. Kennedy and to my daughter. He has young children who are younger than mine, so that shows how vital Africa is.

NOTE: The President spoke at 5:45 p.m. in the Fish Room at the White House. President Nkrumah responded as follows:

May I add this, that meeting you has been a wonderful experience for me, and I really mean that. Thank you.

74 Joint Statement Following Discussions With the President of Ghana. *March* 8, 1961

PRESIDENT John F. Kennedy and President Kwame Nkrumah exchanged views this afternoon regarding the general situation in Africa as well as various aspects of current relations between the United States and the Republic of Ghana.

The two Presidents reviewed economic and political problems of common interest and reaffirmed their desire to work together toward increasing the existing fund of respect and good will shared by the Governments and peoples of Ghana and the United States. The importance of mutual confidence and understanding was emphasized by the two Presidents.

The two Presidents recognized the central importance of the role of the United Nations in Africa and the importance of the African countries and their leaders working together for the peaceful development of that great continent. In particular, they are convinced of the need for unflagging and genuine support, both moral and material, of United Nations efforts to bring peace to the people of the Congo and to promote peace and stability in the continent as a whole. They also agreed that the nations of Africa should be supported in the development of their natural resources so as to benefit the continent as a whole and provide a promising future for their peoples in full and unfettered freedom.

Both expressed gratification at this opportunity occasioned by Dr. Nkrumah's visit to the United Nations, for this informal meeting.

75 Statement by the President Concerning the Interdepartmental Committee for the Voluntary Payroll Savings Plan. *March 9, 1961*

THIS COMMITTEE has carried out its mission in a most commendable way since its inception in April 1942 and has firmly established a widespread thrift program of outstanding merit and popularity in the Federal Government.

It is important to the welfare of our Country that this support of the national debt management function be maintained and fostered to the greatest extent possible. Federal employees, officers and military personnel should be encouraged to show leadership in the purchase of Savings Bonds through the Payroll Savings Plan and thus by example continue to give impetus to the movement throughout the business and industrial structure of the Nation.

NOTE: This statement is part of a White House release announcing the appointment of Mrs. Elizabeth Rudel Smith, Treasurer of the United States, as Chairman of the Committee. The release added that the statement was derived from a letter to the heads of Federal departments and agencies.

76 Special Message to the Congress on Housing and Community Development. *March 9, 1961*

To the Congress of the United States:

Our communities are what we make them. We as a nation have before us the opportunity—and the responsibility—to remold our cities, to improve our patterns of community development, and to provide for the housing needs of all segments of our population. Meeting these goals will contribute to the nation's economic recovery and its long-term economic growth.

In 1949 the Congress, with great vision, announced our national housing policy of "a decent home and a suitable living environment for every American family." We have progressed since that time; but we must still redeem this pledge to the 14 million American families who currently live in substandard or deteriorating homes, and protect the other 39 million American families from the encroachment of blight and slums.

An equal challenge is the tremendous urban growth that lies ahead. Within 15 years our population will rise to 235 million and by the year 2000 to 300 million people. Most of this increase will occur in and around urban areas. We must begin now to lay the foundations for livable, efficient and attractive communities of the future.

Land adjoining urban centers has been engulfed by urban development at the astounding rate of about one million acres a year. But the result has been haphazard and inefficient suburban expansion, and continued setbacks in the central cities' desperate struggle against blight and decay. Their social and economic base has been eroded by the movement of middle and upper income families to the suburbs, by the attendant loss of retail sales, and by the preference of many industrial firms for outlying locations.

Our policy for housing and community development must be directed toward the accomplishment of three basic national objectives:

First, to renew our cities and assure sound

growth of our rapidly expanding metropolitan areas.

Second, to provide decent housing for all of our people.

Third, to encourage a prosperous and efficient construction industry as an essential component of general economic prosperity and growth.

The housing industry is one of the largest employers of labor. Residential construction alone accounts for 30 percent of total private investment in this country. The housing market absorbs more private credit than any other single sector of the economy. Other important industries and services, including those concerned with building materials, appliances, furniture, and home improvement, depend largely and directly on new housing construction.

For some time the nation's homebuilding industry has been depressed and housing output has lagged. Nonfarm private housing starts dropped sharply in 1960 to a volume 18 percent below 1959 and to the lowest level in the past decade. Largely as a result of this decline, one out of every six construction workers was unemployed by the end of 1960, 25 percent more than a year earlier—the highest rate of unemployment in any major American industry. Related industries were also seriously hurt. For example, lumber demand dropped by more than two billion board-feet and roofing demand by nearly three hundred million square feet.

Formerly, this kind of depression in the homebuilding and related industries could be more easily met. But the housing market today is basically different from that of only a few years ago. There is no longer an enormous backlog of economic demand which can be released simply by providing ample credit. Credit devices must now be used selectively to encourage private industry to build and finance more housing in the lower price ranges to meet the unfilled demands of moderate income families. It is these families who offer the largest and the most immediate potential housing market, along with those of still lower incomes who must rely on low-rent public housing.

There are 8 million families today with incomes of less than $2500, 7 million more with incomes between $2500 and $4000. Among the 10 million individuals who live alone, nearly 50 percent have incomes of less than $1500. One-third of the 6 million nonwhite households live in substandard housing. And our older citizens, a group growing at the rate of 500,000 each year, have special housing needs. And in addition to all of this, before this decade is out, a rate of construction of at least 2 million new homes a year will be required merely to meet the needs of new family units being formed.

To build this many houses efficiently, at stable or declining costs of production, requires a steady and progressive rise in the rate of home building, beginning now. To the extent possible, we want to do this by helping private market processes work more effectively—particularly in a period of slump. Thus this Administration has already taken measures:

—to stimulate the flow of mortgage money

—to reduce FHA-insured mortgage interest rates

—to reduce the sale of mortgages from the Federal National Mortgage Association portfolio, in order to help assure that the increasing supply of mortgage money goes directly to new consumer borrowers at lower rates of interest

—to accelerate urban renewal and low-rent public housing projects

—to release additional funds for college housing, farm housing, and housing for the elderly; and

—to remove restrictions and reduce interest rates on community facilities loans.

The combined force of these steps, supported as they have been by the Federal Reserve System's action to encourage a reduction in long-term interest rates, will accelerate housing activity. But much more is needed.

I. HOUSING FOR MODERATE INCOME FAMILIES

Among the basic economic innovations of the Thirties was the development of the Federal Housing Administration mortgage insurance system, which was a precedent for the Veterans loan guaranty program at the end of World War II. These two programs made possible a partnership between industry and government which broadened the housing market and helped make home ownership possible for more than three-fifths of our families.

These programs have aided many families of moderate incomes, but chiefly those with incomes from $5000 to $6000 and more. Many additional families could afford decent housing if it were made available under programs more carefully tailored to their resources.

(a) To the extent possible, we want to meet these needs through private enterprise under the established FHA system of mortgage financing. I am, accordingly, recommending that the present limited FHA insurance of no-downpayment, 40-year mortgages—now available only to families displaced by governmental action—be broadened on a temporary and experimental basis to include any family, and be otherwise amended to make these mortgages more

attractive to private investors. This broader program will offer an opportunity and a challenge to both builders and lenders to meet the needs of middle income families through private enterprise without Government subsidy.

(b) Many families with somewhat lower incomes, however, cannot afford housing at current construction costs and at market interest rates even under the more liberal FHA program. For these families I recommend enactment of a new program of long-term, low interest rate loans for rental and cooperative housing, financed from the special assistance fund of the Federal National Mortgage Association, and processed and supervised by the FHA. These loans would be made to cooperatives, nonprofit associations, limited dividend corporations, and local housing authorities. Occupancy of these projects would be strictly limited to those individuals and families whose incomes exclude them from standard housing in the private market.

II. HELPING LOW INCOME FAMILIES

The housing needs of many families will not be met by the programs outlined above. Government housing subsidies are required for families with very low incomes. Public housing is the only housing they can afford; yet public housing is too often unavailable. Unless we increase the supply of low-rent housing, our communities cannot rid themselves of slums, provide adequate community facilities, and rehouse low income families displaced by clearance operations. I recommend, therefore, that the present limitation upon the use of the remaining authorization in the Housing Act of 1949 for public housing be removed—thus authorizing construction of about 100,000 additional low-rent units.

In addition, both statutory and administrative changes in this program in the light of experience are long overdue. Our program should have maximum flexibility so that it can best be adapted by local communities to their particular requirements. Local housing authorities should have greater freedom in establishing priorities for admission of tenants and to determine design. In addition we need a program of demonstration grants to afford communities greater opportunity to experiment in the field of housing for low income families.

III. HOUSING FOR THE ELDERLY

Sixteen million of our people are 65 years or older. By 1970 this figure will increase to more than 20 million. Most of these elderly people have very limited financial means. More than half of the families headed by a person over 65 have annual incomes below $3000 and four-fifths of all people of this age living alone must subsist on less than $2000 a year.

The housing problem of the elderly is attributable only in part to low incomes—many have physical infirmities limiting their activities; many need access to special community services. Special equipment and apartment designs can make their home life safer and more comfortable.

This country cannot neglect the growing housing needs of the elderly, or rely on the overly limited steps previously taken. Two types of affirmative action are required:

First, I recommend to the Congress legislation increasing the present direct loan authorization for housing for the elderly from $50,000,000 to $100,000,000.

Second, I shall direct the Administrator of the Housing and Home Finance Agency to earmark 50,000 units of low-rent public housing specifically for low-income elderly

persons and families. Because of the special equipment and facilities required in housing for the elderly, and because of the smaller number of rooms per unit, I shall propose to the Congress amendments to the public housing law increasing by $500 per room the cost limitation on housing for the elderly. Furthermore, because many of the elderly have such exceedingly low incomes, payment of an additional subsidy of up to $10 per month for each housing unit occupied by them should be authorized.

IV. REVITALIZING OUR URBAN AND METROPOLITAN AREAS

Seventy-three out of 258 central cities lost population in the decade of the Fifties when our urban population as a whole grew rapidly. Other powerful trends have been eroding the central cities over a much longer period.

1. Improving Our Cities. If the cities are to recapture their economic health, they must offer better opportunities for those commercial, industrial and residential developments for which their central position is a distinct advantage. They must strengthen their cultural and recreational facilities and thus attract more middle- and upper-income residents. They should make space available for suitable light industries, especially those which need close-in locations. And they must improve their transportation systems, particularly rapid transit services.

Urban renewal programs to date have been too narrow to cope effectively with the basic problems facing older cities. We must do more than concern ourselves with bad housing—we must reshape our cities into effective nerve centers for expanding metropolitan areas. Our urban renewal efforts must be substantially reoriented from slum clearance and slum prevention into positive programs for economic and social regeneration.

(a) The Congress has wisely extended the use of urban renewal funds to certain nonresidential renewal projects which the locality deems necessary for sound community development. I recommend that local communities be given even wider discretion in determining renewal areas.

(b) This program, if it is to be truly effective, must help local communities go beyond the project-by-project approach. I have instructed the Administrator of the Housing and Home Finance Agency to work with the local officials in every area to foster this broader approach, in which individual projects will be developed within the framework of an over-all community program, a program which clearly identifies the city's long-term renewal needs and opportunities and the changing shape of the city.

(c) To develop an effective long-range program to arrest and remove blight and revitalize our cities, local communities must be able to count on adequate and continuing support through a long-term Federal commitment. I therefore recommend to the Congress that new authorizations totaling $2,500,000,000 over a 4-year period be made available for urban renewal programs.

(d) We must continue to clear and redevelop slum areas only where suitable housing is elsewhere available for occupants of these areas who can be humanely and fairly relocated. Similarly, small businessmen in clearance areas deserve more consideration. I recommend legislation liberalizing Federal allowances for relocation payments to displaced businessmen, whenever the localities are also prepared to share in larger compensations.

(e) FHA is a major operating agency in the Federal Government's total urban

renewal efforts. It is essential that it perform this function efficiently. I have already issued instructions directing FHA to expedite the processing of applications for insurance on properties in urban renewal areas. This involves both a streamlining of internal procedures and the reassignment of personnel.

2. *Residential Rehabilitation and Conservation.* As we broaden the scope of renewal programs looking toward newer and brighter urban areas, we must move with new vigor to conserve and rehabilitate existing residential districts. Our investment in nonfarm residential real estate is estimated at about 500 billion dollars—the largest single component in our national wealth. These assets must be used responsibly, conserved, and supplemented, and not neglected or wasted in our emphasis on the new.

(a) I recommend to the Congress enactment of new authority for FHA to insure a wide variety of loans for home improvement purposes. Such insurance is needed to help finance the improvement of the nation's housing, especially the backlog of over $300 million in home improvements planned, but not yet started, in existing urban renewal areas.

(b) We must also recognize that some types of rehabilitation, while socially desirable, cannot succeed on a voluntary, self-financing basis. For rehabilitated housing to remain available to moderate income families, public absorption of a portion of the cost may be necessary. I recommend to the Congress legislation permitting the resale of existing housing in urban renewal areas at a realistic price for rehabilitation.

3. *Metropolitan Development.* The city and its suburbs are interdependent parts of a single community, bound together by the web of transportation and other public facilities and by common economic interests.

Bold programs in individual jurisdictions are no longer enough. Increasingly, community development must be a cooperative venture toward the common goals of the metropolitan region as a whole.

(a) This requires the establishment of an effective and comprehensive planning process in each metropolitan area embracing all major activities, both public and private, which shape the community. Such a process must be democratic—for only when the citizens of a community have participated in selecting the goals which will shape their environment can they be expected to support the actions necessary to accomplish these goals. I recommend therefore the enactment of an extended and improved program of Federal aid to urban and metropolitan planning. The draft measure which I shall submit would provide an increase of the Federal share of planning grants to two-thirds and an increase of the authorization from $20 million to $100 million.

(b) As I stated in my Message to the Congress on Highways, I have urged an increase in joint planning between the Administrator of the Housing and Home Finance Agency and the Secretary of Commerce, including the participation of State and local housing and highway officials, as well as private experts.

V. LAND RESERVES

Land is the most precious resource of the metropolitan area. The present patterns of haphazard suburban development are contributing to a tragic waste in the use of a vital resource now being consumed at an alarming rate.

Open space must be reserved to provide parks and recreation, conserve water and other natural resources, prevent building in undesirable locations, prevent erosion and floods, and avoid the wasteful extension of public services. Open land is also needed to provide reserves for future residential development, to protect against undue speculation, and to make it possible for State and regional bodies to control the rate and character of community development.

(a) I am directing the Administrator of the Housing and Home Finance Agency and the Secretary of the Interior to develop a long-range program and policy for dealing with open space and orderly development of urban land.

(b) Nevertheless, this problem is so urgent that we must make a start now. I therefore recommend legislation providing: (1) for $100 million to initiate a program of 20% grants to help public bodies finance the reservation of land—by acquisition or other means—as permanent urban open space in the form of parks and other facilities; and (2) for urban renewal loans to help local agencies finance the acquisition of open space for future public or private development. In both programs a prerequisite for Federal aid will be an effective and comprehensive plan for metropolitan or regional development.

VI. COMMUNITY FACILITIES AND URBAN TRANSPORTATION

(a) The availability and location of community facilities profoundly affect the patterns of urban growth and the cost of serving rapidly growing populations.

Private sources can and should continue to supply most of the credit needed as they have done in the past. However, Federal assistance is required to help communities which do not have ready access to the private capital market to schedule and obtain community facilities construction and to anticipate future needs. To accomplish these objectives, I shall submit legislation to the Congress authorizing an additional $50 million for public facilities loans.

(b) Nothing is more dramatically apparent than the inadequacy of transportation in our larger urban areas. The solution cannot be found only in the construction of additional urban highways—vital as that job is. Other means for mass transportation which use less space and equipment must be improved and expanded. Perhaps even more important, planning for transportation and land use must go hand in hand as two inseparable aspects of the same process.

But to solve the problems of urban transportation will test our ingenuity and put a heavy drain on our resources. While the responsibility for working out these solutions rests primarily with local government and private enterprise, the Federal government must provide leadership and technical assistance.

Accordingly, I have asked the Administrator of the Housing and Home Finance Agency and the Secretary of Commerce to undertake an immediate and extensive study of urban transportation problems and the proper role of the Federal government in their solution.

VII. RURAL HOUSING

Rural housing problems require special attention.

Almost a fifth of the occupied houses in the rural areas of America are so dilapidated that they must be replaced. Hundreds of thousands of other rural homes are far below the level of comfort and convenience considered adequate in our Nation. Both new houses and major repairs, remodeling, and modernization of existing houses are needed throughout our farm and small-town communities. For example, only one-third of

our farm homes have adequate plumbing. A principal factor contributing to this situation is the lack of adequate credit in rural sections.

(a) I therefore recommend that the unused balance of farm housing loan authority of the Secretary of Agriculture, due to expire June 30, 1961, be extended for an additional five years.

(b) In addition, I have directed the Secretary of Agriculture, in cooperation with the Administrators of the HHFA and the VA to develop procedures to assure adequate credit for farm and other housing in rural communities.

(c) Finally, because the existing requirement that every farm home improvement loan be supported by a property mortgage has too often resulted in unnecessary hardship, I recommend legislation permitting farm home improvement loans to be secured either by mortgages or by other acceptable forms of security.

VIII. VETERANS HOUSING

The high interest rates prevailing in the past few years have made it impossible for many veterans to use their right to obtain guaranteed 5¼% loans to purchase housing. At the same time, eligible applications for direct loans in rural areas have substantially exceeded the amount of funds available for such loans.

The basic solution to this problem is to bring down long-term mortgage lending rates—as we are already in process of doing—and thus make guaranteed loans at 5¼% more attractive to private lenders.

But existing Federal programs are also important; and in order to allow sufficient time for planning, I recommend that the Congress now extend the duration of both the loan guarantee and the direct loan programs (which expire, in most cases, in 1962) concentrating on those veterans who have served their country the longest and the most recently—and expand the direct loan authority above the present $150 million to the extent experience should demonstrate that guaranteed loans are still difficult for veterans to obtain.

IX. DEMONSTRATIONS, TRAINING AND RESEARCH

As we proceed in developing a comprehensive housing and community development program we must constantly widen our knowledge of the complex forces which shape our urban way of life. Since the beginning of the century the proportion of our people who live in urban and suburban areas has mounted rapidly. Yet we have lagged badly in mobilizing the intellectual resources needed to understand and improve this important sector of our civilization. The problems related to the development and renewal of our cities and their environs have received comparatively little attention in research and teaching.

To encourage the study of these pressing problems and to train a sufficient supply of skilled manpower will require a substantial commitment of resources. Universities, private research groups, professional and business organizations can all contribute. But the Federal Government must play a key role in support of these activities— through leadership and financial assistance.

(a) The Housing Act of 1948, as amended, and the Housing Act of 1956 both provide broad authority for Federal support of the market analyses and statistics needed by private industry, and for research into housing and urban problems. I shall ask the Congress to appropriate sufficient funds to carry out these programs.

(b) To find ways to improve the technology of homebuilding, and thus to make better homes available at lower cost, is one of the problems most in need of research and experimentation. Therefore, I recommend enactment of a special FHA insurance authorization to be used exclusively to help finance tests and demonstrations of new approaches to home design and construction which give promise of producing substantial savings in cost.

X. A NEW DEPARTMENT OF HOUSING AND URBAN AFFAIRS

Urban and suburban areas now contain the overwhelming majority of our population, and a preponderance of our industrial, commercial and educational resources. The programs outlined above, as well as existing housing and community development programs, deserve the best possible administrative efficiency, stature and role in the councils of the Federal Government. An awareness of these problems and programs should be constantly brought to the Cabinet table, and coordinated leadership provided for functions related to urban affairs but appropriately performed by a variety of Departments and agencies.

I therefore recommend—and shall shortly offer a suggested proposal for—the establishment in the Executive Branch of a new, Cabinet-rank Department of Housing and Urban Affairs.

CONCLUSION

A nation that is partly ill-housed is not as strong as a nation with adequate homes for every family. A nation with ugly, crime-infested cities and haphazard suburbs does not present the same image to the world as a nation characterized by bright and orderly urban development. To achieve our nation's housing goals, to meet our appropriate Federal responsibilities to aid private and local efforts—and at the same time helping to combat the present recession while furthering long-term growth—I commend this program to the Congress and urge its prompt consideration and enactment.

JOHN F. KENNEDY

77 Letter to the President of the Senate and to the Speaker of the House on the Proposed National Cultural Center. *March 9, 1961*

Dear Mr. ————:

Earlier this year President Eisenhower sent to the leadership of the House and the Senate a message urging the enactment of legislation to enlarge the site of the proposed National Cultural Center in Washington. Under the National Cultural Center Act, the site for the Center is to be provided by the federal government. As the President pointed out on January 18th, it is necessary that three parcels of land not now included within the description of the site be added in order to permit construction of the Center in accordance with the approved architectural plan.

I want to renew this recommendation. The National Cultural Center is the most significant cultural undertaking in the history of this city and has enormous importance to the cultural life of the nation as a whole. There is a real and promising opportunity to establish new horizons for the performing arts in this city. There have been many public-spirited citizens participating in the work and planning of the Cultural Center, and I believe that the federal government should take these small additional steps in order to provide a suitable setting and environment for the Center. Moreover, this is an enterprise which has earned the support of membership of both parties in the Congress.

I urge the early enactment of this legislation so that the plans for the National Cultural Center may proceed promptly. This can be an important step in recognizing the vital role of culture in the vigorous development of our country.

Sincerely,

JOHN F. KENNEDY

NOTE: This is the text of identical letters addressed to the Honorable Lyndon B. Johnson, President of the Senate, and to the Honorable Sam Rayburn, Speaker of the House of Representatives.

78 Address at a White House Reception for Members of Congress and for the Diplomatic Corps of the Latin American Republics. *March 13, 1961*

IT IS A GREAT PLEASURE for Mrs. Kennedy and for me, for the Vice President and Mrs. Johnson, and for the Members of Congress, to welcome the Ambassadorial Corps of our Hemisphere, our long time friends, to the White House today. One hundred and thirty-nine years ago this week the United States, stirred by the heroic struggle of its fellow Americans, urged the independence and recognition of the new Latin American Republics. It was then, at the dawn of freedom throughout this hemisphere, that Bolívar spoke of his desire to see the Americas fashioned into the greatest region in the world, "greatest," he said, "not so much by virtue of her area and her wealth, as by her freedom and her glory."

Never in the long history of our hemisphere has this dream been nearer to fulfillment, and never has it been in greater danger.

The genius of our scientists has given us the tools to bring abundance to our land, strength to our industry, and knowledge to our people. For the first time we have the capacity to strike off the remaining bonds of poverty and ignorance—to free our people for the spiritual and intellectual fulfillment which has always been the goal of our civilization.

Yet at this very moment of maximum opportunity, we confront the same forces which have imperiled America throughout its history—the alien forces which once again seek to impose the despotisms of the Old World on the people of the New.

I have asked you to come here today so that I might discuss these challenges and these dangers.

We meet together as firm and ancient friends, united by history and experience and by our determination to advance the values of American civilization. For this New World of ours is not a mere accident of geography. Our continents are bound together by a common history, the endless exploration of new frontiers. Our nations are the product of a common struggle, the revolt from colonial rule. And our people share a common heritage, the quest for the dignity and the freedom of man.

The revolutions which gave us birth ignited, in the words of Thomas Paine, "a spark never to be extinguished." And across vast, turbulent continents these American ideals still stir man's struggle for national independence and individual freedom. But as we welcome the spread of the American revolution to other lands, we must also remember that our own struggle—the revolution which began in Philadelphia in 1776, and in Caracas in 1811—is not yet finished. Our hemisphere's mission is not yet completed. For our unfulfilled task is to demonstrate to the entire world that man's unsatisfied aspiration for economic progress and social justice can best be achieved by free men working within a framework of democratic institutions. If we can do this in our own hemisphere, and for our own people, we may yet realize the prophecy of the great Mexican patriot, Benito Juarez, that "democracy is the destiny of future humanity."

As a citizen of the United States let me be the first to admit that we North Americans have not always grasped the significance of this common mission, just as it is also true that many in your own countries have not fully understood the urgency of the need to lift people from poverty and ignorance and despair. But we must turn from these mistakes—from the failures and the misunderstandings of the past to a future full of peril, but bright with hope.

Throughout Latin America, a continent rich in resources and in the spiritual and cultural achievements of its people, millions of men and women suffer the daily degradations of poverty and hunger. They lack decent shelter or protection from disease. Their children are deprived of the education or the jobs which are the gateway to a better life. And each day the problems grow more urgent. Population growth is outpacing economic growth—low living standards are further endangered—and discontent—the discontent of a people who know that abundance and the tools of progress are at last within their reach—that discontent is growing. In the words of José Figueres, "once dormant peoples are struggling upward toward the sun, toward a better life."

If we are to meet a problem so staggering in its dimensions, our approach must itself be equally bold—an approach consistent with the majestic concept of Operation Pan America. Therefore I have called on all people of the hemisphere to join in a new Alliance for Progress—*Alianza para Progreso*—a vast cooperative effort, unparalleled in magnitude and nobility of purpose, to satisfy the basic needs of the American people for homes, work and land, health and schools—*techo, trabajo y tierra, salud y escuela.*

First, I propose that the American Republics begin on a vast new Ten Year Plan for the Americas, a plan to transform the 1960's into a historic decade of democratic progress.

These 10 years will be the years of maximum progress-maximum effort, the years when the greatest obstacles must be overcome, the years when the need for assistance will be the greatest.

And if we are successful, if our effort is bold enough and determined enough, then the close of this decade will mark the beginning of a new era in the American experience. The living standards of every American family will be on the rise, basic education will be available to all, hunger will be a forgotten experience, the need for massive outside help will have passed, most nations will have entered a period of self-sustaining growth, and though there will be still much to do, every American Republic will be the master of its own revolution and its own hope and progress.

Let me stress that only the most determined efforts of the American nations themselves can bring success to this effort. They, and they alone, can mobilize their resources, enlist the energies of their people, and modify their social patterns so that all, and not just a privileged few, share in the fruits of growth. If this effort is made, then outside assistance will give vital impetus to progress; without it, no amount of help will advance the welfare of the people.

Thus if the countries of Latin America are ready to do their part, and I am sure they are, then I believe the United States, for its part, should help provide resources of a scope and magnitude sufficient to make this bold development plan a success—just as we helped to provide, against equal odds nearly, the resources adequate to help rebuild the economies of Western Europe. For only an effort of towering dimensions can ensure fulfillment of our plan for a decade of progress.

Secondly, I will shortly request a ministerial meeting of the Inter-American Economic and Social Council, a meeting at which we can begin the massive planning effort which will be at the heart of the Alliance for Progress.

For if our Alliance is to succeed, each Latin nation must formulate long-range plans for its own development, plans which establish targets and priorities, ensure monetary stability, establish the machinery for vital social change, stimulate private activity and initiative, and provide for a maximum national effort. These plans will be the foundation of our development effort, and the basis for the allocation of outside resources.

A greatly strengthened IA–ECOSOC, working with the Economic Commission for Latin America and the Inter-American Development Bank, can assemble the leading economists and experts of the hemisphere to help each country develop its own development plan—and provide a continuing review of economic progress in this hemisphere.

Third, I have this evening signed a request to the Congress for $500 million as a first step in fulfilling the Act of Bogotá. This is the first large-scale Inter-American effort, instituted by my predecessor President Eisenhower, to attack the social barriers which block economic progress. The money will be used to combat illiteracy, improve the productivity and use of their land, wipe out disease, attack archaic tax and land tenure structures, provide educational opportunities, and offer a broad range of projects designed to make the benefits of increasing abundance available to all. We will begin to commit these funds as soon as they are appropriated.

Fourth, we must support all economic integration which is a genuine step toward larger markets and greater competitive opportunity. The fragmentation of Latin American economies is a serious barrier to industrial growth. Projects such as the Central American common market and free trade areas in South America can help to remove these obstacles.

Fifth, the United States is ready to cooperate in serious, case-by-case examinations of commodity market problems. Frequent violent change in commodity prices seriously injure the economies of many Latin American countries, draining their resources and stultifying their growth. Together we must find practical methods of bringing an end to this pattern.

Sixth, we will immediately step up our Food for Peace emergency program, help establish food reserves in areas of recurrent drought, help provide school lunches for children, and offer feed grains for use in rural development. For hungry men and women cannot wait for economic discussions or diplomatic meetings—their need is urgent—and their hunger rests heavily on the conscience of their fellow men.

Seventh, all the people of the hemisphere must be allowed to share in the expanding wonders of science—wonders which have captured man's imagination, challenged the powers of his mind, and given him the tools for rapid progress. I invite Latin American scientists to work with us in new projects in fields such as medicine and agriculture, physics and astronomy, and desalinization, to help plan for regional research laboratories in these and other fields, and to strengthen cooperation between American universities and laboratories.

We also intend to expand our science teacher training programs to include Latin American instructors, to assist in establishing such programs in other American countries, and translate and make available revolutionary new teaching materials in physics, chemistry, biology, and mathematics, so that the young of all nations may contribute their skills to the advance of science.

Eighth, we must rapidly expand the training of those needed to man the economies of rapidly developing countries. This means expanded technical training programs, for which the Peace Corps, for example, will be available when needed. It also means assistance to Latin American universities, graduate schools, and research institutes.

We welcome proposals in Central America for intimate cooperation in higher education—cooperation which can achieve a regional effort of increased effectiveness and excellence. We are ready to help fill the gap in trained manpower, realizing that our ultimate goal must be a basic education for all who wish to learn.

Ninth, we reaffirm our pledge to come to the defense of any American nation whose independence is endangered. As its confidence in the collective security system of the OAS spreads, it will be possible to devote to constructive use a major share of those resources now spent on the instruments of war. Even now, as the government of Chile has said, the time has come to take the first steps toward sensible limitations of arms. And the new generation of military leaders has shown an increasing awareness that armies cannot only defend their countries—they can, as we have learned through our own Corps of Engineers, they can help to build them.

Tenth, we invite our friends in Latin America to contribute to the enrichment of life and culture in the United States. We need teachers of your literature and history and tradition, opportunities for our young people to study in your universities, access to your music, your art, and the thought of your great philosophers. For we know we have much to learn.

In this way you can help bring a fuller spiritual and intellectual life to the people of the United States—and contribute to understanding and mutual respect among the nations of the hemisphere.

With steps such as these, we propose to complete the revolution of the Americas, to build a hemisphere where all men can hope for a suitable standard of living, and all can live out their lives in dignity and in freedom.

To achieve this goal political freedom must accompany material progress. Our Alliance for Progress is an alliance of free govern-

ments, and it must work to eliminate tyranny from a hemisphere in which it has no rightful place. Therefore let us express our special friendship to the people of Cuba and the Dominican Republic—and the hope they will soon rejoin the society of free men, uniting with us in common effort.

This political freedom must be accompanied by social change. For unless necessary social reforms, including land and tax reform, are freely made—unless we broaden the opportunity for all of our people—unless the great mass of Americans share in increasing prosperity—then our alliance, our revolution, our dream, and our freedom will fail. But we call for social change by free men— change in the spirit of Washington and Jefferson, of Bolívar and San Martín and Martín—not change which seeks to impose on men tyrannies which we cast out a century and a half ago. Our motto is what it has always been—progress yes, tyranny no— *progreso sí, tiranía no!*

But our greatest challenge comes from within—the task of creating an American civilization where spiritual and cultural values are strengthened by an ever-broadening base of material advance—where, within the rich diversity of its own traditions, each nation is free to follow its own path towards progress.

The completion of our task will, of course, require the efforts of all governments of our hemisphere. But the efforts of governments alone will never be enough. In the end, the people must choose and the people must help themselves.

And so I say to the men and women of the Americas—to the *campesino* in the fields, to the *obrero* in the cities, to the *estudiante* in the schools—prepare your mind and heart for the task ahead—call forth your strength and let each devote his energies to the bet-

174

terment of all, so that your children and our children in this hemisphere can find an ever richer and a freer life.

Let us once again transform the American continent into a vast crucible of revolutionary ideas and efforts—a tribute to the power of the creative energies of free men and women—an example to all the world that liberty and progress walk hand in hand. Let us once again awaken our American revolution until it guides the struggle of

people everywhere—not with an imperialism of force or fear—but the rule of courage and freedom and hope for the future of man.

NOTE: The President spoke in the East Room at the White House. Immediately following his speech, the President's words were translated and broadcast in Spanish, Portuguese, and French, as well as in English, to the nations of the South by the Voice of America.

The text of the Act of Bogotá, adopted September 13, 1960, by a Special Committee to Study the Formulation of New Measures for Economic Cooperation, is published in the Department of State Bulletin (vol. 43, p. 537).

79   Letter to the President of the Senate and to the Speaker of the House on the Interstate Highway Program.   *March 14, 1961*

My dear Mr. —————:

I am transmitting herewith the draft of a bill which will make it possible to complete our interstate highway system by 1972. The program will be financed on a pay-as-you-go basis.

I am convinced that either stretching out or cutting back our highway program would be unwise. It would be particularly unfortunate today, when our economy needs the growth, our people need the safety, and our national defense needs the security that this program helps provide. Unless this legislation is enacted promptly, apportion-

ments to the States will have to be reduced substantially below desired levels.

This is a sound method for resolving the difficulties the program now faces and for meeting our responsibilities to the future.

I am also enclosing a letter from the Secretary of Commerce dealing with the measure.

  Sincerely,

   JOHN F. KENNEDY

NOTE: This is the text of identical letters addressed to the Honorable Lyndon B. Johnson, President of the Senate, and to the Honorable Sam Rayburn, Speaker of the House of Representatives.

80   Statement by the President Concerning the Conference on the Discontinuance of Nuclear Weapon Tests.   *March 14, 1961*

AMBASSADOR Arthur H. Dean leaves on Wednesday for Geneva to head the United States Delegation to the Conference on the Discontinuance of Nuclear Weapon Tests where on March 21 negotiations among the United States, the United Kingdom and the Union of Soviet Socialist Republics will be resumed.

Our Nation is indeed fortunate to have the services of Ambassador Dean at this decisive stage of the sessions. He has accumulated extensive experience in international negotiation of difficult and complex issues. I know that he will present the American point of view with the greatest clarity and skill.

Ambassador Dean and the United States Delegation will be engaged in an enterprise which could not only contribute to halting the proliferation of nuclear weapons but also have important implications for the future of disarmament and arms limitation negotiations and the future peace and security of the world.

The United States Government is determined to do all that is possible to conclude a safeguarded agreement on a sound and equitable basis.

The United States and British Delegations have labored for two and one-half years at the Conference to reach agreement with the USSR on a treaty under which nuclear

weapon tests would be prohibited and an adequate control system established. While much groundwork for a treaty has been laid, critical issues remain to be resolved.

In recent weeks, the United States has undertaken a thorough review of the technical and political problems still outstanding. As a result, the United States Delegation will return to the conference table with proposals which could constitute the basis for a treaty fair to all contracting parties. It is my hope that the proposals will be accepted and that the negotiators will be able to proceed with all appropriate speed toward the conclusion of the first international arms control agreement in the nuclear age.

81   Special Message to the Congress Requesting Appropriations for the Inter-American Fund for Social Progress and for Reconstruction in Chile.   *March 14, 1961*

To the Congress of the United States:

On September 8, 1960, at the request of the Administration, the Congress authorized the sum of 500 million dollars for the Inter-American Fund for Social Progress. On the basis of this authorization the United States, on September 12, 1960, subscribed to the Act of Bogotá along with 18 other American Republics.

In the same bill the Congress authorized 100 million dollars for the long-term reconstruction and rehabilitation of those areas of Southern Chile recently devastated by fire and earthquake.

I now request that Congress appropriate the full amount of 600 million dollars.

_____

The Act of Bogotá marks an historic turning point in the evolution of the West-

ern Hemisphere. For the first time the American nations have agreed to join in a massive cooperative effort to strengthen democratic institutions through a program of economic development and social progress.

Such a program is long overdue. Throughout Latin America millions of people are struggling to free themselves from the bonds of poverty and hunger and ignorance. To the North and East they see the abundance which modern science can bring. They know the tools of progress are within their reach. And they are determined to have a better life for themselves and their children.

The people of Latin America are the inheritors of a deep belief in political democracy and the freedom of man—a sincere faith that the best road to progress is freedom's road. But if the Act of Bogotá becomes just another empty declaration—if we are unwilling to commit our resources and energy to the task of social progress and economic development—then we face a grave and imminent danger that desperate peoples will turn to communism or other forms of tyranny as their only hope for change. Well-organized, skillful, and strongly financed forces are constantly urging them to take this course.

A few statistics will illustrate the depth of the problems of Latin America. This is the fastest growing area in the world. Its current population of 195,000,000 represents an increase of about 30 percent over the past ten years, and by the 1980's the continent will have to support more than 400,000,000 people. At the same time the average per capita annual product is only $280, less than one-ninth that of the United States—and in large areas, inhabited by millions of people, it is less than $70. Thus it is a difficult task merely to keep living standards from falling further as population grows.

Such poverty inevitably takes its toll in human life. The average American can expect to live 70 years, but life expectancy in Latin America is only 46, dropping to about 35 in some Central American countries. And while our rate of infant mortality is less than 30 per thousand, it is more than 110 per thousand in Latin America.

Perhaps the greatest stimulus to our own development was the establishment of universal basic education. But for most of the children of Latin America education is a remote and unattainable dream. Illiteracy extends to almost half the adults, reaching 90 percent in one country. And approximately 50 percent of school age children have no schools to attend.

In one major Latin American capital a third of the total population is living in filthy and unbearable slums. In another country 80 percent of the entire population is housed in makeshift shacks and barracks, lacking the privacy of separate rooms for families.

It was to meet these shocking and urgent conditions that the Act of Bogotá was signed. This Act, building on the concept of operation Pan America initiated by Brazil in 1958, introduced two important new elements to the effort to improve living standards in South America.

First, the nations of Latin America have recognized the need for an intensive program of self-help—mobilizing their domestic resources, and undertaking basic reforms in tax structure, in land ownership and use, and in education, health and housing.

Second, it launches a major Inter-American program for the social progress which is an indispensable condition to growth—a program for improved land use, education, health and housing. This program—supported by the special fund which I am asking Congress to appropriate—will be administered primarily through the Inter-American Bank, and guided by greatly strengthened regional institutions.

The 500 million dollar Inter-American Fund for Social Progress is only the first move toward carrying out the declarations of the Act of Bogotá; and the Act itself is only a single step in our program for the development of the hemisphere—a program I have termed the Alliance for Progress—*Alianza para Progreso.* In addition to the social fund, hemispheric development will require substantial outside resources for economic development, a major self-help effort by the Latin American nations themselves, Inter-American cooperation to deal with the problems of economic integration and commodity markets and other measures designed to speed economic growth and improve understanding among the American nations.

Social Progress and Economic Development.

The fund which I am requesting today will be devoted to social progress. Social progress is not a substitute for economic development. It is an effort to create a social framework within which all the people of a nation can share in the benefits of prosperity, and participate in the process of growth. Economic growth without social progress lets the great majority of the people remain in poverty, while a privileged few reap the benefits of rising abundance. In addition the process of growth largely depends on the existence of beneficial social conditions. Our own experience is witness to this. For much of our own great productivity and industrial development is based on our system of universal public education.

Thus the purpose of our special effort for social progress is to overcome the barriers of geographical and social isolation, illiteracy and lack of educational opportunities, archaic tax and land tenure structures, and other institutional obstacles to broad participation in economic growth.

Self-Help and Internal Reform.

It is clear that the Bogotá program cannot have any significant impact if its funds are used merely for the temporary relief of conditions of distress. Its effectiveness depends on the willingness of each recipient nation to improve its own institutions, make necessary modifications in its own social patterns, and mobilize its own domestic resources for a program of development.

Even at the start such measures will be a condition of assistance from the social fund. Priorities will depend not merely on need,

but on the demonstrated readiness of each government to make the institutional improvements which promise lasting social progress. The criteria for administration of the funds by the Inter-American Development Bank and the ICA will explicitly reflect these principles.

For example: the uneven distribution of land is one of the gravest social problems in many Latin American countries. In some nations 2% of the farms account for ¾ of the total farm area. And in one Central American country, 40% of the privately owned acreage is held in ⅕ of 1% of the number of farms. It is clear that when land ownership is so heavily concentrated, efforts to increase agricultural productivity will only benefit a very small percentage of the population. Thus if funds for improving land usage are to be used effectively they should go only to those nations in which the benefits will accrue to the great mass of rural workers.

Examples of Potential Areas of Progress.

When each nation demonstrates its willingness to abide by these general principles, then outside resources will be focused on projects which have the greatest multiplying effect in mobilizing domestic resources, contributing to institutional reform, and in reducing the major obstacles to a development in which all can share.

In housing, for example, much can be done for middle income groups through improved credit mechanisms. But, since the great majority of family incomes are only $10 to $50 a month, until income levels as a whole are increased, the most promising means of improving mass housing is through aided self-help projects—projects in which the low-income worker is provided with low-cost materials, land, and some technical guidance; and then builds the house with his own labor, repaying the costs of materials with a long-term mortgage.

Education is another field where self-help efforts can effectively broaden educational opportunities—and a variety of techniques, from self-help school construction where the entire village contributes labor, to the use of local people as part-time teachers can be used.

In the field of land use there is no sharp demarcation between economic and social development. Improved land use and rural living conditions were rightly given top place in the Act of Bogotá. Most of the Latin American peoples live and work on the land. Yet agricultural output and productivity have lagged far behind both industrial development and urgent needs for consumption and export.

As a result poverty, illiteracy, hopelessness and a sense of injustice—the conditions which breed political and social unrest—are almost universal in the Latin American countryside.

Thus, there is an immediate need for higher and more diversified agricultural production, better distribution of wealth and income, and wider sharing in the process of development. This can be partly accomplished through establishing supervised rural credit facilities, helping to finance resettlement in new lands, constructing access roads to new settlement sites, conducting agricultural surveys, and research, and introducing agricultural extension services.

Administration of the Inter-American Fund for Social Progress.

It is fundamental to the success of this cooperative effort that the Latin American nations themselves play an important role in the administration of the social fund.

Therefore, the major share of the funds will be administered by the Inter-American Development Bank (IDB)—an organization to which nearly all the American Republics belong.

Of the total $500 million, $394 million will be assigned to the IDB, to be administered under a special Trust Agreement with the United States. The IDB will apply most of these funds on a loan basis with flexible terms, including low interest rates or repayment in local currency. The IDB's major fields of activity will be land settlement and improved land use, housing, water supply and sanitation, and technical assistance related to the mobilizing of domestic financial resources.

In order to promote progress in activities which generally are not self-liquidating and therefore not appropriate for loan financing, the sum of $100 million will be administered by the International Cooperation Administration (ICA). These funds will be applied mainly on a grant basis for education and training, public health projects, and the strengthening of general governmental services in fields related to economic and social development. Funds administered by the ICA will also be available to assist projects for social progress in dependent territories which are becoming independent, but are not yet members of the IDB.

Up to $6 million more is to be used to help strengthen the Organization of American States (OAS). To reinforce the movement toward adequate self-help and institutional improvement, the Inter-American Economic and Social Council (IA–ECOSOC) of the OAS is strengthening its secretariat and its staff. It is also working out cooperative arrangements with the United Nations Economic Commission for Latin America (ECLA) and the IDB.

These three regional agencies will work together in making region-wide studies, and in sponsoring conferences directed toward bringing about tax reform, improved land use, educational modernization, and sound national development programming.

Many of the nations of the Americas have already responded to the action taken at Bogotá by directing attention to their most pressing social problems. In the brief period since the meeting at Bogotá, United States Embassies and Operations Missions, after consultation with Latin American governments, have already reported proposals for social development projects calling for external assistance totalling about $1,225 million. A preliminary selection from this list shows some $800 million worth of projects which are worthy of early detailed examination by the Bank and the ICA.

In the Bank's area of activity these selected projects total $611 million; including $309 million for land use and improved rural living conditions, $136 million in the field of housing, and $146 million for water supply and sanitation.

Selected proposals in fields to be administered by the ICA total $187 million; of which $136 million are for education and training, $36 million for public health, and $15 million for public administration and other assigned responsibilities.

So that each recipient nation will live up to the principles of self-help and domestic reform outlined above, funds will not be allocated until the operating agency receives assurances that the country being aided will take those measures necessary to ensure that the particular project brings the maximum social progress. For the same reason we can make no firm forecast of the rate at which the funds will be committed. Thus,

if they are to be used most efficiently and economically, they must be made available for obligation without limitation as to time.

Urgency of the Need.

Under ideal conditions projects for social progress would be undertaken only after the preparation of integrated country plans for economic and social development. Many nations, however, do not possess even the most basic information on their own resources or land ownership. Revolutionary new social institutions and patterns cannot be designed overnight. Yet, at the same time, Latin America is seething with discontent and unrest. We must act to relieve large scale distress immediately if free institutions are to be given a chance to work out long-term solutions. Both the Bank and the ICA are ready to begin operation immediately. But they must have the funds in hand if they are to develop detailed projects, and stimulate vital measures of self-help and institutional improvement.

The Bogotá conference created a new sense of resolve—a new determination to deal with the causes of the social unrest which afflicts much of the hemisphere. If this momentum is lost, through failure of the United States to act promptly and fully, we may not have another chance.

The Role of Private Organizations.

Inter-American cooperation for economic and social progress is not limited to the actions of government. Private foundations and universities have played a pioneering role in identifying critical deficiencies and pointing the way toward constructive remedies. We hope they will redouble their efforts in the years to come.

United States business concerns have also

played a significant part in Latin American economic development. They can play an even greater role in the future. Their work is especially important in manufacturing goods and providing services for Latin American markets. Technical expertness and management skills in these fields can be effectively transferred to local enterprises by private investment in a great variety of forms—ranging from licensing through joint ventures to ownership.

Private enterprise's most important future role will be to assist in the development of healthy and responsible private enterprise within the Latin American nations. The initiation, in recent years, of strikingly successful new private investment houses, mutual investment funds, savings and loan associations, and other financial institutions are an example of what can be done. Stimulating the growth of local suppliers of components for complex consumer durable goods is another example of the way in which domestic business can be strengthened.

A major forward thrust in Latin American development will create heavy new demands for technical personnel and specialized knowledge—demands which private organizations can help to fill. And, of course, the continued inflow of private capital will con-

tinue to serve as an important stimulus to development.

Chilean Reconstruction and Rehabilitation.

Last May more than 5000 Chileans were killed when fire and earthquake devastated the Southern part of that Republic. Several of the American Republics, including the United States, provided emergency supplies of food, medicine and clothing to the victims of this disaster. Our country provided almost 35 million dollars in emergency grants and loans.

However, these emergency efforts did not meet the desperate need to rebuild the economy of an area which had suffered almost 400 million dollars worth of damage. In recognition of this need, Congress authorized 100 million dollars for long-term reconstruction and rehabilitation. Since then the people of Chile have been patiently rebuilding their shattered homes and communications facilities. But reconstruction is severely hampered by lack of funds. Therefore, I am asking the Congress to appropriate the 100 million dollars so that the task of rebuilding the economy of southern Chile can proceed without delay.

JOHN F. KENNEDY

---

82   Letter to the President of the Senate and to the Speaker of the House on Interest Rates on Time Deposits of Foreign Governments.   *March* 15, 1961

[Released March 15, 1961. Dated March 14, 1961]

Dear Mr. ————:

I am transmitting herewith a draft of legislation which would amend existing law by permitting banks in this country to pay different rates of interest on time deposits held

here by foreign governments than are paid to domestic depositors. Also transmitted is a memorandum from the Secretary of the Treasury describing the draft bill and its impact in detail.

The draft bill implements a recommendation contained in my message to the Congress dated February 6, 1961, relating to the balance of payments problem. It also complements and supports my directive to the Secretary of the Treasury to issue securities at special rates for exclusive holding by foreign central banks or governments.

If commercial banks are permitted to offer foreign governments higher rates of interest in competition with those existing abroad, those governments will be encouraged to maintain dollar accounts in this country rather than require the United States to convert their dollar accounts to gold for withdrawal. In this connection, it is only these foreign governments and their agencies which can directly purchase gold from the reserve stocks of the United States. However, as stated in my message of February 6, the proposed amendment is but one of a series of actions to be taken to alleviate the gold drain. Indeed, the factors which influence any central bank or government to prefer dollar accounts to gold are many and complex. Interest rates are only one. If we pursue policies of stability and growth inspiring world confidence, foreign govern-ments should respond to higher interest rates on time deposits thereby aiding our gold outflow problem.

This inducement to foreign central bank deposits will have practically no impact on domestic market rates of interest. Moreover, any such impact would be confined to the short-term sector of the market and thus be consistent with national policy objectives.

In the interest of orderly procedure, the draft bill also permits similar treatment of deposits of international financial institutions of which the United States is a member.

I will appreciate it if you will lay the draft legislation before the House of Representatives (the Senate). A similar draft has been transmitted to the President of the Senate (the Speaker of the House of Representatives). I urge that the Congress act promptly and favorably on the proposal.

Sincerely,

JOHN F. KENNEDY

NOTE: This is the text of identical letters addressed to the Honorable Lyndon B. Johnson, President of the Senate, and to the Honorable Sam Rayburn, Speaker of the House of Representatives.

Secretary Dillon's memorandum, dated March 8, and the draft bill were released with the President's letter.

83 The President's News Conference of *March 15, 1961*

THE PRESIDENT. I have several brief announcements to make.

[1.] First, the Secretaries of the military departments have been instructed by the Deputy Secretary of Defense to take steps to provide a greater percentage of defense contracts for small business. Specifically, the military departments have been asked to set a goal increasing individually in fiscal year 1962 small business participation by 10 percent over the year for fiscal 1960.

Contracts for small business in fiscal year 1960 amounted to $3,440 million, or 16 percent. We are going to try to increase that by at least 10 percent.

In addition, we are going to provide an increase for small business participation in research and development contracts. During that year this category of contracting amounted to only $180 million, or 3.4 percent of the total. In addition, we are asking the Department of Defense to examine how additional contracts can be steered into distressed areas. At the present time we are not doing as much of that as I hope we can in the future.

[2.] Secondly, I am sending to Congress a request for funds to resume detailed planning of our largest remaining damsite in the Upper Columbia—the Libby Dam in Montana. It will be the first step in the development of the Columbia River Basin in coordination with Canada on an international basis. Yesterday the Foreign Relations Committee reported out unanimously the treaty that will make this dam possible. The Libby Dam will provide the power that we desperately need in the Northwest United States. It will help control the floods that are devastating northern Idaho. And it will prevent the projected power shortage for that area.

The beginning of this project will give impetus to a new period of cooperation with Canada.

[3.] Next I want to announce that the Export-Import Bank is authorizing $25 million credit in favor of the Government of Israel, to purchase agricultural machinery in the United States, to help consolidate Israel's agricultural settlements, and electrical power equipment and construction items for the expansion of Israeli seaports.

This decision, I think, will help speed the development of Israel's economy.

[4.] And then lastly, I want to announce that we will hold a President's Conference on Heart Disease and Cancer, which will be held at the White House beginning April 22. The Department of HEW will then invite a number of distinguished medical leaders throughout the country to participate in this program.

Thank you.

[5.] Q. Mr. President, would you tell us, please, if you have any plans to appear personally at the United Nations General Assembly currently in session and, if so, when you might go up?

THE PRESIDENT. I have no plans to and I do not expect to appear at the Assembly.

[6.] Q. Could you give us your views, sir, about the possibility of reaching some accord with the Soviet Union on general disarmament as well as nuclear test bans, and would you be willing to meet with Mr. Khrushchev face to face if you felt this was necessary to reach a truly genuine agreement?

THE PRESIDENT. Well, as you know, this matter is now being discussed, at least the procedural matters leading up to what we hope will be progress in the area of general disarmament. It is now being discussed at the United Nations, and Ambassador Stevenson has been discussing with the State Department the American position.

We—now that Mr. Dean has left to resume the discussions in Geneva, Mr. McCloy is working full time on developing an American position on disarmament. We have indicated before that we may not have completed our analysis until this summer, and we have suggested that we will be prepared to resume either the Ten-Nation Conference or some other similar structure, conference structure, in, we first suggested, September, and now we have suggested August at the latest. So we are going to concentrate our attention on disarmament now. We hope progress can be made, and we will—I will consider what usefully could be done to advance progress.

[7.] Q. Mr. President, in addition to the $700-odd million in highway money that you have instructed the Commerce Department to make available to the States ahead of time, Governor Rockefeller has asked whether it would be possible for the States to get an advance on the money for highways for fiscal 1962. Have you any ideas on the subject?

THE PRESIDENT. Yes. I received a letter from Governor Rockefeller and we are considering what action can be taken. We have to—the Congress has taken a very clear position on pay as you go, and we have to consider what funds can be made available between now and next July, and we have to consider what action the Congress is going to take on our request for additional funds in order to keep the program going.

So that all this is now being considered and an answer will be given to Governor Rockefeller after we have made a judgment as to what funds will be available, which depends in part upon what our response will be in the Congress.

[8.] Q. Mr. President, you have stressed the constitutional issues in the school-aid fight. Regardless of the constitutional question, do you think it is wise public policy to make Federal loans to parochial and private schools below the college level?

THE PRESIDENT. Well, I have stated my views in the previous White House conferences, and what I hope would be the procedure followed by the Congress, which continues to be my view. We will—when we see proposals, and what form they take, because as the previous press conference developed, loans take many different forms, and I indicated some fall within one category and some within another, and this administration will be glad to cooperate with the Congress in considering the matter.

But I am hopeful that, as I have said before, that the view taken by the administration of the desirability of passing the public school matter first—I am hopeful that that will be the decision which the Congress will adopt. But this is a matter that they are considering and we will consider with them.

[9.] Q. Mr. President, Cardinal Spellman in a statement this week indicated that tax exemptions for the parents who pay tuition for their children to go to private schools might be one possible approach. Do you think, sir, that this would be a constitutional way of perhaps compromising the issue?

THE PRESIDENT. I think that all this matter should be examined carefully by the Congress. The Senator from Oregon, Mr. Morse, has asked the Secretary of HEW to send up a brief on all the various kinds of assistance which are given to nonpublic schools and colleges, which the Secretary is preparing to do. The committees then of the House and Senate, and the House of Representatives, can consider what kind of program they wish to put forward and at that time we can consider what the constitutional problems might be. But it is very difficult as new proposals are made for me or for anyone else to be giving constitutional opinions on each of them as they come up, without seeing the definite language. That obviously is not my function.

I would be glad to have the departments of Government participate in considering these matters with the Congress. But my view on procedures which I hope the Congress will follow are well known. I am hopeful we can get the program which we sent to the Hill out of the way. Then the Congress will have to consider what it wants to do in this other area. And the administration will be delighted to cooperate. But I could not possibly, unless I saw exactly what kind of language, give even a private opinion as to its constitutionality.

[10.] Q. Mr. President, are you able at this time to tell us something of Ambassador Thompson's report on his meeting with Premier Khrushchev?

THE PRESIDENT. No, I have no statement on it at the present time.

[11.] Q. Mr. President, Prince Souvanna Phouma, a representative of the Laotian rebels, said after a visit to the rebel area, that Moscow had provided 20 times as many weapons to the pro-Communist side as we have provided to the Royal Laotian Government. Can you tell us whether we are considering a step-up in such shipments as part of a new look at this?

THE PRESIDENT. Well, we have been watching Laos with the closest attention. As I have frequently said, and as the Secretary has said, it is our hope that from all of these negotiations will come a genuinely independent and neutral Laos, which is the master of its own fate. The purpose of these discussions among the various people who participate in them at Pnom Penh is to make this possible. However, recent attacks by rebel forces indicate that a small minority backed by personnel and supplies from outside is seeking to prevent the establishment of a neutral and independent country. We are determined to support the government and the people of Laos in resisting this attempt.

[12.] Q. Mr. President, labor unions want a shorter workweek to cope with the automation and unemployment. Your Secretary of Labor is against that. Are you for it and if so, would you prefer a shorter workday or a 4-day week? I don't mean yourself, personally, but the——

THE PRESIDENT. I prefer it for myself— [*laughter*]—but I would say that I am opposed to a shorter workweek. I am hopeful that we can have employment high at 5 days a week and 40 hours, which is traditional in this country, and which is necessary if we are going to continue economic growth, and maintain our commitments at home and abroad.

So, I would be opposed to any arbitrary reduction of the workweek. And I am unhappy when I see the workweek reduced artificially, in the sense that the pressures of a declining economy reduce it so that we get averages of 38.5 hours a week instead of the 40 hours a week. In any case, to answer your question, I would be opposed to reducing the workweek.

[13.] Q. Mr. President, your Latin American statement the other day was quite sweeping in calling for political and social reforms in those countries. Have you had any indications before or since of how much acceptance there is in Latin American countries for this kind of reform?

THE PRESIDENT. I think that it would be premature to make a judgment as to what the response will be in Latin America. I am hopeful it will be favorable; I am hopeful that we can begin discussions throughout the hemisphere which will lead to the kind of internal and external planning which will provide for a steady rate of economic growth throughout the hemisphere, which would be a cooperative effort. So that as of today I couldn't tell you what the response will be. I am hopeful it will be favorable, and I am hopeful that it will result in a joint effort of the kind that we saw in Western Europe in the late forties.

[14.] Q. Mr. President, recent public opinion polls and other reports indicate a high degree of public acceptance of your acts since you have become President, and of your program, at the same time that certain basics of the New Frontier legislative program are in considerable trouble in Congress. How do you go about translating public approval into congressional support?

THE PRESIDENT. Well, that is a matter, of course, on which every Member of Congress must reach his judgment. I think that the people are interested in high minimum wage, they are interested in improving our schools, they are interested in medical care for the aged, they are interested, I believe, in fiscal responsibility and the development of the highway program. Now, the problem, of course, is that there are—and they are interested in an agricultural program which provides some more adequate return for the farmer.

Now, I recognize that there are important and powerful and well-organized interest groups in this country which oppose all of these programs, and that they are extremely active, and that they have been successful in developing mail campaigns of one kind or another which tend to give an impression that there is widespread opposition to increasing, for example, the minimum wage.

Now Mr. Gallup's poll the other day showed that over 75 percent of the people were in favor of increasing the minimum wage. I think that increase in the minimum wage is highly desirable. I don't think that anyone should be expected to work for 80 and 85 cents an hour in some of these jobs. We have seen them particularly in retail stores, in a business which makes over $1 million a year.

I think the more orderly way to finance medical care for the aged is through the social security system. I am hopeful that when these matters are brought to the floor of the House and Senate that a majority of the Members will support them. I think that a majority of the people support them.

I know, however, that we face very vigorous opponents who are well organized, and who bring a good deal of pressure to bear on this administration and on the Congress. But we are going to continue to work for these programs, and I am very hopeful that before the year is out they will have passed.

The members of the committees of the House and Senate, I think, have done very well. And I am hopeful that an opportunity will be given to each Congressman to vote on these basic programs this year, and then the people can make a judgment as to what—how their interests are being represented. But I am confident that we are going to get a favorable response.

[15.] Q. Mr. President, what do you think of the Air Force and other branches of Government organizing these side-bar corporations and using taxpayers' money to circumvent the Civil Service and pay large salaries to get scientists and others? Isn't this sort of incongruous with the call for volunteers for your Peace Corps?

THE PRESIDENT. I think a subcommittee of the Congress has been looking into this matter. One of the problems, of course, is that valuable technicians are required to make a substantial economic sacrifice when they come with the Government. Therefore, the services, faced with this problem of where these men who are essential can secure much greater pay outside the Government than inside, have had to resort to the devices to which you refer. And we are looking at the matter, but I would not want to give an opinion today which would deny the services of these valuable scientists. On the other hand, we want to make sure that the way the matter is being conducted is in the public interest. So we will have to say, Mrs. McClendon, that it requires a further examination because it is not an easy matter to solve.

I don't know anyone who has come to work with the Government that I am familiar with that has not taken a—has not made a financial sacrifice in doing so. But most of them have been willing to meet that sacrifice. And we are going to examine the particular problem that you have suggested.

[16.] Q. Mr. President, your election in November was widely hailed as among other things a victory over religious prejudice. Do you think, as some speculation has already indicated in print, that the seemingly inflexible stand on the part of some spokesmen for the Catholic hierarchy on the school legislation may provoke more religious prejudice?

THE PRESIDENT. I am hopeful that it will not. I stated that it is a fact that in recent years when education bills have been sent to the Congress, we have not had this public major encounter. I don't know why that was, but now we do have it.

But everyone is entitled to express their views. The Catholic, Protestant, and Jewish clergy are entitled to take their views. I think it is quite appropriate that they should not change their views merely because of the religion of the occupant of the White House. I think that would be unfortunate if they— I think they ought to state what they think. They ought to express their views, they are entitled to do that. Then I will express mine, and Congress will express its.

I am very hopeful that though there may be a difference of opinion on this matter of Federal aid to education, I am hopeful that when the smoke is cleared there will continue to be harmony among the various religious groups in the country. And I am going to do everything that I can to make sure that that harmony exists because it reaches far beyond the question of education and goes in a very difficult time of the life of our country to an important ingredient of our national strength. So that I am confident that the people who are involved outside the Government, and Members of Congress and the administration, will attempt to conduct the discussion on this sensitive issue in such a way as to maintain the strength of the country and not to divide it.

[17.] Q. Mr. President, there has been some speculation that in order to finance some of your aggressive programs you may possibly seek a national sales tax or even possibly a penny a bottle tax on soft drinks. Could you comment on that, sir?

THE PRESIDENT. No, I have no such plan.

[18.] Q. Mr. President, there has been a controversy in recent days between the Chairman of the Federal Reserve Board and the Chairman of your Council of Economic Advisers as to what constitutes a reasonable expectable level of unemployment. What is your view on this matter?

THE PRESIDENT. Well, there has been—I am not so sure that the controversy is as significant as perhaps it has been reported in the paper. Mr. Martin has made the point that a good deal of structural unemployment exists and I think we have to say that in coal, steel, and perhaps some in aviation, it does exist, structural unemployment, and will continue to be a problem even if you had a substantial economic recovery. It would be far less if you had a substantial economic recovery. I do not see that there is a basic clash between these two views. But I think that they are both important and both ought to be considered. In other words, I do not think that regardless of whether the unemployment we now have is structural or not, and some of it is structural and some of it is not, I do not believe we should accept the present rate of unemployment as a percentage that we should live with. In other words, we have to reduce that percentage. I hope that we can reduce it down to 4 percent, but we are going to have to reduce it. But I do agree with Mr. Martin that even as we attempt to overcome unemployment in this country we are faced with a very serious and important structural unemployment which results from technological change, which the Canadians have also, and which even in good times would cause us serious concern.

In other words, even in eastern Kentucky, West Virginia, southern Illinois, and Pennsylvania, and even in 1959 and in 1957, you still had serious pockets of unemployment which were concentrated, even though the overall national figure was rather limited. It is my understanding that the Joint Committee on the Economic Report may call back Mr. Martin and Mr. Heller to discuss this further. I think that would be useful. It is a very important national problem, but I don't think from my conversations with both of them that there is a serious disagreement between them.

[19.] Q. Mr. President, in connection with the farm bill now in conference in Congress, the principal fight seems to be over the section which would allow the Secretary of Agriculture to sell grain into the market to hold the market price down. Do you feel that this enforcement feature is an absolute requirement in connection with the bill?

THE PRESIDENT. Well, I am hopeful that the conference will reach a decision which gives the Secretary powers in this area, if not the specific language of title III, at least language which will protect, provide protection for the bill. If we don't—if the Secretary lacks power—this bill isn't going to be successful, and a good many people from the urban areas who voted for the program with title III in it, in the House of Representatives, have a right, it seems to me, to expect that the Secretary will be given sufficient powers to protect the program from noncompliers who, if they are—who may use the program, if title III is out, for speculative and exploitive purposes. So that I consider it most important that title III

remain in, or otherwise some alternate language which will give the Secretary substantial powers provided in title III should be provided by the conference. Otherwise, we are not going to have any relief.

I am sorry to see the important agricultural leaders opposing giving us the protection which is required. You cannot have the Federal Government supporting agriculture in important ways unless there is some control over production and if there is some limitation, some provision for cross-compliance. Otherwise, the program will continue to cost a lot of money, the farmers' income will continue to drop, and we will have a gradual deterioration of agriculture in this country. The program we suggested and sent to the Hill in my opinion was one that was well balanced, and I am hopeful that a well-balanced program will come out of the considerations of the House and the Senate.

[20.] Q. Mr. President, this has to do with the labor-management conference which is scheduled for March 21. The past history of such conferences has shown a high percentage of failures, except at times of national crisis. Do you feel the present state of urgency is great enough to anticipate some success, and how do you plan to go about communicating that sense of urgency?

THE PRESIDENT. Well, I think it is. One reason alone I think makes it extremely important, and that is the problem of our being able to be competitive abroad. There are some indications that last year's favorable balance of trade which protected to some degree our gold supply—that we may not have as successful a year abroad. And I would think both manufacturers and labor unions, and certainly the public, would want to see American industry remain competitive. If we are not able to be competitive with a very strong and thriving industrial economy in Western Europe, we are going to find ourselves in serious trouble. There are also serious domestic matters, automation, technological change, unemployment, the wage-price spiral. I am extremely concerned about all these matters. I am sure they are. They live with them. And I am hopeful that we can encourage a public interest philosophy among all the groups which will provide progress. We have not been successful in the past, but I don't—these are the only things we can do. We lack any other powers.

Q. Sir, may I ask whether you plan to have the first meeting of the labor-management conference at the White House?

THE PRESIDENT. Yes. Yes.

[21.] Q. Mr. President, have you sent Ambassador Dean back to Geneva with authority to lower our demand for inspection sites within the Soviet Union, to bring it closer to the Soviet figure?

THE PRESIDENT. Mr. Dean goes back to Geneva with the hope, the administration's hope, that it will be possible for the United States, the British, and the Russians to come to an agreement on nuclear—for a nuclear test ban, which would provide adequate security to all the countries involved.

[22.] Q. Mr. President, is it a fair inference from your answer to Mr. Knebel's earlier question that the constitutional issue aside for the moment, you do not have a personal opinion as to whether it would be wise public policy to expend Federal funds on elementary and secondary nonpublic schools?

THE PRESIDENT. Well, I have—my previous discussions have rested on the constitutional questions.

Q. And you do not wish to speak on the other question?

THE PRESIDENT. Well, I would have to see what kind of loans they were, Mr. Roberts.

As I said before, in 1958 I did vote the loans for education, science, and technology. I voted for that program. I voted against, as a Senator, across the board loans.

So that I have looked over recently the number of programs which the Federal Government has in these areas, impacted areas, aid to particular kinds of colleges— we sent up a program providing for actual grants to medical schools for private colleges, which could be sectarian. So that there is a whole spectrum of programs, some of which raise constitutional questions and some of which do not.

So it is difficult to give an across the board answer. Across the board loans, I have indicated the constitutional question which it raises. There may be other programs which do not raise a constitutional question, which may be socially desirable, and there may be other programs which do not raise a constitutional question which may be socially undesirable.

All I could say is that because of the complexity of the issue it would be better to consider this as a separate matter, and when we have an actual bill before us, this administration could give its views on both the constitutional and the socially desirable elements of the program.

[23.] Q. Mr. President, a study was made recently by the Michigan Law School that recommended that the regulatory responsibility for atomic industry be under an agency other than that which is responsible for its development. The study indicates there is a dangerous paradox in allowing both regulation and development responsibilities to remain within the Atomic Energy Commission. What are your views on this? This has come up during your time in Congress, too, this question of separating health and regulation from——

THE PRESIDENT. Health and regulation?

Q. ——from development of the industry itself.

THE PRESIDENT. Well, there has been some separation of the health with the Public Health having responsibilities in this area, and I think that members of the Atomic Energy Commission agree that there should be some external check on their research and development programs, and I think that there is a fair balance today. It was a matter which was discussed when I was at the Atomic Energy Commission.

[24.] Q. Mr. President, before your inaugural, you expressed the hope that you would be able to use former President Eisenhower in some capacity in your administration. Are you still of that opinion, sir, and do you have any plans in that regard?

THE PRESIDENT. I have no plans at the present time. I have not been——I have not discussed the matter with the President, and if we do have an area where he could be helpful and where he felt he could be helpful, then I would discuss it with him. At the present time I think he is still continuing his vacation, to which he is very much entitled.

[25.] Q. Mr. President, Adrian, Mich., is deeply concerned over what disposition the Government will make of the surplus

Air Force metal extrusion plant there. Twice, when GSA has received bids, a firm which reputedly would dismantle the plant has been high bidder while the firm which ultimately might employ as many as 2,500 has been second highest. Appeals for retention of the plant for the local industry have been directed to you. Would you comment on what you have done or plan to do?

THE PRESIDENT. Well, I have talked to Mr. Moore about it. I have expressed my hope that an arrangement could be worked out to transfer the plant so that employment can be permitted. One of the problems, of course, is that it would require the transfer of the plant at a price which—at least what is now being examined is whether the transfer of the plant could be made at a price which would be justified. But I quite agree that if it is possible to use this plant for employment, it should be done. I am hopeful, and I am glad that you reminded me of the matter. I am hopeful that we could perhaps get a decision out of Mr. Moore's agency this week, and I will press for that.

Reporter: Thank you, Mr. President.

NOTE: President Kennedy's seventh news conference was held in the State Department Auditorium at 10 o'clock on Wednesday morning, March 15, 1961.

84   Remarks on the Occasion of the Celebration of the Centennial of Italian Unification.   *March 16, 1961*

Congressman Anfuso, Your Excellency, the Vice President, Mr. Speaker, Ambassador Dr. Martino, Mr. Secretary, Senator Pastore, distinguished Members of Congress, Ambassadors, and ladies and gentlemen:

Many of us who are here today are not Italian by blood or by birth, but I think that we all have a more than passing interest in this anniversary. All of us, in a large

sense, are beneficiaries of the Italian experience.

It is an extraordinary fact in history that so much of what we are and so much of what we believe had its origin in this rather small spear of land stretching into the Mediterranean. All in a great sense that we fight to preserve today had its origins in Italy, and earlier than that in Greece. So that it is an honor as President of the United States to participate in this most important occasion in the life of a friendly country, the Republic of Italy.

In addition, it is one of the strange facts of history, that this country of ours, which is important to Western civilization, was opened up first by a daring feat of navigation of an Italian, Christopher Columbus. And yet this country was nearly a century old when modern Italy began.

So we have the old and the new bound together and inextricably linked—Italy and the United States, past, present, and we believe future.

The Risorgimento which gave birth to modern Italy, like the American Revolution which led to the birth of our country, was the re-awakening of the most deeply-held ideals of Western civilization: the desire for freedom, for protection of the rights of the individual.

As the Doctor said, the state exists for the protection of those rights, and those rights do not come to us because of the generosity of the state. This concept which originated in Greece and in Italy I think has been a most important factor in the development of our own country here in the United States.

And it is a source of satisfaction to us that those who built modern Italy received part of their inspiration from our experience here in the United States—as we had earlier received part of our inspiration from an older Italy. For although modern Italy is only a century old, the culture and the history of the Italian peninsula stretches back over two millenia. From the banks of the Tiber there rose Western civilization as we know it, a civilization whose traditions and spiritual values give great significance to Western life as we find it in Western Europe and in the Atlantic community.

And to this historic role of Italian civilization has been added the strengthening in the life of this country of millions of Italians who came here to build their homes and who have been valued citizens—and many of their most distinguished sons sit on this platform today.

These ancient ties between the people of Italy and the people of the United States have never been stronger than they are today, and have never been in greater peril. The story of postwar Italy is a story of determination and of courage in the face of a huge and difficult task. The Italian people have rebuilt a war-torn economy and nation, and played a vital part in developing the economic integration of Western Europe.

Surely, the most inspiring experience of the postwar era: Italy has advanced the welfare of her own people, bringing them hope for a better life, and she has played a significant role in the defense of the West.

As we come to this great anniversary in 1961, we realize that once again new and powerful forces have arisen which challenge the concepts upon which Italy and the United States have been founded. If we are to meet this new challenge, we—Italy and the United States—must demonstrate to our own people and to a watching world, as we sit on a most conspicuous stage, that men acting in the tradition of Massini and Cavour and Garibaldi and Lincoln and Washington can best bring man a richer and fuller life.

This is the task of the new Risorgimento, a new re-awakening of man's ancient aspirations for freedom and for progress, until the torch lit in ancient Torino one century ago guides the struggle of men everywhere—in Italy, in the United States, in the world around us.

NOTE: The President spoke at 11:13 a.m. in the Department of State Auditorium. In his opening words he referred to Victor L. Anfuso, U.S. Representative from New York, who presided over the celebration; His Excellency Manlio Brosio, Italian Ambassador to the United States; Vice President Lyndon B. Johnson; the Honorable Sam Rayburn, Speaker of the House of Representatives; Ambassador Gaetano Martino, head of the Italian delegation to the United Nations Assembly and former Italian Foreign Minister; Secretary of State Dean

Rusk; and John O. Pastore, U.S. Senator from Rhode Island.

A White House release dated March 15 announced that the Centennial Celebration would be held under the joint sponsorship of the Italian Embassy and the American Honorary Committee, consisting of Members of Congress and Governors of Italian descent, under the chairmanship of Congressman Anfuso, with Senator Pastore as honorary chairman.

85   Special Message to the Congress on Agriculture. *March 16, 1961*

To the Congress of the United States:

In recent times, it has become customary to speak of American agriculture in terms of distress and failure, as a burden on the taxpayers and a depressant on the economy. But this is only one part of the picture. As the provider of our food and fiber, American agriculture is a highly successful and highly efficient industry. In no other country, and at no other time in the history of our own farm economy, have so many people been so well provided with such abundance and variety at such low real cost.

Nor is this bounty confined to our own people. We are today the world's largest exporter of food and fiber. Seventy percent of these exports are sales for dollars, one of the principal bulwarks of our export trade. The other thirty percent is made available under special programs to promote economic development abroad and to relieve hunger and suffering—efforts that are fundamental to our world leadership and security.

In short, our farmers deserve praise, not condemnation; and their efficiency should be a cause for gratitude, not something for which they are penalized. For their very efficiency and productivity lies at the heart of the distress in American agriculture which—while it represents only a part of the picture—constitutes that part to which our efforts must be devoted. The steady

and continuing decline in income has been most serious for the seven million people engaged in farming operations, and substandard conditions on the farms—which are so important to our economy—lead directly to substandard conditions in all segments of the national economy. Farming remains our largest industry—it employs 12 times as many people as work in steel and 9 times as many as in the automobile industry. It employs, in fact, more people than steel, automobiles, public utilities and the transportation industry combined. The farmer is a consumer as well as a producer, and other economic groups are affected by the continued drop in farm purchasing power. Some $40 billion is spent each year for production goods and services needed on our farms and for the consumer goods used by farm families. Six million people are employed in the manufacture and distribution of the supplies that farmers use. Each year farm families spend from $2.5 to $3.0 billion for new automobiles, trucks, tractors and other farm machinery; and $3.5 billion for fuel, lubricants and maintenance of motor vehicles and machinery. It is deeply in the interest of all Americans that our agriculture be not only progressive but prosperous.

Yet as our farm families enter the 1960's, their incomes are lower relative to the rest of our population than at any time since the

1930's. Although there has been a continuous rise in consumer prices during the past ten years, farm income has steadily declined. Abundant production has filled our bins and warehouses, but one out of ten American households have diets so inadequate that they fall below two-thirds of the standard nutrition requirements.

These paradoxes are of concern to all of us—the farmer, the taxpayer and the consumer. They affect the vitality of our nation, the strength of our most basic industry, agriculture, and the economic health of every community in the land.

Much of the current problem results from four factors:

First. The inability of millions of separate producers to control either output or price of their products. Acting individually the farmer can neither plan his production to meet modern requirements, and shift away from commodities for which there is limited demand, nor bargain effectively for a fair return.

Second. A technological revolution in agricultural production, which is still under way, that has resulted in generally increased yield from a reduced input of acreage and manpower—so that today each farmer produces the food and fiber necessary for 25 people, while at the turn of the century each farmer produced the food and fiber for only 7 people.

Third. A faulty system of distribution, which allows one-half of the people of the free world to suffer from malnutrition at the very same time our surpluses have reached a point where the availability of adequate storage facilities has become a real problem.

Fourth. The steady and continued increase in farm costs. The average farm requires an investment of $36,000. The farmer's interest costs have increased over 300

percent in the past decade. His equipment costs have increased seventy-five percent.

The solution lies not so much in severe restrictions upon our talent to produce as upon proper channeling of our abundance into more effective and expanded uses. American agricultural abundance can be forged into both a significant instrument of foreign policy and a weapon against domestic hardship and hunger. It is no less our purpose to insure that the farm family that produced this wealth will have a parity in income and equality in opportunity with urban families—for the family farm should be protected and preserved as a basic American institution.

Our intention is to accomplish these goals while eventually reducing the cost of our programs to the taxpayer. This can be accomplished in part because it is cheaper to use our agricultural products than to store them. Present storage costs total over $500 million a year or $1.4 million every day.

But it must also be our purpose to see that farm products return a fair income because they are fairly priced. No farm program should exploit the consumer. But neither can it subsidize the consumer at the cost of subnormal incomes to the farmer. We cannot tolerate substandard conditions on the farm any more than we can in industry. A fair return is a necessity for labor, capital and management in industry. It is equally necessary for those who produce our food and fiber.

It must be our purpose to provide an agricultural program that will eventually eliminate the vast farm surpluses that overhang the market and overburden the economy; that will permit effective economies of administration; that will recognize the right of the consumer to fair prices; and that will permit the farmer to receive a fair return for his labor. This will be neither simple nor easy. It will require the cooperation and effort of the farmer, government, and the urban dweller. But the alternative is not alone a substandard rural economy—it is a weakened nation.

I. A WIDER RANGE OF TOOLS TO BOOST FARM INCOME

This Administration's studies to date on how to meet our responsibilities in agriculture have led us to the following conclusions:

—There is no single farm problem, and no single solution. Each commodity requires a somewhat different approach.

—Swift and frequent changes in weather, acreage, yield, and international market conditions require federal programs alert and sensitive to change.

—The Secretary of Agriculture is now equipped with broad responsibilities for the maintenance of farm income. In order to fully and effectively meet these responsibilities he has had authority to set and adjust the level of support prices, set the level and terms of loans, prescribe acreage allotments, specify conservation payments, establish marketing agreements and orders, and take other steps to adjust supplies and protect the prices and incomes of farmers. But these powers have not been fully employed in recent years; and neither are they sufficiently flexible for all contingencies.

I am deeply concerned—and I believe the Congress shares that concern, along with most of our consumers, taxpayers and the farmers themselves—that our farm program is drifting into a chaotic state, piling up surpluses, penalizing efficiency, rewarding inertia and noncompliance, and constantly being torn and weakened by disputes and conflicting pressures. This is not a situation that can be ended by any one sweeping act of magic. It will require diligent study,

hard work, imaginative initiative, and sound, constructive leadership. But I believe that the decline in farm income and the drift in farm policy can both be gradually reversed by the program I recommend.

This will require that the Secretary of Agriculture make full and effective use of all the responsibilities now reposed in him; and that the Congress establish guidelines to enable the Administration to exercise responsible leadership in consultation with those farmers most concerned in establishing sound programs for each commodity for which they are needed.

A generation ago, Congress enacted the Reciprocal Trade Agreements Act to place in the Executive Branch the authority for a tariff-by-tariff approach that could be more effectively and equitably handled there instead of in the halls of Congress. The Reorganization Act similarly shifted the initiative in that complex field to the Executive Branch. Now agriculture needs a commodity-by-commodity approach, fitting each program to the pertinent problems, initiated by the Secretary of Agriculture under Presidential direction, subject to the approval of the farmers voting in referenda and to final review by the Congress.

The authority Congress has previously granted to the Secretary for the management of farm supply and the stabilization of farm income requires additional adjustment. A variety of gaps must be filled before all necessary administrative tools are available for every commodity. I am therefore asking the Congress to enact legislation to be submitted shortly and to be known as the Agricultural Enabling Amendments Act of 1961, covering the following matters:

1. The Agricultural Marketing Agreement Act of 1937, which now authorizes marketing orders for milk, certain fruits and vegetables, tobacco, soybeans, and some

specialized crops, should be amended to permit marketing orders to be used for a wider range of commodities, to make it more flexible in dealing with commodities for which a national or area program may be devised, and to permit, subject to the approval of producers and acceptance of the Congress as noted below, the establishment of quotas and allotments for individual producers. This will enable the valuable tool of the marketing order to be extended and combined with effective production control where the latter is essential.

2. The Agricultural Adjustment Act of 1938 should be amended to permit supply adjustment through marketing quotas for any agricultural commodity for which quotas might be most effective in achieving our goals and subject to affirmative approval by producers and acceptance of the Congress as indicated below. Quotas should be authorized either in quantitative terms— pounds, bushels, or bales—or in terms of production for individual farm acreage allotments. This will insure effective supply adjustment where this is indicated under proper safeguards. Such adjustment in turn is our best assurance against excessive costs to the taxpayers.

3. The Agricultural Act of 1949 should be modified to permit, subject to similar producer approval and Congressional acceptance, the method of supporting producer income that is most appropriate to the competitive and international position of the commodity, the nature of the supply adjustment needed, and economy to the taxpayer. There should be authorization of compensatory payments as well as commodity loans, commodity purchases, diversion programs, incentive payments, and export payments as circumstances require. All of these measures, properly safeguarded as to use, have proven their value in practice and are essential if the programs are to be adjusted to needs of individual commodities. As a part of payment programs the Secretary of Agriculture should be authorized to make payments in kind in cases where producers prefer such payments and where the Secretary determines that the goal of reduction of available stocks makes such payments feasible.

4. The Soil Conservation and Domestic Allotment Act of 1936 should be amended to provide for the establishment of national farmer advisory committees for every commodity or group of related commodities for which a new supply adjustment program is planned. Members of the committees would be elected by the producers of the commodities involved or their appropriate representatives. In consultation with the Secretary of Agriculture, they would be charged with the responsibility for considering and recommending individual commodity programs. To make it possible for farmers to participate in the work and consultation necessary for the development and implementation of sound proposals, the bill should authorize the payment of expenses for the members of these farmer committees.

In order to insure effective farmer participation in the administration of farm programs on the local level, the Secretary of Agriculture is being directed to revitalize the county and local farmer committee system and to recommend such amendments as may be necessary to safeguard such farmer participation.

5. Programs formulated in accordance with the enabling legislation here proposed and involving controls over production and marketing should not go into effect until approved by a majority of two-thirds of the producers voting under regularly authorized voting procedures and there should be legislation to this end. Such voting will be after

full opportunity for debate and discussion and will insure that the producers of no commodity will be asked to accept programs to which they have not given strong affirmative approval.

6. All comprehensive programs prepared under existing and requested authority will be duly submitted to the Congress of the United States not less than sixty days before taking effect. If within the sixty-day period the program is rejected by either House of the Congress, the program will not go into effect. Thus no agricultural program will be adopted if it is regarded adversely by a majority of either House of the Congress.

Agricultural programs must always involve an effort to take the best of the available alternatives. Our task, building on past experience and present authority, is to find a simple and rapid accommodation to changing circumstances which is both effective and consistent with our democratic traditions. I believe that the present proposals will go a long way toward achieving these goals.

II. EXPANDING THE USE OF OUR FARM ABUNDANCE

A. *To Improve Distribution and Nutrition at Home.*

We have already taken a number of steps toward greater utilization of our agricultural abundance at home as well as abroad. I have directed the Secretary of Agriculture to increase both the quantity and quality of our surplus food distribution to the needy; and under this program the amount of food going to each needy family has already been doubled. In addition, pilot food stamp programs are being launched in eight areas to provide emergency aid where the distress is particularly acute. These pilot plans will furnish operating experience necessary for

our determination of the most effective kind of food allotment program.

To improve further our system of distribution I recommend:

1. An expansion of the school lunch program, with the increase going to those schools providing a high proportion of free lunches because of the high level of unemployment in their localities, and with a change in the allocation formula to include, in addition to school age population and per capita income, the number of children who actually receive school lunches. In this way the best possible nutrition will be made available to every school child, regardless of the economic condition of his family or his local school district.

2. Extension and improvement of the special school milk program. Existing authorization for this program expires June 30. No lapse should be permitted.

B. *To Improve Nutrition Among Needy Peoples Abroad.*

We have barely begun to explore the ways in which our abundance can advance the cause of peace and freedom around the world, and contribute to the well-being and stability of undeveloped nations whose peoples eye our storage stockpiles with hungry dissatisfaction. I have already dispatched a series of missions to such areas to ascertain how we can best use our food in a helpful fashion. In addition, I ask the Congress:

1. As previously requested, to authorize an additional $2 billion for this calendar year under Title I of the Agricultural Trade Development and Assistance Act of 1954, which permits the sale for local currencies of our surplus agricultural products. The need for this legislation is urgent, for the funds now available under this Title are virtually exhausted. Until Congress acts we will be unable to process new requests now

coming in from friendly governments.

2. To extend and expand the Agricultural Trade Development and Assistance Act of 1954 for a period of five years. Unless there is some assurance of a continuing program we can neither make the advance plans best suited to an effective instrument of foreign policy nor gauge its long-term effect upon our domestic program. Title I sales should be authorized at a higher level; and our contributions of food and fiber to voluntary agencies such as CARE for use abroad should be liberalized.

C. *Improved Research.*

We should not only continue our research activities directed toward better production and lower costs, but we must expand research into marketing, nutrition and especially utilization. Today approximately two-thirds of our agricultural research is directed toward improved production and only one-third toward utilization. Yet these small expenditures have resulted in the past in developing such items as frozen orange juice, potato flakes, and other foods which have vastly increased food demand and made possible the use of an estimated 500 million pounds of additional animal fats in livestock feed, an additional 250 million pounds of additional animal fats in the manufacture of plastics, and an additional 800,000 bales of cotton for washable cotton fabrics. The proportion of our effort directed at food and fiber utilization should be increased.

In addition, I am directing the Secretary of Agriculture to survey the nutritional needs of our Nation and to formulate plans for helping achieve optimum nutrition goals for all Americans. The Secretary and the Food for Peace Director have already initiated a study of the food and fiber needs of other free countries. With completion of these studies we will be in a position to press forward vigorously to eliminate malnutrition and starvation as a common experience.

D. *Expanded Exports.*

I am directing the Secretary of Agriculture and all other appropriate departments and agencies of the Government to intensify our efforts to expand dollar sales of agricultural products. The Foreign Agricultural Service's assignment of market promotion specialists and agricultural attachés to critical areas will be encouraged. This will strengthen our overseas programs of trade fair exhibits and trade centers, improve information services and market news to the United States trade, and supply us with vitally needed information about agricultural developments abroad and the competition our products face in world markets.

In our progress toward a trade liberalization program, there has been a marked lag in convincing other nations to reduce barriers on agricultural products. Especially at this time, it is important that we redouble our efforts to gain access for more of our agricultural products to the markets of foreign countries.

III. ENCOURAGEMENT OF COOPERATIVES

One of the methods by which farmers can increase their bargaining power and thus remedy to some extent their weakness in the market place is through the effective operation of their own cooperatives.

To this end I recommend legislation to reaffirm and protect the right of farmers to act together through their cooperatives in the processing and marketing of their products, the purchasing of supplies, and the furnishing of necessary services. This legislation should specifically permit farmers' cooperatives to purchase, acquire and build processing plants and related facilities and to merge with other cooperatives so long as such activities do not tend to create a monopoly or substantially lessen competition.

IV. LOW INCOME FARMS

In those areas where farms are predominantly in the lowest income group, entire rural communities have suffered severe economic damage. The small businesses are liquidating, the community facilities are deteriorating and community institutions are weakened. These present a special problem.

The Area Redevelopment Bill now under consideration by the Congress is needed by farmers as urgently as it is needed in cities and towns. I reiterate my urgent recommendation for the speedy enactment of this bill, and thus enhance the resources available to the Secretary of Agriculture as he mobilizes all the services available to him, such as FHA, REA, Forest and Extension Services, to assist in the development of better levels of living, better income opportunities, and better communities in our rural depressed areas.

V. FARM CREDIT AND REA

One of the features of modern agriculture that poses an increasing problem to farmers, especially during periods of low income, is the need for increased capital investment, accompanied by the high cost of credit.

I am directing the Secretary of Agriculture to liberalize and extend the lending operations of the Farmers Home Administration so that any needy farmer can obtain loans for operating capital and for farm home improvements at low cost, and I rec-

ommend that the present legislation be amended to permit farm improvement loans to be secured either by mortgages or by other acceptable forms of security.

I have further directed the Secretary of Agriculture to initiate two measures that will encourage the storage of grain on the farm and strengthen economic activity in farming areas:

(a) Modifying present farm credit regulations to permit farmers to borrow up to 95 percent (instead of the present 80 percent limit) of the cost of materials for building farm storage facilities and equipment; and

(b) Guaranteeing that farmers will be able to earn two full years' storage payments for continuing to store 1960 crop wheat, corn and grain sorghum, and at least one year's storage payments for continuing to store other 1960 crops.

The loans are for 5 years at an interest rate of 4 percent. The effect of this directive will be to increase the demand for steel, wood, and other building materials, to procure the additional farm storage needed for 1960 crops, and to place an estimated $40 million in credit funds in the rural economy in the months ahead.

I have also directed that the Rural Electrification Act be administered in accordance with the original intent and purpose of that program, which has done so much to advance agriculture throughout the Nation. Over 95 percent of our farms now have electricity. But much remains to be done. There are constantly increasing demands for additional power. Only one-third of our farms have modern telephone installations. The cooperatives which so successfully brought light and power to the farm can make an enormous contribution to the continued development of our rural communities.

VI. FOREST RESOURCES

One of our most important natural resources, and one of our most neglected, is our forest land.

We need to give special emphasis to the improvement of the 256 million acres of small, privately owned farm woodlands and other small forests. This is an important sector of our agricultural economy in which the rate of progress and production is far from satisfactory. Yet here is a crop which is not in surplus and to which many farmers should turn, for their benefit and the Nation's. If our grandchildren are to have only the same continuous supply of timber products as we now have, growth of timber on these farm woodlots and other small holdings will have to be doubled within the next forty years. To insure adequate forest resources in the future by sound, effective programs relating to privately-owned woodlands as well as our National Forest, the following administrative and legislative measures are needed:

1. Rejuvenate the Forest Service's long-range program for the development and improvement of our National Forests—a program already returning substantial revenues to the Treasury and designed eventually to return $500 million a year. Accompanying measures were requested in my earlier message on Resources.

2. Accelerate, through a larger Federal grant, the present Federal-State cooperative assistance program to farm and small forest owners for the application of scientific forestry techniques.

3. Expand tree planting funds, in order to make productive fifty million acres that will not restock naturally within a reasonable time, and to increase the timber stand on another one hundred million acres.

4. Increase protection against losses caused by fire, forest insects, and tree diseases. The Federal Government's share of the burden in preventing and controlling forest fires has not been met, even though the states contribute the greater share.

5. Emphasize our incentive cost-sharing programs with owners for tree planting, timber stand improvement, and certain other practices under the Agricultural Conservation Program.

6. Expand forestry research, too long neglected.

7. Encourage the establishment of management and marketing forest cooperatives.

VII. SOIL AND WATER CONSERVATION

We have so taken soil conservation for granted in this generation that we forget it is a task which is barely under way. By June 30, 1960, the Soil Conservation Service had helped 1,301,450 farmers and ranchers to complete basic conservation plans and an additional 500,000 were being assisted. But this represents only twenty-seven percent of all farms and ranches in soil conservation districts. Nearly three-fourths of this important job remains to be done.

I am requesting the Congress to provide the funds necessary to accelerate this program for permanent soil conservation practices and to increase our efforts for small watersheds as well. These smaller projects, now being planned and developed, may well hold the key to our future water and soil requirements at a time of rapidly growing population.

CONCLUSION

The measures I have recommended are not directed solely to the purpose of aiding the farmer. Nor are they simple prescriptions for Federal assistance to a harried segment of our population. Rather they are directed toward broad goals of achieving agricultural production geared to meet needs for food and fiber at home and in the free world, under programs that will enable the farmers of this nation to earn a fair income.

We cannot expect to solve the farm problem in a day or in a year, or perhaps even in this administration. But we can and must adopt a new approach based on a clear recognition of the goals we seek, a realistic appraisal of the problems involved, and a firm determination to solve these problems and attain these goals.

The bills I have suggested will be debated and discussed in terms of general Administration policies and powers. Various portions will undoubtedly be challenged as restrictive upon the farmer or inconsistent with complete freedom in the market. But

I am convinced that the objectives of these programs will, when accomplished, provide for a reasonable balance between supply and demand. They will eliminate the hardship and suffering which inadequate returns force upon so many of our farm families; they will reduce our surpluses to manageable proportions; they will relieve the taxpayer of the unnecessary drain upon the Federal budget; they will spur our national economy, and they will assure the consumer of stable price levels.

Responsibility must be accompanied by the authority to accomplish these goals. If we move forward along the lines I have recommended, the entire Nation will benefit. The farmer can join the city-dweller in the march toward economic health.

JOHN F. KENNEDY

86 Letter to Secretary Ribicoff Concerning Assistance to Exiled Cuban Scholars and Professional Leaders. *March* 17, 1961

Dear Secretary Ribicoff:

I have studied and am in full accord with your recommendations of tangible assistance for Cuban scholars and professional leaders who have temporarily fled their country and are now living here in the United States. Immediate action should be taken on behalf of your proposals, and every possible personal encouragement given to this courageous and remarkable group.

I want to make unmistakably clear that we believe in a free Cuba. The presence in this country of two-thirds of the faculty of the University of Havana, as well as many more educational and professional leaders from the island, attests that an essential part of a free Cuba is now here with us. In community with them, we know that "only the mind cannot be sent into exile."

I will appreciate receiving by July 1 a report on the progress made in this program and the opportunities it opens up in teaching, medicine, economic development work, and other fields for the benefit of all of the Western Hemisphere.

Sincerely,   JOHN F. KENNEDY

NOTE: Secretary Ribicoff's recommendations, made in response to the President's request of February 3 (Item 19), were included in a letter dated March 14, released with the President's reply. Secretary Ribicoff recommended that a grant be made to the University of Miami for (1) the creation of research and teaching opportunities for exiled scholars, (2) for the provision of specialized programs for exiled doctors, lawyers, and judges, including intensive instruction in the English language, and (3) for the maintenance of a roster of academically trained refugees for the use of U.S. colleges and universities seeking additions to their faculties and of Federal agencies in need of assistance on Latin American projects.

87   Remarks at a Meeting of the President's Advisory Committee on Labor-Management Policy.   *March* 21, 1961

Mr. Secretary, Governor Hodges, and fellow members:

The purpose of this Committee is to give direction to the general movement of wages and prices so that the general welfare of this country can be served. We are breaking new ground. Other Presidents have, of course, attempted at different stages to intervene in the wage-price matter with general exhortations from the White House. These exhortations have not had a very great effect but with your help I intend to get a look at this situation before there is a crisis. I do not want the White House to have to come in at the last minute. Since we are breaking new ground, I am not sure how much we can accomplish but I do think it is extremely important that we move ahead.

Our competitive position abroad is affected by the wage-price structure here at home, so this is most important in national survival. The problems of structural unemployment, long range unemployment is a matter of utmost concern now. It is quite possible that we could have a recovery this summer and still have six or seven percent of our people unemployed in the fall.

The question is what we should do about it, or what we can do about it. How many governmental powers have we to effect them? I think it would be helpful if you could give your attention to that. It is extremely serious—steel, coal, automobiles, airplanes, these are all being affected by changes in demand, as well as in production techniques, and I would think that we should as a country be considering the long-range implications of these changes, and we should also consider the relationship be-

tween labor and management as far as collective bargaining goes, particularly in the basic directions which affect our national well being.

I could not possibly—I don't know the answer to these questions, and I am sure none of us does, but I think together we ought to consider them. We are going into a critical phase of our national life. We want to keep our economy free—we want labor to be free—we want management to be free—and we want to keep the Federal Government in its proper role. But we all, regardless of our politics—we all have to come to the conclusion that the general welfare is involved in every act we take. And I would like to see you gentlemen consider how best your interests can be served and also the national interest, which is a matter that concerns the Vice President and myself.

So I want to express my thanks to you and to say to you that this is your work and you will be given the closest support by this Administration. We have two outstanding Members of the Cabinet, Mr. Goldberg and Mr. Hodges. They will alternate which indicates I think that this is a completely objective study from the point of view of labor and management. I am going to be particularly interested in it myself. And we want to have all your suggestions and ideas so that we are able to compete, so that we are able to maintain employment, so we are able to develop policies which strengthen the economy of the United States, and I hope that you can give us some thoughts about it.

We have picked, I think, the finest group that could possibly be brought to bear on this subject, representing important national interests and also men who have a public sense. We are very grateful to you for your helping us, and I am sure there cannot be any precise guidelines at this point—I think that what you do will be very valuable.

NOTE: The President spoke at 10 a.m. in the Cabinet Room at the White House. His opening words "Mr. Secretary, Governor Hodges" referred to the Secretary of Labor, Arthur J. Goldberg, Chairman of the Committee; and the Secretary of Commerce, Luther H. Hodges.

88 Letter to President Eisenhower Upon Signing Bill Restoring His Military Rank. *March* 22, 1961

Dear Mr. President:

It gives me a great deal of pleasure to inform you that I have today approved the Act of Congress authorizing your appointment to the active list of the Regular Army as General of the Army with your former date of rank in such grade. I have directed that a commission be prepared immediately.

The legislation constitutes a reaffirmation of the affection and regard of our Nation for you.

I have arranged to have an exact copy of the Enrolled Bill made, and it is enclosed herewith.

With every good wish, I am

Sincerely,   JOHN F. KENNEDY

NOTE: The Act of Congress referred to is Public Law 87–3 (75 Stat. 5).

89 Statement by the President Upon Signing Bill Providing for an Emergency Feed Grain Program. *March* 22, 1961

I HAVE TODAY signed into law H.R. 4510, providing an emergency feed grain program for the 1961 crop. I am gratified that the Congress moved so promptly in enacting this legislation. Congressmen from the North, East, South and West voted for this program for agriculture which serves the best interests of all the American people.

The emergency feed grain act will enable us to make headway this year toward stemming the flow of feed grains while giving us time to develop more satisfactory permanent legislation. It is a very important step toward learning to live with our agricultural abundance.

This new law will help us to accomplish the following objectives:

1. An increase in farm income.

2. An abundant supply of meat, eggs and dairy products at fair and stable prices.

3. A reduction in the cost of the farm program to the government.

4. A curtailment of the surplus in feed grains which has reached almost unmanageable proportions.

The Congress has given us a workable program for moving toward these objectives. The extent to which this program will succeed in meeting its goals depends upon the degree of participation in the program by farmers. It is in the interest of every eligible farmer to participate in this program.

It will bring him additional income this year. But even more important, it will lay the groundwork for a long range program that will assure increasing prosperity for

American farmers in the years ahead.

It requires the cooperation of every farmer to make it work. And it is to this task that we now must hasten. I urge every farmer who can do so to participate in the program both in his own interest and for the sake of the whole country.

NOTE: As enacted, H.R. 4510 is Public Law 87-5 (75 Stat. 6).

90   Special Message to the Congress on Foreign Aid. *March 22, 1961*

To the Congress of the United States:

This nation must begin any discussion of "foreign aid" in 1961 with the recognition of three facts:

1. Existing foreign aid programs and concepts are largely unsatisfactory and unsuited for our needs and for the needs of the underdeveloped world as it enters the Sixties.

2. The economic collapse of those free but less-developed nations which now stand poised between sustained growth and economic chaos would be disastrous to our national security, harmful to our comparative prosperity and offensive to our conscience.

3. There exists, in the 1960's, an historic opportunity for a major economic assistance effort by the free industrialized nations to move more than half the people of the less-developed nations into self-sustained economic growth, while the rest move substantially closer to the day when they, too, will no longer have to depend on outside assistance.

I.

Foreign aid—America's unprecedented response to world challenges—has not been the work of one party or one Administration. It has moved forward under the leadership of two great Presidents—Harry Truman and Dwight Eisenhower—and drawn its support from forward-looking members of both political parties in the Congress and throughout the nation.

Our first major foreign aid effort was an emergency program of relief—of food and clothing and shelter—to areas devastated by World War II. Next we embarked on the Marshall Plan—a towering and successful program to rebuild the economies of Western Europe and prevent a communist takeover. This was followed by Point 4—an effort to make scientific and technological advances available to the people of developing nations. And recently the concept of development assistance, coupled with the OECD, has opened the door to a united free world effort to assist the economic and social development of the less-developed areas of the world.

To achieve this new goal we will need to renew the spirit of common effort which lay behind our past efforts—we must also revise our foreign aid organization, and our basic concepts of operation to meet the new problems which now confront us.

For no objective supporter of foreign aid can be satisfied with the existing program—actually a multiplicity of programs. Bureaucratically fragmented, awkward and slow, its administration is diffused over a haphazard and irrational structure covering at least four departments and several other agencies. The program is based on a series of legislative measures and administrative procedures conceived at different times and for different purposes, many of them now obsolete, inconsistent and unduly rigid and thus unsuited for our present needs and purposes. Its weaknesses have begun to undermine confidence in our effort both here and abroad.

The program requires a highly professional skilled service, attracting substantial numbers of high caliber men and women capable of sensitive dealing with other governments, and with a deep understanding of the process of economic development. However, uncertainty and declining public prestige have all contributed to a fall in the morale and efficiency of those employees in the field who are repeatedly frustrated by the delays and confusions caused by overlapping agency jurisdictions and unclear objectives. Only the persistent efforts of those dedicated and hard-working public servants who have kept the program going, managed to bring some success to our efforts overseas.

In addition, uneven and undependable short-term financing has weakened the incentive for the long-term planning and self-help by the recipient nations which are essential to serious economic development. The lack of stability and continuity in the program—the necessity to accommodate all planning to a yearly deadline—when combined with a confusing multiplicity of American aid agencies within a single nation abroad—have reduced the effectiveness of our own assistance and made more difficult the task of setting realistic targets and sound standards. Piecemeal projects, hastily designed to match the rhythm of the fiscal year are no substitute for orderly long-term planning. The ability to make long-range commitments has enabled the Soviet Union to use its aid program to make developing nations economically dependent on Russian

support—thus advancing the aims of world communism.

Although our aid programs have helped to avoid economic chaos and collapse, and assisted many nations to maintain their independence and freedom—nevertheless it is a fact that many of the nations we are helping are not much nearer sustained economic growth than they were when our aid operation began. Money spent to meet crisis situations or short-term political objectives while helping to maintain national integrity and independence has rarely moved the recipient nation toward greater economic stability.

II.

In the face of these weaknesses and inadequacies—and with the beginning of a new decade of new problems—it is proper that we draw back and ask with candor a fundamental question: Is a foreign aid program really necessary? Why should we not lay down this burden which our nation has now carried for some fifteen years?

The answer is that there is no escaping our obligations: our moral obligations as a wise leader and good neighbor in the interdependent community of free nations—our economic obligations as the wealthiest people in a world of largely poor people, as a nation no longer dependent upon the loans from abroad that once helped us develop our own economy—and our political obligations as the single largest counter to the adversaries of freedom.

To fail to meet those obligations now would be disastrous; and, in the long run, more expensive. For widespread poverty and chaos lead to a collapse of existing political and social structures which would inevitably invite the advance of totalitarianism into every weak and unstable area. Thus our own security would be endangered and our prosperity imperiled. A program of assistance to the underdeveloped nations must continue because the nation's interest and the cause of political freedom require it.

We live at a very special moment in history. The whole southern half of the world—Latin America, Africa, the Middle East, and Asia—are caught up in the adventures of asserting their independence and modernizing their old ways of life. These new nations need aid in loans and technical assistance just as we in the northern half of the world drew successively on one another's capital and know-how as we moved into industrialization and regular growth.

But in our time these new nations need help for a special reason. Without exception they are under Communist pressure. In many cases, that pressure is direct and military. In others, it takes the form of intense subversive activity designed to break down and supersede the new—and often frail—modern institutions they have thus far built.

But the fundamental task of our foreign aid program in the 1960's is not negatively to fight Communism: Its fundamental task is to help make a historical demonstration that in the twentieth century, as in the nineteenth—in the southern half of the globe as in the north—economic growth and political democracy can develop hand in hand.

In short we have not only obligations to fulfill, we have great opportunities to realize. We are, I am convinced, on the threshold of a truly united and major effort by the free industrialized nations to assist the less-developed nations on a long-term basis. Many of these less-developed nations are on the threshold of achieving sufficient economic, social and political strength and self-sustained growth to stand permanently on their own feet. The 1960's can be—and must be—the crucial "Decade of Develop-

ment"—the period when many less-developed nations make the transition into self-sustained growth—the period in which an enlarged community of free, stable and self-reliant nations can reduce world tensions and insecurity. This goal is in our grasp if, and only if, the other industrialized nations now join us in developing with the recipients a set of commonly agreed criteria, a set of long-range goals, and a common undertaking to meet those goals, in which each nation's contribution is related to the contributions of others and to the precise needs of each less-developed nation. Our job, in its largest sense, is to create a new partnership between the northern and southern halves of the world, to which all free nations can contribute, in which each free nation must assume a responsibility proportional to its means.

We must unite the free industrialized nations in a common effort to help those nations within reach of stable growth get underway. And the foundation for this unity has already been laid by the creation of the OECD under the leadership of President Eisenhower. Such a unified effort will help launch the economies of the newly developing countries "into orbit"—bringing them to a stage of self-sustained growth where extraordinary outside assistance is not required. If this can be done—and I have every reason to hope it can be done—then this decade will be a significant one indeed in the history of free men.

But our success in achieving these goals, in creating an environment in which the energies of struggling peoples can be devoted to constructive purposes in the world community—and our success in enlisting a greater common effort toward this end on the part of other industrialized nations—depends to a large extent upon the scope and continuity of our own efforts. If we encourage recipient countries to dramatize a series of short-term crises as a basis for our aid—instead of depending on a plan for long-term goals—then we will dissipate our funds, our good will and our leadership. Nor will we be any nearer to either our security goals or to the end of the foreign aid burden.

In short, this Congress at this session must make possible a dramatic turning point in the troubled history of foreign aid to the underdeveloped world. We must say to the less-developed nations, if they are willing to undertake necessary internal reform and self-help—and to the other industrialized nations, if they are willing to undertake a much greater effort on a much broader scale—that we then intend during this coming decade of development to achieve a decisive turn-around in the fate of the less-developed world, looking toward the ultimate day when all nations can be self-reliant and when foreign aid will no longer be needed.

However, this will not be an easy task. The magnitude of the problems is staggering. In Latin America, for example, population growth is already threatening to outpace economic growth—and in some parts of the continent living standards are actually declining. In 1945 the population of our 20 sister American Republics was 145 million. It is now greater than that of the United States, and by the year 2000, less than forty years away, Latin American population will be 592 million, compared with 312 million for the United States. Latin America will have to double its real income in the next thirty years simply to maintain already low standards of living. And the problems are no less serious or demanding in the other developing areas of the world. Thus to bring real economic progress to Latin America and to the rest of the less-developed world will require a sustained and united effort on the part of the Latin American Republics, the United States and our free world allies.

This will require leadership, by this country in this year. And it will require a fresh approach—a more logical, efficient and successful long-term plan—for American foreign aid. I strongly recommend to the Congress the enactment of such a plan, as contained in a measure to be sent shortly to the Congress and described below.

III.

If our foreign aid funds are to be prudently and effectively used, we need a whole new set of basic concepts and principles:

1. Unified administration and operation—a single agency in Washington and the field, equipped with a flexible set of tools, in place of several competing and confusing aid units.

2. Country plans—a carefully thought through program tailored to meet the needs and the resource potential of each individual country, instead of a series of individual, unrelated projects. Frequently, in the past, our development goals and projects have not been undertaken as integral steps in a long-range economic development program.

3. Long-term planning and financing—the only way to make meaningful and economical commitments.

4. Special emphasis on development loans repayable in dollars—more conducive to business-like relations and mutual respect than sustaining grants or loans repaid in local currencies, although some instances of the latter are unavoidable.

5. Special attention to those nations most willing and able to mobilize their own resources, make necessary social and economic reforms, engage in long-range planning, and make the other efforts necessary if these are

to reach the stage of self-sustaining growth.

6. Multilateral approach—a program and level of commitments designed to encourage and complement an increased effort by other industrialized nations.

7. A new agency with new personnel—drawing upon the most competent and dedicated career servants now in the field, and attracting the highest quality from every part of the nation.

8. Separation from military assistance—our program of aid to social and economic development must be seen on its own merits, and judged in the light of its vital and distinctive contribution to our basic security needs.

IV.

I propose that our separate and often confusing aid programs be integrated into a single Administration embracing the present Washington and Field operations of

A. The International Cooperation Administration (ICA) and all its technical assistance (Point 4) and other programs;

B. The Development Loan Fund (DLF);

C. The Food-for-Peace Program (P.L. 480) in its relations with other countries, while also recognizing its essential role in our farm economy;

D. The local currency lending activities of the Export-Import Bank;

E. The Peace Corps, recognizing its distinctive contribution beyond the area of economic development;

F. The donation of non-agricultural surpluses from other national stockpiles of excess commodities or equipment;

G. All other related staff and program services now provided by the Department of State as well as ICA.

The field work in all these operations will be under the direction of a single mission chief in each country reporting to the Ameri-can Ambassador. This is intended to remove the difficulty which the aided countries and our own field personnel sometimes encounter in finding the proper channel of decision-making. Similarly, central direction and final responsibility in Washington will be fixed in an Administrator of a single agency—reporting directly to the Secretary of State and the President—working through Washington directors for each major geographical area, and through the directors of the constituent resource units whose functions are drawn together in each national plan: a development lending organization, Food-for-Peace, the Peace Corps, and a unit for technical and other assistance stressing Education and Human Resources—initiating a program of research, development and scientific evaluation to increase the effectiveness of our aid effort; and in addition, the Secretary of State will coordinate with economic aid the military assistance program administered by the Department of Defense, the related operations of the Export-Import Bank, and the role of the United States in the Inter-American Fund for Social Progress and activities of international organizations.

Under the jurisdiction of both the Secretary of State in Washington and the Ambassadors in the field, foreign aid can more effectively play its part as an effective instrument of our over-all efforts for world peace and security. The concentration of responsibilities and increased status will both require and attract high-caliber personnel. Programs such as the Peace Corps and Food-for-Peace, far from being submerged, will be used more effectively and their distinctive identity and appeal preserved—and Food-for-Peace will continue to be based on availabilities determined by the Department of Agriculture.

But I am not proposing merely a reshuffling and relabeling of old agencies and their personnel, without regard to their competence. I am recommending the replacement of these agencies with a new one—a fresh start under new leadership.

v.

But new organization is not enough. We need a new working concept.

At the center of the new effort must be national development programs. It is essential that the developing nations set for themselves sensible targets; that these targets be based on balanced programs for their own economic, educational and social growth—programs which use their own resources to the maximum. If planning assistance is required, our own aid organization will be prepared to respond to requests for such assistance, along with the International Bank for Reconstruction and Development and other international and private institutions. Thus, the first requirement is that each recipient government seriously undertake to the best of its ability on its own those efforts of resource mobilization, self-help and internal reform—including land reform, tax reform and improved education and social justice—which its own development requires and which would increase its capacity to absorb external capital productivity.

These national development programs—and the kind of assistance the Free World provides—must be tailored to the recipients' current stage of development and their foreseeable potential. A large infusion of development capital cannot now be absorbed by many nations newly emerging from a wholly underdeveloped condition. Their primary need at first will be the development of human resources, education, technical assistance and the groundwork of basic facilities and institutions necessary for further growth. Other countries may possess the necessary human and material resources to move toward status as developing nations, but they need transitional assistance from the outside to enable them to mobilize those resources and move into the more advanced stage of development where loans can put them on their feet. Still others already have the capacity to absorb and effectively utilize substantial investment capital.

Finally, it will be necessary, for the time being, to provide grant assistance to those nations that are hard pressed by external or internal pressure, so that they can meet those pressures and maintain their independence. In such cases it will be our objective to help them, as soon as circumstances permit, make the transition from instability and stagnation to growth; shifting our assistance as rapidly as possible from a grant to a development loan basis. For our new program should not be based merely on reaction to communist threats or short-term crises. We have a positive interest in helping less-developed nations provide decent living standards for their people and achieve sufficient strength, self-respect and independence to become self-reliant members of the community of nations. And thus our aid should be conditioned on the recipients' ability and willingness to take the steps necessary to reach that goal.

To meet the varied needs of many nations, the new aid Administration will have a flexible set of tools, coordinated and shaped to fit each national development program: the grant or sale (for either local currency or dollars with special repayment terms) of surplus foods, equipment and other items; technical assistance; skilled manpower from the Peace Corps; development grants; transitional, sustaining or emergency grants; development loans repayable in local currency; and development loans repayable in dollars, with special terms of repayment that will meet the needs of the recipient country. These tools will be coordinated with the activities of the Export-Import Bank, and with loan and investment guarantees to private enterprise.

The instrument of primary emphasis—the single most important tool—will be long-term development loans at low or no rates of interest, repayable in dollars, and designed to promote growth in those less-developed nations which have a real chance for ultimate self-reliance but which lack the ability to service loans from normal lending institutions. The terms of repayment will vary from as long as 50 years for those countries just starting on the road to development, to a much shorter period of time for those countries that are nearing the stage of self-sufficient growth.

Such long-term loans are preferable to outright grants, or "soft loans" repayable in local currencies that are of little benefit to the American taxpayer. The emphasis on low or interest-free loans is not designed to undercut other institutions. The objective is to rely on flexibility in the repayment period and the requirement of ultimate dollar repayment for insuring strict accountancy while meeting individual needs in an area not met by suppliers of capital on normal terms.

Lending on these terms is not normal banking practice. We are banking on the emergence over coming years and decades of a group of independent, growing, self-reliant nations.

VI.

A program based on long-range plans instead of short-run crises cannot be financed on a short-term basis. Long-term authorization, planning and financing are the key to the continuity and efficiency of the entire program. If we are unwilling to make such a long-term commitment, we cannot expect any increased response from other potential donors or any realistic planning from the recipient nations.

I recommend, therefore, an authorization for the new aid agency of not less than five years, with borrowing authority also for five years to commit and make dollar repayable loans within the limits spelled out below. No other step would be such a clear signal of our intentions to all the world. No other step would do more to eliminate the restrictions and confusions which have rendered the current foreign aid program so often ineffective. No other step would do more to help obtain the service of top-flight personnel. And in no other way can we encourage the less-developed nations to make a sustained national effort over a long-term period.

For, if we are to have a program designed to brighten the future, that program must have a future. Experience has shown that long-range needs cannot be met evenly and economically by a series of one-year programs. Close consultation and cooperation with the Congress and its Committees will still be essential, including an annual review of the program.

And we will still need annual appropriations of those amounts needed to meet requirements for which dollar repayable loans would be unsuitable. These appropriations should be available until spent in order to avoid any wasteful rush to obligate funds at the end of a fiscal year.

The new continuity and flexibility this kind of long-term authority will bring cannot help but result in more productive criteria, a greater effort on the part of the developing nations, greater contributions from our more prosperous allies, more solid results and real long-run economy to the taxpayers. The new emphasis on long-term plans and realistic targets will give both the Congress and the Executive a better basis for evaluating the validity of our expenditures and progress.

VII.

A long-term program and borrowing authority, even though limited, will enable us to demonstrate the seriousness of our intentions to other potential donors and to the less-developed world. Over the next five years, the economic program here proposed, together with an expanded Food for Peace Program as recommended in my Agricultural Message, and project loans by the Export-Import Bank, will constitute direct U.S. economic assistance activity of considerable magnitude.

It will, however, take time to institute the new concepts and practices which are proposed. Thus, during this initial year, while we will need to make the necessary long-term commitments for development lending, it is unnecessary to ask the Congress for any additional funds for this year's program.

Consequently, while the funds requested by my predecessor will be sharply shifted in terms of their use and purpose, I am asking the Congress for a total foreign aid budget of new obligational authority no greater than that requested in the rock-bottom Budget previously submitted ($4 billion) despite the fact that the number of new nations needing assistance is constantly increasing; and, though increasing such authority for non-military aid while reducing military assistance, this Budget provides for a level of actual expenditures on non-military aid no greater than reflected in the previous Budget ($1.9 billion). (These figures do not, of course, reflect P.L. 480 operations.)

In deciding on this program, I have also carefully considered its impact on our balance of payments. We are now putting maximum emphasis, in both our development lending and grant aid programs, on the procurement of goods and services of United States origin. As I pointed out in my message on the balance of payments, under present procedures not more than 20% of foreign economic aid expenditures will affect our balance of payments. This means that approximately $2 billion out of the requested $2.4 billion in economic aid will be spent directly for goods and services benefiting the American economy.

This is important. For not only do we have the highest gross national product, both total and per capita, of any country in the world, thus making clear both our obligations and our capacity to do our full part, but we are currently underutilizing our great economic capacity because of economic recession and slack. Less than 80% of our industrial capacity is now in use, and nearly seven percent of our labor force is unemployed. Under these circumstances cutbacks in the foreign aid program would be felt not only in loss of economic progress and hope abroad but in loss of markets and income for business, labor, and agriculture at home.

In short, this program will not in whole or in part unbalance the previous budget in any fashion. Its impact on our balance of payments will be marginal. And its benefits for our domestic economy should not be overlooked.

The $4 billion previously requested for Fiscal Year 1962 will be reallocated under this new program as follows:

—Military assistance will be reduced from the $1.8 billion requested to $1.6 billion, as discussed below.

—Economic assistance, with a much greater portion going to development loans, a small increase in development grants, and a reduction in sustaining grants, will total $2.4 billion.

—Of this, $1.5 billion will be contained in the usual annual appropriation of new obligational authority to finance the part of the program that is not suitable for dollar development loans: grants for education, social progress and institutional development, the Peace Corps, and sustaining aid; $900 million will be available for long-term low or interest-free development loans to be repaid in dollars, financed through an authorization of public debt borrowing authority which would also provide no more than $1.6 billion for each of the succeeding four years. Also to be made available for such loans under the new system of full coordination will be the unappropriated dollar funds now coming in in repayment of the principal and interest on certain previous loans to foreign governments (United Kingdom, E.C.A., G.A.R.I.O.A. and others—but not the Export-Import Bank).

VIII.

The economic programs I am recommending in this message cannot succeed without peace and order. A vital element toward such stability is assurance of military strength sufficient to protect the integrity of these emerging nations while they are advancing to higher and more adequate levels of social and economic well-being.

I shall therefore request the Congress to provide at this time $1.6 billion for provision of Military Assistance. This figure is the amount required to meet the U.S. share in maintaining forces that already exist, and to honor firm existing commitments for the future.

I am frank to say that we cannot now say with precision whether this amount will meet the minimum level of military aid which our basic security policy might demand this year. The emergence of new crises or new conflicts may require us to make an even greater effort.

However, while I have mentioned in this message the amount to be allocated to military assistance, those funds, while coordinated with the policies of the new Agency, will not be administered by it and should not be included in its appropriation. In order to make clear the peaceful and positive purposes of this program, to emphasize the new importance this Administration places on economic and social development quite apart from security interests, and to make clear the relation between the Military Assistance Program and those interests, I shall propose a separate authorization for military assistance with appropriations as part of the Defense budget. Moreover, to the extent that world security conditions permit, military assistance will in the future more heavily emphasize the internal security, civil works and economic growth of the nations thus aided. By this shift in emphasis, we mean no lessening of our determination to oppose local aggression wherever it may occur. We have demonstrated our will and ability to protect Free World nations—if they so desire—from the type of external threat with which many of them are still confronted. We will not fall short on this.

IX.

The levels on which this new program is based are the minimum resulting from a hard reappraisal of each type of assistance and the needs of the less-developed world. They demonstrate both to the less-developed nations and to the other industrialized nations that this country will meet its fair share of effort necessary to accomplish the desired objective, and their effort must be greater as well. These are the rock-bottom minimum of funds necessary to do the job. To provide less would be wasteful, perhaps more wasteful, than to provide more. Certainly it would be wasteful to the security interest of the free world.

But I am hopeful that the Congress will not provide less. Assistance to our fellow nations is a responsibility which has been willingly assumed and fashioned by two great Presidents in the past, one from each party—and it has been supported by the leaders of both parties in both houses who recognized the importance of our obligations.

I believe the program which I have outlined is both a reasonable and sensible method of meeting those obligations as economically and effectively as possible. I strongly urge its enactment by the Congress, in full awareness of the many eyes upon us—

the eyes of other industrialized nations, awaiting our leadership for a stronger united effort—the eyes of our adversaries, awaiting the weakening of our resolve in this new area of international struggle—the eyes of the poorer peoples of the world, looking for hope and help, and needing an incentive to set realistic long-range goals—and, finally, the eyes of the American people, who are fully aware of their obligations to the sick, the poor and the hungry, wherever they may live. Thus, without regard to party lines, we shall take this step not as Republicans or as Democrats but as leaders of the Free World. It will both befit and benefit us to take this step boldly. For we are launching a Decade of Development on which will depend, substantially, the kind of world in which we and our children shall live.

JOHN F. KENNEDY

91   Statement by the President Following Ratification of Convention Establishing the Organization for Economic Cooperation and Development.   *March 23, 1961*

IN BEHALF of the United States, I have ratified the convention establishing the Organization for Economic Cooperation and Development. I have done so with great satisfaction, and with expectations that the Organization for Economic Cooperation and Development will become one of the principal institutions through which we pursue the great aim of consolidating the Atlantic Community. As I said in my Inaugural Address, "United, there is little we cannot do in a host of cooperative ventures. Divided, there is little we can do—for we dare not meet a powerful challenge at odds and split asunder."

In giving its advice and consent to this act of ratification, the United States Senate

has affirmed the intention of the United States to enter upon a new era of cooperative enterprise with our Atlantic partners. We face a broad spectrum of common economic problems.

And OECD should prove a useful forum in which the member states can consider and act together on a number of the vital questions.

Among these challenging problems, none is more urgent than that of helping the less developed countries in their quest for economic growth and stability. The countries represented in OECD have a common interest, and a common responsibility in this task. For they are among those fortunate enough to have earned the capital and the skills required for such programs. And they share with all humanity the hope and determination that the less developed peoples will succeed in their valiant efforts to achieve sustained economic progress.

Next week the Development Assistance Group, which is soon to become the Development Assistance Committee of the OECD, will meet in London. As an indication of the importance I attach to all phases of the work of OECD, I have instructed George W. Ball, our Under Secretary of State for Economic Affairs, to represent the United States at this meeting.

The subject matter of this meeting represents one of the central tasks of OECD. I look forward to the development of joint approaches, and joint solutions, in which each of the member countries will assume its fair share of our common responsibility. I am confident that this meeting will represent a substantial forward step in this effort.

NOTE: The text of the convention is published in the Department of State Bulletin (vol. 44, p. 11).

92   The President's News Conference of *March* 23, 1961

THE PRESIDENT. [1.] I want to make a brief statement about Laos. It is, I think, important for all Americans to understand this difficult and potentially dangerous problem. In my last conversation with General Eisenhower, the day before the inauguration on January 19, we spent more time on this hard matter than on any other thing. And since then it has been steadily before the administration as the most immediate of the problems that we found upon taking office. Our special concern with the problem in Laos goes back to 1954. That year at Geneva a large group of powers agreed to a settlement of the struggle for Indochina. Laos was one of the new states which had recently emerged from the French union and it was the clear premise of the 1954 settlement that this new country would be neutral—free of external domination by anyone. The new country contained contending factions, but in its first years real progress was made towards a unified and neutral status. But the efforts of a Communist-dominated group to destroy this neutrality never ceased.

In the last half of 1960 a series of sudden maneuvers occurred and the Communists and their supporters turned to a new and greatly intensified military effort to take over. These three maps [*indicating*] show the area of effective Communist domination as it was last August, with the colored portions up on the right-hand corner being the areas held and dominated by the Communists at that time; and now next, in December of 1960, 3 months ago, the red area having expanded; and now from December 20 to the present date near the end of March the Communists control a much wider section of the country.

In this military advance the local Communist forces, known as the Pathet Lao, have had increasing support and direction from outside. Soviet planes, I regret to say, have been conspicuous in a large-scale airlift into the battle area—over 100—1,000 sorties since last December 13th, plus a whole supporting set of combat specialists, mainly from Communist North Viet-Nam, and heavier weapons have been provided from outside, all with the clear object of destroying by military action the agreed neutrality of Laos.

It is this new dimension of externally supported warfare that creates the present grave problem. The position of this administration has been carefully considered and we have sought to make it just as clear as we know how to the governments concerned.

First, we strongly and unreservedly support the goal of a neutral and independent Laos, tied to no outside power or group of powers, threatening no one, and free from any domination. Our support for the present duly constituted government is aimed entirely and exclusively at that result. And if in the past there has been any possible ground for misunderstanding of our desire for a truly neutral Laos, there should be none now.

Secondly, if there is to be a peaceful solution, there must be a cessation of the present armed attacks by externally supported Communists. If these attacks do not stop, those who support a truly neutral Laos will have to consider their response. The shape of this necessary response will, of course, be carefully considered, not only here in Washington, but in the SEATO conference with our allies, which begins next Monday.

SEATO—the Southeast Asia Treaty Organization—was organized in 1954, with strong leadership from our last administration, and all members of SEATO have undertaken special treaty responsibilities towards an aggression in Laos.

No one should doubt our resolutions on this point. We are faced with a clear and one-sided threat of a change in the internationally agreed position of Laos. This threat runs counter to the will of the Laotian people, who wish only to be independent and neutral. It is posed rather by the military operations of internal dissident elements directed from outside the country. This is what must end if peace is to be achieved in Southeast Asia.

Thirdly, we are earnestly in favor of

constructive negotiation among the nations concerned and among the leaders of Laos which can help Laos back to the pathway of independence and genuine neutrality. We strongly support the present British proposal of a prompt end of hostilities and prompt negotiation. We are always conscious of the obligation which rests upon all members of the United Nations to seek peaceful solutions to problems of this sort. We hope that others may be equally aware of this responsibility.

My fellow Americans, Laos is far away from America, but the world is small. Its two million people live in a country 3 times the size of Austria. The security of all Southeast Asia will be endangered if Laos loses its neutral independence. Its own safety runs with the safety of us all—in real neutrality observed by all.

I want to make it clear to the American people and to all of the world that all we want in Laos is peace, not war; a truly neutral government, not a cold war pawn; a settlement concluded at the conference table and not on the battlefield.

Our response will be made in close cooperation with our allies and the wishes of the Laotian Government. We will not be provoked, trapped, or drawn into this or any other situation; but I know that every American will want his country to honor its obligations to the point that freedom and security of the free world and ourselves may be achieved.

Careful negotiations are being conducted with many countries at the present time in order to see that we have taken every possible course to insure a peaceful solution. Yesterday the Secretary of State informed the members and leaders of the Congress— the House and Senate—in both parties, of the situation and brought them up to date. We will continue to keep them and the country fully informed as the situation develops.

Q. Mr. President, can you tell us what reaction you may have had from the Russians, either directly or indirectly, perhaps through the British, with respect to the approach you suggest on this problem?

THE PRESIDENT. The British have had a conversation with the Russians, but I think that it's impossible at the present time to make any clear judgment as to what the nature of the response will be. We are hopeful that it will be favorable to the suggestion that we have made—the suggestion that the British have made for a cease-fire and for negotiations of the matter.

[2.] Q. Mr. President, a number—or several, rather—relatively highly placed economists in Government have said recently that the state of the economy is improving and that an upturn may be expected in April or May. How do you, sir, view the current state of the economy?

THE PRESIDENT. Well, I think that there are evidences of some improvement in the economy. The question, of course, is whether the upturn which usually comes in the spring will be sufficient to reduce the unemployment percentage, which is high today, to a figure which is more in accordance with a full employment in our society.

We also have to consider whether the upturn will bring us to the use of our national capacity and whether that upturn will be the beginning of a sustained economic growth this year and in the immediate years to come. It is impossible to make any judgment at this time in March on these factors with any precision.

[3.] Q. Mr. President, there have been reports that some portions of our Navy, some portions of our Marines, have been alerted and are moving toward that area. Could you tell us something of that, sir, and would it be safe to assume that we are preparing to back up our words as you have outlined them here?

THE PRESIDENT. I think that my statement is clear and represents the views I wish to express at the present time, and I'm hopeful that it will be possible for us to see a peaceful solution arrive in a difficult matter, and I would let the matter rest at this point with that.

Q. Is there any kind of indicated deadline or time limit by which this Government will consider that further action is necessary unless hostilities have ceased in Laos?

THE PRESIDENT. No time limit has been given, but quite obviously we are anxious to see an end to overt hostilities as soon as possible so that some form of negotiations can be carried on. And we are—but there has been no precise time limit set.

Q. Sir, I did not mean an ultimatum. I did mean in terms of an indicated time limit in our own minds if this drags on for a week or two weeks or three weeks, is there some time in there?

THE PRESIDENT. Well, I think the matter, of course, becomes increasingly serious as the days go by, and that's why we're anxious to see if it's possible at the present time to reach an agreement on a cease-fire. The longer it goes on, the less satisfactory it is.

Q. Mr. President, that map would indicate that the Communists have taken over a good part of Laos. Have your advisers told you what the—how dangerous the military situation is there? Is there a real danger that the Communists will take over the whole kingdom?

THE PRESIDENT. Well, quite obviously progress has been made on the—substantial progress has been made by the Communists towards that objective in recent weeks. And the capital—royal capital of Luang Prabang—has been in danger, and progress has been made southward towards the administrative capital of Vientiane. So that it is for this reason that we are so concerned and have felt the situation to be so critical.

Q. Yes, sir. Is there any—do you know how much time the supporters of the Laos Government might have for diplomacy? In other words, is there a danger of a quick takeover by the Communists in a matter of——

THE PRESIDENT. I would say that we are hopeful that we can get a quick judgment as to what the prospects are going to be there. I think that every day is important.

Q. Mr. President, you mentioned earlier in your statement that there were dissident elements in Viet-Nam who were carrying on this warfare. There have been many reports of North Vietnamese troops involved. Do we have any intelligence or information that would bear out these reports?

THE PRESIDENT. The phrase "dissident elements," I believe, referred to the internal group, and I also stated that there have been, has been evidence of groups from Viet Minh or North Viet-Nam who have been involved.

[4.] Q. Mr. President, have the events of the past week changed your view on the advisability of a meeting between you and Mr. Khrushchev?

THE PRESIDENT. No.

[5.] Q. Mr. President, we're getting conflicting reports in the Capitol as to your willingness to accept a compromise on this minimum wage bill, particularly in regard to coverage. Can you give us a little information on what your position is on this?

THE PRESIDENT. Well, I'm anxious—I've supported the bill that came out of the committee for $1.25 with the expanded coverage over a period of time and also expanded coverage of nearly 4 million. I'm hopeful that that bill will pass, or a bill as close as

possible to it would pass.

I find it difficult to know why anyone would oppose seeing somebody, by 1963, paid $1.25 in interstate commerce. And in the new coverage we're talking about businesses which make over $1 million a year. And I find it difficult to understand how anybody could object to paying somebody who works in a business which makes over $1 million a year, by 1963, $50 a week. I think that anyone who is paid less than that must find it extremely difficult to maintain themselves and their family.

I consider it to be a very minimum wage. So that I'm hopeful that the House will pass legislation as close to the bill that came out of the committee as possible, and—because I must say we are talking about a standard for fellow Americans, and millions of them—and I must say I think that it is in the public interest to pass that bill as closely as possible to the House committee bill.

[6.] Q. Mr. President, there appears to be some national unawareness of the importance of a free Laos to the security of the United States and to the individual American. Could you spell out your views on that a little further?

THE PRESIDENT. Well, quite obviously, geographically Laos borders on Thailand, to which the United States has treaty obligations under the SEATO Agreement of 1954, it borders on South Viet-Nam—or borders on Viet-Nam to which the United States has very close ties, and also which is a signatory of the SEATO Pact. The aggression against Laos itself was referred to in the SEATO Agreement. So that, given this, the nature of the geography, its location, the commitments which the United States and obligations which the United States has assumed toward Laos as well as the surrounding countries—as well as other signatories of the SEATO Pact, it's quite obvious that if the Communists were able to move in and dominate this country, it would endanger the security of all, and the peace of all, of Southeast Asia. And as a member of the United Nations and as a signatory of the SEATO Pact, and as a country which is concerned with the strength of the cause of freedom around the world, that quite obviously affects the security of the United States.

Q. Mr. President, the United States has made the position all the way through on this that we want a neutral Laos. But isn't it true that Laos has a nonviable economy and it can't exist as an independent country?

THE PRESIDENT. Well, I think it can exist. That was the premise under which the 1954 agreements were signed. It may require economic assistance, but there are many countries which are neutral which have received economic assistance from one side or the other and many of those countries are in Southeast Asia and some of them are geographically quite close to Laos, so that I don't think that the final test of a neutral country is completely the state of its economy. The test of a neutral country is whether one side or another dominates it and uses it, a phrase I referred to, as a pawn in the cold war. We would like it to occupy a neutral category as does Cambodia.

Q. Mr. President, what is your evaluation of the theory that perhaps the Russians are so active in Laos to keep the Chinese Communists out?

THE PRESIDENT. Well, I wouldn't attempt to make a judgment about a matter on which we have incomplete information. I think that the facts of the matter are that there has been external activity and that it has helped produce the result you see on the map, and this is of concern to us. I'm hopeful that those countries which have been supporting this effort will recognize that this is a matter of great concern to us and that they will be agreeable to the kind of proposals which we have made in the interests of peace.

[7.] Q. Mr. President, are you planning a visit to Venezuela or any other areas of Latin America within the next several months?

THE PRESIDENT. To Latin America?

Q. Yes, sir.

THE PRESIDENT. No, I'm not.

Q. Caracas?

THE PRESIDENT. No, I have no plans for a trip.

[8.] Q. Mr. President, the Civil War Commission has decided it has no authority to provide hotel rooms for Negroes who attend sessions in the South. What is your reaction to that decision?

THE PRESIDENT. Well, the Centennial is an official body of the United States Government, Federal funds are contributed to sustaining it, there have been appointments made by the Federal Government to the Commission, and it's my strong belief that any program of this kind in which the United States is engaged should provide facilities and meeting places which may—do not discriminate on the grounds of race or color. I have received the response to my original letter to General Grant, and I am in contact, going to be in contact again with General Grant to see if we can work out a solution which recognizes the principle that I've just enunciated, because we cannot leave the situation as it is today.

[9.] Q. Mr. President, in the event that your strong efforts to reach a neutral Laos go unheeded, would you possibly consider it necessary then for SEATO to intervene, or would you spell out a little more clearly what would have to take place?

THE PRESIDENT. I think a careful reading of my statement makes clear what the various prospects are and the critical nature of them.

[10.] Q. Mr. President, your foreign aid message, particularly the provision for long-term borrowing, has had a rather mixed reception on the Hill. I wonder, sir, could you tell us, in view of the traditional congressional abhorrence of long-term commitments, what steps you are planning to persuade the country that this is necessary?

THE PRESIDENT. Well, I think that it provides far more effective use of the funds that are available. It's very hard for us to say to x country that "We are prepared to join you in economic development if you will make the following contributions towards your own development: investment, tax changes, and all the rest," if we are only able to say that we can do this only on a 12-month basis. If we could say "We will join on a 5-month—over a 5-year period of development for the economy of this country which will give you some hope of improving the standard of living of your people and maintaining freedom," it seems to me that's a far more effective use of our money.

One of the reasons why so much money, I think, has been wasted in mutual security programs in recent years has been because they are financed on a year-to-year basis and no evident progress is made within the countries towards a viable economy. So that I must say that I recognize that the Congress has clear responsibilities for annual appropriations. We are only talking about long-term funding for loans. The Congress would still continue to have its annual appropriations for any other funds, including those which involve military grants. And I would feel that the kind of program we suggested offers the best use of the dollar in these areas. I think progress can be made this way. If we don't get it, I think we'll

continue to see some of the drift we've seen in these programs in the past.

[11.] Q. Mr. President, what are your plans for coordinating our transportation to save the railroads and keep them running, especially to move missiles?

THE PRESIDENT. I think—I've seen no evidences that the missile, the movement of missiles has been—is endangered at the present time or in prospect. The problem of commuters, the problem of the financial integrity of the railroads and their movement is in danger—is in critical position in some areas. It's a matter of concern to the Congress and this administration and we are examining what we can usefully do.

[12.] Q. Mr. President, during the campaign you made a pledge, I believe, that if you became President you would issue an Executive order to ban segregation in Federal housing projects. I wondered if you had any plans to implement that pledge anytime in the near future?

THE PRESIDENT. We are considering those areas. We've already, as you know, in one area, the area of employment by Government contractors, issued an extremely strong, the strongest Federal order that's ever been issued, with detailed facilities for implementation. We are considering other Executive orders that could be usefully issued. In addition, we are—the Department of Justice is moving ahead in carrying out the congressional mandate in regard to voting. So this matter of use of Executive authority in order to establish equality of opportunity in all areas is a matter which will have the continuing attention of this administration.

[13.] Q. Mr. President, taking the aggressive Communist attitude on Laos together with the negative Russian posture at the opening, the reopening of negotiations in Geneva on test ban, does this combination of circumstances disappoint you about the prospect of really improved relations with the Soviet Union?

THE PRESIDENT. I am hopeful that it will be possible for the United States to make progress towards lessening tension in our relations with the Soviet Union. Quite obviously this is a critical area, and I think the kind of response that we get to our efforts for peace in this area will tell us something about what kind of a future our world is going to have. We'll have to wait and see what that response will be, and then I could perhaps give you a better answer as to what our long-range prospects will be after we see what happens here.

Q. Mr. President, if these responses aren't forthcoming and aren't favorable on your proposals here, would you—and we have to shoot—would you use your Executive orders and authority, or is the purpose of Mr. Rusk going to the Senators in preparation of asking for a declaration of war in case it really becomes a shooting matter out there?

THE PRESIDENT. I think that it would be best to consider it as I stated it in my statement. The prospects, alternative responsibilities—I've stated them, I think, as clearly as today they can be stated. We will know a good deal more in the coming days.

[14.] Q. Mr. President, concerning another aspect of this Communist threat, Russia and Red China publish an estimated 3 to 4 billion books a year, sending a large proportion to the noncommitted nations, and an AP story says that our USIA was able to send only a trifling fraction to these countries—last year, I guess less than 5 million. Does this book gap—doesn't this present a tremendous obstacle to our winning the minds of the uncommitted peoples, and does our administration plan to close this gap?

THE PRESIDENT. Well, I agree that both the Chinese Communists and the Russians have poured large sums of money into subsidizing cheap book publications which have poured into many sections of the world and is a matter of concern. I think the point is excellent. Mr. Murrow has been considering what we could do in an expanded way in this area. There are other areas where they've also made a greater effort, radio broadcasts to Africa and so on as well as exchanges. So that we have the whole problem, of which books is a part, in this struggle between freedom and control.

[15.] Q. Mr. President, I have a question about conventional forces in relation to the Laos situation. You have been reviewing the recommendations of your Secretary of Defense on conventional forces. Have you come to any decision on building them up, and have you found them adequate to deal with the Laos situation in case of——

THE PRESIDENT. We will be sending a message on Monday or Tuesday on those changes we are going to make in defense and at that time we'll give, I think, a more adequate response than I could give here to your question, because we're going to discuss the entire military budget. Quite obviously, we are stretched around the world with commitments to dozens of countries and it does raise the question of our— whether a greater effort should not be made.

Q. Mr. President, could you tell us what in your opinion this country has obtained out of its roughly $310 million worth of aid sent in the past 6 or 7 years to Laos?

THE PRESIDENT. Well, Laos is not yet a Communist country and it's my hope that it will not be.

[16.] Q. Mr. President, are you contemplating a further—a meeting with Soviet Foreign Minister Gromyko within the next week or have you one scheduled with him?

THE PRESIDENT. A further meeting? I've

not seen Mr. Gromyko.

Q. *A* meeting.

THE PRESIDENT. No, I have no plans for a meeting.

[17.] Q. Mr. President, because it was such an obvious move, could you tell us what Mr. Salinger handed you just then? [*Laughter*]

THE PRESIDENT. Well, he handed me—I will not draw the cloak of Executive privilege around it. The point was made that Viet-Nam—these are the sort of things he knows—that Viet-Nam is not a signatory of the SEATO Pact, but is a protocol country of—under the SEATO Pact. [*Laughter*]

[18.] Q. Mr. President, do you agree with Secretary Dillon's estimate that the corporate profits for fiscal '62 will be about $3 billion under President Eisenhower's

estimate, and, if so, will your budget take these lower revenue estimates into account?

THE PRESIDENT. The budget estimates will be lower than were estimated in January, substantially lower than they were last October, and a good deal lower than they were estimated to be a year ago. We are sending a budget message up tomorrow which gives our opinion on what those receipts will be. But the economy, as it has slowed down, of course, the profit squeeze has been on, and the returns to the Government have been lessened, which have affected the budget picture.

Reporter: Thank you, Mr. President.

NOTE: President Kennedy's eighth news conference was held in the State Department Auditorium at 6 o'clock on Thursday evening, March 23, 1961.

93   Statement by the President Upon Signing the Temporary Extended Unemployment Compensation Act.   *March* 24, 1961

THE TEMPORARY Extended Unemployment Compensation Act of 1961, which I have just signed into law, is the first major bill proposed by this Administration to deal with the present recession which has passed the Congress. This program will immediately provide economic help for some 700,000 jobless workers and their families whose rights to receive regular unemployment insurance benefits under State law are exhausted. Within the next year it will provide benefit payments to an additional two-and-a half-million workers who are expected to exhaust their benefits.

This Temporary Extended Unemployment Compensation Act will add almost a billion dollars to the nation's purchasing power in the next fifteen months. These dollars will be hard-working dollars. They will be spent almost immediately—for food,

for shelter, for the bare necessities. These dollars will flow into our stores, into our factories, onto our farms.

This Act is important because it will provide much needed help to over 3 million American workers and their families. It is important also because it will add hard-working dollars to the nation's purchasing power. But important as it is, it is but a temporary measure to alleviate an immediate need. We must move forward with other and more permanent programs to invigorate our economy so that our free enterprise system can reach the level of production and employment which is its obligation and which its capacity and tradition promise.

NOTE: The Temporary Extended Unemployment Compensation Act of 1961 is Public Law 87–6 (75 Stat. 8).

94   Special Message to the Congress on Budget and Fiscal Policy. *March 24, 1961*

To the Congress of the United States:

I. BASIC FISCAL POLICIES

This Administration intends to adhere during the course of its term of office to the following basic principles:

(1) Federal revenue and expenditures levels must be adequate to meet effectively and efficiently those essential needs of the nation which require public support as well as, or in place of, private effort. We can afford to do what must be done, publicly and privately, up to the limit of our economic capacity—a limit we have not even approached for several years.

(2) Federal revenues and expenditures—the Federal Budget—should, apart from any threat to national security, be in balance over the years of the business cycle—running a deficit in years of recession when revenues decline and the economy needs the stimulus of additional expenditures—and running a surplus in years of prosperity, thus curbing inflation, reducing the public debt, and freeing funds for private investment.

(3) Federal expenditure and revenue programs should contribute to economic growth and maximum employment within a setting of reasonable price stability. Because of the limits which our balance of payments deficit currently places upon the use of monetary policy, especially the lowering of short-term interest rates, as a means of stimulating economic growth and employment, fiscal policy—our budget and tax policies—must assume a heavier share of the responsibility.

(4) Each expenditure proposed will be evaluated in terms of our national needs and priorities, consistent with the limita-tions and objectives described above and compared with the urgency of other budgetary requirements. We will not waste our resources on inefficient or undesirable expenditure simply because the economy is slack—nor, in order to run a surplus, will we deny our people essential services or security simply because the economy is prosperous.

(5) As the nation, its needs and their complexity continue to grow, Federal non-defense expenditures may also be expected to increase, as predicted by a 1960 Bureau of the Budget study, and as indicated by the nearly 45% increase from fiscal 1953 to fiscal 1961 in expenditures other than national security. But we must not allow expenditures to rise of their own momentum, without regard to value received, prospective revenues, economic conditions, the possibilities of closing out old activities when initiating new ones, and the weight of current taxes on the individual citizen and the economy. It is my determined purpose to be a prudent steward of the public funds—to obtain a dollar's worth of results for every dollar we spend.

II. THE FISCAL 1961 BUDGET INHERITED BY THIS ADMINISTRATION

While this Message is concerned primarily with the Budget for fiscal 1962 now before the Congress, necessary perspective and background are supplied by a re-examination of the fiscal 1961 Budget, adopted by the Congress last year, reviewed in my predecessor's January Budget Message and inherited in its final stage by this Administration.

When originally submitted in January of

1960, the Fiscal 1961 Budget showed a surplus of $4.2 billion. By the time of the mid-year Budget Review, the estimated surplus had shrunk to $1.1 billion. In the final Budget Message in January, it was estimated to be less than $80 million. Without any change in substantive content or policy, that Budget upon later examination proved to be substantially out of balance. These changes reflect the Recession—induced decline in revenues as well as the difficulty always present in making Budget and economic forecasts. The January restatement of the 1961 Budget, simply in terms of its own programs and estimates and without regard to any new decisions or policies by this Administration.

—Optimistically estimated fiscal 1961 tax revenues by assuming a much rosier economy;

—Unrealistically assumed that the Congress would enact a record (though necessary) postal rate increase totalling some $843 million a year in time to take effect April first and provide $160 million additional in the current fiscal year;

—Substantially underestimated the normal flow of defense expenditures under the then-existing policies and commitments by at least half a billion dollars; and

—Similarly underestimated the amount of funds which would be required to pay unemployment benefits to ex-servicemen and Federal employees, to meet the demand for authorized veterans' housing loans, and to fulfill the existing commitments of the Export-Import Bank.

The deficit thus inherited by this Administration for fiscal 1961, augmented by the essential anti-recession and national security steps already taken or recommended to the Congress, is now estimated to total over $2 billion (in contrast with the $4.2 billion surplus originally predicted). But it must be remembered that fiscal 1961 is clearly a recession year, with all of the consequent effects upon both revenues and expenditures. The deficit of nearly $12.5 billion in fiscal 1959 serves as a recent reminder of the difficulties of balancing the budget in a recession year.

III. BALANCING THE BUDGET FOR FISCAL 1962

On January 30th I made the following pledge to the Congress:

". . . a new Administration must of necessity build on the spending and revenue estimates already submitted. Within that framework, barring the development of urgent national defense needs or a worsening economy, it is my current intention to advocate a program of expenditures which, including revenue from a stimulation of the economy, will not of and by themselves unbalance the earlier Budget."

This message is designed to review my recommended budgetary revisions within the framework of that pledge. Omitting any increase in the defense budget too urgent to be denied by budgetary restrictions, and assuming that our review of the economy late in April does not require either a reduction in taxes or additional increases in expenditures, enactment of the new non-defense programs and appropriations I have transmitted will not unbalance the Budget previously submitted by my predecessor.

—if the Congress enacts or continues in effect all the revenue measures requested in that earlier Budget, or preferably the alternative measures that I am requesting to achieve the same amount of revenue;

—if that earlier Budget contained accurate

estimates of the revenue to be produced by those measures, based on accurate assumptions about prospective economic conditions;

—if the Congress enacts no spending measures committing the Executive Branch to outlays in excess of those requested; and

—if the earlier Budget contained accurate estimates of those expenditures which must necessarily be incurred in fiscal 1962 under existing commitments covered by that Budget, regardless of Congressional or Executive decisions—for example, entirely apart from any policy changes, a large proportion of the Department of Agriculture Budget depends upon the effects of economic, crop and weather conditions which must be predicted in advance.

I have already indicated in my message on the State of the Union that my predecessor's Budget for fiscal 1962 "will remain in balance only if . . . an earlier and sharper up-turn in the economy than my economic advisers now think likely produces the tax revenues estimated." Nevertheless the present message, and the fiscal 1962 Budget revisions it summarizes, are based upon a commitment of balancing revenue and expenditures under an assumption that the January predictions with respect to these four conditions are a valid starting basis for a new Administration.

The point I wish to stress in this message is that any Budgetary unbalance at the close of fiscal 1962 will not be the result of any non-defense programs I have submitted, for they have been carefully limited to a pattern of expenditures no greater than the revenues estimated by the earlier Budget, as supplemented by those additional revenues which enactment of this program can reasonably be expected to stimulate, according to Treasury estimates, in fiscal 1962. Other measures I have requested—such as improve-

ments in unemployment compensation, highway construction, Social Security, and health insurance for the aged—are all accompanied by their own self-financing provisions. In short, new defense recommendations aside, should there be a deficit in 1962, it will be the consequence of the over-estimation of revenues and under-estimation of expenditures in the January budget, and not the result of new policies or programs proposed by this Administration.

In summary, the total expenditures estimated in the January budget were $80.9 billion. My proposals, apart from Defense, will add about $2.3 billion for a total of $83.2 billion. The effects of my economic program on the economy would be reflected in additional revenues of about $900 million which, added to the January budget figures, would make a total of $83.2 billion of receipts, and leave the Budget in balance.

At the same time, it would be unrealistic to fail to recognize that the January Budget estimate of receipts was over-optimistic. Based on a more realistic economic outlook and including the effect of my economic proposals, it appears more likely that the revenues for fiscal year 1962 will be about $81.4 billion. However, as the economy returns to satisfactory high levels of economic activity, the position of budget balance will be restored. Indeed, given full recovery, the present tax system would generate revenues substantially in excess of the proposed levels of budget expenditure. This, then, is the revised budget—apart from defense additions—that I now present to the Congress:

—a budget that is in balance in terms of my pledge of January 30;

—a budget that is likely to be in deficit unless economic conditions rapidly improve to meet the levels predicted in the January 16th Budget;

—a budget that would be in surplus if the economy were operating at or near its full potential.

IV. OMISSIONS AND ASSUMPTIONS IN THE
PREVIOUS BUDGET FOR FISCAL 1962

For Fiscal 1962, however, the January Budget submitted by my predecessor assumed a higher rate of economic activity during this calendar year than is presently in sight, and thus a balanced budget. As already stated, that earlier Budget and its assumptions are necessarily the starting point for a new administration. It was on this basis that I made to the Congress on January 30 the commitment quoted earlier in this Message.

But before any new programs or budget increases could even be considered by this Administration—and wholly apart from the overly optimistic economic assumptions of the January Budget—we found upon a closer scrutiny of that Budget that it omitted provision for substantial expenditures for which that Administration was committed, and was based upon fundamental policy and program assumptions which neither this Administration nor the Congress could possibly accept, and which had to be altered at considerable cost to what little budgetary leeway remained.

For example:

(1) The previous administration committed itself, as we have also, to extend $100 million in assistance to Chile for reconstruction and rehabilitation in the wake of a devastating earthquake. But no estimate of expenditures to meet this commitment was included in the Budget.

(2) The earlier Budget recommended, as I do also, the construction of a new $114 million linear electron accelerator for high energy physics research. But appropriations to initiate this project were not specifically recommended in the Budget.

(3) The earlier Budget based its estimate of expenditures for the Department of Agriculture's Commodity Credit Corporation on the assumption that price supports on every major commodity would be reduced to the lowest level permitted by law—reductions which were never formally recommended by the then Secretary of Agriculture, which would never be permitted by the Congress and which would have been absolutely ruinous to our farm economy. Without having to actually take such a move, the earlier Budget assumed a reduction of cotton price supports from 75% to 70% of parity, a reduction of milk from 80% to 76%, rice from 75% to 70% and peanuts from 78.6% to 75%. Compared to the average levels of the last five years, which indicate how far the former Secretary of Agriculture was actually able and willing to push supports down when in office, these recommendations are down some 9.3 parity points for cotton, 5.5 for peanuts, 2.4 for milk and 7.9 for rice.

(4) The earlier Budget recommended a program of Federal aid to public schools, limited to aid for construction. But, under a highly unusual fiscal proposal, the Budget itself included practically no expenditures for this activity. Instead it proposed that states and localities float loans which Federal taxpayers would help pay off through installment payments of school bond interest as well as principal over the next 30 years.

(5) Similarly, aid to higher education was contained in the earlier program, as in mine. But again the effect on that Budget was deferred by the device of a 20–35 year period of installment payments.

(6) The earlier Budget assumed, completely contrary to our urban and economic needs, Congressional termination of the

Federal farm housing loan programs; no new authority for low-income housing; a cut-back in veterans' and college housing loans; and no expansion in urban renewal. In short, before funds could be found to finance new and urgently needed housing programs, merely meeting the needs of existing programs required further additions to the Budget.

(7) The Federal Government, under the previous Administration as well as this, has an obligation to meet the educational needs of Indian children on reservations. The fact is that several thousand such children in New Mexico, Arizona and Alaska have been without any schools at all—but wholly inadequate funds to meet this obligation were included in the earlier Budget.

(8) The earlier Budget proposed that the Congress would cut back sharply on its program for constructing airports, on the electric and telephone loan programs of the REA and on the loan programs of the Farmers Home Administration. I do not believe the Congress would have or should now cut back these essential programs, and I have recommended their expansion.

V. CHANGES IN THE FISCAL 1962 BUDGET

This Message is not intended to present a wholly new budget. For reasons already stated that is not possible for this fiscal year. Nor is it intended to propose any new programs or expenditures in the non-defense area. With but a few exceptions, the items covered by this message and the attached table have been previously communicated, with full explanation, to the Congress. This message is primarily intended to share with the Congress my review of the non-defense changes in Federal activities and expenditures already recommended to meet our nation's needs.

The funds previously recommended for each Department and Agency have been scrutinized as carefully as time would permit, from the viewpoint of both the needs of the nation and the adequacy and efficiency with which these needs are being met. With the exception of the national defense program, that review is now largely complete, and the new programs and amendments resulting therefrom have been transmitted to the Congress or will be shortly.

As already emphasized, these changes of themselves will not unbalance the earlier budget—i.e., their cost in fiscal 1962, assuming the accuracy of the previous expenditure estimates, will be covered by the revenue previously estimated and the new revenues generated by the program. But despite this restraint and the further limitations imposed by the assumptions or omissions already mentioned, these changes nevertheless represent what we regard to be advances in areas of high priority. While the entire list is summarized on the attached table, among the most significant are the following:

Aid to Education. The largest single increase is in the field of education. Our educational needs have become too urgent to overlook. The Federal Government must do more to help finance improvements in this field—both for elementary and secondary education, and for higher education.

Funds for Scientific Research. My recommendations, largely in the form of amendments to the 1962 budget, provide a series of increases for scientific research—for oceanography, for high energy physics, for saline water conversion, for medical research, for National Science Foundation grants for basic research and science education, and for various other purposes. These increases reflect my strong belief that advances in scientific research are of the utmost importance to the growth of our economy, to the welfare of our people, and to the pre-eminence of our scientific achievements, and my conviction that the Federal Government must of necessity play a sizeable role in supporting such research.

Health. I have proposed significant measures to strengthen, improve and lower the cost of health care—with self-financed health insurance for the aged under Social Security at a net savings to the Budget, assistance to medical schools and students, and grants to the States for expanded community health services and facilities.

Housing and Community Development. I have recommended enactment of a program designed to greatly strengthen urban renewal and other existing programs, and add needed new authority in such important areas as moderate-income housing, rehabilitation and improvement of existing housing, and the preservation of open spaces. We are also obliged to increase Federal assistance for local airport construction. The additional expenditures thus entailed, in my judgment, are necessary in our Nation's future.

Area Redevelopment. The tragedy of our chronically depressed areas, and the enormity of their challenge to our economy, require no less than the very reasonable program for aid to depressed areas which I have recommended and which I am confident that the Congress will soon enact.

Natural Resource Development. It is not economical to be foolishly wasteful rather than prudently conservationist toward the country's natural resources. I have proposed modest but symbolic increases in funds for conservation and development of forests and public domain lands, for the national park system and seashore recreational areas, and for navigation and flood control activities; and reprogramming of other funds will permit additional reclamation activities.

Agriculture. In the field of Agriculture we propose to move vigorously in a wholly new direction, to alter fundamentally the pattern of the Nation's agricultural economy with an eventual reduction of governmental outlays. Meanwhile, in the short run, it is necessary to take various actions which will increase the 1962 expenditures over those seriously understated in the January budget, as already discussed. The increases are for price supports, Rural Electrification Administration and Farmers' Home Administration loans, the school lunch program and special milk program, and surplus food distribution at home and abroad. These expenditures will raise farm income and increase the use of our surplus agricultural commodities.

Veterans. I am recommending that the Congress enact a selective increase in compensation rates for veterans with the more severe service-connected disabilities, to offset rises in the cost of living since the last increase in 1957 and to adjust rates in some categories which are out of line. My budget estimates include provision for this purpose.

Budgetary Transfer Authority. To achieve greater effectiveness and savings in the use of the taxpayers' funds, the heads of the several Government Departments and agencies should have the authority to exercise some flexibility in the course of a fiscal year to meet new situations or changing circumstances. Therefore, I am asking the Congress, in enacting appropriations for each Department and agency, to provide the necessary authority for the transfer of a modest amount or percentage of the funds and personnel available to an agency head for operating expenses, to be used only as needed to meet unforeseen high priority requirements, and to be controlled by the Bureau of the Budget through the regular budgetary apportionment process. In this way, the funds appropriated by the Congress can be utilized with the utmost efficiency.

VI. FEDERAL REVENUES

Mention has already been made of the revenue estimates for fiscal 1962 and the necessity for Congressional enactment of all measures necessary to produce those revenues. My earlier message on Highways contained recommendations for the user taxes needed to assure a satisfactory rate of progress on highway construction at levels previously recommended by my predecessor. This Administration will not permit funds for this program to be diverted from general revenues. Other tax recommendations, designed to stimulate modernization of plant and equipment, and to achieve greater tax equity without any material change in over-all revenues, will be contained in a subsequent message.

Three additional points are more appropriately contained in this message:

(1) *Postal Rates.* The January Budget submitted by my predecessor called for an additional $843 million in postal revenues to eliminate the deficit in that Department's operations. Such an increase must be effective July 1 to close the gap between postal expenditures and postal revenues; and, building on the previous Budget, this Administration's Budget requires an equal amount. I urge the Congress to close this gap; and I have directed the Postmaster General to review carefully and intensively all services and activities of the Post Office with a view toward improving efficiency and reducing costs.

(2) *Tax Enforcement.* I want to re-emphasize my earlier request to the Congress for additional funds for the Internal Revenue Service. More and better qualified agents can both increase the collection of Federal revenues and help curb corruption in and out of government, racketeering and organized crime.

(3) *The Debt Limit.* My predecessor's message in January, even in assuming balanced budgets in both fiscal 1961 and 1962, pointed to the seasonal pattern of tax collections as necessitating another increase in the debt limit. The permanent debt limit of $285 billion, presently exceeded, has been superseded by a temporary limit of $293 billion which expires next June 30.

Inasmuch as the federal debt will exceed $285 billion on June 30th, a new increase in the ceiling will be required before that date.

I urge the Congress to enact an increase that will provide sufficient flexibility to permit sound management of the debt and of our budget expenditures. I am delaying the specific recommendation until early May so that we may have the advantage of the very latest estimates of revenues and expenditures.

CONCLUSION

This message reviews the current budget outlook and describes my philosophy concerning budget and fiscal policy. We seek to achieve the vigorous and sustained growth of the economy that will make possible a balance in the Federal budget. If we use our fiscal resources wisely, we can make tangible progress toward the achievement of our national and international objectives. Toward this end, I ask the cooperation of the Congress and the American people.

JOHN F. KENNEDY

NOTE: The table submitted with the President's message, showing changes in the 1962 budget and estimated receipts, is printed in House Document 120 (87th Cong., 1st sess.).

95 Statement by the President on the Inter-American Development Bank. *March* 25, 1961

I MET THIS MORNING with Dr. Felipe Herrera, President of the Inter-American Development Bank, and Robert Cutler, the United States Director. We discussed the role of the Bank in helping to carry out the Alliance for Progress. Dr. Herrera informed me of the Bank's current programs as well as the policies that will guide its future activities.

I am convinced that the Inter-American Bank will play a vital role in the development of the hemisphere. It certainly will be one of the major instruments of our own effort; and the Latin American nations themselves have already indicated their willingness to use the Bank as a principal force in the implementation of the Alliance for Progress. Thus this liberal and progressive institution guided, as it is, by men with a deep understanding of the problems of Latin America can be of major assistance in fulfilling the hemisphere's desire for social change and economic progress.

96 Telegram to the Kenosha, Wisconsin, Housing Authority Concerning an Action for the Eviction of Needy Families. *March* 26, 1961

[Released March 26, 1961. Dated March 25, 1961]

Kenosha Housing Authority
Kenosha, Wisconsin

I have had brought to my attention your pending court action to evict 40 families. I will appreciate every possible effort being made to provide alternative temporary housing for these needy families without means to find other quarters. I understand the plight of some of those being evicted is most unfortunate and that they can still be provided for consistent with step-by-step private development of the property. In order to be of every possible assistance, I have today directed the Federal Housing and Home Finance Agency that the loan previously approved for you to build new public housing facilities be made available promptly upon your optioning a site. In the midst of the present economic downturn and widespread unemployment, I hope that diligent efforts will be made in every community in the nation to avoid eviction of families genuinely in need and seeking to the extent of their means to meet their obligations. Understanding and real help is needed on their behalf by all of us.

JOHN F. KENNEDY

97 Joint Statement With Prime Minister Macmillan Following an Exchange of Views on Laos. *March* 26, 1961

PRESIDENT KENNEDY and Prime Minister Macmillan have had a most valuable exchange of views about the situation in Laos. This will be of great assistance to the representatives of the two countries in the discussions at the SEATO meeting which is due to begin in Bangkok tomorrow.

They agree that the situation in Laos cannot be allowed to deteriorate.

They also agree that the recent British note to the Soviet Union contains proposals which, if implemented, would bring to an end the warfare in Laos and would pave the way for Laos to become the truly neutral country, which it is their joint wish to see.

They strongly hope, therefore, that the Soviet Union will make a positive and constructive reply to these proposals.

NOTE: The joint statement was released at Key West, Fla.

98   Letter to the Chairman, Tennessee Valley Authority, on the Labor Surplus Problem in the Valley Area.   *March 27, 1961*

[Released March 27, 1961.   Dated March 25, 1961]

Dear Mr. Vogel:

I have your letter of March 17th and have studied the reasons which led the TVA Board to locate its new steam plant at the Edgemoor site. The main one you cite— the capital saving of $30 million—would seem to provide a firm base for your decision.

I am of course anxious to utilize every weapon of government to attack the labor surplus problem in places like East Kentucky. The TVA is in the business of resource development and I want to feel that in your future thinking on the continuing problems of the valley region, you will be giving thought to the problems which go beyond the production and sale of power.

We need much creative thinking in this area and the TVA has stood in the past for original and bold thinking. This vigorous and imaginative momentum must be continued.

Sincerely yours,

JOHN F. KENNEDY

[Herbert D. Vogel, Chairman, Board of Directors, Tennessee Valley Authority, Knoxville, Tennessee]

NOTE: Mr. Vogel's letter was released with the President's reply.

99   Special Message to the Congress on the Defense Budget.   *March 28, 1961*

To the Congress of the United States:

In my role as Commander-in-Chief of the American Armed Forces, and with my concern over the security of this nation now and in the future, no single question of policy has concerned me more since entering upon these responsibilities than the adequacy of our present and planned military forces to accomplish our major national security objectives.

In January, while ordering certain immediately needed changes, I instructed the Secretary of Defense to reappraise our entire defense strategy, capacity, commitments and needs in the light of present and future dangers. The Secretary of State and others have been consulted in this reappraisal, and I have myself carefully reviewed their reports and advice.

Such a review is obviously a tremendous task and it still continues. But circumstances do not permit a postponement of all further action during the many additional months that a full reappraisal will require. Consequently we are now able to present the most urgent and obvious recommendations for inclusion in the fiscal 1962 Budget.

Meaningful defense budget decisions, however, are not possible without preliminary decisions on defense policy, reflecting both current strategic assumptions and certain fundamental principles. These basic policies or principles, as stated below, will constitute the essential guidelines and standards to be followed by all civilian and military personnel who work on behalf of our nation's security. The Budget which follows, if enacted by the Congress under its own solemn duty "to provide for the common defense," is designed to implement these assumptions as we now see them, and to chart a fresh, clear course for our security in a time of rising dangers and persistent hope.

I. BASIC DEFENSE POLICIES

1. The primary purpose of our arms is peace, not war—to make certain that they will never have to be used—to deter all wars, general or limited, nuclear or conventional, large or small—to convince all potential aggressors that any attack would be futile—to provide backing for diplomatic settlement of disputes—to insure the adequacy of our bargaining power for an end to the arms race. The basic problems facing the world today are not susceptible to a military solution. Neither our strategy nor our psychology as a nation—and certainly not our economy—must become dependent upon the permanent maintenance of a large military establishment. Our military posture must be sufficiently flexible and under control to be consistent with our efforts to explore all possibilities and to take every step to lessen tensions, to obtain peaceful solutions and to secure arms limitations. Diplomacy and defense are no longer distinct alternatives, one to be used where the other fails—both must complement each other.

Disarmament, so difficult and so urgent, has been much discussed since 1945, but progress has not been made. Recrimination in such matters is seldom useful, and we for our part are determined to try again. In so doing, we note that, in the public position of both sides in recent years, the determination to be strong has been coupled with announced willingness to negotiate. For our part, we know there can be dialectical truth in such a position, and we shall do all we can to prove it in action. This budget is wholly consistent with our earnest desire for serious conversation with the other side on disarmament. If genuine progress is made, then as tension is reduced, so will be our arms.

2. Our arms will never be used to strike the first blow in any attack. This is not a confession of weakness but a statement of strength. It is our national tradition. We must offset whatever advantage this may appear to hand an aggressor by so increasing the capability of our forces to respond swiftly and effectively to any aggressive move as to convince any would-be aggressor that such a movement would be too futile and costly to undertake. In the area of general war, this doctrine means that such capability must rest with that portion of our forces which would survive the initial attack. We are not creating forces for a first strike against any other nation. We shall never threaten, provoke or initiate aggression—but if aggression should come, our response will be swift and effective.

3. Our arms must be adequate to meet our commitments and ensure our security, without being bound by arbitrary budget

ceilings. This nation can afford to be strong—it cannot afford to be weak. We shall do what is needed to make and to keep us strong. We must, of course, take advantage of every opportunity to reduce military outlays as a result of scientific or managerial progress, new strategic concepts, a more efficient, manageable and thus more effective defense establishment, or international agreements for the control and limitation of arms. But we must not shrink from additional costs where they are necessary. The additional $650 million in expenditures for fiscal 1962 which I am recommending today, while relatively small, are too urgent to be governed by a budget largely decided before our defense review had been completed. Indeed, in the long run the net effect of all the changes I am recommending will be to provide a more economical budget. But I cannot promise that in later years we need not be prepared to spend still more for what is indispensable. Much depends on the course followed by other nations. As a proportion of gross national product, as a share of our total Budget, and in comparison with our national effort in earlier times of war, this increase in Defense expenditures is still substantially below what our citizens have been willing and are now able to support as insurance on their security—insurance we hope is never needed—but insurance we must nevertheless purchase.

4. Our arms must be subject to ultimate civilian control and command at all times, in war as well as peace. The basic decisions on our participation in any conflict and our response to any threat—including all decisions relating to the use of nuclear weapons, or the escalation of a small war into a large one—will be made by the regularly constituted civilian authorities. This requires effective and protected organiza-

tion, procedures, facilities and communication in the event of attack directed toward this objective, as well as defensive measures designed to insure thoughtful and selective decisions by the civilian authorities. This message and budget also reflect that basic principle. The Secretary of Defense and I have had the earnest counsel of our senior military advisers and many others—and in fact they support the great majority of the decisions reflected in this Budget. But I have not delegated to anyone else the responsibilities for decision which are imposed upon me by the Constitution.

5. Our strategic arms and defenses must be adequate to deter any deliberate nuclear attack on the United States or our allies—by making clear to any potential aggressor that sufficient retaliatory forces will be able to survive a first strike and penetrate his defenses in order to inflict unacceptable losses upon him. As I indicated in an address to the Senate some 31 months ago, this deterrence does not depend upon a simple comparison of missiles on hand before an attack. It has been publicly acknowledged for several years that this nation has not led the world in missile strength. Moreover, we will not strike first in any conflict. But what we have and must continue to have is the ability to survive a first blow and respond with devastating power. This deterrent power depends not only on the number of our missiles and bombers, but on their state of readiness, their ability to survive attack, and the flexibility and sureness with which we can control them to achieve our national purpose and strategic objectives.

6. The strength and deployment of our forces in combination with those of our allies should be sufficiently powerful and mobile to prevent the steady erosion of the Free World through limited wars; and it is

this role that should constitute the primary mission of our overseas forces. Non-nuclear wars, and sub-limited or guerrilla warfare, have since 1945 constituted the most active and constant threat to Free World security. Those units of our forces which are stationed overseas, or designed to fight overseas, can be most usefully oriented toward deterring or confining those conflicts which do not justify and must not lead to a general nuclear attack. In the event of a major aggression that could not be repulsed by conventional forces, we must be prepared to take whatever action with whatever weapons are appropriate. But our objective now is to increase our ability to confine our response to non-nuclear weapons, and to lessen the incentive for any limited aggression by making clear what our response will accomplish. In most areas of the world, the main burden of local defense against overt attack, subversion and guerrilla warfare must rest on local populations and forces. But given the great likelihood and seriousness of this threat, we must be prepared to make a substantial contribution in the form of strong, highly mobile forces trained in this type of warfare, some of which must be deployed in forward areas, with a substantial airlift and sealift capacity and prestocked overseas bases.

7. Our defense posture must be both flexible and determined. Any potential aggressor contemplating an attack on any part of the Free World with any kind of weapons, conventional or nuclear, must know that our response will be suitable, selective, swift and effective. While he may be uncertain of its exact nature and location, there must be no uncertainty about our determination and capacity to take whatever steps are necessary to meet our obligations. We must be able to make deliberate choices in weapons and strategy, shift the tempo of our production and alter the direction of our forces to meet rapidly changing conditions or objectives at very short notice and under any circumstances. Our weapon systems must be usable in a manner permitting deliberation and discrimination as to timing, scope and targets in response to civilian authority; and our defenses must be secure against prolonged re-attack as well as a surprise first-strike. To purchase productive capacity and to initiate development programs that may never need to be used—as this Budget proposes—adopts an insurance policy of buying alternative future options.

8. Our defense posture must be designed to reduce the danger of irrational or unpremeditated general war—the danger of an unnecessary escalation of a small war into a large one, or of miscalculation or misinterpretation of an incident or enemy intention. Our diplomatic efforts to reach agreements on the prevention of surprise attack, an end to the spread of nuclear weapons—indeed all our efforts to end the arms race—are aimed at this objective. We shall strive for improved communication among all nations, to make clear our own intentions and resolution, and to prevent any nation from underestimating the response of any other, as has too often happened in the past. In addition our own military activities must be safeguarded against the possibility of inadvertent triggering incidents. But even more importantly, we must make certain that our retaliatory power does not rest on decisions made in ambiguous circumstances, or permit a catastrophic mistake.

It would not be appropriate at this time or in this message to either boast of our strength or dwell upon our needs and dangers. It is sufficient to say that the budgetary recommendations which follow, together with other policy, organizational and related changes and studies now underway administratively, are designed to provide for an increased strength, flexibility and control in our defense establishment in accordance with the above policies.

II. STRENGTHENING AND PROTECTING OUR STRATEGIC DETERRENT AND DEFENSES

A. *Improving our missile deterrent.* As a power which will never strike first, our hopes for anything close to an absolute deterrent must rest on weapons which come from hidden, moving, or invulnerable bases which will not be wiped out by a surprise attack. A retaliatory capacity based on adequate numbers of these weapons would deter any aggressor from launching or even threatening an attack—an attack he knew could not find or destroy enough of our force to prevent his own destruction.

1. *Polaris*—the ability of the nuclear-powered Polaris submarine to operate deep below the surface of the seas for long periods and to launch its ballistic, solid fuel nuclear-armed missiles while submerged gives this weapons system a very high degree of mobility and concealment, making it virtually immune to ballistic missile attack.

In the light of the high degree of success attained to date in its development, production and operation, I strongly recommend that the Polaris program be greatly expanded and accelerated. I have earlier directed the Department of Defense, as stated in my State of the Union Message, to increase the fiscal year 1961 program from 5 submarine starts to 10, and to accelerate the delivery of these and other Polaris submarines still under construction. This action will provide 5 more operational submarines about nine months earlier than previously planned.

For fiscal year 1962, I recommend the construction of 10 more Polaris submarines, making a total of 29, plus one additional tender. These 10 submarines, together with the 10 programmed for fiscal year 1961, are scheduled to be delivered at the rate of one a month or twelve a year, beginning in June 1963, compared with the previous rate of 5 a year. Under this schedule, a force of 29 Polaris submarines can be completed and at sea two months before the present program which called for 19 boats, and two years earlier than would be possible under the old 5-a-year rate. These 29 submarines, each with a full complement of missiles, will be a formidable deterrent force. The sooner they are on station, the safer we will be. And our emphasis upon a weapon distinguished primarily for its invulnerability is another demonstration of the fact that our posture as a nation is defensive and not aggressive.

I also recommend that the development of the long-range Polaris A-3 be accelerated in order to become available a year earlier at an eventual savings in the procurement of the A-2 system.

This longer range missile with improved penetration capability will greatly enhance the operational flexibility of the Polaris force and reduce its exposure to shore-based anti-submarine warfare measures. Finally, we must increase the allowance of Polaris missiles for practice firing to provide systematic "proving ground" data for determining and improving operational reliability.

The increases in this program, including $15 million in new obligational authority for additional crews, constitute the bulk of the budget increases—$1.34 billion in new obligational authority on a full funded basis, over a 4 year period though only $270 million in expenditures in fiscal 1962. I consider this a wise investment in our future.

2. *Minuteman*—another strategic missile

system which will play a major role in our deterrent force, with a high degree of survivability under ballistic missile attack, is the solid fuel Minuteman. This system is planned to be deployed in well-dispersed, hardened sites and, eventually, in a mobile mode on railroad cars. On the basis of the success of tests conducted to date and the importance of this system to our over-all strategy, I recommend the following steps:

(1) Certain design changes to improve the reliability, guidance accuracy, range and re-entry of this missile should be incorporated earlier than previously planned, by additional funding for research and development.

(2) A more generous allotment of missiles for practice firing should, as in the case of the Polaris, be provided to furnish more operational data sooner.

(3) The three mobile Minuteman squadrons funded in the January budget should be deferred for the time being and replaced by three more fixed-base squadrons (thus increasing the total number of missiles added by some two-thirds). Development work on the mobile version will continue.

(4) Minuteman capacity production should be doubled to enable us to move to still higher levels of strength more swiftly should future conditions warrant doubling our production. There are great uncertainties as to the future capabilities of others; as to the ultimate outcome of struggles now going on in many of the world's trouble spots; and as to future technological breakthroughs either by us or any other nation. In view of these major uncertainties, it is essential that, here again, we adopt an insurance philosophy and hedge our risks by buying options on alternative courses of action. We can reduce lead-time by providing, *now,* additional standby production capacity that may never need to be used, or

used only in part, and by constructing additional bases which events may prove could safely have been postponed to the next fiscal year. But that option is well worth the added cost.

Together, these recommendations for Minuteman will require the addition of $96 million in new obligational authority to the January budget estimate.

3. *Skybolt*—another type of missile less likely to be completely eliminated by enemy attack is the air-to-ground missile carried by a plane that can be off the ground before an attack commences. Skybolt is a long-range (1000 mile) air-launched, solid-fuel nuclear-warhead ballistic missile designed to be carried by the B–52 and the British V bombers. Its successful development and production may extend the useful life of our bombers into the missile age—and its range is far superior to the present Hound Dog missiles.

I recommend that an additional $50 million in new obligational authority be added to the 1962 budget to enable this program to go forward at an orderly rate.

B. *Protecting our bomber deterrent.* The considerably more rapid growth projected for our ballistic missile force does not eliminate the need for manned bombers—although no funds were included in the January budget for the further procurement of B–52 heavy bombers and B–58 medium bombers, and I do not propose any. Our existing bomber forces constitute our chief hope for deterring attack during this period prior to the completion of our missile expansion. However, only those planes that would not be destroyed on the ground in the event of a surprise attack striking their base can be considered sufficiently invulnerable to deter an aggressor.

I therefore recommend the following steps to protect our bomber deterrent:

1. *Airborne alert capacity.* That portion

of our force which is constantly in the air is clearly the least vulnerable portion. I am asking for the funds to continue the present level of indoctrination training flights, and to complete the stand-by capacity and materials needed to place one-eighth of our entire heavy bomber force on airborne alert at any time. I also strongly urge the re-enactment of Section 512(b) of the Department of Defense Appropriation Act for 1961, which authorizes the Secretary of Defense, if the President determines it is necessary, to provide for the cost of a full airborne alert as a deficiency expense approved by the Congress.

2. *Increased ground alert force and bomb alarms.* Strategic bombers standing by on a ground alert of 15 minutes can also have a high degree of survivability provided adequate and timely warning is available. I therefore recommended that the proportion of our B–52 and B–47 forces on ground alert should be increased until about half of our total force is on alert. In addition, bomb alarm detectors and bomb alarm signals should be installed at key warning and communication points and all SAC bases, to make certain that a dependable notification of any surprise attack cannot be eliminated. $45 million in new obligational authority will pay for all of these measures.

C. *Improving our continental defense and warning systems.* Because of the speed and destructiveness of the intercontinental ballistic missile and the secrecy with which it can be launched, timely warning of any potential attack is of crucial importance not only for preserving our population but also for preserving a sufficient portion of our military forces—thus deterring such an attack before it is launched. For any attacker knows that every additional minute gained means that a larger part of our retaliatory force can be launched before it can be de-

stroyed on the ground. We must assure ourselves, therefore, that every feasible action is being taken to provide such warning.

To supplement the Ballistic Missile Early Warning System (BMEWS), on which construction is now proceeding as fast as is practical, the satellite-borne Midas system, now under development, is designed to provide about 30 minutes of warning by detecting missiles immediately after launching. Together with BMEWS, Midas would greatly increase the assurance and reliability of timely warning. I recommend that an additional $60 million in new obligational authority be added to the 1962 budget to accelerate completion of the development phase of the Midas program, with the goal of achieving an operational system at an earlier date.

For the next several years at least, however, we shall have to continue to provide a defense against manned bomber attack. Such an attack is most likely to coincide with, or follow, a ballistic missile attack seeking to incapacitate our anti-bomber defense system. Measures must therefore be taken to enhance the ability of the air defense system to cope with a combined attack. I recommend $23 million in new obligational authority be added to the 1962 budget for this purpose.

D. *Improving the command and control of our strategic deterrent.* The basic policies stated at the beginning of this message lay new emphasis on improved command and control—more flexible, more selective, more deliberate, better protected and under ultimate civilian authority at all times. This requires not only the development and installation of new equipment and facilities, but, even more importantly, increased attention to all organizational and procedural arrangements for the President and others. The invulnerable and continuous command posts and communications centers provided in these recommendations (requiring an additional $16 million in new obligational authority) are only the beginning of a major but absolutely vital effort to achieve a truly unified, nationwide, indestructible system to insure high-level command, communication and control and a properly authorized response under any conditions.

E. There are a number of other space and research programs related to our stategic and continental air defense forces which I find require additional support. These include missile defense and penetration aids, Dynasoar, Advent, Defender, Discoverer and certain other programs. An additional $226 million in new obligational authority is requested to finance them.

III. STRENGTHENING OUR ABILITY TO DETER OR CONFINE LIMITED WARS

The Free World's security can be endangered not only by a nuclear attack, but also by being slowly nibbled away at the periphery, regardless of our strategic power, by forces of subversion, infiltration, intimidation, indirect or non-overt aggression, internal revolution, diplomatic blackmail, guerrilla warfare or a series of limited wars.

In this area of local wars, we must inevitably count on the cooperative efforts of other peoples and nations who share our concern. Indeed, their interests are more often directly engaged in such conflicts. The self-reliant are also those whom it is easiest to help—and for these reasons we must continue and reshape the Military Assistance Program which I have discussed earlier in my special message on foreign aid.

But to meet our own extensive commitments and needed improvements in conventional forces, I recommend the following:

A. *Strengthened capacity to meet limited and guerrilla warfare*—limited military adventures and threats to the security of the Free World that are not large enough to justify the label of "limited war." We need a greater ability to deal with guerrilla forces, insurrections, and subversion. Much of our effort to create guerrilla and antiguerrilla capabilities has in the past been aimed at general war. We must be ready now to deal with any size of force, including small externally supported bands of men; and we must help train local forces to be equally effective.

B. *Expanded research on non-nuclear weapons.* A few selected high priority areas—strategic systems, air defense and space—have received the overwhelming proportion of our defense research effort. Yet, technology promises great improvements in non-nuclear armaments as well; and it is important that we be in the forefront of these developments. What is needed are entirely new types of non-nuclear weapons and equipment—with increased fire-power, mobility and communications, and more suited to the kind of tasks our limited war forces will most likely be required to perform. I include here anti-submarine warfare as well as land and air operations. I recommend, therefore, an additional $122 million in new obligational authority to speed up current limited warfare research and development programs and to provide for the initiation of entirely new programs.

C. *Increased flexibility of conventional forces.* Our capacity to move forces in sizable numbers on short notice and to be able to support them in one or more crisis areas could avoid the need for a much larger commitment later. Following my earlier direction, the Secretary of Defense has taken steps both to accelerate and increase the production of airlift aircraft. A total of 129 new, longer range, modern airlift aircraft will be procured through fiscal year 1962, compared with the 50 previously programmed. An additional $172 million new obligational authority will be required in the 1962 budget to finance this expanded program.

These additional aircraft will help to meet our airlift requirements until the new specially designed, long-range, jet powered C–141 transport becomes available. A contractor for this program has been selected and active development work will soon be started. Adequate funds are already included in the January budget to finance this program through the coming fiscal year.

I am also recommending in this message $40 million in new obligational authority for the construction of an additional amphibious transport of a new type, increasing both the speed and the capability of Marine Corps sealift capacity; and $84 million in new obligational authority for an increase in the Navy's ship rehabilitation and modernization program, making possible an increase in the number of ship overhauls (as well as a higher level of naval aircraft maintenance).

But additional transport is not enough for quick flexibility. I am recommending $230 million in new obligational authority for increased procurement of such items as helicopters, rifles, modern non-nuclear weapons, electronics and communications equipment, improved ammunition for artillery and infantry weapons, and torpedoes. Some important new advances in ammunition and bombs can make a sizeable qualitative jump in our limited war capabilities.

D. *Increased non-nuclear capacities of fighter aircraft.* Manned aircraft will be needed even during the 1965–75 missile era for various limited war missions. Target recognition, destruction of all types of targets when extreme accuracy is required, and the control of air space over enemy territory will all continue to be tasks best performed by manned aircraft.

Expected phase-out of Navy and Air Force fighters by 1965, together with reduced numbers and increasing obsolescence of the remaining aircraft, make necessary the development of an advanced tactical fighter emphasizing non-nuclear capabilities. I am requesting $45 million in new obligational authority for this purpose.

Meanwhile, I am recommending $25 million in new obligational authority for the modification of the F–105 tactical fighter to improve its capability to handle conventionally armed ordnance items, and to increase its suitability for airstrips of all types of areas.

E. *Increased personnel, training and readiness for conventional forces.* I am recommending $39 million in new obligational authority for increases in Army personnel strength to expand guerrilla warfare units and round out other existing units, and an increase in the Marine Corps to bring it up closer to authorized strength levels. (In addition, personnel is being added to the Navy for Polaris crews, and to the Air Force for the ground alert expansion.) The sum of these personnel additions is 13,000 men. I am also recommending $25 million additional in new obligational authority for pay of retired personnel of the military forces.

But more personnel alone is not enough. I am recommending an additional $65 million in new obligational authority for increased readiness training of Army and Air Force units. These funds will provide for additional field training and mobility exercises for the Army and test exercises for the composite air strike forces and MATS unit. We recognize the role of exercises and deployments in demonstrating to our friends and opponents our ability to deploy forces rapidly in a crisis.

IV. SAVINGS MADE POSSIBLE BY PROGRESS

The elimination of waste, duplication and outmoded or unjustifiable expenditure items from the Defense Budget is a long and arduous undertaking, resisted by special arguments and interests from economic, military, technical and other special groups. There are hundreds of ways, most of them with some merit, for spending billions of dollars on defense; and it is understandable that every critic of this Budget will have a strong preference for economy on some expenditures other than those that affect his branch of the service, or his plant, or his community.

But hard decisions must be made. Unneeded facilities or projects must be phased out. The defense establishment must be lean and fit, efficient and effective, always adjusting to new opportunities and advances, and planning for the future. The national interest must be weighed against special or local interests; and it is the national interest that calls upon us to cut our losses and cut back those programs in which a very dim promise no longer justifies a very large cost.

Specifically:

1. Our decision to acquire a very substantial increase in second-generation solid-fuel missiles of increased invulnerability (Polaris and Minuteman) enables us to eliminate safely the last two squadrons of Titan originally contemplated. These would not have become operational until 1964, and at a cost of $270 million—a cost several times that of the Minuteman missiles we are purchasing for the same period and could increase with our stand-by facility. $100 million in the 1962 budget can be saved by this adjustment.

2. The phase-out of a number of B–47 medium bomber wings already planned will be accelerated to provide promptly the trained crews required for the expanded ground alert program. (Fiscal 1962 savings: $35 million.)

3. Additional personnel will also be made available by the immediate phase-out of the subsonic Snark airbreathing long-range missile, which is now considered obsolete and of marginal military value in view of ICBM developments, the Snark's low reliability and penetrability, the lack of positive control over its launchings, and the location of the entire wing at an unprotected site. (Fiscal 1962 savings: $7 million.)

4. The acquired missile capability programmed by this message also makes unnecessary and economically unjustifiable the development of the B–70 Mach 3 manned bomber as a full weapons system at this time. The B–70 would not become available in operational numbers until well beyond 1965. By that time we expect to have a large number of intercontinental ballistic missiles, fully tested and in place, as well as a substantial manned bomber force mostly equipped with air-to-ground missiles. In view of the extremely high cost of the B–70 system, its lesser survivability as a ground-based system and its greater vulnerability in the air compared to missiles, its capabilities as a second strike system do not appear to have sufficient advantages over a much less expensive missile, or even a B–52 or successor bomber equipped with Skybolt, to justify a request in fiscal 1962 for $358 million.

We recognize, however, that there are still uncertainties with respect to the operational characteristics of our planned missile force. We also recognize that there are certain advantages inherent in a controlled force of manned bombers. To preserve the option of developing this manned bomber weapon system, if we should later determine such a system is required, I recommend that the B–70 program be carried forward essentially to explore the problems of flying at three times the speed of sound with an airframe potentially useful as a bomber, with the development of a small number of prototype aircraft and related bomb-navigation systems. We should also explore the possibility of developing a manned bomber system specifically designed to operate in an environment in which both sides have large ICBM forces.

Even on this more limited basis, the B–70 project will cost $1.3 billion before it is completed in 1967. Approximately $800 million has already been provided, $220 million is now requested for 1962—$138 million less than the amount included in the January budget—and the balance will be required in subsequent years. The total development program which I am recommending will cost $1.4 billion less than that previously planned.

5. Nearly fifteen years and about $1 billion have been devoted to the attempted development of a nuclear-powered aircraft; but the possibility of achieving a militarily useful aircraft in the foreseeable future is still very remote. The January budget already recommended a severe curtailment of this project, cutting the level of effort in half by limiting the scope to only one of the two different engines under development, although not indicating which one. We believe the time has come to reach a clean-cut decision in this matter. Transferring the entire subject matter to the Atomic Energy Commission budget where it belongs, as a non-defense research item, we propose to terminate development effort on both approaches on the nuclear powerplant, comprising reactor and engine, and on the airframe; but to carry forward scientific research and development in the fields of high temperature materials and high performance reactors, which is re-lated to AEC's broad objectives in atomic reactor development including some work at the present plants, making use of their scientific teams. This will save an additional $35 million in the Defense budget for fiscal 1962 below the figure previously reduced in January, and will avoid a future expenditure of at least $1 billion, which would have been necessary to achieve first experimental flight.

6. The January budget did not include funds for the continued development of the Navy's "Missileer" fleet defense aircraft, but funds were included for the continued development of the Eagle missile—designed for use by the Missileer—in the hope that it could be adapted for use by some other aircraft. I am now advised that no such alternative use is in prospect; and I have directed the cancellation of that project, with a saving estimated at almost $57 million in 1961 and 1962.

7. The plan to install Polaris missiles on the Cruiser Long Beach has been canceled. For effectiveness in a nuclear war, the money would be better spent on the far less vulnerable Polaris submarines. In a limited war, the cruiser's utility would be reduced by the presence of the missiles. (Savings in fiscal 1962: $58 million.)

8. Finally, technological progress causes obsolescence not only in military hardware but also in the facilities constructed for their deployment. We must continually review our nearly 7,000 military installations in the light of our needs now and in the event of emergency. Those bases and installations which are no longer required must be inactivated, and disposed of where feasible, and I have so directed the Secretary of Defense. He has already taken steps to have 73 domestic and foreign installations discontinued as excess to our needs now and at any time in the future; and studies are continuing

now to identify additional facilities which are surplus to our requirements.

I am well aware that in many cases these actions will cause hardships to the communities and individuals involved. We cannot permit these actions to be deferred; but the Government will make every practicable effort to alleviate these hardships, and I have directed the Secretary of Defense to take every possible step to ease the difficulties for those displaced. But it is difficult, with so many defense and other budgetary demands, to justify support of military installations, with high operating and payroll costs and property values, which are no longer required for the defense of the nation. The closing of excess installations overseas will in many cases help alleviate our balance of payments deficit.

No net savings are expected to be realized in 1962 from these inactivations because of the added costs involved in closing, and no reductions in the 1962 budget are proposed on that account. Substantial savings, approximately $220 million per year, will be realized, however, in subsequent years.

(I am also proposing that $320 million of the obligational authority required be provided by transfer from the current bal-ances of working capital funds in the Defense Department.)

CONCLUSION

Our military position today is strong. But positive action must be taken now if we are to have the kind of forces we will need for our security in the future. Our preparation against danger is our hope of safety. The changes in the Defense program which I have recommended will greatly enhance the security of this Nation in the perilous years which lie ahead. It is not pleasant to request additional funds at this time for national security. Our interest, as I have emphasized, lies in peaceful solutions, in reducing tension, in settling disputes at the conference table and not on the battlefield. I am hopeful that these policies will help secure these ends. I commend them to the Congress and to the Nation.

JOHN F. KENNEDY

NOTE: The tables submitted with the President's message, "Summary by Program of Proposed Adjustments in New Obligational Authority in Fiscal Year 1962 Budget" and "Summary of Defense Department Budget," are published in House Document 123 (87th Cong., 1st sess.).

---

100   Letter to the President of the Senate on Increasing the National Effort in Oceanography.   *March 29, 1961*

My dear Mr. President:

The seas around us, as I pointed out in my message to the Congress on February 23, represent one of our most important resources. If vigorously developed, this resource can be a source of great benefit to the Nation and to all mankind.

But it will require concerted action, purposefully directed, with vision and ingenuity. It will require the combined efforts of our scientists and institutions, both public and private, and the coordinated efforts of many Federal agencies. It will involve substantial investments in the early years for the construction and operation of ship and shore facilities for research and surveys, the development of new instruments for charting the seas and gathering data, and the training of new scientific manpower.

We are just at the threshold of our knowledge of the oceans. Already their military importance, their potential use for weather predictions, for food and for minerals are evident. Further research will undoubtedly disclose additional uses.

Knowledge of the oceans is more than a matter of curiosity. Our very survival may hinge upon it. Although understanding of our marine environment and maps of the ocean floor would afford to our military forces a demonstrable advantage, we have thus far neglected oceanography. We do not have adequate charts of more than one or two percent of the oceans.

The seas also offer a wealth of nutritional resources. They already are a principal source of protein. They can provide many times the current food supply if we but learn how to garner and husband this self-renewing larder. To meet the vast needs of an expanding population, the bounty of the sea must be made more available. Within two decades, our own nation will require over a million more tons of seafood than we now harvest.

Mineral resources on land will ultimately reach their limits. But the oceans hold untapped sources of such basic minerals as salt, potassium and magnesium in virtually limitless quantities. We will be able to extract additional elements from sea water, such as manganese, nickel, cobalt and other elements known to abound on the ocean floor, as soon as the processes are developed to make it economically feasible.

To predict, and perhaps some day to control, changes in weather and climate is of the utmost importance to man everywhere. These changes are controlled to a large and yet unknown extent by what happens in the ocean. Ocean and atmosphere work together in a still mysterious way to determine our climate. Additional research is necessary to identify the factors in this interplay.

These are some of the reasons which compel us to embark upon a national effort in oceanography. I am therefore requesting funds for 1962 which will nearly double our government's investment over 1961, and which will provide $23 million more for oceanography than what was recommended in the 1962 budget submitted earlier. A summary and comparison of the 1960, 1961 and 1962 budgets is contained in two tables which are enclosed with this letter.

1. *Ship Construction.*

The proposed program for 1962 includes $37 million for ship construction, an increase of $23 million over 1961. This will provide for 10 oceanographic vessels. Only two will replace existing ships. The others will be used to meet needs that have long existed in Federal agencies and other oceanographic institutions conducting research for the Government.

The present United States oceanographic fleet is composed of 27 research ships and 17 survey vessels. All but two were constructed prior to the end of World War II; many are over thirty years old. Only two of the ships were designed specifically for research purposes; the remainder has been converted from a variety of ships designed for other uses. Thus the success of the national oceanographic program will depend heavily on the construction of the new specially designed vessels proposed for 1962.

2. *Shore Facilities and Data Center.*

Shore facilities are urgently required to provide laboratory space for analysis and interpretation of data and to train new oceanographers. In oceanographic research about five scientists and technicians are required ashore for each scientist aboard ship.

For 1962, $10 million is being requested for laboratories and wharfside facilities.

241

This represents a five-fold increase over 1961. It includes, for example, funds for a new Bureau of Commercial Fisheries laboratory to replace a forty-year old structure and additional laboratory space at universities and other oceanographic institutions.

An essential part of the shore establishment is the new National Oceanographic Data Center which will begin its first full year of operation in 1962. This Center will make available to the scientific community oceanographic data collected throughout the world.

3. *Basic and Applied Research.*

The conduct of research is the central purpose of our whole national effort in oceanography. New ships and shore facilities are essential tools of scientific research, but it is the research itself that will yield new knowledge of the earth's "inner space", and new uses of the sea. The proposed program includes $41 million for basic and applied research in oceanography. This is an increase of $9 million over the 1961 level.

Basic research is the cornerstone on which the successful use of the seas must rest. Progress here is largely dependent on the work of scientists at many universities and laboratories throughout the United States and on ships at sea. Their investigations cover all aspects of the marine environment, the motion and composition of ocean waters, the evolution and distribution of marine plants and animals, the shape and composition of the ocean bottom, and many other geophysical and biological problems. Of timely significance is the attempt to penetrate to the earth's mantle to better our understanding of the origin and history of our planet. This undertaking, known as Project Mohole, involves the development of new drilling methods that can be used in the deep seas. This project has recently resulted

in a spectacular achievement. Samples from nearly a thousand feet beneath the sea floor were obtained by drilling in three thousand feet of water.

Considerable attention will also be given to applied problems in the marine sciences. Oceanographers will be studying such problems as sound propagation in water, the effects of changes in ocean conditions on the movement of ships, weather forecasting, and fisheries management. Methods of predicting changes in ocean conditions also are being developed. Eventually they may lead to maps of "weather within the sea" much like the atmospheric weather maps of today.

Many advances are being made in methods of exploring the seas. Oceanographers are now able to descend to the great depths in bathyscaphes. New electronic equipment will allow them to probe the ocean and to "see" with sound pulses what before has been opaque. Using these new techniques, our scientists already have discovered vast currents below the ocean surface a thousand times larger than the flow of the Mississippi.

4. *Training of Oceanographers.*

The most important part of our long-range program in oceanography is the training of young scientists. Scientific manpower of every sort will be needed—technicians, college graduates, and post-graduate researchers—and they must be trained in many scientific disciplines. This training should go hand in hand with the conduct of research at universities and other oceanographic institutions. By their support of these institutions, the programs of the National Science Foundation, the Office of Naval Research, and the Department of Health, Education and Welfare will be of major importance to an expanding program in oceanography; for they can result in the education of new young scientists as well

242

as in the production of new knowledge. In the coming year, these agencies are undertaking to increase the number of fellowship awards and graduate student research contracts, and they also will encourage the development of new university programs in oceanography.

5. *Ocean Surveys.*

World-wide surveys of the oceans—their properties, their contents and boundaries—are needed to make charts and maps for use of scientists in their research programs and for a variety of commercial and defense applications. The United States' ocean survey program for FY 1962 is being increased within the limits of ships available for this purpose. I am requesting additional funds to allow the Coast and Geodetic Survey to extend the operating season of its existing ships, thus making the maximum use of limited ship resources. As already mentioned, funds are included for a new survey ship which will increase our deep-sea survey capability.

6. *International Cooperation.*

Oceanography is a natural area of opportunity for extensive international cooperation. Indeed, systematic surveys and research in all the oceans of the world represent tasks of such formidable magnitude that international sharing of the work is a necessity.

Our present maps of the oceans are comparable in accuracy and detail to maps of the land areas of the earth in the early part of the 18th century. Precise methods of measuring ocean depths have become available during the last ten years, and these, when combined with new developments in navigation, should make possible for the first time modern maps of the topography of the entire sea floor. An accurate mapping of the oceans will require international cooperation in ship operations and in establishing a world-wide system of navigation. In these endeavors the United States can play a leading part.

This year an Intergovernmental Oceanographic Commission is being established under UNESCO to provide a means whereby interested countries can cooperate in research and in making surveys and maps of the deep sea floor, the ocean waters, and their contained organisms. Membership on the Commission is open to all countries of the UN family that desire to cooperate in oceanography. The United States intends to participate fully in the activities of the Commission.

The United States also will participate in the International Indian Ocean Expedition. Many nations, including the Soviet Union, are cooperating in this expedition under the non-governmental sponsorship of the International Council of Scientific Unions. Over a quarter of the world's people live in the countries surrounding the Indian Ocean. If more can be learned of the Indian Ocean's extensive food resources, these nations can be helped to develop and expand their fishing industries as part of their general economic development.

7. *The Coast Guard.*

At present, the Coast Guard enabling legislation limits the extent to which the Coast Guard can engage in scientific research. Only the International Ice Patrol is authorized to make such studies. I recommend that the statutory limitations restricting the participation by the Coast Guard in oceanographic research be removed. With ocean weather stations, deep sea thermometers, and other data collection devices, our

Coast Guard can make a valuable contribution to the oceanographic program.

CONCLUSION

Knowledge and understanding of the oceans promise to assume greater and greater importance in the future. This is not a one-year program—or even a ten-year program. It is the first step in a continuing effort to acquire and apply the information about a

part of our world that will ultimately determine conditions of life in the rest of the world. The opportunities are there. A vigorous program will capture those opportunities.

Sincerely,

JOHN F. KENNEDY

NOTE: The two tables summarizing the national oceanographic program budget for 1960, 1961, and 1962, referred to in the President's message, were also released.

101   Letter to the President of the Senate and to the Speaker of the House Transmitting a Housing and Urban Improvement Bill. *March* 29, 1961

Dear Mr. ————:

I am pleased to transmit to you, for consideration by the Congress, a bill including the principal legislative recommendations of this Administration for housing and urban improvement.

These measures are intended to carry out the proposals set forth in my message to the Congress on March 9. They are, I feel, essential steps the Government should take to enable the housing industry to return to full production as soon as possible.

They will provide the help necessary to reverse the steady deterioration of our cities. And they will make it possible for private enterprise to meet the housing needs of millions of Americans who today live under conditions this Nation can no longer afford.

We must resume with full vigor the forward movement toward a better life for all Americans. Essential to such a better life is housing available to all at a cost all can afford. And just as important, to the increasing number of us who choose to live in and near cities, is an orderly and healthy urban environment.

The provisions of this bill, I believe, will help us to move in this direction.

The bill includes the extension of a number of programs previously approved by Congress, and found by experience to be both a prudent and beneficial investment of our resources.

It also proposes vigorous new lines of action for which strong support has developed in recent years. These include greater assistance to private builders in providing housing for those of retirement age; more liberal financial assistance for those who would rehabilitate deteriorating urban property; greater incentives for the use of new materials and methods to reduce the cost of our housing.

S. 858—now pending before the Senate Committee on Banking and Currency—relates to another new area where vigorous action is needed—the reserve of open spaces near our expanding cities. The objectives of this bill accord with the proposals outlined in my message of March 9. A report giving in detail the Administration views on this bill will shortly be sent to the Congress.

I fully believe the enactment of these measures will start us once again toward providing decent housing for all Americans and halting the blanket of blight which has been spreading over our cities. I hope these proposals will have the early and serious consideration of the Congress so they may soon be put to work for the benefit of all the people.

Sincerely,

JOHN F. KENNEDY

NOTE: This is the text of identical letters addressed to the Honorable Lyndon B. Johnson, President of the Senate, and to the Honorable Sam Rayburn, Speaker of the House of Representatives.

102   Statement by the President on the Progress of the Food for Peace Programs in Latin America.   *March* 29, 1961

IN MY SPEECH of March 13, 1961, I promised immediately to step up food for peace programs in Latin America.

Pursuant to that pledge, a Food for Peace Mission, which recently visited South America, has submitted a series of specific recommendations and begun negotiations to carry out those recommendations in a number of Latin American nations. Some of them have already been acted on.

Throughout the hemisphere millions of men and women suffer from critical protein deficiencies. By using our surplus feed grains to increase the production of protein-rich poultry and livestock, we can help meet this problem. I am sending Mr. Jonathan Garst—a Food for Peace consultant, and one of the nation's top experts on the use of feed grains—to Brazil to discuss the conversion of surplus feed grains into scarce protein. This will be only the first step, a pilot project, in a hemisphere-wide effort to eliminate protein deficiency and provide a decent diet for all the people of the Americas.

In addition we have offered a million tons of wheat to Brazil for sale for local currencies to be used in Brazilian economic and social development. This wheat program is presently under negotiation with the Brazilian government, and delivery should be scheduled shortly.

103   Statement by the President Following Ratification of the 23d Amendment to the Constitution.   *March* 29, 1961

RATIFICATION of the 23d amendment giving the residents of the District of Columbia the right to vote in Presidential elections by the required 38 States is a major step in the right direction. The speed with which this Constitutional amendment was approved by the required number of States demonstrates the interest of the nation at large in providing to all American citizens the most valuable of human rights— the right to share in the election of those who govern us. Hearings on enabling legislation to implement the amendment will be held shortly by the District of Columbia Commissioners and a legislative proposal will be submitted to the Congress at the earliest possible time.

It is equally important that residents of the District of Columbia have the right to select the officials who govern the District.

I am hopeful that the Congress, spurred by the adoption of the 23d amendment, will act favorably on legislative proposals to be recommended by the Administration providing the District of Columbia the right of home rule.

104 Letter to Secretary Stahr Concerning Discontinuance of Commercial Operations by the Panama Line. *March 31, 1961*

[Released March 31, 1961. Dated March 29, 1961]

Dear Mr. Secretary:

I have reviewed the report on the Panama Line, prepared by the Bureau of the Budget in consultation with you and other responsible authorities. I am in accord with the views expressed that continued commercial operations of the Panama Line would not be in the public interest. You should, therefore, take appropriate measures to discontinue the Line's commercial operations by April 20, 1961.

It is my desire that you investigate fully alternative transportation resources in order to select the course of action which would best serve the Government's interest and most adequately and economically meet the Canal Zone's particular transportation requirements. It is my further desire that you render appropriate assistance to those employees displaced by this action in finding other employment.

Sincerely,

JOHN F. KENNEDY

NOTE: The letter was released at Palm Beach, Fla.

105 Recorded Greetings to the President and People of Brazil. *April 3, 1961*

Murillo Neri (Rio de Janeiro announcer): Mr. President, as you know, our President, Janio Quadros is a big admirer of Abraham Lincoln. You have right on your desk a document that was given us by Lincoln's Museum. I would like to very much if you can sign this document or put a dedicatory for our President, Janio Quadros.

PRESIDENT KENNEDY: It is a great pleasure for me to have this opportunity to inscribe a copy of the Gettysburg Address to the President of Brazil.

Abraham Lincoln does not, I think, merely belong to the United States now, he belongs to all those who believe in freedom, who believe in the rights of man. And therefore it is a great pleasure for me to inscribe this copy of Lincoln's Gettysburg Address to your vigorous, dynamic new President, who seeks for Brazil what we seek for the United States and indeed for the people of all our hemisphere: a better life under freedom and justice.

Mr. Neri: Mr. President, we thank you very, very much. And I would like to ask you another thing, if it is possible for you to say some words to our Brazilian people, Mr. President, please.

PRESIDENT KENNEDY: It is a great pleasure for me to have the opportunity to extend my greetings to the people of Brazil.

Over 20 years ago, as a young man, I journeyed to your country. I know something of its history, and I know that its people share the same basic aspirations for a more happy and just life that my own people here in the United States have.

I hope Brazil and the United States, which have been fast friends in the past, will have a warm comradeship in the future.

We shall do our best to join with Brazil in strengthening our hemisphere, and pro-

viding for our people.

It is a great pleasure, through television and films, to have a chance to visit Brazil.

Mr. Neri: Thank you, Mr. President.

NOTE: The program was recorded on film and tape in the President's office at the White House for broadcast to the Brazilian people.

106   Message to the Secretary General of NATO on the 12th Anniversary of the Signing of the North Atlantic Treaty. *April 3, 1961*

APRIL 4th marks the 12th Anniversary of the signing of the North Atlantic Treaty.

We are justified in taking pride in our achievements in NATO and in those other cooperative endeavors in which we are engaged. But this day also reminds us of our obligations to the future. The years ahead will demand of us all courage, sacrifice and the will to seize every opportunity to secure and to advance human liberty. In cooperation with one another, and all those around

the globe who believe in the freedom of man, we can and we will succeed.

Let us on this Anniversary look to the future in this spirit. If we do the cause of freedom will prevail.

JOHN F. KENNEDY

[His Excellency Alberico Casardi, Acting Secretary General, North Atlantic Treaty Organization, Paris]

NOTE: The message was released at Palm Beach, Fla.

107   Message to the Conference of Chiefs of State of African Nations Meeting in Yaoundé. *April 6, 1961*

[Released April 6, 1961. Dated March 25, 1961]

IT GIVES ME deep pleasure to send the greetings of the Government and people of the United States to you who are gathered at Yaoundé to consult on matters of high importance in your mutual interest.

It is a particular pleasure because your consultations represent the kind of regional cooperation that strengthens hope in a world too often divided and torn by dispute. Yours is an association of free and sovereign nations, dedicated to constructive action for the welfare of your peoples. It is this partnership in freedom that is most impressive

to my country and it deserves the emulation of us all. I congratulate you and pledge the readiness of my country to provide concrete support, if you so desire, for your efforts to make effective a permanent organization to foster your economic cooperation and development. You have our warmest good wishes for every success.

NOTE: The chiefs of state of 12 African nations participated in the conference, during which the African and Malagasy Organization for Economic Cooperation was formed.

108   Letter to the President of the Senate and to the Speaker of the House Concerning Preservation of Ancient Monuments in the Nile Valley.   *April 7, 1961*

[Released April 7, 1961.   Dated April 6, 1961]

Dear Mr. ————:

Pursuant to Section 502(c) of the Mutual Security Act of 1954, as amended, I transmit herewith my recommendations for participation by the United States in the international campaign initiated by UNESCO to preserve the ancient temples and other monuments in the Nile Valley which are now threatened with inundation as a result of the construction of the Aswan High Dam.

I consider it to be in the interests of the United States to assist in rescuing these historic remains of a former civilization from destruction—and to join the international effort to conduct exploration and research in the threatened area of Nubia, before it is submerged for all time.

The significance of these ancient monuments has been discussed by President Nasser of the U.A.R. who recently said ". . . we pin our hopes on the preservation of the Nubian treasures in order to keep alive monuments which are not only dear to our hearts—we being their guardians— but dear to the whole world which believes that the ancient and the new components of human culture should blend in one harmonious whole." Reflecting similar sentiments, President Abboud recognized Sudan's responsibility to the rest of the world for the ancient monuments within its borders ". . . since the history of the Sudan is but a part of the history of Mankind."

The United States, one of the newest of civilizations, has long had a deep regard for the study of past cultures, and a concern for the preservation of man's great achievements of art and thought. We have also had a special interest in the civilization of ancient Egypt from which many of our own cultural traditions have sprung—and a deep friendship for the people who live in the valley of the Nile. In keeping with this tradition, and this friendship, I recommend that we now join with other nations through UNESCO in preventing what would otherwise be an irreparable loss to science and the cultural history of Mankind.

The international effort now under way to save the many ancient temples in the United Arab Republic and Sudan is an operation of a magnitude that cannot be borne by one or even a few nations. Its total cost is estimated at 75–100 million dollars. Because of the immense size of the task, the Director General of UNESCO, at the request of the Governments of the United Arab Republic and of the Sudan, has appealed to all nations and peoples to join in a common undertaking to save these historic monuments from destruction.

In return for assistance, the Governments of the United Arab Republic and of the Sudan, in declarations of October 1, 1959 and October 24, 1959, respectively, have offered to cede, with certain exceptions, at least half of the finds to parties carrying out excavations in Nubia. The U.A.R. Government has also declared its willingness to authorize excavations outside the threatened area at sites in Lower, Middle and Upper Egypt, and has stated it is prepared to cede, with a view to their transfer abroad, certain Nubian temples and a large collection of antiquities which are now part of Egyptian state collections. It is also my understanding

248

that the Government of the United Arab Republic is prepared to extend the above privileges and benefits to American museums and institutions if effective financial assistance from the U.S. Government is forthcoming.

The United Arab Republic has itself pledged the Egyptian pound equivalent of $10 million for the UNESCO campaign, to be paid over the next seven years. Seven other nations have either paid in or pledged contributions. Still others are furnishing assistance in kind, have sent expeditions to the area, or are seriously considering financial assistance. To date the United States Government has made no financial contribution to the program, and only modest funds have been forthcoming from private sources.

It is important to note that all United States contributions to this international campaign can be in the form of U.S. owned Egyptian currency generated under P.L. 480. The total of all the contributions recommended below can be met from the portion of these currencies available for U.S. use which is determined to be in excess of U.S. prospective requirements.

The task of saving the Nubian monuments can be conveniently divided into two parts: (A) the preservation of the massive temples of Abu Simbel; and (B) the preservation of the temples on the Island of Philae and the remaining lesser temples in the threatened area.

(a) The cost of preserving Abu Simbel—dedicated to Rameses II and Queen Nefertari, and built in the 13th century B.C.—has been estimated at approximately 60 to 80 million dollars. Two major plans have been advanced for saving these monuments: One recommends building a coffer dam around them; and the other proposes to sever the temples from the rock cliff of which they are a part and lift them 200

feet to the future level of the Nile. Each of these plans entails serious difficulties, and further studies are being made. Therefore I feel it would be premature to recommend, at the present time, that any U.S. funds be provided for this purpose.

(b) The preservation of the Philae Temples, the lesser temples, and also the exploration of the threatened region.

1. The second most important group of monuments are the temples on the Island of Philae—known as the "Pearl of Egypt." Recent engineering studies have indicated that these monuments can be saved at a cost of approximately 6 million dollars. There would be no more effective expression of our interest in preserving the cultural monuments of the Nile Valley than an American offer to finance the preservation of these temples. I am directing that the Egyptian pound equivalent of 6 million dollars be set aside for this purpose. When required an appropriation to cover the use of this sum will be sought.

2. The cost of preserving the lesser temples in the U.A.R. and in the Sudan will be approximately 9.6 million dollars. I recommend an appropriation covering the use of the Egyptian pound equivalent of 2.5 million dollars as the U.S. contribution toward the removal of these temples.

3. In addition to preserving these monuments there is a pressing need for extensive archeological and prehistory research in the Nubia. Much of the threatened area, particularly in the Sudan, still remains unexplored by archeologists. Therefore, a large-scale program of investigation and exploration must be undertaken if the undiscovered treasures and antiquities of this region are not to be lost forever. For this purpose the Egyptian and Sudanese Governments have thrown open the Nubia to archeological teams from other countries, and several in-

stitutions in the United States have either sent expeditions to the area or have expressed their desire to do so. I recommend an appropriation covering the use of the Egyptian pound equivalent of 1.5 million dollars for grants to American archeological expeditions and groups doing related research in Nubia which are prepared to meet their own dollar requirements. These grants will be administered by the United States.

4. Of course Egyptian pounds cannot be used to finance either the preservation of temples or exploration and research in the Sudan. However, the Government of the U.A.R. has indicated its willingness to permit the conversion of the Egyptian pound equivalent of $500,000 into Sudanese currency. Therefore I will set aside this amount to be converted for use in the Sudan from the sums I am requesting for research and for preservation of the lesser temples.

5. I intend to appoint a commission of government officials and leading Egyptologists to make plans for the acquisition and distribution of the antiquities ceded to the United States as a result of our contribution.

In making these funds available the United States will be participating in an international effort which has captured the imagination and sympathy of people throughout the world. By thus contributing to the preservation of past civilizations, we will strengthen and enrich our own.

Sincerely,

JOHN F. KENNEDY

NOTE: This is the text of identical letters addressed to the Honorable Lyndon B. Johnson, President of the Senate, and to the Honorable Sam Rayburn, Speaker of the House of Representatives.

On September 30 the President approved the Supplemental Appropriation Act, 1962 (75 Stat. 733), which included an appropriation of $4 million for the preservation of the ancient Nubian monuments.

109 Message to Chancellor Raab of Austria on the Occasion of His Retirement From Office. *April 8, 1961*

[Released April 8, 1961. Dated April 6, 1961]

Dear Mr. Chancellor:

The American people cherish the bonds of friendship, mutual respect, and devotion to common democratic ideals which unite our two countries. These bonds have grown in strength and vitality during the years of your leadership. Your dedicated service to Austria and to the principles and institutions of Western democracy have earned the respect and gratitude of free men everywhere. Under your stewardship Austria has stead-

fastly executed her mission as a bastion of freedom, a refuge for the oppressed, and an exemplar of the noblest traditions of Western civilization. As you prepare to lay down the demanding duties of the Chancellorship, please accept on my own behalf, and on the behalf of the people of the United States, our sincere best wishes.

Sincerely,

JOHN F. KENNEDY

110 Message to Detlev W. Bronk and Alan T. Waterman
Regarding the Success of the First Phase of Project Mohole.
April 8, 1961

I HAVE BEEN following with deep interest the experimental drilling in connection with the first phase of Project Mohole. The success of the drilling in almost 12,000 feet of water near Guadalupe Island and the penetration of the oceanic crust down to the volcanic formations constitute a remarkable achievement and an historic landmark in our scientific and engineering progress.

The people of the United States can take pride not only in the accomplishment but in the fact that they have supported this basic scientific exploration.

I extend to you my congratulations and ask that you pass them on to the special committee and the staff of the National Academy of Sciences, the National Science Foundation, the Global Marine Exploration Company, and especially to all those on board the *Cuss I* and attendant vessels who have combined their talents and energies to achieve this major success.

JOHN F. KENNEDY

NOTE: This is the text of identical messages addressed to Dr. Detlev W. Bronk, President of the National Academy of Sciences, and Dr. Alan T. Waterman, Director of the National Science Foundation.

111 Statement by the President on the Extension of the
Reorganization Act. *April 8, 1961*

THE REORGANIZATION ACT restores a long accepted and useful procedure for transmitting to the Congress plans for accomplishing Executive reorganizations. It places responsibility for initiating needed action upon the Executive without affecting the right of Congress to scrutinize and legislate in this area. It should result in promoting improvements in government organization and it should make possible more economical operation.

NOTE: On April 7, 1961, the President approved an amendment to the Reorganization Act of 1949 extending it to June 1, 1963 (Public Law 87–18, 75 Stat. 41).

112 Remarks at the Reading of the Joint Statement Following
Discussions With Prime Minister Macmillan. *April 8, 1961*

I WILL READ this Joint Statement of the Prime Minister and myself, and perhaps the Prime Minister might have a word to say:

We have had a series of candid and friendly talks. We have discussed the present world situation in general, and in particular the major issues of international relations which affect our two countries. We have reached a very high level of agreement on our estimate of the nature of the problems which we face. We realize all too well that to meet these problems will require from us many sacrifices.

Open and friendly discussions have served

to clarify and confirm our common commitment to those who care for freedom. We are in complete agreement as to the gravity and depth of the dangers in the present world situation for those nations who wish to retain their independence and the priceless right of choice.

While we recognize that the core of Western security against armed aggression continues to be the North Atlantic Alliance, we also discussed how our countries can help to strengthen the Free World as a whole.

We have considered what measures it might be advisable to take, together with our allies, to ensure the cohesion, effectiveness and adaptability of the Atlantic community in a changing world.

To this end we have examined the world economic and financial situation, including the problems of imbalance and short-term capital movements; the need for coordination to meet these problems by increased utilization of existing international machinery; the need for more effective assistance to nations in an earlier stage of economic development; and the need for maintenance of world trade at the highest possible level. We have recognized both the urgency and the importance of further steps toward the economic and political unity of Europe.

We reaffirm our vigorous support of the United Nations and our determination to oppose the attempts currently being made to undermine its authority as an instrument for peace and security in the world.

We have given close attention to South East Asia and specifically to the critical problems of Laos and Vietnam.

We are agreed upon both the importance and the difficulty of working towards satisfactory relations with the Soviet Union.

We also reaffirm the determination of our governments to do their utmost to bring to a successful conclusion within a reasonable period of time the negotiations in Geneva for the cessation of nuclear weapons tests under effective inspection and control.

We have talked as partners, but with a full awareness of the rights and interests of the other nations with whom we are closely associated.   [*Ends reading.*]

I want to say, speaking personally, and also as President of the United States, that it has been a source of great satisfaction to me to have the Prime Minister visit this country again.   He has enjoyed the closest relations and the fullest confidence with three of my predecessors, President Roosevelt, President Truman, and President Eisenhower; and it is therefore as the fourth in this series of American Presidents it has been the greatest possible pleasure to have had this opportunity to establish close and I think highly satisfactory personal and public relations with him during these last few days.

We are delighted that I had a chance to see him again after our very satisfactory talk in Florida.   Each one of our meetings I think has increased the degree of cohesion which exists and must exist between his country and the United States, and therefore I must say, as these talks come to a conclusion, I think I express the sentiment of all of the Americans who participated, our great appreciation to the Prime Minister, to his Secretary of State, Lord Home, and to the other delegates for another happy milestone in the long series of meetings which have existed between the United States and Great Britain in previous years.

NOTE: The President spoke before a group of newsmen assembled in the Rose Garden at the White House.

The Prime Minister's remarks follow:

Mr. President, I want to thank you very much for the words that you have used. On behalf of myself, of the Secretary of State, and all my colleagues, thank you and Mr. Secretary Rusk for the kindness and courtesy which you have shown us in the last few days.

This has been a very happy visit. I am delighted that we have been able in your own words, to make a friendship both private and public which I feel certain will be good for both our countries and for the future of all the free world.

You, Mr. President, have shown me in particular so many acts of kindness in these days that I really hardly know how to thank you. It has been quite an experience over the last 10 days. I came to lunch with you at Key West, 3,600 miles altogether—very good lunch it was, though. And then, come a week after, here you have given me helicopters and every possible convenience—taken me boating—and everything.

But the point is we have had just friendly talks, sometimes in private and sometimes with our collaborators, which is the basis of confidence that I hope and feel is established between us. And on that friendship I trust that we shall long be able to work for the benefit of our countries and for all the world.

I thank you most warmly.

113   Statement by the President on the Emergency Feed Grain Program. *April* 10, 1961

WITHIN A FEW DAYS farmers will have an opportunity to sign up and cooperate in the 1960 emergency feed grain program. I urge all feed grain producers to give careful and serious consideration to the opportunities offered them by this program.

The response to these opportunities by the farmers will undoubtedly have considerable influence upon future agricultural legislation. Members of Congress from both rural and urban sections of the country supported this program, for it provides an opportunity to improve farm income while reducing the cost of the farm program to the Federal Government; to curtail the surplus stocks of basic commodities while insuring an abundant supply of meat, eggs, and dairy products; and to provide fair and stable prices to consumers.

The program is voluntary. Each farmer must choose for himself. But by joint action we can bring order to a chaotic segment of our economy.

I believe this will constitute a major step forward toward a sound and rational program for all agriculture.

114   Letter to the President of the Senate and to the Speaker of the House on the National Aeronautics and Space Council. *April* 10, 1961

Dear Mr. ————:

I transmit herewith, for the consideration of the Congress, a draft bill relating to the National Aeronautics and Space Council.

I contemplate making the Council an active and useful instrumentality. To achieve that end it is necessary, in my view, to amend existing law providing for the Council.

As you know, it is now the duty of the President to preside over meetings of the Council. As has been previously announced, I desire to place the Council under the chairmanship of the Vice President.

The primary effect of the attached amendatory bill, if enacted, will be to make that possible.

I believe that the Vice President can contribute importantly to, and give me valuable counsel and assistance with respect to, space programs, and that the chairmanship of the National Aeronautics Space Council will materially enhance his opportunity and capability to render maximum service.

I therefore recommend that the Congress enact legislation along the lines of the attached draft bill.

Sincerely,

JOHN F. KENNEDY

NOTE: This is the text of identical letters addressed to the Honorable Lyndon B. Johnson, President of the Senate, and to the Honorable Sam Rayburn, Speaker of the House of Representatives.

The draft bill was released with the President's letter.

115 Remarks at the Opening Session of the Meeting of the Military Committee of NATO. *April* 10, 1961

Lord Mountbatten, members of the Military Committee, and Gentlemen:

I want to express my appreciation to you for your generous welcome this morning, and also to extend to you the warm greetings of the United States Government to the Chiefs of Staff of the nations of NATO as you assemble here for a meeting of the Military Committee. We of course take satisfaction in having your representatives with us regularly, in permanent session, but it is especially good, today, to have in Washington the Military Committee itself. Moreover, it is for me much more than a ceremonial pleasure to meet with you.

You hold a critical responsibility in the affairs of NATO, and I want to talk with you about the substance of the task and about the necessary relation between you as military officers and others of us as political leaders.

NATO, as you gentlemen know, is at a turning point in military planning. In Supreme Headquarters and in many of the capitals of the alliance, work on our future needs is going ahead. As part of this effort, we in the Government of the United States are now well advanced in a careful study of our own view of the military policy of NATO.

Vice President Johnson explained last week in Paris our belief that there should be a reenforcement of the capabilities of NATO in conventional weapons. NATO needs to be able to respond to any conventional attack with conventional resistance which will be effective at least long enough, in General Norstad's phrase, to force a pause. To this end, we ourselves mean to maintain our own divisions and supporting units in Europe and to increase their conventional capabilities.

In addition to strengthened conventional forces, we believe that NATO must continue to have an effective nuclear capability. We hope to consult closely with our allies on the precise forms which the nuclear deterrent should take in future years. In his address last week, Prime Minister Macmillan pointed out the urgency of this question. The United States means to do its full share in working toward an effective solution of this problem, and we believe that the clarity and firmness of our own commitment to the full defense of Europe can be helpful in this direction.

The proper first forum on these matters is of course the North Atlantic Council, and moreover questions of this importance also require careful discussions in each country at the very highest levels of government.

But before I turn to other matters, let me comment briefly on one further military point. In our studies we have found a serious need for a sensitive and flexible control of all arms, and especially over nuclear weapons. We propose to see to it, for our part, that our military forces operate at all times under continuous, responsible command and control from the highest authorities all the way downward—and we mean to see that this control is exercised before, during, and after any initiation of hostilities against our forces, and at any level of escalation. We believe in maintaining effective deterrent strength, but we also believe in making it do what we wish, neither more nor less.

In stating this doctrine, I am reaffirming principles to which the responsible military leaders of NATO have always adhered—but I am also assuring you that the political leadership of the United States will apply both energy and resources in this direction.

And this brings me to my second main point. NATO is remarkable among the alliances of history in its combination of political, military, economic, and even psychological components. What NATO is, at any time, depends not only upon its forces in being, but upon the resolution of its leaders, the state of mind of its people, and the view of all these elements which is held by those who do not always wish us well.

In this situation, it is clearly necessary that there should be close understanding between political leaders and the senior military officers. In our countries, of course, final responsibility always rests with political authorities, and we also have a tradition of respect for the professional judgment of professional soldiers. But in NATO, from the very beginning, it has been essential that neither class of men should accept any arbitrary division of our problems into "the political" and "the military" spheres. The crucial problems have always been mixed. Political leaders have had a duty to share with their senior officers a full understanding of the political purposes of the alliance, and military leaders for their part have had to recognize that in NATO all the important military problems are political problems also.

This recognition of the interconnection between policy and force is an even more compelling necessity today, especially in all the questions which relate to the command, the deployment, and the possible use of nuclear weapons.

In the months ahead, as we share in the framing of NATO's policy and in new decisions which must guide us safely toward the future, we shall need to have the closest and most understanding communication not only from country to country, but from soldier to civilian. Political planning must be aware of military realities, and military plans in turn must be responsive to political considerations—among them such varied and important matters as resource capabilities, national attitudes, and other alliance objectives like our common purpose to advance the economic welfare of the whole free world. Our force goals, our military policy, our deployments, and our war plans themselves must all reflect the purposes and spirit of our great community. Military and political problems are not separable, and military and political men must work ever more closely together.

I hold an office which by our very Constitution unites political and military responsibility, and therefore it is no more than my duty to pledge my own best effort to keep these two kinds of problems together in my mind. I ask the same of you.

In ending, gentlemen, let me turn for one moment from our problems to our accomplishment. NATO has kept the peace of Europe and the Atlantic through 12 dangerous years, and in that time our community has grown in strength and in well-being. This is no small accomplishment. I offer to you, and through you to all of NATO's armed forces, the thanks and congratulations of the people and the Government of the United States of America. Let us continue from this bright past to a future which offers us the high task of guarding a free community's peace, and its security, and its freedom.

Thank you.

NOTE: The President spoke at 10 a.m. in the International Conference Room at the State Department. His opening words "Lord Mountbatten" referred to Admiral of the Fleet Earl Mountbatten, Chief of Britain's Defense Staff. Later in his remarks he referred to General Lauris Norstad, Supreme Allied Commander in Europe.

Another text of this address was released by the White House prior to its actual delivery.

116   Remarks at the First Meeting of the President's Committee on Equal Employment Opportunity.   *April 11, 1961*

THE PRESIDENT'S Committee on Equal Employment Opportunity is meeting for the first time today. I am hopeful and confident that from this time forward the Committee will exercise the great powers given to it by Executive order to permanently remove from Government employment and work performed for the Government every trace of discrimination because of race, creed, color, or place of national origin.

The Executive order creating this committee and granting to it powerful sanctions, is both an announcement of our determination to end job discrimination once and for all, and an effective instrument to realize that objective.

Vice President Lyndon Johnson, Chairman of the Committee, Secretary of Labor Arthur Goldberg, and Assistant Secretary of Labor Jerry Holleman, Executive Vice Chairman, and the other distinguished public officials and private citizens who make up the Committee, will carry the responsibility for implementing equal employment policies in Government and work under Government contracts.

This responsibility I know will be dis-charged with fairness, with understanding, with an open mind, and a generous spirit of cooperation—and also with firmness. There is no intention to make this a harsh or unreasonable mandate for those sincerely and honestly seeking compliance, nor is there any intention to compromise the principle of equality in employment. American citizens unjustly denied the opportunity to work for the Government, or for those doing business with the Government, will have that opportunity.

This is not only just in itself; it is one of the purposes for which we stand before the world. All Americans can be satisfied today that that high moral purpose is in excellent hands.

Let me just say, speaking personally, that I am grateful to all of you for taking on this responsibility. The Federal Government spends billions of dollars a year and therefore this is a most powerful instrument for accomplishing the objectives which we all seek. All of us agree that Federal money should not be spent in any way which encourages discrimination, but rather should be spent in such a way that it encourages the national goal of equal opportunity. And when Federal budgets are as large as they are, when they cover such a large percentage of employed people of this country, directly or indirectly, this quite obviously can be a very effective instrument to carry out a national objective.

I think that we are particularly fortunate to have the Vice President, who in his high position has undertaken to give this Committee leadership. We are also very fortunate to have Arthur Goldberg, using the agency which he heads as a supporting hand in this effort, and Jerry Holleman, who is the Assistant Secretary of Labor and who already has begun working to implement this objective.

I want to thank all of you. This is an important work. I don't think there's any more important domestic effort in which we could be engaged. This is the way it can be done.

The Vice President has just come back from a trip to Senegal, and in conversation with him about it, he indicated the importance of our establishing our image in accordance with our constitutional promise.

So this is the best way I know to do it. This is not going to be an honorary committee. This is not going to be a committee which issues a number of statements and relies upon exhortation. This Committee has powers and it has responsibilities, and I think when those powers and responsibilities are put together, we'll be moving along a very important and useful national road.

Thank you very much.

NOTE: The President spoke in the Cabinet Room at the White House.

117   Statement by the President on the Orbiting of a Soviet Astronaut.   *April* 12, 1961

THE ACHIEVEMENT by the USSR of orbiting a man and returning him safely to ground is an outstanding technical accomplishment. We congratulate the Soviet scientists and engineers who made this feat possible. The exploration of our solar system is an ambition which we and all mankind share with the Soviet Union and this is an important step toward that goal. Our own Mercury man-in-space program is directed toward that same end.

NOTE: The President's statement followed an announcement by the Soviet Government that the Russian astronaut, Maj. Yuri Gagarin, had completed an orbital flight around the earth in 1 hour and 48 minutes.

118   Message to Chairman Khrushchev Concerning the Flight of the Soviet Astronaut.   *April* 12, 1961

THE PEOPLE of the United States share with the people of the Soviet Union their satisfaction for the safe flight of the astronaut in man's first venture into space. We congratulate you and the Soviet scientists and engineers who made this feat possible. It is my sincere desire that in the continuing quest for knowledge of outer space our nations can work together to obtain the greatest benefit to mankind.

JOHN F. KENNEDY

[N. S. Khrushchev, Chairman, Council of Ministers, Union of Soviet Socialist Republics]

119 The President's News Conference of
April 12, 1961

THE PRESIDENT. I have several announcements.

[1.] Today is the 16th anniversary of the death of President Franklin D. Roosevelt. It is also the anniversary of the announcement of the vaccine which has been discovered to prevent paralytic polio. Today over 90 million Americans have been vaccinated with the Salk vaccine. Over 80 million remain unvaccinated. Almost 4,800,000 children have not been vaccinated and a majority of these are under 5 years of age. I hope that the renewed drive this spring and summer to provide vaccination for all Americans, and particularly those who are young, will have the wholehearted support of every parent in America. I hope that they will, knowing some of the long-range suffering which comes from an attack of polio, with this miraculous drug, I hope that everyone takes advantage of it.

[2.] Secondly, I wish to announce the formation of an advisory group, the members of which will be assisting Mr. Labouisse and other governmental officials in bringing about the much needed change in our foreign aid program which we announced in March. Mr. Eugene Black, President of the International Bank, and other distinguished members of the banking community who are familiar with the problems of development assistance abroad will be working with us. We have also secured the services of a distinguished member of the New York Bar, Mr. Theodore Tannenwald, who has agreed to assist us in the drafting of the new legislation; and Mr. George Gann of the Ford Foundation, who is giving us the benefit of his experience in the organizational aspects of the work. And finally, and in the most important phase of the effort, we are fortu-

nate to have the services of Robert Blum of the Asia Foundation, William Dale of the Stanford Research Institute, and Samuel P. Hayes, of the University of Michigan, Don Humphrey of the Fletcher School in Massachusetts, and Professor Arthur Smithies of Harvard, who will work with Dr. Max Millikan of MIT, and Mr. Frank Coffin, Director of the Development Loan Fund, to shift the aid to a sound and economical basis.

[3.] Thirdly, I wish to announce that the U.S. Naval Ordnance Plant at South Charleston, W. Va., will be sold to the Food Machinery and Chemical Corporation of New York City. The General Services Administration has accepted the bid of $4,320,000, and this company is proposing to provide a development which will, they hope, stimulate the economy in this area and in this State, which is a matter of particular interest.

[4.] Q. Mr. President, has a decision been reached on how far this country will be willing to go in helping an anti-Castro uprising or invasion of Cuba? What could you say with respect to recent developments as far as the anti-Castro movements in Cuba are concerned?

THE PRESIDENT. First, I want to say that there will not be, under any conditions, an intervention in Cuba by the United States Armed Forces. This Government will do everything it possibly can, and I think it can meet its responsibilities, to make sure that there are no Americans involved in any actions inside Cuba.

Secondly, the Justice Department's recent indictment of Mr. Masferrer, of Florida, on the grounds that he was plotting an invasion of Cuba, from Florida, in order to establish a Batista-like regime should indicate the feelings of this country towards those who wish to re-establish that kind of an administration inside Cuba.

Third, we do not intend to take any action with respect to the property or other economic interests which American citizens formerly held in Cuba, other than formal and normal negotiations with a free and independent Cuba.

The basic issue in Cuba is not one between the United States and Cuba. It is between the Cubans themselves. I intend to see that we adhere to that principle and as I understand it this administration's attitude is so understood and shared by the anti-Castro exiles from Cuba in this country.

[5.] Q. Could you give us your views, sir, about the Soviet achievement of putting a man in orbit and what it would mean to our space program, as such?

THE PRESIDENT. Well, it is a most impressive scientific accomplishment, and also I think that we, all of us as members of the race, have the greatest admiration for the Russian who participated in this extraordinary feat. I have already sent congratulations to Mr. Khrushchev, and I send congratulations to the man who was involved.

I indicated that the task force which we set up on space way back last January, January 12th, indicated that because of the Soviet progress in the field of boosters, where they have been ahead of us, that we expected that they would be first in space, in orbiting a man in space. And, of course, that has taken place. We are carrying out our program and we expect to—hope to make progress in this area this year ourselves.

[6.] Q. Mr. President, your white paper,[1] last week, referred in very diplomatic language to the takeover by communism in

Cuba. Is it your view that Fidel Castro is personally a Communist?

THE PRESIDENT. Well, he has indicated his admiration on many occasions for the Communist revolution; he has appointed a great many Communists to high positions. A great many of those, I think, in the white paper—well, rather, the state paper—he indicated that two-thirds of those who had been members of his first government had fled Cuba, people who had a strong feeling for the revolution but who did not propose to see it come under the domination of the Communists.

So I would not want to characterize Mr. Castro except to say that by his own words he has indicated his hostility to democratic rule in this hemisphere, to democratic liberal leaders in many of the countries of the hemisphere who are attempting to improve the life of their people, and has associated himself most intimately with the Sino-Soviet bloc, and has indicated his desire to spread the influence of that bloc throughout this hemisphere.

[7.] Q. Mr. President, in your talks with Prime Minister Macmillan, did you come to some common understanding on the best way to handle the problem of Red China in the United Nations next fall?

THE PRESIDENT. Well, we discussed the problem. We also discussed the differing approach which the United States has followed. We discussed the problem of the admission of Red China. We also discussed the fact that there was a difference in approach between the British and ourselves. I made it very clear that the United States was going to continue to meet its commitments to the people on Formosa—the government on Formosa—and I also did discuss the fact that the vote on the moratorium was very close. And that we had no—cannot make a final judgment as to what the vote

---

[1] "Cuba" (Department of State Publication 7171, Inter-American Series 66, April 1961).

on the moratorium will be on the admission of Red China. But I must say that the report I saw this morning of that conversation from London was not accurate in that it indicated that the United States had changed its position on the moratorium. That we have not done. And I want to take this opportunity to emphasize that the United States supports the Taiwan, Formosa, Government in its membership in the United Nations and is exploring with all interested parties what the position will be in the discussions at the United Nations next fall. The Prime Minister made his own position clear and that of his government.

[8.] Q. Mr. President, how do you reconcile your concern with unemployment in connection with the closing of about 50 military installations, which will throw thousands of civilian employees out of work?

THE PRESIDENT. I might say just to make it perfectly clear, in response to Mr. Hightower's question, in conclusion I would say that the United States is opposed under present conditions—continues to be opposed under present conditions to the admission of Red China.

Now, on your question, we stated in the— we have asked for a substantial increase in expenditures for the national defense. This will affect, beneficially, employment. I think we said in our statement very clearly that we did not think that defense bases should be kept going when they no longer had a—when there was no longer a need for them in order to maintain the defensive strength of the United States. I think that is a traditional position and one which this administration will follow. We will attempt to the best of our ability to maintain jobs for the people who are involved, but we cannot get a strong national defense if we continue defense systems or bases which are archaic and outmoded, and which no longer

represent a real need. I am hopeful that the country's economy generally will be strong enough to absorb those who may be thrown out of work because of structural changes in our defense system. But I think it is a serious problem; as we change from planes to missiles you affect employment not only in the bases but in the defense industries themselves. This is a serious matter for the Government, but we cannot permit ourselves— we are paying in the $40 billions for national defense, which represents a heavy burden, and we have to make it as efficient as possible. So we will try to do that with due regard to the needs of people who are involved. But I am hopeful we can meet their needs on a broader national basis, and not merely maintaining bases for which we no longer have a need in our defense structure.

[9.] Q. Mr. President, do you have any indication that the Russians may be about to release the U–2 pilot, Francis Gary Powers?

THE PRESIDENT. No, I do not. I have seen the story, but we do not have any information on the matter.

[10.] Q. Mr. President, the Russians seem to be taking their time in replying to the urgent call for a cease-fire in Laos. In the meantime, there are reports that they have stepped up their airlift of weapons to the rebels. How long can you afford to wait before the Soviets reply?

THE PRESIDENT. I am not sure that there is evidence that a step-up—there may have been an increase of 1 or 2 days, but over a period of 10 days or so, or 2 weeks, I don't think that there is any evidence that there has been very marked increase in their supplies. The supplies have continued, but I don't think it is fair to say, or accurate to say, that there has been a sharp step-up in the last few days.

I am hopeful that we are going to get an answer, I hope, this week, shortly, so that we can get a cease-fire and so that the supplying of forces on both sides could be ended. Our supplies to the government forces are continuing.

[11.] Q. Mr. President, Senator Kefauver and Representative Celler say that we must have legislation to bring down the prices of medicines for sick people and protect the purity of drugs. They have introduced legislation to do that by amending the patent and antitrust laws. Are you for that? Can you do anything executively, or can you do it through the Department of Justice?

THE PRESIDENT. Well, I think that it may be that we can take some action executively without the Congress, and I will be glad to look into that. The Federal Trade Commission also, I am sure, will concern itself with this problem and with other related problems. Mr. Dixon was the counsel for that committee, who is the new chairman of the Federal Trade Commission.

I will be looking with interest to Mr. Kefauver's efforts in this area because the prices are high. I do think, moving away from your point, which I think is a good one, that all this effort would be useful and I think it would also be useful to provide medical care for the aged tied to social security as another facet of the problem of helping our people pay for—afford good health.

[12.] Q. Sir, will you help, actively, Senator William Blakley of Texas to get elected? He is running in the primary on the Democratic ticket, and he has opposed your program quite a bit, and also opposed some of your nominees.

THE PRESIDENT. He has been nominated by the party, but to the best of my knowledge I haven't heard—he hasn't asked for me, my assistance, as yet. If he does, I will certainly be glad to do what I think is useful.

[*Laughter*] But I'm for Democrats in these fights between—I have read Mr. Tower's speech and so I think probably the people of Texas can decide these things. It isn't very useful, ordinarily, for people to come from out of State, whether it is the President or Senator Goldwater or anyone else, and I think probably the people of Texas can make a very effective judgment without external advice. But I would be glad to give it, if asked.

[13.] Q. Mr. President, this question might better be asked at a history class than a news conference, but here it is, anyway. The Communists seem to be putting us on the defensive on a number of fronts—now, again, in space. Wars aside, do you think that there is a danger that their system is going to prove more durable than ours?

THE PRESIDENT. Well, I think that we are in a period of long drawn-out tests to see which system is, I think, the more durable, not better, but more durable. And we have had a number of experiences with this kind of competition—a dictatorship enjoys advantages in this kind of competition over a short period by its ability to mobilize its resources for a specific purpose. We have made some exceptional scientific advances in the last decade, and some of them—they are not as spectacular as the man-in-space, or as the first sputnik, but they are important. I have said that I thought that if we could ever competitively, at a cheap rate, get fresh water from salt water, that it would be in the long-range interests of humanity which would really dwarf any other scientific accomplishments. I am hopeful that we will intensify our efforts in that area.

I think that if we could increase the techniques for improving education in uneducated sections of the world—by using the latest devices of science—that that would be an extraordinary accomplishment. I do not regard the first man in space as a sign of the weakening of the free world, but I do regard the total mobilization of man and things for the service of the Communist bloc over the last years as a source of great danger to us. And I would say we are going to have to live with that danger and hazard through much of the rest of this century.

My feeling is that we are more durable in the long run. These dictatorships enjoy many short-range advantages, as we saw in the thirties. But in the long run I think our system suits the qualities and aspirations of people that desire to be their own masters. I think our system suits better. Our job is to maintain our strength until our great qualities can be brought more effectively to bear. But during the meantime, it is going to require a united effort.

[14.] Q. Mr. President, one aspect of the problem you have just been discussing is the strength of our economy. There has been increasing comment from both within your own administration and outside to the effect that even when we pull out of the current recession, we are going to be left with a very large, serious amount of unemployment. It has been suggested that measures quite different in character from what you have proposed, more far reaching, will be necessary to cure that. And I wonder whether you have anything further in mind?

THE PRESIDENT. Well, in the first place, I would like to see the measures that we have suggested be passed. We haven't yet secured the passage of the depressed area bill. We haven't yet secured the passage of the aid to dependent children, which has passed the House and I hope will pass the Senate shortly.

We have not yet secured the passage of the social security changes, one of which provides for earlier retirement which will, I think, provide some relief. But these

steps—the unemployment compensation which is going to begin to flow into the hands of people in need in the next week, the aid to dependent children, the early retirement, the aid to depressed areas—all these will be useful.

Now, we are also considering what longer range steps could be taken. In some of them which involve different changes in monetary policy, of course, we are rather limited because of the effect on the outflow of gold. Where for our domestic needs we might want to proceed differently, we are limited, because we don't want to start to stimulate the gold outflow again. But we are giving it a good deal of consideration.

These matters are not easy. You want to affect this hard core of unemployment which may continue after we have had a recovery without providing for inflation, without providing for an outflow of our gold. But we are now, in the administration, considering what other measures could be recommended to the Congress which would assist in this area. But I must say it is one of great complexity.

[15.] Q. Mr. President, a Member of Congress said today that he was tired of seeing the United States second to Russia in the space field. I suppose he speaks for a lot of others. Now, you have asked Congress for more money to speed up our space program. What is the prospect that we will catch up with Russia and perhaps surpass Russia in this field?

THE PRESIDENT. Well, the Soviet Union gained an important advantage by securing these large boosters which were able to put up greater weights, and that advantage is going to be with them for some time. However tired anybody may be, and no one is more tired than I am, it is a fact that it is going to take some time and I think we have to recognize it.

They secured large boosters which have led to their being first in sputnik and led to their first putting their man in space. We are, I hope, going to be able to carry out our efforts with due regard to the problem of the life of the man involved this year. But we are behind and I am sure that they are making a concentrated effort to stay ahead.

We have provided additional emphasis on Saturn; we have provided additional emphasis on Rover; we are attempting to improve other systems which will give us a stronger position—all of which are very expensive, and all of which involve billions of dollars.

So that in answer to your question, as I said in my State of the Union Message, the news will be worse before it is better, and it will be some time before we catch up. We are, I hope, going to go in other areas where we can be first and which will bring perhaps more long-range benefits to mankind. But here we are behind.

[16.] Q. Mr. President, the White House News Photographers Association bars Negro members. Do you feel that a group attached to the White House should follow such a policy?

THE PRESIDENT. No, I don't. I hope they will let everyone in. Everyone comes into the White House and I would hope that those who are involved in that organization—I am sure when the matter is brought to their attention that they will permit everyone who is accredited and is a photographer to come to the White House. Anyway, I'd certainly like to see it.

[17.] Q. Mr. President, Mr. Gomulka said in a speech released yesterday that persons who are now high in your administration, unnamed, had given some assurance during the campaign last fall that if elected you would consider the present Polish-German frontier to be final. Have you given any such assurance?

THE PRESIDENT. Well, I saw the story but I am not informed as to who had the conversation with Mr. Gomulka. In fact, I haven't been able to determine who that might be. But in answer to the—and quite obviously at that time we were not in any position—in any case I was not informed of any conversation then or since then. It may have taken place with Mr. Gomulka. In regard to the question itself, I think that the satisfactory solution of the line should be part of a general solution of the problem of Germany, of the question of Germany, involving the peace treaty with Germany and all the rest.

[18.] Q. Mr. President, in connection with the domestic economy and the lag in Congress on the real program, how do you feel that a greater sense of urgency can be developed among the American people generally? Apparently some Congressmen feel that back home at Eastertime there was not enough push and drive and interest among the people there to give them that interest in your program.

THE PRESIDENT. Well, when you have 7 percent unemployed, you have 93 percent working, and therefore it is a fact that you have these pockets of unemployment, which are extremely serious. Some Congressmen can come back who represent West Virginia and some parts of Pennsylvania, and Gary, Ind., and southern Illinois, and all of the rest, and eastern Kentucky, and tell you that there is a great sense of urgency in this matter. Others who represent other areas may not feel it. But I think it is a serious matter. When you look at the rate of economic growth in Italy, Germany, and France this year, and our economic growth, I would say that it is a matter of the greatest urgency. And in addition, anyone who honestly is seeking a job and can't find it deserves the attention of the United States Government and the people, particularly those who are fortunate enough to work, and that includes us all.

[19.] Q. Sir, the United States administration—your administration—has resisted with vigor, especially through its Ambassador to the U.N., Soviet attempts to change the structure of the world organization. Will the administration, now that General de Gaulle has indicated his displeasure with the structure of the U.N., resist with equal vigor any French attempts to change its structure?

THE PRESIDENT. Well, we would not favor the change in the structure. I am not sure that there is an agreement—there is certainly not an agreement. They may both disapprove of the structure, but their disagreements are based on different factors, General de Gaulle and the Soviet. I would be opposed to changing the United Nations in the way the Soviets proposed. I support the United Nations and its present organization. We can, I think, perhaps provide more effective representation among the civil servants structure of the United Nations among all countries and all continents. And we also, I hope, can consider how the newly joined countries can play a greater, have a greater voice in the Security Council. But these are the kinds of improvements I would like to see in the United Nations— not tripartitism of the kind suggested by the Soviet Union, which would make it impossible for the United Nations to function. And I regret that this same principle has been suggested in the Geneva talks.

[20.] Q. At the beginning of the news conference, sir, you told us what the United States cannot do in Cuba. Last night in the broadcast you said, "I think Latin America is in a more critical period in its relations

with us. Therefore, if we don't move now, Mr. Castro may become a much greater danger than he is to us today." Can you explore, sir, what we can or are doing in the line of that now?

THE PRESIDENT. Well, I think that we attempted to indicate some of the areas where I hoped we could take affirmative action, in the speech I made to the ambassadors in March. Mr. Dillon is in Rio at the meeting of the Inter-American Bank. And we are, in the months of April and May and June, going to attempt in other ways to implement the concept behind *alianza para progresso*. I hope that the Congress will appropriate as quickly as possible the $500 million suggested by the Act of Bogotá. That would be at least an important start. We will have other proposals to make, but I think that it's important that we seize the initiative and do not permit those who are not friends of freedom to become the spokesmen for the material aspirations of the people of Latin America. So that I hope we identify ourselves with both the social, political or the social and the material aspirations of the people of Latin America.

Q. Mr. President, in that same question, you said that—you pointed out that this Government has indicted a pro-Batista Cuban. But I am not clear from your answer, sir, whether this Government will oppose any attempt to mount an offensive against Castro from this country. Could you clarify that?

THE PRESIDENT. If your phrase "to mount an offensive" is as I understand it, I would be opposed to mounting an offensive.

Q. Are we barred by our own neutrality acts or by the OAS treaty from giving any aid or arms to anti-Castro elements in the country?

THE PRESIDENT. Well, there are, of course, as I stated—there is a revolutionary committee here which is, of course, extremely anxious to see a change in government in that country. I am sure that they have— that they are very interested in associating with all those who feel the same way. Mr. Castro enjoyed some support here in the United States and received some assistance when he was attempting to carry out his revolution. In fact, some Americans were involved in the military actions with him. That latter is what we are particularly anxious to——

[21.] Q. Would you say, sir, to what extent the United States can lend its good offices to disputes that arise between some of the new countries and their former colonial countries? I am thinking particularly of the West New Guinea dispute between Indonesia and the Netherlands.

THE PRESIDENT. Well, we are going to see Mr. Sukarno, and I am sure that that will be one of the matters we will discuss. I did not have a chance to—that was one of the matters touched upon by the Foreign Minister of the Netherlands. It is rather difficult for the United States to offer its good offices unless we were asked by both parties to do

so. To the best of my knowledge, we have not been asked by both parties to mediate that dispute.

[22.] Q. Mr. President, returning to that Texas election for a moment, what significance, if any, do you see in the vote there in terms of enacting your congressional programs? In other words, was this purely a local election or did it reflect some sort of a reaction to the administration?

THE PRESIDENT. Well, I would think it would be probably unwise—I don't know how profitable it would be then, let's say that—to attempt to make a judgment. You could—each side can claim some comfort out of the Texas election. But I think that Senator Blakley runs as a Democrat, and I think that his prospects are—I think that he will probably run an active and vigorous campaign. And we will see what happens. But I wouldn't attempt, in the divided field with over 71 candidates, to make any judgments about which way Texas is going.

Reporter: Thank you, Mr. President.

NOTE: President Kennedy's ninth news conference was held in the State Department Auditorium at 4 o'clock on Wednesday afternoon, April 12, 1961.

---

120   Joint Statement and Remarks Following Discussions With Chancellor Adenauer of Germany.   *April* 13, 1961

THE PRESIDENT [*reading*]: During the past two days the President and the Chancellor have had a most cordial and useful exchange of views on a number of subjects of interest to their two Governments.

Their informal conversations have included among other things, discussions of; the problem of a divided Germany including Berlin; the current nuclear test ban talks; political and military developments pertaining to NATO; aid to developing

countries; European economic cooperation; East-West relations; and the situation in some critical areas of world politics.

Also participating in the talks were Secretary of State Dean Rusk and German Foreign Minister Heinrich von Brentano.

The President and the Chancellor reaffirmed the position of their Governments that only through the application of the principle of self-determination can a just and enduring solution be found for the problem of Germany including Berlin. They renewed their pledge to preserve the freedom of the people of West Berlin pending the reunification of Germany in peace and freedom and the restoration of Berlin as the capital of a reunified country.

The President and the Chancellor agreed that intensified political cooperation in NATO is indispensable in order to coordinate the efforts of the Allies for the preservation of peace and security in the world.

The President and the Chancellor reaffirmed their support of NATO as the keystone of the common defense of the North Atlantic area. They underlined the conviction of their Governments as to the necessity for the Alliance to maintain and develop further all military means required to enable them to deter effectively a potential aggressor from threatening the territorial integrity or independence of any ally.

Furthermore, the problems of general and controlled disarmament were discussed. The President and the Chancellor are convinced that reasonable, freely negotiated measures to reverse the growth of uncontrolled national armaments will serve to lessen the danger of war and that concurrently measures should be negotiated to secure a life in freedom to all nations. The goal is a general and total peace.

The President and the Chancellor agreed on the importance of a concerted aid effort by the industrialized free world nations in an amount commensurate with their resources and on a basis corresponding to the magnitude of the task. They pledged the support of the United States and the Federal Republic to the fulfillment of the objectives adopted by the member nations of the Development Assistance Group at their meeting in London two weeks ago.

The President and the Chancellor welcomed the prospective establishment of the Organization for Economic Cooperation and Development as constituting a step of vital importance in the development of an Atlantic Community. The new possibilities which it opens for economic cooperation and economic policy coordination and the means of achieving closer interdependence were also discussed.

In this connection, the President and the Chancellor agreed that continuing attention should be paid to the balance of payments problem.

The important role of the European Economic Community as a powerful and cohesive force in the core of the Atlantic Community was stressed. The dynamic political and institutional potential of the EEC was agreed to be an important element of present strength for the Atlantic Community.

The fruitful exchange of views which the President and the Chancellor have had, as well as the frank and cordial atmosphere in which the talks were conducted have contributed significantly to deepening the ties of friendship and understanding between the two countries and to the strengthening of the free world community. [*Ends reading*]

I want to say, speaking as President of the United States, that it has been a great pleasure to welcome to the shores of this country again the Chancellor of the Federal Republic. I don't think that there is any doubt that history will deal most generously with him in writing the history of the Atlantic Community in the years from 1945 to the present. His accomplishments have been extraordinary in binding the nations of Western Europe together, in strengthening the ties which link the United States and the Federal Republic.

Therefore, speaking personally and also

as President of this country, it is a great honor to welcome again to our shores a friend, a great European, a distinguished leader of his country, the Chancellor of the German Republic, Chancellor Adenauer.

NOTE: The President spoke at 5 p.m. before a group of newsmen assembled outside the entrance to the West Lobby at the White House.

Chancellor Adenauer responded as follows:

"Mr. President, I was deeply moved and touched by the kind words which you said after reading out the communique. I should like to assure you, Mr. President, that I feel exactly the same way as you do, that it was an extremely great pleasure for me to have come back again to your country in order to have had the opportunity of sensing the atmosphere which I was able to find over here. I especially felt this atmosphere in the discussions which I had with you, Mr. President, and I also felt it particularly this afternoon when I was welcomed in the Senate.

"This is the ninth time that I have come here to the United States, and every time I feel deeper and closer linked with your country and with your Government. I am very happy indeed, Mr. President, to have had this chance of meeting you—and you, as the great leader of your country, and therefore the personality that carries such a huge responsibility for the fate of all the free world, and you are dealing with this big task with great energy, with great farsightedness.

"Thank you very much, Mr. President."

The text of a communique and two resolutions adopted by the Development Assistance Group during its fourth meeting in London, March 27–29, together with a list of members of the U.S. delegation are published in the State Department Bulletin (vol. 44, p. 553).

121   Special Message to the Congress on the Regulatory Agencies. *April 13, 1961*

To the Congress of the United States:

I. INTRODUCTION

The discharge by the regulatory agencies of this Government of the responsibilities that the Congress has placed upon them must be a constant and continuing concern of both the Congress and the President. The responsibilities with which they have been entrusted permeate every sphere and almost every activity of our national life. Whether it be transportation, communications, the development of our natural resources, the handling of labor-management relationships, the elimination of unfair trade practices, or the flow of capital investment—to take only a few examples—these agencies and their performance have a profound effect upon the direction and pace of our economic growth. If it is in the public interest to maintain an industry, it is clearly not in the public interest by the impact of regulatory authority to destroy its otherwise viable way of life.

Furthermore, the industries subject to their jurisdiction are intertwined with our national defense to such a degree that the health of these industries can well be regarded as an index of both our strength and our power to survive. Thus the capacity of these regulatory agencies to meet their responsibilities, and the efficiency with which they dispatch their business, become a subject of tremendous significance to the entire nation.

A. *The Responsibilities of the Congress.* Both the Congress and the President have a continuing duty to be watchful with respect to the activities of the regulatory agencies. The Congress must see that the statutes under which the agencies are organized and under which they operate adequately set forth the goals that the Congress seeks to achieve. These statutes should neither place responsibilities upon agencies beyond the practical limits of administrative action, nor couch their objectives in such indecisive terms as to leave vast areas open for the free play of agency discretion. The Congress also has the final responsibility to determine from time to time the extent of the influence that these agencies should exert, whether their authority should be withdrawn from or curtailed in one field or extended to and expanded in another. In addition, the Congress has a rightful concern with both the organization of the regulatory agencies and the fairness and efficiency with which they dispatch their business. Finally, inasmuch as the funds for their operations must be appropriated by the Congress, an intimate knowledge of their operations must be acquired if this function is to be discharged intelligently.

Invaluable hearings and investigations have been carried on by the Congress over the years, particularly in recent years, illuminating weaknesses in administration and the intrusion of practices that have undercut those standards of fairness and impartiality that the nation rightly expects its government to maintain. Congressional oversight is thus a spur to the formulation and enactment of necessary remedial measures.

B. *The Responsibilities of the President.* The President also has his responsibilities with respect to the operation of these agencies. In addition to a constitutional duty to see that the laws are faithfully executed, and other inherent Executive powers, it is his duty to staff the regulatory agencies, granted to him, with men and women competent to handle the responsibilities vested in them and dedicated to the goals set forth in the legislation they are appointed to implement. The President, moreover, is charged in many instances by the Congress with the specific responsibility of removing agency members for misfeasance, inefficiency or the neglect of duty. Coupled with this is the discretionary exercise of his duty to reward faithful public service by the reappointment of

agency members, which requires him to form opinions as to the capability of his or his predecessor's appointees to handle the affairs that the Congress has entrusted to them. In short, the President's responsibilities require him to know and evaluate how efficiently these agencies dispatch their business, including any lack of prompt decision of the thousands of cases which they are called upon to decide, any failure to evolve policy in areas where they have been charged by the Congress to do so, or any other difficulties that militate against the performance of their statutory duties.

This does not mean that either the President or the Congress should intrude or seek to intervene in those matters which by law these agencies have to decide on the basis of open and recorded evidence, where they, like the judiciary, must determine independently what conclusion will best serve the public interest as that interest may be defined by law. Intervention, if it be deemed desirable by the Executive or the Congress in any such matter, must be as a party or an intervenor in the particular proceeding; and such intervention should be accorded no special preference or influence.

C. *The Need for Improvement.* I have long felt that too little attention has been given to the overall operation of these agencies by the President, and that too little cooperation between the Congress and the President has characterized the discharge—each in their respective roles—of their appropriate responsibilities with regard to the operation of these agencies. This cannot continue. For it is now clear that some advance in the methods by which the regulatory agencies dispatch their business is essential if they are to become, as Congress originally intended, effective aids to the growth of our private enterprise system.

For these agencies are not merely regulatory; they are designed to further the expansion of certain facets of our economy, as well as the basic tenets that underlie our system of private enterprise. Delays in the disposition of agency business, and the failure to evolve, other than by a slow case-by-case method, policies essential for our national growth seriously handicap their effectiveness in meeting this function.

In certain areas, where large subsidies are involved, such as shipping and aviation, this promotional function is apparent. But it also underlies their regulatory activities. In the banning of unfair labor practices or the designation of employee representatives, the National Labor Relations Board seeks to uphold the right of collective bargaining—a right upon which we, as a nation, base our hopes for peaceful and satisfactory labor-management relationships. In the banning of practices that characterized our security markets in the nineteen twenties, the Securities and Exchange Commission is more than merely regulatory; it seeks, by its emphasis upon fair dealing, to achieve a saner and sounder outflow of savings into investment. In the banning of monopolistic and unfair trade practices, the Federal Trade Commission seeks to defend those fair trade practices which are necessary for the promotion of our system of private competitive enterprise.

D. *The Caliber of Appointed Personnel.* No amount of reorganization or new procedures can be effective without, or substitute for, high quality personnel in charge of these agencies. No other single step can accomplish as much. In the past three months I have had the opportunity to bring to many of these agencies men whom I believe are both competent to handle their complex affairs and dedicated to their statutory aims. The Senate of the United States has cooperated in this effort. I shall continue to pursue

that policy as the occasion demands, drawing from within and without the Government men of competence and imagination, who are anxious to further the ideals and goals that the Congress has formulated.

E. *Coordination of Regulatory Action.* Before turning to a more specific catalog of our administrative ills and suggestive remedial devices to cure them, there is one particular problem in this area that demands the attention of both the Congress and the President—namely, the lack of coordination of regulatory practices. This stems from the fact that the origin of most of our agencies arose out of the practices or the needs of a particular industry. The monopolistic position held by the railroads at the turn of the century brought the Interstate Commerce Commission into being and successively armed it with growing powers. The limitations of the radio spectrum and of our air space called for the creation of the Federal Communications Commission, the Civil Aeronautics Board and the Federal Aviation Agency. The necessities of maintaining an American flag merchant marine for the national defense and the promotion of commerce form the basis for the existence of the Federal Maritime Board.

This history has in many instances resulted in a compartmentalization of regulatory activities—the tendency of each agency to consider only a single industry, or even a single part of an industry. This is wrong. The emphasis must now in the national interest be placed upon the health and the practices of a series of industries, rightfully competitive but which—from a national standpoint—must be viewed as a whole. The problem of mass metropolitan transportation is not merely that of the railroads, but of highways and busses, of housing and even of helicopters. The Transportation Act of 1940 sought, so far as surface transportation was concerned, to describe as a goal a national policy that would give each method of transportation its appropriate role in our economy. It is disturbing, however, to note that, for example, our common carrier inland waterway traffic, our Great Lakes traffic, our intercoastal and coastal traffic have been withering away, at a pace far more rapid than appears desirable in the light of the low-cost nature of this method of transportation and its potential role in the event of war. Of course, no method of transportation should outlive its useful life; but the *absence* of a firm and comprehensive policy as to what role, if any, existing methods should play in our national economy actually is a policy in itself. It is a policy, as a Senate Subcommittee only recently observed, of unrestrained and destructive competition guided by private interests rather than that of the public as a whole.

In broad areas where the interdependence of industries is apparent, and where we have assumed regulatory functions over all or a portion of them, new and careful articulation of our regulatory efforts is essential. For the pattern now is increasingly one of fragmentation of treatment rather than articulation. Economic effort encouraged by one agency may find discouraging treatment by another. Iron curtains are drawn between agencies operating in the same general area. Their concern is only with the particular segment of the industry over which they have been given jurisdiction, rather than its inter-relation to the whole. Indeed, a lack of cooperative effort often characterizes divisional efforts within a single agency. To correct these regulatory imbalances calls for the shaping of attainable goals and the cessation within agencies and among agencies of jurisdictional strife. Both the Congress and the President can

and should play a part in this effort.

I have already initiated programs in the field of aviation to frame the goals we should set for ourselves for this decade. The attainment of these goals will involve careful, detailed and foresighted coordination on a large scale within the Government and several of its agencies. Similarly, a coordinated effort is underway to provide a better method for the allocation among governmental and nongovernmental users of the radio spectrum, and to improve the regulation over the method of their use. In the field of surface transportation, efforts are being made to work out positions that the administration as a whole should take towards the many remedial measures that have been and are being suggested with respect to its ills. The results of all these efforts will naturally be put before the Congress with such recommendations as they may contain.

II. SHARPENING OF AGENCY RESPONSIBILITY

A. *The Responsibility of the Chairman.* But all this is not enough. It is essential, first of all, for both the Congress and the President to fix responsibility for the overall operation of an agency on an individual rather than on a group or a committee where responsibility can too easily be dissipated. A movement, now demonstrably valuable, was initiated in this respect by a series of reorganization plans proposed by President Truman in 1950. These plans sought to focalize responsibility within the agencies themselves by giving broad managerial powers to the chairman of each agency and in turn holding that chairman responsible, not with respect to his tenure as a member of that agency, but with respect to those managerial powers that attach to his authority as chairman. Nothing in these plans impinged upon the ability of the members of the agencies to act independently with respect to controversies that might be before them for decision, or to participate freely and independently in the shaping of policies that the agency as a whole might seek to pursue. They did, however, pinpoint for the industries subject to their jurisdiction, for the President and for the Congress and the nation the managerial competence displayed by the agency under the guidance and leadership of its chairman.

These reorganization plans of the 1950's did not succeed in covering all the agencies. Too little authority, moreover, was granted to most agency chairmen. I urge that the chairman's role be more clearly defined and his responsibility fixed in every agency. Each chairman should be charged with the authority to staff the agency, subject, of course, to civil service requirements, and, in the important posts, to the advice and consent of his colleagues. Each chairman should be made responsible, subject to statutory requirements, for the form of his agency's organization, so as to enable it effectively to dispatch the business before it. It should be his business to review its budget estimates and subsequently to distribute appropriated funds according to major programs and purposes. In the performance of these managerial duties the chairman should be responsible to the President and serve as chairman at his pleasure, as is explicitly provided with regard to several of the major agencies.

This centralization of responsibility for the managerial functions of the agency will significantly further their ability to deal with the business before them, and better enable both the President and the Congress to reach more informed judgments with respect to the effectiveness with which an agency pursues its designated programs, and the most wise and efficient use of its personnel. As a first step I shall shortly send to the Congress a series of recommendations which will carry out this concept.

B. *Responsibility for Agency Decisions*. One internal administrative device, capable of being immediately adopted by every regulatory agency and already adopted by four important agencies, three since the beginning of this year, needs still wider adoption. This is the practice of assigning to individual agency members the responsibility of being individually responsible for the formulation of the rationale underlying important agency decisions, its quality and its release to the public under the individual member's name. The practice of rendering anonymous decisions, which has hitherto generally prevailed, has served as a means of escaping precision and responsibility. When the actual source of the opinion is unknown save only that it is issued in the name of the agency, it not only impairs its value as a precedent, but also makes for that very dissipation of responsibility that we are trying to reduce in our administrative action.

Fortunately, from the beginning of American law, our judges assumed an individual responsibility for uttering the bases which underlay their decisions. This practice has made not only for conscientiousness in undergoing the travail of decision, but has invited examination of each proffered brick that would seek a place in the structure of our law. The adoption of this practice by the regulatory agencies would, in my opinion, tend to develop the law that they administer, as well as be a continual challenge to each agency member to make his contribution to the advancement of administrative justice. I am requesting a wider adoption of this practice.

III. THE REDUCTION OF EXCESSIVE DELAYS AND
WORKLOADS

A. *Allocation of Agency Activities.* The reduction of existing delays in our regulatory agencies requires the elimination of needless work at their top levels. Because so many of them were established in a day of a less complex economy, many matters that could and should in large measure be resolved at a lower level required decision by the agency members themselves. Even where, by the force of circumstance, many of these matters are now actually determined at a lower level they still must bear the *imprimatur* of the agency members. Consequently, unnecessary and unimportant details occupy far too much of the time and energy of agency members, and prevent full and expeditious consideration of the more important issues.

The remedy is a far wider range of delegations to smaller panels of agency members, or to agency employee boards, and to give their decisions and those of the hearing examiners a considerable degree of finality, conserving the full agency membership for issues of true moment. Such delegation would not be an abnegation of responsibility if the agency retained a discretionary right of review of all such decisions, exercisable either upon its own initiative or upon the petition of a party demonstrating to the agency that the matter in issue is of such substantial importance that it calls for determination at the highest agency level. (Nothing in such a procedural change would, of course, disturb the existing rights of a party to seek judicial review of administrative action.)

A similar procedure—the petition for certiorari—succeeded in clearing up the overburdened docket of the Supreme Court of the United States when it was evolved by the Congress in the Judiciary Act of 1925. Some progress in this direction has already been made by the Interstate Commerce Commission in the past two months, which has delegated to intra-agency boards some 18,000 matters which otherwise would have required the attention of a Commissioner, a panel of that Commission, or the Commission as a whole. But more progress in this agency and other agencies can be made if such a program is supported by concrete measures. I shall shortly submit a series of such measures to the Congress.

B. *The Federal Power Commission.* One situation, however, is not amenable to this general treatment. This is the condition that exists in the Federal Power Commission. In that Commission some 4,000 rate increases by independent natural gas producers and pipe lines are pending and are still unresolved. Under the existing law, these rate increases are suspended but nevertheless go into effect within six months after their filing, subject to the provision that such sums as are collected in excess of the rate ultimately found to be reasonable are to be refunded to the consumer. This incredible backlog of cases, consisting frequently of rate increases piled upon rate increases, involves hundreds of millions of dollars deemed ultimately refundable to the consumer. Indeed the annual amount of rate increases so suspended is over $500,000,000. The total amount of rates collected pursuant to such increases is well over one billion dollars.

This situation is paralleled by another just as serious. Under existing procedures and methods for processing applications for pipeline construction, some 193 applications, proposing construction of 5,761 miles of pipeline at a total estimated cost of some $850,000,000 were pending before the Federal Power Commission as of the end of February 1961.

It is not to be assumed that all these applications would be granted; but it can safely be assumed that more prompt handling of these matters would release hundreds of millions of dollars for construction, giving substantial employment throughout the country and making firm commitments out of orders for materials that are now merely contingent—orders that in turn would provide jobs for men and women in mills, factories and foundries.

(1) *Exemptions.* The cause and cure of this administrative log jam—directly responsible for the exclusion of millions of dollars of construction funds from our economy and potentially responsible for an inordinate rise in the price of natural gas—go far beyond the organization and procedures of the F.P.C. I urge the Congress to enact new legislation reducing the Agency's work-load in the natural gas area in two ways:

—The Commission should be authorized to exempt from rate regulation up to 100% of the small individual producers of natural gas (under two billion cubic feet per year) whose sales in interstate commerce to pipelines account for but 10 per cent of the total. The price which the small producers can charge must of necessity be generally in line with those of the larger producers, and thus they cannot individually affect the general level of prices to the consumer. Such a step must be followed up in the Commission by a vigorous handling of all rate cases in the remaining area of jurisdiction, involving hardly more than 270 producers but affecting some 90 per cent of our natural gas production.

—With respect to the processing of pipeline construction permits, the Commission should be authorized to exempt from all or part of its procedures up to 100% of those applications by interstate pipeline companies which seek merely to enlarge, extend or re-place existing facilities for the benefit of existing customers only, whenever it is assured that its action will not impair the preservation of reserves necessary to supply those consumers, or permit the indiscriminate invasion of one supplier's territory by another.

The formulation of these standards will require creative imagination; but the alternative is to defend bureaucracy for bureaucracy's sake.

(2) *Additional Members.* I also urge, because of the crucial situation in the Federal Power Commission, the increase of that Commission by the addition of two members. Normally, increasing the members of an agency adds little to its efficiency and may instead only handicap its function. But the situation in the Federal Power Commission is unique. That Commission possesses on the one hand jurisdiction over electric power projects and, on the other, under a wholly separate statute—the Natural Gas Act—jurisdiction over the production and transmission for sale in interstate commerce of natural gas. The techniques necessary for the handling of problems in the fields of electric power and natural gas are different. An understanding of one industry does not guarantee a background for dealing with the other. And the chaos and delay now characterizing the gas regulation field may soon increase in the electric power area, where in the coming years the problems surrounding the future of hydro-electric generation will call for re-appraisal and hence for added attention.

With the addition of two more members and the clear discretion to allocate or delegate decision-making to smaller panels as previously mentioned, the Commission's flexibility would be greatly increased. For example, the Chairman could establish three panels of two other members and himself, two working with gas and one with electricity or, one panel of three members could work in one area, while another panel of three covered the other, freeing the Chairman for administrative matters. Provision should also be made for the handling of the lesser matters coming before that Commission by single commissioners, hearing examiners and employee boards, subject always to the right of the Commission as a whole in its discretion to review any decision.

C. *Protection of Consumers.* In its hearings the Senate Subcommittee on Administrative Practice and Procedure has called attention to the inadequacy of consumer protection in those cases where a requested rate increase goes into effect subject to its subsequent approval by the regulatory agency, with a return to the consumer of any amounts later determined to be in excess. Where these requests are overstated the consumer is required to furnish to the utility the very capital on which he is also required to provide the return, the utility's credit standing is damaged by such a large contingent liability, and the actual return to each individual ultimate consumer is often impractical, if not impossible, of achievement.

I, therefore, strongly endorse the Subcommittee's informal recommendation to give increased authority to the Federal Power Commission and to any other regulatory agency where this is a major problem, to make sure that any excess rate which is ultimately disallowed will be returned to the consumer—particularly the power to require the deposit of any such collections in escrow until the rate is finally approved.

IV. THE IMPROVEMENT OF ADMINISTRATIVE PROCEDURES

A. *An Administrative Conference.* This nation has had 15 years of experience under the Administrative Procedure Act of 1946. That Act sought to achieve standards of due process and fairness in the handling of controversies before the regulatory agencies both with respect to adjudication and the issuance of regulations. That aim naturally should be maintained and refined. A large amount of work pointed toward objectives of this nature has been undertaken by the legal profession and by various commissions, as well as by committees of the Congress.

The process of modernizing and reforming administrative procedures is not an easy one. It requires both research and understanding. Moreover, it must be a continuing process, critical of its own achievements and striving always for improvement. Judicialization—the method of determining the content of a controversy by processes akin to those followed by the judiciary—may well be the answer in many cases. But new procedures for the analysis of facts, based upon more informal methods and mobilizing the techniques of other disciplines, can be the answer in other cases, provided always that the fundamentals of due process of law are maintained. There can be no single set of conclusive and abiding formulas appropriate for the effective dispatch of all the diverse and ever-changing issues that these agencies are called upon to resolve.

It is for this reason that I have today issued an Executive Order[1] calling at the earliest practicable date an Administrative Conference of the United States, to be organized and headed by an illustrious jurist and a distinguished council of lawyers and other experts from the Administrative agencies of this government, the bar, and university faculties. This council will consider the questions I have discussed, along with the desirability of making this Conference,

---

[1] Executive Order 10934, 26 F.R. 3233.

if it proves itself, a continuing body for the resolution of these varied and changing procedural problems.

Meanwhile its organization can under the Executive Order be largely modeled upon the Judicial Conference of the United States created in 1922, which has been effective in unifying the judicial system of the United States and modernizing its procedures. Like that Conference, it should bring together the leading members of our regulatory agencies, outstanding practitioners, scholars and other experts. It can meet under the leadership of its Chairman and Council, and consider and propose changes in administrative procedure and organization that will make our regulatory processes more effective. It will be provided through the Department of Justice with a Secretariat, enabling it to become a day-by-day forum for concern with our many administrative problems.

The results of such an Administrative Conference will not be immediate but properly pursued they can be enduring. As the Judicial Conference did for the courts, it can bring a sense of unity to our administrative agencies and a desirable degree of uniformity in their procedures. The interchange of ideas and techniques that can ensue from working together on problems that upon analysis may prove to be common ones, the exchanges of experience, and the recognition of advances achieved as well as solutions found impractical, can give new life and new efficiency to the work of our administrative agencies.

B. *Hearing Examiners.* None of the regulatory agencies can be completely efficient and effective unless they are staffed by capable hearing examiners. The hearing examiner can relieve the agency of protracted adjudicatory processes, speed the disposition of the cases, and serve as a valuable aide in the decisional process. The importance of

his position should be recognized by adequate provisions for responsibility and compensation.

The standards for appointments, compensation, promotion, and removal of Hearing Examiners are set forth in Section 11 of the Administrative Procedure Act of 1946. But the application of those standards has been a continuing source of controversy. The examining procedures permit broad discretion without sufficient assurances of high qualifications. The determination of the proper grade and pay levels has been burdensome, involving almost continuing review of individual positions since 1946. The promotion process is inexact and has led to a concentration of almost all the positions in grade GS–15, the highest regular grade in the Classification. At the same time, further promotion has become virtually impossible.

In order to improve the stature and quality of hearing examiners I recommend the following:

1. Section 11 of the Administrative Procedure Act should be amended to remove the requirement that hearing examiners receive compensation in accordance with the Classification Act. Instead, they should receive salaries equivalent to that prescribed for a grade GS–16 or a grade GS–14. The higher salary would apply to examiners in the major regulatory agencies, whose decisions have a broad economic impact on the national welfare.

2. In order to recognize the administrative management responsibility of the Chief Hearing Examiner in each agency I recommend that he receive $500 per annum additional compensation.

3. The Civil Service Commission should review and raise its current examining standards and practices for hearing examiners. The increased responsibilities recommended

in other sections of this message will require the most qualified people for these key positions.

It is my hope that raising the selection standards and increasing the compensation of the hearing examiners will improve both their stature and their general level of competence.

CONCLUSION

The preservation of a balanced competitive economy is never an easy task. But it should not be made more difficult by administrative delays which place unnecessary obstacles in the path of natural growth or by administrative incompetence that has a like effect.

These reasons alone justify the President and the Congress in having a continuous concern with the operations of our regulatory agencies. The cure for a particular ill may lie in legislation; it may, on the other hand, lie in administration. But given a lack of watchfulness on the part of both the President and the Congress maladministration or ill-conceived policies can endure and multiply to the consequent detriment of our economic and social welfare. It is our task to cooperate in achieving those legislative and administrative steps necessary to enable these agencies to fulfill more effectively their roles of promoting and protecting the national interest.

JOHN F. KENNEDY

122 Remarks at the Protocolary Session of the Council of the Organization of American States. *April* 14, 1961

Mr. Chairman, members of the Council of the Organization of American States, Mr. Secretary General, ladies and gentlemen:

A number of Presidents of the United States have visited the Pan American Union since President Theodore Roosevelt shared with Ambassador Nabuco of Brazil the honor of laying the cornerstone of this building over one-half a century ago. It is an honor for me today, as President of the United States, to share the platform with another distinguished Ambassador from Brazil, Ambassador Lobo.

I doubt whether anyone in all those years has had the privilege of listening to a more thoughtful and wise speech than the one we have just heard from the Chairman of the Council of the Organization of American States.

He has defined our task and our responsibility with both precision and feeling.

There is in this last decade, or in the last few years, in the organizations of the hemisphere and in western Europe of the Atlantic Community, a strong pressure to develop new institutions which will bind us all closer together. I sometimes feel that it is our function and responsibility to use in a more effective manner the institutions we now have.

The Organization of American States represents a great dream of those who believe that the people of this hemisphere must be bound more closely together. It seems to me it is our function and our responsibility, in our day, to make this organization alive, to make it fulfill its function, to make it meet its responsibilities, and not divert ourselves always with developing new institutions, when we have one which was nurtured in time, which has served well in the past and which can, if we give it our lasting support, serve us well in the future.

Ambassador Lobo has suggested in his speech that we stand on the threshold of a new epoch in the development of the American Hemisphere. Science, and all the other things which have sprung from science, have brought a better life into the reach of every man and woman in our hemisphere.

The 20th century has given mankind the tools to make abundance not the gift of a privileged few but a practical possibility for all who live within our frontiers.

The other change which our century has given us is even more important.

That change lies in the new attitude of the mass of our people.

For too long, poverty and inequality and tyranny were accepted as the common lot of man.

Today people everywhere are demanding—and are rightly demanding—a decency of life and opportunity for themselves and their children.

This new attitude has produced an immense surge of hope throughout the entire Western Hemisphere.

Our common purpose today is to harness these new aspirations and these new tools in a great inter-American effort—an effort to lift all the peoples of the Americas, including the people of my own country of the United States, into a new era of economic progress and social justice.

Seventy-one years ago the new American nations were exploring new frontiers of international organization when they formed the International Union of the American Republics for regular consultation to solve common problems.

Today, as the Organization of American States, we constitute the oldest organization of nations now in existence.

Already the OAS—our OAS—has moved ahead to meet the new challenges of the 20th century. The Act of Bogotá is our charter for economic and social advance. Many of the provisions of this Act are Latin American in their inspiration. I am glad that this should be so, because the OAS will thrive and grow only as it derives its vitality from all its members—and only as its members strengthen their own capacity for choice and decision.

The time has come to transform these pledges of social and economic concern into a concrete and urgent collaboration for hemisphere development.

The grand concept of Operation Pan-America has already offered inspiration for such an effort. One month ago I proposed a new cooperative undertaking—an *Alianza para el Progreso*—a 10-year program to give substance to the hopes of our people. I asked all the free republics of the hemisphere to join together to make the 1960's a decade of unexampled progress—progress in wiping out hunger and poverty, ignorance, and disease, from the face of our hemisphere.

This is surely the contemporary mission of Pan-Americanism—to demonstrate to a world struggling for a better life that free men working through free institutions can best achieve an economic progress to which all of us aspire.

But, if we are to succeed, we must take specific steps to realize our common goals—and we must take these steps without delay.

This very week, in Rio de Janeiro, the assembled Governors of the Inter-American Development Bank—representing 20 American Republics—endorsed the principle that development planning on a country-by-country basis was vital to the success of an Alliance for Progress.

Now we may take the next step—to establish the machinery, to adopt the plans and to accept the commitments necessary to speed the pace of hemisphere development.

Therefore I will shortly instruct the United States delegation to this Council to request a meeting of the Inter-American Economic and Social Council at the ministerial level. I will suggest that this meeting be held at a mutually agreeable date this summer. This will give us all the time for the extensive preparation that will be necessary.

This meeting should have three fundamental purposes.

First, it should encourage all the free states of the hemisphere to set deadlines for the completion of preliminary plans for national economic development—as well as to begin long-range planning to meet the development needs of the rest of the decade.

Second, it should set up inter-American machinery to aid participating countries in the rapid formulation of realistic economic plans. The OAS Secretariat, the Economic Commission for Latin America, and the Inter-American Bank are already preparing a joint recommendation for a hemisphere planning-for-progress staff. I hope that a group of economists, drawn from all parts of the hemisphere, will soon be available to offer assistance to all nations preparing development programs.

Third, the meeting should outline basic development goals. This means elaborating the objectives of the Act of Bogotá in all the key areas of economic and social betterment—in education, in land use and tenure, in taxation, in public health, in the mobilization of resources, in the development of self-help programs, in the stabilization of commodity markets, and in regional economic integration.

These details of procedure may seem dry and technical. But they are the basis for the development of the life for our people to which all of us aspire. They should not obscure the exciting prospects for human

growth and liberation which lie within our group.

Our task is to build a society of men and women conscious of their individual identity, of their national aspirations, and also of their common hemisphere interest.

This means re-creating our social systems so that they will better serve our nations and our people.

It means social legislation for workers, and agrarian legislation for those who labor on the land. It means abolishing illiteracy, it means schools for children and adults as well, and it means strengthened institutes of higher education, technical as well as humane. It means doctors and hospitals for the sick. It means roads linking the interior frontiers with the markets and the ports of the coast. It means the spread of industry and the steady increase of both industrial and agricultural production. And it means, above all, the assurance that the benefits of economic growth will accrue, not just to the few, but to the entire national community.

Is this not the new ideal of Pan-Americanism? On the OAS rests much of the hope of realizing these possibilities—on the OAS rests the duty of giving the people of this hemisphere their long-awaited goal of self-fulfillment. Either the OAS will demonstrate a capacity for practical action in the next years, or else it will become an artificial and legalistic body, without substance, without purpose, and finally without a future.

If we are a united hemisphere, we have no choice but to make the OAS the instrument of our common purpose. And the social and economic programs represent only one part of the OAS agenda. For material growth is not an end in itself. It is rather a means—a means of strengthening the dignity and freedom of the individual. This faith in freedom is the enduring essence of our hemisphere cooperation.

This year, six of our sister Republics complete the 150th anniversary of their independence. The memory of past struggles for freedom must confirm our resolution to enlarge the area of freedom every year in our hemisphere. In the end, our moral unity as a family of nations rests on the ultimate faith that only governments which guarantee human freedoms, respect human rights, and vindicate human liberties can advance human progress.

Franklin Roosevelt, at an Inter-American Conference in Buenos Aires 25 years ago, spoke of our common faith in freedom and its fulfillment. He said it had proved a mighty fortress, beyond reach of successful attack in half the world. That faith, he said, arises from a common hope and a common design given us by our Fathers—in differing form, but with a single aim: freedom and security of the individual.

That is our task. That is our responsibility—and that, gentlemen, is our opportunity.

NOTE: The President spoke at 11:10 a.m. at the Pan American Union Building. In his opening words he referred to Ambassador Fernando Lobo, Chairman of the Council of the Organization of American States, and Mr. José A. Mora, Secretary General of the OAS.

123   Statement by the President Upon the Departure of the U.S. Delegation to the Meeting of the Economic Policy Committee of OEEC. *April* 14, 1961

THE UNITED STATES delegation leaves this weekend to participate in the Paris meeting of the Economic Policy Committee of the Organization for European Economic Cooperation (OEEC), April 18–19. Now that the U.S. has ratified the convention establishing the Organization for Economic Cooperation and Development (OECD)— the body which will succeed OEEC—the Paris meeting takes on a high and symbolic significance. It will be the first meeting of the Economic Policy Committee to be conducted within the new spirit of the OECD— a spirit which the United States has undertaken to foster by assuming the responsibilities of full membership.

We are entering a new era in which the day-to-day economic affairs of the western nations are becoming more and more closely intertwined. We face problems and opportunities to which we must respond in full awareness of the common stake in sound decisions. To overcome recession and unemployment, to achieve and maintain high rates of growth, to encourage world economic development—these are no longer merely independent national goals to be pursued by each of our twenty member countries in isolation from the others. They are also common goals which call for sustained common action through economic policies which reflect our common interests.

The strength of the delegation which will represent us at the EPC meeting underscores the importance which we attach to this new departure in our economic relations with Western Europe and Canada and the seriousness with which we have accepted our obligations in the new organization. The delegation includes Walter W. Heller, Chairman of the Council of Economic Advisers, as head of the delegation; Robert V. Roosa, Under Secretary of the Treasury; Ambassador John W. Tuthill, Alternate U.S. Permanent Representative to the OEEC; William McChesney Martin, Jr., Chairman

279

of the Board of Governors of the Federal Reserve System; and Edwin M. Martin, Assistant Secretary of State for Economic Affairs.

It is our hope to develop in the OECD a continuous working partnership in a spirit of flexibility and mutual accommodation among the officials responsible for economic policy in these twenty countries. The Paris meetings will be the first of many designed to build and strengthen relationships for dealing with common economic problems as they unfold.

The American people will follow with deep interest and high hopes the progress of this new venture in Western cooperation and unity.

NOTE: A list of the members of the U.S. delegation was released with the President's statement. In addition to those referred to in the third paragraph, the membership list included the following names: Manuel Abrams, Officer in Charge, Economic Organization Affairs, Office of European Regional Affairs, Department of State; Weir M. Brown, United States Representative to the EMA Board of Management; J. Dewey Daane, Assistant to the Secretary of the Treasury; Dixon Donnelley, Assistant to the Secretary of the Treasury; Mortimer D. Goldstein, Deputy Chief, International Finance Division, Department of State; Alfred Reifman, Economic Policy Adviser, United States Mission to the OEEC; James Tobin, Member of the Council of Economic Advisers; Robert Triffin, Consultant to the Council of Economic Advisers; George H. Willis, Director, Office of International Finance, Department of the Treasury; Ralph A. Young, Adviser to the Board of Governors of the Federal Reserve System.

124 Message to President Olympio of Togo on the Occasion of His Inauguration. *April 15, 1961*

[Released April 15, 1961. Dated April 13, 1961]

Dear Mr. President:

I take great pleasure in extending to you, both personally and officially, my very warm greetings and heartiest congratulations upon the occasion of your inauguration as the first President of the Republic of Togo.

The overwhelming majority by which you were elected reflects the Togolese people's admiration and appreciation for the enlight-

ened leadership you have given during the achievement and consolidation of your country's independence.

May your years in office be marked by peace and prosperity for the Togolese people and by increasingly friendly relations between Togo and the United States.

Sincerely,

JOHN F. KENNEDY

125 Remarks at a Reception Marking African Freedom Day. *April 15, 1961*

Mr. Secretary, Ambassadors, Members of the United States Congress, ladies and gentlemen:

I want to say, speaking personally and as President of the United States, that it is the

greatest possible pleasure to join with you today in celebrating this most important occasion. I think the fact that there are so many Members of the House and Senate here from the Hill, and so many members of the United States Government, indicates our great interest, our profound attachment to the great effort which the people of Africa are making in working towards political freedom, and also working towards a better life for their people.

We also are a revolutionary country, and a revolutionary people, and therefore though many thousands of miles of space may separate our continent from the continent of Africa, today we feel extremely close.

I think that the preoccupation of the United States with the cause of freedom not only here but around the world has been one of the most important facets of our national life. All of our early revolutionary leaders I think echoed the words of Thomas Jefferson that "the disease of liberty is catching." And some of you may remember the exchange between Benjamin Franklin and Thomas Paine. Benjamin Franklin said, "Where freedom lives, there is my home." And Thomas Paine said, "Where freedom is not, there is my home." I think all of us who believe in freedom feel a sense of community with all those who are free, but I think we also feel an even stronger sense of community with those who are not free but who some day will be free.

I must say as an American that I can think that all of us in this country can find continued inspiration and I think all of you who are citizens of countries who have newly emerged to freedom, can find some inspiration in the Farewell Address of George Washington.

Washington wrote the address in 1796, in order to eliminate himself as a candidate for a third term, but most importantly to give some guidance to our new Republic. His text, his speech, is alive with the spirit of liberty. It speaks of a union of States as a political fortress against the batteries of internal and external enemies. It counsels against adopting hasty improvisations at the expense of principles which thus might undermine what cannot be directly overthrown.

There is wisdom and foresight in Washington's instructions to cherish public credit and to promote as an object of primary importance institutions for the general diffusion of knowledge. Washington told our forefathers in this country to reject permanent, inveterate antipathies against particular nations and passionate attachments for others, and said any nation failing in this is in some degree a slave. He warned against foreign influences which seek to tamper with domestic factions, to practice the arts of seduction, to mislead public opinion. His rule for commercial relations was to have with them as little political connection as possible.

Every year in the United States Senate we read his speech, and we still get great benefit from it. I hope that in your experiences you will also get benefit from it. I want to stress today that we look to the future with the greatest degree of confidence and hope, and I hope that the people of your continent recognize that we wish to be associated intimately with them, that we wish for them the same things we wish for ourselves: peace, the opportunity to develop our own institutions in our own way, to be independent not only politically but in all of the other kinds of independence which make up important national security.

Your brightest days are still ahead. I believe ours are, also. And I hope when the history of these times is written—when the history of the decade of the Sixties will be written, they will record a more intimate and closer attachment year by year between your countries of Africa and this country of the United States.

NOTE: The President spoke at 11:37 a.m. in the Drawing Room of the State Department Auditorium. His opening words "Mr. Secretary" referred to Secretary of State Dean Rusk.

The diplomatic reception was held by Secretary Rusk for African ambassadors accredited to Washington and their staffs. Among the guests were Members of Congress and the Supreme Court and Government officials.

African Freedom Day was originally proclaimed in a resolution of the first Conference of Independent African States at Accra in April 1958.

126   Statement by the President on the Occasion of National Library Week. *April* 16, 1961

BOOKS AND LIBRARIES and the will to use them are among the most important tools our nation has to diffuse knowledge and to develop our powers of creative wisdom. It is, however, a fact that there is an important gap in the availability of books and libraries to our citizens. As many as 25 million people have no library service, and nearly 50 million have inadequate services. There is a great imbalance of resources among the great educational institutions of our country. A majority of elementary schools has no libraries at all.

The community public library is one of the richest and more enduring aspects of our historical heritage. I hope very much that National Library Week will have widespread citizen participation and that it will serve to encourage all of us to improve libraries and to stimulate reading throughout the nation.

127   Letter to the President of the Senate and to the Speaker of the House Transmitting a Farm Bill. *April* 17, 1961

Dear Mr.————:

Transmitted herewith, for consideration by the Congress, is a draft of a bill which would carry out the principal recommendations set forth in my message to the Congress on March 16, 1961. I believe that the legislation will provide the basis for a sound and healthy agricultural economy.

It will enable the farmer, in cooperation with the government, to adjust his production to meet our domestic needs and our international commitments for food and fiber. It is directed toward assuring that the farmer has an opportunity to achieve an income comparable to that enjoyed by other segments of our economy for comparable

investments in labor and capital. At the same time, it makes provision for the consideration and protection of the interests of consumers. The programs established under the legislation should gradually reduce the burden imposed by large storage costs and high surpluses.

Included in the bill is an extension of the Agricultural Trade Development and Assistance Act of 1954, together with additional amendments to enable us to correlate our programs in agriculture more effectively with our foreign aid programs. This will permit us to make maximum use of our agricultural productivity to further economic development, peace and freedom in the world. Other provisions in the bill are directed toward the encouragement of farm cooperatives, the expansion of commercial exports of agriculture products, and the liberalization and extension of farm credit services.

This legislation will offer the farmer an opportunity to share directly in the framing of the programs that determine the marketing of his products. It permits the producers of food and fiber to assert their views upon the management of their production. Final authority over the policies and programs to be adopted continues to reside in the Congress.

Although the proposed legislation deals with agricultural problems, it will have beneficial effects upon both agriculture and industry, both the farmer and the city dweller, both rural and urban workers. The interrelation between prosperity on the farm and economic health of the city has never been more apparent. I urge that the Congress give these proposals prompt consideration.

Sincerely,

JOHN F. KENNEDY

NOTE: This is the text of identical letters addressed to the Honorable Lyndon B. Johnson, President of the Senate, and to the Honorable Sam Rayburn, Speaker of the House of Representatives.

128 Toasts of the President and Prime Minister Caramanlis of Greece. *April* 17, 1961

Mr. Prime Minister, Mrs. Caramanlis, ladies and gentlemen:

It is a great pleasure for me to welcome you to the shores of the United States once again. Someone once said everyone is either an Athenian or a Spartan—in any case, we are all Greeks in the great sense of recognizing the wellspring from which all of our efforts began.

I am sure that sometimes the Greeks get tired of hearing about ancient history, because they are concerned with making history today. But we look to ancient Greece for inspiration, and we look to modern Greece for comradeship.

And it is a source of pleasure to me today, as President, to welcome them, and also to recall that I was a Member of Congress in 1947 when President Truman put forward the Truman Doctrine. Congressman Halleck who is now Minority Leader of the House was then I believe Majority Whip, and the Majority Leader at that time was Congressman Martin—one of the few oc-

casions when Mr. Rayburn was not the Speaker—but they did indicate their strong support. While there were some questions in dispute in the 80th Congress, that was not one of them. But the immediate support which President Truman as the President received from Members of Congress on both sides—Republican and Democratic—indicates our awareness of the vital role that Greece has to play in the life of Europe, our common obligation to Greece and our common hope for the future.

So that I must say, on a day in which I believe we celebrate the birthday of the Foreign Minister—this first luncheon we have had at the White House where ladies have been permitted to be present, attended by distinguished citizens of my own country, many of whom are of Greek extraction, and all of whom are great citizens of this country and have been greatly interested in furthering good relations between the United States and Greece—it is a great pleasure to welcome you both here, and I ask you all to rise and drink with me a toast to the King of Greece.

NOTE: The President proposed this toast at a state luncheon at the White House. Prime Minister Caramanlis responded as follows:

Mr. President, I am particularly happy of the opportunity offered me by your courteous invitation to be with you today. My assistants and myself consider that this invitation is a manifestation of the interest borne by the United States to Greece, to its people and to its problems. I wish to assure you that the Greek Nation deeply appreciates this interest and has for your great country feelings of admiration and confidence.

We Greeks often forget the evil that many, at times, have done to us. But we never forget those friends who helped us in difficult times, and granted us their effective support. For this reason, we gratefully remember the Truman Doctrine and the practical interest subsequently displayed by the United States for preserving Greek independence and developing our economy.

We know that our friends do not forget Greece's contribution in the creation of those spiritual and moral values which are the heritage of modern civilization. They do not forget, either, the sacrifices undergone by the Greek Nation through thousands of years, in the defense of freedom and justice.

Even in the most recent past, at the conclusion of a war at the price of immense sacrifice to Greece, the Greeks were confronted with a dire and bloody 3-year struggle, when international communism launched its attack for the enslavement of their country. This struggle was won, thanks to Allied assistance and the valuable American aid, with Greek blood only.

Mr. President, Greece lies at one of the most sensitive areas of the world and has felt the consequences of international upheavals, even when she has not been their center. More than any other country, she needs peace because in addition to the scarcity of her natural resources she was subjected to the heaviest destruction as a result of repeated enemy aggressions.

Greece is following a sincere policy towards all, a policy based on the faithful observance of the Charter of the United Nations and honest fulfillment of international obligations. She believes that international legality is the best way to secure the maintenance of peace and at the same time the safeguard of freedom.

Mr. President, now, as the elected leader of the American people, you assume the responsibility of governing this great country and dealing with the tremendous problems emanating from the present international situation. In this high mission, the hopes of all free men are turned to you with confidence and with optimism.

In coping with present day difficulties Greece will be found steady on the side of her NATO allies, contributing to their endeavors for peace, for freedom, and for justice.

True to her history, Greece always stands guard vigilantly of those political, moral, and spiritual values, in which she believes.

I raise my glass to you, Mr. President, to Mrs. Kennedy, and to the prosperity of the American Nation.

---

129   Letter to the President of the Senate and to the Speaker of the House Recommending an Additional Assistant Secretary of Health, Education, and Welfare. *April* 18, 1961

[Released April 18, 1961. Dated April 17, 1961]

Dear Mr. —————:

The vast increase in the international responsibilities of the Secretary of Health, Education, and Welfare in recent years has made this a major activity of that Department. It is important and requires continuing attention at a high level. I, therefore, recommend that there be established in the Department a position of Assistant Secretary of Health, Education, and Welfare, and that this Assistant Secretary have primary responsibility for advising and assisting the Secretary in the field of international affairs. Transmitted herewith is a draft of a bill which would carry out this purpose.

It may be necessary, from time to time, to assign additional functions to this Assistant Secretary. He should not be precluded from assuming such additional functions.

I am convinced that the United States must make full use of its professional and technical skills and resources to assist other nations, particularly those newly emerging. The new Assistant Secretary would provide the necessary assistance to the Secretary to meet this need.

Enclosed is a letter from the Secretary of Health, Education, and Welfare describing the proposal in more detail.

Sincerely,

JOHN F. KENNEDY

NOTE: This is the text of identical letters addressed to the Honorable Lyndon B. Johnson, President of the Senate, and to the Honorable Sam Rayburn, Speaker of the House of Representatives.

130 Letter to the President of the Senate and to the Speaker of the House Transmitting Bill for a New Department of Urban Affairs and Housing. *April 18, 1961*

Dear Mr. ————:

I am transmitting for consideration by the Congress draft legislation to carry out the recommendation in my March ninth message on housing and community development calling for the creation of a new cabinet Department of Urban Affairs and Housing.

Two problems standing near the top of our national priority list are first, preventing the appalling deterioration of many of our country's urban areas and rehabilitating the cities of our nation which currently contain 70% of our people—a figure that is constantly growing—and second, insuring the availability of adequate housing for all segments of our population. Since the National Housing Agency was established in 1942, the activities of the Federal Government in housing and in working with States and local communities in the rebuilding of our urban areas and in preventing their deterioration has increased steadily. The importance of this area of Federal activity merits recognition by the establishment of the De-partment of Urban Affairs and Housing. Thus, the new Secretary of Urban Affairs and Housing will be in a position to present the nation's housing and metropolitan development needs to the Cabinet and will by virtue of his position provide the necessary leadership in coordinating the many Federal programs in these fields.

In addition to the draft bill, I am enclosing a letter from the Director of the Bureau of the Budget describing the legislation in detail. A letter identical to this one is being sent to the Speaker of the House of Representatives (President of the Senate).

I hope that prompt action can be scheduled on this important legislation and that the Congress will act favorably on the proposal.

Sincerely,

JOHN F. KENNEDY

NOTE: This is the text of identical letters addressed to the Honorable Lyndon B. Johnson, President of the Senate, and to the Honorable Sam Rayburn, Speaker of the House of Representatives.

131   Statement by the President on the Occasion of the First
        Anniversary of the Revolution in Korea.   *April 18, 1961*

TODAY the Korean Government and people are celebrating the first anniversary of the April 19 Revolution in the Republic of Korea. I should like to salute the Korean Government and people on this important occasion and express the respect and admiration which the American people have in their hearts for the Korean people who have so courageously demonstrated their devotion to the cause of political democracy and social progress.

On this significant anniversary I should like to affirm to the Korean people once again that the United States shares their hopes and ideals and that my Government intends to continue to assist the Korean Government in every possible and appropriate way in its efforts to lead the Korean people toward the better life they so greatly desire and deserve.

132   Message to Chairman Khrushchev Concerning the Meaning of
        Events in Cuba.   *April 18, 1961*

Mr. Chairman:

You are under a serious misapprehension in regard to events in Cuba. For months there has been evident and growing resistance to the Castro dictatorship. More than 100,000 refugees have recently fled from Cuba into neighboring countries. Their urgent hope is naturally to assist their fellow Cubans in their struggle for freedom. Many of these refugees fought along side Dr. Castro against the Batista dictatorship; among them are prominent leaders of his own original movement and government.

These are unmistakable signs that Cubans find intolerable the denial of democratic liberties and the subversion of the 26th of July Movement by an alien-dominated regime. It cannot be surprising that, as resistance within Cuba grows, refugees have been using whatever means are available to return and support their countrymen in the continuing struggle for freedom. Where people are denied the right of choice, recourse to such struggle is the only means of achieving their liberties.

I have previously stated, and I repeat now, that the United States intends no military intervention in Cuba. In the event of any military intervention by outside force we will immediately honor our obligations under the inter-American system to protect this hemisphere against external aggression. While refraining from military intervention in Cuba, the people of the United States do not conceal their admiration for Cuban patriots who wish to see a democratic system in an independent Cuba. The United States government can take no action to stifle the spirit of liberty.

I have taken careful note of your statement that the events in Cuba might affect peace in all parts of the world. I trust that this does not mean that the Soviet government, using the situation in Cuba as a pretext, is planning to inflame other areas of the world. I would like to think that your government has too great a sense of responsibility to embark upon any enterprise so dangerous to general peace.

I agree with you as to the desirability of

steps to improve the international atmosphere. I continue to hope that you will cooperate in opportunities now available to this end. A prompt cease-fire and peaceful settlement of the dangerous situation in Laos, cooperation with the United Nations in the Congo and a speedy conclusion of an acceptable treaty for the banning of nuclear tests would be constructive steps in this direction. The regime in Cuba could make a similar contribution by permitting the Cuban people freely to determine their own future by democratic processes and freely to cooperate with their Latin American neighbors.

I believe, Mr. Chairman, that you should recognize that free peoples in all parts of the world do not accept the claim of historical inevitability for the Communist revolution. What your government believes is its own business; what it does in the world is the world's business. The great revolution in the history of man, past, present and future, is the revolution of those determined to be free.

JOHN F. KENNEDY

[N. S. Khrushchev, Chairman, Council of Ministers, Union of Soviet Socialist Republics]

133   Transcript of Remarks During an Interview for British Television. *April 19, 1961*

THE PRESIDENT [*answering question on the meaning of the phrase "The New Frontier"*]: Well, the phrase expressed our feeling that the 1960's—this coming decade—was going to be a period of entirely new material changes, that science had brought the means of a much better life for people, not only in the United States, but all around the world and, therefore, we were crossing that frontier. In addition, we were crossing frontiers which involve the struggle for freedom here in the United States and around the world. So that, although the United States is an old country—at least its Government is old as governments now go today—nevertheless I thought we were moving into a new period, and the new frontier phrase expressed that hope.

Q. Sir, I believe that the American Government probably centers more on its leader than any other democratic government in the world. How are you trying to bring it into more manageable proportions? I believe you've reorganized your staff?

THE PRESIDENT. That's right. I think sometimes we overstate the administerial difficulties of the Presidency. I think really, in many ways, it's a judicial function, where alternatives are suggested which involve great matters, and finally the President must make a decision. That is really the most onerous and important part of the burdens of being President. President Truman used to have a sign on this desk which said: "The buck stops here"—these matters which involve national security and our national strength finally come to rest here—but the matter of our staff, therefore, should serve only to make sure that these important matters are brought here in a way which permits a clear decision after alternatives have been presented. Occasionally, in the past, I think the staff has been used to get a pre-arranged agreement which is only confirmed at the President's desk, and that I don't agree with.

Q. I believe your biggest domestic problem, sir, is the recession. How do you see this going?

THE PRESIDENT. It is. We have about 7 percent unemployed. We have the highest number of people working that have ever worked, but we do have this serious economic situation which our friends in Canada also have had, but in a more intensive way. Part of that has come because of the tremendous productive capacity of the United States which is able to quickly produce and catch up with demand. We also have a serious problem because of technological and structural changes in coal, steel, basically, and, even if we have a recovery this summer, we're still going to have serious problems in some of our coal fields where the demand has been lessened and where the new machinery has produced extraordinary productive feats with very few people working. We're producing more coal than we've ever produced before with far less men, and it's difficult for a coal miner who's spent 20 years underground, who's lived around the coal fields, to move and train. So I would say that that's going to be a serious problem for us, and I'm sure you're going to have it.

Q. Your social welfare plans are running into a certain amount of opposition here. How do you hope to get around that?

THE PRESIDENT. Well, any time you try to do anything, there's a lot of people like it the way it used to be. And I just think that the United States has to continue to make it possible for everyone to realize their talents. We have to provide greater emphasis on education. The first people thrown out of work today are those with the least education, so we have to provide the best education. Secondly, we have to provide greater security for our older people. You do much more than we do here in the United States. What we are trying to do conservative governments did—well, at least Lloyd George as a liberal started it before World War I, and conservative governments endorsed it. What we propose to do, which is to provide medical care for the aged on social security, would be regarded as hopelessly reactionary in England, but nevertheless it's new here. We are also attempting to provide equality of opportunity so that all citizens, regardless of their race, have a chance to participate fully in our life. But change is always pleasant to some people and unpleasant to others, and we will make progress, not as much as we would hope, but we're going to move.

NOTE: The remarks were recorded on March 17 during an interview between the President and Ian Trethowen of the Associated TeleVision Limited of London. The program was broadcast in London on April 19.

134 Remarks Upon Awarding the National Geographic Society Gold Medal to Jacques-Yves Cousteau. *April* 19, 1961

I WANT TO SAY that it is a great pleasure and honor to participate in this event sponsored by the National Geographic, which has been a great American institution, and which has advanced our information on a whole variety of horizons in the last years.

And I can think of no more felicitous award than this to the Captain. We have learned in the last 60 years how to fly better than the birds—or at least higher and longer. And the Captain has given us a possibility that some day we may swim as well as the fish—or at least deeper. And he is, therefore, one of the great explorers of an entirely new dimension, and I can imagine his satisfaction in having opened up the ocean floor to man and to science.

And therefore I present the National Geographic Society Gold Medal Award to Captain Jacques-Yves Cousteau, undersea pioneer to earth-bound man, who gave the key to the silent world, April 19, 1961.

I congratulate also your wife, the representatives of France, the Ambassador, Mrs.

Alphand, and your country, and you, and the Geographic.

NOTE: The presentation was made in the Rose Garden at the White House. At the conclusion of his remarks the President referred to Hervé Alphand, the French Ambassador, and Mme. Alphand.

135   Joint Statement Following Discussions With Prime Minister Caramanlis of Greece.   *April* 20, 1961

DURING HIS VISIT in Washington, April 17–20, the Greek Prime Minister and the President of the United States held cordial and friendly talks upon subjects of mutual interest. The same atmosphere characterized the talks of the Prime Minister with the Secretary of State, the Secretary of Defense, and other members of the Cabinet and personalities of the United States administration.

The Greek Prime Minister expressed his thanks for President Kennedy's invitation to visit the United States officially and for the generous hospitality accorded to him and his party.

With regard to the relationship between the two countries it was agreed that it is based upon solid and sincere friendship, mutual confidence and loyalty to common ideals and the common purpose of maintaining peace and safeguarding liberty and justice. It was agreed that cooperation between the two countries in the political, economic and cultural fields should be broadened. It was also agreed that Greek-American ties, which have been steeled in common struggles, should be further tightened in the face of common dangers.

The Greek Prime Minister reviewed the problems in which Greece is vitally interested. These problems, which include the difficult tasks facing the Greek people in achieving economic development and in

raising the standard of living, met with the wholehearted interest of United States officials. Mr. Caramanlis expressed the grateful appreciation of the Greek people for United States aid in the past and for the determination of the United States to continue to support the efforts of Greece in carrying out its programs of economic development.

The Americans expressed admiration for the stability and progress prevailing in Greece and recognized that these are invaluable assets for the free world.

Special attention was devoted to common defense problems within the framework of the North Atlantic Treaty Organization. The need to strengthen the defense of the Atlantic community was recognized, as well as the importance of promoting solidarity and the fulfillment by each member of its obligations.

In this connection the situation in the Balkans, and other areas of immediate interest for Greece, were given particular attention because of their importance in the maintenance of international stability and peace. It was agreed that the two governments would continue to consult closely with each other regarding developments in these areas and elsewhere.

It was recognized that progress toward world security and peace would be advanced greatly by reliable, controlled international disarmament agreements and by agreed procedures for the maintenance of peace and the settlement of disputes in accordance with the principles of the United Nations Charter. To uphold those principles, determination was expressed to strengthen the United

Nations Organization.

The emergence of the new African states was welcomed by both sides. Both countries recognized their responsibility to assist those new states in their growth and development.

136 Special Message to the Congress on Taxation. *April 20, 1961*

To the Congress of the United States:

A strong and sound Federal tax system is essential to America's future. Without such a system, we cannot maintain our defenses and give leadership to the free world. Without such a system, we cannot render the public services necessary for enriching the lives of our people and furthering the growth of our economy.

The tax system must be adequate to meet our public needs. It must meet them fairly, calling on each of us to contribute his proper share to the cost of government. It must encourage efficient use of our resources. It must promote economic stability and stimulate economic growth. Economic expansion in turn creates a growing tax base, thus increasing revenue and thereby enabling us to meet more readily our public needs, as well as our needs as private individuals.

This message recognizes the basic soundness of our tax structure. But it also recognizes the changing needs and standards of our economic and international position, and the constructive reform needs to keep our tax system up to date and to maintain its equity. Previous messages have emphasized the need for prompt Congressional and Executive action to alleviate the deficit in our international balance of payments—to increase the modernization, productivity and competitive status of American indus-

try—to stimulate the expansion and growth of our economy—to eliminate to the extent possible economic injustice within our own society—and to maintain the level of revenues requested in my predecessor's Budget. In each of these endeavors, tax policy has an important role to play and necessary tax changes are herein proposed.

The elimination of certain defects and inequities as proposed below will provide revenue gains to offset the tax reductions offered to stimulate the economy. Thus no net loss of revenue is involved in this set of proposals. I wish to emphasize here that they are a "set"—and that considerations of both revenue and equity, as well as the interrelationship of many of the proposals, urge their consideration as a unit.

I am instructing the Secretary of the Treasury to furnish the Committee on Ways and Means of the House a detailed explanation of these proposals in connection with their legislative consideration.

I. LONG-RANGE TAX REFORM

While it is essential that the Congress receive at this time this Administration's proposals for urgent and obvious tax adjustments needed to fulfill the aims listed above, time has not permitted the comprehensive review necessary for a tax structure which is so complicated and so critically important to so many people. This message is but a first though urgent step along the road to constructive reform.

I am directing the Secretary of the Treasury, building on recent tax studies of the Congress, to undertake the research and preparation of a comprehensive tax reform program to be placed before the next session of the Congress.

Progressing from these studies, particularly those of the Committee on Ways and Means and the Joint Economic Committee, the program should be aimed at providing a broader and more uniform tax base, together with an appropriate rate structure. We can thereby work toward the goal of a higher rate of economic growth, a more equitable tax structure, and a simpler tax law. I know these objectives are shared by—and, at this particular time of year, acutely desired by—the vast majority of the American people.

In meeting the demands of war finance, the individual income tax moved from a selective tax imposed on the wealthy to the means by which the great majority of our citizens participates in paying for well over one-half of our total budget receipts. It is supplemented by the corporation income tax, which provides for another quarter of the total.

This emphasis on income taxation has been a sound development. But so many taxpayers have become so preoccupied with so many tax-saving devices that business decisions are interfered with, and the efficient functioning of the price system is distorted.

Moreover, special provisions have developed into an increasing source of preferential treatment to various groups. Whenever one taxpayer is permitted to pay less, someone else must be asked to pay more. The uniform distribution of the tax burden is thereby disturbed and higher rates are made

necessary by the narrowing of the tax base. Of course, some departures from uniformity are needed to promote desirable social or economic objectives of overriding importance which can be achieved most effectively through the tax mechanism. But many of the preferences which have developed do not meet such a test and need to be reevaluated in our tax reform program.

It will be a major aim of our tax reform program to reverse this process, by broadening the tax base and reconsidering the rate structure. The result should be a tax system that is more equitable, more efficient and more conducive to economic growth.

II. TAX INCENTIVE FOR MODERNIZATION AND EXPANSION

The history of our economy has been one of rising productivity, based on improvement in skills, advances in technology, and a growing supply of more efficient tools and equipment. This rise has been reflected in rising wages and standards of living for our workers, as well as a healthy rate of growth for the economy as a whole. It has also been the foundation of our leadership in world markets, even as we enjoyed the highest wage rates in the world.

Today, as we face serious pressure on our balance of payments position, we must give special attention to the modernization of our plant and equipment. Forced to reconstruct after wartime devastation, our friends abroad now possess a modern industrial system helping to make them formidable competitors in world markets. If our own goods are to compete with foreign goods in price and quality, both at home and abroad, we shall need the most efficient plant and equipment.

At the same time, to meet the needs of a growing population and labor force, and to achieve a rising per capita income and employment level, we need a high and rising level of both private and public capital formation. In my preceding messages, I have proposed programs to meet some of our needs for such capital formation in the public area, including investment in intangible capital such as education and research, as well as investment in physical capital such as buildings and highways. I am now proposing additional incentives for the modernization and expansion of private plant and equipment.

Inevitably, capital expansion and modernization—now frequently under the name of automation—alter established modes of production. Great benefits result and are distributed widely—but some hardships result as well. This places heavy responsibilities on public policy, not to retard modernization and capital expansion but to promote growth and ameliorate hardships when they do occur—to maintain a high level of demand and employment, so that those who are displaced will be reabsorbed quickly into new positions—and to assist in retraining and finding new jobs for such displaced workers. We are developing, through such measures as the Area Redevelopment Bill and a strengthened Employment Service, as well as assistance to the unemployed, the programs designed to achieve these objectives.

High capital formation can be sustained only by a high and rising level of demand for goods and service. Indeed, the investment incentive itself can contribute materially to achieving the prosperous economy under which this incentive will make its maximum contribution to economic growth. Rather than delaying its adoption until all excess capacity has disappeared and unemployment is low, we should take this step now to strengthen our anti-recession pro-

gram, stimulate employment and increase our export markets.

Additional expenditures on plant and equipment will immediately create more jobs in the construction, lumber, steel, cement, machinery and other related capital goods industries. The staffing of these new plants—and filling the orders for new export markets—will require additional employees. The additional wages of these workers will help create still more jobs in consumer goods and service industries. The increase in jobs resulting from a full year's operation of such an incentive is estimated at about half a million.

Specifically, therefore, I recommend enactment of an investment tax incentive in the form of a tax credit of

—15% of all new plant and equipment investment expenditures in excess of current depreciation allowances

—6% of such expenditures below this level but in excess of 50% of depreciation allowances; with

—10% on the first $5,000 of new investment as a minimum credit.

This credit would be taken as an offset against the firm's tax liability, up to an overall limitation of 30% in the reduction of that liability in any one year. It would be separate from and in addition to depreciation of the eligible new investment at cost. It would be available to individually owned businesses as well as corporate enterprises, and apply to eligible investment expenditures made after January 1 of this year. To remain a real incentive and make a maximum contribution to those areas of capital expansion and modernization where it is most needed, and to permit efficient administration, eligible investment expenditures would be limited to expenditures on new plant and equipment, on assets located in the United States, and on assets with a life of six years or more. Investments by public utilities other than transportation would be excluded, as would be investment in residential construction including apartments and hotels.

Of the eligible firms, it is expected that many small firms would be able to take advantage of the minimum credit of 10% on the first $5000 of new investment which is designed to provide a helpful stimulus to the many small businesses in need of modernization. Other small firms, subject to a 30% tax rate, would strive to be eligible for the full 15% credit—the equivalent for such firms of a deduction from their gross income for tax purposes of 50% of the cost of new investment. Among the remaining firms, it is expected that a majority would be induced to make new investments in modern plant and equipment in excess of their depreciation in order to earn the 15% credit. New and growing firms would be particularly benefited. The 6% credit for those whose new investment expenditures fall between 50% and 100% of their depreciation allowances is designed to afford some substantial incentive to the depressed or hesitant firm which knows it cannot yet achieve the 15% credit.

In arriving at this form of tax encouragement to investment, careful consideration was given to other alternatives. If the credit were given across-the-board to all new investment, a much larger revenue loss would result from those expenditures which would have been undertaken anyway or represent no new level of effort. Our objective is to provide the largest possible inducement to new investment which would not otherwise be undertaken. Thus the plan recommended above would involve the same revenue loss—approximately $1.7 billion—as only a 7 percent credit across-the-board to all new investment.

The use of current depreciation allowances as the threshold above which the higher rate of credit would apply recommends itself for a number of reasons. Depreciation reflects the average level of investment over the past, but is a less restrictive and more stable test than the use of an average of investment expenditures for a period such as the preceding five years. In addition, the depreciation allowances themselves in effect supply tax-free funds for investment up to this level. We now propose a tax credit—which would help to secure funds needed for the additional investment beyond that level.

The proposed credit, in terms of the revenue loss involved, will also be much more effective as an inducement to investment than an outright reduction in the rate of corporation income tax. Its benefits would be distributed more broadly, since the proposed credit will apply to individuals and partnerships as well as corporations. It will also be more effective as a direct incentive to corporate investment, and increase available funds more specifically in those corporations most likely to use them for additional investment. In short, whereas the credit will have the advantage of focusing on the profitability of new investment, much of the revenue loss under a general corporate rate reduction would be diverted into raising the profitability of old investment.

It is true that this advantage of focusing entirely on new investment is shared by the alternative strongly urged by some—a tax change permitting more rapid depreciation of new assets (be it accelerated depreciation or an additional depreciation allowance for the first year). But the proposed investment credit would be superior, in my view, for a number of reasons. In the first place, the determination of the length of an asset's life and proper methods of depreciation have a normal and important function in determining taxable income, wholly apart from any considerations of incentive; and they should not be altered or manipulated for other purposes that would interfere with this function. It may be that on examination some of the existing depreciation rules will be found to be outmoded and inequitable; but that is a question that should be separated from investment incentives. A review of these rules and methods is underway in the Treasury Department as a part of its overall tax reform study to determine whether changes are appropriate and, if so, what form they should take. Adoption of the proposed incentive credit would in no way foreclose later action on these aspects of depreciation.

In the second place, an increase in tax depreciation tends to be recorded in the firm's accounts, thereby raising current costs and acting as a deterrent to price reduction. The proposed investment credit would not share this defect.

Finally, it is clear that the tax credit would be more effective in inducing new investment for the same revenue loss. The entire credit would be reflected immediately in the increased funds available for investment without increasing the company's future tax liability. A speed-up in depreciation only postpones the timing of the tax liability on profits from the investment to a later date—an increase in profitability not comparable to that of an outright tax credit. Yet accelerated depreciation is much more costly in immediate revenues.

For example, on an average investment, a tax credit of 15% would bring the same return to the firm as an additional first year depreciation of over 50% of the cost of the investment. Yet the immediate revenue loss to the Treasury from such additional depreciation would be twice as much, and would

remain considerably higher for many years. The incentive to new investment our economy needs, and which this recommendation would provide at a revenue loss of $1.7 billion, could be supplied by an initial write-off only at an immediate cost of $3.4 billion.

I believe this investment tax credit will become a useful and continuous part of our tax structure. But it will be a new venture and remain in need of review. Moreover, it may prove desirable for the Congress to modify the credit from time to time, so as to adapt it to the needs of a changing economy. I strongly urge its adoption in this session.

III. TAX TREATMENT OF FOREIGN INCOME

Changing economic conditions at home and abroad, the desire to achieve greater equity in taxation, and the strains which have developed in our balance of payments position in the last few years, compel us to examine critically certain features of our tax system which, in conjunction with the tax system of other countries, consistently favor United States private investment abroad compared with investment in our own economy.

1. *Elimination of tax deferral privileges in developed countries and "tax haven" deferral privileges in all countries.* Profits earned abroad by American firms operating through foreign subsidiaries are, under present tax laws, subject to United States tax only when they are returned to the parent company in the form of dividends. In some cases, this tax deferral has made possible indefinite postponement of the United States tax; and, in those countries where income taxes are lower than in the United States, the ability to defer the payment of U.S. tax by retaining income in the subsidiary

companies provides a tax advantage for companies operating through overseas subsidiaries that is not available to companies operating solely in the United States. Many American investors properly made use of this deferral in the conduct of their foreign investment. Though changing conditions now make continuance of the privilege undesirable, such change of policy implies no criticism of the investors who so utilize this privilege.

The undesirability of continuing deferral is underscored where deferral has served as a shelter for tax escape through the unjustifiable use of tax havens such as Switzerland. Recently more and more enterprises organized abroad by American firms have arranged their corporate structures—aided by artificial arrangements between parent and subsidiary regarding intercompany pricing, the transfer of patent licensing rights, the shifting of management fees, and similar practices which maximize the accumulation of profits in the tax haven—so as to exploit the multiplicity of foreign tax systems and international agreements in order to reduce sharply or eliminate completely their tax liabilities both at home and abroad.

To the extent that these tax havens and other tax deferral privileges result in U.S. firms investing or locating abroad largely for tax reasons, the efficient allocation of international resources is upset, the initial drain on our already adverse balance of payments is never fully compensated, and profits are retained and reinvested abroad which would otherwise be invested in the United States. Certainly since the postwar reconstruction of Europe and Japan has been completed, there are no longer foreign policy reasons for providing tax incentives for foreign investment in the economically advanced countries.

If we are seeking to curb tax havens, if we recognize that the stimulus of tax deferral is no longer needed for investment in the developed countries, and if we are to emphasize investment in this country in order to stimulate our economy and our plant modernization, as well as ease our balance of payments deficit, we can no longer afford existing tax treatment of foreign income.

I therefore recommend that legislation be adopted which would, after a two-step transitional period, tax each year American corporations on their current share of the undistributed profits realized in that year by subsidiary corporations organized in economically advanced countries. This current taxation would also apply to individual shareholders of closely-held corporations in those countries. Since income taxes paid abroad are properly a credit against the United States income tax, this would subject the income from such business activities to essentially the same tax rates as business activities conducted in the United States. To permit firms to adjust their operations to this change, I also recommend that this result be achieved in equal steps over a two-year period, under which only one-half of the profits would be affected during 1962. Where the foreign taxes paid have been close to the U.S. rates, the impact of this change would be small.

This proposal will maintain United States investment in the developed countries at the level justified by market forces. American enterprise abroad will continue to compete with foreign firms. With their access to capital markets at home and abroad, their advanced technical know-how, their energy, resourcefulness and many other advantages, American firms will continue to occupy their rightful place in the markets of the world. While the rate of expansion of some American business operations abroad may be reduced through the withdrawal of tax deferral such reduction would be consistent with the efficient distribution of capital resources in the world, our balance of payments needs, and fairness to competing firms located in our own country.

At the same time, I recommend that tax deferral be continued for income from investment in the developing economies. The free world has a strong obligation to assist in the development of these economies, and private investment has an important contribution to make. Continued income tax deferral for these areas will be helpful in this respect. In addition, the proposed elimination of income tax deferral on United States earnings in industrialized countries should enhance the relative attraction of investment in the less developed countries.

On the other hand, I recommend elimination of the "tax haven" device anywhere in the world, even in the underdeveloped countries, through the elimination of tax deferral privileges for those forms of activities, such as trading, licensing, insurance and others, that typically seek out tax haven methods of operation. There is no valid reason to permit their remaining untaxed regardless of the country in which they are located.

2. *Taxation of Foreign Investment Companies.* For some years now we have witnessed substantial outflows of capital from the United States into investment companies created abroad whose principal justification lies in the tax benefits which their method of operation produces. I recommend that these tax benefits be removed and that income derived through such foreign investment companies be treated in substantially the same way as income from domestic

investment companies.

3. *Taxation of American Citizens Abroad.* It is no more justifiable to provide tax exemptions for individuals living in the developed countries than it is to provide tax inducements for capital investment there. Nor should we permit totally unjustified tax benefits to be obtained by those Americans whose choice of residence is dictated primarily by their desire to minimize taxes.

I, therefore, recommend:

—that the total tax exemption now accorded the earned income of American citizens residing abroad be completely terminated for those residing in economically advanced countries;

—that this exemption for earned income be limited to $20,000 for those residing in the less developed countries; and

—that the exemption of $20,000 of earned income now accorded those citizens who stay (but do not reside) abroad for 17 out of 18 months also be completely terminated for those living or travelling in the economically advanced countries.

4. *Estate Tax on Property Located Abroad.* I recommend that the exclusion from the estate tax accorded real property situated abroad be terminated. With the adoption several years ago of the credit for foreign taxes under the estate tax, there is no justification for the continued exemption of such property.

5. *Allowance for Foreign Tax on Dividends.* Finally, the method by which the credit for foreign income taxes is computed in the case of dividends involves a double allowance for foreign income taxes and should be corrected.

These proposals, along with more detailed and technical changes needed to improve the taxation of foreign income, are expected to reduce substantially our balance of payments deficit and to increase revenues by at least $250 million per year.

I next recommend a number of measures to remove other serious defects in the income tax structure. These changes, while making a beginning toward the comprehensive tax reform program mentioned above, will provide sufficient revenue gains to offset the cost of the investment tax credit and keep the revenue-producing potential of our tax structure intact.

1. *Withholding on Interest and Dividends.* Our system of combined withholding and voluntary reporting on wages and salaries under the individual income tax has served us well. Introduced during the war when the income tax was extended to millions of new taxpayers, the wage-withholding system has been one of the most important and successful advances in our tax system in recent times. Initial difficulties were quickly overcome, and the new system helped the taxpayer no less than the tax collector.

It is the more unfortunate, therefore, that the application of the withholding principle has remained incomplete. Withholding does not apply to dividends and interest, with the result that substantial amounts of such income, particularly interest, improperly escape taxation. It is estimated that about $3 billion of taxable interest and dividends are unreported each year. This is patently unfair to those who must as a result bear a larger share of the tax burden. Recipients of dividends and interest should pay their tax no less than those who receive wage and salary income, and the tax should be paid just as promptly. Large continued avoidance of tax on the part of some has a steadily demoralizing effect on the compliance of others.

This gap in reporting has not been appreciably lessened by educational programs. Nor can it be effectively closed by intensified enforcement measures, except by the expenditure of inordinate amounts of time and money. Withholding on corporate dividends and on investment type interest, such as interest paid on taxable government and corporate securities and savings accounts, is both necessary and practicable.

I, therefore, recommend the enactment of legislation to provide for a 20% withholding rate on corporate dividends and taxable investment type interest, effective January 1, 1962, under a system which would not require the preparation of withholding statements to be sent to recipients. It would thus place a relatively light burden of compliance on the payers of interest and dividends—certainly less than that placed on payers of wages and salaries—while at the same time largely solving the compliance problem for most of the taxpayers receiving dividends and interest. Steps will also be taken to avoid hardships for recipients who are not subject to tax.

The remaining need for compliance, largely in the high income group subject to a higher tax rate, would be met through the concentration of enforcement devices on taxpayers in these brackets. Introduction of equipment for the automatic processing of information returns would be especially helpful for this purpose and would thus supplement the extension of withholding.

Enactment of this proposal is estimated to increase revenue by $600 million per year.

2. *Repeal of the Dividend Credit and Exclusion.* The present law provides for an

exclusion from income of the first $50 of dividends received from domestic corporations and for a 4% credit against tax of such dividend income in excess of $50. These provisions were enacted in 1954. Proponents argued that they would encourage capital formation through equity investment, and that they would provide a partial offset to the so-called double taxation of dividend income. It is now clear that they serve neither purpose well; and I, therefore, recommend the repeal of both the dividend credit and exclusion.

The dividend credit and exclusion are not an efficient stimulus to capital expansion in the form of plant and equipment. The revenue losses resulting from these provisions are spread over a large volume of outstanding shares rather than being concentrated on new shares; and the stimulating effects of the provisions are thus greatly diluted, resulting in relatively little increases in the supply of equity funds and a relatively slight reduction in the cost of equity financing. In fact, such reduction as does occur is more likely to benefit large corporations with easy access to the capital market, while being of little use to small firms which are not so favorably situated. Insofar as raising the profitability of new investment in plant and equipment is concerned, the tax investment credit proposed above would be far more effective since it is offered to the corporation, where the actual investment decision is made.

The dividend credit and exclusion are equally inadequate as a solution to the so-called problem of double taxation. Whatever may be the merits of the arguments respecting the existence of double taxation, the provisions of the 1954 Act clearly do not offer an appropriate remedy. They greatly overcompensate the dividend recipient in the high income bracket, while giving either insufficient or no relief to shareholders with smaller income.

This point deserves emphasis. For viewed simply as a means of tax reduction, the dividend credit is wholly inequitable. The distribution of its benefits is highly favorable to the taxpayers in the upper income groups who receive the major part of dividend income. Only about 10 percent of dividend income accrues to those with incomes below $5,000; about 80 percent of it accrues to that 6.5% of taxpayers whose incomes exceed $10,000 a year. Similarly, dividend income is a sharply rising fraction of total income as we move up the income scale. Thus, dividend income is about 1 percent of all income from all sources for those taxpayers with incomes of $3,000 to $5,000; but it constitutes more than 25 percent of the income for those with $100,000 to $150,000 of income, and about 50 percent for those with incomes over $1,000,000.

The role of the dividend credit should not be confused with the broader question of tax rates applicable to high incomes. These high rates deserve re-examination; and this is one of the problems which will be examined in the context of next year's tax reform. But if top bracket rates were to be reduced, the dividend credit is not the way to do it. Rate reductions, if appropriate, should apply no less to those with high incomes from other sources, such as professional and salaried people whose tax position is particularly difficult today.

If the credit is eliminated, the $50 exclusion should also be discarded for similar reasons. The tax saving from the exclusion is substantially greater for a dividend recipient with a high income than for a recipient with low income. Moreover, on equity grounds, there is no reason for giving tax reduction to that small fraction of low income tax payers who receive dividends in contrast to those who must live on wages, interest, rents or other forms of income.

The 1954 formula therefore is a dead-end and should be rescinded, effective December 31 of this year. The estimated revenue gain is $450 million per year.

3. *Expense Accounts.* In recent years widespread abuses have developed through the use of the expense account. Too many firms and individuals have devised means of deducting too many personal living expenses as business expenses, thereby charging a large part of their cost to the Federal Government. Indeed, expense account living has become a byword in the American scene.

This is a matter of national concern, affecting not only our public revenues, our sense of fairness, and our respect for the tax system, but our moral and business practices as well. This widespread distortion of our business and social structure is largely a creature of the tax system, and the time has come when our tax laws should cease their encouragement of luxury spending as a charge on the Federal treasury. The slogan—"It's deductible"—should pass from our scene.

Tighter enforcement of present legislation will not suffice. Even though in some instances entertainment and related expenses have an association with the needs of business, they nevertheless confer substantial tax-free personal benefits to the recipients. In other cases, deductions are obtained by disguising personal expenses as business outlays. But under present law, it is extremely difficult to separate out and disallow such pseudo-business expenditures. New legislation is needed to deal with the problem.

I, therefore, recommend that the cost of such business entertainment and the maintenance of entertainment facilities (such as yachts and hunting lodges) be disallowed in full as a tax deduction and that restric-

tions be imposed on the deductibility of business gifts, expenses of business trips combined with vacations, and excessive personal living expenses incurred on business travel away from home.

I feel confident that these measures will be welcomed by the American people. I am also confident that business firms, now forced to emulate the expense account favors of their competitors, however unsound or uneconomical such practices may be, will welcome the removal of this pressure. These measures will strengthen both our tax structure and the moral fibre of our society. These provisions should be effective as of January 1, 1962 and are estimated to increase Treasury receipts by at least $250 million per year.

4. *Capital Gains on Sale of Depreciable Business Property.* Another flaw which should be corrected at this time relates to the taxation of gains on the sale of depreciable business property. Such gains are now taxed at the preferential rate applicable to capital gains, even though they represent ordinary income.

This situation arises because the statutory rate of depreciation may not coincide with the actual decline in the value of the asset. While the taxpayer holds the property, depreciation is taken as a deduction from ordinary income. Upon its resale, where the amount of depreciation allowable exceeds the decline in the actual value of the asset so that a gain occurs, this gain under present law is taxed at the preferential capital gains rate. The advantages resulting from this practice have been increased by the liberalization of depreciation rates.

Our capital gains concept should not encompass this kind of income. This inequity should be eliminated, and especially so in view of the proposed investment credit. We should not encourage through tax incentives the further acquisition of such property as long as this loophole remains.

I therefore recommend that capital gains treatment be withdrawn from gains on the disposition of depreciable property, both personal and real property, to the extent that depreciation has been deducted for such property by the seller in previous years, permitting only the excess of the sales price over the original cost to be treated as a capital gain. The remainder should be treated as ordinary income. This reform should immediately become effective as to all sales taking place after the date of enactment. It is estimated to raise revenue by $200 million annually.

5. *Cooperatives and Financial Institutions.* Another area of the tax laws which calls for attention is the treatment of cooperatives, private lending institutions, and fire and casualty insurance companies.

Contrary to the intention of Congress, substantial income from certain cooperative enterprises, reflecting business operations, is not being taxed either to the cooperative organization itself or its members. This situation must be corrected in a manner that is fair and just to both the cooperatives and competing businesses.

The present inequity has resulted from court decisions which held patronage refunds in certain forms to be non-taxable. I recommend that the law be clarified so that all earnings are taxable to either the cooperatives or to their patrons, assessing the patron on the earnings that are allocated to him as patronage dividends or refunds in scrip or cash. The withholding principle recommended above should also be applied to patronage dividends or refunds so that the average patron receiving scrip will, in effect, be given the cash to pay his tax on his patronage dividend or refund. The cooperatives should not be penalized by the as-

sessment of a patronage tax upon dividends or refunds taxable to the patron but left in the business as a substitute for the sale of securities to obtain additional equity capital. The exemption for rural electric cooperatives and credit unions should be continued.

The tax provisions applicable to fire and casualty insurance companies, originally adopted in 1942, need to be reviewed in the light of current conditions. Many of these companies, organized on the mutual or reciprocal basis are now taxed under a special formula which does not take account of their underwritings gains and thus results in an inequitable distribution of the tax burden among various types of companies. Consideration should be given to taxing mutual or reciprocal companies on a basis similar to stock companies, following the pattern of similar treatment of stock and mutual enterprise in the life insurance field.

Some of the most important types of private savings and lending institutions in the country are accorded tax deductible reserve provisions which substantially reduce or eliminate their Federal income tax liability. These provisions should be reviewed with the aim of assuring non-discriminatory treatment.

Remedial legislation in these fields would enlarge the revenues and contribute to a fair and sound tax structure.

V. TAX ADMINISTRATION

One of the major characteristics of our tax system, and one in which we can take a great deal of pride, is that it operates primarily through individual self-assessment. The integrity of such a system depends upon the continued willingness of the people honestly and accurately to discharge this annual price of citizenship. To the extent that some people are dishonest or careless in their dealings with the government, the majority is forced to carry a heavier tax burden.

For voluntary self-assessment to be both meaningful and productive of revenues, the citizens must not only have confidence in the fairness of the tax laws, but also in their uniform and vigorous enforcement of these laws. If non-compliance by the few continues unchecked, the confidence of the many in our self-assessment system will be shaken and one of the cornerstones of our government weakened.

I have in this message already recommended the application of withholding to dividends and interest and revisions to halt the abuses of expense accounts. These measures will improve taxpayer compliance and raise the regard of taxpayers for the fairness of our system. In addition, I propose three further measures to improve the tax enforcement machinery.

1. *Taxpayer Account Numbers.* The Internal Revenue Service has begun the installation of automatic data processing equipment to improve administration of the growing job of tax collection and enforcement. A system of identifying taxpayer account numbers, which would make possible the bringing together of all tax data for any one particular taxpayer, is an essential part of such an improved collection and enforcement program.

For this purpose, social security numbers would be used by taxpayers already having them. The small minority currently without such numbers would be assigned numbers which these persons could later use as well for social security purposes if needed. The numbers would be entered on tax returns, information returns, and related documents.

I recommend that legislation be enacted to authorize the use of taxpayer account numbers beginning January 1, 1962 to iden-

tify taxpayer accounts throughout the processing and record keeping operations of the Internal Revenue Service.

2. *Increased Audit Coverage.* The examination of tax returns is the essence of the enforcement process. The number of examining personnel of the Internal Revenue Service, however, has been consistently inadequate to cope with the audit workload. Consequently, it has been unable to audit carefully many of the returns which should be so examined. Anticipated growth in our population will, of course, increase this enforcement problem.

Related to broadened tax audit is the criminal enforcement program of the Revenue Service. Here, the guiding principle is the creation of a deterrent to tax evasion and to maintain or, if possible, increase voluntary compliance with all taxing statutes. This means placing an appropriate degree of investigative emphasis on all types of tax violations, in all geographical areas, and identifying violations of substance in all income brackets regardless of occupation, business or profession.

Within this framework of a balanced enforcement effort, the Service is placing special investigative emphasis on returns filed by persons receiving income from illegal sources. I have directed all Federal law enforcement agencies to cooperate fully with the Attorney General in a drive against organized crime, and to utilize their resources to the maximum extent in conducting investigations of individuals engaged in criminal activity on a major scale. With the foregoing in mind, I have directed the Secretary of the Treasury to provide through the Internal Revenue Service a maximum effort in this field.

To fulfill these requirements for improved audits, enforcement and anti-crime investigation, it is essential that the Service be provided additional resources which will pay their own cost many times over. In furthering the Service's long-range plans, the prior Administration asked additional appropriations of $27.4 million to hire about 3,500 additional personnel during fiscal 1962, including provisions for the necessary increases in space and modern equipment vital to the efficient operation of the Service. To meet the commitments described above, this Administration reviewed these proposals and recommended that they be increased by another $7 million and 765 additional personnel to expedite the expansion and criminal enforcement programs. The pending alternative of only 1,995 additional personnel, or less than one-half of the number requested, this Administration would constitute little more than the additional employees needed each year during the 1960's just to keep up with the estimated growth in number and complexity of returns filed. Thus I must again strongly urge the Congress to give its full support to my original request. These increases will safeguard the long-term adequacy of the nation's traditional voluntary compliance system and, at the same time, return the added appropriations several times over in added revenue.

3. *Inventory Reporting.* It is increasingly apparent that the manipulation of inventories has become a frequent method of avoiding taxes. Current laws and regulations generally permit the use of inventory methods which are acceptable in recognized accounting practice. Deviations from these methods, which are not always easy to detect during examination of tax returns, can often lead to complete non-payment of taxes until the inventories are liquidated; and, for some taxpayers, this represents permanent tax reduction. The understating of the valuation of inventories is the device most frequently used.

I have directed the Internal Revenue Service to give increasing attention to this area of tax avoidance, through a stepped-up emphasis on both the verification of the amounts reported as inventories and an examination of methods used in arriving at their reported valuation.

VI. TAX RATE EXTENSION

As recommended by my predecessor, it is again necessary that Congress enact an extension of present corporation income and excise tax rates otherwise scheduled for reduction or termination on July 1, 1961. Such extension has been adopted by the Congress on a number of previous occasions, and our present revenue requirements make such extension absolutely necessary again this year.

In the absence of such legislation, the corporate tax rate would be decreased 5 percentage points, from 52 percent to 47 percent, excise tax rates on distilled spirits, beer, wines, cigarettes, passenger automobiles, automobile parts and accessories, and the transportation of persons would also decline; and the excise tax on general telephone service would expire. We cannot afford the loss of these revenues at this time.

VII. AVIATION FUEL

The last item on the agenda relates to aviation fuel. The two previous Administrations have urged that civil aviation, a mature and growing industry, be required to pay a fair share of the costs of operating and improving the Federal airways system. The rapidly mounting costs of these essential services to air transportation makes the imposition of user charges more imperative now than ever before. The most efficient method for recovering a portion of these costs equitably from the airway users is through a tax on aviation fuel. Present law provides for a net tax of 2 cents a gallon on aviation gasoline but no tax on jet fuel. The freedom from tax of jet fuel is inequitable and is resulting in substantial revenue losses due to the transition to jet power and the resulting decline in gasoline consumption.

My predecessor recommended a flat 4½ cent tax for both aviation gasoline and jet fuels. Such a request, however, appears to be unrealistic in view of the current financial condition of the airline industry.

Therefore, I recommend:

—extending the present net 2-cent rate on aviation gasoline to jet fuels;

—holding this uniform rate covering both types of fuel at the 2-cent level for fiscal 1962; and

—providing for annual increments in this rate of ½ cent after fiscal year 1962 until the portion of the cost of the airways properly allocable to civil aviation is substantially recovered by this tax.

The immediate increase in revenue from this proposal is modest in comparison with anticipated airways costs; and the annual gradation of further increases is intended to moderate the impact of the tax on the air carrier industry. Should future economic or other developments warrant, a more rapid increase in the fuel tax will be recommended. The decline from the revenues estimated by my predecessor is not large, and will be met by the reforms previously proposed. I repeat my earlier recommendation that, consistent with the user charge principle, revenues from the aviation fuels tax be retained in the general fund rather than diverted to the highway trust fund.

CONCLUSION

The legislation recommended in this message offers a first step toward the broader objective of tax reform. The immediate need is for encouraging economic growth through modernization and capital expansion, and to remove tax preferences for foreign investment which are no longer needed and which impair our balance of payments position. A beginning is made also toward removing some of the more glaring defects in the tax structure. The revenue gain in these proposals will offset the revenue cost of the investment credit. Finally, certain rate extensions are needed to maintain the revenue potential of our fiscal system.

These items need to be done now; but they are a first step only. They will be followed next year by a second set of proposals, aimed at thorough income tax reform. Their purpose will be to broaden and unify the income tax base, and to review the entire rate structure in the light of these revisions. Let us join in solving these immediate problems in the coming months, and then join in further action to strengthen the foundations of our revenue system.

JOHN F. KENNEDY

137 Memorandum on Racial or Other Discrimination in Federal Employee Recreational Associations. *April 20, 1961*

[Released April 20, 1961.   Dated April 18, 1961]

Memorandum for the Heads of all Executive Departments and Agencies:

Executive Order Number 10925, promulgated March 6, 1961, reaffirms that "discrimination because of race, creed, color or national origin is contrary to the Constitutional principles and policies of the United States" and that "it is the policy of the Executive Branch of the Government to encourage by positive measures equal opportunity for all qualified persons within the Government."

I want immediate and specific action taken to assure that no use is made of the name, sponsorship, facilities, or activity of any Executive Department or Agency by or for any employee recreational organization practicing discrimination based on race, creed, color, or national origin. Current practices in each Department are to be brought into immediate compliance with this policy, and a report by the head of each Executive Agency filed to that effect before May 1, 1961.

JOHN F. KENNEDY

138 Address Before the American Society of Newspaper Editors. *April 20, 1961*

Mr. Catledge, members of the American Society of Newspaper Editors, ladies and gentlemen:

The President of a great democracy such as ours, and the editors of great newspapers such as yours, owe a common obligation to the people: an obligation to present the facts, to present them with candor, and to present them in perspective. It is with that obligation in mind that I have decided in the last 24 hours to discuss briefly at this time the recent events in Cuba.

On that unhappy island, as in so many other arenas of the contest for freedom, the news has grown worse instead of better. I have emphasized before that this was a struggle of Cuban patriots against a Cuban dictator. While we could not be expected to hide our sympathies, we made it repeatedly clear that the armed forces of this country would not intervene in any way.

Any unilateral American intervention, in the absence of an external attack upon ourselves or an ally, would have been contrary to our traditions and to our international obligations. But let the record show that our restraint is not inexhaustible. Should it ever appear that the inter-American doctrine of non-interference merely conceals or excuses a policy of nonaction—if the nations of this Hemisphere should fail to meet their commitments against outside Communist penetration—then I want it clearly understood that this Government will not hesitate in meeting its primary obligations which are to the security of our Nation!

Should that time ever come, we do not intend to be lectured on "intervention" by those whose character was stamped for all time on the bloody streets of Budapest! Nor would we expect or accept the same outcome which this small band of gallant Cuban refugees must have known that they were chancing, determined as they were against heavy odds to pursue their courageous attempts to regain their Island's freedom.

But Cuba is not an island unto itself; and our concern is not ended by mere expressions of nonintervention or regret. This is not the first time in either ancient or recent history that a small band of freedom fighters has engaged the armor of totalitarianism.

It is not the first time that Communist tanks have rolled over gallant men and women fighting to redeem the independence of their homeland. Nor is it by any means the final episode in the eternal struggle of liberty against tyranny, anywhere on the face of the globe, including Cuba itself.

Mr. Castro has said that these were mercenaries. According to press reports, the final message to be relayed from the refugee forces on the beach came from the rebel commander when asked if he wished to be evacuated. His answer was: "I will never leave this country." That is not the reply of a mercenary. He has gone now to join in the mountains countless other guerrilla fighters, who are equally determined that the dedication of those who gave their lives shall not be forgotten, and that Cuba must not be abandoned to the Communists. And we do not intend to abandon it either!

The Cuban people have not yet spoken their final piece. And I have no doubt that they and their Revolutionary Council, led by Dr. Cardona—and members of the families of the Revolutionary Council, I am informed by the Doctor yesterday, are involved themselves in the Islands—will continue to speak up for a free and independent Cuba.

Meanwhile we will not accept Mr. Castro's attempts to blame this nation for the hatred which his onetime supporters now regard his repression. But there are from this sobering episode useful lessons for us all to learn. Some may be still obscure, and await further information. Some are clear today.

First, it is clear that the forces of communism are not to be underestimated, in Cuba or anywhere else in the world. The advantages of a police state—its use of mass terror and arrests to prevent the spread of free dissent—cannot be overlooked by those who expect the fall of every fanatic tyrant. If the self-discipline of the free cannot match the iron discipline of the mailed fist—in economic, political, scientific and all the other kinds of struggles as well as the military—then the peril to freedom will continue to rise.

Secondly, it is clear that this Nation, in concert with all the free nations of this hemisphere, must take an ever closer and more realistic look at the menace of external Communist intervention and domination in Cuba. The American people are not complacent about Iron Curtain tanks and planes less than 90 miles from their shore. But a nation of Cuba's size is less a threat to our survival than it is a base for subverting the survival of other free nations throughout the hemisphere. It is not primarily our interest or our security but theirs which is now, today, in the greater peril. It is for their sake as well as our own that we must show our will.

The evidence is clear—and the hour is late. We and our Latin friends will have to face the fact that we cannot postpone any longer the real issue of survival of freedom in this hemisphere itself. On that issue, unlike perhaps some others, there can be no middle ground. Together we must build a hemisphere where freedom can flourish; and where any free nation under outside attack of any kind can be assured that all of our resources stand ready to respond to any request for assistance.

Third, and finally, it is clearer than ever

that we face a relentless struggle in every corner of the globe that goes far beyond the clash of armies or even nuclear armaments. The armies are there, and in large number. The nuclear armaments are there. But they serve primarily as the shield behind which subversion, infiltration, and a host of other tactics steadily advance, picking off vulnerable areas one by one in situations which do not permit our own armed intervention.

Power is the hallmark of this offensive—power and discipline and deceit. The legitimate discontent of yearning people is exploited. The legitimate trappings of self-determination are employed. But once in power, all talk of discontent is repressed, all self-determination disappears, and the promise of a revolution of hope is betrayed, as in Cuba, into a reign of terror. Those who on instruction staged automatic "riots" in the streets of free nations over the efforts of a small group of young Cubans to regain their freedom should recall the long roll call of refugees who cannot now go back—to Hungary, to North Korea, to North Viet-Nam, to East Germany, or to Poland, or to any of the other lands from which a steady stream of refugees pours forth, in eloquent testimony to the cruel oppression now holding sway in their homeland.

We dare not fail to see the insidious nature of this new and deeper struggle. We dare not fail to grasp the new concepts, the new tools, the new sense of urgency we will need to combat it—whether in Cuba or South Viet-Nam. And we dare not fail to realize that this struggle is taking place every day, without fanfare, in thousands of villages and markets—day and night—and in classrooms all over the globe.

The message of Cuba, of Laos, of the rising din of Communist voices in Asia and Latin America—these messages are all the same. The complacent, the self-indulgent, the soft societies are about to be swept away with the debris of history. Only the strong, only the industrious, only the determined, only the courageous, only the visionary who determine the real nature of our struggle can possibly survive.

No greater task faces this country or this administration. No other challenge is more deserving of our every effort and energy. Too long we have fixed our eyes on traditional military needs, on armies prepared to cross borders, on missiles poised for flight. Now it should be clear that this is no longer enough—that our security may be lost piece by piece, country by country, without the firing of a single missile or the crossing of a single border.

We intend to profit from this lesson. We intend to reexamine and reorient our forces of all kinds—our tactics and our institutions here in this community. We intend to intensify our efforts for a struggle in many ways more difficult than war, where disappointment will often accompany us.

For I am convinced that we in this country and in the free world possess the necessary resource, and the skill, and the added strength that comes from a belief in the freedom of man. And I am equally convinced that history will record the fact that this bitter struggle reached its climax in the late 1950's and the early 1960's. Let me then make clear as the President of the United States that I am determined upon our system's survival and success, regardless of the cost and regardless of the peril!

NOTE: The President spoke at the Statler Hilton Hotel in Washington. His opening words "Mr. Catledge" referred to Turner Catledge, President of the American Society of Newspaper Editors, and Managing Editor of the New York Times. Later in his remarks the President referred to Dr. José Miró Cardona, President of the Cuban Revolutionary Council.

139   The President's News Conference of *April 21, 1961*

THE PRESIDENT. Gentlemen, I have several announcements to make.

[1.] I know that many of you have further questions about Cuba. I made a statement on that subject yesterday afternoon. We are continuing consultations with other American Republics. Active efforts are being made by ourselves and others on behalf of various individuals, including any Americans who may be in danger. I do not think that any useful national purpose would be served by my going further into the Cuban question this morning. I prefer to let my statement of yesterday suffice for the present.

[2.] I am pleased to announce that the United States has offered concrete support to a broad scale attack by the United Nations upon world hunger. I have instructed the Food for Peace Director to offer $40 million in food commodities towards an initial United Nations reserve of $100 million. This will be administered by the United Nations Food and Agricultural Organization. I am informed that other United Nations members will also make similar contributions. The food will then be used to relieve hunger and to improve nutrition in underdeveloped countries of the world. Our participation in this project will complement rather than diminish our existing Food for Peace program.

[3.] Third, I am pleased to announce that the Veterans Administration will pay a special insurance dividend of $230 million, in a decision made this morning, to approximately 5 million holders of GI life insurance, beginning July 1. These dividends have been speeded up in order to assist the economy.

[4.] And lastly, I am pleased to announce that the Peace Corps is proceeding with its first project. At the request of the Government of Tanganyika, an African country that will gain its first independence on December 28, the Peace Corps will send to that country a party of surveyors, geologists, and civil engineers to help Tanganyika's own technicians map and construct roads. Twenty surveyors, 4 geologists, and 4 civil engineers will provide some of the skills needed to accelerate the development plan. There is nothing more important in Tanganyika than the development of roads to open up the country, and I am delighted that some Americans have volunteered to help in this important effort.

[5.] Q. Mr. President, can you tell us anything about your talk with Vice President Nixon last night?

THE PRESIDENT. I brought—the Vice President came to the White House at my invitation, and I informed him of—brought him up to date, on the events of the past few days.

[6.] Q. Mr. President, can you tell us the status of the mid-April economic review you promised?

THE PRESIDENT. Yes. I stated at a previous conference at the end of I think 75 days we were going to undertake a review of the economy. That is now under way under the direction of Dr. Heller, and I hope when that survey is completed that we will have a statement to make on it.

[7.] Q. Mr. President, respecting your feeling of not going beyond your statement of yesterday on Cuba, there still is in print this morning, quite widely distributed, a published report that you took the decision to continue training Cuban refugees with arms provided by this Government and for releasing ships and fuel for launching the current operations in Cuba.

Furthermore, this report says that you reached this decision against the advice of Secretary Rusk and Mr. Bowles. Now, is this true?

THE PRESIDENT. I think that the facts of the matter involving Cuba will come out in due time. I am sure that an effort will be made to determine the facts accurately. As for me, I am confining myself to my statement for good reason.

Q. Mr. President, this is not a question about Cuba; it's a question about Castro.

Could you tell us whether any intelligence that you have received can shed any light on the reports that the Prime Minister has been incapacitated, that he has not been heard from since Monday or Tuesday, or reports to that effect?

THE PRESIDENT. No, I cannot. I saw some, I think some reference was on the ticker this morning that Mr. Castro was seeing some members of the press today, so I suppose we will have a better idea of that later on.

[8.] Q. Mr. President, the leaders of House and Senate Republicans told us yesterday at a press conference that they are setting up special study committees on the effect of automation and technological improvements in agriculture as well as industry.

Are you hoping that your Democrats in Congress will set up similar study committees? Do you need them?

THE PRESIDENT. Well, I do think that on the Subcommittee on Labor, a subcommittee headed by Congressman Holland, of Pennsylvania, has been conducting studies on the effect of automation for some months.

In regard to the effect of automation on agriculture, I think it is—some of our most serious problems which have arisen in agriculture have been because of research combined with automation, which have brought an extraordinary increase in production, with far less manpower, so that I know that this problem is a matter of substantial concern to all of us.

I am glad that the Republicans are conducting this study, because I think all the attention we can get by both parties into what I consider to be a genuine national problem, automation—what happens to the people who are thrown out of work—I think will be most useful. And agriculture, where we have a great increase in production, with around 4 million people less than we had several years ago, some years ago, in many ways is one of the most extraordinary and admirable facets of our national life.

I think it is unfortunate that we are not able to bring it more to the attention of the world where so many people, including in the Soviet Union and in China, are spending most of their time on subsistence agriculture, that we are able to have this extraordinary production with very few people. But like all blessings, they bring problems with them. And I am glad they are conducting the studies.

[9.] Q. Mr. President, at your last news conference you expressed hope that the Soviets would agree within a few days to a cease-fire in Laos. More than a week has gone by since then and the Soviets have not agreed yet. Could you tell us how much longer you will wait before contemplating other kinds of action?

THE PRESIDENT. I understand that the British and the Soviets are conferring at the present time, using it in a general sense, and we are hopeful that a cease-fire can be obtained in Laos. We continue to be hopeful.

[10.] Q. Mr. President, Mr. Nixon, on the Ev and Charlie Show yesterday said that he was going to give you 10 days' grace to produce on your campaign promises that certain things would be done by 90 days. Did he go into this or other domestic politics in your White House meeting?

THE PRESIDENT. No, there was nothing stated about—on politics. Mr. Nixon and I discussed matters of national concern, and it was done in a wholly nonpolitical way. Mr. Nixon's response was most helpful.

[11.] Q. Mr. President, I wonder if you would tell us what your grounds, your investigations of the Maj. Gen. Ted Walker incident in Europe—if you will please tell us what grounds you found for relieving him of his command for allegedly teaching troops anti-Communist doctrine?

THE PRESIDENT. When I saw the stories in regard to the things which had been said, or at least alleged to have been said in regard to General Walker, I called Secretary McNamara and asked him to investigate. Secretary McNamara then, I believe, suspended General Walker—and my term may not be precise—"pending a completion of investigation," but no decision has been made in regard to General Walker until the investigation has been completed, to find out exactly what was going on.

I do not believe that Secretary McNamara took even that limited action, however, merely because he felt that General Walker was teaching—talking against the Communists. That was not the ground for concern. But no final decision, to the best of my information, has been made on the matter of General Walker. He will be given every opportunity, and those who have been critical of him will be given every opportunity, to present their case. And a final decision will then be made by Mr. McNamara, who will then bring the matter to my attention and I will then review it, without prejudice to General Walker.

[12.] Q. Mr. President, you don't seem to be pushing the space program nearly as energetically now as you suggested during the campaign that you thought it should be pushed. In view of the feeling of many people in this country that we must do everything we can to catch up with the Russians as soon as possible, do you anticipate applying any sort of crash program, or doing anything that would——

THE PRESIDENT. We have added, I think it was $130 million to the budget on space several weeks ago, which provides some speedup for Saturn, some speedup for Nova, some speedup for Rover. And I will say that the budget for space next year will be around $2 billion. Now, we are now and have been for some time attempting to make a determination as to developing larger boosters, whether the emphasis should be put on chemical, nuclear rockets or liquid fuel, how much this would cost. And some of these programs have been estimated to be between 20 and 40 billion dollars.

We are attempting to make a determination as to which program offers the best hope before we embark on it, because you may commit a relatively small sum of money now for a result in 1967, '68, or '69, which will cost you billions of dollars, and therefore the Congress passed yesterday the bill providing for a Space Council which will be chaired by the Vice President. We are attempting to make a determination as to which of these various proposals offers the best hope. When that determination is made we will then make a recommendation to the Congress.

In addition, we have to consider whether there is any program now, regardless of its cost, which offers us hope of being pioneers in a project. It is possible to spend billions of dollars in this project in space to the detriment of other programs and still not be successful. We are behind, as I said before, in large boosters.

We have to make a determination whether there is any effort we could make in time or money which could put us first in any new area. Now, I don't want to start spending the kind of money that I am talking about without making a determination based on careful scientific judgment as to whether a real success can be achieved, or whether because we are so far behind now in this particular race we are going to be second in this decade.

So I would say to you that it's a matter of great concern, but I think before we break through and begin a program which would not reach a completion, as you know, until the end of this decade—for example, trips to the moon, may be 10 years off, maybe a little less, but are quite far away and involve, as I say, enormous sums—I don't think we ought to rush into it and begin them until we really know where we are going to end up. And that study is now being undertaken under the direction of the Vice President.

Q. Mr. President, don't you agree that we should try to get to the moon before the Russians, if we can?

THE PRESIDENT. If we can get to the moon before the Russians, we should.

Q. Mr. President, isn't it your responsibility to apply the vigorous leadership to spark up this program?

THE PRESIDENT. When you say "spark up the program," we first have to make a judgment based on the best information we can get whether we can be ahead of the Russians to the moon. We are now talking about a program which may be—which is many years away.

Q. The Saturn is still on a 40-hour week, isn't it, Mr. President?

THE PRESIDENT. We have, as I say, appro-priated $126 million more to the Saturn and we are attempting to find out what else we can do. The Saturn is still going to put us well behind. Saturn does not offer any hope of going to the—being first to the moon. The Saturn is several years behind the Soviet Union. I can just say to you that regardless of how much money we spend on Saturn, the Saturn is going to put us—we are still going to be second.

The question is whether the nuclear rocket or other kinds of chemical rockets offer us a better hope of making a jump forward, but we are second, and the Saturn will not put us first.

I want, however, to speed up, if we can, the Saturn, and the Vice President is now leading a study to see what we ought to do in this area.

[13.] Q. Mr. President, do you anticipate that there will be a vote in both Houses of Congress this year on your medical care program?

THE PRESIDENT. I don't know. If we had a vote in the House it would depend, of course, on the action of the Ways and Means Committee, so that I'm not—I haven't any information yet as to whether we will get a vote in the House. It is possible that there will be one in the Senate, which is not restricted by the same rules.

Q. There have been reports on Capitol Hill that this administration has reconciled itself to no vote on medical care this year.

THE PRESIDENT. In either body; in either House?

Q. Yes, sir.

THE PRESIDENT. Well, I haven't seen the reports and I would not make that assumption. I am hopeful that—we are dependent in the House on committee action. There can't be a vote in the House without action by the committee because of the rules of germaneness. In the Senate, however, there is a somewhat different situation, but there is no rule of germaneness.

So it's possible that somebody might offer the bill in the Senate as an amendment to another bill. I don't know that yet, but it is very possible that you could get a vote in the Senate this year.

The House is a different problem. You can't get a vote unless the Ways and Means Committee acts.

[14.] Q. Mr. President, your order to investigate General Walker suggests that you look askance at the teachings of the John Birch Society. Can you tell us how you feel about that organization?

THE PRESIDENT. Well, I don't think that their judgments are based on accurate information of the kinds of challenges that we face. I think we face an extremely serious and intensified struggle with the Communists. But I'm not sure that the John Birch Society is wrestling with the real problems which are created by the Communist advance around the world.

I would hope that all those who are strongly concerned about it would address themselves to the kinds of problems which are created by Laos, Viet-Nam, by internal subversion, by the desperate life lived by so many people in this hemisphere and in other places which the Communists exploit.

These are the kinds of problems that we are dealing with. I said something about them yesterday. The use which the Communists make of democratic freedoms and the success which they are able to—once they have seized power—success with which they are able to maintain their power against dissent.

This seems to me to be the problem. We have talked about and read stories of 7,000 to 15,000 guerrillas operating in Viet-Nam, killing 2,000 civil officers a year and 2,000 police officers a year—4,000.

Now, there's been an election in Viet-Nam in which 75 percent of the people, or 80 percent, endorse the government. And yet we read how Viet-Nam is in danger because of guerrilla operations carried on by this small well disciplined, well supplied, across the border group of guerrillas.

How we fight that kind of a problem which is going to be with us all through this decade seems to me to be one of the great problems now before the United States. And I would hope all those who are concerned about the advance of communism would face that problem and not concern themselves with the loyalty of President Eisenhower or President Truman or Mrs. Roosevelt or myself or someone else.

[15.] Q. Mr. President, was your speech yesterday before the editors intended to suggest another approach or a new departure in the administration's dealing with the Russians?

THE PRESIDENT. No—I didn't—no.

Q. You have practiced what has been described as the quiet diplomacy approach and your speech yesterday seemed to suggest that you have perhaps decided upon another approach.

THE PRESIDENT. No, I wouldn't attempt to make a judgment or response to that. I think that—I am concerned about the kind of problem which I just described. I don't feel satisfied that we have an effective answer to it yet and I think it's a matter of greatest possible concern to all of us because I think events have been moving with some speed.

The use which the Communists make of democracy, and then when they seize power, the effectiveness with which they manage the police apparatus so that dissent cannot arise and so that the people can no longer express their will—liquidation by gunfire of the opposition or by forcing them out of the country to be refugees—this suggests the kind of a problem which we are going to have in this decade.

And in my judgment it's an extremely difficult matter for the free nations to deal with. But I must say that it's a matter to which we must address all of our energy and all of our attention.

[16.] Q. Mr. President, how would you evaluate the present state of your domestic program in Congress?

THE PRESIDENT. I think we've done better recently. Yesterday the Senate passed the $1.25 minimum wage. There was action on aid to dependent children and on social security. The vote in the Senate was very ample on the minimum wage. I think there were only 28 votes against it so I think that at least yesterday there was—we made progress.

Q. How much more, sir, do you think needs to be done in order to give you a satisfactory score on your hoped-for legislative program?

THE PRESIDENT. Well, I'm hopeful that we can move ahead on the various other parts of the program, including education and housing. We are making progress on social security, distressed areas, and minimum wage. There may be other proposals which we might make to the Congress after we've considered—completed our review of the economy and made a judgment as to exactly what peak or plateau the economy is going to reach this year. And that is what we're attempting to do now and to see whether any additional Government programs may be necessary to encourage it.

[17.] Q. Sir, since last Saturday a certain foreign policy situation has given rise to many conflicting stories. During that time reporters in Washington have noticed that there's been a clamming up of information from formerly useful sources. To my knowledge the State Department and the White House have not attempted to take a representative group of reporters and say, "These are the facts as we know them," and this morning we are not permitted to ask any further questions about this foreign policy situation. In view of the fact we are taking a propaganda lambasting around the world, why is it not useful, sir, for us to explore with you the real facts behind this, or our motivations?

THE PRESIDENT. Well, I think, in answer to your question, that we have to make a judgment as to how much we can usefully say that would aid the interest of the United States. One of the problems of a free society, a problem not met by a dictatorship, is this problem of information. A good deal has been printed in the paper and I wouldn't be surprised if those of you who are members of the press will be receiving a lot of background briefings in the next day or two by interested people or interested agencies.

There's an old saying that victory has 100 fathers and defeat is an orphan. And I wouldn't be surprised if information is poured into you in regard to all of the recent activities.

Now, I think we see some of the problems, to move from this particular case into the problem of space where in the Soviet Union no reports were made in regard to any experiments that they carried out on "our man in space." I saw in a national magazine about some student who said the Americans talk a good deal about their man in space, the Soviet Union says nothing and yet it wins. That is one of the problems of a democracy competing and carrying on a struggle for survival against a dictatorship.

But I will say to you, Mr. Vanocur, that I have said as much as I feel can be usefully said by me in regard to the events of the past few days. Further statements, detailed discussions, are not to conceal responsibility because I'm the responsible officer of the Government—and that is quite obvious—but merely because I do not believe that such a discussion would benefit us during the present difficult situation.

But as I say, I think you'll be informed and some of the information, based on what I have seen, will not be accurate.

[18.] Q. Mr. President, have you any assurance your tax investment incentive plan will be supported in Congress?

THE PRESIDENT. No, I think it will be a hard fight because the plan when it was sent up was intended to secure as much revenue as may have been lost because of the tax credit plan. The tax credit plan puts special emphasis on stimulating new industry and therefore new employment, but in order to make up the revenues we lost by the tax credit plan we have had to take control of other revenues, and of course those people are going to object—the expense accounts and the dividend credits and so on, so that I think we will have a hard fight.

Q. You asked for it at this session—do you think your educational program will be persuasive this session?

THE PRESIDENT. I hope so because I really believe that the tax credit program, in fact, the whole tax bill, was carefully considered by people in the Treasury as well as the Council of Economic Advisers. It had the strong support of Mr. Dillon and others who have given this matter great consideration. I am hopeful that Congress will respond favorably. But it is a technical matter, it involves important interests. And I think it will have a—be very soberly considered, which I hope it will be. But I am hopeful that it will pass and I think it would be useful if it would.

[19.] Q. Mr. President, are you contemplating visiting any other countries besides France on your trip at the end of May to see General de Gaulle?

THE PRESIDENT. I am planning—my only present plan is to go to France.

Q. There had been some talk that you're going to London, I understand, to christen the Radziwill baby.

THE PRESIDENT. Well, that has been considered but I've not reached any judgment on it. I think there is some interest by the family and it would really be a question of whether we could—whether it would be the best thing to do.

[20.] Q. Mr. President, would you explain the reason for the dropping of espionage charges in Chicago recently against the Russian spy Melekh, and was that a part of a bargain for the RB-47 fliers?

THE PRESIDENT. In answer to the last part of the question, it was not. There was no connection. The dropping of the charges was made after an examination of the details of the case and of the national interest and it was felt that it would be useful to take the action we took. I am sorry I can't be more responsive but I will say it was not in regard to the RB-47 fliers.

[21.] Q. Mr. President, we have demonstrated a great capability in space and communications and meteorology. While these are not as dramatic as a man orbiting in space, there has been a strong feeling among scientists the world over that the country that would first develop a space telecommunications system to bring communications within the reach of every nation in the world at the price they could afford would make an even greater impact than the country that orbited man first in space.

Are you considering putting more funds, because you have cut some, in both communications and meteorology—are you considering adding more funds to the budget?

THE PRESIDENT. Yes, I believe that we

have, or are about to, if we haven't already done so, put an additional—and I just have to go from memory now, of a decision made several weeks ago—I am under the impression that we decided to put another 25 to 27 million dollars into a communication satellite as part of this general program.

Q. Yes, but industry also has been interested in putting its funds in it, and there was a statement by Mr. Webb that we weren't going to at this point put any of this program into industry's hands until we had investigated further. Since they're willing to spend money, are you considering perhaps allowing them to share the cost and advance this program?

THE PRESIDENT. Well, I don't know enough about the matter to give you a detailed answer, except I do know that we did put an additional sum of money for a communications satellite, amounting to the sum that I suggested there. Now if there are any other further things that can be done, or if anyone else wants to put their money into it, I am sure that Mr. Webb would be agreeable. But I must say from examining this and other programs, I find that the Government puts most of the money into them.

[22.] Q. Mr. President, do you intend to send Vice President Johnson to Southeast Asia soon?

THE PRESIDENT. We have been considering the Vice President going to Southeast Asia, and I think a decision will be reached on that in the next—perhaps over the weekend or the next few days.

[23.] Q. Given the stress that you've put this morning and in recent days on this problem of fighting the indirect Communist tactics, do you still—and also given the rather harsh language out of Moscow, including Mr. Khrushchev's note to you— do you still feel that it is useful to go ahead

with efforts at the diplomatic level to negotiate formal agreements with the Soviet Government?

THE PRESIDENT. Well, we still continue to hope that some agreement could be reached on the cessation of nuclear tests. We are, of course, very discouraged by the newest insistence of the Soviets on a veto. It's quite obvious that the Senate would not accept such a treaty nor would I send it to the Senate, because the inspection system then would not provide any guarantees at all.

Now, I noticed the language used by Mr. Khrushchev himself, not merely one of his representatives, in Mr. Lippmann's article, a strong insistence on the tripartite and on unanimous agreement in regard to the inspection system. I am hopeful that there may be a change in that. But if there isn't a change in that position, it is going to be very hard to get an agreement. But I believe that Mr. Dean should continue because if these test conversations should break up, then of course our hopes of getting any agreement on disarmament would be substantially lessened and we could look for a proliferation of atomic testing in other countries.

So that I feel that Mr. Dean should continue, though we have been discouraged by the Russian position.

Q. Do you feel, sir, that it is possible to have really a two-level operation here, an undeclared kind of warfare which you have been talking about, and yet a formalized effort not only in the test ban negotiations but in terms of exchanges and other types of negotiations? Are these two things compatible?

THE PRESIDENT. The incompatability may rest in the fact that it's hard to get an agreement on any matter when there is suspicion between the two systems and when one of the systems are pressing their interest with great vigor around the world.

It makes the chances of getting any agreement far less. I thought the best hope was the nuclear testing, even though it was always true that the obstacles were large.

But if there is any chance at all of getting an agreement on a cessation of nuclear tests, regardless of what appear to be the obstacles,

I think we should press on.

So in answer to your question, I still believe that Mr. Dean should continue to work at Geneva.

Reporter. Thank you, Mr. President.

NOTE: President Kennedy's tenth news conference was held in the State Department Auditorium at 10 o'clock on Friday morning, April 21, 1961.

140   Exchange of Messages With President de Gaulle of France. *April 24, 1961*

[Released April 24, 1961. Dated April 23, 1961]

Dear General de Gaulle:

In this grave hour for France, I want you to know of my continuing friendship and support as well as that of the American people. Your personal achievements in bringing the resurgence of France as a great champion of freedom have won the esteem of all those who cherish liberty. The course you have chosen to settle the tragic problem of Algeria cannot but meet the approval of those who believe in the principles of democracy and who seek a durable understanding

among nations of the world. With warm personal wishes,

Sincerely,

JOHN F. KENNEDY

NOTE: General de Gaulle's reply, dated April 24, follows:

Dear Mr. President:

I was deeply touched by the message which you sent me and I thank you very sincerely for the sentiments which you expressed to me in your name and in the name of the American people.

Be assured, dear Mr. President, of my profoundly cordial sentiments.

CHARLES DE GAULLE

141   Letter to the President of the Senate and to the Speaker of the House Proposing Extension of the Federal Airport Act. *April 24, 1961*

Dear Mr. ————:

I am transmitting herewith for consideration by the Congress a draft of legislation to amend the Federal Airport Act.

Without this legislation, authority under that Act would expire on June 30 of this year. The proposed bill authorizes additional obligations for a period of 5 years, ending June 30, 1966.

Continuing the program of Federal assistance to airports is essential to our national

security, passenger safety, and economic growth. Air commerce, since the enactment of the Federal Airport Act in 1946, has grown so rapidly that many existing airport facilities are both overburdened and underequipped. The increase in the speed, weight, and capacity of jet age aircraft has already antiquated many existing airports and threatens to outmode many more.

In addition, the expansion in general aviation has created a special need for the development of general aviation airports, particularly where this is necessary to relieve congestion at airports having a high density of traffic and serving other segments of aviation. For this reason, I have recommended that funds be specifically allocated to the development of such airports.

The bill has six major features:

1. The bill provides for a 5-year extension of the Federal Airport Act, with a $75 million per year obligational authority. Of that amount, $1,500,000 would be made available for projects in Puerto Rico and the Virgin Islands and $7 million for certain general aviation airports.

2. Funds apportioned under the Act but not obligated by grant agreements at the end of each fiscal year would be transferred to the discretionary fund.

3. In addition to high intensity runway lighting, there is Federal participation in the cost of land for approach light systems, in runway lighting and runway distance markers. This is an ever increasing safety need.

4. Instead of the requirement that a sponsor provide free space for air traffic control,

weather reporting and communications activities, there is a provision that the Government be furnished without cost such interests in land as the Administration may consider necessary or desirable for the construction of facilities for such purposes. This permits greater flexibility and more efficient utilization.

5. The cost of constructing any part of an airport building is disallowed as a project cost except when a building is constructed to house facilities or activities directly related to safety of persons at the airport.

6. Alaska and Hawaii are permitted to participate for the first time on the same basis as other States.

This legislation is consistent with the current national airport plan for which provision is made in the Federal Airport Act.

Sincerely,

JOHN F. KENNEDY

NOTE: This is the text of identical letters addressed to the Honorable Lyndon B. Johnson, President of the Senate, and to the Honorable Sam Rayburn, Speaker of the House of Representatives.

---

142   Letter to the President of the Senate and to the Speaker of the House Concerning Secret Service Protection of Persons in Line for the Presidency. *April 24, 1961*

Dear Mr. ————:

I am transmitting herewith a draft of a proposed bill to provide penalties for threats against the successors to the Presidency, to authorize their protection by the Secret Service, and for other purposes.

The purpose of the proposed legislation is to: (1) close gaps that exist in present law with respect to threats against, and Secret Service protection for, the person who is next in line to the Presidency; (2) authorize full-time protection of the Vice President; and

(3) authorize the protection of a former President for a reasonable period of time after he leaves office.

The existing law governing threats against and protection for the person next in line to the Presidency applies only to the President-elect and the Vice President of the United States. It does not apply to the person next in line to the Presidency when a President has died and the Vice President has become President or when some disability has resulted in the succession of the

Vice President to the Presidency. Nor does existing law make any provision for the protection of the Vice President-elect between Election Day and the date he assumes his office. Since it is the purpose of the law to provide protection for both the President and the person next in line to succeed him, there appears to be an obvious gap in the existing statutes. The proposed legislation would close that gap.

The bill, when enacted, will also provide for protection of the Vice President at all times. At present, he must request the attendance of Secret Service agents. The proposed legislation would remove the necessity for such a request.

Finally, the proposed legislation would specifically authorize the Secret Service to continue to provide a staff of five or six agents for a period of six months to the former President immediately after he leaves office. Although no longer the Chief Executive, he continues to be exposed to harmful acts by mentally deranged individuals or persons bearing grudges for a short time after he leaves office. The furnishing of such protection would, however, be left to the discretion of the former President.

It would be appreciated if you would lay the proposed bill before the Senate (House of Representatives). A similar proposed bill has been transmitted to the Speaker of the House of Representatives (President of the Senate).

Sincerely,

JOHN F. KENNEDY

NOTE: This is the text of identical letters addressed to the Honorable Lyndon B. Johnson, President of the Senate, and to the Honorable Sam Rayburn, Speaker of the House of Representatives.

The draft bill was released with the President's letter.

143   Remarks of Welcome to President Sukarno of Indonesia at Andrews Air Force Base. *April 24, 1961*

I WANT TO TAKE this opportunity to welcome the President of the Republic of Indonesia. His country has always held the imagination of the people of the United States. Near to my own city of Boston—the town of Salem—its seal is a ship and the words are "To the farthest island of the Indies." From the beginning of our country, from the first voyage of Columbus, which was intended to reach his country, down through the 18th century and the 19th century, his country has attracted the youngest and the bravest of our countrymen who have sailed to those islands.

We have, however, an even greater interest in his country today, and it is a source of satisfaction to me that the United States played, I think, a useful and helpful role in the early days when his country was first becoming established.

We wish that the relations between his country and the United States should be intimate and close. We seek for our country what he seeks for his country—a better life for his people, a life of independence, a life of security.

I am particularly glad also to welcome him here because he is in a very real sense the father of his country. Throughout his life he has devoted himself to the independence of his country. He occupies the unique role in the life of his country and his people that was occupied by the early founders of this country. And therefore, in welcoming him once again to the shores of the United States, we welcome a distinguished national leader, father of his country, and a leader in the world.

Therefore, Mr. President, it is a great honor for me to welcome you here to the United States and to tell you that the people of this country are happy to have you here again.

NOTE: President Sukarno responded as follows:

Mr. President, I am happy to be on American soil again for the fifth time. I think America is the only country in the world which I have visited so often, of course for certain reasons.

When I came here the first time in 1956, in my speech I said that I had come to see for myself the center of an idea. And 2 years ago in Los Angeles I said, "This time I come to the United States to see for myself one of the centers of action."

The United States occupies a very distinguished part, a very distinguished place, in the hearts of the Indonesian people. And really I am very grate-

ful to the President of the United States, President Kennedy, that he has invited me to call on Washington to see him, to have talks with him.

President Kennedy called me 2 minutes ago the father of the Indonesian Nation, and it is to my opinion not true. I am not the father of the Indonesian Nation. I am just a small mouthpiece of the Indonesian Nation. I express the aspirations, the longings, the wishes of the Indonesian Nation. I am not the father of the Indonesian Nation. Without my nation I am nothing. Without my nation, I am just the man next door. But, yes, I have together with my nation, struggled for freedom, and I am now working hard, together with my nation, for the establishment of a just and prosperous society in Indonesia, and for peace in the world, for cooperation amongst nations in the world.

And it is my vivid hope that America and Indonesia shall always be close friends.

Thank you, Mr. President, for the invitation to come, and my best wishes for you, for the prosperity of the American Nation.

Thank you.

144 Letter to the President of the Senate and to the Speaker of the House on the National Defense Education Act. *April 25, 1961*

Dear Mr. —————:

Three years ago, the Congress declared, in enacting the National Defense Education Act, that "the security of our Nation requires the fullest development of the mental resources and technical skills of its young men and women." The principal objective of that Act was to correct serious imbalances in the American educational system by assisting and encouraging improved education and training in science, mathematics, modern foreign languages, and technology. It also included measures to strengthen our elementary and secondary school system and to help our young people to obtain college and graduate education.

That program has served the Nation well. It has made a significant contribution toward education in fields which were suffering from lack of attention but which were important to our national security and progress. It has helped improve foreign language in-

struction, testing and counseling programs, and education in science and mathematics. The student loan and fellowship provisions have assisted more than 200,000 students in their quest for higher education.

But the need today to improve and strengthen our educational system is still great. There are still critical shortages of teachers. Loan funds for college students are still needed. The importance of scientific and technological advance is increasing. It will take the combined efforts of both our public and our private school systems to meet the challenges facing us.

Almost all of the programs of the National Defense Education Act will terminate on June 30, 1962. Steps should be taken immediately to make provision for the continuation and expansion of these programs. Our national strength and welfare demand a strong and balanced educational system. Many proposals have been made by both public and private organizations to achieve this strength and balance, including the Report of the Consultants to the Secretary of Health, Education and Welfare and the U.S. Commissioner of Education, the recommendations of the Chief State School Officers, the American Council on Education, the American Library Association, and the Modern Language Association.

I am transmitting herewith draft legislation to amend, improve and extend the National Defense Education Act. Some of the recommendations of these organizations are included in the draft legislation. It is also appropriate that the Congress consider other proposals contained in these and other reports.

The legislation herewith proposed is an integral part of the proposals sent to the Congress for strengthening the basic elements of our educational system. It complements legislation already being considered to authorize general aid to public, elementary and secondary schools, to provide funds for construction of college facilities, and to authorize a college scholarship program.

I recommend that the student loan, fellowship, language and statistical improvement programs be made permanent. Equipment grants, grants for testing, guidance and counseling and educational media research should be extended for three years to permit reappraisal after the general education aid programs have gone into operation. The vocational education program should be extended pending completion of the reevaluation of all national vocational education programs, to which I referred in my message of February 20. Major programs authorized by the existing Act have already proved their value and should be expanded and improved.

The proposed legislation is described in more detail in the enclosed letter from the Secretary of the Department of Health, Education and Welfare.

Sincerely,

JOHN F. KENNEDY

NOTE: This is the text of identical letters addressed to the Honorable Lyndon B. Johnson, President of the Senate, and to the Honorable Sam Rayburn, Speaker of the House of Representatives.

145   Remarks Before the National Academy of Sciences. *April 25, 1961*

Dr. Bronk, Dr. Wiesner, ladies and gentlemen:

I want to express my appreciation for your generous invitation to be here. It has always been a source of interest to me that in the earliest days of the founding of our country there was among some of our Founding Fathers a most happy relationship, a most happy understanding of the ties which bind science and government together.

I am sure that even some of our English friends who may be here today would probably agree that the two most exceptional men of the 18th century, both in this country and

I think probably in Western Europe, would have been Benjamin Franklin and Thomas Jefferson—both leading political figures of their time, both scientists, social as well as natural.

This Academy was founded in the administration of another President who though not a scientist himself did understand the intimate ties which must exist between science and government. This Academy is I think now about a hundred years old. I don't suppose there has ever been a time, even during the days of World War II, when the relationship between science and government must be more intimate. Nearly every question which we approach—those of us who hold political office—has scientific overtones.

We are a free society in this country, therefore all of you are able to pursue your own private interests. But it is a fact that the members of this Academy have also recognized, probably as much if not more than any other group in our society, their obligations to society, to the public interest. And therefore, though all of you either teach or work in private industry—some of you in Government—all of you have been willing to give your time and your talent to the service of society as a whole. We are on the threshold of a good many new frontiers. The work which some of you have done on oceanography, the work which we hope we can carry through to fruition in the next months and years on desalinization, the work under Dr. Bronk which you have recently undertaken on an analysis of our natural resources, the work which we must try to undertake on the problems of our urban society, all these problems are political problems, are social problems, are scientific problems.

And therefore, as President of the United States, I would like to emphasize again the message which all of you have heard in other days: we need your help.

This country must move forward. Most of the areas where we move forward involve most sophisticated problems, which your experience and training can help us to solve. One of the problems, it seems to me, of a free society is the fact that all of the questions which we must decide now are extremely sophisticated questions. It's difficult enough for those who hold office, either in the administration or in the Congress, to attempt to make a determination between alternate courses of action—fiscal policy,

monetary policy, agricultural policy, international policy, disarmament, arms control, all the rest, all of these involve questions to confound the experts. For those of us who are not expert and yet must be called upon to make decisions which involve the security of our country, which involve the expenditures of hundreds of millions or billions of dollars, we must turn, in the last resort, to objective, disinterested scientists who bring a strong sense of public responsibility and public obligation. So this Academy is most important.

Speaking personally as President, I am called upon to make decisions, for example, in the field of space which involve many billions of dollars, where men are committed to one program or another. This Academy serves as a great natural resource, then, for those of us who are called upon to make these decisions, when we can turn to you and ask your view, ask your advice. You are motivated by desire to see the public interest expanded. It is the same desire that we have.

And therefore, I think that in the long history of this Academy, stretching back over a hundred years, never during that time has there been a greater need for understanding and support by the Government, the scientific community, and by the public at large.

So I was anxious to come here today to express my appreciation to you, to ask your help in the days and months to come, because I think together we can build a stronger society here in this country.

Thank you.

NOTE: The President spoke at the annual meeting of the National Academy in the National Academy of Sciences Building. His opening words "Dr. Bronk, Dr. Wiesner" referred to Dr. Detlev W. Bronk, President of the National Academy of Sciences, and Dr. Jerome B. Wiesner, Special Assistant to the President for Science and Technology.

146   Joint Statement Following Discussions With President Sukarno
    of Indonesia.   *April 25,* 1961

PRESIDENT KENNEDY and President Sukarno completed today in Washington a series of discussions on a wide range of matters of mutual interest.   First Deputy First Minister of Indonesia, Johannes Leimena; the Secretary of State, Dean Rusk; Indonesian Foreign Minister Subandrio; the Acting Assistant Secretary of State for Far Eastern Affairs, John M. Steeves; the United States Ambassador to Indonesia, Howard P. Jones; and Indonesian Ambassador to the United States, Zairin Zain, participated in the discussions.

The two Presidents welcomed this opportunity to renew their friendship and to re-affirm the spirit of cooperation and confidence which has characterized the relations between their two countries.

The two Presidents discussed the recent emergence of the new nations in Asia and Africa.   Both Presidents welcomed the newly found freedom of these countries and agreed that their genuine aspirations can best be fulfilled through mutual cooperation both within and without the United Nations.   Both Presidents recognize that these new countries must be alert to any attempts to subvert their cherished freedom by means of imperialism in all its manifestations.

President Kennedy stated that the Indo-nesian Eight-Year Development Plan provides further opportunity for the two nations to work together.   He offered to provide the services of a top-level economic team to consult with their Indonesian counterparts regarding the best way in which the United States might assist in achieving the goals of this plan.

Both Presidents expressed gratification at the high degree of cooperation between their countries and noted, in illustration, the successful visit to Indonesia of the hospital ship, the S. S. *Hope,* sponsored by the People-to-People Health Foundation.

Both Presidents recognize that the disarmament problem must be considered in relation to the general world situation. Both men agreed that the successful conclusion of a treaty ending nuclear tests, while not in itself a solution to the problem of disarmament, would be a first and most significant step.

Both Presidents strongly and unreservedly support the goal of a neutral and independent Laos.

Both Presidents expressed pleasure that President Sukarno's travel schedule had provided an opportunity for them to meet for this informal and worthwhile exchange of views.

147   Statement by the President Upon Signing Bill Amending the
    Aeronautics and Space Act.   *April 25,* 1961

I HAVE TODAY signed HR 6169, amending the Aeronautics and Space Act to place the Vice President of the United States at the head of the Space Council.

Enactment of this measure is symbolic of our Government's intention to translate leadership and determination into action. I congratulate the Congress—all the Members—and particularly the Space Committees of both Houses, for their speed and understanding in passing this bill.

HR 6169 is a key step toward moving the

United States into its proper place in the space race. Prior to this, I have sent to the Congress a request for additional funds to accelerate the large booster development, which is essential to our moving ahead in space.

The Vice President brings to the leadership of our space program 30 years' experience in constructive action in government. He was the author of the Space Resolution in the Congress, the Chairman of the Special Senate Committee which played such an important role in developing space legislation, and the Chairman of the permanent Committee of Aeronautical and Space Sciences. He was Chairman of the Senate Preparedness Committee which as far back as 1958 urged immediate action for the development of a million pound rocket booster.

Working with the Vice President, I intend that America's space effort shall provide the leadership, resources, and determination necessary to step up our efforts and prevail on the newest of man's physical frontiers.

NOTE: As enacted, H.R. 6169 is Public Law 87–26 (75 Stat. 46).

148   Message to the Government and People of Sierra Leone on the Occasion of Their Independence.   *April 26, 1961*

ON THE OCCASION of their independence, I wish to extend to the Government and people of Sierra Leone the heartiest congratulations and warmest wishes of the people of the United States.

We in the United States have watched with sympathy and admiration the progress of the people of Sierra Leone toward this historic and welcome event, which is the result of fruitful cooperation between the people of Sierra Leone and the Government and people of the United Kingdom. We are confident that this spirit of cooperation will inspire Sierra Leone's future relationships with all who hold freedom dear.

In expressing the best wishes of my country, I speak for a people who cherish individual liberty and independence, and who have made great sacrifices so that these vital principles might endure. It is with special pleasure, therefore, that we witness the assumption by this new nation of its sovereign place in the world community.

I am keenly conscious of the friendship which has marked the relations of our two countries, and, for the future, all Americans stand ready to work with the people of Sierra Leone to reach the goals we all share of health, enlightenment and material well-being. I am confident that in years to come our two countries will stand as one in safeguarding the greatest of all bonds between us, our common belief in a free and democratic way of life.

149   Letter to President Frondizi of Argentina Concerning the Alliance for Progress.   *April 27, 1961*

[Released April 27, 1961.   Dated April 18, 1961]

Dear Mr. President:

I am grateful for your letter of April 3 with its eloquent statement of the principles and aims of your government in the field of hemispheric relations. I am especially heartened to be assured of your support in the determination to make the Alliance for Progress an undertaking of transcendent spiritual and material consequence for all the people of the Americas.

Many problems beset the effort to enlarge economic abundance, cultural opportunity and social justice for all the people of the hemisphere. You have masterfully analyzed the demoralizing and disruptive consequences of persisting underdevelopment. I share your belief that we must all work together at the earliest possible time and with the utmost resolution and vigor to overcome this condition.

I have great sympathy for your view that the "initial impetus" should be concentrated on the establishment and expansion of basic industries and services. Industrialization provides the vital means by which the hemisphere can move forward toward a greater and more equitably shared abundance. It is our hope that the *Alianza* will provide a means of raising and generating the capital necessary to stimulate such industrial development.

And I am sure—from your reference to the overcoming of illiteracy and disease and to the need for opportunities corresponding to talent and character—that you agree equally that capital by itself is not enough to do the job.

Experience has shown that capital investment is only one of the conditions of economic growth. Other conditions include an increasingly literate and healthy population, an expanding supply of administrative and managerial talent, an ever more mobile society and, above all, a growing commitment to social justice so that the returns of growth accrue, not to a single class, but to an entire community. For this reason we believe that social progress has an indispensable role to play in helping create the conditions in which capital investment will lead to meaningful economic growth. Far from being in conflict, economic and social development are essential partners in the task of modernization.

You correctly state that underdevelopment is not limited to grave material need. Economic abundance, agreeable as it may be, is not itself the end of life. A full life, as you wisely note, must be defined in a cultural and spiritual sense. Our concern with economic abundance is precisely to provide the foundation on which our hemisphere may strive for higher cultural and spiritual fulfillment.

The goals of development are simple; the means of development infinitely ramified. I see the process as one of intimate cooperation among the free republics of the hemisphere, in which each will pool his ideas and experience in order to promote the growth of all. I see the Alliance for Progress as a great release of the creative energies of our peoples in a hemisphere defined by freedom, social justice and mutual self-respect.

I warmly welcome your desire for continued consultations between our Governments and for the pooling of our efforts and ideas as we move forward to make the Alliance for Progress a dynamic reality.

Sincerely,

JOHN F. KENNEDY

NOTE: President Frondizi's letter of April 3, released by the White House April 4, is published in the Department of State Bulletin (vol. 44, p. 815).

150 Special Message to the Congress Transmitting Reorganization Plan 1 of 1961. *April 27, 1961*

To the Congress of the United States:

I transmit herewith Reorganization Plan No. 1 of 1961, prepared in accordance with the Reorganization Act of 1949, as amended, and providing for reorganization in the Securities and Exchange Commission.

This Reorganization Plan No. 1 of 1961 follows upon my message of April 13, 1961 to the Congress of the United States. It is believed that the taking effect of the reorganizations included in this plan will provide for greater efficiency in the dispatch of the business of the Securities and Exchange Commission.

The plan provides for greater flexibility in the handling of the business before the Commission, permitting its disposition at different levels so as better to promote its efficient dispatch. Thus matters both of an adjudicatory and regulatory nature may, depending upon their importance and their complexity, be finally consummated by divisions of the Commission, individual Commissioners, hearing examiners, and, subject to the provisions of Section 7(a) of the Administrative Procedure Act of 1946 (60 Stat. 241), by other employees. This will relieve the Commissioners from the necessity of dealing with many matters of lesser importance and thus conserve their time for the consideration of major matters of policy and planning. There is, however, reserved to the Commission as a whole the right to review any such decision, report or certification either upon its own initiative or upon the petition of a party or intervenor demonstrating to the satisfaction of the Commission the desirability of having the matter reviewed at the top level.

Provision is also made, in order to maintain the fundamental bipartisan concept explicit in the basic statute creating the Commission, for mandatory review of any such decision, report or certification upon the vote of a majority of the Commissioners less one member.

Inasmuch as the assignment of delegated functions in particular cases and with reference to particular problems to divisions of the Commission, to Commissioners, to hearing examiners, to employees and boards of employees must require continuous and flexible handling, depending both upon the amount and nature of the business, that function is placed in the Chairman by section 2 of the plan.

By providing sound organizational arrangements, the taking effect of the reorganizations included in the accompanying reorganization plan will make possible more economical and expeditious administration of the affected functions. It is, however, impracticable to itemize at this time the reductions of expenditures which it is probable will be brought about by such taking effect.

After investigation, I have found and hereby declare that each reorganization included in the reorganization plan transmitted herewith is necessary to accomplish one or more of the purposes set forth in section 2(a) of the Reorganization Act of 1949, as amended.

I recommend that the Congress allow the reorganization plan to become effective.

JOHN F. KENNEDY

NOTE: Reorganization Plan 1 of 1961 is published in House Document 146 (87th Cong., 1st sess.).

151   Special Message to the Congress Transmitting Reorganization
      Plan 2 of 1961.   *April 27, 1961*

To the Congress of the United States:

I transmit herewith Reorganization Plan No. 2 of 1961, prepared in accordance with the Reorganization Act of 1949, as amended, and providing for reorganization in the Federal Communications Commission.

This Reorganization Plan No. 2 of 1961 follows upon my message of April 13, 1961, to the Congress of the United States. It is believed that the taking effect of the reorganizations included in this plan will provide for greater efficiency in the dispatch of the business of the Federal Communications Commission.

The plan provides for greater flexibility in the handling of the business before the Commission, permitting its disposition at different levels so as better to promote its efficient dispatch. Thus matters both of an adjudicatory and regulatory nature may, depending upon their importance and their complexity, be finally consummated by divisions of the Commission, individual Commissioners, hearing examiners, and, subject to the provisions of Section 7(a) of the Administrative Procedure Act of 1946 (60 Stat. 241), by other employees. This will relieve the Commissioners from the necessity of dealing with many matters of lesser importance and thus conserve their time for the consideration of major matters of policy and planning. There is, however, reserved to the Commission as a whole the right to review any such decision, report or certification either upon its own initiative or upon the petition of a party or intervenor demonstrating to the satisfaction of the Commission the desirability of having the matter reviewed at the top level.

Provision is also made, in order to main-tain the fundamental bipartisan concept explicit in the basic statute creating the Commission, for mandatory review of any such decision, report or certification upon the vote of a majority of the Commissioners less one member. In order to substitute this principle of discretionary review for the principle of mandatory review pursuant to exceptions that may be taken by a party, functions of the Commission calling for the hearing of oral arguments on such exceptions under subsection (b) of section 409 of the Communications Act of 1934 (66 Stat. 721), as amended, are abolished.

Inasmuch as the assignment of delegated functions in particular cases and with reference to particular problems to divisions of the Commission, to Commissioners, to hearing examiners, to employees and boards of employees must require continuous and flexible handling, depending both upon the amount and nature of the business, that function is placed in the Chairman by section 2 of the plan.

Section 3 of the plan also abolishes the "review staff" together with the functions established by section 5(c) of the Communications Act of 1934 (66 Stat. 712), as amended. These functions can be better performed by the Commissioners themselves, with such assistance as they may desire from persons they deem appropriately qualified.

By providing sound organizational arrangements, the taking effect of the reorganizations included in the accompanying reorganization plan will make possible more economical and expeditious administration of the affected functions. It is, however, impracticable to itemize at this time the re-

325

ductions of expenditures which it is probable will be brought about by such taking effect.

After investigation, I have found and hereby declare that each reorganization included in the reorganization plan transmitted herewith is necessary to accomplish one or more of the purposes set forth in section 2(a) of the Reorganization Act of 1949, as amended.

I recommend that the Congress allow the reorganization plan to become effective.

JOHN F. KENNEDY

NOTE: Reorganization Plan 2 of 1961 is published in House Document 147 (87th Cong., 1st sess.).

152   Special Message to the Congress on Conflict-of-Interest Legislation and on Problems of Ethics in Government. *April 27, 1961*

To the Congress of the United States:

No responsibility of government is more fundamental than the responsibility of maintaining the highest standards of ethical behavior by those who conduct the public business. There can be no dissent from the principle that all officials must act with unwavering integrity, absolute impartiality and complete devotion to the public interest. This principle must be followed not only in reality but in appearance. For the basis of effective government is public confidence, and that confidence is endangered when ethical standards falter or appear to falter.

I have firm confidence in the integrity and dedication of those who work for our government. Venal conduct by public officials in this country has been comparatively rare—and the few instances of official impropriety that have been uncovered have usually not suggested any widespread departure from high standards of ethics and moral conduct.

Nevertheless, in the past two decades, incidents have occurred to remind us that the laws and regulations governing ethics in government are not adequate to the changed role of the Federal Government, or to the changing conditions of our society. In addition, many of the ethical problems confronting our public servants have become so complex as to defy easy common sense solutions on the part of men of good will seeking to observe the highest standards of conduct, and solutions have been hindered by lack of general regulatory guidelines. As a result many thoughtful observers have expressed concern about the moral tone of government, and about the need to restate basic principles in their application to contemporary facts.

Of course, public officials are not a group apart. They inevitably reflect the moral tone of the society in which they live. And if that moral tone is injured—by fixed athletic contests or television quiz shows—by widespread business conspiracies to fix prices—by the collusion of businessmen and unions with organized crime—by cheating on expense accounts, by the ignoring of traffic laws, or by petty tax evasion—then the conduct of our government must be affected. Inevitably, the moral standards of a society influence the conduct of all who live within it—the governed and those who govern.

The ultimate answer to ethical problems in government is honest people in a good ethical environment. No web of statute or regulation, however intricately conceived, can hope to deal with the myriad possible challenges to a man's integrity or his devotion to the public interest. Nevertheless formal regulation is required—regulation which can lay down clear guidelines of policy, punish venality and double-dealing, and set a general ethical tone for the conduct of public business.

Such regulation—while setting the highest moral standards—must not impair the ability of the government to recruit personnel of the highest quality and capacity. Today's government needs men and women with a broad range of experience, knowledge and ability. It needs increasing numbers of people with top-flight executive talent. It needs hundreds of occasional and intermittent consultants and part-time experts to help deal with problems of increasing complexity and technical difficulty. In short, we need to draw upon America's entire reservoir of talent and skill to help conduct our generation's most important business—the public business.

This need to tap America's human resources for public purposes has blurred the distinctions between public and private life. It has led to a constant flow of people in and out of business, academic life and government. It has required us to contract with private institutions and call upon part-time consultants for important public work. It has resulted in a rapid rate of turnover among career government employees—as high as twenty per cent a year. And, as a result, it has gravely multiplied the risk of conflicts of interest while seriously complicating the problem of maintaining ethical standards.

These new difficulties and old problems led me to appoint, immediately after my inauguration, three distinguished lawyers to review our existing conflict of interest laws and regulations. This panel was composed of Judge Calvert Magruder, retired chief judge of the First Judicial Circuit; Dean Jefferson B. Fordham of the University of Pennsylvania Law School; and Professor Bayless Manning of the Yale Law School. The proposals put forward in this message are in large measure based upon their work and that of others who have considered the problems in recent years.

The recommendations of this panel were arrived at after careful study and review of the work of other groups, particularly the 1958 staff report of the Anti-Trust Subcommittee of the House Judiciary Committee under Congressman Celler; the pioneering study in 1951 by a subcommittee of the Senate Committee on Labor and Public Welfare under Senator Douglas; the recent report of the staff of the Senate subcommittee on National Policy Machinery of the Committee on Government Operations headed by Senator Jackson; and valuable appraisals conducted during the last administration by the executive branch, and by the Association of the Bar of the City of New York.

All of these studies have emphasized the seriousness of the problem encountered. All have recommended that our outmoded and hodge-podge collection of statutes and regulations be amended, revised and strengthened to take account of new problems. If the proposals have varied in their details, all have underscored the need for legislative and executive action in a commonly agreed direction.

I. STATUTORY REFORM

There are seven statutes of general application termed "conflict-of-interest" statutes. Many others deal with particular offices or very limited categories of employees. These latter usually exempt officials from some or all of the general restrictions. Occasionally

327

they impose additional obligations.

The seven statutes cover four basic problems:

—The Government employee who acts on behalf of the Government in a business transaction with an entity in which he has a personal economic stake. (18 U.S.C. 434)

—The Government employee who acts for an outside interest in certain dealings with the Government. (18 U.S.C. 216, 281, 283)

—The Government employee who receives compensation from a private source for his government work. (18 U.S.C. 1914)

—The former Government employee who acts in a representative capacity in certain transactions with the Government during a two-year period after the termination of his Government service. (18 U.S.C. 284, 5 U.S.C. 99)

Five of these statutes were enacted before 1873. Each was enacted without coordination with any of the others. No two of them use uniform terminology. All but one impose criminal penalties. There is both overlap and inconsistency. Every study of these laws has concluded that, while sound in principle, they are grossly deficient in form and substance.

The fundamental defect of these statutes as presently written is that: On the one hand, they permit an astonishing range of private interests and activities by public officials which are wholly incompatible with the duties of public office; on the other hand, they create wholly unnecessary obstacles to recruiting qualified people for government service. This latter deficiency is particularly serious in the case of consultants and other temporary employees, and has been repeatedly recognized by Congress in its enactment of special exemption statutes.

Insofar as these statutes lay down the basic law restricting the private economic activities of public officers and employees they constitute a sound and necessary standard of conduct. The principle which they embody in varying form—that a public servant owes undivided loyalty to the government—is as important today as when the first of these statutes was enacted more than a century ago. However, the statutory execution of this principle in the seven statutes of general application was often directed to specific existing evils which at the time of their enactment were important political issues. As a result large areas of potential conflict of interest were left uncovered.

For example, where some of these conflict-of-interest statutes are restricted to "claims of money and property"—as the courts have said—they do not protect the government against the use of official position, influence or inside information to aid private individuals or organizations in government proceedings which involve no claims for money or property. Yet the danger of abuses of government position exist to an equal if not greater degree in proceedings such as license applications for TV or radio stations, airline routes, electric power sites, and similar requests for government aid, assistance or approval.

Thus, literally read, it would be a crime punishable by fine or imprisonment under these statutes for a postal clerk to assist his mother in filing a routine claim for a tax refund, but it would be permissible for a Cabinet officer to seek to influence an independent agency to award a license for a valuable TV station to a business associate in a venture where he shared the profits.

There are many other technical inadequacies and statutory gaps. Section 434 of title 18, born of the Civil War procurement scandals, prohibits a Government official interested in the pecuniary profits of a business entity from acting as an officer or agent of the United States for the transaction of business with that business entity. By limiting its scope to "business entities" the statute does not cover the many other organizations which deal with the Government. In addition, the concept of "transacting business," if narrowly construed—as would be likely in a criminal prosecution—would exclude many dealings with the government, such as the clearance or rejection of license applications in the executive branch or before an independent agency.

Similar defects exist in the case of government officials who have left government service. Clearly such an official should be prohibited from resigning his position and "switching sides" in a matter which was before him in his official capacity. But for technical reasons the statutes aimed at this situation do not always hit the mark. There is nothing in the criminal statutes which would prevent the General Counsel of the Federal Power Commission from resigning to represent an unsuccesful license applicant who is contesting the Commission's decision in the courts (although such conduct might be grounds for disbarment). And, a Commission employee who was not a lawyer could, in the present state of the law, unscrupulously benefit in such a case from his "inside information" without fear of sanctions.

But if the statutes often leave important areas unregulated, they also often serve as a bar to securing important personal services for the government through excessive regulation when no ethical problem really exists. Fundamentally, this is because the statutes fail to take into account the role in our government of the part-time or intermittent adviser whose counsel has become essential but who cannot afford to be deprived of private benefits, or reasonably requested to deprive themselves, in the way now required

by these laws. Wherever the government seeks the assistance of a highly skilled technician, be he scientist, accountant, lawyer, or economist, such problems are encountered.

In general, these difficulties stem from the fact that even occasional consultants can technically be regarded as either "officers or employees" of the government, whether or not compensated. If so, they are all within the prohibitions applicable to regular full-time personnel.

A few examples illustrate some of the difficulties:

Section 281 of the Criminal Code forbids public employees from providing services to outsiders for compensation in connection with any matter in which the United States is interested and which is before a department, agency or commission.

This section makes it almost impossible for a practicing lawyer to accept a part-time position with the Government. He would be in violation of Section 281 if he continued to receive compensation for cases before government agencies, or even if his law partnership receives such compensation, though he personally has no connection with any case. It is usually impractical for the law firm to withdraw from all transactions involving the government. And almost all law firms have some tax matters, for example, as part of their normal business. The same prohibition unfairly affects accountants.

In addition, the two existing postemployment statutes raise serious problems in terms of recruiting non-career personnel (particularly lawyers). Enacted at different times, they employ different terms and are totally uncoordinated in language or in policy.

The criminal statute (18 U.S.C. 284) forbids a former employee for two years after his government employment ceases to prosecute in a representative capacity any claim against the government involving a "subject matter" directly connected with his government job. The civil statute (5 U.S.C. 99) forbids employees of an executive department for two years after the end of their government service from prosecuting in a representative capacity any claim against the United States if the claim was pending before "any department" while he was an employee.

These prohibitions are unnecessarily broad. They should be confined to "switching sides." For example, they now prohibit a lawyer who worked for the Department of Labor from subsequently representing a client in a wholly unrelated tax matter which had been before the Treasury during his government service.

These restrictions prove an even more formidable barrier to the part-time consultant who works in a partnership since he and his partners would be excluded from participation in many if not all claims against the Government—a severe and unnecessary penalty for contributing to public service. It is possible to cite many other examples of excessive restrictions which serve no ethical purpose, but effectively bar government from using available talent.

It is true that a large number of statutory exemptions passed at various times over the years have mitigated some of the adverse effects of these statutes upon certain specific individuals and certain categories of employees. However, no uniform standard of exemption has ever been adopted by the Congress in enacting these exemptions. Many of the exemptions are inconsistent. Some exemptions are subject to so many limitations as practically to nullify them. Some statutes unqualifiedly exempt categories of employees from all of the conflict statutes. Others exempt them from some

but not all of the restrictions. The resulting hodge-podge of exemptions seriously weakens the integrity of the Government personnel system.

To meet this need for statutory reform, I am transmitting to the Congress a proposed Executive Employees' Standards Act—a comprehensive revision of existing conflict-of-interest statutes. I believe that this bill maintains the highest possible standards of conduct, eliminates the technical deficiencies and anachronisms of existing laws, and makes it possible for the government to mobilize a wide range of talent and skill.

First, the bill closes gaps in regulation of the type discussed above, and eliminates many of the pointless differences in treatment. For example, no longer will some former government employees be subject to more severe restrictions simply because they once worked for one of the ten executive "departments" rather than in an agency which is not technically a department.

Secondly, the bill overrules existing judicial interpretation that only when a claim for money or property is involved is a former government employee prohibited from working for a private interest in a matter for which he once had governmental responsibility. The basic issue of integrity is the same if the matter relates to government regulation rather than to a property or money claim.

Third, the bill establishes special standards for skilled individuals whose primary activity is in private professional or business life, but whose skills are used by the government on a part-time or advisory basis. By permitting such individuals to carry on private business, even business with the government, as long as there is no direct conflict between their private and public work, ethical principles are maintained and a wide range of abilities are made available to government.

330

Fourth, this bill adds to the traditional criminal sanctions by permitting agency heads to adopt implementing regulations and impose disciplinary measures. Most of the existing laws are criminal statutes. As such they have been strictly construed and, because of their harshness, infrequently invoked. By granting this added flexibilty we help to ensure more effective enforcement. In addition, the regulations which are adopted will permit more specific adaptation of the general prohibitions tailored to the activities of particular agencies.

Fifth, the bill deals only with employees involved in executive, administrative and regulatory functions. It does not apply to either the judicial or legislative branch of government. Existing laws relating to the judiciary are deemed adequate. The adequacy and effectiveness of laws regulating the conduct of Members of Congress and Congressional employees should be left to strictly congressional determination.

Sixth, the proposed bill covers the District of Columbia and its employees. However the District—essentially a municipal government—has its own distinctive problems. I will submit legislation dealing with these problems in the near future.

II. EX-PARTE CONTACTS WITH OFFICIALS OF INDEPENDENT AGENCIES

Some of the most spectacular examples of official misconduct have involved *ex parte communication*—undisclosed, informal contact between an agency official and a party interested in a matter before that official. Such covert influence on agency action often does basic injury to the fairness of agency proceedings, particularly when those proceedings are judicial in nature.

This problem is one of the most complex in the entire field of government regulation.

It involves the elimination of ex parte contacts when those contacts are unjust to other parties, while preserving the capacity of an agency to avail itself of information necessary to decision. Much of the difficulty stems from the broad range of agency activities—ranging from judicial type adjudication to wide-ranging regulation of entire industries. This is a problem which can best be resolved in the context of the particular responsibilities and activities of each agency.

I therefore recommend that the Congress enact legislation requiring each agency, within 120 days, to promulgate a code of behavior governing ex parte contacts within the agency specifying the particular standard to be applied in each type of agency proceeding, and containing an absolute prohibition against ex parte contact in all proceedings between private parties in which law or agency regulation requires that a decision be made solely on the record of a formal hearing. Only in this manner can we assure fairness in quasi-judicial proceedings between private parties. The statute should make clear that such codes when approved by Congress will have the force of law, and be subject to appropriate sanctions.

III. EXECUTIVE ORDERS AND PRESIDENTIAL ACTION

There are several problems of ethics in government which can be dealt with directly by Presidential Order, Memoranda or other form of action.

First, I intend to prohibit gifts to government personnel whenever (a) the employee has reason to believe that the gift would not have been made except for his official position; or (b) whenever a regular government employee has reason to believe that the donor's private interests are likely to be affected by actions of the employee or his agency. When it is impossible or inappropriate to refuse the gift it will be turned over to an appropriate public or charitable institution.

Such an order will embody the general principle that any gift which is, or appears to be, designed to influence official conduct is objectionable. Government employees are constantly bothered by offers of favors or gratuities and have been without any general regulation to guide their conduct. This order will attempt to supply such guidelines, while leaving special problems including problems created by gifts from foreign governments, to agency regulation.

Secondly, I intend to prohibit government employees from using for private gain official information which is not available to the public. This regulation will be drawn with due regard for the public's right to proper access to public information. A government employee should not be able to transform official status into private gain, as is done, for example, if a government employee speculates in the stock market on the basis of advance knowledge of official action.

Third, I am directing that no government employee shall use the authority of his position to induce another to provide him with anything of economic value whenever the employee has reason to believe that the other person's private interests may be affected by the actions of the employee or his agency.

This regulation is an effort to deal with the subtler forms of extortion; where an employee acquiesces in the gift of an economic benefit, or gives a delicate indication of receptivity. The criminal law deals with outright extortion. Beyond this the problem is too elusive for the criminal law and must be dealt with by administrative regulation, and by the sound judgment of the administrator.

Fourth, I am directing that no government employee should engage in outside employment which is "incompatible" with his government employment.

The outside employment of government employees is one of the most complex and difficult of all ethical problems. It is clear that some forms of employment may have benefits to the government or society (e.g. teaching in universities); or be beneficial to the employee and not inconsistent with his government work. On the other hand, some types of outside work may involve exploitation of official position or be incompatible with the best interests of the agency to which the employee owes his first allegiance.

Since "incompatibility" of employment will depend on many varied factors, its definition will be left to agency and department regulation and case-by-case rulings.

Fifth, I will shortly issue an Executive Order regulating in more detail the conduct of those officials who are appointed by the President. These high level officials owe a special responsibility to the government and to the employees of their departments to set a high standard of ethical and moral behavior. Therefore the Executive Order (a) prohibits outside employment or activity of any sort incompatible with the proper discharge of official responsibility; (b) prohibits outside compensation for any activity within the scope of official duty; (c) prohibits the receipt of compensation for any lecture, article, public appearance, etc., devoted to the work of the department or based on official information not yet a matter of general knowledge.

Sixth, In carrying out the provisions of law, I will apply government-wide standards to the continuance of property holdings by appointees to the Executive branch. The law prohibits any conflict of the public and private interests of employees of the government. The Senate, in the exercise of its power of confirmation, has taken the lead in requiring that Presidential appointees sell their property holdings in cases where retention of property might result in such a conflict of interest. The problem of property ownership by executive appointees is properly a matter of continuing congressional concern, and I welcome the initiative taken by the Jackson Subcommittee on Conflict of Interest. At the same time, the Executive Branch has an obligation to ensure that its appointees live up to the highest standard of behavior. It is to carry out this responsibility that I will apply general standards governing the ownership of property by Presidential appointees—standards which will ensure that no conflict of interest can exist. It is my hope that these regulations will aid the Senate in the uniform exercise of its own responsibility.

IV. THE ADMINISTRATION OF ETHICAL STANDARDS

Criminal statutes and Presidential orders, no matter how carefully conceived or meticulously drafted, cannot hope to deal effectively with every problem of ethical behavior or conflict of interest. Problems arise in infinite variation. They often involve subtle and difficult judgments, judgments which are not suited to generalization or government-wide application. And even the best of statutes or regulations will fail of their purpose if they are not vigorously and wisely administered.

Therefore I am instructing each Cabinet Member and Agency Head to issue regulations designed to maintain high moral and ethical standards within his own department.

These regulations will adapt general principles to the particular problems and activity of each agency. To aid in the administration of these regulations each agency will establish an ad hoc committee to serve in an advisory capacity on ethical problems as they arise.

Although such agency regulation is essential, it cannot be allowed to dissolve into a welter of conflicting and haphazard rules and principles throughout the government. Regulation of ethical conduct must be coordinated in order to ensure that all employees are held to the same general standards of conduct.

Therefore I intend to designate, in the Executive Office of the President, a single officer charged with responsibility for coordinating ethics administration and reporting directly to the President. This officer will:

—prepare, for Presidential proclamation, general regulations as needed;

—develop methods of informing government personnel about ethical standards;

—conduct studies and accumulate experience leading to more effective regulation of ethical conduct, including the formulation of rules in areas which are not yet regulated, such as government use of outside advisers and the contracting of government services to private institutions or firms; and

—clear and coordinate agency regulations to assure consistent executive policy.

Such an officer will not only provide central responsibility for coherent regulation, but will be a means through which the influence of the Presidency can be exerted in this vital field.

V. CONCLUSION

Ultimately, high ethical standards can be maintained only if the leaders of government provide a personal example of dedication to the public service—and exercise their leadership to develop in all government employees an increasing sensitivity to the ethical and moral conditions imposed by public service. Their own conduct must be above reproach. And they must go beyond the imposition of general regulations to deal with individual problems as they arise—offering informal advice and personal consideration. It will often be difficult to assess the propriety of particular actions. In such subtle cases honest disclosure will often be the surest solution, for the public will understand good faith efforts to avoid improper use of public office when they are kept informed.

I realize, too, that perhaps the gravest responsibility of all rests upon the office of President. No President can excuse or pardon the slightest deviation from irreproachable standards of behavior on the part of any member of the executive branch. For his firmness and determination is the ultimate source of public confidence in the government of the United States. And there is no consideration that can justify the undermining of that confidence.

JOHN F. KENNEDY

NOTE: On May 5 the President signed Executive Order 10939 "To Provide a Guide on Ethical Standards to Government Officials" (26 F.R. 3951).

---

153   Address "The President and the Press" Before the American Newspaper Publishers Association, New York City. *April 27, 1961*

Mr. Chairman, ladies and gentlemen:

I appreciate very much your generous invitation to be here tonight.

You bear heavy responsibilities these days and an article I read some time ago reminded me of how particularly heavily the burdens of present day events bear upon your profession.

You may remember that in 1851 the New York Herald Tribune, under the sponsorship and publishing of Horace Greeley, employed as its London correspondent an obscure journalist by the name of Karl Marx.

We are told that foreign correspondent Marx, stone broke, and with a family ill and undernourished, constantly appealed to Greeley and Managing Editor Charles Dana for an increase in his munificent salary of $5 per installment, a salary which he and Engels ungratefully labeled as the "lousiest

petty bourgeois cheating."

But when all his financial appeals were refused, Marx looked around for other means of livelihood and fame, eventually terminating his relationship with the Tribune and devoting his talents full time to the cause that would bequeath to the world the seeds of Leninism, Stalinism, revolution and the cold war.

If only this capitalistic New York newspaper had treated him more kindly; if only Marx had remained a foreign correspondent, history might have been different. And I hope all publishers will bear this lesson in mind the next time they receive a poverty-stricken appeal for a small increase in the expense account from an obscure newspaper man.

I have selected as the title of my remarks tonight "The President and the Press." Some may suggest that this would be more naturally worded "The President Versus the Press." But those are not my sentiments tonight.

It is true, however, that when a well-known diplomat from another country demanded recently that our State Department repudiate certain newspaper attacks on his colleague it was unnecessary for us to reply that this Administration was not responsible for the press, for the press had already made it clear that it was not responsible for this Administration.

Nevertheless, my purpose here tonight is not to deliver the usual assault on the so-called one-party press. On the contrary, in recent months I have rarely heard any complaints about political bias in the press except from a few Republicans. Nor is it my purpose tonight to discuss or defend the televising of Presidential press conferences. I think it is highly beneficial to have some 20,000,000 Americans regularly sit in on these conferences to observe, if I may say so, the incisive, the intelligent and the courteous qualities displayed by your Washington correspondents.

Nor, finally, are these remarks intended to examine the proper degree of privacy which the press should allow to any President and his family.

If in the last few months your White House reporters and photographers have been attending church services with regularity, that has surely done them no harm.

On the other hand, I realize that your staff and wire service photographers may be complaining that they do not enjoy the same green privileges at the local golf courses which they once did.

It is true that my predecessor did not object as I do to pictures of one's golfing skill in action. But neither on the other hand did he ever bean a Secret Service man.

My topic tonight is a more sober one of concern to publishers as well as editors.

I want to talk about our common responsibilities in the face of a common danger. The events of recent weeks may have helped to illuminate that challenge for some; but the dimensions of its threat have loomed large on the horizon for many years. Whatever our hopes may be for the future—for reducing this threat or living with it—there is no escaping either the gravity or the totality of its challenge to our survival and to our security—a challenge that confronts us in unaccustomed ways in every sphere of human activity.

This deadly challenge imposes upon our society two requirements of direct concern both to the press and to the President—two requirements that may seem almost contradictory in tone, but which must be reconciled and fulfilled if we are to meet this national peril. I refer, *first,* to the need for far greater public information; and, *second,* to the need for far greater official secrecy.

I.

The very word "secrecy" is repugnant in a free and open society; and we are as a people inherently and historically opposed to secret societies, to secret oaths and to secret proceedings. We decided long ago that the dangers of excessive and unwarranted concealment of pertinent facts far outweighed the dangers which are cited to justify it. Even today, there is little value in opposing the threat of a closed society by imitating its arbitrary restrictions. Even today, there is little value in insuring the survival of our nation if our traditions do not survive with it. And there is very grave danger that an announced need for increased security will be seized upon by those anxious to expand its meaning to the very limits of official censorship and concealment. That I do not intend to permit to the extent that it is in my control. And no official of my Administration, whether his rank is high or low, civilian or military, should interpret my words here tonight as an excuse to censor the news, to stifle dissent, to cover up our mistakes or to withhold from the press and the public the facts they deserve to know.

But I do ask every publisher, every editor, and every newsman in the nation to re-examine his own standards, and to recognize the nature of our country's peril. In time of war, the government and the press have customarily joined in an effort, based largely on self-discipline, to prevent unauthorized disclosures to the enemy. In time of "clear and present danger," the courts have held that even the privileged rights of the First Amendment must yield to the public's need for national security.

Today no war has been declared—and however fierce the struggle may be, it may never be declared in the traditional fashion. Our way of life is under attack. Those who make themselves our enemy are advancing around the globe. The survival of our friends is in danger. And yet no war has been declared, no borders have been crossed by marching troops, no missiles have been fired.

If the press is awaiting a declaration of war before it imposes the self-discipline of combat conditions, then I can only say that no war ever posed a greater threat to our security. If you are awaiting a finding of "clear and present danger," then I can only say that the danger has never been more clear and its presence has never been more imminent.

It requires a change in outlook, a change in tactics, a change in missions—by the government, by the people, by every business-man or labor leader, and by every newspaper. For we are opposed around the world by a monolithic and ruthless conspiracy that relies primarily on covert means for expanding its sphere of influence—on infiltration instead of invasion, on subversion instead of elections, on intimidation instead of free choice, on guerrillas by night instead of armies by day. It is a system which has conscripted vast human and material resources into the building of a tightly knit, highly efficient machine that combines military, diplomatic, intelligence, economic, scientific and political operations.

Its preparations are concealed, not published. Its mistakes are buried, not headlined. Its dissenters are silenced, not praised. No expenditure is questioned, no rumor is printed, no secret is revealed. It conducts the Cold War, in short, with a war-time discipline no democracy would ever hope or wish to match.

Nevertheless, every democracy recognizes the necessary restraints of national security—and the question remains whether those restraints need to be more strictly observed if we are to oppose this kind of attack as well as outright invasion.

For the facts of the matter are that this nation's foes have openly boasted of acquiring through our newspapers information they would otherwise hire agents to acquire through theft, bribery or espionage; that details of this nation's covert preparations to counter the enemy's covert operations have been available to every newspaper reader, friend and foe alike; that the size, the strength, the location and the nature of our forces and weapons, and our plans and strategy for their use, have all been pinpointed in the press and other news media to a degree sufficient to satisfy any foreign power; and that, in at least one case, the publication of details concerning a secret mechanism whereby satellites were followed required its alteration at the expense of considerable time and money.

The newspapers which printed these stories were loyal, patriotic, responsible and well-meaning. Had we been engaged in open warfare, they undoubtedly would not have published such items. But in the absence of open warfare, they recognized only the tests of journalism and not the tests of national security. And my question tonight is whether additional tests should not now be adopted.

That question is for you alone to answer. No public official should answer it for you. No governmental plan should impose its restraints against your will. But I would be failing in my duty to the Nation, in considering all of the responsibilities that we now bear and all of the means at hand to meet those responsibilities, if I did not commend this problem to your attention, and urge its thoughtful consideration.

On many earlier occasions, I have said— and your newspapers have constantly said— that these are times that appeal to every citizen's sense of sacrifice and self-discipline. They call out to every citizen to weigh his rights and comforts against his obligations to the common good. I cannot now believe that those citizens who serve in the newspaper business consider themselves exempt from that appeal.

I have no intention of establishing a new Office of War Information to govern the flow of news. I am not suggesting any new forms of censorship or new types of security classifications. I have no easy answer to the dilemma that I have posed, and would not seek to impose it if I had one. But I am asking the members of the newspaper profession and the industry in this country to reexamine their own responsibilities, to consider the degree and the nature of the

present danger, and to heed the duty of self-restraint which that danger imposes upon us all.

Every newspaper now asks itself, with respect to every story: "Is it news?" All I suggest is that you add the question: "Is it in the interest of the national security?" And I hope that every group in America— unions and businessmen and public officials at every level—will ask the same question of their endeavors, and subject their actions to this same exacting test.

And should the press of America consider and recommend the voluntary assumption of specific new steps or machinery, I can assure you that we will cooperate whole-heartedly with those recommendations.

Perhaps there will be no recommendations. Perhaps there is no answer to the dilemma faced by a free and open society in a cold and secret war. In times of peace, any discussion of this subject, and any action that results, are both painful and without precedent. But this is a time of peace and peril which knows no precedent in history.

II.

It is the unprecedented nature of this challenge that also gives rise to your second obligation—an obligation which I share. And that is our obligation to inform and alert the American people—to make certain that they possess all the facts that they need, and understand them as well—the perils, the prospects, the purposes of our program and the choices that we face.

No President should fear public scrutiny of his program. For from that scrutiny comes understanding; and from that understanding comes support or opposition. And both are necessary. I am not asking your newspapers to support the Administration, but I am asking your help in the tremendous task of informing and alerting the American people. For I have complete confidence in the response and dedication of our citizens whenever they are fully informed.

I not only could not stifle controversy among your readers—I welcome it. This Administration intends to be candid about its errors; for, as a wise man once said: "An error doesn't become a mistake until you refuse to correct it." We intend to accept full responsibility for our errors; and we expect you to point them out when we miss them.

Without debate, without criticism, no Administration and no country can succeed—and no republic can survive. That is why the Athenian law-maker Solon decreed it a crime for any citizen to shrink from controversy. And that is why our press was protected by the First Amendment—the only business in America specifically protected by the Constitution—not primarily to amuse and entertain, not to emphasize the trivial and the sentimental, not to simply "give the public what it wants"—but to inform, to arouse, to reflect, to state our dangers and our opportunities, to indicate our crises and our choices, to lead, mold, educate and sometimes even anger public opinion.

This means greater coverage and analysis of international news—for it is no longer far away and foreign but close at hand and local. It means greater attention to improved understanding of the news as well as improved transmission. And it means, finally, that government at all levels, must meet its obligation to provide you with the fullest possible information outside the narrowest limits of national security—and we intend to do it.

III.

It was early in the Seventeenth Century that Francis Bacon remarked on three recent inventions already transforming the world: the compass, gunpowder and the printing press. Now the links between the nations first forged by the compass have made us all citizens of the world, the hopes and threats of one becoming the hopes and threats of us all. In that one world's efforts to live together, the evolution of gunpowder to its ultimate limit has warned mankind of the terrible consequences of failure.

And so it is to the printing press—to the recorder of man's deeds, the keeper of his conscience, the courier of his news—that we look for strength and assistance, confident that with your help man will be what he was born to be: free and independent.

NOTE: The President spoke at the annual dinner of the Association's Bureau of Advertising held at the Waldorf-Astoria Hotel in New York City. His opening words "Mr. Chairman" referred to Palmer Hoyt, Editor and Publisher of the Denver Post, who acted as chairman of the dinner.

154 Remarks Recorded for Broadcast During the Annual Civil Defense Exercises. *April 28, 1961*

Fellow Americans:

The annual civil defense exercise of which this broadcast is a part is a test of our program of peaceful preparedness. We do not expect war. However, common prudence demands that we take all necessary measures to protect our homes, our institutions, and our way of life, so that they can survive should an enemy thrust war upon us.

Should the United States ever be subjected to direct enemy attack Conelrad and the National Emergency Broadcasting System will be vital to our defense. This carefully planned program would prevent an enemy from using our radio stations to assist him, and yet permits emergency broadcasting such as you now hear. The voluntary participation of the radio and television broadcasters of the nation at their own expense is a commendable example of individual responsibility which is so essential to the survival of this Nation.

In the whole area of civil defense there is the same requirement. It is true that your government, too, must fulfill its responsibility in civil defense with vigorous leadership. To this end I have directed an intensive study of the whole subject of emergency planning. It is also true, however, that individual preparedness, which is beyond the province of government, is essential to an effective civil defense. For unless individual Americans plan to protect their own families—the most ambitious and carefully organized activities of government will prove inadequate.

We are a people of strong faith in ourselves and in our institutions. We believe that our freedom and our liberty are worth protecting.

Therefore, I ask you to support civil emergency planning in your local communities.

To those participating in this 3-day exercise, I express my appreciation for your active response to the obligations of citizenship in a free country.

NOTE: The President's remarks were broadcast at 4 p.m. on the two Conelrad channels while all commercial TV and radio stations were silent.

155   Address in Chicago at a Dinner of the Democratic Party of Cook County. *April* 28, 1961

Mayor Daley, Governor Kerner, Senator Douglas, Congressman Dawson, Chairman Cullerton, Alderman Keane, Members of the Congress, ladies and gentlemen:

I appreciate your generous welcome. This year I expect to attend two Democratic dinners, one in my home of Boston, Massachusetts, and the other in my second home of Chicago, Illinois.

I would not be here tonight without the strong support of your Mayor at the Convention, and your Senator and Governor during the campaign—your State Chairman. I do not know whether to thank you or not, but I am here and I expect to do my duty.

Some years ago, in the city of Fall River, Massachusetts, the Mayor was elected by one vote, and every time he went down the street, everyone would come up to him and say, "Dan, I put you in office." I feel a little like that in Chicago tonight. If all of you had voted the other way—there's about 5500 of you here tonight—I would not be the President of the United States. I campaigned downstate with the Senator and Governor and also with the Lieutenant Governor. Politics is a rather humbling experience. I introduced Sam Shapiro all over Illinois and I figured that I was really going to help him along, and he told me tonight that he won by 250 thousand—I grabbed Sam Shapiro's coat-tail and he dragged me in. In any case, I am delighted to be here tonight. I owe your Mayor a good deal. He is a valued friend. I have been proud of his support, and I am proud to be here with him tonight.

I am grateful for the generous words of Paul Douglas, who serves this State and country, and I know that he feels as I do about the passage of a bill on which he has worked for many years, which has now passed the United States Senate on three separate occasions, has now passed the House of Representatives and which I will look forward to signing into law next week—the Area Redevelopment Bill, which will mean much to the State of Illinois, and which he made possible.

And then Congressman Dawson, who speaks for this District and also for the country, and who is Chairman of a most important Committee of the House which recently sent to the desk of the President the reorganization bill which will make it possible for us to improve our Government. I am proud to share the program with him.

Above me is the Seal of the President of the United States, and in my State of the Union Address, I called attention to the fact that the American Eagle holds in his right hand the olive branch of peace and he holds in his left hand a bundle of arrows. I said in my State of the Union Address that we intended to give equal attention to both— and we intend to do so.

We live in a hazardous and dangerous time. I do not think it's possible to over- state it. We live in a world which has changed tremendously in our lifetime—his- tory only will secure a full perspective on that change. But here is Africa, which was held by Western European powers for several centuries, now independent—which holds within its countries masses of people, many of them illiterate, who live on average in- comes of 50 or 60 or 75 dollars a year, who want a change, who now are the masters of their own house but who lack the means of building a viable economy, who are im- pressed by the example of the Soviet Union and the Chinese, who—not knowing the meaning of freedom in their own lives—

wonder whether the Communist system holds the secret of organizing the resources of the state in order to bring them a better life.

And what is true of Africa is true of Asia, and what is true of Africa and Asia is true in some degree of Latin America. The Communists move among them, disciplined, organized, subject to an international dis- cipline, promising under their system that all will be well, knowing that if they can win just once, then the iron grip of the totali- tarian state goes upon the population—those who resist become refugees, or are shot— and they manage to control the population.

Tonight, in Viet-Nam, where the Presi- dent was reelected recently in the last 2 weeks by a majority of 75 to 80 percent, yet a small army of guerrillas, organized and sustained by the Communist Viet Minh in the north, control most of the countryside in the nighttime—in the last 12 months have assassinated over four thousand civil officers, two thousand state employees and two thou- sand police, believing if they can "spill the wine," that then they can win control of the population. And when they have won, they do not intend to give way.

Now our great responsibility is to be the chief defender of freedom, in this time of maximum danger. Only the United States has the power and the resources and the determination. We have committed our- selves to the defense of dozens of countries stretched around the globe who look to us for independence, who look to us for the defense of their freedom.

We are prepared to meet our obligations, but we can only defend the freedom of those who are determined to be free themselves. We can assist them—we will bear more than our share of the burden, but we can only help those who are ready to bear their share of the burden themselves.

The Russians and the Chinese, containing within their borders nearly a billion people, totally mobilized for the advance of the Communist system, operating from narrow, interior lines of communication, pressuring on Southeast Asia with the masses of the Chinese armies potentially ready to move— of the Russians who hold great power potentially in the Middle East and Western Europe—the United States stands as the chief defender of freedom.

I said in my Inaugural Address that no group of people in any generation since democracy was first developed by the ancient Greeks nearly twenty-four or -five hundred years ago, have ever borne a responsibility as great as ours. And I welcome it—and I welcome it tonight.

There is no easy answer to the dilemmas that we face. Our great ally is the fact that people do desire to be free, that people will sacrifice everything in their desire to maintain their independence. And as the true nature of the Communist conspiracy becomes better known around the globe, when people come to realize—as they surely will— that the Communist advance does not represent a means of liberation but represents a final enslavement, then I believe that they will rally to the cause to which we have given our support and our commitment.

I believe that we must build our country well, also. Senator Douglas described what we are attempting to do. The burdens are heavy upon us. We have to make this society an example to the world, strong enough to serve not only as an example but strong enough to maintain the commitments that we have assumed.

I am not satisfied, as an American, to see people who want to work can't find a job. I do not believe it saps the initiative of any American to pay him $1.25 minimum wage. I am not impressed by the argument that

we are softening our society when we make it possible for older people to contribute to their own maintenance in their older age through medical care under social security. These are the things that any society must do, if it deserves its name. And I am particularly anxious that a free society of which we rightfully boast so much, that it does it better than anyone else does it.

I want our educational system to be the best in the world, because the responsibility upon the graduates of our schools is greater than it is upon any other society.

Mr. Khrushchev and the members of the Presidium make the final, ultimate decisions for the Soviet Union, and a similar group for the Chinese Communists. They are talented and able men, who have risen in a hard school to their present eminence.

A majority of the people—not a select few—a majority of the people make the final decision for us, and we want that majority to be well-educated, to be self-disciplined, to understand the true nature of our challenge, to be able to find work to strengthen themselves and their families, to build in this country a prosperous society which can demonstrate what free men and women can do.

I believe that our future can be bright. I do not take a depressed view of our society here, or of our prospects around the world. I believe we live in a hard and difficult era of history. I believe that we are going to fail as well as succeed, but I believe that we are at least going to make the effort. I believe that we are going to try, and we will take our setbacks as well as our successes, and we will continue to move here, and around the world. We will continue to demonstrate that we desire for other people what we desire for ourselves: the chance to build in this country a free society and under the shelter of our effort to permit others to do likewise.

The next decade offers us challenges enough—and opportunities enough, but I believe that we will meet our responsibilities.

So I come here to this city, which in its own way has demonstrated its confidence in the future—to the State of Illinois, which stands on the prairies of this country, in the heart of the Middle West—I come here as a citizen of the great Republic, and I believe that the future can belong to those who are free, because I believe it must belong to those who are free.

If we put our power and wealth, and capacity and courage and determination, to the single-minded service of freedom, then I

believe with Francis Bacon "that there is hope enough and to spare, not only to make a bold man try, but also to make a sober-minded and wise man believe."

That is our opportunity, and that is our responsibility.

NOTE: The President spoke at 9:30 p.m. at the McCormick Place Exposition Center in Chicago. In his opening words he referred to Richard J. Daley, Mayor of Chicago; Otto Kerner, Governor of Illinois; Paul H. Douglas, U.S. Senator, and William L. Dawson, U.S. Representative, from Illinois; P. J. Cullerton, Assessor of Cook County and chairman of the fund-raising dinner; Thomas Keane, Chairman of the Finance Committee of the City Council of Chicago; and Lieutenant Governor Sam Shapiro, President of the Illinois State Senate.

Another text of this address was released by the White House prior to its actual delivery.

156   Message From the President on the Occasion of the Dedication of the Inter-Faith Chapel, Kings Point, New York.   *May 1, 1961*

IT IS FITTING that the Inter-Faith Chapel in memory of the American seamen of all faiths who gave their lives at sea be established at Kings Point.

Erected to the Glory of God, this edifice commemorating the memory of these men, will stand as a national monument on the grounds of the United States Merchant Marine Academy where young Americans prepare to serve their country in the American Merchant Marine.

Our Nation has ever sought Divine guid-

ance in its hours of thanksgiving and its moments of peril.

On the high seas, between heaven and the deep, men of all faiths feel a sense of brotherhood with the infinite.

May this Chapel ever inspire those who pause here to dedicate themselves to the service of their fellow men.

NOTE: The message, addressed to Rear Adm. Gordon McLintock, USMS, Superintendent of the U.S. Merchant Marine Academy, was read by John S. Stillman, Assistant to the Under Secretary of Commerce.

157   Remarks to the Joint Conference of Regional Commissioners and District Directors of the Internal Revenue Service.   *May 1, 1961*

Commissioner, Mr. Secretary:

I came over here this morning to express my great interest in the work that you are doing. I don't know any other society which attempts what this country attempts

to do, which requires really the good will and support of the citizens of the United States in contributing a large share of their income to the maintenance of the American society.

You are the point of contact with them, the people who work for you, and therefore the kind of spirit which you are able to inculcate into your people has a good deal to do with the success or failure of this great national effort.

Heavy burdens are placed upon the American society today. Over half of the money that is collected under taxes goes to our national defense. A good deal of the rest goes to other programs of great importance to our national security. Out of a total national income of $500 billion, nearly $90 billion are collected in taxes by the Federal Government. Other billions are collected by the cities and the States. That is a tremendous burden to place upon any society, and yet the American people have been willing to assume it.

I think it is our responsibility to make sure here in the national Government that every dollar that is collected by the Internal Revenue Service, every dollar that is paid by our people, is spent wisely, for a useful national purpose, for a purpose which advances our national interest.

I want to commend you for the efforts that you are making to improve our service, to make it easier for people to understand exactly what their responsibility is. I hope that you will impress upon the agents of the Internal Revenue Service how much we are dependent upon them, on their courtesy, on their efficiency, on their integrity, on their fairness.

I hope that here in Washington we will continue to work so that the burdens of the tax system become as fairly distributed as possible, so that they are distributed in a way which stimulates our economy and stimulates our growth to the extent that is possible, and not retards it.

This is a matter which is receiving great concern under the direction of the Commissioner, under the leadership of the Secretary of the Treasury, under the counsel of the Assistant Secretary of the Treasury, Mr. Surrey—and it is a matter of great personal interest to me.

This is a civil service area. It is going to be directed and administered in that fashion. I want you to understand that we are strongly behind you. We expect the best from you, and I can assure you that we will do the best we can here.

This is a difficult time in the life of our country. Our obligations spread around the world. It is becoming more obvious that the United States is the great source of strength not only to the people of this area of the world but also to people stretched all around the globe. They all look to us. And therefore the obligations upon us are many.

I commend you for your work. I express the hope that in the future we can all of us constantly improve our responsibilities to the public interest.

NOTE: The President spoke at 10:30 a.m. in the Internal Revenue Building in Washington. His opening words "Commissioner, Mr. Secretary" referred to Mortimer M. Caplin, Commissioner of the Internal Revenue Service, and Douglas Dillon, Secretary of the Treasury. He later referred to Assistant Secretary Stanley S. Surrey.

158   Remarks Upon Signing the Area Redevelopment Act. *May 1, 1961*

I WANT TO EXPRESS my great pleasure in signing this bill, which has been before the Congress and before the people for many years. It passed both the House and Senate on several occasions, and it is a great satisfaction now to have it finally signed into law.

This bill will help make it possible for thousands of Americans who want to work, to work. It will be of special help to those areas which have been subjected to chronic unemployment for many months, and in some cases for many years.

In this free society we want to make it possible for everyone to find a job who wants to work and support their families, and this bill is an important step in that direction.

This bill has become law because of the devoted efforts of a number of Members of the House and Senate, on both sides of the aisle, who have persevered at times against obstacles—substantial obstacles. And as a result of their efforts we now see it become law.

I want to commend the Members of the House and Senate who've been identified

with this issue for a number of years—and they surround me here on both sides. I want to congratulate them and to say that there's no piece of legislation which has been passed which gives me greater satisfaction to sign.

I want to announce that the Secretary of Commerce, in whose Department the responsibility is placed, is going right to work now in organizing this matter.

And I want to announce the appointment of William Batt of Pennsylvania, who has probably more experience in working in this matter than any other American—who has been working in the State of Pennsylvania on the same subject, who was a member of Senator Douglas' task force in the investigation of the problem in West Virginia, who is very familiar with the problems in Eastern Kentucky, Southern Illinois, and parts of Ohio. So that he will take on the responsibility of administering this act.

I think we are fortunate to have him, and glad he is with us today.

NOTE: The Area Redevelopment Act is Public Law 87–27 (75 Stat. 47).

159   Letter to the President of the Senate and to the Speaker of the House on Compensation Rates for Veterans Injured in the Service. *May 2, 1961*

[Released May 2, 1961. Dated April 27, 1961]

Dear Mr. ————:

In my recent message on budget and fiscal policy I recommended that the Congress enact selective increases in compensation rates for veterans with service-connected disabilities, to offset rises in the cost of living since the last increase in 1957 and to adjust rates

in categories which are out of line. The American people have traditionally insisted that those veterans who were injured in the service of their Nation be treated justly and humanely—a policy which will be carried out by this Administration.

The Administrator of Veterans Affairs has

prepared and submitted to me a draft of legislation which implements the recommendation in my message. I believe this approach which gives greater increases to those veterans with the more severe injuries is fair and reasonable. I am, therefore, transmitting the Administrator's letter of justification and the accompanying draft bill. I

strongly recommend early enactment of this legislation by the Congress.

Sincerely,

JOHN F. KENNEDY

NOTE: This is the text of identical letters addressed to the Honorable Lyndon B. Johnson, President of the Senate, and to the Honorable Sam Rayburn, Speaker of the House of Representatives.

160 Statement by the President Upon Appointing Teodoro Moscoso of Puerto Rico as U.S. Ambassador to Venezuela. *May 2, 1961*

I HAVE TODAY met with Mr. Teodoro Moscoso whom it has been my pleasure to name to the very important post of Ambassador to Venezuela. I expect him to depart for his new post within the next few days.

Ambassador Moscoso has a brilliant record as Administrator of the Economic Development Administration of Puerto Rico in carrying out what has come to be known throughout the world as "Operation Bootstrap," that dramatic effort through which economic diversification and development have brought a high degree of social benefits and equitable shares of economic returns

to our fellow citizens in that island. I believe that Ambassador Moscoso's experience in this field will enhance his ability to treat sympathetically and knowingly the Government and people of Venezuela and to ensure maximum effectiveness for the common efforts to provide a better life for the people of Venezuela and the entire Western Hemisphere.

I am confident that Ambassador Moscoso will be warmly welcomed among our friends in Venezuela as my personal envoy and as a particularly appropriate representative of the people of the entire United States.

161 Statement by the President Announcing a Program of Assistance to the Textile Industry. *May 2, 1961*

THE PROBLEMS of the textile industry are serious and deep-rooted. They have been the subject of investigation at least as far back as 1935, when a Cabinet committee was appointed by President Roosevelt to investigate the conditions in this industry. Most recently these problems were the subject of a special study by the Interdepartmental Committee headed by Secretary of Commerce Luther H. Hodges. I believe it is time for action.

It is our second largest employer. Some 2 million workers are directly affected by conditions in the industry. There are another 2 million persons employed in furnishing requirements of the industry at its present level of production. Two years ago, the Office of Defense Mobilization testified that it was one of the industries essential to our National security. It is of vital importance in peacetime and it has a direct effect upon our total economy. All the studies have

345

shown that unemployment in textile mills strikes hardest at those communities suffering most from depressed conditions.

I propose to initiate the following measures:

First, I have directed the Department of Commerce to launch an expanded program of research, covering new products, processes and markets. This should be done in cooperation with both union and management groups.

Second, I have asked the Treasury Department to review existing depreciation allowances on textile machinery. Revision of these allowances, together with adoption of the investment incentive credit proposals contained in my message to the Congress of April 20, 1961, should assist in the modernization of the industry.

Third, I have directed the Small Business Administration to assist the cotton textile industry to obtain the necessary financing for modernization of its equipment.

Fourth, I have directed the Department of Agriculture to explore and make recommendations to eliminate or offset the cost to United States mills of the adverse differential in raw cotton costs between domestic and foreign textile producers.

Fifth, I will shortly send to the Congress a proposal to permit industries seriously injured or threatened with serious injury as a result of increased imports to be eligible for assistance from the Federal Government.

Sixth, I have directed the Department of State to arrange for calling an early conference of the principal textile exporting and importing countries. This conference will seek an international understanding which will provide a basis for trade that will avoid undue disruption of established industries.

Seventh, In addition to this program, an application by the textile industry for action under existing statutes, such as the escape clause or the national security provision of the Trade Agreements Extension Act, will be carefully considered on its merits.

I believe this program will assist our textile industry to meet its basic problems, while at the same time recognizing the national interest in expansion of world trade and the successful development of less developed nations. It takes into account the dispersion of the industry, the range of its products, and its highly competitive character. It is my hope that these measures will strengthen the industry and expand consumption of its products without disrupting international trade and without disruption of the markets of any country.

NOTE: On October 11 the White House announced that the Treasury Department had completed its review of existing depreciation allowances on textile machinery and that a new depreciation schedule had been adopted. The release stated that the estimated average useful life for most textile machinery and equipment had been reduced from 25 years or longer to 15 years and in some cases to 12 years. The release added that the resulting speeding up of depreciation deductions, reflecting current technological conditions, would be of significant help to the industry in enabling it to modernize, meet foreign competition, and provide jobs.

The release further stated that a study of depreciation allowances with respect to all industries was under way, but that, in accordance with the President's directive, the study with respect to the textile industry had been accelerated.

See also Item 428.

162   Remarks at George Washington University Upon Receiving an Honorary Degree. *May 3, 1961*

Mr. President:

I want to express my appreciation to the President and to the Fellows of this University for the honor that they have bestowed upon me. My wife beat me to this honor by about 8 or 9 years. It took her 2 years to get this degree and it took me 2 minutes, but in any case we are both grateful.

I am also glad to be here because this University bears the distinguished name of the father of our country, George Washington. It is a matter of great interest that there has been an intimate relationship between the great political leaders of our country and our colleges and universities.

This University bears the name of George Washington, which showed his understanding in his day of the necessity of a free society to produce educated men and women. John Adams and John Quincy Adams from my own State of Massachusetts had an intimate relationship with Harvard University. Both of them, I believe, were members of the board of overseers. In both of their lives, Harvard and its development played a major part.

Washington and Lee shows an intimate relationship, for General Lee, the fact that he was willing to devote his life at the end of the war to educating the men and women of the South, indicated his understanding of this basic precept. Woodrow Wilson, Theodore Roosevelt—and all the rest.

I don't think that there has ever been a time when we have had greater need for those qualities which a university produces. I know that many people feel that a democracy is a divided system, that where the Communists are certain in purpose and certain in execution, we debate and talk and are unable to meet their consistency and their perseverance.

I do not hold that view. There are many disadvantages which a free society bears with it in a cold war struggle, but I believe over the long run that people do want to be free, that they desire to develop their own personalities and their own potentials, that democracy permits them to do so. And that it is the job of schools and colleges such as this to provide the men and women who will with their sense of discipline and purpose and understanding contribute to the maintenance of free societies here and around the world.

A hundred years ago, George William Curtis of my own State asked a body of educators during the Kansas-Nebraska controversy, "Would you have counted him a friend of ancient Greece who quietly discussed the theory of patriotism on that hot summer day through whose hopeless and immortal hours Leonidas and the three hundred stood at Thermopylae for liberty? Was John Milton to conjugate Greek verbs in his library when the liberty of Englishmen was imperiled?" No, quite obviously, the duty of the educated man or woman, the duty of the scholar, is to give his objective sense, his sense of liberty to the maintenance of our society at a critical time.

This is our opportunity, as well as our responsibility; and I am particularly glad to be here today when we are witnessing the swearing-in of a new President. Many years ago, as most of you know, at Harvard University somebody came around and asked for President Lowell. They said, "He's in Washington seeing Mr. Taft." I know that some other day, when they are asking for the President of your University, they will say that he is over at the White House seeing Mr. Kennedy.

They understood at Harvard, and you

347

understood here, the relative importance of a University President and a President of the United States.

Thank you.

NOTE: The President spoke at 10:50 a.m. at a ceremony marking the inauguration of Dr. Thomas Henry Carroll 2d as President of the University.

The President was awarded the degree of Doctor of Laws. Mrs. Kennedy received a Bachelor of Arts degree from the University in 1951.

163 Special Message to the Congress Transmitting Reorganization Plan 3 of 1961. *May 3, 1961*

To the Congress of the United States:

I transmit herewith Reorganization Plan No. 3 of 1961, prepared in accordance with the Reorganization Act of 1949, as amended, and providing for reorganization in the Civil Aeronautics Board.

This Reorganization Plan No. 3 of 1961 follows upon my message of April 13, 1961 to the Congress of the United States. It is believed that the taking effect of the reorganizations included in this plan will provide for greater efficiency in the dispatch of the business of the Civil Aeronautics Board.

The plan provides for greater flexibility in the handling of the business before the Board, permitting its disposition at different levels so as better to promote its efficient dispatch. Thus matters both of an adjudicatory and regulatory nature may, depending upon their importance and their complexity, be finally consummated by divisions of the Board, individual Board members, hearing examiners, and, subject to the provisions of Section 7(a) of the Administrative Procedure Act of 1946 (60 Stat. 241), by other employees. This will relieve the Board members from the necessity of dealing with many matters of lesser importance and thus conserve their time for the consideration of major matters of policy and planning. There is, however, reserved to the Board as a whole the right to review any such deci-

sion, report or certification either upon its own initiative or upon the petition of a party or intervenor demonstrating to the satisfaction of the Board the desirability of having the matter reviewed at the top level.

Provision is also made, in order to maintain the fundamental bipartisan concept explicit in the basic statute creating the Board, for mandatory review of any such decision, report or certification upon the vote of a majority of the Board less one member.

Inasmuch as the assignment of delegated functions in particular cases and with reference to particular problems to divisions of the Board, to Board members, to hearing examiners, to employees and boards of employees must require continuous and flexible handling, depending both upon the amount and nature of the business, that function is placed in the Chairman by section 2 of the plan.

By providing sound organizational arrangements, the taking effect of the reorganizations included in the accompanying reorganization plan will make possible more economical and expeditious administration of the affected functions. It is, however, impracticable to itemize at this time the reductions of expenditures which it is probable will be brought about by such taking effect.

After investigation, I have found and hereby declare that each reorganization included in the reorganization plan transmitted herewith is necessary to accomplish one or more of the purposes set forth in section 2(a) of the Reorganization Act of 1949, as amended.

I recommend that the Congress allow the reorganization plan to become effective.

JOHN F. KENNEDY

NOTE: Reorganization Plan 3 of 1961 is published in the Federal Register (26 F.R. 5989). It became effective on July 3, 1961.

164 Remarks of Welcome to President Bourguiba of Tunisia at the Washington National Airport. *May 3, 1961*

IT IS a great pleasure for me as President of the United States and also as a citizen of our country to welcome the President of a friendly country and a distinguished world statesman.

Long before I occupied this present responsibility, I had become familiar with the long struggle in the life of President Bourguiba for his country's independence. He spent years in prison. He spent years in struggle. He is given in his own country the name of the Supreme Combatant, because he had one goal always in mind: the independence and freedom of his country.

And now that that independence and freedom has been won, he has put before his people another goal, and that is to build a better life for themselves, to make it possible for all of the people of his country to share in a more fruitful and abundant existence.

I think that it's most proper that the first head of state to pay an official state visit to this country in this administration should be President Bourguiba.

We welcome him. I think he knows that the people of this country admire those who stand for principle, those who fight for freedom. We have among us today a man who has fought for freedom and fought for principle.

It is a great honor to welcome him to the United States.

NOTE: President Bourguiba responded (through an interpreter) as follows:

Mr. President, ladies and gentlemen:

I am deeply touched by the kind words which you have just expressed towards Tunisia and towards myself. The warm welcome which has been extended to the members of my party and to myself constitutes the most eloquent possible proof of the traditional long friendship which has never ceased to exist between our two nations.

This is my way of telling you, Mr. President, the profound joy which I experience in being once again in your country, land of liberty and democracy, and the joy I feel in bringing to the noble American nation a message of friendship and consideration on the part of the Tunisian nation. Our common devotion to the great values of civilization, our devotion to the principles of justice and liberty, constitute the most firm basis for friendship which unites our two peoples. And the surest possible pledge of the development and strengthening of such friendship, the understanding and the support of the Government of the United States and of Your Excellency in particular, have never failed us, and authorize the trust that we have in the happy outcome of the meetings that we are to have.

That is why, Mr. President, I should like to express to you my deep gratitude for your kind invitation and to tell you my conviction that it will contribute to strengthening still further the bonds of friendship and cooperation which exist between our two countries.

I should like to conclude by expressing my most sincere good wishes for the happiness and prosperity of the noble people of the United States.

165   Toasts of the President and President Bourguiba. *May 3, 1961*

Ladies and gentlemen:

I want to express on behalf of our country our great pleasure in having President Bourguiba here. I think it is most appropriate that today he visited the home of George Washington, because in many ways his own life is comparable to the experiences of the father of our country, General Washington. Like President Washington, President Bourguiba is a revolutionary, and like President Washington he also, when the revolution was won, had the sense of judgment, self-discipline and strength to attempt to bring good will and peace among his people and to the people of the former occupiers of his country and his surrounding neighbors.

I think we are extremely fortunate to have President Bourguiba here tonight. As we look back in our own history, there is a glow around the names of Washington, Hamilton, Jefferson, and all the others who contributed to the founding of our country. We are in the presence tonight of a man who has played a comparable role in the life of his own country. He spent many months and years in prison, and yet under great pressure and with great temptation to take the easy way, he continued to fight for the independence of his country, the peace of North Africa, for the well-being of his people.

This, I think, represents an extraordinary achievement in the life of any man, and I must say it was a great satisfaction to me to see the warm response which the people of our country gave to the President this morning.

This is the first state dinner that we have had for a chief of state since Mrs. Kennedy and I have come to the White House, and I must say, speaking personally and as President, there is no dinner that gives me greater satisfaction.

I hope that you all will join with me in drinking a toast to President Bourguiba.

NOTE: Following the toast President Bourguiba responded (through an interpreter) as follows:

Mr. President, ladies and gentlemen:

I am most honored and very proud of the remarks of sympathy shown to me by President Kennedy, and the remarks of sympathy expressed to me and my people by the people of the District of Columbia.

Just now President Kennedy was good enough to recall the fact that I paid a visit today to the home of the first President of the United States, George Washington, and he was even good enough to go so far as to say that my life to a certain extent has resembled that of George Washington.

That is a very flattering comparison, for which I thank you. But I would really feel that George Washington did a good deal more for his country, for America, than it has been possible for me to do for the people of Tunisia.

But I might say that today I also have had a chance to enter into the past of another President, who is long known to us, and that is to say President Lincoln, whose Memorial I visited today. We look upon him as President of the Union. And if I have played a part in Tunisia in gaining independence for my people, I feel that I did so because I was able to achieve union among the Tunisian people, around a certain doctrine, around certain ideals, and to that extent, therefore, perhaps my role was similar to that of your President Lincoln in the history of the United States. And perhaps it may be said that the part Lincoln played was as great as that played by George Washington in the history of the United States.

I, for myself, found great inspiration for my own work in the work and life of Lincoln, because I found my country deeply divided—divided by ideas, by traditions, by ancient rancors, passions, feelings of all sorts; and for 25 years I have struggled to achieve the unification of my people.

But to my mind the greatest piece of work is to bring about an understanding among peoples and mutual comprehension. That is the great task in the world. Peace, to my mind, can be achieved only through a rapprochement of people, just as within a nation it is necessary to bring people together. That is a difficult task, and because not all people are inspired by the same good intentions.

But it is a task which has to be performed, and it cannot succeed—or rather, if this task does not succeed, it will mean that we will be simply giving way to hatred, to distrust, to evil ambitions, and the world will be running backwards—it will be a retrogression away from peace.

President Kennedy has often spoken of the example of George Washington. We have spoken of the example of President Lincoln. It seems to me that President Kennedy has here, in his hands, the opportunity himself to facilitate a "rapprochement," a greater understanding among peoples. We all must work together for good or for ill. It is only thus that we can develop in harmony, in peace and in happiness.

I should like to thank President Kennedy in the name of my country, in the name of my people, for his kindness. I should like to thank Mrs. Kennedy for the kindness she has shown to my wife and to me personally when we were chatting this evening. I should like to thank the people of the United States and the people of the District of Columbia for the warm welcome given to us today—and I should like to ask you to drink a Toast to President Kennedy.

---

166   Letter to the President of the Senate and to the Speaker of the House Transmitting Bill To Provide for an Additional Assistant Secretary of Labor.   *May* 4, 1961

Dear Mr. ————:

I am transmitting herewith a bill to provide for an Assistant Secretary of Labor in the Department of Labor. This bill will better enable the Department of Labor to meet its increasing responsibilities in connection with the growing role of women in the work force of the Nation. In the next decade it is estimated that there will be an increase in that work force of 25 percent. This will require special attention and special emphasis upon the programs devoted to them.

I am enclosing, also, a letter from the Secretary of Labor describing the need for the bill.

Sincerely,

JOHN F. KENNEDY

NOTE: This is the text of identical letters addressed to the Honorable Lyndon B. Johnson, President of the Senate, and to the Honorable Sam Rayburn, Speaker of the House of Representatives.

The President approved a bill providing for an additional Assistant Secretary of Labor on August 11, 1961 (Public Law 87–137, 75 Stat. 338).

Secretary Goldberg's letter was also released.

---

167   Letter to President Dacko Concerning U.S. Assistance to the Central African Republic.   *May* 4, 1961

[Released May 4, 1961.   Dated April 19, 1961]

Dear Mr. President:

I appreciated your letter on your desire to make plans for the economic and social development of your country. The United States, as you know, has always made clear its wish to assist the newly independent African countries to establish strong and stable economies, to the extent that our heavy commitments permit us to contribute to this goal. I can, therefore, assure you of my country's desire to be of assistance.

In the immediate future, if you wish, I am prepared to send to your country representatives from the United States International Cooperation Administration to discuss with you and your government ways in which the United States can best respond to your request.

In the meantime, may I suggest you and other appropriate officials of your government make available to our Charge d'Affaires, Mr. Lukens, more details of your thinking on an economic program for the Central African Republic. I shall read his reports and recommendations with great interest.

Sincerely,

JOHN F. KENNEDY

[His Excellency David Dacko, President, Central African Republic, Bangui, Central African Republic]

NOTE: President Dacko's letter is published in the Department of State Bulletin (vol. 44, p. 766).

168 Letter to Members of the President's Foreign Intelligence Advisory Board. *May 4, 1961*

Dear —————:

I am delighted that you have consented to serve as a member of the President's Foreign Intelligence Advisory Board which is being reactivated pursuant to the Executive Order which I approved on May 4, 1961.

I am establishing this Board for the purpose of providing me periodically with independent evaluations of the objectives and conduct of U.S. foreign intelligence activities and of the performance of the several agencies engaged in foreign intelligence and related efforts.

It is my desire that the Board should meet periodically to analyze objectively the work of the Government's foreign intelligence agencies. While the review by the Board will be concerned with all U.S. foreign intelligence activities, I would expect particular attention to be devoted to the performance of those civilian and military intelligence elements of key importance to the Government in the fields of national security and foreign relations. I am especially anxious to obtain the Board's views as to the over-all conduct and progress of the foreign intelligence effort as well as its advice as to any modifications therein which would enhance the acquisition of intelligence essential to the policy making branches of the Government in the areas of national security and foreign relations.

It is my hope that you and the others whom I have invited to serve on the Board will be able to meet with me on May 15, 1961, to discuss in detail the scope of the work which you have so generously agreed to undertake.

I know that you and your fellow Board members can make a real contribution to the national interest by your service with this body.

Sincerely,

JOHN F. KENNEDY

NOTE: This is the text of identical letters addressed to Dr. James R. Killian, Jr., Chairman of the Board; Dr. William O. Baker, Vice President, Research, Bell Telephone Laboratories; Lt. Gen. James H. Doolittle, USAF (ret.), Chairman of the Board, Space Technology Laboratories, Inc.; Dr. William L. Langer, Professor of History, Harvard University; Robert D. Murphy, President, Corning Glass International; and Gen. Maxwell Taylor, USA (ret.), President, Lincoln Center for the Performing Arts, Inc. Later, on May 15, Clark M. Clifford and Gordon Gray were appointed members of the Board.

169 Remarks Upon Signing the Minimum Wage Bill.
May 5, 1961

I WANT TO EXPRESS my great satisfaction in signing the bill to increase the minimum wage to a dollar twenty-five cents an hour, and to extend the coverage to three million, six hundred thousand people today who are not covered by this most important piece of national legislation.

This is the first time since the act came into existence under the administration of President Franklin Roosevelt in 1938 that we have been able to expand the coverage. I don't believe that there's any American who believes that any man or woman should have to work in interstate commerce, in companies of substantial size, for less than a dollar twenty-five cents an hour, or fifty dollars a week. That itself is a very minimum wage, and I therefore want to commend the Members of the Congress in the House and the Senate, the Chairmen of the Subcommittees who were particularly involved, under the leadership of the House and Senate, for their untiring efforts.

I also want to commend the leaders of organized labor, the AFL–CIO, who are here today with Mr. Meany, for their long interest. Every member, pretty much, of their unions is paid more than a dollar and a quarter, but they have been concerned about unorganized workers who have been at the bottom of the economic ladder who have not benefited from our growing prosperity in this country as a nation over the long number of years and who need our help.

This doesn't finish this job, but it is a most important step forward, and as a former Member of the Senate who is particularly interested in it, I must say that I am delighted to sign it. I congratulate those who worked for it. They are one group of our citizens who deserve our assistance more, and I think that we can move from this improvement into greater gains in the months and years to come.

NOTE: The bill, entitled "Fair Labor Standards Amendments of 1961," is Public Law 87–30 (75 Stat. 65).

170 Statement by the President on the Flight of Astronaut Alan B. Shepard. *May 5, 1961*

ALL AMERICA rejoices in this successful flight of Astronaut Shepard. This is an historic milestone in our own exploration into space. But America still needs to work with the utmost speed and vigor in the further development of our space program. Today's flight should provide incentive to everyone in our nation concerned with this program to redouble their efforts in this vital field. Important scientific material has been obtained during this flight and this will be made available to the world's scientific community.

We extend special congratulations to Astronaut Shepard and best wishes to his family who lived through this most difficult time with him. Our thanks also go to the other Astronauts who worked so hard as a team in this project.

171 The President's News Conference of May 5, 1961

THE PRESIDENT. I have several announcements to make.

[1.] This week Ambassador Arthur H. Dean has reported to me upon the status of the nuclear test ban conference at Geneva. On the opening day of the resumed conference, the United States in closest cooperation with the United Kingdom presented a series of new proposals, and on April 18, 1961, presented a complete nuclear test ban draft treaty. The new U.S. position represents an earnest and reasonable effort to reach a workable agreement. It constitutes a most significant overall move in these negotiations. Unfortunately, the Soviet Union has introduced a new proposition into the negotiations which amounts to a built-in veto of an inspection system.

The Soviet proposal calls for a three-man administrative council to direct inspection operations and other activities of the control arrangements. This proposal reverses a position to which the Soviet Union had previously agreed. In earlier negotiations before this session in Geneva, it had been agreed that the inspection system would be headed by a single administrator, operating within a mandate clearly defined in the treaty. The Soviet Union would substitute a directorate, representing the Communist bloc, the Western Nations, and uncommitted countries. Each member of this triumvirate would have to agree with every other member before any action could be taken. Even relatively detailed elements of the inspection system would be subject to a veto or a debating delay.

We recognize that the Soviet Union put forward its proposition before it had considered our new proposals. It is now considering our draft treaty, and we hope it will do so in a positive manner, as of course we are most anxious to secure an agreement in this vital area—a responsible and effective agreement.

Ambassador Dean is leaving for Geneva today to resume the negotiations. The United States will continue to strive for a reliable and workable agreement. I have asked Ambassador Dean to report to me within a reasonable time on the prospects for a constructive outcome.

[2.] Secondly, I have asked Vice President Johnson to undertake a special fact-finding mission to Asia. The Vice President has agreed to do this. I consider this an extremely important assignment and I will be looking forward to receiving the Vice President's firsthand reports when he returns.

The Vice President will report directly to me upon his return. It is expected that the State Department will make public the itinerary and the technicians who will accompany the Vice President as soon as possible. It is anticipated that in the course of his trip the Vice President will consult with top governmental officials and conduct discussions on the highest level relating to the situations in those countries.

[3.] Next, I have today instructed the United States representatives on the Council of the Organization of American States to propose the convocation on July 15th of an extraordinary meeting of the Inter-American Economic and Social Council to be held at the ministerial level. The purposes of this meeting should be to initiate and develop planning and arrangements related to realistic economic development in the Americas, as well as to elaborate the objectives of the Act of Bogotá in all key areas of economic and social betterment. This will be an important aspect of the cooperative program which I have set forth in the concept of the Alliance for Progress.

[4.] Finally, I was asked at a previous press conference what the Government was going to do about the aluminum extrusion plant that it owns in Adrian, Mich. I am pleased to announce that the General Services Administration has completed negotiations for the sale of the plant to the Harvey Aluminum Company of California and one of the conditions of the sale was that the plant be kept in production.

[5.] Q. Mr. President, you said earlier today that today's space flight should provide incentive to everyone in our Nation concerned with this program to redouble their efforts in this vital field. Do you have any specific proposals as to how these efforts should be redoubled, and would you want more money for space now than you have already asked from Congress?

THE PRESIDENT. The answer to the question is yes, we are going to send an additional request for appropriations for space, which I hope will have a beneficial effect on the program. We are going to make a substantially larger effort in space.

[6.] Q. Mr. President, in the speech prepared for delivery in Chicago last Friday which you did not read, you said that the principal adversary was not the Russians but rather our own unwillingness to do what must be done. Could you clarify for us your thinking on that and indicate some field in which the American people have not done what their governmental leaders asked?

THE PRESIDENT. Well, the latter is not the correct—I said "our," not to make a distinction between the Government and the people. I was talking about the common problems of our free society.

I do wish that some of the speeches I give would get as much attention as the speeches which I do not give. [*Laughter*]

I do think there are a number of things that can usefully be done. We are going to require a larger effort in space. We are going to require a larger effort in other areas of the national security and we will be making our suggestions to the Congress.

I will say that this is a free society and it is not—it really requires a good deal of voluntary effort. On the matter of space, I've asked Secretary Goldberg to cooperate closely with Senator McClellan, to see if we can get a responsible, consistent effort by labor and management in the field of production of our missile program.

What is true there is true of other programs essential to our national defense. We have meeting at the White House, under the leadership of Secretary Goldberg and Secretary Hodges, a panel composed of the leading business and labor leaders of this country and public members, to see if we can persuade labor and management to come to useful national conclusions on problems of price and wages which will affect our balance of payments, and also address themselves to the problems of automation.

Now the Federal Government cannot compel that. All we can do is indicate the need. We are asking the people of this country to spend a good deal of money on mutual security and foreign assistance, which is not a popular program but which I believe to be essential. We have asked the people to support a greater effort—both of the National Government and in their own communities—to improve education. We are asking the people of this country to try, regardless of their own personal views, to reach—to come closer to the constitutional concept of equality of opportunity for all Americans, regardless of their race or creed.

There are a good many of these areas which are within the private sector where each person can contribute usefully to strengthen education, to improve the opportunity for all Americans, to pay heavy burdens as they do in taxation to maintain programs which they may not always wholly agree with but which at least many of us feel to be in the national interest. In their own private work they consider the national needs, and we will continue to try to point out where we need a national effort.

Q. May I ask one followup question, sir? When you use the word "our," are you suggesting that it's the unwillingness of Government *and* people to do what must be done?

THE PRESIDENT. I had not subjected that sentence to the—but what I do think is a problem is to, in a free society, to attempt to come to actions which permit us to compete successfully with the discipline of the Communist state. And I think it's probably not only true using the "our"—I would use it not only in the national sense, but also in the international sense.

There isn't any doubt, reading today's news from one country and another, that the forces of freedom are in many areas on the defense, partly because they have not always been willing to take those progressive steps which will associate the governments with the progressive aspirations of the people so that when I use "our," I use it really in the sense of speaking of the common purpose of the free world, which affects other countries besides ourselves. But as time goes on, I think the point made in the question is a good one.

I think we should continue as much as we can to indicate where the people, other than in the payment of taxes or in their acceptance of military obligations, where they can usefully contribute to the advancement of

the national interest. I have suggested several areas, and I will suggest others in time.

[7.] Q. Mr. President, there have been reports that you would be prepared to send American forces into South Viet-Nam if that became necessary to prevent Communist domination of that country. Could you tell us whether that is correct, and also anything else you have regarding plans for that country?

THE PRESIDENT. Well, we have had a group working in the Government and we have had a Security Council meeting about the problems which are faced in Viet-Nam by the guerrillas and by the barrage which the present government is being subjected to. The problem of troops is a matter— the matter of what we are going to do to assist Viet-Nam to obtain its independence is a matter still under consideration. There are a good many which I think can most usefully wait until we have had consultations with the government, which up to the present time—which will be one of the matters which Vice President Johnson will deal with: the problem of consultations with the Government of Viet-Nam as to what further steps could most usefully be taken.

[8.] Q. Mr. President, is the administration satisfied that the Indian Chairman of the International Control Commission in Hanoi has pressed as vigorously as he might have the right of the Commission to go to the Hanoi airfield, where the Soviet planes have been putting down on the way to Laos? Specifically, has he at times declined to have the Commission do that?

THE PRESIDENT. There has been, as you know, some disagreement as to the authority of the International Control Commission. I would hope that—and after all, this is a matter which the British have, and the Indian Government, as well as the other two members of the Control Commission, the

Canadians and the Poles—I would hope that they would use maximum influence to make the Control Commission as effective as possible. And we would be—this Government would cooperate in every way to make it effective.

[9.] Q. Mr. President, is it anticipated that the United States will continue to train and arm the Cuban exiles in this country or elsewhere, or will that operation be disbanded?

THE PRESIDENT. We have no plans to train Cuban exiles as a Cuban force in this country or in any other country at this time. There are, of course, Cubans who live in this country or have the opportunity to serve in the Armed Forces of the United States. But if your question means are we planning now to train a Cuban force, as I understand your question, we are not now training and are not now planning to train a Cuban force of the kind that your question would suggest.

[10.] Q. Mr. President, are you embarrassed or is the Government harmed in any way by the rather frank statements that Senator Fulbright has made on foreign policy?

THE PRESIDENT. Am I embarrassed—and what was the other word?

Q. Or is the Government harmed in any way in its foreign relations by a member of your party speaking as he has?

THE PRESIDENT. No. Senator Fulbright and I spent an hour together last evening, and we've had—I've talked to Senator Fulbright, I think, at least on five different occasions in the last 4 or 5 weeks, and I expect to continue to confer with him. He is Chairman of the Senate Foreign Relations Committee and he is a valuable citizen, and I think his counsel is useful and I think that he should say what he thinks. And if he has indicated disagreement on occasions, then he has indicated general sup-

port on a good many other occasions, although that has not become as newsworthy.

[11.] Q. Mr. President, about 10 days ago you sent a message to Congress on the conflict of interest laws and in that message you mentioned that public confidence is the basis for effective government, and that when that confidence appears to falter or does falter then we are in some sort of trouble. Since that time one of your Cabinet members, Secretary of the Interior Udall, has been involved in a situation in which one of his friends, believing to have acted on his suggestion, solicited members of the oil and gas industry for contributions to a $100-a-plate Democratic Rally.

Now, in this instance, do you believe that ethical standards have appeared to falter or have you had any advice for your Secretary in this case?

THE PRESIDENT. Well, I know that the Secretary attempted, I believe, according to what I read of his press conference and the conversations that I have had with him myself, did—when he heard of the letter that had gone out which he had not envisioned—did attempt to have those letters recalled.

I think this whole question of trying to raise funds for campaigns is a very difficult one and it leads to embarrassments. I wish and I hope that before we get into another presidential campaign that we can work out some system by which the major burdens of presidential campaigns on both sides would be sustained by the National Government, as suggested by Theodore Roosevelt, as suggested by Senator Neuberger—Dick Neuberger—when he was here. Because, to try to raise $6 million or $7 million, which a presidential campaign must, from people, is a very difficult task and leads to embarrassing situations. I made it clear in the campaign, and I make it clear again, that no one should contribute—that while we are glad to have support, no one should contribute to any campaign fund under the expectation that it will do them the slightest bit of good, and they should not stay home from a campaign fund or dinner or campaign under the slightest expectation that it will do them a disservice.

I'm satisfied that that's Mr. Udall's view, from my knowledge of him. But I do think that every member of the Cabinet, every member of this administration, should bend over backwards to make sure that there are no misunderstandings of the kind that could have arisen from this incident.

Secretary Udall understands that. I hope everybody else does. But I think the best way to prevent an embarrassment to a Cabinet officer—and I think that Mr. Udall was embarrassed by this incident—and embarrassment to an administration, would be to try to work out some other way of raising funds for these presidential campaigns, because there isn't any doubt that people give—and I am talking now not about this incident, but about generally—under the expectation that they should, or it is expected of them. As long as we can't get broader citizen participation, I think it ought to be done through the National Government, and I would support that strongly if the Congress would move in that direction.

Q. Have you spoken to Mr. Udall about this, sir?

THE PRESIDENT. I have.

[12.] Q. Mr. President, has the administration made any determination with respect to an embargo on trade with Cuba?

THE PRESIDENT. We had a meeting of the National Security Council in which we discussed the problems of Cuba. As you know, the only kinds of supplies that are now being sent to Cuba involve food and medicine, so that we have to consider carefully all of the implications of further action and that is being done.

Q. Is a decision imminent?

THE PRESIDENT. That will be considered carefully.

[13.] Q. Mr. President, in addition to the statement you issued earlier, will you here give your evaluation and reaction to today's successful launching of an American astronaut into space and back?

THE PRESIDENT. Well, I first would like to repeat what I said about Major Gagarin, which was that as a human accomplishment and as a demonstration of courage, I think everyone, whether they are citizens of this country or citizens of another country, take the greatest personal satisfaction in the accomplishment of another member of the human race.

As an American, I am, of course, proud of the effort that a great many scientists and engineers and technicians have made, of all of the astronauts, and, of course, particularly of Commander Shepard and his family.

We have a long way to go in the field of space. We are behind. But we are working hard and we are going to increase our effort. In addition, we are making available the scientific information which we have gathered to other scientists in the world community and people who share our view that the probe into space should be peaceful, and should be for the common good, and that will continue to motivate us.

[14.] Q. Mr. President, leaving aside the matter of the space trip today, I think many of us are concerned by the relentless knelling of the gong of gloom and doom by some of the administration officials who participate in foreign affairs. I was wondering, sir, if you could tell us if there are any bright spots on the international horizon?

THE PRESIDENT. Well, I think that we have grounds for encouragement. I am hopeful that NATO will be strengthened by the meeting in Oslo, and that we will make a more determined effort. I believe that as other situations become more difficult, that there is a common recognition of the need for closer collaboration. That is true of NATO.

Secondly, I am hopeful that our ties with Japan can become strengthened as the weeks and months pass, and I have a good deal of encouragement from the effort which India is making on its third 5-year plan, which if successful could make a tremendous difference in the cause of freedom throughout all of Asia.

Then I feel that there is a greater recognition in this hemisphere of—I don't think that there is any doubt about this—that there is a greater recognition of the urgency of a common hemispheric approach to the problems of poverty and a common hemispheric effort to improve the life of the people. In addition, I think there is a common hemispheric awareness now that there is cause for alarm in the determined effort which Communists are making to seize control of the liberal revolutionary movements which are endemic to the Western Hemisphere, and turn them to their own ends.

And, quite obviously, I think that we are happy about what happened this morning. I am not a pessimist about the future, but I think that we have a good many problems, but that doesn't——

[15.] Q. Mr. President, you have emphasized on several occasions in public the necessity to find new nonmilitary ways to assert and support our foreign policy. Can you suggest to us this afternoon any ways in the immediate future that we might do that in meeting the Communist threat in Southeast Asia, specifically?

THE PRESIDENT. Well, I think the United States can play an important role. And I think in considering the problems in our own hemisphere we have to remember that the United States is holding back—is protecting the integrity by its guarantees of a good many countries which are in the direct line of hazard in the Middle East, in Asia, and in Western Europe—and that in itself is a substantial accomplishment. We can assist these countries by our guarantees or at least we can protect these countries by our guarantees against outright military invasion. We can assist them through economic assistance to improve the life of their people. We can assist them through defense support in strengthening their armed forces against internal guerrilla activity. But in the final analysis they have to—and we cannot do it for them—they have to organize the political and social life of the country in such a way that they maintain the support of their people.

There is a limit beyond which our efforts cannot go. I think that I have described what our efforts can do. In the final analysis, then, the responsibility rests with the people involved to maintain the support of the people, to identify their government with the people.

One of the reasons why it has been a satisfaction to have the President of Tunisia here, Mr. Bourguiba, is that he has done that. He has stood for freedom; he has identified himself with a common effort—national effort—by the people under freedom, and that's what we need to do around the globe.

[16.] Q. Mr. President, what are you and the Defense Department doing to better prepare the one-half million dependents, more than half of whom are wives, sons, and daughters, of Peace Corps qualifications, for their roles while living overseas with their husbands, in the case of wives, and fathers, in the case of sons and daughters?

359

THE PRESIDENT. Well, I don't think the Defense—did you say the Defense Department?

Q. I asked what you and the Defense Department, because I was referring primarily to Armed Forces wives and sons and daughters who are of Peace Corps qualification.

THE PRESIDENT. Well, that really is a responsibility of the Peace Corps, which is to—I may not be——

Q. Perhaps I did not make myself clear. [*Laughter*] We have at least 485,000 dependents of our Armed Forces——

THE PRESIDENT. In order to make themselves more effective?

Q. Yes.

THE PRESIDENT. Well, I see. I think that is a good—I don't know whether we are doing enough. I am not informed about the matter. I think it is a good point, and I think that the Defense Department and the State Department and the White House should see if there is anything more effective we can do, so we will.

[17.] Q. Mr. President, in view of the communistic declarations of Cuba's Castro, what is the position of the United States now on the Monroe Doctrine and how do we expect to enforce it?

THE PRESIDENT. Well, the Monroe Doctrine and other treaties which the United States has committed itself to, of course, govern the foreign policy of the United States in this hemisphere. I have discussed the problem, and the Secretary of State has made other references to it. It is a matter of some concern now on an individual and hemispheric basis.

[18.] Q. Mr. President, how would you appraise your first 100 days in office?

THE PRESIDENT. Well, I feel I can read what you gentlemen write about it and I wouldn't attempt to contradict you.

[19.] Q. Mr. President, speaking of ties with Japan, as you did, do you think it might still be useful for General Eisenhower to visit Tokyo in the fall, or is that still under consideration?

THE PRESIDENT. Well, I think whatever the judgment would be of the President, I would accept, and——

Q. The State Department has asked him not to, if I recall correctly.

THE PRESIDENT. I have looked into it and it is—I saw that statement and I have talked to the State Department, and we are attempting to come to a more definitive conclusion as to what we might suggest to him, though, of course, what we would do is give him all the information we have and then see what his best judgment was. I think that President Eisenhower could very usefully travel abroad as an individual and also, of course, as a respected citizen of this country. When and where he should go is a matter on which he would make a judgment. But we would, in the meanwhile, provide him with all the information we had as to the appropriateness—as, really, to the wisdom of exactly when those trips should be taken and where. The final decision will be made by the President—President Eisenhower—but we will make available to him all the information that we have.

[20.] Q. Mr. President, during the campaign you repeatedly mentioned the plight of laundry workers in some of our big cities, being paid substandard wages. How do you feel about both Houses having passed a minimum wage bill which specifically excludes them from coverage?

THE PRESIDENT. I wish we could include them in the coverage. I am hopeful that we will not settle with what we now have, but that we will get the laundry workers in. One of the problems with laundry workers, of course, is that they are paid quite badly now. I would say they are among the lowest group—almost the lowest group in the American economy. Laundries are not a prosperous business at the present time. The passage of the minimum wage of $1.25 would increase the cost of the laundry owners by a substantial sum because manpower represents a high percentage of their cost, and they are competing with home laundries, which now have become a rather easy alternative in many cases, so that the argument is made that we would liquidate a substantial percentage of the industry and throw them out of work. So it is not the easiest problem. But, nevertheless, considering all that, in my judgment they should be covered. And that goes for hotel and restaurant workers, too—it was necessary to drop them in order to get the coverage we did. The coverage we passed, which was 3,600,000, is the first time that we expanded the coverage since 1938. It's a hard fight, but I am hopeful that we will come back to them and get those groups covered.

[21.] Q. Mr. President, does your administration have plans for further spending in public works as an attack on unemployment, and do your remarks that a substantially larger effort is needed in the space program indicate that you prefer to channel any extra spending into the military field?

THE PRESIDENT. Well, I think we can make a judgment as to what additional efforts should be made in retraining or public works, and so on, based on our judgment of the economy, and also what other expenditures we have to make in the fields of national security and related—we are making a study of what greater effort should be made in the field of conventional forces at the present time. All these will be completed before the end of the month, and will be made public. So that we are trying to make a judgment on the state of the economy, of what usefully could be done, of the international and national needs. I cannot today give you an answer to the——

[22.] Q. Mr. President, is there any evidence that the Soviet Union is making available to the scientists in other countries the knowledge which it recently acquired from its man in space?

THE PRESIDENT. I have not heard it. Now, I don't want to be inaccurate. It is possible they have, but it has not been brought to my attention. And there was our statement this morning in which we spoke of the fact that we were going to disseminate it to other scientists. We did. It was suggested that others who have pioneered in this field have not made that information available.

[23.] Q. Mr. President, in that connection, were you satisfied with the coverage given today of the space shot, and if you were, and it was not a successful thing, would we be back in the orphanage?

THE PRESIDENT. Back in the what?

Q. In the orphanage.

THE PRESIDENT. I agree that if it had failed, having had some experience with that, it would be a very difficult time for NASA and for us all. But fortunately, it succeeded. I have not got the answer, however, to the question of the buildup.

What I think is somewhat unfair is when pressmen themselves, or editorial writers, criticize NASA for attempting a big buildup with all of the implications it would have to our prestige and standing if there is a failure. We are not responsible, at least we are making every effort not to be responsible, for encouraging a press concentration on this event, because quite obviously if we fail we are humiliated here and around the world.

But in a free society, if a newspaperman asks to be represented, and to come, then he can come. So I think everybody ought to understand that we are not going to do what the Russians did, of being secret and just hailing our successes. If they like that system, they have to take it all, which means that you don't get anything in the paper except what the government wants. But if you don't like that system, and I don't, then you have to take these risks. And for people to suggest that it is a publicity circus, when at the same time they are very insistent that their reporters go down there,

does seem to me to be unfair.

What is fair is that we all recognize that our failures are going to be publicized and so are our successes and there isn't anything that anyone can do about it or should.

Reporter: Thank you, Mr. President.

NOTE: President Kennedy's eleventh news conference was held in the State Department Auditorium at 3:30 o'clock on Friday afternoon, May 5, 1961.

172   Exchange of Remarks in the Rose Garden With President Bourguiba of Tunisia.   *May 5, 1961*

WE ARE going to have a communique which will be ready in 3 or 4 minutes, which represents the views of the President and myself.

I do want to say, speaking personally, that as President Bourguiba's visit here in Washington comes to an end, and as he sets out for his visit to the Tennessee Valley, to Texas, to New York, that this country and the Government, Members of the Congress, and speaking as the President, have taken the greatest possible satisfaction in his visit here.

As I stated when the President arrived, he represents, personifies, and is in fact a national leader who has spent his life fighting for the freedom of his people. And now as leader and as President, their having achieved their freedom, spends his life fighting for their well-being.

It is the greatest source of satisfaction to me as an American who is interested in the spread of liberty, to be host over here to a man of President Bourguiba's quality and

character. And we have developed extremely friendly personal ties during this visit. I have admired him for a great many years, and I must say that he leaves Washington with the full knowledge that he holds a memorable place in the hearts of all Americans who value fortitude, perseverance, and vision.

NOTE: President Bourguiba responded (through an interpreter) as follows:

I am most proud of the kind words just spoken by President Kennedy, proud of the esteem shown me by President Kennedy. This is something of which I can be proud, of which the people of Tunisia can be proud.

We have fought for liberty and we continue to struggle to obtain the conditions for the full exercise of that freedom. And in this second phase of our struggle, we have as a supporter President Kennedy and the people of the United States, whose welcome has gone straight to our heart. And we have gained in this work of rapprochement and friendship an agreement and a unanimity on the part of the executive and the legislative branches, and the people, so that this work cannot fail to succeed.

We are sure of victory, since we share it—share in this task with the American people.

173 Joint Statement Following Discussions With President Bourguiba. *May 5, 1961*

PRESIDENT BOURGUIBA concludes tomorrow the Washington portion of the State visit he is making to the United States at the invitation of President Kennedy. The two Presidents have had very cordial, frank and fruitful talks on a broad range of subjects. Their conversations have been characterized by the same spirit of mutual understanding and respect which has been responsible for the friendly and positive relations which have evolved between the two countries.

President Bourguiba defined his policy of non-alignment and friendship with all countries desiring good relations with Tunisia. President Kennedy expressed the support of the United States for the inviolate right of peoples and countries to exercise freedom of choice in the organization of their societies and in the definition of their political attitudes. They agreed that the retention by all countries of this freedom of choice is essential to the existence of a peaceful and harmonious world of freedom and justice.

The two Presidents found themselves in agreement as to the political, economic and social problems that confront many new countries, particularly in Africa. They share the conviction that the orderly process of decolonization is essential to the promotion of human welfare, the consolidation of peace and the encouragement of the striving African peoples. They are in basic accord that political progress and economic development will be hindered if the continent of Africa becomes an arena for the so-called cold war. They believe that the independent states of Africa should be free to follow their own policies without outside interference and that they should at the same time strive for a closer harmonization of African viewpoints.

The two Presidents discussed the problem of Algeria. They believe that negotiation and that peaceful application of the principle of self-determination are the key to peace in Algeria and to stability in North Africa and the Mediterranean.

The two Presidents also examined the problem of the Congo. They feel strongly that all nations should give wholehearted support to the efforts of the United Nations and particularly of the Secretary General in carrying out the pertinent General Assembly and Security Council resolutions on the Congo, and should refrain from unilateral actions contrary to those resolutions.

In the social and economic fields, President Bourguiba stressed the importance which Tunisia attaches to the full realization of its human and material potential through a well-conceived national program. President Kennedy expressed his full sympathy with these objectives and made clear the desire of the United States to enter into partnership relationships with the developing countries, based on social justice, self-help and long-range planning. The two Presidents agreed that cooperative efforts of their two countries toward these ends should be continued and expanded. They directed their advisers to explore without delay and in greater detail the means whereby these efforts could be rendered more effective in support of accelerated economic and social growth on a long-range basis.

President Bourguiba extended to President and Mrs. Kennedy a cordial invitation to visit Tunisia. President Kennedy expressed their sincere thanks and indicated they look forward to the opportunity.

174 Message to Prime Minister Lefevre of Belgium. *May 7, 1961*

[Released May 7, 1961. Dated May 3, 1961]

Dear Mr. Prime Minister:

Although there is a long tradition of friendship and cooperation between the United States and Belgium, today's pressing need for free-world solidarity calls for ever-closer ties between our two countries. I am convinced that through our common efforts the partnership which the United States and Belgium have built over the years will continue to serve not only the best interests of our two countries, but the cause of free men everywhere. I have asked Ambassador MacArthur, in whom I place full confidence, to devote his energies to these ends. I am confident that full and frank discussion will strengthen mutual understanding and thus also serve to strengthen the partnership between our two countries. I would like you to know that for our part we will greatly value your views on all matters of mutual interest.

My fellow Americans join me in extending to you congratulations and best wishes on your assumption of the office of Prime Minister.

Sincerely,

JOHN F. KENNEDY

[His Excellency Theo M. Lefevre, Prime Minister of Belgium]

175 Message to President Tubman of Liberia on the Occasion of the Monrovia Conference of African States. *May 8, 1961*

Dear Mr. President:

I want to extend to you and to the delegates to the Monrovia Conference the best wishes of the Government and the people of the United States for the success of your conference.

When the leaders of the African nations meet together to discuss the freedom, the security and the economic well-being of their people, all friends of Africa rejoice. We greatly applaud the determination of African leaders to come to grips with their own problems. They are African problems and they must be solved, first of all, in African terms. Solutions thus arrived at advance not only the interest of the African peoples; they contribute also to international understanding and world peace.

The United States of America welcomes African moves toward greater regional or continent-wide cooperation. It strongly hopes for the success of African arrangements designed to keep the peace in Africa, which can serve as an inspiration for other parts of the world community.

It is our further hope that your conference, through discussion of economic and social problems of the African peoples, may arrive at understandings and decisions which will promote economic growth. I assure you that the United States is anxious to assist in promoting that growth because of our conviction that no nation in the world today can live in peace and prosperity while others are denied the full realization of social progress and human dignity.

To you, your fellow Chiefs of State, and the Foreign Ministers and other representatives at the Monrovia Conference, I express in my own name and in the name of the American people our most sincere hope that this Conference will achieve a full measure of practical success, contributing thereby to the further strengthening of freedom in Africa and throughout the world.

JOHN F. KENNEDY

[His Excellency, William V. S. Tubman, President of the Republic of Liberia, Monrovia]

176   Statement by the President Following a Meeting With the Conference of Appalachian Governors. *May* 8, 1961

WE DISCUSSED at a meeting this morning, and at lunch, the economic problems faced by the Appalachian region. Here many of the economic problems that face our nation find special emphasis.

Certainly, there is an urgent need for development of this region to utilize its full resources. To achieve this objective, I have directed that:

1. The Area Redevelopment Administration focus particular attention upon the opportunities—as well as the problems—of the Appalachian region along the lines of my discussion with the Appalachian Governors.

2. The re-training program for workers be expanded.

3. The Defense Department review its policies with regard to the placement of contracts in areas of substantial unemployment.

4. A special liaison be established within the Area Redevelopment Administration to evaluate, and where possible, to put into effect, suggestions by the Conference of Appalachian Governors. The Conference of Appalachian Governors will be constituted as an advisory group to work closely with the Area Redevelopment Administration.

The Appalachian Governors are to be complimented upon their resourcefulness in the treatment of unusual multi-State regional problems. It is the first time an entire section of a Nation has been organized to develop an important regional program of this magnitude.

The meeting has been productive and I am confident that cooperation between State and Federal governments will lead the way toward a prosperous Appalachian region.

NOTE: In a White House release of the same date the Governors stated that they had urged early action on highways, water resource and forestry development, and education and special training programs. They also stated that they had proposed the establishment of a Federal Appalachian Regional Commission to focus available information and programs for more effective application in the region. The Governors added that the new area redevelopment legislation would not reach full effectiveness unless the more basic problems causing regional underdevelopment were dealt with.

Participating in the meeting were Governors from the States of Alabama, Kentucky, Maryland, North Carolina, Pennsylvania, Tennessee, Virginia, and West Virginia.

177   Remarks at the Presentation of NASA's Distinguished Service
Medal to Astronaut Alan B. Shepard.   *May 8, 1961*

Ladies and gentlemen:

I want to express on behalf of all of us the great pleasure we have in welcoming Commander Shepard and Mrs. Shepard here today. I think they know as citizens of this great country how proud we are of him, what satisfaction we take in his accomplishment, what a service he has rendered our country. And we are also very proud of Mrs. Shepard.

I know that the other members of this team who are astronauts know that our pride in them is equal. They have been part of this effort from the beginning. Commander Shepard has pointed out from the time that this flight began and from the time this flight was a success, that this was a common effort in which a good many men were involved. I think it does credit to him that he is associated with such a distinguished group of Americans whom we are all glad to honor today, his companions in the flight into outer space, so I think we want to give them all a hand. They are the tanned and healthy ones—the others are Washington employees!

I also want to pay particular tribute to some of the people who worked on this flight: Robert Gilruth, Director of the Space Task Force at Langley Field; Walter Williams, the Operations Director of Project Mercury; the NASA Deputy Administrator, Dr. Hugh Dryden; Lt. Col. John H. Glenn, Jr.—and of course, James Webb, who is head of NASA.

Most of these names are unfamiliar, but if this flight had not been an overwhelming success, these names would be very familiar to everyone. So I think it is very appro-

priate that in this success that their work should be acknowledged.

And I also want to take cognizance of the fact that this flight was made out in the open with all the possibilities of failure, which would have been damaging to our country's prestige. Because great risks were taken in that regard, it seems to me that we have some right to claim that this open society of ours which risked much, gained much.

Now I want to give this award.

"The National Aeronautics and Space Administration awards to Alan B. Shepard, Jr., the NASA Distinguished Service Medal for outstanding contributions to space technology. His flight as the first United States astronaut was an outstanding contribution to the advancement of human knowledge of space technology, and a demonstration of man's capabilities in sub-orbital space flight. Signed and sealed in Washington this fifth day of May, 1961. James E. Webb, the Administrator of NASA, and Hugh L. Dryden, the Deputy Administrator of NASA."

This is a civilian award for a great civilian accomplishment, and therefore I want to again express my congratulations to Alan Shepard. We are very proud of him, and I speak on behalf of the Vice President, who is Chairman of our Space Council and who bears great responsibilities in this field, and the Members of the House and Senate Space Committee who are with us today.

NOTE: The President spoke in the Rose Garden at the White House.

178   Address at the 39th Annual Convention of the National Association of Broadcasters.   *May 8, 1961*

Governor Collins, Bishop Hannan, ladies and gentlemen:

We have with us today the Nation's number one television performer, who I think on last Friday morning secured the largest rating of any morning show in recent history. [*Laughter*]

I must say, I think all of us as citizens of the free world are extremely proud not only of Commander Shepard, but also of Mrs. Shepard—and perhaps with the Vice President they would come forward. [*Loud and prolonged applause*]

Commander Shepard: How do you get them to stop? We only have time for a few words here, because I understand we have a rather busy day ahead of us. I just want to say, thank you very much for such a warm welcome.

THE PRESIDENT: I must say I think the presence of Commander Shepard and also Mrs. Shepard who I think is—I must say, when I saw her on television, I had great satisfaction as a fellow citizen. I must say we are delighted to have them all. It's a great source of satisfaction and pride to us.

I said this morning, when I read off the names of some of the other people who have been involved in this flight—Mr. Webb, who is head of NASA, and Dr. Dryden, and all the rest—I said that they were names which were rather unknown. If this flight had not been successful, however, they would have been among the best known names in the United States. So that even I, who had nothing to do with the flight, would have become very much identified with it.

So that I do express my commendation to Commander Shepard and also his fellow astronauts who all involved themselves in the hazards and the discipline of the work,

but also those who were involved with the program. Because this is a free society, and because we therefore take our chances out in the open, of success or failure, all those who were part of the program, who were involved in the decisions which made the program possible, who were involved in the very public decision which made the very public flight possible on Friday morning, were also in hazard. And while their task did not in any manner approach that of the Commander, nevertheless it is a very real one, and it is the kind of risk which members of a free society must take.

There had been before the flight, as you know, a good many members of our community who felt that we should not take that chance. But I see no way out of it. I don't see how it's possible for us to keep these matters private, unless we decide on the highest national level that all matters which are risky, which carry with them the hazard of defeat, which could be detrimental to our society—that none of them will be printed in the paper or carried on radio and television.

The essence of free communication must be that our failures as well as our successes will be broadcast around the world. And therefore we take double pride in our successes.

I am delighted that there are members here of your profession who are not citizens of this country but who come from our hemisphere. I hope that they understand that we share a fraternal feeling with them, that we are engaged in a common effort to maintain freedom here in this hemisphere, and to assist freedom throughout the world.

And it has been our fortune to be placed in positions of responsibility—all of us—at a time when freedom is under its greatest attack.

I know that to those who live in some parts of this country and some parts of the world, that the discipline of the totalitarian system has some attraction. I called attention at my press conference more than a week ago to a comment made by a student in Paris, an African student, after the extraordinary flight of Major Gagarin, in which the student said, "The Russians don't talk about things, they do them, and then we hear about them."

It is difficult for me to believe that any young man or woman, or any citizen who understands the real meaning of freedom, who recognizes that freedom is at issue around the globe, could possibly hold that view.

I feel, as a believer in freedom, as well as President of the United States, that we want a world in which the good and the bad, successes or failures, the aspirations of people, their desires, their disagreements, their dissent, their agreements, whether they serve the interest of the state or not, should be made public, should be part of the general understanding of all people.

And that is why I was particularly anxious to come here today. There is no means of communication as significant as that in which you are involved: to hear, to see, to listen.

And you have the opportunity to play a significant role in the defense of freedom all around the globe.

Our adversaries in this struggle against freedom—and they are not national adversaries, we have no national disagreements, what is involved is the great struggle for freedom, and our adversaries in that struggle possess many advantages. Their forces press down upon us, on the borders of the Middle East, Southeast Asia, and Western Europe. They use the secrecy of the totalitarian state and the discipline to mask the effective use of guerrilla forces secretly undermining independent states, and to hide a wide international network of agents and activities which threaten the fabric of democratic government everywhere in the world. And their single-minded effort to destroy freedom is strengthened by the discipline, the secrecy, and the swiftness with which an efficient despotism can move. In addition, the ability of a totalitarian state to mobilize all of its resources for the service of the state, whatever the human cost, has great attraction for those who live on the marginal edge of existence, fired with a strong feeling of ancient wrongs and grievances, a feeling which is tirelessly exploited by our adversaries—the people who live on an income of sixty or seventy or eighty dollars a year—the example of the Soviet Union which in the short space of forty years has transformed itself from being among the most backward countries of Europe to being a leader in space, has powerful attraction.

Once a state succumbs, however, to this attraction, to the lure of communism, to the lure of totalitarianism—even for a moment—resistance is then crushed, opposition is destroyed, and despotic power is maintained even when finally the people may realize they have been cruelly misled—and the steady stream of refugees out of Viet-Minh in the north, out of Eastern Germany, out of Cuba, all indicate the real nature of their society once it has assumed control.

On this path thus far there has been no turning back. There can be no doubt, therefore, that this determined and powerful system will subject us to many tests of nerve and will in the coming years—in Berlin, in Asia, in the Middle East, in this hemisphere.

We will face challenge after challenge, as the communists armed with all the resources and advantage of the police state attempt to shift the balance of power in their direction.

But despite this, I do not believe that the tide of history is on the side of despotism. I do not believe that the tide of history necessarily is on either side. It is only what we decide ourselves we will do—which direction we will turn the tide of history—that we can be successful.

For we bring to the battle our own resources, the particular advantages of a free society—advantages which our adversaries cannot match, advantages which if vigorously used offer hope for the ultimate triumph of freedom.

On our side is the simple and all-important fact that men want to be free, and nations want to be their own masters. It is this fact that helps to explain why no nation in the past decade—with the possible exception of Cuba, where a social revolution was betrayed, and where the story is not yet finally ended—has fallen under communist rule without being subdued by armed force.

It is this fact that explains the courageous revolution against hopeless odds in Poland, and East Germany, and Hungary, and Tibet—revolutions that would have succeeded if alien armies had not been present to put them down.

It is this fact that explains why the poverty-stricken nations of this hemisphere and Africa, filled with discontent in some cases, and social tensions, bearing the memory of past wrongs, have still not succumbed to the lure of communism.

And it is this fact that is man's best hope. For our nation is on the side of man's desire to be free, and the desire of nations to be independent. And thus we are allied, if we are true to ourselves and true to our destiny, with the strongest force in the world today.

The great inner resource of freedom, the resource which has kept the world's oldest democracy continually young and vital, the resource which has always brought us our greatest exploits in time of our greatest need, is the very fact of the open society.

Thus, if we are once again to preserve our civilization, it will be because of our freedom, and not in spite of it. That is why I am here with you today. For the flow of ideas, the capacity to make informed choices, the ability to criticise, all the assumptions upon which political democracy rests, depend largely upon communication. And you are the guardians of the most powerful and effective means of communication ever designed.

In the rest of the world this power can be used to describe the true nature of the struggle, and to give a true and responsible picture of a free society. And in addition, broadcasting has new and untried possibilities for education, for helping to end illiteracy, which holds back so much of the world and which denies access to the information so vital to a free and informed choice. The full development of broadcasting as an instrument of education is one of the most significant challenges which confronts your industry. And here in our own country this power can be used, as it is being used, to tell our people of the perils and the challenges and the opportunities that we face—of the effort and painful choices which the coming years will demand. For the history of this nation is a tribute to the ability of an informed citizenry to make the right choices in response to danger, and if you play your part, if the immense powers of broadcasting are used to illuminate the new and subtle problems which our nation faces—if your strength is used to reinforce the great strengths which freedom brings, then I am confident that our people and our nation, and all other people and all other nations will again rise to the great challenges of the sixties.

No man can hope to prophesy with precision the outcome of the great struggle in which our generation is now engaged. Yet we do know that the cause of human freedom has been threatened on many occasions since the system of free choice and democracy was developed in sunlit Greece more than twenty-four hundred years ago. And yet from each threat and indeed from each defeat, as well as from each success, it has ultimately emerged unconquered.

That is why in the face of an ominous

future we can share that faith which Winston Churchill expressed more than a half-century ago, "Humanity will not be cast down."

We are going along, along the same high road, and already behind the distant mountains the sun can be seen—and will be seen again.

That is your opportunity—and that is a responsibility which all of us who are citizens of the free world must once again meet.

NOTE: The President spoke at the Sheraton-Park Hotel in Washington. His opening words "Governor Collins, Bishop Hannan" referred to LeRoy Collins, former Governor of Florida, President of the National Association of Broadcasters, and The Most Reverend Philip M. Hannan, Auxiliary Bishop of Washington, D.C.

179 Greetings Telephoned to President Truman on the Occasion of His 77th Birthday. *May 8, 1961*

PRESIDENT KENNEDY: Hello, Mr. President, how are you?

PRESIDENT TRUMAN: Well, I'm all right. Having a great time and they're giving me too much to eat and too much to do.

PRESIDENT KENNEDY: Listen—I want to congratulate you on this great anniversary——

PRESIDENT TRUMAN: Well, you're very kind indeed——

PRESIDENT KENNEDY: Well, I must say that——

PRESIDENT TRUMAN: ——I've always hoped that after I was 70, they would forget about these birthdays, but they don't seem to do it.

PRESIDENT KENNEDY: I don't understand how you can look so well, after having spent 7 years here.

PRESIDENT TRUMAN: Well, I'll tell you how I did that. I did just what you are doing, try to make the right decision and forget about it, and that's what you have to do. And then sleep over it at night and forget about it.

PRESIDENT KENNEDY: Well, listen—I'm delighted—I had lunch with the Vice President and some of your friends who are Governors, Governor Lawrence and the rest, and they all wanted to join me in congratulating you. We are all great rooters of yours, Mr. President.

PRESIDENT TRUMAN: You are just as kind as you can be, and I more than appreciate it.

PRESIDENT KENNEDY: Well, you take——

PRESIDENT TRUMAN: You're better to me than I deserve.

PRESIDENT KENNEDY: Well, you take care of yourself, and we look forward to seeing you soon here in Washington.

PRESIDENT TRUMAN: I'll be there.

PRESIDENT KENNEDY: We're taking good care of your House.

PRESIDENT TRUMAN: Thank you, goodbye.

NOTE: The President's call was made from the Signal Corps studios at the White House at 3:36 p.m. President Truman was being honored by more than 200 friends at a birthday party in the grand ballroom of the Muehlebach Hotel in Kansas City, Mo.

180   Special Message to the Congress Transmitting Reorganization Plan 4 of 1961.   *May 9, 1961*

To the Congress of the United States:

I transmit herewith Reorganization Plan No. 4 of 1961, prepared in accordance with the Reorganization Act of 1949, as amended, and providing for reorganization in the Federal Trade Commission.

This Reorganization Plan No. 4 of 1961 follows upon my message of April 13, 1961 to the Congress of the United States. It is believed that the taking effect of the reorganizations included in this plan will provide for greater efficiency in the dispatch of the business of the Federal Trade Commission.

The plan provides for greater flexibility in the handling of the business before the Commission, permitting its disposition at different levels so as better to promote its efficient dispatch. Thus matters both of an adjudicatory and regulatory nature may, depending upon their importance and their complexity, be finally consummated by divisions of the Commission, individual Commissioners, hearing examiners, and, subject to the provisions of section 7(a) of the Administrative Procedure Act (60 Stat. 241), by other employees. This will relieve the Commissioners from the necessity of dealing with many matters of lesser importance and thus conserve their time for the consideration of major matters of policy and planning. There is, however, reserved to the Commission as a whole the right to re-

view any such decision, report or certification either upon its own initiative or upon the petition of a party or intervenor demonstrating to the satisfaction of the Commission the desirability of having the matter reviewed at the top level.

Provision is also made, in order to maintain the fundamental bi-partisan concept explicit in the basic statute creating the Commission, for mandatory review of any such decision, report or certification upon the vote of a majority of the Commission less one member.

Inasmuch as the assignment of delegated functions in particular cases and with reference to particular problems to divisions of the Commission, to Commissioners, to hearing examiners, to employees and boards of employees must require continuous and flexible handling, depending both upon the amount and nature of the business, that function is placed in the Chairman by section 2 of the plan.

By providing sound organizational arrangements, the taking effect of the reorganizations included in the accompanying reorganization plan will make possible more economical and expeditious administration of the affected functions. It is, however, impracticable to itemize at this time the reductions of expenditures which it is probable will be brought about by such taking effect.

After investigation, I have found and

hereby declare that each reorganization included in the reorganization plan transmitted herewith is necessary to accomplish one or more of the purposes set forth in section 2(a) of the Reorganization Act of 1949, as amended.

I recommend that the Congress allow the reorganization plan to become effective.

JOHN F. KENNEDY

NOTE: Reorganization Plan 4 of 1961 is published in the Federal Register (26 F.R. 6191). It became effective on July 9, 1961.

181 Remarks on the White House Lawn at a Reception for Foreign Students. *May* 10, 1961

Ladies and gentlemen—students:

I want to express on behalf of Mrs. Kennedy and myself our great appreciation to you for coming and joining us today on this old lawn before this old house, and to also tell you what a pleasure it is and honor it is for us that you have chosen to come and study in the United States.

You represent, really, the seed for your country. In every case all of you represent a sacrifice not only on behalf of yourselves but in behalf of your country and the people within your country who were responsible for sending you here to study.

When you go back you will become among the future leaders of your country. In the last 2 months I have been honored by a visit from two visitors who are leaders of their country, both of whom studied as young men here in the United States—President Nkrumah and Dr. Banda, both from Africa—and I am confident that in other days other Presidents of the United States will be visited by Presidents and other leaders of their country, who will be you who will have studied here and who will, I hope, have gotten a better understanding not only of our country and its aspirations but also of the meanings of a free society.

We are an open and free society. All of our strengths and all of our weaknesses are on display. They are a matter of discussion.

Those of us who hold high office and high responsibilities are subject to all of the scrutiny—the careful scrutiny—which comes from a free press and a free people, operating within an open society.

That is the way this country was planned, and I hope that those of you who study here will come to realize that this diversity, this division, in some cases this dissension, is not a source of weakness but is a source of strength.

Upon it rests the security of each individual in this country, so that when you come here and when you study and when you teach us, I hope that you will go away not merely expressing doubts because we have been unable to reach our high aspirations, but also recognizing that those high aspirations represent the ultimate goals of our society. And where we fall short, we know it—and we mean to do better.

The Chinese have an old proverb that to begin a voyage of a thousand miles requires the first step. I believe that we've taken more than the first step in this country, that we are moving ahead. But I realize we have a long way to go to build a free and open country here, and free and open societies around the world.

We want you to enlist yourselves in that great effort for your own people. That is what we hope you will go from here back home understanding what we are trying to do, and getting a better understanding of what your countries themselves must do.

We want for you freedom—we want for you a better life—we want for you friendship with our people. So today we welcome you here. You are going to teach us a good deal more in the time you are here than you will learn. You are our guests, and you benefit us—and you are welcome among us today.

The last great visit we had was—this house has, I suppose, had many invasions, including that of the British when they burned it down. Today we seek to build.

We want you to know that we are proud to have you here.

NOTE: The President spoke from a bandstand erected on the South Lawn at the White House. The guests included about 1,000 foreign students, representing 73 nations, who were attending colleges in the Washington, D.C., area.

In the course of his remarks the President referred to President Kwame Nkrumah of Ghana and Dr. Hastings K. Banda of Nyasaland.

182   Letter to the Speaker of the House of Representatives Concerning Measures To Combat Juvenile Delinquency. *May 11, 1961*

Dear Mr. Speaker:

I have received reports indicating that there has been an increase in the amount of juvenile delinquency in both urban and rural communities. This delinquency seems to occur most often among school drop-outs and unemployed youth faced with limited opportunities and from broken families.

I view the present trend with serious concern. Juvenile delinquency and youth offenses diminish the strength and the vitality of our Nation; they present serious problems to all the communities affected; and they leave indelible impressions upon the people involved which often cause continuing problems.

Many steps have already been taken to broaden the available opportunities for learning and work and to remove barriers to the full utilization of our young people. I am, today, issuing an Executive Order directing the Attorney General, the Secretary of Health, Education, and Welfare and the Secretary of Labor to coordinate their efforts in the development of a program of Federal leadership to assist the States and local communities in their efforts to reduce juvenile delinquency. But with our greatly increased teenage population, further measures are necessary. The social, educational, economic, and law enforcement aspects of delinquency must all be considered in any effective program to combat this condition in our society.

In order to accomplish these objectives, I am transmitting herewith legislation to enable the Federal Government to undertake projects designed to demonstrate and evaluate the most effective ways of using our resources to combat juvenile delinquency within local communities. Measures must be taken to reach deeply into the experiences of everyday life in deprived families and local communities. We must undertake a program integrating specific remedies into a total attack upon the prevention and control of youth offenses.

By means of the proposed legislation, the Federal Government will be able to provide assistance to those dedicated persons in local communities throughout the Nation who are striving in many ways to create the social conditions that will ensure the growth of a skilled and resourceful population of young men and women who are firm in character and committed to the development of a democratic way of life.

The enclosed letter from the Secretary of Health, Education, and Welfare explains in detail the proposed legislation.

Sincerely,

JOHN F. KENNEDY

NOTE: The letter was addressed to the Honorable Sam Rayburn, Speaker of the House of Representatives.

Executive Order 10940 "Establishing the President's Committee on Juvenile Delinquency and Youth Crime" is published in the Federal Register (26 F.R. 4136).

Secretary Ribicoff's letter was also released.

183   Message to Cuban Mothers Assembled in Miami.
May 14, 1961

TO YOU who have gathered today in Miami, I send greetings. You have personally encountered the sorrow and pain which accompany the fight for freedom.

The mothers and fathers who in every generation have seen their sons fight for freedom have understood and lived through this grief.

But today, I send you a message of hope. The American people will never forget the people of Cuba—the American people will always associate themselves with your fight for freedom. And freedom will come—for tyranny can never in the long run overcome the legitimate ambitions of people to be free.

Sincerely,

JOHN F. KENNEDY

NOTE: The envelope containing this message was addressed to "The Cuban Mothers" and was delivered by the Secret Service to Dr. Luis Conte Aguero, 10276 Northeast 12th Avenue, Miami, Florida.

184   Letter to President Paz Estenssoro Concerning a Long-Range Program for the Development of Bolivia. *May 15, 1961*

Excellency:

The Government of the United States has long had a deep concern for the welfare of the people of Bolivia; and a close friendship for your country. We believe it is essential to work with you in helping the Bolivian people satisfy their aspirations for a better life and for increased social justice. This means rapidly stimulating the growth of your economy in order to raise the standard of living of the Bolivian people.

To this end I recently sent a special economic mission to Bolivia to explore, with the Bolivian government, ways in which the United States and its free world allies could effectively aid the intensified development of Bolivia. That mission has returned, and on the basis of its reports we are prepared to take some immediate steps which have been in preparation for several weeks.

However, we must realize that these steps are just the beginning in the development of a long-range plan for the steady growth of the Bolivian economy. Bolivia is a country rich in resources, and in the skill and courage and determination of its people.

As these riches are liberated and used to the benefit of the Bolivian people, we can help eliminate poverty from your land. This will require the combined efforts of the Bolivian government and people and the industrial nations of the West.

First, we commit ourselves to help in the long-range, systematic development of the Bolivian economy—looking on Bolivia as a full partner in the Alliance for Progress— working toward the day when all Bolivians can enjoy a higher standard of living and external assistance is no longer required.

Secondly, we will cooperate with the Bolivian National Planning Commission, the United Nations Advisory Group and the Inter-American Economic and Social Council to work together in developing a long-range program of economic development— and in preparing the necessary technical studies needed to implement this plan. Such a plan can be the guide to the contributions and loans of all resource supplying institutions.

Third, if you believe it will be helpful, I am prepared to send a special representative to assist in carrying forward the Program and especially to try to insure that United States assistance—from all sources—contributes effectively to the long-term development of the Bolivian economy. With your approval this representative can be dispatched in the very near future.

We are also willing to begin immediately on a series of projects important to the economic development of Bolivia. These are projects which are already in an advanced state of preparation and which will make an immediate contribution to national welfare. Other urgent projects—such as low-cost worker and *campesino* housing—can be undertaken as soon as planning and programming are complete.

Fourth, a loan agreement was signed with the Bolivian Government on March 24, providing $3.5 million to finance the purchase of urgently needed machinery and equipment to improve the operating efficiency of the state-owned mining enterprise, COMIBOL. This amount constitutes the United States contribution to the first phase of a "triangular" program for the rehabilitation of the Bolivian mining industry. The Federal Republic of Germany has also made a similar sum available for this purpose. It is expected that the Inter-American Development Bank will announce its contribution to the triangular agreement soon. The loan arrangements also provide for new geological explorations and research for improved recovery facilities under a management-consultant contract with the expert West German firm of Salzgitter. Urgent discussions with the two latter partners in this operation are currently in progress to complete working arrangements for the first phase of this project and to consider the total investment eventually to be required.

Fifth, the YPFB has recently made application to Washington lending agencies for a loan to finance the import purchase of essential repair and replacement equipment urgently needed to restore oil production to former levels. In response to this request the International Cooperation Administration will extend an immediate loan for YPFB of $6 million for this purpose.

Sixth, the diversification of the Bolivian economy urgently requires the extension of its existing road network to open up new areas for settlement. I propose that steps be immediately taken to accelerate the use of counterpart over and above the Bs 16 billion now earmarked for road construction. In addition we will, as soon as plans are complete, loan $2 million to finance the equipment costs of this road program.

Seventh, pursuant to the objectives of our "Food for Peace" program, and in agreement with your Government, $1,350,000 of surplus agricultural products are being allocated for a school lunch and family relief program to be administered by voluntary relief agencies under PL 480 Title III. To cover the transportation and distribution costs incurred in this program, a sum of $500,000 is being made available from United States dollar funds.

Eighth, in addition, several other projects to be financed by counterpart funds have already been agreed on.

As a result of these special measures, existing programs, loans already committed to Bolivia by such agencies of the United States government as the Development Loan Fund (for the El Alto airport and the La Esperanza Sugar Mill, for example), and funds committed by the Federal Republic of Germany and such agencies as the Inter-American Development Bank, a total of some $50 million in free world assistance is pledged to Bolivia. The projects to be financed through this assistance are regarded by my Government as initial steps towards the re-alization of the longer-range program of economic development to which I have already referred.

With these steps I believe we can begin to help the Bolivian nation move toward its ultimate destiny as a strong and prosperous country. Bolivia has a vital role to play in the task of developing our hemisphere and in the preservation of the values of American civilization. This great revolution has blazed a path for others to follow. And I believe that if we work together the horizons of your people and mine will be unlimited—and that the next ten years will see the fulfillment of the hopes of the American people for economic progress with social justice.

My best personal good wishes,

JOHN F. KENNEDY

[His Excellency, Victor Paz Estenssoro, President of the Republic of Bolivia]

NOTE: President Paz Estenssoro's letter, dated May 14 and released May 17, is published in the Department of State Bulletin (vol. 44, p. 921).

A White House release dated August 14 announced that the President had designated Dr. Rowland A. Egger, university professor and international consultant, to serve as his special representative to the Government of Bolivia to assist in carrying forward the long-range economic program.

185 Letter to Mrs. Alicia Patterson, Editor and Publisher of Newsday, Concerning the Nation's Response to the Cold War. *May 16, 1961*

[Released May 16, 1961. Dated May 11, 1961]

Dear Mrs. Patterson:

Many thanks for your wire of May fourth. I appreciate your interest in our nation's needs and the spirit that motivates your telegram.

Apparently the demands of the "cold war" are not as dramatic, and thus not as well-identified, as the demands of the traditional "shooting war"—such as rationing (which we do not need), a doubling of draft quotas (which would not help), or an increase in personal income taxes (which would only impede the recovery of our economic strength).

But that does not mean that nothing is being asked of our citizens. The facts of the matter are that all the programs I am seeking—to strengthen our economy, our defenses, our image abroad, our balance of payments position and our foreign policy tools—all make demands upon one or more groups of Americans, and most often upon all Americans jointly. All of them involve some effort, some inconvenience or some sacrifice—and, indeed, they are being opposed in some quarters on that basis.

For example: I have asked that we provide a leaner, more efficient defense establishment by terminating certain projects and closing a good many bases, although there are many protests from those who want economy practiced in someone else's community. I have asked that a major effort in Foreign aid to other nations be maintained for many years to come, as burdensome as some regard it. I have asked young Americans to serve without pay or comfort in a Peace Corps for under-developed countries; I have asked many talented individuals to give up a higher income to serve their country in public office (and not all have been willing to do so); and I have asked all government officials to give up any incompatible financial interests.

I have asked that our excise and corporation tax rates not be permitted to fall as scheduled by law—that trucking companies and jet airline companies pay a higher tax for the highways and airways they use—that our business corporations pay a higher payroll tax for improved Social Security, unemployment compensation and health insurance—and that certain taxpayers give up their privileges of expense account living, in yachts, hunting lodges, night-clubs and all the rest. I have asked all Americans to help meet our deficit through higher postal rates.

These requests for sacrifice are being strongly resisted by some unwilling to pay the price of national greatness.

I have asked other Americans to contribute to the strengthening of our economy by paying a decent minimum wage—or to give up their rights to purchase as many duty-free goods when they are travelling abroad—or, if they are farmers, to accept the limitations of our feed grain program. I have asked our businessmen and labor leaders, through my Advisory Committee, to adopt price and wage levels consistent with our economic goals and need to compete; and, more directly, I have asked them to take steps that will avoid harmful work stoppages in our missile and space effort.

I have asked the newspaper industry, without much success, to exercise more self-restraint in publishing intelligence data helpful to any enemy. My messages on education, urban affairs and natural resources have all stressed the role the local community must assume if we are to make the most of our schools, our cities and our water and other resources. We have made clear our very strong request to employers, labor unions and indeed all citizens for an end to racial discrimination.

I have tried to make the whole tone and thrust of this office and this Administration one that will demand a higher standard of excellence from every individual in his private life—in his education, his physical fitness, his attitudes toward foreign visitors, his obligations as a citizen, and all the rest.

And finally, each time we make any move or commitment in foreign affairs, I am in need of the support of the American people, their understanding, their patience, their willingness to endure set-backs and risks and hardships in order that this country can regain leadership and initiative.

So I have asked quite a lot of the American people—and I have been gratified at their response. There is much more to be done. But I do not wish to be misinterpreted. I think we have the will as well as the re-sources to prevail. And I think we will.

Sincerely,

JOHN F. KENNEDY

[Mrs. Alicia Patterson, Editor and Publisher, Newsday, Garden City, Long Island, New York]

---

186 Letter to the President of the Senate and to the Speaker of the House Transmitting Bill Implementing the 23d Amendment to the Constitution. *May 16, 1961*

[Released May 16, 1961. Dated May 14, 1961]

Dear Mr. —————:

I am pleased to transmit to the Congress draft legislation implementing the 23d Amendment to the Constitution, providing for voting by the residents of the District of Columbia in Presidential elections.

The passage of the 23d Amendment by the Congress and its remarkably prompt ratification by the required number of States reaffirms the belief of the people of the entire Nation in the basic principle that government must be responsible to those governed. I take special pride, therefore, in submitting this proposal to permit the greatest possible number of citizens of the District of Columbia to share with their fellow Americans the basic right to vote for President and Vice President of the United States.

I hope that prompt and favorable action will be taken by the Congress on the proposed legislation so that the long-standing aspirations of the citizens of the District of Columbia to participate in national elections finally will become a reality.

In addition to the draft bill, I am enclosing a letter from the President of the Board of Commissioners of the District of Columbia describing this legislation in detail. A similar letter has been sent to the Speaker (President of the Senate).

Sincerely,

JOHN F. KENNEDY

NOTE: This is the text of identical letters addressed to the Honorable Lyndon B. Johnson, President of the Senate, and to the Honorable Sam Rayburn, Speaker of the House of Representatives.

The President approved the bill on October 4, 1961 (Public Law 87–389, 75 Stat. 817).

---

187 Statement by the President Announcing a Peace Corps Project in Colombia. *May 16, 1961*

SOME WEEKS AGO, I announced the first project of the newly-organized Peace Corps. It was to assist the Tanganyikan Government in its farm-to-market road surveying program. Today, I am pleased to announce the second project of the Peace Corps: this time in Colombia. The Colombian project will train and assign some sixty-four volunteers in small farming, handicraft, rural construction, and sanitation. They will work with already trained Colombian counterparts in a joint program sponsored by the private voluntary agency, CARE, and Colombia's Department of Community Development. There they will assist small rural communities to develop their own economic resources and educational and sanitary facilities.

I am particularly pleased to announce that the second project of the Corps will be in Latin America, because of the many ties of mutual respect and mutual ideals which bind us together as brother republics in this traditionally free and democratic hemisphere. It is also gratifying that the Peace Corps is entering a joint venture with Colombia, with which we have long and historic ties of friendship.

I am particularly pleased with the high quality of the 7,000 people who have volunteered for the Peace Corps. And I strongly urge each one of them to take the entrance test given on May 27th—or for those interested in being secondary school teachers on June 5th. The tests will be given at 330 cities throughout the country and in Puerto Rico. The first projects will be staffed from the candidates who qualify from this exam.

188   Message to the Addis Ababa Conference of African States on the Development of Education.   *May 16, 1961*

IT IS a great pleasure, both personally and officially, to extend the best wishes of the Government and the people of the United States to the Conference of African States on the Development of Education under the auspices of UNESCO and the Economic Commission for Africa.

This conference of African States can perform an important function in establishing an inventory of educational needs and a program to meet those needs. In this endeavor, the United States stands ready to assist wherever it can, if such assistance is desired. For in the monumental task of educational development, there is much to be learned, and I am confident, we can learn it together.

The U.S. Observer Delegation, which we are honored to send, will lay primary stress on the full development of human resources. I believe this general emphasis is sound for our own education as well as for yours. For unless education aims at elevating the motives of men we can find no basic answer to the division and troubles of our times.

We need evaluations and plans, but we need in the planners a passion to create through education what Governor General Azikiwe of Nigeria called for in his Inaugural Address: "a hate-free, fear-free, greed-free world, peopled by free men and women." We seek citizens and statemen whose guiding principle is not *who* is right but *what* is right. We seek an education that gives wisdom as well as knowledge.

The American people applaud the leaders of Africa whose vision assigns to education a primary role in the achievement of stability and progress.

It is in this spirit, then, that I wish to express on behalf of the American people and myself our most sincere hope that this Conference bringing together your leaders and educators attains every possible measure of success.

NOTE: The message was read by A. J. Dowuona Hammond, Minister of Education of Ghana and President of the Conference, held May 15–25. Philip H. Coombs, Assistant Secretary of State for Educational and Cultural Affairs, served as Chairman of the U.S. Observer Delegation.

189 Joint Statement Following Meeting With Dr. Walter Hallstein, President of the European Economic Community. *May 16, 1961*

THE PRESIDENT and Dr. Walter Hallstein, President of the Commission of the European Economic Community, met at the White House on May 16.

The President took the occasion to reaffirm the strong support of the U.S. Government for the European Economic Community and the movement toward European integration as envisaged by the Treaty of Rome. The President and Dr. Hallstein were in full agreement that the European integration movement of the six signatory countries of the Treaty of Rome complements and reinforces the progressive development of a true Atlantic Community which will be given new impetus by the coming-into-force of the OECD.

The President and Dr. Hallstein discussed the current state of relations between the the U.S. and the European Economic Community. The President took the occasion to reiterate the interest of the U.S. in the preliminary discussions now under way looking toward the establishment of a common agricultural policy within the European Economic Community. While fully endorsing the establishment of a common agricul-

tural policy as an essential prerequisite to the implementation of the Rome Treaty, the President expressed the hope that a common agricultural policy would take into account the importance of agricultural commodities in the overall pattern of free world trade and the interest of the United States and other agricultural exporting countries.

The President and Dr. Hallstein also discussed the tariff negotiations now in progress in Geneva within the framework of the GATT. The President and Dr. Hallstein are agreed that these negotiations should be conducted in such a manner as to assist the adjustment of non-member countries to the coming into effect of the European Economic Community. In this connection, the President and Dr. Hallstein discussed in particular the effect of the coming into existence of the EEC upon trade with the Latin-American countries.

With regard to the association of African States with the EEC, the President and Dr. Hallstein also discussed the need for a sustained, increased and coordinated flow of development and technical assistance to the less-developed countries.

190 Remarks Upon Arrival at the Royal Canadian Air Force Uplands Airport in Ottawa. *May 16, 1961*

Your Excellency Governor General, Madame Vanier, Prime Minister, Mrs. Diefenbaker, ladies and gentlemen:

I want to express the heartfelt thanks of my wife and myself for your generous welcome today. This easy voyage of less than 2 hours, from Washington to this capital,

this great country, indicates I think more than anything the cordial and intimate relations which exist between Canada and the United States.

I am somewhat encouraged in saying a few words in French, from having had a chance to listen to the Prime Minister.

[*Prolonged laughter*] It's an unfortunate division of labor, that my wife who speaks so well should sit there without saying a word, while I get up and talk.

Ce voyage est le premier que je fais hors des États-Unis depuis mon élection à la Présidence de mon pays et il est juste que c'est au Canada, le plus ancien de nos voisins et l'un de nos amis les plus chers.[1]

I do want to say that I am here to repay the visit which your distinguished Prime Minister made to the United States, the first visit which I received as a new President. And I must say that his counsel and friendship were of great value to us all in the early days of a new administration.

The tide of foreign affairs flows swiftly in and out. New nations arise, old empires vanish, alliances come and go, but through it all the historic friendship of your nation and mine has stood firm. Together we have worked for peace, together we have stood in war, and now in this long twilight era that is neither peace nor war, we must stand together even more firmly than ever before.

In the effort to build a continent of economic growth and solidarity, in the effort to build a hemisphere of freedom and hope, in the effort to build an Atlantic community of strength and unity of purpose, and in the effort to build a world of lasting peace and justice, Canada and the United States, the Red Ensign and Old Glory, must be found, and I am certain will be found, standing where we have always stood—together.

I am delighted to be here today. Back in 1812 one of our distinguished speakers, John Randolph, attacked the Members of the Congress for saying one word only, Canada, Canada, Canada. I think at different times many of us in Canada and the United States, conscious of the problems that we face, of the differences which may exist between us, have indulged ourselves in the luxury of criticising the shortcomings of each other, forgetting how important it is that a strong and intimate understanding should exist between the United States and Canada, sharing as we do a great continent bound together by history and by geography.

The generous trip of your Prime Minister I think reminded many of my fellow Americans of how important that relationship is. This trip which I take I hope will remind the people of my own country and of Canada of how essential it is in the coming days—and many of them will be difficult—that this friendship should continue.

Therefore, Mr. Prime Minister—therefore Governor General—therefore all your countrymen—we are proud and honored to be with you today.

Thank you.

---

[1] The following translation appears in the White House release of this address:

This is my first trip away from the United States since I succeeded to the Presidency. It is fitting that I should come here to Canada, the oldest of our neighbors and among the closest of our friends.

NOTE: The President spoke at 4:56 p.m. In his opening words he referred to Governor General George P. Vanier and Madame Vanier, and Prime Minister John G. Diefenbaker and Mrs. Diefenbaker.

191 Remarks at the U.S. Embassy in Ottawa.
May 17, 1961

Ambassador and Mrs. Merchant, ladies and gentlemen:

I want to express my appreciation to you for your generous welcome. I also want to express our country's appreciation to you for the work that you are doing, representing our country in this friendly country of Canada.

I must say that those of you who work for the State Department may frequently feel that they are relatively unappreciated. I must say Presidents sometimes have that feeling also. But I do feel that in these very difficult and hazardous days that the work that you are doing, which involves very intimately the security of the country, that you are fulfilling your responsibility as citizens to the highest. And I think that anyone who has that opportunity in these days is to be envied.

So I express to you our commendation. It is not always pleasant to move from sta-

tion to station around the world, especially if you have young children, which I am happy to say you have. But nevertheless I think you serve not only our country but the cause of freedom.

I also want to express our appreciation to the Canadians. I hope that they feel that they are serving their own country when they come and help us here in this Embassy.

The ties that bind Canada and the United States are so intimate, are so long-based in history and a common interest, that I am sure that you feel a sense of mutual service to the cause of this great North American continent.

So, thank you for your generous reception, and I must say I am glad to be here.

NOTE: The President spoke at 9:20 a.m. In his opening words he referred to Livingston T. Merchant, U.S. Ambassador to Canada, and Mrs. Merchant.

192 Address Before the Canadian Parliament in Ottawa.
May 17, 1961

Mr. Speaker of the Senate, Mr. Speaker of the House, Mr. Prime Minister, Members of the Canadian Houses of Parliament, distinguished guests and friends:

I am grateful for the generous remarks and kind sentiments toward my country and myself, Mr. Prime Minister. We in the United States have an impression that this country is made up of descendants of the English and the French. But I was glad to hear some applause coming from the very back benches when you mentioned Ireland. [*Laughter*] I am sure they are making progress forward.

Je me sens vraiment entre amis.[1]

It is a deeply felt honor to address this distinguished legislative body. And yet may I say that I feel very much at home with you here today. For one-third of my life was spent in the Parliament of my own country—the United States Congress.

There are some differences between this body and my own, the most noticeable to me is the lofty appearance of statesmanship which is on the faces of the Members of the—Senators who realize that they will

_____
[1] I feel that I am truly among friends.

382

never have to place their cause before the people again!

I feel at home also here because I number in my own State of Massachusetts many friends and former constituents who are of Canadian descent. Among the voters of Massachusetts who were born outside the United States, the largest group by far was born in Canada. Their vote is enough to determine the outcome of an election, even a Presidential election. You can understand that having been elected President of the United States by less than 140 thousand votes out of 60 million, that I am very conscious of these statistics!

The warmth of your hospitality symbolizes more than merely the courtesy which may be accorded to an individual visitor. They symbolize the enduring qualities of amity and honor which have characterized our countries' relations for so many decades.

Nearly forty years ago, a distinguished Prime Minister of this country took the part of the United States at a disarmament conference. He said, "They may not be angels but they are at least our friends."

I must say that I do not think that we probably demonstrated in that forty years that we are angels yet, but I hope we have demonstrated that we are at least friends. And I must say that I think in these days where hazard is our constant companion, that friends are a very good thing to have.

The Prime Minister was the first of the leaders from other lands who was invited to call upon me shortly after I entered the White House; and this is my first trip—the first trip of my wife and myself outside of our country's borders. It is just and fitting, and appropriate and traditional, that I should come here to Canada—across a border that knows neither guns nor guerrillas.

But we share more than a common border. We share a common heritage, traced back to those early settlers who traveled from the beachheads of the Maritime Provinces and New England to the far reaches of the Pacific Coast. Henry Thoreau spoke a common sentiment for them all: "Eastward I go only by force, Westward I go free. I must walk towards Oregon and not towards Europe." We share common values from the past, a common defense line at present, and common aspirations for the future— our future, and indeed the future of all mankind.

Geography has made us neighbors. History has made us friends. Economics has made us partners. And necessity has made us allies. Those whom nature hath so joined together, let no man put asunder.

What unites us is far greater than what divides us. The issues and irritants that inevitably affect all neighbors are small indeed in comparison with the issues that we face together—above all the somber threat now posed to the whole neighborhood of this continent—in fact, to the whole community of nations. But our alliance is born, not of fear, but of hope. It is an alliance that advances what we are for, as well as opposes what we are against.

And so it is that when we speak of our common attitudes and relationships, Canada and the United States speak in 1961 in terms of unity. We do not seek the unanimity that comes to those who water down all issues to the lowest common denominator—or to those who conceal their differences behind fixed smiles—or to those who measure unity by standards of popularity and affection, instead of trust and respect.

We are allies. This is a partnership, not an empire. We are bound to have differences and disappointments—and we are equally bound to bring them out into the the open, to settle them where they can be settled, and to respect each other's views

383

when they cannot be settled.

Thus ours is the unity of equal and independent nations, co-tenants of the same continent, heirs of the same legacy, and fully sovereign associates in the same historic endeavor: to preserve freedom for ourselves and all who wish it. To that endeavor we must bring great material and human resources, the result of separate cultures and independent economies. And above all, that endeavor requires a free and full exchange of new and different ideas on all issues and all undertakings.

For it is clear that no free nation can stand alone to meet the threat of those who make themselves our adversaries—that no free nation can retain any illusions about the nature of the threat—and that no free nation can remain indifferent to the steady erosion of freedom around the globe.

It is equally clear that no Western nation on its own can help those less-developed lands to fulfill their hopes for steady progress.

And finally, it is clear that in an age where new forces are asserting their strength around the globe—when the political shape of the hemispheres are changing rapidly—nothing is more vital than the unity of the United States and of Canada.

And so my friends of Canada, whatever problems may exist or arise between us, I can assure you that my associates and I will be ever ready to discuss them with you, and to take whatever steps we can to remove them. And whatever those problems may be, I can also assure you that they shrink in comparison with the great and awesome tasks that await us as free and peace-loving nations.

So let us fix our attention, not on those matters that vex us as neighbors, but on the issues that face us as leaders. Let us look southward as part of the Hemisphere with whose fate we are both inextricably bound. Let us look eastward as part of the North Atlantic Community upon whose strength and will so many depend. Let us look westward to Japan, to the newly emerging lands of Asia and Africa and the Middle East, where lie the people upon whose fate and choice the struggle for freedom may ultimately depend. And let us look at the world in which we live and hope to go on living—and at the way of life for which Canadians—and I was reminded again of this this morning, on my visit to your War Memorial—and Americans alike have always been willing to give up their lives in nearly every generation, if necessary to defend and preserve freedom.

First, if you will, consider our mutual hopes for this Hemisphere. Stretching virtually from Pole to Pole, the nations of the Western Hemisphere are bound together by the laws of economics as well as geography, by a common dedication to freedom as well as a common history of fighting for it. To make this entire area more secure against aggression of all kinds—to defend it against the encroachment of international communism in this Hemisphere—and to see our sister states fulfill their hopes and needs for economic and social reform and development—are surely all challenges confronting your nation, and deserving of your talents and resources, as well as ours.

To be sure, it would mean an added responsibility; but yours is not a nation that shrinks from responsibility. The Hemisphere is a family into which we were born—and we cannot turn our backs on it in time of trouble. Nor can we stand aside from its great adventure of development. I believe that all of the free members of the Organization of American States would be heartened and strengthened by any increase in your Hemispheric role. Your skills, your resources, your judicious perception at the council table—even when it differs from our own view—are all needed throughout the inter-American Community. Your country and mine are partners in North American affairs—can we not now become partners in inter-American affairs?

Secondly, let us consider our mutual hopes for the North Atlantic Community.

Our NATO alliance is still, as it was when it was founded, the world's greatest bulwark of freedom. But the military balance of power has been changing. Enemy tactics and weaponry have been changing. We can stand still only at our peril.

NATO force structures were originally devised to meet the threat of a massive conventional attack, in a period of Western nuclear monopoly.

Now, if we are to meet the defense requirements of the 1960's, the NATO countries must push forward simultaneously along two lines:

First, we must strengthen the conventional capability of our Alliance as a matter of the highest priority.

To this end, we in the United States are taking steps to increase the strength and mobility of our forces and to modernize their equipment. To the same end, we will maintain our forces now on the European Continent and will increase their conventional capabilities. We look to our NATO Allies to assign an equally high priority to this same essential task.

Second, we must make certain that nuclear weapons will continue to be available for the defense of the entire Treaty area, and that these weapons are at all times under close and flexible political control that meets the needs of all the NATO countries. We are prepared to join our Allies in working out suitable arrangements for this purpose.

To make clear our own intentions and commitments to the defense of Western Europe, the United States will commit to the NATO command five—and subsequently still more—Polaris atomic-missile submarines, which are defensive weapons, subject to any agreed NATO guidelines on their control and use, and responsive to the needs of all members but still credible in an emergency. Beyond this, we look to the possibility of eventually establishing a NATO sea-borne force, which would be truly multi-lateral in ownership and control, if this should be desired and found feasible by our Allies, once NATO's non-nuclear goals have been achieved.

Both of these measures—improved conventional forces and increased nuclear forces—are put forward in recognition of the fact that the defense of Europe and the assurances that can be given to the people of Europe and the defense of North America are indivisible—in the hope that no aggressor will mistake our desire for peace with our determination to respond instantly to any attack with whatever force is appropriate—and in the conviction that the time has come for all members of the NATO community to further increase and integrate their respective forces in the NATO command area, coordinating and sharing in research, development, production, storage, defense, command and training at all levels of armaments. So let us begin. Our opponents are watching to see if we in the West are divided. They take courage when we are. We must not let them be deceived or in doubt about our willingness to maintain our own freedom.

Third, let us turn to the less-developed nations in the southern half of the globe— those who struggle to escape the bonds of mass misery which appeals to our hearts as well as to our hopes. Both your nation and mine have recognized our responsibilities to these new nations. Our people have given generously, if not always effectively. We could not do less. And now we must do more.

For our historic task in this embattled age is not merely to defend freedom. It is to extend its writ and strengthen its covenant— to peoples of different cultures and creeds and colors, whose policy or economic system may differ from ours, but whose desire to be free is no less fervent than our own. Through the Organization for Economic Cooperation and Development and the Development Assistance Group, we can pool our vast resources and skills, and make available the kind of long-term capital, planning and know-how without which these nations will never achieve independent and viable economies, and without which our efforts will be tragically wasted. I propose further that the OECD establish a Development Center, where citizens and officials, and students and professional men of the Atlantic area and the less-developed world can meet to study in common the problems of economic development.

If we in the Atlantic Community can more closely coordinate our own economic policies—and certainly the OECD provides the framework if we but use it, and I hope that you will join as we are seeking to join to use it—then surely our potential economic resources are adequate to meet our responsibility. Consider, for example, the unsurpassed productivity of our farms. Less than 8 percent of the American working force is on our farms; less than 11 percent of the Canadian working force is on yours. Fewer men on fewer acres than any nation on earth—but free men on free acres can produce here in North America all the food that a hungry world could use—while all the collective farms and forced labor of the communist system produce one shortage after another. This is a day-to-day miracle of our free societies, easy to forget at a time when our minds are caught up in the glamor of beginning the exploration of space.

As the new nations emerge into independence, they face a choice: Shall they develop by the method of consent, or by turning their freedom over to the system of totalitarian control. In making that decision they should look long and hard at the tragedy now being played out in the villages of Communist China.

If we can work closely together to make our food surpluses a blessing instead of a curse, no man, woman or child need go hungry. And if each of the more fortunate nations can bear its fair share of the effort to help the less-fortunate—not merely those with whom we have traditional ties, but all who are willing and able to achieve meaningful growth and dignity—then this decade will surely be a turning-point in the history of the human family.

Finally, let me say just a few words about the world in which we live. We should not misjudge the force of the challenge that we face—a force that is powerful as well as insidious, that inspires dedication as well as fear, that uses means we cannot adopt to achieve ends we cannot permit.

Nor can we mistake the nature of the struggle. It is not for concessions or territory. It is not simply between different systems. It is an age old battle for the survival of liberty itself. And our great advantage—and we must never forget it—is that the irresistible tide that began five hundred years before the birth of Christ in ancient Greece is *for* freedom, and *against* tyranny. And that is the wave of the future—and the iron hand of totalitarianism can ultimately neither seize it nor turn it back. In the words of Macaulay: "A single breaker may recede, but the tide is coming in."

So we in the Free World are not without hope. We are not without friends. And we are not without resources to defend ourselves and those who are associated with us. Believing in the peaceful settlement of disputes in the defense of human rights, we are working throughout the United Nations, and through regional and other associations, to lessen the risks, the tensions and the means and opportunity for aggression that have been mounting so rapidly throughout the world. In these councils of peace—in the UN Emergency Force in the Middle East, in the Congo, in the International Control Commission in South East Asia, in the Ten Nations Commission on Disarmament—Canada has played a leading, important, and constructive role.

If we can contain the powerful struggle of ideologies, and reduce it to manageable proportions, we can proceed with the transcendent task of disciplining the nuclear weapons which shadow our lives, and of finding a widened range of common enterprises between ourselves and those who live under communist rule. For, in the end, we live on

one planet and we are part of one human family; and whatever the struggles that confront us, we must lose no chance to move forward towards a world of law and a world of disarmament.

At the conference table and in the minds of men, the Free World's cause is strengthened because it is just. But it is strengthened even more by the dedicated efforts of free men and free nations. As the great parliamentarian Edmund Burke said, "The only thing necessary for the triumph of evil is for good men to do nothing." And that in essence is why I am here today. This trip is more than a consultation—more than a good-will visit. It is an act of faith—faith in your country, in your leaders—faith in the capacity of two great neighbors to meet their common problems—and faith in the cause of freedom, in which we are so intimately associated.

NOTE: The President spoke in the House of Commons chamber at 3:27 p.m. His opening words referred to the Honorable Mark Robert Drouin, Speaker of the Senate, the Honorable Roland Michener, Speaker of the House of Commons, and Prime Minister John G. Diefenbaker.

193   Joint Statement Following Discussions With Prime Minister Diefenbaker of Canada. *May* 18, 1961

PRESIDENT KENNEDY and Prime Minister Diefenbaker stated that they had had a welcome opportunity of renewing the personal contact they established during the Prime Minister's visit to Washington in February and of examining together questions of concern to both their governments. Their discussions covered broad international issues as well as specific Canadian-United States questions.

United Nations. The President and Prime Minister stated their confidence in the United Nations as an organization dedicated

to the peaceful settlement of differences and the defense of national and human rights.

Disarmament. They reaffirmed that the goals sought by both countries is a secure world order in which there can be general disarmament under effective controls. They agreed, in particular, that the negotiation of a nuclear test ban treaty with effective provisions for inspection was a basic step in the process of moving towards disarmament.

Defense. The President and Prime Minister examined certain aspects of U.S.-Canadian defense arrangements and the international defense commitments which both countries have assumed, notably in NATO. They expressed the conviction that a strong defense must be maintained until such time as effective disarmament measures can be secured under proper safeguards. They agreed that it is more than ever necessary that the strength and unity of NATO be reinforced.

Western Hemisphere. The President and Prime Minister discussed the need for accelerating economic progress and social reform throughout the hemisphere, as well as the need to strengthen the strong hemispheric trend away from dictatorship and towards democracy. They recognized that these objectives are closely related. They were in accord that the alignment of a regime in the Western hemisphere with Communist leadership abroad was a matter for serious concern, threatening as it did the peaceful and democratic evolution of the Latin-American peoples. The Prime Minister assured the President of Canada's continued and increasing interest in inter-American affairs.

Laos. The President and Prime Minister examined the problem of Laos. They reaffirmed the objective of negotiating at Geneva a truly independent and neutral Laos. In this connection they examined the experience of the International Control and Supervisory Commission created by the Geneva Accords of 1954. They agreed that the development of and general support for effective control machinery represented a key element in a settlement of the Laos situa-

tion and an essential ingredient in achieving peace and stability in South East Asia.

O.E.C.D. Noting that both countries are now members of the Organization for Economic Cooperation and Development and are participating in the Development Assistance Group, the President and Prime Minister examined the continuing responsibility of their countries to assist under-developed nations. Both countries have had active programs of economic assistance to under-developed nations for many years. It was agreed that the new machinery would enable the policies and contributions of the two countries in this field to be more closely related than in the past.

Trade. The President and Prime Minister noted the efforts which their two governments had been making in the tariff negotiations in Geneva to work out satisfactory trading relations with the European Economic Community and exchanged views on how this broad objective of importance to both countries can best be achieved. They emphasized the interest of both countries in promoting employment and a general expansion of world trade.

To banish the scourge of war, to improve the human lot, to defend and to enlarge the area of freedom, to assist peoples less privileged than our own—these are aims that bind together Canada and the United States and which, with other allies and friends, our two countries will, jointly and steadfastly, pursue.

NOTE: The statement was released in Ottawa.

194 Letter to the President of the Senate and to the Speaker of the House Transmitting Bill Amending the Welfare and Pension Plans Disclosure Act. *May 19, 1961*

Dear Mr.————:

Since the enactment of the Welfare and Pension Plans Disclosure Act of 1958 we have had an opportunity to study its operation and effect. This has disclosed several serious deficiencies. I am transmitting herewith for appropriate consideration by the Congress a draft bill designed to correct these deficiencies.

The proposed legislation will give the Secretary of Labor the investigative and enforcement authority which he needs to implement the legislation and make it effective. In addition, it will authorize the Secretary of Labor to provide uniform interpretations and clarify existing ambiguities.

The Welfare and Pension Plans Disclosure Act is designed to prevent repetition of abuses and irregularities in the administration of employee benefit plans. I believe these amendments are necessary to carry out that purpose.

The enclosed letter from the Secretary of Labor and the explanatory statement attached to the proposal describe the measure in detail.

Sincerely,

JOHN F. KENNEDY

NOTE: This is the text of identical letters addressed to the Honorable Lyndon B. Johnson, President of the Senate, and to the Honorable Sam Rayburn, Speaker of the House of Representatives.

195 Statement by the President Upon Signing Bill Providing for an Increase in the Federal Judiciary. *May 19, 1961*

I AM DELIGHTED to sign this needed legislation. It authorizes 73 new judicial positions in the District Courts and in the Courts of Appeal.

I believe it will permit a major improvement in the effectiveness of our judicial system. The present congestion in the Federal courts has seriously delayed the prompt administration of justice. In a Nation like ours, which lives by the rule of law—not men—the effectiveness of the Judicial Branch of the Government is of critical importance—and nothing contributes more toward ineffectiveness than delay.

From the earliest days of the Nation, all administrations, of every political shade,

have been mindful of the importance of nominating and confirming judges who will be a credit to our citizenry, and an assurance to our litigants of a high standard of professional performance.

I want to take this opportunity to say that for our Federal courts I shall choose men and women of unquestioned ability. I want for our courts individuals with respected professional skill, incorruptible character, firm judicial temperament, the rare inner quality to know when to temper justice with mercy, and the intellectual capacity to protect and illuminate the Constitution and our historic values in the context of a society experiencing profound and rapid change.

This is the first increase in the Federal judiciary since 1954. It resulted largely from the study and recommendations of the Judicial Conference. I am grateful to the Conference for its contribution and to the

House and Senate leadership for the dispatch with which this legislation was handled.

NOTE: The bill (S. 912) as enacted is Public Law 87–36 (75 Stat. 80).

196 Statement by the President Upon Transmitting to Congress Plans for Small Watershed Protection Projects in 15 States. *May 19, 1961*

THE SMALL Watershed Program has been lagging. More than 1,400 communities have applied for assistance under this legislation but only 303 projects have been authorized for operations. Today's action is tangible evidence that this Administration is determined to move ahead vigorously on badly needed natural resource programs that are in the public interest.

NOTE: This statement was part of a White House release announcing that the President had transmitted to the Congress for approval work plans for 20 small watershed protection and flood prevention

projects in 15 States, the largest number of such projects presented to Congress at one time since the Small Watershed Program was authorized in 1954 (Watershed Protection and Flood Prevention Act, Public Law 566, 83d Congress, 68 Stat. 666). The release stated that small watershed projects were an integral part of the Nation's soil and water conservation program, that they were initiated by local people and financed cooperatively with local governments, and that it was expected that they would stimulate the economy of the communities affected.

On July 12 and August 14 the White House announced the transmittal to Congress of work plans for 34 additional projects, making a total of 54 projects to be located in 30 States and in the Commonwealth of Puerto Rico.

197 Letters to the Secretary of State and to the Secretary of the Interior Concerning the Passamaquoddy Tidal Power Project. *May 20, 1961*

To the Secretary of State:

My dear Mr. Secretary:

I am informed that you have requested the comments of interested Federal agencies on the report of the International Joint Commission, United States and Canada, on the Passamaquoddy Tidal Power Project.

This project has challenged engineers and students of water resources for many years, and I am hopeful that the current report and related studies can be as useful as possible in formulating a sound policy for the development of resources in the area covered by the report. I have, therefore, asked the Secretary of the Interior to advise me on the

power and natural resource aspects of the report. A copy of my request to Secretary Udall is enclosed for your information.

I wish you would give particular attention to his views on these matters prior to submitting your report to the Bureau of the Budget for clearance.

Sincerely,

JOHN F. KENNEDY

To the Secretary of the Interior:

My dear Mr. Secretary:

As you know, the International Joint Commission, United States and Canada, has submitted its report on the International Passamaquoddy Tidal Power Project to the Governments of the United States and Canada. I am informed that the report has now been circulated by the Secretary of State to the interested Federal agencies, including the Department of the Interior, for comment.

This project has challenged engineers and students of water resources for many years, and I am hopeful that the current report and the related studies of the International Passamaquoddy Engineering Board and the New England-New York Inter-agency Committee can be as useful as possible in formulating a sound policy for the development of resources in the area covered by the report. I would, therefore, appreciate it if, following

your review and evaluation of the report, you would advise me of your judgment about what changes in fuel, engineering and financing costs might result in making the project economically feasible. I would also appreciate your advice on the advisability of hydroelectric power development on the upper St. John River at this time and on any other relevant matters relating to the report.

I have notified the Secretary of State of my request for your advice on this project and have asked that he give particular attention to your views on these matters in his report on the project.

Sincerely,

JOHN F. KENNEDY

198   Statement by the President Concerning Interference With the "Freedom Riders" in Alabama.   *May 20, 1961*

THE SITUATION which has developed in Alabama is a source of the deepest concern to me as it must be to the vast majority of the citizens of Alabama and other Americans. I have instructed the Justice Department to take all necessary steps based on their investigations and information. I call upon the Governor and other responsible State officials in Alabama as well as the Mayors of Birmingham and Montgomery to

exercise their lawful authority to prevent any further outbreaks of violence. I would also hope that any persons, whether a citizen of Alabama or a visitor there, would refrain from any action which would in any way tend to provoke further outbreaks. I hope that state and local officials in Alabama will meet their responsibilities. The United States Government intends to meet its.

199   Remarks to the National Advisory Council for the Peace Corps.   *May 22, 1961*

THE FOREIGN POLICY of the United States is founded upon concern for the welfare of man. The Peace Corps is a new dimension of that policy and I consider your presence in Washington today a demonstration of our moral purpose.

I am pleased to announce at this time the third Peace Corps project, which will be to

send 300 teaching assistants to the Philippines. The Peace Corps already has stated it will send surveyors and engineers to Tanganyika and a group of community development workers to Colombia.

I believe Peace Corps volunteers will give a fresh personal meaning to our diplomacy. There can be no better evidence of our good will than days of honest work in behalf of our neighbors.

In the few months the Peace Corps has been operating it has received requests for volunteers from more than two dozen countries. Mr. Shriver, during his recent visit to Africa and Southeast Asia, received enthusiastic approval of the program from the highest levels of government.

I am delighted with this response abroad and I am equally delighted with the response from our own country. Next Saturday the first tests for Peace Corps volunteers will be given in cities throughout the Nation. I understand that more than 8000 applications for service have been received and that new applications are arriving at the rate of 500 a week.

These applications range through the whole spectrum of our culture and our skill. Doctor, farmer, mechanic, typist, teacher, engineer, student—all have asked to work with their fellowmen against poverty, disease and hardship.

In these days of international tension the response of these volunteers stands as a light to all who seek a peaceful world.

NOTE: In another release of the same date the White House stated that the group assigned to the Philippines would serve in the elementary schools. The release added that their primary task would be to assist in the instruction in general science and in English, and that they would work under Filipino supervisors.

---

200 Special Message to the Congress Transmitting Reorganization Plan 5 of 1961. *May 24, 1961*

To the Congress of the United States:

I transmit herewith Reorganization Plan No. 5 of 1961, prepared in accordance with the Reorganization Act of 1949, as amended and providing for reorganization in the National Labor Relations Board.

This Reorganization Plan No. 5 of 1961 follows upon my message of April 13, 1961 to the Congress of the United States. It is believed that the taking effect of the reorganizations included in this plan will provide for greater efficiency in the dispatch of the business of the National Labor Relations Board.

The plan provides for greater flexibility in the handling of the business before the Board, permitting its disposition at different levels so as better to promote its efficient dispatch. Thus matters both of an adjudicatory and regulatory nature may, depending upon their importance and their complexity, be finally consummated by divisions of the Board, individual Board members, hearing examiners, and, subject to the provisions of section 7(a) of the Administrative Procedure Act (60 Stat. 241), by other employees. This will relieve the Board members from the necessity of dealing with many matters of lesser importance and thus conserve their time for the consideration of major matters of policy and planning. There is, however, reserved to the Board as a whole the right to review any such decision, report or certification either upon its own initiative or upon the petition of a party or intervenor demonstrating to the satisfaction of the Board the desirability of having the matter reviewed at the top level.

Provision is also made, in order to maintain the fundamental bipartisan concept explicit in the basic statute creating the Board, for mandatory review of any such decision, report or certification upon the vote of a majority of the Board less one member.

By providing sound organizational arrangements, the taking effect of the reorganizations included in the accompanying reorganization plan will make possible more economical and expeditious administration of the affected functions. It is, however, impracticable to itemize at this time the reductions of expenditures which it is probable will be brought about by such taking effect.

After investigation, I have found and hereby declare that each reorganization included in the reorganization plan transmitted herewith is necessary to accomplish one or more of the purposes set forth in section 2(a) of the Reorganization Act of 1949, as amended.

I recommend that the Congress allow the reorganization plan to become effective.

JOHN F. KENNEDY

NOTE: Reorganization Plan 5 of 1961 is published in House Document 172 (87th Cong., 1st sess.).

201   Statement by the President on the Tractors-for-Freedom Movement. *May* 24, 1961

THE TRACTORS - FOR - FREEDOM movement is a wholly private humanitarian movement aimed at saving the lives of several hundred men. It is supported by free men and women throughout the Americas.

When Fidel Castro first made his offer to "exchange" the lives and liberty of 1,200 prisoners for 500 agricultural tractors, the American people responded with characteristic compassion. A number of private committees were organized to raise the necessary funds, and many private citizens, in this country and throughout the Hemisphere, inquired as to where they could contribute. My concern was to help make certain that a single, representative group of citizens headed this effort in the United States. And I am grateful to Mrs. Roosevelt, Walter Reuther and Dr. Milton Eisenhower for their leadership.

The United States government has not been and can not be a party to these negotiations. But when private citizens seek to help prevent suffering in other lands through voluntary contributions—which is a great American tradition—this government should not interfere with their humanitarian efforts.

Neither law nor equity calls upon us to impose obstacles in their path as they seek to save those who fought to restore freedom in our Hemisphere. I am advised that the Logan Act is not involved, inasmuch as it covers only negotiations "in relation to any disputes or controversies with the U.S., or to defeat the measures of the U.S."; that tax exemption is granted as a matter of course to any "charitable" organizations engaged in the rehabilitation and assistance of needy refugees; and that export licenses are routinely granted for humanitarian reasons, to ship farm produce and medicines to Cuba, and would thus be granted for a humanitarian shipment of farm implements.

While this government is thus putting forward neither obstacles nor assistance to this wholly private effort, I hope that all citizens will contribute what they can. If they were our brothers in a totalitarian prison, every American would want to help. I happen to feel deeply that all who fight for freedom—particularly in our Hemisphere— are our brothers.

393

202 Statement by the President Following a Meeting With Roberto T. Alemann, Minister of Economy of Argentina. *May 24, 1961*

THE UNITED STATES has long had deep ties of friendship with the people of Argentina. In the past we have worked together to raise living standards and to defend the freedom of all of the American States. If the 1960's are to be a decade of progress for the Americas—if we are to bring increasing economic progress and social justice under freedom to our entire hemisphere—then we must rely, in substantial part, on the future cooperative efforts of the governments of Argentina and the United States.

We in the United States hope to work with the Argentine government in its heroic effort to improve the welfare of its people, for we are committed to the long range economic development of Argentina. Even more important, we are committed to a continuing relationship of friendship, partnership and mutual respect.

Together Argentina and the United States can work not only to solve their own problems but to improve the life of free men in this hemisphere and throughout the world. For the United States and the cause of freedom has no stronger or more respected friends than the people of Argentina.

203 Remarks of Welcome to Vice President and Mrs. Johnson on Their Return From Southeast Asia. *May 24, 1961*

I WANT TO EXPRESS our great pride and satisfaction in having the Vice President and Mrs. Johnson back with us. And I also want to join our fellow countrymen in commending the people who went with them— Mr. Suffridge who is head of the Retail Clerks, who had a chance to communicate with some of the labor people in the countries which were visited by the Vice President; also Dr. Cain of the Mayo Clinic, who was a valuable participant in this voyage; and also my sister Jean and her husband Steve.

We are most grateful to the Ambassadors of the countries which the Vice President and his wife visited for coming today to join in this reception. I received today a communication from one of our Ambassadors, addressed to me, in which the first sentence was—this is from an American Ambassador

in one of the countries which the Vice President visited—which I think reflects the reports we received from every country visited by the Vice President: "I believe the Vice President's timely and gallant enterprise of purpose accomplished the missions originally conceived in Washington."

I want to express, and I know he will, our great appreciation to the countries and to the people of the countries, their leaders, for the courtesy with which they received the Vice President, Mrs. Johnson and the members of their family. From all the information we received, there was not a single discordant note in their generous hand of welcome which they extended to this group of distinguished Americans.

Therefore I want to take this opportunity to express our thanks to the Ambassadors here, and through them to their countries, for their very kind action to a group of Americans in whom we have great confidence.

I think the Vice President's journey represented a great public service. There are members from both parties here today to greet him. There were members of both parties in his group going around the world. This was an American effort to indicate our great concern for the cause of freedom in significant and important countries around the world.

So Mr. Vice President, we're glad to have you back. We don't quite understand why all of you should look so well while those of us who are here resting look so pale, but nevertheless, we're glad to have you back, and we appreciate very much what you did.

NOTE: The President spoke at 11:20 a.m. in the Rose Garden at the White House.

Vice President Johnson responded as follows:

"Thank you, Mr. President. The easiest way for you to understand why we are not pale is to spend 2 or 3 days in 110 degree temperature in India.

"This is one of the most challenging trips that I have ever taken. When we left, we said that it would be a trip of hope and a mission of purpose, and we return considerably strengthened and with much greater hope. We visited in several countries where the population would add up to more than three quarters of a billion people. We did not see all of those people but we saw a good many of them as well as their leaders. We never heard a hostile voice and we never shook a hostile hand. We went to listen and learn and to seek their counsel and to give them the benefit of the judgments of this country as expressed by the President in his letter and by our distinguished Secretary of State.

"Everywhere we went we found that the leader-

ship and the government had great respect for our country, for our President, for our Secretary of State and for the policies pursued by our government. We received their suggestions and their recommendations and they will be given to the President in a report this afternoon.

"I will have a chance a little later to answer your questions and to talk to you about details of the trip.

"We are deeply indebted to the Speaker and the Majority and Minority leadership, and particularly to Chairman Fulbright and Dr. Morgan and the leaders of the House and Senate Foreign Relations Committee for their warm welcome here. I shall ask for an opportunity to visit with them this afternoon and tomorrow, and to ask their judgments before completing a detailed report to the President. We will have an interim memorandum for him before the day is over.

"I want to thank the Ambassadors who represent the countries we visited. They saw me away when we left on our journey, and they are here to receive me when we return.

"I believe that we will march closer together, that we will remain more united, that we will be a stronger force for freedom than we were when we last met.

"I am very grateful to all who took the time to come out here and welcome us home, and we are mighty glad to be back."

Following a request of the President that she tell something of her trip, Mrs. Johnson responded as follows:

"Well, after twenty-eight thousand miles in 13 days, my chief impression is that I have seen a world of people on the move. I did more people-seeing than sightseeing. It was the most marvelous two weeks I have ever spent, and I am so grateful that I had a little opportunity to serve as one additional link between the United States and all of those countries to which we went."

In his opening remarks the President referred to Mr. James A. Suffridge, President of the Retail Clerks International Association; Dr. James C. Cain, Specialist in Internal Medicine at the Mayo Clinic; and the President's sister and her husband, Mr. and Mrs. Stephen E. Smith.

204   Statement by the President Upon the Signing of a Joint Statement by Lockheed Aircraft Corporation and the President's Committee on Equal Employment Opportunity.   *May 25, 1961*

ONE OF MY EARLY ACTIONS as President was the creation by Executive Order of the President's Committee on Equal Employment Opportunity. I directed this Committee to work toward the elimination of discrimination because of race, creed, color or national origin in Federal employment and on contract work performed for the government.

Here today we are witnessing the signing of a joint statement by the Lockheed Aircraft Corporation, represented by Mr. Courtlandt Gross, president of the company, and the Committee, represented by Vice President Lyndon B. Johnson. This statement is a forward-looking program. It is voluntary action, appropriately named the "Plan for Progress" for the Lockheed Aircraft Corporation. This program is a long-range commitment by the Lockheed Corporation and by the United States government to work together in improving and expanding the job opportunities available to members of minority groups. I believe that this plan is a milestone in the history of civil rights

in this country. The Lockheed Corporation—through its voluntary action—is setting a pattern which can open new doors and expanded employment opportunities for members of minority groups throughout this country. Through voluntary action such as this men of good will can, together, make real and measurable progress toward the goal of equal opportunity in employment for all Americans. No goal is more important for us as Americans and as leaders of the free world. Few actions of my administration have been more significant than the signing of this document.

I feel that through the development of this joint statement the Committee, under the leadership of Vice President Johnson, as chairman, and Secretary of Labor Goldberg, as vice chairman, has demonstrated that it is vigorously working to fulfill its tasks. I congratulate the Committee and the Lockheed Aircraft Corporation on this positive, constructive step toward elimination of discrimination.

205   Special Message to the Congress on Urgent National Needs.   *May 25, 1961*

[Delivered in person before a joint session]

Mr. Speaker, Mr. Vice President, my copartners in Government, gentlemen—and ladies:

The Constitution imposes upon me the obligation to "from time to time give to the Congress information of the State of the Union." While this has traditionally been interpreted as an annual affair, this tradition

has been broken in extraordinary times.

These are extraordinary times. And we face an extraordinary challenge. Our strength as well as our convictions have imposed upon this nation the role of leader in freedom's cause.

No role in history could be more difficult or more important. We stand for freedom.

That is our conviction for ourselves—that is our only commitment to others. No friend, no neutral and no adversary should think otherwise. We are not against any man—or any nation—or any system—except as it is hostile to freedom. Nor am I here to present a new military doctrine, bearing any one name or aimed at any one area. I am here to promote the freedom doctrine.

I.

The great battleground for the defense and expansion of freedom today is the whole southern half of the globe—Asia, Latin America, Africa and the Middle East—the lands of the rising peoples. Their revolution is the greatest in human history. They seek an end to injustice, tyranny, and exploitation. More than an end, they seek a beginning.

And theirs is a revolution which we would support regardless of the Cold War, and regardless of which political or economic route they should choose to freedom.

For the adversaries of freedom did not create the revolution; nor did they create the conditions which compel it. But they are seeking to ride the crest of its wave—to capture it for themselves.

Yet their aggression is more often concealed than open. They have fired no missiles; and their troops are seldom seen. They send arms, agitators, aid, technicians and propaganda to every troubled area. But where fighting is required, it is usually done by others—by guerrillas striking at night, by assassins striking alone—assassins who have taken the lives of four thousand civil officers in the last twelve months in Vietnam alone—by subversives and saboteurs and insurrectionists, who in some cases control

whole areas inside of independent nations.[1]

With these formidable weapons, the adversaries of freedom plan to consolidate their territory—to exploit, to control, and finally to destroy the hopes of the world's newest nations; and they have ambition to do it before the end of this decade. It is a contest of will and purpose as well as force and violence—a battle for minds and souls as well as lives and territory. And in that contest, we cannot stand aside.

We stand, as we have always stood from our earliest beginnings, for the independence and equality of all nations. This nation was born of revolution and raised in freedom. And we do not intend to leave an open road for despotism.

There is no single simple policy which meets this challenge. Experience has taught us that no one nation has the power or the wisdom to solve all the problems of the world or manage its revolutionary tides—that extending our commitments does not always increase our security—that any initiative carries with it the risk of a temporary defeat—that nuclear weapons cannot prevent subversion—that no free people can be kept free without will and energy of their own—

---

[1] At this point the following paragraph, which appears in the text as signed and transmitted to the Senate and House of Representatives, was omitted in the reading of the message:

They possess a powerful intercontinental striking force, large forces for conventional war, a well-trained underground in nearly every country, the power to conscript talent and manpower for any purpose, the capacity for quick decisions, a closed society without dissent or free information, and long experience in the techniques of violence and subversion. They make the most of their scientific successes, their economic progress and their pose as a foe of colonialism and friend of popular revolution. They prey on unstable or unpopular governments, unsealed, or unknown boundaries, unfilled hopes, convulsive change, massive poverty, illiteracy, unrest and frustration.

and that no two nations or situations are exactly alike.

Yet there is much we can do—and must do. The proposals I bring before you are numerous and varied. They arise from the host of special opportunities and dangers which have become increasingly clear in recent months. Taken together, I believe that they can mark another step forward in our effort as a people. I am here to ask the help of this Congress and the nation in approving these necessary measures.

II. ECONOMIC AND SOCIAL PROGRESS AT HOME

The first and basic task confronting this nation this year was to turn recession into recovery. An affirmative anti-recession program, initiated with your cooperation, supported the natural forces in the private sector; and our economy is now enjoying renewed confidence and energy. The recession has been halted. Recovery is under way.

But the task of abating unemployment and achieving a full use of our resources does remain a serious challenge for us all. Large-scale unemployment during a recession is bad enough, but large-scale unemployment during a period of prosperity would be intolerable.

I am therefore transmitting to the Congress a new Manpower Development and Training program, to train or retrain several hundred thousand workers, particularly in those areas where we have seen chronic unemployment as a result of technological factors in new occupational skills over a four-year period, in order to replace those skills made obsolete by automation and industrial change with the new skills which the new processes demand.

It should be a satisfaction to us all that we have made great strides in restoring world confidence in the dollar, halting the outflow of gold and improving our balance of payments. During the last two months, our gold stocks actually increased by seventeen million dollars, compared to a loss of 635 million dollars during the last two months of 1960. We must maintain this progress—and this will require the cooperation and restraint of everyone. As recovery progresses, there will be temptations to seek unjustified price and wage increases. These we cannot afford. They will only handicap our efforts to compete abroad and to achieve full recovery here at home. Labor and management must—and I am confident that they will—pursue responsible wage and price policies in these critical times. I look to the President's Advisory Committee on Labor-Management Policy to give a strong lead in this direction.

Moreover, if the budget deficit now increased by the needs of our security is to be held within manageable proportions, it will be necessary to hold tightly to prudent fiscal standards; and I request the cooperation of the Congress in this regard—to refrain from adding funds or programs, desirable as they may be, to the Budget—to end the postal deficit, as my predecessor also recommended, through increased rates—a deficit incidentally, this year, which exceeds the fiscal 1962 cost of all the space and defense measures that I am submitting today—to provide full pay-as-you-go highway financing—and to close those tax loopholes earlier specified. Our security and progress cannot be cheaply purchased; and their price must be found in what we all forego as well as what we all must pay.

III. ECONOMIC AND SOCIAL PROGRESS ABROAD

I stress the strength of our economy because it is essential to the strength of our nation. And what is true in our case is true in the case of other countries. Their strength in the struggle for freedom depends on the strength of their economic and their social progress.

We would be badly mistaken to consider their problems in military terms alone. For no amount of arms and armies can help stabilize those governments which are unable or unwilling to achieve social and economic reform and development. Military pacts cannot help nations whose social injustice and economic chaos invite insurgency and penetration and subversion. The most skillful counter-guerrilla efforts cannot succeed where the local population is too caught up in its own misery to be concerned about the advance of communism.

But for those who share this view, we stand ready now, as we have in the past, to provide generously of our skills, and our capital, and our food to assist the peoples of the less-developed nations to reach their goals in freedom—to help them before they are engulfed in crisis.

This is also our great opportunity in 1961. If we grasp it, then subversion to prevent its success is exposed as an unjustifiable attempt to keep these nations from either being free or equal. But if we do not pursue it, and if they do not pursue it, the bankruptcy of unstable governments, one by one, and of unfilled hopes will surely lead to a series of totalitarian receiverships.

Earlier in the year, I outlined to the Congress a new program for aiding emerging nations; and it is my intention to transmit shortly draft legislation to implement this program, to establish a new Act for International Development, and to add to the figures previously requested, in view of the swift pace of critical events, an additional 250 million dollars for a Presidential Contingency Fund, to be used only upon a Presidential determination in each case, with regular and complete reports to the Congress in each case, when there is a sudden and extraordinary drain upon our regular funds which we cannot foresee—as illustrated by recent events in Southeast Asia—and it makes necessary the use of this emergency reserve. The total amount requested—now raised to 2.65 billion dollars—is both minimal and crucial. I do not see how anyone who is concerned—as we all are—about the growing threats to freedom around the globe—and who is asking what more we can do as a people—can weaken or oppose the single most important program available for building the frontiers of freedom.

IV.

All that I have said makes it clear that we are engaged in a world-wide struggle in which we bear a heavy burden to preserve and promote the ideals that we share with all mankind, or have alien ideals forced upon them. That struggle has highlighted the role of our Information Agency. It is essential that the funds previously requested for this effort be not only approved in full, but increased by 2 million, 400 thousand dollars, to a total of 121 million dollars.

This new request is for additional radio and television to Latin America and Southeast Asia. These tools are particularly effective and essential in the cities and villages of those great continents as a means of reaching millions of uncertain peoples to tell them of our interest in their fight for freedom. In Latin America, we are proposing to increase our Spanish and Portuguese broadcasts to a total of 154 hours a week, compared to 42 hours today, none of which is in Portuguese, the language of about one-third of the people of South America. The Soviets, Red Chinese and satellites already broadcast into

Latin America more than 134 hours a week in Spanish and Portuguese. Communist China alone does more public information broadcasting in our own hemisphere than we do. Moreover, powerful propaganda broadcasts from Havana now are heard throughout Latin America, encouraging new revolutions in several countries.

Similarly, in Laos, Vietnam, Cambodia, and Thailand, we must communicate our determination and support to those upon whom our hopes for resisting the communist tide in that continent ultimately depend. Our interest is in the truth.

V. OUR PARTNERSHIP FOR SELF-DEFENSE

But while we talk of sharing and building and the competition of ideas, others talk of arms and threaten war. So we have learned to keep our defenses strong—and to cooperate with others in a partnership of self-defense. The events of recent weeks have caused us to look anew at these efforts.

The center of freedom's defense is our network of world alliances, extending from NATO, recommended by a Democratic President and approved by a Republican Congress, to SEATO, recommended by a Republican President and approved by a Democratic Congress. These alliances were constructed in the 1940's and 1950's—it is our task and responsibility in the 1960's to strengthen them.

To meet the changing conditions of power—and power relationships have changed—we have endorsed an increased emphasis on NATO's conventional strength. At the same time we are affirming our conviction that the NATO nuclear deterrent must also be kept strong. I have made clear our intention to commit to the NATO command, for this purpose, the 5 Polaris submarines originally suggested by President

Eisenhower, with the possibility, if needed, of more to come.

Second, a major part of our partnership for self-defense is the Military Assistance Program. The main burden of local defense against local attack, subversion, insurrection or guerrilla warfare must of necessity rest with local forces. Where these forces have the necessary will and capacity to cope with such threats, our intervention is rarely necessary or helpful. Where the will is present and only capacity is lacking, our Military Assistance Program can be of help.

But this program, like economic assistance, needs a new emphasis. It cannot be extended without regard to the social, political and military reforms essential to internal respect and stability. The equipment and training provided must be tailored to legitimate local needs and to our own foreign and military policies, not to our supply of military stocks or a local leader's desire for military display. And military assistance can, in addition to its military purposes, make a contribution to economic progress, as do our own Army Engineers.

In an earlier message, I requested 1.6 billion dollars for Military Assistance, stating that this would maintain existing force levels, but that I could not foresee how much more might be required. It is now clear that this is not enough. The present crisis in Southeast Asia, on which the Vice President has made a valuable report—the rising threat of communism in Latin America— the increased arms traffic in Africa—and all the new pressures on every nation found on the map by tracing your fingers along the borders of the Communist bloc in Asia and the Middle East—all make clear the dimension of our needs.

I therefore request the Congress to provide a total of 1.885 billion dollars for Military Assistance in the coming fiscal year—an amount less than that requested a year ago—but a minimum which must be assured if we are to help those nations make secure their independence. This must be prudently and wisely spent—and that will be our common endeavor. Military and economic assistance has been a heavy burden on our citizens for a long time, and I recognize the strong pressures against it; but this battle is far from over, it is reaching a crucial stage, and I believe we should participate in it. We cannot merely state our opposition to totalitarian advance without paying the price of helping those now under the greatest pressure.

VI. OUR OWN MILITARY AND INTELLIGENCE SHIELD

In line with these developments, I have directed a further reinforcement of our own capacity to deter or resist non-nuclear aggression. In the conventional field, with one exception, I find no present need for large new levies of men. What is needed is rather a change of position to give us still further increases in flexibility.

Therefore, I am directing the Secretary of Defense to undertake a reorganization and modernization of the Army's divisional structure, to increase its non-nuclear firepower, to improve its tactical mobility in any environment, to insure its flexibility to meet any direct or indirect threat, to facilitate its coordination with our major allies, and to provide more modern mechanized divisions in Europe and bring their equipment up to date, and new airborne brigades in both the Pacific and Europe.

And secondly, I am asking the Congress for an additional 100 million dollars to begin the procurement task necessary to re-equip this new Army structure with the most modern material. New helicopters, new armored personnel carriers, and new howitzers, for example, must be obtained now.

Third, I am directing the Secretary of Defense to expand rapidly and substantially, in cooperation with our Allies, the orientation of existing forces for the conduct of non-nuclear war, para-military operations and sub-limited or unconventional wars.

In addition, our special forces and unconventional warfare units will be increased and reoriented. Throughout the services new emphasis must be placed on the special skills and languages which are required to work with local populations.

Fourth, the Army is developing plans to make possible a much more rapid deployment of a major portion of its highly trained reserve forces. When these plans are completed and the reserve is strengthened, two combat-equipped divisions, plus their supporting forces, a total of 89,000 men, could be ready in an emergency for operations with but 3 weeks' notice—2 more divisions with but 5 weeks' notice—and six additional divisions and their supporting forces, making a total of 10 divisions, could be deployable with less than 8 weeks' notice. In short, these new plans will allow us to almost double the combat power of the Army in less than two months, compared to the nearly nine months heretofore required.

Fifth, to enhance the already formidable ability of the Marine Corps to respond to limited war emergencies, I am asking the Congress for 60 million dollars to increase the Marine Corps strength to 190,000 men. This will increase the initial impact and staying power of our three Marine divisions and three air wings, and provide a trained nucleus for further expansion, if necessary for self-defense.

Finally, to cite one other area of activities that are both legitimate and necessary as a means of self-defense in an age of hidden perils, our whole intelligence effort must be reviewed, and its coordination with other elements of policy assured. The Congress and the American people are entitled to know that we will institute whatever new organization, policies, and control are necessary.

VII. CIVIL DEFENSE

One major element of the national security program which this nation has never squarely faced up to is civil defense. This problem arises not from present trends but from national inaction in which most of us have participated. In the past decade we have intermittently considered a variety of programs, but we have never adopted a consistent policy. Public considerations have been largely characterized by apathy, indifference and skepticism; while, at the same time, many of the civil defense plans have been so far-reaching and unrealistic that they have not gained essential support.

This Administration has been looking hard at exactly what civil defense can and cannot do. It cannot be obtained cheaply. It cannot give an assurance of blast protection that will be proof against surprise attack or guaranteed against obsolescence or destruction. And it cannot deter a nuclear attack.

We will deter an enemy from making a nuclear attack only if our retaliatory power is so strong and so invulnerable that he knows he would be destroyed by our response. If we have that strength, civil defense is not needed to deter an attack. If we should ever lack it, civil defense would not be an adequate substitute.

But this deterrent concept assumes rational calculations by rational men. And the history of this planet, and particularly the history of the 20th century, is sufficient to remind us of the possibilities of an irra-

tional attack, a miscalculation, an accidental war, [or a war of escalation in which the stakes by each side gradually increase to the point of maximum danger] which cannot be either foreseen or deterred. It is on this basis that civil defense can be readily justifiable—as insurance for the civilian population in case of an enemy miscalculation. It is insurance we trust will never be needed—but insurance which we could never forgive ourselves for foregoing in the event of catastrophe.

Once the validity of this concept is recognized, there is no point in delaying the initiation of a nation-wide long-range program of identifying present fallout shelter capacity and providing shelter in new and existing structures. Such a program would protect millions of people against the hazards of radioactive fallout in the event of large-scale nuclear attack. Effective performance of the entire program not only requires new legislative authority and more funds, but also sound organizational arrangements.

Therefore, under the authority vested in me by Reorganization Plan No. 1 of 1958, I am assigning responsibility for this program to the top civilian authority already responsible for continental defense, the Secretary of Defense. It is important that this function remain civilian, in nature and leadership; and this feature will not be changed.

The Office of Civil and Defense Mobilization will be reconstituted as a small staff agency to assist in the coordination of these functions. To more accurately describe its role, its title should be changed to the Office of Emergency Planning.

As soon as those newly charged with these responsibilities have prepared new authorization and appropriation requests, such requests will be transmitted to the Congress for a much strengthened Federal-State civil defense program. Such a program will provide Federal funds for identifying fallout shelter capacity in existing structures, and it will include, where appropriate, incorporation of shelter in Federal buildings, new requirements for shelter in buildings constructed with Federal assistance, and matching grants and other incentives for constructing shelter in State and local and private buildings.

Federal appropriations for civil defense in fiscal 1962 under this program will in all likelihood be more than triple the pending budget requests; and they will increase sharply in subsequent years. Financial participation will also be required from State and local governments and from private citizens. But no insurance is cost-free; and every American citizen and his community must decide for themselves whether this form of survival insurance justifies the expenditure of effort, time and money. For myself, I am convinced that it does.

VIII. DISARMAMENT

I cannot end this discussion of defense and armaments without emphasizing our strongest hope: the creation of an orderly world where disarmament will be possible. Our aims do not prepare for war—they are efforts to discourage and resist the adventures of others that could end in war.

That is why it is consistent with these efforts that we continue to press for properly safeguarded disarmament measures. At Geneva, in cooperation with the United Kingdom, we have put forward concrete proposals to make clear our wish to meet the Soviets half way in an effective nuclear test ban treaty—the first significant but essential step on the road towards disarmament. Up to now, their response has not been what we hoped, but Mr. Dean returned last night to

Geneva, and we intend to go the last mile in patience to secure this gain if we can.

Meanwhile, we are determined to keep disarmament high on our agenda—to make an intensified effort to develop acceptable political and technical alternatives to the present arms race. To this end I shall send to the Congress a measure to establish a strengthened and enlarged Disarmament Agency.

IX. SPACE

Finally, if we are to win the battle that is now going on around the world between freedom and tyranny, the dramatic achievements in space which occurred in recent weeks should have made clear to us all, as did the Sputnik in 1957, the impact of this adventure on the minds of men everywhere, who are attempting to make a determination of which road they should take. Since early in my term, our efforts in space have been under review. With the advice of the Vice President, who is Chairman of the National Space Council, we have examined where we are strong and where we are not, where we may succeed and where we may not. Now it is time to take longer strides—time for a great new American enterprise—time for this nation to take a clearly leading role in space achievement, which in many ways may hold the key to our future on earth.

I believe we possess all the resources and talents necessary. But the facts of the matter are that we have never made the national decisions or marshalled the national resources required for such leadership. We have never specified long-range goals on an urgent time schedule, or managed our resources and our time so as to insure their fulfillment.

Recognizing the head start obtained by the Soviets with their large rocket engines, which gives them many months of lead-time, and recognizing the likelihood that they will exploit this lead for some time to come in still more impressive successes, we nevertheless are required to make new efforts on our own. For while we cannot guarantee that we shall one day be first, we can guarantee that any failure to make this effort will make us last. We take an additional risk by making it in full view of the world, but as shown by the feat of astronaut Shepard, this very risk enhances our stature when we are successful. But this is not merely a race. Space is open to us now; and our eagerness to share its meaning is not governed by the efforts of others. We go into space because whatever mankind must undertake, free men must fully share.

I therefore ask the Congress, above and beyond the increases I have earlier requested for space activities, to provide the funds which are needed to meet the following national goals:

First, I believe that this nation should commit itself to achieving the goal, before this decade is out, of landing a man on the moon and returning him safely to the earth. No single space project in this period will be more impressive to mankind, or more important for the long-range exploration of space; and none will be so difficult or expensive to accomplish. We propose to accelerate the development of the appropriate lunar space craft. We propose to develop alternate liquid and solid fuel boosters, much larger than any now being developed, until certain which is superior. We propose additional funds for other engine development and for unmanned explorations—explorations which are particularly important for one purpose which this nation will never overlook: the survival of the man who first makes this daring flight. But in a very real sense, it will not be one man going to the moon—if

we make this judgment affirmatively, it will be an entire nation. For all of us must work to put him there.

Secondly, an additional 23 million dollars, together with 7 million dollars already available, will accelerate development of the Rover nuclear rocket. This gives promise of some day providing a means for even more exciting and ambitious exploration of space, perhaps beyond the moon, perhaps to the very end of the solar system itself.

Third, an additional 50 million dollars will make the most of our present leadership, by accelerating the use of space satellites for world-wide communications.

Fourth, an additional 75 million dollars—of which 53 million dollars is for the Weather Bureau—will help give us at the earliest possible time a satellite system for world-wide weather observation.

Let it be clear—and this is a judgment which the Members of the Congress must finally make—let it be clear that I am asking the Congress and the country to accept a firm commitment to a new course of action—a course which will last for many years and carry very heavy costs: 531 million dollars in fiscal '62—an estimated seven to nine billion dollars additional over the next five years. If we are to go only half way, or reduce our sights in the face of difficulty, in my judgment it would be better not to go at all.

Now this is a choice which this country must make, and I am confident that under the leadership of the Space Committees of the Congress, and the Appropriating Committees, that you will consider the matter carefully.

It is a most important decision that we make as a nation. But all of you have lived through the last four years and have seen the significance of space and the adventures in space, and no one can predict with certainty what the ultimate meaning will be of mastery of space.

I believe we should go to the moon. But I think every citizen of this country as well as the Members of the Congress should consider the matter carefully in making their judgment, to which we have given attention over many weeks and months, because it is a heavy burden, and there is no sense in agreeing or desiring that the United States take an affirmative position in outer space, unless we are prepared to do the work and bear the burdens to make it successful. If we are not, we should decide today and this year.

This decision demands a major national commitment of scientific and technical manpower, materiel and facilities, and the possibility of their diversion from other important activities where they are already thinly spread. It means a degree of dedication, organization and discipline which have not always characterized our research and development efforts. It means we cannot afford undue work stoppages, inflated costs of material or talent, wasteful interagency rivalries, or a high turnover of key personnel.

New objectives and new money cannot solve these problems. They could in fact, aggravate them further—unless every scientist, every engineer, every serviceman, every technician, contractor, and civil servant gives his personal pledge that this nation will move forward, with the full speed of freedom, in the exciting adventure of space.

X. CONCLUSION

In conclusion, let me emphasize one point. It is not a pleasure for any President of the United States, as I am sure it was not a pleasure for my predecessors, to come before the Congress and ask for new appropriations which place burdens on our people. I came

to this conclusion with some reluctance. But in my judgment, this is a most serious time in the life of our country and in the life of freedom around the globe, and it is the obligation, I believe, of the President of the United States to at least make his recommendations to the Members of the Congress, so that they can reach their own conclusions with that judgment before them. You must decide yourselves, as I have decided, and I am confident that whether you finally decide in the way that I have decided or not, that your judgment—as my judgment—is reached on what is in the best interests of our country.

In conclusion, let me emphasize one point: that we are determined, as a nation in 1961 that freedom shall survive and succeed—and whatever the peril and set-backs, we have some very large advantages.

The first is the simple fact that we are on the side of liberty—and since the beginning of history, and particularly since the end of the Second World War, liberty has been winning out all over the globe.

A second great asset is that we are not alone. We have friends and allies all over the world who share our devotion to freedom. May I cite as a symbol of traditional and effective friendship the great ally I am about to visit—France. I look forward to my visit to France, and to my discussion with a great Captain of the Western World, President de Gaulle, as a meeting of particular significance, permitting the kind of close and ranging consultation that will strengthen both our countries and serve the common purposes of world-wide peace and liberty. Such serious conversations do not require a pale unanimity—they are rather the instruments of trust and understanding over a long road.

A third asset is our desire for peace. It is sincere, and I believe the world knows it.

We are proving it in our patience at the test-ban table, and we are proving it in the UN where our efforts have been directed to maintaining that organization's usefulness as a protector of the independence of small nations. In these and other instances, the response of our opponents has not been encouraging.

Yet it is important to know that our patience at the bargaining table is nearly inexhaustible, though our credulity is limited—that our hopes for peace are unfailing, while our determination to protect our security is resolute. For these reasons I have long thought it wise to meet with the Soviet Premier for a personal exchange of views. A meeting in Vienna turned out to be convenient for us both; and the Austrian government has kindly made us welcome. No formal agenda is planned and no negotiations will be undertaken; but we will make clear America's enduring concern is for both peace *and* freedom—that we are anxious to live in harmony with the Russian people—that we seek no conquests, no satellites, no riches—that we seek only the day when "nation shall not lift up sword against nation, neither shall they learn war any more."

Finally, our greatest asset in this struggle is the American people—their willingness to pay the price for these programs—to understand and accept a long struggle—to share their resources with other less fortunate people—to meet the tax levels and close the tax loopholes I have requested—to exercise self-restraint instead of pushing up wages or prices, or over-producing certain crops, or spreading military secrets, or urging unessential expenditures or improper monopolies or harmful work stoppages—to serve in the Peace Corps or the Armed Services or the Federal Civil Service or the Congress—to strive for excellence in their schools, in their cities and in their physical fitness and that of their children—to take part in Civil Defense—to pay higher postal rates, and higher payroll taxes and higher teachers' salaries, in order to strengthen our society—to show friendship to students and visitors from other lands who visit us and go back in many cases to be the future leaders, with an image of America—and I want that image, and I know you do, to be affirmative and positive—and, finally, to practice democracy at home, in all States, with all races, to respect each other and to protect the Constitutional rights of all citizens.

I have not asked for a single program which did not cause one or all Americans some inconvenience, or some hardship, or some sacrifice. But they have responded—and you in the Congress have responded to your duty—and I feel confident in asking today for a similar response to these new and larger demands. It is heartening to know, as I journey abroad, that our country is united in its commitment to freedom—and is ready to do its duty.

206   Remarks by Telephone to the Conference on Peaceful Uses of Space Meeting in Tulsa. *May 26, 1961*

Gentlemen, ladies:

I appreciate this opportunity, at the invitation of Senator Kerr, who is Chairman of the Space Committee of the Senate, to open the first national conference on peaceful uses of space, and I regret very much that I am unable to participate personally in this conference and in the discussions in which you will be engaged.

Your conference subject deals with the

very heart of our national policy in space research and explorations, to which I devoted a good deal of my speech yesterday before the Congress. All of us in the United States and in all nations can derive many benefits from the peaceful application of space technology. The impact of this new science will be felt in our daily lives. It can bring all people closer together, improve communications; it can help control the weather and the climate around us. We can safely predict that the impact of the space age will have a far-ranging effect within industry and in our labor force, on medical research, education, and many other areas of national concern.

The keystone of our national policy is space research, as defined in the act which established the National Aeronautics and Space Administration, whose function is the preservation of the role of the United States as a leader in aeronautical and space science and technology, and in the application thereof to the conduct of peaceful activities within and outside the atmosphere.

These are the words in the act of the Congress, "the preservation of the role of the United States as a leader," and it is to meet that great responsibility that I have suggested a great national effort in the field of space for the American people.

We are dedicated to the accomplishment of this objective, and are determined that this nation will continue to be a pioneer in the new frontier of space.

I am delighted that the people of Tulsa have taken the initiative in the heart of our country in making this important meeting possible, and that the response has been so widespread. It indicates the forward spirit of this city and this State—and our country. And I hope this conference will establish a precedent as the people of America move forward into space.

NOTE: The President spoke at 11:35 a.m. from the Signal Corps Recording Studios at the White House. The conference was held at the Fair Grounds in Tulsa, Okla.

207   Letter to the President of the Senate and to the Speaker of the House Transmitting Bill Implementing the Message on Foreign Aid. *May 26, 1961*

Dear Mr. ————:

Transmitted herewith for consideration by the Congress is a draft of a bill which would carry out the principal recommendations set forth in my message on foreign aid of March 22, 1961.

The legislation is drafted to provide for aid to social and economic development under an Act for International Development and to provide for military assistance under an International Peace and Security Act. It is designed to provide the concepts, the means, and the organization for programs of foreign aid attuned to the needs of the decade ahead.

The Act for International Development seeks authorization for appropriations of $1.690 billion for four major purposes:

a. To assist and support nations whose independence or stability depends upon such help and is important to our own security;

b. To provide for our share in certain programs under multilateral auspices;

c. To provide grant assistance to less-developed countries primarily to assist in the development of their human resources; and

d. To establish a Presidential Contingency Fund to meet the unpredictable exigencies with which we will doubtless be confronted during the forthcoming year.

The Act for International Development also seeks authorization by the Congress to make loans, repayable in U.S. dollars, to promote the economic development of less-developed countries and areas with emphasis upon long-term plans and programs designed to develop economic resources and increase productive capacities. For this purpose I am asking the Congress for long-term authority in the form of public debt transactions which would make available for this purpose $900 million in Fiscal Year 1962 and $1.6 billion in each of the following four years. Additionally, repayments of previous foreign loans of about $300 million annually would be made available for development lending. Authority to make firm long-term commitments is of paramount importance. Real progress in economic development cannot be achieved by annual, short-term dispensations of aid and uncertainty as to future intentions. To make investments in economic development more effective, the terms and conditions of the investment should be related to the establishment of sound long-term development plans and the achievement of specific targets. While the methods proposed represent a departure from previous patterns in economic aid programs, they conform to the traditional techniques of numerous other governmental operations. These methods are essential to our new approach to development assistance and to the effectiveness of that approach.

The International Peace and Security Act will continue the program of military assistance which constitutes an integral part of our whole security and defense posture. It is essential that this program be maintained and continued in the present international climate. Appropriations will be sought to provide for the United States' share of maintaining forces that already exist, to complete undertakings initiated in earlier years, to give increased emphasis to internal security, and to provide for a limited and selected modernization of forces in areas under particular duress. I envisage a continuous review and assessment of the needs for military assistance around the world and continuing discussions with our allies and associated nations to determine the extent to which expenditures for defense can safely be lessened. Such adjustments necessarily may not be accomplished overnight, and, in any case, neither we nor our allies can afford a relaxation in the maintenance of an effective collective deterrent to armed aggression. The increasing problems of internal security with which we are confronted reflect an expanded utilization of the technique of indirect subversion which demands new and more vigorous counter measures if the spread of international communism is to be prevented. Assisting developing countries to create and maintain an environment of security and stability is essential to their more rapid social, economic, and political progress.

The achievement of our goals requires effective organizational arrangements to execute these programs. In this regard, Section 604 of the Mutual Security Act of 1960 placed two requirements upon the President: (1) To have a study made of the functions of, and the degree of coordination among, agencies engaged in foreign economic activities, with a view to providing the most effective means for the formulation and implementation of United States foreign economic policies and (2) to include in his presentation of the fiscal year 1962 mutual security program to the Congress his findings and recommendations resulting from that study.

To fulfill the first requirement, at the request of the President the Bureau of the Budget conducted a study of the existing situation and prepared a descriptive and analytical staff report. That report and the results of studies initiated by this administration have been available to executive branch officials concerned with foreign economic affairs. The recommendations which follow constitute my response to the second requirement.

My decisions on foreign affairs organization are predicted on the following principles:

First, authority for the conduct of activities which advance our foreign policy objectives should be vested in the President or other officials primarily concerned with foreign affairs.

Second, international activities of domestic agencies should be clearly either (i) necessary extensions of their normal domestic missions or (ii) undertaken on behalf of and in support of programs and objectives of the appropriate foreign affairs agencies.

These guidelines are particularly important for our foreign development assistance program. Domestic agencies can and should make a substantial contribution to the success of this program, and I will expect the foreign affairs agencies to make maximum use of their resources, skills, and experience.

My proposals for the organization and coordination of foreign aid are based also on the concepts and principles set forth in my March 22 message to the Congress—specifically, the critical necessity for unified administration and operation of foreign development assistance activities carried out in accordance with integrated country plans.

These proposals will be put into effect by appropriate executive action.

FOREIGN ASSISTANCE PROGRAMS

Responsibility and authority for the formulation and execution of the foreign development aid programs will be assigned to a single agency—the Agency for International Development—within the Department of State. It will replace the International Cooperation Administration and the Development Loan Fund, which will be abolished. The new agency—AID—will be headed by an Administrator of Under Secretary rank reporting directly to the Secretary of State and the President. The internal organization of AID will be geographically focused to give operational meaning to the country plan concept. Thus, the line authority will run from the Administrator to the Assistant Administrators heading four regional bureaus and, through the Ambassadors, to the chiefs of AID missions overseas. The four Assistant Administrators will be equal in rank to the geographical Assistant Secretaries of State and will work closely with them.

The proposed rank of the AID Administrator and the relationship between AID and other elements of the Department of State highlight a fundamental fact: Economic development assistance can no longer be subordinated to, or viewed simply as a convenient tool for meeting, short-run political objectives. This is a situation we can ill afford when long-range, self-sustained economic growth of less developed nations is our goal. Development assistance, therefore, must—and shall—take its place as a full partner in the complex of foreign policy.

The new agency will develop the full potential of the use of agricultural commodities as an instrument of development assistance. The Department of Agriculture will continue its active role in respect to commodity availability, the disposal of surplus stocks, international marketing, and the relationship of domestic agricultural production to world food needs. In view of the interrelationship of domestic agricultural products and their use for foreign policy purposes, I shall rely on the Director of the food-for-peace program, Mr. George McGovern, to advise me in the formulation of policies for the constructive use of our agricultural abundance as well as to assist in the overall coordination of the program.

The Peace Corps, too, has a special significance in our international development efforts. It will continue as an agency within the Department of State, and its Director will have the rank of Assistant Secretary of State. The Secretary of State will establish arrangements to assure that Peace Corps activities are consistent and compatible with the country development assistance plans. These arrangements will assure that the Peace Corps activities and AID programs are brought into close relation and at the same time preserve the separate identity and the unique role and mission of the Peace Corps.

The principal assignments of authority for the administration of military assistance are satisfactory and will remain unchanged. The Department of Defense has operational responsibility for approved programs. In recognition of the fact that military assistance should clearly serve the foreign policy objectives and commitments of the United States, the Secretary of State provides continuous supervision and general direction of the program, including the determination as to whether there should be a program for a country and the value of that program.

TRADE, AID, AND FOREIGN ECONOMIC POLICY

The self-help efforts of less developed nations, together with coordinated external assistance from economically advanced nations, must be coupled with a constructive approach in dealing with international commodity problems and barriers to international trade. Each of these approaches is needed if the goals of economic growth and stability are to be reached.

The relationship of trade, aid, and other aspects of foreign economic policies involve the interests of many agencies of Government, particularly when both foreign and domestic economic considerations are an issue. It is, therefore, essential that interagency consultation and coordination be as meaningful and productive as possible and that the Secretary of State become the focal point of responsibility for the coordination of foreign economic policies. With these requirements in mind, I abolished the Council on Foreign Economic Policy, which had been chaired by a Special Assistant to the President. I have assigned the functions of the Council to the Secretary of State. I shall expect him—in facilitating executive branch coordination—to choose whatever mechanisms he finds appropriate, including the formation of interagency working groups. This assignment will strengthen the affirmative leadership role of the Secretary of State in the development and integration of foreign economic policies. I have every confidence that the views of agencies concerned will be brought to bear on such matters early and fully.

ROLE OF CHIEFS OF UNITED STATES DIPLOMATIC
MISSIONS

The ambassador, as representative of the President and acting on his behalf, bears ultimate responsibility for activities of the United States in the country to which he is accredited. His authority will be commensurate with his major responsibilities. Presidential action has already been taken to strengthen the role of our ambassadors, and further executive action is being undertaken to clarify their responsibility and authority.

In light of the above recommendations and in the earnest hope and expectation that the United States will meet its challenges and responsibilities in this decade of development in a forthright, affirmative manner which can engender the respect and cooperation of the community of free nations, I urge the early consideration and enactment of this legislative proposal.

Respectfully yours,

JOHN F. KENNEDY

NOTE: This is the text of identical letters addressed to the Honorable Lyndon B. Johnson, President of the Senate, and to the Honorable Sam Rayburn, Speaker of the House of Representatives.

For the President's statement upon signing the Act for International Development, see Item 969.

208 Remarks Upon Signing Bill Appropriating Funds for Inter-American Cooperation and for Reconstruction in Chile. *May 27, 1961*

IT IS a great honor in the company of distinguished Members of the Congress and our friends from this hemisphere, to sign this bill which implements the Act of Bogotá.

This proposal was originally put forward by my predecessor, and it is a source of satisfaction to us all that we are now able to make a substantial contribution to the betterment of the life of the people who share the great adventure of living in the Western Hemisphere.

The cooperation between the countries, north and south, their efforts to make a better life for their people, their willingness to advance, their common willingness to take the necessary steps which will insure a more fruitful existence, all these are essential if this hemisphere is to move forward in a true Alliance for Progress.

This is an effort made by the people of the United States to participate in this effort. I think in the coming months and years we can build a stronger and more prosperous hemisphere, a hemisphere in which all people from the top down to the bottom of the globe share in hopes for a better life.

So it is a great pleasure for me to sign this act in the presence of the Members of the Congress, whose actions made this bill possible, and in the presence of a distinguished predecessor of mine, President Truman, who in his administration carried out the efforts to improve relations substantially in this hemisphere.

NOTE: The President spoke at 9:50 a.m. in his office at the White House. The bill (H.R. 6518) as enacted is Public Law 87–41 (75 Stat. 86).

209 Remarks at the Democratic National Committee Dinner in Honor of the President's 44th Birthday. *May 27, 1961*

Chairman John Bailey, my friend the Vice President, Mr. Speaker Rayburn, President Truman, Mrs. Wheeler, Mr. Gardner, Mrs. Price, fellow Democrats:

It is a great pleasure to be here, and I want to express my appreciation to the members of the committee who made this dinner such a success, to all who participated in it: Mrs. Wheeler, Mr. Gardner—and Stew Udall who handled the publicity [*laughter*]—and all the others. I am glad to be here with the Vice President. When I was away recently, somebody called the White House and said, "I would like to speak to the President." And they said, "Well, he's in Canada." "Well, I'd like to speak to the Vice President." And they said, "Well, he's in Southeast Asia." "Well then, I would like to speak to the Secretary of State." They said well he was in Geneva. "Well," they said, "who's running that store?" And the operator said, "The same man who has been running it for years—Sam Rayburn!"

I must say that I thought one point in Lyndon's very fine speech, which I think is worthy for us all to—who are Democrats, and that is, the success of any President of the United States who has the distinction of being a Democrat is due to the fact that he is supported by a strong, democratic, progressive party.

Woodrow Wilson once said in 1913, "What good is the success of a political party unless it's used by the nation for a great national purpose?" And I believe in the administration of Woodrow Wilson and Franklin Roosevelt and Harry Truman, and now today—the Democratic Party has a great national purpose, to move this country forward.

I will say on becoming President that the only thing that really surprised us when we got into office was that things were just as bad as we had been saying they were; otherwise we have been enjoying it very much.

In 1783, the first American official to visit France, Benjamin Franklin, signed in Paris the treaty declaring that His Britannic Majesty acknowledged the United States to be free, sovereign, and independent. When we became free, sovereign, and independent, there was a King of France, a Czar of Russia, an Emperor in Peking. They've all gone, and this country remains.

Today, 178 years later, I return to the place where the United States was born, and my trip next week—the ground for that trip was laid in the administration of a predecessor of mine, Harry Truman, whose vision and activity in the 1940's helped make it possible to build a Europe which is our strong ally in difficult days.

I must say I do not go to Europe in a difficult time in the life of our country with any feeling of historic inevitability. I suppose when historians come to write about the 1940's and 1950's with the perspective which history will give them, they will say that this was a time when the power of the Sino-Soviet bloc increased. But I think that they will also note an even more remarkable event, and that is that from 1945 to 1961 was the most extraordinary growth in the individual liberty of individual countries that the world has ever seen. And it is my judgment that when the time comes to write the story of the 20th century, the dominant fact will be that liberty grew and spread around the world.

And that's why I go to Europe, and with confidence and hope, because the United States is associated with that great cause.

I do not believe that meetings between heads of state, either allies or those whose purposes make them our adversaries, are designed to solve a series of specific problems or bring about a fundamental change in relationships. For only changes in the realities which underlie the relations between nations, shifts in power, the pressure of events, revisions of policies which reflect new needs, fresh assessments, and the change in power balances within the countries—only such changes as these leave a permanent mark on the prospects for peace. And while meetings of Presidents and Premiers can sometimes help in fulfilling such changes, they rarely initiate them.

We do not lack for communication with France or the Soviet Union, or any other nation. The Vice President with distinction has carried our message to Southeast Asia in recent days. The Secretary of State has already met with our allies and adversaries around the globe. Capable and dedicated Ambassadors maintain a constant flow of information and judgment between foreign capitals and Washington. Representatives of nearly all countries work here in the United States.

Nevertheless, meetings of those who bear the responsibility of leadership in states, viewed as an instrument of policy and not as a substitute for policy—these meetings can play a real and helpful role in the quest for peace.

In a fast-moving and revolutionary world where new crises and threats occur almost daily, where the power to make decisive and perhaps irrevocable decisions rests in a few hands, where calculation of how others will react is often a decisive factor in decisions—

in such a world I believe it is indispensable for leaders of nations to have an understanding of men with whom they must deal.

In addition, there is no real substitute for the attempt to explore general areas of accommodation and mutual interest, to ward off danger and clarify intention at the highest level. And as long as we realize that there is no substitute for the long and painful process of diplomatic negotiation, necessary to translate general principles into specific agreements, these meetings can be useful.

Moreover, such meetings are symbolic. In the case of our allies they symbolize the deep unity of the Western World, the fixed determination by which we guide our policy, unalterable under any conditions, to marshal our common strength for the defense of freedom.

And the meeting with Mr. Khrushchev is also a symbol: an expression of our intention to leave no path to peace unexplored, to neglect no opportunity to ease world tensions or to lessen the dangers into which our adversaries may plunge us and themselves.

Thus I go to Europe, seeking not solutions to all our problems, but insight into the conditions which must guide our policies in the coming difficult months. I go as the representative of the great nation of the United States. I shall tell our allies that the United States is embarking on an effort to muster the energy and resources of the strongest nation in history—in the world—in defense of our common heritage. I shall tell those who do not agree with us that our desire for peace is matched by our determination to resist all those who seek the destruction of freedom. And I shall tell the world that here in this country American men and women are calling forth all the great resources and untapped power of this country, providing strength for that faith in the freedom of man which will be the silent guest at every conference table.

NOTE: The President spoke at the National Guard Armory in Washington. In his opening words he referred to John M. Bailey, Chairman of the Demo-

cratic National Committee, Vice President Lyndon B. Johnson, Speaker of the House of Representatives Sam Rayburn, former President Harry S. Truman, Mrs. George Y. Wheeler 2d and Ralph W. Gardner, co-chairmen of the dinner, and Mrs. Margaret Price, Vice Chairman of the Democratic National Committee.

210 Statement by the President Concerning Adlai Stevenson's Special Mission to South America. *May 29, 1961*

I HAVE ASKED Ambassador Adlai E. Stevenson to undertake a special mission on my behalf to the countries of South America. He will consult with officials of the Governments of the South American continent about what can be done to perfect and accelerate our Inter-American program for social and economic development as well as our cooperation in other respects. I am delighted that Governor Stevenson has agreed to undertake this mission.

Governor Stevenson plans to leave very soon and will be away for about three weeks. We are consulting the governments concerned and our embassies, and the itinerary has not yet been finally worked out. But I can say that Governor Stevenson hopes to visit all the countries in South America. He regrets, and I do also, that he will not be able to visit all the other American Republics with which we have diplomatic relations.

It seems to us that this is an especially appropriate time for Governor Stevenson to visit South America again. The American Governments are preparing for the Ministerial Meeting of the Inter-American Economic and Social Council which is to be held beginning on July 15 in Uruguay. The United States Government views this meeting as one of great potential significance and promise for strengthening the free and independent nations of this hemisphere and

both national and Inter-American institutions for social progress and economic development.

Our Latin American neighbors and we are also bound together under the United Nations Charter in worldwide arrangements for peace and security, for economic cooperation, and for the protection of human rights. As the United States Representative in the United Nations, Governor Stevenson is in an excellent position to canvass with our South American friends the relationship between our hemispheric arrangements and our common interest in an effective United Nations. He will assuredly speak for me as well as for himself in expressing admiration for the magnificent record of liberal leadership which the Latin American Governments continue to exert in the work of the United Nations.

On March 13 I suggested to the people of this hemisphere an "Alliance for Progress, a vast cooperative effort . . . to satisfy the basic needs of the American people, for homes, work and land, health and schools." While the name, Alliance for Progress, might be new, the ideas I put forward are not the monopoly of any single American state, but flow naturally from our long tradition of Inter-American cooperation. On April 14 I stated that "Our common purpose today is to harness these new aspirations and these new tools in a great Inter-

American effort—an effort to lift all the peoples in the Americas . . . into a new era of economic progress and social justice." I said that the OAS, the oldest organization of nations in existence, should move ahead to meet this new challenge. I asked all the free republics of the hemisphere to join this cooperative undertaking to eliminate hunger and poverty, ignorance and disease from our hemisphere. I believe these aspirations are common to the Americas and that there exists a firm will and determination to move ahead with this great work. Inter-American machinery must be strengthened. We need to outline basic development goals. It is essential that each government individually and cooperating with others, define objectives in the key areas of economic and social betterment such as education, land use and tenure, taxation, public health. And we must do it while enlarging, not restricting, the area of freedom, while guaranteeing, not destroying, the human rights and the dignity of the individual.

In this effort each country needs first of all to help itself. But we must also help each other and move together.

Governor Stevenson will be ready to explain our ideas as to how we believe this can be done. And he will seek the ideas of our good neighbors. These exchanges of ideas about our new plans and responsibilities will be a useful part of the preparations for our meeting in Uruguay.

In my statement of March 13 I also emphasized that our cooperation in this hemisphere should not be only in economic and social fields. We need to explore methods of obtaining closer relationships in the cultural field as well—between our schools and universities, our teachers and students, in our scientists and artists, our writers and thinkers—in short each manifestation of the diversity of the culture and tradition of our peoples. I think there are few people in the United States better qualified than Adlai Stevenson to examine and discuss all these possibilities. I am sure that his journey will contribute immeasurably to our preparations for the Montevideo conference and to the strengthening of the Inter-American system.

211   Letter to the President of the Senate and to the Speaker of the House Concerning the Training of Workers in New Occupational Skills. *May 29, 1961*

Dear Mr. —————:

I am transmitting herewith a draft of a bill designed to carry out the recommendation contained in my Message of May 25 to the Congress providing for the training and retraining of several hundred thousand workers in new occupational skills over a 4-year period.

The need for prompt enactment of this legislation is clear. As I stated in my Message, this measure is of special importance in abating unemployment and achieving full use of our resources, as well as in meeting the occupational demands of our Nation's expanded defense, space, aid, and trade programs.

The unemployed whose skills have been rendered obsolete by automation and other technological changes must be equipped with new skills enabling them to become productive members of our society once again. The skills of other workers must also be improved to enable them to meet the more demanding requirements of modern industry.

Also enclosed is a letter sent me by the Secretary of Labor describing the legislation more fully, and a memorandum explaining the draft bill in detail. A similar

letter is being sent the Speaker of the House of Representatives.

Sincerely,

JOHN F. KENNEDY

NOTE: This is the text of identical letters addressed to the Honorable Lyndon B. Johnson, President of the Senate, and to the Honorable Sam Rayburn, Speaker of the House of Representatives.

212 Remarks at the President's Birthday Dinner in Boston. *May 29, 1961*

Congressman McCormack, your Eminence, Governor Volpe, Mr. Mayor, distinguished guests, ladies and gentlemen:

I first of all want to express my appreciation to our distinguished Majority Leader, Congressman McCormack. He and I and the leadership of the House and Senate have breakfast every Tuesday morning and what he does with me he did with President Truman and he did before that with President Roosevelt. So Congressman McCormack has been identified with the great decisions which this country has made in the Thirties, the Forties, the Fifties, and now the Sixties, and he has been a source of strength, and I appreciate the support in the past and tonight. I want to state how gratified I am that his Eminence is with us tonight. He married us, he christened my daughter, he inaugurated me, he's prayed over me and I hope he'll continue to do so. Thank you.

And we all pray for Governor Volpe, that now that he's seen how pleasant it is to be a Democrat, he will come over with us. I want to express my thanks to Pat Lynch, our distinguished Chairman, who undertook this great responsibility of running this dinner. To Judge Melen, to the Mayor of Boston for his generous reception tonight, to the members of Congress from our State and Senator Smith, and also to our friends

from other states of New England, Senator Pastore, my friend and valued colleague, Ed Muskie, who is with us from Maine, Governor Notte from Rhode Island, Governor Dempsey from Connecticut. Actually, I must say that I had something to do with making Governor Dempsey the Governor of Connecticut. When we brought Abe Ribicoff down to Washington we did two good things. And also, we don't have any Democratic Governors in New Hampshire and Vermont, but we have Representatives and we appreciate their being here.

Most of all, I want to thank all of you. I have been informed that with this dinner I am now responsible as the leader of the Democratic Party for a debt of only one million dollars. Now, did anybody ever get a birthday present like that? One million dollars. I don't know—they spent it like they were sure we were going to win. But I'm most grateful to you. This has been a series of shocks which you've endured on my behalf, in '52, in '58, the primaries, the election, and I'm sure you're wondering when it's all going to be over. But the great thing is, of course, it never ends. We'll get this paid off and then we'll start all over again. I'm indebted to you all. This is a tremendous dinner. It is the greatest possible help to us. And I want you to know that I am—even though we have many things in

416

our mind, this is on our mind, and it's on John Bailey's mind and I'm greatly in your debt tonight. Thank you.

I want to also thank Mr. Frost for saying an Irish poem over us. He spoke very highly of Harvard, but I do think it appropriate to reveal that on the morning after the Inaugural when he came to the White House, he said, "You're something of Irish and I suppose something of Harvard. My advice to you as President is to be Irish." So we're going to do the best we can.

I leave tomorrow night on a trip to France. The United States is, as President de Gaulle has said, the daughter of Europe, and in a special way we have the most intimate relations with France. Paul Revere, who's regarded as a good Yankee, was of French descent. Benjamin Franklin spent 7 years in France and played a leading role in bringing France to our assistance in a moment of need and emerged from France in 1783 bearing the treaty with the British which proclaimed us a sovereign and independent nation. Americans in the 19th Century went back to Europe, this time on peaceful missions, and particularly to France, and gained from France some of its great understanding of the past and its view of the future. And twice in this century Americans have gone to France, this time not on a peaceful mission, but on behalf of the new world in its efforts to redress the balance of the old, in 1917 and again in 1944. I go to France on this occasion not in order to invoke old memories, even though those memories are important, but to look to the future, of the close relationship which must exist between France and the United States if the cause of Freedom in the Atlantic community is to be preserved. And I go to pay a visit to a distinguished captain of the West, General de Gaulle, who has been involved for more than 20 years in a struggle to protect the integrity of Western Europe; and therefore I go with the good wishes of all of our citizens of our country as we pay a visit to an old friend.

I go also to Vienna, and I know there are some Americans who wonder why I take that journey. I am only 44, but I have lived in my 44 years through three wars, the First World War, the Second World War, and the Korean War. No one can study the origins of any of those three struggles without realizing the serious miscalculations, the serious misapprehensions, about the possible actions of the other side which existed in the minds of the adversaries which helped bring about all those wars. The War of 1914, where the Austrians gave an ultimatum to Serbia and the Russians then mobilized and the French then in alliance with Russia then mobilized and then the Germans mobilized, and then when the Germans saw the French and the Russians mobilizing attacked through Belgium which brought the British in. One week before the British never would have dreamed they would be at war and I doubt that the French would. No one would have dreamed that two years later the United States would be involved in a war on the continent. In 1939 and 1940, after the loss of Austria and Czechoslovakia, finally the British guaranteed Poland, but there is certainly some evidence that Hitler never believed that the British would come to the assistance of Poland, and he never believed that the United States would again become involved in a great struggle on the plains of Europe. Certainly in the War of 1950 in Korea, the North Koreans never imagined that the United States would come to the assistance, by war-like means, of the Republic of South Korea, and we on our part did not imagine that the Chinese Communists would intervene as we approached to the north of North Korea.

Now we live in 1961, where freedom is in battle all around the globe, where the United States has intimate alliances with more than 40 countries, and where the communists in their meeting in Moscow and in the speech of the Chairman of the Communist Party, in his speech of January 6th, enunciated the Doctrine of the Wars of Liberation, where the possibility of escalation is always with us. I see value in talking to those with whom we're allied, but I also think it valuable at a time when both sides possess weapons of mutual destruction and annihilation—I think it's also valuable that there should be understanding and communication and a firm realization of what we believe.

So I go to see Mr. Khrushchev in Vienna. I go as the leader of the greatest revolutionary country on earth. I know that there is in some areas of the world, and even in some parts of the United States an image of us as a fixed society. Bernard DeVoto once said New England is a finished place, and some people may think that of the United States. That is not my view. When John Quincy Adams went to call on the British Governor, before the Revolution, about the problem of the British here in this state, they had an amiable conversation until finally Adams

mentioned the word "revolution," and then he wrote in his diary "It was then I saw his knees tremble." Now, our knees do not tremble at the word "revolution." We believe in it. We believe in the progress of mankind. We believe in freedom, and we intend to be associated with it in the days to come.

So I come back to this old city, to express my thanks to all of you who are my oldest friends, beginning with Dr. Good, to express my appreciation for your confidence and support tonight, on past occasions, and I hope in the future, and I carry with me a message which is written on one of our statues by a distinguished and vigorous New Englander, William Lloyd Garrison, "I am in earnest, I will not equivocate, I will not excuse, I will not retreat a single inch, and I will be heard."

Thank you.

NOTE: The President spoke at the Boston Armory. In his opening remarks he referred to John W. McCormack, U.S. Representative from Massachusetts; His Eminence Richard Cardinal Cushing, Archbishop of Boston; Governor John A. Volpe of Massachusetts; and John F. Collins, Mayor of Boston. Later in his remarks he referred to John M. Lynch, Massachusetts Democratic State Chairman; James Melen, District Court Judge of Massachusetts; poet Robert Frost; and Dr. Frederick L. Good of Boston.

213 Letter to the President of the Senate and to the Speaker of the House Proposing the Establishment of a Permanent Peace Corps. *May 30, 1961*

Dear Mr. ————:

I have the honor to transmit herewith for the consideration of the Congress a legislative proposal to authorize the establishment of a Peace Corps in fiscal year 1962, as I recommended on March 1, 1961. Enactment of this legislation will provide authority for the recruitment, training, and service overseas of American men and women

whose skills and knowledge can contribute in a most valuable and practical way to the achievement of social and economic development goals of developing countries.

Simultaneously with my Special Message to the Congress of March 1, I directed the undertaking of a Peace Corps pilot program to serve as a source of information and experience in formulating plans for a more permanent organization. The Peace Corps has already announced projects to be undertaken in Tanganyika, Colombia, and the Philippines, and others will be announced soon. Progress and planning to date has confirmed that there is a genuine and immediate need in many parts of the world for skilled manpower which the Peace Corps will be able to furnish. Moreover, the governments and peoples of many developing countries have enthusiastically received the idea of a Peace Corps.

Americans as well are responding to this opportunity to serve their country. More than 8,500 Peace Corps Volunteer Questionnaires have been returned, and additional questionnaires are being received at a rate of more than 100 every day.

This legislative proposal requests that Congress authorize $40 million for this program for the fiscal year 1962. This should enable the Peace Corps to have 500–1,000 volunteers abroad by the end of this calendar year, to have approximately 2,700 abroad or in training by June 1962 and to provide for the training during the summer of 1962 of volunteers expected to be enrolled in June and July 1962.

Under the proposed legislation volunteers will receive a living allowance and subsistence adequate to maintain a modest standard of living overseas. In addition, their health is carefully provided for. In return for service, each volunteer will receive a modest monthly payment which, in most cases, will be accumulated to be paid upon the termination of his duty.

I have further requested the Secretary of State to establish arrangements to assure that Peace Corps activities are consistent and compatible with country development assistance plans. These arrangements will assure that the Peace Corps and the Agency for International Development programs are brought into close relationship, while at the same time preserving the separate identity and unique role of the Peace Corps.

The Peace Corps offers a special and timely opportunity to put dedicated Americans to work for the cause of world peace and human understanding. Therefore, I urge the early consideration and enactment by the Congress of the proposal.

Respectfully yours,

JOHN F. KENNEDY

NOTE: This is the text of identical letters addressed to the Honorable Lyndon B. Johnson, President of the Senate, and to the Honorable Sam Rayburn, Speaker of the House of Representatives.

For the President's remarks upon signing the Peace Corps bill, see Item 380.

214   Transcript of Interview With the President Recorded for French TV and Radio. *May 30, 1961*

THE PRESIDENT. I am very happy to welcome you to the White House.

Q. Mr. President, what is your view of Europe's political and economic unity, and what role will the United States play in it?

THE PRESIDENT. Well, one of the most encouraging post-war developments in the entire free world has been the economic and increasing political unity of Europe. The United States has supported strongly this movement, because we feel that a strong Europe strengthens freedom, and we have been much impressed by the leadership which France has given to that movement. We hope it will spread through Europe. I think it offers the greatest security for us all in the years to come. So we are very much behind your efforts in that regard.

Q. Do you think, Mr. President, that the disarmament talks will be resumed in July and that they have a chance of succeeding?

THE PRESIDENT. Well, I'm most hopeful that the conversations which are taking place now at Geneva, on the matter of securing an agreement with the Soviet Union on the cessation of nuclear tests, will be successful. This is the easiest kind of agreement to reach, because it's possible to patrol it most effectively. So far, however, we have not made the progress we had hoped to make. The insistence on a veto on all inspections makes it extremely difficult for us to set up any realistic, effective inspection—and responsible inspection—system. So that we have not been as encouraged as we hoped we would be. But we will keep working at Geneva, if we can make a success there, then we can move with greater confidence into the disarmament conversations in July and August. If we fail at Geneva, on nuclear testing, then our problem of disarmament will be that much more serious. So, this is a very critical time for these efforts.

Q. Mr. President, do you intend to establish a geographic limitation on Communist penetration in Southeast Asia and not to let it go beyond that?

THE PRESIDENT. Well, the French know more about Southeast Asia perhaps than certainly any Western people and they know the difficulty of the problems involved there. The danger in Southeast Asia—as we have seen in Laos and we see now in Vietnam— is not of overt aggression across boundary lines by foreign armies but rather by the effective use of guerrillas, which have—for example in Vietnam—have assassinated in the last twelve months two thousand civil officers of the government and two thousand local policemen, and are carrying on a very vigorous effort to seize control of the Government by guerrilla means. But it's true

there; we've seen in Laos and we will see in other parts of Southeast Asia as time goes on. So we will attempt to assist the governments which want to remain free to maintain themselves, but it's going to be a very hard and difficult road for us all in Southeast Asia.

Q. More specifically with regard to aid to underdeveloped countries, Mr. President, what are the general lines of your policy following your special message to the Congress on March 22?

THE PRESIDENT. Well, I think there are three points to it. First, that I think that all of us who live in the prosperous areas of the West must make a concerted national and international effort to assist the people of the underdeveloped world—who have their political independence but who live on the marginal edge of existence in many cases—to move toward a better life. Because, if they feel they cannot do it under a system of freedom, then they will turn to a totalitarian system. So that I think we all have to make a greater effort—in the United States, in Western Europe, in all free countries that are moving ahead themselves.

Secondly, I think that this effort should be based in part upon the willingness of the countries themselves to make effective long-range economic plans which will provide, over a period of years, a better life for their people. So that we make sure that our aid is given to countries that can use it effectively and use it for the people.

And third, the aid should be committed over a long period of time. One of our troubles has been that we have appropriated money by the year and it makes it difficult to have the kind of economic planning which will bring success.

A greater effort by us all; second, a greater effort by the underdeveloped countries themselves; and third, a commitment of aid over a longer period of time to permit long-range economic planning. Those are the three principles for which we now stand.

Q. Lastly, Mr. President, what do you expect from your talks with Mr. Khrushchev?

THE PRESIDENT. Well, I think it's important—when there are so many serious issues which involve us both, involve the West with the Sino-Soviet bloc—that we should have some communication with Mr. Khrushchev. This is a dangerous time for us all, and if we can, by having a communication, lessen the chance of miscalculation—which could lead to a very dangerous situation, and hazard for all people—I think that we should have those conversations. If we can reach greater understanding, on the question of testing and disarmament, perhaps on Laos, perhaps on the general matters which divide us, I think that it would make it easier for us to look forward with hope for the future. So, I have not met Mr. Khrushchev, and we meet in Vienna.

Q. Well, Mr. President, I should like to thank you and, on behalf of my fellow countrymen, to wish you a good trip and a pleasant stay in France.

THE PRESIDENT. Merci beaucoup.

NOTE: The interview was conducted on May 20 by Pierre Crenesse, Director in North America for Radiodiffusion-Télévision Française.

215 Remarks at a Dinner of the Eleanor Roosevelt Cancer Foundation in New York City. *May 30, 1961*

Mr. Rosenhaus, Mrs. Roosevelt, General Bradley, Mayor Wagner, Vice President Johnson, Ambassador Stevenson, Mr. Baruch, my colleague Congressman Roosevelt, ladies and gentleman:

I recognize that tonight I bear a heavy responsibility of having kept a distinguished group of Americans who paid $125 for this dinner from that dinner for an hour and 30 minutes. But I will say that, if I may quote an old East Side expression, "that what you have lost on the bananas you are going to make up on the apples." Because this could have been one of the longest dinners in the history of these occasions. Lyndon is good for 45 minutes when he is given a chance. Ambassador Stevenson has been known to go for a very long time. Frank Pace has a long story to tell—and Bob Hope will, if called upon. So this might have gone to 1 or 2 in the morning. But because of my imminent journey to Paris, you will be out—hungry, rather unhappy—but you will be home early tonight.

It is now 1:30 in Paris and I am due there at 10:30, and I do not believe it would be a good start to keep the General waiting. So I shall be brief.

I don't think that it's at all inappropriate that I should come from this meeting to go to see President de Gaulle and Chairman Khrushchev. The figures which disturb our lives in regard to cancer—one out of every four, or two out of every three families—are not American figures. They are the same figures that can be found in the country of General de Gaulle. They are the same statistics which will bring death in the country of Chairman Khrushchev. And therefore I feel it most appropriate to go from this dinner with a group of Americans who have given great effort to conquering this disease—to go from here on my journey across the sea.

[215]

...nce said that every ...es—his own country ...am sure that in this ...take that I bring to ...dent de Gaulle the ap- ...ct and esteem of all of the ...country who value his courage over a period of 20 years in which he has served as one of the great Captains of the West.

And I am glad to be at this dinner to pay tribute to a former comrade-in-arms of his—General Bradley—whose conduct throughout all of his life has been governed by the motto of the Corps whose young men we now see with us tonight, "Duty, honor, and country."

This service which he renders in this cause is only the most recent in a long series of causes, a long series of efforts which he has made on behalf of our country and the free countries of the earth. So General, I am proud to be here tonight to honor you.

And also Mrs. Roosevelt. She has lent her name and her efforts and her talents and her generosity to so many causes, and all of us here, individually and collectively, have been the beneficiary of them in one way or another.

So ladies and gentlemen, I want to express my thanks for your invitation to me tonight.

The great strength of our country is the willingness of people such as yourselves to undertake this kind of work. The Vice President and I are conscious always of the fact that we appropriate in Washington from forty-five to fifty billion dollars a year in the defense of the great Republic. And we spend a fraction of that in the fight for cancer. If in any way it will make it possible for us to make a greater effort on this cause and no longer have to build our strength constantly, then the trip which I am about to make, the trip which the Vice President made a week ago, the trip which Ambassador Stevenson will make next week are all worthwhile.

We go to many countries but we sing the same song. And that is, this country wants peace and this country wants freedom.

Therefore in going tonight across the sea I recognize that all of you, as citizens of the great Republic, come with me.

Thank you.

NOTE: The President spoke at the Waldorf-Astoria Hotel in New York City. In his opening words he referred to Matthew B. Rosenhaus, chairman, Executive Committee of the American Cancer Foundation, of which the Eleanor Roosevelt Cancer Foundation is an affiliate; Mrs. Eleanor Roosevelt; Gen. Omar N. Bradley, chairman, Board of Trustees of the Eleanor Roosevelt Cancer Foundation; Robert F. Wagner, Mayor of New York City; Vice President Lyndon B. Johnson; Adlai E. Stevenson, U.S. Representative to the United Nations; Bernard Baruch; and James Roosevelt, U.S. Representative from California and president of the Eleanor Roosevelt Cancer Foundation. Later in his remarks the President referred to Frank Pace, general chairman of the dinner.

216 Remarks Upon Arrival at Orly Airport in Paris. *May 31, 1961*

General de Gaulle, members of his government, Madame de Gaulle:

I want to express on behalf of my wife and myself our most generous appreciation of your welcome today.

I come from America, "the daughter of Europe," to France, which is America's oldest friend. But long before my country was born, French influence, French philosophy, French culture led the Western World to such a degree that the first American Ambassador to Paris, Benjamin Franklin, could say, "Every man has two countries: France and his own."

But I come today not merely because of past ties and past friendship, but because the present relationship between France and the United States is essential for the preservation of freedom around the globe. I come also because of the grandeur of France's present mission, the productivity of her workers, the brilliance of her universities, the vigor of her leaders. In my office, in recent weeks, I've received many envoys of new countries.

Many of them spoke French, the language of free men.

So, General, it is an honor to come and visit you today. You have been a captain in the field in the defense of the West for more than 20 years. Your vigor, your leadership, your long sense of history, are needed now more than ever in the past. France and the United States have been associated in the past in many great causes, but I can think of no more happy cause than to be associated together in the climactic moment in the defense of freedom.

NOTE: The President spoke at 10:30 a.m.

217   Toasts of the President and President de Gaulle at the Formal Dinner in the Elysée Palace.   *May 31, 1961*

President de Gaulle, ladies and gentlemen:
It is naturally a great honor for any President of the United States to come to Paris. In this city in 1783, Benjamin Franklin signed the treaty which made us sovereign, independent and equal, and in addition, it is not difficult for this President of the United States to come to France. I sleep in a French bed. In the morning my breakfast is served by a French chef. I go to my office, and the bad news of the day is brought to me by my Press Secretary, Pierre Salinger, not in his native language, and I am married to a daughter of France. But I do not believe that sentiment is sufficient to explain the close relations which exist between the United States and France. There is no doubt that the early Revolutionary leaders paid due tribute to France, George Washington and the others, for the role which France played in the independence of our country. But it is an interesting fact in history that John Adams, who was also a Minister to France, and a successor to General Washington, should want

as his epitaph to be written, "He kept the peace with France." So changes the times, and where once General Washington and Mr. Adams paid tribute to France, Mr. Adams could claim as his great contribution that he did not engage in war with this country. So that sentiment and friendship which come and go are not sufficient to explain the enduring ties which exist between France and the United States. It is something more substantial.

I live in a part of America which is the most eastern part, and I look across the ocean and the nearest country I can see is France. It has been in this century a strong conviction of the Presidents and the people of the United States that the security of my country would be directly threatened if France were not independent, strong, and sovereign. And so in this century, on two occasions, young men from my country have come to contribute to the maintenance of that independence and that sovereignty. And now in the most difficult era in the life of our two countries, this next decade,

I believe the ties should be even more intimate. Benjamin Franklin once wrote in his diary, Poor Richard's Almanac, about a snake, which had one body and two heads and going to the river to get a drink it ran into a twig. One head went in one direction and one head went in the other, and ultimately he died of thirst.

I believe that we are one body. And it is my hope that on this visit we can contribute to the uniformity of view which will permit us to go to the river of peace and gain satisfaction from it. As an American I take pleasure in seeing people around the world salute the American Revolution and the principles for which we fought. As Frenchmen, I know that you take satisfaction that people around the world invoke your great motto of Liberty, Equality and Fraternity. What counts, of course, is not merely the words, but the meaning behind them. We believe in liberty and equality and fraternity. We believe in life and liberty and the pursuit of happiness. And we believe that the rights of the individual are preeminent, not merely the slogans and the mottoes which are invoked across the globe by those who make themselves our adversary. We believe in the significance behind these great ideas. Therefore, I think it quite natural that in this most difficult decade of the 1960's France and the United States should be once again associated together.

It is a particular source of satisfaction to me as President of the United States that we should be associated with President de Gaulle. He stands now as the only great leader of World War II who occupies a position of high responsibility. The others have gone and he remains, and he stands true to the same concept which he fought for during the Second World War, the sovereignty of France, the community of the Western Nations. And therefore, as a junior

figure on this field, which he has occupied for more than 20 years, I ask you to drink to the great Captain of the West, your President, General de Gaulle.

NOTE: A translation of General de Gaulle's response follows:

Mr. President:

France congratulates herself on your visit and fully realizes its meaning. Indeed, through your presence she feels directly linked with the United States, first because you are its President, but also because you seem to her to symbolize the great American Nation as it faces the harsh issues of our time.

For the United States—uniquely among the great powers—has never from its birth to this day found itself in conflict with France, nor has it seen even a momentary weakening of the deep friendship between our two countries, which share a common view of man's destiny.

And who among us has forgotten the glorious contribution of Americans to the victory which ended the First World War—or, in the Second, to the liberation and salvation of Europe which marked the triumph of our cause?

Nor are we in France unmindful of your own valiant combat service to that cause in the Pacific theater. These are for us as Frenchmen the strongest of reasons for happiness in welcoming you—reasons to which are added the honor and pleasure of seeing, joined to your energy and drive, the charm of Mrs. Kennedy.

Yet, great as have been the successes of the recent past, they cannot forever provide the answer to everything and everyone. In a world shaken by the gigantic forces of modern times and by totalitarian ambitions aimed at domination, America and France, together with the entire free world, are assailed by hard and dangerous problems.

How fitting it is—and, may I add, how gratifying—that you have wished to come and discuss them in person with us. Of course no one on either side can in the least question the necessary solidarity which joins our two peoples for good or ill. But our common objective of peace in freedom calls as well for the fullest possible mutual understanding and for effective harmony of concepts and actions. Such is the endeavor, Mr. President, to which you and I wish to devote ourselves, and it is one to which France assents with all her mind and heart.

Finally, if we value so highly the presence in Paris of a President of the United States, it is also because that President is yourself. Let me tell you how greatly Frenchmen have admired your intelligence and courage since you first grasped, in your turn and in today's heavy seas, the helm of the

American ship of state. Already we have discerned in you the philosophy of the true statesman, who chooses his goal, who holds his course, who is neither halted nor diverted by vicissitudes, and who looks to no easy formula or expedient to lighten the responsibility which is his burden and his honor.

I raise my glass in honor of Mr. John Kennedy, the President of the United States of America, in honor of Mrs. Kennedy, in honor of the United States, whose steadfast and resolute friend and ally France has been, is now, and will remain.

218   Remarks to the Staff of the U.S. Embassy in Paris. *June 1, 1961*

Ambassador Gavin, Mr. Bohlen, Mr. Nitze, members of the Embassy:

I want to express my pleasure at being here this morning. I tried to get assigned to the Embassy in Paris myself, and unable to do so, I decided that I would run for President. But this represents the ultimate. I want to express my appreciation to all of you for the efforts that you are making on behalf of the United States, and also, I believe it quite appropriate to say, on behalf of France and Europe and the Free World. I said last night in my toast that the United States interest in France is not based on mere sentiment. I know it is customary on these visits to recall Lafayette and all the rest. But I also said last night that in the administration after that of General Washington, the United States came close to an open break with France, so swiftly had the sentimental memories of the Revolutionary War disappeared. Our interest here is more substantial, and I believe it goes to the common interests of both the United States and France. We are closely associated and are allies, because it helps protect the interest of our country and because it protects the interests of freedom around the world. I do not believe that there is any Embassy in the world more important to the United States than the Embassy in Paris, because the influence of this city and country goes far beyond its borders. When Mrs. Kennedy and I went to Ottawa 2 weeks ago, we were greeted in

the Parliament by a speech by the President of the Senate in French. When the Vice President of the United States was welcomed in Saigon 2 weeks ago, he was welcomed in a speech in French. The long tradition of this country, stretching back to a position of leadership for so many years, gives the representatives of this country a special voice, a special prestige, a special distinction, in their work around the world. France is larger than the total of its parts, and its past, its present, and its future makes your assignment here at this Embassy of the greatest possible importance to our common cause. The security of Europe, its freedom, is essential to the security of the United States, and we plan to take every measure, we plan to continue to devote every energy, to strengthening the common ties which bind us.

You play a great role in that. This country is extremely vital to the success of our common cause, and, therefore, when you speak for the United States here, and when the French people who comprehend under their distinguished leader the long movement of history, I believe you have a unique opportunity to be of service.

I want to express my special appreciation to those of you who are of French extraction. I do not believe it inopportune to say that in serving the United States in this Embassy, I hope that you feel also that you are serving France.

So, ladies and gentlemen, we are indebted

to you. This is an important post. You serve our country, and I know together that we will continue to press forward for the causes in which we believe.

Thank you.

NOTE: The President's opening words referred to James M. Gavin, American Ambassador to France, Charles E. Bohlen, Special Assistant to the Secretary of State, and Paul H. Nitze, Assistant Secretary of Defense for International Security Affairs.

219   Remarks at a Civic Reception for President Kennedy at the Hôtel de Ville. *June 1, 1961*

President Tardieu, members of the Council, members of the City Government of Paris, Mr. Minister, Mr. Ambassador, President of the Assembly, ladies and gentlemen:

I want to express in behalf of my wife and myself our appreciation for your generous welcome today. I am a descendant, on both sides, of two grandparents who served in the City Council of Boston, and I'm sure they regarded that as a more significant service than any of their descendants have yet rendered. You are closest to the people. Their judgment of the efficacy of government comes in large part because of their contacts with you. And it is a source, I know, of satisfaction to you that you should bear a position of responsibility in this ancient City of Light.

There are many in the West who, taking the long view of Mr. Spengler and others, talk of the decline, and they search, hither and yon, in order to document their case. I believe the events of recent years have proved them wrong. I do not believe the West is in decline. I believe the West is in the ascendancy. And what has happened in this country and the other communities of Western Europe, I believe reinforces that view. Even in the last 15 years, the strongest tides in the direction of the affairs of the world have been the rise of independent states, the desire of people to be independent. And it is a felicitous fact that the slogans which have governed your country in the past and at present, in the future, of Liberty, Equality and Fraternity, and the ideals by which my country has been directed from its earliest days, are in accordance with the basic aspirations of people all around the globe.

As President of the United States, I said at the airport, I have received in recent weeks ambassadors from many countries who are associated with France by language and culture and who represent countries who are independent. This desire for freedom, this desire for liberty, wherever it may be on the globe, in my opinion is the strongest tide of the 20th century, and it is a happy fact that the interests and policies of France and the United States are directed towards encouraging this growth.

I come to this ancient city which was a community when *omnia Gallia est divisa in tres partes*. This city stands today and I think it is evidence of the continuity of history.

This city is no stranger to me. A Parisian designed the City of Washington, Pierre L'Enfant, who laid out our broad boulevards after living here in this community. When he had finished his generous designs he presented a bill to the Congress for $90,000, and the Congress of the United States in one of those bursts of economic fervor for which they are justifiably famous awarded him the munificent sum of $3000. Some people have been so unkind as to suggest that your clothes designers have been collecting his bill ever since!

I am delighted to be here today. You have been extremely generous, and the people of Paris, to my wife and myself. I was in Canada 2 weeks ago. France has not been in military possession of Canada for more than two centuries, and yet the debate in the Parliament of Canada is bilingual. Thirty percent of the people of Canada speak French. More people speak French in my own section of New England than any other language except English. These descendants of Frenchmen who have been separated from this country for more than two centuries maintain in their lives the faith, the tradition, the culture, the understanding, which that language and that background give them. And they send their sons to Assumption College in Worcester, Massachusetts, which teaches in French. That is why I

said at the American Embassy this morning that France is more than the sum of its parts. This long influence which stretches around the globe, which is a part of your tradition, is a source of strength to us today, and that great interest in common, more than any of the ties of the past, that great hope for the future is what makes inevitable the intimate and constant association of France and the United States.

I salute this city and I salute your country, and I salute your distinguished President. And I express in behalf of the American people our thanks to you all.

NOTE: In his opening words the President referred to Julien Tardieu, President of the Paris Municipal Council, Roger Frey, Minister of the Interior, Hervé Alphand, French Ambassador to the United States, and Jacques Chaban-Delmas, President of the National Assembly.

Another text of this address was released by the White House prior to its actual delivery.

220   Remarks in Paris Before the North Atlantic Council. *June 1, 1961*

Gentlemen:

I am grateful for your invitation to be here today. I consider it an honor, and it does give me an opportunity to once again restate the basic conviction of the people of the United States that our security is inevitably tied up with the security of Europe. The United States cannot look forward to a free existence if Western Europe is not free. And we believe in my country, as I am happy to see the people of your country also believe, that this independence must continue and grow.

The circumstances which brought about the birth of the NATO Council and the NATO Alliance in some degree have changed. In some ways the hazards have increased. In some ways we give attention

to other areas which were not under direct attack in 1949. But the basic fact still remains, that the power and productivity of this section of the world is a source of vital strength to the security of freedom all around the globe. The United States and Canada in combination with the people of Western Europe form together the most powerful group of people in the world, with long experience, great productive capacity, a high degree of commitment, a high degree of education, and a comprehension of the issues which now divide the world. In many ways, the experience of Europe in the last 10 years has confounded all of those who believed that the tide of history was running against us. I think our problem is to give new life to the NATO Council and to the organization, to transfer its attention and interests not only to the immediate security of this area, to which we are all committed, and will be in the future, but also to consider jointly how we can play a more significant role in those other areas of the world which are subjected to increasing pressure. We have an historic responsibility, and it is a matter of vital strategic significance to the future of your countries and mine that we concern ourselves with the whole southern half of the globe where we are now in danger, and where freedom is now in danger, and where those who place themselves on the opposite side of the table from us seek to make their great advances.

The strength of Western Europe, the strength of my country, the strength of Canada, the association of Japan, the countries in Asia and Africa, the countries in my hemisphere, where we share a great common tradition—all these people desire to be free and independent. I am not an historical determinist, but I do believe that history is not moving against us, but in the long run is moving with us.

There is no doubt that in our time we will see different groups assume positions of responsibility within each state, different groups assume power. But the whole experience of the last years has shown the desire of people to be free and independent,

to maintain their national sovereignty and independence. And I believe that when our times come to be recorded this will be noted as the outstanding fact. This serves us because that is our ambition. Even the experience of those countries behind the Iron Curtain in their own relations show a strong desire to be free and independent. This is going to be true increasingly in Africa. It is true in Latin America. It is true in Asia. So while new groups may come to power in many of these countries in the next decade, these groups inevitably, themselves, will want to maintain their independence.

So I do not look to the future with any degree of discouragement. What has happened here in the last 10 years shows what free men can do. And I want to restate again the strong commitment of my country to the defense of Western Europe. We believe it vital to the security of the United States and we intend to honor our commitments. We want to see this association become more intimate. We want to see it play an expanded and greater part throughout the world.

So I welcome your invitation today. And I sit here, speaking for a country which is separated from yours by many hundreds of miles, but which is totally involved with your destiny.

Thank you.

221   Remarks at SHAPE Headquarters in Paris. *June 2, 1961*

General Norstad, Ambassador Finletter, officers, ladies and gentlemen:

I want to express my thanks to all of you for having been kind enough to come out in the rain and to express your good will to my country. The United States made a de-

termination on three different occasions in this century, in 1917, in 1941, in 1948 and '49, that the security of my country must inevitably be linked with the security of a free Europe. We believe that strongly in 1961. It is for this reason that we have determined to maintain and strengthen the forces which we now have stretched across Europe, joined with you in the common defense of the freedom of this historic section of the world, whose security inevitably affects the well-being of my own country.

We are here with you, and as long as you are determined that our association with you is useful in the common cause, we shall remain, and we shall meet our commitments to the full, and we shall maintain our strength, and we shall continue to insist that here in this most ancient section of the civilized world springs the force, the vigor, the strength, and the commitment which can

provide freedom, not only for this section of Europe, but also radiate around the globe.

I salute all of you who are participating in this great common event, and I hope in the years that are now ahead that this communal alliance will have even greater strength and force than it has had in past years. And I can assure you that the United States of America intends to bear its full part.

Thank you.

NOTE: The President's opening words referred to Gen. Lauris Norstad, Supreme Commander of Allied Forces in Europe, and Thomas K. Finletter, U.S. Permanent Representative on the Council of the North Atlantic Treaty Organization.

222 Remarks and Question and Answer Period at the Press Luncheon in Paris. *June 2, 1961*

Distinguished guests, ladies and gentlemen:

I do not think it altogether inappropriate to introduce myself to this audience. I am the man who accompanied Jacqueline Kennedy to Paris, and I have enjoyed it.

I am also happy to have an opportunity to express publicly my appreciation to President and Mrs. de Gaulle for the hospitality and kindness which they have shown to us since our visit to Paris. I must say also, as I said to the General, that my most vivid impression of my visit here was not even the extraordinary spectacle which we all witnessed last night, which reminded us of the long reach into history which this country possesses, but rather was the sense of vigor and vitality and force possessed by the French people themselves. I do not say that riding in a car through rainy streets is the best method of making a determination of national character, but I have ridden through many streets and I must say it is a most effective method of determining the quality of the people. And I think any American who

shared the experiences which we have had during the past 2 days in the sunshine on occasion, in the rain more often, would come away from this country with a feeling of confidence and hope.

I come on the same mission which occupied many of my predecessors, stretching all the way back to President Wilson at the conclusion of the First World War, and that is how it is possible to bind more intimately for the common interest France and the United States, Europe and the United States. This is not altogether a new effort. I recall in my first days in the Congress of the United States in 1947, '48, and '49, when the great steps which were proposed on a bipartisan basis by the American people to assist in the restoration of Europe were among the most foresighted and farsighted actions in which my country has been engaged, the Truman doctrine, the British loan, the aid for Greece and Turkey, the Marshall plan and later NATO. The United States, I believe, can be proud of these programs, and of the great results that they helped to produce. Without them it is possible that the whole history of Western Europe since 1945 would now be entirely different. Even today the basic concepts suggested in these programs form the essential part of the foreign policy of the United States. But these concepts alone are not adequate for our European policies in the 1960's. All of the power relationships in the world have changed in the last 15 years, and therefore our policies must take these changes into account. First is the change in Europe, itself. In the 1940's Europe—much of it was destroyed, its productive capacity liquidated, divided by a bitter war, inflation rampant, and only those who were optimists of the most extreme sort could have ever predicted the astonishing renaissance of Western Europe today. Its people have energy and confidence. Its economic growth rate is higher than that of the new world, either Canada or the United States. Its dollar shortages have been converted into balances which have even disturbed the monetary stability of the United States.

There were those who said that Europe after the war would be a prisoner again of its ancient rivalries. Today this continent offers the world the most outstanding examples of strength through unity. After 15 years of extraordinary creative effort and administrative invention, the development of the OEEC, the European Payments Union, the Coal and Steel Community, Euratom, the Common Market, and the OECD, and all of these have only laid the foundation for an even closer economic and political unity.

At the same time, the wise and sympathetic policies followed by France and Great Britain towards those countries which were formerly dependencies have strengthened the free world, the globe around us, and

have also increased the prestige, influence, and stature of the countries themselves.

The second great change is the change in weaponry. The United States no longer has a nuclear monopoly. The Soviet Union's possession of atomic and hydrogen weapons has increased its willingness to test and probe and push the West. In addition, the intercontinental ballistic missile has made my own country vulnerable to attack and it has also reinforced our view that your defense and ours is indivisible, that in terms of potential destruction, Washington today is closer to Moscow than this city was to any other city in any other country before the outbreak of World War II. We must in short be constantly strengthening all of our forces of all kinds, at all levels, deterring war, and keeping the peace by making certain that those who would oppose us know that we are determined to resist aggression, whatever its force, and whatever kind of force is needed to resist it.

The new change in weaponry presents new challenges, with possession by both the United States and the Soviet Union of an atomic and hydrogen capacity, with the great masses of armies that are available to the Sino-Soviet bloc, to the close lines of communication which they have at their service in Western Europe, in the Middle East, in Asia, in Southeast Asia. It indicates the kind of difficult problems that we face in planning for a secure future. But while we keep our arms so strong that no antagonist can believe that he can secure an easy or shortcut road to world domination, man's inventive power for keeping the peace has not kept pace. We still have strong hopes that it will be possible for us to reach an agreement at Geneva on a cessation of nuclear tests. If we cannot reach an agreement on this subject, which is relatively easy to patrol because of the flow of radiation, how is it going to be possible for us to set up the kind of inspection system for the control of other weapons which could lead to disarmament, and, therefore, to a world peace?

I consider this to be a most essential, realistic step, and those of you who in this audience may have reported on the proceedings in Geneva in the 1920's and '30's, when many months and years and energy of a great many different countries were engaged in the subject under far better conditions of good will then prevailing, the subject of how to secure an adequate disarmament system which provided security, can judge how difficult it will be for us to do so in the future if we cannot make successfully this step.

Third and most important is the change in the location and the nature of the threat. The cause of freedom is under pressure all over the world. But because of the extraordinary rebirth of Western European strength, the struggle has been switched to other areas where the security of your countries and mine are now being directly threatened. The whole southern half of the globe where the attack potentially comes not from massive land armies but from subversion, insurrection, and despair. Europe has conquered her own internal problems. Those that remain are on the way to solution. The time has now come for us to associate more closely together than ever in the past in a massive and concerted attack on poverty, injustice, and oppression, which overshadow so much of the globe. When the threat of military aggression was the primary one, our posture was defensive. But where the contest is one of human liberty and economic growth—and I tie them both together as we must always do so because the slogans with which we have associated ourselves have significance and force when they are bound together with a recognition that economic growth and productivity and

material well-being are the handmaidens of liberty—we have the resources in this most extraordinary section of the world, the oldest, and in many ways now among the youngest, allied with the United States and Canada, associated with the countries of Latin America and Africa and Asia, we have an opportunity in our time to fulfill our responsibilities.

In 1779, before France came into the War of Independence, someone said to Benjamin Franklin, "It is a great spectacle that you are putting on in America," and Benjamin Franklin said, "Yes, but the trouble is, the spectators do not pay."

We are not spectators today. We are all contributing, we are all involved, here in this country, here in this community, here in Western Europe, here in my own country, here all around the globe, where it is our responsibility to make a maximum contribution.

[*A question and answer period followed.*]

[1.] Q. In case of the failure of talks at Evian, would the United States be led to intervene more directly in settling the Algerian question, for example, in case of massive support by the Soviet Union and China?

THE PRESIDENT. It is, of course, our hope that the talks now proceeding at Evian will be successful, and I can think of no useful purpose at the present time in planning for the eventuality which was suggested by the question. We should look forward to the present, we should look forward to the effort which is being made to work out a peaceful solution. If that effort should fail, then of course all of us who are concerned would be expected to participate in appropriate consultations. But for the present and certainly as we look to the future, we look with hope towards those talks.

431

[2.] Q. Question from the Los Angeles Times: Will the President indicate how, and how soon he hopes to induce the negligent European member states of the North Atlantic Alliance to fulfill their accepted force goals for NATO's European shield forces?

THE PRESIDENT. Without accepting the presumptions upon which the Los Angeles Times places the question, I am hopeful that all members of the NATO Alliance will fulfill the goals to which they are committed. I think it important that in making these goals we make them realistic, that we do not make plans that we have no intentions of keeping. So quite obviously I think it would be in the interests of all that we meet our commitments, and I can assure you that the United States of America will make every effort on its part to carry out its obligations. I will say also that I am interested in the effort which Western Europe and the United States and Canada are making through the OEEC, through DAG, to play a more substantial role in economic assistance to the southern part of the globe. This is a great challenge for Western Europe. So that we hope that all of us will be willing to bear the burdens that free people must in dangerous days.

[3.] Q. [*In French*] Did you discuss with General de Gaulle the French atomic tests and the attitude of France with regard to the Geneva conference on suspension of nuclear tests? At what stage of the atomic development of France will the McMahon law no longer prevent the President of the United States from giving her American secrets? Who in the United States is the judge as to whether this stage has been reached or not?

THE PRESIDENT. In answer to the first part of the question, the answer was we have discussed these matters. In answer to the second, the determination or the interpretation of the McMahon Act is a matter of concern to the Executive and also a matter of great concern to the Joint Committee on Atomic Energy of the Congress. And I'm sure that if a question were raised in regard to the interpretations that the United States Government would attempt to make an appropriate determination.

The third part of the question is—to what degree—the responsibility falls most immediately on the President. It is a matter, of course, which—it's a statute of the Congress, it is a matter of great concern to many members of the Congress who have given this matter long attention. There are varying views on how it would be interpreted. And I would say that the United States Government would make a judgment if a judgment were required after consulting with our partners in the Congress.

May I say that on some of these matters my answers will be less than full and less than satisfactory to you. When this press conference was first planned, I expected to be at the end of my voyage. It comes at a time before General de Gaulle and I have concluded our talks, before a communique has been issued, and beginning tomorrow I face new responsibilities. Therefore, I hope that those who I leave less than satisfied will at least be sympathetic.

[4.] Q. Mr. President, a question by Serge Fleigers of the Hearst Newspapers: What in your opinion, Mr. President, is the principal aim of a meeting with Mr. Khrushchev at this time and do you feel that you are meeting him with enough cards in your hands?

THE PRESIDENT. To answer the second part of the question first, I consider the power of the United States, plus those countries that are associated with it in the common defense, to give every form of encouragement to any Western leader who discusses matters which concern us with those who occupy positions of responsibility in other parts of the globe. I think Mr. Khrushchev has the same view. And to the first part of the question, I would say, as I have said before, that the purpose of this meeting is to permit me to make a more precise judgment on those matters which involve the interests of the United States, and the Soviet Union, and those countries which are associated with us and those countries which are members of the Sino-Soviet bloc. We are involved in two conferences at Geneva. We hope that more progress can be made at both of them. And if there is anything that may be said in the meetings Saturday and Sunday which may improve that prospect, then, of course, that makes the trip worthwhile. There are other matters also on which we have not come to an agreement with Mr. Khrushchev, and I think it important that we understand fully his viewpoint and all of its implications, and that in return he has the same understanding of our viewpoint.

I said recently that in my lifetime I had been present, alive, during three world wars, and it is impossible to study the origins of each of these struggles without realizing the serious miscalculations which were made by the leaders on both sides. The most recent example was in our own experience in Korea, where the North Koreans did not seem certain that we would respond immediately upon the occasion of their invasion into South Korea, and where there was serious doubt on the part of the United States that the Chinese Communists would intervene as we moved to the north. In the experience of Europe, you have had similar circumstances. Therefore, when responsibility is pressed heavily on anyone to make a judgment, it seems to me useful to have as close

an understanding of the view of each side as possible. I think that it is most valuable to talk to those with whom we are allied. I also think it is important that we talk to those who are separated from us, because in the final analysis, heavy decisions rest, constitutionally, upon the President of the United States. He must under some conditions make the final judgment himself, and if my judgment may be more lucid, may be based more on reality as a result of this exchange, then I think the trip will be useful.

[5.] Q. [*In French*] Would you interpret for us your understanding with General de Gaulle on Berlin? What is the real meaning and scope of this understanding?

THE PRESIDENT. The matter of Berlin, of course, will be a matter, I am sure, of discussion tomorrow and Sunday and, therefore, I do not think that this is a particularly appropriate time to go into details on the position which we occupy in Berlin as it is a matter, of course, which will be discussed by Mr. Khrushchev and myself. Let me therefore sum it up by saying that I think that neither General de Gaulle nor I would feel it appropriate to have our rights, statutory rights, in West Berlin changed by force or the threat of force.

[6.] Q. Crosby Noyes, Washington Evening Star: Mr. President, in view of the attitude shown by the Soviet and Chinese delegations at the Geneva conference on Laos, do you now feel that the neutrality and independence of that country can be established and insured by an international agreement?

THE PRESIDENT. I think that the prospects are not easy of securing an independent and neutral Laos as we understand it, but we intend to continue to discuss this matter, and we will stay at the conference for as long as we feel that there is some hope of success. The Soviet Union has stated on occasions that it wishes a neutral and independent Laos. If we can come to an agreement on the exact, precise definition of these words, then our progress should be swift. I will say that the first and most essential step at the present time is to provide an effective mechanism for controlling the cease-fire. If we can secure a cease-fire, then we can move on to those other matters which must be settled by the conference. It is a difficult area. It presents us with many difficult decisions. But I cannot believe that anyone would imperil the peace by failing to recognize the importance of reaching an agreement in this country, by breaking up a conference and refusing to agree to a cease-fire and a government and a people which can maintain their neutrality against outside intervention from whatever source.

[7.] Q. [*In French*] Question of Mme. Geneviève Tabouis together with question annexed by a colleague: How does President Kennedy view the role of France in Europe? Do you think that closer consultations may take place between Washington, London, and Paris, on the political and military problems of the world?

THE PRESIDENT. Yes, I do, and the reason I came to Paris was to participate in that kind of consultation. Consultation does not always, regardless of how long it may go on, does not always provide unanimity at the end of the consultation. But there is a more precise understanding of those areas where there is agreement and there is a more precise understanding of the reasons for positions which may be taken on which there is not agreement. So I regard conversations such as I have had for the last 2 days, and they have been more than 8 hours with President de Gaulle, I regard them as most valuable. And I believe that more than talking about consulting it is important to

consult. And we have done that and will continue to do it, I hope with increasing intimacy, in the months ahead.

[8.] Q. Question of Thomas Cadett, of the BBC, and Christopher Johnson of the Financial Times: Mr. President, did you discuss Britain's entry into the Common Market with President de Gaulle, and what did he say? And does the United States advise the French Government to facilitate the entry of Britain into the Common Market as a full member?

THE PRESIDENT. I cannot believe that Mr. Cadett or Mr. Johnson have been in Paris less time than I have, but nevertheless I am sure that even if they had been here only in the last few hours they would know that on those matters on which—regarding General de Gaulle's views, that the most authoritative place to secure them is General de Gaulle.

[9.] Q. [*In French*] What can the United States and her allies do to be again regarded in the world as a whole as the true defenders of liberty, of justice, when in the eyes of underdeveloped countries they all appear today as the defenders of the unique privileges which the whites enjoy because of their high standard of living? Can you tell us, for Africa and Latin America, what means the United States is thinking of to help the peoples of these continents in their revolution for peace, for equality—for an "independent order" as you yourself have said.

THE PRESIDENT. I think the question suggests a basic problem which is not easy to solve. We are a prosperous people. Some of us in the Atlantic Community have held colonial possessions and we, therefore, have not always experienced, in my own hemisphere, in Africa, or Asia, the happiest relations with the people who are involved. But I will say on the other hand, that the record of the last 15 years is an extraordinary one, as country after country has gained its independence, by free means in many cases—in fact, in the majority of cases—who were once held as colonial possessions. This is an extraordinary record for the Western World and one not matched by the Eastern World, which continues to hold areas under its control, not by free means. I think that it is not enough, as I said in my speech, that we give our slogans, though the slogans cloak very basic principles, but I feel we must make a greater concerted effort than we have made in the past on a long-term basis, to demonstrate to these people that through free choice they may be able to solve their material problems. I do not want to see the United States, and I am sure that those of you who are Europeans do not want to see Europe, associated with reactionary groups within these countries who seek only to maintain their own position. We want to assist and be associated with those groups who look to the future, who are identified with the aspirations of their people. Otherwise, our days in some of these areas are on the yellow leaf. I will say that one of the matters which I discussed with General de Gaulle was the great hope which we had in the Western Hemisphere that Europe would play an increasingly larger role. Its traditional ties, its cultural affinities, its ties of language—of Latin America—are extremely intimate with Europe, and I believe that there is a great opportunity for Europe, not only to serve the general cause, not only in Africa and Asia, but also in the hemisphere of the Americas. And it was a source of great satisfaction to me that General de Gaulle, as he demonstrated in his speech of some weeks ago, shares strongly that view of the obligation of this area.

[10.] Q. Question by Joseph Barry, of the New York Post: Mr. President, has there been an investigation of the case of the reports circulated about alleged Central Intelligence Agency involvement in the April 22 Algiers revolt of the generals, and would you care to comment on this?

THE PRESIDENT. I feel that the good will of this visit may be rapidly diminishing. Let me say that I have not been informed, and all my information is to the contrary, that there was any involvement by members of the CIA or any other members of the American Government. I think that the foreign minister discussed that matter quite clearly in his report of some weeks ago, and I think that the statements which our Government has made in regard to its association with this country and its government I think obviously answer it. So in answer to your question, I know of no basis for such a charge. I have never received information on it. I assume I would have and, therefore, I regard the matter as not in fact true.

[11.] Q. [*In French*] Mr. President what impressed you most, first about France, and then concerning General de Gaulle?

THE PRESIDENT. In France, as I said, I think the vitality of a very old race, which the French people are. In General de Gaulle, I am having a conversation with the only active figure who played a major role in the Second World War who is now involved in major policy matters affecting the security of the Western World. President Roosevelt, Prime Minister Churchill, Marshal Stalin have all disappeared from the positions of responsibility. General de Gaulle remains. And he is faithful to the same concepts of the strength of France and the unity of Europe as he has been for many years. It has been my hope in these conversations that he has a renewed appreciation of how seriously we consider our ties with France and Western Europe. I hope from our conversations that he understands how

435

our new government in the United States is firmly committed to the security of this area and means to implement its commitments.

[12.] Q. Question by L. E. Micey, of the United Press International: Mr. President, how can Communist China normalize her relations with the West and be admitted to United Nations membership?

THE PRESIDENT. I would say that the normalization of relations which—of course, peaceful relations—which is in the common interest of us all, between China and the West—I would hope that they would be brought about. But we desire peace and we desire to live in amity with the Chinese people. But I will say that since long before I assumed office and in the first days of our new administration, before really any actions were taken, the attacks upon our Government and the United States were constant, immediate, and in many cases malevolent. The debate which took place last fall between Communist parties indicated that the Chinese planned to take an extremely belligerent attitude and role towards us and those with whom we are associated. We hope that policy changes. We want good will. But it takes two to make peace, and I am hopeful that the Chinese will be persuaded that a peaceful existence with its neighbors represents the best hope for us all. We would welcome it. But I do not see evidence of it today.

[13.] Q. [*In French*] If you were in the place of Mr. Khrushchev——

THE PRESIDENT. If I were—I suppose if I were in Mr. Khrushchev's place, it would be because I was Mr. Khrushchev and had lived his life, and therefore, I would look to the West and I would see a good deal of reports of disagreement. I would see where all Western leaders may not agree on every issue. I would see where distinguished American correspondents who speak with great influence take a different view on what actions the United States should take. I would see Mr. Kennedy under critical attack by many of his fellow countrymen, as well as those who live across the ocean. I would look at my own country, where everything on the surface is serene, where nobody criticizes or opposes, and everyone is united behind me. And, therefore, I would draw a conclusion that the tide of history was moving with me.

If I were Mr. Khrushchev, however, and had spent some time in the West, I would take a somewhat different view of the tide of history. I would read those distinguished spokesmen who had prophesied the imminent collapse of Europe in 1947 and '48. I would read those others who had felt it would be impossible for us to associate more closely together and I would also recognize that dissent and controversy brings a kind of vitality and also protects individual liberty. And I would consider that possibly we could improve Russian society. I will say that I don't agree very basically with one of the assumptions which a good many Communists put forward, and that is from the events of the last 15 years they have made the judgment that the tide is determined and in their favor. You cannot look at the relations between the countries behind the Iron Curtain. For example, the rather strange relationship between Albania and China, or between Yugoslavia and Albania and Russia, or between all the other countries of the bloc, to feel that if time were permitted to pass and the Communists were permitted to be successful, that there would not inevitably be the same rivalries which we now see already in evidence. The difficulty, of course, is that Caesar and Pompey and Antony and Octavius and the others did not fall out until they were successful. We cannot afford the luxury of permitting them the kind of success which will prove them wrong finally in the kind of world which they were witness. We have to maintain our position. And therefore, I hope Mr. Khrushchev is not misled by those signs of democracy which we understand but they do not, but instead recognizes that the United States of America, divided as it may be on many important questions, including governmental spending, is united in its de-termination to fulfill its commitments and to play the role that history and its own free choice have brought upon it in these years.

So I may say, as I said at the beginning, I go to Vienna with a good deal of confidence, and I go to Vienna with more confidence as a result of my last 2 days.

NOTE: The President's twelfth news conference was held at 1:15 p.m. at the Palais de Chaillot in Paris.

223 Joint Statement Following Discussions With President de Gaulle. *June 2,* 1961

THE PRESIDENT of the United States of America paid a state visit to Paris from May 31 to June 2. This visit itself is evidence of the close and friendly relations traditionally characteristic of the history of the two countries.

During the visit there have been long talks between General de Gaulle, President of the French Republic, and President Kennedy.

The two presidents discussed the principal issues in the present international situation with regard both to relations between the United States and France, and to their policies in all parts of the world. In the course of these discussions, which were both direct and searching, they examined the position of the two countries with regard to the Soviet Union and the communist world; and the activities of these two countries in Africa, Asia, and Latin America, including aid to under-developed countries. They also examined means for strengthening the At-lantic Alliance, that fundamental association of free nations.

These conversations have shown the fundamental agreement which exists between the two presidents. In particular, President de Gaulle and President Kennedy confirmed the identity of their views on their commitments and responsibilities towards Berlin.

The conversation which has just taken place allowed the President of France and the President of the United States to know each other and to set forth fully the respective position of the two countries, taking into account the interests and responsibilities incumbent upon each of them.

Thus the talks have made an essential contribution to the development of relations between France and the United States.

The deep solidarity which binds the two nations together in the tradition of Franco-American friendship remains the basis of these relations.

NOTE: The statement was released in Paris.

224 Remarks Upon Arrival at the Schwechat Airport in Vienna. June 3, 1961

Mr. President:

I want to express my appreciation for your very generous welcome. Twenty years ago, 21 years ago, I spent nearly a month in Klagenfurt on the Wörthersee in your beautiful country and, therefore, I am delighted to have an opportunity to visit here again. We are very grateful to the city of Vienna and to the Government of Austria for the hospitality which they have afforded

us, for permitting us to meet on this most important occasion in an effort to improve the prospects for more general understandings between people.

So I wish to thank you again on behalf of my wife and myself and to say that we are proud to be in your country.

Thank you.

NOTE: The President was greeted at the airport by President Adolf Schärf.

225 Joint Statement Following Discussions With Premier Khrushchev in Vienna. June 4, 1961

PRESIDENT KENNEDY and Premier Khrushchev have concluded two days of useful meetings, during which they have reviewed the relationships between the U.S. and the USSR, as well as other questions that are of interest to the two States. Today, in the company of their advisers, they discussed the problems of nuclear testing, disarmament, and Germany. The President and the Chairman reaffirmed their support of a neutral and independent Laos under a government chosen by the Laotians themselves, and of international agreements for insuring that neutrality and independence, and in this connection they have recognized the

importance of an effective cease-fire. The President and the Chairman have agreed to maintain contact on all questions of interest to the two countries and for the whole world.

NOTE: During their meeting Premier Khrushchev handed the President an aide memoire on Berlin and another dealing with the testing of nuclear weapons. On June 17 the White House released the text of the U.S. reply to the latter. Stating that the positions taken by the Soviet delegation at Geneva and at Vienna made it appear that the Soviet Union did not want an agreement banning nuclear weapons testing, the U.S. note urged the adoption of an effective test ban treaty (Department of State Bulletin, vol. 45, pp. 18, 22, 231).

For the President's statement concerning the U.S. reply to the aide memoire on Berlin, see Item 292.

226 Remarks at the Airport in Vienna Upon Leaving for London. June 4, 1961

Mr. President:

I want on behalf of my wife and myself and also the people of the United States to express our great appreciation to the Government of Austria, to you, sir, personally, and to the Mayor and to the people of Vienna.

Twenty-one years elapsed between my only two visits to this ancient city. I hope that less time will be in between the next visit.

I was anxious to come to this city and to this country because the experience of this country demonstrated how it was possible for problems to be solved in such a way that the interests of the people concerned could be protected. And therefore I thought it most appropriate that we meet in this city.

I want to again express my thanks to the people of Austria. They were extremely generous to my wife and to myself. I had not only the opportunity to see Mr. Khru-shchev, the members of your government, but also to hear played the Tales of the Vienna Woods, so that it has been a very pleasant trip—and, unlike Marie Antoinette, I came from Versailles to Schönbrunn.

Thank you.

NOTE: The President's opening words referred to President Schärf.

227   Remarks Upon Arrival at the London Airport.
June 4, 1961

Mr. Prime Minister:

I want to express on behalf of my wife and myself our appreciation for the generous welcome accorded us by Her Majesty the Queen, and by you, sir, and Lady Dorothy Macmillan and the members of your government.

We have had a long and varied journey, and it is a great pleasure to come to this ancient country from which so many of our great traditions in my own country have sprung.

I hope I may say that I come not to Great Britain as a stranger. I spent many months here in the days before the Second War. Two of my sisters had the good judgment to marry citizens of Great Britain, and to-morrow I am about to assume my most sober responsibility, which is to become the god-father of a new English citizen. So I am glad to be here.

I am especially glad, Mr. Prime Minister, to have an opportunity to counsel with you, and I must say that I consider it to be a fitting climax to a journey which has taken us from Washington to Paris, to Vienna, and to London. So, Mr. Prime Minister, I hope you will permit me to say to the citizens of your country that we are very glad to be among them.

NOTE: The President's opening words referred to Prime Minister Harold Macmillan.

228   Remarks to the Staff of the U.S. Embassy in London.
June 5, 1961

AMBASSADOR, I want to express my thanks to you, and also to express my appreciation to those of you who are representing the United States here in this country.

I worked at the American Embassy—not too hard—but I worked here for a few months before the outbreak of World War II and therefore I know this square on which this new building is ranged as well as I do my own street at home.

I want to express how important I believe your responsibility is here in this great country. Our friendship with Great Britain goes back to our earliest beginnings. Our obligations to them for the beneficial influences that they have had in the development of our great political structure I think are known to every American.

But it is not merely sentiment and affection for past associations that makes your assignment so important now. This country, while no longer a far-ranging empire, is a great commonwealth composed of independent nations who are associated with this country. This country is an island which in the standards, physically, of the United States is not large. But nevertheless it has influence, it is persuasive throughout much of the world. The actions it has taken to assist the freedom of people after people around the globe have given it a special prestige. Its diplomats speak with a long tradition of over a thousand years behind them.

And therefore, when you work here in this country, you are working not only with a country of 47 or 50 million people, you are working with a country which, associated with us, believing in the same principles in which we believe, standing for the same things for which we stand, having demonstrated that it stands behind its convictions on many occasions, a people of courage and energy whose judgment is respected. All this makes your assignment especially important.

And it is because of that that I asked Ambassador Bruce, after his long experience, to accept this new responsibility.

There are some of you, I imagine, here who may be citizens of Great Britain, and I do want to express the hope that in working here in the United States Embassy for the United States Government, that you also feel that you are working for the very best interests of your own country.

So I express my thanks to you all, and tell you that having gone just about around the circle from Washington, that I am particularly glad to be in this country where the prospects are so pleasing.

Thank you.

NOTE: The President's opening words referred to David K. E. Bruce, American Ambassador to Great Britain.

229   Transcript of Interview by a Correspondent of the British Broadcasting Company. *June 5, 1961*

THE PRESIDENT [*replying to a question regarding his stay in England*]: Oh well, we have had a great trip here. In addition, as I said, we successfully baptized a godchild, and I had a chance to talk to the Prime Minister for nearly 4 hours, so it was very useful.

Q. Do you feel that because your meeting with Mr. Khrushchev was one in which Mr. Macmillan didn't take part, that the influence of this country in world affairs is very much less than what it was?

THE PRESIDENT. Oh, no—this was not intended to be a summit meeting. Mr. Macmillan himself, the Prime Minister, has seen Mr. Khrushchev on several occasions. But I bear the responsibilities as President of the United States, and I felt it important to have an exchange of views with Mr. Khrushchev, and also to make clear our position; and particularly I was—after that conversation I was anxious to see the Prime Minister.

But this was not a summit meeting but it was an opportunity to make a more precise judgment as to our future course.

Q. It has been a very short stay. I hope you will come back, sir.

THE PRESIDENT. Well, I am delighted. I appreciate that very much indeed.

Correspondent: Thank you very much.

NOTE: The interview was held as the President was leaving the residence of Prince and Princess Radziwill, where he stayed during his visit in London. The President referred to the baptism at Westminster Cathedral of his infant niece, Anna Christina Radziwill.

230 Joint Statement Following Discussion With Prime Minister Macmillan. *June 5,* 1961

AFTER HIS VISITS to Paris and Vienna, President Kennedy paid a short private visit to London on June 4 and 5. This gave the President the opportunity to review the world situation with the Prime Minister in the light of his talks with President de Gaulle and Mr. Khrushchev. The President and Mr. Macmillan were thus able to continue the close personal contact begun in Washington two months ago.

Their discussion covered the major problems, both economic and political, and revealed once again the close agreement of the two governments in pursuing their common purposes.

Occasion was given to review the need for economic collaboration and expansion in the general interest of developed and under-developed countries alike.

On Laos, the President and the Prime Minister noted with satisfaction the agreement in Vienna on the need for an effective cease fire which, in their opinion, should lead to progress in Geneva towards an agreement permitting the establishment of a neutral and independent Laos.

Particular attention was also given to the nuclear tests conference and to the question of disarmament.

The situation in regard to Germany was reviewed and there was full agreement on the necessity of maintaining the rights and obligations of the allied governments in Berlin.

NOTE: The statement was released in London.

231 Radio and Television Report to the American People on Returning From Europe. *June 6,* 1961

[Delivered from the President's Office at 7 p.m.]

Good evening, my fellow citizens:

I returned this morning from a weeklong trip to Europe and I want to report to you on that trip in full. It was in every sense an unforgettable experience. The people of Paris, of Vienna, of London, were generous in their greeting. They were heartwarming in their hospitality, and their graciousness to my wife is particularly appreciated.

We knew of course that the crowds and the shouts were meant in large measure for the country that we represented, which is regarded as the chief defender of freedom. Equally memorable was the pageantry of European history and their culture that is very much a part of any ceremonial reception, to lay a wreath at the Arc de Triomphe, to dine at Versailles, and Schönbrunn Palace, and with the Queen of England. These are the colorful memories that will remain with us for many years to come. Each of the three cities that we visited—Paris, Vienna, and London—have existed for many centuries, and each serves as a reminder that the Western civilization that we seek to preserve has flowered over many years, and has defended itself over many centuries. But this was not a ceremonial trip. Two aims of American foreign policy, above all others, were the reason for the trip: the unity of the free world, whose strength is the security of us all, and the eventual achievement of a lasting peace. My trip was devoted to the advancement of these two aims.

To strengthen the unity of the West, our journey opened in Paris and closed in London. My talks with General de Gaulle were profoundly encouraging to me. Certain differences in our attitudes on one or another problem became insignificant in view of our common commitment to defend freedom. Our alliance, I believe, became more secure; the friendship of our nation, I hope—with theirs—became firmer; and the relations between the two of us who bear responsibility became closer, and I hope were marked by confidence. I found General de Gaulle far more interested in our frankly stating our position, whether or not it was his own, than in appearing to agree with him when we do not. But he knows full well the true meaning of an alliance. He is after all the only major leader of World War II who still occupies a position of great responsibility. His life has been one of unusual dedication; he is a man of extraordinary personal character, symbolizing the new strength and the historic grandeur of France. Throughout our discussions he took the long view of France and the world at large. I found him a wise counselor for the future, and an informative guide to the history that he has helped to make. Thus we had a valuable meeting.

I believe that certain doubts and suspicions that might have come up in a long time—I believe were removed on both sides. Problems which proved to be not of substance but of wording or procedure were cleared away. No question, however sensitive, was avoided. No area of interest was ignored, and the conclusions that we reached will be important for the future—in our agreement on defending Berlin, on working to improve the defenses of Europe, on aiding the economic and political independence of the underdeveloped world, including Latin America, on spurring European economic unity, on concluding successfully the conference on Laos, and on closer consultations and solidarity in the Western alliance.

General de Gaulle could not have been more cordial, and I could not have more confidence in any man. In addition to his individual strength of character, the French people as a whole showed vitality and energy which were both impressive and gratifying. Their recovery from the postwar period is dramatic, their productivity is increasing, and they are steadily building their stature in both Europe and Africa, and thus, I left Paris for Vienna with increased confidence in Western unity and strength.

The people of Vienna know what it is to live under occupation, and they know what it is to live in freedom. Their welcome to me as President of this country should be heartwarming to us all. I went to Vienna to meet the leader of the Soviet Union, Mr. Khrushchev. For 2 days we met in sober, intensive conversation, and I believe it is my obligation to the people, to the Congress, and to our allies to report on those conversations candidly and publicly.

Mr. Khrushchev and I had a very full and frank exchange of views on the major issues that now divide our two countries. I will tell you now that it was a very sober 2 days. There was no discourtesy, no loss of tempers, no threats or ultimatums by either side; no advantage or concession was either gained or given; no major decision was either planned or taken; no spectacular progress was either achieved or pretended.

This kind of informal exchange may not be as exciting as a full-fledged summit meeting with a fixed agenda and a large corps of advisers, where negotiations are attempted and new agreements sought, but this was not intended to be and was not such a meeting, nor did we plan any future summit meetings at Vienna.

But I found this meeting with Chairman Khrushchev, as somber as it was, to be immensely useful. I had read his speeches and of his policies. I had been advised on his views. I had been told by other leaders of the West, General de Gaulle, Chancellor Adenauer, Prime Minister Macmillan, what manner of man he was.

But I bear the responsibility of the Presidency of the United States, and it is my duty to make decisions that no adviser and no ally can make for me. It is my obligation and responsibility to see that these decisions are as informed as possible, that they are based on as much direct, firsthand knowledge as possible.

I therefore thought it was of immense importance that I know Mr. Khrushchev, that I gain as much insight and understanding as I could on his present and future policies. At the same time, I wanted to make certain Mr. Khrushchev knew this country and its policies, that he understood our strength and our determination, and that he knew that we desired peace with all nations of every kind.

I wanted to present our views to him directly, precisely, realistically, and with an opportunity for discussion and clarification. This was done. No new aims were stated in private that have not been stated in public on either side. The gap between us was not, in such a short period, materially reduced, but at least the channels of communications were opened more fully, at least the chances of a dangerous misjudgment on either side should now be less, and at least the men on whose decisions the peace in part depends have agreed to remain in contact.

This is important, for neither of us tried to merely please the other, to agree merely to be agreeable, to say what the other wanted to hear. And just as our judicial system relies on witnesses appearing in court and on cross-examination, instead of hearsay testimony or affidavits on paper, so, too, was this direct give-and-take of immeasurable value in making clear and precise what we considered to be vital, for the facts of the matter are that the Soviets and ourselves give wholly different meanings to the same words—war, peace, democracy, and popular will.

We have wholly different views of right and wrong, of what is an internal affair and what is aggression, and, above all, we have wholly different concepts of where the world is and where it is going.

Only by such a discussion was it possible for me to be sure that Mr. Khrushchev knew how differently we view the present and the future. Our views contrasted sharply but at least we knew better at the end where we both stood. Neither of us was there to dictate a settlement or to convert the other to a cause or to concede our basic interests. But both of us were there, I think, because we realized that each nation has the power to inflict enormous damage upon the other, that such a war could and should be avoided if at all possible, since it would settle no dispute and prove no doctrine, and that care should thus be taken to prevent our conflicting interests from so directly confronting each other that war necessarily ensued. We believe in a system of national freedom and independence. He believes in an expanding and dynamic concept of world communism, and the question was whether these two systems can ever hope to live in peace without permitting any loss of security or any denial of the freedom of our friends. However difficult it may seem to answer this question in the affirmative as we approach so many harsh tests, I think we owe it to all mankind to make every possible effort. That is why I considered the Vienna talks to be useful. The somber mood that they conveyed was not cause for elation or relaxation, nor was it cause for undue pessimism or fear. It simply demonstrated how much work we in the free world have to do and how long and hard a struggle must be our fate as Americans in this generation as the chief defenders of the cause of liberty. The one area which afforded some immediate prospect of accord was Laos. Both sides recognized the need to reduce the dangers in that situation. Both sides endorsed the concept of a neutral and independent Laos, much in the manner of Burma or Cambodia.

Of critical importance to the current conference on Laos in Geneva, both sides recognized the importance of an effective cease-fire. It is urgent that this be translated into new attitudes at Geneva, enabling the International Control Commission to do its duty, to make certain that a cease-fire is enforced and maintained. I am hopeful that progress can be made on this matter in the coming days at Geneva for that would greatly improve international atmosphere.

No such hope emerged, however, with respect to the other deadlocked Geneva conference, seeking a treaty to ban nuclear tests. Mr. Khrushchev made it clear that there could not be a neutral administrator—in his opinion because no one was truly neutral; that a Soviet veto would have to apply to acts of enforcement; that inspection was only a subterfuge for espionage, in the absence of total disarmament; and that the present test ban negotiations appeared futile. In short, our hopes for an end to nuclear tests, for an end to the spread of nuclear weapons, and for some slowing down of the arms race have been struck a serious blow. Nevertheless, the stakes are too important for us to abandon the draft treaty we have offered at Geneva.

But our most somber talks were on the subject of Germany and Berlin. I made it clear to Mr. Khrushchev that the security of Western Europe and therefore our own security are deeply involved in our presence and our access rights to West Berlin, that those rights are based on law and not on sufferance, and that we are determined to maintain those rights at any risk, and thus meet our obligation to the people of West Berlin, and their right to choose their own future.

Mr. Khrushchev, in turn, presented his views in detail, and his presentation will be the subject of further communications. But we are not seeking to change the present situation. A binding German peace treaty is a matter for all who were at war with Germany, and we and our allies cannot abandon our obligations to the people of West Berlin.

Generally, Mr. Khrushchev did not talk in terms of war. He believes the world will move his way without resort to force. He spoke of his nation's achievements in space. He stressed his intention to outdo us in industrial production, to outtrade us, to prove to the world the superiority of his system over ours. Most of all, he predicted the triumph of communism in the new and less developed countries.

He was certain that the tide there was moving his way, that the revolution of rising peoples would eventually be a Communist revolution, and that the so-called wars of liberation, supported by the Kremlin, would replace the old methods of direct aggression and invasion.

In the 1940's and early fifties, the great danger was from Communist armies marching across free borders, which we saw in

444

Korea. Our nuclear monopoly helped to prevent this in other areas. Now we face a new and different threat. We no longer have a nuclear monopoly. Their missiles, they believe, will hold off our missiles, and their troops can match our troops should we intervene in these so-called wars of liberation. Thus, the local conflict they support can turn in their favor through guerrillas or insurgents or subversion. A small group of disciplined Communists could exploit discontent and misery in a country where the average income may be $60 or $70 a year, and seize control, therefore, of an entire country without Communist troops ever crossing any international frontier. This is the Communist theory.

But I believe just as strongly that time will prove it wrong, that liberty and independence and self-determination—not communism—is the future of man, and that free men have the will and the resources to win the struggle for freedom. But it is clear that this struggle in this area of the new and poorer nations will be a continuing crisis of this decade.

Mr. Khrushchev made one point which I wish to pass on. He said there are many disorders throughout the world, and he should not be blamed for them all. He is quite right. It is easy to dismiss as Communist-inspired every anti-government or anti-American riot, every overthrow of a corrupt regime, or every mass protest against misery and despair. These are not all Communist-inspired. The Communists move in to exploit them, to infiltrate their leadership, to ride their crest to victory. But the Communists did not create the conditions which caused them.

In short, the hopes for freedom in these areas which see so much poverty and illiteracy, so many children who are sick, so many children who die in the first year, so many

families without homes, so many families without hope—the future for freedom in these areas rests with the local peoples and their governments.

If they have the will to determine their own future, if their governments have the support of their own people, if their honest and progressive measures—helping their people—have inspired confidence and zeal, then no guerrilla or insurgent action can succeed. But where those conditions do not exist, a military guarantee against external attack from across a border offers little protection against internal decay.

Yet all this does not mean that our Nation and the West and the free world can only sit by. On the contrary, we have an historic opportunity to help these countries build their societies until they are so strong and broadly based that only an outside invasion could topple them, and that threat, we know, can be stopped.

We can train and equip their forces to resist Communist-supplied insurrections. We can help develop the industrial and agricultural base on which new living standards can be built. We can encourage better administration and better education and better tax and land distribution and a better life for the people.

All this and more we can do because we have the talent and the resources to do it, if we will only use and share them. I know that there is a great deal of feeling in the United States that we have carried the burden of economic assistance long enough, but these countries that we are now supporting—stretching all the way along from the top of Europe through the Middle East, down through Saigon—are now subject to great efforts internally, in many of them, to seize control.

If we're not prepared to assist them in making a better life for their people, then I believe that the prospects for freedom in those areas are uncertain. We must, I believe, assist them if we are determined to meet with commitments of assistance our words against the Communist advance. The burden is heavy; we have carried it for many years. But I believe that this fight is not over. This battle goes on, and we have to play our part in it. And therefore I hope again that we will assist these people so that they can remain free.

It was fitting that Congress opened its hearings on our new foreign military and economic aid programs in Washington at the very time that Mr. Khrushchev's words in Vienna were demonstrating as nothing else could the need for that very program. It should be well run, effectively administered, but I believe we must do it, and I hope that you, the American people, will support it again, because I think it's vitally important to the security of these areas. There is no use talking against the Communist advance unless we're willing to meet our responsibilities, however burdensome they may be.

I do not justify this aid merely on the grounds of anti-Communism. It is a recognition of our opportunity and obligation to help these people be free, and we are not alone.

I found that the people of France, for example, were doing far more in Africa in the way of aiding independent nations than our own country was. But I know that foreign aid is a burden that is keenly felt and I can only say that we have no more crucial obligation now.

My stay in England was short but the visit gave me a chance to confer privately again with Prime Minister Macmillan, just as others of our party in Vienna were conferring yesterday with General de Gaulle and Chancellor Adenauer. We all agreed that there is work to be done in the West and from our conversations have come agreed steps to get on with that work. Our day in London, capped by a meeting with Queen Elizabeth and Prince Philip was a strong reminder at the end of a long journey that the West remains united in its determination to hold to its standards.

May I conclude by saying simply that I am glad to be home. We have on this trip admired splendid places and seen stirring sights, but we are glad to be home. No demonstration of support abroad could mean so much as the support which you, the American people, have so generously given to our country. With that support I am not fearful of the future. We must be patient. We must be determined. We must be courageous. We must accept both risks and burdens, but with the will and the work freedom will prevail.

Good night, and thank you very much.

232 Remarks at Annapolis to the Graduating Class of the United States Naval Academy. *June 7, 1961*

Admiral, Mr. Secretary, members of the Joint Chiefs of Staff, members of the faculty, members of the Graduating Class and their families:

I am proud as a citizen of the United States to come to this institution and this room where there is concentrated so many men who have committed themselves to the defense of the United States. I am honored to be here.

In the past I have had some slight contact with this Service, though I never did reach the state of professional and physical perfection where I could hope that anyone would ever mistake me for an Annapolis graduate.

I know that you are constantly warned during your days here not to mix, in your Naval career, in politics. I should point out, however, on the other side, that my rather rapid rise from a Reserve Lieutenant, of uncertain standing, to Commander-in-Chief, has been because I did not follow that very good advice.

I trust, however, that those of you who are Regulars will, for a moment, grant a retired civilian officer some measure of fellowship.

Nearly a half century ago, President Woodrow Wilson came here to Annapolis on a similar mission, and addressed the Class of 1914. On that day, the graduating class numbered 154 men. There has been, since that time, a revolution in the size of our military establishment, and that revolution has been reflected in the revolution in the world around us.

When Wilson addressed the class in 1914, the Victorian structure of power was still intact, the world was dominated by Europe, and Europe itself was the scene of an uneasy balance of power between dominant figures and America was a spectator on a remote sideline.

The autumn after Wilson came to Annapolis, the Victorian world began to fall to pieces, and our world one-half a century later is vastly different. Today we are witnesses to the most extraordinary revolution, nearly, in the history of the world, as the emergent nations of Latin America, Africa, and Asia awaken from long centuries of torpor and impatience.

Today the Victorian certitudes which were taken to be so much a part of man's natural existence are under siege by a faith committed to the destruction of liberal civiliza-

tion, and today the United States is no longer the spectator, but the leader.

This half century, therefore, has not only revolutionized the size of our military establishment, it has brought about also a more striking revolution in the things that the Nation expects from the men in our Service.

Fifty years ago the graduates of the Naval Academy were expected to be seamen and leaders of men. They were reminded of the saying of John Paul Jones, "Give me a fair ship so that I might go into harm's way."

When Captain Mahan began to write in the nineties on the general issues of war and peace and naval strategy, the Navy quickly shipped him to sea duty. Today we expect all of you—in fact, you must, of necessity—be prepared not only to handle a ship in a storm or a landing party on a beach, but to make great determinations which affect the survival of this country.

The revolution in the technology of war makes it necessary in order that you, when you hold positions of command, may make an educated judgment between various techniques, that you also be a scientist and an engineer and a physicist, and your responsibilities go far beyond the classic problems of tactics and strategy.

In the years to come, some of you will serve as your Commandant did last year, as an adviser to foreign governments; some will negotiate as Admiral Burke did, in Korea, with other governments on behalf of the United States; some will go to the far reaches of space and some will go to the bottom of the ocean. Many of you from one time or another, in the positions of command, or as members of staff, will participate in great decisions which go far beyond the narrow reaches of professional competence.

You gentlemen, therefore, have a most important responsibility, to recognize that your education is just beginning, and to be

447

prepared, in the most difficult period in the life of our country, to play the role that the country hopes and needs and expects from you. You must understand not only this country but other countries. You must know something about strategy and tactics and logic—logistics, but also economics and politics and diplomacy and history. You must know everything you can know about military power, and you must also understand the limits of military power. You must understand that few of the important problems of our time have, in the final analysis, been finally solved by military power alone. When I say that officers today must go far beyond the official curriculum, I say it not because I do not believe in the traditional relationship between the civilian and the military, but you must be more than the servants of national policy. You must be prepared to play a constructive role in the development of national policy, a policy which protects our interests and our security and the peace of the world. Woodrow Wilson reminded your predecessors that you were not serving a government or an administration, but a people. In serving the American people, you represent the American people and the best of the ideals of this free society. Your posture and your performance will provide many people far beyond our shores, who know very little of our country, the only evidence they will ever see as to whether America is truly dedicated to the cause of justice and freedom.

In my inaugural address, I said that each citizen should be concerned not with what his country can do for him, but what he can do for his country. What you have chosen to do for your country, by devoting your life to the service of our country, is the greatest contribution that any man could make. It is easy for you, in a moment of exhilara-

tion today, to say that you freely and gladly dedicate your life to the United States. But the life of service is a constant test of your will.

It will be hard at times to face the personal sacrifice and the family inconvenience, to maintain this high resolve, to place the needs of your country above all else. When there is a visible enemy to fight, the tide of patriotism in this country runs strong. But when there is a long, slow struggle, with no immediate visible foe, when you watch your contemporaries indulging the urge for material gain and comfort and personal advancement, your choice will seem hard, and you will recall, I am sure, the lines found in an old sentry box at Gibraltar, "God and the soldier all men adore in time of trouble and no more, for when war is over, and all things righted, God is neglected and the old soldier slighted."

Never forget, however, that the battle for freedom takes many forms. Those who through vigilance and firmness and devotion are the great servants of this country—and let us have no doubt that the United States needs your devoted assistance today.

The answer to those who challenge us so severely in so many parts of the globe lies in our willingness to freely commit ourselves to the maintenance of our country and the things for which it stands.

This ceremony today represents the kind of commitment which you are willing to make. For that reason, I am proud to be here. This nation salutes you as you commence your service to our country in the hazardous days ahead. And on behalf of all of them, I congratulate you and thank you.

NOTE: The President spoke at 11:04 a.m. at the Field House. His opening words "Admiral, Mr. Secretary" referred to Rear Adm. John F. Davidson, Superintendent of the Naval Academy, and John B. Connally, Jr., Secretary of the Navy.

233 Letter to the President of the Senate and to the Speaker of the House on Youth Employment Opportunities and Training.
June 7, 1961

My dear Mr. ————:

I am transmitting herewith a draft bill to provide useful employment and training on a pilot basis for young men and women between the ages of 16 and 22.

As set forth in more detail in the enclosed letter to me from the Secretary of Labor and the accompanying memorandum, this legislation would provide pilot programs over a three-year period, designed to develop the most effective methods of assisting our young people in acquiring the skills necessary for productive employment. The draft legislation would establish three different pilot programs through which young people can equip themselves for suitable employment: (1) on-the-job training; (2) a Youth Conservation Corps, and (3) local public service and public works programs performed in the areas in which the youths reside.

The progress we make as a Nation depends upon the use we make of our resources, including manpower. And it is especially important that our young people—the real key to our National future—be prepared to contribute to our economic growth.

Forecasts of the difficulty they can expect to meet in the next few years in finding suitable employment make it clear that we must act without delay. The approaches to this problem proposed in the attached draft will provide a solid base upon which an effective program can be built. We believe, too, that they will stimulate action by all elements of our communities, both public and private, in developing employment opportunities and training for our youth.

A letter similar to this is being sent to the Speaker of the House (President of the Senate).

Sincerely,

JOHN F. KENNEDY

NOTE: This is the text of identical letters addressed to the Honorable Lyndon B. Johnson, President of the Senate, and to the Honorable Sam Rayburn, Speaker of the House of Representatives.

234 Remarks at a Dinner of the Big Brothers of America.
June 7, 1961

Mr. Pearson, Mr. Vice President, Mr. Foley, Mr. Donohue, Judge Youngdahl, Mrs. Boggs, Justice Clark, ladies and gentlemen:

I hope it was only a tradition that prevented Drew Pearson from launching into a more generous eulogy in that introduction.

I wanted to get you on the record but we'll have to wait.

I was anxious to come here tonight for two reasons. First, because this dinner honored an outstanding citizen, Ed Foley, whose speech tonight, once again, I think indicates and illustrates why he is held in high regard by so many of the people here, by President Truman and others with whom he has lived and worked. And also because I think this cause which has brought together a good many busy people who have many other obligations and many other interests, is a most important cause to this country.

Drew Pearson had in his article this morning some statistics which I would hope every American would read. And I have three statistics here which I think are important.

449

In the next 10 years 7½ million American young people will drop out of school before they graduate. Two and a half million will not have finished the eighth grade. In the next 10 years 26 million men and women, boys and girls, 25 years or under will come under the labor market and be looking for jobs. And during that same period of time the jobs available to those who are only semiskilled, who are not well-educated, who are not well-adjusted, who are not well-motivated, those jobs will become less and less.

Now, I feel that we are a city on a hill and that one of our great responsibilities during these days is to make sure that we in this country set an example to the world not only of helping and assisting them to fulfill their own destiny, but also demonstrating what a free people can do. We cannot possibly permit, therefore, the waste of hundreds and thousands of young boys and girls, who grow up in underprivileged areas, many of them in our northern cities, ignored in many cases by their families and their community, who drift into life without hope of ever developing their talents and who ultimately may end up, as so many do, in a life of crime when they're young, which stains their life from then on.

This is a free society, and many people write to me once in a while and say, "Will you say what can we do for America? What are we supposed to do?" Well, I suppose they feel that it might be easier if you could write back and say that you want them to go ashore on a bombarded beach, or to take some action one afternoon which would make a significant difference in the life and survival of our country. But those are not really the responsibilities, the kind of responsibilities which we're going to have to meet in the coming days and years. It's a much

slower and more gradual task. There is no final definite responsibility or commitment which we must accept, and if accept, fulfill our responsibility. We must do all the gradual things which are unspectacular and in many cases seem unrewarding—to help a foreign student or to do what you are doing here tonight.

No one in the United States other than those who are associated in your work will possibly recognize that the effort that you make here tonight or, more importantly, that is made week by week, year by year, to assist one, two, or three boys or girls—no one could possibly feel that that represents a significant contribution to the maintenance of our country. But if it's done by enough people for enough periods of time it will represent a significant contribution.

The Government of the United States, the Vice President, or the President, cannot possibly in a free society command, or should they, those actions for the benefit of the state which our adversaries are able to do with ease. These things must be done in a voluntary manner. And they must be done by our own individual impulse. Therefore, I think this work that you are doing is work which is most important in a most important time in the life of our country.

If in that effort you are able by the passage of some hours of a busy life to make a significant difference in the life of one of our fellow Americans, who might, without your help slip into an experience which could prevent him from ever fulfilling his responsibilities to the maximum as a participant in our society, then I would hope you would feel that you've not only met your own obligations as an individual but also as a participating member of a great society.

So I congratulate you tonight and those

who are joined with you. This is the sort of thing that I mean when I say what we can do for America.

NOTE: The President spoke at the Mayflower Hotel in Washington. His opening words referred to Drew Pearson, President of the Big Brothers of the National Capital Area, Vice President Lyndon B. Johnson, Edward H. Foley, one of the founders of the Big Brothers of the National Capital Area, F. Joseph Donohue, member of the Board of Directors of the Big Brothers of the National Capital Area, Luther W. Youngdahl, Judge of the District Court for the District of Columbia, Mrs. Hale Boggs, chairman of the women's division for the dinner, and Tom C. Clark, Associate Justice of the Supreme Court.

235 Remarks of Welcome to President Youlou of the Republic of Congo at the Washington National Airport. *June 8*, 1961

Mr. President, Mr. Secretary, Lieutenant Sita:

I wish to express my great pleasure at this country being honored by your visit. You have played a most important and significant role in the most important event in the life of any country. And that is its emergence into a free, sovereign and independent status.

It is therefore a particular source of satisfaction to welcome you to the United States, which also many years ago passed through a similar experience, which has a comprehension of the things for which you stand and the things for which your country stands.

It is therefore a particular source of pleasure to me, Mr. President, to inform you that we recognize in your life and in your efforts and in your commitments, a strong passion for freedom for your own people and for people everywhere.

And therefore, Mr. President, you come to us today from a distant continent, but you come as a statesman whom we admire as a friend of freedom and as one who believes in increasing the cordial relations between your distinguished country and this country.

Mr. President, we're proud to have you here.

NOTE: The President's opening words referred to President Fulbert Youlou of the Republic of Congo, Secretary of State Dean Rusk, and Lt. Albert Sita of the Congolese Army, Aide-de-Camp to President Youlou.

236 Joint Statement Following Discussions With President Youlou. *June 8*, 1961

PRESIDENT KENNEDY and President Youlou met today and discussed problems of joint interest to their governments. The ties that bind the Republic of Congo to the United States were stressed including their common links with the European continent and western civilization.

President Youlou stressed that his visit to the United States was not for the purpose of securing immediate financial assistance but the two Presidents entered into a discussion of the economic problems of the Congo and long-range economic development of that country. A great part of the economic discussion between President Kennedy and President Youlou centered on the future hydro-electric development of the Congo which will provide the basis of a planned industrial expansion.

In discussing the affairs of the Congo and

451

of the world, they found that they had a common approach to the problems of the free world.

President Youlou gave President Kennedy

his impressions on the way of preserving and developing the traditional heritage of the western civilization in Africa.

237   Special Message to the Congress Transmitting Reorganization Plan 6 of 1961.   *June 12, 1961*

To the Congress of the United States:

I transmit herewith Reorganization Plan No. 6 of 1961, prepared in accordance with the provisions of the Reorganization Act of 1949, as amended, and providing for reorganizations in the Federal Home Loan Bank Board.

Reorganization Plan No. 6 of 1961 relates to my message of April 13, 1961, to the Congress regarding regulatory agencies and, in particular, to that portion of the message advocating the fixing of responsibility for the overall administration of multi-headed agencies in their chairmen. The reorganization plan also is in keeping with actions begun by President Truman, largely through reorganization plans, to strengthen the internal management of multi-headed agencies by making their chairmen, rather than the boards or commissions as a whole, responsible for day-to-day administration.

The first Commission on Organization of the Executive Branch of the Government concluded that purely executive duties can be performed far better by a single administrative official and stated: "Administration by a plural executive is universally regarded as inefficient." Also, as a matter of sound organization, the Congress and the President should be able to hold a single official rather than a group accountable for the effective management of an agency. The reorganization plan will meet both of those needs by placing responsibility and authority for the administration of the activities of the

Federal Home Loan Bank Board in the Chairman of the Board. By relieving the Board of day-to-day managerial functions, the reorganization plan will significantly further the ability of the Board to deal more effectively with regulatory and policy matters before it.

Action to strengthen the management of the Federal Home Loan Bank Board and to relieve the Board of day-to-day operating responsibility is particularly needed because of the phenomenal growth of the Board's activities in recent years. By way of example, the number of institutions that are members of the Federal home loan bank system and subject to the Board's supervision has increased from 3898 in 1950 to 4552 at present. In the same period, the assets of those institutions have increased almost fivefold from $15.4 billion to $71.0 billion. In fiscal year 1950, the Board examined 2450 institutions; in fiscal 1961, about 4224 examinations will be conducted. The personnel of the Board have more than doubled in number in the last decade to handle the increased workload.

Pursuant to Reorganization Plan No. 3 of 1947, the Chairman of the Home Loan Bank Board was made the chief executive officer of the Board, and there was transferred to him the authority to appoint and direct the personnel necessary to perform the functions of the Board, the Chairman and the agencies under the Board. The Chairman's authority with respect to personnel was returned to the whole Federal Home Loan Bank Board by the Housing Amendments of 1955. The reorganization plan herewith transmitted would restore that authority of the Chairman and further increase his management functions.

Specifically, the reorganization plan will transfer to the Chairman of the Federal Home Loan Bank Board the Board's functions with respect to the overall management, functioning and organization of the agency; the appointment, removal and direction of personnel; the distribution of business among, and communication of Board policies to, such personnel; and the enforcement of policies and the general improvement of staff support. There are also transferred to the Chairman functions relating to preparation, review, presentation and justification of budget estimates and other fund authorizations and those relating to the allocation, use and expenditure of funds available for administrative expenses.

Nothing in the plan impinges upon the ability of the members of the Board to act independently with respect to substantive matters that come before them for decision, or to participate in the shaping of Board policies. In carrying out his managerial functions, the Chairman will be governed by the policies of the Board and the determina-

tions it is authorized to make. The Board will have the authority to approve the Chairman's appointments of the heads of major administrative units, and the other members of the Board will retain their present control over the personnel in their immediate offices.

The taking effect of the reorganizations included in the accompanying reorganization plan will provide sound organizational arrangements and will make possible more economical and expeditious administration of the affected functions. It is, however, impractical to itemize at this time the reductions in expenditures which it is probable will be brought about by such taking effect.

After investigation, I have found and hereby declare that each reorganization included in the reorganization plan transmitted herewith is necessary to accomplish one or more of the purposes set forth in section 2(a) of the Reorganization Act of 1949, as amended.

I recommend that the Congress allow the reorganization plan to become effective.

JOHN F. KENNEDY

NOTE: Reorganization Plan 6 of 1961 is published in the Federal Register (26 F.R. 7541). It became effective on August 12, 1961.

238   Special Message to the Congress Transmitting Reorganization Plan 7 of 1961. *June 12, 1961*

To the Congress of the United States:

I transmit herewith Reorganization Plan No. 7 of 1961, prepared in accordance with the Reorganization Act of 1949, as amended, and providing for the reorganization of maritime functions.

The basic objective of the plan is to strengthen and revitalize the administration of our Federal programs concerned with the

promotion and development of the United States merchant marine by concentrating responsibility in separate agencies for the performance of regulatory and promotional functions. The plan provides, therefore, for the creation of a separate Federal Maritime Commission, composed of five commissioners, which would be charged with the regulatory functions of the present Federal

Maritime Board. There would be transferred from the Federal Maritime Board to the Secretary of Commerce the award of subsidies and related promotional functions. The Secretary of Commerce would retain the functions transferred to him by Reorganization Plan No. 21 of 1950 which reorganized the United States Maritime Commission into a Federal Maritime Board and a Maritime Administration in the Department of Commerce. The plan retains the present Maritime Administration, provides for an Administrator as head thereof, retains a Deputy Maritime Administrator, and effects no change in the Office of the Under Secretary of Commerce for Transportation. The Federal Maritime Board is abolished.

Existing organizational arrangements have not proved to be satisfactory. The development and maintenance of a sound maritime industry require that the Federal Government carry out its dual responsibilities for regulation and promotion with equal vigor and effectiveness. Intermingling of regulatory and promotional functions has tended in this instance to dilute responsibility and has led to serious inadequacies, particularly in the administration of regulatory functions. Recent findings by Committees of the Congress disclose serious violations of maritime laws and point to the urgent need for a reorganization to vest in completely separate agencies responsibility for (1) regulatory functions and (2) promotional and operating functions.

The plan would provide the most appropriate organizational framework for each of the functions concerned. Regulation would be made the exclusive responsibility of a separate Commission organized along the general lines of other regulatory agencies. On the other hand, non-regulatory functions, including the determination and award of subsidies and other promotional and operat-

ing activities, would be concentrated in the head of the Department of Commerce. The Secretary of Commerce is best qualified to coordinate these activities with other transportation and related economic programs.

The vesting of all subsidy functions in the Secretary of Commerce will make it possible for the Congress and the President to hold a single official responsible and accountable for the effective conduct of all aspects of this program, including the size and character of the fleet under the United States flag, the need for Government assistance and requirements for appropriations to support subsidy programs. Furthermore, the placing of these functions in the Secretary of Commerce will assure essential supervision and review of subsidy awards.

The taking effect of the reorganizations included in the accompanying reorganization plan will result in a modest increase in expenditures. The improved organizational alignments provided by the plan will, however, make possible a more effective and expeditious administration of the statutory objectives to foster and promote a United States merchant marine capable of meeting the Nation's needs in peace and war. Failure to meet these objectives would be far more costly than the anticipated increase in expenditures under the plan.

After investigation, I have found and hereby declare that each reorganization included in Reorganization Plan No. 7 of 1961 is necessary to accomplish one or more of the purposes set forth in section 2(a) of the Reorganization Act of 1949, as amended.

I have also found and hereby declare that it is necessary to include in the accompanying reorganization plan, by reason of reorganizations made thereby, provisions for the appointment and compensation of new officers specified in sections 102 and 201 of the plan. The rates of compensation fixed for these officers are, respectively, those which I have found to prevail in respect of comparable officers in the executive branch of the Government.

I recommend that the Congress allow the

reorganization plan to become effective.

JOHN F. KENNEDY

NOTE: Reorganization Plan 7 of 1961 is published in the Federal Register (26 F.R. 7315). It became effective on August 12, 1961.

239   Toasts of the President and Prime Minister Fanfani of Italy. *June* 12, 1961

I WOULD LIKE to express on behalf of us all our great pleasure in having the Prime Minister here today.

I had the opportunity to meet the Prime Minister when he came to the two conventions of our political parties of 1956. I think maybe he and Congressman Anfuso may have come together but in spite of having visited the Democratic Convention of 1956, he politically has been able to maintain— unlearn all the lessons he learned there— maintain his political power and influence and prestige in his own country.

I want to say that we are very appreciative to the Prime Minister for coming here. Our countries are closely allied and associated. His country occupies, as history has shown us for the last two thousand years, a most important strategic position. And although the geography of the world may be somewhat different than it was when his country began its great rise, nevertheless the basic fact of the commanding position of Italy in the Mediterranean, the southern part of Europe, is an influence which stretches all the way across the Mediterranean into Africa, the Middle East. All these things have helped make his country play a paramount role in the days, certainly of all of our years, and particularly since the end of the Second War. So that I think at a time when the Western Alliance and the Atlantic Alliance is faced with most serious and critical problems of decisions, I think that it's

very appropriate that we should have the advice and counsel of the Prime Minister and also be able better to coordinate the two policies of our two countries.

May I say also, Prime Minister, that those who become fainthearted about our problems today I think might consider the extraordinary record of your own country: the tremendous increase in its economic growth, which has been at a higher percentage than ours has; the real, the successful, effort which your country has made to meet its internal economic problem, which was serious after the war; the fact that it's played an increasing important role in NATO. It has more than met its commitments to NATO for an increase in its forces each year. It has been willing to accept and participate greatly in the strengthening of the European community, as one of the six, and also in the Atlantic Community and also NATO, and its influence, particularly in areas such as Latin America, which go far beyond its geography. I think all these things make us particularly glad to have you here. And for those Americans who have failed to realize the extraordinary rise of Italian strength and vigor, I would remind them of a newspaper story which appeared around February or March this year which said Italy had assisted the United States to get some of its gold back and was helping the United States economically now. So we are very appreciative.

So I hope that you all will join with me in expressing our great pleasure at having at our side as a country, the people of Italy, and having the advantage of having the Prime Minister and the Foreign Minister, the Ambassador, members of the Government, here at a time when we commonly face, as we have so many times in the past, serious problems and decisions. So I hope you will join in drinking to the President of the Republic of Italy.

NOTE: The President proposed the toast at a luncheon at the White House. The Prime Minister responded as follows:

Mr. President:

Allow me at this time to express my profound gratitude, first for your kind invitation that you extended to me to come to your country and indeed for the warm welcome that you have bestowed upon me, upon Foreign Minister Segni and members of our party.

You have also seen fit to remember the occasion on which we met at the convention in Chicago in 1956.

In fact it was right after the conversation I had with you, Mr. President, Ambassador Stevenson called me apart. He asked me on that occasion in his capacity as Secretary of the Democratic Party how the propaganda machinery was set up in a political party in Italy.

I explained to him how this was done and he thereafter called one of his colleagues over to him and said, "See how they do it." Then he turned to me and said, "For the time being we will keep doing things as we have. But if we lose this election we will come to Italy and settle down."

You expressed the hope that I unlearned what I had picked up at the convention after my return to Italy, but the fact is that there are many things that I have indeed learned.

And then you will remember how in our convention that transpired in October 1956 we introduced a few little grassroots in administrative and organizational twists that we had picked up in Chicago and San Francisco.

Then in the summer of 1958 Mr. Stevenson came to my summer home to pay me a visit. At that time we set him up with a little cart being pulled by a Sardinian donkey. Mr. Stevenson asked me if I thought it would be good for the next election and I said I thought it would. "But suppose Eisenhower comes here, what are you going to put him on?" I said I would put him on an elephant!

All joking aside, Mr. President, as you see I did learn some very useful things from what I observed at your political conventions and from my observations of the democratic way of life of your people.

You can imagine how overjoyed I am at after having once met you in Chicago I could now—I have been able to come here now today and meet you and find you at the head of this great Nation and to be able to express to you how glad we are to see you at the head of this Nation—strong, democratic, and free.

And I should also like to bring to mind with great pleasure the common fight which we have maintained together in favor of peace and freedom. The United States—the people of the United States and the people of Italy march forward together in this fight, especially since the Second World War.

And I am glad that you recalled that on the basis of this inspiration the people of Italy since that time has permitted its government beginning with the policies of de Gasperi to operate in such a way that the people on the basis of his operations were able to pursue in peace all blessings of liberty.

This year on the 16th of March for the first time ever the United States and the President of the United States have celebrated the first centennial of Italian unity. We should like to express our profoundest appreciation for this testimony—this testimony to the world, to the closeness which binds our two people together.

We are also very gratified to be able to say now that in the last 15 years of our history as out of 100, Italy has been able to realize more progress than it ever did during all these preceding 85 years.

And the other day a public statement by the President of the Bank of Italy revealed that income in Italy over the last 100 years has increased threefold. Half of this increase has been accomplished during the last 10 years.

We hope that this will serve as eloquent testimony as to what can be accomplished under democracy and liberty.

Now it is our duty to disseminate, to distribute this prosperity throughout the various regions and to all the families of our people. And especially we must use this prosperity and this opportunity to disseminate the blessings of liberty, especially in the field of education. And in this way we are confident that we will be able to increase the prospect of concrete freedom for each of our citizens who will have every reason on this basis to live and progress in peace.

The progress which we have been able to achieve of course increases our responsibility on the international scene. Our people, by reason of its tradition, its religious principles, and its civic convictions feel the duty to extend these blessings to all the people of the earth. We have witnessed the great generosity of the American Government during the last several years. And you have seen fit to recall the various evidences of our progress. But we have said nothing about this. We did not mention this because we thought it was more our duty to simply reciprocate the feeling—the spirit of friendship and fraternity; with which you dealt with us.

We are glad to have had the opportunity to come here to this capitol and say to the American people that the Italian people fully restored to their national unity and integrity have every intention of contributing everything it can to great effort to extending the blessings of liberty throughout the world.

Because of course if peace is for all people and freedom is not to be the blessing of the few and prosperity is to be widespread, then there will be a decreasing number of attempts against freedom and peace.

We should like to express our great pride in what the United States has done in this respect and we should like to modestly request that you allow us to associate ourselves in this pride with you for what little we have done in this direction.

But we must consider what is still to be done in order to maintain freedom and to extend liberty to all men. And we must reaffirm with great conviction the propositions which we defend and the methods—the instruments which have been at our command to maintain peace and spread liberty and defend them against all threats from the outside. And we must consider these things and consider ways of using them, polishing them and adapting them to new ways so that we can ever increase these benefits to all mankind.

We should like to congratulate you, Mr. President, in your great efforts and your actions which have been so effective and long-seeing and to assure you that Italy and the alliance which joins us, which brings us together and in our common values, we will do everything along with you to consolidate progress in freedom towards the permanence of peace.

With this, Mr. President, I should like to drink to your health, to the success of your actions, and to the lasting prosperity and well-being of the people of the United States.

240 Statement by the President on the Appointment of deLesseps Morrison as U.S. Ambassador to the Organization of American States. *June* 13, 1961

I AM PLEASED and gratified to announce that Mayor deLesseps Morrison, of New Orleans, has agreed to serve as United States Ambassador to the Organization of American States.

In accepting this post Mayor Morrison has agreed to undertake one of our most important and difficult diplomatic posts. For the future of this hemisphere—the progress of its people and the maintenance of freedom—will largely depend on the vigor and effectiveness of the Organization of American States. The OAS is the principal instrument through which the American Republics—acting together—can attack their common problems: the elimination of social injustice, the attack on economic stagnation, the alleviation of the discontent which flows from poverty and hunger, and the maintenance of free society against the attacks of

those who are bent on its destruction. If the OAS can help perform these tasks and solve these problems then the future strength and welfare of the Americas will be assured. If the OAS should falter—if it fails to take the lead—then our freedom, and our security itself, will be in danger.

I have asked Mayor Morrison to assume this most critical post—at this critical time—as a service to his nation and to the hemisphere. His experience and ability will help us to build an OAS capable of meeting the new demands of the coming decade. He has been active in Latin American affairs for more than fifteen years. During that period he has won the respect and friendship of the people and leaders of Latin America. His presence in the OAS will symbolize the great importance which this government attaches to that organization. And his skill will assure the United States of dynamic and effective representation.

Mayor Morrison will be one of the leaders of the American delegation to the IA–ECOSOC meeting to be held in Montevideo, Uruguay in mid-July.

241 Letter to the President of the Senate and to the Speaker of the House Transmitting Bill on Unemployment Compensation. *June 13, 1961*

Dear Mr. —————:

I am transmitting herewith a bill which would provide permanent improvements to the Federal-State unemployment compensation system. You will recall that in my message to the Congress of February 2nd, which recommended a program of temporary extended unemployment compensation, I pointed out the need for permanent improvements in the system.

The bill would strengthen the Federal-State system by increasing the number of workers covered, by requiring adequate benefit amounts, by improving financing, and by providing a Federal program of additional compensation, on a stand-by basis, for workers who exhaust their regular benefits during economic recessions and at all times for workers who have had a long attachment to the labor force.

Although the bottom of the recession has been passed, there are still 4.8 million Americans out of work and 900,000 of them have been unemployed for more than six months. A number of legislative measures have al-

ready been proposed to the Congress aimed at providing both jobs and the skills needed to meet current industrial requirements—and we shall continue our efforts to reduce unemployment. It is apparent, however, that there will be those who will be unemployed at various times. Enactment of the draft bill will to some extent alleviate the suffering of unemployed workers and their families, and will help stabilize the economy by increasing the purchasing power of such workers. I hope it will have prompt and favorable consideration by the Congress.

Also enclosed is a letter from the Secretary of Labor together with an explanatory statement describing the draft legislation in detail. A letter similar to this is being sent today to the President of the Senate (Speaker of the House).

Sincerely,

JOHN F. KENNEDY

NOTE: This is the text of identical letters addressed to the Honorable Lyndon B. Johnson, President of the Senate, and to the Honorable Sam Rayburn, Speaker of the House of Representatives.

242 Joint Statement Following Discussions With Prime Minister Fanfani of Italy. *June 13, 1961*

PRESIDENT Kennedy and Prime Minister Amintore Fanfani today concluded a cordial and constructive two day series of consultations on a broad range of international problems and matters of interest to the governments and peoples of the United States and Italy who are engaged in the work of defending freedom and strengthening peace. The two reviewed the important role which Italy has played in the rebuilding of post-war Europe and the extraordinary rise of Italian strength and vigor in this era.

They reaffirmed the strong ties of friendship and heritage which bind the two countries.

The President and the Prime Minister met alone for a period of time and were later joined in discussions by Foreign Minister Antonio Segni, Secretary of State Dean Rusk, Ambassador Sergio Fenoaltea, Ambassador G. Frederick Reinhardt and other high officers of the foreign ministries of both countries. President Kennedy informed the Prime Minister in detail concerning his recent conversations with Premier Khrushchev in Vienna and views were exchanged on the principal issues involved, including Berlin and disarmament. The President and the Prime Minister found themselves in complete agreement on the need for strengthening the Atlantic community both as an instrument of defense and in its political and economic aspects and for maintaining and developing the closest Western consultations on all major international questions.

There was concurrence on the need for continuing international efforts to reach a workable agreement on disarmament with adequate safeguards. They also agreed on the importance and utility of further progress towards European integration and on the need for continuing Western solidarity in the face of the unremitting Communist challenge to the cause of freedom.

The two leaders also discussed in detail the problems related to economic and technical assistance to the newly-emerging and developing countries of the world with particular reference to the countries of the Mediterranean area, Latin America and Africa—

areas where Italy has especially close ties based on history, culture and economic association.

Prime Minister Fanfani stated in this regard that the Italian Government—within the limits of Italy's capabilities and of the engagements already undertaken for the development of Italy's southern regions—is ready to participate with its contribution to the implementation of these programs which will be agreed upon. It was agreed that in making plans for the further elaboration of the program for assisting emerging and developing nations the two governments should maintain contact between themselves and with the many other friendly governments as well as the governments concerned whose support and participation are essential to the success of the program.

Prime Minister Fanfani also had meetings during his visit with Secretary of State, Mr. Dean Rusk, the Secretary of the Treasury, Mr. Douglas Dillon. Foreign Minister Segni also met with Secretary of Defense Robert S. McNamara. The Italian leaders also met with leaders of both Houses of Congress.

This meeting again confirmed the profound and intimate relations between the two countries and the common aspirations of these governments to maintain peace and security and freedom in the promotion of the welfare of the peoples of the world.

Prime Minister Fanfani is expected to leave Washington by car tomorrow morning, June 14, for further visits in Baltimore, Philadelphia, and New York before his return to Italy on June 16. Foreign Minister Segni will return to Italy on June 14.

243 Remarks Upon Presenting the Collier Trophy to Admiral William F. Raborn, Jr. *June 15, 1961*

I WANT to say what a great pleasure it is to welcome you here and to have an opportunity to participate in this ceremony honoring Admiral Raborn. It is a strange fact that this trophy which was designed 50 years ago to further the cause of aviation should now go to a man who has perhaps done more to further the cause of the defense of the United States through submarines, which shows where technology is taking us.

We are glad you're an aviator, Admiral. We are delighted that you are associated with a most important project. I think the

fact that so many Americans from the Congress and from all the branches of our national defense are here today indicates the high regard in which they hold you.

We're very grateful to you for your work and it's most appropriate that this trophy should be presented to you and through you to the men who have developed the Polaris programs in both the Navy and industry. We're glad to see you, Admiral.

NOTE: The presentation ceremony was held in the Rose Garden at the White House.

244 Remarks at the Eighth National Conference on International Economic and Social Development. *June 16, 1961*

Governor Kerner, Mr. Chairman, Secretary Dillon, Secretary McNamara, Secretary Ribicoff, Senator Humphrey, distinguished Members of Congress, Mr. Black, Mr. Day, ladies and gentlemen:

I was most anxious to come here today because I think that the work that you are doing and effort that you are making represents a fulfillment of your responsibilities as citizens at the highest level.

There is no work in which you could be engaged in these days that is more important to the welfare of your country, to the security of the cause of freedom. There is no work, probably, more thankless, there is no work, probably, that may be less appreciated, but I hope the very fact that all those matters may be true gives you a sense of satisfaction. The easy work and the popular work, I think, can be left to many hands. But this work requires the effort of committed and dedicated citizens. So I was extremely anxious to come here today to express my

appreciation to you for the effort that you have made, and the hope the work in which you are engaged will be understood by our fellow citizens across the country; that from this meeting a new understanding of this great national commitment and effort will pass through the country so that in the coming weeks we'll be able to commit ourselves to a program in the coming months and years that will give us a greater degree of security.

As I said in my speech the other night, I cannot understand those who are the most vigorous in wishing to stem the tide of communism around the world and who are at the same time bombarding the Congress and the Administration with attacks on this program. We all get used to paradoxes, but I must say that in all my political life that is one of the most extreme. This is a program which does offer hope of stemming the advance. I know of no program at the present time other than those that go to the actual military security of the United States and the strengthening of the Armed Forces of this country that offer a comparable return. And therefore we should recognize the close identification of this effort—the effort to protect those societies which wish to be free—because it involves directly our own security.

This is not an effort even though it brings about beneficial results and fulfills responsibilities that we have as human beings to those who are less fortunate, this is a program that involves very importantly the security of the United States. And it is therefore, in my opinion, a program that deserves the support of every American who recognizes the real nature of the struggle in which we're engaged.

Now I know that there are those who are tired of carrying what they regard as a burden—and it is a burden. But if they say that, then they mean they're tired of the struggle. And the struggle is reaching its climax in the sixties. And as I am not tired of the struggle, and you're not tired of the struggle, and this country isn't tired of the struggle, we should be willing to pay and bear our burdens in this regard for a longer period of time. And if we are tired of it, then we should recognize the implication of that fatigue.

In 1952, when foreign aid was developed in this scale it was regarded as a period of transition and trial. In 1952, the Communists were seeking to expand their influence primarily through military means. In 1952, the United States was concerned about Korea-type control and invasions with actual military forces. Now, however, we have seen an entirely different concept, which the Communists have very frankly and generously explained to us at great length: Mr. Khrushchev's speech in January—he reiterated it again in Vienna—the so-called war of liberation, which is not the Korean type of war, where an armed force of one side passes across en masse the frontier of another country, but instead the seizure of power internally by what he considers the forces of liberation but which are, as we know in many cases, forces which are Communist controlled and which are supported from outside the country, but which are internal in their operation. It is for these reasons and because of this change in the Communist strategy which they believe offers them the best hope of success that this work is more important today than it's ever been before.

I think that we should recognize that the efforts to seize power in these countries, particularly those that are bordering the periphery of the Communist bloc, can be stemmed only—particularly in those countries where poverty and ignorance and illiteracy are the order of the day—can be stemmed only by one thing. And that is governments which are oriented and directed towards assisting the people and identified with causes which mean a better life for the people of those countries.

Quite obviously we cannot stem any tide which is inevitable. But I do not believe it inevitable that the governments in those areas should adopt policies which are reactionary. I think it's inevitable that they will adopt policies which are progressive and I think we should assist them. If we're not prepared to assist them, then quite obviously they cannot carry this burden, in many cases, by themselves. And if we're not prepared to assist them, whatever efforts they make will be doomed to failure. So I think that what we want to see in these areas are governments which are concerned with the life of their people, which are making a genuine effort, which are making and putting forward programs which over a period of time promise a better life for the people. And then we should be prepared to play our part and that is what we are suggesting in this program, and that in my opinion is in the best interest of our country at this time.

Now I know it's possible to go through foreign aid in the past and show the mistakes that have been made. But as Hubert Humphrey and all of us know, who've been through this, we can go through any section of the Government and show where mistakes have been made in the past and where money has been wasted. It isn't just in foreign aid. It is difficult to spend the people's money in an effective way, always wisely, always with judgment, always with integrity, and we find errors which have been made in many sections of governmental spending in the past. The Hoover commissions were only one indication of things that they unveiled in waste in Government. It's done every day in the military establishment, in the White House, in the Congress. There is waste. There's waste in our private expenditures. What we've got to do is to try to make sure that there is as little waste as possible, that we have the best people directing these programs that we can; that we do it as well as we can.

When I talked with Ambassador Bunker who is in India and who has a distinguished record there, the other day, and he said he did not believe in his long experience as head of one of the most important companies in the United States—he did not believe that he had ever seen money as usefully and as wisely spent as the American assistance which he saw in India. We can show the obvious examples of the waste but we can show many, many countries which if we had not helped them in the past 10 years would have long ago collapsed. My trip through

Western Europe indicates the extraordinary success of one facet of this program.

Now I think if we're going to talk about the mistakes we should also talk about the successes. Western Europe is an obvious one, and there are others. The effort we made in India, that we're making in Pakistan, have also been most helpful. There isn't any doubt in my mind that if we had not played a role in other countries, in the Middle East, in Asia, and in Southeast Asia, and up through the Island chain, the countries would have collapsed.

So that you may say that Laos is an unfortunate example, and perhaps it was, and perhaps it is, and perhaps the money was not wisely spent; and there have been other examples. But I can show you also examples of countries that would today be Communist dominated if it had not been for this effort, and I think we should consider the program in totality—even though we must recognize that mistakes have been made in the past and that a real effort is being made in this program to improve it. First, we are attempting to reorganize the agency so that there is one man in charge of all the aid programs in each country, who will have the responsibility instead of the present duplication. Secondly, we're attempting to reorganize so that we get in personnel. We are going to attempt to borrow them from some of our most successful companies. We're attempting to recruit them from all parts of the United States. And anyone of talent and experience in this field who wishes to serve is invited now to join us in a position which may not have great public acclaim, but which will make a measurable contribution in this area. And thirdly, we are attempting, and we think this most important, to provide long-range financing for this program. If we say to a country which is attempting an economic program, "If you do such and so over a period of 5 years, devote so much to public investment; do so much in tax reform, do so much in agriculture and all the rest, then we are prepared to support you year-by-year to the amount of X assistance." Now, that's far better than our being able to say, "Well, we can do this in 12 months, and after that we don't know if we can do anything." What incentive is there for them to devote a percentage of their national income to a particular area unless they're sure that we are going to play a supporting role.

Mr. Black in the World Bank has seen the effectiveness of this kind of long-range planning on a responsible basis, which has been the secret of the World Bank success. And no bank could function either locally or through the world if it only loaned for 12 months on any program which required a 5 or 10 year development period. So that I think that the Congress will have under the proposal we've suggested great authority in case the money is in any way wasted. They continue to maintain their control of it. But they do, I think—would permit us under this program to provide a more effective use of the taxpayers' money.

And let me say finally, that since my return from abroad, I've found in Washington and about the country a desire to do something to stop the spread of communism, to bolster the cause of freedom, to exercise initiative in world affairs; and I've heard talk about new military commitments and troop deployments, and there have been extra funds to be made available to our military purposes. But all of this is important. But the so-called war of liberation which Mr. Khrushchev has described cannot be stopped by a new B–58 squadron. They cannot be deterred—these internal movements cannot be deterred by military guarantees. They

cannot for the most part be resisted by American intervention in the absence of outside Communist troop intervention.

I therefore urge those who want to do something for the United States, for this cause, to channel their agencies behind this new foreign aid program to help prevent the social injustice and economic chaos upon which subversion and revolt feed; to encourage reform and development; to stabilize new nations and weak governments; train and equip the local forces upon whom the chief burden of resisting local Communist subversion rests. Those who oppose foreign economic and military assistance should know that the Communists do not oppose it; that their aid to less-developed countries is rising sharply; that they have already sent some 8,000 technicians into these areas; that they make credits available on a long-term basis without subjecting the recipient country to the perils of annual legislative review. Even in our own hemisphere, Communist bloc aid is dangled before the eyes of those who have long been devoted to freedom but have longed for an end to their poverty. We've read in recent weeks about the proposal which grandiosely states, but which is somewhat incompletely filled in—but at least it is proposed—to give Bolivia a loan of $150,000,000, a steel mill with supporting equipment—in our own hemisphere, by the Soviet Union. In short, there's no point in speaking out against the spread of communism unless we are willing to do our part in giving those who are fighting communism the weapon to fight it. There's no point in calling for vigorous action to protect our security if we're unwilling to pay the price and maintain the burden which are necessary for that security, and as the late Arthur Vandenberg said long ago, "There is no point in throwing a drowning man 20 feet off the beach a 10-foot rope."

I don't say that our program will be free from error. Mistakes will be made and setbacks will be suffered. But I'm more concerned about the waste to our security which will result from too small a program in this critical year and too short a period of authority than I am about anything else. I'm less concerned about the dangers of meeting our full responsibility and about—in a crucial year, and this well may be the crucial year of 1961—of doing too little and too late.

I therefore want to say to all of you that I am most grateful to your coming. I hope that your example of support will be followed by citizens across the country. It is difficult for me to believe that in the climactic period of this great era, that the United States is going to fail to meet its responsibility to itself and to those who look to it. I believe that we have an opportunity to play our part. I'm confident that we're going to do so. And I think it's most important—those who are burdened and those who are fatigued and those who feel that we have been through this so much for so many years—I would think that they should realize that that challenge will be with us for a long time to come. This is an obligation and an opportunity. And there's more than self-interest and anti-communism involved. I want it to be said that this generation of Americans, jealous of its rights, conscious of its responsibilities, met its responsibility in the year 1961 and in the years to come—met it with all the resources and all the wisdom and all the judgment, and meeting it, prevailed.

NOTE: The President spoke at a luncheon meeting at the Shoreham Hotel in Washington. In his opening words he referred to Otto Kerner, Governor of Illinois, Charles P. Taft, chairman of the 1961 conference, C. Douglas Dillon, Secretary of the Treasury, Robert S. McNamara, Secretary of Defense, Abraham A. Ribicoff, Secretary of Health, Education, and Welfare, Hubert H. Humphrey, U.S. Senator from Minnesota, Eugene R. Black, President, International Bank for Reconstruction and Development, and J. Edward Day, Postmaster General.

245   Remarks to the Members of the Commission on Money and Credit. *June 19, 1961*

I AM PLEASED to receive this report from the Commission on Money and Credit. I have been well aware of the wide-ranging work that the Commission has had under way during the past 3 years. As you know, three members of my administration have come from among your distinguished membership.

I congratulate the Commission on the effort it has spent in devising ways and means to improve our private and public system of money and credit—and thus to strengthen the Nation's economic health.

I should also like to express my appreciation to the Committee for Economic Development for originating this project, and to the Ford Foundation and the Merrill Foundation for financing it.

The Commission on Money and Credit has presented a program of monetary and fiscal reforms that could make an important contribution to the health and strength of our economy. The Commission—drawn mainly on business and banking, but also of labor and the professions—has submerged the special interests of its members in a laudable effort in the public interest.

Their report, which points the way to improve coordination of financial and economic policy, deserves the attention of every American. I commend particularly those who have the responsibility for the maintenance of conditions of high employment and rapid growth in the American economy.

It dramatizes how private citizens, regardless of their committed points of view, can, and sometimes do, dedicate themselves to work in the public interest. It demonstrates also the constructive role that private philanthropic institutions play in providing financial support for such activities.

This private, voluntary study cannot fail to stimulate and inform the national discussion of those grave economic problems that this Nation faces from day to day. As a

consensus of people in many walks of life, this report should bring others to study and discuss the problems of national coordination of the governmental and private institutions which together guide our complex money and credit system.

I hope that people everywhere in the Nation, as well as those who represent them in Congress, will read this report for the information, analysis, and recommendations it contains, whether or not they agree with its numerous and provocative proposals.

NOTE: The President spoke in his Office at the White House. The Commission's report is entitled "Money and Credit: Their Influence on Jobs, Prices, and Growth" (282 pp., Prentice Hall, 1961).

246   Letter to the Speaker of the House of Representatives on Federal Assistance for Urban Transportation Planning. *June* 19, 1961

Dear Mr. Speaker:

As stated in my message to the Congress on Housing and Community Development, "nothing is more dramatically apparent than the inadequacy of transportation in our larger urban areas." We are pledged to assist in the sound development of our cities, and believe Federal financial assistance should be provided to help plan and develop the comprehensive and balanced transportation systems which they so desperately need. Such assistance will not only directly benefit our cities, but will also make more effective use of Federal funds spent for other urban development programs.

As a first step, I am submitting with this letter a proposed bill to provide increased authority for Federal assistance to urban transportation planning. The assistance to be provided would include grants for surveys, studies, planning, and experimental demonstrations.

Because mass transportation is a distinctly urban problem and one of the key factors in shaping community development, the proposed bill assigns the administration of the program to the Housing and Home Finance Agency. This responsibility, together with the other functions of the Agency, will be transferred to the new Department of Urban Affairs and Housing upon enactment of legislation which I have previously proposed.

Following the directive in my message on Housing and Community Development, the Secretary of Commerce and the Housing and Home Finance Administrator are undertaking an extensive study—due to be completed this fall—on methods and the extent of Federal financial assistance for the actual development and improvement of mass transportation systems. The proposed bill would require the Housing Administrator to submit to the Congress, early in the next session, a report and recommendation based

465

on the findings of the study group. Non-Federal government financing will have to provide the preponderant share of the new capital funds needed for mass transportation, and Federal assistance should therefore encourage and supplement rather than supplant such investment.

But the time required to complete the study and translate its recommendations into a legislative proposal should not be wasted. Enactment this session of the proposed bill will permit the planning and demonstration programs to be set up and will also stimulate urban areas to establish area-wide agencies empowered to plan, develop and operate transportation systems. These steps are essential to an effective transit program since two absolute requisites to Federal aid are (1) an approved comprehensive transit plan and, (2) the existence of a suitable organization representing all, or substantially all, of the local governmental units in the metropolitan area.

Although final decision on the exact nature of a Federal program of loans, loan guarantees, or grants for the purchase or modernization of transit facilities and equipment must await the results of this Executive Branch study, immediate emergency assistance to finance transportation equipment

and facilities in a few metropolitan areas with especially urgent problems may be warranted to assure continuation of essential services. While Federal funds should not be used solely to salvage obsolete systems, emergency loans may be essential for projects found by the Administrator to be consistent with the probable comprehensive transit plan for the area, if financing is not available on reasonable terms from private sources or elsewhere in the Federal Government. Consistent with these strictly limited conditions, the Congress may wish to enact, as a part of the bill, a temporary one-year authority for emergency loans.

Since the Senate has already concluded its consideration of the Omnibus Housing Bill and has adopted an amendment containing a mass transportation program, I hope it will be possible for the House to hold hearings on the subject in order that a satisfactory program can be enacted during the current session.

Sincerely,

JOHN F. KENNEDY

NOTE: On June 30 the President approved the Housing Act of 1961 (Public Law 87–70, 75 Stat. 149), which provided for Federal assistance for urban transportation planning.

247 Statement by the President on the Garrison Diversion Irrigation Development in the Upper Missouri River Basin. *June 21, 1961*

AS INDICATED in my message to the Congress on Natural Resources, "wise investment in a resource program today will return vast dividends tomorrow, and failures to act now may be opportunities lost forever." The Garrison Diversion project is an excellent illustration of the principle. The

investment to be made now in the Upper Missouri River Basin will in the future bring to the people of the Dakotas and the Nation at large great benefits in the form of a sound agricultural economy, improved recreational facilities, and perhaps most important of all, the region will be able to retain and support its greatest resource, the young people who have in recent years been forced to leave farms in the areas in alarming numbers.

NOTE: The White House release of which the President's statement was a part noted that administration approval of the project was transmitted to the Congress in a report by Secretary Udall and in testimony before a Senate subcommittee by Assistant Secretary Kenneth Holum. The release added that the irrigation project, located principally in North Dakota, would enable farmers to change from dry farming of wheat, which is in surplus, to varied crops including those which would support cattle raising and yield higher incomes.

248   Remarks Upon Activating by Remote Control the Saline Water Conversion Plant at Freeport, Texas.   *June* 21, 1961

Ladies and gentlemen:

The dedication of the conversion plant at Freeport, Texas, today is an important step towards the achievement of one of man's oldest dreams: securing fresh water from salt water.

The Government of the United States and the people of this country take pride in this research enterprise which holds such high promise for meeting one of man's basic needs in areas where nature has not been generous.

I want to express the congratulations of the people of this country to the men and women who've been involved in this work, to the Dow Chemical Company, to those who work in Freeport, Texas, to scientists and engineers who've been involved in this enterprise.

I might say that I can think of no cause and no work which is more important, not only to the people of this country but to people all around the globe, especially those who live in deserts or on the edge of oceans.

I am hopeful that the United States will continue to exert great leadership in this field, and I want to assure the people of the world that we will make all the information that we have available to all people. We want to join with them, with the scientists and engineers of other countries, in their efforts to achieve one of the great scientific break-throughs of history.

I'm sure that before this decade is out, that we will see more and more evidence of man's ability at an economic rate to secure fresh water from salt water, and when that day comes then we will literally see the deserts bloom.

This is a work which in many ways is more important than any other scientific enterprise in which this country is now engaged. It serves the interests of men and women every place. It can do more to raise men and women from lives of poverty and desperation than any other scientific advance.

It's a matter of great interest to me. It's a matter of the greatest interest to the Vice President who, living as he does in the State of Texas, has seen throughout his life how important it is that fresh water be secured. And it is for that reason that he is there today in Freeport, participating in this dedication.

I congratulate you all, and I think that you serve very well the interests of our country and the cause of humanity in general; and therefore it is a great pleasure for me, on behalf of the people of this country, to press this button which will cause this project to begin to work. In addition to getting fresh water from salt water, we will also get minerals from the sea as a result of this effort. One of the minerals which we believe will be secured is magnesium, and I think that it's part of this button and helps establish the current, which indicates where science is now taking us.

NOTE: The President's remarks, spoken in the Fish Room at the White House, were carried by telephone to the ceremonies at Freeport, Tex.

249 Toasts of the President and Prime Minister Ikeda of Japan. *June 21, 1961*

IT IS a great pleasure and honor to welcome the Prime Minister and his wife here to the White House. A year ago the President of the United States and Mrs. Eisenhower welcomed the Crown Prince and his wife who visited the United States on the occasion of the one hundredth anniversary of the relations between the United States and Japan.

It is therefore most appropriate that we should on this occasion welcome the Prime Minister and his wife to America, and also to welcome back to the White House President and Mrs. Eisenhower.

I think the fact that they are here today among this group of distinguished Americans indicates the extraordinary importance that we place on the Prime Minister's visit, and also the great significance which this country attaches to its relations with Japan.

We believe in this country that the Pacific Ocean does not separate Japan and the United States. Rather, it unites us. And we have the greatest admiration for this extraordinary people, who have conquered the sea and the land and in the most energetic and productive way have built a life for themselves.

Their influence in Asia, their influence in the Pacific, their friendship for us, all these things are basic to the security and prosperity of the people of this country. Therefore, Prime Minister, in welcoming you here we want you to know that we welcome you as a distinguished spokesman for the free world, as the leader of an outstanding nation that is playing a most important role at a climactic time in the life of our two countries and in the life of the cause of freedom.

We welcome you because of your own distinguished service to your country, and we welcome you both also because you have been generous enough to entrust to us several hostages of fortune in the case of your daughters who have come to the United States to teach as well as to learn.

So that I hope that all of you will join me in drinking a toast to the Emperor of Japan.

NOTE: The President proposed the toast at a state luncheon at the White House. Prime Minister Ikeda responded (through an interpreter) as follows:

Thank you, Mr. President. Your remarks reflect an extraordinary insight, and it is for this characteristic of your leadership that the people of all countries have come to regard you with special esteem. The words of wisdom you addressed to the American people reach us, too, with undiminished force as they echo throughout the world.

Please be assured, Mr. President, that we share your determination to preserve world peace, as well as your faith in the ultimate triumph of the free way of life.

Toward this end, and to reexamine matters affecting our relations, I look forward to further meetings with you and the members of your administration.

And we are encouraged, Mr. President, by the warmth of the hospitality extended by you and the charming and gifted First Lady, and by a series of what I believe are highly fruitful talks.

I am also grateful, Mr. President, for the honor you have accorded my wife and myself by the presence at this luncheon of the esteemed citizen of the United States, General Eisenhower and Mrs. Eisenhower.

Ladies and gentlemen, may I now propose a toast to the President of the United States.

250   Memorandum on Employee-Management Relations in the Federal Service.   *June* 22, 1961

Memorandum for the Heads of Departments and Agencies:

The right of all employees of the federal government to join and participate in the activities of employee organizations, and to seek to improve working conditions and the resolution of grievances should be recognized by management officials at all levels in all departments and agencies. The participation of federal employees in the formulation and implementation of employee policies and procedures affecting them contributes to the effective conduct of public business. I believe this participation should include consultation by responsible officials with representatives of employees and federal employee organizations.

In view of existing policy relating to equal employment opportunity, management officials will maintain relationships only with those employee organizations which are free of restrictions or practices denying membership because of race, color, religion, or national origin. Further, such officials shall refrain from consultation or relationships with organizations which assert the right to strike against or advocate the overthrow of the government of the United States.

Further steps should be explored fully and promptly. We need to improve practices which will assure the rights and obligations of employees, employee organizations and the Executive Branch in pursuing the objective of effective labor-management cooperation in the public service. I know this is not a simple task. The diversity of federal programs, the variety of occupations and skills represented in federal employment, the different organizational patterns of federal departments and agencies, and the special obligations of public service complicate the task of formulating government-wide policy guidance. Nevertheless, this important subject requires prompt attention by the Executive Branch. With that objective in mind, I am designating a special task force to review and advise me on employee-management relations in the federal service, composed of the following officials:

The Secretary of Defense

The Postmaster General

The Secretary of Labor

The Director of the Bureau of the Budget

The Chairman of the Civil Service Commission

The Special Counsel to the President

The Secretary of Labor will serve as Chairman of this task force. This study will cover the broad range of issues relating to federal employee-management relations, including but not limited to definition of appropriate employee organizations, standards for recognition of such organizations, matters upon which employee organizations may be appropriately consulted, and the participation of employees and employee representatives in grievances and appeals. In the course of this study employees and employee organization representatives, department and agency officials, consultants in labor-management relations, and interested groups and citizens shall be given an opportunity to present their views for the consideration of the task force. In view of the need for decisions on this important issue at a reasonably early date, I am asking the task force to report their findings and recommendations to me not later than November 30, 1961.

All department and agency heads and their staffs are directed to cooperate fully

with the task force in the accomplishment of this study.

JOHN F. KENNEDY

NOTE: See also the President's statement upon receiving the task force report (Item 494).

251   Memorandum on Minimum Wage Rates for Government Employees.   *June 22, 1961*

Memorandum for the Heads of Departments and Agencies:

In response to my urgent request, Congress has recently enacted legislation to raise minimum wages which must be paid by private employers in interstate commerce. Although this legislation specifically exempts the federal government as an employer, I believe that the social and economic reasons underlying this Congressional action are equally compelling and applicable to wage earners employed by federal departments and agencies.

In my view it is both desirable and in the public interest to establish the same minimum rates of $1.15 an hour, effective September 3, 1961, and $1.25 an hour, effective

September 3, 1963, for all regular federal employees paid from appropriated funds. I want to make clear these minimum rates should apply to federal laundry workers, even though such workers in private employment are specifically exempted by the law.

These new minimum rates should be applied to federal employees in the United States not later than the effective dates specified in the legislation. It is my wish that the head of each department and agency review this matter promptly and take appropriate action unless clearly prevented from doing so by law.

JOHN F. KENNEDY

252   Joint Statement Following Discussions With Prime Minister Ikeda of Japan.   *June 22, 1961*

PRESIDENT KENNEDY and Prime Minister Ikeda concluded today a constructive and friendly exchange of views on the present international situation and on relations between the United States and Japan. Secretary Rusk, Foreign Minister Kosaka, and other U.S. and Japanese officials participated in the conversations.

The President and the Prime Minister discussed various problems confronting the peoples of the world who are resolved to defend their freedom, and they reaffirmed the deter-

mination of the two countries to intensify their efforts toward the establishment of world peace based on freedom and justice. The President and the Prime Minister stressed that the common policy of the two countries is to strengthen the authority of the United Nations as an organ for the maintenance of world peace.

The President and the Prime Minister expressed their concern over the unstable aspects of the situation in Asia and agreed to hold close consultations in the future with a view to discovering the ways and means by which stability and well-being might be achieved in that area. Their discussion of the Asian situation included an examination of various problems relating to Communist China. They also exchanged views concerning the relations of their respective countries with Korea.

The President and the Prime Minister recognized the urgent need for an agreement on a nuclear test ban accompanied by effective inspection and control measures, agreeing that it is of crucial importance for world peace. They also expressed their conviction that renewed efforts should be made in the direction of general disarmament.

The President and the Prime Minister reviewed the world economic situation. They agreed on the need for continued close cooperation among the free countries of the world, particularly in promoting the growth of international trade and financial stability. They agreed that both countries should pursue liberal trade policies looking to an orderly expansion of trade between the two countries.

The President and the Prime Minister stressed the importance of development assistance to less developed countries. The Prime Minister expressed a particular interest in this connection in development assistance for East Asia. They agreed to exchange views on such assistance and agreed that both countries would make positive efforts to the extent of their respective capacities.

The President and the Prime Minister expressed satisfaction with the firm foundation on which the United States-Japanese partnership is established. To strengthen the partnership between the two countries, they agreed to establish a Joint United States-Japan Committee on Trade and Economic Affairs at the cabinet level, noting that this would assist in achieving the objectives of Article II of the Treaty of Mutual Cooperation and Security. The President and the Prime Minister also recognized the importance of broadening educational, cultural and scientific cooperation between the two countries. They therefore agreed to form two United States-Japan committees, one to study expanded cultural and educational cooperation between the two countries, and the other to seek ways to strengthen scientific cooperation.

The President and the Prime Minister exchanged views on matters relating to the Ryukyu and Bonin Islands, which are under United States administration but in which Japan retains residual sovereignty. The President affirmed that the United States would make further efforts to enhance the welfare and well-being of the inhabitants of the Ryukyus and welcomed Japanese cooperation in these efforts; the Prime Minister affirmed that Japan would continue to cooperate with the United States to this end.

253 Statement by the President Upon the Entry Into Force of the Antarctic Treaty. *June 23*, 1961

I WISH to express my profound satisfaction on the occasion of the entry into force today of the Antarctic Treaty. This Treaty has now been ratified by all of the 12 countries which participated in the Conference on Antarctica held in Washington in 1959—Argentina, Australia, Belgium, Chile, France, Japan, New Zealand, Norway, South Africa, the Soviet Union, the United Kingdom and the United States—all of which signed the Treaty at the conclusion of the Conference on December 1, 1959.

This is a significant treaty in several respects. First and foremost it provides that the vast Antarctic continent shall be used for peaceful purposes only. Accompanying this provision is the important provision whereby the parties have the right to send observers anywhere in Antarctica at any time to see that the Treaty is not being violated, and the right of overflight of all areas of Antarctica. It could very well provide valuable practical experience in the field of international inspection in other situations.

The Treaty also provides for freedom of scientific investigation and international cooperation in science in Antarctica. Nuclear explosions throughout the area are banned, pending general international agreement on the subject, although the use of nuclear energy for such purposes as heat and power is permitted.

The difficult question of territorial claims in Antarctica is in effect set aside by the Treaty, which states that nothing in the Treaty shall be interpreted as either a re-

nunciation or recognition of claims or bases of claims. The United States has never asserted a territorial claim in Antarctica, nor has it ever recognized the claims of others. By this Treaty the United States continues to reserve its rights throughout the whole of Antarctica.

The Antarctic Treaty was conceived by the United States and the Conference at which it was drawn up was called by the United States, after nearly two years of patient and skillful preliminary negotiations. It has been signed and ratified by countries representing all of the world's six continents, many of which held divergent views on Antarctica. That this was possible I find very encouraging.

I earnestly believe that the Antarctic Treaty represents a positive step in the direction of world-wide peace, and am genuinely gratified to announce its entry into force today.

NOTE: The text of the treaty is printed in Treaties and Other International Acts Series 4780 (Government Printing Office), and in the Department of State Bulletin (vol. 41, p. 912).

254 Letter to the Vice President on the Need for Developing Operational Communications Satellites. *June 24, 1961*

[Released June 24, 1961. Dated June 15, 1961]

Dear Lyndon:

I will appreciate your having the Space Council undertake to make the necessary studies and government-wide policy recommendations for bringing into optimum use at the earliest practicable time operational communications satellites. The Federal agencies concerned will provide every assistance which you may request.

I am anxious that this new technology be applied to serve the rapidly expanding communications needs of this and other

nations on a global basis, giving particular attention to those of this hemisphere and newly developing nations throughout the world. Such communications needs include both governmental and non-governmental requirements. Throughout this analysis, public interest objectives should be given the highest priority.

Policy proposals should include recommendations not only as to the nature and diversity of ownership and operation of communications systems and parts thereof, but also proposed objectives. Effective utilization of both our public and private resources needs to be assured, as well as close cooperation with other countries and their communications systems. Continuing coordination of the governmental agencies responsible for regulatory, space, military, and other aspects of this field is essential.

I will appreciate receiving recommendations from you on these and other matters bearing on the development and use of communications satellites just as promptly as possible. Research and development should proceed at an accelerated pace while this study is in progress.

Sincerely,

JOHN F. KENNEDY

NOTE: For the President's statement following the receipt of the Vice President's recommendations, see Item 299.

255 Message to the Members of the National Education Association Meeting in Atlantic City. *June 25, 1961*

I AM DELIGHTED to have this opportunity to extend greetings to the members of the National Education Association and, through you, to your fellow teachers throughout the Nation. I wish you success in your convention, in your professional endeavors which are so vital to our future, and in your efforts to improve the quality and support of American education.

It is fitting that this message is conveyed to you by my friend, Frank Thompson, co-sponsor of the Administration's Morse-Thompson bill for assisting our public schools. The most crucial period for this legislation is still ahead. But it is a sound measure. It is a just measure. It is an urgently needed measure—and I have every reason to believe that, with the help of organizations such as yours, and with the help of Congressmen such as Frank Thompson, I will sign into law before the summer is out this Nation's first Federal Aid to Education program.

That will be the end of a forty-year battle. But more than an end, it will be a beginning. For mere money alone is not enough. Enactment of this bill will not improve the excellence of education overnight. Our goal—our objective in obtaining these funds—is not simply to provide an adequate educational system—or even a merely good educational system. Our goal must be an educational system that will permit the maximum development of the talents of every American boy and girl.

This will require continued leadership and stimulation by the Federal Government— including the enactment of other educational measures already proposed. It will require increased effort by our state and local school systems, by school boards and parents and individual citizens.

But perhaps the greatest responsibility of all will rest with you, the teachers of America. In the last analysis, no amount of federal aid, no amount of new classrooms, no amount of state and local support can succeed without your daily efforts to improve the minds of our children. That is why you bear a responsibility for the Nation's future that is as heavy as that of any office-holder—and that is also why I think it imperative that our Federal Aid to Education program include funds for teacher's salaries.

No man who sits in the White House can fail to be sobered by the problems which will face future generations as well as our own. Whatever decisions we make, whatever

473

events occur in our time, the students of to-day and tomorrow will face in their time a host of decisions so critical and complex as to demand a degree of wisdom and dedication never previously reached. Thus, to a large extent, the success of freedom *then* depends upon the success of free education *now*.

Holding fast to basic concepts while discarding outmoded practices, recognizing the progress that has been made as well as the problems we face, and justifying educational excellence on its own merits and not simply in terms of "cold war" competition, let us work together, make every effort and meet every challenge to build this Nation's most fundamental resource: the human mind.

NOTE: The message was read by Frank Thompson, Jr., U.S. Representative from New Jersey.

256 Statement by the President on Establishing a Board of Inquiry in the Maritime Strike. *June 26, 1961*

I AM ESTABLISHING a Board of Inquiry to inquire into the labor dispute in the maritime industry.

The shutdown in this industry has continued now for eleven days. It involves virtually all American companies, 70,000 men, and the commerce at every Atlantic, Pacific and Gulf port.

There have already been serious interruptions in the movement of food, oil and other essential commodities. The supply lifelines to the State of Hawaii and to Puerto Rico have been cut. There have been delays in the shipments of military cargoes.

The law provides for establishment of a Board of Inquiry whenever, in the opinion of the President, a strike affecting a substantial part of an industry will, if permitted to continue, imperil the national health and safety. It is my opinion that we have reached this stage in this dispute.

I am aware of the suggestions some of the parties to this dispute have made for minimizing its effect upon the national health and safety. These suggestions appear, on first impression, more tactical than substantial. I request the Board of Inquiry to consider these suggestions, however, and to include findings of fact regarding them in the report the Board will submit to me.

I am also keenly aware of the desirability of so conducting the Government's participation in this dispute as to recognize the continuing importance here of collective bargaining. For this dispute will eventually be settled by collective bargaining. The law provides no alternative settlement process. The report the Board of Inquiry submits to me is limited, by law, to a statement of the facts.

I therefore urge the parties to continue their bargaining, and to use the offices of the Federal Mediation and Conciliation Service, as well as the Board of Inquiry, toward the end of achieving *now* the settlement of this dispute which will in any event come eventually by and through their efforts.

I note the desirability in situations of this kind of more flexible statutory procedures. I have urged in the past the adoption of such procedures. The Secretary of Labor has sought, in the course of this dispute, to develop such procedures; but has not been able to obtain consent of all of the parties.

This dispute presents new evidence of the imperative need for modifications in the present law.   I propose to make suggestions to the Congress along these lines very shortly.

In the meantime, this particular dispute must be met with the procedures at hand.

I have appointed to the Board: Mr. David L. Cole, of Paterson, New Jersey, as Chairman; Judge Samuel I. Rosenman, of New York; and Professor James J. Healy, of Boston.

I am asking the Board to report to me as quickly as possible, hopefully by Friday of this week.

NOTE: Executive Order 10949, creating the Board of Inquiry, was amended on June 29 by Executive Order 10951, which extended to July 3 the time for the Board to submit its report.

The Board's report and supplement, dated July 2, 1961, and its final report of September 1, 1961, were made available through the Federal Mediation and Conciliation Service.

257   Letter to the President of the Senate and to the Speaker of the House Transmitting Bill on Saline Water Research. *June 26, 1961*

My dear Mr. ————:

I am transmitting for the consideration of the Congress a draft bill to carry out the recommendations on saline water research in my Natural Resources Message.

Water—one of the most familiar and abundant compounds on the earth's surface—is rapidly becoming a limiting factor on further economic growth in many areas of this Nation and the world.   As time goes on, more and more communities will be faced with the prospect of economic distress and stagnation unless alternative sources of suitable water are developed.

It is essential, therefore, that we make every effort at this time to search for low-cost processes for converting sea and brackish water into fresh water to meet our future water needs and those of our neighbors throughout the world.   I know of no Federal activity that offers greater promise of making a major contribution to the ultimate economic well-being of all mankind than this program.

This bill will provide the Department of the Interior with a wide variety of tools to attack the saline water conversion cost barrier.   It contemplates a major acceleration of current programs of basic and applied research, and permits the construction of conversion plants far larger than any now in existence to test the feasibility of known and yet to be developed processes.   I am confident that the Congress will share my view that we must move ahead with this important program, and I urge that favorable and prompt consideration be given this legislation.

I am enclosing a letter from the Secretary of the Interior describing this legislation in greater detail.   A letter identical to this is being sent to the Speaker of the House of Representatives (President of the Senate).

Sincerely,

JOHN F. KENNEDY

NOTE: This is the text of identical letters addressed to the Honorable Lyndon B. Johnson, President of the Senate, and to the Honorable Sam Rayburn, Speaker of the House of Representatives.

For the President's statement upon signing a bill to expand and extend the saline water conversion program, see Item 381.

258 The President's News Conference of *June 28, 1961*

THE PRESIDENT. Good morning.

[1.] I want to first of all express my regret at the information I've just received in regard to the death of our colleague in these press conferences and a fine newspaper man, Ed Koterba, who, I understand, was killed in a plane crash last night.

He was a most—he was an outstanding newspaperman who was associated with Scripps-Howard, and we want to express our sympathy to members of his family and also to the papers with which he was associated. I want to say personally that I'm extremely sorry to have heard the news.

[2.] Secondly, I should like to comment briefly on Germany and Berlin.

Soviet and East German leaders have followed the recent Soviet aide memoire with speeches which were apparently designed to heighten tension. It is of the greatest importance that the American people understand the basic issues involved and the threats to the peace and security of Europe and of ourselves posed by the Soviet announcement that they intend to change unilaterally the existing arrangements for Berlin.

The "crisis" over Berlin is Soviet-manufactured.

The Soviets illegally blockaded the city in 1948 and lifted the blockade in the spring of 1949. From that time until November 1958, almost a decade, the situation in Berlin was relatively peaceful.

The peoples of West Berlin developed a thriving and vital city. We carried out our responsibilities and exercised our rights of access to the city without serious incident, although we were never completely free from irritating difficulties that were put in our way.

In November 1958, the Soviets began a new campaign to force the Allied Powers out of Berlin, a process which led up to the abortive summit conference in Paris of May last year.

Now they have revived that drive. They call upon us to sign what they call a "peace treaty," with the regime that they have created in East Germany. If we refuse, they say that they themselves will sign such a treaty.

The obvious purpose here is not to have peace but to make permanent the partition of Germany.

The Soviets also say that their unilateral action in signing a "peace treaty" with East Germany would bring an end to Allied rights in West Berlin and to free access for that city.

It is clear that such unilateral action cannot affect these rights, which stem from the surrender of Nazi Germany.

Such action would simply be a repudiation by the Soviets of multilateral commitments to which they solemnly subscribed and have repeatedly reaffirmed.

About the exercise of the rights of the principal powers associated in World War II: If the Soviets thus withdraw from their own obligations, it is clearly a matter for the other three allies to decide how they will exercise their rights and meet their responsibilities.

But the Soviets say that when we do so, we will be subject to the designs of the East German regime and that these designs will be backed by force.

Recent statements by leaders of this regime make it very plain that the kind of "free city" which they have in mind is one in which the rights of the citizens of West Berlin are gradually but relentlessly extinguished—in other words, a city which is not free.

No one can fail to appreciate the gravity of this threat. No one can reconcile it with the Soviet professions of a desire to coexist peacefully.

This is not just a question of technical legal rights. It involves the peace and the security of the peoples of West Berlin. It involves the direct responsibilities and commitments of the United States, the United Kingdom, and France. It involves the peace and the security of the Western world.

In the interests of our own vital security, we and other Western countries entered in a defense arrangement in direct response to direct Soviet moves following World War II.

These alliances are wholly defensive in nature. But the Soviets would make a grave mistake if they suppose that Allied unity and determination can be undermined by threats or fresh aggressive acts.

There is peace in Germany and in Berlin. If it is disturbed, it will be a direct Soviet responsibility.

There is danger that totalitarian governments not subject to vigorous popular debate will underestimate the will and unity of democratic societies where vital interests are concerned.

The Soviet Government has an obligation to both its own people and to the peace of the world to recognize how vital is this commitment.

We would agree that there is unfinished business to be settled as concerns Germany. For many years, the Western nations have proposed a permanent and peaceful settlement of such questions on the basis of self-determination of the German people.

Moreover, we shall always be ready to discuss any proposals which would give increased protection to the right of the people of Berlin to exercise their independent choice as free men.

The proposals which have now been placed before us move in the opposite direction and are so recognized throughout the world.

Discussions will be profitable if the Soviets will accept in Berlin, and indeed in Europe, self-determination which they profess in other parts of the world, and if they will work sincerely for peace rather than an extension of power.

[3.] I have a second statement. The Soviet Union's refusal to negotiate seriously on a nuclear test ban at Geneva is disheartening to all those who have held high hopes of stopping the spread of nuclear weapons and the pace of the arms race. It also raises a serious question about how long we can safely continue on a voluntary basis a refusal to undertake tests in this country without any assurance that the Russians are not now testing.

Consequently, I have directed that the President's Science Advisory Committee convene a special panel of eminent scientists to take a close and up-to-date look at the serious questions involved, including two questions in particular.

First, what is the extent of our information on whether the Soviet Union has been or could be engaged in secret testing of nuclear weapons?

Second, to the extent that certain types of tests can be concealed by the Soviet Union, what technical progress in weapons could be under way in that area without our knowledge?

These answers will be received and reviewed by myself, by the Joint Chiefs of Staff, and the National Security Council in the light of what they mean to the security of the free world.

In the meantime, our negotiating team will remain at Geneva, our draft treaty is on the table there, and I urge the leaders of the Soviet Union to end their intransigence and to accept a reasonable and enforceable treaty which is our wholehearted desire.

[4.] And lastly, Chairman Khrushchev has compared the United States to a worn-out runner living on its past performance and stated that the Soviet Union would outproduce the United States by 1970.

Without wishing to trade hyperbole with the Chairman, I do suggest that he reminds me of the tiger hunter who has picked a place on the wall to hang the tiger's skin long before he has caught the tiger. This tiger has other ideas.

Premier Khrushchev states that the Soviet Union is only 44 years old but his country is far older than that, and it is an interesting fact that in 1913, according to the best calculations I can get from governmental and private sources, the Russian gross national product was 46 percent of the United States gross national product.

Interestingly enough, in 1959 it was 47 percent. Because, while the Soviet Union was making progress and improving the material standards of her people in the ensuing years, so was the tiredout runner, and, on a per capita basis, the Soviet product in 1959 was only 39 percent of ours.

If both countries sustain their present rate of growth, 3½ percent in the United States and 6 percent in the Soviet Union, Soviet output will not reach two-thirds of ours by 1970 and our rate will be far easier to sustain or improve than the Soviet rate, which starts from a lower figure.

Indeed, if our growth rate is increased to even 4½ percent, which is well within our capability, it is my judgment that the Soviet Union will not outproduce the United States

at any time in the twentieth century.

This faster growth rate is a primary object of the various measures I've submitted and will submit in the future, tax incentives, education, resource development, research, area redevelopment, and all the rest.

Mr. Khrushchev obviously sees the future differently than we do and he has urged his people to work hard to develop that future. We in the United States must work hard, too, to realize our potential.

But I believe that we can maintain our productive development and also our system of freedom. We invite the U.S.S.R. to engage in this competition which is peaceful and which could only result in a better living standard for both of our people.

In short, the United States is not such an aged runner and, to paraphrase Mr. Coolidge, "We do choose to run."

[5.] Q. Would you care to comment on recurrent reports that the administration is considering a partial mobilization to meet the threat in Berlin?

THE PRESIDENT. No such proposal has been placed before me at the present time. As you know this matter of what steps we would take to implement our commitments to Berlin have been a matter of consideration. Mr. Acheson, the former Secretary of State, was named to consider this matter in the middle of April. His report will be coming in—we're going to discuss it this week and we will be considering other proposals which might be put forward in order to make meaningful our commitment. But the proposals are still—have not still come to the White House officially and I'm therefore not able to comment because we have not seen any such proposal as you suggested at the present time, though of course we will be considering a whole variety of measures which might be taken.

[6.] Q. Mr. President, in some retrospect, how do you now view the Cuban tractor deal? It seems pretty well off. What's the next move there? How do you plan to get those prisoners out of there now?

THE PRESIDENT. Well, the tractors—the committee offered Mr. Castro, as I understand it, the 500 agricultural tractors which he mentioned in the original speech. Mr. Castro has not accepted these agricultural tractors but is insisting on a different kind of tractor—far larger, which could be used for other purposes besides agriculture. The committee has therefore felt that Mr. Castro is not interested in permitting these prisoners to be released in return for agricultural tractors and, unless he changes his view, the situation will remain as it is.

I wish the prisoners could be free. I wish that it had been possible to secure their release because they are, as I said at my first statement, men in whom we have great interest and who are devoted to the cause of freedom. But I think the committee did everything that reasonable men and citizens could do. They were motivated by humanitarian interests. I think that they demonstrated, by exploring with Castro in detail, exactly the nature of Castro's interest.

If the—our first response had been negative, it might have been possible for Mr. Castro to say that we had refused to send agricultural tractors in return for these men. This committee went to every conceivable length in order to demonstrate their good faith. Mr. Castro did not accept it.

[7.] Q. Mr. President, I think we'd like to hear you say how you are feeling now.

THE PRESIDENT. Very well, very well. I'm feeling better, even, than Pierre Salinger.

[8.] Q. Mr. President, with respect to the Cuban operation, would you tell us what General Taylor's findings were and what reorganization or adjustment in our intelli-

gence activities you contemplate as a result of this report?

THE PRESIDENT. General Taylor made an oral report to me, which I asked him to make and which I think will be useful to me. In addition, of course, General Taylor has been—is now a member of the staff of the White House as our military representative with special responsibilities in the field of defense matters and intelligence and coordination in those areas.

[9.] Q. Mr. President, will you tell us about the reorganization plan, if any, with respect to our intelligence activities because of his appointment?

THE PRESIDENT. No, that matter will—has not been completely—completed. In addition, we—the Killian committee is looking at the same matter and when the Killian committee has finished its preliminary surveys, we may have some changes.

[10.] Q. Mr. President, approximately 200 Members of Congress have protested to you regarding the Department of State plan for distributing low-priced textile imports among other Western nations. They urge abandonment of the plan because they feel it commits the United States to an unreasonable high level of low-priced imports in the future. Could you tell us whether this State Department plan has your unqualified support or whether you would favor modifying it to meet congressional objections?

THE PRESIDENT. In the first place, there's no plan yet. No solution has been devised to this problem of how we're going to provide for an orderly flow of textiles from the newly emerging countries which concentrate on this kind of commodity and how we're going to provide for an orderly flow between those countries and the consuming countries so that we protect the interests of the producing countries and the consuming countries.

It's an extremely complicated task. No decision has been reached as to what the formula would be. It is proposed that we discuss the formula, and I think that the conference should go on and we should discuss it. If we come to any conclusion about what should be done, and we have not reached that conclusion, as yet, we will inform the American people and the members of the Congress.

I do want to point out that we do export nearly 7 million bales of cotton every year. We sell more cotton to Japan than we import in textiles from all over the world. This is not a matter on which we can say we'll take no imports and at the same time feel that we can continue to provide this tremendous outflow of cotton.

We export nearly 7 million bales of cotton every year. We import a total of about 600,000 bales of cotton, manufactured into textiles a year. So that we have to consider the economic interests of the United States as well as other people. We sell Japan—I think last year we sold them $150 million more than they bought from us, totally. So that while I'm concerned about, and I *am* concerned about the problem of the textile industry, which is one of the reasons why this conference was called, as a result of the protests which were made by members of Congress because the imports have increased in the textile industry, and it is hard hit. I think it came, it increased in recent months and recent years from around 4½ to 7 percent and therefore the trend is against, has been sharply—has provided for increases.

I do feel that we ought to take into account that this is a balance matter. In addition, some of the States which sell cotton overseas which may be adversely affected by textile imports—we also export a lot of

textiles. We also, for example, export tobacco, which is an export product, so that we have to consider the general economic interest. We cannot expect that we're going to be able to cut off completely the importation of textiles and then think that we're going to have anything but ruin for our cotton exporters.

So it all has to be balanced, and one of the ways that the economic interests of all can be balanced is in this conference, and I support it.

[11.] Q. Mr. President, without respect to the current maritime strike, do you plan to take any action on the American-owned flags of convenience, or runaway ships, as you once described them?

THE PRESIDENT. Well, we are concerned about the—as I have said before—about the problem of runaway ships in the sense that ships who are put by American owners under other flags in order to avoid paying the wage scale which we have for our American merchant marine, the United States Government pays a large share of the bill for important segments of the American merchant marine, including these wages. So when these ships leave us and compete against us, in a sense it affects not only the welfare of the seamen involved but also affects governmental policy and governmental obligations. So we are concerned about the matter.

But in regard to the actual details, I would prefer for the present to wait until the Cole committee makes its report in regard to Taft-Hartley. And we are also considering what we could do to see if we can work out some solutions which will ease the burden of the people involved.

There is also an obligation, let me say, on the representatives of the American merchant marine, an obligation of Mr. Curran and Mr. Hall to make sure that the problems of the American merchant marine in its competition with other areas are taken into consideration. They cannot merely consider it isolated. This is a competitive business. And we could very well find, instead of flags of convenience or so-called runaway ships, that the ships were actually put under the—which, and in those cases the American, the United States Government has some control over the ships. They could actually put them under the flags or have contractual relationship with the British or the Norwegians and then we would not have the control in case of a national emergency and we would still be being undercut.

So it's an extremely complicated question to which Secretary Goldberg and the Secretary of Commerce and the members of the committee are giving a good deal of attention.

[12.] Q. Mr. President, in considering the resumption of nuclear testing, have you requested or do you propose to request a report and recommendation from the Federal Radiation Council regarding the consequences of fallout that may result from such a resumption of tests?

THE PRESIDENT. All these matters, of course, would be considered before any decision were reached.

[13.] Q. Mr. President, how do you feel now in retrospect about summit meetings and do you foresee any more of them in the future?

THE PRESIDENT. Well I've never described the meeting in Vienna as a summit meeting. I think the meeting in Vienna was useful to—certainly to me in meeting my responsibilities, and perhaps it was also to Mr. Khrushchev. Because, as I've said from the beginning, these issues which we're now talking about are extremely serious issues

which involve the well-being of a great many people besides even the people of the United States, and decisions have to be made on the basis of the best information we can get, and they involve the security of the United States and they involve also the peace of the world, and therefore if those decisions can be made more educated by such a meeting it was useful. Now there are no plans to have any further meetings that I know of.

[14.] Q. Mr. President, Vice President Nixon seems to be taking a dim view of your administration. He said in a speech yesterday that never in American history has a man talked so big and acted so little. Do you have anything to say about this?

THE PRESIDENT. No, I wouldn't comment on Mr. Nixon. He has been engaged and busy and I sympathize with the traveling problems he has and his other problems but—[*laughter*]—I don't have any response to make. We're doing the best we can and will continue to do so until 1964 and then we can see what the situation looks like. [*Laughter*]

[15.] Q. Mr. President, you said that if the United States can attain a rate of growth of 4½ percent, that Russia will not catch up with us in the twentieth century. What is our rate of growth now, sir?

THE PRESIDENT. Well, culling it from 1953 to today, it's about 3½ percent.

[16.] Q. What are we doing to attain a rate of growth?

THE PRESIDENT. Well, we're going to have a sharp—from the recession of 1960, winter of '61, we ought to have a substantial rate of increase. The big problem will be to sustain it over a period of time and that will require—I mentioned some of the things—a tax system which provides a stimulation to growth, education, and research, also the development of the natural resources of this country and also monetary and fiscal policies which will recognize the necessity of preventing a recurrence of these successive dips.

Now we had a recession in '54, we had a recession in '58, we had a recession in '60. The '60 recession came right on the heels of the '58 recession. Two of the reasons why it may have contributed—it was the movement from a $12 billion deficit in '58–59 to a prospective $4 billion surplus, which was a change of more than $16 billion in the potential receipts of the Government, which did have a restraining influence on the recovery.

Secondly, of course, the long-term interest rates were extremely high. Now we have to—the Federal Reserve will meet with Mr. Martin frequently. It's a very uncertain science, but we have to figure out what steps we can take—with this free economy—that will provide not only a recovery now, and we hope a reduced unemployment rate, but will also sustain it, not just through '62 but over a period of time. That we have to do if we're going to defeat Mr. Khrushchev, but it's within our potential and, therefore, I think, my judgment is that if the United States considers this problem and the people of the United States and the Government working together attempt to master this uncertain science in a more precise way, that we will remain not only ahead on a per capita basis but also on a national income basis in this century.

We have to recognize, of course, that the Soviet Union is working extremely hard and enjoys some advantages in being able to mobilize its resources for this purpose in the sense that a totalitarian society enjoys that advantage. What we wish was that they would do it under a system of freedom, but that is their decision.

[17.] Q. Mr. President, there's been some criticism of our handling of inter-American affairs, particularly on grounds

that you have a multiplicity of advisers in the White House duplicating and sometimes overruling people in the State Department. I wonder if you could define for us the relationship of policymakers on your staff as against those in State and perhaps in the Pentagon?

THE PRESIDENT. Well, we have in the White House a number of people who have responsibilities in various areas. And one of the areas in which we're particularly interested is Latin America. Now I've read the—I think it's—I was sorry that we did not secure a replacement for Mr. Mann more quickly. I did talk to almost eight people. We had assurances in a number of cases which lasted some days, but we finally did not—in every case we were not successful. I think we were very fortunate to have Mr. Woodward and perhaps maybe we should have started with Mr. Woodward. That's the first point.

Secondly, we are particularly interested in Latin America. My experience in government is that when things are noncontroversial, beautifully coordinated, and all the rest it may be that there isn't much going on. I've never heard of any criticism of—I do not hear any criticism of our organizational structure in several areas of the world which I know are rather inactive as far as anything being done. So if you really want complete harmony and good will, then the best way to do it is not to do anything.

Now we haven't done so much in Latin America in the last decade. It has not been a matter of great priority. We are attempting to do something about it. And we've been fortunate to have the services of Mr. Berle who is completing the work of his task force. Mr. Goodwin from the White House has given it a great deal of attention, particularly the meeting of the IAECOSOC in Montevideo through the end of July.

The whole refinancing of the Brazil debt, which could have been a most serious crisis in that very vital country, was handled in cooperation between the Treasury, the White House, the State Department, the Export-Import Bank, Food for Peace and ICA. We've also given particular attention to the economic problems of Bolivia.

So we are attempting to do something about Latin America and there's bound to be a ferment. If the ferment produces useful results then it will be worthwhile. But I must say I don't think—my experience is you can't get very much done if—when things are very quiet and beautifully organized, I think it's the time to be concerned, not when there is some feelings and interest and concern.

In addition, Governor Stevenson went down and made a tour there as a prelude to our meeting at Montevideo, which I think was useful. So I would say we have given more thought in this administration to the problem of Latin America than on almost any matter involving our foreign policy.

In answer to your question, when Mr. Woodward comes here next week he will be the responsible officer in the State Department and will work closely, I'm sure, with the Secretary of State and with me.

[18.] Q. Do you feel that the Berlin threat is serious enough for you to plan a personal meeting with the British and French to map our strategy there if the situation becomes indeed very hot?

THE PRESIDENT. It is a matter which we discussed with General de Gaulle and Mr. Macmillan. In addition, they've had—Lord Home was here—the French Government has had a representative, as well as the British Government, talking about the response in the aide memoire. I've no doubt that we will have close exchanges with Mr. Macmillan and General de Gaulle and when the

matter reaches a point where a meeting would be useful, we would have it.

[19.] Q. On your statement this morning about a committee to go into the extent of information on Soviet testing, is there any suggestion here, sir, that we have an intelligence gap in this field? Or to specify, did not the Eisenhower administration and does not your administration pretty well know what the Soviets have been doing in nuclear testing during this——

THE PRESIDENT. No, there's—in what way?

Q. I just wondered if you had information about what testing they may have been doing.

THE PRESIDENT. No, we do not—this is a matter which the committee will look into. But in answer to your question, I have not seen any information, nor did the previous administration have any knowledge, which would state that the Soviet Union had been testing—information either by seismography or by any other means. What is of concern is, is it possible to test without those evidences being secured? Is it possible to test underground, for example, without a determination being made that such a test is being carried on? That's the matter which we wish to have explored. But it would be inaccurate to state that we have information that would indicate to us that the Soviet Union is now testing. What we're concerned about is that our information is quite incomplete and we want to know whether it's possible that they could be testing without our knowing and what the chances are that that might be true.

[20.] Q. It has been almost 6 weeks, sir, since the conference on Laos has been under way. There seems to have been little progress, at least little understanding, between the two sides. Do you consider it worthwhile to continue the conference?

THE PRESIDENT. Yes, the cease-fire is generally in operation. What we're now concerned about are the details of the ICC's power, and I'm hopeful that we can secure effective instruction for the ICC, so that it can meet its responsibilities. I would continue the conversations to see if that can be obtained.

[21.] Q. Realizing that the Acheson and other contingency reports have not yet been finished, could you, nevertheless, give us at least a hint this morning in what areas the public may be involved in supporting your strong stand on Germany? I ask that question against this background: that it's generally considered that your words to Mr. Khrushchev in Vienna were highly impressive, but it's necessary to follow them up with decisions and deeds.

THE PRESIDENT. Yes, well, that's the matter which is now engaging the attention of the United States Government; it is one of the matters which will be discussed at the Security Council tomorrow. But as of now, no report of the deliberations of the Pentagon and others as to what actions might be usefully taken have officially—have been finalized.

In addition, I would point out that we are talking about matters of extreme serious-ness and I think that we should wait until a judgment has been reached as to what action we should take before it's useful to discuss it publicly. As of today, these considerations and recommendations have not yet come to the White House. One of the matters which will be discussed, as I say, tomorrow will be this matter at the Security Council.

[22.] Q. Mr. President, can something be done to require mortgage bankers to quit enriching themselves off of the FHA system of making loans? I refer to the many complaints that are coming in to FHA on this matter from widows and poor people who—buyers and sellers—who are losing, say, several hundred dollars on the sale of a small house to these mortgage bankers who laugh at the people and say FHA and your Government condones this system whereby we charge side payments for financing these loans.

THE PRESIDENT. Well, I think—I will look into it and Mr. Salinger will have a statement to make on it by tomorrow afternoon.

Reporter: Thank you, Mr. President.

NOTE: President Kennedy's thirteenth news conference was held in the State Department Auditorium at 10 o'clock on Wednesday morning, June 28, 1961.

259 Memorandum on the United Fund and Community Chest Campaigns. *June 28, 1961*

To the Heads of Executive Departments and Agencies:

United Funds and Community Chests this fall will make their annual appeals throughout the country and among Federal civilian and military personnel for the support of more than 28,000 health, welfare and recreation organizations. Many of these campaigns will include such national agencies as the Red Cross, USO, and others working to eliminate disease and secure the health of us all. Altogether they will be seeking to raise more than $470,000,000 in the largest of all voluntary fund-raising appeals.

We who work in the Government want to assume our full citizen's share of the voluntary support of health and welfare services. The United Fund and Community Chest campaigns provide us with an opportunity to contribute to a wide variety and a large number of organizations through a single appeal.

The Honorable Robert S. McNamara, Secretary of Defense, will serve as Vice Chairman for the Federal Government of United Community Campaigns of America. I am confident everyone will extend full cooperation to the Vice Chairman in these campaigns. Such cooperation should, under the Federal policy on voluntary fund-raising, include the effective solicitation of all employees, the acceptance of equitable unit goals, and the setting up of an adequate collection method for the convenience of those who wish to make contributions on an installment basis.

It is my hope that employees of your department in each community where it conducts its operations will give thoughtfully and generously to these campaigns.

JOHN F. KENNEDY

NOTE: On August 1 the White House announced the appointment by the President of Secretary of Commerce Luther B. Hodges as chairman of the Government Unit for the United Givers Fund campaign. In a memorandum to the departments and agencies announcing Secretary Hodges' appointment, the President stated that "our Nation's Capital can and should be an example to the Nation in building a healthy and strong community through the American tradition of voluntary giving to assist those less fortunate. The UGF agencies that provide comfort to the aged, help to those afflicted with mental illness or crippling disease, counsel and guidance to those beset with family and personal problems, and character building youth activities are truly dedicated to this great tradition. Meeting these human needs requires the support of all Government personnel and I have complete confidence that they will meet this opportunity and responsibility."

---

260   Remarks at the Presentation of the Distinguished Service Medal to General Thomas D. White. *June* 28, 1961

IT'S A GREAT PLEASURE for me personally and on behalf of the people of the United States to award this decoration to General White who has served this country, who has served the people of this country for most of his life, whose career has been an example of duty, honor and country, and who has placed his obligations to the national security at the hazard of his life. He is an example to all citizens of those qualities which insure the survival of this country, and will in the future.

Therefore it's most appropriate at the conclusion of this phase of his career, of his life, that he come here to the White House and receive at least a small token of the recognition which is properly his.

We want him to know that in the months that I've been President I have leaned very heavily on his advice. I have found that on all occasions it has been directed to the best interests of our country.

He is succeeded, fortunately, by a man of his own qualities, General LeMay, and he's been associated with distinguished Chiefs of Staff, under the chairmanship of General Lemnitzer, and we are fortunate to have their service continue.

Therefore, I want to read this citation.

"Citation to accompany the award of the Distinguished Service Medal (First Oak Leaf Cluster) to Thomas D. White:

"General Thomas D. White distinguished himself by exceptionally meritorious service to the United States as Chief of Staff, United States Air Force from 1 July 1957 to 30 June 1961. Throughout this time, General White discharged with great distinction the tremendous responsibility of assuring strong, effective deterrent forces in being while simultaneously integrating into the Air Force the new military systems which are the product of modern technology. As airman, strategist and military statesman, General White has contributed immeasurably to the deliberations of the United States Joint Chiefs of Staff and to the senior military councils of the Free World. The selfless dedication, integrity, outstanding

foresight and objectivity demonstrated by General White during this period, which have characterized his career of forty-one years in the service of his country, reflect the highest credit upon himself and the United States Air Force."

I present this to you, General, and also this decoration which we'll place right here to go with all the others.

NOTE: The presentation ceremony was held in the Rose Garden at the White House.

261 Remarks Upon Signing the Federal-Aid Highway Act. *June 29, 1961*

IT IS with the greatest pleasure that I today sign into law the Highway Act of 1961. The House Ways and Means Committee, the Senate Finance Committee, the Public Works Committees of both Houses, and the Congress as a whole, accepted the challenge imposed by the perils facing our Federal pay-as-you-go highway program, and have enacted a bill providing the increased authorizations and revenues required to permit completion of the vital national system of interstate and defense highways in time to meet the traffic for which it was designed.

Earlier this year, I presented to the Congress a plan for financing the highway program and equitably distributing the tax burden among the various highway users. There are many honest differences of opin-

ion on how this should best be done, but the resolution of the problems—and there are problems of great complexity involving great interest—in the Highway Act presented to me, is a tribute to the diligent and conscientious work that was done by the Members of Congress.

With the support provided by this act, the States and the Federal Government can continue with the construction of the new highway system, a system which will increase our defense readiness, decrease the appalling highway accident toll, lower transportation costs, and stimulate economic development.

And therefore it is a great pleasure to sign this bill into law.

NOTE: The Federal-Aid Highway Act of 1961 is Public Law 87–61 (75 Stat. 122).

262 Letter to the President of the Senate and to the Speaker of the House Proposing the Establishment of a United States Disarmament Agency. *June 29, 1961*

Dear Mr. ————:

I am transmitting herewith, for consideration by the Congress, a draft of legislation to carry out the recommendation contained in

my May twenty-fifth Message, for the establishment of a strengthened and enlarged disarmament agency to make an intensified effort to develop acceptable political and technical alternatives to the present arms race.

Today, ability of man to master his environment threatens to outpace his ability to control himself. The world is more and more interdependent, and the people of the earth can now look beyond this planet to a new age of discovery, but they have not yet been able to banish the primitive threat of war. The ingenuity that has made the weapons of war vastly more destructive should be applied to the development of a system of control of these weapons.

But peace cannot be brought about by concentrating solely on measures to control and eliminate weapons. It must also encompass measures to sustain and strengthen international institutions and the rule of law. A disarmament program must take into account the national security; our foreign policy; the relationships of this country to international peace-keeping agencies, including the United Nations; and our domestic economic and other policies. It should drive toward the creation of a peaceful world society in which disarmament, except for the forces needed to apply international sanctions, is the accepted condition of international life.

For the past five months, Mr. John J. McCloy, my adviser on disarmament matters, has been conducting, at my request, an extensive study of the governmental effort and organization necessary to give effect to our national purpose in this field. He has had available to him the results of searching studies by individual members and committees of the Congress, the agencies of Goverment principally concerned, national and international organizations and eminent private individuals. During the course of his study, Mr. McCloy has consulted closely with Secretary Rusk, Secretary McNamara, Chairman Seaborg and other high officials. All of these studies and consultations have inescapably pointed to the conclusion that a new effort, considerably larger than our present effort, in terms of size, range of skills and authority will be necessary. This can best be accomplished by the creation of a new United States agency.

Following Mr. McCloy's recommendations, I am therefore proposing that a new United States Disarmament Agency for World Peace and Security be established. Enactment of the proposed legislation will permit this agency to deal broadly with the whole range of disarmament matters, including research, policies, and programs.

The importance and broad scope of disarmament matters require continuing Presidential attention. The complex inter-relationships between disarmament activities, foreign affairs, and national security also require that close working-level coordination and cooperation be established between the new agency and the Departments of State and Defense, the Atomic Energy Commission, and other agencies.

The proposed legislation provides that the Director of the new agency function under the direction of the President and the Secretary of State. This arrangement will permit coordination of disarmament matters within the purview of the various agencies; it will give special recognition to the need for intermeshing disarmament policies and programs with the broad conduct of foreign affairs; and it will provide a focal point at the highest level of Government for the consideration of disarmament matters.

In the light of these unique relationships the Director, as the principal adviser to the President in the disarmament field, will have direct access to him but will, of course, notify the Secretary of State as to the occasion and substance of the advice he offers. In addition, the Director will report to the Secretary of State without going through intermediate authority, and he will act as the agent of the Secretary of State with authority under his direction, to act in his name. Also, I intend that he participate in all meetings of the National Security Council having to do with disarmament.

I am enclosing a letter from Mr. McCloy

describing the legislation in more detail.

Sincerely,

JOHN F. KENNEDY

NOTE: This is the text of identical letters addressed to the Honorable Lyndon B. Johnson, President of the Senate, and to the Honorable Sam Rayburn, Speaker of the House of Representatives.

Mr. McCloy's letter of June 23 and the text of the draft bill are printed in the Congressional Record (vol. 107, June 29, 1961, p. 10855).

For the President's statement upon signing the Arms Control and Disarmament Act, see Item 288.

263 Statement by the President Upon Signing the Social Security Amendments of 1961. *June 30, 1961*

IT IS with great satisfaction that I have signed into law the Social Security Amendments of 1961. They represent an additional step toward eliminating many of the hardships resulting from old age, disability, or the death of the family wage-earner.

A nation's strength lies in the well-being of its people. The Social Security program plays an important part in providing for families, children, and older persons in times of stress. But it cannot remain static. Changes in our population, in our working habits, and in our standard of living require

constant revision.

I am pleased that the Congress has acted so promptly this year to modernize the program. It has done so with commendable regard for the sound principles on which social insurance must be based—for the legislation is both financially sound and socially responsible.

With these amendments, the Social Security program will be a more effective instrument.

NOTE: The Social Security Amendments of 1961 is Public Law 87–64 (75 Stat. 131).

264 Remarks Upon Signing the Housing Act. *June 30, 1961*

I WANT to express our pleasure in signing S. 1922, the Housing Act of 1961. This bill is the most important and far-reaching Federal legislation in the field of housing since the enactment of the Housing Act of 1949. For the communities of the Nation, large and small, it provides an opportunity for a giant step toward better cities and improved housing. And I think the beneficial effects of this legislation will be felt by every American.

It makes available, for the first time, Federal aid to preserve rapidly disappearing open land and to improve inadequate public transportation in our growing urban and metropolitan areas. It recognizes, through a new program of low interest loans, the forgotten families—those who are ineligible for public housing on the one hand and those whose incomes will not allow them to pay for decent housing on the other. It provides, at the same time, expanded opportunities for private industry to meet the housing needs of families of moderate income. It authorizes new tools long needed to cope with blighted housing and neighborhoods. And finally, it extends the principle of experiment and research to the problems of mass transportation and both public and private housing.

The legislation also provides greatly expanded authorizations and funds for major existing programs of assistance for housing and community development. Moreover, for key programs—mortgage insurance, urban renewal, college housing, low rent public housing, and farm housing— long term authorizations will assure continuity without the uncertainties and interruptions which have plagued these programs in the past.

These programs, old and new, offer our communities and private builders and lenders the opportunity and the challenge to build the cities of tomorrow where families can live in dignity, free from both the squalor of the slums and the unbroken monotony of suburban sprawl—in many cases of housing which is not built with an eye to the long-term development of this country.

I want to express our great thanks to the members of the committees of the Con-

gress—the Banking and Currency Committee, Congressman Spence, Chairman—the Banking and Currency Committee of the Senate—and to also express our great appreciation to Senator Sparkman who shepherded this bill through the Senate, and to Congressman Rains who carried it on under Congressman Spence's leadership in the House.

Having this bill signed without them here is somewhat like having Hamlet played without the Prince, but we will go ahead anyway. But I did want to express our great thanks to them. They both did an extraordinary job, and I am delighted to have the Members of Congress here. Also Dr. Weaver, head of the Housing organization in the Government. And to Mrs. McGuire, head of the various sections of the Housing agency dealing with urban housing. Also Mayor Dilworth, representing the mayors of the United States, who have been extremely interested in this legislation.

NOTE: The Housing Act of 1961 is Public Law 87–70 (75 Stat. 149).

In his remarks, the President referred to Brent Spence, U.S. Representative from Kentucky; John J. Sparkman, U.S. Senator from Alabama; Albert Rains, U.S. Representative from Alabama; Robert C. Weaver, Administrator, Housing and Home Finance Agency; Mrs. Marie C. McGuire, Commissioner, Public Housing Administration; and Richardson Dilworth, Mayor of Philadelphia.

265 Remarks at the Swearing In of General Curtis LeMay as Chief of Staff, U.S. Air Force. *June 30, 1961*

I WANT to express our great pleasure at the assumption of this responsibility by General LeMay. He was one of the most distinguished combat commanders in World War II. He played a most instrumental role in developing SAC into its present high peak as the great shield of the United States in the free world.

He brings to the responsibilities of the Chief of Staff long experience in the Air Force, and also a wide recognition of the challenges and responsibilities and opportunities which face the United States in meeting our commitments around the globe.

It's a source of satisfaction to me personally as President, to be able to rely on his counsel as a member of a group of distinguished Americans, the Joint Chiefs of Staff; and I think the fact that so many Members of the Congress are here from both parties indicates the wide respect which he has in the country.

So, General, we want to say that, speaking personally, and also as President, that it's a great pleasure to welcome you as the new Chief of Staff of the United States Air Force and member of the Joint Chiefs of Staff.

NOTE: The President spoke at 3:15 p.m. in the Rose Garden at the White House.

266 Statement by the President on the 10th Anniversary of the Colombo Plan. *July 1, 1961*

I WANT to pay tribute today on its tenth anniversary to the Colombo Plan for co-operative economic development in South and Southeast Asia, a great international organization of which the United States has proudly been a member almost from its inception. The Colombo Plan is being honored at this time in some twenty countries which make up its membership. The countries of South and Southeast Asia which comprise the Colombo area are all struggling to free themselves from the ageless burden of poverty. Their economic development is the central objective of the Colombo Plan. They are helped in this by the non-area members—Australia, New Zealand, Japan, Canada, the United Kingdom and the United States.

The Colombo Plan seeks through friendly consultation to aid South and Southeast Asian countries in their individual efforts to develop themselves and encourages the fullest possible cooperation among all members to achieve this objective.

While the Colombo Plan is not in itself an operating agency, it nourishes intimate multilateral consultations on development problems and plans and stimulates practical economic cooperation among its members through bilateral arrangements. The Colombo Plan has become a symbol of the economic aspirations of hundreds of millions of people in South and Southeast Asia.

On behalf of the United States I congratulate the Colombo Plan on its first decade of dedicated service to the noble cause of a better life for the peoples of Asia. We are proud to be associated in this effort. It illustrates well the type of self-reliance and mutual cooperation—learning to help each other—which the United States particularly endeavors to further through its own foreign aid program. We hope the constructive influence of the Colombo Plan will grow with the years.

NOTE: The statement was released at Hyannis, Mass.

267 Statement by the President Concerning Economic Cooperation Between the United States and Pakistan. *July 1, 1961*

THE COMPLETION of ten years of economic cooperation between Pakistan and the United States stands as firm evidence of the friendly relations existing between our two countries. In observing this significant milestone, we are proud to have the privilege of working with the people of Pakistan, and it is our firm intention to continue in a joint effort to secure peace and progress for the community of free nations.

We have made known our deep interest in the success of the Second Five-Year Plan, and we intend to support the determined effort of the Pakistan Government and people to insure its success.

I wish particularly to offer congratulations to President Ayub and the Government and people of Pakistan for the vigor which characterizes their efforts to build a still stronger nation. The achievement of greater human well-being motivates free men everywhere. We in the United States admire Pakistan for her steady adherence to the goal of human betterment. We join her in facing the future with inspiration and confidence.

NOTE: The statement was released at Hyannis, Mass.

268   Statement by the President on the Death of Ernest Hemingway. *July 2, 1961*

FEW AMERICANS have had a greater impact on the emotions and attitudes of the American people than Ernest Hemingway.

From his first emergence as one of the bright literary stars in Paris during the twenties—as a chronicler of the "Lost Generation," which he was to immortalize—he almost single-handedly transformed the literature and the ways of thought of men and women in every country in the world.

When he began to write—the American artist had to look for a home on the Left Bank of Paris. Today, the United States is one of the great centers of art. Although his journeys throughout the world—to France, to Spain and even to Africa—made him one of the great citizens of the world, he ended life as he began it—in the heartland of America to which he brought renown and from which he drew his art.

NOTE: The statement was released at Hyannis Port, Mass.

269   Statement by the President Following Receipt of Report of Board of Inquiry in the Maritime Strike. *July 3, 1961*

THE BOARD of Inquiry in the maritime dispute has reported to me that although there has been agreement between some of the parties, full accord has not been achieved and the strike continues with respect to a majority of American ships.

Reports I have received clearly manifest that a continuation of this strike imperils the national health and safety.

I have therefore directed the Attorney General to seek an injunction against this strike under the national emergency provisions of the Taft-Hartley Act.

While an injunction will restore the maritime industry to full operation and return the striking members to work for a period of 80 days, it should not interfere in any way with efforts toward settlement. In the last several days, progress has been made toward such a settlement and I hope the parties will exert the necessary effort to achieve it quickly. However, the public interest does not permit further delay in applying for an injunction. Consequently, I have made the decision to direct the Attorney General to apply for the appropriate order.

The circumstances of this dispute present new evidences for the imperative need of improvements of the national emergency section of the Taft-Hartley Act. I have directed the Secretary of Labor promptly to prepare for submission to the Congress proposals for improving our mechanism of dealing with national emergency strikes.

In addition, this dispute also points up the necessity for reviewing our procedures for improving collective bargaining in the maritime industry. I shall likewise deal with this in submitting proposals to the Congress.

I wish to commend the members of the board of inquiry for their untiring efforts in this matter in the public interest.

NOTE: The statement was released at Hyannis, Mass. For the President's directive to the Attorney General, see Item 270.

270   Letter to the Attorney General Directing Him To Petition for an Injunction in the Maritime Strike. *July 3, 1961*

Dear Mr. Attorney General:

On June 26, 1961, by virtue of the authority vested in me by Section 206 of the Labor Management Relations Act, 1947 (29 U.S.C. 176), I issued Executive Order No. 10949, creating a Board of Inquiry to inquire into the issues involved in a labor dispute between certain ship owners and operators in the United States foreign and domestic trades and certain of their employees represented by: the National Maritime Union of America; the Seafarers International Union of North America; the National Marine Engineers' Beneficial Association; the International Organization of Masters, Mates, and Pilots; the American Radio Association; the Radio Officers Union; and the Staff Officers Association of America.

On July 3, 1961, I received the Board's written report in the matter. I understand you have a copy of that report.

In my opinion this unresolved labor dispute has resulted in a strike affecting a substantial part of the maritime industry, an industry engaged in trade, commerce, and transportation among the several States and with foreign nations, which strike, if permitted to continue, will imperil the national health and safety.

Therefore, in order to remove a peril to the national health and safety and to secure a resumption of trade, commerce, and transportation among the several States and with foreign nations, I direct you, pursuant to the provisions of Section 208 of the Labor Management Relations Act, 1947, to petition in the name of the United States any District Court of the United States having jurisdiction of the parties to enjoin the continuance of such strike and for such other relief as may in your judgment be necessary or appropriate.

Very sincerely yours,

JOHN F. KENNEDY

NOTE: On July 3 the Attorney General sought and obtained in the District Court for the Southern District of New York a temporary injunction against continuation of the strike, which was made permanent in a decision of July 10.

Terms of various contracts were agreed upon during the course of the injunction, the terms of the final contract being reached on October 11. The Board's reports of July 2 and September 1, 1961, were made available through the Federal Mediation and Conciliation Service.

The letter was released at Hyannis, Mass.

271   Exchange of Greetings on Independence Day Between the United States and the Soviet Union.   *July 4, 1961*

Leonid I. Brezhnev
Chairman, Presidium of the Supreme Soviet,
U.S.S.R.
N. S. Khrushchev
Chairman, Council of Ministers, U.S.S.R.

I wish to thank you personally and on behalf of the American people for your greetings on the occasion of the 185th Anniversary of the Independence of the United States.

It is a source of satisfaction to me that on our 185th Anniversary the United States is still committed to the revolutionary principles of individual liberty and national freedom for all peoples, which motivated our first great leader. I am confident that given a sincere desire to achieve a peaceful settlement of the issues which still disturb the world's tranquillity we can, in our time, reach that peaceful goal which all peoples so ardently desire. A special responsibility at this time rests upon the Soviet Union and the United States.

I wish to assure the people of your country of our desire to live in friendship and peace with them.

JOHN F. KENNEDY

NOTE: The message, dated July 3, 1961, from Mr. Khrushchev and Mr. Brezhnev follows:

Dear Mr. President:

Personally and on behalf of the Soviet people we send to the American people, and to you personally, our sincere congratulations on the occasion of this important date in the life of the American people, namely, the 185th Anniversary of achieving their independence. While sending our congratulations to you today, we want to express the hope that the recent Vienna meeting, and the exchange of opinions which took place there on questions of interest to both countries, will further the mutual efforts of our governments directed to the urgent solution of problems which long ago became pressing and which the last war left to us after the defeat of the aggressors. History imposed on our peoples, on their governments, and on their leaders an enormous share of the responsibility for the preservation of peace, for the future of humanity. In order to carry out this great historical mission it is necessary to commence building, from both sides, enduring bridges of trust, of mutual understanding and of friendship. The Soviet Union has always striven and strives now to achieve this aim. The Soviet and the American peoples by right must go down in history as the two great peoples who made a decisive contribution to the cause of ensuring permanent peace on earth.

N. KHRUSHCHEV
L. BREZHNEV

The messages were released at Hyannis, Mass.

272   Remarks at Ceremonies Marking the 150th Anniversary of Venezuelan Independence.   *July 5, 1961*

Mr. Secretary, Your Excellency the Ambassador of Venezuela, and other Representatives of the Governments in our hemisphere, ladies and gentlemen:

We celebrate today the liberation, 150 years ago, of a great American nation, Venezuela. We do so before a statue of its liberator, Simón Bolívar, an American illustrious—an American who is held in common

regard by all the sister Republics of this great neighborhood. By this act, we give double testimony: of our friendship for the land that gave him birth and that he launched on the road to freedom; and of our own rededication to the ideal of which he was the first and perhaps the greatest prophet—the unity of the Americas.

Fifteen years ago this month, President

Betancourt of Venezuela said before another statue of Bolívar: "Today our concern and interest is to make his [Bolívar's] message live, to incorporate his ideology in our concepts, to follow loyally his luminous example in our daily tasks as governors and governed." It is as important today to do all of these things.

Bolívar with his insight and genius pursued goals then that we strive to attain today. His greatest dream was of a mutually defensive union of all the Republics of the hemisphere against the aggression of foreign philosophies. Its substance inspires the determination of today's statesmen of the Americas to protect their heritage of freedom from alien encroachment; to realize to the fullest the spiritual and material greatness of our nations; to extend to all the Americas the benefits of freedom and social justice; to make common war against poverty and sickness and man's inhumanity to man.

This determination is today's expression of the great world revolution whose principles were clarioned from Philadelphia 185 years ago yesterday, again from Caracas 150 years ago today, and whose aims must never be considered to be finally finished or accomplished. It was and is a revolution based on the ideals of human equality and dignity; a revolution that inspires men—as long as man aspires to be free—as they must be eternally; a revolution so flexible that it answers the needs of all of our countries, of all of our races, of all of our cultures. Like all great movements in the history of man, it has followed an uneven course. Men have tried to stem it, to divert it. Its ideals have been distorted and redefined to sap them of its essence, which is freedom. But always when this revolution has been imperiled men have risen to strengthen others' faith in it, to inspire them to its defense. In our

lifetime we of the Americas must be such men and women. And I am confident that this generation who hold positions of responsibility in this great area of the world, the Western Hemisphere, will meet their responsibilities—not merely yesterday, the Fourth of July, and not merely today, which is another equally important anniversary, but every day of every month of every year during the great decade of the 1960's.

Allied for progress, for a determined effort to realize the dreams of those who made our countries free, we are on the eve of great undertakings in our own hemisphere. May Bolívar's words be a beacon for all of us today: "The freedom of the new world is the hope of the universe."

As the Secretary of State said, the man we honor today played a significant and vital role in the liberation of six countries. It is a source of pride to those of us who live in my country that the Founding Fathers of this country played a role not only in the liberation of the United States, but by the standard that they raised played a great role in the liberation of other countries, even down to the present day.

Every action that we take for freedom has implications far beyond the frontiers of our own country. This hemisphere seeks a better life for its people. It is committed to progress, and it is committed to that progress through freedom.

It's a source of great satisfaction as President of the United States to salute a hero of our hemisphere from whose life and example we gather in this country, and in all the countries that share our commitment to freedom, great inspiration today.

NOTE: The President spoke at 11 a.m. at wreath-laying ceremonies at the Simón Bolívar Monument near the Pan American Union. His opening words referred to Secretary of State Dean Rusk and Dr. José Antonio Mayobre, Venezuelan Ambassador to the United States.

273 Letter to President Nkrumah of Ghana Concerning the Volta
     River Authority.   *July 6, 1961*

[Released July 6, 1961.   Dated June 29, 1961]

Dear Mr. President:

I was glad to receive your letter regarding the selection of a Chief Executive for the Volta River Authority. I think it was an excellent idea to ask Prime Minister Diefenbaker to propose a candidate. We have been in touch with our Canadian friends, and I am advised that the Prime Minister is giving this problem his personal attention and hopes to be able to suggest a suitable candidate soon.

I have asked my advisers to try to develop some alternative suggestions in the event that others do not prove available. At the same time, we have been in touch with Mr. Eugene Black of the International Bank for Reconstruction and Development, and I know that he is continuing to look over the field for possible candidates.

I am delighted to be able to advise you that all major issues involved in negotiations for the United States Government's share of the financing of the dam and smelter have now been resolved. The United States Government representatives are now working with your representatives here to develop the necessary documentation for signature and final closing.

Of course, as we all appreciate, our signing is contingent upon your bringing your negotiations with the International Bank for Reconstruction and Development to a successful conclusion.

It is a source of satisfaction to me that we have been able to join with your Government in helping to make this great project possible. It is a good omen that this major initial step has been accomplished during the first year of your Republic and it is a satisfaction to me that this was achieved during the first year of my Administration. I send you my congratulations on Republic Day and my sincere hope for the continued progress of your nation.

With kindest personal regards.

Sincerely,

JOHN F. KENNEDY

NOTE: The White House announced on October 20 that Clarence B. Randall, consultant to the U.S. Government on special foreign assistance projects, would lead a special mission to review U.S. participation in the Volta River project, and that he would be accompanied by Abram Chayes, Legal Adviser, Department of State, and Harry Shooshan, Assistant Deputy Managing Director for Operations, Development Loan Fund.

274 Remarks to the Executive Board of the United Steelworkers of
     America.   *July 6, 1961*

I AM GLAD to learn, President McDonald, that you and the members of the executive board of your great union have been meeting today with the Secretary of Labor and Under Secretary of Commerce to discuss the problems concerning employment and unemployment which face our Nation.

These problems were highlighted yesterday when the Department of Labor reported that although economic recovery had pushed employment to an alltime record level in June the percentage of unemployed remained at the same high level it has held for the past 7 months. Certainly, as representatives of workers in the steel industry who experienced the greatest curtailment of employment of any group of workers during the recent recession, you are well aware of the need for the Nation's economy to provide more jobs.

I can assure you that we in this administration will continue to devote ourselves to seeking ways to make sure that eventually every one of our fellow citizens who is willing and able to work can find a job.

In attempting to carry out this task I am most grateful for the support given my Executive actions and legislative program by the United Steelworkers of America. Without the help of organizations such as yours we would not have been able to achieve passage of the temporary extended unemployment insurance program or the Area Redevelopment Act, to name but two vital areas where your support was important

And I am especially pleased that the support you gave was predicated on a recognition of the public interest.

You have also shown this public responsibility in your support of our foreign policy.

That time in our history is passed when our relations with other nations, conditioned by great geographical barriers between us, represented the exclusive concern of governments and diplomats. It is now a matter of personal involvement for every citizen and for the free institutions that our citizens have built to express and protect their interests. The support of such institutions, like labor unions, is vital to the successful execution of our policy. I am happy to have this opportunity to thank you and your membership personally for the support you have given.

NOTE: The President spoke at the White House. In the opening paragraph he referred to David J. McDonald, President, United Steelworkers of America, Secretary of Labor Arthur J. Goldberg, and Under Secretary of Commerce Edward Gudeman.

275 Exchange of Messages With President Paz Estenssoro of Bolivia. *July* 8, 1961

[Released July 8, 1961. Dated June 22, 1961]

Dear Mr. President:

I have asked Ambassador Stephansky to convey to you my personal best wishes.

The program of cooperation which we have already initiated will, I trust, be only the first step in a continuing relationship of mutual respect and assistance. The government of the United States regards the economic and social development of Bolivia as one of the principal goals of the Alliance for Progress. We are firmly committed to continue to assist your efforts to promote the welfare of the Bolivian people and to achieve in freedom the fundamental aspiration of this historic Bolivian revolution.

I have requested Ambassador Stephansky to relay my deep admiration for your courage and vision in confronting the difficulties which your nation is now undergoing, and to wish you every success.

With warmest personal regards, I am

Sincerely,

JOHN F. KENNEDY

NOTE: President Paz' reply, dated June 29, follows:
Dear Mr. President:

I have had the pleasure of receiving from Ambassador Stephansky your cordial and thoughtful letter.

I see that you understand the aspirations of the Bolivian people, and I share your idea that the program of cooperation already initiated is only the beginning of a new and auspicious period of closer collaboration between Bolivia and the United States, within a friendly relationship of mutual respect and assistance.

The joint effort of our two nations can make a success, in my country, of the plan of the Alliance for Progress which the continent has received with lively enthusiasm, seeing in it the hope of overcoming underdevelopment in a climate of freedom and social justice.

I value your accurate appraisal of the struggle in which my people are engaged to achieve a better and more fitting standard of living. My government is resolved steadfastly to continue the process of the Bolivian revolution, surmounting all existing obstacles, to the end of achieving fully its aims of collective well-being and emancipation.

In my first personal contact with Ambassador Stephansky, upon the occasion of receiving his letters of credence, I was able to recognize his high intellectual qualities as well as his sincere concern for our problems. I am confident that his mission will be fruitful for both our countries.

I reciprocate your thoughtful greetings with the expression of my sincere friendship.

Cordially yours,

VICTOR PAZ ESTENSSORO

---

276   Letter to Adolf Berle on Receiving Final Report of the President's Task Force on Latin America.   *July* 8, 1961

[Released July 8, 1961.   Dated July 7, 1961]

Dear Professor Berle:

I have read with great interest and appreciation your final report as Chairman of the President's Task Force on Latin America. Helping the passage of the 500 million dollar social fund appropriation, securing critically needed financial assistance for Brazil, expediting urgent economic aid projects in Venezuela and Colombia, formulating revised hemispheric defense policies and assembling an emergency program for Bolivia, are among the many substantial accomplishments of your group. This record is one of which you and your fellow task force members should be proud.

Your group has fulfilled, in an outstanding manner, its purpose of helping to coordinate and direct the formulation and conduct of new Latin American policies during the transition period immediately following the inauguration. In addition, your pre-inauguration task force—primarily devoted to the formulation of policy—laid the groundwork for many aspects of the Alliance for Progress.

I intend to give careful and serious study to your recommendations for future policy, including the expansion of our educational-information-propaganda program in Latin America.

Let me extend to you my warmest expressions of deep personal gratitude for the time, energy and talent you have devoted to the work of the task force—work which has made a lasting contribution to the cause of freedom in the hemisphere. It is another example of the devotion to public service which you have displayed throughout your long and brilliant career in government and in private life. In unhesitatingly giving up your scholarly and legal work to come to Washington you have furnished an outstanding example of dedication and sacrifice in the public interest. And I hope I can continue to feel free to call upon your services from time to time as problems arise in which your many skills can be of use.

Sincerely,

JOHN F. KENNEDY

[Honorable Adolf A. Berle, Jr., Chairman, Task Force on Latin America, Department of State, Washington 25, D.C.]

277 Remarks to the Citizens Committee for International Development. *July 10, 1961*

MR. PIERSON, I want to express my thanks to you, and to the other members of the committee, who are outstanding public and private citizens, for their effort to assist us in securing the passage of the mutual security bill through this session of the Congress.

I consider this bill to be probably the most vital piece of legislation in the national interest that may be before the Congress this year. It involves the effort by this country for its own security, for its own well-being, to assist other countries in maintaining their security.

All of us have been concerned, rightfully, when one or another country passes behind the Iron Curtain. I can say, as my predecessor President Eisenhower said before me, that if the United States were not engaged in this program, if we fail to meet our responsibilities in this area this year, and in the days to come—the years to come—then other countries must inevitably fall.

The Communists are making a great effort to expand their influence, to move their center of power outward. The thing that stands between them and their objective are these governments and these people.

I believe that we have an opportunity to assist them to maintain their countries' independence. They depend in a large degree upon us. This country is a free country, it has great resources, and I think we have to recognize that freedom for ourselves and for others is not purchased lightly. It requires an effort by each of us. This is a matter of the greatest national importance. It is a matter which has engaged the attention of the United States since the end of the Second World War. We have seen the assistance which we gave to Western Europe

permit Western Europe to be rebuilt into a strong and vital area upon which our security depends. We see ourselves heavily engaged in Latin America. We see ourselves involved in a great effort in Africa, in Asia, to maintain the independence of these countries.

It is not an easy matter for our people to again support this kind of assistance abroad, but I want to make it very clear that it is assistance to the United States itself. We cannot live in an isolated world. And I would much rather give our assistance in this way—and a large part of it consists of food, defense support as well as long-term economic loans—I would much rather have us do it this way than have to send American boys to have to do it.

We believe in this program. One of the most important parts of it now is the provision providing long-term authorizations and commitments. That means that we will say to a country that if you will do "one, two, three" on taxes and land reform and capital investment, then the United States along with other prosperous countries of Western Europe will be prepared to meet their responsibilities over a longer period.

Now when we move from year to year without having any idea what we can do in the future, the country's programing, the country's organization for its advance is bound to be haphazard. And I think that is one of the reasons why the program has not always been successful in the past, and one of the reasons why we have had waste in the past.

We are bringing new people into this organization. We are reorganizing it. We are getting the best talent we can get. I hope that we are going to get long-term authorizations to permit us to move ahead over a period of time.

I want to express my thanks to you, Mr. Pierson, for your efforts, and to the members of your committee. You are now engaged in a most important public service. And I want to ask the American people to support this program as a vital one in the fight for our own security and in the fight for peace.

NOTE: The President spoke in the Rose Garden at the White House. His opening words "Mr. Pierson" referred to Warren Lee Pierson, chairman of the Citizens Committee for International Development, a volunteer group of business, labor, and educational leaders working in support of the President's foreign aid bill.

278   Remarks at Ceremonies Honoring George W. Norris on the 100th Anniversary of His Birth. *July 11, 1961*

FIRST, let me tell you that I am sorry to keep my former colleagues waiting. Secondly, I am glad to have this visit from the Board of Directors of the TVA because of TVA's national and international importance. Perhaps Mr. Vogel would like to say something to us here.

[*At this point Herbert D. Vogel, Chairman of the Board of Directors of TVA, paid a tribute to Senator Norris and announced a reduction in the TVA rate schedule to be known as the Norris Centennial Rate. The President then called on Senator Lister Hill of Alabama and Representative Clifford Davis of Tennessee for remarks, after which he resumed speaking.*]

I want to express again my appreciation. I always thought it was a most interesting thing about Senator Norris, that he actually lived so far from it that he would get no benefit at all for his own State, but he and the people of his State still made this great effort.

The second thing is, I am conscious, sitting here, of the tremendous international implications of TVA and the fact that the TVA effort not only affects TVA but also reflects similar efforts in Pakistan, India, Iran, Colombia, other parts of Africa and Latin America. Every economic mission that comes here from Africa always comes first to see what they can do about a dam and power, and the TVA has always been their great inspiration. So that this is one of the most important international assets, as well as national assets, that we have.

And I want to say, General, that this Government, and the Members of both parties, this administration is extremely anxious to see TVA go forward, not rest on its laurels. For instance, we have had correspondence about certain tributaries of the Tennessee River, and it seems to me this should receive greater attention in the TVA, as well as by the national Government. Local flood control projects in the Valley can be emphasized. Experiments in conjunction with the Atomic Energy Commission can be worked out to see about cheaper power from atomic energy at rates that will make it competitive, and that more intensive effort will now be made in soil conservation, particularly coal mines.

I want to express my thanks to Members of Congress for coming, because this is not only a substantive act in honoring Senator Norris, but shows our continuing interest by the Valley people and also by the people of the United States in further development of the TVA.

We have here Members almost all of whom served—and Mrs. Reece—who have been responsible over a period of many years in securing support from the Congress for the TVA. And this announcement from the TVA today, I have become more and more conscious of the role it plays. So that we are delighted to have you all here, and the Members of Congress, and to tell you that I hope when you next have a Norris Day, that additional progress will have been reported.

I happen to have one of my staff members here who was a former employee of the TVA, therefore I hear a good deal about it. I want to thank you—I don't want to hold anybody up, because I know many of you have Committee meetings, it's just that I appreciate your coming. Sorry I kept you, but I want to say that I think this matter is much more important than just an ordinary White House ceremony, because of the significance of this project in many different ways.

NOTE: The President spoke in his office at the White House. In the concluding paragraphs he referred to Mrs. Louise G. Reece, U.S. Representative from Tennessee, and Lee C. White, Assistant Special Counsel to the President.

279   Remarks of Welcome to the President of Pakistan at Andrews Air Force Base. *July 11, 1961*

Mr. President, your daughter the Begum, the Ambassador of Pakistan, members of your party, ladies and gentlemen:

It is a great pleasure and great honor for me to welcome our distinguished visitor, the President of Pakistan. I do not know if he realizes that many generations of young boys, of which I was one in this century, found the same excitement, the same adventure in the history of his country that young men, young boys find in my own country in Laramie, Fort Dodge, Tombstone, and all the rest.

The Khyber Pass, the fact that Alexander's troops moved through your country so many years ago in extending their control into the far reaches of the known earth, the great struggles of the 19th and 20th century on your frontiers—all this had a great effect upon at least one young American growing up, and I'm sure it was shared by many of my contemporaries.

We are also glad to have you here because Americans in private and in their public life appreciate the value of friendship and the constancy of friends. And it is a fact which is remembered by every citizen of this country, that during the difficult days which faced our country at the time of the war in Korea, one of the first to offer us assistance was your country, and one of those who played a most significant role during the whole years of the long struggle was the country of Pakistan.

Thirdly, we are glad to have you here because even in my short months as President of the United States I have had my own opportunity to make a judgment of the vigor, of the friendship, of the people of your country. And during the difficult days which we have already had, the support and friendship which your country has extended to us has caused you to be especially welcome today.

Most of all, we're glad to have you here because you come as the head of an important and powerful country which is allied with us in SEATO, which is associated with us in CENTO, which represents a powerful force for freedom in your area of the world.

I want to say that the President originally had intended to come in November, but after the Vice President's trip there, where he was most impressed with the exchange of views which he had with the President, he suggested that we impose upon the President and ask him to move his trip ahead, because of the importance of consultation on great issues during these summer months. He was kind enough to do it, and I want to say, Mr. President, that we appreciate your coming now.

We are looking forward to having a chance to talk with you on the great issues which face both of our countries. Your leadership in your country, your stand for freedom, your efforts to build a better life for your people, your efforts to harness science in order to defeat nature, in the whole effort to reclaim your land and make it fruitful—all these things have made you a figure which causes us to be extremely grateful to have you here.

I want you to know, Mr. President, and I hope your countrymen know, that you come with the warmest welcome from the people of this country, and the warmest welcome from the Government, the warmest welcome from the Congress—as you will see tomorrow.

I want to say, Mr. President, that in these difficult days it is a pleasure to welcome a friend of immediacy and constancy, the President of Pakistan.

NOTE: President Ayub Kahn responded as follows: *Mr. President, Secretary of State, General Lemnitzer, and other friends:*

I am overwhelmed by the warmth of the reception, Mr. President, you have given me, and the very kind words you have expressed about my country and its relationship with your country.

We in Pakistan take deep interest in the thinking, policies, and actions of the United States of America, although we are a long way away from you and you are a long way away from us; but the world has shrunk and we feel that our safety and our security and our independence is endurably linked with yours. And I hope that you also feel that your interests in the regions in which we live are an identification with our interest.

We therefore naturally take deepest interest in what goes on in this country and especially what you do, sir. We watch you very carefully, for the simple reason that what you do affects our future. And so therefore, Mr. President, I have come here to see you especially, to exchange views with you, for the simple reason that your country and my country are so close to each other. And when in the near future very far-reaching events may overtake us, it is necessary that we should all have our minds clear as to the work that has to be done. At the same time I have heard of your great dynamic personality, and the people that are around you, and it is so nice and refreshing to hear that somebody has the wisdom, the drive, and the go, that at least it does my heart a lot of good. I am looking forward to having the opportunity of exchanging views with you and the other members of your team, and I shall be presenting before you the views of the people of Pakistan right on the other side of the world—and it is a good thing to know what goes on, on the other side of the hill.

And at the same time I shall be anxiously listening to what you have to say, and I have no doubt that our area of understanding will enlarge as a result of it, and our friendship will get stronger.

Before I finish I would like to perform one more pleasant duty, and that is this: Mr. President, I bring to you the greetings—through you to the people of the United States of America—the greetings of the people of Pakistan. They wish you all well.

Thank you.

280   Toasts of the President and President Ayub Khan at the State Dinner at Mount Vernon. *July 11, 1961*

Ladies and gentlemen:

I want to express, first, the appreciation of us all to our hosts, and I would not want the President of Pakistan and his party to think that he was being entertained by the United States Government, or the President. We are all guests here tonight—the Americans and our visitors from abroad—of a somewhat obscure group, but nevertheless extremely powerful and significant, the Ladies of Mount Vernon.

It is a source of great satisfaction to my wife, far surpassing anything else that has happened to her, that she is related by marriage to Connecticut, which is the title given to the Lady of Mount Vernon who comes from that State.

We are also, though Members of Congress never probably realized it, we also have in Congress, Ohio—which is Mrs. Bolton, who is the Lady who is very active in politics but hides many of the things that she does under a bushel, and has labored long for Mount Vernon and for many other causes, and as usual none of us knows about it. So we want to express our great satisfaction in having a member of our lowly profession so honored by the Ladies.

I want to express our thanks to the Regent, Mrs. Beirne, who has been so generous, and to Mr. Wall, who is the Director of Mount Vernon. I want to say, and I am sure I speak on behalf of my fellow countrymen and women, the great pride and satisfaction that we have in Mount Vernon. This is the first time, I am sure, that any of us have dined here. This is a great object of regard and respect by our fellow citizens. It is intensely felt by the Members of the Congress and members of the Government,

and therefore for all of us, not only from abroad but from home who come to Mount Vernon, we feel the greatest pride in it.

Mr. President, we feel a special satisfaction because you are our guest tonight and because we feel that what Mount Vernon stands for is understood by you. Mount Vernon means to us not merely a beautiful home, but it also is, we hope, the symbol of the United States—in the past, the present, and we hope the future.

This country was developed by an extraordinary group of men who had wide talent, who came from among the most prosperous group in our country, and yet were revolutionaries, and who made this country's independence possible. And we hope that the same principles with which our hosts tonight honor President Washington, we hope this country stands for today.

We recognize in you a leader who stands for those things in his own country, who recognizes that the independence of his own country is not enough, that there is a link which binds your country and ours all the way across the globe. And it is a particular source of satisfaction to my wife and to myself that this dinner here honors you who, as I said at the airport this morning, has been a friend of our country long before I became the President; but even in the short time that I have been President, I have seen a most particular manifestation of your country's willingness to commit itself for the cause of freedom.

George Washington once said, "I would rather be at Mount Vernon with a friend or two about me than be attended at the seat of government by the officers of state and the representatives of every power in Europe."

We have got a friend or two about us tonight. We nevertheless feel that Washington would be glad we are here, and would be glad that we are his guests and particularly, I believe, that you brought your daughter and her husband here, and the members of your party. And I hope you realize that among both Republicans and Democrats, and among all the Americans here tonight, that no one could be a more welcome guest.

I hope that you will all join with me in drinking a toast to the President of Pakistan and the people of his country.

NOTE: The President proposed the toast at a state dinner given in a pavilion overlooking the Potomac River at Mount Vernon. President Ayub Khan responded as follows:

"Mr. President, ladies and gentlemen:

"I am very grateful to the President for the kind words he said about me and my country. And I am also very grateful for our hosts. I thought Mrs. Kennedy was our host. I thought that it was her idea, and that may well be right, even now. After what the President has said, I must thank the Ladies of Mount Vernon—I hope they are here—for this magnificent arrangement which they have made.

"I have been most inspired to come to this place, because the man who built it, your first President, he certainly was a very distinguished soldier. And it seems that history keeps on repeating itself. The poor soldiers!—having to first of all defend their country; when they get into a mess they have also got to put it right, too. And when they do that, people call them dictators. That is a very poor consolation for an honest effort to serve one's kith and kin and one's future generations.

"I think the history of a country like mine is probably passing through a similar phase as the history of your country did at the time of George Washington. And I think, too, that it will be correct to say that our problems are probably more pressing and more immediate, and we have to fight against time.

"Life has never been easy for anybody who wants to do things above the normal. But today, for instance, a country like mine that got its independence 14 years ago, found itself all of a sudden pitched forth into a very competitive and fast-moving world, whilst the people had not been prepared, through foreign domination, through the accident of history, to be able to fit into today's world, to be able to move with today's world. And if those people don't move in today's world, they are not only going to be left behind, but they will find no place in this world.

"So we not only have to have the task of getting rid of all those legacies that accumulate as a result of that type of history, but we have the task of shaking our people out of stagnation, we have the task of educating them, and bringing them up to the common line of starting, from which they can start moving out into the world of today. We have got to shed our prejudices, we have got to carry out all sorts of information, in order to psychologically, physically, and otherwise to prepare our people to move and be of some consequence in the life of today.

"And that is happening, especially in Asia, an extremely dangerous and difficult environment. And any country that falters in Asia, for even a year or two, will find itself subjugated to communism. And that threat is always present. And to say that in any country the number of Communists is limited, and so on, is not a true guide. Once you have weak governments, once you have people at the helm of affairs who are incapable of giving the right decisions, and in time, and not be able to make your people move forward—you have got to make, sometimes, harsh decisions, certainly unpleasant decisions—the creeping forward of communism begins.

"So in one way or another we are carrying out a similar sort of exercise George Washington did, in his time, under perhaps more difficult circumstances. But I think if people have a certain amount of vision, a certain amount of determination and courage, I don't see any reason why one should not be able to overcome this problem.

"Now during this period of trying to develop the people and make them progress, and make their lives a little better than they have been in the past, we have to spare all our resources we can to sink into the country, and at the same time expect our friends to assist us to be able to develop our country; because no country in the world, to my knowledge, has been able to develop or obtain a higher standard of living without some sort of outside assistance. But I am sure that our friends are conscious of it, and at the same time I can assure them that we are determined, and I think our people are determined. They are getting conscious, they are getting ready to make a real effort to move forward by breaking through that period of stagnation, in order to make secure their freedom, in order to secure for themselves a better living condition.

"So as I say, it is really a source of great inspiration to me to come to a place like this. And I am very grateful to you, Mr. President, for bringing them here, at the same time all the ladies who are our hosts, and I see quite a number of my old friends here—and really, in one way or another, it has been a lovely evening—indeed one which I shall never forget.

"Now I will ask you to rise, please, in a toast to the health of the President and Mrs. Kennedy, and the well-being and happiness of your great country."

In his remarks the President referred to Mrs. Francis F. Beirne, Regent of the Mount Vernon Ladies Association, and Charles C. Wall, Resident Director of Mount Vernon.

281 Statement by the President on the Signing of Equal Opportunity Agreements by Major Government Contractors. *July 12, 1961*

THIS MORNING'S signing—by officials of the eight largest government contractors—of the Plans for Progress marks an historic step forward in the effort to secure equal employment opportunity for every American of every race, color and belief.

More than 800,000 jobs are covered by these agreements—agreements for continuous, systematic and vigorous action to open new job opportunities to members of minority groups. They have been the result of completely voluntary and cooperative action between the United States Government and its largest contractors. Yet they hold greater promise of tangible measurable progress than all our previous efforts to secure equal employment opportunity for Americans.

With the addition of these eight companies to the one which has already signed such an agreement a significant portion of American business is now covered by voluntary equal opportunity agreements. During the next several months we hope to secure the adherence of many more of the Nation's largest employers to similar agreements. In this way we can move toward the day when American business, in cooperation with American government, will have abolished all artificial barriers to a man's effort to secure a decent life for himself and his family.

NOTE: Equal opportunity agreements were signed by Boeing Airplane Company; North American Aviation, Inc.; United Aircraft Corporation; Western Electric Company; Martin Company; General Electric Company; Radio Corporation of America; and Douglas Aircraft Company. For the President's statement upon the signing of the first such agreement, with Lockheed Aircraft Corporation, see Item 204.

282 Remarks to a Group of American Field Service Students. *July 13, 1961*

I WANT, first of all, to say that I'm a great admirer of the American Field Service. A good many young Americans whom I knew in the days of the Second World War served with distinction, showed the hand of, I hope, compassion—certainly friendship—to those on both sides, and what is more important, they learned from that experience a valuable lesson. And because of that, and their continued interest in our country and in the cause of peace, you are here.

I hope that your experience here has taught you a valuable lesson, and that is that there are no simple problems, that as we look, in the United States, around the world at so many different people and so many different countries, we build up in our own minds stereotypes and prejudices, and sympathies and affections—and I'm sure you have learned how far removed we may be from our real understanding of the life of your people.

You will go back to your countries, and they have stereotypes and prejudices and ideas about the United States. It is going to be your destiny, I hope, to serve in the interests of peace as a bridge between the best parts of my country and your people.

I hope that you go from here not merely as a friend but understanding our faults and our assets, but most of all understanding what we're trying to do, and what we're trying to be—and that we recognize that we have in this country great unfinished business.

We want your friendship, and I hope that you 1200 will be the seed which will build a better life for all of our people.

This house belongs to the American people, and we are temporary residents. It has housed a good many Americans who I am glad to say have served as inspirations to your own people—Washington, Jefferson, Lincoln, the Roosevelts, Wilson, and the others.

We are now occupying a position of responsibility in a most difficult time—all of us—and therefore once again it is an honor as President of the United States to welcome you, who will in the coming months and years bear the great burdens of leadership in your country.

And I hope it will be possible that a future President of the United States will greet a President or a Prime Minister, some years from now, who stood in July 1961 on the lawn of the White House.

Thank you.

NOTE: The President spoke from the Rose Garden to a group of students from 50 countries studying in the United States under the auspices of the American Field Service.

283 Joint Statement Following Discussions With the President of Pakistan. *July* 13, 1961

PRESIDENT KENNEDY and President Ayub have had a cordial and frank exchange of views over the past three days on topics of mutual interest to their Governments. The visit afforded a timely opportunity for the two Presidents to establish a personal acquaintance and to carry forward the exchange of views which has taken place by correspondence over the past several months.

The two Presidents reviewed at length the international situation with emphasis upon events in areas in which the dangers of conflict have become a cause of deep concern to the community of nations. The talks on these subjects again underlined the importance of close cooperation and understanding between nations of the free world in order to provide the greatest possible unity in protecting the independence of states and in preserving international peace and security.

They considered the dangers arising out of recent events in Berlin and in Southeast Asia, especially in Laos.

The two Presidents examined together the threats to the free people of the subcontinent of South Asia and agreed that this area is a primary target of international Communism; that the integrity and independence of each country in this area depend heavily upon friendship and cooperation among all of them; and that solutions of divisive issues, which call for farsighted statesmanship on all sides, are a clear and present need.

President Ayub reaffirmed the desire and objective of his Government to maintain friendly relations with all neighboring states based on mutual respect and the integrity of Pakistan's borders. He reviewed his Government's position on the Kashmir issue and stressed the great importance attached to this issue by the people of Pakistan. He stated that current developments in South Asia had made an early resolution of this issue imperative. President Kennedy affirmed the desire of the United States to see a satisfactory solution of the Kashmir issue and expressed the hope that progress toward a settlement would be possible at an early date.

The coincidence of President Ayub's visit with the tenth anniversary of economic cooperation between the United States and Pakistan afforded a unique opportunity for a thorough review of Pakistan's economic development program. The two Presidents discussed the substantial advances that have been made in agriculture, industrial production, communications, education and other programs designed to bring a better life to the people of Pakistan. They agreed upon the need for outside aid to fulfill the financing requirements of the current Five Year Plan, and discussed the forthcoming Consortium meeting sponsored by the International Bank for Reconstruction and Development to provide needed assistance. President Ayub was assured of firm United States interest in the finding of adequate funds so that this program will be implemented with the greatest possible effectiveness.

They examined the serious problem of water-logging and salinity which is rapidly taking vast areas of land out of cultivation. It was agreed that the United States would send to Pakistan in the very near future a mission of highly qualified scientists and engineers with a view to making suggestions to the Government of Pakistan for speeding up progress in combating this problem which is recognized to be of greatest importance to the people of that country. Efforts will then be made with friendly countries to work out the provision of the necessary external financing.

President Kennedy expressed keen interest in President Ayub's description of the needs of Pakistan relating to scientific and technical facilities.

The two Presidents reaffirmed the solemn purpose of the bilateral agreements signed by the two Governments on March 5, 1959 which declares among other things that "The Government of the United States of America regards as vital to its national interest and to world peace the preservation of the independence and integrity of Pakistan . . ." They also reaffirmed the value of existing collective security arrangements as an instrument for defense against aggression.

They reviewed the progress of United States' military assistance to Pakistan which is being extended in order to assist that nation to maintain forces for the preservation of its security.

President Ayub described the progress which has been made toward the development of a new constitution suitable to the requirements of the people of Pakistan.

The two Presidents agreed that this, their first meeting, has greatly enhanced the understanding between the Governments of Pakistan and the United States and has contributed substantially to continuing close cooperation between the two nations.

284   Letter to the President of the Senate and to the Speaker of the House Transmitting a Water Resources Planning Bill.
July 13, 1961

Dear Mr. ————:

I am transmitting herewith a draft of legislation designated as the "Water Resources Planning Act of 1961." This draft supersedes the proposal transmitted with the letter of January 16, 1961, from the former Director of the Bureau of the Budget and now pending before the Committee on Interior and Insular Affairs.

In my message to the Congress on natural resources, I stated that:

"Our Nation has been blessed with a bountiful supply of water; but it is not a blessing we can regard with complacency. We now use over 300 billion gallons of water a day, much of it wastefully. By 1980 we will need 600 billion gallons a day.

"Our supply of water is not always consistent with our needs of time and place. Floods one day in one section may be countered in other days or in other sections by the severe water shortages which are now afflicting many eastern urban areas and are particularly critical in the West. Our available water supply must be used to give maximum benefits for all purposes—hydroelectric power, irrigation and reclamation, navigation, recreation, health, home and industry. . ."

Maximum beneficial use of water rests upon comprehensive and coordinated planning by both Federal agencies and States. This draft legislation will encourage and make possible such planning.

Legislation already introduced in the Senate and the House manifests congressional recognition of the need for comprehensive planning for water and related land resources. The draft legislation adopts principles and procedures included in a number of these pending bills. Implementing the recommendations on comprehensive planning and grants to States for such planning made by the Senate Select Committee on National Water Resources, the proposed legislation brings together in a single bill authorizations for complementary planning activities by Federal agencies and State governments.

The regional or river basin commissions authorized by the bill will prepare and keep up to date comprehensive, integrated, joint plans for Federal, State, and local development of water and related land resources. Existing laws will not be modified or superseded. The preparation of detailed plans and specifications for individual projects, and the construction and operation of works of improvement will continue to be the responsibility of appropriate Federal agencies, States, or local groups.

Another important feature of the bill is the establishment of an interdepartmental group in the Executive Branch for coordinating river basin plans and for maintaining a continuing study of water supply, requirements, and management. The Water Resources Council will be composed of the Secretary of the Interior, the Secretary of Agriculture, the Secretary of the Army, and the Secretary of Health, Education, and Welfare. Other departments and agencies with interest in the water resources field, will participate in the work of the Council on an ad hoc basis. The draft legislation provides that the chairman of the Council shall be designated by the President. I propose to designate the Secretary of the

507

Interior as the first chairman of the Council.

The first major task of the Water Resources Council will be to establish, subject to my approval, standards for formulating and evaluating water resources projects. These standards will replace those currently in effect.

Finally, the proposed legislation would authorize financial assistance to the States enabling them to play a more effective role in planning for the development and conservation of water and related land resources. This is an essential element in promoting sound, comprehensive water resources planning.

We have a national obligation to manage our basic water supply so it will be available when and where needed and in acceptable quality and quantity—and we have no time to lose. The planning authorized by this legislation will provide a vital tool for achieving effective water resources management.

Also enclosed is a section-by-section analysis of the bill. A similar letter is being sent to the President of the Senate.

Sincerely,

JOHN F. KENNEDY

NOTE: This is the text of identical letters addressed to the Honorable Lyndon B. Johnson, President of the Senate, and to the Honorable Sam Rayburn, Speaker of the House of Representatives.

285   Statement by the President Concerning a Plan for the Development of Northeast Brazil.   *July 14, 1961*

NO AREA in this hemisphere is in greater or more urgent need of attention than Brazil's vast Northeast. Covering more than 600,000 square miles and containing almost 25 million people, Northeast Brazil is one of South America's most crowded and poverty-stricken regions. The average per capita income barely reaches $100, in 18 Northeastern cities infant mortality is between 25 and 35 percent, and the area as a whole suffers from overpopulation, recurrent drought, food shortages, and high illiteracy. To these problems is added a yearly population increase of 600,000.

This area with its poverty, hunger and consequent discontent is a crucible of social, economic and political problems—problems which have unmistakable implications for the future development of Brazil and the security of the entire hemisphere.

To study cooperative methods of dealing with these problems the United States invited Dr. Celso Furtado—Director of the Development Agency for Northeast Brazil (SUDENE)—to come to Washington and review projected plans for the development of the Northeast. Dr. Furtado has prepared—through the agency of SUDENE—a five year plan for the Northeast designed to reconstruct the economy of that area and bring hope for a better life to its people. The plan is the result of two years' study, and has the firm support of President Quadros and the Brazilian Congress.

The plan envisages a total cost of $900 million dollars over a five year period; $500 million to be supplied by the Brazilians; and $126 million by international institutions such as the Inter-American Bank or IDA. Of the remainder, the plan permits providing almost half through the supply of surplus foodstuffs. High officials of the United States Government—in meetings chaired by Milton Barall of the Department of State—have spent this week in preliminary discussions of the program with Dr. Furtado.

Certainly a plan of this magnitude, with its wealth of technical detail, will require a great deal of further study. And the United States intends to dispatch a group of economists and technicians to Brazil to participate with SUDENE in such studies. However, although the details of the plan and the magnitude of resources involved need further examination, the overall objectives of SUDENE appear to be substantially sound, realistic, and in harmony with those of the Alliance for Progress; which itself is an outgrowth of the Brazilian concept of Operation Pan-America.

Therefore, the United States is prepared to cooperate with SUDENE to help it realize the objectives embodied in this program. Together the United States and Brazil will work with international agencies and other Western nations in an effort to mobilize the external resources which may be necessary. The United States is prepared to cooperate with SUDENE, on a continuing basis, to help solve the problems of the Northeast and to bring economic and social progress to that hard-pressed region.

The Governments of Brazil and the United States have already cooperated in providing a great deal of assistance to Northeast Brazil just as we have cooperated in providing substantial assistance this year to the entire country. And the ICA, on request by the Brazilian Government, is prepared to immediately provide technicians for research and technical assistance in river valley development, soil utilization, water supply, basic education and other fields to which SUDENE is giving priority attention.

In the course of Dr. Furtado's visit we have concluded initial agreements for the supply—as part of the Food for Peace Program—of grain and lard as an emergency reserve for flood or drought. In addition, food will be used to aid the resettlement of emigrants from the Northeast area. Negotiations are also continuing for the donation of U.S. foodstuffs to be used as partial wages in connection with economic development projects.

The visit of Dr. Furtado has helped to increase our understanding of the problems of Northeast Brazil. The systematic study, planning and concern which the Goverment of Brazil has devoted to the area holds high promise for the betterment of the living conditions of its 25 million people. And the United States intends to play a continuing role in helping our sister Republic of Brazil meet this urgent challenge.

286   Letter to the President of the Senate and to the Speaker of the House Concerning Local Self-Government in the District of Columbia. *July* 15, 1961

Dear Mr. ————:

I am transmitting for consideration by the Congress a proposed District of Columbia Charter Act. The draft bill would restore to District residents the basic right to local self-government through the elective process, a right enjoyed by all other American citizens. Restoration of suffrage and the responsibility to the people of the District for dealing with their municipal problems is long overdue. It is time to eliminate the last legal and constitutional anomaly in the United States and to reaffirm our belief in the principle that government should be responsible to the governed.

The draft bill authorizes (1) a locally

elected mayor, a seven-member legislative council and a non-voting delegate to the House of Representatives; (2) full participation by District residents in election campaigns; (3) a specific formula for regular annual payments by the Federal Government to pay its proper share of the expenses of the District government and to permit the District government to stabilize its long-range fiscal plans and its tax and borrowing programs; and (4) transfer to the District of certain independent agencies which perform essentially municipal functions and are closely related to other functions directly carried out by the District government.

The District of Columbia is the seat of the Nation's legislative and executive branches of government, the Supreme Court, the headquarters of most of the executive agencies and a showcase for diplomatic missions, international visitors and our own citizens, as well as the residence of over three-fourths of a million citizens. The draft bill therefore authorizes the President to review and disapprove District legislative actions which would adversely affect a Federal interest; and obviously the Congress

would retain authority to enact legislation to override any action taken by the District government.

In addition to the draft bill, I am enclosing a letter from the President of the Board of Commissioners to the District of Columbia, describing the legislation in some detail. A letter identical to this is being sent to the Speaker of the House of Representatives (President of the Senate).

I believe that enactment of the proposed legislation will again vest in the residents of the District the fundamental right of self-government and will offer the Nation's Capital city the opportunity for more effective governmental organization and management. I hope therefore that early hearings can be held and that favorable action will be taken by the Congress on this important legislation.

Sincerely,

JOHN F. KENNEDY

NOTE: This is the text of identical letters addressed to the Honorable Lyndon B. Johnson, President of the Senate, and to the Honorable Sam Rayburn, Speaker of the House of Representatives.

The letter was released at Hyannis, Mass.

287 Remarks at the Swearing-In Ceremonies for deLesseps Morrison and Robert F. Woodward. *July 17, 1961*

I WANT to express our great pleasure—of everyone here, particularly the citizens of Louisiana, the two Senators, Senator Ellender and Senator Long, and the Members of Congress and the other friends of our new Ambassador to the Organization of American States, at his assumption of this responsibility.

Ambassador Morrison left a most significant position as Mayor of New Orleans, a position he's occupied for a number of years. He did so only because he considered

it in the vital interests of the United States to assume his present position. The fact that we were so anxious to have him become our Ambassador to the Organization of American States and the fact that he was willing to do so indicate the extraordinary interest which this country has in the relations in our hemisphere, and also the great hopes we put in the Organization of American States. This Organization of sister Republics, which has been built and developed in order to maintain the security of the hemisphere, will face responsibilities and problems of greater importance in the coming months and years than it's ever faced in the past.

And it is for that reason that I'm particularly glad to have as the representative of the United States a valued public servant who has served his city, his State, and his country on many occasions, and who brings to this new position of trust great energy and great interest in the welfare of our entire hemisphere.

So, Ambassador, it is a great pleasure to welcome you into the sacred ranks of Ambassadors, and to express the hope that it will serve our country and also our hemisphere.

[*The President spoke in the Cabinet Room following the taking of the oath of office by Mr. Morrison as Representative to the Organization of American States with the rank of ambassador. After Mr. Woodward took the oath of office as Assistant Secretary of State for Inter-American Affairs the President resumed speaking.*]

It is a great pleasure to participate in the assumption of responsibility by the new Assistant Secretary of State. He felt that he was safely hidden from all attention in Chile, that he was many thousands of miles away, and that the long hand of the Government would fall on someone else besides him and he would be permitted to live out his years in seclusion. But nevertheless I think we are most fortunate to have him. This is a most demanding post.

It is a matter of primacy to this Government that our relations with the countries of this hemisphere should be increasingly intimate and increasingly fruitful, and therefore we now have as our Assistant Secretary a valued officer of the Foreign Service, who brings to this position long experience, understanding, and also a great acquaintance with all of the leaders of Latin America and all of the powerful forces that run throughout our hemisphere.

So, Mr. Secretary, I'm sure I speak on behalf of the Secretary of State, your colleagues in the ambassadorial group from this hemisphere, the Members of Congress, in welcoming you as the center of responsibility for our policy in this area of the world.

288   Joint Statement Following Discussions With Prime Minister Nyerere of Tanganyika.   *July 17, 1961*

PRIME MINISTER NYERERE today concluded a series of talks with the President, the Secretary of State, the Secretary of Commerce and the Director of the International Cooperation Administration. The Prime Minister came to Washington on an informal visit following discussions last week at the Trusteeship Council of the United Nations.

The talks covered African problems of common interest and Tanganyika's economic development plan. Prime Minister Nyerere emphasized that his country's political and social future depended upon the attainment of the development plan's objectives.

President Kennedy expressed the friendly interest of the United States in Tanganyika's future and made clear the intention of the United States to join the UK and others in helping Tanganyika to meet the objectives of its three-year development plan.

289 Letter to the President of the Senate and to the Speaker of the House Concerning the Need for Additional Institutes Within the Public Health Service. *July 18, 1961*

Dear Mr.————:

I am enclosing for consideration by the Congress a draft bill to authorize the Surgeon General to establish within the Public Health Service a National Institute of Child Health and Human Development and a National Institute of General Medical Sciences.

At present, there are seven separate Institutes within the Public Health Service. Each Institute focuses its attention on a major disease problem. Each Institute organizes, arranges for financing, and stimulates a wide range of studies in its field. They have all made important contributions to our knowledge of the dangers in crippling diseases and advanced the frontiers of medicine.

It is now both appropriate and timely to elevate two additional areas of medical research activity to the level of Institutes. In this way, the kind of research effort that is needed to improve the health of the children and to stimulate basic studies in the biological sciences will be assured. One of these two Institutes will deal with child health and human development. It will include a Center for Research in Child Health, as well as other activities not now covered by the existing Institutes. It is my belief that this concentration of attention in this field will help us discover some of the secrets of the aging process. In time, it will help us live happier and more useful lives.

The other proposal will convert the Division of General Medical Sciences in the Public Health Service into an Institute, thus recognizing the importance of its program. This new Institute will be an important center for research in the general medical sciences.

The purposes and functions of both of the new Institutes are outlined in detail in the attached letter from the Secretary of Health, Education, and Welfare. I urge the favorable consideration of the proposal.

Sincerely,

JOHN F. KENNEDY

NOTE: This is the text of identical letters addressed to the Honorable Lyndon B. Johnson, President of the Senate, and to the Honorable Sam Rayburn, Speaker of the House of Representatives.

290 Letter to the President of the Senate and to the Speaker of the House Relating to the Research Functions of the Children's Bureau. *July 18, 1961*

Dear Mr.————:

Transmitted herewith is a draft bill to authorize cooperative arrangements for research relating to maternal and child health services and crippled children's services. It complements the proposed legislation which I am submitting to you in a separate letter today, establishing an Institute of Child Health and Human Development.

The proposed legislation will enable the

Children's Bureau to carry out more effectively its responsibilities pertaining to the welfare of children.   At present, the Bureau may conduct its own research, but it may not make grants or enter into other cooperative financial arrangements with other institutions.   The proposed legislation will provide the necessary flexibility to enable the Children's Bureau to use either its own facilities or those of others.   The need for this authority is outlined in the attached letter from the Secretary of Health, Education, and Welfare.

Without this legislation, the Children's Bureau is handicapped.   I believe that handicap should be removed.

Sincerely yours,

JOHN F. KENNEDY

NOTE: This is the text of identical letters addressed to the Honorable Lyndon B. Johnson, President of the Senate, and to the Honorable Sam Rayburn, Speaker of the House of Representatives.

291   The President's News Conference of *July* 19, 1961

THE PRESDENT. [1.]   I have a statement on Germany and Berlin.   I'll read a few paragraphs of it and it will be available for distribution right after the press conference.

The Soviet aide memoire is a document which speaks of peace, but threatens to disturb it.   It speaks of ending the abnormal situation in Germany, but insists on making permanent its abnormal division.   It refers to the Four Power Alliance of World War II, but seeks the unilateral abrogation of the rights of the other three powers.   It calls for new international agreements, while preparing to violate existing ones.   It offers certain assurances, while making it plain that its previous assurances are not to be relied upon.   It professes concern for the rights of the citizens of West Berlin, while seeking to expose them to the immediate or eventual domination of a regime which permits no self-determination.   Three simple facts are clear:

1. Today there is peace in Berlin, in Germany, and in Europe.   If that peace is destroyed by the unilateral actions of the Soviet Union, its leaders will bear a heavy responsibility before world opinion and history.

2. The people of West Berlin are free.   In that sense it's already a "free city"—free to determine its own leaders and free to enjoy the fundamental human rights reaffirmed in the United Nations Charter.

3. Today the continued presence in West Berlin of the United States, the United Kingdom, and France is by clear legal right, arising from war, acknowledged in many agreements signed by the Soviet Union, and strongly supported by the overwhelming majority of the people of that city.   Their freedom is dependent upon the exercise of these rights—an exercise which is thus a political and moral obligation as well as a legal right.   Inasmuch as these rights, including the right of access to Berlin, are not held from the Soviet Government, they cannot be ended by any unilateral action of the Soviet Union.   They cannot be affected by a so-called "peace treaty," covering only a part of Germany, with a regime of the Soviet Union's own creation—a regime which is not freely representative of all or any part of Germany, and does not enjoy the confidence of the 17 million East Germans.   The steady stream of German refugees from

East to West is eloquent testimony to this fact.

The real intent of the June 4 aide memoire is that East Berlin, a part of a city under four power status, would be formally absorbed into the so-called German Democratic Republic while West Berlin, even though called a "free city," would lose the protection presently provided by the Western Powers and become subject to the will of a totalitarian regime. Its leader, Herr Ulbricht, has made clear his intention, once this so-called "peace treaty" is signed, to curb West Berlin's communications with the free world and to suffocate the freedom it now enjoys.

The world knows that there is no reason for a crisis over Berlin today—and that if one develops it will be caused by the Soviet Government's attempt to invade the rights of others and manufacture tensions.

A city does not become free merely by calling it a "free city." For a city or a people to be free requires that they be given the opportunity, without economic, political, or police pressure, to make their own choice and live their own lives. The people of West Berlin today have that freedom. It is the objective of our policy that they will continue to enjoy it.

Peace does not come automatically from a "peace treaty." There is peace in Germany today even though the situation is "abnormal." A "peace treaty" that adversely affects the lives and rights of millions will not bring peace with it. A "peace treaty" that attempts to affect adversely the solemn commitments of three great powers will not bring peace with it. We again urge the Soviet Government to reconsider its course, to return to the path of constructive cooperation it so frequently states it desires, and to work with its World War II Allies in concluding a just and enduring settlement of issues remaining from that conflict.

[2.] Secondly, preliminary estimates of the gross national product in the second quarter of this year have been completed. The Nation's output of goods and services rose sharply to an annual rate of $515 billion, a $14 billion increase over the first quarter, reversing three consecutive quarters of decline.

Total personal income has risen steadily. In June it reached nearly $417 billion, $10½ billion above its recession low of last February, and as you know the Federal Reserve Board Index of Production increased 2 points in June to reach a level of 110.

There are still, however, serious problems of unemployment in this country. As I said some time ago, unemployment is bad enough when there's a recession, but it is intolerable when there is prosperity, and I believe it important, therefore, that the country, the administration, and the Congress remember as we move into a period of advance that there are still 5 million Americans who are unemployed, a million who are employed part time, and we have to develop programs and actions that will make it easier for them to secure their jobs.

[3.] Finally, as you know, I had hoped to be able to attend the forthcoming meeting of the Inter-American Economic and Social Council at Montevideo. However, during early August the Congress will be dealing with many of the most important issues of this session, including the foreign aid bill itself. Therefore, I consider it in the best interest of the Alliance for Progress that I remain here and work for those proposals on which our Latin American program and, indeed, our future relations with the entire free world so largely depend.

The delegation that I'm sending to Montevideo will be led by Secretary of the Treasury Dillon, and will consist of high-level, responsible people from other departments of the Government. They carry with them proposals to which I've given a good deal of personal attention and which have occupied the attention of the Government for some months, and which will, I believe and hope, mark an historic turning point in the life of the Americas.

Our task at Montevideo will be to build the framework of procedures and goals within which we can construct an American community of democratic states moving towards a better life for their people. This conference is the most important international gathering since the beginning of this administration, for on its success very largely depends the future of freedom in this hemisphere.

[4.] Q. Mr. President, are you now considering a declaration of national emergency, limited or otherwise, in order to call up National Guard or Reserve units?

THE PRESIDENT. We are concluding this afternoon our review of what actions we might take towards strengthening the military position of the United States. Those decisions will be brought to the attention of our allies this week, who also bear heavy responsibilities in this area. They will be part of a speech which I will make to the country next Tuesday evening, and will be presented to the Congress a week from today, and at that time the details of what we now plan to do will be made public.

[5.] Q. Mr. President, some months ago you suggested that our allies could contribute to Western security by increasing the strength of their conventional forces. Since then, nothing much seems to have happened in this direction. Could you tell us whether you are satisfied with the pace of developments in this field?

THE PRESIDENT. We will this week be talking with our allies about what we intend to do, and we will also have consultations with them about what we can in common do. There is going to be a foreign ministers conference in early August in Paris which will be preceded by preliminary consultations and at that time this will be one of the matters which will be before the foreign ministers. We have the problem of concerting our activities with 14 other countries.

Napoleon once said that he won all his successes because he fought allies. We are anxious that we make the consultations between our allies on all these questions—military, political, information, economic—that we try to work out procedures which will permit close harmony in the actions of all the countries which bear responsibility as members of NATO. Therefore, in answer to your question, we will be discussing—this will be one of the subjects which will be discussed in the next 2 weeks.

[6.] Q. Mr. President, in the note on Berlin yesterday, it said on several occasions that we are not wedded to the present situation in Berlin. In view of that, are we now planning to take an active lead in bringing about orderly and beneficial developments on Berlin and, specifically, how do you look upon the idea of an international peace conference on this subject?

THE PRESIDENT. The statement of yesterday plus the statement of today represents the view I want to express at this time on Germany and Berlin, and other views will be expressed, of course, as the time moves on. But this is where I stand for the present.

[7.] Q. Mr. President, if your proposals for meeting the Berlin situation require substantial additional defense outlays, would you favor taxing to pay for this, rather than adding it to deficit spending? The Senate majority whip has suggested that we ought to meet this kind of cost with higher taxes.

THE PRESIDENT. As you know, our budget—if the economy is proceeding at what we hope will be a steady rate of growth the present tax structure would bring in very substantial resources. I think we discussed at a previous conference that that tax structure is so strong that it contributed to strangling the recovery after the '58 recession. Therefore, the judgment on taxes and on expenditures will be made in light of what will produce the best economic situation for the United States in the coming months. We will make it clear at the time that we complete our review and announce them—as to what exactly we propose on taxes.

I will suggest, however, while we're on it, that both the previous administration and this administration recommended nearly $840 million of tax increase in postal payments. That amount has been steadily scaled down, and yet we've been unable to get a vote in the House of Representatives on the issue, and no hearings have been held in the Senate. This is a matter which I'm hopeful that Congress will deal with, because it represents an agreement between this administration and the last administration that we should not permit nearly $1 billion in deficit in the Postal Service. And a bill has just passed the Senate providing increased benefits for the employees, which will add another 60 or 70 million dollars to the deficit, which will take it over $1 billion if passed and signed by the President. So that here is at least one area, preliminary to a decisive answer to your question, which will come in the next few days, that I think we should move on.

[8.] Q. Mr. President, the whole bundle of your school legislation was torpedoed in the House Rules Committee yesterday, and it's clear that one of the things that largely helped to sink it was the religious issue. Will you discuss that problem, including the report that you have just about given up on passing school legislation in this first session of this Congress?

THE PRESIDENT. Well, I know that we were defeated in the Rules Committee by a vote of 8 to 7. I will say that 7 out of those 8 votes came from members of Congress who were not sympathetic to the legislation nor supported me in the last election. They have, of course, their responsibility to meet. But the fact of the matter is that there are procedures available to the House of Representatives to adopt this bill, in spite of the action of yesterday, before the session ends.

Now the Senate passed it by a generous majority and it came out of the House Committee with support. I consider it to be probably the most important piece of domestic legislation. I'm hopeful that the members of Congress who support this will use those procedures which are available to them under the rules of the House to bring this to a vote, and that a majority of the members of Congress will support it. Every study that we make indicates the need for the legislation. There is broad general support, in my opinion, for improving our educational system. Anyone who has a child wants that child to be educated to the extent of its talents. This program is most important.

In addition, included within that bill is a provision for the so-called impacted areas, and the July 1st date is past and those impacted areas are working on an emergency basis. So I feel that the impacted area part should stay in this bill, that it should be, I'm hopeful, considered by the House and that a majority of the members will vote "aye" or "nay" on it.

This matter has been involved. Education is a very important part of the life of this country and there are strong feelings—the matter of religion has been brought into it, other issues have. My view is that assistance for public education should be passed by this session. I'm hopeful a majority of the members of the House will agree, because I think it would be a most important step forward and I'm confident that Congressman Thompson and others in the House, Senator Morse in the Senate, who've been working on it, will continue to use all of their energies to get this bill by. I would sign it with the greatest possible pleasure.

[9.] Q. Mr. President, could you give us a broad estimate of approximately how much more defense funds you might be asking next week?

THE PRESIDENT. No, Mr. Lawrence. We are meeting in the National Security Council this afternoon, at which a final judgment will be reached; we do have an obligation to communicate our views to—particularly those who are involved with us in Berlin. It will be presented to the Congress early next week and to the American people early next week.

[10.] Q. Mr. President, will you give us your view of the Freedom Riders movement?

THE PRESIDENT. I think the Attorney General has made it clear that we believe that everyone who travels, for whatever reason they travel, should enjoy the full constitutional protection given to them by the law and by the Constitution. They should be able to move freely in interstate commerce.

Now, I'm hopeful that that will become the generally accepted view, and if there are any legal doubts about the right of people to move in interstate commerce, that that legal position will be clarified. We naturally want those rights to be developed in a way which will permit them to be lasting and which will permit them to meet the needs of those people who have—who wish to travel.

In my judgment, there's no question of the legal rights of the freedom travelers—Freedom Riders, to move in interstate commerce. And those rights, whether we agree with those who travel, whether we agree with the purpose for which they travel, those rights stand, providing they are exercised in a peaceful way. We may not like what people print in the paper, but there's no question of their constitutional right to print it. So that follows, in my opinion, for those who move in interstate commerce.

So the basic question is not the Freedom Riders. The basic question is that anyone who moves in interstate commerce should be able to do so freely. That's a more substantive question, not the question merely of the Freedom Riders.

[11.] Q. Mr. President, in your consideration of the military requirements now in dealing with the Berlin situation, and of the allied military reevaluation, are you basing your judgment on the assumption that it is conceivable that we might fight a ground war in Europe over Berlin?

THE PRESIDENT. I'm making my judgment on what I consider to be the relative power balance between the Communist bloc and ourselves, the attitude which the Communist bloc is now taking, and what possible needs we might have in protecting our commitments and vital interest. I think that we have to realize that we are—our commitments are far flung. We operate at the end of a long supply line, and others in some cases operate at the end of a short supply line. All this indicates the needs, the very heavy burdens, placed upon this country. We have commitments in Southeast Asia and we have commitments in Berlin, and we are being very vigorously challenged.

Now, in answer to your question, I think that we'll make public—and you can make perhaps a better calculation after we give our figures—and as I said before those figures should not be discussed, in my opinion, until at least those who share this burden with us have a chance to be informed.

This alliance—NATO alliance—is going to move through very difficult periods in the coming months. Every country has its own strategic and tactical problems and carries particular burdens which other countries do not. If this alliance is going to move in concert, in my opinion we have to improve our consultation.

It took us, as you know, some time before we were able to come to a conclusion on the language of the aide memoire. We're going to have to improve our consultation so that we can come to decisions more quickly. But I think we should realize—as anyone who has studied the history of alliances—how enormous a task it is to have 15 countries moving down a stream all together over an issue which involves the security of them all. So we will inform them, and then the Congress, of what we plan to do, and the Congress will make the final judgment.

[12.] Q. Mr. President, can you give us some details of the speech that you plan for the Nation next Tuesday?

THE PRESIDENT. The speech will be a discussion of what our responsibilities are, and what our hazards are, and what I think the situation appears to be at the present time, what its consequences could be, and what we must do and what our allies must do to move through not merely the present difficulties but I would say we have to look forward to many challenges in the coming months and years.

So, we'll try to discuss at least the general problem that the United States faces in the security field in the summer of 1961, not merely that tied to Berlin, but generally.

[13.] Q. Mr. President, could you tell us whether the space program—the launching of a man into orbit—is going to come a bit faster than we might have expected in view of the fact that a second short ballistic flight was scheduled for today? I don't know whether it's come off or not.

THE PRESIDENT. I'm not familiar with—that there's been any step-up in the previously announced schedule. If there has been I'll speak to Mr. Webb. But as I understood it, it was at the end of this year that we were talking about the orbit, but that may not be a precise date now. I'll have to look into it.

[14.] Q. Mr. President, many countries receiving foreign aid from us are concerned because their expanding populations nullify the aid. The President of Pakistan referred to this in his speech to the joint session of Congress and also in his speech at the Press Club. Since you are asking billions of dollars more in foreign aid, will you help countries control their expanding populations if they ask you?

THE PRESIDENT. I've said before, Mrs. Craig, that this is a decision which goes very much to the life of a country, and it is a personal decision and a national decision which these nations must make. The problem is not altogether an economic one. We help countries which carry out different policies in this regard and it's a judgment, in my opinion, which they should make.

[15.] Q. Although the White House has commented on the fact that Under Secretary of State Bowles is remaining in his job at this time, there still remains some doubt as to your own confidence in him, sir, and your own ideas on how the administration of the State Department is proceeding.

THE PRESIDENT. Well, in the first place, I've never, contrary to some reports, never asked Mr. Bowles for his resignation, nor has he ever offered it. I have always expected that he would be part of this administration until it concluded its responsibilities.

I have a high regard for Mr. Bowles. He was my adviser on foreign policy last year. And all my conversations with the members of the State Department, the members of the Defense Department, and the members of the intelligence community have gone to the question of how we can best organize our talents—in the White House—how we can best organize our talents so that everyone is being used in a way which makes maximum use of their abilities.

Now, when General Taylor was appointed it was regarded as a diminution of the responsibilities of the Joint Chiefs, which it is not. But it came about as a result of conversations between the Joint Chiefs and Secretary McNamara. We have the Killian committee now examining the structure of the intelligence community. We have been talking about how we can make more effective the structure and the personnel of the State Department. We'll continue to do so, because they're faced with unprecedented hazards.

As I said, when Mr. Rusk is going to be meeting with the foreign ministers on the very vital question, Berlin, Secretary Dillon will be meeting at Montevideo and this puts great burdens on the Department of State, which is the arm of the President in foreign policy.

Mr. Bowles has my complete confidence. He is going on the trip which will take him to Africa and Asia, consulting with heads of states and with allies, and I expect that his trip will be most valuable and I'm confident that everyone who talks to him, Americans or heads of other states, will recognize that Mr. Bowles will be, I hope, a valuable part of this administration as

long as it continues, and that he has the confidence of the President and the Secretary of State.

Q. Mr. President, does your answer mean that there is a possibility that he may be shifted, though, to some other responsibilities more in keeping with his talents?

THE PRESIDENT. We have reached no judgment on how we're going to organize any of these departments or people. I've put the general principle forward that we are going to attempt to maximize the abilities of everyone working in the Government. If I came to the conclusion that Mr. Bowles could be more effective in another responsible position, I would not hesitate to ask him to take that position, and I am confident Mr. Bowles would not hesitate to take it.

My judgment is now that he should stay as Under Secretary of State and if there's going to be any change, I'll make it very clear at the time. But he will continue as Under Secretary of State, and I have no plan to ask him to assume a new responsibility. But any time I think that he or anyone else in the administration can do their job better in another way, I will certainly ask them, because as long as I'm going to bear the responsibility of the Presidency I'm going to attempt to make sure that it's implemented to the best, at least, of my ability.

[16.] Q. Congressman Powell said yesterday, sir, that it's your intention to veto any bill that may be passed for aid to education in federally impacted areas unless the general Federal aid bill is approved. Would you veto a bill for impacted areas if the general aid bill isn't——

THE PRESIDENT. My judgment is that the impacted school bill should be part of general public assistance. That's the position of the administration. Therefore, I'm hopeful that the Members of Congress who are anxious to secure the passage of this legislation should also recognize that we are not meeting our responsibilities if we merely pass the impacted area, that we should pass them both together and that's what we're working towards doing. As far as what action we'd take, of course, we have to wait until Congress has made its judgment. But my view is that the best way to secure the passage of that bill is to treat this as a unit, which I believe it is.

[17.] Q. Mr. President, in your reply to the Soviet aide memoire, you stressed several times the lack of the right of self-determination among the peoples of Eastern Europe, and within the week you have issued a proclamation looking to the freedom of captive nations. Can you conceive in the event of any popular uprisings in Eastern Europe of a more active role for the United States in support of those uprisings than was the case in Hungary in 1956?

THE PRESIDENT. I think—I'll stand on the statement which we made at this time.

[18.] Q. Mr. President, do you personally favor passage of aid to private schools as part of the National Defense Education Act, as part of the school package, which Congress should enact this year?

THE PRESIDENT. Well, as you know—the bill which we sent to the Congress continued the previous assistance given to nonpublic schools to meet certain technical and defense requirements. The Office of HEW, I think, indicated to the House committee that the amendments which they added were not unconstitutional. Whether they are in public policy or not, and whether that would affect the final passage would be a judgment we would reach. They're not unconstitutional because they do not go across the board in a way which in my opinion is clearly unconstitutional. But the program which we support and which we hope the

Congress will pass is the program we sent up there. Now, the Congress has to make its judgment on those bills. But in my judgment the best bills were the ones that—the most effective in meeting the problem was the legislation that we sent up there.

[19.] Q. Mr. President, Soviet Ambassador Menshikov is reported to have said that he did not think the United States people were either prepared or ready to go to war over Berlin. Do you think Ambassador Menshikov is sending back a correct assessment of the mood and temper of the American people?

THE PRESIDENT. Well, I saw that this report came out of some function. I don't know how accurate it is, and whether that represents Mr. Menshikov's view. But I don't think that it's possible that anyone could read the aide memoire or the other statements which have been made by other governments and this Government without realizing that this is a very basic issue, the question of West Berlin, and that we intend to honor our commitments.

[20.] Q. Mr. President, tomorrow as you doubtless know marks the end of your first 6 months in the Presidency. In view of Laos, Cuba, and now Berlin, I wonder if there is anything you would care to tell us about the vicissitudes of the Presidency.

THE PRESIDENT. Well, I will say that we've had a—I think I said in the State of the Union address about the news will be worse instead of better. I would also say that Mr. Khrushchev would probably agree with that, in the sense that I think we are always conscious of the difficulties that we have. But there are a good many difficulties which should be taken into calculation in considering future bloc actions, in considering their own problems—whether it's the food shortage in China or the difficulties in other parts of the bloc empire, relations between certain bloc countries, and all the rest.

Now, as far as the United States, we've been pleased with the progress we've made internally, as far as the economy, the progress the country has made. We do feel we still have this problem of rather chronic unemployment. I'm glad that some of these bills which have been discussed for a number of years have passed. I'm hopeful that we can add education to that and long-term borrowing authority for foreign aid. My judgment is that the American people and this Government and the Congress must realize that we're in a long struggle which we'll be involved with for a great many years against very powerful countries, nearly a billion people in them, with strong economies in some cases, and that we cannot look for success on every occasion.

But I think if we have the patience and willingness to take some setbacks without taking unwise actions, recognizing that there are also other successes which may not be as dramatic to us but certainly come within Mr. Khrushchev's calculations, that we can move through this period, I hope, protecting our vital interests and our commitments and also maintaining the peace. But no one should think that it's going to be easy.

Reporter: Thank you, Mr. President.

NOTE: President Kennedy's fourteenth news conference was held in the State Department Auditorium at 10 o'clock on Wednesday morning, July 19, 1961.

292   Statement by the President Concerning the U.S. Reply to the Soviet Government's Aide Memoire on Germany and Berlin. *July* 19, 1961

IN CONSULTATION and full agreement with its British and French allies, and with the benefit of the views of the Federal Republic of Germany, and after consultation with the other member governments of the North Atlantic Treaty Organization, the United States on Monday delivered through its Embassy in Moscow its reply to the aide memoire on Germany and Berlin received from the Soviet Government on June 4. Our reply speaks for itself and advances what I believe to be an irrefutable legal, moral and political position. In this statement I should like to convey to the American people and the people of the world the basic issues which underlie the somewhat more formal language of diplomacy.

The Soviet aide memoire is a document which speaks of peace but threatens to disturb it. It speaks of ending the abnormal situation in Germany but insists on making permanent its abnormal division. It refers to the Four Power Alliance of World War II but seeks the unilateral abrogation of the rights of the other three powers. It calls for new international agreements while preparing to violate existing ones. It offers certain assurances while making it plain that its previous assurances are not to be relied upon. It professes concern for the rights of the citizens of West Berlin while seeking to expose them to the immediate or eventual domination of a regime which permits no self-determination. Three simple facts are clear:

(1) Today there is peace in Berlin, in Germany and in Europe. If that peace is destroyed by the unilateral actions of the

Soviet Union, its leaders will bear a heavy responsibility before world opinion and history.

(2) Today the people of West Berlin are free. In that sense it is already a "free city"—free to determine its own leaders and free to enjoy the fundamental human rights reaffirmed in the United Nations Charter.

(3) Today the continued presence in West Berlin of the United States, the United Kingdom and France is by clear legal right, arising from war, acknowledged in many agreements signed by the Soviet Union, and strongly supported by the overwhelming majority of the people of that city. Their freedom is dependent upon our exercise of these rights—an exercise which is thus a political and moral obligation as well as a legal right. Inasmuch as these rights, including the right of access to Berlin, are not held from the Soviet Government, they cannot be ended by any unilateral action of the Soviet Union. They cannot be affected by a so-called "peace treaty," covering only a part of Germany, with a regime of the Soviet Union's own creation—a regime which is not freely representative of all or any part of Germany, and does not enjoy the confidence of the 17 million East Germans. The steady stream of German refugees from East to West is eloquent testimony to that fact.

The United States has been prepared since the close of the war, and is prepared today, to achieve, in agreement with its World War II allies, a freely negotiated peace treaty covering all of Germany and based on the freely expressed will of all of the German people. We have never suggested that, in violation of international law and earlier Four Power agreements, we might legally negotiate a settlement with only a part of Germany, or without the participation of the other principal World War II allies. We know of no sound reason why the Soviet Government should now believe that the rights of the Western Powers, derived from Nazi Germany's surrender, could be invalidated by such an action on the part of the Soviet Union.

The United States has consistently sought the goal of a just and comprehensive peace treaty for all of Germany since first suggesting in 1946 that a special commission be appointed for this purpose. We still recognize the desirability of change—but it should be a change in the direction of greater, not less, freedom of choice for the people of Germany and Berlin. The Western Peace Plan and the All-Berlin solution proposed by the Western Allies at Geneva in 1959 were constructive, practical offers to obtain this kind of fair settlement in Central Europe. Our objective is not to perpetuate our presence in either Germany or Berlin— our objective is the perpetuation of the peace and freedom of their citizens.

But the Soviet Union has blocked all progress toward the conclusion of a just treaty based on the self-determination of the German people, and has instead repeatedly heightened world tensions over this issue. The Soviet Blockade of Berlin in 1948, the Soviet note of November 27th, 1958, and this most recent Soviet aide memoire of June 4, 1961, have greatly disturbed the tranquility of this area.

The real intent of the June 4 aide memoire is that East Berlin, a part of a city under 4-Power status, would be formally absorbed into the so-called German Democratic Republic while West Berlin, even though called a "free city," would lose the protection presently provided by the Western Powers and become subject to the will of a totalitarian regime. Its leader, Herr Ulbricht, has made clear his intention, once this so-called "peace treaty" is signed, to curb West Berlin's communications with the free world and to suffocate the freedom it now enjoys.

The area thus newly subjected to Soviet threats of heightened tension poses no danger whatsoever to the peace of the world or to the security of any nation. The world knows that there is no reason for a crisis over Berlin today—and that, if one develops, it will be caused by the Soviet Government's attempt to invade the rights of others and manufacture tensions. It is, moreover, misusing the words "freedom" and "peace." For, as our reply states, "freedom" and "peace" are not merely words—nor can they be achieved by words or promises alone. They are representative of a state of affairs.

A city does not become free merely by calling it a "free city." For a city or a people to be free requires that they be given the opportunity, without economic, political or police pressure, to make their own choice and to live their own lives. The people of West Berlin today have that freedom. It is the objective of our policy that they shall continue to have it.

Peace does not come automatically from a "peace treaty." There is peace in Germany today even though the situation is "abnormal." A "peace treaty" that adversely affects the lives and rights of millions will not bring peace with it. A "peace treaty" that attempts to affect adversely the solemn commitments of three great powers will not bring peace with it. We again urge the Soviet Government to reconsider its course, to return to the path of constructive cooperation it so frequently states it desires, and to work with its World War II allies in concluding a just and enduring settlement of issues remaining from that conflict.

NOTE: The text of the U.S. note in reply to the Soviet aide memoire of June 4 was released by the White House on July 18 together with the text of the three-power agreement of 1944 on the zones of occupation in Germany and the administration of "Greater Berlin." The documents are published in the Department of State Bulletin (vol. 45, pp. 224–233).

293   Remarks on the Youth Fitness Program.
July 19, 1961

THE STRENGTH of our democracy and our country is really no greater in the final analysis than the well-being of our citizens. The vigor of our country, its physical vigor and energy, is going to be no more advanced, no more substantial, than the vitality and will of our countrymen.

I think in recent years we have seen many evidences in the most advanced tests, comparative tests, that have been made that many of the boys and girls who live in other countries have moved ahead of younger people in this country in their ability to endure long physical hardship, in their physical fitness and in their strength.

This country is going to move through difficult days, difficult years. The responsibilities upon us are heavy, as the leader of the free world. We carry worldwide commitments. People look to us with hope, and if we fail they look to those who are our adversaries.

I think during this period we should make every effort to see that the intellectual talents of every boy and girl are developed to the maximum. And that also their physical fitness, their willingness to participate in physical exercise, their willingness to participate in physical contests, in athletic contests—all these, I think, will do a good deal to strengthen this country, and also to contribute to a greater enjoyment of life in the years to come.

This is a responsibility which is upon all of us—all of us who are parents—to make sure that we stress this phase of human life and human existence. It is also the responsibility of our schools—and our schools have been doing a great deal to meet this responsibility—of our school administrators and school committees, and communities, and states. And also, of course, it is a matter of vital interest to our national Government.

To members of school boards, school administrators, teachers, the pupils themselves, and their parents, I am directing this urgent call to strengthen all programs which contribute to the physical fitness of our youth.

I strongly urge each school in the United States to adopt the three specific recommendations of our National Council on Youth Fitness.

First, to identify the physically underdeveloped pupil and work with him to improve his physical capacity. And if he will work and the school will work together, a great deal can be done.

Two: Provide a minimum of 15 minutes of vigorous activity every day for all of our school students, boys and girls alike.

Three: Use valid fitness tests to determine pupil physical abilities and to evaluate their progress.

The adoption of these recommendations by our schools will insure the beginning of a sound basic program of physical development, exercise, and achievement.

I want to urge that this be a matter of great priority. "A sound mind and a sound body" is one of the oldest slogans of the Western World. I am hopeful that we will place a proper weight on intellectual achievement, but in my judgment, for the long-range happiness and well-being of all of you, for the strengthening of our country, for a more active and vigorous life, all of you as individuals and as groups will participate in strengthening the physical well-being of young American boys and girls.

This is a matter of importance, and I am hopeful that we can move ahead in the coming months.

Thank you very much.

NOTE: Shortly after the end of his news conference of July 19 the President returned to the rostrum and spoke to the members of the press who remained for the occasion. His remarks were recorded on film and tape for distribution to schools and to other interested groups. An abridged revision of the remarks appears as a foreword to the pamphlet "Youth Physical Fitness—Suggested Elements of a School-Centered Program" published by the President's Council on Youth Fitness (Government Printing Office, July 1961).

294 Remarks Upon Signing the Federal Water Pollution Control Act Amendments. *July 20, 1961*

IT IS a great pleasure for me to sign H.R. 6441, the Federal Water Pollution Control Act Amendments of 1961. It is especially gratifying to sign this Act in the presence of the Members of Congress whose labors made this legislation possible.

I think this affords a more comprehensive and precise definition of the Federal government's role in controlling the pollution of our country's rivers and streams.

I think it is very important to all of us in this generation to pass on and perhaps even better the position of all the natural resources that we have, and this is particularly true with water.

I think only through an intensified attack by our communities, our States and by the national government, can we make real progress on this most vital national problem.

I therefore ask the Governors, our Mayors and our industrial leaders of the nation to pursue in close cooperation with all of us,

the important work in this area, and I know that all of us in Congress and in the Administration will continue to devote a good deal of attention to this matter. And I know that under the leadership of Secretary Ribicoff of HEW, that HEW will also continue to meet its responsibilities.

NOTE: As enacted, H.R. 6441 is Public Law 87–88 (75 Stat. 204).

295   Statement by the President Upon Issuing Order Assigning Major Responsibility for Civil Defense to the Secretary of Defense. *July 20, 1961*

MORE THAN EVER, a strong civil defense program is vital to the Nation's security. Today, civil defense is of direct concern to every citizen and at every level of government.

In calling upon the resources of the Department of Defense to stimulate and invigorate our civil defense preparations, I am acting under the basic Federal premise that responsibility for the accomplishment of civil defense preparations at the Federal level is vested in me. In the States and localities, similar responsibilities are vested in the governors and local executives. It is my hope that they, too, will redouble their efforts to strengthen our civil defense and will work closely with the Department of Defense in its new assignment.

Civil defense, like other elements of the

total non-military defense program, reaches into virtually every phase of our government and of our national life. I shall accordingly be actively concerned with the problem of coordinating our civil defense preparations with other non-military defense preparations required to achieve a strong position for our Nation. In this, I shall be represented and assisted by the Director of the Office of Civil and Defense Mobilization.

NOTE: The White House release of which this statement is a part summarized the civil defense responsibilities of the Secretary of Defense and the Director of the Office of Civil and Defense Mobilization as set forth in Executive Order 10952 "Assigning Civil Defense Responsibilities to the Secretary of Defense and Others" (26 F.R. 6577). Also released the same day was the text of a memorandum dated July 7 from the Director of OCDM, containing recommendations with respect to the civil defense and defense mobilization programs.

296   Remarks Upon Signing Bill Providing for an Expanded Space Program. *July 21, 1961*

IT IS a pleasure to sign today the authorization bill for the National Aeronautics and Space Administration. This bill has been approved by the Congress in an overwhelm-

ing manner and demonstrates united support for a new and vigorous space program, submitted to our country by the Vice President as Chairman of the National Aeronautics and Space Council, sent to the Congress by me as President, and given overwhelming support by Members of both of our parties who are committed, as we all are, to seeing to it that the United States occupies an important position in the race into the far reaches of Space.

It is especially fitting that this bill should be signed on the day that our second Astronaut, Captain Virgil Grissom, with whom I spoke this morning, after he had made his successful flight. I think it's most important that we should have once again this emphasis on the leadership which our fellow Americans are showing in this field—their courage, and also the strong scientific support that they've received from the entire American scientific community.

It's significant, also, that this flight was made before the eyes of the watching world, with all the hazards that that entails.

As our space program continues on even more ambitious missions, it will continue to be this Nation's policy to use space for the advancement of all mankind, and to make free release of all scientific and technological results.

And therefore it is with great pleasure that we sign it today.

NOTE: The President spoke in the Fish Room at the White House.

As enacted, the bill authorizing appropriations for the National Aeronautics and Space Administration is Public Law 87-98 (75 Stat. 216).

297   Letter to the President of the Senate and to the Speaker of the House Proposing Reorganization and Reenactment of Refugee Aid Legislation. *July 21, 1961*

Dear Mr. ————:

For a number of years the continuing refugee and migration programs in which the United States participates have been authorized and funded by the Congress through the Mutual Security Program. The precise objectives of all but one of these programs are not consonant with the philosophy and purposes of the proposed new foreign aid legislation. For this reason they have been excluded from the proposed Act for International Development. The decision not to include these programs in the proposed aid legislation in no way detracts from their importance or the conviction of this Administration that they should be continued. I believe, however, that the statutory structure for them can be simplified and consolidated into one law. Accordingly, I transmit herewith for consideration by the Congress a draft of a bill which is designed

to centralize the authority to conduct and to appropriate funds to support United States programs of assistance to refugees, escapees, migrants, and selected persons.

In transmitting the proposed legislation I should like to reemphasize the fact that refugee problems often develop initially as emergencies resulting from severe political or economic crises or from natural disasters. It is sound, therefore, to obtain a renewed and positive authorization from the Congress to support both the current programs now in operation, for which specific appropriation requests will be made, and such emergency programs as may be required in the future.

The proposed bill seeks authorization in support of the following principles:

1. The United States, consistent with the traditional humanitarian regard of the American people for the individual and for

his right to a life of dignity and self-fulfillment, should continue to express in a practical way its concern and friendship for individuals in free-world countries abroad who
are uprooted and unsettled as the result of
political conditions or military action.

2. The successful re-establishment of refugees, who for political, racial, religious or
other reasons are unable or unwilling to return to their country of origin or of national-
ity under conditions of freedom, dignity, and
self-respect, is importantly related to free
world political objectives. These objectives
are: (a) continuation of the provision of
asylum and friendly assistance to the oppressed and persecuted; (b) the extension of
hope and encouragement to the victims of
communism and other forms of despotism,
and the promotion of faith among the captive populations in the purposes and processes of freedom and democracy; (c) the
exemplification by free citizens of free countries, through actions and sacrifices, of the
fundamental humanitarianism which constitutes the basic difference between free and
captive societies.

3. Some refugee problems are of such
order of magnitude that they comprise an
undue burden upon the economies of the
countries harboring the refugees in the first
instance, requiring international assistance
to relieve such countries of these burdens.

4. It is important to assist in the movement of persons to developing countries in
need of manpower—the most valuable asset
of the free world. The contributions of the
United States, together with other free
nations, to international migration assistance programs, not only helps build
and strengthen developing countries and
thus the free world, but it enlarges the opportunities of individuals to live useful,
productive lives.

Consistent with the four principles just

enumerated, the proposed bill provides authorization for continuation of the United
States membership in and contributions to
the Intergovernmental Committee for
European Migration (ICEM) and for contributions to the Office of the United Nations
High Commissioner for Refugees. It also
includes a general authorization for the
United States Escapee Program, the program for assisting Cuban refugees, and similar programs for refugees, escapees, and
selected persons whom the President may
determine from time to time should be
helped in the interest of the United States.
It does not make provision for assistance to
such groups as refugees in Palestine—a program closely tied to problems of economic
development in the Middle East, and for that
reason included in the proposed foreign aid
legislation.

The bill intends that the extension of
United States assistance shall be in a form
designed to meet the varying needs of particular refugee problems at home and
abroad, i.e., through cash in dollars or local
currencies; through surplus commodities;
through loans, grants or contracts; through
international organizations, private voluntary organizations, or direct United States
operations. It will be necessary to provide
varying types of aid to meeting the varying
needs which refugee situations present, including interim care, housing, welfare assistance, training, rehabilitation, job placement,
local re-establishment, and overseas resettlement. Other technical provisions of the bill
are designed to provide the necessary operational flexibility to meet the unusual and
emergency features of refugee problems.
There is also provision for a special emergency fund, subject to Presidential determination, to meet unexpected refugee and
migration developments.

I am sure that the Congress shares with

me and with the people of America our pride in the generous and successful efforts of the United States in helping the homeless and stateless victims of war and political oppression to live again as free men. The leadership which the United States has given to this great humane task has helped to generate wide participation by private citizens and governments in voluntary and international programs in behalf of the uprooted. It is altogether fitting that the United States should do this. From the earliest days of our history, this land has been a refuge for the oppressed and it is proper that we now, as descendants of refugees and immigrants, continue our long humanitarian tradition of helping those who are forced to flee to maintain their lives as individual, self-sufficient human beings in freedom, self-respect, dignity, and health. It is, moreover, decidedly to the political interests of the United States that we maintain and continue to enhance our prestige and leadership in this respect.

Great strides have been made in alleviating many of the world's refugee and migration problems. Through the efforts of the free world in its continued support of international assistance programs, with the added impetus of the World Refugee Year and of the improving European economy, many of the refugee camps in Europe have been closed and much has been done to improve the lot of thousands of other refugees in Europe who have been living in substandard conditions.

Yet millions of refugees are still in desperate want in many parts of the world and the foreboding atmosphere of political conditions and the oppression of communism gives continuing warning of more refugees to come. The United States must be prepared at all times to act promptly and effectively to help these new refugee groups as they emerge and to show our humanitarian concern for those who seek freedom as the unwilling and unfortunate victims of war and violence.

With the enactment by the Congress of the requisite authorization and appropriation legislation for these programs, the Department of State will continue its responsibilities for overseas refugee activities and the assistance programs for Cuban refugees in the United States will continue to be a responsibility of the Department of Health, Education, and Welfare.

I am confident that these proposals will be given the full and sympathetic support of the Congress. This country has always served as a lantern in the dark for those who love freedom but are persecuted, in misery, or in need. We must and will continue to show the friendship of the United States by doing our share in the compassionate task of helping those who are refugees today as were so many of our forefathers in the years past.

Sincerely,

JOHN F. KENNEDY

NOTE: This is the text of identical letters addressed to the Honorable Lyndon B. Johnson, President of the Senate, and to the Honorable Sam Rayburn, Speaker of the House of Representatives.

298 Telephone Conversation With the Prime Minister of Canada on the Opening of a New Mutual Defense Communication System. *July 22, 1961*

THE PRESIDENT. Hello—Prime Minister Diefenbaker?

THE PRIME MINISTER. Hello, how are you, Mr. President?

THE PRESIDENT. Prime Minister, I am delighted to talk to you again.

THE PRIME MINISTER. I am very pleased at this opportunity to welcome you again on behalf of the people of Canada. This is a very great occasion. I wish you could have been here. Here we have representatives of the United States, the Consul General representing the Ambassadors; Colonel White, the Commander of the Alaska Force connected with this project, and I only wish that you, instead of being at the Atlantic post, were here in Northern Canada with us, to meet not only with the Canadians but generally with Americans who are present here.

THE PRESIDENT. Well, thank you, Prime Minister. I am delighted to speak to you all the way across from the coast of New England to the western part of Canada and reaching into Alaska. I want to congratulate you and the people of Canada upon adding a great new link to the communications system that binds this continent together, and I know that the Governor of Alaska and all of the people in our 49th State welcome this great addition to their contact with Canada and the rest of the United States.

THE PRIME MINISTER. Yes, Mr. President. This is a fine illustration—what I have just spoken of—the practical cooperation of the Canadian-American partnership. As I conclude, may I say this, Mr. President: If you give us leadership in the world contest for the hearts of men, we wish you all good fortune, we wish you that vision which will bring about peace for all mankind.

THE PRESIDENT. Well, Prime Minister, I want to express my congratulations to you again. This great new effort I think can show us what can be done once again by the people of Canada and the United States. I want to congratulate you personally and also to express our very best wishes to you and the vigorous people of western Canada.

THE PRIME MINISTER. Thank you very much, Mr. President. The best to you.

THE PRESIDENT. Thank you, Prime Minister.

NOTE: The President spoke from his residence in Hyannis Port, Mass., to Prime Minister John G. Diefenbaker in Whitehorse, Yukon Territory. The ceremony marked the opening of a broadband microwave system through Canada linking the missile detection and alarm systems of the North American Continent.

299 Statement by the President on Communication Satellite Policy. *July 24, 1961*

SCIENCE and technology have progressed to such a degree that communication through the use of space satellites has become possible. Through this country's leadership, this competence should be developed for global benefit at the earliest practicable time.

To accomplish this practical objective, increased resources must be devoted to the task and a coordinated national policy should guide the use of those resources in the public interest. Consequently, on May 25, 1961 I asked the Congress for additional funds to accelerate the use of space satellites for worldwide communications. Also, on June 15, I asked the Vice President to have the Space Council make the necessary studies and policy recommendations for the optimum development and operation of such system. This has been done. The primary guideline for the preparation of such recommendations was that public interest objectives be given the highest priority.

I again invite all nations to participate in a communication satellite system, in the interest of world peace and closer brotherhood among peoples throughout the world.

The present status of the communication satellite programs, both civil and military, is that of research and development. To date, no arrangements between the government and private industry contain any commitments as to an operational system.

A. *Policy of Ownership and Operation*

Private ownership and operation of the U.S. portion of the system is favored, provided that such ownership and operation meet the following policy requirements:

1. New and expanded international communications services be made available at the earliest practicable date;

2. Make the system global in coverage so as to provide efficient communication service throughout the whole world as soon as technically feasible, including service where individual portions of the coverage are not profitable;

3. Provide opportunities for foreign participation through ownership or otherwise, in the communications satellite system;

4. Non-discriminatory use of and equitable access to the system by present and future authorized communications carriers;

5. Effective competition, such as competitive bidding, in the acquisition of equipment used in the system;

6. Structure of ownership or control which will assure maximum possible competition;

7. Full compliance with antitrust legislation and with the regulatory controls of the government;

8. Development of an economical system, the benefits of which will be reflected in overseas communication rates.

B. *Policy of Government Responsibility*

In addition to its regulatory responsibilities, the U.S. Government will:

1. Conduct and encourage research and development to advance the state of the art and to give maximum assurance of rapid and continuous scientific and technological progress;

2. Conduct or maintain supervision of international agreements and negotiations;

3. Control all launching of U.S. spacecraft;

4. Make use of the commercial system for general governmental purposes and establish separate communications satellite systems when required to meet unique government needs which cannot, in the national interest, be met by the commercial system;

5. Assure the effective use of the radio-frequency spectrum;

6. Assure the ability to discontinue the electronic functioning of satellites when required in the interest of communication efficiency and effectiveness;

7. Provide technical assistance to newly developing countries in order to help attain an effective global system as soon as practicable;

8. Examine with other countries the most constructive role for the United Nations, including the ITU, in international space communications.

C. Coordination

I have asked the full cooperation of all agencies of the government in the vigorous implementation of the policies stated herein. The National Aeronautics and Space Council will provide continuing policy coordination and will also have responsibility for recommending to me any actions needed to achieve full and prompt compliance with the policy. With the guidelines provided here, I am anxious that development of this new technology to bring the farthest corner of the globe within reach by voice and visual communication, fairly and equitably available for use, proceed with all possible promptness.

300   Letter to the Chairmen of the Senate and House Committees on Agriculture Urging Approval of Wheat and Feed Grain Programs. *July 25, 1961*

[Released July 25, 1961.   Dated July 24, 1961]

Dear Mr. Chairman:

First, I wish to thank you for your diligent and effective efforts in guiding the Agricultural Act of 1961 (S. 1643–H.R. 8230) through the Committee on Agriculture and Forestry (the Committee on Agriculture). This bill, as approved by the Committee, will substantially strengthen the laws designed to meet the problems which beset American agriculture. Although it omits some of the provisions which I recommended, the bill nevertheless is a very important and constructive piece of farm legislation.

I wish to emphasize especially the need for prompt approval of programs for the 1962 crops of wheat and feed grains along the general lines included in these bills.

These programs will accomplish the following results:

(1) Increase the income of producers of these grains above that which they would receive under existing law—probably in the neighborhood of $600 to $800 million in the 1962 crop year;

(2) Reduce the ultimate costs to the Government resulting from the 1962 crops to a point far below the costs of the programs for these grains which would be required under existing law—probably about $750 million to $1 billion;

(3) Prevent a further build-up and achieve a moderate reduction in the excessive stocks of these grains now on hand; and

(4) Assure the continued availability of abundant stocks of these grains to meet the needs of consumers at reasonable and stable prices, and to provide adequate reserves for peacetime and emergency purposes.

Early action on the wheat program is especially needed so that production can be reduced, and wheat carryovers decreased substantially in 1962–63, following the pattern being set by the Emergency Feed Grain Program this year.

Extension of the 1961 Emergency Feed Grain Program is equally important. Corn stocks are expected to be reduced by 400 million bushels in the coming year. Total feed grain stocks will be reduced by about 15 percent—the first reduction in nearly a decade. But feed grains on hand when the 1962 harvest begins will still be equivalent to around 2,500 million bushels of corn, higher than at any time except 1960 and 1961, and far above our needs for reserve stocks.

If the Emergency Feed Grain Program is not extended, acreage and production in 1962 would increase to pre-1961 levels. Stocks of grain and costs to the Government would increase once more. Farm income would decline, both because of lower livestock prices which inevitably follow excessive grain supplies, and because the price support levels effective in 1961 could not be justified in 1962 without substantial adjustment of feed grain acreage and production.

The feed grain program should be passed

now—not postponed until 1962. This will avoid the inconvenience to growers which results from emergency actions, will permit producers of fall-seeded barley to participate, and will provide time for a thorough review of administrative procedures.

With every good wish, I am

Sincerely,

JOHN F. KENNEDY

NOTE: This is the text of identical letters addressed to the Honorable Allen J. Ellender, Chairman, Senate Committee on Agriculture and Forestry, and to the Honorable Harold D. Cooley, Chairman, House Committee on Agriculture.

On August 8 the President approved Public Law 87–127 (75 Stat. 293) extending the emergency feed grain program.

301 Greetings to the People of Puerto Rico on the Ninth Anniversary of the Commonwealth. *July 25, 1961*

MY CORDIAL GREETINGS and best wishes go to Governor Muñoz Marin and the people of Puerto Rico on this ninth anniversary of the establishment of the Commonwealth.

The great social and economic accomplishments of the Commonwealth have evoked the admiration of your fellow-citizens throughout the United States, and, indeed, of freedom loving Americans throughout the Hemisphere.

In achieving the transition from a stagnant, low income society to a dynamic, prospering community, Puerto Rico has been a source of hope and inspiration to those of us deeply concerned with charting new courses of social progress for our Hemisphere.

What we seek to accomplish in our *Alianza para el Progreso* has already been accomplished to a remarkable measure in Puerto Rico. That the people of Puerto Rico have pioneered in translating objectives of social advancement, long range economic planning, equitable tax structures, improved land use and vigorous investment in education, into visible realities is undeniable proof to all citizens of the Americas of the strength and creativeness of democratic ideals.

NOTE: On the same day the President addressed a memorandum to the heads of executive departments and agencies calling attention to the unique status of Puerto Rico and pointing out that all actions affecting the Commonwealth should be consistent with its structure and basic principles.

The memorandum is published in the Federal Register (26 F.R. 6695).

302 Radio and Television Report to the American People on the Berlin Crisis. *July 25, 1961*

[Delivered from the President's Office at 10 p.m.]

Good evening:

Seven weeks ago tonight I returned from Europe to report on my meeting with Premier Khrushchev and the others. His grim warnings about the future of the world, his aide memoire on Berlin, his subsequent speeches and threats which he and his agents have launched, and the increase in the Soviet military budget that he has announced, have all prompted a series of decisions by the Administration and a series of consultations with the members of the NATO organization. In Berlin, as you recall, he intends to bring to an end, through a stroke of the pen, *first* our legal rights to be in West Berlin—and *secondly* our ability to make good on our commitment to the two million free people of that city. That we cannot permit.

We are clear about what must be done— and we intend to do it. I want to talk frankly with you tonight about the first steps that we shall take. These actions will require sacrifice on the part of many of our citizens. More will be required in the future. They will require, from all of us, courage and perseverance in the years to come. But if we and our allies act out of strength and unity of purpose—with calm determination and steady nerves—using restraint in our words as well as our weapons— I am hopeful that both peace and freedom will be sustained.

The immediate threat to free men is in West Berlin. But that isolated outpost is not an isolated problem. The threat is worldwide. Our effort must be equally wide and strong, and not be obsessed by any single manufactured crisis. We face a challenge in Berlin, but there is also a challenge in Southeast Asia, where the borders are less guarded, the enemy harder to find, and the dangers of communism less apparent to those who have so little. We face a challenge in our own hemisphere, and indeed wherever else the freedom of human beings is at stake.

Let me remind you that the fortunes of war and diplomacy left the free people of West Berlin, in 1945, 110 miles behind the Iron Curtain.

This map makes very clear the problem that we face. The white is West Germany—the East is the area controlled by the Soviet Union, and as you can see from the chart, West Berlin is 110 miles within the area which the Soviets now dominate— which is immediately controlled by the so-called East German regime.

We are there as a result of our victory over Nazi Germany—and our basic rights to be there, deriving from that victory, include both our presence in West Berlin and the enjoyment of access across East Germany. These rights have been repeatedly confirmed and recognized in special agreements with the Soviet Union. Berlin is not a part of East Germany, but a separate territory under the control of the allied powers. Thus our rights there are clear and deep-rooted. But in addition to those rights is our commitment to sustain—and defend, if need be—the opportunity for more than two million people to determine their own future and choose their own way of life.

II.

Thus, our presence in West Berlin, and our access thereto, cannot be ended by any act of the Soviet government. The NATO shield was long ago extended to cover West Berlin—and we have given our word that an attack upon that city will be regarded as an attack upon us all.

For West Berlin—lying exposed 110 miles inside East Germany, surrounded by Soviet troops and close to Soviet supply lines, has many roles. It is more than a showcase of liberty, a symbol, an island of freedom in a Communist sea. It is even more than a link with the Free World, a beacon of hope behind the Iron Curtain, an escape hatch for refugees.

West Berlin is all of that. But above all it has now become—as never before—the great testing place of Western courage and will, a focal point where our solemn commitments stretching back over the years since 1945, and Soviet ambitions now meet in basic confrontation.

It would be a mistake for others to look upon Berlin, because of its location, as a tempting target. The United States is there; the United Kingdom and France are there; the pledge of NATO is there—and the people of Berlin are there. It is as secure, in that sense, as the rest of us—for we cannot separate its safety from our own.

I hear it said that West Berlin is militarily untenable. And so was Bastogne. And so, in fact, was Stalingrad. Any dangerous spot is tenable if men—brave men—will make it so.

We do not want to fight—but we have fought before. And others in earlier times have made the same dangerous mistake of assuming that the West was too selfish and too soft and too divided to resist invasions of freedom in other lands. Those who threaten to unleash the forces of war on a dispute over West Berlin should recall the words of the ancient philosopher: "A man who causes fear cannot be free from fear."

We cannot and will not permit the Communists to drive us out of Berlin, either gradually or by force. For the fulfillment of our pledge to that city is essential to the morale and security of Western Germany, to the unity of Western Europe, and to the faith of the entire Free World. Soviet strategy has long been aimed, not merely at Berlin, but at dividing and neutralizing all of Europe, forcing us back on our own shores. We must meet our oft-stated pledge to the free peoples of West Berlin—and maintain our rights and their safety, even in the face of force—in order to maintain the confidence of other free peoples in our word and our resolve. The strength of the alliance on which our security depends is dependent in turn on our willingness to meet our commitments to them.

III.

So long as the Communists insist that they are preparing to end by themselves unilaterally our rights in West Berlin and our commitments to its people, we must be prepared to defend those rights and those commitments. We will at all times be ready to talk, if talk will help. But we must also be ready to resist with force, if force is used upon us. Either alone would fail. Together, they can serve the cause of freedom and peace.

The new preparations that we shall make to defend the peace are part of the long-term build-up in our strength which has been underway since January. They are based on our needs to meet a world-wide

534

threat, on a basis which stretches far beyond the present Berlin crisis. Our primary purpose is neither propaganda nor provocation—but preparation.

A first need is to hasten progress toward the military goals which the North Atlantic allies have set for themselves. In Europe today nothing less will suffice. We will put even greater resources into fulfilling those goals, and we look to our allies to do the same.

The supplementary defense build-ups that I asked from the Congress in March and May have already started moving us toward these and our other defense goals. They included an increase in the size of the Marine Corps, improved readiness of our reserves, expansion of our air and sea lift, and stepped-up procurement of needed weapons, ammunition, and other items. To insure a continuing invulnerable capacity to deter or destroy any aggressor, they provided for the strengthening of our missile power and for putting 50% of our B–52 and B–47 bombers on a ground alert which would send them on their way with 15 minutes' warning.

These measures must be speeded up, and still others must now be taken. We must have sea and air lift capable of moving our forces quickly and in large numbers to any part of the world.

But even more importantly, we need the capability of placing in any critical area at the appropriate time a force which, combined with those of our allies, is large enough to make clear our determination and our ability to defend our rights at all costs—and to meet all levels of aggressor pressure with whatever levels of force are required. We intend to have a wider choice than humiliation or all-out nuclear action.

While it is unwise at this time either to call up or send abroad excessive numbers of these troops before they are needed, let me make it clear that I intend to take, as time goes on, whatever steps are necessary to make certain that such forces can be deployed at the appropriate time without lessening our ability to meet our commitments elsewhere.

Thus, in the days and months ahead, I shall not hesitate to ask the Congress for additional measures, or exercise any of the executive powers that I possess to meet this threat to peace. Everything essential to the security of freedom must be done; and if that should require more men, or more taxes, or more controls, or other new powers, I shall not hesitate to ask them. The measures proposed today will be constantly studied, and altered as necessary. But while we will not let panic shape our policy, neither will we permit timidity to direct our program.

Accordingly, I am now taking the following steps:

(1) I am tomorrow requesting the Congress for the current fiscal year an additional $3,247,000,000 of appropriations for the Armed Forces.[1]

(2) To fill out our present Army Divisions, and to make more men available for prompt deployment, I am requesting an increase in the Army's total authorized strength from 875,000 to approximately 1 million men.

(3) I am requesting an increase of 29,000 and 63,000 men respectively in the active duty strength of the Navy and the Air Force.

(4) To fulfill these manpower needs, I am ordering that our draft calls be doubled

---

[1] A letter to the President of the Senate transmitting amendments to the Department of Defense budget was released by the White House on July 26. On August 17 the President approved the Department of Defense Appropriation Act, 1962 (Public Law 87–144 ; 75 Stat. 365).

and tripled in the coming months; I am asking the Congress for authority to order to active duty certain ready reserve units and individual reservists, and to extend tours of duty; [2] and, under that authority, I am planning to order to active duty a number of air transport squadrons and Air National Guard tactical air squadrons, to give us the airlift capacity and protection that we need. Other reserve forces will be called up when needed.

(5) Many ships and planes once headed for retirement are to be retained or reactivated, increasing our airpower tactically and our sealift, airlift, and anti-submarine warfare capability. In addition, our strategic air power will be increased by delaying the deactivation of B–47 bombers.

(6) Finally, some $1.8 billion—about half of the total sum—is needed for the procurement of non-nuclear weapons, ammunition and equipment.

The details on all these requests will be presented to the Congress tomorrow. Subsequent steps will be taken to suit subsequent needs. Comparable efforts for the common defense are being discussed with our NATO allies. For their commitment and interest are as precise as our own.

And let me add that I am well aware of the fact that many American families will bear the burden of these requests. Studies or careers will be interrupted; husbands and sons will be called away; incomes in some cases will be reduced. But these are burdens which must be borne if freedom is to be defended—Americans have willingly borne them before—and they will not flinch from the task now.

IV.

We have another sober responsibility. To recognize the possibilities of nuclear war in the missile age, without our citizens knowing what they should do and where they should go if bombs begin to fall, would be a failure of responsibility. In May, I pledged a new start on Civil Defense. Last week, I assigned, on the recommendation of the Civil Defense Director, basic responsibility for this program to the Secretary of Defense, to make certain it is administered and coordinated with our continental defense efforts at the highest civilian level. Tomorrow, I am requesting of the Congress new funds for the following immediate objectives: to identify and mark space in existing structures—public and private—that could be used for fall-out shelters in case of attack; to stock those shelters with food, water, first-aid kits and other minimum essentials for survival; to increase their capacity; to improve our air-raid warning and fall-out detection systems, including a new household warning system which is now under development; and to take other measures that will be effective at an early date to save millions of lives if needed.

In the event of an attack, the lives of those families which are not hit in a nuclear blast and fire can still be saved—*if* they can be warned to take shelter and *if* that shelter is available. We owe that kind of insurance to our families—and to our country. In contrast to our friends in Europe, the need for this kind of protection is new to our shores. But the time to start is now. In the coming months, I hope to let every citizen know what steps he can take without

---

[2] On July 26 the White House released the text of identical letters to the President of the Senate and to the Speaker of the House of Representatives transmitting a request for authority to call reservists and to extend tours of duty. Also released was the text of a proposed joint resolution granting such authority, which was enacted on August 1, 1961 (Public Law 87–117; 75 Stat. 242).

delay to protect his family in case of attack. I know that you will want to do no less.

v.

The addition of $207 million in Civil Defense appropriations brings our total new defense budget requests to $3.454 billion, and a total of $47.5 billion for the year. This is an increase in the defense budget of $6 billion since January, and has resulted in official estimates of a budget deficit of over $5 billion. The Secretary of the Treasury and other economic advisers assure me, however, that our economy has the capacity to bear this new request.

We are recovering strongly from this year's recession. The increase in this last quarter of our year of our total national output was greater than that for any postwar period of initial recovery. And yet, wholesale prices are actually lower than they were during the recession, and consumer prices are only ¼ of 1% higher than they were last October. In fact, this last quarter was the first in eight years in which our production has increased without an increase in the overall-price index. And for the first time since the fall of 1959, our gold position has improved and the dollar is more respected abroad. These gains, it should be stressed, are being accomplished with Budget deficits far smaller than those of the 1958 recession.

This improved business outlook means improved revenues; and I intend to submit to the Congress in January a budget for the next fiscal year which will be strictly in balance. Nevertheless, should an increase in taxes be needed—because of events in the next few months—to achieve that balance, or because of subsequent defense rises, those increased taxes will be requested in January.

Meanwhile, to help make certain that the current deficit is held to a safe level, we must keep down all expenditures not thoroughly justified in budget requests. The luxury of our current post-office deficit must be ended. Costs in military procurement will be closely scrutinized—and in this effort I welcome the cooperation of the Congress. The tax loopholes I have specified—on expense accounts, overseas income, dividends, interest, co-operatives and others—must be closed.

I realize that no public revenue measure is welcomed by everyone. But I am certain that every American wants to pay his fair share, and not leave the burden of defending freedom entirely to those who bear arms. For we have mortgaged our very future on this defense—and we cannot fail to meet our responsibilities.

vi.

But I must emphasize again that the choice is not merely between resistance and retreat, between atomic holocaust and surrender. Our peace-time military posture is traditionally defensive; but our diplomatic posture need not be. Our response to the Berlin crisis will not be merely military or negative. It will be more than merely standing firm. For we do not intend to leave it to others to choose and monopolize the forum and the framework of discussion. We do not intend to abandon our duty to mankind to seek a peaceful solution.

As signers of the UN Charter, we shall always be prepared to discuss international problems with any and all nations that are willing to talk—and listen—with reason. If they have proposals—not demands—we shall hear them. If they seek genuine understanding—not concessions of our rights—we shall meet with them. We have previously indicated our readiness to remove any actual irritants in West Berlin, but the freedom of that city is not negotiable. We cannot negotiate with those who say "What's mine is mine and what's yours is negotiable." But we are willing to consider any arrangement or treaty in Germany consistent with the maintenance of peace and freedom, and with the legitimate security interests of all nations.

We recognize the Soviet Union's historical concern about their security in Central and Eastern Europe, after a series of ravaging invasions, and we believe arrangements can be worked out which will help to meet those concerns, and make it possible for both security and freedom to exist in this troubled area.

For it is not the freedom of West Berlin which is "abnormal" in Germany today, but the situation in that entire divided country. If anyone doubts the legality of our rights in Berlin, we are ready to have it submitted to international adjudication. If anyone doubts the extent to which our presence is desired by the people of West Berlin, compared to East German feelings about their regime, we are ready to have that question submitted to a free vote in Berlin and, if possible, among all the German people. And let us hear at that time from the two and one-half million refugees who have fled the Communist regime in East Germany—voting for Western-type freedom with their feet.

The world is not deceived by the Communist attempt to label Berlin as a hot-bed of war. There is peace in Berlin today. The source of world trouble and tension is Moscow, not Berlin. And if war begins, it will have begun in Moscow and not Berlin.

For the choice of peace or war is largely theirs, not ours. It is the Soviets who have stirred up this crisis. It is they who are trying to force a change. It is they who have opposed free elections. It is they who

have rejected an all-German peace treaty, and the rulings of international law. And as Americans know from our history on our own old frontier, gun battles are caused by outlaws, and not by officers of the peace.

In short, while we are ready to defend our interests, we shall also be ready to search for peace—in quiet exploratory talks—in formal or informal meetings. We do not want military considerations to dominate the thinking of either East or West. And Mr. Khrushchev may find that his invitation to other nations to join in a meaningless treaty may lead to *their* inviting *him* to join in the community of peaceful men, in abandoning the use of force, and in respecting the sanctity of agreements.

VII.

While all of these efforts go on, we must not be diverted from our total responsibilities, from other dangers, from other tasks. If new threats in Berlin or elsewhere should cause us to weaken our program of assistance to the developing nations who are also under heavy pressure from the same source, or to halt our efforts for realistic disarmament, or to disrupt or slow down our economy, or to neglect the education of our children, then those threats will surely be the most successful and least costly maneuver in Communist history. For we can afford all these efforts, and more—but we cannot afford *not* to meet this challenge.

And the challenge is not to us alone. It is a challenge to every nation which asserts its sovereignty under a system of liberty. It is a challenge to all those who want a world of free choice. It is a special challenge to the Atlantic Community—the heartland of human freedom.

We in the West must move together in

building military strength. We must consult one another more closely than ever before. We must together design our proposals for peace, and labor together as they are pressed at the conference table. And together we must share the burdens and the risks of this effort.

The Atlantic Community, as we know it, has been built in response to challenge: the challenge of European chaos in 1947, of the Berlin blockade in 1948, the challenge of Communist aggression in Korea in 1950. Now, standing strong and prosperous, after an unprecedented decade of progress, the Atlantic Community will not forget either its history or the principles which gave it meaning.

The solemn vow each of us gave to West Berlin in time of peace will not be broken in time of danger. If we do not meet our commitments to Berlin, where will we later stand? If we are not true to our word there, all that we have achieved in collective security, which relies on these words, will mean nothing. And if there is one path above all others to war, it is the path of weakness and disunity.

Today, the endangered frontier of freedom runs through divided Berlin. We want it to remain a frontier of peace. This is the hope of every citizen of the Atlantic Community; every citizen of Eastern Europe; and, I am confident, every citizen of the Soviet Union. For I cannot believe that the Russian people—who bravely suffered enormous losses in the Second World War—would now wish to see the peace upset once more in Germany. The Soviet government alone can convert Berlin's frontier of peace into a pretext for war.

The steps I have indicated tonight are aimed at avoiding that war. To sum it all up: we seek peace—but we shall not surrender. That is the central meaning of this crisis, and the meaning of your government's policy.

With your help, and the help of other free men, this crisis can be surmounted. Freedom can prevail—and peace can endure.

I would like to close with a personal word. When I ran for the Presidency of the United States, I knew that this country faced serious challenges, but I could not realize—nor could any man realize who does not bear the burdens of this office—how heavy and constant would be those burdens.

Three times in my life-time our country and Europe have been involved in major wars. In each case serious misjudgments were made on both sides of the intentions of others, which brought about great devastation.

Now, in the thermonuclear age, any misjudgment on either side about the intentions of the other could rain more devastation in several hours than has been wrought in all the wars of human history.

Therefore I, as President and Commander-in-Chief, and all of us as Americans, are moving through serious days. I shall bear this responsibility under our Constitution for the next three and one-half years, but I am sure that we all, regardless of our occupations, will do our very best for our country, and for our cause. For all of us want to see our children grow up in a country at peace, and in a world where freedom endures.

I know that sometimes we get impatient, we wish for some immediate action that would end our perils. But I must tell you that there is no quick and easy solution. The Communists control over a billion people, and they recognize that if we should falter, their success would be imminent.

We must look to long days ahead, which if we are courageous and persevering can bring us what we all desire.

In these days and weeks I ask for your help, and your advice. I ask for your suggestions, when you think we could do better.

All of us, I know, love our country, and we shall all do our best to serve it.

In meeting my responsibilities in these coming months as President, I need your good will, and your support—and above all, your prayers.

Thank you, and good night.

303 Remarks at the Presentation of the Distinguished Service Medal to Admiral Arleigh A. Burke. *July 26, 1961*

Ladies and gentlemen, Admiral and Mrs. Burke, General Lemnitzer, Members of the Congress, Members of the Naval Establishment:

I want to welcome you all here to the White House, and also express appreciation that you have come to join us in paying honor to an American who wholly deserves this award and this tribute as he finishes a lifetime of service to the United States.

I have served with Admiral Burke in the Government as President—he is a member of the Joint Chiefs of Staff—for only 6 months but I must say that in that period I have come to have the same opinion of him that my predecessors have had, and that is that I know of no American who is more devoted to his country, who is more willing to make any contribution that he can make to its welfare, and who more appropriately typifies the best qualities in the American serviceman.

So Admiral, I'm sure you realize that personally and speaking also as President, that your departure is greatly missed. We are fortunate to have as your successor Admiral Anderson, whom you recommended, but I do say that in the very difficult times that are ahead we will continue to count upon you as an ex officio member of the Joint Chiefs of Staff.

I will therefore read this citation for the Distinguished Service Medal. This is not the most overwhelming honor we could pay the Admiral, as I find that he has two others—this is his third—but he deserves them all.

The citation says:

"The President of the United States takes pleasure in presenting the Distinguished Service Medal (Gold Star in lieu of Third Award) to Admiral Arleigh A. Burke, United States Navy, for service as set forth in the following citation:

"For exceptionally meritorious service to the Government of the United States while serving as Chief of Naval Operations and member of the Joint Chiefs of Staff from August 1955 to August 1961. In this demanding and exacting position, Admiral Burke has displayed the same superb leadership, the same vigor and outstanding professional competence, that marked his courageous and highly successful combat operations in the Pacific Theater during World War II.

"With broad vision and an untiring devotion to duty, he has done much to increase the strength of United States naval forces, as well as to promote the cause of justice and order throughout the world. Admiral Burke's distinguished achievements on behalf of the Navy and his country, are in keeping with the highest traditions of the United States Naval Service."

NOTE: The presentation ceremony was held in the Rose Garden at the White House. In his opening remarks the President referred to Gen. Lyman L. Lemnitzer, Chairman of the Joint Chiefs of Staff. Later he referred to Adm. George W. Anderson, Jr.

304 Joint Statement Following Discussions With the Prime Minister of Nigeria. *July 27, 1961*

PRIME MINISTER BALEWA concludes tomorrow the Washington portion of the official visit he is making to the United States at the invitation of President Kennedy. The President and the Prime Minister have had very cordial and frank discussions on a wide range of subjects of interest to their governments. These talks have been conducted in a spirit of mutual understanding and respect characteristic of the friendly relations existing between Nigeria and the United States.

The President and the Prime Minister consulted together on the general international situation, giving special attention to disarmament and to the problems of Berlin and Bizerte.

The two leaders reviewed recent developments in Africa. The President expressed his pleasure at the success of the Conference of African and Malagasy States, held in Monrovia last May, and congratulated the Prime Minister and his delegation on their constructive contribution to its deliberations. The President conveyed his hope that the second meeting of these States, to be convened in Lagos, would be equally harmonious and productive.

The President and the Prime Minister reaffirmed their support for the principle of self-determination for dependent peoples and their unalterable opposition to racial discrimination under any name or in any guise.

The President and the Prime Minister reiterated their strong support for the United Nations as an instrument for world peace. The two leaders agreed that there should be greater opportunities for African representation in UN organs and agencies. They are opposed, however, to any proposals which would compromise the integrity and effectiveness of that organization or its subsidiary bodies.

With respect to the Congo, the President praised the strenuous and effective efforts made by Nigerian statesmen toward a peaceful solution of the problems of that country, and the exemplary performance of Nigerian troops and police serving with the United Nations in the Congo. The Prime Minister and the President agreed that the Congo problem was largely a political one and that the United Nations should use its best endeavors, with the maximum assistance of the African States, to enable the Congolese themselves to provide a solution to that problem, thus avoiding a major confrontation in the heart of Africa. The two leaders also agreed that the Congo's political and economic problems must not be used for cold war purposes.

On the subject of economic aid to Nigeria, the President reiterated the desire of the United States Government to assist Nigeria in its social and economic development pointing out that it was this sincere desire that prompted the sending of a Special Economic Mission to Nigeria last May for the purpose of discussing with Nigerian officials their forthcoming Five Year Plan. The President expressed his gratification at the report of the Mission which speaks highly of the extent to which Nigeria is committing its own resources to well-conceived development plans, its ability to absorb foreign assistance and the sense of social justice that pervades its planning. Under the circumstances, the United States Government regards these preliminary findings as most encouraging and it can say at this time that it is prepared in principle to assist Nigeria in a substantial way in the implementation of its Five Year Plan. The exact extent and manner of United States support will depend upon a further study of the Plan, which is expected to be sufficiently refined in October of this year, and upon the action taken by the United States Congress on the Administration's request for aid funds.

The President and the Prime Minister expressed their pleasure at the opportunity afforded by the Prime Minister's visit to become personally acquainted, and their confidence that their exchange of views had further strengthened the bonds of friendship between their two countries. They agreed the bonds would be strengthened more by a greater interchange of knowledge and by increased contacts between the peoples of the two countries in all spheres.

305   Telegram to the Leader of the Italian Mount McKinley Expedition. *July 27*, 1961

[Released July 27, 1961.   Dated July 26, 1961]

Mr. Riccardo Cassin, Leader
The Italian Mount McKinley Expedition
Anchorage, Alaska

I want to send my warmest congratulations to you and to the other members of the Italian team who have achieved such a splendid mountaineering feat on Mount McKinley. This outstanding accomplishment under the most hazardous of conditions is a fine testimonial to your superb skill and fortitude. Our nation is proud to have witnessed within its own borders this conquest which has served to strengthen the ties between the United States and Italy and to earn the admiration of all of the world.

JOHN F. KENNEDY

306   Toasts of the President and Vice President Chen Cheng of the Republic of China. *July 31*, 1961

I WANT to express our great pleasure at being honored by the visit of the Vice President of the Republic of China and his wife, the Foreign Minister, and the members of his party who are here with our good friend, their Ambassador and his wife.

We are delighted to have him for several reasons. First, because he represents a distinguished country, a leader with whom this country of ours is most intimately associated in very difficult times and also because in his own right, his own character, his own

542

qualities of leadership in good times and bad in his country's fortunes have won him the admiration and respect of all of my countrymen who have seen him. His own military leadership on the mainland, the efforts he has made to maintain the life of his country during recent years, the great contribution which he has made, which was described to me by our Vice President on his recent trip there to rebuild the economy of the island, all these things have won for him a special position in the minds and hearts of all of us.

So we are glad to have him for what he is himself, and we are glad to have him also because he represents and has the complete confidence of the President of his country.

His country and ours are intimately associated. I believe that the visit of the Vice President can do much to make sure that both his country and ours move on parallel lines in the difficult days and months and years ahead. So for every reason, Mr. Vice President, we are very proud to have you here. You are surrounded by friends. Some Members of the Congress had to leave, though they are coming back. But they left to vote for a cause in which all of us are committed, and therefore they serve us better on the Hill than they would here.

The Vice President informed me that Congressman Judd came from a part of China which is known for its tight hold on the dollar, where some of the most famous financiers of China come from, which illuminates the scene you have here today.

So we are glad to have you, Mr. Vice President, and I know that all the people here today are devoted to you and your country. You have also sent to us three of your children who have come before you who are, I think, the most obvious indication of your regard for us.

I know that you will all join with me in drinking a toast to the President of the Republic of China who has sent us this fine emissary.

NOTE: The President proposed the toast at a state luncheon in the East Room at the White House. Vice President Chen Cheng responded (through an interpreter) as follows:

"Mr. President, it is my great honor to be invited to visit the United States. This is the high point in my personal life, especially this morning in the conversation with Your Excellency, that left me with a very deep impression that this will be a great contribution to our national policy so determined to fight against international communism.

"I am very much impressed by the remarks you made, but I would like to say at this time that whatever progress the Republic of China, my country, has achieved, an important factor is the encouragement and the aid given by the Government and the people of the United States.

"With our two countries together, we can march toward our common goal, and with your leadership over the entire free world, Mr. President, I am sure that the future of the world will be greatly benefited.

"All actions taken by our country will be coordinated with the leadership of you, Mr. President.

"Last May, Mr. President, when you sent the able Vice President to Asia, it was a very important and lasting event in Asia, because it not only constituted a stabilizing force so far as Asia was concerned, but it gave tremendous encouragement to the people of Asia.

"I would like to propose a toast at this time to your health, and to the continued prosperity of the United States of America."

In his opening remarks the President referred to Shen Chang-Huan, Foreign Minister of the Republic of China, and George K. C. Yeh, the Chinese Ambassador.

307   Remarks at Ceremonies Marking the 15th Anniversary of the Fulbright Exchange Program.   *August 1, 1961*

WE WANT to express our great pleasure at having this opportunity to celebrate the 15th anniversary today of the signing of the legislation which led to the Fulbright program.

Of all the examples in recent history of beating swords into plowshares, of having some benefit come to humanity out of the destruction of war, I think that this program in its results will be among the most preeminent.

As a result of this program, which permits this exchange of representative scholars, students, educators, artists, from our country to countries around the world, from their countries to our country—as a result of this program and the related Smith-Mundt program, over 50,000 people have been permitted to come to a greater understanding of the benefits of our culture and civilization, and the culture and the civilization of other countries.

This program has been most important in bettering the relations of the United States with other parts of the world. It has been a major constructive step on the road to peace. And therefore in a most troubled time in the life of our country and in the history of the world, I think it's most appro-

priate that we celebrate the 15th anniversary of the Fulbright program.

I want to express our great appreciation to Senator Fulbright who created this program, and who has carefully guarded its integrity since its founding.

We are delighted that Senator Smith is with us today again and Senator Mundt who have also shown great interest in the related program, and members of the Department of State.

And it is particularly fortunate that at this time Senator Fulbright and the members of the Foreign Relations Committee are working on a major program to improve and to move this great effort ahead over the next years.

So, Senator Fulbright, we want to congratulate you, and I hope that by this ceremony that we emphasize this most important phase of our international relations.

NOTE: The ceremonies were held in the Rose Garden at the White House. In his remarks the President referred to J. W. Fulbright, U.S. Senator from Arkansas, H. Alexander Smith, former U.S. Senator from New Jersey, and Karl E. Mundt, U.S. Senator from South Dakota.

Remarks by Senator Fulbright and former Senator Joseph C. O'Mahoney of Wyoming were also released.

308   Remarks on Secretary Dillon's Mission to the Punta del Este Conference of the Inter-American Economic and Social Council.   *August 2, 1961*

TOMORROW MORNING Secretary Dillon leads an American delegation to the conference at Montevideo. This conference is of vital importance to this hemisphere. Our hopes go with Secretary Dillon, and our strong support.

I consider this conference to be the most important international conference which has been held since this administration assumed responsibility on January 20th.

If it were not that we were deeply involved and heavily committed in the legislation which is now being considered by the Congress on mutual security, legislation which is an integral part of the whole program for this hemisphere, I would be attending the conference myself.

In Secretary Dillon we have selected a man who has participated in related negotiations before. He leads a high-level conference, and it is my great hope that this conference will be a success, and it will begin a new period in the hemisphere in the development of a better life for our people. So that we wish him every success.

NOTE: The President spoke to newsmen in the Fish Room at the White House. A list of the members of the delegation is published in the Department of State Bulletin (vol. 45, p. 318).

309 Joint Statement Following Discussions With the Vice President of the Republic of China. *August 2, 1961*

PRESIDENT KENNEDY and Vice President Chen have concluded a series of cordial and constructive talks on a broad range of international problems and matters of common interest to the governments and peoples of the United States and the Republic of China. Foreign Minister Shen, Secretary Rusk, Ambassador Yeh, Ambassador Drumright, and other Chinese and U.S. officials participated in the conversations, which were characterized by a spirit of understanding and mutual interest consonant with the deep and lasting friendship between the two countries.

The President, who at his personal initiative had invited the Vice President to the United States for these discussions, welcomed this opportunity to reaffirm the close ties between the Governments and peoples of the United States and the Republic of China.

In their review of the world situation, the President and the Vice President agreed that while Berlin is the current focus of world attention, this problem can be evaluated only against the background of the world-wide Communist challenge. They agreed that although the free world has made serious efforts to relax world tensions, the belligerency of the Communist bloc has thus far rendered these efforts fruitless. They further agreed that free world interests require the continued presence of free world forces in West Berlin and the maintenance of the security and the viability of West Berlin.

The President and the Vice President discussed at length the present situation in Asia and expressed their concern over the future of Laos. The President stated that while he is hopeful that the Geneva Conference on Laos will result in the emergence of a truly neutral and independent Laos, the United States will not approve any arrangement which would result in Communist domination of that country. The President stated that the United States is determined that the Republic of Viet-Nam shall not be lost to the Communists for lack of any support which the United States Government can render.

The President and the Vice President welcomed the announced policies of the new Korean Government to continue its partnership with the free world, to oppose communism, and to combat the economic problems that face the Korean people.

In their discussion of Chinese representation in the United Nations there was a candid and comprehensive exchange of views on all relevant issues including the pending applications for United Nations membership of Outer Mongolia and Mauritania. The President reiterated firm United States support for continued representation of the Republic of China in the United Nations, of which she is a founding member. He also reaffirmed the U.S. determination to continue to oppose admission of the Chinese Communist regime to the United Nations.

The President and the Vice President expressed their intention to support the admission to the United Nations of the nations emerging into independence which meet the qualifications set forth in the Charter. In this connection they noted with concern the Soviet veto which has frustrated the admission of Mauritania. The Vice President declared that the Republic of China has consistently supported admission of the newly independent states and that it will continue to support the deserved admission of Mauritania.

The President and the Vice President reviewed conditions on the China mainland. In the economic field, they noted that Communist mismanagement, unworkable agricultural policies, and the Commune system have brought serious food shortages and grave hardships to the Chinese people. They noted that reports from refugees and visitors indicate the magnitude of the apathy, discontent, and disillusionment on the main-

land of China. They agreed that these developments provide vivid proof that the Communist regime cannot meet the genuine needs and desires of the Chinese people for economic and social progress.

The President and the Vice President discussed United States assistance for the continued economic growth of free China. The President noted the remarkable achievements of the past ten years in Taiwan, which have brought unprecedented improvements in the standard of living, in public health and education, and in industrial and agricultural output. He noted that, in contrast with the disregard for human rights manifested by the Chinese Communist regime, this record was accomplished without violence to the great traditions and human values which have been cherished throughout history by the Chinese people. The President confirmed the intention of the United States Government to continue its military aid program in the Republic of China and to provide substantial assistance to the Republic of China in support of its economic development program designed to achieve accelerated social and economic progress for the welfare of the people of free China.

In conclusion, the President and the Vice President recognized the importance of further strengthening the close cooperation and coordination of both countries in matters affecting their common security interests.

310 Letter to Secretary Hodges Requesting Recommendations for Dealing With the Problems of the Transportation Industry. *August 2, 1961*

Dear Mr. Secretary:

It is becoming increasingly clear that the current difficulties facing all segments of the transportation industry will require increased

leadership and additional actions on the part of the Federal Government.

I would appreciate it if you would take the lead in developing for my consideration recommendations which could be made to the next session of Congress on this subject. These recommendations should include both long range and short range actions necessary to achieve and maintain healthy and efficient transportation systems.

Since the Department of Commerce has the statutory authority for the development of a national transportation policy, I am placing the primary responsibility for this task in the Department. Under your direc-

tion, I will expect full cooperation and participation of all other Federal agencies with functions and interests in the transportation area. Copies of this letter are being transmitted to these agencies.

It is my desire that you complete this task and have your recommendations in my hands by November 1, 1961.

Sincerely,

JOHN F. KENNEDY

---

311   Message to Admiral Richmond on the Occasion of the 171st Anniversary of the U.S. Coast Guard. *August* 4, 1961

IT GIVES ME great pleasure to extend my warmest congratulations to the United States Coast Guard on the occasion of its 171st birthday.

Throughout its long history the Coast Guard has served our Nation in peace and war with valor and distinction. Both as a military force and as our chief agency for promoting maritime safety it is making a vital contribution to our economic well-being and our national security.

As one who is personally familiar with

the work of your fine service, I should like to express my admiration for an outstanding record of performance that has not been surpassed in the annals of our country. May you have many additional years of service to our country and to humanity.

JOHN F. KENNEDY

[Admiral Alfred C. Richmond, Commandant, United States Coast Guard, 1300 E Street NW., Washington 25, D.C.]

NOTE: The message was released at Hyannis, Mass.

---

312   Telegrams of Commendation Following the Capture of High-Jackers of a Jet Airliner in El Paso, Texas. *August* 4, 1961

Honorable J. Edgar Hoover
Director, Federal Bureau of Investigation
Washington, D.C.

I would like to commend the Federal Bureau of Investigation for its key role in helping to bring about the capture of the two high-jackers of the Continental Airlines 707 jet in El Paso, Texas, effecting the safe rescue of the passengers and crew. Your Special-Agent-in-Charge Francis Crosby is especially to be commended for the level-

headed and courageous manner in which he led the rescue operation.

JOHN F. KENNEDY

General J. M. Swing
Commissioner, Immigration and Naturalization Service
Washington, D.C.

I would like to commend Leonard Walter Gilman, Assistant Regional Commissioner for Enforcement of your Service in San

Pedro, California for his courageous and level-headed manner in which he helped effect the capture of the two high-jackers of the Continental Airlines jet in El Paso, Texas under the most difficult circumstances.

JOHN F. KENNEDY

313 Message to the Inter-American Economic and Social Conference at Punta del Este, Uruguay. *August 5, 1961*

[Read by Robert A. Conrads, Assistant Secretary General of the Conference]

Fellow citizens of the Americas:

Twenty-five years ago one of the greatest of my predecessors, Franklin Roosevelt, addressed the Inter-American conference for the maintenance of peace, meeting at Buenos Aires—a conference called to protect the peace and freedom of the hemisphere.

That conference was a great success. Its accomplishments were in Roosevelt's words, "Far-reaching and historic." New molds of friendship and cooperation were forged. A new day in the history of the Americas had begun.

Yet, on his return from the conference, President Roosevelt stopped in Montevideo just a few miles from your meeting place to warn that "We have not completed our task. That task is a continuing one. We seek new remedies for new conditions. New conditions will continue to arise but the net result is that we move forward."

Today a quarter century later, we meet to carry on that task to demonstrate anew that freedom is not merely a word or an abstract theory, but the most effective instrument for advancing the welfare of man. We face new conditions and we must devise new remedies to meet them, and we are confident that we will move forward.

Those of you at this conference are present at an historic moment in the life of this hemisphere. For this is far more than an economic discussion, or a technical conference on development. In a very real sense it is a demonstration of the capacity of free nations to meet the human and material problems of the modern world. It is a test of the values of our own society, a proving ground for the vitality of freedom in the affairs of man.

The views of the United States on the important social and economic questions encompassed by the agenda will be fully explained by Secretary C. Douglas Dillon. Underlying those views are the simple and basic principles of the Alliance for Progress.

We live in a hemisphere whose own revolution has given birth to the most powerful forces of the modern age—the search for the freedom and self-fulfillment of man. We meet to carry on that revolution to shape the future as we have the past.

This means that all of our countries—nations of the north and nations of the south—must make new efforts of unparalleled magnitude.

Self-fulfillment. For the developing nations it means careful national planning, the orderly establishment of goals, priorities, and long-range programs.

It means expanded export markets, closer economic integration within Latin America and greater market stability for the major primary products.

548

It means the dedication of a greatly increased proportion of national resources and capital to the cause of development.

And it means full recognition of the right of all the people to share fully in our progress. For there is no place in democratic life for institutions which benefit the few while denying the needs of the many even though the elimination of such institutions may require far-reaching and difficult changes such as land reform and tax reform and a vastly increased emphasis on education and health and housing. Without these changes our common effort cannot succeed.

The Alliance for Progress also means a greatly increased effort by the United States both in terms of material resources and deeper comprehension of the basic needs of Latin America. My country has already begun its contribution. During the year which began on March 13 with the announcement of the Alliance for Progress the United States will allocate more than one billion dollars in development assistance to Latin America. This amount is more than three times that made available last year. It includes less than half of the 500 million dollars appropriated under the Act of Bogotá. It does not include the additional resources which will be made available through the World Bank, other international institutions and private sources.

This rapid increase in the level of our assistance is only the first step in our continuing and expanding effort to help build a better life for the people of the hemisphere, an effort to which I am devoting my personal attention. And as the nations of Latin America take the necessary steps, as they formulate the plans, mobilize the internal resources, make the difficult and necessary social reforms, and accept the sacrifice necessary if their national energy is to be fully directed to economic development—then I believe that the United States should supplement this effort by helping to provide resources of a scope and magnitude adequate to realize the bold and elevated goals envisaged by the Alliance for Progress. For, as I have said before, only an effort of towering dimension—an effort similar to that which was needed to rebuild the economies of Western Europe—can ensure fulfillment of our Alliance for Progress.

This heroic effort is not for governments alone. Its success demands the participation of all our people—of workers and farmers, businessmen and intellectuals and, above all, of the young people of the Americas. For to them and to their children, belongs the new world we are resolved to create.

The tasks before us are vast, the problems difficult, the challenges unparalleled. But we carry with us the vision of a new and better world, and the unlimited power of free men guided by free governments. And I believe that our ultimate success will make us proud to have lived and worked at this historic moment in the life of our hemisphere.

With warmest personal regards.

JOHN F. KENNEDY

NOTE: The message was released at Hyannis, Mass.

314   Letter to the Director, Bureau of the Budget, Concerning
Contracts With Private Enterprises for the Government's
Scientific and Technical Work.   *August 6, 1961*

[Released August 6, 1961.   Dated July 31, 1961]

Dear Mr. Bell:

Since the end of World War II, the Federal Government has been making extensive use of contracts with private institutions and enterprises to provide for the operation and management of research and development facilities and programs, for analytical studies and advisory services, and for technical supervision of weapons systems and other programs administered on a systems basis. Through such contracts the Government has been able to accomplish scientific and technical work essential to urgent public purposes.

In part, the use of such contracts has been made necessary by the Government's entry into new fields, such as atomic energy, missile development and space exploration, and the need for talents and services not previously employed. In part, the use of contracts has also been induced by the recommendations of the second Hoover Commission and other groups that the Government terminate activities which could better be performed for it by private enterprise. Present Federal policies with respect to contracting-out Government activities are outlined generally in Bureau of the Budget Circular No. A-49, "Use of management and operating contracts," and Bureau of the Budget Bulletin No. 60-2, "Commercial-industrial activities of the Government providing products or services for governmental use."

After a decade or more of experience with such contracts, I think it would be desirable to review the effectiveness of this means of accomplishing the Government's purposes.

Some of the questions that require review have been posed recently in studies and reports by several committees of Congress. I would like to have you undertake, with the assistance and cooperation of the other Federal officials most concerned, a review of the experience with respect to the types of contracts mentioned above. I am requesting the following officials to participate in the study: the Secretary of Defense, the Chairman of the Atomic Energy Commission, the Chairman of the United States Civil Service Commission, the Administrator of the National Aeronautics and Space Administration, and the Special Assistant to the President for Science and Technology.

The product of the review should be recommendations to guide future executive branch action. While there is a consensus that the use of contracts is essential and appropriate to carry on certain types of Federal operations, it also appears that use of the contract device has been made necessary in part by the limitations which exist with respect to direct Federal operations.

I would like to have you explore the circumstances and conditions under which contractor operations provide the most effective means for accomplishing the Government's objectives in the areas under review. I would also like to have full consideration given to the limitations which make direct Federal operations difficult, and to the development of proposals for adjustments and new concepts in direct Federal operations which would provide the Government with greater flexibility in determining whether the public interest would best be served by the use of contractor or direct Government operations.

The review should focus on the following matters: (1) the effect of the use of contractors on direct Federal operations, the Federal personnel system, and the Government's own capabilities, including the capability to review contractor operations and carry on scientific and technical work in areas where the contract device has not been used, and policies and actions needed to increase the Government's capabilities in these respects; (2) the policies, if any, that the Government should follow in controlling the salaries and fringe benefits of personnel working under a contract, and the appointment, management and dismissal of such personnel; (3) the criteria to be used in determining whether to perform a service or function through a contractor or through direct Federal operations, including any spe-

cial considerations to be given to the nature of the contractor and his relationship to production contractors; (4) the policies which should apply in selecting contractors, including the organization of institutions for the sole purpose of entering into contracts with the Government; (5) the means for reviewing and supervising contractor operations, and for achieving maximum efficiency in such operations; and (6) the policies which should apply with respect to contractor fees and cost reimbursement practices on items such as overhead, facilities and equipment, and advertising.

The results of the review should be available not later than December 1.

Sincerely,

JOHN F. KENNEDY

[Honorable David E. Bell, Director, Bureau of the Budget, Washington 25, D.C.]

NOTE: The letter was released at Hyannis, Mass.

315   Remarks Upon Signing Bill Authorizing the Cape Cod National Seashore Park. *August 7*, 1961

I WOULD LIKE to make a brief statement. Today, in signing S. 857, an act to authorize the establishment of the Cape Cod National Seashore Park, I join the Congress and hope that this will be one of a whole series of great seashore parks which will be for the use and benefit of all of our people.

This act makes it possible for the people of the United States through their Government to acquire and preserve the natural and historic values of a portion of Cape Cod for the inspiration and enjoyment of people all over the United States.

This is a wise use of our natural resources, and I am sure that future generations will benefit greatly from the wise action taken by

the Members of the Congress who are here today.

I commend the Congress for giving very careful judgment in balancing off public needs in the interests of people who live in this section of the Cape, and I think that they have done an admirable job in serving both interests in this piece of legislation.

I cosponsored, as a Member of the Senate, a similar bill. It is a very old part of the United States, and I must say that from personal knowledge I realize very well how useful this is going to be for the people of the Cape and Massachusetts and New England and the entire United States.

There are Members of Congress here today from Texas and Colorado and Utah who have seen in their own States the tremendous contribution which these national parks can make. If we are going to double the population in another 50 years or so, we can get some idea of how important preserving this section for all the people will be.

I think we are going to need a good deal more effort like this, particularly in the more highly developed urban areas, where so many millions of people now live, and work out the means of securing the advantages of recreation and leisure which these areas can bring. So I know that the Government and the Congress will work together in seeing how they can carry on similar projects in other parts of the country.

This is a matter of great interest to me, and I express my appreciation to the Members of the Congress and to the chairmen of the committees, and to those Members of Congress particularly, as I said, from not only Massachusetts who worked hard on it in a bipartisan spirit but from all sections of the country who strongly supported this legislation.

NOTE: As enacted, S. 857 is Public Law 87–126 (75 Stat. 284).

316   Remarks Upon Signing the Agricultural Act of 1961.
August 8, 1961

THE AGRICULTURAL ACT of 1961 is a major step toward a sound agricultural economy and a better life for the farmers of this country. It is designed to improve farm income, expand the markets for agricultural products, reduce our stocks of grains and wheat, and relieve our taxpayers of carrying some of the cost of carrying these stocks. I believe these objectives are in the best interests of our farmers and our country.

Of particular significance is the extension of the use of marketing orders to additional farm commodities. This will offer producers an opportunity to influence the market and offer the consumers advantage in quality, regularity of supply, and stability of prices. I am also pleased that the act permits us to increase the present scope of our program for the distribution of agricultural commodities abroad, and extends the school lunch program to assure millions of our children better nutrition and better health.

These programs have long proved their merit and in these critical times and days they do assume significance for the welfare of our Nation. The benefits of the farm program that will result from this act are all in the right direction. They should help us toward the achievement of our goals for American agriculture, because American agriculture is of concern to us all, whether we live on the farm or in the city, and of concern to hundreds of millions of people around the world who look to this tremendous capacity which we have, with a relatively limited number of people, to produce food for ourselves and a good portion of the world. This is really a most outstanding accomplishment of our civilization in this century, to produce more food with less people than any country on earth. And it contrasts to the efforts of those behind the Iron Curtain in Russia and China where by entirely different systems they have had great difficulty. We wish for them well in this area because we want food available for all people.

We do point with pride to the record the American farmers have made and I hope that this legislation—I am sure and I know it will help to increase that record.

So that in this bill today we serve our people, our farmers, and also people around the globe.

NOTE: The Agricultural Act of 1961 is Public Law 87–128 (75 Stat 294).

317 Remarks on Presenting a Trophy to the Winner of the 1960 President's Cup Regatta. *August 9, 1961*

I WANT to express my great pleasure at having an opportunity to present to the winner of last year's race, Mr. "Chuck" Thompson, who directed his boat *Miss Detroit* to win the President's Cup during the race here last summer, this trophy.

Mr. Thompson informed me that his average speed was around 98 miles per hour and that he had had this boat up to as high as 185 miles per hour.

I have been interested all my life in boats, and it's therefore a great personal pleasure to award this Cup to Mr. Thompson.

I think what is most impressive is the effort and courage of all those who run their boats at high speed. John Paul Jones once said, "Give me a fast boat and I'll go in harm's way." And you have a fast boat and we're very proud of you as Americans, and it's a great pleasure for me as President to present to you this Cup—and also to greet the other members of the committee who've been responsible for carrying on the tradition of this great race.

NOTE: The President presented the award to Charles ("Chuck") Thompson, Sr., at a ceremony in the Rose Garden at the White House.

318 The President's News Conference of *August 10, 1961*

THE PRESIDENT. Good morning. I have three announcements.

[1.] I read last week with great interest the statement by Prime Minister Macmillan, calling for negotiations looking toward Great Britain's entry as a full member in the European Common Market. I am gratified that this statement has been well received by the governments that are already members of the Common Market, and by the Commission of the European Economic Community. The United States Government, under the leadership of both parties, has steadfastly supported the political and economic integration of Western Europe.

We are convinced that the continuing progress of this movement can bring new vitality to the Atlantic Community, and mounting strength to the free world. We welcome the prospect of Britain's participation in the institutions of the Treaty of Rome and in the economic growth that is the achievement and promise of the Common Market.

During the progress of the negotiations, the United States will of course give close attention to all developments affecting our own economic interests, and those of other friendly states in this hemisphere and elsewhere.

553

The enlargement of the European Community will necessarily result in some changes in the pattern of trade, but the necessary adjustments can be greatly facilitated if the European Community builds on the principle of broad and increasing trade relations with all other nations. It is our hope that progress towards this end can be made during the tariff negotiations under way in Geneva, in which both the European Economic Community and the United Kingdom are participating.

[2.] Secondly, I now have a report from the special panel on nuclear testing. This panel has examined a broad range of issues concerning our capabilities to detect and identify nuclear explosions. It has also gone into certain technical questions relating to nuclear weapons development. Although the report is made up of highly classified materials and cannot be released for that reason, I can say that as far as I am concerned this report has made me feel more urgently than ever that without an inspection system of the kind proposed by the United States and the United Kingdom at Geneva no country in the world can ever be sure that a nation with a closed society is not conducting secret nuclear tests.

In view of this report and in view of the deep longing of the people of the world for an effective end to nuclear testing, I am asking Ambassador Dean to return to Geneva on August 24 in an effort to ascertain whether the Soviet Union is now prepared to bring a safeguarded test ban agreement into being. It is my hope that he will succeed in convincing the Soviet representatives that the test ban treaty which we have proposed and stand ready to use as a basis for serious negotiations is a necessary and rational means of reducing the likelihood of nuclear war, and if we were successful,

would be an admirable beginning in the long road towards general disarmament.

His return to Geneva is with our hopes and prayers, and I believe with the hopes and prayers of all mankind who are most concerned about further developments of this deadly weapon. This meeting is most important, most critical, and I am hopeful that we will find a favorable response by those who will participate in this negotiation.

[3.] Finally, I would like to say that while we face many problems about the world, one of the most encouraging features of recent months has been the wholehearted response which so many young men and women have given to the proposal for the Peace Corps.

We have an opportunity, particularly in the area of teaching, to send hundreds and hundreds of young men and women who are skilled in this area throughout the world, teaching them English. And English opens up not only a key of communication, but also opens up all of the great cultural, historical, judicial areas which have become identified with the Anglo-Saxon world, and which are so vital in these difficult days.

I am hopeful, therefore, that the Congress will support this effort. It has had a most promising beginning, and we have an opportunity, if the amount requested by the Peace Corps is approved by the Congress, of having over 2700 volunteers serving the cause of peace in 1962, fiscal year.

[4.] Q. Mr. President, in your reading of Mr. Khrushchev's recent speech and statements, have they increased, reduced, or left unchanged the chances for a peaceful settlement of the German problem?

THE PRESIDENT. I thought Mr. Khrushchev restated the position which he took at Vienna and which he took in the Soviet aide memoire, and that there were no new proposals in that speech. He did state his desire, as I have done before, to have negotiations on these matters which are in dispute, and I can say that it is the strong conviction of the United States Government that every means should be employed, every diplomatic means, to see if a peaceful solution to this difficult matter can be achieved.

I think that we will, in the coming months, as I have said, use every device available to us to see if we can reach an equitable solution, and to see if we can get a more precise definition of the phrases and words and thoughts which the Soviet Union has expressed in the matter of Berlin, Germany, and Central Europe.

Q. Mr. President, I would like to ask your judgment on a passage in Mr. Khrushchev's speech. He says that in connection with a peace treaty between the Soviet Union and the East German Government: "We do not intend to infringe upon any lawful interests of the Western powers. Barring of access to Berlin, blockade of West Berlin, is entirely out of the question." Is there a catch in this, Mr. President?

THE PRESIDENT. I think you have to read the speech in total. I believe it was stated that we should engage in negotiations with the East German Government in order to achieve the result which has been suggested. There have been a number of proposals about the rights of the East German Government to control access, and also to control the territory of West Berlin, and, therefore the speech should be read in total.

But I do believe that we should use, as I have said, every means available to us to make a determination whether a peaceful solution can be reached which will protect the rights of the people of West Berlin and our own rights.

[5.] Q. As a former member of the House of Representatives and the Senate, sir, how do you feel about proposals to increase the size of the House from the present number of 437?

THE PRESIDENT. Well, as a former member of the House, I would feel that it should be left to the members of the House of Representatives. [*Laughter*]

[6.] Q. Mr. President, as a matter of prudence in these tense times, have you given any thought to making formal arrangements for the exercise of Presidential power in the event that you might become unable to function?

THE PRESIDENT. Yes, I have entered into the same kind of an agreement with the Vice President that my predecessor, President Eisenhower, entered into with Mr. Nixon in the case of Presidential incapacity or inability to fulfill his constitutional functions, and I will ask Pierre if he could, at his noon briefing, put out a statement on what that agreement consists of.

[7.] Q. Mr. President, recently you have appealed to our allies to make a greater effort in the conventional force field. In the light of that, are you satisfied with the results of the Paris conference which just concluded?

THE PRESIDENT. Well, Mr. Rusk, after the Paris conference, went to Rome to talk to the Prime Minister of Italy, and I think was going to see Dr. Adenauer in Italy also and should be back very shortly, and then I think we could—I could give a precise answer.

That was one of the subjects which was discussed, and I think that I'll suspend any precise answer until Mr. Rusk has returned. In addition, those who participated at the Paris conference, the French Foreign Minister and, of course, Lord Home, have an obligation to report back to their governments to find out what the policy will be, as well as the members of NATO.

So I think it's still premature to make a determination. I am hopeful that the members of NATO will carry out the commitments which have been made in NATO on previous occasions, and particularly during these difficult days.

[8.] Q. Mr. President, in the event that Mr. Dean fails in his mission in Geneva, do you have in mind any deadline—any possibility of setting a certain date when you will decide to resume nuclear testing?

THE PRESIDENT. I think we will be able to tell almost immediately whether the Soviet Union has made any change in its insistence upon the Troika, and therefore a unilateral veto on any inspection system. That of course is the fundamental issue which has up till now made it impossible to secure the acceptance of a treaty. Quite obviously, if that were written into any treaty, the treaty would be self-policing, and we would have no treaty, and as I've said in my statement, it's impossible to make a precise determination without inspection of whether nuclear testing is going on. We'll be able, therefore, to tell quite quickly whether there is any prospect for success, and if there is not, Mr. Dean will come home and I will then make the appropriate decisions.

Q. Is this our last try, then, Mr. President?

THE PRESIDENT. We will try always if there's any genuine hope of success. But as I have indicated, this is probably a decisive meeting, because we will now find out whether there's any prospect of bringing an end to nuclear testing. And if we cannot agree on a system for effective inspection system on nuclear testing, which is really the easiest kind because of the various mechanisms that are available to determine testing—which is the easiest kind of dis-

armament in a sense, or at least limitations on arms, to police—how possibly can any country which will refuse to accept an effective inspection system on nuclear testing, how can they possibly say and argue in the General Assembly or anyplace else, that they're really for disarmament?

[9.] Q. Mr. President, there has been considerable argument in Congress in recent weeks about the proper role of military officers in educating the public on the dangers of communism. Senator Fulbright wrote a memorandum on it. There have been some orders issued in the Defense Department on the subject of proper conduct of military officers in this matter. I wonder if you could give us your views on this subject?

THE PRESIDENT. Well, Senator Fulbright sent a memorandum to the Secretary of Defense at the request of the Secretary of Defense and expressed his views about a matter which is of course of concern to the Department of Defense. The United States military, due to one of the wisest actions of our Constitutional Founders, have been kept out of politics, and they continue their responsibilities regardless of the changes of administration. I have no idea what the politics are of the members of the Joint Chiefs of Staff. I've appointed two of them since I've been President, and I have no idea what their views of politics are. This is a most important protection for our country, and it's equally important protection for the military. It prevents them from being exploited or discriminated by political people in either party. So therefore the problem always is, is how can the military remain removed from political life and how can civilian control of the military be effectively maintained and at the same time the military have the right and the necessity to express their educated views on some of the great problems that face us around the world. So I think this is a continuing matter which the Secretary of Defense is giving attention to. There is no desire to restrain or prevent any military man from speaking. What we are concerned about, however, always is that they not be exploited for any partisan purpose.

And I think basically it's for their own protection as well as the protection of the country. So in answer to your question, some of this arose because of an NSC decision in 1958, which placed special responsibilities upon them. And I think that it's therefore an obligation upon those who place those responsibilities upon them to clarify it in such a way that the common interest is protected.

So in my judgment, Senator Fulbright performed a service in sending his viewpoint to the Department of Defense and I am hopeful that every member of the Senate on this and every other matter will continue to give the administration the benefit of their judgment. That is why we are all up here.

[10.] Q. Mr. President, some members of your administration and others have privately expressed concern that the continued large flight of East German refugees to the West might result in an act of violence. Senator Fulbright suggested that the border might be closed. Could you give us your assessment of the danger and could you tell us whether this Government has any policy regarding the encouragement or discouragement of East German refugees moving West?

THE PRESIDENT. No, I don't think we have attempted to encourage or discourage the movement of refugees, in answer to the last part of the question. Of course, we're con-

cerned about the situation in Eastern Germany, and really in Eastern Europe. There has been a tremendous passage from East to West which, of course, I know is a matter of concern to the Communists because this tremendous speedup of people leaving the Communist system to come to the West and freedom, of course, is a rather illuminating evidence of the comparative values of free life in an open society, and those in a closed society, under a Communist system. In answer to your question, however, the United States Government does not attempt to encourage or discourage the movement of refugees and I know of no plans to do so.

[11.] Q. Mr. President, are you satisfied that the United States compromises in the agreement at Punta del Este on the public information program and the committee of experts will not weaken your Alliance for Progress program?

THE PRESIDENT. Well, we haven't concluded the negotiations. So far I have been very satisfied with what has been done, and I have the greatest possible hopes for this meeting. I hope that all of us will not get so occupied with other matters occurring in this hemisphere that we forget that perhaps one of the most significant meetings in the history of the Western Hemisphere, in this century, is now taking place in Montevideo, and that if we can reach a successful conclusion we can come out of that meeting, all of these republics, with a real hope that we can move ahead in improving the life of the people of this continent. And that's where the great struggle is going on. If we fail there, and if we fail here in the United States to recognize that this is the issue to which we should now be devoting our attention, then the spread of communism is—and the failure of the free society—is going to be far more assured.

So I am hopeful that the meeting will be successful. I am hopeful that the country and the people of this hemisphere will look at what's going on there, because that is the most significant event of recent weeks.

[12.] Q. Sir, have you asked your aides, or your science aides, to prepare for you some kind of a study on whether a greater focus can be put in our space efforts in some possible arrangement similar to the Manhattan project during the last war?

THE PRESIDENT. We are now attempting to devote—we are spending as much money and devoting as large a percentage of scientific personnel, engineering and all the rest, as we possibly can to the space program. We are constantly concerned with speeding it up. We are making what I consider to be a maximum effort.

It may be possible to improve it as we go along and we will attempt to do so. But we asked for all the money for this program that those in positions of responsibility felt could be usefully employed for this purpose, because beyond this we begin to get into diminishing returns on personnel and all the rest.

We may be able to improve it and if we can, we will, but it is our hope to make the largest possible effort.

[13.] Q. Mr. President, if fighting should break out over Berlin, that is, if peace efforts fail, do you believe it can be limited to a conventional war or would it lead to the use of nuclear weapons?

THE PRESIDENT. Well, we are hopeful that we would be able to reach peaceful solutions to these problems.

[14.] Q. Mr. President, the Budget Director testified at the Capitol a week ago and said that your administration was a little unhappy with the policy planning and the generation of ideas in the State and Defense Departments and cooperation between them.

Can you tell us what that problem is in a little detail and what is being done to improve the situation?

THE PRESIDENT. Well, I think he also expressed satisfaction that some progress was being made. One of the problems, of course, is that nearly every international problem involves several governmental agencies: certainly the Defense Department, State, and in many cases at least one other agency. And therefore, the problem of coordinating these different agencies in an effective way represents a major problem of administration. We have, of course, as you know, on a number of the most important international problems that we faced, set up task forces which meet frequently and render at least weekly reports to the NSC, but it's a matter of constant concern, though I think we have improved our techniques recently.

[15.] Q. Mr. President, several congressional committees have issued reports that were quite critical of the handling of foreign aid in the past in Peru and Laos specifically, and they centered much of their attention on two or three individuals: Mr. Theodore Achilles, Mr. Rollin Atwood, Mr. Graham Parsons, who still have some positions of some responsibility in the Government. I wonder if you contemplate, or your administration contemplates, any action—removal of these individuals from positions of responsibility, or any studies of their role today, and do you have any specific plans for tighter administration of these programs in the light of the past record?

THE PRESIDENT. Yes, I am hopeful, if we are able to secure passage of legislation now before the Congress, that our administration will be more effective. In addition, we hope to bring in, if we are effective in the Congress, 5 new area administrators, and between 45 and 50 new country heads, into the administration of foreign aid. Now, on the three names you gave me, I am familiar with two of them. One of them is an Ambassador now to Sweden, and the other is at work here in the State Department, and I am not informed about the third. I am not aware of anything in their records that throws any question, of course, on their integrity, and we are satisfied that they can meet the responsibilities which they now hold.

[16.] Q. Mr. President, would you give us your views on the latest hijacking plane incidents involving——

THE PRESIDENT. The Cuban one or the American one?

Q. Both. [*Laughter*]

THE PRESIDENT. It's my understanding that the hijacking which took place yesterday of the American plane was done by a— at least the information I had before I came in—by a Frenchman who had been treated earlier this year for mental aberrations at Bellevue. The hijacking a week ago was done once again by two men, one of whom had also been treated for mental weakness. It does indicate that the lunatic fringe, those who are desirous of seeing their names in the paper, and all of the rest, have seized upon this technique.

I am, of course, wholeheartedly opposed to it. I am hopeful that we can make it possible to work out satisfactory procedures so that every government involved takes steps to prevent hijacking which endangers the lives of innocent people.

Now, let me say that we are—have ordered today on a number of our planes a border patrolman who will ride on a number of our flights. We are also going to insist that every airplane lock its door, and that the door be strong enough to prevent entrance by force, and that the possession of

the key be held by those inside the cabin so that pressure cannot be put on the members of the crew outside to have the door opened.

In addition, I am hopeful that governments everywhere will use their maximum influence to discourage this kind of action which endangers the lives of the crew and of the people involved, and which is an exercise in futility. And that is the view of this Government and we will take every means that we can to prevent not only the hijacking of our own planes but the hijacking of other planes. I'm hopeful that all concerned will do the same. It just endangers the lives of people who should be protected.

[17.] Q. Mr. President, there seems to be some doubt in the country as to whether the Russians really did put two men in orbit around the earth, as they have claimed. Are you satisfied from the evidence available to you that they did do what they said they did?

THE PRESIDENT. Yes.

Q. Mr. President, after this latest Soviet space effort, Senator Long of Missouri, among others, said that the real problem was not our present space effort but the lack of young Americans going into science. He pointed out that the Soviets are still graduating three times as many scientists as we are. Can you, sir, see anything that the Government can and is doing to step up this problem?

THE PRESIDENT. Well, we are hopeful that we can secure the passage of the Aid to Education Act as well as the NDEA, both of which offer scholarships to talented young men and women, and that we can increase the number of scientists who may be graduated.

In addition, of course, we have a good many very talented scientists, but we did not make a major effort in this area for many years, and we are now behind and paying the price of having the Soviet Union exploit a great propaganda advantage now on three separate occasions, with the flight of the Sputnik, the flight of Mr. Gagarin, and the most recent one. They are still, as I've said before, many months ahead of us. And therefore, we can look for other evidences of their superiority in this area. We are making a major effort which will cost billions of dollars. But we cannot possibly permit any country whose intentions toward us may be hostile to dominate space. What I would like to see at the United Nations and elsewhere is an effort made to have space insured for peaceful purposes. And the United States delegation to the General Assembly is going to make a major effort in that regard this year.

[18.] Q. Mr. President, there has been a lot of talk recently about the developments of a neutron bomb. Can you give us your estimate of the feasibility of developing a weapon which would destroy human beings without destroying real estate values?

THE PRESIDENT. No.

[19.] Q. Could you tell us, sir, whether your report from the experts on the test situation changes the general belief in this country that while we have no evidence that the Russians are cheating, we have no evidence that they are not cheating?

THE PRESIDENT. I think my statement stated that we could not make a precise determination whether testing was going on in a closed society by present techniques.

[20.] Q. Sir, I wonder what you think of a proposal by Senator Styles Bridges to amend the Mutual Assistance Act whereby we will deny any aid to any country exporting strategic goods to a country dominated by Russia.

THE PRESIDENT. Well, that is a language somewhat similar to the Battle Act, and I'd have to look at the language of Senator Bridges and compare it to the Battle Act before I could give you a judgment on it.

Q. If it's an extension, I think it might hit at some of our allies, mightn't it?

THE PRESIDENT. Well, I'll read the language——

[21.] Q. Mr. President, when you were a Senator, you were actively in favor of legislation to broaden our immigration laws and establish a more liberal and equitable quota system. Under present laws, many of the foreign born scientists and scholars who contributed so largely to our national strength might not be admitted. What plans does the administration now have in this area of immigration?

THE PRESIDENT. We have consulted with Congressman Walter and others as to what we can do to improve our immigration laws and we are going to continue to do so.

[22.] Because yesterday's hijacking aroused such great public excitement, and the week before, even though we now see that neither one of these hijackings was done by Cubans, does, it seems to me, make it important for us to act with the prudence which is worthy of a great power which bears responsibilities for the defense of freedom all around the globe, and not to make determinations on policy until our information is more complete.

In addition, we should realize that over 25 planes have come to the United States, 14 have been returned, 9 have been sold in response to a court order, and that, therefore, we should, I think, concern ourselves with procedures which will prevent a repetition and which will make sure that our own responsibilities are fully met in this regard.

The point I want to make is that what is going on in Montevideo is so important that we should not get overexcited about matters when our information is so faulty, so incomplete.

[23.] Q. Mr. President, in connection with the Berlin crisis, there has been quite a bit of speculation about one or more summit conferences. Would you tell us what your attitude is at this time toward summit negotiations?

THE PRESIDENT. Well, the attitude which I have held and still hold is that no summit between East and West is useful unless the groundwork has been laid beforehand which will insure some success. As far as a summit of Western leaders, I think that if it should prove important in coordinating our policy on any matter, Berlin, I think that that meeting should be held and would be prepared to do so.

[24.] Q. Mr. President, during the foreign aid debate, there has been some concern expressed by legislators based upon the reports from Montevideo that some of the Latin American nations are not, apparently, eager to institute the self-help measures which you've made a condition of your program, and that the administration may not insist upon those conditions. Do you intend to insist upon those conditions?

THE PRESIDENT. We're prepared to make a major effort in this regard and we're hopeful that other countries who also have high living standards will do so. But of course it would be completely useless unless an effort were made by all concerned. One of the proposals which have been made in Montevideo which is of particular interest is that under the aegis of the Inter-American Bank, that a study by independent experts be made of each country's economic planning and progress and commitment, and it seems to me that this is a great basis for a hemispheric effort. We're not interested in making the contributions which I think we have to make unless we feel that they're going to improve the life of the people. And, therefore, there's a responsibility on us all, for us to contribute to the success of this goal and for the countries involved to make sure that this effort helps the people, because otherwise the effort will fail and those societies will inevitably be wiped away—unless some real progress is made.

Reporter: Thank you, Mr. President.

NOTE: The President's fifteenth news conference was held in the State Department Auditorium at 10 o'clock on Thursday morning, August 10, 1961.

---

319   White House Statement and Text of Agreement Between the President and the Vice President on Procedures in the Event of Presidential Inability. *August 10, 1961*

THE PRESIDENT and the Vice President have agreed to adhere to procedures identical to those which former President Eisenhower and Vice President Nixon adopted with regard to any questions of Presidential inability. Those procedures are as follows:

(1) In the event of inability the President would—if possible—so inform the Vice President, and the Vice President would serve as Acting President, exercising the powers and duties of the Office until the inability had ended.

(2) In the event of an inability which would prevent the President from so communicating with the Vice President, the Vice President, after such consultation as seems to him appropriate under the circumstances, would decide upon the devolution

of the powers and duties of the Office and would serve as Acting President until the inability had ended.

(3) The President, in either event, would determine when the inability had ended and at that time would resume the full exercise of the powers and duties of the Office.

After consultation with the Attorney General, it is the understanding of the President and the Vice President that these procedures reflect the correct interpretation to be given to Article II, Section 1, clause 5 of the Constitution. This was also the view of the prior Administration and is supported by the great majority of constitutional scholars.

The relevant constitutional provision is:

"In Case of the Removal of the President from Office, or of his Death, Resignation, or Inability to discharge the Powers and Duties of the said Office, the same shall devolve on the Vice President, and the Congress may by Law provide for the Case of Removal, Death, Resignation or Inability, both of the President and Vice President, declaring what Officer shall then act as President, and such Officer shall act accordingly, until the Disability be removed, or a President shall be elected."

Under this provision, upon a proper determination of Presidential inability, the Vice President succeeds temporarily to the powers and duties of the Presidency until such time as the President is enabled to act again. Unlike the case of removal, death, or resignation, the Vice President does not permanently become President.

Under the arrangement quoted above, the Vice President agrees to serve as Acting President "after such consultation as seems to him appropriate under the circumstances." There is no provision of the Constitution or of law prescribing any procedure of consultation, but the President and Vice President felt, as a matter of wisdom and sound judgment, that the Vice President would wish to have the support of the Cabinet as to the necessity and desirability of discharging the powers and duties of the Presidency as Acting President as well as legal advice from the Attorney General that the circumstances would, under the Constitution, justify his doing so. The understanding between the President and the Vice President authorizes the Vice President to consult with these officials with a free mind that this is what the President intended in the event of a crisis.

Prior to the Eisenhower-Nixon arrangement, there were no similar understandings of a public nature. For this reason, prior Vice Presidents have hesitated to take any initiative during the period when the President was disabled. Obviously, this is a risk which cannot be taken in these times, and it is for that reason that President Kennedy and Vice President Johnson have agreed to follow the precedent established by the past Administration.

NOTE: The Attorney General's opinion upon the construction to be given to the Presidential inability clause of the Constitution was submitted to the President in a letter dated August 2 (27 pp., Government Printing Office, 1961).

320 Letter to the President of the Seneca Nation of Indians
      Concerning the Kinzua Dam on the Allegheny River.
      August 11, 1961

[Released August 11, 1961. Dated August 9, 1961]

Dear Mr. Williams:

I fully appreciate the reasons underlying the opposition of the Seneca Nation of Indians to the construction of Kinzua Dam on the Allegheny River. Involved are very deep sentiments over the loss of a portion of the lands which have been owned by the Seneca Nation for centuries. I therefore directed that this matter be looked into carefully and that a report be submitted to me on the basic issues involved.

I have now had an opportunity to review the subject and have concluded that it is not possible to halt the construction of Kinzua Dam currently under way. Impounding of the funds appropriated by the Congress after long and exhaustive Congressional review, and after resolution by our judicial process of the legal right of the Federal Government to acquire the property necessary to the construction of the reservoir, would not be proper. Moreover, I have been assured by the Corps of Engineers that all of the alternative proposals that have been suggested, including the so-called "Morgan Plan Number Six," have been thoroughly and fairly examined and are clearly inferior to the Kinzua project from the viewpoint of cost, amount of land to be flooded and number of people who would be dislocated. In addition, the need for flood protection downstream is real and immediate—the cessation of construction would, of course, delay the providing of essential protection.

Even though construction of Kinzua must proceed, I have directed the departments and agencies of the Federal Government to take every action within their authority to assist the Seneca Nation and its members who must be relocated in adjusting to the new situation. Included in the items I have directed the Executive departments and agencies to consider are (1) the possibility of the Federal Government securing a tract of land suitable for tribal purposes and uses contiguous to the remaining Seneca lands in exchange for the area to be flooded; (2) a careful review of the recreation potential resulting from construction of the reservoir, and the manner in which the Seneca Nation could share in the benefits from developing this potential; (3) a determination of whether any special damages will be sustained because of the substantial proportion of the total Seneca lands to be taken; and (4) special attention and assistance to be given those members of the Seneca Nation required to move from their present homes, by way of counseling, guidance, and other related means. In the event legislation is required to achieve these objectives, I have asked that recommendations be prepared.

I hope you will convey to the members of the Seneca Nation the desire of the Federal Government to assist them in every proper way to make the adjustment as fair and orderly as possible. I pledge you our cooperation.

Sincerely,

JOHN F. KENNEDY

[Mr. Basil Williams, President, Seneca Nation of Indians, 25 Main Street, Salamanca, New York]

321 Message to Sir Winston Churchill on the 20th Anniversary of the Atlantic Charter. *August 14, 1961*

TODAY marks the 20th Anniversary of the Atlantic Charter. Time has not changed and events have not dimmed the historic principles you there expressed with President Franklin Roosevelt. Our two nations are still united on the common goals you two so eloquently charted at sea. We still believe that all nations must come to the abandonment of the use of force. We still seek a peace in which all the men in all the lands may live out their lives in free-

dom from fear and want. And we are still determined to protect the right of all peoples to choose the form of government under which they will live—and to oppose all territorial changes that do not accord with the freely expressed wishes of the people concerned.

Your own name will endure as long as free men survive to recall these words.

JOHN F. KENNEDY

322 Statement by the President Urging Bipartisan Support for Long-Term Foreign Aid. *August 17, 1961*

[Released August 17, 1961.   Dated August 16, 1961]

LONG-TERM authorization of development loans, as earlier recommended by President Eisenhower, is essential to making certain that our foreign aid program is both efficient and effective. At a time when Secretary Dillon is about to sign our long-range pledge to Latin America, when Asia and Africa are poised between economic development and chaos, when Mr. Khrushchev is probing the West for any sign that our resolve is weakening, I cannot believe that the bipartisan support always given this program is at this crucial moment to be aban-

doned. I strongly urge the members of the House, by reversing this afternoon's vote, to demonstrate that this nation is still united in its determination to meet its responsibilities and halt the spread of Communism and Castroism by every available means. For eight years the Democrats in both Houses gave President Eisenhower overwhelming support in every major vote on foreign policy and foreign aid. It is urgent that this bipartisan principle be maintained in this crucial hour of the nation's history.

323 Letter to Secretary Goldberg Concerning the 25th Anniversary of the First Unemployment Insurance Payment. *August 17, 1961*

Dear Mr. Secretary:

I want to thank you for your letter concerning the 25th Anniversary of the first unemployment insurance payment. The

occasion marks a milestone in the progress of social legislation.

The $28 billion that has been paid out in benefits since the unemployment insurance program was begun in 1936, has eased the financial burden of many millions of workers who lost their jobs through no fault of their own. It has also contributed materially to lessening the impact of economic downturns on business by providing essential purchasing power for our economy. Thus unemployment insurance has not only helped workers and their families, it has also lightened and shortened the recessions we have experienced during the past 25 years.

The contribution that the unemployment insurance program has made to the nation over the years points up the desirability of the improvements in the program I have recommended to the Congress. I hope these will be enacted early in the next session.

Sincerely,

JOHN F. KENNEDY

324   Remarks of Welcome to Secretary Dillon on His Return From the Punta del Este Conference. *August 19, 1961*

Ladies and gentlemen:

I want to express our great satisfaction in welcoming back to the United States the Secretary of the Treasury, Mr. Dillon, who headed our mission to the conference in Uruguay.

I must say I believe that this conference was the most important event which has occurred in the foreign policy of the United States in the last 6 months. I think it offers more hope for the future. I think it represents a more concentrated effort by a great number of Republics and a great number of people in this hemisphere to build a better life for their people.

It is a particular source of satisfaction to all of us that we were represented at that conference by the Secretary of the Treasury, Mr. Dillon, who has represented this country in previous conferences but who represented this country with particular distinction at this conference.

During the last 2 weeks he has carried forward the concepts which motivated the Alliance for Progress with the greatest vigor, the greatest understanding, and the greatest determination. And it is, I think, a source of credit to him and to the other members of the delegation that this conference and this agreement which finally was achieved represented our best hopes and the best hopes of our fellow Republics. So that while we're extremely sorry that I was not able to go, and the Members of the Senate and other members of the Government, the Members of the House, were not able to attend this conference as we had at first hoped—we were engaged in a struggle here—we do feel, however, that Mr. Dillon represented this country with the greatest distinction, the greatest credit. And I want him to know, and all those who were engaged in this conference, that we stand strongly behind the commitments that were made there, that this Government will do everything it possibly can to make sure that these commitments are carried out.

They stretch over a period of 10 years, and I am sure that this administration, and other administrations to follow, will make sure that it devotes the efforts of this country to assisting our fellow Republics in achieving a better life for the people of those countries.

This can be done now, I'm hopeful, by agreeing to legislation which will permit us to make long-range commitments.

I welcome back the Secretary of the Treasury and all the other members of the delegation, which is a most distinguished one.

We have here some stamps which were issued by the country which was our host, on the last day, which were stamps for the opening and the closing of this conference. We want you to know, Mr. Dillon, that you carried with you our best hopes and you have come back with our fondest expectations.

NOTE: The President spoke in the Rose Garden at the White House. At the conclusion of the ceremony, Secretary Dillon handed to the President the text of the agreement entitled "Charter of Punta del Este" which established the Alliance for Progress within the framework of Operation Pan America. The text of the Charter is published in the Department of State Bulletin (vol. 45, p. 463).

Another text of the President's welcoming statement was released by the White House prior to its actual delivery.

325 Remarks Following the Vice President's Report on the Berlin Situation. *August 21, 1961*

THE VICE PRESIDENT has given me a report on his remarkably successful and important trip to West Germany and West Berlin. His report emphasizes the confidence and trust which the people of West Berlin have in this country and in its commitments, and it places a heavy responsibility upon all of us to meet that responsibility.

I want to express my thanks to him for this most important service he has rendered to our country, and to General Clay who accompanied him, who was the Commandant in Berlin during the airlift in the late forties—and to Mr. Bohlen from the State Department.

The Secretary of State, Mr. Rusk, and I are most gratified by their visit, and we are aware—and the Vice President has emphasized this—that we are going to pass through difficult weeks and months in the time ahead in maintaining the freedom of West Berlin, but maintain it we will.

NOTE: The President spoke in the Fish Room at the White House. The Vice President responded as follows:

"I feel very fortunate that the President should have asked me to undertake this assignment in company with such distinguished Americans as General Clay and Ambassador Bohlen. It was a most stimulating and inspiring experience.

"We first went to Bonn and discussed with Chancellor Adenauer the President's views and the views of this Government, and also received suggestions from him. Later we went to Berlin and delivered the President's reply to Mayor Brandt's letter, and further details and views of this Government to Mayor Brandt. The exchanges were useful and fruitful, and I think will be productive.

"No person can see what we saw without deeply feeling the great responsibilities that America has to the people of West Berlin, and to humanity. They look to us for encouragement, for hope, and for leadership—and together we are going to continue to march shoulder to shoulder to the end that freedom is preserved in the world."

In his remarks the President referred to General Lucius D. Clay, his personal representative in Berlin, and to Charles E. Bohlen, Special Assistant to the Secretary of State.

326 Statement by the President on Ambassador Dean's Return to the Geneva Test Ban Conference. *August* 22, 1961

MR. DEAN is leaving to return to Geneva on a most vital mission. He will make a further effort to reach agreement on a treaty for an effective ban on nuclear testing. He goes with my full support and confidence. Our proposed treaty carries hope for our country and for the world, for relief from great dangers, and the United States continues to attach the highest importance to these negotiations. We must all hope that the Soviet Union will make some affirmative response to this renewed effort.

327 Remarks at the White House Concert for Handicapped Children. *August* 22, 1961

I WANT to express our great pleasure at having Dr. Pfohl and the students from his school in North Carolina. I just said to them that I think they played "Hail to the Chief" better than the Marine Corps Band, and we're very grateful to them. I think we have the Governor of North Carolina and Mrs. Sanford, and Governor Hodges and Mrs. Hodges, and also some of the North Carolina delegation with us today.

This is the first in a series of concerts here at the White House, by students of music, by younger people for younger people—and we hope that we will have many during the coming months and years.

As an American I have the greatest possible pride in the work that's being done in dozens of schools stretching across the United States—schools where devoted teachers are studying with interested young men and women and opening up the whole wide horizon of serious music.

I think the program which we're going to hear today is an example of how successful this school and these students have been. I think that sometimes in this country we're not as aware as we should be of the extraor-

dinary work that's being done in this field. Probably the best chamber music in the world is played in Vermont, by young Americans—and here in this school where they have produced extraordinary musicians and teachers, and their work is being duplicated all across the United States. This is a great national cultural asset, and therefore it is a great source of satisfaction to me, representing as I do today my wife, to welcome all of you here today at the White House.

We're particularly glad that you're playing for a group of children from the District, whom we're very happy to welcome here to the White House also.

So, while I will have to go back to my office, I do want to say that I'm going to keep the door open.

Thank you.

NOTE: The President spoke from a stand erected for the occasion on the South Lawn at the White House. The concert, planned and sponsored by Mrs. Kennedy, was given by the symphony orchestra of the Brevard Music Camp of Transylvania County, N.C. The orchestra was conducted by the camp's director, Dr. James Christian Pfohl.

328 Statement by the President Upon Welcoming the Millionth Visitor to the White House in 1961. *August 23, 1961*

IT IS a great pleasure that we welcome Mrs. Jack Sprayberry of Rome, Georgia who is the one-millionth visitor to the White House in the year 1961. This is the first year in the history of the White House that we have welcomed this many visitors. The previous high was 977,142 in 1960.

I believe this indicates a renewed interest in the White House as a great American landmark and virtually the only home of a head of state in the world where the people of the country are welcome as visitors. The White House is alive with history back to the earliest days of our country and I would like to take this opportunity to urge every American when the opportunity presents itself to come to Washington to visit this historic home.

Our young people can be inspired by the history; our older people can have their faith renewed by it. The White House is the home belonging to the United States and it is only fitting that as many visit it as possible.

329 White House Statement Warning the Soviet Union Against Interference With Free Access to Berlin. *August 24, 1961*

THE SOVIET NOTE of August 23, 1961, is clearly but one more step in a deliberate campaign of deception and attempted intimidation designed to distract attention from failures of the Soviet Government and to heighten world tensions.

The charges and allegations contained in this note with respect to the United States and its allies are false, as the Soviet Government well knows. That such statements should be made with respect to activities in the free Western sectors of Berlin at the very moment when the Soviet Government is sealing off the Eastern sector of the city is an act of cynicism and irresponsibility. This act is also a direct violation of the Soviet Government's commitment to "the economic and political unity of Germany" and the pledged word of the Soviet Government to cooperate with the Allied Governments "to mitigate the effects of the administrative division of Germany and Berlin" by "facilitation of the movement of persons and goods and the exchange of information" throughout Germany, including Berlin.

The slanderous remarks of the Soviet Government about the legitimate activities of free men in West Berlin suggest that somehow the Soviet Government supposes the United States to share the Soviet view that subservience to dictatorship is the proper mode of German life. The peaceful commitment to freedom of the people of West Berlin and the restraint of their leaders under great provocation have never been demonstrated more plainly than in recent days. Moreover, it is strange that the Soviet Government should protest against relations between West Germany and West Berlin at a time when it is insisting upon the identity of East Berlin with East Germany.

These charges and allegations can thus not be taken seriously. What must be taken seriously by the whole world, however, is the scarcely veiled threat of aggression against the Allied air routes to and from

West Berlin. The United States must serve a solemn warning to the Soviet Union that any interference by the Soviet Government or its East German regime with free access to West Berlin would be an aggressive act for the consequences of which the Soviet Government would bear full responsibility.

NOTE: A translation of the Soviet note of August 23 is published in the Department of State Bulletin (vol. 45, p. 433).

The commitments of the Soviet Government referred to in the second paragraph of the U.S. statement are contained in a communique released at the close of the sixth session of the Council of Foreign Ministers on June 20, 1949. For text, see Department of State Bulletin of July 4, 1949 (vol. 21, p. 857).

330   Letter of Commendation Following the Settlement of a Dispute Between the Metropolitan Opera Association and the Orchestra. *August 28, 1961*

Gentlemen:

I am extremely pleased that a settlement has been reached in the dispute between the Metropolitan Opera Association and the orchestra, thus assuring a 1961–62 season.

You are to be highly commended for your statesmanship in submitting the issues you have been unable to resolve between yourselves to voluntary and binding arbitration by Secretary of Labor Arthur J. Goldberg, who will serve at your and my request.

By reaching agreement the parties to this dispute have insured that a great cultural resource of the United States will be continued for this season as it has since 1892. The Metropolitan Opera, as a standard of excellence and as a measure of creative vigor

in the performing arts for over half a century, has become, through its travels about the United States and Canada, and through its recordings and broadcasts, a truly international institution, without losing its unique identity with the cultural life of New York City.

The Metropolitan Opera is important to the Nation. I am glad we have all found a way for it to continue.

    Sincerely,

        JOHN F. KENNEDY

NOTE: This is the text of identical letters addressed to Anthony A. Bliss, President, Metropolitan Opera Association; Herman D. Kenin, President, American Federation of Musicians; and Alfred Manuti, President of Local 802 of the Federation.

331   Remarks to a Group of Peace Corps Volunteers Before Their Departure for Tanganyika and Ghana. *August 28, 1961*

I WANT to express my great pleasure at welcoming all of you who are the first members of the Peace Corps to be graduated from these schools and also the first members of the Peace Corps to go overseas.

Those of you who are going to Ghana to teach, I am sure that you realize how important and valuable is the work in which

you are engaged. One of the great problems that the people of Africa face are the comparatively few experienced, educated leaders that they have for positions of responsibility during these first days of their independence.

And to indicate the intimate relationship between teaching and leadership, the President of Ghana, President Nkrumah, studied here in the United States, at Lincoln College in Pennsylvania. The Prime Minister-to-be of Tanganyika, Mr. Nyerere, studied at St. Andrews in Scotland, and both of them of course are among the most vigorous leaders of the new Africa.

I feel a particular satisfaction because this is the most immediate response—the Peace Corps—that I think the country has seen to the whole spirit which I tried to suggest in my inaugural about the contribution which we could make to our country.

The fact that you've been willing to volunteer, that you've gone through very detailed, demanding tests, that you are willing to go to Ghana and Tanganyika, and other countries as time goes on—Americans who are without great compensation, all of you with special skills, which could mean that if you stayed home you could pursue your own private interests with a good deal of assurance of success—the fact that you are willing to do this for our country in the larger sense, as the name suggests, for the cause of peace and understanding, I think should make all Americans proud and make them all appreciative.

There are of course a great many hundreds of millions of people scattered throughout the world. You will come in contact with only a few, but the great impression of what kind of country we have and what kind of people we are will depend on their judgment, in these countries, of you. You will be the personification of a special group of young Americans, and if you can impress them with your commitment to freedom, to the advancement of the interests of people everywhere, to your pride in your country and its best traditions and what it stands for, the influence may be far-reaching and will go far beyond the immediate day-to-day tasks that you may do in the months that are ahead.

So I hope you realize—I know you do—that the future of the Peace Corps really rests with you. If you do well, then the Peace Corps will be developed and more and more Americans will go abroad and will find a greater and greater response to this idea of serving our country.

I'm glad that those who are going to Tanganyika, who are going to take part in surveying—it's desperately needed, it's the kind of skill which I think can bring great benefit to the people that are involved. Tanganyika is gifted with unusual leadership, and I'm particularly glad that you are going there to help open the back land.

So that you're very welcome here, and we're all proud of you. And I must say, we put a good deal of hope in the work that you do.

Thank you.

NOTE: The President spoke in the Rose Garden at the White House. The group leaving for Tanganyika had attended the Peace Corps' first overseas training school, in Puerto Rico, the establishment of which was announced by the White House on July 10.

332 Statement by the President: Labor Day, 1961.
August 29, 1961

WE COMMEMORATE today achievement in human welfare—the economic and social protections our working people enjoy, the wide distribution of our wealth, the access to advancement and education, the strength of our labor organizations, the exercise of individual decision in guiding our institutions.

These are crucial issues in most of the world's societies, especially those with new political identities and modernizing economies. The root of genuine social revolution lies deep in the desire for a life better in material terms and—we believe—freer in spiritual terms.

Thus, this Labor Day again makes the vital distinction between opposing ways of life in the modern world. We celebrate the labor of our people precisely because we believe it to be an essential to man's dignity, performed freely and in good conscience, and commanding by right a just reward. We look upon man's toil as an expression of individual personality and will, not a commodity to be exploited for the benefit of a State or ruling political party. Tyranny deprives a man of the freedom and joy of his work.

These beliefs underlie our system of self-government in economic life. Our free and democratic labor movement is based upon the advancement of individual dignity. Today, as throughout our modern history, we rely upon the men and women of organized labor to help safeguard our democracy whose freedom is inseparably linked with their own.

Now these beliefs and this system face a stern test of history.

Here in America, technological change is altering the structure of industrial production and the content of jobs across a broad range of occupations. Old skills are rapidly outmoded. The demand for new skills outreaches the supply. It is clear that the maintenance of a fully competent labor force requires constant reinvestment in skills so that greater job opportunity, resulting from an expanded economic life, can be capitalized upon.

Especially needful of attention is the situation of the older person who becomes unemployed and finds no market for his ability and the young man or woman who faces a competitive labor force without adequate training.

Perhaps in no other area of our national life is the need to realize our ideal so clearly an economic necessity as in the attainment of genuine equality of opportunity for all. We serve ourselves and the stature of freedom throughout the world by serving our moral commitment to equality. Our government, in its own employment policies, will hold to this commitment and it must predominate in the personnel and membership policies of all organizations whose power or activities affect the public interest.

Full employment through wider opportunity for the occupationally displaced and the minority group member rests ultimately, as do all of our ambitions for higher economic life, upon the ability of the economy to grow. This Labor Day we can find satisfaction that our government, this Administration and the Congress, have been successful in enacting legislation such as the Temporary Extended Unemployment Compensation Act, the new Minimum Wage Law, the Area Redevelopment Act, improved Social Security, and the Housing Act that contributes to the economic welfare of all of our people. The guide-posts to the further and greater progress we seek are these:

Wage and price policies that contribute to expansion without impairing our competitive posture in world markets; great productivity from a wide use of scientific discovery and the exertion of dedicated individual effort; the proper utilization of increased resources for the fulfillment of urgent national needs; statesmanship in collective bargaining that acknowledges the public interest.

We can well earn what we well need in America.

In setting the goal of our society at the realization of human dignity, we reach for the highest of stars and seek the outer limits of human capability. In this, now as always the new world for the spirit, the labor of free men is both the reward and the way.

JOHN F. KENNEDY

333 White House Statement on the Agreement by Senate and House Conferees on Long-Term Development Programs. *August 29, 1961*

THE COMPROMISE which the Senate-House conferees have worked out is wholly satisfactory. It gives the United States government authority to make commitments for long-term development programs with reasonable assurance that these commitments will be met. In providing five years of substantial authorization, the conferees have recognized the magnitude of the need in the developing countries. In ensuring specific authority to enter into commitments with these countries the conferees have recognized the necessity for this government to give assurance that assistance will be forthcoming over a period of years.

The agreement reached by the conferees today is an important decision both for the United States and the Free World.

334 The President's News Conference of *August 30, 1961*

PRESIDENT KENNEDY. I have several announcements to make.

[1.] First, I want to take this opportunity to congratulate Governor Vandiver of Georgia, Mayor Hartsfield of Atlanta, Chief of Police Jenkins, Superintendent of Schools Letson and all of the parents, students and citizens of Atlanta, Ga., for the responsible, law-abiding manner in which four high schools were desegregated today.

This was the result of vigorous effort for months by the officials of Atlanta and by groups of citizens throughout the community. Their efforts have borne fruit in the orderly manner in which desegregation was carried out—with dignity and without incident.

Too often in the past, such steps in other cities have been marred by violence and disrespect for law.

I strongly urge the officials and citizens of all communities which face this difficult transition in the coming weeks and months to look closely at what Atlanta has done, and to meet their responsibilities, as have the officials and citizens of Atlanta and Georgia, with courage, tolerance, and, above all, respect for the law.

[2.] Secondly, as agreed at their recent meeting in Paris, the Foreign Ministers of France, the United Kingdom, and the United States will again be joined by the Foreign Minister of the Federal Republic of Germany, and they will meet in Washington on

September 14. This meeting will constitute a further stage in the process of continuing consultation by the four powers and our NATO allies with respect to Germany and Berlin in light of the Soviet challenge to our position there.

[3.] Three, I am appointing Gen. Lucius Clay to be my personal representative in Berlin with the rank of Ambassador. The situation in Berlin is a serious one, and I wish to have the advantage of having on the scene a person of General Clay's outstanding capacity and experience.

While this appointment will not change the existing responsibilities of our military and diplomatic officers in Germany and Berlin, General Clay will be in close touch with such men as Ambassador Dowling in Bonn and General Watson our Berlin commandant, and the appointment adds to our resources of judgment and action by placing in a most important city an American in whom the Secretary of State and I have unusual confidence.

We are most grateful to General Clay for once again resuming his long career of public service. General Clay will take up his duties on September 15, will proceed then to Berlin, and will serve as long as this special arrangement seems desirable.

[4.] Lastly, I am sending the following message to the conference of unaligned states convening in Belgrade on September 1:

"It is always encouraging when responsible world leaders join together to consider the problems that beset mankind. We recognize that most of the countries at Belgrade do not consider themselves committed on certain of the issues which confront us today, but we do know that they are committed to the United Nations Charter. The people of the United States share this commitment.

"We know that those gathering in Belgrade are committed to finding a way to halt the waste of the earth's resources in the building of the implements of death and destruction, and the people of the United States have constantly pledged themselves to this goal.

"We believe that the peoples represented at this conference are committed to a world society in which men have the right and the freedom to determine their own destiny, a world in which one people is not enslaved by the other, in which the powerful do not devour the weak. The American people share that commitment, and we have pledged the influence of this Nation to the abolition of exploitation in all of its forms.

"The peoples represented at Belgrade are committed to achieving a world at peace in which nations have the freedom to choose their own political and economic systems and to live their own way of life, and since our earliest beginnings this Nation has shared that commitment.

"All this and much more the leaders at Belgrade have in common. This and much more the people of the United States have in common with them. So for myself, and I'm sure for the American people, I express the hope that their deliberations there will bring us all nearer these goals."

[5.] Q. Mr. President, there have been increasing statements on both sides about the prospects for Western negotiations with Russia on the Berlin question. Could you spell out in any specific terms just what areas there are for negotiations and what will you hope to gain in view of recent Communist words and actions?

THE PRESIDENT. No, I don't think that it would be useful at this time to attempt to spell out the areas of negotiation.

We have indicated—and I've said before that we are prepared to participate in any exchange of views, to use all available channels which are open to us to see if a peaceful solution can be reached on the problems in Europe and in Germany—any solution which can provide greater guarantees to the people of West Berlin that they will have the right to live out their lives in a way of their own choosing and that we will be glad to participate in any conversations which we have hopes will advance that prospect. This is particularly true because the situation in this area is so fraught with danger.

Q. Do you think, generally speaking, sir, that the crisis in Berlin has a better chance of being settled through negotiation, as you have suggested, rather than by force, as the Soviets have threatened upon occasion?

THE PRESIDENT. Well, I don't see that there could be any solution—which would serve the world—to Berlin by force, and therefore I'm hopeful that all people involved will realize that in these days of massive forces available on every side that—for the future of the countries involved and for the human race—that we should attempt to work out a peaceful solution and that neither side should attempt to impose its will by brute force because in that case it would be unsuccessful and disaster would be the common result.

[6.] Q. On a domestic question, Mr. President, in view of the House action today on your school aid measure, how do you view the future prospects for such legislation?

THE PRESIDENT: Well, it's very difficult because everyone is for education but they're all for a different education bill. And it's very difficult to get a majority who will support legislation that has a prospect of getting out of the House committee and the Senate committee—and through the House committee and through the Senate committee— and be signed by the President.

So that it's going to require a good deal of good will on all sides, because the only one who loses today is not the administration but schoolchildren who need this assistance.

So we will be back next year. But it's going to require a recognition by all groups that—and our experience this year shows it— that there has to be some recognition that what we're concerned about is advancing education of the young people of this country, which, of course, is our most important asset and responsibility.

I'm hopeful that before the session ends there will be an opportunity for the Congress to vote on our aid to higher education, because that is desperately needed. In the next 10 years we're going to have to build more school buildings than we have built since the beginning of this country.

And the Federal Government, since our earliest beginnings, has had a responsibility in this field. This responsibility continues.

And therefore, though the defeat today was quite clear, and though the defeat today indicates it will be difficult to find a satisfactory formula, we will attempt to do so.

[7.] Q. Mr. President, could you give us your views on the wish of the Senate to question Dick Goodwin? Mr. Hatcher said this morning that he did not think the question of Executive privilege was involved.

THE PRESIDENT. No. I've—Mr.—I think Mr. Goodwin is going to be available to members of the Senate Foreign Relations Committee tomorrow afternoon at 5 in an informal meeting, and will be glad to discuss the entire report on the Punta del Este meeting, and all of its activities. And I'm sure other members of the delegation will be doing likewise.

Q. Sir, if I may pursue that just one second. You spoke of an informal meeting. Does this meet the problem of Executive privilege and not——

THE PRESIDENT. The question of Executive privilege has not been raised.

Q. Would it not be raised if there were formal meetings? is what I'm really getting at.

THE PRESIDENT. Well, the question of Executive privilege has not been raised in the request that was made by Senator Morse for Mr. Goodwin to appear. And Mr. Goodwin attended the Punta del Este meeting as a member of the delegation, and I would be delighted, and I think it would be most helpful, if Mr. Goodwin appeared under the circumstances that I've described. Does that answer your question? [*Laughter*]

[8.] Q. Mr. President, I would like to ask you a two-part question: Do you think that Mr. Nixon should run for Governor of California, and as a politician, Mr. President, what do you think of the advisability of a political party giving a defeated candidate a second chance at the Presidency?

THE PRESIDENT. Well, I would think, in answer to your first question, if Mr. Nixon asked my view as a fellow practitioner of the—follower of the political profession— I'd be glad to give him my opinion, as I do have an opinion on the matter. [*Laughter*]

But, second, I think that history is filled with the case of men who have been defeated for offices who have continued their public service, and I think we've seen it very much in the last few years, and I'm sure we'll see it in the next years.

[9.] Q. Mr. President, do you think the Peace Corps should dismiss Charles Kamen because of the complaints that have been made about him?

THE PRESIDENT. I think the Peace Corps, as Mr. Shriver has said, should make a judgment as they do. I don't think Mr. Kamen is as yet a member of the Peace Corps. He's in training, as a good many other men and women are, and then he will either be accepted or rejected. It's a matter which I'm sure the Peace Corps will deal with in a responsible way. And I've every confidence in the judgment of those who make the selections.

[10.] Q. Mr. President, there's a very hard core of unemployment still. Do you have any special plans now beyond those you've already suggested?

THE PRESIDENT. Well, we are concerned still about unemployment, which is four and a half million and on a seasonally adjusted rate would be about five million, which is still too high.

We have had in the last 2 or 3 months a tremendous economic recovery, but population increases and because of productivity increases and technological changes, we still have a hard core, particularly in some of the major industrialized areas, as well as some of the areas which have had chronic unemployment, we still have this hard core.

I'm hopeful that as the economy begins to move ahead more that there will be a further decrease in the number of those unemployed.

In addition, I am hopeful that Congress will take action before they go home, on job retraining, because some of this is technological and even if we had a complete economic recovery you would still find some men left behind because of the change in skills.

So I do think that legislation would be helpful, and if these programs do not work, then we're going to have to consider what other steps we can take. But we have a large deficit and it's difficult to think that we could usefully increase that in order to effect employment without adversely affecting the cost of living. That's our difficulty there.

[11.] Q. Mr. President, Mr. Nixon has

called the movement of American troops into West Berlin a useless gesture, which Mr. Khrushchev might interpret as weakness rather than strength. At the same time, the Republican National Chairman has said that your administration's attitude in general is one of appeasement toward communism throughout the world. Do you have any comment on this criticism by top spokesmen of the opposition party?

THE PRESIDENT. No, I don't. We are in a situation in Germany which is fraught with peril and I think that anyone who is aware of the nature of the destructive power that's available to both sides should, I would think, be careful in attempting to take any political advantage out of our present difficulties.

Now, in regard to the statement of the Vice President, I'm quite aware that Berlin is, from a military point of view, untenable, if it were subjected to a direct attack by the Soviet Union. What we hope will prevent that direct attack is the awareness of the Soviet Union that we mean to defend our position in West Berlin, and that American troops, who are not numerous there, are our hostage to that intent.

It would seem to me, and I think at the time, that the West Berliners would benefit from a reminder of that commitment, and it was for that reason that those troops were added to the garrison of West Berlin. I don't see really how that weakens our commitment. If troops were withdrawn, would that strengthen it?

[12.] Q. Mr. President, in view of the fact that the economy is recovering, what steps is the administration prepared to take to prevent a breakdown in the auto negotiations in Detroit?

THE PRESIDENT. Well, they're being carried on at the present time between the Auto Workers and the automobile industry, in the hope that they will come to a conclusion which will make it possible for work to be maintained and that it will make it possible for an agreement to be reached that will not provide for an increase in the cost of cars.

This is a matter in which the public interest is involved, quite obviously, but it's a matter which should be left, at this time, to the—those on both sides of the bargaining table, who are bargaining in a free economy.

[13.] Q. Mr. President, I'm not clear from your answer to Mr. Spivak whether we are actively seeking negotiations with the Russians at this time on the question of Berlin, whether Mr. Thompson or any other official of the Government is trying to set a date, time, and place for talks on——

THE PRESIDENT. Well, I think Mr. Thompson is going to be returning, under his regular schedule, in the next few days to Moscow and, as I have said, we will be using those means which are available to us to attempt to exchange views among all the parties that are interested, and see whether a satisfactory solution can be reached. And I feel I should leave it at that point.

[14.] Q. Do you believe that there is anything the Government can or should do to try to head off a hike in steel prices? And if so, what would you plan to do?

THE PRESIDENT. Well, I'm hopeful that the steel companies themselves will reach a conclusion that the October increase in wages can be absorbed without an increase in steel prices.

The inflation which marked our economy before 1958 was, I think, tied very closely to the increases in steel prices. Since 1958 the steel prices have remained relatively stable. And it is a fact that during that same period the cost of living has remained relatively stable.

Now my economic advisers inform me that it would be possible for the steel companies to absorb the increase, without increasing—the increase in wages—without increasing prices, and still insure to the steel companies, and their owners, a good profit.

I am concerned that an increase in steel prices would set off another inflationary spiral, and also make us less competitive abroad, serve as a brake on our recovery, and also affect our balance of payments.

So that I am very hopeful that these private companies will—and I'm sure they will—concern themselves with the public interests that are involved in their decision.

[15.] Q. Mr. President, you described the present session of the Geneva nuclear test ban conference as critical. Does the Soviet reaction to our latest proposals bring us closer then to a resumption of tests, or what is our next step in this area?

THE PRESIDENT. Well, Mr. Dean is going to continue during next week, and I would think that by the end of next week—I think they're meeting every other day—we should have a much—we'll have an answer as to whether it's going to be possible to reach an agreement.

He will then return home, and as I said before, we would then be expected to make the appropriate decisions.

[16.] Q. Mr. President, the language adopted last night by the conference committee on the foreign aid bill gives you authority to make long-term commitments for development lending. If both houses approve this language, would you then think that there is at least a kind of moral obligation upon the part of the Appropriations Committee to honor those commitments with appropriations?

THE PRESIDENT. No, I would think that the Appropriations Committee would have to make their own—meet their own responsibilities. But it would mean that—if the conference report is accepted by the House and Senate—that the House and Senate and

those committees which have particular responsibility for foreign affairs have set this figure.

This figure does represent a cut in both economic assistance and military assistance. And as we do have heavy responsibilities in the coming years in these areas—we've accepted a particularly heavy responsibility and commitment, for example, toward the countries of Latin America—I am hopeful that the Appropriations Committees and the Congress will come as close as possible to the figures that the conference has set, because any cut would diminish by that much our ability to do the job.

I think the compromise, while of course not in the language which was originally suggested, I do think gives us a very valuable tool. And I'm therefore appreciative of the work that was done by the conference.

[17.] Q. Mr. President, everything in the past 3 months that's been said by you and written about you indicates that you have a grave sense of your responsibility for involving this country and the world in a nuclear war over Berlin. Yet everything that's been said by Mr. Khrushchev and written about Mr. Khrushchev indicates he doesn't seem to share this grave responsibility.

Do you think there's been a failure in our diplomacy and our policy that he is not yet convinced about his responsibility in setting off a nuclear war?

THE PRESIDENT. Well, every country operates under different systems and every— Mr. Khrushchev—there has been a good deal of brandishing of nuclear weapons, but I am hopeful, as I've said, that anyone—and I'm sure Mr. Khrushchev knows very well what the effect would be on the people of this world of ours if nuclear weapons were exchanged in a massive way between the countries which possess them—and I'm conscious of this and I'm sure Mr. Khrushchev is—and we will have to wait and see now whether from that consciousness on both sides peace can be achieved, which is our objective.

[18.] Q. Mr. President, what is your view of the interference in the internal political affairs of Brazil by Castro in sending a message of encouragement to the leftist elements there, and what is your general view of the situation?

THE PRESIDENT. I think it's a matter which should be left to the people of Brazil. It is their country, their constitution, their decisions, their government, and I'm confident that they are going to solve the problem themselves without outside interference by any country.

[19.] Q. Mr. President, in view of the Berlin situation and the common threat, you have called up 75,000 reserves and have called in aircraft and naval ships. Can you tell us whether you're satisfied with what our NATO allies are doing to increase their strength, and can you tell us what they are doing and what they are planning to do if you have any knowledge of that?

THE PRESIDENT. There have been some increases, but we do not have a final judgment on what our NATO allies will do nor will we finally, I think, until the end of September. In addition, the United States is going to be considering what other steps it could take.

We have in the meeting of the foreign ministers in early August urged very strongly that the NATO countries commit larger forces to the defense of Europe. It involves their security and it involves peace in this area and I'm hopeful that all the countries that are involved will make the kind of effort which is required.

And I think if they do not, then, Europe has diminished to that degree. I am hopeful that we're going to meet our responsibility and we're asking them to meet theirs. And by the end of September we'll know whether that's going to be done.

[20.] Q. Mr. President, on steel do you have any thoughts or specific plans for meeting the situation if the steel industry does not seem to be persuaded by the arguments that you have been presenting against the price increase?

THE PRESIDENT. Well, I'm hopeful that the view which has been expressed today, and been expressed on other occasions, and the problems—and the public responsibilities of people involved, I'm hopeful that they will have an effect, and I prefer to leave it at that for the present.

[21.] Q. Mr. President, Ambassador Dowling has delivered a message to the Soviet Ambassador in Germany insisting—and that was the word of the note—that the Soviet Union take the necessary steps to insure continued unrestricted access to East Berlin without hindrance as to place or time. The East Germans have restricted some of the entry points into East Berlin for us and for the West Germans. Can you tell us how you intend to follow through on this?

THE PRESIDENT. We—the communication between East and West Berlin is open. And the situation which you've described has existed for a number of days.

Q. Do I understand that we consider the present situation to meet these requirements of unrestricted access?

THE PRESIDENT. We—I don't feel the situation in East Berlin is satisfactory in any way. And we have made clear that we have—do not consider it satisfactory. But it is also a fact that communication does exist between East and West Berlin, and that it's possible for those who have official responsibilities, as well as private citizens, to pass.

It is limited—it is not, in our opinion, in accordance with the agreements; but it does exist. What we are concerned about in addition, of course, is the whole question of access to West Berlin itself.

Q. Mr. President, on Berlin, if one takes the public statements of the two sides at face value, it would seem the U.S. and the U.S.S.R. are on something of a collision course here.

Do you have any feeling from private information, or other sources, that there is somewhere in all this wordage going back and forth, some room for diplomatic negotiation, and possibly a peaceful settlement of this problem?

THE PRESIDENT. I do not have such information at the present time. Though I am hopeful that—as I have said—that negotiations can be successful. There have been some statements which have been made which would indicate that there would be a recognition under all conditions of the rights of the people of West Berlin. Other statements have not been precise.

So we will know as time goes on. As I've said before at a previous press conference, it was important that we try to get at the real meaning of words—dealing with access, and rights, and freedom and the rest.

But in answer to your question, I am—do not have information today which would make me wholly sanguine about present prospects.

[22.] Q. Sir, there has been some indication that in the Cabinet, and elsewhere in the Government, that some of our top officials are deferring to the State Department for matters of decision involving the military and defense. There've even been papers sent from the Defense Department over to the State Department for clearance. I wonder if this is done at your order?

THE PRESIDENT. Well, ma'am, if you would be more precise, I could perhaps tell you.

Q. Well, sir, recently at a press conference, Secretary McNamara was asked several questions about the future in Berlin. He said, I can't answer those questions, you'll have to go to the Secretary of State.

THE PRESIDENT. Well, it depends what questions they were. If the questions dealt with matters which come under the competence of the State Department, then it seems to me Mr. McNamara was quite right.

My judgment and experience has been that Mr. McNamara is fully competent to deal with the military—his military responsibilities, and so does. And Mr. Rusk does.

There are a good many matters that overlap. This is a government which is supposed to communicate. And that's what they're doing. But I've never heard it suggested that Mr. Rusk—that Mr. McNamara was turning over his responsibilities to Mr. Rusk, or vice versa.

But I would think that it would be the height of folly not to have the most intimate communication on a matter as important as Berlin.

[23.] Q. Mr. President, can you at this time discuss with us some of the contents of the letter you received from Chancellor Adenauer this morning?

THE PRESIDENT. No, the main thrust of the letter was in regard to what measures might be taken by the countries which have responsibilities in the area to any further steps which might be taken by the Soviet Union or the East German regime to limit access of the people of West Berlin or our access to West Berlin, and it dealt with that matter of countermeasures.

[24.] Q. Mr. President, what is your view of the bitter Democratic primary fight in New York City, and do you favor one

579

Democratic group over another?

THE PRESIDENT. No. [*Laughter*]

[25.] Q. Mr. President, there has been some concern expressed over the amount of time it takes the allies to consult on the specific steps necessary to handle the Berlin situation. I think you, in one of your press conferences, recently indicated you weren't quite satisfied with the amount of time it took to draft a note. Could you tell us whether you are satisfied with the present tempo of such consultations?

THE PRESIDENT. Yes, well they're meeting almost every day—in any case every other day—the ambassadors of the countries that are directly involved. There are four countries that are involved and there is also NATO, so quite naturally it takes a longer time.

When it's a matter of involving a direct interest of the United States, however, we have attempted to make our responses immediate. For example, last week, when there was some suggestion that air traffic might be interfered with, we did get out the same day our response, because we thought the matter was so important.

But there is very—there is daily consultation, and I'm hopeful that through that consultation and through advanced planning we can meet some of the problems that you suggest, but it's difficult to meet them all satisfactorily.

[26.] Q. Time magazine today publishes a version of the Cuban invasion in which they say that Secretary Rusk canceled the air support for the landing force and that you supported his viewpoint. Could you comment on that?

THE PRESIDENT. No, I said from the beginning that I would not comment or attempt to, on the matter because I didn't think it was in the public interest. I'll merely state that this is the most inaccurate of all the articles that have appeared on Cuba. [*Laughter*]

Q. Sir, in a recent interview with Señor Castro he told me that you have said in the inaugural speech that you would not fear to negotiate and will not negotiate in fear.

It was a question I could not answer and maybe you could give us an idea on it because he says that the United States negotiates with the Russians and big powers and seems to be afraid—that was his words—to negotiate with Cubans about all the problems that concern both countries.

THE PRESIDENT. Yes. Well, I've expressed my view that as long as Cuba makes itself a willing—the Cuban Government makes itself a willing accomplice to the Communist objectives in this hemisphere, that we could not have successful negotiations. And that, in my opinion, is what their status is today.

Reporter: Thank you, Mr. President.

NOTE: President Kennedy's sixteenth news conference was held in the State Department Auditorium at 4:10 o'clock on Wednesday afternoon, August 30, 1961.

335 White House Statement on Soviet Resumption of Nuclear Weapons Tests. *August* 30, 1961

THE SOVIET government's decision to resume nuclear weapons testing will be met with deepest concern and resentment throughout the world. The Soviet government's decision to resume nuclear weapons testing presents a hazard to every human being throughout the world by increasing the dangers of nuclear fallout. The Soviet government's decision to resume nuclear weapons testing is in utter disregard of the desire of mankind for a decrease in the arms race. The Soviet government's decision to resume nuclear weapons testing presents a threat to the entire world by increasing the dangers of a thermo-nuclear holocaust. The Soviet government's decision to resume nuclear weapons testing indicates the complete hypocrisy of its professions about general and complete disarmament.

For three years world attention has centered on the negotiations in Geneva for a treaty to secure an end to nuclear testing. Until last March it appeared that slow but encouraging progress had been made. At that time, the Soviet Union reversed its own earlier positions on key issues, refused to discuss seriously the genuine efforts made by the United States and the United Kingdom to meet known Soviet views, and blocked the path toward a nuclear test ban treaty. In order to avoid missing any possible opportunity to arrive at an agreement, the United States and the United Kingdom remained at the negotiating table. Only this week Ambassador Dean has made additional proposals in the hope of moving toward a test ban under effective international control. Urgent discussion of this issue had been scheduled at United States initiative at the forthcoming session of the General Assembly in the hopes that constructive debate could show the way to surmount the impasse at Geneva.

The pretext offered by the announcement for Soviet resumption of weapons testing is the very crisis which they themselves have created by threatening to disturb the peace which has existed in Germany and Berlin. It is not the first time they have made such charges against those who have dared to stand in the way of Soviet aggression. In addition, the announcement links the Soviet resumption of testing with threats of massive weapons which it must know cannot intimidate the rest of the world.

The purpose and motivation of this Soviet behavior now seems apparent: The Soviet Government wished to abandon serious negotiations in order to free its hand to resume nuclear weapons testing.

The United States continues to share the view of the people of the world as to the importance of an agreement to end nuclear weapons tests under effective safeguards. Such an agreement would represent a major breakthrough in the search for an end to the arms race. It would stop the accumulation of stock piles of even more powerful weapons. It would inhibit the spread of nuclear weapons to other countries with its increased risks of nuclear war.

These results, with their prospects for reducing the possibility of a nuclear war, have been blocked by the Soviet unilateral decision to resume nuclear testing. The Soviet Union bears a heavy responsibility before all humanity for this decision, a decision which was made in complete disregard of the United Nations. The termination of the moratorium on nuclear testing by the Soviet unilateral decision leaves the United States under the necessity of deciding what its own national interests require.

Under these circumstances, Ambassador Arthur Dean is being recalled immediately from Geneva.

336   Statement by the President Upon Signing Resolution Deferring Drainage Payments on the Columbia Basin Project. *August 30, 1961*

I AM PLEASED to sign Senate Joint Resolution 76 which will provide deferment of 1962 drainage payments for users of water in the Columbia Basin Project.

This legislation is fully in accord with the Administration's objectives and I know that the Secretary of the Interior will, with proper consultation with all interested parties, attempt to obtain a permanent solution of these repayment problems. Our goal is a rate schedule which is fair to those water users who make their living from the land and which will permit the Columbia Basin Project to go forward on a sound financial basis.

NOTE: As enacted, Senate Joint Resolution 76 is Public Law 87–169 (75 Stat. 408).

337   Letter to Representative Harris on Pending Legislation Relating to the Federal Trade Commission. *August 31, 1961*

[Released August 31, 1961. Dated August 28, 1961]

Dear Congressman Harris:

I want to express my strong support for pending legislation to authorize the Federal Trade Commission to issue temporary cease-and-desist orders against the continuance of unfair practices while cases concerned with permanent relief from such practices are pending before that agency. I understand measures to accomplish that purpose are now pending before the House Committee on Interstate and Foreign Commerce: H.R. 1233 and H.R. 1817, introduced by Congressmen Steed and Patman.

Effective law enforcement by the Federal Trade Commission has long been hampered by delays in litigation and an increasing backlog of cases. Despite a concerted effort to decrease these delays through recent revision of the Commission's organization and procedures, the basic difficulty requires additional remedies. At present, the Commission is powerless to halt allegedly illegal practices until the termination of frequently protracted proceedings. As a consequence, small businessmen who are so often the target of discriminatory and monopolistic activities are often irreparably injured or destroyed long before the lengthy process of adjudication has been completed. The proposed legislation will provide means to prevent such injury during that interim period. It will thus provide important protection for the small business community and, indeed, all those who are confronted by violations of the laws which seek to sustain our competitive economy. Such orders should, of course, be subject to the protection of appropriate due process, including the safeguards of judicial review.

The White House Committee on Small Business which I established in April and which includes representatives of the major Government agencies, has studied the proposed legislation and recommended its approval.

I have concluded that such legislation will

provide essential protection for small businessmen and thus strengthen competition throughout the nation's economy. I am hopeful that Congressional action on behalf of the objectives of this legislation will be both expeditious and favorable.

Sincerely,   JOHN F. KENNEDY

[Honorable Oren Harris, Chairman, Committee on Interstate and Foreign Commerce, The House of Representatives, Washington 25, D.C.]

338   Statement by the President on Traffic Safety. *August 31, 1961*

JUST AHEAD of us is Labor Day, a great American holiday. As usual Americans will be traveling the highways by the millions—visiting, sightseeing, recreating.

This enjoyable opportunity also brings into sharp focus the traffic accident problem—the problem of nearly 40,000 deaths and more than a million disabling injuries in traffic accidents each year.

This is a most acute problem in our modern society. It is a problem resulting in needless economic waste of millions of dollars and of untold hardship and sorrow to families of America.

Certainly we appreciate our freedom of movement in this country. We should also appreciate the right to live as long and as well as we can and respect this right for others.

I express the concern of the government, the President's Committee for Traffic Safety and of the entire safety movement in asking every American to drive this holiday time with patience and a clear head, with consideration for the rights of others, giving exemplary support to effective traffic enforcement.

339   Remarks on the 50th Anniversary of the First State Workmen's Compensation Law. *August 31, 1961*

Mr. Vice President, Governor Freeman, Postmaster General Day, and members of the Cabinet:

I want to express our great pleasure at being here this morning and having this opportunity to salute the State of Wisconsin, the State Legislature of that State, for the action it took in 1911, 50 years ago, in passing the first State workmen's compensation law. And the leadership shown in that State on that occasion was followed in later years by other actions which that State took in the twenties, which led directly to passage in the thirties of the National Social Security Act.

This first step, to provide security for American working men who may have been injured, to provide security for their families if they may have been fatally injured, represents one of the great landmarks of social legislation on our books in the long history of this country. That promising beginning has meant security to millions of Americans, and it represents the kind of forward-looking action on State and national level, the need for which faces us in our own day in 1961.

We look back today, but we also look forward, and we recognize that in our time, in the States and in the National Government, there is still a good deal of unfinished business: to provide more security for our younger people who want jobs and can't find them; to provide more security for those who are unemployed—for those particularly who are unemployed chronically and who have families who depend upon them, who exhaust their unemployment compensation, who have exhausted in recent weeks the emergency unemployment compensation, and who now want to work and find themselves having to turn to inadequate public assistance.

And we also recognize the great need that lies before us to deal more satisfactorily with the question of health in our society; most particularly and immediately is the health of our older citizens, those who are chronically ill, those who come to the end of their working lives with inadequate resources stored away in spite of many years of devoted labor—inadequate resources to meet their medical bills.

I believe it is the national responsibility in the sixties, and the national opportunity, as it was the responsibility and opportunity of the Wisconsin State Legislature in 1911, for us to meet this problem of medical care for our older citizens, and better medical

care for all our citizens.

So I want to congratulate the Post Office for this memorial to progress. I'm delighted that the Governor—a distinguished Governor and progressive Governor of the State of Wisconsin, to which we all owe much— that he has come here today and participated in this ceremony. And I'm sure that his presence here—this stamp—that when all of us look at this stamp and put it on any letter, or see it on any letter we receive, that we remember that all of us, in our time and generation, have as great an opportunity as the State Legislature of 1911, and we mean to take advantage of that opportunity and meet that responsibility in the areas I've described. I'm grateful to all of you for coming today.

NOTE: The President spoke at ceremonies held on the South Lawn at the White House. His opening words referred to Vice President Lyndon B. Johnson; Orville L. Freeman, Secretary of Agriculture and former Governor of Minnesota; and Postmaster General J. Edward Day. At the close of his remarks the President referred to Gaylord Nelson, Governor of Wisconsin.

Attending the ceremonies, as announced by the White House on August 28, were members of the Wisconsin congressional delegation, and the only living members of the 1911 Wisconsin Legislature— Judge Edward T. Fairchild of Madison and Theodore Brazeau of Wisconsin Rapids.

---

340 White House Statement Following the President's Meeting With the National Security Council and Congressional Leaders on the Resumption of Nuclear Tests by the U.S.S.R.   *August 31, 1961*

THE PRESIDENT met this morning with members of the National Security Council and with Congressional leaders to discuss the resumption of nuclear testing by the Soviet Union. It was recognized that the Soviet announcement was primarily a form of atomic blackmail, designed to substitute terror for reason in the present international scene.

What the Soviet Union is obviously testing is not only nuclear devices but the will and determination of the free world to resist such tactics and to defend freedom.

The President is entirely confident that the size of the U.S. nuclear weapons stockpile and the capabilities of individual weapons and delivery systems are wholly adequate for the defense needs of the United

States and of the free world.

The President shares the disappointment registered throughout the world that serious and sustained attempts to ban nuclear testing have come to this abrupt end.

NOTE: On September 1 the White House released the following statement by Ambassador Arthur Dean:

"In recent weeks, Chairman Khrushchev has been boasting about a hundred megaton bomb, a weapon far too large for military objectives. Two days ago the Soviet government announced its intention to resume nuclear tests.

"These events, at a time when the world could have had a workable treaty banning nuclear explosions, show a determined Soviet purpose to rest its future policy on the terrorization of humanity.

"The Soviet policy is the policy of over-kill. But the Soviet government under-estimates the people of the world, if it thinks they will capitulate to a strategy of blackmail and terror."

---

341   Letter to the Chairman, Senate Special Committee on Aging, Concerning Health Insurance Legislation.   *September* 1, 1961

[Released September 1, 1961. Dated August 31, 1961]

Dear Pat:

I consider adequate health care for our seventeen million senior citizens one of our most important responsibilities. Medical costs represent the greatest of all threats to economic security in old age. The financial burden of illness and incapacity in later years constitutes an ever-present specter to almost every family. Inability to meet the costs of hospitalization or home care can destroy self-respect and deny the right to dignity and comfort after retirement.

Although everyone recognizes the threat presented by the possibility of serious illness in later years, savings for this purpose are often inadequate. Nine out of ten persons over 65 are hospitalized at least once. The duration of their hospitalization averages two and one-half times longer than that of those under 65. I am convinced that only the Social Security system can furnish satisfactory protection against the costs of these illnesses. Small retirement incomes are usually inadequate to cover the premiums required to obtain a sufficient amount of private insurance.

The theory of using earnings during the most productive years to purchase protection during retirement years has been tested and proved. This is the Social Security approach. I know you share my view that it is the only mechanism that can satisfy the need, insure protection, and be financially sound.

I have followed with considerable interest the hearings held by the Committee on Ways and Means of the House of Representatives on this subject. The testimony incontrovertibly establishes the need for the legislation. Our national responsibilities require prompt and effective action.

I wholeheartedly agree with your belief in the importance of this legislation to our Nation. It will relieve some of the most serious hardships of old age, it will enable the worker to look forward with confidence to his ability to take care of himself, it will help solve many problems of family living. I consider the proposal to provide health insurance for the aged under Social Security one of the most important measures I have advocated. Your support is very much appreciated and I assure you that I intend to recommend that this legislation be given the highest priority at the next session of Congress.

Sincerely,

JOHN F. KENNEDY

NOTE: The President wrote in response to a letter from Senator Pat McNamara, dated August 30,

expressing his interest in a health insurance program financed through Social Security, and stating his belief that an assurance from the President of his determination to pursue the matter vigorously in the next session of Congress would be welcomed by supporters of the measure and by those benefiting from it. Senator McNamara's letter was released with the President's reply.

342 Statement by the President on the Discovery of the Omega Particle. *September 1, 1961*

I HAVE just been advised of the discovery, by the University of California's Lawrence Radiation Laboratory, of a new elementary particle of matter which gives important insight into the structure and behavior of the atomic nucleus. I wish to commend the responsible researchers, Drs. Luis W. Alvarez, B. C. Maglic, Arthur H. Rosenfeld, and M. L. Stevenson, for this important contribution to the advancement of scientific knowledge. This discovery, I am told, is but one of a series of important

scientific contributions in this field by scientists at the University of California, starting with Professor Lawrence's development of the cyclotron.

I understand that one of the responsible researchers, Dr. B. C. Maglic, is a visiting scientist from Yugoslavia. We are indebted to him and his other colleagues at Berkeley for their important scientific contribution and pleased that he could participate in these researches at one of our great universities.

343 Statement by the President Urging the Congress To Appropriate Requested Foreign Aid Funds. *September 2, 1961*

I URGE the Congress to appropriate foreign aid funds of a magnitude as close as possible to the original request—a request which in the opinion of both President Eisenhower and myself represented the minimum amount necessary to meet our basic commitments and responsibilities in the years ahead.

The fight for freedom throughout the world is in a climactic hour. The developing nations of the world—and especially of our own hemisphere—are engaged in an urgent effort to bring a better life to their people. They are looking to the United States as their only hope for leadership and assistance in this effort. For they realize, as do we, that their failure will inevitably bring the dissolution of democratic governments

and greatly increase the threat of the Communist advance.

The countless billions of dollars which we spend for essential military defenses will, in the long run, be unable to ensure our security if we lose the battle to demonstrate to the hungry and impoverished of all lands that free and independent nations have the capacity to meet our basic needs. We must not lose this battle.

Therefore, I again ask the Congress for the tools to carry on this vital task.

NOTE: On September 30, 1961, the President approved the Foreign Assistance and Related Agencies Appropriation Act, 1962 (Public Law 87–329, 75 Stat. 717).

The President's statement was released at Hyannis, Mass.

344 Statement by the President on the Increase in the Minimum Wage. *September 3, 1961*

TODAY the legal minimum wage for millions of American workers increases. Some will receive higher minimum protection than before, and others will be protected for the first time.

This advance in one of our great pieces of social legislation is one of the most important domestic accomplishments so far of this Administration. It represents the most significant advance in the Federal Wage and Hour Law since it was first passed 23 years ago.

While the new minimums of $1.15 per hour for workers presently covered by the law and of $1.00 per hour for those newly covered are admittedly inadequate to provide the full material well-being that this great nation is capable of giving to each of its citizens, they still provide for millions of workers a chance to enjoy a greater share of our nation's general economic progress.

I congratulate the Congress and all men of good will who worked so hard for this social gain. All fair employers know that a minimum wage does not harm the economy, but on the contrary helps eliminate unfair competition. In the months and years to come, I can see important gains for the whole economy resulting from this improvement to the living and working standards of our people.

NOTE: The statement was released at Hyannis, Mass. For the President's remarks upon signing the minimum wage bill, see Item 169.

345 Joint Statement With Prime Minister Macmillan Proposing a Three-Power Agreement To End Atmospheric Nuclear Tests. *September 3, 1961*

THE PRESIDENT of the United States and the Prime Minister of the United Kingdom propose to Chairman Khrushchev that their three governments agree, effective immediately, not to conduct nuclear tests which take place in the atmosphere and produce radioactive fallout.

Their aim in this proposal is to protect mankind from the increasing hazards from atmospheric pollution and to contribute to the reduction of international tensions.

They urge Chairman Khrushchev to cable his immediate acceptance of this offer and his cessation of further atmospheric tests.

They further urge that their representatives at Geneva meet not later than September 9 to record this agreement and report it to the United Nations. They sincerely hope that the Soviet Union will accept this offer, which remains open for the period indicated.

They point out that with regard to atmospheric testing the United States and the United Kingdom are prepared to rely upon existing means of detection, which they believe to be adequate, and are not suggesting additional controls. But they reaffirm their serious desire to conclude a nuclear test ban treaty, applicable to other forms of testing as well, and regret that the Soviet Government has blocked such an agreement.

NOTE: The joint statement was released at Hyannis, Mass.

346   Statement by the President Upon Signing the Foreign Assistance Act.   *September 4, 1961*

WITH THE SIGNING into law of this bill, a Decade of Development begins. The long-term commitment of development funds, which the bill authorizes, will assist the under-developed countries of the world to take the critical steps essential to economic and social progress.

The bill also continues our support of world-wide collective security arrangements essential to free world defense.

I am hopeful that the Congress will provide the funds necessary to fulfill the commitments it undertook in enacting this legislation.

Our adversaries are intensifying their efforts in the entire under-developed world. Those who oppose their advance look to us and I believe, at this dangerous moment, we must respond.

It is my belief that in the administration of these funds we should give great attention and consideration to those nations who have our view of the world crisis.

NOTE: The Foreign Assistance Act of 1961 is Public Law 87–195 (75 Stat. 424).

The President's statement was released at Hyannis, Mass.

347   Message to the Conference on Science and World Affairs Meeting at Stowe, Vermont.   *September 4, 1961*

I HAD LOOKED forward to sending my best wishes to the Conference on Science and World Affairs under happier and more optimistic conditions than now prevail. The somber turn of events within the past week, a course against which your past Conferences have strongly counseled, makes all the more urgent the matters you meet to discuss. As you take up the problems of scientific cooperation and disarmament, I urge that you search with renewed diligence and imagination for practical ways in which to set forth on both these paths to peace.

Science remains universal, and the fruits of science, if wisely chosen, provide a means by which humanity can realize a full and abundant life. Yet the vitality of science, its ability to enrich our culture and our understanding, and the material benefits it promises all depend in large measure upon international pooling of knowledge and

effort. National leaders who share this view must look to scientists such as yourselves for the initiative and guidance to transform the desire to cooperate into actual achievement. We hope that out of the suggestions and proposals that you make, new ways can be found to extend the benefits of science, and to foster the trust and mutual understanding that is essential to a prospering world.

In the other area of your discussions, you will have an opportunity to advance the world-wide search for a solution to the central threat of our time, nuclear war. Your past Conferences have revealed that special knowledge and concern make you particularly sensitive to the meaning of this threat. The task of disarmament is not easy, and progress, the world has found, is not inevitable. But, when men of good will meet in such frankness as your discussions typify, the door to peace is open, reason can guide us forward, and all nations can begin to face their full responsibilities to mankind.

I am hopeful that your deliberations, in their quiet and beautiful Vermont setting, will be informed by the objectivity of your science and inspired by the desire of men everywhere for peace. Despite setbacks,

there is no more noble or urgent cause than the development of practical ways to bring closer the goal of reliable disarmament.

JOHN F. KENNEDY

NOTE: The message was addressed to Professor Paul Doty, c/o Smugglers Notch Hotel in Stowe, Vt., where the conference opened on September 5. The message was released at Hyannis, Mass.

348   Statement by the President on the Physical Fitness of Young Americans. *September* 5, 1961

I HAVE, on many occasions, expressed my concern over the physical fitness of our youth and I want to stress again the importance of a strong and vital nation—of a physically fit young America.

I am informed by General Hershey, Director of the Selective Service System, that since October 1948 of some 6 million young men examined for military duty, more than a million have been rejected for *physical reasons alone.* General Hershey likewise has told me that a very substantial number of these physically-unacceptable men were in the preventable category.

The number of these men in the preventable category—men who would not have been rejected had they participated in adequate physical developmental programs—

represents more soldiers than we now have stationed in Berlin and West Germany ready to defend freedom.

The situation grows steadily worse. In the last year, more than a thousand men per month—an all-time high—were in the preventable category among those rejected for physical reasons.

I again urge school administrations to implement the basic physical fitness program developed by my Council on Youth Fitness, or a similar one, this fall.

Young Americans must be made fit—to serve our nation in its hour of need—fit to face the future with confidence and strength.

NOTE: The statement was released at Hyannis, Mass.

349   Statement by the President on Ordering Resumption of Underground Nuclear Tests. *September* 5, 1961

IN VIEW of the continued testing by the Soviet Government, I have today ordered the resumption of nuclear tests, in the laboratory and underground, with no fallout. In our efforts to achieve an end to nuclear testing, we have taken every step that reasonable men could justify. In view of the

acts of the Soviet Government, we must now take those steps which prudent men find essential. We have no other choice in fulfillment of the responsibilities of the United States Government to its own citizens and to the security of other free nations. Our offer to make an agreement to end all fallout tests remains open until September 9.

NOTE: Following the resumption of underground nuclear tests by the United States on September 15, the White House released the following statement:

President John F. Kennedy announced that the United States conducted an underground nuclear weapons development test of low yield at the Nevada Test Site at 1 p.m. The detonation has produced no fallout. This is in marked contrast to Soviet nuclear tests in the atmosphere.

The United States was forced reluctantly to make the decision to resume testing after years of attempting to reach a nuclear test ban with the Soviet Union when the Soviet Union without warning but after a great deal of preparation resumed testing in the atmosphere. We have announced ten such

Soviet tests—three of them in the megaton range.

Today's test was the first in the joint Atomic Energy Commission-Department of Defense program to strengthen the defense of the free world. The resumption of extensive Soviet testing has made this action necessary to fulfill the responsibilities of the United States Government to its own citizens and to the security of other free nations.

In addition, as the program progresses, tests will be utilized to provide information in support of the U.S. programs to improve means of detecting and identifying nuclear explosions for possible use in an international nuclear test control system (Vela), and to study the use of nuclear detonations for peaceful purposes (Plowshare).

The United States once again affirms its readiness to negotiate a controlled test ban agreement of the widest possible scope.

350 Telegram to Labor and Management Leaders Urging a Just Settlement in the General Motors Negotiations. *September 5, 1961*

I WISH to emphasize to you, the parties participating in the automobile negotiations, the high degree of responsibility you bear to the country to achieve a settlement before the deadline. While the hour is late, I am confident that you can, by exercising industrial statesmanship, achieve a settlement which is fair and reasonable to both shareholders and workers and which preserves price stability in the industry.

I urge that in the hours that remain before the deadline, you, the representatives of

the General Motors Corporation and the UAW make an all out effort to achieve a just settlement. Our country at this juncture in our affairs can ill afford a shutdown in this important segment of our economy.

JOHN F. KENNEDY

NOTE: This is the text of identical telegrams addressed to Louis Seaton, Vice President, General Motors Corporation, Detroit, Mich., and Walter P. Reuther, President, United Automobile, Aircraft and Agricultural Implement Workers of America, Detroit, Mich.

351 Statement by the President: The Jewish High Holy Days. *September 6, 1961*

I AM HAPPY to extend to millions of our fellow citizens of the Jewish faith, now celebrating Rosh Hashanah, my warm greetings and every good wish for the New Year.

In every celebration of ending and beginning there is both the remembrance of

tribulation and the anticipation of good. There is, too, the knowledge that suffering must make both a people and a man more certain of the right, while triumph brings with it the command to respect that right.

This is the hard wisdom of the centuries, marked again with the turning of each new season. We in the United States have found our way as a free people because we have gathered in our own traditions the experience of many peoples and lives. We have learned that tolerance and cooperation are the ways to true national strength.

Americans of the Jewish faith have given to their country a great gift in this regard.

I know that all Americans, of every faith, join with me in this greeting and wish for an abundant and peaceful year.

JOHN F. KENNEDY

352   Statement by the President on the Peaceful Integration of Schools in the South and Southwest. *September 6, 1961*

THE PEACEFUL INTEGRATION of many schools in the South and Southwest yesterday and today, following similar developments in Atlanta last week, is a dramatic demonstration of the progress that the United States is making in improving the position of Negroes in our society. The important thing is that there is progress and that law and order and dignity have prevailed.

In Dallas, Texas, the Citizens Council, working closely with Negro leaders, has shown again how responsible, level-headed leadership can weld a whole community together to solve a difficult problem in race relations. Little Rock and Dallas and other communities in Arkansas, Texas, Florida, Virginia, North Carolina and Tennessee have given the world a convincing demonstration of the American people's respect for the law which is fundamental in the maintenance of our rights as free men and women.

I wish to congratulate the officials of these cities and states and parents and citizens who have given so much time, effort and leadership in moving their communities and America forward. But most of all I would like to congratulate the children of both races for their mutual tolerance, good will and exemplary conduct.

353   Letter to the Secretary of State and to the Heads of Other Agencies Concerning the Publication of U.S. Diplomatic Papers. *September 7, 1961*

[Released September 7, 1961. Dated September 6, 1961]

Dear————:

The effectiveness of democracy as a form of government depends on an informed and intelligent citizenry. Nowhere is the making of choices more important than in foreign affairs; nowhere does government have a more imperative duty to make available as swiftly as possible all the facts required for intelligent decision.

As many of these facts as possible should be made public on a current basis. But, because of the inherent need for security in the current conduct of foreign affairs, it is obviously not possible to make full immediate disclosure of diplomatic papers. However, delay in such disclosure must be kept to a minimum.

It has long been a pride of our government

591

that we have made the historical record of our diplomacy available more promptly than any other nation in the world. The Department of State has the responsibility within the Executive Branch for putting out this permanent record in the series "Foreign Relations of the United States." The discharge of this responsibility requires the active collaboration of all departments and agencies of our Government in the submission and clearance of papers necessary for the completeness of this record.

In recent years the publication of the "Foreign Relations" series has fallen farther and farther behind currency. The lag has now reached approximately twenty years. I regard this as unfortunate and undesirable. It is the policy of this Administration to unfold the historical record as fast and as fully as is consistent with national security and with friendly relations with foreign nations.

Accordingly I herewith request all departments, agencies and libraries of the Government to collaborate actively and fully with the Department of State in its efforts to prepare and publish the record of our diplomacy. In my view, any official should have a clear and precise case involving the national interest before seeking to withhold from publication documents or papers fifteen or more years old.

Sincerely yours,

JOHN F. KENNEDY

NOTE: This is the text of identical letters addressed to Dean Rusk, Secretary of State, Robert S. McNamara, Secretary of Defense, C. Douglas Dillon, Secretary of the Treasury, and John L. Moore, Administrator of General Services.

354 Letter to Leaders of the Steel Industry on the Need for Price Stability. *September 7, 1961*

[Released September 7, 1961. Dated September 6, 1961]

Dear————:

I am taking this means of communicating to you, and to the chief executive officers of 11 other steel companies, my concern for stability of steel prices.

In the years preceding 1958, sharply rising steel prices and steel wages provided much of the impetus to a damaging inflation in the American economy. From the beginning of 1947 to the end of 1958, while industrial prices as a whole were rising 39 percent, steel mill product prices rose 120 percent. Steel wage rates also rose rapidly, causing employment costs per ton of steel to rise by about 85 percent. The international competitive position of American producers was impaired, and our balance of payments was weakened. Our iron and steel export prices from 1953 to 1958 rose 20 percent more than the export prices of our principal foreign competitors, and our share of world exports of iron and steel fell from 19 percent to 14 percent.

Since 1958, our price performance has substantially improved. Steel prices have been stable since 1958, as has the Wholesale Price Index. Industrial prices have not risen since 1959. The rise in consumer prices has been held within tolerable limits.

This record of price stability was purchased, however, at the cost of persistent unemployment and underutilized productive capacity. In the steel industry itself, the rate of utilization of capacity for the last three years has averaged under 65 percent. In consequence of our recent price experience, many persons have come to the conclusion that the United States can achieve price stability only by maintaining a substantial margin of unemployment and excess capacity and by accepting a slow rate of economic growth. This is a counsel of despair which we cannot accept.

For the last three years, we have not had to face the test of price behavior in a high-employment economy. This is the test which now lies ahead.

Under the collective bargaining contract signed in January 1960, steel industry wages and other employment costs will increase at the end of this month. The amount of the increase in employment costs per man-hour is difficult to measure in advance with precision. But it appears almost certain to be outweighed by the advance in productivity resulting from a combination of two factors—the steady long-term growth of output per man-hour, and the increasing rate of operations foreseen for the steel industry in the months ahead.

The Council of Economic Advisers has supplied me with estimates of steel industry profits after October 1, calculated on an assumption that prices are not increased. These estimates indicate that the steel industry will be earning 7 to 9 percent on net worth after taxes if the rate of operations is around 70 percent; 10 to 12 percent if the operating rate is at 80 percent; and 13 to 15 percent if the operating rate is at 90 percent. The steel industry, in short, can look forward to good profits without an increase in prices.

The owners of the iron and steel companies have fared well in recent years. Since 1947, iron and steel common stock prices have risen 393 percent; this is a much better performance than common stock prices in general. Likewise, dividends on iron and steel securities have risen from $235 million

in 1947 to $648 million in the recession year of 1960, an increase of 176 percent.

A steel price increase in the months ahead could shatter the price stability which the country has now enjoyed for some time. In a letter to me on the impact of steel prices on defense costs, Secretary of Defense McNamara states: "A steel price increase of the order of $4 to $5 a ton, once its effects fanned out through the economy, would probably raise military procurement costs by $500 million per year or more."

Steel is a bellwether, as well as a major element in industrial costs. A rise in steel prices would force price increases in many industries and invite price increases in others. The consequences of such a development might be so grave—particularly on our balance of payments position—as to require the adoption of restrictive monetary and fiscal measures which would retard recovery, hold unemployment at intolerable levels, and hamper growth. The depressing effect of such measures on the steel industry's rate of operations might in the long run more than offset the profit-raising effect of a price increase.

In emphasizing the vital importance of steel prices to the strength of our economy, I do not wish to minimize the urgency of preventing inflationary movements in steel wages. I recognize, too, that the steel industry, by absorbing increases in employment costs since 1958, has demonstrated a will to halt the price-wage spiral in steel. If the industry were now to forego a price increase, it would enter collective bargaining negotiations next spring with a record of three and a half years of price stability. It would clearly then be the turn of the labor representatives to limit wage demands to a level consistent with continued price stability. The moral position of the steel industry next spring—and its claim to the support of public opinion—will be strengthened by the exercise of price restraint now.

I have written you at length because I believe that price stability in steel is essential if we are to maintain the economic vitality necessary to face confidently the trials and crises of our perilous world. Our economy has flourished in freedom; let us now demonstrate again that the responsible exercise of economic freedom serves the national welfare.

I am sure that the owners and managers of our nation's major steel companies share my conviction that the clear call of national interest must be heeded.

Sincerely,

JOHN F. KENNEDY

NOTE: This is the text of identical letters addressed to the following steel officials: Logan T. Johnston, President, Armco Steel Corporation; Arthur B. Homer, Chairman of the Board, Bethlehem Steel Corporation; Alwin F. Franz, President, Colorado Fuel and Iron Corporation; Joseph L. Block, Chairman of the Board, Inland Steel Company; Avery C. Adams, Chairman of the Board, Jones and Laughlin Steel Corporation; J. L. Ashby, President, Kaiser Steel Corporation; Merlin A. Cudlip, President, McLouth Steel Corporation; Thomas E. Millsop, Chairman of the Board, National Steel Corporation; Thomas F. Patton, President, Republic Steel Corporation; Roger M. Blough, Chairman of the Board, United States Steel Corporation; William A. Steele, Chairman of the Board, Wheeling Steel Corporation; and J. L. Mauthe, Chairman of the Board, Youngstown Sheet and Tube Company.

Several of the replies to the President's letter were made public by the White House on September 22.

See also Item 366.

355   Special Message to the Congress Transmitting Agreement With France for Cooperation on Uses of Atomic Energy for Mutual Defense. *September 7, 1961*

To the Congress of the United States:

For some time members of the North Atlantic Treaty Organization have been taking steps toward the introduction of the most modern weapons into NATO forces. Among these measures is the introduction into forces of our NATO Allies of weapons capable of delivering nuclear warheads. Such steps have been proceeding for some time following the considered judgment and agreement of the NATO Governments. The objective is to achieve the most effective pattern of NATO military defensive strength. In view of the well known purely defensive purposes of the Alliance, the introduction of modern weapons into NATO forces to take account of technological developments is in no way a cause for legitimate concern on the part of other countries.

Article III of the North Atlantic Treaty calls upon the members of the Alliance to maintain their capacities to resist armed attack through effective self-help and mutual aid. As part of its contribution to the strength of the Alliance, the United States has entered into a number of agreements through which we cooperate with NATO Allies in the uses of atomic energy for mutual defense purposes. These agreements have been concluded pursuant to the Atomic Energy Act of 1954, as amended. All of these agreements are designed to implement the NATO objectives for maintaining the most modern weapons and techniques in NATO forces.

We have just concluded an agreement with the Government of France which is essentially the same as agreements previously

594

concluded with a number of other NATO Allies for cooperation in the uses of atomic energy for mutual defense purposes. This agreement will make possible effective cooperation with France in NATO mutual defense planning and in the training of French NATO forces. Training of certain French NATO forces which play a significant role in European defense cannot proceed to conclusion until this agreement becomes effective. This agreement should be brought into effect as quickly as possible, in order that we can promptly and fully utilize the potential of French military forces in the development of our NATO defensive strength. In light of the probable time remaining for this session of the Congress and in view of the provisions of Sec. 123d of the Atomic Energy Act of 1954, as amended, it appears that normally it would not be possible to bring this agreement into effect until the next session of the Congress. Accordingly, I would appreciate action by the Congress during the current session which would permit the agreement to come into force promptly.

I understand and respect the importance of mature consideration in the Congress of agreements of this sort, but I believe that in the present case there are compelling reasons for rapid action. The gravity of the international situation, and in particular the Soviet threat to the freedom of West Berlin, have made it a matter of first importance that the unity of the North Atlantic nations should be sustained. The Government of France, in this crisis, has behaved with great firmness, and the staunch and determined position of President de Gaulle, in particular, has reinforced the West. In these circum-

stances, I deem it of great importance that we should proceed promptly with such a joint undertaking as this one, carefully matured in prolonged negotiation. As has already been explained in informal discussions with interested Members of the Congress, the present agreement provides for a limited release of information to carefully selected personnel. Careful arrangements have been made to insure that all necessary security requirements are met, and the inclusion of France among NATO countries participating in this general undertaking is an important step forward at a moment in which such a step has a wider significance than usual. It is for these reasons that I urge upon the Congress appropriate special actions to permit the agreement to come into force.

In accordance with the Atomic Energy Act of 1954, as amended, I am submitting to each House of the Congress an authoritative copy of the agreement with the Government of France. I am transmitting also a copy of the letter from the Secretary of State which forwarded to me an authoritative copy of the agreement, a copy of the joint letter from the Deputy Secretary of Defense and the Chairman of the Atomic Energy Commission recommending my approval of the agreement, and a copy of my memorandum in reply thereto which contained my approval.

JOHN F. KENNEDY

NOTE: On October 4 the President approved H.J. Res. 568 (Public Law 87–363; 75 Stat. 782) waiving certain provisions of the Atomic Energy Act of 1954 so as to permit the agreement to be made immediately effective.

The text of the agreement and related documents, also released, is published in the Department of State Bulletin (vol. 45, p. 556).

356 Statement by the President in Support of Bill Providing for Payment of Philippine War Damages. *September* 8, 1961

I REGRET that the bill (H.R. 8617) to compensate Philippine citizens for World War II damage to their property has been held over until next year by the House because of the press of other business.

We had hoped that this long-delayed recognition of the staunch contribution of our Philippine allies, through the satisfaction of their claims, would receive Congressional approval this year. However, the Administration continues to give wholehearted support to such legislation and is hopeful that it will be approved by the Congress early in the next session.

357 Joint Statement With Prime Minister Macmillan on Soviet Rejection of Proposal To End Atmospheric Nuclear Tests. *September* 9, 1961

PRESIDENT KENNEDY and Prime Minister Macmillan note with deepest regret that the Soviet Union has not accepted their proposal of September 3, that tests in the earth's atmosphere producing fall-out be stopped without delay.

This action contrasts vividly with the Soviet Union's own repeated expressions of concern as to the health hazards of such testing.

The President and the Prime Minister reaffirm the readiness of the United States and the United Kingdom to negotiate a controlled nuclear test ban agreement of the widest possible scope.

NOTE: The joint statement was released at Hyannis, Mass.

358 Remarks at the Swearing In of the U.S. Delegation to the United Nations. *September* 12, 1961

WELL, Governor, I want to express my appreciation to all of you. This is, as you have said, a delegation with a good deal of experience. A good many of you have already been representing the United States at the United Nations.

I think this is going to be a most significant session, also one fraught with more responsibility, probably, for our country and the delegation than we have ever had before.

We are faced with—and have been, really, for the last few years, but certainly of a more intense kind—a different or differing situation than we faced in earlier days, with the admission into the United Nations of new countries with all their problems and all their hopes.

And it is therefore a particular source of satisfaction to me that this delegation of ours represents so much collective experience, and also that it is led by you, Governor.

I think that the United Nations will be called upon to play a key role in some of the vital areas in the next 2 or 3 months, involving not only the security of the United

States and the free world but also possibly the peace of the world.

Therefore, I want you to know that our hopes very much go with you, and our confidence. And also, that we look to you not only to implement the policy of the United States, but also to participate in forming that policy. And I can think of no more important assignment for any American, especially now, in the field of foreign policy and in the field of our responsibilities around the world for the next 2 or 3 months, than in New York City at the United Nations.

So I congratulate you on the opportunity, really, that you have to serve the country, and also to say that we want to work in the closest and most intimate way with you—the Secretary of State, and Harlan Cleveland, and here at the White House. We want to make sure that it flows two ways, and that

you will not merely be instructed by us, but also instruct us.

So that I appreciate your coming this morning. We look forward to swearing you in. I am very glad we have two distinguished Members of Congress, Church and Burleson, and I know that they will help a good deal. We are glad to have the supporting members of the cast here.

NOTE: The President spoke in his office at the White House. In his opening words he referred to Adlai E. Stevenson, U.S. Representative to the United Nations and former Governor of Illinois. Later in his remarks he referred to Harlan Cleveland, Assistant Secretary of State for International Organization Affairs; Mrs. Marguerite Stitt Church, U.S. Representative from Illinois; and Omar Burleson, U.S. Representative from Texas.

Other members of the delegation were Francis T. P. Plimpton and Arthur H. Dean. Alternate members of the delegation were Charles W. Yost, Clifton R. Wharton, Philip M. Klutznick, Jonathan B. Bingham, and Mrs. Gladys A. Tillett.

359   Remarks of Welcome to President Sukarno of Indonesia and President Keita of Mali at Andrews Air Force Base. *September* 12, 1961

I TAKE great pleasure in welcoming once again to the United States President Sukarno. We appreciated the opportunity of your visit with us last spring, and we're delighted that you have come to visit us again.

It is a great pleasure and satisfaction to welcome President Keita to the United States for the first time, and we hope that though his visit may not be long he will come to understand our country and our people better for his visit with us.

On behalf of the people of the United States and the Government of the United States, I extend a warm welcome to our two distinguished visitors who come repre-

senting the leaders, the states, and the people who were assembled at the recent conference in Belgrade, Yugoslavia.

We realize that they come on a mission of peace, and we want them to know that the people of this country share their great desire that the problems which disturb the tranquility of the world be settled in a peaceful manner, in a manner which represents the desires of the people who are involved to live their own lives in freedom, a peace which is real, which permits an orderly settlement of difficult problems, a peace which represents the basic aspirations of people everywhere—a matter of such great importance, quite rightly, to the people who met in Yugoslavia—to live out their own lives in the way they choose.

So we are delighted, Mr. President, to welcome you. We are grateful to you for making the long voyage. We recognize that in coming, as you have, around the world to visit us here in the United States, that your objectives are those which you share with us: a desire that the world may continue to move forward, and that the people of the world may live out their lives in the way they wish, and in the peace they want.

Mr. President.

NOTE: President Sukarno responded as follows:

"My dear President Kennedy:

"Today I am again in Washington, and for the fourth time. It was indeed, as you said, a long voyage from Belgrade to Washington, but it was a very pleasant one.

"I thank you, Mr. President, for the kind reception, and for your kind words. We both—President Keita and I—have come here, as you said, emissaries of the Belgrade conference of nonalined nations. The previous times I came here as a representative of the Indonesian Republic, a representative of 92 million people. But today I have come here, together with President Keita, as an envoy of the Belgrade conference, representing about 750 million people.

"Our task is not a task of mediation. No, our task is to communicate the thoughts and concerns of the Belgrade conference to you, Mr. President— our thoughts and concerns about the present situation in the world.

"The world in which we are living now is a world in transition, and a world in transition to a new world is always full of conflicts—minor conflicts, medium conflicts, big conflicts—big conflicts especially when big powers are involved.

"I spoke about our thoughts and our concerns of the Belgrade conference about the present situation. We, members of the Belgrade conference, 25 nations, we do not command physical power, we do not command military power, we do not command big economic power. But we nonalined nations are the least inhibited in developing our thoughts and conceptions for the formation of a

new world, a new world of freedom, of prosperity, of friendship, and cooperation and brotherhood amongst nations.

"I am sure that, as you said, Mr. President, also the American people and you, yourself, Mr. President, you also are very concerned about the world situation. And that is why I express the hope that our talks will bear fruit, in order to save this world from calamity and catastrophe.

"Thank you."

President Keita responded (through an interpreter) as follows:

"Mr. President, I come here as representative of the Belgrade conference with my friend, President Sukarno. I come here for my first contact with this great country and the great people of the United States, people and country about whom I have heard so much for so many years.

"And yet I come here at a moment which is extremely serious. I come here to bring to you, Mr. President, and to the American people, the greetings not only of the 25 nations of the Belgrade conference, but also of the people which I represent myself, the people of Mali.

"And we are bringing to you a grave burden, Mr. President. We are bringing to you a message of trust, because we are quite certain that the people of the United States wish to live in peace and only in peace.

"We bring to you also a message of brotherhood, because we know that man, whatever be the color of the skin, wants to live together and work together in this common civilization—the civilization of the universe.

"We bring to you also, Mr. President, a message of peace. We bring to you this message because the young countries need peace. We need peace even more than the great countries and the great powers need it, because, as President Sukarno said, we have neither military nor economic power. And moreover, we have the need of the help of the great nations to build up our own countries, to build up our own economies.

"However, as I said, we need more than anything peace, and that is why we need the peace and peace alone even more than the great powers need it.

"I would take advantage of my presence here, Mr. President, to establish a contact with the great people of the United States, the people whose struggle for its own development we have followed. Thank you."

360   Statement by the President on the Need for Federal Power
        Transmission Lines for the Upper Colorado and Trinity
        Projects. *September 12, 1961*

I APPROVE wholeheartedly the action of the House Appropriations Committee last week in approving funds requested by the Administration to construct Federal backbone transmission lines to market power generated at the Upper Colorado Project and the Trinity Project in California. In order to insure that the Federal investment in these projects will benefit the general public and to insure that the generated power will be delivered to points where both public and private agencies are able realistically to purchase and distribute this power, Federal transmission lines are necessary.

The breadth of the support for this principle is evidenced by the strong Congressional action in authorizing the Upper Colorado Transmission System of 1956, by the recommendation of the Eisenhower Administration in January of this year, and by the vigorous advocacy of the same concept by this Administration through the Secretary of the Interior.

I believe this project to be fundamental to a sound power policy and sincerely hope the Congress will approve the appropriations items recommended by the House Appropriations Committee.

361   Letter to the Chairman, Atomic Energy Commission,
        Concerning the Dedication of the Brookhaven Synchrotron.
        September 13, 1961

[Released September 13, 1961. Dated September 12, 1961]

Dear Dr. Seaborg:

I understand that on Wednesday, September 13, 1961, the new Alternating Gradient Synchrotron at the Brookhaven National Laboratory will be dedicated. The completion of this machine—the largest high energy particle accelerator in the world—represents a significant scientific accomplishment on the part of Brookhaven National Laboratory. The nation is justly proud of this achievement. By means of this and similar instruments of science, the United States, in cooperation with scientists throughout the world, is making substantial strides toward man's greater understanding of the properties and interactions of fundamental particles from which all matter is composed.

I am informed that the Commission will be represented at the dedication ceremonies by Commissioner Leland Haworth. Perhaps he would be kind enough to convey to Dr. Maurice Goldhaber, Director of the Brookhaven National Laboratory, and to all the scientists and engineers who participated in this great step forward, my sincere congratulations.

        Sincerely yours,

                JOHN F. KENNEDY

[The Honorable Glenn T. Seaborg, Chairman, United States Atomic Energy Commission, Washington 25, D.C.]

NOTE: The Brookhaven National Laboratory, located at Upton, Long Island, N.Y., is a research and development facility operated by the Atomic Energy Commission.

362   Remarks Upon Signing Bills To Combat Organized Crime and Racketeering.   *September 13, 1961*

IT IS a pleasure to sign these three important bills which we hope will aid the United States Government and the people of this country in the fight against organized crime.

These pieces of legislation are the culmination, in these three areas, of years of effort by the Federal Government and by the Congress to place more effective tools in the hands of local, State, and national police.

And therefore it is a pleasure to sign them, and in the presence of the representative of the Justice Department, Mr. Hoover—and

Members of the Congress of both parties who have given this legislation strong bipartisan support—most particularly Senator McClellan whose recent hearings indicate great need for this kind of legislation.

NOTE: As enacted the three bills, S. 1653, S. 1656, and S. 1757 are Public Laws 87–228 (75 Stat. 498), 87–216 (75 Stat. 491), and 87–218 (75 Stat. 492).

At the close of his remarks the President referred to J. Edgar Hoover, Director, Federal Bureau of Investigation, and John L. McClellan, U.S. Senator from Arkansas and Chairman of the Permanent Subcommittee on Investigations of the Senate Committee on Government Operations.

363   Toasts of the President and the President of Mali.   *September 13, 1961*

I WANT to express our great appreciation to President Sukarno and President Keita for—as I said yesterday—coming halfway around the world to visit us on behalf of the seven hundred million people gathered together in Belgrade.

We are delighted to see them, because we recognize the vital interest which the nations assembled at Belgrade, and indeed all nations, including the Soviet Union and the United States, have in maintaining peace in the world.

And, therefore, though the trip is far, I am sure that the two Presidents both feel that any contribution that they can make to the relaxation of tensions is well worth the longest journey.

In addition, we are glad to see them because of the countries they represent. They represent countries which have become newly independent in the years since the end of the Second World War. We recognize the desire and the necessity of the people of those countries to build their own societies,

to build a life of freedom and associate themselves with their own tasks and their own future.

I do want them both to know that that is the basic objective of the policy of this country towards Mali and Indonesia. Thirdly, we are proud to have them because of their own leadership, because they played leading parts in the liberation of their own two countries, and because they represent the living aspirations of their people in their own personalities.

We are very glad to have here also the Ambassadors from some of the countries that were represented at Belgrade—the Ambassador of Yugoslavia, the Ambassador of the UAR—the Chargé d'Affaires of India, and the others who were associated in the conference that was held a week ago.

So as you leave us this afternoon, President Sukarno—and President Keita, as you leave us tomorrow—to take your journeys home, we hope that you will carry with you a message: That this country wants peace, and that it will go to any effort, that those of us who hold official responsibility in our Nation will undertake any journey and meet with any group that promises to advance peace and the aspirations, the legitimate aspirations, of people everywhere.

We are also very proud to have the son and daughter of the President of Indonesia with us—he has let them study in the United States, to teach us as well as to learn. And also the young lady—she represents the ladies of the unalined world today.

So will you join me in drinking a toast to the two Presidents.

NOTE: The President proposed the toast to President Sukarno of Indonesia and President Keita of Mali at 2:20 p.m. at a state luncheon at the White House. President Keita responded (through an interpreter) as follows:

"Mr. President, Excellencies:

"In the name of President Sukarno and myself, I should like especially to thank President Kennedy, and through his person the people of the United States, for the welcome which we have received here today.

"In undertaking this mission, we were certain we would not be disappointed by the welcome which we have received in this country, always attached to liberty and whose present policies have evolved from the fight for liberty and independence.

"We also knew that the President and the people of the United States would share fully our concern for the peace of the world and the welfare of all, that we know that you are determined to use all means to find a peaceful solution for the tensions in which the world now finds itself.

"As for me, this is my first visit to the United States. I have not had before the pleasure of meeting President Kennedy and the American people—unlike President Sukarno who has been here before. But I can say that my first appreciation and first impression talk with frankness and directness of the American people.

"I am sure that they will use all means at their disposal to see that the crisis in which we are now passing through will be peacefully resolved.

"Therefore, I should like to ask you to raise your glasses to the President of the United States, and God willing that we may have peace in the world."

During his remarks the President referred to Marko Nikezic, Ambassador of Yugoslavia; Mostafa Kamel, Ambassador of the United Arab Republic; and D. N. Chatterjee, Minister and Chargé d'Affaires ad interim of India, who represented their countries at the Conference of Nonaligned Nations held at Belgrade, Yugoslavia, September 1–6, 1961. The President also referred to Mohammed Guntar Sukarnoputra and Megawati Sukarnoputri, the son and daughter of President Sukarno.

364   Statement by the President Following the Visit of President Sukarno and President Keita. *September* 13, 1961

WE HAVE welcomed the visit of President Sukarno and President Keita on behalf of the nations which recently met in Belgrade, because we have viewed with growing concern the heightening tension in world affairs. Statesmen everywhere have an urgent responsibility to make every effort to preserve the peace and to solve their differences by peaceful means. This can be done if all approach these differences with full understanding of the rights, obligations and vital interests of others.

The situation in Berlin is filled with danger. I have made it clear that the position of the West and of the West Berliners will be defended. I have also made it clear that we are ready to discuss these matters with other governments, including the Government of the Soviet Union, and to search for the means to preserve an honorable peace. If that is the purpose on all sides, there is no need for resort to force.

The Foreign Ministers of the Western powers are meeting in Washington tomorrow. Next week the Secretary of State will head the United States Delegation to the General Assembly of the United Nations. We understand that Foreign Minister Gromyko will also be present. This will provide an opportunity for serious talks about Germany and other problems if the Soviet side proves willing. The channels of diplomacy are open for the exploration of constructive steps toward a reduction of tension. Other means are available when they can serve a useful purpose. Meanwhile, it is clearly of the utmost importance that there be no unilateral acts which will make peaceful progress impossible.

365 Letter to the Presidents of Indonesia and Mali Concerning the Message and Declaration of the Belgrade Conference. *September 14, 1961*

[Released September 14, 1961. Dated September 13, 1961]

Dear Mr. President:

I have studied with care the message from the Conference of Nonaligned Nations which you were good enough to present in person. The United States Government is aware that the nonaligned powers assembled at Belgrade represent an important segment of world opinion, and, especially, that their peoples share with ours a vital stake in the maintenance of the peace. In our continuing deliberations within the United States Government and with our Allies, we will give the message from the conference most careful consideration.

As regards the proposal that I enter into direct negotiations with Premier Khrushchev, we are prepared to use existing and appropriate channels to establish the possibility of surmounting the present impasse. It has been and continues to be our policy to seek to settle our problems with others by peaceful means. We have not attempted to create crises, and we believe it is incumbent upon all responsible governments to explore all possible avenues, including negotiations at the highest levels, for mutually acceptable solutions of current international problems. However, unless such negotiations are carefully prepared beforehand they risk failure and may lead to deterioration of the situation. We therefore feel that a time of great tension it is particularly necessary that negotiations of the kind proposed by the Belgrade Conference not only have careful preparation but also a reasonable chance of success.

The Foreign Ministers of the Western powers are meeting in Washington tomorrow. Next week the Secretary of State will head the United States delegation to the General Assembly of the United Nations. We understand that Foreign Minister Gromyko will also be present. This will provide an opportunity for serious talks about Germany and other problems if the Soviet aide proves willing. The channels of diplomacy are open for the exploration of constructive steps toward a reduction of tension. Other means are available when they can serve a useful purpose. Meanwhile, it is clearly of the utmost importance that there be no unilateral acts which will make peaceful progress impossible.

Given a realistic approach and a sincere desire on the other side as well as ours to reach a mutually acceptable solution, we see no reason why eventual negotiations should not be successful in coping with the present crisis. However, we do not intend to enter into negotiations under ultimata or threats.

It is also clear that we do not propose to discuss either abdication of our responsibility or renunciation of the modalities for carrying out those responsibilities.

Nevertheless, we believe it possible to find a solution which can accommodate vital interests on both sides of the crisis.

The United States has carefully noted the statements in the Belgrade Declaration recognizing that the Berlin and German situations are of vital importance to future developments in international relations. It has consistently been, and will continue to be, our policy to settle differences with realism and responsibility. We would note that this crisis has been initiated by Soviet not by American action. We endorse the Declaration's reference to the rights of all nations to unity, self-determination, and independence, and its condemnation of intimidation, intervention, and interference in the exercise of the right of self-determination. We presume that these principles apply equally to the people of Germany and Berlin.

Our policies in this area have sought to respect these principles. We have absolutely no intention of resorting to force or threats of force to solve the Berlin and Germany problems, but we are determined to honor our commitments and are prepared to meet force with force if it is used against us. While the United States and its Allies are all agreed there must be negotiations on the problem, the Soviet Union must give indication of a readiness to engage in discussion based on mutual respect. The only conditions it has yet exhibited any willingness to consider are conditions which involve the surrender of Western rights.

The United States continues to believe that conclusion of an adequately controlled test ban agreement is a matter of greatest urgency. We wish to reaffirm, however, our belief that test ban negotiations should be resumed separately from negotiations on general and complete disarmament. The Soviet resumption of atmospheric testing has increased the urgency which attaches to the signature of a complete treaty test ban. Complex negotiation on general disarmament should not be permitted to delay the achievement of this significant step forward.

I would emphasize again my regret that the Soviet Union has rejected the offer of the United Kingdom and the United States Governments to halt atmospheric tests creating fallout.

Only after a searching review of vital U.S. security interests and after the utmost provocation did we announce our intent to resume underground tests. The non-aligned nations may be assured of our continued willingness to negotiate an effective treaty; but, meanwhile, the national security interests of our country and of our Allies in the Free World must be protected. The United States looks forward to full consideration of the test ban issue in the forthcoming United Nations General Assembly which we hope will move the Soviet Union to abandon its opposition to effective controls and toward acceptance of a test ban agreement.

The United States is pleased to note that the participants in the recent conference in Belgrade mentioned the importance of an effective system of inspection and control. This is the crux of the matter. It is clear from United States proposals in the nuclear test negotiations that the United States contemplates inspection and control procedures in the disarmament field in which the nonaligned countries, as well as others, would participate.

For some months the United States has been conducting an intensive study of the problem of general disarmament which resulted in a request to Congress to create a disarmament agency. The study has also resulted in the development of a comprehensive plan for general and complete disarmament which is in the final stage of preparation for public presentation. This plan provides for a program which will insure that the disarmament is general and complete; that war is no longer an instrument for settling international disputes; and that disarmament is accompanied by the creation of reliable procedures for peaceful settlement of disputes and maintenance of peace in accordance with the principles of the United Nations Charter.

The American commitment to these objectives goes deep. Our colleagues in the world community will not find us fainthearted in this cause.

Talks between the United States and the Soviet Union resumed September 6 in New York in a further effort to bring the two sides closer together and to work out a satisfactory disarmament forum. The proposals put forth by the United States by these talks provide for participation of non-aligned countries in future broad disarmament negotiations. They also provide for negotiations under the auspices of the United Nations if the Soviet Union will agree. The United States believes the Gen-

eral Assembly will have an opportunity to go into the matter since a Committee of the Whole exists in the form of the Disarmament Commission, which can be convened at any time.

In conclusion let me say, Mr. President, that we found elements in the message and in the Declaration which reflected a genuine desire to bring about a relaxation of tensions and which, if applied in a truly neutral and objective manner, could be of positive benefit in easing world tensions.

We respect, as always, the desire of other nations to remain non-aligned. We understand with sympathy and share their passion for peace. We are, as always, prepared to cooperate with all initiatives to bring about an improvement in the world situation. We look forward to continued friendly relations with the governments and peoples participating in the Belgrade meeting.

Sincerely,

JOHN F. KENNEDY

NOTE: This is the text of identical letters addressed to His Excellency Dr. Sukarno, President of the Republic of Indonesia, and His Excellency Modibo Keita, President of the Republic of Mali.

The text of the message from the Belgrade Conference is published in the Department of State Bulletin (vol. 45, p. 543).

For the President's message to the Conference, see Item 334 [4].

366 Letter to the President, United Steelworkers of America, on the Importance of Price Stability. *September* 14, 1961

Dear Mr. McDonald:

I appreciate very much your letter of September 8 in which you pledge the cooperation of the Steelworkers Union in the negotiations next year with the steel industry, to make sure that full weight and recognition is given to the public interest.

I am sure that you agree with me that the

public interest requires responsible price and wage policies in this basic industry and throughout the American economy. The Steelworkers Union can make a significant contribution to the public interest by following, in the forthcoming negotiations, policies that will ensure that their collective bargaining proposals are fashioned so that, in meeting the needs of workers in the industry, the interests of stockholders are safeguarded and the public interest in price stability is protected. This implies a labor settlement within the limits of advances in productivity and price stability.

No one, including workers in the industry, can profit by inflation and by advances in the cost of living. Nor can America as a whole maintain its position in the world if our balance of payments is jeopardized by price and wage policies that make our goods less competitive in the world markets. The whole nation has benefited from the price stability in steel for the last three years. We

count on all concerned to maintain this stability.

I am confident that on the basis of your letter, we can rely upon the leadership and members of the Steelworkers Union to act responsibly in the wage negotiations next year in the interests of all of the American people.

Sincerely,

JOHN F. KENNEDY

[Mr. David J. McDonald, President of the United Steelworkers of America, 1500 Commonwealth Building, Pittsburgh, Pa.]

NOTE: Mr. McDonald's letter was released with the President's reply.

367　Message to Prime Minister U Nu on the Flood Disaster in Burma. *September 16, 1961*

His Excellency U Nu:

On behalf of the Government and the people of the United States I express deepest sympathy for losses suffered by victims of the severe floods which have devastated large areas of your country. Ambassador Everton has already made certain funds available for relief and I have asked him to discuss

with your government other emergency measures which the United States Government might be able to take to help relieve suffering.

JOHN F. KENNEDY

NOTE: In his message, released at Hyannis, Mass., the President referred to the American Ambassador to Burma, John S. Everton.

368　Statement by the President on the Death of Dag Hammarskjold. *September 18, 1961*

I KNOW that I am speaking for all of my fellow Americans in expressing our deep sense of shock and loss in the untimely death of the Secretary-General of the United Nations, Mr. Dag Hammarskjold.

Dag Hammarskjold's dedication to the cause of peace, his untiring labors to achieve it, his courage under attack, his willingness to accept all responsibility in trying to strengthen the United Nations and make it

a more effective instrument for the aspirations of the hundreds of millions of people around the globe who desire to live out their lives—those efforts of his are well known.

It is tragic and ironic that his death came during a mission he was undertaking in order to bring about a cease-fire in Katanga.

I am hopeful that the members of the United Nations, recognizing his untiring labors, will attempt in the coming sessions

605

and in the years to come to try to build the United Nations into the effective instrument for peace which was Dag Hammarskjold's great ambition.

I express my sympathy to his country, the Government of Sweden, and I hope that all of us will recognize the heavy burdens that his passing places upon us.

NOTE: The President read the statement to members of the press in the Fish Room at the White House where it was also recorded for broadcast by radio and television. In addition, he issued Proclamation 3430 (26 F.R. 8877) which provided that, in honor and tribute to Mr. Hammarskjold, the National Flag should be flown at half-staff on all Government buildings of the United States until the interment.

Another text of the statement was released by the White House prior to its actual delivery.

369   Statement by the President Upon Signing Bill for the Relief of the Princess Anne County School Board, Virginia. *September* 19, 1961

I HAVE signed H.R. 1627, "For the relief of the Princess Anne County School Board, Virginia." The noise and potential danger from jet aircraft using the Oceana Naval Air Base has made certain school buildings belonging to the Board largely unusable, and this bill directs that the Board be compensated for them in an amount to be determined by the Court of Claims.

The courts provide a remedy in cases such as this, and I believe judicial remedies, rather than legislative determinations, should be pursued when they are available.

Because the Board's claim is obviously meritorious, I did not withhold approval of H.R. 1627. However, I wish to make it clear at this first opportunity that I do not approve the concept of Congressional action when adequate relief is available in judicial proceedings.

NOTE: H.R. 1627, approved by the President on September 15, 1961, is Public Law 87–251 (75 Stat. 520).

370   Statement by the President Upon Signing Bill Amending the Shipping Act of 1916. *September* 19, 1961

I HAVE today signed S. 1368, "To amend the Shipping Act, 1916, to provide for licensing independent ocean freight forwarders, and for other purposes."

The bill is designed to correct some undesirable practices described in detail in reports by Congressional committees and by the Federal Maritime Board. The Federal Maritime Board has sought, by regulations issued in June, to correct these practices. This legislation will require those regulations to be modified so that the same result can be achieved under a licensing procedure. It is my hope that the law and the regula-

tions will increase the efficiency of the maritime industry. Certainly, as a product of long and careful consideration, it should be given a trial.

If experience should show, however, that this legislation is inadequate either to deal with the abuses or to provide necessary assistance to the shippers and carriers, I intend to recommend further remedial legislation. In the meantime, I am requesting the Federal Maritime Commission to keep this subject matter under review.

NOTE: As enacted, S. 1368 is Public Law 87–254 (75 Stat. 522).

371   Statement by the President Announcing the First Public Housing Loan for Families on an Indian Reservation. *September* 19, 1961

I CONGRATULATE the Oglala Sioux Housing Authority and Mrs. McGuire, the Public Housing Commissioner, and Housing Administrator Robert Weaver, in working out this project to enable Federal assistance to be used for the decent housing of our Indian families as it has been used for so many others.

This is the first use of public housing aid to meet the needs of our Indians and it is long overdue. It expresses our determination to extend the benefits of Federal Housing aids to all Americans. And certainly these Indian families are the first who can claim their rights as Americans.

The extension of the public housing program to our Indian reservations is a practical fulfillment of the promise I made last October to the Association of American Indian Affairs. I said then that, if elected, I intended to "make the benefits of the Federal housing programs available to Indians." At that time I said: "Housing conditions on Indian reservations are a national shame."

The Public Housing Administration, in approving this project, has opened the door to better housing for many of our low-income Indian families at prices and interest rates they can afford, and I hope that similar developments will in due time be planned by other Indian reservations.

NOTE: In the third paragraph the President referred to statements made in a letter, dated October 28, 1960, to Mr. Oliver La Farge, President of the Association of American Indian Affairs. The text is published in "The Speeches of Senator John F. Kennedy, Presidential Campaign of 1960" (Senate Report 994, Part 1, p. 801, 87th Cong., 1st sess.).

372   Remarks of Welcome to President Prado of Peru at the Washington National Airport.   *September* 19, 1961

President and Señora Prado:

I want to express my great pleasure on behalf of the people of the United States in welcoming you here.

History has a strange rhythm. History does repeat itself, even if sometimes in a slightly different form. And it is a striking fact that in 1942 President Prado was one of the first, if not the first, of the democratically elected leaders of the Latin American Republics to visit the United States on an official visit.

The United States was then engaged in war, and yet President Roosevelt wanted President Prado of Peru to come to our country in order to express our appreciation and esteem for him for the leadership which he had taken in this hemisphere in the fight against the Axis.

His strong support in many public forums, his willingness to commit his country to this great struggle, all of these facts are remembered now, as in 1961, nearly 20 years later, President Prado of Peru comes again to the United States on an official visit.

The Presidents are different. The times have changed. The adversaries take a different form. But I believe in a very real sense that both Peru and the United States, still standing shoulder to shoulder, fight for the same things, and that is: a world at peace, a world of law, a world which permits us to develop in our respective countries a better life for our people, which uses the advantages of science to build life instead of to destroy it.

President Prado is the first leader of a Latin American Republic to come to this country in this new administration. The good-neighbor policy has passed into history. We have sought to replace it by a partnership, North and South, an alliance for the progress of our people.

We in this country esteem our friends. We have a long memory, Mr. President. And therefore, standing as I do where 20 years ago my distinguished predecessor stood, I extend to you a warm personal welcome, and I hope in extending this welcome to you that the people of your country will realize that we hold them in the strongest bonds of friendship.

NOTE: President Prado responded as follows:

I sincerely appreciate, Mr. President, the very warm greetings which you have just extended to me, in which you express the noble sentiments of the American people for Peru.

This is not the first time that I have had the privilege of visiting the United States as the President of my country. I came to Washington initially in 1942 as the guest of my friend, President Roosevelt. I arrived here during the most difficult days of World War II, and I was pleased to bear a message of solidarity from my country.

I return today, almost 20 years later, under circumstances in which we are faced with a new crisis in history. I am in spirit as before, with the same ideals of liberty and respect for human dignity. I am equally moved by a desire to fortify hemisphere solidarity and fraternal relations between the United States and Peru.

I also seek means of closing ground against aggression from abroad, and against infiltration by foreign and disruptive ideologies.

Most of all I want my greeting to the people of the United States to contain a sense of faith in democratic institutions, and an expression of conviction that through the cooperation of the free nations we shall succeed in defeating the attempt at Communist domination, and in turn assure the world a future of peace, justice, and progress.

Mr. President, I want to thank you very much for your noble words about my international policies and for my personal actions in my country, and the international support with your country and the allies in the Second World War; and now in this moment you and your people can be sure that Peru is solidly on your side.

373 Toasts of the President and President Prado. *September 19, 1961*

Ladies and gentlemen:

I know that I speak on behalf of all of you in expressing our warm welcome to our distinguished guests from our sister Republic of Peru. We are delighted to welcome President Prado and Señora Prado for many reasons. One of the reasons is because I do not think that we in the United States have been as conscious as we should be of the common inheritance which we in this country have with Spaniards who came not only to the United States but also to Peru. We regard ourselves as descendant from mostly Europeans, but I think that that is only because we have failed to recognize the extraordinary adventure and courage of these Spaniards who came to Florida and Louisiana and Texas and all through the Southwest United States, and whose confreres also went and established their life in Peru. So that we feel, Mr. President, that we are also descendants. While from a mixed culture, we also, I hope, can claim that we are descendants in a sense from the same strains and cultures which have distinguished your own country.

We are delighted that your Ambassador is also here, occupying a special place in the life of our city and country. I have been looking forward to your retaining him long enough to permit him to succeed the Ambassador of Nicaragua. This is an honor which he wishes to have passed from him, but we expect to see him at every plane and welcoming the visiting dignitaries.

Also, Mr. President, we are glad to have you and the Minister here because, as I said, you really are in a sense the only leader of the free world who occupied a position of responsibility during the Second World War, and who now today at this most crucial moment occupies a position of commanding responsibility.

I do not know anyone in the free world, with the possible exception of General de Gaulle, who played a leading role in the Second World War who was a most active figure in mobilizing the Republics of this hemisphere in the fighting against Fascism, and who now bears the great responsibility, almost 20 years later.

As I said at the airport, you were if not the first among the very first of the democratically elected Presidents of the Latin American Republics who came to this country. It is a great pleasure that you should also come as the first state visitor from this hemisphere in this new administration.

And finally, Mr. President, may I say that your life has had a consistency which is not always true of those of us who follow our profession. You were a revolutionary figure in your youth. You spent almost a decade in exile in Paris. You were a leader in the fight against Fascism. You have been a leader in the fight against communism, and you are where you began: a defender of your country's stature, a defender of the cause in which we all believe. You stand

for what you stood for as a young man in Peru. You stand for the Western World. You have in the Prado doctrine carried out the most important principles of the ties between the Atlantic Community and the American Republics.

Therefore, Mr. President, here tonight we honor you, as you were honored by President Roosevelt 20 years ago. We honor your country. We are delighted to have you in this year of 1961.

As my American colleagues will all testify, we have a particular appreciation for our friends, and therefore I hope that all of you will join me in drinking to the people of Peru and to the President of Peru and Señora Prado.

NOTE: The President proposed the toast at a state dinner at the White House.

President Prado responded as follows:

"Mr. President, Mrs. Kennedy:

"Mrs. Prado and I wish to extend to you both our appreciation for this magnificent reception. Your warm hospitality is a reflection of the sincere cordiality with which the American people are receiving us.

"Your very kind invitation for a state visit to the country of Washington and Lincoln provides me with an opportunity to tell you, Mr. President, and through you to your fellow citizens, that my government is devoted to the democratic way of life. It is loyal to its international commitments and to the cause of peace. It remains allied with the United States of America.

"It is prepared to share in the common effort to raise the standard of living of the hemisphere, and to promote economic and social development. Furthermore, it is determined to contribute toward repelling aggression from abroad, and combating Communist infiltration in the Western Hemisphere. It is equally resolved to help countries in other continents resist firmly the daily threat of totalitarian domination.

"The identity of ideals, which you and I are defending, gives my visit all of the aspects of a frank and firm friendship. I am sure, Mr. President, that the results will be beneficial for both countries and will open a new stage of understanding and cooperation between the United States and Peru, and which will be ever closer and ever more fruitful.

"I thank you again, Mr. President, for your very kind and generous expressions about my personality. I thank you very much.

"Ladies and gentlemen, I propose a toast to the United States, to its increasing greatness within a free America, and to President Kennedy and to the charming First Lady."

During the President's remarks he referred to the Peruvian Ambassador, Fernando Berckemeyer, to succeed the Nicaraguan Ambassador, Dr. Guillermo Sevilla-Sacasa as Dean of the Diplomatic Corps; and to Arturo Garcia, Minister Counselor at the Peruvian Embassy.

374 Statement by the President Upon Signing Bill Extending the Federal Airport Act. *September 20, 1961*

I AM HAPPY to approve this extension of the Federal Airport Act. This program is vital to our economy, our defense, and the growth and safety of our aviation industry.

I am particularly gratified by the action of Congress in providing the Administrator of the Federal Aviation Agency with the funds necessary to execute grant agreements over a three-year period. Such long-term assurance is essential if the States and local communities are to plan their airport programs effectively.

The bill also includes many new safety provisions. Airport landing aids will now be required in airport projects; and there is a special fund to develop airports to serve private flying and thus relieve congestion at busy airports serving commercial airlines.

Ever-increasing safety of transportation must be a continuing goal. I have directed the Administrator of the Federal Aviation Agency to establish priorities among projects based on safety considerations and to develop a classification system for civil airports based on suitability for safe use by various kinds of traffic as a part of the national system.

NOTE: The bill extending the Federal Airport Act is Public Law 87–255 (75 Stat. 255).

375 Remarks Recorded for the Opening of the United Community Campaigns. *September 20, 1961*

My fellow Americans:

I welcome the opportunity to speak to you in behalf of the United Campaign across the country. No value is more deeply ingrained in our national life than that of community responsibility. In our earliest days of the nation, in the small communities of Jamestown and Plymouth, all the way to the western frontier, Americans helped each other build their lives, their communities, their homes. This has been a valuable part of our national experience. This country grew great by individual effort, but it was combined with a generous response to the needs of our neighbors. Now life in America has become more complicated. Our country has grown so large, people move so frequently from home to home, community to community, that we have lost some of this tradition. I believe that one of the most valuable ways that we can maintain it, one of the most valuable means by which we can help our fellow Americans, is through the United Community Campaigns.

This year there are over 2200 United Funds and Community Chests in 50 States. They are attempting to raise $478 million for nearly 30,000 State and local voluntary services, services that will help our fellow Americans in many, many ways: day nurseries, services for homeless children, special care for our aging citizens, care of the sick and the handicapped, help for young men and women in uniform, in many communities help for the Red Cross. I attach particular importance to those programs which will help young people meet their problems today so that they can build a better life for the future. The United Campaign brings together Americans of all races and all creeds in a great national effort. They work together, they plan together and by this means I think they renew a sense of community concern. The United Campaign can become not merely an expression of community will but it's also a means of building the strength and future of our Nation. William Bradford who helped found the Plymouth Colony, way back in the beginning

of this country, nearly three and a half centuries ago in Massachusetts Bay, said, "As one small candle may light a thousand, so the light here kindled has shone unto many, yea, in some sort to the whole nation." I hope this year we can light many candles. This is the emblem for the Community Funds across the Nation this year—a young child who needs your help. I'm confident that in these great days of our country that all Americans will respond to this request. I congratulate Mr. Ford, the national chairman. I wish him and all those who are working so hard in this great cause the best possible success.

NOTE: The President's remarks were broadcast over the major networks at approximately 9:55 p.m. At the close of his remarks the President referred to Benson Ford, vice president of the Ford Motor Company, who served as national chairman of the United Community Campaigns of America.

376   Joint Statement Following Discussions With the President of Peru. *September 21, 1961*

DR. MANUEL PRADO, President of the Republic of Peru, is making a state visit to the United States at the invitation of President Kennedy, with a view to strengthening the already friendly relations prevailing between the two countries. In keeping with this objective, the two Presidents have held conversations characterized by a spirit of cordiality, frankness and understanding. They discussed a number of matters of bilateral interest as well as other important problems in international relations.

The Presidents in their discussions affirmed their adherence to the principles of the Alliance for Progress. They stressed the great importance of the economic and social development of Latin America in order to achieve growing economies, with effective

and continuing improvement in living standards, and thus to satisfy the urgent aspirations of its peoples for a more equitable participation in the life of their countries. Each Latin American country must therefore concentrate increasing efforts and make greater sacrifice toward such basic development. The United States for its part is prepared to assist in the realization of this objective in accordance with the principles established in the Charter of Punta del Este. With this in mind the Presidents considered various projects of importance to Peru's economic and social development. The United States will participate in emergency projects being initiated by the Peruvian Government in the critical Puno area.

The Presidents agreed that such development in Latin America would be facilitated by the formulation by each country of a national development plan to establish its own goals, priorities and reforms.

They also agreed that only by instituting reforms in such fields as land tenure, tax structure and the utilization of national income can the objective of integrated social and economic development be achieved.

President Prado emphasized that one of the essential problems in the case of Peru is the integration of the Indian population into the life of the country.

The Presidents agreed to the need for stimulating private investment in Peru and in all of Latin America. President Prado emphasized that Peru, because of its raw materials, its advanced legislation, its policy of free trade, monetary stability and the absence of exchange controls, offers excellent opportunities for foreign capital interested in participating with Peruvian capital in the growth of its promising economy. In order to encourage such investment, he stressed the desirability of eliminating double taxation.

Following a review of the international situation, the Presidents agreed on the need for a firm policy to confront the unceasing conspiracy of international Communism against the peace of the hemisphere and of the world, recognizing that the successes or failures of Communism wherever they may occur have direct or indirect repercussion in each and every nation.

The Presidents emphasized the importance of hemispheric unity for the preservation of peace and the development of harmonious relations among nations. Because of their traditions of liberty, faith in the human being and encouragement of individual initiative in all aspects of life, the Americas must serve as a bastion of these

principles and a force for harmony in the world. Such unity is firmly founded upon long historic ties and a community of purpose of the nations of the hemisphere and on recognition and respect for the distinctive national character of each member of the American family.

As guiding principles governing the peaceful relationship of nations, fundamental to the Inter-American system, the Presidents reiterated the importance of nonintervention in the domestic affairs of other states and the right of self-determination of peoples by means of periodic, free and democratic elections to guarantee the rule of liberty, justice and individual social and human rights. They agreed that when an alien ideology establishes a foothold in the hemisphere or when its official and unofficial agents engage subversively in undermining constitutional order, this constitutes both a violation of the principle of nonintervention and a threat to all the nations of the hemisphere.

The Presidents reasserted their adherence to the principles of the United Nations and of the Organization of American States, which are the embodiment of the fundamental precepts of the rule of law and justice, the faithful observance of international obligations and agreements, and the respect for national independence, identity and dignity. They call on all nations to reaffirm in their actions their adherence to the high principles of those two organizations.

The Presidents also discussed the similarity of the principles, particularly the principle of reciprocal assistance, which characterize the Organization of American States and the North Atlantic Treaty Organization. They agreed that it is more than ever essential that these regional organizations be alert to maintain and defend the civilization that is common to their members.

In conclusion, the two Chiefs of State reiterated their unwavering determination to foster and perfect the close cooperation that exists between their nations in matters of common interest both of regional consequence and of world importance.

377   Letter to the President of the Senate and to the Speaker of the House Transmitting a National Forests Development Program. *September 21, 1961*

Dear Mr. —————:

I am pleased to transmit to the House of Representatives (the Senate) a report prepared by the Department of Agriculture setting forth "A Development Program for the National Forests."

This report is the response of the Department of Agriculture to the request I made in my messages to the Congress on natural resources and on American agriculture that forest development on public lands be accelerated. The developmental program recommended in the report modifies and supplements the 1959 National Forest Program submitted by the preceding Administration. The principal components of the new program are (1) substantially broadened and intensified recreation resource management, (2) acceleration of timber harvesting and management, (3) adjustment of the road and trail program to provide needed multiple-purpose roads and, (4) acquisition of needed tracts within national forests boundaries, especially those having recreational values.

As our nation's population increases and our industrialization grows, the obligation to preserve and to protect our nation's forests becomes greater. The forward-looking program outlined in this report holds great hope. Congressional interest in our national forests has always been high—an interest this Administration shares. I am confident that this program will be carefully reviewed by the appropriate Congressional committees and that significant progress can be made in this important field.

Sincerely,

JOHN F. KENNEDY

NOTE: This is the text of identical letters addressed to the Honorable Lyndon B. Johnson, President of the Senate, and to the Honorable Sam Rayburn, Speaker of the House of Representatives.

The 19-page report (Government Printing Office, 1961), prepared by the Forest Service, was released by the U.S. Department of Agriculture.

378   Statement by the President: National Science Youth Month. *September 21, 1961*

SCIENTIFIC PROGRESS is the concern of each of us. The growth of our scientific effort has placed the growth of the Nation's strength in terms of health, economy, and security, and has contributed benefits to all mankind. The diversity, vitality, and high standards of American science today are one of our brightest promises for the future.

Fulfilling that promise depends to a large extent on our efforts in encouraging the scientific interests of young persons of ability. Scientific talent is a resource which must be developed to the fullest. Observance of National Science Youth Month which recognizes the achievements of high school students and their teachers, is sponsored by 38 national scientific, educational, industrial, and governmental groups.

I hope the observance will further stimulate young people in every area of education, and encourage all citizens to help develop a vital national asset.

JOHN F. KENNEDY

379   Remarks Upon Signing the Mutual Educational and Cultural Exchange Act.   *September 21, 1961*

I AM DELIGHTED to sign the new Fulbright-Hays Act. This ceremony has historic significance because it marks full recognition by the Congress of the importance of a more comprehensive program of educational and cultural activities as a component of our foreign relations.

The varied pieces of legislation, beginning with the Fulbright Act of 1946, following through with the Smith-Mundt bill and others, have now been gathered together and expanded to form for the first time a solid base for more effective activity in this most essential field.

I want to congratulate and express my appreciation to Senator Fulbright, whose name has long been a household symbol in the world for this great phase of our national and international life, and to Congressman Wayne Hays who has so skillfully and conscientiously steered this legislation through the House.

NOTE: The Mutual Educational and Cultural Exchange Act of 1961 is Public Law 87–256 (75 Stat. 527).

380   Remarks Upon Signing the Peace Corps Bill.   *September 22, 1961*

WITH THE ENACTMENT of this legislation, an avenue is provided by which Americans can serve their country in the cause of world peace and understanding and simultaneously assist other nations toward their legitimate goals of freedom and opportunity.

I want particularly to express pleasure at the bipartisan effort and support in the shaping of this new agency.

Already more than thirteen thousand Americans have offered their services to the Peace Corps. By the end of the year almost one thousand will be serving overseas or completing their training in the United States. By July of next year we hope to have twenty-seven hundred in training or abroad.

These men and women are going overseas at the request of the host nations. They will be doing specific, needed jobs. They will be working at a level and living at a level comparable to the citizens of the foreign nations. They will be farmers and teachers, craftsmen and nurses, doctors and technicians of all kinds. They will be a cross-section of the finest men and women that this Nation has to offer.

The sure sign of a good idea is that you can follow it, and I am pleased that several other nations have decided to establish Peace Corps agencies of their own.

Much credit for what has been done must go to congressional leaders like the men and women in this room, and the scores of other dedicated Americans who have given their advice and counsel.

Also I want to express my esteem for the most effective lobbyist on the Washington scene, Mr. Sargent Shriver.

NOTE: The Peace Corps Act is Public Law 87–293 (75 Stat. 612).

In his remarks the President referred to the Director of the Peace Corps, Sargent Shriver.

---

381   Remarks Upon Signing Bill To Expand and Extend the Saline Water Conversion Program. *September 22, 1961*

I AM GLAD to approve H.R. 7916, which expands and extends the saline water conversion program being conducted by the Department of the Interior. This act authorizes the appropriation of $75 million for research and development over the next 6 years, and extends the 1958 Demonstration Plant Act to 1970.

The enactment of this bill into law is very important to the future of our country. Present shortages of water are already adversely affecting industrial development in important sections of the United States. Unless these necessary steps are taken now, within 15 years these shortages will become a serious handicap. This bill opens the door to development of a means whereby low-cost water can be made available from limitless sources.

Cheap conversion of saline and brackish water is a goal within our reach, and dedicated efforts will answer the hopes which have attracted the attention of mankind for many centuries. In less than a decade, the cost of converting salt water has been reduced from about $5 per thousand gallons to almost $1 per thousand gallons. While this progress is significant and encouraging, our objective, which is to make fresh water secured from salt or brackish water competitive with other fresh water, is still to be achieved.

There is nothing, really, that we can do in this country that can mean more in the long run to our people and to people all around the world than to be able to make an important and significant scientific breakthrough in this area. This legislation helps and moves us towards that goal, and we want to express America's appreciation and thanks to everyone in the country and to the Members of Congress who have concerned themselves in this matter over the years.

NOTE: As enacted, H.R. 7916 is Public Law 87–295 (75 Stat. 628).

382   Remarks Upon Signing the Juvenile Delinquency and Youth Offenses Control Act.   *September 22, 1961*

I AM HAPPY to approve S. 279, Juvenile Delinquency and Youth Offenses Control Act of 1961.

The future of our country depends upon our younger people who will occupy positions of responsibility and leadership in the coming days. Yet for 11 years juvenile delinquency has been increasing. No city or State in our country has been immune. This is a matter of national concern and requires national action.

With this legislation the Federal Government becomes an active partner with States and local communities to prevent and control the spread of delinquency. Though initiative and primary responsibility for coping with delinquency reside with families and local communities, the Federal Government can provide leadership, guidance and assistance.

The Secretary of HEW will administer the

act. He will, however, work closely with the Committee on Juvenile Delinquency and Youth Crime, which I have appointed to bring about a more effective coordination of Federal resources in this field. This Committee includes the Attorney General as Chairman, and the Secretary of Labor, along with the Secretary of HEW.

The resources provided under this program will help local communities in their efforts to stem the tide of juvenile delinquency and youthful offenses, and thus contribute to the preservation of human resources in this vital area of the life of our Nation.

I want to express my appreciation to the Members of both parties of both Houses for their efforts in this area which are of concern to us all.

NOTE: As enacted, S. 279 is Public Law 87–274 (75 Stat. 572).

383   Veto of Bill Increasing Retirement Benefits of Certain Policemen and Firemen.   *September 22, 1961*

I RETURN herewith, without my approval, S. 1528 "To increase the relief or retirement compensation of certain former members of the Metropolitan Police force, the Fire Department of the District of Columbia, the United States Park Police force, the White House Police force, and the United States Secret Service; and of widows and children of certain deceased former officers and members of such forces, department or service."

This bill is a re-enactment of a similar proposal in the last Congress which President Eisenhower expressed disapproval of on September 24, 1959.

I find objectionable that portion of the bill which increases by 10% the annuities of certain former members of the Police, Fire Department and Secret Service.

Already, as a result of the Equalization Act of 1923, which gives an automatic proportionate increase in annuities whenever active duty policemen and firemen receive them, a significant number of these retirees now receive a larger pension than their annual salaries while on active duty. The record also indicates that this group is much more generously treated than other District Government annuitants who are covered by other retirement programs. The proposal would compound the existing disparity and is inconsistent with essential objectives of fairness and impartiality to all employees.

The provisions of the bill affecting widows and surviving minor children of deceased policemen and firemen who retired prior to October 1, 1956, are a different matter. Their annuities were last adjusted in 1949,

and, in the years since, this fixed income has diminished in value with each increase in the cost of living. S. 1918, which has passed the Senate, provides for an early increase in these annuities and I am hopeful that the House of Representatives will pass this bill promptly.

JOHN F. KENNEDY

384 Statement by the President Upon Signing Bill Amending the Railroad Retirement Act. *September 22, 1961*

I HAVE TODAY signed S. 2395, amending the Railroad Retirement Act to permit early retirement on a reduced annuity by male railroad workers.

This bill contains provisions similar in most respects to those contained in the recent amendments to the Social Security Act, providing railroad employees with benefits similar to those enjoyed by those under the Social Security Act.

I have approved the legislation because I believe that it is appropriate and desirable to furnish railroad employees with such comparable benefits. I am concerned, however, with the actuarial deficiency in the railroad retirement system. It is already $73 million a year. This legislation adds an

additional $2 million to this deficiency. In addition, the railroad unemployment insurance system is in such financial difficulty it has had to borrow more than $200 million in recent years.

I urge the Congress, in the next session, to take those steps which are necessary to restore these systems to healthy financial self-sufficiency. I am instructing the Chairman of the Railroad Retirement Board, in consultation with representatives of the industry and of the labor organizations, to develop recommendations to assist the Congress to take the necessary action.

NOTE: As enacted, S. 2395 is Public Law 87–285 (75 Stat. 585).

The statement was released at Hyannis, Mass.

385 Letter to the Chairman, Railroad Retirement Board, on the Financial Condition of the Railroad Retirement and Unemployment Compensation Systems. *September 22, 1961*

Dear Mr. Chairman:

In my signing statement on S. 2395, the bill providing early retirement for railroad workers, I informed the Congress of my serious concern over the financial conditions

of the railroad retirement and unemployment compensation systems. I know you, and the other members of the Board, share my concern in this matter, and I noted with satisfaction your recent statement to Chairman Harris during the hearings on this legislation that the Board would take up its responsibilities to keep the system financially sound.

I also indicated to the Congress my hope that we might soon have some recommendations designed to remedy the financial situation of these systems. Accordingly I would like you to undertake immediately a review of the situation and to develop recommenda-

tions which I can consider for presentation to the Congress.

Sincerely,

JOHN F. KENNEDY

[Honorable Howard W. Habermeyer, Chairman, Railroad Retirement Board, 44 Rush Street, Chicago 11, Illinois]

NOTE: For the President's statement upon signing S. 2395, see Item 384.

In his letter the President referred to U.S. Representative Oren Harris from Arkansas, Chairman of the Interstate and Foreign Commerce Committee.

386   Statement by the President Upon Signing Bill Relating to the Office of Emergency Planning.   *September 22, 1961*

I HAVE TODAY approved H.R. 8406, a bill "To Change the Name of the Office of Civil and Defense Mobilization to Office of Emergency Planning."

Effective August 1, I assigned to the Secretary of Defense major Federal responsibilities for civil defense. The remaining responsibilities can more accurately be described as emergency planning functions, for they deal with responsibilities for investigation, advice, coordination, and policy

formulation in connection with our preparedness effort.

These functions of the Office of Emergency Planning may be of critical importance to our very survival. The national security requires that there be soundly conceived and well-tested plans for every emergency.

NOTE: As enacted, H.R. 8406 is Public Law 87–296 (75 Stat. 630). See also Item 295.

The statement was released at Hyannis, Mass.

387   Address in New York City Before the General Assembly of the United Nations.   *September 25, 1961*

Mr. President, honored delegates, ladies and gentlemen:

We meet in an hour of grief and challenge. Dag Hammarskjold is dead. But the United Nations lives. His tragedy is deep in our hearts, but the task for which he died is at the top of our agenda. A noble servant of peace is gone. But the quest for peace lies before us.

The problem is not the death of one man—the problem is the life of this organization. It will either grow to meet the

challenges of our age, or it will be gone with the wind, without influence, without force, without respect. Were we to let it die, to enfeeble its vigor, to cripple its powers, we would condemn our future.

For in the development of this organization rests the only true alternative to war—and war appeals no longer as a rational alternative. Unconditional war can no longer lead to unconditional victory. It can no longer serve to settle disputes. It can no longer concern the great powers alone. For a nuclear disaster, spread by wind and water and fear, could well engulf the great and the small, the rich and the poor, the committed and the uncommitted alike. Mankind must put an end to war—or war will put an end to mankind.

So let us here resolve that Dag Hammarskjold did not live, or die, in vain. Let us call a truce to terror. Let us invoke the blessings of peace. And, as we build an international capacity to keep peace, let us join in dismantling the national capacity to wage war.

II.

This will require new strength and new roles for the United Nations. For disarmament without checks is but a shadow—and a community without law is but a shell. Already the United Nations has become both the measure and the vehicle of man's most generous impulses. Already it has provided—in the Middle East, in Asia, in Africa this year in the Congo—a means of holding man's violence within bounds.

But the great question which confronted this body in 1945 is still before us: whether man's cherished hopes for progress and peace are to be destroyed by terror and disruption, whether the "foul winds of war" can be tamed in time to free the cooling winds of reason, and whether the pledges of our Charter are to be fulfilled or defied—pledges to secure peace, progress, human rights and world law.

In this Hall, there are not three forces, but two. One is composed of those who are trying to build the kind of world described in Articles I and II of the Charter. The other, seeking a far different world, would undermine this organization in the process.

Today of all days our dedication to the Charter must be maintained. It must be strengthened first of all by the selection of an outstanding civil servant to carry forward the responsibilities of the Secretary General—a man endowed with both the wisdom and the power to make meaningful the moral force of the world community. The late Secretary General nurtured and sharpened the United Nations' obligation to act. But he did not invent it. It was there in the Charter. It is still there in the Charter.

However difficult it may be to fill Mr. Hammarskjold's place, it can better be filled by one man rather than by three. Even the three horses of the Troika did not have three drivers, all going in different directions. They had only one—and so must the United Nations executive. To install a triumvirate, or any panel, or any rotating authority, in the United Nations administrative offices would replace order with anarchy, action with paralysis, confidence with confusion.

The Secretary General, in a very real sense, is the servant of the General Assembly. Diminish his authority and you diminish the authority of the only body where all nations, regardless of power, are equal and sovereign. Until all the powerful are just, the weak will be secure only in the strength of this Assembly.

Effective and independent executive action is not the same question as balanced representation. In view of the enormous change in membership in this body since its founding, the American delegation will join in any effort for the prompt review and revision of the composition of United Nations bodies.

But to give this organization three drivers—to permit each great power to decide its own case, would entrench the Cold War in the headquarters of peace. Whatever advantages such a plan may hold out to my own country, as one of the great powers, we reject it. For we far prefer world law, in the age of self-determination, to world war, in the age of mass extermination.

III.

Today, every inhabitant of this planet must contemplate the day when this planet may no longer be habitable. Every man, woman and child lives under a nuclear sword of Damocles, hanging by the slenderest of threads, capable of being cut at any moment by accident or miscalculation or by madness. The weapons of war must be abolished before they abolish us.

Men no longer debate whether armaments are a symptom or a cause of tension. The mere existence of modern weapons—ten million times more powerful than any that the world has ever seen, and only minutes away from any target on earth—is a source of horror, and discord and distrust. Men no longer maintain that disarmament must await the settlement of all disputes—for disarmament must be a part of any permanent settlement. And men may no longer pretend that the quest for disarmament is a sign of weakness—for in a spiraling arms race, a nation's security may well be shrinking even as its arms increase.

For 15 years this organization has sought the reduction and destruction of arms. Now that goal is no longer a dream—it is a practical matter of life or death. The risks inherent in disarmament pale in comparison to the risks inherent in an unlimited arms race.

It is in this spirit that the recent Belgrade Conference—recognizing that this is no longer a Soviet problem or an American problem, but a human problem—endorsed a program of "general, complete and strictly an internationally controlled disarmament."

It is in this same spirit that we in the United States have labored this year, with a new urgency, and with a new, now statutory agency fully endorsed by the Congress, to find an approach to disarmament which would be so far-reaching yet realistic, so mutually balanced and beneficial, that it could be accepted by every nation. And it is in this spirit that we have presented with the agreement of the Soviet Union—under the label both nations now accept of "general and complete disarmament"—a new statement of newly-agreed principles for negotiation.

But we are well aware that all issues of principle are not settled, and that principles alone are not enough. It is therefore our intention to challenge the Soviet Union, not to an arms race, but to a peace race—to advance together step by step, stage by stage, until general and complete disarmament has been achieved. We invite them now to go beyond agreement in principle to reach agreement on actual plans.

The program to be presented to this assembly—for general and complete disarmament under effective international control—moves to bridge the gap between those who insist on a gradual approach and those who talk only of the final and total achievement. It would create machinery to keep the peace as it destroys the machinery of war. It would proceed through balanced and safeguarded stages designed to give no state a military advantage over another. It would place the final responsibility for verification and control where it belongs, not with the big powers alone, not with one's adversary or one's self, but in an international organization within the framework of the United Nations. It would assure that indispensable condition of disarmament—true inspection—and apply it in

stages proportionate to the stage of disarmament. It would cover delivery systems as
well as weapons. It would ultimately halt
their production as well as their testing,
their transfer as well as their possession.
It would achieve, under the eyes of an international disarmament organization, a steady
reduction in force, both nuclear and conventional, until it has abolished all armies
and all weapons except those needed for
internal order and a new United Nations
Peace Force. And it starts that process now,
today, even as the talks begin.

In short, general and complete disarmament must no longer be a slogan, used to
resist the first steps. It is no longer to be
a goal without means of achieving it, without means of verifying its progress, without
means of keeping the peace. It is now a
realistic plan, and a test—a test of those only
willing to talk and a test of those willing to
act.

Such a plan would not bring a world free
from conflict and greed—but it would bring
a world free from the terrors of mass destruction. It would not usher in the era of
the super state—but it would usher in an
era in which no state could annihilate or be
annihilated by another.

In 1945, this Nation proposed the Baruch
Plan to internationalize the atom before
other nations even possessed the bomb or
demilitarized their troops. We proposed
with our allies the Disarmament Plan of
1951 while still at war in Korea. And we
make our proposals today, while building
up our defenses over Berlin, not because we
are inconsistent or insincere or intimidated,
but because we know the rights of free men
will prevail—because while we are compelled
against our will to rearm, we look confidently beyond Berlin to the kind of disarmed
world we all prefer.

I therefore propose, on the basis of this
Plan, that disarmament negotiations resume
promptly, and continue without interruption until an entire program for general and
complete disarmament has not only been
agreed but has been actually achieved.

IV.

The logical place to begin is a treaty assuring the end of nuclear tests of all kinds,
in every environment, under workable controls. The United States and the United
Kingdom have proposed such a treaty that
is both reasonable, effective and ready for
signature. We are still prepared to sign that
treaty today.

We also proposed a mutual ban on atmospheric testing, without inspection or controls, in order to save the human race from
the poison of radioactive fallout. We regret that that offer has not been accepted.

For 15 years we have sought to make the
atom an instrument of peaceful growth
rather than of war. But for 15 years our
concessions have been matched by obstruction, our patience by intransigence. And
the pleas of mankind for peace have met
with disregard.

Finally, as the explosions of others be-
clouded the skies, my country was left with
no alternative but to act in the interests of
its own and the free world's security. We
cannot endanger that security by refraining
from testing while others improve their
arsenals. Nor can we endanger it by another
long, uninspected ban on testing. For three
years we accepted those risks in our open
society while seeking agreement on inspection. But this year, while we were negotiating in good faith in Geneva, others were
secretly preparing new experiments in
destruction.

Our tests are not polluting the atmosphere. Our deterrent weapons are guarded against accidental explosion or use. Our doctors and scientists stand ready to help any nation measure and meet the hazards to health which inevitably result from the tests in the atmosphere.

But to halt the spread of these terrible weapons, to halt the contamination of the air, to halt the spiralling nuclear arms race, we remain ready to seek new avenues of agreement, our new Disarmament Program thus includes the following proposals:

—First, signing the test-ban treaty by all nations. This can be done now. Test ban negotiations need not and should not await general disarmament.

—Second, stopping the production of fissionable materials for use in weapons, and preventing their transfer to any nation now lacking in nuclear weapons.

—Third, prohibiting the transfer of control over nuclear weapons to states that do not own them.

—Fourth, keeping nuclear weapons from seeding new battlegrounds in outer space.

—Fifth, gradually destroying existing nuclear weapons and converting their materials to peaceful uses; and

—Finally, halting the unlimited testing and production of strategic nuclear delivery vehicles, and gradually destroying them as well.

v.

To destroy arms, however, is not enough. We must create even as we destroy—creating worldwide law and law enforcement as we outlaw worldwide war and weapons. In the world we seek, the United Nations Emergency Forces which have been hastily assembled, uncertainly supplied, and inadequately financed, will never be enough. Therefore, the United States recommends

that all member nations earmark special peace-keeping units in their armed forces—to be on call of the United Nations, to be specially trained and quickly available, and with advance provision for financial and logistic support.

In addition, the American delegation will suggest a series of steps to improve the United Nations' machinery for the peaceful settlement of disputes—for on-the-spot fact-finding, mediation and adjudication—for extending the rule of international law. For peace is not solely a matter of military or technical problems—it is primarily a problem of politics and people. And unless man can match his strides in weaponry and technology with equal strides in social and political development, our great strength, like that of the dinosaur, will become incapable of proper control—and like the dinosaur vanish from the earth.

vi.

As we extend the rule of law on earth, so must we also extend it to man's new domain—outer space.

All of us salute the brave cosmonauts of the Soviet Union. The new horizons of outer space must not be driven by the old bitter concepts of imperialism and sovereign claims. The cold reaches of the universe must not become the new arena of an even colder war.

To this end, we shall urge proposals extending the United Nations Charter to the limits of man's exploration in the universe, reserving outer space for peaceful use, prohibiting weapons of mass destruction in space or on celestial bodies, and opening the mysteries and benefits of space to every nation. We shall propose further cooperative efforts between all nations in weather prediction and eventually in weather control.

We shall propose, finally, a global system of communications satellites linking the whole world in telegraph and telephone and radio and television. The day need not be far away when such a system will televise the proceedings of this body to every corner of the world for the benefit of peace.

VII.

But the mysteries of outer space must not divert our eyes or our energies from the harsh realities that face our fellow men. Political sovereignty is but a mockery without the means of meeting poverty and illiteracy and disease. Self-determination is but a slogan if the future holds no hope.

That is why my Nation, which has freely shared its capital and its technology to help others help themselves, now proposes officially designating this decade of the 1960's as the United Nations Decade of Development. Under the framework of that Resolution, the United Nations' existing efforts in promoting economic growth can be expanded and coordinated. Regional surveys and training institutes can now pool the talents of many. New research, technical assistance and pilot projects can unlock the wealth of less developed lands and untapped waters. And development can become a cooperative and not a competitive enterprise—to enable all nations, however diverse in their systems and beliefs, to become in fact as well as in law free and equal nations.

VIII.

My Country favors a world of free and equal states. We agree with those who say that colonialism is a key issue in this Assembly. But let the full facts of that issue be discussed in full.

On the one hand is the fact that, since the close of World War II, a worldwide declaration of independence has transformed nearly 1 billion people and 9 million square miles into 42 free and independent states. Less than 2 percent of the world's population now lives in "dependent" territories.

I do not ignore the remaining problems of traditional colonialism which still confront this body. Those problems will be solved, with patience, good will, and determination. Within the limits of our responsibility in such matters, my Country intends to be a participant and not merely an observer, in the peaceful, expeditious movement of nations from the status of colonies to the partnership of equals. That continuing tide of self-determination, which runs so strong, has our sympathy and our support.

But colonialism in its harshest forms is not only the exploitation of new nations by old, of dark skins by light, or the subjugation of the poor by the rich. My Nation was once a colony, and we know what colonialism means; the exploitation and subjugation of the weak by the powerful, of the many by the few, of the governed who have given no consent to be governed, whatever their continent, their class, or their color.

And that is why there is no ignoring the fact that the tide of self-determination has not reached the Communist empire where a population far larger than that officially termed "dependent" lives under governments installed by foreign troops instead of free institutions—under a system which knows only one party and one belief—which suppresses free debate, and free elections, and free newspapers, and free books and free trade unions—and which builds a wall to keep truth a stranger and its own citizens prisoners. Let us debate colonialism in full—and apply the principle of free choice and the practice of free plebiscites in every corner of the globe.

IX.

Finally, as President of the United States, I consider it my duty to report to this Assembly on two threats to the peace which are not on your crowded agenda, but which causes us, and most of you, the deepest concern.

The first threat on which I wish to report is widely misunderstood: the smoldering coals of war in Southeast Asia. South Viet-Nam is already under attack—sometimes by a single assassin, sometimes by a band of guerrillas, recently by full battalions. The peaceful borders of Burma, Cambodia, and India have been repeatedly violated. And the peaceful people of Laos are in danger of losing the independence they gained not so long ago.

No one can call these "wars of liberation." For these are free countries living under their own governments. Nor are these aggressions any less real because men are knifed in their homes and not shot in the fields of battle.

The very simple question confronting the world community is whether measures can be devised to protect the small and the weak from such tactics. For if they are successful in Laos and South Viet-Nam, the gates will be opened wide.

The United States seeks for itself no base, no territory, no special position in this area of any kind. We support a truly neutral and independent Laos, its people free from outside interference, living at peace with themselves and with their neighbors, assured that their territory will not be used for attacks on others, and under a government comparable (as Mr. Khrushchev and I agreed at Vienna) to Cambodia and Burma.

But now the negotiations over Laos are reaching a crucial stage. The cease-fire is at best precarious. The rainy season is coming to an end. Laotian territory is being used to infiltrate South Viet-Nam. The world community must recognize—and all those who are involved—that this potent threat to Laotian peace and freedom is indivisible from all other threats to their own.

Secondly, I wish to report to you on the crisis over Germany and Berlin. This is not the time or the place for immoderate tones, but the world community is entitled to know the very simple issues as we see them. If there is a crisis it is because an existing peace is under threat, because an existing island of free people is under pressure, because solemn agreements are being treated with indifference. Established international rights are being threatened with unilateral usurpation. Peaceful circulation has been interrupted by barbed wire and concrete blocks.

One recalls the order of the Czar in Pushkin's "Boris Godunov": "Take steps at this very hour that our frontiers be fenced in by barriers. . . . That not a single soul pass o'er the border, that not a hare be able to run or a crow to fly."

It is absurd to allege that we are threatening a war merely to prevent the Soviet Union and East Germany from signing a so-called "treaty" of peace. The Western Allies are not concerned with any paper arrangement the Soviets may wish to make with a regime of their own creation, on territory occupied by their own troops and governed by their own agents. No such action can affect either our rights or our responsibilities.

If there is a dangerous crisis in Berlin—and there is—it is because of threats against the vital interests and the deep commitments of the Western Powers, and the freedom of West Berlin. We cannot yield these interests. We cannot fail these commitments. We cannot surrender the freedom of these people for whom we are responsible. A "peace treaty" which carried with it the provisions which destroy the peace would be a fraud. A "free city" which was not genuinely free would suffocate freedom and would be an infamy.

For a city or a people to be truly free, they must have the secure right, without economic, political or police pressure, to make their own choice and to live their own lives. And as I have said before, if anyone doubts the extent to which our presence is desired by the people of West Berlin, we are ready to have that question submitted to a free vote in all Berlin and, if possible, among all the German people.

The elementary fact about this crisis is that it is unnecessary. The elementary tools for a peaceful settlement are to be found in the charter. Under its law, agreements are to be kept, unless changed by all those who made them. Established rights are to be respected. The political disposition of peoples should rest upon their own wishes, freely expressed in plebiscites or free elections. If there are legal problems, they can be solved by legal means. If there is a threat of force, it must be rejected. If there is desire for change, it must be a subject for negotiation and if there is negotiation, it must be rooted in mutual respect and concern for the rights of others.

The Western Powers have calmly resolved to defend, by whatever means are forced upon them, their obligations and their access to the free citizens of West Berlin and the self-determination of those citizens. This generation learned from bitter experience that either brandishing or yielding to threats can only lead to war. But firmness and reason can lead to the kind of peaceful solution in which my country profoundly believes.

We are committed to no rigid formula. We see no perfect solution. We recognize that troops and tanks can, for a time, keep a nation divided against its will, however unwise that policy may seem to us. But we believe a peaceful agreement is possible which protects the freedom of West Berlin and allied presence and access, while recognizing the historic and legitimate interests of others in assuring European security.

The possibilities of negotiation are now being explored; it is too early to report what the prospects may be. For our part, we would be glad to report at the appropriate time that a solution has been found. For there is no need for a crisis over Berlin, threatening the peace—and if those who created this crisis desire peace, there will be peace and freedom in Berlin.

x.

The events and decisions of the next ten months may well decide the fate of man for the next ten thousand years. There will be no avoiding those events. There will be no appeal from these decisions. And we in this hall shall be remembered either as part of the generation that turned this planet into a flaming funeral pyre or the generation that met its vow "to save succeeding generations from the scourge of war."

In the endeavor to meet that vow, I pledge you every effort this Nation possesses. I pledge you that we shall neither commit nor provoke aggression, that we shall neither flee nor invoke the threat of force, that we shall never negotiate out of fear, we shall never fear to negotiate.

Terror is not a new weapon. Throughout history it has been used by those who could not prevail, either by persuasion or example. But inevitably they fail, either because men are not afraid to die for a life worth living, or because the terrorists themselves came to realize that free men cannot be frightened by threats, and that aggression would meet its own response. And it is in the light of that history that every nation today should know, be he friend or foe, that the United States has both the will and the weapons to join free men in standing up to their responsibilities.

But I come here today to look across this world of threats to a world of peace. In that search we cannot expect any final triumph—for new problems will always arise. We cannot expect that all nations will adopt like systems—for conformity is the jailor of freedom, and the enemy of growth. Nor can we expect to reach our goal by contrivance, by fiat or even by the wishes of all.

But however close we sometimes seem to that dark and final abyss, let no man of peace and freedom despair. For he does not stand alone. If we all can persevere, if we can in every land and office look beyond our own shores and ambitions, then surely the age will dawn in which the strong are just and the weak secure and the peace preserved.

Ladies and gentlemen of this Assembly, the decision is ours. Never have the nations of the world had so much to lose, or so much to gain. Together we shall save our planet, or together we shall perish in its flames. Save it we can—and save it we must—and then shall we earn the eternal thanks of mankind and, as peacemakers, the eternal blessing of God.

NOTE: The President spoke at 11:30 a.m. His opening words "Mr. President" referred to Mongi Slim, President of the General Assembly and U.N. Representative from Tunisia.

388   Remarks in New York City Upon Signing Bill Establishing the U.S. Arms Control and Disarmament Agency. *September 26, 1961*

WITH THE SIGNING of H.R. 9118, there is created the United States Arms Control and Disarmament Agency. This act symbolizes the importance the United States places on arms control and disarmament in its foreign policy.

The creation for the first time by act of Congress of a special organization to deal with arms control and disarmament matters emphasizes the high priority that attaches to our efforts in this direction.

Our ultimate goal, as the act points out, is a world free from war and free from the dangers and burdens of armaments in which the use of force is subordinated to the rule of law and in which international adjustments to a changing world are achieved peacefully. It is a complex and difficult task to reconcile through negotiation the many security interests of all nations to achieve disarmament, but the establishment of this agency will provide new and better tools for this effort.

I am pleased and heartened by the bipartisan support this bill enjoyed in the Congress. The leaders of both political parties gave encouragement and assistance. The new agency brings renewed hope for agreement and progress in the critical battle for the survival of mankind.

I want to express my thanks to the Members of the Congress, particularly who are here, who were specially interested. I am extremely sorry that Senator Humphrey, who was a particularly vigorous proponent of this legislation for many years in the Senate, is obliged to remain in Washington. And I want to add a special word of thanks to Mr. McCloy, the disarmament adviser, who has given this entire matter his most constant attention.

I want to take this opportunity to announce that the Director of the United States Arms Control and Disarmament Agency, set up by this legislation, will be Mr. William Foster. He has been a consultant to Mr. McCloy in preparing the American plan which was submitted to the United Nations General Assembly yesterday, and he and a group have been working for many months, full time, on this most important assignment.

I think that Mr. Salinger can give, this afternoon, to any members of the press some of the biographical material. Mr. Foster has been a distinguished public servant for many years in the Congress as a most active and leading official in the Marshall Plan. He is a Republican, and I think his appointment indicates the bipartisan, national concern of both parties—and really, in a sense, all Americans—for this effort to disarm mankind with adequate safeguards.

So I want to express our appreciation to you, Mr. Foster, for taking on this assignment, and Mr. Salinger perhaps can fill in some of the details. Mr. Foster, as Director of this, has the rank of an Under Secretary of State, and his work will be most closely coordinated with the Secretary of State, with me and the White House, and with our representatives in the General Assembly.

NOTE: The President spoke at signing ceremonies at the Carlyle Hotel in New York City. During his remarks he referred to Hubert H. Humphrey, U.S. Senator from Minnesota; John J. McCloy, Adviser to the President on Disarmament; and Pierre E. G. Salinger, Press Secretary to the President.

As enacted, H.R. 9118 is Public Law 87–297 (85 Stat. 631).

389 Joint Statement Following Discussion With the President of Argentina. *September 26, 1961*

THE MEETING between the Presidents of the United States and of the Republic of Argentina was held in the spirit of deep friendship and mutual respect which unites the two countries and which finds this expression in the fruitful cooperation and close solidarity in ideals and aims that are common to the two nations.

On the basis of this spirit of understanding and common interest the two Presidents joined in conversation for four hours, during which time they considered subjects of the greatest relevance in the field of cooperation between the two countries—questions relating to political solidarity and the economic and social development of the American continent, as well as serious world problems.

This frank understanding has made it possible to reaffirm the deep and unchangeable identity of purpose of the two nations, which, being based on a common historic tradition, has reached an unprecedented level, thanks to the work and effort of the two governments.

President Frondizi expressed to President Kennedy the full adherence of Argentina to the untiring efforts on the part of the United States directed toward the maintenance of world peace, the preservation and broadening of the full exercise of freedom, representative democracy and the dignity of man, as well as toward the fuller development of

627

the economically underdeveloped countries. President Frondizi made especially clear to President Kennedy the extent to which Argentina looks favorably upon President Kennedy's effort to give United States international cooperation policies a dynamic, far reaching, realistic and effective content, which answers the pressing needs of the present serious situation.

President Kennedy, in turn, expressed to President Frondizi the importance that the United States gives to the firm and sincere adherence on the part of Argentina to those common ideals and aims which, being characteristic of Western civilization, are the intrinsic and inherent values of the two nations. At the same time President Kennedy reiterated his firm decision to cooperate with President Frondizi, in the latter's effort to consolidate, once and for all, effective democratic institutions in Argentina, and to speed up at an unprecedented rate, the economic development of his country. He expressed his assurance that these efforts contain a deep historic significance for this South American nation and constitute, by the same token, a decisive factor in the stabilization of democracy and the consolidation of social and economic progress in the entire Hemisphere.

President Frondizi informed President Kennedy of the progress attained by his country in transforming its economic structure and the solid foundation of a modern nation. He reiterated the gratitude of his government for the extensive aid received from the United States towards that end.

President Frondizi also explained his country's basic current problems and needs which require an immediate solution so that gains already achieved can be consolidated and national development can be carried out in a progressive manner. In this connec-

tion, he pointed out to President Kennedy the importance of United States cooperation, and emphasized the renewed determination derived from the formulation of the Alliance for Progress, as approved at Punta del Este.

President Kennedy reiterated to President Frondizi the terms of the declaration that was formulated at the White House on May 24 of this year. He stated that the present experience in Argentina constitutes an essential part of the Free World's effort to demonstrate, in a practical fashion, the capacity of the democratic countries to work for the rapid economic and social development while reaffirming human rights and denying those violent methods, which are inconsistent with the way of life of either country and which destroy human dignity and individual freedom.

For all these reasons, the government of the United States will continue to collaborate with the efforts of Argentina.

President Frondizi and President Kennedy discussed various aspects of the Argentina development plan which—in addition to projects already submitted for United States consideration—include the El Chocón-Los Colorados project, the modernization of the meat packing industry, development of the fishing industry, expansion of housing programs, and water development. The Presidents agreed that these programs were consistent with the basic aims of the Alliance for Progress. President Kennedy expressed his great admiration for the impressive efforts and sacrifices which Argentina has already made in order to speed up its economic and social development; and his recognition of the effort being made to mobilize domestic resources for future development. Therefore, President Kennedy welcomed the opportunity to reaffirm his government's firm commitment to assist the government of Argentina in its development program in order to help in bringing as rapidly as possible higher standards of living and increased social welfare to all the people of Argentina. He spoke of his government's intention to examine carefully the specific project applications for the above program and to consider them as rapidly as possible in view of their great importance for the people of Argentina.

President Kennedy was particularly impressed by the significance of the El Chocón-Complex project in view of its potential for the transformation of a vast region of the country. He noted that it was similar in concept to the highly successful TVA project in the United States.

President Kennedy stated that he would join with the Argentine government in seeking to expedite the completion of the survey of the project which is being undertaken by the Inter-American Development Bank. As sound plans are developed the United States government will consult with the Argentine government with respect to financing of the project. In this connection this large and important project, which can be of such widespread benefit for the Argentine people and which is receiving such a major impulse from the Argentine government, will clearly require for its successful execution the full cooperation of European countries as well as the United States government and major international financial institutions.

Among the problems of economic cooperation, special attention was given to those arriving at commercial interchange. There was full agreement concerning the need to continue joint efforts to promote the expansion of commerce between the two countries in which Argentina at present has an unfavorable balance. Likewise, it was agreed that it is necessary to press vigorously in international forums such as GATT to achieve our common purposes. This will require a more intense effort to reduce restrictions on international trade that are obstructing the expansion of commerce with other countries. The importance to both countries that the European regional agreements grant fair treatment to imports from third countries was noted in this connection.

The major issues in the present world political situation were thoroughly examined. During the exchange of views on problems such as the Berlin question, the resumption of nuclear tests, the maintenance of peace, the Cuban situation and other situations and threats emerging from the Cold War, the President of the United States and the President of Argentina evidenced agreement on fundamental goals and President Kennedy stressed during the discussion his awareness of the significance of the growing Argentine participation in world affairs.

The topics of political solidarity and economic cooperation in the American hemisphere received special attention. Both Presidents agreed as to the need for strengthening and revitalizing multi-lateral and bi-lateral machinery of the Inter-American system so as to guarantee, in a definitive manner, the prevalence of the principles of cooperation, the principle of non-intervention by foreign powers in the affairs of this hemisphere, the principle of self-determination and non-intervention, political solidarity, mutual respect, effective exercise of representative democracy and economic and social development in each and every one of the countries of this hemisphere.

NOTE: President Kennedy and President Frondizi met in the President's suite in the Carlyle Hotel, New York City. The joint statement was released at Newport, R.I.

390   Statement by the President on Making Additional Uranium-235 Available for Peaceful Uses. *September 26, 1961*

PROGRESS in using atomic energy for peaceful purposes is evident in the numerous national and international programs for scientific research and for the development of nuclear power and other applications. Many of the current projects and those contemplated for the future are based on the use of enriched uranium. I am announcing today a further step by the United States to meet the prospective needs for this material.

I have determined under Section 41–b of the Atomic Energy Act of 1954 that the amount of enriched uranium to be made available for peaceful uses at home and abroad will be increased to a total of 165,000 kilograms of contained Uranium-235. Of this total 100,000 kilograms is to be available for distribution within the United States under Section 53 of the Atomic Energy Act and 65,000 kilograms for distribution to other countries under Section 54. These amounts have been recommended by the Atomic Energy Commission with the concurrence of the Secretaries of State and Defense. The material will be distributed as required over a period of years and will be subject to prudent safeguards against unauthorized use.

This action increases the amounts of Uranium-235 made available by previous determination announced on February 22, 1956, and July 3, 1957. The new amounts are estimated to cover present commitments and those expected to be made during the next few years under domestic licenses and foreign agreements. The purpose of this announcement is to provide continuing assurance of the availability of enriched uranium for peaceful programs contemplated at home and abroad. As those programs develop in the future, it will undoubtedly be necessary to make further determinations to meet their requirements. The capacity of the United States for producing enriched uranium is sufficient to meet all foreseeable needs for peaceful uses in addition to our defense needs.

A discussion of the new determination is contained in the attached statement by the Chairman of the Atomic Energy Commission.

NOTE: The statement by the Chairman of the Atomic Energy Commission, Glenn T. Seaborg, was released with the President's statement at Newport, R.I.

For Presidential determinations of February 22, 1956, and July 3, 1957, see *Public Papers of the Presidents, Dwight D. Eisenhower, 1956* volume, p. 258, and *1957* volume, p. 528.

391   Statement by the President Upon Signing Bill Relating to Determining Gross Income From Mining in the Brick and Tile Industry. *September 26, 1961*

I HAVE TODAY approved H.R. 7057 entitled "An Act Relating to the determination of gross income from the property for taxable years prior to 1961 in the case of certain clays and shale which were used in the manufacture of certain clay products."

To determine the percentage depletion allowance, it is necessary to apply the percentage rate, determined by Congress, against the gross income from the mining property. H.R. 7057 provides, in the case of brick and tile clay, and shale used in making certain clay products, that the gross income from mining shall, at the election of the taxpayer, be equal to 50 percent of the total amount for which the manufactured products are sold during the year but not more than $12.50 per ton of clay or shale used in such manufactured products. This provision would apply retroactively to all taxable years beginning before January 1, 1961, which are not barred by the statute of limitations on the date of enactment of the bill. It has no application to taxable years beginning after December 31, 1960.

There is a basic policy against retroactive amendments to the tax laws. However, there may be circumstances in specific cases which justify departure from this well founded policy. The question of how gross income from mining is to be determined in the brick and tile industry has had a complex and involved history dating back to 1951 and culminating in 1960 when the Supreme Court decided in the *Cannelton* case that gross income from mining means the gross income attributable to the raw materials rather than the manufactured products. This history contains factors which, taken together, justify some measure of retroactive relief for the brick and tile industry from the full application of the principles set forth by the *Cannelton* decision. Although other methods of providing relief would have been appropriate, the

particular relief provided by the bill is not so questionable as to warrant withholding my approval.

I do not understand that the use in this bill of an arbitrary percentage of the sales price of the end product as gross income from mining constitutes acceptance by Congress of a principle that mineral depletion in general should be based on the value of the manufactured product. Moreover, the factors present in the record serve to distinguish the brick and tile industry from the various other mineral industries. Therefore, my approval of this bill should not be viewed as establishing a precedent for the enactment of similar legislation for other mineral industries. Nor does my decision indicate any willingness to approve retroactive legislation which is applicable to any particular industry unless very unusual circumstances exist. There are always pending before Congress a large number of retroactive measures which would create substantial administrative problems, loss of revenue, and discrimination between taxpayers. Therefore, approval of any one of these measures must be premised upon peculiar circumstances justifying departure from the fundamental policy against this special type of legislation.

NOTE: As enacted, H.R. 7057 is Public Law 87–312 (75 Stat. 674).

The statement was released at Newport, R.I.

---

392 Remarks in Newport Upon Announcing the Appointment of John McCone as Director of the Central Intelligence Agency. *September 27, 1961*

Admiral, Mr. Dulles, Mr. McCone:

I want to express, first, our appreciation to you, Admiral, for your hospitality this morning and that of the U.S. Navy.

I have just one announcement. I have asked Mr. John McCone to accept the responsibility of being the Director of the Central Intelligence Agency and Chairman of the Joint Intelligence Board, and have asked him to assume this responsibility later in the fall.

When Mr. Allen Dulles and I had our conversation last November, and when I asked him to continue on in his responsibility as Director of the Central Intelligence Agency, he agreed to do so for a year. He and I have been concerned this summer that this agency should continue to serve as an effective instrument of our country's policy, and we have been most anxious that we would secure the services of an experienced public servant, and that the transition which would be made this fall should be as smooth and effective as possible.

We are both extremely pleased and satisfied that Mr. John McCone, who has served his country in important positions of responsibility, as Under Secretary of the Air Force in the administration of President Truman, as Chairman of the Atomic Energy Commission in the administration of President Eisenhower, has agreed to once more come and accept a position of high responsibility.

He has had broad experience. Coming once again to Washington represents a real sacrifice for him. I know that all of us who are concerned with our present responsibilities are extremely happy to have his counsel, extremely happy to have him associated with us.

He will come in about 2 weeks and work with Mr. Dulles, and in November will assume the responsibility.

I would like to say one word about my very strong feelings of appreciation and regard for the present Director of the Central Intelligence Agency. He has a record almost unique, if not unique, in the history of this country. He has served under eight Presidents of the United States, beginning with President Wilson in World War I— Presidents of different parties, serving during different times with different problems. He has brought to their service on each occasion and in each administration a unique regard for the public interest.

I know of no man who is a more courageous, selfless, public servant than Mr. Allen Dulles, and I, therefore, in expressing pleasure at having secured the services of Mr. McCone, want to express my profound regret that at the age of 68, after 10 years in this responsibility, that Mr. Dulles should be retiring. He has agreed to continue to serve as a consultant to me on intelligence matters, and therefore his long experience will be available to the people of this country.

NOTE: The President spoke at the Naval War College, U.S. Naval Base, Newport, R.I. In his opening words he referred to Vice Admiral Bernard L. Austin, President of the College.

393   Letters to the Vice President Relating to His Trip to Sweden To Attend the Funeral of Dag Hammarskjold.
September 27, 1961

[Released September 27, 1961.   Dated September 26, 1961]

Dear Lyndon:

I am very grateful to you for undertaking to serve as my representative at the funeral of Dag Hammarskjold. I would have liked

to make this journey myself, and I am most grateful that you will act as the senior representative for the United States in my place. I am sure you will convey to the Hammarskjold family and to the appropriate officials of the Swedish government my own profound sympathy and respect of the American government and the American people.

Sincerely,

JOHN F. KENNEDY

Dear Lyndon:

I know that your trip to Sweden will perhaps be brief and that you might find it necessary to come back immediately after the Hammarskjold funeral because of previous engagements, but if circumstances make it possible I shall be glad if you can find time for a brief stop in Paris on your way back. There is much going on in our discussions with our major European allies and I shall be glad to have the advantage of your own account of discussions which you might have in Paris with our senior people there—men like Gavin, Finletter and General Norstad, if he has not already left to come back here for direct discussions in Washington.

Sincerely,

JOHN F. KENNEDY

NOTE: In the second letter the President referred to the American Ambassador to France, James M. Gavin; the U.S. Permanent Representative on the Council of NATO, Thomas K. Finletter; and the Supreme Commander of Allied Forces in Europe, General Lauris Norstad.

The letters were released at Newport, R.I.

394 Message to Governor General Azikiwe on the First Anniversary of the Independence of Nigeria. *October 2, 1961*

[Released October 2, 1961. Dated October 1, 1961]

Dear Governor General:

It gives me the greatest pleasure to extend to you and the people of Nigeria cordial greetings and heartfelt congratulations on the first anniversary of your country's independence.

This first year of your nationhood has been a highly auspicious one. It has seen Nigeria take its place with distinction among the family of free nations. It has seen the emergence of wise and far-reaching plans for the social and economic betterment of the Nigerian people. In essence, it has been a period in which firm foundations have been laid for the future of a great nation. The people of the United States join me in the hope that the peace and prosperity of this first year will continue and that the succeeding anniversaries of Nigeria's independence will be equally happy and fruitful.

Sincerely,

JOHN F. KENNEDY

[His Excellency, The Governor General, Dr. Nnamdi Azikiwe, Lagos, Nigeria]

NOTE: The message was released at Newport, R.I.

395 Remarks at the Swearing In of Fowler Hamilton as Administrator of the Agency for International Development. *October 3, 1961*

I WANT to express our great pleasure at participating in the swearing in of Mr. Fowler Hamilton to be the head of the new AID program. And it is a great pleasure to have the Justice join us in making this ceremony legal.

Mr. Hamilton assumes a major responsibility, and I am delighted that he has accepted it. Our hopes are very high for this Agency, and I think that his assumption of responsibility gets us off to a most promising start.

I am glad that the members of his family are here also.

NOTE: The President spoke in the Fish Room at the White House. In his opening remarks he referred to Justice Charles E. Whittaker, Associate Justice of the Supreme Court.

396 Memorandum of Disapproval of Bill Relating to Longevity Step Increases for Postal Employees. *October* 3, 1961

I AM withholding my approval from S. 1459, a bill "To amend the provisions of law relating to longevity step increases for postal employees."

While the supporters of this legislation are well-intentioned and its objectives sound—improvement of the within-grade provisions of the postal pay structure, and better correlation of these provisions with the related provisions affecting employees paid under the Classification Act—this bill does not achieve these objectives, despite its $60 million annual cost. Moreover, the Congress failed to provide—through enactment of the postal rate increases recommended by this Administration and its predecessor—the revenues necessary to cover the current postal deficit, much less a deficit

of even greater magnitude. Without new revenues this bill would increase the postal deficit to over 800 million dollars.

The classified and postal pay structures, including the longevity and within-grade provisions are in need of extensive revision, and will receive the sympathetic consideration of this Administration, with recommendations to be forthcoming at the next session of the Congress. The reforms needed are fundamental and sweeping and will require the most careful consideration by both the Executive Branch and the Congress. However, budgetary needs are too urgent to permit approval of this measure unattended by revenue increases, at this time.

JOHN F. KENNEDY

397 Remarks at a Luncheon Marking the Publication of the First Four Volumes of the Adams Papers. *October* 3, 1961

Mr. Wiggins, Mr. Butterfield, Dr. Boyd, Mr. Adams, distinguished guests, ladies and gentlemen:

First of all, I want to say to Mr. Adams, that it is a pleasure to live in your family's old house, and we hope that you will come by and see us.

I suppose a number of things attract us all here today. Some of us think it wise to associate as much as possible with historians

and cultivate their good will, though we always have the remedy which Winston Churchill once suggested in the House of Commons, when he prophesied during World War II that history would deal gently with us. And then in an afterword he said, "Because I intend to write it."

And then I think we like to be here because all of us as Americans are constantly bemused and astounded by this extraordinary golden age in our history which produced so many men of exceptional talent. I have not heard, nor I suppose is there a rational explanation for the fact that this small country, possessed of a very limited population, living under harsh circumstances, produced so many, many, many brilliant and extraordinary figures who set the tone for our national life and who really represent the most extraordinary outpouring of human ability devoted to government, really, than any time since the days of Greece. And any touch which we may have in our lives with that period attracts us all.

And then I think we are here because of our regard for the extraordinary record of the Adams family. I have in my office at the White House one of the few papers which got out of the hands of the Adamses, which is a report of a committee of the Congress which Mr. John Quincy Adams as Senator headed, which supported Thomas Jefferson's embargo which ruined Massachusetts commerce, and which cost John Quincy Adams his seat.

This tremendous devotion to the public interest, this vitality which goes from generation to generation down to the present is really the most exceptional scarlet thread which runs throughout the entire tapestry of American political life.

It is an interesting fact that Mr. Charles Francis Adams who was the Secretary of the Navy was also probably the best sailor that this country ever produced. This ability to do things well and to do them with precision and with modesty attracts us all. And therefore, as an honorary member of the Massachusetts Historical Society, I was delighted and proud of the fine speech made by our President, Mr. Adams, today.

Thomas Jefferson and Adams exchanged one bit of correspondence which I think is rather illuminating. In a letter to Jefferson

in 1815, Adams wrote: "Who shall write the history of the American Revolution? Who can write it? Who will ever be able to write it?" And Jefferson replied: "Nobody, except merely its external facts. All its councils, designs and discussions having been conducted by Congress with closed doors. . . . These, which are the life and soul of history must forever be unknown."

These books, these volumes, do something to open those doors. But I am impressed by the difficulty, even with these contemporary records of the Adamses, the Jeffersons, Madisons, Franklins, and all the others, of really getting to the historical truth. Even with the most complete reporting which we now have, even with the most accurate contemporary record which may be kept, I still am impressed, from personal experience as well as observation, with how difficult it ever is to feel that we've finally gotten to the "bone" of truth on any great historical controversy.

But this does open the doors. This does bring us closer to the tables where the record was written. And for this reason it serves as a most valuable chronicle of a long series of lives which stretch down to the present date. And therefore this formidable record of a formidable family deserves the kind of great editorial support which it's now receiving.

I have no doubt that Lyman Butterfield and Thomas Adams are breathing heavy sighs of relief—4 volumes out, and only 80 or 100 more to go. Obviously the worst is over.

In a different field, I sometimes feel that way myself, until I read the somber words of Mr. Wiggins in the morning papers and realize how far we have to go.

It is interesting that in John Adams' prepresidential days, he once wrote, "The Deliberations of the Congress are spun out to an immeasurable Length. There is so much Wit, Sense, Learning, Acuteness, Subtilty, Eloquence, etc., among fifty Gentlemen, each of whom has been habituated to lead and guide in his own Province, that an immensity of Time is spent unnecessarily." Which shows how times do change.

Reading about the Presidency in those days does bring us a certain nostalgia. John Adams used to spend every summer in Quincy, and during the undeclared war with Spain he spent a substantial time away from Washington. I suppose for one who has spent, in the words of the AP, 14 straight weekends at Hyannis Port, we should not be too critical. But it does indicate that there was a different and more satisfactory pace in those times.

I feel that the Adams family intimidates us all, and what it has been, their extraordinary contribution to the public service, I have examined with some care. It is a source of interest to me that this extraordinarily able group of public servants, President Adams and his son, were the only two Presidents of the United States who were not reelected during the first 50 years of our country's service. So when posterity gives them something better than reelection, it does present a heart-warming thing to some of us who face the hazards of public life. And I'm sure they would have felt that way, too.

I think the other quality which I find interesting in the Adamses is their constant dissatisfaction with their own record. John Adams' son, John Quincy Adams, could write after having been Minister to Holland and Russia, England—worked for us in France, taking part in the Treaty ending the War of 1812—he could still write in his diary, "Two-thirds of a long life have passed, and I have done nothing to distinguish it by usefulness to my country and to man-

kind." And in his 70th year, after having held more offices than any other American in the history of our country, he could pronounce his life a whole succession of disappointments. "I can scarcely recollect a single instance of success in anything that I ever undertook."

This high regard for his own position, his own qualities, which led him into constant frustration and disappointment that he could never achieve in his own mind the goal that he and his wife and his family had set for themselves, represents a most extraordinary prod, and I think explains the tremendous contribution which he and his successors have made to our country.

In a sense it was their self-love and self-esteem, rather than any synthetic sense of their inadequency, that made them work so hard, and yet made them all feel that they had failed to achieve what they were capable of and what the times demanded.

I think therefore that we can consider that they have bequeathed to us two extraordinary and important qualities: conscience, Puritan conscience, and courage—the courage of those who look to other days and other times.

A few days before John Adams in 1826 died, his fellow townsmen of Quincy asked him to send them a toast for the Fourth of July. His response was brief but comprehensive. His toast stands both for the Adamses and for America.

He recommended that the patriots of Quincy drink to a simple sentiment: independence forever.

I congratulate all those gentlemen who have labored so long to produce these volumes. I congratulate Dr. Boyd who was a pioneer in this field. I congratulate those Presidents of the United States who in recent days have been most concerned that effective, contemporary records be kept. I congratulate us—I congratulate this country— I congratulate us all—in being part of the legacy which President John Adams left to us.

Thank you.

NOTE: The luncheon, held at the Statler-Hilton Hotel in Washington, was sponsored by the Washington Post in honor of the publication of "The Adams Papers: Diary and Autobiography of John Adams" (Harvard University Press, 1961).

In his opening words the President referred to J. R. Wiggins, editor and executive vice president of the Washington Post; Lyman H. Butterfield, editor of the Adams Papers; Dr. Julian P. Boyd, editor of the Jefferson Papers; and Thomas B. Adams, president of the Massachusetts Historical Association and a great-great-great grandson of John Adams.

398   Statement by the President Upon Signing an Education Bill. *October 3, 1961*

IT IS with extreme reluctance that I am signing S. 2393, which extends for two years: (1) the National Defense Education Act of 1958 and (2) the expired provisions of Public Laws 815 and 874 of the 81st Congress, which provides Federal assistance to "Federally impacted" schools—districts furnishing free public education to children whose parents reside or work on Federal property, or whose presence due to other Federal activity causes a sudden and substantial increase in enrollment.

(1) The extension of the NDEA without the amendments submitted by this Administration merely continues the current program, without urgently needed improvements, for two more years—years which are crucial to the training of more teachers and the strengthening of this nation's teaching of science, mathematics, foreign language and other essential subjects. Particularly undesirable is the continuation of the discriminatory and ineffective non-Communist disclaimer affidavit. I hope the Congress can renew its consideration of these NDEA amendments next year, regardless of the new expiration date.

(2) Far more undesirable is the continuation for two more years of the current aid to impacted areas program, which gives more money to more schools for more years than either logic or economy can justify. This Administration recommended a reduction in the cost of this program, an increase in its eligibility requirements and local participation, its extension for only one year instead of two, and its eventual absorption in a general aid-to-education program. The rejection of all of these requests highlights the air of utter inconsistency which surrounds this program.

Communities which beseeched the Federal Government to maintain nearby installations, however uneconomical, now demand that the Federal Government rescue them from the fiscal burdens these installations allegedly create. School districts originally entitled to temporary Federal assistance, during a transition period in which the costs of these Federally connected children could be absorbed, now demand that the aid be continued indefinitely, without any reduction for absorption, and without regard to the local taxes paid by those parents who entered the community to work on, but not reside on, Federal property. Individuals who profess opposition to Federal aid to education on grounds of states rights, racial or religious controversy, budgetary economy or academic freedom do not hesitate to demand this Federal aid to build school houses and pay teachers' salaries in their own areas.

I am not unmindful of the problems this program is designed to meet: overcrowded and hazardous classrooms in communities whose financial resources are strained to educate these Federally connected children. But I believe that overcrowded and hazardous classrooms are undesirable anywhere, whether filled by the children of Federal employees or by the children of other Federal taxpayers, and whether the local resources are strained by the location of a Federal facility or by any other cause. A quality education is a necessity for all American children, not merely those who by good fortune live in a district covered by this program.

It ill becomes those who insist that we cannot afford the expenditure of Federal funds to aid the public education of all children, to insist with equal fervor upon the passage of this unsound and uneconomical measure which aids the education of only some.

The Department of Health, Education and Welfare advises me that a refusal to ex-

tend this program at this time, thus deferring action until the next session of the Congress, would jeopardize the entire educational effort of a substantial number of school districts dependent in large measure on these funds, and unable to find substitute sources of revenue in time to meet current outlays. Many districts are legitimately in need of this aid in order to educate a substantial majority of their students whose parents both reside and work on tax-exempt Federal property. A veto would not distinguish between those properly entitled to this assistance and those who should be making more of an effort locally. I am therefore signing this bill. But the need to improve the standards of education in this country will still be before the Congress next year; and that need must be met on a basis which, for every dollar spent, goes much further to attack our most critical deficiencies than the measure I am required to approve today.

NOTE: As enacted, S. 2393 is Public Law 87–344 (75 Stat. 759).

399 Statement by the President Upon Signing Bill Creating the Woodrow Wilson Memorial Commission. *October 4, 1961*

I HAVE a short statement I would like to make, that I am happy to have the opportunity to sign this bill establishing the Woodrow Wilson Memorial Commission— and I am particularly happy to have the privilege of doing so in the presence of Mrs. Wilson and the members of the Wilson family, and with Senator Williams who has been responsible for this legislation in the Senate.

We have a continuing commitment, in the words of President Wilson, to the service of humanity. His life, his actions, and his ideals serve as an inspiration today to the

achievement of the goals that he articulated so well more than 40 years ago.

I hope the Commission will plan a memorial that expresses the faith in democracy and President Wilson's vision of peace and a dedication to international understanding that President Wilson himself did so much to advance.

He called for a New Freedom at home, and a world of unity and peace, and we are still striving to achieve these objectives. "Democratic institutions are never done," he once wrote, "they are, like the living tissue, always a-making. It is a strenuous thing, this of living the life of a free people; and we cannot escape the burden of our inheritance."

It is therefore most appropriate that this Commission is established, whose function it will be to formulate the plans for the design and construction and the location of a permanent memorial to Woodrow Wilson in Washington, D.C., or this immediate area.

NOTE: The joint resolution creating the Woodrow Wilson Memorial Commission is Public Law 87–364 (75 Stat. 783).

During his remarks the President referred to Harrison A. Williams, Jr., U.S. Senator from New Jersey.

400   Statement by the President Upon Signing Bill Governing Recruitment of Mexican Agricultural Workers. *October* 4, 1961

I HAVE signed H.R. 2010, legislation governing recruitment of agricultural workers from the Republic of Mexico. I have done so despite the failure to include in the legislation provisions which I believe necessary to protect domestic farm workers.

Studies of the operation of the Mexican labor program have clearly established that it is adversely affecting the wages, working conditions and employment opportunities of our own agricultural workers, large numbers of whom are unemployed or underemployed. The workers most seriously affected are from those underprivileged groups which are already at the bottom of our economic scale; the conditions under which these people work and live are a matter of grave concern to me.

The Secretary of Labor, on the basis of the studies that have been made of the Mexican labor program, proposed amendments to Title V of the Agricultural Act of 1949 designed to provide needed safeguards for our workers and to prescribe more specific standards. While the enactment includes some of these safeguards, a number of the more significant ones have been omitted.

I am aware, however, that some Mexican workers will still be needed next year, in some areas, to supplement our agricultural labor force. I am also aware of the serious impact in Mexico if many thousands of workers employed in this country were summarily deprived of this much-needed employment. These considerations impel me to sign H.R. 2010 despite its shortcomings.

Present law, however, provides broad authority to regulate the conditions under which Mexican workers are to be employed. In particular, existing law authorizes, and indeed requires, the Secretary of Labor to permit the employment of Mexican workers only when he can determine that their admission will not adversely affect the wages and working conditions of domestic agricultural workers. This comprehensive, general authority was not changed by H.R. 2010 and its availability was clearly recognized during the legislative consideration of the bill.

The adverse effect of the Mexican farm labor program as it has operated in recent years on the wage and employment conditions of domestic workers is clear and is cumulative in its impact. We cannot afford to disregard it. We do not condone it. Therefore I sign this bill with the assurance that the Secretary of Labor will, by every means at his disposal, use the authority vested in him under the law to prescribe the standards and to make the determinations essential for the protection of the wages and working conditions of domestic agricultural workers.

NOTE: As enacted, H.R. 2010 is Public Law 87–345 (75 Stat. 761).

401 Statement by the President Upon Signing Bill Amending the Shipping Act. *October 4, 1961*

I HAVE signed H.R. 6775, "An Act to amend the Shipping Act, 1916, as amended, to authorize ocean common carriers and conferences thereof serving the foreign commerce of the United States to enter into effective dual rate contracts with shippers and consignees, and for other purposes."

The bill is designed to accomplish two necessary and important objectives. First, it legalizes, subject to several limitations, the use of so-called "dual rate" systems, whereby a common carrier, or conference of common carriers, in foreign commerce give a rate reduction of up to 15 percent to shippers or consignees who agree to give all or any fixed portion of their patronage to such carrier or conference. Secondly, it provides for advance filing of rate increases and otherwise buttresses and enlarges the Commission's regulatory responsibilities over common carriers by water in the foreign commerce of the United States.

The safeguards established in the legis-

lation to protect shippers and carriers against any abuses that might arise from agreements made under the authority of this bill will be fully enforced. The bill requires the Federal Maritime Commission to disapprove conference agreements it finds unjustly discriminatory, detrimental to the United States commerce, contrary to the public interest or in violation of the Shipping Act of 1916. These standards will permit the Maritime Commission to insure the continuing competition and service among carriers without undue prejudice to those operating independently of the conference. If experience under the law demonstrates that additional protection or additional regulatory authority is necessary, it will be requested. In the meantime, I am requesting the Federal Maritime Commission to keep the subject matter under continuing consideration.

NOTE: As enacted, H.R. 6775 is Public Law 87–346 (75 Stat. 762).

402 Remarks of Welcome to President Abboud of the Republic of the Sudan at Andrews Air Force Base. *October 4, 1961*

Mr. President, members of your party, ladies and gentlemen:

I wish to express on behalf of the people of the United States our great satisfaction in welcoming you to our country.

This is the first occasion in the history of the Sudan that a leader of your country has

come to visit the United States and we're particularly glad that this should happen in this most significant year of 1961.

Your flag, like the flag of the United States, tells us a good deal about your country. The blue for the Nile River, the yellow for the desert, the green for what you have been able to do with the combination of the desert and the Nile.

We welcome you also because you have set an example of a country with eight neighbors, all of whom live at peace with you and with each other. You have set a standard for your continent and indeed in that sense for the world.

So, Mr. President, we welcome you to Washington. We are extremely happy that you will visit the United States, that you will see something of our country and something of our people. We are a young country. You are the leader of a country which is even younger, but in a very real sense is perhaps the oldest part of the known world.

So for many reasons, Mr. President, we welcome you here. We value the fact that you have chosen to visit us. We want you to know that your Ministers and yourself will be most welcome, and we hope that when you depart you will carry with you a very real appreciation of the warm feeling of friendship that our country feels for yours.

NOTE: President Abboud responded (through an interpreter) as follows:

Mr. President John F. Kennedy, President of the United States of America:

At this moment when we begin our visit to your great country to make direct contact with your friendly nation, we feel overwhelmed by a deep sense of joy and happiness. This joy is derived from your bright history and on behalf of the Sudan I present to you and to the great American Nation our most sincere congratulations on the occasion of the 183rd anniversary of the memorable Valley Forge—that great event which marked a chapter in the book of heroism and the gospel of principles written by your great Revolution under that outstanding leader, George Washington. Then they scored the first victory for the cause of independence and freedom. Your people presented this historical achievement to the world, that inspired and still inspires many nations for all these years to follow suit and be guided by its principles.

It is a good omen, Mr. President, that our visit to the United States of America coincides with this dear occasion to you and to me. It enables us to couple our congratulations to you and to the American people with our sincere thanks and appreciation for your kind invitation which we were so fortunate to be able to accept on behalf of the Sudan. This invitation will further strengthen our friendship and cooperation. We shall always remember that you and the American people have readily shown to the Sudan, even before they achieved independence, sincere friendship and fraternity by sending missions of good will, by supporting our candidacy for membership in the United Nations, of cooperation between the two nations on an exemplary and disinterested basis.

I have no doubt that this visit which we make on behalf of the Sudan will remain as a landmark in the history of our relations. The warm reception accorded me by you, Mr. President, and by the honorable members of your administration, demonstrates once more those kind feelings and sincere friendship extended towards the Sudan.

Indeed, this visit will be of great significance because it came at a time when many nations, particularly Africans, have achieved independence and become full members of the international family. They have awakened to shoulder their responsibilities for the welfare of their people within a happy and peaceful world.

For all these considerations, Mr. President, we are happy to be able to accept your kind invitation, which is a good example of cooperation between members of the international family and the establishment of close relations on the basis of mutual respect and confidence, especially during this troubled period of human history.

It gives me great pleasure, Mr. President, to convey to you and to the great American people on this occasion a message from the Sudanese people, a message of good will and true friendship stemming out of the genuine desire to further these friendly relations and strengthen them on the basis on which they started: mutual confidence and respect for the interests of our countries and the world at large.

In spite of the long distances that separate our two countries, we have many things in common. The system of government derived from the principles of your Revolution and our Revolution. We now devote our efforts to establish a system of our own, based on our traditions and aiming at the fulfillment of the wishes of our people for freedom and social justice in the true Sudanese pattern—again similar to the situation of your great country in the American continent. The Sudan stretches from the Arab world into the heart of Africa and is adjacent to no less than eight countries. We are fully aware that this situation imposes on us the declaration and application of a clearly cut policy based on sincerity and cooperation inside as well as outside the continent—that we have to stand for eradication of what remains of foreign domination and for developing the economic and social life of the Africans.

Thus we safeguard freedom in Africa, and hence the peace of the world. In this spirit, which we feel is shared by the American people, we look forward, Mr. President, to the forthcoming meetings. I am confident from what we already know of your personal courage and frankness that our deliberations will have far-reaching results in the fulfillment of the objectives of our two nations, and in strengthening world peace and prosperity.

Finally, to the captain and crew of this magnificent and efficient aircraft which the President has so kindly placed under our disposal, as an indication of honoring the Sudan, in my person, to them I wish to express my deep thanks and appreciation for all that they have done to make the journey most comfortable.

I wish also to congratulate them for the confidence of their people in charging them with the history-making feat, the landing of the first Boeing 707 at Khartoum Airport, a feat which in fact they have performed with distinguished success.

Thank you.

403 Statement by the President on Establishing the President's Commission on Campaign Costs. *October 4, 1961*

ELECTION of the President of the United States is the supreme test of the democratic process in this country. Because the duly nominated candidates of both our national parties must campaign throughout the country, carrying their views to all the nation's voters, there are great financial burdens in conducting Presidential campaigns. To have Presidential candidates dependent on large financial contributions of those with special interests is highly undesirable, especially in these days when the public interest requires basic decisions so essential to our national security and survival. The financial base of our Presidential campaigns must be broadened.

Among the services which must be paid for are staff assistance, transportation and communication facilities, radio and television time. Under present circumstances these items are enormously expensive, and thus the ability of candidates to carry on campaigns is, in large measure, governed by their success as fund raisers.

Traditionally, the funds for national campaigns have been supplied entirely by private contributions, with the candidates forced to depend in the main on large sums from a relatively small number of contributors. It

is not healthy for the democratic process—or for ethical standards in our government—to keep our national candidates in this condition of dependence. I have long thought that we must either provide a Federal share in campaign costs, or reduce the cost of campaign services, or both.

My Commission on Campaign Costs will take a fresh look at this problem, and will make such recommendations as it deems appropriate, looking toward proposals for the next session of Congress.

A Federal share in Presidential campaign costs has been under public discussion for a great many years. President Theodore Roosevelt was among the first to propose that Presidential campaigns be assisted by the government. Comparable proposals have been advocated subsequently by private citizens and by Members of the Congress, notably by the late Senator Neuberger of Oregon. Several such proposals are contained in bills pending in the current Congress. I am asking the Commission to inform itself on all of these as it conducts its study. In addition, I am asking the Commission to examine programs actually employed by the Commonwealth of Puerto Rico and by several democratic countries overseas in which governments participate in financing political campaigns.   Finally, I expect that the Commission will consider a variety of other measures used in this country and elsewhere for facilitating campaigns, among them the permissive legislation which made possible last year's television debates without cost to the candidates.

As I made plain in a press conference last May, I regard the inquiry to be undertaken by this Commission as a matter of great importance.   I am grateful to the distinguished members of the Commission for their willingness to serve.   I look forward to the results of their inquiry.

NOTE: The statement was issued as part of a White House release announcing that the President had named Alexander Heard, Dean of the Graduate School at the University of North Carolina, to serve as Chairman of the Commission on Campaign Costs. Other members of the Commission were listed in the release as follows: V. O. Key, Cambridge, Mass., Professor of Government, Harvard University; Dan Kimball, Los Angeles, Calif., President, Aerojet-General Corporation, former Secretary of the Navy; Malcolm Moos, New York City, Adviser to the Rockefeller Brothers on Public Affairs, Professor of Political Science, Johns Hopkins University, former Administrative Assistant to President Eisenhower; Paul Porter, Washington, D.C., member of law firm of Arnold, Porter, and Fortas, former Chairman, Federal Communications Commission; Neil Staebler, Ann Arbor, Mich., small businessman, Democratic National Committeeman from Michigan, former Chairman, Michigan Democratic State Central Committee; Walter Thayer, New York City, President, New York Herald-Tribune, former Chairman, United Republican Finance Committee of New York, National Finance Chairman of Volunteers for Nixon-Lodge; John Vorys, Columbus, Ohio, member of law firm of Vorys, Sater, Seymour and Pease, former Member of the United States House of Representatives; James Worthy, Chicago, Ill., President, Republican Citizens of Illinois, former President, United Republican Fund of Illinois, former Assistant Secretary of Commerce in the Eisenhower Administration, former Vice President, Sears Roebuck and Company.

On November 9 the White House announced that the members of the Commission had met with the President, and that the President had asked the Commission to report to him not later than April 30, 1962.   The release also stated that Dr. Herbert E. Alexander, Director of the Citizens Research Foundation, Princeton, N.J., would serve as the Commission's Executive Director.

404   Toasts of the President and President Abboud.
October 4, 1961

SPEAKING on behalf of all of us here, and also on behalf of all of our countrymen, Mr. President, I want to express the welcome of the oldest of the Republics and the youngest of the people to the youngest of the Republics and the oldest of the people.

It is a source of interest to those of us who are the beneficiaries of the Anglo-American system of culture, that on the day that you left your country there was buried the grandson of the Mahdi who led the charge against Winston Churchill as a young man in your country, about 30 miles from Khartoum—many Americans' only connection with your country.

But I think that your visit here, and the visit of your Ministers, is a most important event for us.   You occupy—your country—a most significant geographic position in Africa, a continent which has been relatively unknown to most of us in this country in the last decade, and which we have now come to realize is a most vital area of the world.   And therefore, Mr. President, it is a great pleasure to welcome you here, and in welcoming you here to indicate to our people and indeed to the whole Western World the significance of your country, the willingness of your country to bear the burdens which go with sovereignty, with independence, and also your willingness to bear the responsibilities which go with leadership in your continent.

I have not been to your country, but I have been impressed by the fact that one of our most distinguished predecessors came to your capital, Theodore Roosevelt—whose picture hangs outside—who said, "I speak of Africa and golden joys. It is the strong attraction of silent places, the wide, vast spaces of the earth, unmourned of man and changed only by the slow change of ages through time everlasting."

The only other time that Theodore Roosevelt ever got so excited was when he visited the Western United States. Therefore, Mr. President, I think he would have gotten as excited by visiting the Western United States today and by visiting your country today, to see a new country, newly independent, playing in the year 1961—the spring of 1961 and the winter of 1961 especially—a most significant role in the maintenance of freedom in your continent, and the maintenace of freedom throughout the world.

Therefore, I hope that all of you here who are my fellow countrymen will drink to the country, and most particularly to the President, who has demonstrated in difficult times the courage and reliance and character of the people of the Sudan, the people of Africa.

Ladies and gentlemen, the President of the Republic of the Sudan.

NOTE: The President proposed this toast at a state dinner at the White House. President Abboud responded (through an interpreter) as follows:

Mr. President and Mrs. Kennedy:

During these pleasant hours in the White House, which I feel is both a historic shrine and very much a home to which Mrs. Kennedy has added so much, I have felt the presence of such great men as Adams, Jefferson, Madison and others who put their names to your Declaration of Independence—of Lincoln, whose spirit still shines as a beacon light of compassion to all those throughout the world who cherish freedom and strive to realize it—of Jackson, Wilson, and of all the great men who have occupied this Mansion, some of whom were, like myself, soldiers. Perhaps it is not too much to suggest that with the present occupant, there may be starting a new tradition of distinguished service in Naval uniform prior to occupancy of the Executive Mansion.

It is my warm wish that one day you, Mr. President, and Mrs. Kennedy may sense the antiquity which is also felt in our capital city of Khartoum where the White Nile and the Blue Nile meet to form the river which gave rise to our civilization.

I would like to suggest that our host has demonstrated not alone the courage of action in uniform, but the courage of principle in his valorous adherence to the cause of individual freedom and national sovereignty. Not only since he was elected to the Presidency, but in his years in the Congress where he consistently displayed an interest in the emerging nations. Not only in his adherence to principle, but in his specific contributions as Chairman of the African Affairs Subcommittee of the Senate Foreign Relations Committee.

I would like to say that in recognizing the sincerity of purpose of those nations which like my own honestly feel that they must look first to their own struggle at home against poverty and social injustice as their contribution to international stability, President Kennedy has opened a New Frontier in foreign policy which bespeaks the very highest order of courage on his part, and on the part of your great nation.

405 Statement by the President Announcing Further Progress in the Voluntary Desegregation of Schools. *October 5, 1961*

FOR THE third time this fall I have the good fortune to call the attention of the nation to the progress which is being made in the peaceful and voluntary desegregation of our schools in compliance with the mandate of the Constitution.

This week, after months of work by the school board and other officials in Memphis,

Tennessee, four schools in that city were peacefully desegregated in compliance with the law and without disorder. This was again the fruit of mutual respect and cooperation by the leaders of both races and by public and forthright support by the Mayor, the Commissioner of Police, business leaders, and other citizens for the action of the Memphis School Board.

In New Orleans last month, following the developments in Atlanta, Dallas, Little Rock and many other cities in the South, there was a new demonstration by the people of that city of their respect for law and of their acceptance of the necessity and wisdom of orderly compliance with the command of the law.

The way in which our citizens are meeting their responsibilities under the law in Memphis, New Orleans and elsewhere reflects credit on the United States throughout the world.

406   Statement by the President Upon Signing the Community Health Services and Facilities Act.   *October 5, 1961*

IN MY Health Message to Congress, I called for Federal action to help communities develop organized out-of-hospital health services and expand health care facilities, particularly for the care of the chronically ill and aged. The bill I have just signed—the Community Health Services and Facilities Act of 1961—is a strong, affirmative response by the Congress to this request.

The bill authorizes special project grants to develop improved methods of providing out-of-hospital care so that many aged people and chronically ill patients can be spared the high cost of hospital care and can spend more time with their families. It authorizes increased Federal aid in the construction of health research facilities. It steps up support for research on the construction and equipment design of hospitals in a search for ways to improve services and cut costs. It encourages, by Federal grants, the construction of nursing homes to help relieve the existing shortage of these facilities. It will help place the best available knowledge in public health methods and new research knowledge in health care at the disposal of communities by increasing Federal assistance to State and local public health services.

Effective public health measures and medical care depend, in the last analysis, on action at the community level. This legislation will provide stimulation for improvement in local organized health services and facilities for home, nursing home, and hospital care, and particularly care for the aged. It will help to meet the objective of making quality health care available on an economical basis. I hope the State and community leaders and members of the health professions will take immediate advantage of the new opportunities provided by this legislation.

NOTE: The Community Health Services and Facilities Act of 1961 is Public Law 87–395 (75 Stat. 824).

407 Letters to Mayor Wagner and to Robert Moses Concerning the New York World's Fair. *October 5, 1961*

Dear Mayor Wagner:

I appreciated having your letter of September 29 and to learn of the excellent progress being made in preparation for the New York World's Fair of 1964–65. Pledges of participation on the part of 64 nations is indeed gratifying. I am fully aware of your own personal interest and efforts on behalf of a fair which will do credit not only to New York City but to the Nation.

As you know, the Congress has considered legislation in the last session which would authorize studies as to the nature and extent of participation in the New York World's Fair by the Federal Government. Both the Secretary of State and the Secretary of Commerce supported this legislation before the Committees of Congress. In anticipation of favorable action on this legislation I transmitted to the Congress an appropriation request to make a thorough study of this matter. I know that the Congress will give this matter its fullest consideration at the next session.

A fair of the magnitude and character which you have planned has great potential for promoting international good will and understanding and should do much to promote additional travel from foreign countries. These are objectives in which both the City of New York and the Federal Government can join.

Best wishes.

Sincerely,

JOHN F. KENNEDY

[Honorable Robert F. Wagner, Mayor of New York, New York, New York]

Dear Mr. Moses:

I have written the Mayor assuring him of my support of the World's Fair, which under your direction and leadership will be, I am sure, most successful. You can be certain of my continued interest and the support of the Administration.

I hope to be with you at the ribbon cutting.

Sincerely,

JOHN F. KENNEDY

[Mr. Robert Moses, President, New York World's Fair 1964–65 Corporation, Administration Building, World's Fair, Flushing, New York]

408 Letter of Commendation to John J. McCloy, Adviser to the President on Disarmament. *October 6, 1961*

Dear Mr. McCloy:

I would like to extend my hearty thanks to you for the work you have done as my Adviser on disarmament and arms control. You have made a notable contribution to the country and to the world in this most important area.

Through your service the Government has been able to table at Geneva a workable, effective and understandable draft treaty for the banning of nuclear weapons tests.

In the field of general disarmament, your discussions with Mr. Zorin concerning the principles which should guide future disarmament negotiations have cleared away many of the misunderstandings and misconceptions which have clouded this difficult subject.

At the same time, your development of the United States Program for General and

Complete Disarmament in a Peaceful World has set forth clearly the proposals of the United States for an effective disarmament agreement with the Soviet Union and other countries.

You have also performed a valuable service in connection with the establishment of a permanent agency of the Government to deal with the problems of disarmament and arms control. After giving this matter the most thorough consideration, you arrived at a recommendation with respect to the organization of the Government in the field of arms control and disarmament which I transmitted to the Congress. The substantial majority by which the Congress has recently enacted the Arms Control and Disarmament Act is a tribute to the soundness of your recommendations and the diligence and persuasiveness with which you presented them to the Congress.

In all of these steps you have assisted in clarifying the position of the United States as a country which is seeking realistic, mutually balanced and beneficial steps to reduce

the dangers of war and to obtain the kind of disarmed world we all prefer. These tasks have been carried out at a time when the intransigence of others, especially on the issue of control over nuclear testing, has brought disappointment to the world. But we must not be discouraged, and I am confident that in the longer view what you have done will be recorded as a major contribution to the great task of achieving disarmament.

In expressing my thanks, I know I am expressing the thanks of our country also. I am very glad that we shall continue to have the benefit of your advice in this most important field.

Sincerely,

JOHN F. KENNEDY

NOTE: The President wrote in response to a letter from Mr. McCloy, dated October 6, reporting on his special mission and transmitting a series of papers relating to U.S. activities in the field of disarmament. Mr. McCloy's letter and the related papers were released with the President's reply. They are published in the Department of State Bulletin (vol. 45, pp. 763 et seq., 589 et seq., 650).

409   Message to President Paz Estenssoro of Bolivia Concerning U.S. Disposal of Tin. *October 6, 1961*

Excellency:

I wish to acknowledge your telegram of September 16, 1961, expressing your serious concern at the announcement that the United States Government had requested the Congress to grant authority to dispose of a part of its stockpile of tin.

Please be assured that my Government retains a deep interest and concern in the rapid development of the Bolivian nation and the economic and social progress of the Bolivian people. We are committed to assist you in carrying forward the historic aims of the Bolivian revolution; and we

intend to continue to fulfill that commitment. I assure you that we will not take any action—in regard to tin or any other matter—which will tend to frustrate our mutual goal of a better life for the people of Bolivia.

We fully understand the great importance of tin to the Bolivian economy. Even now we are engaged in an effort of unparalleled vigor and dimension to help modernize your tin mines and increase their productivity. You can be sure, therefore, that we will sell no tin from our stockpile without first consulting with your government and the governments of other tin producing nations. In this way we can help ensure that the interests of all nations are protected.

The course of action which we have suggested is the sale of small lots of tin over a period of several years. This tin would come from the 50,000 tons which we now have in excess of our strategic requirements. We do not intend to depress the price of tin through these sales; they would be initiated at a time of world-wide shortage and would have the effect of discouraging tin consumers from substituting other materials for their normal tin consumption. In this way we can protect the long-run stability and continued prosperity of the tin market.

We have consulted continuously with officials of your government concerning this problem and such consultations will continue. We hope to work with Bolivia toward a long-term solution to the problem of tin prices. It is to further this aim that we are now studying the terms of our accession to the International Tin Agreement to which Bolivia belongs and which the United States has not previously joined.

I have taken, from the very beginning of my Administration, a deep personal interest in the development of Bolivia and in your own heroic efforts to raise the standard of living of the Bolivian people. It was this interest which led to our early exchange of letters, the sending of a special economic mission to Bolivia, the conclusion of several economic aid agreements including the Triangular Operation for the rehabilitation of COMIBOL, and the stationing of a special economic representative in your country. Therefore, I am certain that our proposal to dispose of small lots of tin over several years, only after prior consultation with your government, will not be counter to the interests of Bolivia or inconsistent with the abiding friendship of our two peoples.

With warmest personal regards,

JOHN F. KENNEDY

NOTE: President Paz Estenssoro's telegram of September 16, 1961, is published in the Department of State Bulletin (vol. 45, p. 773).

410   Letter to the Members of the Committee on Civil Defense of the Governors' Conference.   *October 6, 1961*

Gentlemen:

I was gratified to learn of the productive meeting of the Committee on Civil Defense of the Governors' Conference on September 17 in the Pentagon. The basis was well laid for continuing and close cooperation between your committee and all of us concerned with the federal civil defense program.

There is need for a nationwide understanding of what each level of government, each private organization and each citizen can do to bring about and maintain the best attainable protection for the civilian population against the major effects of a thermo-nuclear attack. Information is in preparation which I will use to inform the American people on what individuals should know and can do for their own protection. In the meantime, your committee may wish to inform the Governors of the goal towards which the Federal Government, the state governments, industry and other institutions in the United States should work.

In simple terms, this goal is to reach for fallout protection for every American as rapidly as possible. Radioactive fallout, extending down-wind for as much as several hundred miles, could account for the major part of the casualties which might result from a thermonuclear attack on an unprotected population. Protection against this threat is within reach of an informed America willing to face the facts and act.

The Federal Government is moving forward to bring into operation fallout shelter space for large groups of people under very austere conditions. Many homeowners, communities and business firms can and will provide more adequate and better located shelter space for their own needs. The Federal Government is backing this effort with a massive dissemination of technical information. In addition, we will inform those who cannot afford costly structures on low-cost methods of improvising shielding against fallout radiation. The people of this country will be urged, by me, by the Governors and by other leaders to do what is within their means.

The state governments have a vital role to play in accelerating attainment of the goal of full fallout protection. Shelter can be provided in new construction of state and local public buildings. State and municipal laws and ordinances can be adapted to encourage private initiative in this effort. State and local leadership in organizing people to prepare, and communities to cooperate, during and immediately after an attack is a cornerstone of any successful civil defense effort.

I look forward to the closest cooperation between all levels of government in the United States to move rapidly towards this goal. Your committee is making a major contribution in stimulating participation by the state governments in the nationwide civil defense effort.

Sincerely,

JOHN F. KENNEDY

NOTE: The letter was read by Stewart Pittman, Assistant Secretary of Defense for Civil Defense, at a meeting of State Civil Defense Directors held at the Sheraton Park Hotel in Washington at 1 p.m.

---

411   Joint Statement Following Discussions With President Abboud of the Sudan. *October 6, 1961*

PRESIDENT Abboud and President Kennedy have had a most cordial exchange of views on a variety of subjects of interest to the Sudan and to the United States. Their talks revealed that the two Presidents shared a common concern for the preservation of world peace, and a common reliance on the United Nations as the most effective instrument for maintaining peace.

The two Presidents considered that the current international situation underscored the importance of reaching through negotiation mutually acceptable solutions to existing disputes, especially when moral issues are involved, such as the right of self-determination, which belongs to the peoples of every continent. President Abboud stressed the importance of rapidly implementing the right of self-determination throughout the African continent. President Kennedy expressed satisfaction with the political gains which had been achieved by the African peoples and confirmed his hopes and expectations for further progress to this end.

President Abboud explained that the policy of non-alignment followed by the Republic of the Sudan was designed to strengthen and consolidate the independence of the Sudan and to enable it to play a constructive role in the resolution of situations which are sources of international tensions. President Kennedy confirmed that the

649

United States fully endorsed the determination of the newly-independent countries of Africa to maintain their independence. He noted that the support given by the Sudan to the mission of the United Nations in the Congo had contributed to an important extent to the maintenance of that country's independence and territorial integrity.

President Kennedy drew attention to the courageous struggle of the people of West Berlin to preserve their independence and to the determination of the United States to support them in their efforts to live in peace and freedom. President Abboud confirmed that the Republic of the Sudan also attached great importance to a peaceful resolution of the Berlin question on terms which are consistent with the legitimate expectations of the people of Berlin and of the German people as a whole.

The two Presidents were in complete agreement as to the importance of the early conclusion of a nuclear test ban agreement based on an effective system of inspection and control. They also agreed that efforts should be continued in the field of general

disarmament with a view to reducing international tensions and the increased application of the resources of the world to the task of economic and social development.

President Abboud explained to President Kennedy the steps the Sudan was taking to promote economic development and social justice. He confirmed the Sudan's intentions to mobilize its human and material resources in accordance with an integrated national plan to be executed by a planning organization with the requisite authority, and outlined the steps the Sudan was taking to achieve this goal.

The two Presidents agreed that talks would continue between their advisers with respect to expanding and expediting their cooperation in key areas in which the United States can most effectively assist the self-help efforts of the Republic of the Sudan.

President Abboud extended to President and Mrs. Kennedy a cordial invitation to visit the Sudan. President Kennedy said that he and Mrs. Kennedy look forward to such a visit whenever his presidential duties permit.

---

412 Message to President Chiang Kai-shek on the 50th Anniversary of the Chinese Revolution. *October 9, 1961*

[Released October 9, 1961. Dated October 5, 1961]

Your Excellency:

The people of the United States join me in offering congratulations on China's National Day which this year marks the 50th Anniversary of the Chinese Revolution. On this occasion we recall vividly the long, arduous struggle Free China has waged under your valiant leadership against foreign aggression and Communist tyranny and for the realization of the noble aspirations of Dr. Sun Yat-Sen. Our alliance, based on ties of historic friendship and unity of pur-

pose, has withstood the tests of the past. May it grow ever stronger in the years ahead.

Your Excellency, the American people share your abiding faith in the ultimate triumph of justice over evil. We look confidently toward the day when the great people of China will again take their place in the struggle for those principles of freedom and progress espoused by Dr. Sun Yat-Sen.

JOHN F. KENNEDY

NOTE: The message was released at Newport, R.I.

413   Statement by the President on the Need for a National Program
      To Combat Mental Retardation.   *October* 11, 1961

THE MANNER in which our Nation cares for its citizens and conserves its manpower resources is more than an index to its concern for the less fortunate.   It is a key to its future.   Both wisdom and humanity dictate a deep interest in the physically handicapped, the mentally ill, and the mentally retarded.   Yet, although we have made considerable progress in the treatment of physical handicaps, although we have attacked on a broad front the problems of mental illness, although we have made great strides in the battle against disease, we as a nation have for too long postponed an intensive search for solutions to the problems of the mentally retarded.   That failure should be corrected.

What is Mental Retardation?

The term mental retardation itself is often misunderstood.   It is confused with mental illness.   Simply stated, mental retardation is a condition resulting from a basic abnormality of the human mind.   It refers to the lack of intellectual ability resulting from arrested mental development.   It interferes with the ability to adjust to the demands of environment.   It manifests itself in poor learning, inadequate social adjustment, and delayed achievement.   Usually this condition is either present at birth or begins during childhood.   The causes are many and obscure.   Some have already been determined and are easy to highlight; others are beyond our present knowledge and would yield only to research.

Mental retardation is not a disease.   Rather, it is a symptom of a disease, of an injury, of some obscure failure of development, even of inadequate opportunity to learn.   Just as a fever is a symptom of an infection, mental retardation is a symptom of mongolism, birth injury or infection, or even inadequate stimulation in early childhood.   It can be so severe that the afflicted person never leaves protective care, or so mild that it is detected only under stress or through special tests.

In most instances, it can be clearly distinguished from mental illness, for mental illness strikes and incapacitates after there has been normal development up to the time of the affliction.   The younger the child the more difficult it is to distinguish between the two.   However, accurate diagnosis is an essential prelude to treatment.   Unfortunately, the present limitations of our knowledge in this field make this diagnosis extremely difficult when the very young are involved.

I. The Scope of the Problem

The scope of the problem and its effect upon us is apparent in the large numbers affected by the condition.   Approximately 5 million persons in this country are retarded.   It strikes those least able to protect themselves—our children.   It affects by its nature their relationships to all members of their families and their friends.   Thus, mental retardation is a serious personal matter to at least one out of every twelve people.   It disables ten times as many as diabetes, twenty times as many as tuberculosis, twenty-five times as many as muscular dystrophy, and six hundred times as many as infantile paralysis.

By 1970, at this rate we will have at least one million more retarded persons than there are at present.   Over half will be children under nine, many of whom will suffer from both physical and mental handicaps.   This growth in mental retardation is particularly anomalous in view of the advances in the medical sciences. Deaths at the time of birth have been reduced 75 percent in 20 years, tuberculosis 30 percent in 5 years, and such scourges as whooping cough, diphtheria and scarlet fever have been almost completely eliminated. But the prevalence of mental retardation has steadily increased. Today, one out of four beds in State institutions is assigned to a mentally retarded person. Nevertheless, all public facilities have long waiting lists. Children needing service cannot obtain it. Our State institutions are overcrowded. The average State hospital has 367 patients more than its rated capacity. Its waiting list numbers 340.

Many retarded persons never reach a hospital. Their impairment, though mild, is a matter of serious concern. Over 700,000 draftees were rejected as unfit during World War II because they were mentally deficient or illiterate. The number of retarded who could not participate in the war effort was even greater. In many instances, illiteracy and mental retardation are indistinguishable.

Every year 126,000 babies are born who will be mentally retarded. Neither the rich nor the poor, the urban dweller or the farmer, the captain of industry or the manual laborer, or any other part of our society is exempt from the threat. It is a national problem and it requires a national solution.

There are no reliable estimates of the cost to each family for the care of the mentally retarded. Community costs of the 4 percent confined to institutions total approximately $300 million annually. The other 96 percent live in private homes. The financial strain of providing for them represents a staggering burden to each family that has this responsibility.

But the financial hardships are not the most serious aspect of the problem. It is the emotional strain, the problems of adjust-

ment, training, schooling and vocation—the attempt to make possible a full life for the child, that represents the major impact of retardation. Our goal should be to prevent retardation. Failing this, we must provide for the retarded the same opportunity for full social development that is the birthright of every American child.

In addition to research, the current problems are those of diagnosis, evaluation, care, appropriate training and education, family guidance, the need for sympathetic environment, a lack of public understanding and a dearth of private and public facilities. There are difficult issues involving not only our social responsibility for adequate care of the retarded, but the extent of the responsibility of the retarded individual himself, as, for example, when he gets into trouble with the law. For a long time we chose to turn away from these problems. The standard treatment consisted of commitment to institutions, segregation from society, and silence about the affliction.

In this vast reservoir of children and adults who need various degrees of assistance to enable them to adjust to the demands of our complex society, we have a largely unused resource. As society becomes more complex, the problems will of necessity increase both in size and in seriousness.

It is just as important to integrate the mentally retarded within our modern society and make full use of their abilities as it is to make a special effort to do this for the physically handicapped. The grim struggle for survival does not allow us the luxury of wasting our human resources.

II. Present Programs

Some forms of mental retardation can be prevented; in others the degree of incapacity can be reduced; and in still others it may be possible to obtain a completely satisfactory adjustment. Steps taken thus far have concentrated upon improvements in environment and understanding. These are important and should be expanded. But real improvement will require a major effort along new lines.

Prior to 1950 relatively little attention was directed to the problem of mental retardation by either the Federal or State governments or, in fact, by private groups. During the past decade, however, increased interest and activity have been stimulated by a few foundations, by the demands of parents, by interested lay and professional groups, and by members of legislative bodies who have been convinced of the urgent need for progress in this field.

Until 1954, no State health department offered any special services for mentally retarded children or their families. The welfare services were directed largely to long-term institutional care. Today almost every State has a special demonstration, service or training project in mental retardation as a part of its maternal and child health service program. Last year the National Institute of Mental Health spent over $2.5 million on research, technical assistance and grants in the mental retardation area, and the National Institute of Neurological Diseases and Blindness spent over $8 million on mental retardation. Next year's budget requests will double these figures. And the number of mentally retarded persons rehabilitated should also increase.

Today, the effort to help the mentally retarded takes six basic forms:

(1) Diagnostic and clinical services for the retarded are being expanded. There are over 80 clinics specializing in services to the retarded. Well over half were established within the past five years. These services need still greater expansion. The 20,000 children aided in 1960 represent only a small fraction of those who need the service.

(2) There has been an increase in the beds in residential institutions. Today there are over 200,000 mentally retarded patients in such institutions, approximately 10 percent more than there were five years ago. But the average waiting list continues to grow, and the quality of the service often suffers from limited budgets and salary levels. In the public institutions, there are less than 500 full-time physicians for 160,000 patients. The limited resources of the State institutions have been taxed beyond the breaking point. Additional increases in both facilities and manpower are necessary.

(3) The number of mentally retarded enrolled in special educational classes has been doubled over the past decade. In spite of this record, we are not yet meeting our existing requirements, and more such facilities must be provided. Less than 25 percent of our retarded children have access to special education. Moreover, the classes need teachers specially trained to meet the specialized needs of the retarded. To meet minimum standards, at least 75,000 such teachers are required. Today there are less than 20,000, and many of these have not fully met professional standards.

(4) Parent counselling is now being provided by private physicians, clinic staffs, social workers, nurses, psychologists, and school personnel. Although this service is still in an experimental stage of development, it offers bright prospects for helping parents to meet their social and emotional problems.

(5) Child welfare agencies are attempting to meet some of the needs of the mentally retarded. It is estimated that 10 percent of the 375,000 children brought to the attention of the agencies through such pathways as neglect, dependency and delin-

quency are retarded. The social workers and other personnel tending to the needs of these children should be trained specifically in the area of retardation.

(6) Finally, the preparation of the mentally retarded for a useful role in society and industry must receive more attention. In the past five years the number of mentally retarded rehabilitated through State vocational agencies has more than tripled—going from 756 to 2500—but in terms of potential, it is little more than a gesture. The problem is complex. Neither special education nor special rehabilitation procedures furnish the complete answer to employment of the retarded. New knowledge and new techniques are needed, for over 25 percent of those coming out of the special classes still cannot be placed.

III. *Present Opportunities for New Scientific Solutions*

In terms of the enormity of the challenge, all these efforts represent only a modest approach along limited lines. The central problem remains unsolved, for the causes and treatment of mental retardation are largely untouched. An attack on these questions justifies the talents of our best minds.

A moon-shot is not possible without prior discoveries in aero-dynamics, propulsion physics, astronomy, and other sciences. A successful attack on a complex problem like mental retardation also requires a host of prior achievements, trained scientific personnel, tools and techniques, profound understanding of the behavioral sciences, a spirit of devotion to the underprivileged, and a free, democratic atmosphere of inquiry. Fortunately, ours is a country in which these ingredients abound. Our leadership in these fields is unchallenged.

Much of the world's population still struggles for mere survival; others for domination of the weaker. Our aim is individual and national dignity. Our fortune is scientific and technological ability. Our obligation is to search for the secrets of the human mind and to share our knowledge throughout the world.

Discoveries of the wheel, the internal combustion engine and principles of thermodynamics have liberated mankind from much physical labor. Two hundred years ago man demonstrated, through the discoveries of Lavoisier and Harvey, that human life is governed by universal physical laws. Major progress in science and medicine can be measured from that date. Until the last two decades, however, little research was concentrated on the nature of the living cell and its reproduction. But great strides have been made in that direction through the understanding of the chemical basis of genes and chromosomes and their governing role in life itself.

The future belongs to those who can carry forward these achievements. It is now possible to attack the causes and prevention, as well as the treatment, of mental retardation. This will require new break-throughs, but it will pay enormous dividends in knowledge about ourselves, for the functions of the brain represent an almost completely uncharted frontier. The basic research entailed in such an effort will probe the essence of human development, and its results may far exceed its objectives. Exploration and discovery in this field may uncover the secrets of life and man's capacities, and the answers to many mysteries of social behavior. Perhaps even more important, an understanding of the motivation and effect of human behavior offers the hope of fostering the rational behavior of nations.

Progress in the natural sciences during the past 15 years has been impressive, but achievements in the prevention and therapy of mental retardation can be even more spectacular and can bring important benefits to mankind.

IV. The Task of the Panel

We must undertake a comprehensive and coordinated attack on the problem of mental retardation. The large number of people involved, the great cost to the nation, the striking need, the vast area of the unknown that beckons us to increased research efforts—all demand attention.

It is for that reason that I am calling together a panel of outstanding physicians, scientists, educators, lawyers, psychologists, social scientists and leaders in this field to prescribe the program of action. I am sure that the talent which has led to progress in other fields of medicine and the physical sciences can enlarge the frontiers of this largely ignored area.

It shall be the responsibility of this panel to explore the possibilities and pathways to prevent and cure mental retardation. No relevant discipline and no fact that will help achieve this goal is to be neglected.

The panel will also make a broad study of the scope and dimensions of the various factors that are relevant to mental retardation. These include biological, psychological, educational, vocational and socio-cultural aspects of the condition and their impact upon each state of development—marriage, pregnancy, delivery, childhood and adulthood.

The panel will also appraise the adequacy of existing programs and the possibilities for greater utilization of current knowledge.

There are already many devoted workers in this field, trained in diagnosis, treatment, care, education and rehabilitation. The panel should ascertain the gaps in programs and any failure in coordination of activities.

The panel will review and make recommendations with regard to:

1. The personnel necessary to develop and apply the new knowledge. The present shortage of personnel is a major problem in our logistics. More physicians, nurses, social workers, educators, psychologists, and other trained workers are needed.

2. The major areas of concern that offer the most hope; and the means, the techniques and the private and governmental structures necessary to encourage research in these areas.

3. The present programs of treatment, education and rehabilitation.

4. The relationships between the Federal Government, the States and private resources in their common efforts to eliminate mental retardation.

I am asking the panel to report on or before December 31, 1962.

NOTE: On October 16 a White House release concerning the panel announced that Leonard Mayo, Executive Director of the Association for the Aid of Crippled Children, New York City, would serve as chairman, and that Dr. George Tarjan, Superintendent of the Pacific State Hospital, Pomona, Calif., would serve as vice chairman. The release also listed 22 other members, and stated that the President would meet with the panel on October 18.

A later release, dated October 28, listed three additional members and stated that the President had also appointed Mrs. Robert Sargent Shriver, Jr., as a consultant to the panel. Mrs. Shriver is a member of the Chicago Commission on Youth Welfare and of the Board of Governors of the Menninger Foundation, Topeka, Kans.

414   Telegram Commending the AFL–CIO Campaign for the Eleanor Roosevelt Cancer Foundation.   *October 11, 1961*

Mr. George Meany, President
American Federation of Labor and
   Congress of Industrial Organizations
Hotel Commodore
New York, New York

I was delighted to learn today that the AFL–CIO and its member unions have pledged to raise $1 million for the Eleanor Roosevelt Cancer Foundation. Your decisions to undertake this special effort on behalf of the general welfare, at a time when you are also confronted with many problems of direct and immediate concern to your members, exemplifies again the spirit of public service that is traditional in the American labor movement. I wish your campaign every success.

JOHN F. KENNEDY

415   The President's News Conference of *October 11, 1961*

THE PRESIDENT. I have several announcements to make.

[1.] You will recall that in my recent address to the United Nations General Assembly I expressed concern of this Government over the situation in southeast Asia, particularly in the attacks on the people of South Viet-Nam.

With this situation in mind I've asked General Taylor, with the wholehearted endorsement of Secretary McNamara and General Lemnitzer, to go to Saigon this week to discuss with the President and American officials on the spot ways in which we can perhaps better assist the Government of Viet-Nam in meeting this threat to its independence.

General Taylor will be accompanied by a small staff from the various departments of Government which are concerned.

[2.] Secondly, I have today announced my intention to appoint a panel of outstanding scientists, doctors, and others to prescribe a program of action in the field of mental retardation.

This condition strikes those least able to protect themselves from it. It affects not only the people involved but also the members of their family.

It is a serious personal matter to at least 1 out of every 12 persons, disables 10 times as many as diabetes, 20 times as many as tuberculosis, 25 times as many as muscular dystrophy, and 600 times as many as infantile paralysis.

At one time, there was practically no effective program in the field of mental retardation. Wherever possible the children were committed to institutions. They were segregated from normal society and forgotten except by the members of their family. Only in isolated cases was an effort made to bring them back into useful lives in the community. They suffered from lack of public understanding and they suffered from lack of funds.

The situation today is better. Most attempts still take the form of therapeutic research and treatment. The central problems of cause and prevention remain unsolved. And I believe that we, as a country, in association with scientists all over the world, should make a comprehensive attack. It is a matter of the greatest possible interest to me, and I am going to meet with the panel next week. Thank you.

[3.] Q. Mr. President, at our last news conference you were hopeful but not, as I recall, wholly sanguine about prospects for a Berlin settlement. In the meantime, have there been any developments, including the Gromyko talks, or any new information in hand, to raise hopes for a solution?

THE PRESIDENT. No. I would say that we are still anxious to have a solution which will lessen the threat of war and which, we would hope, could improve the security of the people of West Berlin. We have had not negotiations but exploratory talks—Mr. Rusk with Mr. Gromyko on three occasions, and I had a talk with him and the Prime Minister yesterday—in an attempt to determine the precise position of the Soviet Union on the various questions dealing with access, the free city, the question of boundaries, and all the rest. We have not, as I have said, carried out any negotiations, nor will we.

We will now continue the talks with Ambassador Thompson in Moscow, I hope. He is back here for that purpose and will be returning shortly. And we are going to be now in the process of consulting with our allies in order to determine a common Western position on these matters which are at issue.

So that I don't think that we can come to any conclusion as to what the ultimate outcome will be, though the talks which we had with Mr. Gromyko did not give us immediate hope that this matter would be easily settled.

[4.] Q. Mr. President, I believe recently you spoke to a group of New Jersey publishers about your forthcoming plan involving fallout shelters that might be quite economical. In this general range of interest, sir, do you have personally fallout shelters in any of the residences that you frequently

use? I'm thinking particularly of your house in Hyannis or in Middleburg or in Palm Beach or at Newport.

THE PRESIDENT. Well, they're not all my residences, I'm sorry to say—[*laughter*]—but I would say that there are naturally provisions for the protection of those in the Presidency and in the Joint Chiefs of Staff and others who would have to maintain responsibility in case of a military action. Though of course there's no sure answer for anybody.

We—obviously you cannot build a shelter in the accepted sense of the word for the kind of money which we have talked about. But we can provide directions whereby a family can take steps to protect themselves on a minimum basis and give them—members of the family—some hope that if they're out of the blast area they could survive the fallout. And by the middle of November we hope to suggest some of the steps that every homeowner could take.

My own feeling is that these shelters are most useful and most important, and we're going to live through a long period of constant tension with these dangerous weapons which will be proliferating, and, therefore, anything that we can do to increase the chances of protection for our families ought to be done.

[5.] Q. Mr. President, a recent public opinion poll showed that a majority of the American people are more worried about a war breaking out now than they have been in any time in recent years. Would you address yourself to this poll, sir, and whether you share that view or just how do you feel about it?

THE PRESIDENT. Well, I think that they're naturally and quite correctly concerned because there is a collision in the points of view which the Western powers have taken in NATO with that of the Soviet Union and the Warsaw bloc countries over Berlin, and this area is extremely vital.

Western Europe is an area of great resources and the Soviet Union has long had policy ambitions in this area, so that this is a very, very serious matter unless we can reach a peaceful accommodation.

In addition, there are other areas where we can become involved. And as the weapons now are so annihilating, it causes the American people to be quite rightfully concerned.

Our ambition is to protect our vital interests without a war which destroys and doesn't really represent a victory for policy.

But we happen to live—because of the ingenuity of science and man's own inability to control his relationships one with another, we happen to live in the most dangerous time in the history of the human race.

[6.] Q. Mr. President, Communist China's Foreign Minister has indicated that high-level talks at the foreign minister level with the United States would be, as he says, acceptable, provided the United States took the initiative. How do you feel about this?

THE PRESIDENT. Well I—we are, of course, having conversations at the present time at Geneva. The Chinese Communists are represented at the conference over Laos, and there are therefore many channels through which any exchange of views could flow.

We have been meeting periodically, for the last 3 or 4 years, for a period at Geneva and, of course, most recently at Warsaw in which we talked about the question of the exchange of prisoners, or rather the release of prisoners, and other matters. So that I would feel that these efforts will continue at Geneva and they will continue at Warsaw.

But we have not seen any evidence as yet that the Chinese Communists wish to live in comity with us, and our desire is to live in friendship with all people. But we have

not seen that attitude manifested. In fact, just a few days ago there was a statement about Berlin that was quite bellicose.

[7.] Q. There have been charges that we have not adequately maintained the strength or the credibility of our nuclear deterrent and that we also have not fully convinced the leaders of the Soviet Union that we are determined to meet force with force in Berlin or elsewhere. What is your reaction to those charges?

THE PRESIDENT. Well, we have made many statements. I have made them and they've been as precise as I could make them. The Secretary of State, the Secretary of Defense, other Western people in positions of responsibility have all talked of our determination to maintain our vital interests in this area.

I think probably—aside from any domestic reasons for this kind of criticism—it's that everyone realizes that these weapons are, as I said, extremely dangerous and that the Soviet Union has a long-range bomber and missile capacity, as we do, and that, as I've said, we move through a period of maximum hazard. So that naturally anyone would be reluctant, unless all else had failed, to destroy so much of the world.

But we have indicated that we will meet our commitments with whatever resources are necessary to meet them and we also add that we hope it will be possible that accords can be reached which will protect the interests and freedom of the people involved without having to go to this—these extreme weapons.

Now I would like to point out two or three details about the effort we've made in the field of national security and national defense.

Since January, we have added more than $6 billion to the national defense budget, which is more than a 14-percent increase over the previous budget.

In strategic forces, which are the nuclear forces, we have ordered a 50-percent increase in the number of Polaris submarines to be on station—battle station—by the end of 1964; a 50-percent increase in the number of strategic bombers on 15-minute ground alert at the end of runways, which is already in effect; a 100-percent increase in our capacity to produce Minuteman missiles against the day when that production capacity may be needed, and a similar increase in Skybolt and other programs which affect our strategic arm.

Now to strengthen our nonnuclear forces—and I think this is important—we have called up two additional divisions and many thousands more—particularly in the air; we've increased by 75 percent our modern long-range airlift capacity; we've increased our antiguerrilla forces by 150 percent; we've stepped up the delivery of the M–14 rifle from a maximum of 9,000 a month to 44,000 a month and taken other steps to bring the Army, Navy, and Marine units to full strength in terms of manpower and equipment. And we still have someway to go.

But it does indicate our feeling that we should be stronger and also that there should be a balance in the forces that we have.

[8.] Q. Mr. President, following up this same subject, sir, it has been reported that you have been angered or at least disturbed by what has been described as partisan criticism of your foreign policy.

It has also been reported that some members of your administration, possibly including yourself, have felt that sharp Republican warnings against appeasement have constricted the room that you may have to negotiate with the Russians. Would you discuss these points?

THE PRESIDENT. No—I'm going to attempt to, as I have said, to protect our vital interests and see whether it's possible for us to reach an agreement in this matter which will not necessitate a war which could mean so much destruction for so many millions and millions of people in this country and elsewhere.

Now, I'm going to continue to do that and we'll do the best we can and we'll see what happens.

Everyone is free to make any attacks they want. I think what would be most helpful to the Nation today would be constructive and frequently critical alternatives—suggestions for alternative courses of action—and not merely rather generalized statements which throw very little light on very complicated and dangerous matters.

But I would never suggest that the battle of the mimeograph machines between the Republican Committee and the Democratic Committee should cease, only that it should perhaps be wiser.

[9.] Q. Mr. President, in your July speech you said that you didn't want to negotiate on a basis of what's mine is mine and what's yours is negotiable. In your talks with Mr. Gromyko, sir, what did you talk about that was theirs?

THE PRESIDENT. Well, I don't think really it's particularly useful at this time to attempt to go into precise detail. Most of the—a good deal of the information in the talks has already been printed in the press. These talks, if they're not going to turn into merely exchanges of propaganda, should at least have the value of some degree of privacy.

I've stated that we have not been engaged in negotiations, no agreements have been reached but merely an attempt to explore what are the positions of the various powers.

I've already characterized my view of these talks and I think that with the information, which has been quite lucid and only slightly inaccurate, I think we can proceed on to additional talk.

[10.] Q. Mr. President, in reference to your decision to send General Taylor to Viet-Nam, there may be some interpretation of that decision as implying confirmation of reports that you intend to send American forces to Viet-Nam or to Thailand or to Laos. Can you give us your appraisal of the conditions under which you might find it necessary to send troops in?

THE PRESIDENT. Well, we're going to wait till General Taylor comes back and brings an up-to-date description of the situation, particularly in Viet-Nam. As you know, in the last 2 or 3 months there has been a large increase in the number of the forces that have been involved. There has been evidence that some of these forces have come from beyond the frontiers. And General Taylor will give me—and the Joint Chiefs of Staff—an educated military guess as to what the situation that the government there faces. Then we can come to conclusions as what is best to do.

[11.] Q. Mr. President, if it becomes necessary for the House to elect a new Speaker, would you be likely to express, either publicly or privately a preference for any candidate?

THE PRESIDENT. The House has a Speaker; and the House will elect its next Speaker; and I would think it would be unwise for anyone outside the House to attempt to indicate a preference. This is a matter for the House. I'm sure they'll choose wisely.

[12.] Q. Mr. President, in addition to the criticism that's been heard in some quarters of your foreign policy, there's also been some criticism of your domestic program and it encountered some trouble in Congress. Does your decision to make speak-

ing engagements in the West and the announced series of appearances of some of your Cabinet members indicate a feeling that it's now time to take your program to the country?

THE PRESIDENT. Well, on the last part, we are having the members of our Cabinet speak at nonpartisan meetings upon invitation in various parts of the country to talk to them about some of the domestic programs that we have worked on and could work on in the future.

My own trip is very limited. I'm going to speak in Washington at the 100th anniversary of the University of Washington, and also at a dinner—the 25th anniversary of Senator Magnuson's service in the Senate—and will then go the next night to speak at the 50th anniversary of Senator Hayden's coming to the Congress, in Arizona. And those are my only speeches.

[13.] Q. Mr. President, going back to Berlin, I think the American people are confused by what they read and hear about Berlin. One day they read or they're told that American officials are encouraged by the outlook. Another day they read that they're not encouraged, that they're gloomy. One day we're going ahead, the next day we're going back. Mr. President, does the real situation fluctuate that much? As a one-time journalist who became President, how does it look to you?

THE PRESIDENT. Well, a lot of journalists had bad luck—[*laughter*]—and I know these stories based on recent conversations that there have been, I think, from New York, exchanges between Mr. Rusk and Mr. Gromyko.

There seemed to be more hope in the stories that came out of my meeting with Mr. Gromyko.

I think it would be—I see no evidence as

yet that there is any clear solution to Berlin. There still seems to—there still are very major differences of view.

Now I feel that the three talks he had and the talk I had at least helped to make more precise those differences.

We now will continue some more and in addition—and I think this is most important—the Germans will have a new government shortly and be able to participate with perhaps more vigor in making Allied policy with the other NATO countries, and then we can get a better idea as to how it's all going to end up.

There is—I would say that there have been, as I have said, no negotiations in the sense that we made proposals and they made them.

What there has been is a description of the kind of solution that they would like to see. And I must say that I have not found substantial changes in that policy as it was previously expressed some months ago.

There has been, and I think this may explain the stories, a desire to discuss these matters and a—statements about a desire to reach a peaceful accord. But on the substance we are not in sight of land.

[14.] Q. Mr. President, do you have any feeling about whether members of your administration should belong to the Metropolitan Club here in Washington?

THE PRESIDENT. It seems to me that where everyone eats and the clubs that they belong to—private clubs—is a matter that each person must decide himself, though I personally approved of my brother's action—the Attorney General.

[15.] Q. Mr. President, written into the foreign aid bill is a clause which says that there should be more stress on giving aid to friendly countries, countries that share our view on major world problems. In view of

the decision to review aid to Ghana's Volta River project, could you elaborate on how far you think a country should go towards agreeing with us on these major issues?

THE PRESIDENT. Well, I think that they should—what—we're not attempting to use our aid in order to secure agreement by these countries with all of our policies. The phrase that was used in signing the mutual security bill was that we should give particular attention to the needs of those countries which share our view of the world crisis.

Our view of the world crisis is that countries are entitled to national sovereignty and independence. That is all we ever suggested. That is the purpose of our aid—to make it more possible.

Now if a country has ceased to choose national sovereignty or ceased to choose national independence, then, of course, our aid becomes less useful. But that is a different matter from suggesting that in order to be entitled to our assistance, particularly as a good percentage of our assistance today is in the form of loans, that they must agree with us, because quite obviously these people in the underdeveloped world are newly independent. They want to run their own affairs.

They would rather not accept assistance if we have that kind of string attached to it. Therefore, I think we ought to make an educated guess. But it's not an easy matter. These countries are passing through very difficult times and they're going to swing one way and then another. But in general, our object is that they maintain their independence. We hope it's theirs.

[16.] Q. Mr. President, considering what we may know now about the—may have learned now from the Russians on nuclear shots and what we do know now about our own underground explosion, do you think it's probable, in order to keep up with the state of this art, that we'll have to go to atmospheric testing in the near future?

THE PRESIDENT. Well, quite obviously if at the conclusion of this immediate series of tests, the Soviet Union was to propose an uninspected moratorium—that would not be very helpful in view of the experience we've gone through this year. We will be glad to negotiate, but we will not feel that the moratorium will be extended during the period of negotiation.

As to what kind of tests we will operate, we—I am extremely sorry that we were not able to get the Soviet Union to accept the proposal to ban atmospheric testing by the Prime Minister and myself.

They've made over 20 tests in the atmosphere, and we have to make a judgment as to what is in the best interests of our security, and that is a matter which is being studied. For the present, our tests are underground, and we feel that's in accordance with our security.

[17.] Q. Mr. President, do you feel that the Nation has reacted positively to your May 25 appeal to send a man to the moon? And do you feel that progress is being made on Projects Mercury and Apollo?

THE PRESIDENT. Well, until we have a man on the moon, none of us will be satisfied. But I do believe a major effort is being made. But as I said before, we started far behind, and we're going to have to wait and see whether we catch up.

But I would say that I will continue to be dissatisfied until the goal is reached. And I hope everyone working on the program shares the same view.

[18.] Q. Mr. President, did you make the decision for us not to use force to stop the building of the wall in Berlin? And if you had it to do over again, would you make

the same decision? Or what would have been the alternative if you had not made that decision?

THE PRESIDENT. As you know, Eastern Berlin and East Germany have been under the control of the Soviet Union, really, since 1947 and '48. There's not been four-power control and they have controlled this area.

There are many things that happen in Eastern Europe, as I said in my United Nations speech, which we consider to be wholly unsatisfactory—the denial of liberties, the denial of political freedom, national independence, and all the rest.

And that is a matter of equal concern in the action which you described. These are areas which the Soviet Union has held since the end of World War II, for over 16 years.

Q. Mr. President, you spoke of seeking a common Western position. Are we far apart and at what level do we have to seek it?

THE PRESIDENT. Well, I think we're going to be meeting next week in Washington and by those who are particularly competent here among—we've had almost daily conversations, and as I say I'm hopeful that when the new German Government assumes its responsibility we can come to more final conclusions as to what our next approach should be to the Soviet Union.

I believe there are basic agreements among the Western Allied powers, but these are matters which should be carefully explored and I think we can only explore them with success since the talks with Mr. Gromyko because I think they've helped illuminate the matters which we must decide.

[19.] Q. We are told that your defense expenditures this year and next year will be vastly increased. Will they be increased so much that they will curtail your legislative program, especially for revision of the tax structure?

THE PRESIDENT. Yes, in answer to the last part of your question, we had hoped before the Berlin crisis came out that we might have a, if business came back, we might have a $3 billion surplus which would have permitted a tax reduction. As you know since the July callup decision, which was $3,500 million we've lost that hope.

We still have a strong desire to balance our budget. But I cannot predict what extra military demands may be made in the next month or two which may lessen that chance. But our present intention is to balance our budget unless military increases—and only military increases—threaten that object.

Q. Mr. President, in your July speech on this same subject, you said that if it was necessary to balance the budget you would increase taxes. Do you still feel that way?

THE PRESIDENT. I would, if we can—for example, there isn't any doubt that if we had been able to persuade the Congress to accept the $600 million or $700 million increase in postal rates it would have assisted us in our responsibility. We will increase—we will secure sufficient revenue to balance the budget unless there is excessive and substantial— and they may come, because of the events in southeast Asia or Western Europe.

Whether we should—at that time we will then make a judgment as to how much we can cut from nondefense expenditures and, secondly, how much of a tax burden can be sustained without strangling the recovery.

We don't want to—which I think is one of the difficulties—the recovery of '58 which was aborted in 1960, so that we don't want to provide a tax structure which already is very heavy—and brings in tremendous receipts at full employment—we don't want it to result in waste of resources and manpower. So that's the judgment we must make.

[20.] Q. Mr. President, could you give us your assessment of the vigor of the economic recovery, particularly in the light of statements by organized labor that we may have five and a half million unemployed by next February?

THE PRESIDENT. Well, we've had a 10-percent increase in the second quarter and a 5-percent increase in the third quarter, and we are going to continue to have a substantial increase in the next quarter.

I think we're producing more cars this quarter probably than any year since 1950 and we've had less increase in the cost of living in a recovery than we've had in 10 or 12 years. So that the private sector is moving ahead.

The problem of unemployment continues because of technological changes and increases in the population and we do not have—unemployment is now at about 4 million. We do not—I am still as concerned as they are that we could have a great boom and still have the kind of unemployment they describe.

[21.] Q. Sir, do you believe your letter to the steel companies has had the desired effect that there will not be a steel price increase this fall?

THE PRESIDENT. I think that the steel companies are going to make a judgment based on what they consider to be in the public interest and in line with their own responsibilities, and I think it's their judgment and I'm hopeful that they will make a judgment which will assist our economy.

[22.] Q. Mr. President, on Berlin, the Russians seem to be making a considerable effort to cut any relationship between West Berlin and West Germany, even the relationship which now exists. Do you consider that any settlement of the Berlin issue will have to include free access for West Germans and West Berliners back and forth and other relationships between the city and the country as well as access to the Allied forces themselves?

THE PRESIDENT. Well, I think that without going into the details, as I said at the beginning, it's quite obvious that we're not only talking about the freedom of the city but also its viability, economic as well as political, and it operates under the greatest possible difficulties, 100 miles within an area controlled by the Soviet Union, so that this tie with the West—West Germany and other sections of the west—is very vital to its remaining more than just a shell, so that we will be concerned with the viability and vitality—economic vitality—of the city in any agreement that we're able to make—if we can make an agreement.

Reporter. Thank you, Mr. President.

NOTE: President Kennedy's seventeenth news conference was held in the State Department Auditorium at 4:30 o'clock on Wednesday afternoon, October 11, 1961.

416 Remarks Recorded at the Raleigh-Durham Airport for the Opening of the North Carolina Trade Fair at Charlotte. *October 12, 1961*

Governor Sanford, Members of the Congress, Secretary Hodges:

I want to express my pleasure at again being back in North Carolina. The last time was a year ago, though the conditions were somewhat different.

I do want to say that it's a great satisfaction to me to join you in opening this fair. North Carolina has a great story to tell. Its progress in recent years has been among the most vigorous of any State in the United States. And this effort to tie together in a place where this State and country and world can see the products of this State, I think can mean increased development and well-being for the people of this State in the future.

What Governor Sanford and the officials and the people of this State are attempting to do in developing the economy of North Carolina, and in providing a better life for the people, we with the help of the Secretary of Commerce, Governor Sanford's predecessor, are attempting to do in the Nation.

This country cannot stand still. It must move forward. North Carolina has not stood still. It is moving forward, and I think together we can show what North Carolina and the United States can and must do.

And therefore, as President of the United States, it is a high honor to open this fair and with it to show the world what North Carolina stands for.

Thank you.

NOTE: In his opening words the President referred to Governor Terry Sanford of North Carolina and Secretary of Commerce Luther H. Hodges, former Governor of North Carolina.

417   Statement by the President Announcing a Contract for a
        Materials Research Laboratory at the University of North
        Carolina.   *October* 12, 1961

RESULTS of more specialized materials research in recent years have indeed had a revolutionary impact in a number of existing non-military technologies, that of the communications industry being a prime example. Application of new materials and processes has contributed greatly to the explosive growth of such vital new industries as electronic data processing and computers. They have also made feasible the development of essential hardware for unprecedented technical advances under extreme environmental conditions such as space exploration and new rocket components.

Recognizing that critical qualities of national programs in defense and space exploration would depend on strong reinforcement of national capabilities for materials research and development, the Defense Department, acting on the advice of the Federal Council for Science and Technology and the President's Science Advisory Committee, has already established eight interdisciplinary laboratories at universities. These new ventures in which the universities have undertaken to assemble faculties and students and to create advanced facilities, will for the first time combine modern progress in solid state physics, chemistry, metallurgy, mechanics, applied mathematics and other related fields. Accordingly, the programs will also train unprecedented numbers and kinds of materials specialists who have previously been offered higher education only specifically as metallurgists, solid state physicists, inorganic chemists, or experts in ceramics. Each of these new generations of students produced by the interdisciplinary laboratories will correspondingly have a broader competency in the challenging materials problems of the missile and space age than ever before.

Three important additions are now being made to the eight laboratories previously established. The University of North Carolina, along with the University of Maryland and Purdue University, comprise these latest three. The University of North Carolina was one of the first in its geographical region and one of the first State universities to qualify for this new national strengthening of science, technology and education. A particular feature of the interdisciplinary materials research laboratory program is its full observance of the long-term qualities of basic research. Accordingly, the University of North Carolina has received, along with the others, a novel four year support commitment so that full values of the continuing nature of research and education can be properly combined in this new venture.

NOTE: The statement was part of a White House release announcing a $1 million contract between the University of North Carolina and the Advanced Research Projects Agency of the Department of Defense. The release also recorded the President as saying that the contract had been awarded to the university "in recognition of its notable faculty and student body. The State of North Carolina can well be proud of the accomplishments of this great university, the first State University in the land."

418   Address at the University of North Carolina Upon Receiving an Honorary Degree.   *October* 12, 1961

Mr. Chancellor, Governor Sanford, members of the faculty, ladies and gentlemen:

I am honored today to be admitted to the fellowship of this ancient and distinguished university, and I am pleased to receive in the short space of 1 or 2 minutes the honor for which you spend over 4 years of your lives. But whether the degree be honorary or earned, it is a proud symbol of this university and this State.

North Carolina has long been identified with enlightened and progressive leaders and people, and I can think of no more important reason for that reputation than this university, which year after year has sent educated men and women who have had a recognition of their public responsibility as well as in their private interests.

Distinguished Presidents like President Graham and Gray, distinguished leaders like the Secretary of Commerce, Governor Hodges, distinguished members of the congressional delegation, carry out a tradition which stretches back to the beginning of this school, and that is that the graduate of this university is a man of his Nation as well as a man of his time. And it is my hope, in a changing world, when untold possibilities lie before North Carolina, and indeed the entire South and country, that this university will still hew to the old line of the responsibility that its graduates owe to the community at large—that in your time, too, you will be willing to give to the State and country a portion of your lives and all of your knowledge and all of your loyalty.

I want to emphasize, in the great concentration which we now place upon scientists and engineers, how much we still need the men and women educated in the liberal traditions, willing to take the long look, undisturbed by prejudices and slogans of the moment, who attempt to make an honest judgment on difficult events.

This university has a more important function today than ever before, and therefore I am proud as President of the United States, and as a graduate of a small land grant college in Massachusetts, Harvard University, to come to this center of education.

Those of you who regard my profession of political life with some disdain should remember that it made it possible for me to move from being an obscure lieutenant in the United States Navy to Commander-in-Chief in 14 years, with very little technical competence.

But more than that, I hope that you will realize that from the beginning of this country, and especially in North Carolina, there has been the closest link between educated men and women and politics and government. And also to remember that our nation's first great leaders were also our first great scholars.

A contemporary described Thomas Jefferson as "a gentleman of 32 who could calculate an eclipse, survey an estate, tie an artery, plan an edifice, try a cause, break a horse, dance the minuet, and play the violin." John Quincy Adams, after being summarily dismissed by the Massachusetts Legislature from the United States Senate for supporting Thomas Jefferson, could then become Boylston Professor of Rhetoric and Oratory at Harvard University, and then become a great Secretary of State.

And Senator Daniel Webster could stroll down the corridors of the Congress a few steps, after making some of the greatest speeches in the history of this country, and dominate the Supreme Court as the foremost lawyer of his day.

This versatility, this vitality, this intellectual energy, put to the service of our country, represents our great resource in these difficult days.

I would urge you, therefore, regardless of your specialty, and regardless of your chosen field or occupation, and regardless of whether you bear office or not, that you recognize the contribution which you can make as educated men and women to intellectual and political leadership in these difficult days, when the problems are infinitely more complicated and come with increasing speed, with increasing significance, in our lives than they were a century ago when so many gifted men dominated our political life. The United States Senate had more able men serving in it, from the period of 1830 to 1850, than probably any time in our history, and yet they dealt with three or four problems which they had dealt with for over a generation.

Now they come day by day, from all parts of the world. Even the experts find themselves confused, and therefore in a free society such as this, where the people must make an educated judgment, they depend upon those of you who have had the advantage of the scholar's education.

I ask you to give to the service of our country the critical faculties which society has helped develop in you here. I ask you to decide, as Goethe put it, "whether you will be an anvil or a hammer," whether you will give the United States, in which you were reared and educated, the broadest possible benefits of that education.

It's not enough to lend your talents to deploring present solutions. Most educated men and women on occasions prefer to discuss what is wrong, rather than to suggest alternative courses of action. But, "would you have counted him a friend of ancient Greece," as George William Curtis asked a body of educators a century ago, "would you have counted him a friend of ancient Greece who quietly discussed the theory of patriotism on that hot summer day through whose hopeless and immortal hours Leonidas and the three hundred stood at Thermopylae for liberty? Was John Milton to conjugate Greek verbs in his library when the liberty of Englishmen was imperiled?"

This is a great institution with a great tradition and with devoted alumni, and with the support of the people of this State. Its establishment and continued functioning, like that of all great universities, has required great sacrifice by the people of North Carolina. I cannot believe that all of this is undertaken merely to give this school's graduates an economic advantage in the life-struggle.

"A university," said Professor Woodrow Wilson, "should be an organ of memory for the State, for the transmission of its best traditions." And Prince Bismarck was even more specific. "One third of the students of German universities," he once said, "broke down from over-work, another third broke down from dissipation, and the other third ruled Germany." I leave it to each of you to decide in which category you will fall.

I do not suggest that our political and public life should be turned over to college-trained experts, nor would I give this university a seat in the Congress, as William and Mary was once represented in the Virginia House of Burgesses, nor would I adopt from the Belgian constitution a provision giving three votes instead of one to college graduates—at least not until more Democrats go to college. But I do hope that you join us.

This university produces trained men and

women, and what this country needs are those who look, as the motto of your State says, at things as they are and not at things as they seem to be.

For this meeting is held at an extraordinary time. Angola and Algeria, Brazil and Bizerte, Syria and South Viet-Nam, Korea or Kuwait, the Dominican Republic, Berlin, the United Nations itself—all problems which 20 years ago we could not even dream of.

Our task in this country is to do our best, to serve our Nation's interest as we see it, and not to be swayed from our course by the faint-hearted or the unknowing, or the threats of those who would make themselves our foes.

This is not a simple task in a democracy. We cannot open all our books in advance to an adversary who operates in the night, the decisions we make, the weapons we possess, the bargains we will accept—nor can we always see reflected overnight the success or failure of the actions that we may take.

In times past, a simple slogan described our policy: "Fifty-four-forty or fight." "To make the world safe for democracy." "No entangling alliances." But the times, issues, and the weapons, all have changed—and complicate and endanger our lives. It is a dangerous illusion to believe that the policies of the United States, stretching as they do world-wide, under varying and different conditions, can be encompassed in one slogan or one adjective, hard or soft or otherwise—or to believe that we shall soon meet total victory or total defeat.

Peace and freedom do not come cheap, and we are destined, all of us here today, to live out most if not all of our lives in uncertainty and challenge and peril. Our policy must therefore blend whatever degree of firmness and flexibility which is necessary to protect our vital interests, by peaceful means if possible, by resolute action if necessary.

There is, of course, no place in America where reason and firmness are more clearly pointed out than here in North Carolina. All Americans can profit from what happened in this State a century ago. It was this State, firmly fixed in the traditions of the South, which sought a way of reason in a troubled and dangerous world. Yet when the War came, North Carolina provided a fourth of all of the Confederate soldiers who made the supreme sacrifice in those years. And it won the right to the slogan, "First at Bethel. Farthest to the front at Gettysburg and Chickamauga. Last at Appomattox."

Its quest for a peaceful resolution of our problems was never identified in the minds of its people, of people today, with anything but a desire for peace and a preparation to meet their responsibilities.

We move for the first time in our history through an age in which two opposing powers have the capacity to destroy each other, and while we do not intend to see the free world give up, we shall make every effort to prevent the world from being blown up.

The American Eagle on our official seal emphasizes both peace and freedom, and as I said in the State of the Union Address, we in this country give equal attention to its claws when it in its left hand holds the arrows and in its right the olive branch.

This is a time of national maturity, understanding, and willingness to face issues as they are, not as we would like them to be. It is a test of our ability to be far-seeing and calm, as well as resolute, to keep an eye on both our dangers and our opportunities, and not to be diverted by momentary gains, or setbacks, or pressures. And it is the long view of the educated citizen to which the graduates of this university can best contribute.

We must distinguish the real from the illusory, the long-range from the temporary, the significant from the petty, but if we can be purposeful, if we can face up to our risks and live up to our word, if we can do our duty undeterred by fanatics or frenzy at home or abroad, then surely peace and freedom can prevail. We shall be neither Red nor dead, but alive and free—and worthy of the traditions and responsibilities of North Carolina and the United States of America.

NOTE: The President spoke on University Day at Kenan Stadium, Chapel Hill, immediately after receiving an honorary degree of Doctor of Laws. His opening words "Mr. Chancellor, Governor Sanford" referred to William B. Aycock, Chancellor at the University, and Terry Sanford, Governor of North Carolina. Later in his remarks the President referred to former presidents of the University of North Carolina, Frank P. Graham and Gordon Gray.

419   Remarks to the 82d Airborne Division at Fort Bragg, North Carolina. *October 12, 1961*

Secretary Stahr, General Trapnell, General Conway, General Decker:

I want to express my appreciation to the officers and men of the 82d Airborne for this opportunity to see a group of Americans who do in peacetime what other men do in war, and that is, live hazardously in defense of their country.

I saw this Division first in July of 1945, secondly when it marched up Fifth Avenue later that year for the Victory Parade. And now I come here on this occasion, when this Division with its long and illustrious history of combat leadership in World War I and World War II is performing a most vital function.

The United States of America has obligations and alliances which stretch around the world. Millions of people look to us. In many of those countries there are few Americans and no American soldiers, but out beyond the sight of land there are the ships of the United States Navy.

Here at Fort Bragg there is this Division and our other STRAC Divisions, and in Omaha, Nebraska, and other cities there are the wings of our Air strength.

It is all of this that makes it possible for freedom to maintain its position. So I hope that those of you who serve here, during these days of a cold peace, will recognize that every day that you are on duty and in a position of preparedness, you are maintaining freedom all around the globe.

So on behalf of my fellow citizens of this country we express our pride in you, and our appreciation to you. This is a Division which is "All-American"—and as an American I am proud of it.

NOTE: The President spoke at a combat readiness and weapons demonstration. His opening words referred to Elvis J. Stahr, Jr., Secretary of the Army; Lt. Gen. Thomas J. H. Trapnell, Commanding General of the 3d U.S. Army; Maj. Gen. Theodore J. Conway, Commanding General, 82d Airborne Division; and General George H. Decker, Chief of Staff, U.S. Army.

669

420 Statement by the President in Support of UNICEF.
October 13, 1961

THE WORLD'S children offer our greatest promise for the future. It gives me great pleasure to send a message of congratulations and support to UNICEF again this year.

The United Nations Children's Fund has worked tirelessly and effectively across national boundaries to help children escape the threat of hunger and disease. Their program of education in disease prevention, medical care and nutrition has already had a real impact upon today's children, and its benefits will be felt even more keenly by the millions of children to come. We can feel proud of the cooperative effort which has enabled UNICEF to carry out its work.

UNICEF has caught the imagination of our people—especially our nation's children whose Halloween collections have become a symbol of concern and an expression of tangible aid. I urge all my fellow citizens, young and old, to support UNICEF generously again this year.

JOHN F. KENNEDY

421 Remarks of Welcome to the President of Finland at Andrews Air Force Base. *October* 16, 1961

Mr. President, Mr. Minister:

I want to express on behalf of the people of the United States our great satisfaction at your visit here. As President of your country, I think you must realize that Finland and the Finnish people are identified in the minds of the people of the United States with those qualities of courage and fortitude and perseverance which have made the reputation of your country and people second to none here in the United States.

They are the qualities which we have found in those Finns who have come among us and raised their families, and it is a source of personal pleasure to us all that during your visit here you will, in Michigan, have a chance to visit one of those families who are related to you.

In addition, throughout the long history of the Finnish people, and especially today, we have come to recognize in the actions of her people her outlook on life, her determination to maintain her own freedom, her own integrity.

So, Mr. President, no visitor could be more welcome. We are delighted to have you here personally. Your last visit to the United States was when you led the Olympic Team from Finland to Los Angeles in 1932. Much has changed in this country since then, and much has changed in your own country. But I am confident that the same warm ties which were in existence then, many years ago in other days, are strengthened today.

Mr. President, though you have come from a far north country here to the United States to Washington, you have come to a country which is warm in its welcome to you and in our admiration for your people.

NOTE: President Kekkonen responded as follows:
"Mr. President and Mrs. Kennedy:

"I wish to express my very sincere thanks for the friendly and warm welcome with which you have received me and my wife. The invitation you extended to us has been greatly appreciated in Finland as an expression of friendship toward the Finnish people.

"We have both very much looked forward to this visit to the United States, and to this opportunity of meeting you personally, Mr. President and Mrs. Kennedy. It is at the same time a great pleasure for us to be able to see your beautiful Capital and to visit also other parts of your great country and to meet with American people. Our attention will be directed especially to your powerful economy, your splendid scientific achievements and the progress you have made in the social sphere.

"This moment when I step on American soil gives me occasion to remember those hundreds of thousands of Finns who have settled in this country and who with their toil and labor have made themselves a place in the American community. They are a living bond between our two peoples.

"Mr. President, we Finns are keenly aware of the friendship of the people of the United States towards the people of Finland. I hope that my visit to the United States will further develop and strengthen the good and friendly relations which have always existed between our two countries."

In his opening words the President referred to Ahti Karjalainen, Finland's Minister of Foreign Affairs.

422 Toasts of the President and President Kekkonen. *October 16, 1961*

MR. PRESIDENT, I want to express again our great welcome to you and Madame Kekkonen, your Foreign Minister, and the members of your Cabinet, your son, and our great pleasure at having you here at the White House.

As you said in your address at the airport, the thing which has bound Finland and the United States perhaps closest together in the past has been the hundreds of thousands of Finnish men and women who have come to this country, who are loyal Americans but also look with affectionate regard to the land from whence they came.

They have been among our finest citizens. When I was a Member of the Congress, I represented Massachusetts, which includes many thousands of Finns within its borders, and I must say my experience and the experience of all Americans who have dealt with your countrymen ensures you a warm welcome as you travel through the United States.

In addition, we are glad to have you here because we feel that Finns have understood the very close connection between physical well-being and strength and mental and spiritual well-being. I remember, perhaps my very first memory as a boy, being taken to a stadium in Boston, Massachusetts, and watching Paavo Nurmi run around the track in a way which made a lasting impression on me, and of your country.

Your own experience as an athlete, as head of your Olympic Team in 1932, and now as President who today skis over 35 miles a day without pausing for breath, you set a dangerous precedent for all of us. All these things make you particularly welcome.

We are gathered here because we admire your country—we admire its courage in war, and we admire its courage in peace. I am particularly glad that you are going to travel throughout the United States. We are a prosperous country and people, who are very content with our own country. We do not desire anything but peace and to be let alone. And yet the American people, under different leaderships under different political parties since 1945, have assumed broad burdens stretching around the world, which we are glad to assume because we believe it is in a most important cause.

We believe that the strength of this country contributes to the independence of countries thousands of miles away, and while the ties which may bind these countries and the direct connection between them may not always be immediate and obvious, we believe that the willingness of the American people to show their responsibilities and to shoulder the burden in the cause of freedom helps the cause of freedom all around the globe—and we hope contributes to the cause of freedom within your own country.

Mr. President, in the days ahead, the challenge which faces Finland and the United States, varying as they do in location and in size, in many ways is equally great, and it is my hope that the relations between our two countries will continue to be warm and friendly, that the freedom of our two peoples will continue to be maintained, and that you, Mr. President, in the future as you have so well in the past, will continue to speak for Finland and speak for freedom.

And therefore, Mr. President, it is a great honor for us to welcome you to this ancient house, and to welcome your wife—and on behalf of the American people to drink to you and the people of Finland.

NOTE: The President proposed the toast at a luncheon in the state dining room at the White House. President Kekkonen responded as follows:

"Mr. President and Mrs. Kennedy:

"I thank you for that very warm welcome we have had in this country and in your home, the White House.

"I also wish to thank you, Mr. President, for the friendly sentiments you have just expressed toward my country. The friendship and understanding that Finland has always met with in the United States is greatly appreciated by us. And it is my hope that my visit here, and the tour I will be making through this great country, will convey to the American people the feelings of friendship of the Finnish people, our admiration for your great achievements and our respect for the principles and ideals on which your Republic was founded and for which you stand.

"In their outlook our two peoples have much in common. We Finns have an ancient tradition of Scandinavian democracy which has its roots in the society of free yeomen. It is based on respect for the individual and freedom under law. Our faith in these values has undergone severe tests, and I am convinced it will never falter. The main purpose of our policy is the maintenance of our independence and the safeguarding of our national way of life.

"For security, Finland cannot rely on military power. We have sought, and I believe found, security through the policy of neutrality. We wish to stay outside conflicts and disputes between the great powers, and to have friendly relations with all countries. With determination, we faithfully fulfill all obligations undertaken. By such means we have been able to live in peace and friendship with our neighbors and with the world, and to develop our country without having to ask for outside help. It is our hope that we will be able to continue to live in this way. However, such a policy depends on the confidence of all powers in the sincerity of our purpose.

"This is the aim in all our actions, and I believe we have succeeded.

"But we must have peace in the world. Without peace all our hopes will be shattered. In decisions affecting world peace, Finland has but a modest part to play. We on our part try to live up to the principle of the United Nations Charter which tells member states to live in peace as good neighbors; and we shall always support, as we have done until now, every proposal or action designed to promote conciliation between nations.

"I am aware of the great difficulties that stand in the way of an understanding between the great powers on which peace primarily depends. But we have faith in the sincere desire of the American people, and in your will, Mr. President, to work untiringly for the cause of peace.

"I hold my glass to you, Mr. President."

President Kekkonen's party included his wife and his son, Taneli K. Kekkonen, and his wife.

423   Message Marking the Observance of International Credit Union Day.   *October 16, 1961*

To Credit Union Members Everywhere:

You and millions of your fellow Americans have been showing for years your recognition of the importance of thrift by your participation in your credit union. You and many others understand the role of credit unions in encouraging both regular saving and the wise use of credit.

More recently, credit unions have undertaken new and valuable work in spreading overseas their encouragement of thrift. In newly developing countries, and particularly in Latin America, the Credit Union National Association and its World Extension Department are helping spread knowledge of this valuable instrument of economic democracy.

Credit unions are now operating in more than fifty countries of the free world, and in addition to helping their members economically are also furnishing an example of democratic control through their principle that each member has one vote, regardless of the size of his share in or his debt to his credit union.

For these reasons, on this day, the fourteenth annual celebration of International Credit Union Day, I salute all the people in the United States and throughout the free world who are taking an active part in the credit union movement.

JOHN F. KENNEDY

424 Joint Statement Following Discussions With the President of Finland. *October 17, 1961*

THE PRESIDENT of Finland and Mrs. Urho K. Kekkonen were guests yesterday of President and Mrs. Kennedy at a White House luncheon. Following the luncheon the two presidents exchanged views with regard to current international developments.

President Kennedy paid tribute to the many common ties between Finland and the United States and the democratic ideals the two nations share. Regarding Finland's position on the world scene the American President took account of Finland's treaty commitments and expressed American understanding for the reasons why Finland follows a policy of neutrality. He stated the United States will scrupulously respect Finland's chosen course. President Kennedy emphasized that all nations must avoid interference in the affairs of Finland.

President Kekkonen expressed his appreciation for the long-standing friendship between Finland and the United States, and for the understanding shown in the United States for Finland. Asserting that the purpose of Finland's foreign policy is to safeguard the security and independence of the nation, the Finnish President reaffirmed his country's intention to remain neutral while maintaining the confidence and friendship of all nations.

Presidents Kennedy and Kekkonen discussed recent world events. They agreed it was essential for both countries to support the United Nations as firmly as ever, since that body offers all men their greatest hope for achievement of the noble causes envisioned in the Charter.

Presidents Kennedy and Kekkonen discussed economic and cultural relations. The outlook for European economic development and the implications for other countries of possible enlargement of the European Common Market were reviewed. There was agreement between the presidents that current exchanges of students, teachers, leaders in various fields, and cultural and artistic presentations should be fostered. Exchanges of this nature were commended as a fundamental aid in developing understanding of each other's problems as well as consolidating existing friendship between the peoples of the United States and Finland.

Presidents Kennedy and Kekkonen expressed their mutual hopes that peace and justice would prevail in the world. All nations, large and small, have a grave responsibility toward civilization in that they must constantly search for a formula to bring true and universal peace, said the two presidents.

Only a sustained effort in pursuit of this great objective, using all available human talents and resources of nations, can assure progress toward realization of this goal, one of man's oldest and most basic desires.

425   Statement by the President Following Receipt of a Supplementary Report on the Airline Labor Problem. *October 17, 1961*

I HAVE today received the supplemental report of the Commission I established to consider the airlines controversy which tied up practically all major air carriers earlier this year. This report contains detailed recommendations for settlement of the dispute amplifying the Commission's May 24, 1961 report.

This report is a result of long, diligent, and objective study. The recommendations are concurred in by the Secretary of Labor and appear to me to be fair and equitable to the parties, and an honorable way to a peaceful settlement of a difficult inter-union dispute which has plagued the airline industry for years.

I am sure that the public joins with me in urging the pilots, the flight engineers, and the carriers to seriously consider and follow the Commission's recommendations so that a new era of labor peace can be achieved in the industry.

I should deeply appreciate it if the Commission will remain available to receive reports from the parties as to their progress in implementing the Commission's recommendations and transmitting such reports to me with the Commission's observations.

Professor Nathan P. Feinsinger, the Commission chairman, and his associates, Professors Richard A. Lester and J. Keith Mann, are to be commended for their work on a most difficult and taxing problem. They have performed an outstanding public service.

NOTE: The "Report to the President by the Commission Established by Executive Order 10921, dated February 21, 1961 [26 F.R. 1553], as Amended, To Consider Differences That Have Arisen Between Certain Air Carriers and Certain of Their Employees," dated May 24, 1961 (31 pp.), and the supplemental report, dated October 17, 1961 (15 pp.), were published by the Government Printing Office.

426   White House Statement Concerning Soviet Plans To Test a 50-Megaton Bomb. *October 17, 1961*

IT IS REPORTED that the Soviet Union plans to explode a giant nuclear bomb—the equivalent to 50 million tons of TNT.

We call upon the Soviet Union to recon-

sider this decision, if in fact it has been made. We know about high-yield weapons. Since 1957 the United States has had the technical know-how and materials to produce bombs in the 50–100 megaton range and higher. But we also know that such weapons are not essential to our military needs. Furthermore, full-scale tests are not necessary to develop 50 megaton bombs. Such an explosion could only serve some unconfessed political purpose.

We believe the peoples throughout the world will join us in asking the Soviet Union not to proceed with a test which can serve no legitimate purpose and which adds a mass of additional radioactive fallout to that which has been unleashed in recent weeks.

427 Remarks to the Members of the Panel on Mental Retardation. *October* 18, 1961

I WANT to express my appreciation to the members of this panel who have agreed to serve on a most important subject. I am especially glad that this is not merely a national effort but will attempt to coordinate our research and information and results with those of other countries who have been working on this problem for some years.

This is a matter which I think should be brought out into the sunlight and given a full national commitment, and I want to express my thanks to all the members of this panel who have been willing to serve, because I think that we can make easier the lives of many, many thousands of people and their families. It is high time that the country gives its time and attention to this.

I want to express my thanks to all the doctors on the panel, and to the Secretary of HEW and to Secretary Goldberg, who is in a related field, and to the members of the institutes of health who have shown what can be done by a concentrated national commitment. So that we want to do the same in this area, which is one of the most heartrending tragedies of life, and we want to do something about it.

We are all much in your debt.

NOTE: The President spoke in the Rose Garden at the White House.

428 Memorandum Implementing the International Textile Agreement. *October* 18, 1961

Memorandum to the Secretary of State, the Secretary of Commerce, and the Secretary of Labor:

In view of the International Textile Agreement reached ad referendum at Geneva on July 21, 1961, which I signed September 7, 1961:

A.

I am asking the Secretary of Commerce, as Chairman of the President's Cabinet Textile Advisory Committee, to convene that Committee for the purpose of creating an Interagency Textile Administrative Committee to carry out the rights and obligations of the United States under the "Short-Term Arrangement" provided for in the International Textile Agreement of July 21, 1961, at Geneva. The Interagency Textile Administrative Committee is to be established under the Chairmanship of a designee of the Secretary of Commerce; will be located, for administrative purposes, in the Department of Commerce; and will be composed of the Chairman and one representative each, from the Departments of State, Treasury, Agriculture, and Labor. The President's Cabinet Textile Advisory Committee will, at the request of any member of the interagency Textile Administrative Committee, consider any question of policy relating to the administration of the "Short-Term Arrangement."

B.

I am asking the Secretary of State to undertake, in accordance with policies established by the President's Textile Advisory Committee, the negotiations contemplated by the International Textile Agreement of July 21, 1961, including bilateral textile agreements. The Secretary of State will request the Secretaries of Commerce and Labor to appoint representatives of these Departments to the delegation on the Provisional Cotton Textile Committee of GATT, contemplated under the International Textile Agreement of July 21, 1961, toward the end that the United States representation on this GATT Committee shall include designees of the Secretaries of State, Commerce,

and Labor, with the Chairman being the designee of the Secretary of State.

C.

I am asking the President's Cabinet Textile Advisory Committee to form a Management-Labor Textile Advisory Committee to provide continuing advice on Textile problems to it, the Interagency Textile Administrative Committee, the United States representation on the GATT Committee, and the United States negotiators on bilateral agreements.

JOHN F. KENNEDY

NOTE: A White House release of September 7, 1961, announced that the President had accepted, on behalf of the United States, the international cotton textile agreement reached at a July 17–21 meeting in Geneva of the major textile importing and exporting countries.

The meeting, the release further stated, was called by the Executive Secretary of the General Agreement on Tariffs and Trade at the request of the United States, a request based on point 6 of President Kennedy's 7-point program of assistance to the textile industry, announced on May 2 (item 161, above).

The text of the Agreement is published in the Department of State Bulletin (vol. 45, p. 337).

429 Remarks of Welcome to the President of Liberia at Washington National Airport. *October* 19, 1961

MR. PRESIDENT, it is a great honor to welcome you and the members of your government here on a visit to Washington and the United States.

You have occupied a position of the highest responsibility in your country since 1943, a record unprecedented at this time any place in the world. You are the only surviving political leader of those days long ago during the days of the Second World War.

You have come on many occasions to the United States, and you come again on this

occasion at a time of great change in Africa, a time of great progress within your own country. You, Mr. President, are a symbol of stability and also of change, and it is a particular pleasure to welcome to this country the leader of a country with which the United States has enjoyed the closest and most intimate relations stretching back over a century, to welcome a leader who has been identified in his own life and in his own country with the great causes of freedom and progress and well-being of his people. And therefore, Mr. President, I welcome you to the United States once again. I express particular pleasure in having you here at this time and in having an opportunity to discuss with you the great changes which are occurring in Africa and throughout the world. With your long view, your long experience, you are a most welcome guest.

Mr. President, the people of the United States once again wish to join in welcoming you to our country.

NOTE: President Tubman responded as follows:

Mr. President, the fact that you have extended us an invitation to visit you and your great country at a time like this, a time of crisis, a time of tension, is reassuring and another manifestation of a century old friendship and intimacy that has existed between our two countries from the time of our incipiency as a nation until the present.

Through the years we have identified ourselves with your system of government. Our own Constitution was patterned after that of the United States of America, and that immortal document was written and prepared by one of your fellow countrymen, Mr. Greenleaf, and I could go on for many hours showing the cordial and very friendly close ties that have existed between our countries.

I am very happy to be here. As you well said, I have come here on several occasions, and particularly now that I know the burdens and responsibilities that you carry, it is a great expression of affection, not for me so much as for my country, of which I am particularly proud and grateful.

430 Joint Statement Following Discussions With President Tubman. *October* 21, 1961

AT THE INVITATION of President Kennedy, President Tubman paid a visit to Washington beginning October 19th. The two Presidents exchanged views on the present international situation and on relations between the United States and Liberia. This visit afforded a timely opportunity for the two Presidents to establish a personal acquaintance.

The two Presidents reaffirmed the strong ties of friendship and heritage which bind the two countries.

They reviewed the international situation with emphasis on developments in the United Nations. The two leaders agreed African representation in the United Nations should be given greater opportunity for participation. The two Presidents are opposed to any proposal which would compromise the integrity and effectiveness of the United Nations organization.

The two leaders reviewed recent developments in Africa. The President congratulated President Tubman and his delegation on their leadership and contribution to the success of the meetings of African and Malagasy States held in Monrovia last May. The President expressed the hope that the second meeting to be convened in Lagos in January would be equally harmonious and productive.

On the subject of economic aid to Liberia, the President reiterated the desire of the United States government to assist Liberia in its social and economic development, pointing out that it was this sincere desire that prompted the sending of a special economic mission to Liberia earlier in October to consult with the Liberian government on its development program. The President expressed his gratification that the consultations in Monrovia revealed a determination on the part of the Liberian government to pursue a program for an accelerated expansion of the Liberian economy. It was agreed that top priority in United States assistance would be given to establishment of a strong central planning agency as the basis for more

677

extensive assistance in all development areas.

The United States government will give serious consideration to participation in a long-term loan for the Mount Coffee hydro-electric project should further site engineering studies provided for in a pending Export-Import Bank loan confirm the project's feasibility.

The President also assured President Tubman that the United States government is prepared to give immediate increased assistance in the expansion of Liberia's educational program and the provision of additional health facilities with special reference to para-medical training facilities. The United States government will further give prompt consideration to means for participating in Liberia's plan to build a new hospital and medical training center in the city of Monrovia.

The conversation confirmed to the two leaders the profound and intimate relations between the two countries and their common aspirations to maintain peace and security and freedom in the promotion of the welfare of the peoples of the world.

NOTE: The joint statement was released at Newport, R.I.

---

431 Letter to Pablo Casals Inviting Him To Give a Concert at the White House. *October 24, 1961*

[Released October 24, 1961. Dated October 10, 1961]

Dear Mr. Casals:

Mrs. Kennedy and I would like to extend an invitation to you to give a concert at The White House on Monday evening, November 13th. We feel that your performance as one of the world's greatest artists would lend distinction to the entertainment of our invited guests. I do hope you will honor us with your presence.

Sincerely,

JOHN F. KENNEDY

[Mr. Pablo Casals, c/o Mr. Abe Fortas, 3025 N Street, N.W., Washington, D.C.]

NOTE: Mr. Casals' letter of acceptance, dated October 16, 1961, was also released.

---

432 Remarks to an International Group Attending the Inter-American Archival Seminar. *October 24, 1961*

Ladies and gentlemen:

I want to express our great pleasure and satisfaction at having all of you here.

In the Archives Building here in Washington you have probably seen the phrase "What is past is prologue," and your ability to guard and make possible the interpretation of the past I think will insure a stronger future.

I am hopeful that the meeting here will improve the techniques which we all have for preserving the record of the past, but that it will do more than that, that it will make it more possible for you and for us to make meaningful this past to our present citizens.

There's no sense in having the papers of the past beautifully kept unless they have an impact on the lives of our people. I have, for example, always felt that one of the great lacks among Americans of this country, in their knowledge of the past, has been their knowledge of the whole Spanish influence and exploration and development in the 16th century in the Southwest United States, which is a tremendous story.

Unfortunately, too many Americans think that America was discovered in 1620 when the Pilgrims came to my own State, and they forget the tremendous adventure of the 16th century and the early 17th century in the Southern and Southwest United States. But what is true here is true in your own country.

The Doctor was telling me that in Mexico you keep some of the records of Cortez in his country, and I am sure that stretching through all your countries are the most extraordinary records of courage and fortitude and perseverance—and I am hopeful that we can get all that into the light of day.

NOTE: The President spoke in the Rose Garden at the White House. In his closing remarks he referred to Dr. Jorge Ignacio Rubio Mañé, Director of the National Archives of Mexico, who spoke on behalf of the visiting group.

---

433   Message to Walter P. Marshall on the Occasion of the Transcontinental Telegraph Centennial.   *October 24, 1961*

Mr. Walter P. Marshall, President
The Western Union Telegraph Company
Omaha, Nebraska

I am happy to send my greetings and cordial good wishes to the Governors, Mayors, officials, members of patriotic and historical societies, educators and others participating in the observance of the transcontinental telegraph centennial.

It has been my pleasure to receive, over a line linking ceremonies at cities along the original transcontinental route, copies of the historic messages received by President Abraham Lincoln on October 24, 1861.

Those messages, so eloquently assuring Lincoln of the loyalty of Western states to the Union, then divided in Civil War, are proof of the vital importance of the first transcontinental line to the preservation of our nation.

Rapid communications play a vital role today in our national security, as they did in 1861, and have a great part as they did then in the development and carrying on of business and industry.

I join with all of you in saluting the pioneer telegraph men who built the line a century ago, and also those who are building and operating the great communications systems of today.

JOHN F. KENNEDY

NOTE: Mr. Marshall's message dated October 24, 1961, and the messages received by President Lincoln on October 24, 1861, were also released.

---

434   Letter to Henry B. Gonzalez in Support of His Candidacy in Texas.   *October 26, 1961*

[Released October 26, 1961.   Dated October 25, 1961]

Dear Senator Gonzalez:

It gives me great pleasure to join with Vice President Johnson and your other friends and good Democrats in Texas, in expressing my confidence in your candidacy for U.S. Representative for the 20th Texas district. Your awareness of national responsibilities, your concern with the problems and opportunities of the people of your district, and your courage in performing the duties of public office are well known to your friends.

Through the years the people of San Antonio and Bexar County have repeatedly called upon men of our Party to serve them in the United States Congress. You are indeed fortunate to aspire to succeed a distinguished public servant, whom I have had the honor to appoint a judge, a fine son of Texas and exemplary citizen, Paul J. Kilday. Vice President Johnson and I will always

be most grateful for the confidence shown to our Party by the citizens of the 20th district.

I want to wish you every success in your campaign and extend my warmest regards to yourself and your family.

Sincerely,

JOHN F. KENNEDY

[Honorable Henry B. Gonzalez, Houston Building, San Antonio, Tex.]

NOTE: Mr. Gonzalez was elected to the U.S. House of Representatives on November 4, 1961.

---

435   Letter to President Ngo Dinh Diem on the Sixth Anniversary of the Republic of Viet-Nam. *October* 26, 1961

[Released October 26, 1961. Dated October 24, 1961]

Dear Mr. President:

On the sixth anniversary of the Republic of Viet-Nam, the United States of America is proud to pay tribute to the courage of the Vietnamese people. We have seen and marked well the anguish—and the glory—of a nation that refuses to submit to Communist terror. From the people that twice defeated the hordes of Kublai Khan, we could expect no less. America, and indeed all free men, must be grateful for the example you have set.

Mr. President, in 1955 we observed the dangers and difficulties that surrounded the birth of your Republic. In the years that followed, we saw the dedication and vigor of your people rapidly overcoming those dangers and difficulties. We rejoiced with you in the new rice springing again from fields long abandoned, in the new hospitals and roads and schools that were built, and in the new hopes of a people who had found peace after a long and bitter war. The record you established in providing new hope,

shelter and security to nearly a million fleeing from Communism in the North stands out as one of the most laudable and best administered efforts in modern times.

Your brave people scarcely tasted peace before they were forced again into war. The Communist response to the growing strength and prosperity of your people was to send terror into your villages, to burn your new schools and to make ambushes of your new roads. On this October 26, we in America can still rejoice in the courage of the Vietnamese people, but we must also sorrow for the suffering, destruction and death which Communism has brought to Viet-Nam, so tragically represented in the recent assassination of Colonel Hoang Thuy Nam, one of your outstanding patriots.

Mr. President, America is well aware of the increased intensity which in recent months has marked the war against your people, and of the expanding scale and frequency of the Communist attacks. I have read your speech to the Vietnamese National Assembly in which you outline so clearly the threat of Communism to Viet-Nam. And I have taken note of the stream of threats and vituperation, directed at your government and mine, that flows day and night from Hanoi. Let me assure you again that the United States is determined to help Viet-Nam preserve its independence, protect its people against Communist assassins, and build a better life through economic growth.

I am awaiting with great interest the report of General Maxwell Taylor based on his recent talks and observations in Viet-Nam, supplementing reports I have received from our Embassy there over many months. I will then be in a better position to consider with you additional measures that we might take to assist the republic of Viet-Nam in its struggle against the Communist aggressors.

Mr. President, we look forward in these perilous days to a future October 26, when Viet-Nam will again know freedom and peace. We know that day is coming, and we pray that it may be soon. I speak for the American people when I say that we are confident of the success of the Vietnamese nation, that we have faith in its strength and valor, and that we know that the future of the Vietnamese people is not Communist slavery but the freedom and prosperity which they have defended and pursued throughout their history.

Sincerely,

JOHN F. KENNEDY

436   Statement by the President to Cabinet Officers and Agency Heads on the 1962 and 1963 Budget Outlook. *October 26, 1961*

I HAVE ASKED you to meet with me today to discuss the current outlook for the Federal budget.

The budget reflects national policy. This year our national policy has emphasized: strengthening the defenses against threats to world peace in Berlin, Southeast Asia, and elsewhere; bringing about recovery from economic recession; and laying firmer foundations for long-term growth in national welfare and security.

Our accomplishments have been substantial.

In the military field, the 6.4 billion dollar increase in appropriations over the previous administration's budget provides for a 50 percent higher production target for Polaris missile-carrying submarines; a doubling of our capacity to produce Minuteman intercontinental missiles; many more strategic bombers placed on ground alert; an increase by nearly one-half in the number of combat-ready Army divisions; and increases in air and sea lift capacity, tactical air power, stocks of weapons and ammunition, and many other aspects of our military strength.

In the vital area of United States assistance to the economic and military strength of other countries to buttress their independence from communism, I regret that the Congress did not support my request for additional appropriations (and in fact appropriated 90 million dollars less than the previous administration's proposal of 4 billion dollars). Nevertheless the new AID legislation accomplishes major improvements in the organization and management of these programs. A new AID Administrator is giving unified leadership to the entire effort, and new and stronger criteria

681

of self-help and long-range planning are being applied to aided countries.

With respect to the recession, strong action by the Government, coupled with the recuperative forces in the private economy, reversed the downward trend of jobs and incomes early in the year and brought steady and strong recovery. The annual rate of national output has risen from a low of 501 billion dollars in the first quarter of calendar 1961 to 526 billion dollars in the third quarter. There is every indication that this strong rise will continue into 1962. Direct budgetary costs for anti-recession purposes will be about 600 million dollars in fiscal 1962 above the previous administration's budget—providing for temporary extended unemployment compensation benefits, aid to dependent children of the unemployed, increases in surplus food distribution (including the pilot food stamp program), and the area redevelopment program. More than half of these funds will later be returned to the Treasury in special unemployment taxes authorized when the extended benefits were enacted.

In the field of housing and community development, new and more effective legislation has been enacted, carrying forward tested programs such as urban renewal to attack blighted and slum areas, and adding new programs such as aid for the acquisition of open space in urban areas and assistance to urban mass transit. Expenditures are up 350 million dollars in fiscal 1962 over the proposals of the previous administration; were it not for the necessity to devote so much of our resources to defense, a strong case could be made for more rapid increases in Federal participation in the joint Federal-State-local effort to meet the enormous and growing problems of community development in cities and towns.

In agriculture, we can take pride in the resurgence this year of farm income. Beginning steps have been taken—although thus far with inadequate legislative tools—in the intricate and necessarily time-consuming process of adjusting our impressive agricultural productive capacity to the needs of domestic and foreign requirements. Our new programs for feed grains and wheat are preventing substantial unneeded production and although costs are high this year, these programs are expected to avoid the heavy future costs that would have accompanied the continuation of previous programs. We have stepped up the Food for Peace program. However, the effects of exceptionally good weather and rising farm productivity have brought higher than anticipated crops and added to the cost of price support programs in the present fiscal year. We still have much to do to achieve effective adjustments in agricultural output.

While I regret very much the failure of the Congress to enact legislation for general aid to education, expenditures for scientific research (including medical research) and education will rise by 170 million dollars over the proposals of the previous administration, even excluding the large increases in funds for military and space research. The scientific and technological gains that will be achieved as a result of the national research effort (including military and space research) will be of the utmost importance to the future growth and strength of our Nation.

Looking at these and other fields of national effort, it is clear that the increases in the budget this year are yielding important returns; that our military security has increased sharply; that the vigor of the recovery from the recent recession has been strengthened; that wages, farm income, corporate profits and the gross national product have all risen sharply; and that in areas of health, natural resources, science and other activities strong gains are being made.

From the beginning this administration has followed a prudent budget policy in meeting national needs. With your cooperation it was possible to send to the Congress appropriation requests more than one billion dollars below the amounts originally asked by your departments and agencies. Furthermore, we have taken steps during the present year to save tens of millions of dollars by actions to improve efficiency. Modern cost-saving machines have been installed; field offices have been merged or closed; interdepartmental and advisory committees have been abolished; publications and exhibits have been curtailed; procurement practices have been tightened; greater use has been made of scrap and surplus material; wasteful duplications and variations have been eliminated; administrative structures have been streamlined; and other operations have been reorganized, pooled, consolidated or abolished.

Special efforts have been made to achieve substantial savings by making our defense establishment lean, fit, and efficient. The Defense budget submitted in March reflected savings in this fiscal year alone of over 700 million dollars in projects, programs and installations which were either unproven or unnecessary in the light of our new missile buildup and general defense posture. A new central supply agency for the Department of Defense has been established and is already saving significant sums.

In both the defense and non-defense fields, this administration resisted attempts to increase expenditures beyond the level justified in budget requests. Our proposals in the area of social insurance were all self-financed.

We sought to make the highway program self-supporting, without a drain on general revenues.

Now that the Congress has adjourned, the budget has been reviewed in the light of congressional actions and other events since the budget proposals and estimates were made. The current outlook re-emphasizes the necessity to conduct the necessary work of the Government at the lowest possible cost, to eliminate or defer low priority activities, and to limit the number of Government employees to the absolute minimum.

The position on the revenue side is essentially unchanged from the estimates of some months ago. Revenues being collected in fiscal 1962 reflect incomes earned during calendar 1961 and therefore are depressed by the effects of the recent recession. Indeed, had there been no recession in 1960–61 the budget would today be in surplus even with all the additional expenditures for defense and other purposes.

On the expenditure side, there are a number of increases compared with the position some months ago. The Congress failed to increase postal rates to meet a postal deficit of some three-quarters of a billion dollars. The necessity of calling up two additional divisions and thousands of other servicemen, as well as the general speedup in procurement and construction which accompanies an increase in military readiness, have brought about a sharper rise in defense expenditures than was previously foreseen. Excellent weather conditions, and increased productivity from machines and fertilizer, have boosted this year's crops and the accompanying price support costs to large proportions which will be difficult to reduce until the Congress enacts adequate farm legislation.

With these increases in expenditures the

estimated deficit for the current year has risen. There is general agreement that under the present conditions of high unemployment and recession-reduced tax receipts, a deficit is normally to be expected. It is important to make sure that the deficit is kept within reasonable limits and reflects only essential expenditures.

The present deficit—reflecting the 1960–61 recession—is expected to be much smaller than the 12.4 billion dollar deficit incurred in fiscal year 1959—reflecting the 1958–59 recession—despite the far greater increases in defense and space expenditures in the current year. The increase in domestic civilian expenditures is less than three-fifths the increase that took place during the 1958–59 recession.

More than 80 percent of the additions this administration proposed to the previous administration's budget were for strengthening the national security or for combating the recession, or included other sums to be repaid to the Treasury.

There is no evidence that the currently-estimated deficit presents serious risk to the domestic price level or the U.S. balance of payments. Moreover, considering the economic effect of the budget on a month-by-month basis, as contrasted to the annual totals, the current impact of Government operations is expected to change early in calendar 1962 from a net stimulative to a net restraining influence on the economy.

While the recent rises in the estimates of expenditures and the deficit, therefore, are compatible with the sound fiscal and budget policies we have been following, they are further grounds for insistence on economy in executing Government programs. This is the reason I have asked each of you to follow a most careful and frugal policy with respect to commitments and expenditures under the 1962 budget as enacted by the

Congress. The Congress has on many occasions made it clear that appropriations are only a ceiling, not a mandate to spend, and that department and agency heads are not required to spend every dollar appropriated. Accordingly, I have asked each of you to exercise the maximum care in scrutinizing all expenditures, tightening requirements, postponing the initiation of deferrable projects, and phasing out any acceleration of spending which was instituted as an anti-recession measure.

I am especially desirous that new programs or expansions of existing programs be undertaken with caution and deliberation, to make sure that sound criteria are used, careful plans are laid, and minimum funds are spent. I much prefer that obligational authority remain uncommitted where there is any doubt that expenditures would yield substantial returns to the national interest.

I am also especially desirous that the number of Government employees be limited to the minimum consistent with getting the job done. There is no question that employment can be held substantially below the levels which would be possible under the funds authorized by the Congress, if strong efforts are made to achieve increases in productivity and efficiency, to use better techniques of management and production, and to staff each activity with only the minimum number of employees needed to carry out our objectives. I expect each of you to make such efforts.

The Director of the Bureau of the Budget informs me that the estimated expenditures for fiscal 1962 which will appear in the autumn budget review, reflect the judgment of each of you as to what will actually be spent during this fiscal year under the policies I have outlined, and that total outlays will be substantially less than they might have been under the authority enacted by the Congress.

I appreciate your continued efforts to keep uncommitted any funds, the expenditure of which is not absolutely necessary to the national interest at this time. While I know that these actions represent a cutback or postponement in many functions to which each of you attaches great importance, I congratulate you on this recognition of the overriding requirements of a budget policy reflecting the total national interest.

Let me add a word about the 1963 budget. In view of the prospective gains in the economy, it is my intention to propose a balanced budget for that year, barring extraordinary and unforeseen defense requirements. As you know, we can expect a substantial increase in revenues under existing tax laws in fiscal 1963, reflecting the economic recovery now taking place. However, it is already clear that expenditures for the military and other elements of our national security programs will necessarily rise next year. In these circumstances it will plainly be necessary to defer or limit increases in many programs which in more normal times would be thoroughly desirable, and to shift present staffs and resources to the maximum extent from work of lower to work of higher priority. I will appreciate your cooperation in putting these policies into effect in planning the 1963 budget.

437   Statement by the President Concerning Export Credit Facilities. *October 27, 1961*

IN MY MESSAGE to the Congress on Balance of Payments and Gold earlier this year, I directed the President of the Export-Import Bank to initiate measures designed to give American exporters full equality with their competitors in other countries in order to help boost the total volume of United States exports. I also asked the Secretary of the Treasury to undertake a study of methods through which private financial institutions could participate more broadly in providing export credit facilities.

These two studies have been closely coordinated and carried out under the immediate supervision of the Export-Import Bank, with policy guidance from the Secretary of the Treasury and the National Advisory Council. I am pleased to announce two fundamental and complementary steps to achieve the objectives of stimulating American exports, strengthening the balance of payments of our country, and enlisting maximum cooperation of private credit facilities.

The new programs are intended to be fully comparable with those offered abroad, particularly with respect to small and medium sized export concerns and with respect to assistance in the financing of consumer goods exports.

The first new program consists of a system of export credit insurance to exporters. This will be operated through the newly organized Foreign Credit Insurance Association—a voluntary, unincorporated group of major United States insurance companies. The FCIA has entered into an agreement with the Export-Import Bank to issue coverage against commercial foreign credit risks in partnership with Eximbank, which will cover political risks.

The second program consists of a new system of guarantees to be issued by Eximbank directly to commercial banks and affiliated financial institutions undertaking the financing of exports. It is designed to encourage these banks to provide non-recourse financing of medium term credits, and to speed up these transactions by permitting the exporter to deal with his bank, rather than with Eximbank in Washington.

The objective of both programs is to assure that U.S. exporters will not lose sales because of a lack of credit facilities where the extension of credit is appropriate. I believe that American exporters will be more disposed to extend credit to their customers if they hold an export credit insurance policy issued through the FCIA, and that commercial banks will be prepared to discount such insured paper. Accordingly, our exporters,

through use of the insurance and bank guarantee programs, will be better able to compete successfully with exporters in other countries on sales where credit is required by the customers overseas.

I am deeply appreciative of the splendid response of private industry in furthering the national interest in this area. Both the participating insurance companies and the commercial banks have rendered a public service through their cooperation in making these export credit facilities available as part of the national effort to improve the balance of payments to the United States.

438 Proclamation 3438: Thanksgiving Day, 1961. *October 28, 1961*

By the President of the United States of America a Proclamation:

"It is a good thing to give thanks unto the Lord."

More than three centuries ago, the Pilgrims, after a year of hardship and peril, humbly and reverently set aside a special day upon which to give thanks to God for their preservation and for the good harvest from the virgin soil upon which they had labored. Grave and unknown dangers remained. Yet by their faith and by their toil they had survived the rigors of the harsh New England winter. Hence they paused in their labors to give thanks for the blessings that had been bestowed upon them by Divine Providence.

This year, as the harvest draws near its close and the year approaches its end, awesome perils again remain to be faced. Yet we have, as in the past, ample reason to be thankful for the abundance of our blessings. We are grateful for the blessings of faith and health and strength and for the imperish-

able spiritual gifts of love and hope. We give thanks, too, for our freedom as a nation; for the strength of our arms and the faith of our friends; for the beliefs and confidence we share; for our determination to stand firmly for what we believe to be right and to resist mightily what we believe to be base; and for the heritage of liberty bequeathed by our ancestors which we are privileged to preserve for our children and our children's children.

It is right that we should be grateful for the plenty amidst which we live; the productivity of our farms, the output of our factories, the skill of our artisans, and the ingenuity of our investors. But in the midst of our thanksgiving, let us not be unmindful of the plight of those in many parts of the world to whom hunger is no stranger and the plight of those millions more who live without the blessings of liberty and freedom. With some we are able to share our material abundance through our Food-for-Peace Program and through our support of the United

Nations Freedom-from-Hunger Campaign. To all we can offer the sustenance of hope that we shall not fail in our unceasing efforts to make this a peaceful and prosperous world for all mankind.

Now, THEREFORE, I, JOHN F. KENNEDY, President of the United States of America, in consonance with the joint resolution of Congress approved December 26, 1941, which designates the fourth Thursday in November of each year as Thanksgiving Day, do hereby proclaim Thursday, the twenty-third day of November of this year, as a day of national thanksgiving.

I urge all citizens to make this Thanksgiving not merely a holiday from their labors, but rather a day of contemplation. I ask the head of each family to recount to his children the story of the first New England Thanksgiving, thus to impress upon future generations the heritage of this nation born in toil, in danger, in purpose, and in the conviction that right and justice and freedom can through man's efforts persevere

and come to fruition with the blessing of God.

Let us observe this day with reverence and with prayer that will rekindle in us the will and show us the way not only to preserve our blessings, but also to extend them to the four corners of the earth. Let us by our example, as well as by our material aid, assist all peoples of all nations who are striving to achieve a better life in freedom.

IN WITNESS WHEREOF, I have hereunto set my hand and caused the Seal of the United States of America to be affixed.

DONE at the City of Washington this twenty-seventh day of October in the year of our Lord nineteen hundred and [SEAL] sixty-one, and of the Independence of the United States of America the one hundred and eighty-sixth.

JOHN F. KENNEDY

By the President
DEAN RUSK
   Secretary of State

---

439   Message to President Gürsel Following His Election Under the New Turkish Constitution.   *October 29, 1961*

Dear Mr. President:

I congratulate you on your election as President of the Republic of Turkey. I also wish to congratulate, in the name of the United States Government and its people, the Turkish Government and people for their success in promulgating a new constitution and in establishing a freely-elected Grand National Assembly.

As you assume your Presidential responsibilities, let me assure you of my country's dedication to the firm friendship and co-

operation which have consistently characterized Turco-American relations. We are united in our aims of preserving the security of our homelands and creating a world where mankind can live in peace and freedom. In these cherished causes, we are proud to work side by side with the Government and people of Turkey.

Please accept my warmest greetings and best wishes.

   Sincerely,

JOHN F. KENNEDY

440   Remarks at the Airport at Fort Smith, Arkansas. *October 29, 1961*

Governor, Mr. Mayor, Commissioners, Senator McClellan, Senator Fulbright, Jim Trimble, and Members of Congress:

I want to express my thanks to Fort Smith and to Arkansas for a welcome today. It is a year since I used to make airport speeches, and while I'm here for only 8 minutes, I do want to express my appreciation to Arkansas for eight electoral votes.

I am delighted to be here. I served in the Congress of the United States for 6 years, in the House of Representatives, with your distinguished Congressman Jim Trimble— who spoke for this District and also spoke for the country. And I served in the Senate of the United States for 8 years with Senator McClellan as a member of the Rackets Committee—where he spoke for what is best in the United States, and with Senator Fulbright on the Foreign Relations Committee—who has worked for a strong United States in a peaceful world and also spoken for the interests of Arkansas.

I do not believe that there is anything inconsistent in the year 1961, in a critical and dangerous period, in our opening up Fort Chaffee in order to strengthen this country, and in also dredging the river in order to make it navigable by 1970.

This Southwest United States was built by men who carried rifles and plowed their fields. They plowed their fields because

they were building for the future, and they carried their rifles in order that there might be a future.

We believe in a strong country. We believe in a country which is militarily prepared. We have, in the last 6 months, increased our expenditures for defense by over six billion dollars. But we do so because we want this country to be able to fulfill its destiny. We want this country to grow stronger and we do not concentrate only on our military strength. We believe that as you build the river and as you build the ground and reclaim it, and as you strengthen the resources of this country, together they will ensure this country will not only survive but its ideas prevail.

I am proud to come to Fort Smith. When Fort Chaffee was closed in 1959, this community showed what it could do. It has built a great industrial base here. Now Fort Chaffee is open, and we're going to keep it open—and we're going to keep this community and this State and this country moving.

I am proud to be here, and I thank you.

NOTE: In the President's opening words he referred to Orval E. Faubus, Governor of Arkansas; Robert R. Brooksher, Jr., Mayor of Fort Smith; John L. McClellan and J. W. Fulbright, U.S. Senators from Arkansas; and James W. Trimble, U.S. Representative from Arkansas.

441   Remarks at Big Cedar, Oklahoma, on the Opening of the Ouachita National Forest Road. *October 29, 1961*

Ladies and gentlemen, Senator Kerr, Governor, Members of the Congress:

I am proud to come to Oklahoma. During the campaign last year I met many citizens of this State, but not in this State. I met them in Alaska, where many Oklahomans had gone in the thirties to build a new life. I met them in the valleys of

California, where many citizens of this State had gone in the thirties to build a better life. And they left Oklahoma, the State that they loved, because this country had not learned the lessons of land, wood, and water, because they had not recognized that these great national resources can only be maintained for ourselves and those who come after us by dedicated men—men, land, wood, and water.

Now the citizens of Oklahoma stay in Oklahoma. Now they recognize the opportunities that are to be found in this State— and Oklahomans instead of leaving are coming home.

I think in these years of great hazard for our country, where we are faced with many challenges, and also I believe many opportunities, that we take our lesson and our theme from the Bible and the story of Nehemias, which tells us that when the children of Israel returned from captivity they determined to rebuild the walls of Jerusalem, in spite of the threats of the enemy. The wall was built and the peace was preserved. But it was written, "Of them that built on the wall . . . with one of his hands he did the work, and with the other he held the sword."

We hold the sword, and we are determined to maintain our strength and our commitments. But we also hold in our hand the trowel. We are determined to build in our own country, so that those who come after us—as they surely will—will find available to them all of the great resources that we now have.

This forest was preserved for the people of this State and country by the efforts of a Congressman from far away Massachusetts, at the turn of the century, who recognized the importance of building for other generations.

But this forest and these rivers and all that has been done here in Oklahoma has been done by the dedicated men that have represented this State in the National Capital— by Senator Robert Kerr who has helped build this State, by his partner Senator Mike Monroney who speaks for Oklahoma and the country, by Carl Albert who in a relatively short period of time has become the Majority Whip of the House, one of the three leaders with Congressman McCormack and Speaker Rayburn of the Democratic majority in the House of Representatives, which shows their regard for him; and I must say, in fight after fight for the development of the interests of the people of this country this year, Congressman Albert was in front always leading, and always fighting for this country.

And he is associated with distinguished Members who are here today. Congressman Edmondson, and Congressman Jarman, and Congressman Steed, with whom I served once in the House on the Labor and Education Committee. This State has a distinguished Governor, Governor Edmondson, and I am proud that as an old and valued friend of mine he has come here today.

We open this north-south highway, but in a larger sense, this meeting contributes to the education and well-being, in a sense, of the President of the United States. There is nothing more valuable for any occupant of that high office than to leave that city once in a while and come and see this country, and to see what a great asset we have, in these difficult times.

This country will have, by the year two thousand, more than three hundred million people in it. We want them to have the same assets that we have. We want to build for ourselves and for them. And therefore I can assure you, in the 1960's, as the United States carries the standard of freedom everywhere in the world, we will also be carrying the standard of progress, here in Oklahoma, here in the United States, as this country moves ahead.

Thank you.

NOTE: The President spoke at the ribbon-cutting ceremonies. In his opening words he referred to Robert S. Kerr, U.S. Senator from Oklahoma, and J. Howard Edmondson, Governor of Oklahoma.

442 White House Statement Announcing the Explosion by the U.S.S.R. of a 50-Megaton Bomb. *October 30, 1961*

AT THREE THIRTY this morning, the Soviet Union detonated a very large nuclear device. Preliminary evidence indicates that its magnitude is on the order of 50 megatons. The explosion took place in the atmosphere. It will produce more radioactive fallout than any previous explosion.

The Soviet explosion was a political rather than a military act. The device exploded does not add in effectiveness against military targets to nuclear weapons now available both to the Soviet Union and the United States. It does not affect the basic balance of nuclear power. Any such weapon would be primarily a mass killer of people in war— and the testing of this device primarily an incitement to fright and panic in the cold war.

In undertaking this test, the Soviet Union has deliberately overridden the expressed hope of the world as stated in the resolution adopted by the General Assembly of the United Nations on October 28. It has done so because it intends through this display to spread such fear across the world that peace-loving men will accept any Soviet demand. Fear is the oldest weapon in history. Throughout the life of mankind, it has been the resort of those who could not hope to

prevail by reason and persuasion. It will be repelled today, as it has been repelled in the past—not only by the steadfastness of free men but by the power of the arms which men will use to defend their freedom.

There is no mystery about producing a 50-megaton bomb. Nor is there any technical need for testing such a weapon at full-scale detonation in order to confirm the basic design. The United States Government considered this matter carefully several years ago and concluded that such weapons would not provide an essential military capability. The existing United States nuclear arsenal is superior in quantity and quality to that of any other nation. The United States today has ample military power to destroy any nation which would unleash thermonuclear war.

We have no wish ever to use this military power. We are ready, now as ever, to sign the test-ban treaty proposed at Geneva. We are ready, now as ever, to negotiate a treaty for general and complete disarmament. In the meantime, we will continue to take whatever measures are necessary to preserve the security of our country and of others who count on us.

443 Message to a Meeting on the Foreign Student in the United States. *October 30, 1961*

I WOULD LIKE to take this opportunity to express my personal interest in the purpose and plan of your meeting on "The

Foreign Student in the United States." The need for greater effort, to promote international understanding both through the

Government and through non-Governmental organizations, becomes ever more evident as the number of foreign students increases and the attendant responsibilities and opportunities rise. The object of your meeting—to enable the Government to advise and consult with representatives of many of the vital action groups which have long been concerned with providing a better experience for foreign students—emphasizes the essential basis of our total effort.

Government has its role to play: the Department of State has recently indicated a broadened concern for improving the experience of all foreign students regardless of whether they came here under Government programs. But it is on individuals such as you and the voluntary groups you represent, that the Government must depend primarily for the character and quality of the relationships we form with foreign students. This responsibility gives all of you and your organizations a first-hand role in this increasingly important part of our foreign relations. I hope your meeting is a most productive one in outlining ways by which we can, jointly, meet this great and growing opportunity more effectively.

JOHN F. KENNEDY

NOTE: The 2-day meeting was held at the Department of State October 30–31, 1961. The President's message was read by Philip H. Coombs, Assistant Secretary of State for Educational and Cultural Affairs, who addressed the opening meeting.

---

444 Letter to Prime Minister Ikeda of Japan Suggesting an Exchange of Information on the Problem of Mental Retardation. *November 1, 1961*

[Released November 1, 1961. Dated October 27, 1961]

My dear Mr. Prime Minister:

I have recently learned that you have taken steps to initiate a study of the problem of mental retardation and that the Chichibu Gakuen under the leadership of Dr. Osamu Kan is making important advances, and I congratulate you on this undertaking. It presents a universal challenge to all the nations of the world.

Recently I appointed a Panel composed of distinguished scientists, educators, physicians, lawyers, sociologists, and others to organize and chart a program to conquer this disability. It seems to me that it would be useful to exchange information between our nations in our common effort to solve the problems in this field.

Accordingly, I am asking Mr. Myer Feldman, as my personal representative, to request your permission to invite the participation of Dr. Kan, or any other person you may suggest, to the next meeting of the American Panel on Mental Retardation. This is scheduled for December 8th and 9th in Washington, D.C. The attendance at this meeting of Dr. Kan, or any other person you may feel it appropriate to suggest, would be most helpful and deeply appreciated by me.

I feel sure that you share my conviction that the challenge presented by the unsolved problems to which both Japan and the United States are directing their attention in the field of mental retardation offers a great opportunity for service to the cause of humanity. It seems particularly appropriate at this time that our two countries unite in seizing this opportunity. The consequences of our joint endeavors can be much more important to mankind than even the deep concerns over the destructive forces being unleashed in the world today.

Sincerely,

JOHN F. KENNEDY

NOTE: The letter was delivered to Prime Minister Ikeda by Myer Feldman, Deputy Counsel to the President, who was in Japan as the White House representative attending the meetings of the Joint United States-Japan Committee on Trade and Economic Affairs.

In a letter dated November 3 and released by the White House on November 9, Prime Minister Ikeda stated that arrangements were being made for Dr. Kan to participate in the American Panel.

445 Remarks at the Signing of the Delaware River Basin Compact. *November 2, 1961*

TODAY'S formal signing of the Delaware River Basin Compact is a significant event. Its significance lies in the unique character of the Compact and the great hope for comprehensive plans for full and effective development of the Delaware River Valley.

The highly industrialized character of the Basin and the heavy population concentrated in the region presents a real challenge to the Commission in its efforts to devise a water resource program suited to the area's needs.

Included within the Commission's jurisdiction is the control and development of adequate water supplies, pollution control, flood protection, watershed management, recreation, hydroelectric power and the regulation of withdrawals and the diversion of water.

I am designating the Honorable Stewart L. Udall, the Secretary of the Interior, to be the Federal representative on the Commission. I know he will work with and have

the counsel and cooperation of the many departments and agencies of the Federal Government concerned with water and resource development. I am sorry he is not with us today, but as you know, he is out of the country in Japan. He has, however, expressed his willingness to serve in this capacity, and I know he shares the optimism of the four States concerning the future of the Delaware Basin.

We are glad to join with Delaware, New Jersey, New York, and Pennsylvania in this bold venture. The task set for the Commission will not be easy to achieve, but we are confident that the cooperation that has brought forth this Compact will endure, and that working together real progress can be made for the people of the Basin.

NOTE: The signing ceremonies were held in the President's office at the White House. During his remarks the President referred to the Delaware Basin Commission.

446 Statement by the President Concerning the Development and Testing of Nuclear Weapons. *November 2, 1961*

THE UNITED STATES is carefully assessing the current series of nuclear tests being conducted by the Soviet Union. I do not have to dwell on the irresponsible nature

of these Soviet actions. The Soviet Union has shown its complete disregard for the welfare of mankind, first, by breaking off the nuclear test cessation negotiations at Geneva, which had been underway since October 31, 1958, and second, by contemptuously exploding in the atmosphere a large number of nuclear weapons ranging into many megatons, including a device which, by their own admission, exceeded 50 megatons.

I do not suggest that we can dismiss these Soviet nuclear tests as mere bluff and bluster. To a certain extent this does enter into the Soviet campaign of fear, but these tests are, no doubt, of importance to Soviet leaders and scientists in developing and improving nuclear weapons.

This much can be said with certainty now:

1. In terms of total military strength, the United States would not trade places with any nation on earth. We have taken major steps in the past year to maintain our lead—and we do not propose to lose it.

2. The United States does not find it necessary to explode 50 megaton nuclear devices to confirm that we have many times more nuclear power than any other nation on earth and that these capabilities are deployed so as to survive any sneak attack and thus enable us to devastate any nation which initiates a nuclear attack on the United States or its Allies. It is essential to the defense of the Free World that we maintain this relative position.

In view of the Soviet action, it will be the policy of the United States to proceed in developing nuclear weapons to maintain this superior capability for the defense of the Free World against any aggressor. No nuclear test in the atmosphere will be undertaken, as the Soviet Union has done, for so-called psychological or political reasons. But should such tests be deemed necessary to maintain our responsibilities for Free World security, in the light of our evaluation of Soviet tests, they will be undertaken only to the degree that the orderly and essential scientific development of new weapons has reached a point where effective progress is not possible without such tests—and only within limits that restrict the fall-out from such tests to an absolute minimum.

In the meantime, as a matter of prudence, we shall make necessary preparations for such tests so as to be ready in case it becomes necessary to conduct them.

In spite of the evidence which shows very clearly that the Soviet Union was preparing its own tests while pretending to negotiate their cessation at Geneva, the United States maintains its determination to achieve a world free from the fear of nuclear tests and a nuclear war. We will continue to be ready to sign the nuclear test treaty which provides for adequate inspection and control. The facts necessary for such a treaty are all evident—the argument on both sides have all been made—a draft is on the table—and our negotiators are ready to meet.

447 Statement by the President in Support of the Reelection of Robert F. Wagner as Mayor of New York City. *November 2, 1961*

I WANT to take this opportunity to state with the utmost conviction my whole-hearted support for the re-election of Mayor Robert F. Wagner.

His experience in coping with the problems of this great city cannot be matched. I have visited with him many times, not only during this year in the White House but earlier as well—for he was of great help to me in my own campaign. On each occasion I have been impressed with his insight into the needs of this city and the problems and opportunities of all its people.

Moreover, during this past year I have worked closely with Mayor Wagner on a number of federal-city problems; and I am counting on continuing this close relationship in the future. Many of our most important efforts in achieving greater progress for this nation involve the city of New York: providing better housing, ending the pollution of its air and water, attacking the congestion of its major streets and highways, and aiding the employment of all its citizens, to cite only a few examples. I hope I can continue to work with Mayor Wagner who shares my philosophy on these issues.

New York is, moreover, a unique asset to all the country—as a home for the U.N., as a port of entry to visitors and immigrants.

In short, our efforts nationally to strengthen our economy, the opportunities of our citizens and our stature abroad can be complete only if those same efforts are going ahead in this city, under a Mayor with those same convictions. That is why I am glad that you have in the New York Mayor's office a man of Bob Wagner's ability; and I am sure New York will do its duty in keeping him there.

NOTE: The statement was released in New York on the President's arrival in the city.

448   Remarks at a Political Rally in Trenton, New Jersey. *November 2, 1961*

Judge Hughes, Governor Meyner, Thorn Lord, Senator Williams, Congressman Thompson, Congressman Gallagher, ladies and gentlemen:

One year ago at this time I came into this city around dark, after having made about 15 stump speeches. In the last 9 months, I'm happy to say that this is the first stump speech I've made for a candidate and I am glad it's here in New Jersey.

I am somewhat out of practice, but I will say that the last time I came to New Jersey was just after Mr. Nixon had turned down the fifth debate. And I gather that Mr. Mitchell feels that no Republican should ever be caught in a debate again.

I was interested the other day to see where Mr. Nixon suggested that Governor Rockefeller and Senator Goldwater should engage in some debate. I wish he would come over here and suggest that Mr. Mitchell stand up and debate Judge Hughes on the problems of New Jersey.

I am all for debates, because I believe— and I am going to debate when I am a candidate, if I am again—because I believe that this is the way the people of this State or other States or this country can make a judgment as to the competence and knowledge of those who present themselves for office; and whether it's the Governor of New Jersey or the President of the United States, I believe they should all step forward and answer each other.

In President Truman's library at Independence he has a whole exhibit on the five or six responsibilities of the President of the United States. The President is the Commander-in-Chief and he is the head of state, and he has responsibilities as a legislative leader. But one of these responsibilities— and I think all of our Presidents, our great

Presidents, in both of our political parties have recognized it—is also to be head of a political party, because a political party, as Woodrow Wilson so often pointed out, is the means by which the people are served, the means by which those programs of benefit to our country are written into the statutes.

I come here to New Jersey, therefore, not because I do not recognize that the people of this State are fully competent to make their judgment as to their leaders, as they have on so many different occasions—and they have picked able men in both parties—but I have come here tonight as the leader of the Democratic Party, because I believe the Democratic Party under Governor Meyner in this State, and now under Judge Hughes, is committed to the same progress for the United States that we are committed to in the National Capital.

I did not say when I was a candidate, nor do I say now, that all of the problems that face this country at home and abroad are capable of immediate solution, but I do say that it is vitally important that this country, in these days when so much of our attention is turned abroad, should also recognize our obligations to freedom in maintaining a strong and vital country here at home.

We do not know what the future will bring, though we have in the past 9 months spent over $6 billion more in order to strengthen the Armed Forces of the United States, and we have also for the first time made a commitment to be second to none in the area of space.

But this challenge which we face may go on for months, and maybe years, and this country and its capacity and the skill of its people will be the great resource for freedom over a period of years.

I believe in time those forces that we so strongly believe in, which are in every individual's breast, whether he lives here or any other part of the world, will eventually provide the final answer to the challenge of communism.

It is our task to maintain our country as a strong example of what a free society can be, and it is our task to protect our vital interests abroad. And this is what we intend to do.

We have to educate our children here, in these years—not merely look to Berlin and other problems, but also recognize that these challenges will come upon us year after year—and in the meanwhile we educate our children, we provide jobs for our people, we provide medical care for our aged, we provide housing for those who need it, we provide an opportunity for all Americans to live as free men in a powerful and growing country. That is our objective.

And in the last 9 months we have passed legislation which for many months and years was stymied or vetoed—in housing, on a minimum wage of a dollar and a quarter, and increases in Social Security, and aid for those who are unemployed, and aid for those who are elderly who prefer good housing. These are the things that must be done to keep this country moving ahead.

We have to find 25,000 jobs a week—every week for the next 10 years. We're going to have over 300 million people in this country by the turn of the century. Where are they going to live? What are going to be their chances? Where are they going to get decent housing? These are the problems to which we must address ourselves and not become so concerned with the far reaches of the world, where our interests are also vital, that we forget to take care of our problems here.

If we can keep this country moving ahead and keep the people working, give to them and to the world an example of a free society moving ahead, then we meet our responsibilities to freedom. And I believe that that is what we are trying to do in the Nation's Capital. That is what your Governor has tried to do in this State. That is what Judge Hughes will try to do when he is elected Governor of New Jersey on next Tuesday. He has had a long and uphill campaign. He has been written off on more front pages of more papers supporting other candidates than any candidate I know, with the possible exception of myself about 18 months ago. And I believe that day by day, because of his knowledge of the problems of this State, because he runs on a record which he is proud to stand on of a previous Democratic administration, because he recognizes that New Jersey and the country must move ahead, I believe on next Tuesday if you move and do your job from now till then, this State will be in the Democratic column again, and Judge Hughes will succeed Governor Meyner and Governor Wilson and the other distinguished Governors of this State who have meant so much to New Jersey.

I am proud to come here today. I am proud to stand on this platform with him. I am delighted to join him in asking support for the things in which he believes and I

believe, and that is: the States of the Union moving with the country, year in and year out, building here at home so that we can maintain our position abroad, until that day comes when the powerful forces of freedom—in every man as well as in every nation—ultimately bring about liberty here and around the world.

I want you to know that there is no source of strength greater in the free world—and I say this having been President during difficult days for nearly 9 months—there is no source of strength greater than the people of the United States: courageous, persevering, long-sighted.

I salute Judge Hughes—and you—and this country.

Thank you.

NOTE: The President spoke at the War Memorial Building. In his opening words he referred to Richard J. Hughes, former superior court judge and a candidate for Governor of New Jersey; Robert B. Meyner, Governor of New Jersey; Thorn Lord, Democratic State Chairman; Harrison A. Williams, Jr., U.S. Senator from New Jersey; and Frank Thompson and Cornelius E. Gallagher, U.S. Representatives from New Jersey. He later referred to James Mitchell, former Secretary of Labor, also a candidate for Governor of New Jersey; Nelson Rockefeller, Governor of New York; and Barry Goldwater, U.S. Senator from Arizona.

449   Message to Adlai Stevenson Following the Election of U Thant as U.N. Secretary General.   *November 3, 1961*

THE ELECTION of U Thant is a splendid achievement in which the whole world can rejoice.

Please express the congratulations of the United States Government to the UN membership for the unanimous action in electing so distinguished a diplomat to succeed the late Dag Hammarskjold.

In preserving the integrity of the office of the UN Secretary General, they have re-

affirmed this dedication to the UN Charter.

To U Thant, please express my personal congratulations, and assure him on behalf of the people of the United States that, as he begins one of the world's most difficult jobs, he has our confidence and our prayers.

I also wish to thank you and your associates for the devoted and successful service you have given your country during these difficult weeks.

450 Remarks of Welcome to President Senghor of Senegal at the Washington National Airport. *November 3, 1961*

Mr. President, Mr. Prime Minister, members of the Cabinet:

I wish to express our great satisfaction, Mr. President, in welcoming you to Washington.

A famous American once said many years ago that he did not care who wrote his nation's laws as long as he could write this nation's songs. Mr. President, you help write your nation's songs and poems and you also help write your nation's laws. You have been an architect of your country's independence. You have been the poet in the great sense of the aspirations of the people of Africa, and you will come, as you do, to this country, and see millions of men and women who came from Africa to the United States who are building their lives here and making for them a strong place in the American society. They form a valuable link between our country and yours, and your continent.

In addition, you will see millions of other Americans who came from other parts of the world, who came here to build their lives in independence and liberty and fraternity in a free society. So though Senegal and the United States may be separated by thousands of miles, though we occupy different positions and different historical evolutions, nevertheless in a very real sense we wish for the Senegal what you wish for us, which is peace and liberty and national sovereignty, an opportunity to build a better life for your people. So Senegal and the United States,

in that very fundamental sense, are sisters under the skin.

Mr. President, we welcome you as the President of your country. We welcome you as a distinguished contributor to the development of Western culture, and I want you to know—and I speak on behalf of all Americans—that you and the members of your government are most welcome for your counsel and your friendship in the crucial year of 1961.

NOTE: President Senghor responded (through an interpreter) as follows:

"Mr. President, allow me first of all to tell you how deeply touched we are by this welcome, how deeply touched we are to be welcomed by the great Federal Republic of the United States. But if we admire you, we admire you most of all not only for your material power but for your spiritual power. You also were a colony once. We shall never forget your Declaration of Independence. We shall never forget your Declaration of Human Rights. You have indeed carried out the principles of these declarations into the actuality—a great Republic of free men.

"During World War I and World War II the United States fought not only for the freedom of the United States but for the freedom of all the peoples of the world, and we admire you for it.

"Senegal is a small country, but it is a Republic which is inspired by the principles of democracy. We have a parliamentary regime. We have a majority, it is true, but there is also an opposition, and thus the basic rights of the human person are safeguarded. The resemblances between our two political systems help to explain the friendship between our two nations.

"I am very happy to be among you today. Long live the United States!"

In his opening remarks the President referred to Doudou Thiam, the Minister of Foreign Affairs of Senegal.

451   Message to President Kekkonen of Finland on His Departure From the United States. *November 6, 1961*

[Released November 6, 1961.   Dated November 2, 1961]

Dear Mr. President:

Upon the conclusion of your visit to the United States, I wish on behalf of all Americans to extend to you and the Finnish people our most cordial good wishes for the continued prosperity and well-being of Finland.

The reaction of my fellow countrymen to your presence here has once again shown the depth of our feelings of admiration and esteem for Finland. Your nation, though small in size compared with many others, is peopled with lovers of freedom whose hearts are of giant proportion.

As you have journeyed through our land, I trust you have gained greater knowledge of our unrelenting determination. Ameri-cans are united in their resolve to meet with calmness and purpose the problems posed by forces which challenge not only the United States but indeed the whole community of nations sharing democratic institutions. We will never cease our efforts in pursuit of peace with justice for all mankind.

As you depart from our shores, please be assured of our continuing interest in Finland's welfare, and of our awareness of the value of the shared ideals and bonds of friendship linking our countries.

Sincerely,

JOHN F. KENNEDY

[His Excellency, Urho Kekkonen, President of Finland, Ambassador Hotel, Los Angeles, Calif.]

452   Remarks of Welcome to Prime Minister Nehru of India at Andrews Air Force Base. *November 6, 1961*

Prime Minister, Madame Gandhi, Foreign Minister, members of the Indian Cabinet:

I wish to express, Prime Minister, on behalf of the people of the United States, our great satisfaction in welcoming you once more to our country, which you have visited in earlier days.

Some national leaders, and it is a source of pride to us as Americans that some American leaders, have had their fame and their reputation spread across their national frontiers and boundaries, and their reputation and the affection in which they are held have become world-wide—Lincoln, Roosevelt, our earlier leaders. And you, Prime Minister, and your illustrious leader in the fight for Indian independence, Mahatma Gandhi, your reputation, the things for which you have stood, things with which you've been identified in your long career—all these have spread your fame and your reputation beyond the borders of your own country and have been identified with the great aspirations of people all over the world.

India and America are separated by half the globe, but I think that you are aware, as you surely must have been aware, during the long days of your struggle for independence, of the great well of affection and regard for which your country and people are held in this country—a great affectionate regard which belongs to you particularly in these difficult days.

So, Prime Minister, we welcome you here to the shores of this country as a friend, as a great world leader, as one who has in his own life and times stood for those basic aspirations which the United States stands for today.

Prime Minister, you are most welcome here to this country and we hope that when you leave you will find a renewed sense of vigor and purpose here in the United States.

Prime Minister, we are glad to see you again.

NOTE: The President spoke upon his and Prime Minister Nehru's arrival from Newport, R.I., where they had conferred earlier in the day.

Mr. Nehru responded as follows:

"Mr. President, Mrs. Kennedy, I feel deeply honored and happy to be here again, and to receive this great welcome from you. More particularly not for the formal side of it but for the friendship which animated your words. You have been good enough in the past also to refer to my country in terms which evoke a warm response in our hearts.

"This is the fourth time I have come to the United States, and whenever I have come here I have been deeply impressed not only by the magnificent achievements of this great country but, if I may say so, even more so by the popular good will and friendship that I met everywhere here.

"You have referred, sir, to our struggle for freedom. Many countries have struggled for freedom and achieved it. Your own great country was nurtured in freedom and has grown up in that great tradition. In our struggle, as you yourself just mentioned, those leaders who built up this country in the past, and even in the recent past, we were influenced by them, and I think going back to what we used to say in those days, we often refer to them and to the achievements of this country.

"And so when I came here first some 12 years ago, I came with great expectations and fulfilled a long-felt desire of my heart. Those expectations were realized and I went away with greater admiration for the achievements of this country, and with a feeling of almost—if I may say so—warm and personal friendship. They have persisted. Because the relationships of countries are more basic, I think, or should be more basic than temporary political events that happen. If they have that basic quality, they can subsist.

"And so I came again on two or three occasions, and every time I was happy that I came, and re-

newed old friendships and made new ones. This time this is a very special pleasure for me to come, to have occasion and opportunity to talk to you, Mr. President, to understand many things, and to some extent to explain what we have on our own minds.

"Your nation was nurtured in liberty. So also ours, and in a peculiar way rather unlike other countries, in the sense that we had a peculiar leader, to whom you were pleased to refer, Mahatma Gandhi. And our struggle for freedom as always everywhere conditioned us, and Mr. Gandhi's message and the training he gave us also conditioned us. I do not presume to say that we stood up to his teaching, but anyhow it was always on our minds and still continues on our minds, and to some extent still conditions us.

"And among the things that he laid great stress on, as you no doubt know, Mr. President, was on peace and peaceful methods of approach to problems. Even in our struggle with the British Empire of those days we adhered to peaceful methods. And so as a result we were fortunate at the end of that struggle when we achieved freedom to do so in friendship with the British people. The past is not only forgotten, of course, but does not come in the way of our friendly relations with the British people today. That was largely, I think, the result of the whole peaceful approach to those problems and our deliberate attempt not to pile up a mountain of bitterness over the past.

"We face mighty problems in the world today, and you, Mr. President, bear perhaps the greatest responsibility in this world. And so we look up to you and to your country, and seek to learn from you, and sometimes also to express what we have on our minds, so that we can achieve the greatest aim that the world needs today and that is peace and opportunity to grow and flourish in peace.

"Our own country is full of its own problems, more particularly to give a better life to all our innumerable people, and that can only be done if there is peace. And so, for us, peace is a passion—not only a passion but something which all our logic and mind drives us to as essential for our growth. And you stand for peace, I know, Mr. President, and I wish you all success in your efforts to maintain peace and freedom.

"I am grateful to you, sir, for your warm welcome, and to Mrs. Kennedy also."

In his opening words the President referred to Mrs. Indira Gandhi, daughter of Prime Minister Nehru, and M. J. Desai, Foreign Minister of India.

453 Telegram to Chairman Brezhnev on the Anniversary of the November Revolution in Russia. *November 7, 1961*

[Released November 7, 1961.   Dated November 6, 1961]

Leonid Brezhnev,
Chairman, Presidium of the Supreme
Soviet, U.S.S.R.

On the occasion of this national holiday of the Union of Soviet Socialist Republics,

the people of the United States join me in sending to the peoples of the Soviet Union our best wishes for a prosperous future in a secure and peaceful world.

JOHN F. KENNEDY

454 Remarks by Telephone to the First White House Regional Conference Meeting in Chicago. *November 7, 1961*

WELL, MAYOR, I want to thank you and Governor Kerner and the citizens of Chicago and Illinois who are participating in this White House Regional Conference.

On other occasions, as you know, the White House has had conferences here in Washington, but we believe that it is vitally important that the Government remain close to the people, and therefore we have arranged to have representatives of the various agencies and departments of Government travel through some of the major cities of the United States, to talk to informed and interested citizens on the problems that our people are facing and on those governmental actions which might assist our country to move forward.

We have a steadily rising population. We have the problem of maintaining high employment. We want education for our children. We want our families to live in decent housing. We want to keep our employment steadily growing, and to take advantage of the millions of young men and women who are coming into the labor market everywhere. And we want to provide

security for our older citizens.

If we can provide a strong economy here at home, with steadily improving life for all of our people, then we can maintain our position abroad with more effectiveness, and we can demonstrate what a free system can do in this competing world.

So I want to express our thanks to you, Mayor, for serving as host. This is a nonpartisan effort to attempt to bring the people and the Government, which is attempting to serve the people, closer together, and I appreciate very much the efforts by everyone to make this meeting a success.

Thank you, Mayor, and good luck to you, and Chicago, and Illinois.

NOTE: The President's telephoned remarks were amplified over a loud-speaker system. In his opening words he referred to Richard J. Daley, Mayor of Chicago, and Otto Kerner, Governor of Illinois.

The 2-day session held in the grand ballroom of the Sheraton-Chicago Hotel, was the first of 12 White House regional conferences. Other meetings were held in St. Louis, Nashville, Detroit, Cleveland, New York, Philadelphia, San Francisco, Los Angeles, Madison (Wis.), Denver, and Seattle. The series of conferences was first announced by the White House on October 4.

455   The President's News Conference of *November 8, 1961*

THE PRESIDENT. Ladies and gentlemen, I have several statements to make.

[1.] I am delighted to announce that General Eisenhower has agreed to serve as the first chairman of the board of trustees of a new people-to-people organization. The purpose of the new organization will be, and I quote: "To foster contacts between citizens of the United States and people of other lands in every way possible."

The original people-to-people organization was formed in September 1956 by a group of leading American citizens at a White House conference.

The new organization will provide a private, centralized coordination and fund-raising leadership for the activities and projects of the people-to-people program, which has been a matter of great interest to General Eisenhower.

I consider it a great honor to be able to serve as honorary chairman of this outstanding citizens organization.

[2.] Secondly, General Taylor has returned and he and his colleagues have reported their findings to me and to other members of the administration. In the next few days we shall be considering carefully the grave problems which have been posed by both externally supported violence and the natural disaster of a great flood in South Viet-Nam. Our concern is to find the most effective way of sustaining the progress of the people of South Viet-Nam, and obviously this is a matter on which we shall need to coordinate our activities with those of the Government of South Viet-Nam.

Therefore General Taylor's findings will need review not only in this Government but discussion with the Government of South Viet-Nam, and at this stage I have no public announcement to make.

[3.] Third, finally, I want to comment on the success and significance of the first meeting of the joint United States-Japan committee on trade and economic affairs, which was held in Japan last week.

This joint Cabinet group was led by Secretary Rusk on our side and Foreign Minister Kosaka for the Japanese.

It succeeded in extending the concept of American-Japanese partnership to the economic and trade field and, I think, was a most important step forward in the relations between both of our countries.

Japan is our second largest trading partner and we are her largest trading partner.

Moreover, our merchandise export to Japan greatly exceeds the imports that we receive from her. In the first 6 months of this year, our merchandise trade surplus with Japan totaled $433 million.

In addition, Japan also plays a key role in the economy of Asia, and free world economic objectives depend to a very important extent on her cooperation.

This conference was characterized by a frank exchange of views, and I believe that economic cooperation between our two countries can be expanded by further meetings, and we are looking forward to the next annual meeting of the joint committee to be held in Washington in 1962.

Thank you.

[4.] Q. During the past campaign, the political campaign last year, specifically in October, you and others spoke of the serious deterioration of our military strength in relation to that of Russia. In recent weeks, however, you and the top officials of the Pentagon have spoken of our measurable superiority to Russia in military strength. I'd like to ask you, sir, what's happened since the campaign and now? Did you during the campaign possibly not have as much information as you derived later, or do you say, sir, that the improvement in our military position has resulted from the activities solely of your administration?

THE PRESIDENT. Well, I think the phrase that I used in my announcement last week was that the United States would not trade places with anyone.

My statement to which you referred was echoed by a good many members of the previous administration as well as members of my own party. I think President Eisenhower himself said, and I quote him, that we are somewhat behind in the long-range missile field. General LeMay, in testimony before congressional committees, expressed concern that in overall military strength we would be behind in 1959. Admiral Radford expressed concern about the defense of the United States—the continental United States.

We have, as you know, since coming into office made requests for over $6 billion in increase in our national defense, and we have speeded up our Polaris program, our Minuteman standby capability; we've increased the number of SAC which is on a 15-minute alert—now 50 percent of SAC—and we have made important contributions to strengthening our conventional forces.

We attempt to keep our information up to date, and we are doing so to the best of our ability. And, based on our present assessments and our intelligence, we, in my words, would not trade place with anyone in the world. And that represents our judgment as

of now. But it's a matter to which we must give continuing study.

We're going to ask for additional funds for defense next year, and we are going to continue to maintain the most careful assessments of our intelligence and capabilities and that of our adversaries, as well as our commitments, so that statements that I made represented the best of my information based on public statements made by those in a position to know in the late years of the nineteen fifties.

[5.] Q. Mr. President, would you give us your view of the elections Saturday and yesterday—whether they may reflect public reaction to your administration or to the part that you and Mr. Eisenhower took in them? Can this type of election be a political barometer?

THE PRESIDENT. Well, I am always reluctant to claim that what happens in one election with one set of candidates necessarily means it will happen again at a later date with a different set of candidates. But as I believe if Mr. Gonzalez and Mayor Wagner and Judge Hughes had lost, that it would have been interpreted as a stunning setback for this administration. I will break my rule and say that the fact that they all won constitutes a source of satisfaction to us.

They won because they were effective candidates. But they all ran as Democrats. And I believe that it indicates that the American people believe that the candidates and parties in those areas as well as nationally are committed to progress, and that's what they're committed to. So I'm happy and I suppose someday we'll lose and then I'll have to eat those words. [*Laughter*]

[6.] Q. Can you give us the latest, sir, on the Berlin crisis, which seems to have quieted down a bit, and also your views regarding the talk of possible trips to the summit again to discuss this problem?

THE PRESIDENT. No. In answer to your last part of the question—I know of no proposed trips to the summit. In the first matter, this is a matter of continuing, of course, concern. And Chancellor Adenauer is coming to the United States shortly and I think that his trip is of vital importance in our consideration of the entire matter of Berlin, Germany, Europe. We are anxious to get his views. We are anxious to make sure that our policies are concerted, and therefore I'm delighted that he is coming and I'm delighted that he's bringing members of his new administration with him.

[7.] Q. Mr. President, this is the first anniversary of your election last year, and in the campaign that preceded that election there was considerable talk on the part of both candidates and both parties about a number of very specific subjects—Cuba, for instance; the economic growth of the country; the prestige of the Nation with other countries; hard-core unemployment, and an Executive order to end racial discrimination in housing. I wonder if you could assess for us these issues in the light of your year in office and if we might know, if you were campaigning again today, if the emphasis of your campaign might be somewhat different?

THE PRESIDENT. Well, it would be exactly what it was. We have met a good many of these commitments and I'm hopeful before our term is ended that we will meet the others. But we have passed a minimum wage of $1.25 an hour. We have made it possible for men to retire at 62. We did pass the area redevelopment bill for areas of chronic unemployment—which had been vetoed twice. We did pass the most broad-range housing bill that had been passed since 1949. We did provide additional funds for pollution. And we did, I think, in a whole variety of areas, take actions which benefit the people.

The fact of the matter is that since we took office in January, our national income or gross national product has gone up from around $501 billion to—it is our calculation by the—within the two quarters immediately ahead, our gross national product will be $565 billion and—which represents a substantial increase and, I think, is of particular importance in sustaining our many burdens.

Unemployment in October now stands at 3,900,000. There are more people working than ever before—67,800,000. The number of people in industry has gone up 2,000,000 since we took office in January—who have jobs.

Now I am not saying that these problems are solved because, in a sense, they're never solved. And there are areas which are still unfinished. Medical care for the aged, which we are going to recommend to the Congress in the coming session.

We have, I think, made substantial progress in the field of civil rights. To conclude there have been more suits filed to provide for voting and there will continue to be a concentrated effort by this administration to make it possible for every citizen to vote under the laws and the directions provided by Congress.

We have put more people to work, under our Vice President's committee—unemployment—than there was ever done in the previous 8 years—in the last 8 months.

And I think that in voting, in the activities of the Justice Department, in education, in other areas, we are making substantial progress with a good deal left unfinished. And we'll meet our commitments before we're finished.

[8.] Q. Mr. President, in view of our overall military position and your statement that you would not trade places, many people are wondering how you might eventually justify the possible resumption of nuclear testing in the atmosphere.

THE PRESIDENT. Well, I've stated that I felt it incumbent upon us to maintain our lead; that we have not concluded as yet our analysis of Soviet tests, and if we felt that our present position in this very vital area has been endangered by Soviet tests, then we would have to take action to protect our security. So that, I also said, we would not test for political or psychological reasons unless we feel it militarily necessary. And, in the meanwhile, because there is a long time gap, we have ordered preparations to be made.

The Soviet Union tested while we were at the table negotiating with them. If they fooled us once, it's our own fault; if they fool us twice, it's our fault.

Q. On this question of nuclear testing, sir, Soviet officials have asserted in recent days that the United States in total has fired a larger quantity of megatons than all the Soviet tests. Is this statement true?

THE PRESIDENT. The Soviet Union with the most recent tests have put into the air about 170 megatons, the United States and Great Britain combined about 125 megatons, France less than one megaton. What is significant in this area, of course, is the amount of megatons put in the air and the condition under which the bombs may be exploded as it might affect fallout. And I don't think that there is any doubt the Soviet Union is first in that very dubious category.

[9.] Q. Last spring the Secretary of State indicated that an embargo was about to be imposed on imports from Cuba—sugar—not sugar, pardon me—tobacco, molasses, vegetables. Nothing has happened; that's months ago. Could you throw some light on that point, please, sir?

THE PRESIDENT. Yes, when the limitations were put on trade by the previous administration, there was exempted food and drugs which amount to around $12 million a year. And it would be impossible for us to break, to stop, that trade unless we enforce the Trading With the Enemy Act.

This has been a matter continually before us, but we are not anxious to be in the position of declaring war on the Cuban people by denying them essential food and also denying them medicines, and therefore this administration, like the previous administration, has been reluctant to take that action, but it's a matter that will be before us continually, and if it seems like the proper action, we'll take it, but our dispute is not with the Cuban people but with the Communist control of Cuba.

[10.] Q. Could you enlighten us, sir, as to why you're not having these press conferences more frequently, especially as to whether anything in particular you don't like about them or anything we might do on our part to encourage you to meet with us more often?

THE PRESIDENT. Well, I like them. But—sort of—(*laughter*)—but I will—let me just say that I'll hold these—I'm anxious to hold press conferences as often as I believe it to be in the public interest. Now, we do hold—Mr. Salinger holds one or two press conferences a day. We put out a good many statements from the White House, members of the Cabinet speak around the country, we attempt to carry out communications to the extent possible. We're even having these regional meetings.

We are involved in a number of very sensitive matters on the question of Berlin, and I'm—I talk not only to the American people but also to our allies, to those who are opposed to us and our enemies, and those who are neutral, and, therefore, I feel that the schedule as we have recently had it is in the public interest. But I would have no objection to having them two or three times a week if I thought at that time it was in the public interest.

I had them nearly every week and I'm sure I will again when Congress is back. But most of the matters now before us deal with matters of foreign policy, and this seemed to be the most appropriate schedule in view of the public interest.

[11.]   Q. Mr. President, how do you feel about the Postmaster General's statement that he yielded to political pressure to reinstate a postal employee considered unsuitable?

THE PRESIDENT. Well, I think that Mr. Day probably feels that he would like to recast that statement, and, as I understand it, it was submitted to a board of review. The charges, although with the exception of one, were dismissed unanimously. One was considered and there was a 2-to-1 vote. It seems to me that that is the procedure that is best to follow without resort to political pressures of any kind. And I think that's what the Post Office and everyone else should do, and I hope they will. But—and I think that's Mr. Day's view.

[12.]   Q. Mr. President, what significance to the West, in the course of the cold war, do you see in the current open rift between Red China and Russia?

THE PRESIDENT. Well, I think that it's not—that none of us can talk with precision about the details of the relationships between Russia and China. It is a matter of surmise, and on this experts may differ. Therefore, I don't feel that it's probably useful now for us to attempt to assess it. I think we can judge better by actions. And we can—we'll have an opportunity to witness those actions

in the coming weeks and months.

That's what really counts, not the—altogether the dialectics, but what result—the varying philosophies which animate the Communist world—what resultant actions— their different view of Marx and the different interpretation of the Communist doctrine; what action it brings them to, and what threats it poses to the free world. That will give us a more precise answer to your question.

[13.]   Q. Mr. President, there is a great deal of confusion among the public in regard to fallout shelters. Many people—people apparently aren't sold on building home shelters. Do you have any comment that might be helpful today on any aspect of this matter?

THE PRESIDENT. Well, of course, as you know, none of us were really interested—I think that includes us all—in civil defense really until this summer and until we began to recognize the change in weapon technology which gave the Soviet Union the power to reach the United States with missiles as well as bombers, the destructive nature of the weapons, and also the fact that our two systems were in conflict in various areas.

We asked for additional appropriations, therefore, this summer for civil defense. We are—we asked for five times and received five times as much as we had the previous year.

Now, it's very difficult in a large country, with varying problems of geography, with 180 million people, to suddenly organize a civil defense program when so much depends on the cooperation between the Federal Government assigning it its proper responsibility, the State government, the local community, and the individual.

I stated that in July—that we were going to send a book giving the latest information that we had to every household, and I'm hopeful that that book will be completed before the end of this month.

But I'm—we are very conscious of the difficulties. We are very conscious of the desire of people to have accurate and precise information.

But it was not really, in my opinion, until August that this became a matter of great public urgency. The responsibility for shelters was then transferred to the Department of Defense and I believe that the booklet will be helpful, but it will be a—must be recognized that each family, each community, each State, and the Federal Government are all going to have a role, and we desire to interpret that role with precision so that we are moving ahead on it.

[14.] Q. Mr. President, some of the press in your country and India say that our Prime Minister is more pro-Communist and pro-Russian than he is Western. Now that your talks have concluded after the last 3 days, please tell us how you feel? Do you believe that he was either consciously or unconsciously against the interests of the United States or Western countries? Do you believe that he was for the cause of world peace? And please give us some idea of your talk with him?

THE PRESIDENT. In answer to your question, I have never thought, quite obviously, that—to use your phrase—that Mr. Nehru works consciously or unconsciously for the Communist movement, and I know of no rational man in the United States who holds that view. There are matters on which we differ, as the Prime Minister said in "Meet the Press" on Sunday, that "geography dictates a good deal of policy" as well as internal conditions, so that, quite obviously—and tradition, culture, the past, all this affects foreign policy.

So that there are areas where we differ, but I do not know any figure in the world, as I have said on other occasions, who is more committed to individual liberty than Mr. Nehru, and I think the people of India are committed to maintaining their national sovereignty and supporting liberty for the individual as a personal and cultural and religious tradition. We are going to disagree, but I'm sure it's possible for us to disagree in the framework of not charging each other with bad faith.

I have a high regard for the Prime Minister. It has become higher during our conversations. I've attempted to explain to him some of the areas of responsibility which the United States faces, and he has given me his views on a number of important questions, so I regard the talks as most valuable— [*inaudible*]—all matters affecting our countries and the personalities that may be involved.

[15.] Q. Mr. President, as you know, during the recent German crisis there's been a great deal of anxiety both in Germany and in this country about what our views are on the problem. Now that Dr. Adenauer has been invited to this country, can you give us a general idea of what you see as the future role of Germany, including East Berlin and East Germany, and also the question of rearming Germany or arming her with nuclear weapons?

THE PRESIDENT. Well, I think that these are some of the matters which we will discuss with Chancellor Adenauer and involves his country and our country, and I think that it will be better to wait a few days when I will have a chance to see him.

On the question of arming them with nuclear weapons, as you know, Dr. Adenauer has stated West Germany does not intend to do so. And on the general matter of arms,

I know that charges were made in regard to the remilitarization of Western Germany. Western Germany has almost no air force, very limited navy, has now nine divisions. Eastern Germany, which is far less in population, has substantially larger ground forces. And I think the effort to suggest that Dr. Adenauer, who is a distinguished European, who has brought about a reconciliation between France and Germany, who has brought the Common Market—helped bring the Common Market about, who has met his responsibilities under NATO, is a—represents a revanchist attitude, I think is wholly wrong. But on the details, I think this is what we should talk to Dr. Adenauer about.

[16.] Q. Mr. President, recently there have been statements by several people inside and outside the Government that the United States needs a major change in its trade policy, a major liberalization in trade policy. We haven't heard from you on this score during this immediate period of policy formation. What is your feeling about the need for change and, specifically, do you feel that the administration should seek to have the change made next year.

THE PRESIDENT. We have had several meetings in the administration about the matter and we'll be having others and will make recommendations to the Congress at the first of the year. I think that, quite obviously, we have to begin to realize how important the Common Market is going to be to the economy of the United States. One-third of our trade generally is in Western Europe, and if the United States should be denied that market, we will either find a flight of capital from this country to construct factories within that wall, or we will find ourselves in serious economic trouble.

On the other hand, we have obligations, for example, to Japan, and we have concern about our relations with Latin America, and what will happen to them, dependent as they are upon raw materials and on western European markets—where will they be left? These are all matters which we are now considering.

But I think that the people of this country must realize that the Common Market is going to present us with major economic challenges and, I hope, opportunities, and that this country must be ready to negotiate with the Common Market on a position of equality, as far as our ability to negotiate to protect our interests and the interests of those that are associated with us.

I think that one of our problems in the United States—and I think that it's illuminated by the statistics on Japan—we've read a good deal about the threat of Japanese goods coming into the United States, and I can understand where it is a concern. But here is a country where in the last 6 months a half billion dollars has been on our side, a balance of payments contributing to our dollar surplus and our gold balance.

Well, now we cannot just sell and never buy, and if all those who recognize the benefit to the United States—workers, industry—in an almost $5 billion to $6 billion surplus which we have every year, recognize how essential that is to our security, will speak as loudly as those who are hurt, we can get an adjustment, I think of the public interest.

But, in answer to your specific question, we are considering the matter and we will come to the Congress in January and make our recommendations. But the matter is by no means complete. The details of the Common Market, for example, and its effect upon us, will not be obvious probably until '63 or '64, and we have to attempt to go to the Congress at a time when we can be most successful. My judgment is that the time to begin is now, but as a matter of final decision, I think we'll have to wait about 2 or 3 more weeks.

[17.] Q. Mr. President, how much more do you think you will have to do to assure American business leadership that you are not antibusiness and, in fact, do you think they need any special assurance?

THE PRESIDENT. Well, if to be an—to stop them from saying we're antibusiness we're supposed to cease enforcing the antitrust law, then I suppose the cause is lost.

There has been a—nearly a 10 percent increase, as I have said, in our gross national product. We have cut the flow of gold since January 1 even though we still have a serious dollar problem—it was almost $1 billion last year in gold lost, it's $76 million so far this year. We have had a very slight increase in the cost of living. In fact, wholesale prices are down. We've had less strikes than we've had any time in 20 years.

This country cannot prosper unless business prospers. This country cannot meet its obligations—its tax obligations and all the rest—unless business is doing well. Business will not do well and you will not have full employment unless they feel that there's a chance to make profit.

So that there is no long-range hostility between business and the Government. There cannot be. We cannot succeed unless they succeed. But that doesn't mean that we should not meet our responsibilities under antitrust, or that doesn't mean when we attempt to pass a bill on taxes to prevent tax havens abroad or a flood of capital which affects our gold balances—that doesn't mean we're antibusiness. It means that we have to meet our public responsibilities. So that I think in the long run that most businessmen know that we are allied—as we are with labor and the farmer—in trying to keep this country going.

[18.] Q. On nuclear tests, in view of the fact that the Soviets have exploded 31 or more devices in the atmosphere, I think it's generally agreed that they're improving their nuclear weapons technology. Now this means that they're getting stronger in relation to the United States. Wouldn't it also mean that if we do not test in the atmosphere, that we're willing for the United States to become weaker with relation to the Soviet Union than we were, say, last summer?

THE PRESIDENT. Well, I've stated that I thought that the United States was in a position that was powerful—Mr. Gilpatric said "second to none." I said it was our obligation to remain so. And that is what we intend to do. And therefore, as you suggest, these calculations will have to be made and a decision reached. And pending these calculations, we are making our appropriate preparations.

Q. Mr. President, Dr. Pauling said that the biggest Russian bomb would cause 40,000 gross mutations in the next three or four generations. This remark has been criticized by some scientists because he didn't say that this—if this was true—it would be spread over 34 billion people, and that this leads to an exaggerated fear of fallout. Do you think there is in the popular mind an exaggerated fear of fallout, because of statements like that?

THE PRESIDENT. Well, I think that anyone feels that if one individual, whether it's among many billions, is—particularly an individual three generations from now—finds their life warped by radiation, of course it's a concern to anyone. And we should, therefore, approach atmospheric testing with the greatest caution and hesitancy, as I've already indicated.

On the other hand, of course, we have a responsibility to the freedom of hundreds of millions of people—including the citizens of our own country. So we cannot—we have to attempt to balance off our needs. But I've said we would never, because of the reason—whether Mr. Pauling's statistics are accurate or not, one is enough—that we would never test for political or psychological reason, but only if we felt that the security of the United States was endangered, and therefore the free world, which does affect this generation and others to come. So we must balance off our risks.

[19.] Q. Mr. President, the Democratic platform in which you ran for election promises to work for equal rights for women, including equal pay, and to wipe out job opportunity discriminations. Now you have made efforts on behalf of others. What have you done for the women, according to the promises of the platform?

THE PRESIDENT. Well, I'm sure we haven't done enough. [*Laughter*] I must say I am a strong believer in equal pay for equal work, and I think that we ought to do better

than we're doing, and I'm glad that you reminded me of it, Mrs. Craig. [*Laughter*]

[20.] Q. Mr. President, the boys and girls of the high school at Columbus, Ind., sent you a wire a week or so ago in which they reminded you that you had invited them to bring you any problems that they had. Their problem was that Joseph Turk, their Russian instructor—a very hard-to-find gentleman—was being taken off to be a clerk-typist in the Army. Has their request come to your attention and have you taken any action on it?

THE PRESIDENT. No, it hasn't come to my attention, and we will give it to the responsible groups. I agree that the problem of bringing teachers in is a difficult one. But I think we ought to let the Defense Department make that judgment.

Reporter: Thank you, Mr. President.

NOTE: President Kennedy's eighteenth news conference was held in the State Department Auditorium at 4 o'clock on Wednesday afternoon, November 8, 1961.

456 Joint Statement Following Discussions With Prime Minister Nehru. *November 9, 1961*

THE PRESIDENT and the Prime Minister have had four days of especially pleasant and rewarding conversations. These began in Newport, Rhode Island, on Monday, were continued for several hours Tuesday morning with senior Indian and U.S. officials present, with further private discussions Wednesday, and a brief final meeting today. Subjects covered amount almost to a map of the troubled areas of the world. The problems of getting a peaceful settlement in Berlin, of securing the peace and liberties of the people of Southeast Asia, the problems of control of nuclear testing and disarmament, of the Congo, on how to

strengthen the United Nations, and of United States and Indo-Pakistan relations were among the topics. Prime Minister Nehru used the occasion to go deeply into the philosophic and historical background of Indian foreign policy. The President similarly went into the goals and objectives of American foreign policy as they have been molded and shaped over the years.

The President and the Prime Minister examined in particular those areas where peace is threatened. They discussed the dangers inherent in recent developments in Berlin and in Southeast Asia. Concerning Berlin, President Kennedy reaffirmed the

United States commitment to support the freedom and economic viability of the two and one-quarter million people of West Berlin and the President and the Prime Minister concurred in the legitimate and necessary right of access to Berlin. The President also assured the Prime Minister that every effort would be made to seek a solution of the Berlin problem by peaceful means, and underlined the importance of the choices of the people directly concerned.

With respect to Southeast Asia, the President and the Prime Minister confirmed that it is the common objective of the United States and India that Laos be a genuinely neutral state, free of domination by any foreign power, and that each nation in the area have the opportunity to make its own choice of the course it will take in seeking to solve pressing economic and social problems under conditions of peace.

The President and the Prime Minister discussed India's efforts for the improved well-being of her people. The President reaffirmed the United States interest in the success of this great effort.

They exchanged views on the desirability of a cessation of nuclear testing. The President referred in this connection to the recent resumption of tests by the Soviet Union which broke the previous moratorium and reaffirmed the United States unwillingness to accept a further uncontrolled nuclear test moratorium. The Prime Minister and the President agreed on the urgent need for a treaty banning nuclear tests with necessary provision for inspection and control.

The President and Prime Minister stressed the high importance of measures to avoid the risk of war and of negotiations in this connection to achieve agreement on a program of general and complete disarmament.

India and the United States share in the fullest measure their common objective to develop the United Nations as the most effective instrument of world peace. The President and the Prime Minister reviewed the United States and Indian contributions to United Nations operations in the Congo, which they regard as an illustration of how that body, even under extremely difficult conditions, can help bring about conditions for the peaceful resolution of conflict. Both the Prime Minister and the President strongly share the hope that as the result of the efforts of the people of the Congo and the United Nations a peaceful and united Congo will be achieved. The President expressed his special appreciation of the role played by the Indian soldiers in the Congo, who comprise more than one-third of the United Nations force there.

The Prime Minister and the President noted the cooperation and exchange of information between United States and Indian scientists in space science research. They agreed that this activity, which has the aim of peaceful exploitation of outer space for the benefit of mankind, could be usefully developed.

The Prime Minister and the President consider that their talks have been highly useful in the pursuit of their common objectives of an enduring world peace and enhanced understanding between the Governments of India and the United States. They intend to keep closely in touch with each other in the months and years ahead.

457   Telegram to Constantine Caramanlis Following His
       Reappointment as Prime Minister of Greece.
       November 9, 1961

[Released November 9, 1961. Dated November 8, 1961]

Dear Mr. Prime Minister:

I wish to convey my sincere greetings and best wishes to Their Majesties, the Greek people and yourself and to congratulate you on the occasion of your reappointment and investiture as Prime Minister of Greece.

Recalling your recent visit to the United States with pleasure and satisfaction, I am confident that in these troubled times our two nations will continue to work together in the spirit of firm friendship which has traditionally characterized Greek and American relations. As a common aim, we seek a peaceful world based on the ideals of freedom, liberty and democracy which Greece has bequeathed to the world.

Please accept my warmest personal regards.

Sincerely,

JOHN F. KENNEDY

458   Statement by the President Upon Announcing the Appointment
       of a Panel To Review Employment Statistics.
       November 10, 1961

THE STATISTICS of employment and unemployment are of vital importance as measures of the economic health and well-being of the nation. They serve as guides to public policy in the development of measures designed to strengthen the economy, to improve programs to re-employ the unemployed, and to provide assistance to those who remain unemployed. It is my objective to maintain and enhance the quality of our statistics in this and in all other fields of government, so that the public may have the highest degree of confidence in them.

NOTE: The statement was issued as part of a White House release announcing that the President had appointed a committee of technical experts to appraise the status of the information available on employment and unemployment and to make recommendations as to changes or improvements. The release lists the members of the committee as follows: chairman, Robert Aaron Gordon, Chairman of the Department of Economics, University of California; Robert Dorfman, Professor of Economics, Harvard University; Martin R. Gainsbrugh, Chief Economist of the National Industrial Conference Board and President of the American Statistical Association; Albert E. Rees, Professor of Economics, University of Chicago; Stanley H. Ruttenberg, Director of the Research Department, AFL–CIO; and Frederick F. Stephan, Professor of Statistics, Princeton University.

Also released was a letter from the Secretary of Labor, dated November 8, 1961, proposing the establishment of the committee.

459   Remarks Upon Presenting the Merchant Marine Achievement Award to Solon B. Turman.   *November 10, 1961*

I WANT to present, with great pleasure, this trophy, which is significant of the great contributions which you have made to the American Merchant Marine.

I understand that your company is one of the largest dry cargo companies in the world, and that is a great asset to the American Merchant Marine.

Our commerce with the world, and our influence on the seas, are of course essential to us, so I want to congratulate you, and in congratulating you the members of your company, and also the American Legion for its interest.

NOTE: The trophy was presented to Mr. Turman, President of the Lykes Brothers Steamship Company of New York, in the President's office at the White House.

460   Statement by the President Concerning an Educational Consortium To Aid in Developing a Technical Institute in India   *November 11, 1961*

THIS IS the first time such a consortium has been used in United States aid programs in the field of education. I am delighted that these nine major centers of knowledge and learning have been willing to pool their resources, in cooperation with the Agency for International Development, to cooperate in the development of advanced education facilities in India in this important phase of her Third Five Year Plan.

The success of this cooperative enterprise will be a model for other similar efforts on the part of the United States to share our educational and technical resources with the peoples of the developing nations of the world.

I am particularly hopeful that Prime Minister Nehru will consider this project a souvenir of his visit.

NOTE: The statement was issued as part of a White House release announcing the formation of an educational consortium to assist in developing the Indian Institute of Technology at Kanpur, India. The following universities and institutes of technology were listed as participants: California Institute of Technology, Carnegie Institute of Technology, Case Institute of Technology, Massachusetts Institute of Technology, Ohio State University, Princeton University, Purdue University, University of California, and the University of Michigan.

461   Remarks at the Veterans Day Ceremony at Arlington National Cemetery.   *November 11, 1961*

General Gavan, Mr. Gleason, members of the military forces, veterans, fellow Americans:

Today we are here to celebrate and to honor and to commemorate the dead and the living, the young men who in every war since this country began have given testimony to their loyalty to their country and their own great courage.

I do not believe that any nation in the history of the world has buried its soldiers farther from its native soil than we Americans—or buried them closer to the towns in which they grew up.

We celebrate this Veterans Day for a very few minutes, a few seconds of silence and then this country's life goes on. But I think it most appropriate that we recall on this occasion, and on every other moment when we are faced with great responsibilities, the contribution and the sacrifice which so many men and their families have made in order to permit this country to now occupy its present position of responsibility and freedom, and in order to permit us to gather here together.

Bruce Catton, after totaling the casualties which took place in the battle of Antietam, not so very far from this cemetery, when he looked at statistics which showed that in the short space of a few minutes whole regiments lost 50 to 75 percent of their numbers, then wrote that life perhaps isn't the most precious gift of all, that men died for the possession of a few feet of a corn field or a rocky hill, or for almost nothing at all. But in a very larger sense, they died that this country might be permitted to go on, and that it might permit to be fulfilled the great hopes of its founders.

In a world tormented by tension and the possibilities of conflict, we meet in a quiet commemoration of an historic day of peace. In an age that threatens the survival of freedom, we join together to honor those who made our freedom possible. The resolution of the Congress which first proclaimed Armistice Day, described November 11, 1918, as the end of "the most destructive, sanguinary and far-reaching war in the history of human annals." That resolution expressed the hope that the First World War would be, in truth, the war to end all wars. It suggested that those men who had died had therefore not given their lives in vain.

It is a tragic fact that these hopes have not been fulfilled, that wars still more de-

structive and still more sanguinary followed, that man's capacity to devise new ways of killing his fellow men have far outstripped his capacity to live in peace with his fellow men.

Some might say, therefore, that this day has lost its meaning, that the shadow of the new and deadly weapons have robbed this day of its great value, that whatever name we now give this day, whatever flags we fly or prayers we utter, it is too late to honor those who died before, and too soon to promise the living an end to organized death.

But let us not forget that November 11, 1918, signified a beginning, as well as an end. "The purpose of all war," said Augustine, "is peace." The First World War produced man's first great effort in recent times to solve by international cooperation the problems of war. That experiment continues in our present day—still imperfect, still short of its responsibilities, but it does offer a hope that some day nations can live in harmony.

For our part, we shall achieve that peace only with patience and perseverance and courage—the patience and perseverance necessary to work with allies of diverse interests but common goals, the courage necessary over a long period of time to overcome an adversary skilled in the arts of harassment and obstruction.

There is no way to maintain the frontiers of freedom without cost and commitment and risk. There is no swift and easy path to peace in our generation. No man who witnessed the tragedies of the last war, no man who can imagine the unimaginable possibilities of the next war, can advocate war out of irritability or frustration or impatience.

But let no nation confuse our perseverance and patience with fear of war or unwillingness to meet our responsibilities. We cannot save ourselves by abandoning those who are associated with us, or rejecting our responsibilities.

In the end, the only way to maintain the peace is to be prepared in the final extreme to fight for our country—and to mean it.

As a nation, we have little capacity for deception. We can convince friend and foe alike that we are in earnest about the defense of freedom only if we are in earnest—and I can assure the world that we are.

This cemetery was first established 97 years ago. In this hill were first buried men who died in an earlier war, a savage war here in our own country. Ninety-seven years ago today, the men in Gray were retiring from Antietam, where thousands of their comrades had fallen between dawn and dusk in one terrible day. And the men in Blue were moving towards Fredericksburg, where thousands would soon lie by a stone wall in heroic and sometimes miserable death.

It was a crucial moment in our Nation's history, but these memories, sad and proud, these quiet grounds, this Cemetery and others like it all around the world, remind

us with pride of our obligation and our opportunity.

On this Veterans Day of 1961, on this day of remembrance, let us pray in the name of those who have fought in this country's wars, and most especially who have fought in the First World War and in the Second World War, that there will be no veterans of any further war—not because all shall have perished but because all shall have learned to live together in peace.

And to the dead here in this cemetery we say:

> They are the race—
>   they are the race immortal,
> Whose beams make broad
>   the common light of day!
> Though Time may dim,
>   though Death has barred their portal,
> These we salute,
>   which nameless passed away.

NOTE: In his opening words the President referred to Maj. Gen. Paul A. Gavan, Commanding General of the Military District of Washington, and J. S. Gleason, Jr., Administrator of Veterans Affairs.

462 Message Recorded for the Centennial Convocation of the Association of Land-Grant Colleges and State Universities. *November* 12, 1961

IN JULY 1862, in the darkest days of the Civil War, President Abraham Lincoln signed two acts which were to help to mold the future of the Nation which he was then struggling to preserve.

The first of these, the Homestead Act, provided, in Carl Sandburg's words, "a farm free to any man who wanted to put a plow into unbroken sod."

The second, the Morrill Act, donated more than one million acres of Federal land to en-

dow at least one university in every State of the Union.

Thus even as the Nation trembled on the brink of destruction the vast lands of the American West were open to final settlement. A new America of unparalleled abundance began to grow, and the most ambitious and fruitful system of higher education in the history of the world was developed. Today more than 68 land-grant institutions located in each of the 50 States and in Puerto Rico are a monument to the visions of those who built the foundations of peace in a time of war. Over one-half of our Ph.D. degrees in science and engineering are awarded by these schools. Twenty-four out of forty Nobel Prize winners in our country are among their graduates. One-fourth of all high school and elementary teachers and over one-third of our college teachers are their products.

These universities have grown as our Nation's needs have grown. The original endowment called for instruction which emphasized agricultural and mechanized arts, and with their help the strongest agricultural community on earth was built. Today these schools teach subjects ranging from philosophy to science and the conduct of foreign relations—the whole broad spectrum of knowledge upon which the future of this country and freedom depends, and upon which the well-being of Americans who will come after us is so richly intertwined.

In the history of land-grant schools can be read much of the history of our country, a history they have played no small part in shaping. In addition, these schools are one of the finest examples of our Federal system:

the fruitful cooperation between National and State Governments in the pursuit of a decent education for all of our citizens. Founded at Federal initiative, strongly supported by Federal funds—funds which were specifically appropriated for instruction rather than the construction of buildings or facilities—these institutions have built a proud tradition of independence and academic integrity untroubled by governmental interference of any kind. They are a monument to the fact that the cooperative effort of Federal and State Governments is the best way to insure an independent educational system of the highest quality.

I congratulate the land-grant colleges on the centennial of their birth. I assure you of my vigorous and continued support. I bring you the thanks of a grateful Nation for what you have done in the past. And I bring you the hope of all of our people that you will continue to light the way for our country and for future generations.

NOTE: The President's message was recorded on film at the White House. It was presented on November 12 at the opening in Kansas City, Mo., of the Centennial Convocation of Land-Grant Colleges and State Universities.

463 Remarks to the Trustees of the Union of American Hebrew Congregations. *November* 13, 1961

I WANT to express my great satisfaction in welcoming you to the White House again, and to tell you how grateful I am for your generosity. These Torahs I know have special significance for you, and particularly this one, which is so intimately associated with the founder here in the United States, one which is brought from Europe and which has been part of your life. So that I am doubly appreciative to you for being will-

ing to part with it and present it to us here today.

I think, as the Rabbi said, that the significance of this ceremony is not merely a gift of an ancient document, but that in a very real sense the great issue today is between, as he said, the supremacy of the moral law which is initiated, originated, and developed in the Bible, and which has special application here today.

I've never felt that we should attempt to use the great impulse towards God and towards religion, which all people feel, as an element in a cold war struggle. Rather, it's not an arm, it is the essence of the issue—not the organization of economy so much, but as the supremacy of moral law, and therefore the right of the individual, his rights to be protected by the state and not be at the mercy of the state.

In the Inaugural Address, which the Rabbi mentioned, I said that the basic issue was that the rights the citizen enjoyed did not come from the state but rather came from the hand of God. And it's written here [*pointing to the Torah*]. And it is written in the Old and the New Testaments.

So I'm grateful to you, and I want you to

know that in coming here today I think it symbolizes the happy relations which exist between all religious groups, and must continue to exist in this country if we are to be worthy of our heritage.

So, Rabbi, I'm grateful to you. There is no gift which could please me more—and I'm delighted to welcome you to our house.

NOTE: The President spoke in the Rose Garden at the White House, following the presentation of a Sacred Torah by Rabbi Maurice N. Eisendrath, president of the Union of American Hebrew Congregations, and Emil N. Paar, chairman of its board of trustees.

The Torah was brought to the United States from Bohemia in 1846 by Rabbi Isaac Mayer Wise, founder of American Reform Judaism. Dating from the 18th century, the scroll had been in the ark of the Isaac M. Wise Temple in Cincinnati.

464   Remarks of Welcome at the White House Concert by Pablo Casals. *November 13, 1961*

Ladies and gentlemen:

I want to welcome you all to the White House on this occasion. This dinner tonight is in honor of our distinguished guest, Governor Muñoz Marin and his wife and the people of Puerto Rico.

Pablo Casals has honored all of us by consenting to come here and play.

I think that all of us feel a special pride in what the Governor has done, the lessons he has taught us, the link which he has established between us and the most important countries to the south, and for his own efforts to improve the life of his people.

Therefore, Governor, in your coming tonight, we want to pay special tribute to you and your efforts in behalf of the cause to which we are all committed.

I also want to welcome those of you who are in the world of music, and those who support those who are in the world of music.

I think it is most important not that we regard artistic achievement and action as a part of our armor in these difficult days, but rather as an integral part of our free society.

We believe that an artist, in order to be true to himself and his work, must be a free man or woman, and we are anxious to see emphasized the tremendous artistic talents we have available in this country.

I don't think that even our fellow citizens are perhaps as aware as they should be of the hundreds of thousands of devoted musicians, painters, architects, those who work to bring about changes in our cities, whose talents are just as important a part of the United States as any of our perhaps more publicized accomplishments.

So that we welcome you here to the White House—and most especially to welcome you, Maestro, and to tell you what a great honor it is to have you back in the White House.

We are privileged to have Mrs. Nicholas Longworth here with us, who was here in 1904 when Casals played for Theodore Roosevelt—in this room. He also played for Queen Victoria in 1898.

So that we are most glad to have you here, not only because of your long and distinguished career in music but also because you have indicated and demonstrated in your own life what I said earlier, that an artist must be a free man.

We are delighted to have you here in the White House.

NOTE: The President spoke just before the beginning of the concert in the East Room at the White House.

465   Memorandum on the Need for Greater Coordination of Regional and Field Activities of the Government. *November 14, 1961*

[Released November 14, 1961.   Dated November 13, 1961]

Memorandum for Heads of Departments and Agencies

As an integral part of present steps to increase the effectiveness and economy of Federal agencies, I want coordination of government activities outside of Washington significantly strengthened. That is to include improvement of the management and direction of Federal offices throughout the country by the chief departmental officials in Washington, and provision for an inter-agency working group for closer coordination across department and agency lines in important centers of Federal activity outside of the National Capital area.

More than ninety percent of all Federal employees work outside of the Washington area. Decisions affecting the expenditure of tens of billions of dollars are made in the field. Federal programs have their impact on State and local governments largely through the actions of regional and local representatives of our departments and agencies. Most important, Federal officials outside of Washington provide the principal day-to-day contact of the Government with the citizens of this country and generally constitute the actual point of contact of Federal programs with the economy and other phases of our national life.

In the international assistance programs, previously separate U.S. efforts are being brought together in order to provide a common focus on the needs and problems of individual countries. Here at home we must similarly bring more closely together the many activities of the Federal Government in individual states and communities throughout the nation.

Although each Executive agency and its field organization have a special mission, there are many matters on which the work of the departments converge. Among them are management and budgetary procedures, personnel policies, recruitment efforts, office space uses, procurement activities, public information duties, and similar matters. There are opportunities to pool experience and resources, and to accomplish savings. In substantive programs, there are also opportunities for a more closely coordinated approach in many activities, as on economic problems, natural resources development, protection of equal rights, and urban development efforts.

As a first step in bringing Federal officials

63930—62——49

outside of Washington closer together, I have directed the Chairman of the Civil Service Commission to arrange for the establishment of a Board of Federal Executives in each of the Commission's administrative regions. Where associations of Federal regional officials exist in other regional centers they will be continued. Each Executive department and agency is directed to arrange for personal participation by the heads of its field offices and installations in the work of these Federal Executive Boards. These activities are not to require additional personnel but provide means for closer coordination of Federal activities at the regional level.

The cooperative activities of Federal Executive Boards must be undertaken primarily through the initiative of the heads of our field activities. The Chairman of the Civil Service Commission and the Director of the Bureau of the Budget will furnish the Boards from time to time with guides on official goals and objectives in the management field and will arrange for periodic briefings by national executives of the government. Each of the Boards will consider management matters and interdepartmental cooperation and establish liaison with State and local government officials in their regions. A clearinghouse will be provided in the office of the Chairman of the Civil Service Commission on problems and recommendations submitted by the regional Boards.

Following a reasonable period for evaluation of these initial steps, recommendations are to be prepared by the Chairman of the Civil Service Commission and the Director of the Bureau of the Budget for continuing improvement of the management and coordination of Federal activities.

Within each department, I want the chief officers of each agency, particularly the chief operating officials for administrative matters, to make a critical appraisal of pending field management procedures with the principal regional officers of that agency. The Director of the Bureau of the Budget shall provide guidance to department and agency heads on their internal appraisals of field management. Over all, new emphasis shall be placed on management skills in support of improved economy, efficiency, and the substantive effectiveness of the Executive Branch of the Government.

JOHN F. KENNEDY

466 Remarks at the Swearing In of Teodoro Moscoso as Assistant Administrator for Latin America, AID. *November 14, 1961*

MR. AMBASSADOR, I want again to express my great pleasure at your willingness to assume this responsibility, after having been Ambassador to Venezuela. And I think the fact that we asked you to come back from there to assume this new duty indicates the great importance we place on it.

Our economic efforts in this hemisphere will be directed through the Alliance for Progress, and through you, working under the guidance of Mr. Fowler Hamilton and the Secretary of State. We want everyone to know in this hemisphere that we are proceeding ahead and are going to make a major effort to accomplish the task we set out to do.

So that symbolically it's a pleasure to participate in this ceremony with the Secretary of State, the Secretary of Defense, and with the Ambassadors from the countries who are so intimately a part of our lives.

Gentlemen, we're glad you came today,

and we're very grateful that you came under the conditions you did, and Ambassador Woodward I know joins in expressing his satisfaction with this decision.

Thank you very much.

NOTE: The ceremonies were held in the Fish Room at the White House. During his remarks the President referred to Fowler Hamilton, Administrator of the Agency for International Development, and Robert F. Woodward, Assistant Secretary of State for Inter-American Affairs.

467   Remarks to the Trustees and Advisory Committee of the National Cultural Center.   *November 14, 1961*

Mr. Stevens, and ladies and gentlemen:

I want to express my appreciation to all of you for coming down today to discuss with Mr. Stevens this effort that we are making.

Somebody once said that Washington was a city of Northern charm and Southern efficiency. In any case it is a city which is somewhat artificial, unlike most capitals of the world, and therefore lacks the great asset which London and Paris and Rome, to name but three—and Moscow itself—has in being the center not only of Government but also the center of national cultural activities.

I think it is most important that the tremendous work which is being done across this country to develop those skills which make liberty worth while—I think it is very important that there be put a national emphasis on this side of our national life, and this is where it must be done—by making a tremendous effort.

In New York City the Lincoln Center is making a comparable effort, and in different ways across the country, and I think that we have to do that in Washington—which after all is not a city belonging only to the people that live here, but is the Capital of the Nation and belongs to all the people, and was established for that reason.

When George Washington participated in the establishment of Washington, he did emphasize that in addition to being the center of Government it would also be a great cultural center.

Now the Soviet Union does not waste its resources. Of course we do not have to point to them to indicate the importance of this work, but it is of significance that they have made a major effort in this field, because they recognize, even though they manipulate this desire, the tremendous interest that people have in the arts.

Last night we were particularly fortunate to have one of the most distinguished artists in the world, and I am hopeful that it will not be necessary always to have a special stage put in the White House for Shakespeare, or for a special hearing for a distinguished musician, but that in Washington here we can have a great cultural center which expresses the interest of the people of this country in this most basic desire of mankind.

This is a most important national responsibility, and I can assure you that if you will be willing to help, that this administration will give it every possible support. We face many hazards, all of which you have been through before in your own communities, many difficulties in not only building it but maintaining it, but I am confident we can do it. I think it is an issue that we put face forward to the world.

When we had a children's orchestra playing here this last summer, Isaac Stern told me that the best chamber music being played in the world is played in Vermont. There are so many tremendous activities going on across the United States. But I think to dramatize that phase of our Nation, particularly in relation to countries which put so much emphasis on their culture and history and philosophy, it is so important that we indicate what we really feel.

As I said, this represents a basic side of our national life, and I think we should not hide it but should emphasize it, and it will not only be a service to the world but it will be a service to our own people.

Everything that happens here has its influence across the country. Every stone we put here I think will result in other stones in other areas. For example, I am sure we wouldn't be going ahead now with this, if we hadn't seen what they were able to do in organizing the Lincoln Center; and when we do it here and overcome the difficulties and challenges we face, it will come up in other areas.

So I hope that those of you who do not live in Washington will help in this effort and will not feel that it is taking from your own communities, but instead will realize that in building here you are building for the country and you are building for your own communities.

So we are indebted to you. And I want to assure you that Mr. Stevens, while perhaps on occasion he has not had too many failures theatrically, would not have undertaken this without making it succeed. And I would not want to be in this as intimately as I am, unless I was sure it will be successful. So that we are in your debt, and I think that it represents a great national step forward.

We are delighted to have you here today. All of you are busy men and women, and that is why you were asked to give your time to this.

Thank you very much.

NOTE: The President spoke in the movie room of the East Wing at the White House. His opening words "Mr. Stevens" referred to Roger L. Stevens, Chairman of the Board of Trustees of the National Cultural Center. Members of the Board of Trustees and of the Advisory Committee met with the President to discuss plans for enlisting nationwide support for the National Cultural Center, established by the act of September 2, 1958 (Public Law 85-874, 72 Stat. 1698).

468 Joint Statement Following Discussions With Chairman Chung Hee Park of Korea. *November 14, 1961*

CHAIRMAN PARK and President Kennedy concluded today a friendly and constructive exchange of views on the current situation in Korea and the Far East and the various matters of interest to the governments and peoples of the Republic of Korea and the United States of America. Foreign Minister Choi, Secretary Rusk and other officials of the two governments participated in the conversations.

The two leaders reaffirmed the strong bonds of friendship traditionally existing between the two countries and their determination to intensify their common efforts toward the establishment of world peace based on freedom and justice.

The Chairman reviewed the situation in Korea which led to the military revolution of May 16 and set forth the achievements made by the revolutionary Government. He emphasized the positive steps taken by the Government for social reform and economic stability, particularly the new Government's actions to reform the civil service, rationalize tax collections, abolish usury in local areas, increase employment opportunities, stimulate investment, and expand both domestic and foreign trade. He emphasized as well the positive steps taken by the Government in strengthening the nation against Communism and in eliminating corruption and other social evils.

The President welcomed Chairman Park's full exposition of the current situation in the Republic of Korea and expressed his gratification at the many indications of progress made by the new Government of the Republic.

The Chairman reiterated the solemn pledge of the revolutionary government to return the government to civilian control in the summer of 1963, as he declared in the statement made on August 12, 1961. The President particularly expressed his satisfaction with the Korean Government's intention to restore civilian government at the earliest possible date.

The two leaders discussed the position of Korea in the maintenance of peace and security in the Far East, and in this connection reviewed the continuing contribution of United States economic and military assistance to the strengthening of the Korean nation. Recognizing that the successful achievement of Korean economic development in accordance with a long-range plan is indispensable to build a democratic foundation and to maintain a strong anti-Communist posture in Korea, the President expressed great interest in Korea's draft Five Year Economic Development Plan. In this connection, he assured the Chairman that the United States Government would continue to extend all possible economic aid and cooperation to the Republic of Korea, in order to further such long range economic development.

The Chairman and the President discussed the problem of mutual defense against the threat of external armed aggression in the Pacific area. They recognized that the common interest of their two countries as bulwarks of the Free World against Communist expansion is deepened and reinforced by the fact that Korean and United States troops are brothers-in-arms, standing side by side in the United Nations Command for the defense of Korean soil. The President reaffirmed the determination of the United States to render forthwith and effectively all possible assistance to the Republic of Korea, in accordance with the Mutual Defense Treaty between the Republic of Korea and the United States of America signed on October 1, 1953, including the use of armed forces, if there is a renewal of armed attack.

The two leaders recalled that Korea had been successfully defended against armed aggression by the first collective military measures pursuant to the call of the United Nations. They recalled the declarations by United Nations members whose military forces participated in the Korean action, including their affirmation that in the interests of world peace, "If there is a renewal of armed attack, challenging again the principles of the United Nations, we would again be united and prompt to resist." The Chairman and the President reaffirmed their faith in the United Nations, and their determination to seek the unification of Korea in freedom through peaceful means under the principles laid down and reaffirmed by the United Nations General Assembly.

Chairman Park and President Kennedy expressed their deep satisfaction with their meeting and discussions and reiterated their resolve to continue to serve the cause of freedom and democracy, and to strengthen the friendly ties between their two peoples.

469   Letter to President Chiari of Panama Concerning the Canal.
November 15, 1961

[Released November 15, 1961.   Dated November 2, 1961]

Dear Mr. President:

I have read with great interest your letter of September 8, 1961 which your brother delivered to me on September 15th. I am also very pleased to have had a personal conversation with your brother at that time.

I agree with you that an unusual community of interests exists between the Republic of Panama and the United States. Our respective Governments and peoples have been closely associated since the very beginning of your nation. The Panama Canal has been an important element in the development and growth of the relationship between our two countries, and has also contributed to the bonds of unity which link all the American Republics.

The Government of the United States hopes to maintain and strengthen the relations between our two nations on the basis of mutual respect and sincere friendship. I feel sure that the Government of Panama shares this objective.

Once again, on behalf of the Government of the United States, I reaffirm our willingness to cooperate wholeheartedly with the Government of Panama to insure the full enjoyment of the various benefits which the Canal should afford to the two nations that made possible its construction. We also wish to make these benefits available to all nations interested in international trade.

As I pointed out to your brother on September 15, I realize that the historic friendship and cooperation between our two countries has sometimes been marred by differences concerning the interpretation of the rights granted to the United States by the Republic of Panama. In past years, these problems have been resolved in various ways—sometimes through formal treaty negotiations and sometimes through friendly discussions and the subsequent implementation of specific measures agreed upon by representatives of the two Governments.

My Government recognizes that differences will inevitably arise between even the friendliest nations, and believes that these differences must be discussed thoroughly and frankly, in order to clarify the interests and attitudes of both parties. It seems clear, therefore, that when two friendly nations are bound by treaty provisions which are not fully satisfactory to one of the parties, arrangements should be made to permit qualified representatives of both nations to discuss these points of dissatisfaction with a view to their resolution.

I have instructed the various responsible Departments and agencies of the United States Government to make a complete reexamination of our current and future needs with respect to Isthmian Canal facilities. I expect this study to be completed within a very few months, at which time my Government will communicate promptly with the Government of Panama.

I am confident that representatives of our two Governments, after a frank exchange of views and a careful assessment of our mutual needs and interests, can reach fruitful conclusions which will promote the mutual welfare of both countries.

With cordial good wishes.

Sincerely,

JOHN F. KENNEDY

470   Statement by the President Upon Establishing the President's
Committee on Youth Employment.   *November* 15, 1961

OUR LATEST employment figures for October 1961 show that 67,800,000 Americans are at work—the highest number of employed for any October in our history.

The total number of people in industry, business and commerce has gone up by approximately 2 million since we took office in January.   This is 500,000 more than seasonal expectations.

The factory work week has gone up by a full hour since January and weekly earnings stand at more than $94.00 per week, establishing a new earning record.

Unemployment in October stands at 3,900,000.   This is down substantially from the 5,700,000 people who were unemployed when we took office.

Particularly gratifying is the 900,000 decline in the long-term unemployed—4 months or more—since early spring this year.

Although there are these bright spots in the employment situation nationally, I am not satisfied with an unemployment rate which has remained at about 6.8 percent seasonally adjusted for the last 11 months.   We are greatly concerned about unemployment and the Administration is attacking this problem on a broad front.

I am particularly disturbed over the serious plight of the nearly one million out-of-school and out-of-work youth.

Our youth are our greatest resource, and the social and economic implications of pro-tracted unemployment among the one million young job seekers today and the many millions who will enter the labor force in the next few years demand immediate attention and action.

The Secretary of Labor is announcing today a comprehensive program to attack vigorously the mounting problems of jobless youth and to help put youth into jobs.   This program is outlined in a letter to me from the Secretary of Labor.

As an important part of this program, I am today establishing a President's Committee on Youth Employment to bring the nation's attention and resources to bear on this vital national problem.   This Committee will be chaired by the Secretary of Labor and will consist of other members of the Cabinet concerned with youth as well as distinguished public members.   It will be charged with the task of carrying on an active drive to help our young people who seek jobs.   This activity, directed to the special employment problems of youth, will complement the actions already being taken by the Administration to provide jobs for all who seek work.

I know that the Committee will receive the full support of the American people in carrying out its important assignment.

NOTE: In addition to the chairman, Secretary Goldberg, the release listed 22 other members appointed to the Committee.

471 Statement by the President on the Death of Sam Rayburn. *November* 16, 1961

MRS. KENNEDY and I join the nation in mourning the death of Speaker Rayburn. His public service stretched from the administration of Woodrow Wilson to the present day. But it was the quality of that service more than its length that was so distinctive.

A strong defender of constitutional responsibilities of the Congress, he had an instinctive understanding of the American system and was a loyal counselor and friend of Presidents of both parties on the great matters which affected our national interest and security.

I had singular opportunity as a young Congressman, and now more recently as President, to appreciate his temperament and his character, both were bedded in rock and remained unchanged by circumstance.

This country has lost a devoted servant and the citizens of this country, an unflinching friend.

NOTE: Mr. Rayburn was elected to the Congress in 1912 and served continuously until the time of his death. His service included 17 years as Speaker of the House of Representatives.

472 Remarks Upon Arrival at Boeing Airfield, Seattle. *November* 16, 1961

Governor, Mr. Mayor, my colleagues from the Senate:

It is a great pleasure and honor to come to this State, on the 100th anniversary of the University of Washington, the 25th anniversary of Senator Magnuson, and the first anniversary of my election to the Presidency.

It is a source of satisfaction to me to have the opportunity to visit, in that capacity, for

the first time, the Northwest United States, and particularly to come to this State at this time when so many happy occasions are combined.

Thank you.

NOTE: The President's opening words referred to Albert D. Rosellini, Governor of Washington; Gordon S. Clinton, Mayor of Seattle; and Warren G. Magnuson and Henry M. Jackson, U.S. Senators from Washington.

473 Address in Seattle at the University of Washington's 100th Anniversary Program. *November* 16, 1961

President Odegaard, members of the regents, members of the faculty, students, ladies and gentlemen:

It is a great honor on behalf of the people of the United States to extend to you congratulations on the Centennial Anniversary of this University, which represents 100 years of service to this State and country.

This nation in two of the most critical times in the life of our country, once in the days after the Revolution in the Northwest ordinance to which Doctor Odegaard referred, and again during the most difficult days of the Civil War, in the Morrill Act which established our land grant colleges, this nation made a basic commitment to the maintenance of education, for the very reasons which Thomas Jefferson gave, that if this nation were to remain free it could not remain ignorant. The basis of self-government and freedom requires the development of character and self-restraint and perseverance and the long view. And these are qualities which require many years of training and education. So that I think this University and others like it across the country, and its graduates, have recognized that these schools are not maintained by the people of the various States in order to merely give the graduates of these schools an economic advantage in the life struggle. Rather, these schools are supported by our people because our people realize that this country has needed in the past, and needs today as never before, educated men and women who are committed to the cause of freedom. So for what this University has done in the past, and what its graduates can do now and in the future, I salute you.

This University was founded when the Civil War was already on, and no one could be sure in 1861 whether this country would survive. But the picture which the student of 1961 has of the world, and indeed the picture which our citizens have of the world, is infinitely more complicated and infinitely more dangerous.

In 1961 the world relations of this country have become tangled and complex. One of our former allies has become our adversary— and he has his own adversaries who are not our allies. Heroes are removed from their tombs—history rewritten—the names of cities changed overnight.

We increase our arms at a heavy cost, primarily to make certain that we will not have to use them. We must face up to the chance of war, if we are to maintain the peace. We must work with certain countries lacking in freedom in order to strengthen the cause of

freedom. We find some who call themselves neutral who are our friends and sympathetic to us, and others who call themselves neutral who are unremittingly hostile to us. And as the most powerful defender of freedom on earth, we find ourselves unable to escape the responsibilities of freedom, and yet unable to exercise it without restraints imposed by the very freedoms we seek to protect.

We cannot, as a free nation, compete with our adversaries in tactics of terror, assassination, false promises, counterfeit mobs and crises.

We cannot, under the scrutiny of a free press and public, tell different stories to different audiences, foreign and domestic, friendly and hostile.

We cannot abandon the slow processes of consulting with our allies to match the swift expediencies of those who merely dictate to their satellites.

We can neither abandon nor control the international organization in which we now cast less than 1 percent of the vote in the General Assembly.

We possess weapons of tremendous power—but they are least effective in combating the weapons most often used by freedom's foes: subversion, infiltration, guerrilla warfare, civil disorder.

We send arms to other peoples—just as we send them the ideals of democracy in which we believe—but we cannot send them the will to use those arms or to abide by those ideals.

And while we believe not only in the force of arms but in the force of right and reason, we have learned that reason does not always appeal to unreasonable men—that it is not always true that "a soft answer turneth away wrath"—and that right does not always make might.

In short, we must face problems which do not lend themselves to easy or quick or permanent solutions. And we must face the fact that the United States is neither omnipotent or omniscient—that we are only 6 percent of the world's population—that we cannot impose our will upon the other 94 percent of mankind—that we cannot right every wrong or reverse each adversity—and that therefore there cannot be an American solution to every world problem.

These burdens and frustrations are accepted by most Americans with maturity and understanding. They may long for the days when war meant charging up San Juan Hill—or when our isolation was guarded by two oceans—or when the atomic bomb was ours alone—or when much of the industrialized world depended upon our resources and our aid. But they now know that those days are gone—and that gone with them are the old policies and the old complacencies. And they know, too, that we must make the best of our new problems and our new opportunities, whatever the risk and the cost.

But there are others who cannot bear the burden of a long twilight struggle. They lack confidence in our long-run capacity to survive and succeed. Hating communism, yet they see communism in the long run, perhaps, as the wave of the future. And they want some quick and easy and final and cheap solution—now.

There are two groups of these frustrated citizens, far apart in their views yet very much alike in their approach. On the one hand are those who urge upon us what I regard to be the pathway of surrender—appeasing our enemies, compromising our commitments, purchasing peace at any price, disavowing our arms, our friends, our obligations. If their view had prevailed, the world of free choice would be smaller today.

On the other hand are those who urge upon us what I regard to be the pathway of war: equating negotiations with appeasement and substituting rigidity for firmness. If their view had prevailed, we would be at war today, and in more than one place.

It is a curious fact that each of these extreme opposites resembles the other. Each believes that we have only two choices: appeasement or war, suicide or surrender, humiliation or holocaust, to be either Red or dead. Each side sees only "hard" and "soft" nations, hard and soft policies, hard and soft men. Each believes that any departure from its own course inevitably leads to the other: one group believes that any peaceful solution means appeasement; the other believes that any arms build-up means war. One group regards everyone else as warmongers, the other regards everyone else as appeasers. Neither side admits that its path will lead to disaster—but neither can tell us how or where to draw the line once we descend the slippery slopes of appeasement or constant intervention.

In short, while both extremes profess to be the true realists of our time, neither could be more unrealistic. While both claim to be doing the nation a service, they could do it no greater disservice. This kind of talk and easy solutions to difficult problems, if believed, could inspire a lack of confidence among our people when they must all—above all else—be united in recognizing the long and difficult days that lie ahead. It could inspire uncertainty among our allies when above all else they must be confident in us. And even more dangerously, it could, if believed, inspire doubt among our adversaries when they must above all be convinced that we will defend our vital interests.

The essential fact that both of these groups fail to grasp is that diplomacy and defense are not substitutes for one another. Either alone would fail. A willingness to resist force, unaccompanied by a willingness to talk, could provoke belligerence—while a willingness to talk, unaccompanied by a willingness to resist force, could invite disaster.

But as long as we know what comprises our vital interests and our long-range goals, we have nothing to fear from negotiations at the appropriate time, and nothing to gain by refusing to take part in them. At a time when a single clash could escalate overnight into a holocaust of mushroom clouds, a great power does not prove its firmness by leaving the task of exploring the other's intentions to sentries or those without full responsibility. Nor can ultimate weapons rightfully be employed, or the ultimate sacrifice rightfully demanded of our citizens, until every reasonable solution has been explored. "How many wars," Winston Churchill has written, "have been averted by patience and persisting good will! . . . . How many wars have been precipitated by firebrands!"

If vital interests under duress can be preserved by peaceful means, negotiations will find that out. If our adversary will accept nothing less than a concession of our rights, negotiations will find that out. And if negotiations are to take place, this nation cannot abdicate to its adversaries the task of choosing the forum and the framework and the time.

For there are carefully defined limits within which any serious negotiations must take place. With respect to any future talks on Germany and Berlin, for example, we cannot, on the one hand, confine our proposals to a list of concessions we are willing to make, nor can we, on the other hand, advance any proposals which compromise the security of free Germans and West Berliners, or endanger their ties with the West.

No one should be under the illusion that negotiations for the sake of negotiations always advance the cause of peace. If for lack of preparation they break up in bitterness, the prospects of peace have been endangered. If they are made a forum for propaganda or a cover for aggression, the processes of peace have been abused.

But it is a test of our national maturity to accept the fact that negotiations are not a contest spelling victory or defeat. They may succeed—they may fail. They are likely to be successful only if both sides reach an agreement which both regard as preferable to the status quo—an agreement in which each side can consider its own situation to be improved. And this is most difficult to obtain.

But, while we shall negotiate freely, we shall not negotiate freedom. Our answer to the classic question of Patrick Henry is still no—life is not so dear, and peace is not so precious, "as to be purchased at the price of chains and slavery." And that is our answer even though, for the first time since the ancient battles between Greek city-states, war entails the threat of total annihilation, of everything we know, of society itself. For to save mankind's future freedom, we must face up to any risk that is necessary. We will always seek peace—but we will never surrender.

In short, we are neither "warmongers" nor "appeasers," neither "hard" nor "soft." We are Americans, determined to defend the frontiers of freedom, by an honorable peace if peace is possible, but by arms if arms are used against us.

And if we are to move forward in that spirit, we shall need all the calm and thoughtful citizens that this great University can produce, all the light they can shed, all the wisdom they can bring to bear. It is customary, both here and around the world, to regard life in the United States as easy. Our advantages are many. But more than any other people on earth, we bear burdens and accept risks unprecedented in their size and their duration, not for ourselves alone but for all who wish to be free. No other generation of free men in any country has ever faced so many and such difficult challenges—not even those who lived in the days when this University was founded in 1861.

This nation was then torn by war. This territory had only the simplest elements of civilization. And this city had barely begun to function. But a university was one of

their earliest thoughts—and they summed it up in the motto that they adopted: "Let there be light." What more can be said today, regarding all the dark and tangled problems we face than: Let there be light. And to accomplish that illumination, the University of Washington shall still hold high the torch.

NOTE: The President spoke at the Edmundson Pavilion in Seattle. His opening words "President Odegaard" referred to Charles E. Odegaard, President of the University.

474   Remarks in Seattle at the Silver Anniversary Dinner Honoring Senator Magnuson. *November 16, 1961*

Senator Jackson, "Maggy," Governor Rosellini, my former colleagues from the Senate, Mrs. Green, Congressman Magnuson, Congresswoman Hansen, Mike Kirwan, ladies and gentlemen:

I want to express my great pleasure at being with you here tonight in honor of our distinguished friend, Senator Magnuson.

Most Members of the Senate, as you can already judge, have developed the art of speaking with precision and clarity and force. The secret of Senator Magnuson's meteoric Senate career has been the reverse. He may make clear speeches to you on great public questions, but in Washington he speaks in the Senate so quietly that few can hear him. He looks down at his desk—he comes into the Senate late in the afternoon— he is very hesitant about interrupting other Members of the Senate—when he rises to speak, most Members of the Senate have left—he sends his messages up to the Senate and everyone says "What is it?" And Senator Magnuson says, "It's nothing important." And Grand Coulee Dam is built.

Today he drove me through the town and pointed out a $12 million Federal building

at this new scientific center. And he said, "You remember when you voted for that?"

This summer two Senators from the East who had developed the art of speaking clearly asked for a small amount of money in order to have a study made of a possible contribution to their World's Fair. They explained this carefully to Members of the Senate—answered all questions—and it was overwhelmingly rejected.

So it was necessary, therefore, for me to be here tonight. I'm glad to be here also with "Scoop" Jackson, who carries on as a Member of the Senate, as a member of the Armed Services Committee, as chairman of the Subcommittee on the Military Uses of Atomic Energy, for the Atomic Energy Committee, and also for some of its peacetime uses at Hanford and other places, and who has spoken for this State and this country—and with other Senators from the West and from the East.

I was appreciative of what was said about Mike Kirwan, who they said did more for the development of the Northwest United States, perhaps, than any man, but who came, as you noticed, from the State of

Ohio. He recognizes that the Northwest United States is as much a part of Ohio as Ohio is a part of the United States; and therefore it is quite natural that Senator Muskie should come from Maine to Washington tonight, or that I should come from the Capital in Washington to this State of Washington, that Jennings Randolph should come from West Virginia—that friends from all sections of this country should come here and pay tribute to Senator Magnuson—should come here in friendship with Senator Jackson, to join the Members of the Congress from the Northwest United States in re-affirming their commitment to the development of this section of the country and this section of America.

This country from its earliest inception has been divided between those who prophesied doom and gloom for the future and those who recognized that their brightest hopes for this country would be more than fulfilled. That has been true of the career of Senator Magnuson. In the 25 years that he has served in the Congress, he has seen the Northwest United States move steadily ahead.

All those who planned for the future of this section of the country—the power, the wood, the reclamation, the conservation— all of those programs which were so strongly opposed in their inception, have in fact all proved to be inadequate. Those who bet on the United States, in the long run have proved to be correct. Those who have been bold about this country have seen their great predictions and estimations come true.

When he was elected, this State and country was in despair, and a front page story on November 1 by a distinguished newspaper of this city predicted the closest electoral vote in 1936 since 1916—and warned that the people of the United States would be in for a surprise—and so would the Roose-

velt regime. They predicted a gain of 50 to 80 seats for another party. And they said that FDR had made his biggest mistake in the 1936 campaign in discussing social security. But on the following day the Seattle Times reported two noteworthy events, the re-election of Franklin Roosevelt by a landslide majority and the election of King County's prosecuting attorney, Warren G. Magnuson, described in that story as handsome and young, as a Member of the Congress of the United States.

This State was half sagebrush. The Columbia River ran unharnessed to the sea. There was no atomic energy plant at Hanford, no aluminum plants, no dams or locks, no up-river navigation. Today there are more than a million acres of new fertile farmland, more than 50,000 men working in the aluminum plants, millions of kilowatts of electrical energy are produced by a vast complex of hydro-electric power plants—the Columbia has been largely tamed and great ships sail its waters.

Senator Magnuson, Senator Jackson, the Members of the Congress, Presidents of the United States, have committed themselves to this program, because they recognized 10, 15, 20, 25 years ago that this country was going to explode—in people—in resources and things—and that we must plan for them.

I visited today the University of Washington which was founded in this country's darkest days a hundred years ago. It was founded because a hundred years before a group of men who regarded the Northwest United States as Michigan and the States around it, committed themselves to educating the people of this country.

Now that University and your State University and Seattle will in the next 10 years have twice as many young boys and girls applying for admission to those colleges as there are today. In our large universities in every State we are going to have to build more buildings in the next 10 years than have been built in the whole history of this country. And what is true in education is true in power, in land, in housing, and the rest.

And therefore those who say in 1961 "We've had enough," those who wish to stand still, those who wish to stand against all programs which commit us to the growth of this country, are as wrong today as they were 25 years ago.

Those who say that the United States should not commit itself to being a leader in the peacetime use of atomic energy— those who say we should waste those resources which we have now in the Northwest and which have been fought for by Senator Jackson at Hanford—those who say no to this country, I believe are going to find as time goes on, in the next 5, 10, 15, 20, 25 years, that all their predictions of failure and disaster will have been proved as wrong as they have been in the last 25 years.

And when we gather together, old and tired, while "Maggy" is young and handsome on his 50th anniversary, we will realize that this country is moving ahead steadily.

We bet on this country. We believe in its prospects, and we are ready to face what difficulties there are in our time.

Senator Anderson reminded me tonight of an old saying of Thomas Paine, "If there is going to be trouble, let it come in my time, so that my children may live in peace."

We live in a troublesome time, but let it come in our time, so that in this country and around the world our children and their children may live in peace and security.

NOTE: The President spoke in the Grand Ballroom of the Olympic Hotel in Seattle. In his opening words he referred to Henry M. Jackson and Warren G. Magnuson, U.S. Senators from Washington; Albert D. Rosellini, Governor of Washington; Mrs. Edith Green, U.S. Representative from Oregon; Don Magnuson, U.S. Representative from Washington; Mrs. Julia B. Hansen, U.S. Representative from Washington; and Michael J. Kirwan, U.S. Representative from Ohio. Later in his remarks the President referred to U.S. Senators Edmund S. Muskie of Maine, Jennings Randolph of West Virginia, and Clinton P. Anderson of New Mexico.

475 Remarks Upon Arrival at the Airport in Phoenix. *November 17, 1961*

THANK YOU, Governor. I want to express my pleasure at coming back again to Arizona, and particularly coming back on an occasion which I think has so much significance, as this does.

Arizona, which is comparatively speaking a young State, is represented in the United States Senate by a Senator who has been so intimate a part of the life of this State.

So, in saluting Senator Hayden for 50

years of devoted service, we also salute Arizona and the Southwest and the best of the United States.

Thank you for the warm welcome, and I share your pride and satisfaction in the work of this State and in the work of a man so intimately identified with it.

And thank you for coming to the airport.

NOTE: In the President's opening words he referred to Paul Fannin, Governor of Arizona.

476   Remarks in Phoenix at the 50th Anniversary Dinner Honoring Senator Hayden. *November 17, 1961*

Senator Hayden, Vice President Johnson, Governor, Mr. Chairman Tom Chauncey, Members of the Senate, friends of Senator Hayden:

I know that I speak for all of us in expressing our great pleasure at being with Senator Hayden tonight.

Last night some of us were in Seattle, attending the 25th anniversary dinner of Senator Magnuson of that State, and now we are honored to be here in Phoenix to attend this 50th anniversary. This actually is the first anniversary of the election of the Vice President and myself, and while I'm not sure it should be celebrated in Phoenix, nevertheless we are very happy to come here under your protection tonight, Senator, and say what a pleasure it is to be here.

The Vice President made some reference to the oratorical ability of Senator Hayden. In looking at one of his early speeches, before he assumed his present status, he once said in 1914, "I know that Congress does not conduct its business in an efficient manner. If any corporation had a board of directors as inefficient as Congress, it would become bankrupt in a year."

My first contact with the Senator was after I had been in the Senate about 2 months in 1953, and I got up to take part in the debate as a new Member. And after speaking for a few minutes, I sat down near Senator Hayden and said, "Senator, what's the difference between the Senate as you knew it and now?" And the Senator said, "New Members did not speak in those days." So I went back to my seat.

I am very proud to be here. I think it is a remarkable fact that two leading positions in the United States, positions of the greatest responsibility, were held by Speaker Rayburn as the presiding officer of the House and by the President Pro Tem of the Senate from the neighboring State of Arizona.

When a Congressional District or a State sends men back year after year, they may serve themselves, but they may not realize that the seniority system of House and Senate gives those Members a profound influence over the policies of our country at home and abroad. Congressmen or Senators who may serve a district with particular vigor, who may arrange to have its interests particularly well protected, and may be rewarded, and may some day become the great voice of a committee which decides great issues of national security, the size of our force levels, what our actions will be in Space, what our actions will be abroad. So that the District of Bonham, which year after year sent back Sam Rayburn, and this State which sent back year after year Senator Hayden, made one man the Speaker of the House in the most difficult and critical period in the life of our country, and made the other the President Pro Tem of the Senate, and also the Chairman of the Senate Appropriations Committee which provides the funds which makes it possible for all these programs to be carried on. So while I commend the Speaker of the House and Senator Hayden, I also commend the good judgment of the people of Texas and the people of Arizona in recognizing character and patriotism and courage when they found it— and rewarding it.

Pericles once said that if you wanted to see his monument, to look around you, and I think that is particularly true in Arizona. This State has benefited year after year by the constant care and attention which Senator Hayden has given to the development of

731

Arizona and the Southwest. Very few sections of our country have required wider and wiser Federal programs for its development than the State of Arizona—this city—Tucson and the rest. This city and this State live on water and from the days when he was first there, in his fight for reclamation and irrigation and all the rest down to the present time, he has spoken for the country and he has spoken for Arizona. And I am confident that this State which has seen the extraordinary growth which the Governor described, from two hundred odd thousand who were here when he went to Congress to the 1,300,000 people who are here today, and the 2,300,000 people who will be here, I'm sure, by the turn of the century, they must know, the people of this State, how vitally important it is that the leadership of Senator Hayden be continued, so that Arizona and the country may continue to move forward.

Every Federal program which has contributed to the development of the West—irrigation, power, reclamation—bears his mark, and the great Federal highway program which binds this country together, which permits this State to be competitive east and west, north and south, this in large measure is his creation. But as I said at the beginning, his great contribution has been to our country. When he went to the Congress of the United States before World War I, our problems were simple. Now the United States occupies a key position in the arch of freedom all around the globe.

I know that many Americans are often unhappy and concerned about all the problems that the United States faces abroad, but I think you should take pride and satisfaction in realizing that only the United States, and our power and strength and commitment, permits dozens of countries scattered all over the world to maintain their free-

dom; and if we did not bear the heavy burdens we now bear, the United States would be isolated, with only a few of the countries of Western Europe to look to.

It is the United States that carries this great burden, and however dissatisfied you may be, as you look at the troubled world around you, and however you may wish for peace and contentment—as we all do—you should take pride in the fact that under the administrations of both parties, beginning with the days of the close of World War II, it has been the United States—first in Western Europe and now in Latin America, and now in Africa, and now in the Middle East, and now in Asia, and now in SEATO, and now in CENTO, and now in NATO, and now in the OAS—that really does the heavy work that makes it possible for these institutions to survive.

Other countries look to their own interests. Only the United States has obligations which stretch ten thousand miles across the Pacific, and three or four thousand miles across the Atlantic, and thousands of miles to the south. Only the United States—and we are only 6 percent of the world's population—bears this kind of burden.

And as an American, it is a source of satisfaction to me, looking back over 50 years of service, that the people of this frontier State had the good judgment to put their stamp of approval on him, and year after year have given it to him again.

Senator, as one who loves our country, it is a source of pride to me that Arizona and you are so happily matched.

Thank you.

NOTE: The President spoke at the Westward Ho Hotel in Phoenix. In his opening words he referred to Carl Hayden, U.S. Senator from Arizona, Vice President Lyndon B. Johnson, Paul Fannin, Governor of Arizona, Tom Chauncey, chairman of the Hayden Testimonial Dinner Committee, and the following Members of the U.S. Senate: Leverett

Saltonstall of Massachusetts, Clinton P. Anderson of New Mexico, Alan Bible of Nevada, Roman L. Hruska of Nebraska, Edmund S. Muskie of Maine, Jennings Randolph of West Virginia, Ralph Yar- borough of Texas, Stephen M. Young of Ohio, Gale W. McGee of Wyoming, Robert S. Kerr of Okla- homa, E. L. Bartlett of Alaska, Mike Mansfield of Montana, and Gordon Allott of Colorado.

477   Address in Los Angeles at a Dinner of the Democratic Party of California.   *November 18, 1961*

Governor Brown, Attorney General Mosk, Ed Pauley, Members of the Congress, dis- tinguished public officials, and ladies and gentlemen:

After campaigning in New York last month, it's a pleasure to come to a State where the Democrats are all united. I am confident there will be a candidate in this State in 1962 who will unite the Demo- cratic Party, and I refer to Pat Brown. Pat Brown said that I would carry this State by a million votes. He did carry the State by a million votes—and I prophesy that he is going to run—I prophesy that he is going to win.

And I think he's going to win because of some of the reasons that the Attorney General gave. Being a Governor is not an easy job, and being the Governor of Cali- fornia is a particularly difficult job. I think the efforts which Governor Brown has made since he was elected to be Governor of this great State way back in 1958, I think that record which represents the culmination of years of working in this State, which rep- resents the acquired knowledge, year after year, as a dedicated and effective Attorney General of California, I think the people of California know that Governor Brown knows this State and can lead it during the difficult years which are to come.

He is going to be elected Governor of the State because this State, above all others in the Union, must continue to move for- ward—and Governor Brown and the Dem- ocratic Party are committed to progress.

The efforts which he has made in this State alone in the field of education, I be- lieve deserve the wholehearted endorsement of the people of California, and of the country. From the time that the first Col- ony was established in Massachusetts, the people of this country have recognized that the primary responsibility of local govern- ment is to educate our children. And I think California is doing this, and doing a job in this area which I think serves as a good guide to what the Federal Government must do in its own area in the field of education.

You are going to have more than twice as many young men and women applying for admission to these schools in California in 10 years as you do today. And I believe that Governor Brown and the efforts that he has made in junior colleges and univer- sities, and secondary education across this entire State, I believe that he recognizes that this country will be as strong and as free in direct proportion to how well educated and motivated our children are.

And I believe that the evidence that he has given of the fight to provide water for California, which I think must be the basis for the development of the whole West, I believe this effort alone, which has repre- sented one of the most difficult political challenges which this or any other State has faced, I believe this is another reason why he will receive the endorsement of the people of California in 1962.

And thirdly, because of his efforts in the

733

field to provide equality of opportunity for all Americans. I see no reason why it was necessary for California to wait till 1959 before it wrote on the statute books of this State legislation providing for equality of opportunity for every young man and woman in this State—and I hope in the country—regardless of their race or creed.

We met last week in the White House with Doctor Conant and others. One-fourth of all our boys and girls looking for jobs in their teens are unemployed in the United States—and this is concentrated among the Negroes and the Puerto Ricans and those of Mexican extraction in this and other States.

We cannot be satisfied until, first, everyone who wants a job can find it, and also everyone who wants a job will find that job based on their own native ability and desire for work, and not because of their racial or religious extraction.

So Governor Brown will be elected Governor of this State—and that is a prophecy which I believe will come true. He will be elected to your State because of his record, and because he deserves it.

And what he has been attempting to do in the State, we have been attempting to do in the Nation's Capital. We have passed, as we promised we would, the minimum wage of $1.25 an hour, which is little enough. We have provided for the largest extension of housing since the 1949 Act—particularly for those who are old. We have attempted to provide better protection for those who are older. And I can assure you that in January of 1962 this Administration will recommend wholeheartedly that we finally pass a medical care for the aged, which provides them and gives them an opportunity to pay for it themselves under Social Security.

We have made a concentrated effort, and I believe that we are on the brink of a major breakthrough in the coming years, to secure fresh water from salt water at a competitive price, to cleanse our rivers, to develop our resources, to provide jobs for our people, to educate our children, and to provide security for our aged. And we have also attempted to develop the strength of the United States abroad.

When we came into office, of the 14 divisions of the United States, three of them were training divisions, and we have turned them into combat divisions, and we have called up two of our National Guard. We have developed five additional combat divisions, therefore, for the United States in the last 9 months. Now 50 percent of the strategic Air Force in the United States is on a 15-minute alert—we will have a substantially increased number of Polaris submarines by 1963 and 1964 than we would have had.

We have attempted in the field of space, and there is no area—and I say this with complete conviction, there is no area where the United States received a greater setback to its prestige as the number one industrial country in the world than in being second in the field of space in the fifties. And while many may think that it is foolish to go to the moon, I do not believe that a powerful country like the United States, which wishes to demonstrate to a watching world that it is first in the field of technology and science, which represents so basic an aspiration of so many people, I do not believe that we want to permit the Soviet Union to dominate space, with all that it might mean to our peace and security in the coming years.

So in the field of national defense, in the field of space, in the field of our economic growth here at home, which has been over 10 percent in the last 9 months, we have attempted to do in Washington what the Democratic Party has always attempted to do there, and in California, and that is to move the United States forward.

In recent months I have spoken many times about how difficult and dangerous a period it is through which we now move. I would like to take this opportunity to say a word about the American spirit in this time of trial.

In the most critical periods of our Nation's history, there have always been those on the fringes of our society who have sought to escape their own responsibility by finding a simple solution, an appealing slogan or a convenient scapegoat. Financial crises could be explained by the presence of too many immigrants or too few greenbacks.

War could be attributed to munitions makers or international bankers. Peace conferences failed because we were duped by the British, or tricked by the French, or deceived by the Russians. It was not the presence of Soviet troops in Eastern Europe that drove it to communism, it was the sellout at Yalta. It was not a civil war that removed China from the Free World, it was treason in high places. At times these fanatics have achieved a temporary success among those who lack the will or the wisdom to face unpleasant facts or unsolved problems. But in time the basic good sense and stability of the great American consensus has always prevailed.

Now we are face to face once again with a period of heightened peril. The risks are great, the burdens heavy, the problems incapable of swift or lasting solution. And under the strains and frustrations imposed by constant tension and harassment, the discordant voices of extremism are once again heard in the land. Men who are unwilling to face up to the danger from without are convinced that the real danger is from within.

They look suspiciously at their neighbors and their leaders. They call for "a man on horseback" because they do not trust the people. They find treason in our churches, in our highest court, in our treatment of water. They equate the Democratic Party with the welfare state, the welfare state with socialism, socialism with communism. They object quite rightly to politics intruding on the military—but they are very anxious for the military to engage in their kind of politics.

But you and I—most Americans, soldiers and civilians—take a different view of our peril. We know it comes from without, not within. It must be met by quiet preparedness, not provocative speeches. And the steps taken this year to bolster our defenses—to increase our missile forces, to put more planes on alert, to provide more airlift and sealift and ready divisions—to make more certain than ever before that this nation has all the power that it will need to deter any attack of any kind—these steps constitute the most effective answer that can be made to those who would sow the seeds of doubt and of hate.

So let us not heed these counsels of fear and suspicion. Let us concentrate more on keeping enemy bombers and missiles away from our shores, and concentrate less on keeping neighbors away from our shelters. Let us devote more energy to organizing the free and friendly nations of the world, with common trade and strategic goals, and devote less energy to organizing armed bands of civilian guerrillas that are more likely to supply local vigilantes than national vigilance.

Let our patriotism be reflected in the creation of confidence in one another, rather than in crusades of suspicion. Let us prove we think our country great, by striving to make it greater. And, above all, let us remember, however serious the outlook, however harsh the task, the one great irreversible trend in the history of the world is on the side of liberty—and we, for all time to come, are on the same side.

NOTE: The President spoke at the Hollywood Palladium. In his opening words he referred to Edmund G. Brown, Governor of California, Stanley Mosk, Attorney General for California, and Edwin Pauley. Later in his remarks he referred to Dr. James B. Conant, vice chairman of the President's Committee on Youth Employment, which met with the President on November 15.

478   Letter to the Chairman, U.S. Tariff Commission, Requesting an Investigation of Cotton Imports.   *November 21, 1961*

Dear Mr. Dorfman:

I have been advised by the Secretary of Agriculture that there is reason to believe that articles or materials wholly or in part of cotton are being or are practically certain to be imported into the United States under such conditions and in such quantities as to render or tend to render ineffective, or materially interfere with, the programs or operations undertaken by the Department of Agriculture with respect to cotton or products thereof, or to reduce substantially the amount of cotton processed in the United States from cotton or products thereof with respect to which such programs or operations are being undertaken.

The Tariff Commission is requested to make an immediate investigation under Section 22 of the Agricultural Adjustment Act, as amended, to determine whether a fee equivalent to the per pound export subsidy rate on the cotton content of imported articles and materials wholly or in part of cotton is necessary to prevent the imports of such articles from rendering or tending to render ineffective or materially interfering with the Department's programs for cotton and cotton products, or from reducing substantially the amount of products processed in the United States from cotton or products thereof, with respect to which such programs are being undertaken.

The Commission's investigation and report should be completed as soon as practicable.

A copy of the Secretary's letter is enclosed.

Sincerely,

JOHN F. KENNEDY

[Honorable Ben D. Dorfman, Chairman, United States Tariff Commission, Washington, D.C.]

479   Remarks to the Officers of the National Conference of Christians and Jews.   *November 21, 1961*

Gentlemen:

I want to express my great pleasure at having you here today at the White House. I think your efforts in this field represent a very valuable service to our country. It has always seemed to me that when we all—regardless of our particular religious convictions—draw our guidance and inspiration, and really in a sense moral direction from the same general area, the Bible, the Old and the New Testaments, we have every reason to believe that our various religious denominations should live together in the closest harmony.

We have a great advantage, really, in so much of the world, in having such common roots, and therefore though our convictions may take us in different directions in our faith, nevertheless the basic presumption of the moral law, the existence of God, man's relation to Him—there is generally consensus on those questions.

So that we should set a happy model for the world, but like all things, these things cannot be taken for granted. Your efforts, really, over the last period of 30 years, I think have done perhaps more than any other factor in our national life to provide for harmonious living among our different religious groups.

I think there are still important tasks ahead, so I am delighted to hear, Doctor, that your group is committing itself to an intelligent and nonpartisan and open discussion—continued discussion, really—of the relationships between the state and religion.

It, after all, was a matter which occupied our Founding Fathers, and should occupy our attention; and I am hopeful that the fact that you are discussing it will be another evidence of what an open and happy society we live in. So I welcome you here. I congratulate you for the efforts you are making in this area. You are performing a valuable function as citizens. And therefore, speaking as President, and personally, we want to emphasize how much your work is appreciated, how valuable it is, and what a service you're rendering.

Thank you.

NOTE: The President spoke in the Rose Garden at the White House. During his remarks he referred to Dr. Lewis Webster Jones, president of the National Conference of Christians and Jews.

480   Toasts of the President and Chancellor Adenauer. *November* 21, 1961

Gentlemen:

I know that you join me in expressing our great pleasure in having the Chancellor here once again in the United States. We are particularly glad that he has come accompanied by the Foreign Minister and the Minister of Defense, and that in the company of our friend, the Ambassador, and the other members of his party we are extremely glad to have him back on our shores once again.

The Chancellor occupies a very special position in this country, and it is a source, I know, of satisfaction to him that he has enjoyed the confidence of three different Presidents in recent years, and four Secretaries of State—President Truman, President Eisenhower—Secretary Acheson, Secretary Dulles, Secretary Herter, and Secretary Rusk. And I think that in spite of the changes which have taken place in this country from party to party and from administration to administration, they have recognized the Chancellor as being committed, as we are, to the defense of the West and the strengthening of Europe.

He has been generous enough to say that Americans are good Europeans, and he has demonstrated not only that he is a great European, but that also the people of the Federal Republic not only look to the day when Germany can be unified, but also to the West and the development of Europe, in the close association between the Atlantic Community and its members in other parts of the world.

So, Chancellor, there are some in this room who admire you because of your political success, which is extraordinary, and there are others, in fact all, who admire you for the long view that you have taken in the interests of your country. In the confidence which you have had in the United States—which we hope is still maintained—and the recognition which you have had from the beginning, the United States and the Federal Republic must move in harmony together, not only in the forties and fifties, but in the sixties.

I think an alliance is an extremely difficult system to operate. The interests of all must be considered. It is far easier for our adversaries to move with speed, commanding as they do their satellites. We are all sovereign and allied, and we are therefore interdependent as well as independent. And I would therefore consider it most advantageous that you were generous to come and see us again, in order that we might renew our friendship, the friendship which exists between the members of the government and also between the people of our countries.

So I hope that all our guests will join me in drinking to one of the transcendent figures of our time—the Chancellor.

NOTE: The President proposed the toast at a luncheon in the state dining room at the White House.

Chancellor Adenauer responded (through an interpreter) as follows:

"Mr. President, gentlemen:

"This is my tenth visit to the United States of America in my capacity as Federal Chancellor of the Federal Republic of Germany. After the breakdown of my country as a result of the last war, it was very clear to me and to my friends that there was only one way out of this ruin and chaos for my country; namely, to establish inseparable links with the countries of the Free World, and in particular with the United States of America. And my trust and my confidence in the United States of America has never been disappointed.

"I have always considered it to be one of the greatest deeds of the people—the United States of America—that after having won this victory in 1945, under the leadership of the United States of America, that the victors did not rebuff the vanquished, but on the contrary they extended a helping hand to the vanquished—they helped them get back on their feet.

"That, I think, was a great action—a great deed—and rare in history.

"Mr. President, I thank you very much for the very kind words you said, and I also thank you for the spirit which inspired your words, and for the attitude you have always shown towards me.

"You may be sure, Mr. President, that the close ties that existed between your predecessor and myself will continue between you and myself; because we consider both you and your predecessor to be great Americans. And I may assure you, Mr. President, of the great veneration, the great love, and the great affection which the German people have for you.

"I now propose a toast to you, sir, and to the indissoluble friendship between the people of the United States of America and of Germany."

In the first paragraph the President referred to Gerhard Schroeder and Franz Josef Strauss, Foreign Minister and Minister of Defense of the Federal Republic of Germany, respectively, and Wilhelm G. Grewe, German Ambassador to the United States.

481   Joint Statement Following Discussions With Chancellor Adenauer. *November 22, 1961*

THE PRESIDENT and the Chancellor have had an extended exchange of views during the past three days on a number of problems of vital concern to their Govern-

ments. These exchanges took place in a frank and cordial atmosphere and established that there is substantial unanimity of view both on the substance of the problems and how to deal with them.

The visit of the Chancellor afforded an opportunity to the Foreign Ministers and the Defense Ministers of the two countries to participate in the discussion and exchange views among themselves.

Berlin, over which the Soviet Union has created an international crisis, was the subject of earnest consultation. The President and the Chancellor reaffirmed their clear determination to insure the continuance of a free and vigorous life for the population of Berlin. They are in accord on the basic elements which will permit a peaceful resolution of this crisis through negotiation if there is reasonableness on the part of the Soviet Union. They agreed on the measures which should be taken in pursuing this objective in a manner consistent with the legitimate interests of all parties concerned. At the same time they also agreed on the necessity for maintaining and increasing the ability of the NATO Alliance to cope with any military developments. These discussions will be continued through the already announced meetings between Chancellor Adenauer, Prime Minister Macmillan and President de Gaulle and concluded in the Foreign Ministers meeting and the NATO Ministerial Meeting scheduled in mid-December in Paris.

The President and the Chancellor reaffirmed the ultimate goal of their Governments of achieving by peaceful means the reunification of Germany on the basis of self-determination. They were also in agreement that this objective could be realized without prejudice to the legitimate interests of the Soviet Union and Germany's neighbors.

The President and the Chancellor reviewed the state of the North Atlantic Treaty Organization. They welcomed the measures now in progress to strengthen the Alliance, but recognized the need for a sustained effort to further improve the ability of the Alliance to resist aggression.

The President and the Chancellor noted Soviet charges accusing the NATO Alliance of aggressive intent, and singling out the Federal Republic of Germany and its democratically elected government as the principal object of its false and unwarranted attack. In this regard, the President and the Chancellor reaffirmed that:

(1) The North Atlantic alliance is an alliance for defense against aggression which abides fully by the requirements of the Charter of the United Nations. The peaceful characteristics of its members and their freedom from coercion make it manifestly impossible for NATO to commit aggression against anyone.

(2) The Federal Republic of Germany has demonstrated that it looks to its legitimate security interests entirely within the North Atlantic Alliance, and to this end has integrated its entire effective defense establishment into the multinational NATO framework. The Chancellor, in emphasizing the defensive aspects of West German armed forces, noted that the Federal Republic is the only nation of its size all of whose forces are under international command.

While agreeing on the need to take all measures essential to strengthen the defensive posture of NATO, the President and the Chancellor recognized the necessity of not permitting Soviet pressure over Berlin to deflect them from urgently required constructive tasks vital to the welfare of their peoples and those of other nations.

The President reaffirmed the strong support of the United States for the movement toward European unity through the European Economic Community, the European Coal and Steel Community, and EURATOM. The President and the Chancellor agreed on the important role that the development of the European communities can play in further strengthening and complementing the entire Atlantic community. They agreed particularly on the importance and significance of proposals now being considered for a European Political Union pursuant to the Bonn Declaration of July 1961.

They welcomed the recent decision by the OECD Council of Ministers to increase the combined gross national product of the OECD member countries by 50 percent in 1970 and pledged themselves to work toward this goal.

The President and the Chancellor also discussed the urgent need to increase the flow of development assistance to the less-developed countries. They noted that the Development Assistance Committee of the OECD provides an excellent means of stimulating a greater effort in this field. They considered that in many cases the application of combined resources from several capital exporting countries to specific development assistance problems would be a valuable method of assisting the less-developed countries.

It is the view of the President and the Chancellor that the fruitful exchange of views which they have had will facilitate the close cooperation between the United States and the Federal Republic and result in further strengthening the ties of friendship and mutual understanding which have characterized their relations in the post-war period.

482 Remarks in Connection With the United Nations Freedom From Hunger Campaign. *November 22, 1961*

IT IS a great pleasure and honor to welcome to the White House again Mrs. Woodrow Wilson and Miss Marian Anderson as representatives of the United States Freedom From Hunger Foundation.

It is fitting that on tomorrow, Thanksgiving Day, the United States will launch its Freedom From Hunger Campaign in cooperation with the United Nations Food and Agriculture Organization.

As the Pilgrims gave thanks more than three centuries ago for a bountiful harvest, so we give thanks in 1961 for the blessing of our agriculture and the continued opportunity that the great productivity of our farms gives us in sharing our food with the world's hungry.

President Woodrow Wilson responded to that opportunity in 1914, when food was sent to Europe. The American people have answered this call before, in all parts of the world, and they answer it now. Since last January, under the Food for Peace Program directed by Mr. McGovern, nearly 28 million tons of food have been programed for shipment abroad.

The challenge of world hunger is one that we must meet, knowing that the burden is greater today than it's ever been before. But it is heartening to know that we are now joined in a worldwide alliance, the Freedom From Hunger Campaign, to eliminate hunger from the earth.

As long as there are hungry families— mothers, fathers, and children—through the world, we cannot possibly believe or feel that our great agricultural production, in any sense, is a burden. It is a great asset, not only for ourselves but for people all over the world; and I think that instead of using the term "surpluses," and regarding it, in a sense, as a failure, we should regard it as one of the great evidences of our country's capacity, and also as a great resource, in order to demonstrate our concern for our fellow men.

As I've said, as long as any of them are hungry tomorrow, I'm sure that Americans will not sit down at their table without hoping that we can do more to aid those who sit at no table.

NOTE: The President spoke in the Fish Room at the White House. Also present, in addition to Mrs. Wilson and Miss Anderson, was Chancellor Adenauer.

The White House announced on the same day that 33 prominent Americans, including President Truman, Mrs. Wilson, Mrs. Roosevelt, and Adlai E. Stevenson, had been named members of the U.S. Freedom From Hunger Foundation. On December 14 the President announced that President Truman had accepted the honorary chairmanship of the Foundation, and released a statement by the former President.

483   Transcript of Interview With the President by Aleksei Adzhubei, Editor of Izvestia. *November 25, 1961*

Mr. Adzhubei: Mr. President, I am happy to get this interview from you, and I would like to tell you quite frankly that your election to the high post of President of the United States office was met with great hope by public opinion in our country. In connection with this, I would like to ask you the following question——

THE PRESIDENT. May I just say that I appreciate very much your coming to the United States. I also appreciate the opportunity to talk, through you and through your newspaper, to the people of the Soviet Union. I think that communication, an exchange of views, an honest report of what our countries are like and what they want and what the people wish, is in the interests of both our countries and in the interests of peace. So we are delighted to have this opportunity.

Mr. Adzhubei: I would like to ask you the following question. Mr. President, during the election campaign, on several occasions you expressed good intentions with respect to the necessity of improving Soviet-American relations. On the occasion of your Inauguration as President of a great country, Nikita Khrushchev, Chairman of the Council of Ministers of the USSR, and Leonid Brezhnev, Chairman of the Presidium of the Supreme Soviet of the USSR, in their message to you expressed the hope that by their joint efforts our countries can succeed in radically improving our relations and the international situation. They also expressed confidence that we can, step by step, liquidate the existing suspicion and distrust, and thus bring cooperation between our peoples. On its part, the Soviet government is always ready to support any good endeavor in that direction, and to do its best for the establishment of a stable peace in the world, in order that all peoples may live in friendship and without hatred among them.

Mr. President, what do you think about the present state of Soviet-American relations, and what in your opinion must be done by the American as well as the Soviet governments to improve the relations between our two countries?

THE PRESIDENT. Well, I would say that the relations today are not as satisfactory as I had hoped they would be when I first took office. In fact, one of the first things that I did on becoming President was to commit the United States to an earnest effort to achieve a satisfactory agreement with the Soviet Union on the cessation of nuclear tests. As a result of that effort, at the end of March, we sent our representatives, along with Great Britain's, to Geneva for the first time with a complete treaty which we tabled for discussion. I had hoped that this would be one area where we could make real progress. It would lessen the contamination of the air, it would be a first step towards disarmament, and I felt that if we could achieve an agreement in this area, we could then move on to the other areas of disarmament which required action.

We were not successful. And, as you know, we were in fact still at the table in Geneva in August when, still negotiating, the Soviet Union resumed its tests which must have been in preparation for many months, at the very time that the conversations were going on. So that has been a disappointment.

In addition, Berlin and Germany have become, I think, areas of heightened crisis since the Vienna meeting, and I think extremely dangerous to the peace, which I am sure—I know—both of our people want.

I think that the Soviet Union and the United States should live together in peace. We are large countries, energetic people, we are steadily providing in both our countries an increase in the standard of living. If we can keep the peace for 20 years, the life of the people of the Soviet Union and the life of the people of the United States will be far richer and will be far happier as the standard of living steadily rises.

Where we feel the difficulty comes is the effort by the Soviet Union to communize, in a sense, the entire world. If the Soviet Union were merely seeking to protect its own national interests, to protect its own national security, and would permit other countries to live as they wish—to live in peace—then I believe that the problems which now cause so much tension would fade away.

We want the people of the Soviet Union to live in peace—we want the same for our own people. It is this effort to push outward the communist system, on to country after country, that represents, I think, the great threat to peace. If the Soviet Union looked only to its national interest and to providing a better life for its people under conditions of peace, I think there would be nothing that would disturb the relations between the Soviet Union and the United States.

Mr. Adzhubei: That is very interesting. However as a citizen of the Soviet Union, as a member of the Communist Party, I cannot agree with you, in that part of your answer where you are saying that we are trying to "communize" the world. At the 22nd Party Congress, which, in our opinion, was an historic event, we adopted a program of communist development and we said that we are against any export of the revolution, but we are also against any export of counterrevolution. If we turn to facts, there are many countries in the world in the affairs of which, from our point of view the United States is interfering. Yesterday, I saw a TV program which was being shown to millions of Americans, where your commentator asserted that the whole world is under complete threat of the communists to capture the world. We would like to see an end put to this situation.

Our government and our party believe that every people chooses such a system of government as they like. Austria chose the capitalist way of development, although American and Soviet troops were there. But Cuba has chosen another way of development. And we would be happy if you, Mr. President, were to state that the interference in the affairs of Cuba was a mistake. We hope that the Cuban people will consolidate their own way of life—as well as the Dominican Republic, Ecuador, Brazil, and many other countries.

THE PRESIDENT. May I just say, without getting into a debate, that the United States supports the idea that every people shall have the right to make a free choice as to the kind of government they want. In the case of Cuba, let me remind you that the Castro revolution was originally supported by the great majority of the people. When Castro was leading the revolution, the statement was made that there would be free elections, and freedom for the people, and progress for the people. But Castro has not kept that commitment. Until the present government of Cuba will allow free and honest elections, in our opinion, it cannot claim to represent the majority of the people. That is our dispute with Cuba.

Mr. Jagan, on the other hand, who was recently elected Prime Minister in British Guiana is a Marxist, but the United States doesn't object—because that choice was made by an honest election, which he won.

If the people of any country choose to follow a communist system in a free election, after a fair opportunity for a number of views to be presented, the United States would accept that. What we find to be objectionable, and a threat to the peace, is when a system is imposed by a small militant group by subversion, infiltration, and all the rest.

If the Soviet Union and this country could develop their own resources, and if you permitted the peoples of the world to develop in the way they wish to develop, then, if any nation should choose a communist system, we would recognize and and accept that. And if they chose another

system, then we would hope that you would recognize and accept that, too. If we could get that on both sides, I believe the Soviet Union and the United States, which have so much to gain from peace, could live in peace.

Mr. Adzhubei: I understand you, Mr. President, and I am very happy to hear these words from you, because as you know, the future of the world depends in many respects on the relations between the United States and our country. Let the people decide what way of development they want to choose. However I would like to draw your attention to the following historical parallel. When the Bolsheviks, headed by V. I. Lenin, came to power, all the capitalist world was shouting that they were plotters and that there was no freedom in Russia but in 44 years our country became a great power. But this is not the issue. I would like to ask you another question——

THE PRESIDENT. You are a newspaper man and a politician.

Mr. Adzhubei: In our country every citizen is a politician, because we like our country very much. The young and the old like the socialist system of our country and we are ready to fight for it until its victorious end. You are proud of your country, Mr. President, and we are also very much proud of our own country, and we are very proud of our party, and we are proud of V. I. Lenin.

Mr. President, sometimes it's said that in order to improve the relations between our countries, it is necessary to start with the settlement of small problems. Others believe that too many small issues have accumulated and that perhaps it would be better to start with a big act. We believe that such a big act was the visit by Nikita Sergeyevich Khrushchev to the United

States in 1959. But unfortunately the results of that trip were not completely satisfactory.[1] Mr. President, what is your attitude toward the idea of concluding a pact of peace between the United States and the Soviet Union? That would be a great step forward.

THE PRESIDENT. I think we should have not only an agreement between our countries, but take those steps which make peace possible. I don't think that paper, and words on paper, are as significant as looking at those areas which provide tension between our two systems and seeing if we can dispel that tension.

One of those areas now is the problem of Germany and Berlin. If we could make progress there, then in my opinion it would provide a most important step in improving our relations in other areas.

I stated that if we had been able to get an agreement on the nuclear tests cessation, that would lead to other agreements on disarmament. If we can make an agreement successfully which provides peace in Central Europe, if we can conclude our efforts in Laos and insure a government and a country which are neutral and independent, as Chairman Khrushchev and I agreed at Vienna, then we would be able to move into other areas of tension. I believe, as I have said, if we can now make an agreement on a satisfactory basis on Berlin and Germany, which is the most critical area—because it represents a matter of great interest to both our countries, and great concern to our peoples—then we could take other steps. If we can solve the problem of Germany and Berlin, I believe we can find our relations substantially improved.

----

[1] This sentence, as published in Izvestia, reads: "But the positive results of that trip were wrecked and brought to nothing by the well-known actions of the then American administration."

Mr. Adzhubei: Thank you, Mr. President, this is a most worthy thought. Especially because, as I understand you, you intend to talk seriously on these problems with our government. Let me say that the German problem is of great importance to our country, for many reasons. Not only for strictly political reasons, and not only because of prestige considerations. As you know we have allies—Poland, Czechoslovakia, and a number of other countries. However, to date we haven't heard any sober voices from the West affirming the integrity of the borders existing in Europe and it would be very important to hear that. But there is also another aspect to the German problem. In our country, in the Soviet Union, there is not a single family that did not lose some kin in the war. You know we are trying to put out the smouldering coals of the last war in Central Europe. But we do not wish only to play the role of a political fireman, as it were, though it is very important. In the heart of every Soviet citizen, in the soul of every Soviet citizen, there are, as you know, coals still burning from the last war and they are burning his soul and does not let him sleep quietly. Thus, solution of the question of a peace treaty is the hope and tranquillity in the heart of every Soviet man. After all we are still singing songs about those who did not come home from the war. I know that you participated in the war, that you are a hero of the war, and this is why I am talking to you in such lofty words. But this, if you wish, is a sideline.

Mr. President, in 1958, if I am not mistaken, our government suggested to the government of the United States—of course, the previous administration was in power then—that the trade relations between our countries be normalized. Now, as you know, the trade relations between our countries are in a very lamentable condition. Before I left for the United States, I had a conversation with my friends from the Ministry of Foreign Trade, and they asked me to inquire with you whether there are any prospects of improving the trade relations between our countries. After all there is a very old truth: together with goods, together with the exchange of goods, there also come better relations among peoples.

THE PRESIDENT. Let me say that I know that the Soviet Union suffered more from World War II than any country. It represented a terrible blow, and the casualties affected every family, including many of the families of those now in government.

I will say that the United States also suffered, though not so heavily as the Soviet Union, quite obviously. My brother was killed in Europe. My sister's husband was killed in Europe.

The point is that that war is now over. We want to prevent another war arising out of Germany. I think the important thing between the United States and the USSR is not to create the kind of tension and pressure, which in the name of settling World War II increases the chances of a conflict between the Soviet Union and its allies on the one hand and the United States and its allies on the other. What we should attempt to do is work out a solution through negotiation which will make it possible to keep the peace in Central Europe. And that is the aim of this government.

Now in regard to trade, one of the first things I did on becoming President was to change governmental policy which provided for the admission of crab meat. This was not a matter of great dollar value, but had some symbolic importance, and was a matter which Chairman Khrushchev had spoken about on several occasions.

My own judgment is that, if we can solve the problems that we are now talking about, particularly in Berlin, and ease the general tension, trade will then increase. What has diminished trade in recent months has been the difficulty which we have experienced in Germany and Berlin. I would hope that trade could be expanded, and in my judgment it would expand immediately, if we can bring about a peaceful and satisfactory solution to the interests of all in Germany and Berlin.

Mr. Adzhubei: I shall communicate your words to our readers with a feeling of satisfaction. We have always thought and still think of the Americans as the realists. It is your energy, your realistic approach, that has helped you to create such a wealthy country. But now I would like to ask you frankly, Mr. President, because this idea was expressed by you in several instances, whether you seriously think that the social changes which are happening in the world today are the result of actions in which Moscow has its hands? I would like to remind you of one thing. You know, in France when the bourgeois revolution won, the aristocratic Europe accused France of every mortal sin. When the October revolution won, all the world of the rich condemned that revolution. But this revolution won! You mentioned that a Marxist came to power in British Guiana. Do you think that events occurred there according to our instructions? Of course, we can't give you any assurances that there won't be social changes in the world, although you will call it the result of the "hands" of Moscow.

THE PRESIDENT. Let me say, as I indicated, if the people of these countries make a free choice, that they prefer the communist or socialist or any other kind of system, then the United States and the people of the United

States accept that. That is why I gave the example of British Guiana. But of course I do not hold and I do not say that the Soviet Union is responsible for all the changes that are coming in the world. For example, since the end of World War II, the British Empire has been turned into independent states, I think 15 of them. The French community has been turned into 21 independent states. There are many changes in the world. Western Europe has joined closer together in the Common Market. These are not the result of the communists' efforts. There are many changes, as I have said, throughout the world. People want to live in different ways. That is what we want, also. If they have a fair opportunity to make a choice, if they choose to support communism, we accept that. What we object to is the attempt to impose communism by force, or a situation where once a people may have fallen under communism the communists do not give them a fair opportunity to make another choice.

We had been under the impression that the Yalta Agreement and the Potsdam Agreement provided for a free choice for the peoples of Eastern Europe. They do not, in our opinion, today have a free choice. You may argue that they may want to live under communism, but if they do not they are not given the opportunity to change.

We believe that if the Soviet Union—without attempting to impose the communist system—will permit the people of the world to live as they wish to live, relations between the Soviet Union and the United States will then be very satisfactory, and our two peoples, which now live in danger, will be able to live in peace and with a greatly increased standard of living. And I believe we have such vast economic opportunities now in both of our countries that we should consider how we can get along, and not

attempt to impose our views, one on the other or on anyone else.

Mr. Adzhubei: Of course, Mr. President, I did not expect in such a short period of time I would succeed in converting you to another belief—just as you did not expect to convert me. You have talked with our Chairman, the First Secretary of the Central Committee of the Communist Party of the Soviet Union, and he did not succeed in convincing you, nor did he try to do so. This, as you know, is a matter of personal outlook. One man may consider certain elections to be free, while another would consider those elections non-democratic. For example, in a number of countries of Latin America, great revolutionary changes are taking place. For a long period of time you considered that Trujillo was elected in a democratic way. You have been saying the same about the regime of the Shah of Iran as well. But let us not engage in an argument and let us turn to the next question.

Mr. President, may I ask you the following question? It is well known that the Soviet government has declared its readiness to accept any proposal of the Western powers on international control and inspection, if agreement on general and complete disarmament is reached. At the same time, the Soviet government does not exclude the possibility of reaching agreement on a number of measures which may decrease the danger of war and which could be effected in the nearest future. Such proposals are, for instance, the proposals on the freezing of military budgets, renunciation of the use of nuclear weapons, the conclusion of a non-aggression pact between NATO and the Warsaw Pact countries, withdrawal of foreign troops from the territories of other countries, the establishment of a nuclear free zone, or measures against the danger of surprise attack. What, in your views, are the prospects of general and complete disarmament, and of decreasing international tensions?

THE PRESIDENT. Inasmuch as the Soviet Union and the United States agreed in the declaration of principles in September, at the end of the McCloy-Zorin talks, on the goal of general and complete disarmament, the problem now becomes an attempt to implement that goal, stage by stage. The Soviet Union and the United States have a basic disagreement which must be resolved on this question. We believe that there must be adequate inspection, to make sure that each side is disarming and staying in accordance with the agreements which they make. The Soviet Union has stated that it will permit us, or the international body, to inspect those weapons which are destroyed but will not permit us to carry out an inspection to see what weapons remain. One side could destroy a hundred bombers but still have a thousand or two thousand bombers left. If you are really going to provide for orderly disarmament, it seems to me you have to inspect not only those weapons which have been destroyed, but also those weapons that remain. Otherwise we do not have any guarantee of security for either side. If we can agree to an effective inspection system so that each country can know that the other is living up to its agreement, then, in my opinion, we can move into general and complete disarmament.

That is why I thought it so vitally important that we make an agreement on cessation of nuclear testing as the first step, and then proceed step by step through atomic weapons, through missiles, through the level of ground forces, the Navy, and all the rest. If we can get agreement on that, then we can move toward general and complete disarmament.

I think it would be helpful if NATO and the Warsaw pact engaged in a commitment to live in peace with each other. I certainly believe we should take every conceivable step to prevent surprise attack. I believe that if the relations between our countries can be normalized, there will be less military buildup on both sides, but we cannot now withdraw our troops from Europe, way back across the Atlantic Ocean, when you merely withdraw your troops to the Soviet Union which is only a few hundred miles away. That is why we need some understanding of what is going to be the situation in Berlin and in Germany. And that is why I hope negotiations will take place between our governments quickly and will come to a successful conclusion.

The statement has been made on many occasions that we object to the signing of a peace treaty, that we regard that as a belligerent act. That is not the point. It is our view that the statement which the four powers made at Geneva in 1955 providing for the reunification of Germany represents the soundest policy. To divide a country, to divide a city, to put up a wall in a city, we believe, only increases tensions rather than diminish them. And we believe that, if the German people were permitted to be reunified, adequate steps could be taken to protect the security of all involved.

Now we recognize that today the Soviet Union does not intend to permit reunification, and that as long as the Soviet Union has that policy, Germany will not be reunified. The question now is whether the Soviet Union will sign a treaty with the East German authorities which will increase tension rather than diminish it. As I said in my speech at the United Nations, we recognize that the Soviet Union can sign any treaty it wishes with the East German authorities. What we find to be so dangerous, however, is the claim that that treaty will deny us our rights in West Berlin, rights which we won through the war, rights which were agreed to by the Soviet Union, the United States, Britain, and France at the conclusion of the war, and which we believe should be continued. But if you sign a treaty with East Germany and those rights are subject to the wishes of the East German authorities, it seems to me that that is going to increase tension. If the Soviet Union attempts in that treaty to turn over jurisdiction over West Berlin to the East German authorities, against the wishes of the people of West Berlin—if the lines of communication and access, from West Berlin to the outside world and the West, are completely under the control of East German authorities to cut any time they so wish—then this treaty does not bring peace, it only increases the danger.

Now I am hopeful that, in the conversations and negotiations which we hope to have with the Soviet Union, assurances will be given which will permit us to continue to exercise the rights which we now have in West Berlin, as a result of the existing four power agreement, and will permit free access in and out of the city. We do not want to stay in West Berlin if the people there do not want us to stay. But they want us to stay. When they decide that they don't want us, we will leave. But as long as they wish us to stay, it seems to me that the rights which are ours by agreement should be maintained. I am hopeful that the Soviet Union will agree with this, and in particular will agree to permit supplies and people to move in and out of West Berlin freely. Then we can, in my opinion, reach a peaceful settlement in the center of Europe, and if we can reach an agreement on this question, then I believe our relations will greatly improve.

Mr. Adzhubei: You just answered the question I was going to ask. But I cannot agree with you. I am not a specialist in the field of disarmament, but as I understand it, the McCloy-Zorin agreement was a very important step forward, and we hope that the efforts by specialists who will be authorized by our governments will lead to better results. And now a few words about Germany. If I understood correctly the translation, I have heard a very unrealistic term. I have in mind the term "East German authorities." It would be more pleasant to hear "government of the German Democratic Republic." You don't like the German Democratic Republic. We don't like the Federal Republic of Germany, but we have diplomatic relations with the FRG, we have very good trade relations with it. Thus, we are realists. If the government of the United States were not saying "East German authorities" but were to say "government of the GDR," that would be very good and realistic.

And now a second point. We would like to sign a peace treaty together with our World War II allies, and we hope that it will be so. It would be a great happiness not only for our government but also for our people. Nobody intends to turn West Berlin over to East Germany. That does not make sense. There is the GDR and there is the FRG with its capitalist system. Let's sign a peace treaty and let us guarantee freedom for West Berlin by every means— by troops of the four powers, by United Nations troops—and let's thus guarantee its rights. But this is a problem for future negotiation. Now a few words about access to West Berlin. Why complicate such a simple problem? Communication to West Berlin runs over 100 miles through the territory of the German Democratic Republic. If one needs to visit West Berlin, if it is necessary to send people, food or other goods there, then it is very elementary to ask permission for that of the government of the GDR. Sometimes I feel—and I am saying this to you very frankly—that some evil people are attempting to complicate simple things and thus are deliberately creating tension. Yesterday, when I was talking with your closest advisers, I gave this example: if a man has his nervous system extremely strained, he is irritated by every noise, every sound and everything is taken by him very suspiciously. Such a man can create much trouble. We hope that the negotiations which will take place in the near future will be objective, realistic, and will be conducted in an atmosphere of complete calm.

THE PRESIDENT. May I just make one brief response? All Berlin was put under four-power authority by the agreements at Potsdam. East Berlin, which was under the immediate authority of the Soviet Union, has now been turned over to East Germany in violation of those agreements. It is no longer effectively under four-power control. And now the Soviet Union seeks to place Soviet troops in West Berlin. It does not suggest that the troops of the other three powers be placed in East Berlin. In other words, the Soviet Union now seeks to share in the control of West Berlin. That is the first point that is in question. The second is this question of the rights of access in crossing East Germany. As I gather it, you would give the East German authorities—you say East German government—the power to interfere with that traffic. It is stated that they would not do so, but we have no assurances in Mr. Ulbricht's statements which vary from week to week. In my opinion, if such an agreement is signed, if our rights on the communication lines between the West and West Berlin—which are now governed by the Soviet Union—are turned over to the East German authorities,

and if the East Germans should interfere with that right of access, for one reason or another, then this would provide for heightened tension, the Soviet Union might come to the support of East Germany and we would find ourselves, instead of having settled this now, once more face to face.

The reason why we have been reluctant to recognize East Germany as a sovereign power is that we do not recognize the division of Germany. In our opinion the German people wish to have one united country. If the Soviet Union had lost the war, the Soviet people themselves would object to a line being drawn through Moscow and the entire country. If we had been defeated in war, we wouldn't like to have a line drawn down the Mississippi River. The Germans want to be united. I think it should be possible to provide for that under conditions which will protect the interests of all concerned. But the Soviet Union believes that it is more in their interest to keep Germany divided.

Now the question is—given that decision—can we provide for the protection of our rights in West Berlin, which were agreed to in 1945 by the Soviet Union, so that this is not a continuing crisis? In attempting to work out a solution of the problems which came about as a result of World War II, we don't want to increase the chances of World War III. All we wish to do is maintain a very limited—and they are a very limited number of troops of the three powers in West Berlin and to have, for example, an international administration on the Autobahn so that goods and people can move freely in and out. Then we can have peace in this area for years. But if East Germany is going to exercise the right of authority over that access, we are going to have continued tension there—and I simply do not see, given the strong interests of both of us in having peace in this part of Europe, why that is a wise decision. I am hopeful instead that the negotiations which we are anxious to see take place will bring about an agreement on this area which will recognize fairly the interests of all.

Mr. Adzhubei: Mr. President, since I'm talking to you in a very frank and friendly manner, I would like to ask you to imagine, at least for a moment, the following impossible thing. Imagine that you were an officer, a veteran of the Soviet Navy, who fought in World War II. You won the war, and then the very events occurred which are now taking place. One of the parts of Germany—the Federal Republic of Germany—does not recognize the borders which have been established after the war. It is again building up its armed forces. The Chancellor of that country goes to the United States to talk to the President of the United States and they have secret talks. The spirit of revanchism is very high in that part of Germany. What would your attitude be toward this, if you were a veteran of the Soviet Navy?

THE PRESIDENT. If I were a Soviet veteran, I would see that West Germany now has only 9 divisions, which is a fraction of the Soviet forces. Nine divisions. It has no nuclear weapons of its own. It has a very small Air Force—almost no Navy, I think perhaps two or three submarines. So it is not a military threat. Its nine divisions are under the international control of NATO, and subject to the command of the NATO organization, which is made up of 15 countries of Europe which altogether have, in West Germany now, about 22 or 23 divisions—about the same number as the Soviet divisions in East Germany. So that I do not see that this country represents a military threat now to the Soviet Union, even though I recognize how bitter was the struggle in

World War II—in the same way that Japan today represents no threat to the United States, even though 20 years ago there were 4 years of war in the Pacific against the Japanese. The power of countries changes—weapons change—science changes—without missiles, without nuclear capability, with very few divisions today, I don't believe West Germany is a military threat.

Then I would look at the power of the United States, and I would look at the power of the Soviet Union, and I would say that the important thing is for the Soviet Union and the United States not to get into a war, which would destroy both of our systems. So as a Soviet veteran, I would want the Soviet Union to reach an agreement with the United States which recognizes the interests and the commitments of the United States, as well as our own, and not attempt to enforce single-handedly a new situation upon the United States which would be against previous commitments we had made. The Soviet Union made a commitment in regard to Berlin in 1945. Germany today is divided. Germany today is not a threat to the Soviet Union militarily.

The important thing is to attempt to reach an accord which recognizes the interests of all; and I believe that can be done with respect to Germany. I recognize that there are going to be two Germanies as long as the Soviet Union believes that that is in her interest. The problem now is to make sure that, in any treaty which the Soviet Union reaches with East Germany, the rights of the other powers are recognized in Berlin. That's all we're talking about. We are not talking about encouraging revanchism, building a great German military machine, or anything else you mention. In any peace treaty which is signed with East Germany, there must be a recognition of the rights of the United States and the other powers.

Now that does not seem to me to be a threat in any way to the security of the Soviet Union. That does not provide for any increase in the Western military forces, which are rather limited there. I think we could have peace in this century in Central Europe if we can reach an accord over West Berlin. To pursue another course in the name of ending World War II—a course which threatens to increase the chance of World War III—represents a wholly unwise policy, for you and for us.

So, if I were a Soviet officer and wanted peace, I would think peace can be won and my country's security can be assured. The Soviet Union is a strong military power. It has great nuclear capacity. It has missiles, planes—it has a great number of divisions—it has countries associated with it. No one is ever going to invade the Soviet Union again. There is no military power that can do that. The problem is to make an agreement which will permit us to have our interests recognized, as well as yours. That should not be beyond the capacity of us both.

Chairman Khrushchev did not, nor did I, make the arrangements in 1945 in regard to Berlin. Our responsibility, given the situation which is a difficult one, is to bring about peace, and I believe it can be done.

In short, if I were a Soviet naval officer, I would feel that the security of the Soviet Union was well protected, and that the important thing now is to reach an accord with the United States, our ally during that second war.

Mr. Adzhubei: Mr. President, I am about to finish. Of course, you answered this question not as a veteran of the Soviet armed forces but as President of the United States, and that is quite natural. However, as I understand you, Mr. President, you are

against West Germany's having nuclear weapons at her disposal, or in any degree of control over such weapons?

THE PRESIDENT. The United States, as a matter of national policy, as I said at the United Nations, will not give nuclear weapons to any country, and I would be extremely reluctant to see West Germany acquire a nuclear capacity of its own. Chancellor Adenauer stated that they would not, in 1954. That is still the policy of that government, and I think that is the wise policy.

Mr. Adzhubei: But you know perfectly well that many top posts in NATO are occupied by German generals, and you know that Europe is very far from the United States. Don't you think that at some point it might happen that German generals might become too influential in NATO?

THE PRESIDENT. That is why I believe it to be so important to stress the West German army is integrated in NATO. NATO is now commanded by an American; and, in my judgment, as long as German forces are integrated in NATO—and NATO is under the control of the 15 NATO countries, none of which wants another war—there is security for all. And I think that will continue.

Now if this situation changed, if Germany developed an atomic capability of its own, if it developed many missiles, or a strong national army that threatened war, then I would understand your concern, and I would share it. After all, we have had two wars in Europe, as well as you. But the situation today, and the situation for the future, is as I have described it. If it changed, then it would seem to me appropriate for the United States and the Soviet Union and others to consider the situation at that time. But it is not that way now, so why take the risk of having the United States, which is a powerful country, and the Soviet Union, which is also powerful, getting into difficulty with each other, when there is no real threat in Europe to you or to us. I think that we should look at things as they are in 1961.

You have stated that you are realists. This is not 1939, 1940, or 1941. Look what has happened. As I said, in the Far East, Japan's strength was entirely different in those years. China's power was also entirely different. Countries change. Situations change. And we have to be realistic enough to see where the real danger lies. The real danger today is the fact that both of us possess in our nuclear stockpiles the means to impose great devastation upon each other—and we are the ones that have the most to lose from war.

Therefore I think, if we look at it realistically, we should be able to reach an accord which protects the interests of our two great countries, and permits us both to go ahead with increasing our standard of living and meeting other problems. In the United States in the last 14 years our living standard has increased 40 percent. In the Soviet Union it has gone up sharply. Nobody can benefit more from peace than the Soviet Union and the United States.

I would hope that rather than attempting to talk about conditions in Germany as they were 20 years ago, we would look at them as they are today. We have had peace, really, in Europe for 15 years. The problem now is to see if we can reach a negotiation which can settle this matter for another 15 years. Nobody knows what is going to happen in the world over the long run, but at least we ought to be able to settle this matter of Berlin and Germany.

Mr. Adzhubei: I thank you for your at-

tention and this time that I took from your weekend rest.

THE PRESIDENT. I appreciate very much your giving me, as President, this opportunity to talk to the people of the Soviet Union, and your courtesy in coming here. I want to emphasize that to the people of this country there is nothing that would satisfy them more than to see the two countries live at peace, and the people of the two countries enjoying a steadily increasing standard of living. I was in the Soviet Union as a student in 1939, and I understand that there have been many changes, and that the standard of living of the people is rising. The standards of the people of the United States have also risen. I am hopeful that this interview will contribute in some degree to better understanding and to peace. For, I repeat again, our two peoples have the most to gain from peace.

Mr. Adzhubei: Thank you Mr. President.

NOTE: The interview was held in the living room of the President's residence at Hyannis Port, Mass., beginning at 10:20 a.m. Present during the interview were: Alex Akalovsky, interpreter for the President; Georgi Bolshikov, interpreter for Mr. Adzhubei; Pierre Salinger, Press Secretary to the President; and Jack Romagna, official White House reporter.

Printed above is the text as released by the White House. It is not a verbatim record of the interview as recorded on tape, but rather the official translation of the approved Russian text.

In preparing this text the President's words—and the English translation of Mr. Adzhubei's—were transcribed by the official White House reporter. This transcription was translated into Russian, for publication in Izvestia, by the two interpreters and Mr. Adzhubei. The Russian text was then retranslated into English by Mr. Akalovsky for release to the American press.

The Russian text, published in Izvestia on November 28, follows the White House text except for one statement by Mr. Adzhubei (see footnote, p. 744).

484 Letter to the Secretary of the Treasury Concerning Monetary Silver. *November 28, 1961*

Dear Mr. Secretary:

On the basis of your recommendations and the studies conducted by the Treasury and other Departments, I have reached the decision that silver metal should gradually be withdrawn from our monetary reserves.

Simultaneously with the publication of this letter, you are directed to suspend further sales of free silver, and to suspend use of free silver held by the Treasury for coinage. In this way, the remaining stock and any subsequently acquired can be used, at your discretion, to contribute to the maintenance of an orderly market in silver and for such other special purposes as you may determine. In order to meet coinage needs, the amount of silver required for this purpose should be obtained by retirement from circulation of a sufficient number of five-dollar and ten-dollar silver certificates.

Pursuant to this general determination, I intend to recommend to Congress, when it reconvenes, that it repeal the acts relating to silver of June 19, 1934, July 6, 1939, and July 31, 1946. The existing tax on transfers of interest in silver bullion has been necessary only to provide reinforcement for this legislation. I will therefore simultaneously propose that the relevant portion of the Internal Revenue Code also be repealed.

These actions will permit the establishment of a broad market for trading in silver on a current and forward basis comparable to the markets in which other commodities are traded. Our new policy will in effect provide for the eventual demonetization of silver except for its use in subsidiary coinage.

Although the potential supply of silver now embodied in the outstanding five-dollar and ten-dollar certificates will be sufficient to cover coinage requirements for a number of years, I believe this is an appropriate time to provide for the gradual release of the silver now required as backing for one-dollar and two-dollar silver certificates. I shall therefore also recommend that legislation be enacted to accomplish this purpose and authorize the Federal Reserve Banks to include these denominations in the range of notes they are permitted to issue.

Sincerely,

JOHN F. KENNEDY

NOTE: A letter from Secretary Dillon, dated November 27, was also released. The Secretary summarized the changes that had taken place in the world position of silver, and proposed measures to deal with the problems created by the large and growing industrial demand.

485 Remarks Upon Presenting an Award to Allen W. Dulles. *November 28, 1961*

Mr. Dulles, Mr. McCone, General Cabell, members of the Central Intelligence Agency:

I want, first of all, to express my appreciation to you all for the opportunity that this ceremony gives to tell you how grateful we are in the government and in the country for the services that the personnel of this Agency render to the country.

It is not always easy. Your successes are unheralded—your failures are trumpeted. I sometimes have that feeling myself. But I am sure you realize how important is your work, how essential it is—and how, in the long sweep of history, how significant your efforts will be judged.

So I do want to express my appreciation to you now, and I'm confident that in the future you will continue to merit the appreciation of our country, as you have in the past.

I'm also particularly grateful because this ceremony gives us all an opportunity to pay tribute to an outstanding public servant. Allen Dulles' career as a citizen of this country—and as one who has made his vast personal resources available to the country—stretches all the way back to the administration of President Woodrow Wilson. I know of no other American in the history of this country who has served in seven administrations of seven Presidents—varying from party to party, from point of view to point of view, from problem to problem, and yet at the end of each administration each President of the United States has paid tribute to his service—and also has counted Allen Dulles as their friend.

This is an extraordinary record, and I know that all of you who have worked with him understand why this record has been made. I regard Allen Dulles as an almost unique figure in our country. I know of no man who brings a greater sense of personal commitment to his work—who has less pride in office—than he has. And therefore I was most gratified when we were permitted today to come out to the Agency to present this award to him in your presence.

I'd like to read the citation.

"Allen Welsh Dulles is hereby awarded the National Security Medal.

"As principal intelligence adviser to the President of the United States, Mr. Dulles has fulfilled the responsibilities of his office with unswerving purpose and high dedication. His ten years of service in the Central Intelligence Agency have been the climax of a lifetime of unprecedented and devoted public service beginning in the First World War, and stretching through the administrations of seven Presidents.

"The outstanding contributions Mr. Dulles has made to the security of the United States have been based upon a profound knowledge of the role of the intelligence office, a broad understanding of international relations, and a naturally keen judgment of men and affairs. The zestful energy and undaunted integrity of his service to his country will be an enduring example to the profession he has done so much to create."

NOTE: The President presented the National Security Medal to Mr. Dulles at the CIA Building in Langley, Va. In his opening words the President referred to John A. McCone, successor to Mr. Dulles, and Gen. C. P. Cabell, Deputy Director of CIA.

Mr. Dulles served as Director of CIA from February 23, 1953, to November 29, 1961. His letter of resignation was released by the White House on November 29.

---

486   Remarks Upon Presenting the Harmon Trophy to Three Test Pilots of the X–15 Rocket Plane.   *November 28, 1961*

I WANT to express my great pleasure at having an opportunity, as President, to participate in this ceremony which presents this very famous and celebrated award, which is held by some of our most distinguished aviators, to these three fliers who I think in the year 1960 have done what earlier winners of this award have done in their time and generation.

Among the winners of this award are I

think Colonel Lindbergh, Major Balchen, and General LeMay—probably I think Mr. Sikorsky and probably five or six others who are here today, who also won it, who made their contribution to aviation.

I think that this award is particularly gratifying because it is a very exact combination of technical development, engineering skill by the companies involved in manufacturing this plane, by the Air Force, and by the three men, who demonstrate that even though we may be able to make the most advanced contributions in the field of scientific development, the men are required—particularly those that are highly trained and with unusual courage and skill.

I think, as you pointed out, flights of over four thousand miles an hour, at two hundred and fifteen or twenty thousand feet, all this I think is an extraordinary achievement. So

that in presenting it to these three men I think they will also permit us to share their pride and satisfaction as a country.

So gentlemen, on behalf of the trustees, on behalf of the people of this country, I want to present this trophy to you, and to tell you that your achievements give us the greatest possible satisfaction and a sense of pride in knowing that Americans have made this tremendous contribution—and that we produced you three.

NOTE: The ceremonies were held in the Fish Room at the White House. The trophy was presented jointly to Joseph A. Walker, chief engineering test pilot and a physicist with the National Aeronautics and Space Administration; A. Scott Crossfield, development engineer and research test pilot of North American Aviation, Inc.; and Maj. Robert M. White, who set a new speed and altitude record.

During his remarks, the President referred to Col. Charles A. Lindbergh, Col. Bernt Balchen, Gen. Curtis E. LeMay, and Igor I. Sikorsky.

487   Remarks in Connection With the Parvin Foundation Awards.
November 28, 1961

I WOULD LIKE to express my satisfaction at participating in this ceremony. The trustees of the Parvin Foundation made two wise decisions this year. First, was to present the award to Dag Hammarskjold, who so richly deserved it, whose efforts were not for any national victory but rather were for peace, whose efforts to make the United Nations stronger, to develop it in accordance with the needs of our time, to make it not an institution powerless to control great events but a participant in them, in the direction of easing the tensions which are so much of our every-day life. So he richly deserved the award.

And with his untimely and tragic death, I believe the trustees of the Parvin Foundation have made an equally wise decision in awarding the fifty thousand dollars to the

school at Leopoldville so that young men from this most important and vital Republic can play a part in bringing the rule of law to their own lives and have an influence throughout all of Africa.

I think that this is the kind of work which we in this country strongly favor. I'm hopeful that the judgment of the trustees and the suggestion of the trustees—that others will participate in strengthening this school—that that judgment and advice will be followed.

I certainly strongly endorse this initial effort, and I'm gratified that we have here today representatives of the Republic of the Congo, and to have heard their warm endorsement of this work and of this man for whom the Chair is named.

I congratulate those associated with it, and

I think all of us will benefit from the educated young men and women who pass through this school and come to know Dag Hammarskjold and the things for which he stood.

NOTE: The ceremonies marking the establishment of the Dag Hammarskjold Chair of Government and Law at Leopoldville were held in the Fish Room

at the White House. Among those present were Albert Parvin, founder of the Parvin Foundation; Dr. Jaime Benitez, Director of the Foundation; and Associate Justice William O. Douglas. Representing the Republic of the Congo were J. P. Dericoyard, member of the delegation to the United Nations; and Maurice Kasongo, Director of the Information Bureau for the Congo delegation at the United Nations.

488 The President's News Conference of November 29, 1961

THE PRESIDENT. Are there any questions?

[1.] Q. Mr. President, last week we had a show of force off the Dominican Republic. Under what circumstances would these ships and men actually have gone into action and is this an indication of policy in the hemisphere? Would U.S. forces be used to knock out any attempt by Castro, for instance, to overthrow an existing government?

THE PRESIDENT. Well, the United States forces which remained in international waters were there because there was some feeling that steps might be taken in the Dominican Republic which would end any hope that a democratic solution could be achieved. Because events in the Dominican Republic proceeded in the way they did, United States forces have been gradually withdrawn.

It's our hope that, as a result of the conversations now going on in the Dominican Republic, that we can make progress towards achieving the kind of government which will permit the Dominican people to control their own destiny.

As to the broader questions, we would, of course, be concerned and have responsibilities as a member of the Organization of American States, if actions were taken by one state against another state through the use of force, and we would be most concerned

about that whatever its source and particularly if its source came from the one you describe.

[2.] Q. Mr. President, do you plan a trip out of the country any time before the first of the year?

THE PRESIDENT. We have not finalized any plans.

[3.] Q. The Government-controlled press in South Viet-Nam is attacking the United States now, apparently because we are asking for political reforms in exchange for our military and economic assistance. I wonder if this has jeopardized our effort to stop communism there, and if you could throw any light on this situation for us?

THE PRESIDENT. Well, there have been stories in the press there that have been critical of the United States and of course there have been stories in the United States press which may in some cases bear a different relationship to the Government than the press in Saigon does to its government but which nevertheless have suggested that the steps which are being taken within Viet-Nam to counter the Communist threat have not been sufficient. We—of course, our ambition is to permit the Vietnamese people to control their destiny, and we are attempting to work with the Government and encourage steps which will increase the sense of commitment by the people of Viet-Nam to the struggle. These steps are bound to be subject to discussion and controversy, and we are going to continue to have our conversations with the Vietnamese Government.

[4.] Q. Mr. President, what significance do you see in the fact that the Soviet Government at this time permitted you to speak to the Russian people?

THE PRESIDENT. Well, I welcomed it. We had expressed, Mr. Salinger had—I think other newspapermen in the United States had expressed their concern that Mr. Khrushchev had been interviewed at some length by three or four American newspapermen, that all his views were carried in full in the Western world and particularly in the United States, but no similar opportunity had been given to the President of the United States or any other American leaders and this view was presented with vigor to Soviet representatives and I am delighted that they decided to give us that opportunity.

Q. Mr. President, when Mr. Khrushchev visited this country a couple of years ago, he had quite a number of chances to speak to the American people on virtually all of our radio, television, and newspapers. Would you welcome such an opportunity to do so personally in the Soviet Union to speak to the Russian people and see them?

THE PRESIDENT. Well, I would think that Mr. Khrushchev came on invitation of the President of the United States and was a guest of the United States. I have not been given a similar invitation. I think that the important thing now is to attempt to work out a solution to the difficult problems which disturb our relations. The interview mentioned Germany and Berlin. There are also problems in southeast Asia, and that's the immediate task. And I think that probably they hold that view too in regard to any

visit by a President of the United States that there are important problems that must be solved before such a visit would be rewarding to either side. No such invitation has as yet been extended.

Q. Mr. President, in your interview with the Izvestia reporter you said that what we objected to was the deprivation of a political choice, and I wonder if you could discuss with us how this criterion would apply to Finland where apparently the only anti-Soviet candidate and opponent to President Kekkonen has been pressured into retiring from the race.

THE PRESIDENT. Well, I think the general thesis which I expressed on Saturday stands. We—what we desire is that the people of these countries will have a free choice. If they choose to follow under a condition of freedom, as I've said, with sufficient opportunity for alternative views to be presented, then we accept that. We would feel also, of course, that if they should choose the Communist system, then they should also be given the opportunity at another date to make another choice.

That is what we regard as freedom. That is not the view that has been held by the Soviet Union. And I would prefer to make that as a general statement rather than apply it to any particular country because some countries are having difficulties and I'm not sure that any statement that we might make at this time would be of assistance to them.

[5.] Q. Mr. President, you and your wife and other members of your family have declined to go to private clubs and to take part in other functions, even women's benefits at churches, where there was racial segregation. Now I wonder if you don't think it's simply fair that the President of the United States, members of his Cabinet, U.S. Ambassadors and other officers of this Government should decline to speak at and participate in functions where women newspaper reporters are barred?

THE PRESIDENT. I feel that I have many responsibilities and the press has less and I would think that the press should deal with that problem and I'm sure that—I think it would be most appropriate if the members of the Press Club had a meeting and permitted you to come and present your views to them. [*Laughter*]

I will say that as we are expected, as President, to comment on everything, I will say that in my judgment when an official visitor comes to speak to the Press Club, that all working reporters should be permitted in on a basis of equality. That is not a social occasion but a working occasion.

That happens to be my personal view and the members of the Press Club will have to decide it in the way they want. They are entitled to have any arrangement they would want in regards, I would think, to social occasions, but I would think that when there is an official visitor here as part of—the guest of the people of the United States and there's a meeting held, that all reporters should come on a basis of equality. But that—I am not a member of the Press Club except honorary and therefore—but I give my view as an honorary member, not as President of the United States. [*Laughter*]

[6.] Q. Mr. President, in your interview yesterday—published yesterday—you spoke of the possibility of a commitment to peace between NATO and the Warsaw Pact. Senator Mansfield early this month also suggested an exploratory meeting between the members of these two pacts to attempt to work out a better understanding between them.

Are these two ideas, yours and Senator Mansfield's, in the same vein and do you envisage such a meeting?

THE PRESIDENT. Well, as I stated, as we stated at the time of the visit of Chancellor Adenauer, we hoped that negotiations would take place in regard to Berlin and Germany, and of course, this is a question which would be related to that. And at that time we would attempt to improve the relations between the NATO and the Warsaw Pact countries.

I think there are some differences in the view expressed by Senator Mansfield and by me, but the purpose was the same—to provide a lessening of tensions between the two blocs and to improve their relations. I think that the details could best be worked out in negotiation, but we cannot have, of course, an increase in harmony between the two blocs until we've come to some negotiated and mutually satisfactory agreement in regard to Berlin and Germany. After we've done that, then such an arrangement would be meaningful.

[7.] Q. Mr. President, could you tell us what you had in mind when you suggested in your interview with Mr. Adzhubei the creation of an international administration on the Autobahn to Berlin?

THE PRESIDENT. I would think that—what I'm anxious to do is to work out some system which will permit freedom of access for the people of West Berlin without constant pressures and without harassments which endanger their freedom and which increase the tensions between the countries.

One of the suggestions which have been considered is to provide some international authority which will control traffic in the Autobahn and, therefore, guarantee its free movement. I think we would have to wait until negotiations began between the Soviet Union and the Western powers before any precise suggestions in regard to this kind of control might be put forward.

Q. May I ask a subordinate question, sir?

Does this contemplate international control under the United Nations, or something apart from the U.N.?

THE PRESIDENT. The details, I would think, of what kind of an international authority might be arranged could be, I think, better a subject for the negotiations. There could be many different forms that it would take—four-power, U.N., or some other bodies—but it must be one, of course, which is acceptable to both sides. That would be difficult to achieve, but I believe, would be one of the chief points in any negotiations.

[8.] Q. Mr. President, Congressman John Fogarty has criticized as a devastating blow to major areas of medical research, the recent cut of $60 million by the Department of Health, Education, and Welfare from the budget of the National Institutes of Health.

Also, in the name of economy, the Atomic Energy Commission has announced curtailment of its reactor program.

Would you comment on this, and is any consideration being given to restoring these cuts?

THE PRESIDENT. The difficulty—whenever we have a cut, well everyone wants economy and wants cuts. Whenever any cut is made, of course, there are always complaints about it. Now the fact of the matter is that we substantially increased over the Eisenhower budget the amount that we requested for the Department of HEW, including research—including support for the health institutes.

The House of Representatives increased our request and the Senate substantially increased it. Now the figure which Mr. Ribicoff cut to was, I believe, several million dollars above the figure that the House of Representatives themselves passed, and the fact of the matter is that the figure as it now stands in the area of HEW, cancer research and others, is 25 percent now above what it was a year ago.

So that I think that we have funded these programs adequately. We would spend additional funds if we felt they could be usefully spent. And this matter has been very carefully examined.

And let me reiterate: the amount of money being spent is 25 percent above what was spent last year and it is above what was recommended by the House of Representatives itself, as well as being now above what we recommended in our budget, which was substantially above what President Eisenhower recommended in his budget.

[9.] Q. Mr. President, could you discuss the recent personnel changes in your administration and the reasons behind them?

THE PRESIDENT. The question was: would I discuss the recent personnel changes in our administration, and the reasons behind it. I think the first sentence of our announcement on Sunday, which said that we thought the changes would provide a better matching of the men with their tasks and responsibilities explains the change.

One of the problems, of course, is that our attention is focused today on—particularly on Western Europe, Berlin, Germany, the Common Market, and the Soviet and bloc tensions with the NATO Alliance and the United States.

We are, of course, also bearing heavy responsibilities and are extremely concerned with the course of events in South America, Africa, the Middle East and Asia.

Mr. Bowles has traveled a good deal in those areas before and after becoming Under Secretary. He is now going to devote his entire time to our problems and policies in those areas. I believe it's a much more effective use of his extremely—of his obvious talents to use him in this area, rather than

759

using him in the area of day-to-day administration in the Department of State.

I regard this, as I've said, as an increased opportunity for Mr. Bowles, and I think it's vitally important to the United States. We do not want to become so concerned about the problems we face in Western Europe that we ignore the tremendous responsibilities and opportunities that are before the free world in these important sections of the world.

So that I'm encouraged by the changes and I'm grateful to Mr. Bowles for taking on this assignment. I think he can render a real service as he has in the past.

I'm also grateful to Governor Harriman for becoming, after holding probably as many important jobs as any American in our history, with the possible exception of John Quincy Adams, for now taking on the job of Assistant Secretary for the Far East.

[10.] Q. Mr. President, there are reports that the morale among the Reservists who have been called up is bad. They claim they don't have—they say they have nothing to do; the equipment is inadequate. Do you care to comment?

THE PRESIDENT. Well, I have seen the newspaper stories. There isn't any doubt that any newspaper can go out and interview men who've been called up. Their lives are disturbed. Many of them are older. They've all got jobs. For most of them it's a heavy sacrifice. And we are not at war.

And they go to camps which have perhaps been newly opened or where the equipment may not be immediately available. And they're bound to be unhappy. I've seen the stories in some cases where newspapers have reported that the Department of Defense is determined to keep these people in for more than a year.

Then when it was proved that that story was wholly wrong, they then write that the Pentagon has changed its mind and not going to keep them in more than a year and then sent their reporters around to examine and interview servicemen and build up the sense that Americans are not ready to serve their country.

Now let me make it very clear what the reason, that we called these men—the reason we called these men is that there is a direct clash of interest in a major area, which is Berlin and West Germany. There also is increased tension in Viet-Nam.

When we came into office, we did not feel that there was sufficient strength in our conventional forces. Of the 14 Army divisions, 3 were training divisions. And the United States has commitments all around the world.

Now, while we rely on our nuclear weapons, we also, as I've said, want to have a choice between humiliation and a holocaust. And therefore, we believe that calling these men up and their willingness to serve increased the chance of maintaining the peace.

There are countries where leaders have talked very strongly about standing firm in various areas, but do not have the military force to support that statement. We require it. The United States is the strongest power and the leader of the free world, and as such we must have the power to make our commitments good.

These men, who may be serving in a very cold and windy camp in Fort Lewis, in Washington, therefore, are rendering the same kind of service to our country that an airplane standing on a 15-minute alert at a SAC base in Omaha is rendering. We called them in, in order to prevent a war, not to fight a war.

And, if our efforts to hold the peace should fail, then, of course, they would be used in a more direct way. But their function today is to indicate that the United States is serious about its commitments; that it means to meet its commitments; that it wants to negotiate a peaceful settlement if it can, but it does not propose to surrender.

And therefore, I would hope that any serviceman who is sitting in a camp, however unsatisfactory it may be, and I know how unsatisfactory it is, will recognize that he is contributing to the security of his family in a most direct way.

And, in these days when weapons are so terrible, the important thing is to attempt to maintain the peace, and they're helping to do it.

And I think it's up to us to make sure that they do get the equipment. It is up to us to make sure that their training is useful. As I have said, we've sent the Inspector General out to Washington to look at the camp and to talk to the people involved.

But I do think it would be well for us all to recognize that in the first place, these men are not going to be kept in longer than a year. There has never been such a proposal in the Pentagon that I've ever heard of—newspaper reports to the contrary, notwithstanding. This has never been suggested.

Secondly, it is our hope to get these men out before their 12-month period.

Third, these men were called in at the request of the administration and with the approval of the Congress, which gave us the authorization to call them in. In my opinion they're rendering a valuable function. We are going to get them out as quickly as we can. But they are doing a service and I hope they recognize it and I hope that all of us who are in a position to communicate will explain to them and to their families how important their service is today.

Q. Mr. President, now the——

THE PRESIDENT. This chimpanzee who is flying in space took off at 10:08. He reports that everything is perfect and working well. [*Laughter*]

[11.] Q. Mr. President, now that you have met with Chancellor Adenauer and the British Prime Minister Macmillan has met with French President de Gaulle, will you give us your view, sir, of the present state of Western readiness for negotiations on Berlin?

THE PRESIDENT. Well, there is one more step to be taken in that series of meetings, and that is the meeting between Chancellor Adenauer and General de Gaulle which is, was supposed to take place this week but has been delayed a week because of the Chancellor's cold, but which will take place before the meeting of the foreign ministers at the time of NATO. And at that time, then, we should be able more precisely to answer that question.

[12.] Q. Could you clarify your rather mystifying remark about a possible trip abroad? Are you thinking of going to the NATO meeting in December?

THE PRESIDENT. No, I'm not.

Q. Could you tell us anything more about it?

THE PRESIDENT. I will as soon as we've made a decision about whether such a trip would be useful, but I'm not thinking about going to NATO. But I don't mean to be at all unresponsive, but the trip has not been—a trip has not been definitely arranged, and until it is, it would seem to me to be—and it depends on circumstances which may develop in the future and therefore it's really in about the status that I suggested.

[13.] Q. Mr. President, in attempts to clarify your civil defense policy, it's been reported that you favor community shelter, fallout shelters, over the private shelters. If this was so, could you give us some of your reasoning behind that move?

THE PRESIDENT. Well, we have never thought that the Government could engage in the task of building shelters in each home because it would be a diversion of our resources and would vitally affect our deterrent strength which remains our best hope of avoiding a nuclear exchange. So that we have stated from the beginning and the decisions made last spring and summer in regard to the markings of available shelters emphasize the community structure.

We made some decisions in regard to Federal policy in relation to community shelters last Friday. We are now going to talk to some of the Governors who are directly concerned and involved in this matter because it requires cooperation between the Federal Government, the State, and the communities so that we will have a program and a budget to send to the Congress in January.

The emphasis will be on community shelters, and information will be made available to the individual as to what he could do within his own home. But the central responsibility, it seems to me, is for us to provide community shelters. It seems—it seemed the most effective use of our resources and to provide the best security for our people.

[14.] Q. Mr. President, there have been reports of sizable financial contributions to the sort of right-wing extremist groups that you criticized last week. Do you regard this as a danger to the elective process and will you press in the next session for some form of Federal financing of elections?

THE PRESIDENT. Well, as you know we set up a committee to provide for Federal—at least to reconsider the whole problem of financing presidential elections. That was their only responsibility. There is a committee in the Senate which has examined other methods of financing other campaigns. As I understand it, what you're referring to is the contributions by some individuals or groups to right-wing movements, not so much candidates—is that correct?

Q. Yes.

THE PRESIDENT. As long as they meet the requirements of the tax laws, I don't think that the Federal Government can interfere or should interfere with the right of any individual to take any position he wants. The only thing we should be concerned about is that it does not represent a diversion of funds which might be taxable to—for nontaxable purposes. But that is another question and I'm sure the Internal Revenue System examines that. But I would not want to interfere with the right of any individual to give his own finances or support to any movement that he chooses to do so, providing it comes within the laws, the present laws of the United States.

[15.] Q. Mr. President, the General Assembly last night voted to urge all nations to take separate and collective action to force South Africa to abandon its racial policies. What specific steps would you favor the U.S. taking to implement that resolution?

THE PRESIDENT. I've not examined the language of the Assembly resolution so that I'm not able to answer that.

[16.] Q. Sir, last year before the session of Congress began you listed domestic and foreign legislation that would be "must" for that session of Congress. Can you at this time list your priorities for legislation in the upcoming Congress?

THE PRESIDENT. No, I think that the—I should do that in the State of the Union Address and we will. Quite obviously, we've touched on one of the matters which are of importance—civil defense. I talked previous to this about another matter which is medical care for the aged. But the general program I think should wait till January.

[17.] Q. Sir, could you clarify one thing? There seem to be confusion and conflicting reports about whether you are going to press for a more liberal trade policy.

Has the decision been made on that yet?

THE PRESIDENT. A preliminary decision has been made in regard to the matter, yes, and will be announced in January. Once again there are some consultations which must be made and will be made with the members of Congress who have responsibility in the area in the month of December, and then we will go to the Congress in January with our program.

Q. Mr. President, Senator Goldwater has indicated his opposition to us becoming associated with the Common Market. Would you comment on that and perhaps sum up for us the possible effect the Common Market might have on the American economy?

THE PRESIDENT. Yes, I don't know what the word "associated" means in the question. I don't know anyone—I have not heard it proposed that the United States should become a member of the Common Market or associated with the Common Market in the sense that the word is ordinarily used.

What we are concerned about is that we have the power to negotiate with the Common Market to protect our export industry. Now the Common Market will represent a tremendously important market for American production. It is one of our areas where we have concentrated most on in recent years and will—and represents a tremendous potential for us in the future, particularly when Great Britain joins it. But we don't—we want to, therefore, protect our export market.

We want to keep the ratio of exports to imports comparable to what it is today or perhaps even improve it, because if we're not able to export substantially more than we import, we're going to either have to cut off all assistance to countries abroad or begin to withdraw our troops home.

We spend over $3 billion a year in keeping our bases and our troops abroad. That represents a $3 billion drain or potentially gold drain upon us. The only reason we've been able to afford that, of course, has been that we've had a balance of trade in our favor of around $5 billion.

Now in addition we are concerned that American companies who are locked out of the Common Market because of their high tariffs will feel that the only way that they can get into the market will be through investing in Western Europe, and therefore we will have capital leaving, which will cost jobs. Every time an American firm invests in Europe and builds its company there, it hires European workers and not American workers.

Now we believe in the free flow of capital. We do not believe in capital exchange here. Therefore we have to have the ability to negotiate with the Common Market so that American goods can enter the market and we will not have American capital jumping the wall in order to compete.

So that this is a matter of great importance to the American workers and industry and to the American economy, and it is in that—because of that reason, as well as our desire to associate as closely as we can to Europe, which is going to be such an important power and force, that we are considering what our trade program will be. But if you use the word "associate" with the Common Market, or "join" the Common Market, that is not an accurate description of our policy.

[18.] Q. Mr. President, do you favor, and did you urge on Chancellor Adenauer closer ties, particularly political ties between the two halves of Germany?

THE PRESIDENT. No. In answer to your first question, the reason I answer it with some hesitation is the question of "ties." At the present time, for example, as you know, the East Germans and West Germans do negotiate in regard to trade. So that we have to decide—and those negotiations may continue and we will have a clearer idea of what form they will take if we get into negotiation.

Political ties could be defined in so many ways that I think that unless you would be prepared to define it more precisely, I think the wiser thing would be to wait till we got into negotiation with the Soviet Union and then to determine what these relationships would be.

I think my interview on Saturday indicated my general view of the Federal Republic and its actions in the future.

[19.] Q. Mr. President, you have espoused more liberal trade barriers. Yet, the other day, you put machinery in motion that could result in a higher import duty on cotton textiles. Now I understand the Japanese have protested. How do you square your policy on lowering trade barriers with this sort of protectionist action?

THE PRESIDENT. I square it in an attempt to achieve a balance which serves the interest of the United States and those countries which are involved around the world.

I will point out that the United States does sell cotton at a price which is vastly lower than an American manufacturer can buy it for. We sell it at the world price which represents a contribution by the United States to each pound or bale of cotton which is sold abroad, which permits a manufacturer in a country around the world to buy their cotton much lower than our manufacturers, which puts our manufacturers at a competitive disadvantage.

We do that for obvious reasons. But we have to try to balance off those burdens.

[20.] Q. Mr. President, a Republican Congressman making answer to your speech in Los Angeles in which you criticized extremist groups went back to 1949 and got a

speech you made in Salem, Mass., in which you reviewed the loss of mainland China, and found in that what he considered inconsistencies. Would you care to comment on your view then and now?

THE PRESIDENT. Yes. I always have felt that we did not make a determined enough effort in the case of China. Given the problems we now see, I think a more determined effort would have been advisable. I would think that in my speech in '49 I placed more emphasis on personalities than I would today.

And I would say that my view today is more in accordance with the facts than my view in '49. But my—I've always felt, and I think history will record, that the change of China from being a country friendly to us to a country which is unremittingly hostile affected very strongly the balance of power in the world. And while there were—there is still, of course, room for argument as to whether any United States actions would have changed the course of events there, I think a greater effort would have been wiser. I said it in '49, so it isn't totally hindsight.

[21.] Q. Mr. President, earlier you said that information would be made available to private citizens as to what they can do individually to protect against fallout. Do you have an opinion as to whether individuals should build private shelters or not?

THE PRESIDENT. I stated that we are going to send out a booklet when it is ready. I hoped it would be ready by the end of November. The booklet will reflect the decisions we made in November, and I think it will tell them what the Federal policy will be; what we hope to do, and what each individual can do in his own home, which will provide greater assurances if an attack should come.

I want to emphasize that the best defense

still remains the American deterrent.

But I do think that within each individual home that some steps can be taken which are not expensive, but which would, if a disaster should strike us, provide a greater security, though of course, there is no security against blast.

And there is bound to be, particularly as these new weapons increase in power, there are obvious limits to what any of us can do.

But in answer to your question, the booklet which will be sent out, I hope shortly, will inform each individual what he can do within his own home as well as within his community.

Reporter.   Thank you, Mr. President.

NOTE: President Kennedy's nineteenth news conference was held in the State Department Auditorium at 10 o'clock on Wednesday morning, November 29, 1961.

489   Remarks at the Swearing In of John McCone as Director, Central Intelligence Agency.   *November 29, 1961*

I WANT to say what an honor it is and what a pleasure it is to have Mr. McCone back in the national service.

This appointment—I think that he was willing to take it indicates how important it is, and how important I feel it is, as well as members of the Government and Members of Congress believe it to be.

He has not only the responsibility as Director of CIA, but also coordinating the work of all the Intelligence community, and I know that he will give his attention to both these functions upon which so much of our security depends.

We want to welcome you here and to say that you are now living on the bull's-eye, and I welcome you to that spot.

NOTE: The ceremonies were held in the Cabinet Room at the White House.

490   Remarks at the Rockefeller Public Service Award Ceremonies.   *November 29, 1961*

I WANT to say what a pleasure it is to have this opportunity again to give much deserved recognition to our public servants.

I think this program of the Rockefeller Foundation in cooperation with Princeton University and the Woodrow Wilson School is very beneficial to the public service.   And I think this also gives us an opportunity to draw the attention of the country to the very extraordinary number of gifted people who are working for the United States at this time.

One of our honored recipients here today

is head of our Geological Department.   One is most active with the Joint Committee on the Finance Committee of the Senate—the Joint Committee on Taxation.   Mr. Staats with the Budget Bureau has been a career employee for a number of years.   Livingston Merchant has been our Ambassador to Canada and a former Deputy Undersecretary of State.

This gives us a chance to indicate the wide range of talent available to people in the public service, and we hope that their success will encourage others in the Federal service, and also encourage young men and women to come into the government and make it a career.

NOTE: The awarding ceremonies were held in the President's office at the White House. Recipients of the awards were Dr. Robert H. Felix, Assistant Surgeon General, National Institutes of Health; Livingston T. Merchant, Ambassador to Canada; Dr. Thomas B. Nolan, Director, Geological Survey; Elmer B. Staats, Deputy Director, Bureau of the Budget; and Colin F. Stam, Chief of Staff, Joint Committee on Internal Revenue Taxation.

491 Remarks at the Inaugural Meeting of the Inter-American Economic and Social Council. *November 29, 1961*

Ambassadors, representatives, ministers, Mr. Secretary:

Today marks another milestone in the Alliance for Progress. For today we begin to select the Panel of Experts established by the Charter of Punta del Este.

This Panel is an historic innovation, not only in Inter-American relations, but in the effort to develop the economies of half the world. Not since the Marshall Plan has a group of allied nations embarked on a program of regional development guided by a regional body largely selected by the developing nations themselves.

These experts will review the long-term development plans of the Latin American nations—advising them on measures to strengthen the plans and the self-help and the social reform measures which will accompany them. In addition they will provide help in financing agencies to provide external resources in the most effective manner.

I am confident that the skills and ability of the men you select will enable all the nations of the Hemisphere to benefit greatly from their work. And I assure you that the United States will give the greatest possible weight to the conclusions of the experts in the distribution of funds. Similarly, we will instruct our representatives to international agencies to rely heavily on the work of the Panel.

I am confident that this new and im-

aginative creation of the Inter-American system will vastly strengthen our common effort—the Alliance for Progress for all our people.

I have also, today, signed an agreement for the use of $6 million in Alliance for Progress Funds to strengthen the OAS. This money will be used for studies and technical assistance—called for by the Charter of Punta del Este—to help nations in planning the growth of their economies. Thus a pledge of long standing has been fulfilled.

I would also like to express my gratification at the important progress which has been made since the Alliance for Progress was proposed in March.

In August, the American nations drafted the Charter of Punta del Este—the framework for the decade of development—a document whose scope and significance is matched only by the Charter of the OAS itself. The Inter-American Bank, ECLA, and the OAS have agreed to provide development missions to assist nations in their planning—and some of these missions are already in the field. In addition, you have strengthened the machinery of the Inter-American Economic and Social Council, and prepared for today's selection of the Panel of Experts.

For its part the United States has streamlined its own AID program—placing general responsibility for coordination of our effort in the hands of a distinguished administrator with long experience in the work of development—Ambassador Moscoso. And we have already developed new sets of standards to guide our work.

In these—and in many other ways—we have developed the basic structure for our future effort—for the work of the next 10 years. But we have not waited for the establishment of that structure to begin our work.

All over Latin America new development plans are being formulated, and some have already been completed. New tax and land reform programs—basic requirements of social progress—have been instituted or are being prepared. Many of the American nations are now mobilizing their resources, and the energies of their people, for the task of development. And the United States, for its part, has already committed more than $800 million of the more than $1 billion which it pledged to the first year of the Alliance—a year which ends on March 13.

But despite this speed, I am determined to do better, as far as this country goes, in the coming months. The urgent needs of our people in this Hemisphere cannot wait. Their need for food and shelter, for education and relief from poverty, and above all, their need to feel hope for their future and the future of their children, demands attention and toil this year, this month, today.

Measured by the past, we have moved swiftly. Measured by the needs of the future, we must all do much better. And I can assure you that the energies of this Government—and my own personal efforts—will be devoted to speeding up the pace of development. For I share with you a determination that before this decade comes to a close the Americans will have entered upon a new era—when the material progress of American man and woman, and the justice of his society, will match the spiritual and cultural achievements of this Hemisphere.

I am fully aware of the immensity of the task, and of the difficulties that we face. But I know we share the faith of one of the earliest settlers of my country—William Bradford of Massachusetts—who, when told in 1630 that the hazards of settling this part of the United States were too great to overcome, answered:

"All great and honorable actions are accompanied with great difficulties, and must be both enterprised and overcome with answerable courage . . . the dangers were great, but not desperate; the difficulties were many, but not invincible . . . all of them, through the help of God, by fortitude and patience, might either be borne or overcome."

We shall overcome them.

NOTE: The President spoke at the Pan American Union. In his opening words "Mr. Secretary" referred to José A. Mora, Secretary General of the Organization of American States.

---

492   Letter to Secretary Ribicoff Concerning the Role of the Federal Government in the Field of Mental Health. *December 1, 1961*

Dear Mr. Secretary:

As you know, the Report of the Joint Commission on Mental Illness and Health represents a significant assessment of the magnitude of the mental health problem with which we are confronted. As such,

it deserves the close attention of all those responsible for the formulation of public policy in this area.

For this reason, I would like you to analyze the Report with a view to developing courses of action which might be appropriate for the Federal Government. I am also asking the Secretary of Labor and the Administrator of Veterans' Affairs to join with you in this undertaking and to provide assistance in the consideration of the Report and the formulation of possible courses of action.

In developing your proposals, I believe careful attention should be given to the following specific questions:

1. What should be the Federal role in the mental health field and what responsibility should remain with the States, localities, and private groups?

2. If broadened Federal activity is warranted, through what channels should it be directed?

3. What emphasis should be given to Federal activity in the mental health field in relation to support for more general health programs?

4. What rate of expansion in public programs for mental health services and re-

search is consistent with the present and prospective supply of trained manpower?

5. In the mental health field, should relatively greater encouragement be given to strengthening institutional services or non-institutional programs, including means for bringing the cost of non-institutional services within the financial means of a larger number of people?

These questions involve matters of long-standing interest and concern to many parts of the executive branch. I am therefore asking representatives of the Council of Economic Advisers and the Bureau of the Budget to assist you in your consideration of the Report and the development of your proposals.

Sincerely,

JOHN F. KENNEDY

NOTE: The Joint Commission's report is entitled "Action for Mental Health" (Basic Books, Inc., New York City, 1961, 338 pp.).

493   Remarks Upon Presenting the Enrico Fermi Award to Dr. Hans Bethe. *December* 1, 1961

DOCTOR, I want to express my appreciation and pleasure, taking part in this ceremony in which you receive this justly earned award.

This country and I believe the whole free world—in fact, the entire world—has benefited from the number of extraordinarily gifted scientists who came to our country from Western Europe, who played a most important and vital role in the defense of our country in times of danger, and who have also helped make possible for our people the benefits of science—in making their lives easier and happier and more secure.

So that I take pleasure in presenting this award to you, for your own extraordinary

work and also in calling to the minds of our fellow citizens the great debt we owe to so many people who came to this country and made the United States their home.

I congratulate you for the versatility of your work, as well as its significance. I express appreciation to the members of the advisory panel who participated in this selection—and to all those who work in the frontiers of knowledge.

NOTE: The ceremonies were held in the Cabinet Room at the White House.

Dr. Bethe, Professor of Physics at Cornell University, came to the United States from Germany in 1935. The award cited his "contributions to nuclear and theoretical physics, to peaceful uses of atomic energy, and to the security of the United States."

494   Statement by the President on Employee-Management Relations
      in the Federal Service.   *December 5,* 1961

THE TASK FORCE on Employee-Management Relations in the Federal Service which I appointed last June has submitted a report recommending a constructive, forward-looking program of employee-management relations within the Federal establishment keyed to current needs.   The Task Force has done an excellent job in a difficult and complicated field.

While preserving the public interest as the paramount consideration in the administration of employee-management relations in the Federal Service and retaining appropriate management responsibilities, the Task Force report recognizes the right of Federal employees and employee organizations to participate in developing improved personnel policies and working conditions.   In recommending that employee organizations be consulted and that under specified conditions agreements with such organizations may be entered into, the Task Force has urged a proper course of action that should result in increased governmental efficiency as well as improved relations with Federal employees.

The report clearly recognizes that Federal employees do not have the right to strike, that both the union shop and the closed shop are inappropriate to the Federal Government, that where salaries and other conditions of employment are fixed by the Congress these matters are not subject to negotiation, and that all agreements must be consistent with merit system principles.

Additional recommendations of the Task Force call for regularizing arbitration procedures in handling individual employee grievances; extending to nonveterans appeal rights already held by veterans; requesting legislation to authorize voluntary withholding of employee organization dues by the Federal Government, at the expense of the organization; and appointment by the Secretary of Labor, when necessary, of panels of expert arbitrators to make advisory recommendations as to what constitutes appropriate units for negotiating purposes and to supervise elections by employees.

The Task Force reached its conclusions after holding public hearings in cities throughout the country, and after consulting the heads of Federal departments and agencies.   Its recommendations will provide an effective system for developing improved employee-management relations.   As an employer of more than 2,300,000 civilian employees, the Federal Government has long had an obligation to undertake the reappraisal which has now been made so well by the Task Force.

I have directed that an executive order giving effect to the Task Force recommendations be prepared for issuance by the end of the year.

NOTE: For memorandum announcing the appointment of the Task Force, see Item 250.

The report, dated November 30, 1961, is entitled "A Policy for Employee-Management Cooperation in the Federal Service" (Government Printing Office, 1961, 54 pp.).

Executive Order 10988 "Employee-Management Cooperation in the Federal Service" was issued by the President on January 17, 1962 (27 F.R. 551).

495 Statement by the President Upon Establishing Awards for Significant Contributions to the Export Expansion Program. *December 5*, 1961

I AM DELIGHTED to be able to announce the revival of a great national symbol in a new and constructive context of national urgency.

The "E" flag that once flew over plants making notable records in war production now will fly over factories contributing significantly to the goals of international peace and prosperity. I call on both management and labor to exert their utmost efforts toward producing and selling in the world market. Here is the next great frontier we must cross. The United States must in the best traditions of American competitiveness and ingenuity, push forward with the development and sale of goods in all the markets of the world.

An increased level of exports is absolutely essential for a healthy situation in our international balance of payments. Such a healthy situation in turn will enable us to carry our international responsibilities for preservation of freedom.

I hope that all Americans will regard the new "E" symbol as an incentive to their best efforts.

More exports will mean a stronger America; a more prosperous America, and greater assurance of a free world.

NOTE: Executive Order 10978 "Establishing Presidential Awards for Significant Contributions to the Export Expansion Program" was issued by the President on December 5, 1961 (26 F.R. 11714).

496 Address in New York City at the National Football Foundation and Hall of Fame Banquet. *December 5*, 1961

Mr. LaRoche, ladies and gentlemen:

I want to express my thanks to you for this award. Politics is an astonishing profession—it has permitted me to go from being an obscure lieutenant serving under General MacArthur to Commander in Chief in 14 years, without any technical competence whatsoever; and it's also enabled me to go from being an obscure member of the junior varsity at Harvard to being an honorary member of the Football Hall of Fame.

Actually, there are not so many differences between politics and football. Some Republicans have been unkind enough to suggest that my election, which was somewhat close, was somewhat similar to the Notre Dame-Syracuse game. But I'm like Notre Dame,

we just take it as it comes and we're not giving it back.

I'm proud to be here tonight. I think General MacArthur, when he was Superintendent, really spoke about football in the classic way, because on so many occasions, in war and peace, I have seen so many men who participated in this sport—some celebrated and some obscure—who did demonstrate that the seeds had been well sown.

I am delighted to be here tonight and participating with you. This is a great American game. It has given me, personally, some of the most pleasant moments of my life— from last Saturday when I had a chance to see the Army-Navy game to a Harvard-Yale game I saw 40 years before.

And I'm also glad to be here tonight with some men who also gave me some of the most exciting moments of my life. Clint Frank, who I understand is sitting down there, whom I saw score 5 touchdowns against Princeton. Tom Harmon who scored 21 points on my 21st birthday in the first half of a game against California. Cliff Battles who made George Marshall look good at Boston way back in the thirties. And Jay Berwanger who's here tonight, who, when Chicago was tenth in the Big Ten, was on everyone's All-American. And Sam Huff, who campaigned with me through the coal mines of West Virginia—and he's even better at that than he is on Sunday.

So I'm like a good many other Americans who never quite made it—but love it.

I do see a close relationship between sports and our national life and I sometimes wonder whether those of us who love sports have done as much as we should in maintaining sports as a constructive part of this country's existence.

I will not enter into a debate about whether football or baseball is our national sport. The sad fact is that it looks more and more as if our national sport is not playing at all— but watching. We have become more and more not a nation of athletes but a nation of spectators.

Professional athletes—professional athletics—I believe has a great place in our national life, but I must confess that I view the growing emphasis on professionalism and specialization in amateur sports without great enthusiasm. Gibbon wrote two centuries ago that professionalism in amateur sports was one of the early evidences of the decline and fall of the Roman Empire.

Football today is far too much a sport for the few who can play it well. The rest of us—and too many of our children—get our exercise from climbing up to seats in stadi-ums, or from walking across the room to turn on our television sets. And this is true for one sport after another, all across the board.

The result of this shift from participation to, if I may use the word "spectation," is all too visible in the physical condition of our population.

Despite our much-publicized emphasis on school athletics, our own children lag behind European children in physical fitness. And astonishingly enough, when Dr. Kraus and Dr. Weber recently went back, after 10 years, to Europe they found a sharp decline in the physical fitness of European children, because in the last decade mechanization had begun to get at them too.

It's no wonder that we have such a high proportion of rejections for physical reasons in our Selective Service. A short time ago General Hershey told me that since October of 1948, of some six million young men examined for military duty, more than a million were rejected as physically unfit for military service. A good many of these men would not have been rejected if they had had an opportunity, when younger, to take part in an adequate physical development program.

To get two men today, the United States Army must call seven men. Of the five rejected, three are turned down for physical reasons and two for mental disabilities. To get the 196 thousand additional men that we needed for Berlin, the government had to call up, therefore, 750 thousand men—and the rejection rate is increasing each year.

I find this situation disturbing. We are under-exercised as a nation. We look, instead of play. We ride, instead of walk. Our existence deprives us of the minimum of physical activity essential for healthy living. And the remedy, in my judgment, lies in one direction; that is, in developing programs for broad participation in exercise by all of our young men and women—all of our boys and girls.

I do not say this in order to decry excellence in sports or anywhere else. But excellence emerges from mass participation. This is shown by the fact that in some areas of our Olympic Games, we have steadily fallen behind those nations who have stressed broad participation in a great variety of sports.

I believe that as a nation we should give our full support, for example, to our Olympic development program. We will not subsidize our athletes as some nations do, but we should as a country set a goal, not in the way the Soviet Union or the Chinese do, but in the kind of way that Australia and other countries do—perhaps in our own way, to emphasize this most important part of life, the opportunity to exercise, to participate in physical activity, and generally to produce a standard of excellence for our country which will enable our athletes to win the Olympics—but more importantly than that, which will give us a nation of vigorous men and women.

There are more important goals than winning contests, and that is to improve on a broad level the health and vitality of all of our people.

We have begun this year to make progress toward this goal with the new President's Council on Youth Fitness. The idea behind our youth fitness program is to give as many American boys and girls as possible a chance for a healthy physical development.

Coach Bud Wilkinson, who shook off the Washington—after losing his first five games finally got out of our atmosphere and went on to win his next five, and the Council staff, in cooperation with the Nation's leading educators and medical organizations, have worked out a basic physical fitness pro-

gram for our elementary and secondary schools. Pilot projects have been set up in a number of cities.

The results so far show the effectiveness of what can be done and the extent of the need. In Muskogee, Okla., for example, a city which prides itself on athletic achievement, which has had seven All-Americans in recent years, 47 percent of the students failed a minimum physical fitness test. Only a fraction of those who qualified could pass the more comprehensive test of physical capability. Yet only 6 weeks of participation in a daily 15-minute program of vigorous exercise brought about a 24 percent improvement among those who failed the first test.

Throughout the country we have found equally discouraging examples of deficiency—and equally encouraging examples of progress. I hope that every school district in this country will adopt our minimum program. I urge every parent to support the program and his own children's participation in it. I urge our colleges and universities to lay down basic standards of physical fitness. I urge the Nation's community recreation centers to provide more opportunity for those who are no longer attending school. And finally, I urge organizations such as this, with all of the prestige and influence which you bring to American life, to help establish more programs for participation by American boys and girls—by Americans young and old. In short, what we must do is literally change the physical habits of millions of Americans—and that is far more difficult than changing their tastes, their fashions, or even their politics.

I do not suggest that physical development is the central object of life, or that we should permit cultural and intellectual values to be diminished, but I do suggest that physical health and vitality constitute an essential element of a vigorous American community.

No one knew this better than the men of Greece, to whom our civilization owes so much. The Greeks sought excellence not only in philosophy and drama and sculpture and architecture, but in athletics. The same people who produced the poetry of Homer, the wisdom of Plato and Aristotle—they also produced the Olympic Games. The Greeks understood that mind and body must develop in harmonious proportion to produce a creative intelligence. And so did the most brilliant intelligence of our earliest days, Thomas Jefferson, when he said, "Not less than two hours a day should be devoted to exercise." If a man who wrote the Declaration of Independence, was Secretary of State, and twice President could give it 2 hours, our children can give it 10 or 15 minutes.

There's no reason in the world—and we've seen it tonight—why Americans should not be fine students and fine athletes. When I was young, Barry Wood used to play with Ben Ticknor football for Harvard—and hockey and baseball and tennis. He was a ten-letter man—and also the First Marshal of Phi Beta Kappa. And since then he has combined a life of leadership in the medical profession.

I have in Washington, as you know—and he is a friend of many of you—the Deputy Attorney General, Byron White, who was simultaneously a Rhodes scholar and a halfback for the Detroit Lions, and the year that he led the league in ground gained rushing, was also number one man in his class at the Yale Law School. We can combine and must combine intellectual energy and physical vitality.

Theodore Roosevelt once said, "The credit belongs to the man who is actually in the arena—whose face is marred by dust and sweat and blood . . . who knows the great enthusiasms, the great devotions—and spends himself in a worthy cause—who at best if he wins knows the thrills of high achievement—and if he fails at least fails while daring greatly—so that his place shall never be with those cold and timid souls who know neither victory nor defeat."

The athletes in this room—you gentlemen—and your colleagues across the country have known victory and defeat, and have accepted both. I salute you.

NOTE: The President spoke at the Waldorf-Astoria Hotel in New York City. His opening words "Mr. LaRoche" referred to Chester J. LaRoche, President of the National Football Foundation.

The award to which the President referred is the Foundation's gold medal presented annually by the Football Hall of Fame to a person dedicated to propagating the concept of amateur football.

497　Address in New York City to the National Association of Manufacturers.　*December 6, 1961*

Mr. President, and gentlemen:

I understand that President McKinley and I are the only two Presidents of the United States to ever address such an occasion. I suppose that President McKinley and I are the only two that are regarded as fiscally sound enough to be qualified for admission to this organization on an occasion such as this.

I have not always considered the membership of the NAM as among my strongest supporters. I'm not sure you've all approached the New Frontier with the greatest possible enthusiasm, and I was therefore somewhat nervous about accepting this invitation, until I did some studying of the history of this organization. I learned that this organization had once denounced on

one occasion—I'll quote—"swollen bureaucracy" as among the triumphs of Karl Marx,
and decried on another occasion new governmental "paternalism and socialism." I
was comforted when reading this very familiar language to note that I was in very good
company. For the first attack I quoted was
on Calvin Coolidge and the second on Herbert Hoover.

I remind you of this only to indicate the
happy failure of many of our most pessi-
mistic predictions. And that is true of all
of us. I recognize that in the last campaign,
most of the members of this luncheon group
today supported my opponent, except for a
very few—who were under the impression
that I was my father's son. But I hope that
some of your most alarming feelings of a
year ago about the imminent collapse of the
whole business system if I was elected have
been somewhat lessened.

We have selected, I think, able men who
I hope you have come to have a regard for,
to serve in the responsible positions of the
government. One of them here, our dis-
tinguished Secretary of Commerce, Governor
Hodges, who had a long career in business;
Secretary Goldberg, who I think has earned
the respect of business as well as labor; Secretary of the Treasury Dillon and his Under
Secretary Mr. Robert Roosa who was the
Vice President of the Federal Reserve Bank
of New York; Mr. Robert McNamara, whom
many of you know, the Secretary of Defense;
Mr. John McCone, who is the head of the
Central Intelligence Agency succeeding Mr.
Dulles; and Mr. Rusk, Secretary of State—I
think they're all men of experience and also,
I think, they're vitally interested in the maintenance of all kinds of freedom in this
country.

I think that while we may not have been
together a year ago, we are together now,
and I will be the President of the United

States for the next three years, and I am
most anxious that while we may not agree
on all matters, that goodwill at least will prevail among us and that we will both recognize that those of us who work in the national government, and all of you, are motivated by a desire to serve our country.

Our responsibilities are different, but I believe that we can have a period, in the next
few years, of cooperation between business
and government in order to advance the common interest.

I have read about the feeling of some businessmen that we are antibusiness, and I
would think that a moment's thought would
show how really untrue that must be. And
I say it, really, for three reasons.

In the first place, we are committed to the
defense of freedom around the world.
When business does well in this country, we
have full employment, and this country is
moving ahead, then it strengthens our image
as a prosperous and vital country in this
great fight in which we are engaged. When
you do well, the United States does well, and
our policies abroad do well. And when you
do badly, all suffer.

Secondly, we're unable to maintain the
kind of high employment which we must
maintain, unless you are making profits, and
reinvesting, and producing; and therefore as
we are committed to the goal—and we must
all be in this country, of trying to make sure
that everyone who wants a job will find it,
then quite obviously we must make the system work, and the business community
must prosper.

And thirdly, and to put it on its most narrow basis, we are—in the national government, and I know—a rather unpopular
partner in every one of your businesses. Our
revenues come from you. When you are
making profits, then we are able to meet our
bills. When you fail, then we fail. So for

every reason, government and business are completely interdependent and completely involved. And while we may differ on the policies which may bring this country prosperity, there is no disagreement, I am sure, on either side, about the tremendous importance of you gentlemen moving ahead, and prospering, and contributing to the growth of this country.

And I hope, if nothing else, that my presence here today indicates that my remarks represent the views of all of us who occupy a position of responsibility in Washington today.

It's not an exaggeration to say that this endeavor of building a prosperous America, in a world of free and prosperous states, of making the most of our human and material resources and avoiding the harmful effects and fluctuations of inflation and recession, are of course matters of the greatest importance to us all.

And it's not an exaggeration to say that this endeavor proceeds under conditions today more fraught with peril than any in our history.

As communism continues its long-range drive to impose its way of life all around the world, our strongest desire is not unnaturally to seize the initiative, to get off the defensive, to do more than react to the Soviets. But while this is not an unreasonable urge, its concrete application is more difficult. In the military arena, the initiative rests with the aggressor—a role that we shun by nature and tradition—and our alliances are largely, therefore, defensive. In the paramilitary arenas of subversion, intimidation and insurrection, an open and peaceful society is again at a disadvantage.

But there is one area, in particular, where the initiative can and has been ours—an area of strategic importance in which we have the capacity for a still greater effort—

and that is in the area of economic policy.

The Marshall Plan was an example of our initiative in this area. So were Point 4 and OECD and the Alliance for Progress. This year's new long-range program to aid in the growth of the underdeveloped regions of the world, and the unaligned nations can bring us still further gains—not merely as a blow against communism but as a blow for freedom. Of equal if not greater importance is the stunning evolution of Western European economic unity from treaty to concrete reality. And it is the success of this still-growing movement which presents the West, at this time, with an historic opportunity to seize the initiative again. The United States is, in fact, required to do so for its own self-interest and progress.

The Communist Bloc, largely self-contained and isolated, represents an economic power already by some standards larger than that of Western Europe and gaining to some degree on the United States. But the combined output and purchasing power of the United States and Western Europe is more than twice as great as that of the entire Sino-Soviet Bloc. Though we have only half as much population, and far less than half as much territory, our co-ordinated economic strength will represent a powerful force for the maintenance and growth of freedom.

But will our strength be combined and coordinated—or divided and self-defeating? Will we work together on problems of trade, payments and monetary reserve—or will our mutual strength be splintered by a network of tariff walls, exchange controls, and the pursuit of narrow self-interest in unrelated if not outright hostile policies on aid, trade, procurement, interest rates and currency?

This is not a debate between "deficit" nations and "surplus" nations. It is not speculation over some "grand design" for the future. It is a hard, practical question for every member of the Western community—involving most immediately for this nation our policies in two mutually dependent areas: our balance of payments and our balance of trade.

I. OUR BALANCE OF PAYMENTS

While exaggerated fears can be harmful, we would not inspire needed confidence abroad by feigning satisfaction with our international balance of payments position. In essence, that position reflects the burden of our responsibilities as the Free World's leader, the chief defender of freedom and the major source of capital investment around the world. As the cost of these responsibilities grows, and is not offset by foreign expenditures here, the monetary deficit in our relations with the rest of the world grows, except to the extent that our trade surplus (of exports over imports) can increase with it. During the previous three years, as competition in international markets increased, in spite of the fact that we had a generous balance in our favor in trade, our trade surplus did not keep pace with our needs. At the same time, higher interest rates in other countries as well as speculation in the price of gold attracted some American short-term capital away from our shores. Our balance of payments was in deficit at a rate of nearly 4 billion dollars a year; and, with its consequences extended by a weakened confidence in the dollar, we suffered over that 3-year period a net loss of 5 billion dollars in our gold reserve.

The complete elimination of this problem is clearly some time off—but so are any ultimately dangerous consequences. The United States still holds some 43% of the Free World's monetary gold stock, a proportion far larger than our share of its trade

and clearly sufficient to tide us over a temporary deficit period—and I emphasize the words *temporary deficit period*—while we mount an offensive to reverse these trends. Our exports and export surplus have both been rising. The net claims of Americans against foreigners have doubled during the last decade, and the annual increase in the value of our assets abroad—which now total nearly 45 billion dollars and must always be put in the balance sheet, when we're considering the movement of gold and dollars in the value of our assets abroad—has regularly exceeded our payments deficit. Contrary to the assertion that this nation has been living beyond its means abroad, we have been increasing those means instead.

This year, moreover, our wholesale prices have been steady. In fact, in spite of the recovery, our wholesale prices are a fraction less than they were in February, and in a very real sense, for the last three years, the United States has had generally stable prices. Confidence in the dollar has been upheld—the speculation fever against the dollar has ceased—the outflow of gold has been reduced from 2 billion dollars in the ten months before February 1961, to 450 million dollars in the last ten months and, due partly to the temporary decline in imports that accompanied the recession, our general payments deficit in 1961 will be less than half of the 1960 deficit.

There is cause for concern, in short, but I do not believe that there is cause for alarm. We should be blind neither to our basic strengths nor to our basic problems. A long-term deficit requires long-term solutions, and we must not be panicked by setbacks of a short-run nature or the inevitable results of a reviving economy which has increased our imports and therefore leaves us in a less favorable position than we might have expected two or three months ago.

For negative, shortsighted remedies will do more to weaken confidence in the dollar than strengthen it; and this Administration, therefore, during its term of office, and I repeat this, and make it as a flat statement— has no intention of imposing exchange controls, devaluing the dollar, raising trade barriers, or choking off our economic recovery.

What we will do, and have been doing, is to take a series of positive steps to reduce our outpayments and to increase our receipts from abroad.

First of all, we recognize, as already stressed, that this country cannot solve this problem alone. Our Allies have a vital interest in its solution. Because, let me repeat, if it were not for our national security commitments abroad, which defends our own interests and that of our Allies, the United States would have gold pouring in, rather than pouring out. It is this commitment which is extremely large and constant which gives us our problem, and should be so recognized. Our Allies, therefore, have a vital interest in the solution. Thus we have sought to increase the share of the contribution which other industrialized states are making to the less-developed world; and are seeking their assumption of a larger share of the cost of our joint defense requirements.

We lose three billion dollars a year because of our defense expenditures. It costs us hundreds of millions of dollars to keep our troops in Western Germany. We lose nearly three hundred million dollars a year to France alone because of our defense expenditures in those areas. That three billion dollars, therefore, represents a charge in the interests of our national security, which is vitally important. That drain is serious. And it was because of that reason that President Eisenhower last year suggested the exceptional step of bringing back our dependents from Western Europe which would

have saved two hundred and fifty million dollars. But three billion dollars represents the contribution which we make to our defense establishments abroad.

The reason why the British, as you know, have been considering withdrawing some of their troops from bases stationed around the world is because of their balance of payments difficulty. The reason that they have been reluctant to station additional troops in Western Germany has been because of the same reason. In other words, therefore, the matter which we are now discussing, of trade, involves not only our economic well-being but the basic commitments of the United States to dozens of countries around the world.

Unless our balance of trade, and our surplus, is sufficient, for example, to pay for this three billions of dollars, then we have no remedy but to start pulling back. So that for those who address themselves to this subject in the coming months, they must realize that it goes to the heart of our survival as well as our economic vitality.

We are working with foreign governments now and central banks on new techniques for dealing in foreign currencies; on coordinating our development aid, fiscal, debt management, monetary and other policies through the OECD; on preparing a new stand-by lending authority for the International Monetary Fund; on the prepayment of our Allies' long-term debts during this period of adverse trends; and on increasing the proportion of their own military procurement in the United States, a very important move, because of the arrangements that have been recently made, that is expected to cut our payments deficit by at least another half a billion dollars next year.

Secondly, to hold our own outlays abroad to the absolute essentials, we have emphasized procurement in this country for our military aid and overseas defense, and insisted upon it for three-quarters of our economic aid. This means that our economic aid to these countries does not go as far as it once did. The South Koreans can buy fertilizer from Japan at half the cost that they can buy it here in the United States, and much less shipping. But because we are determined to protect our gold, and therefore our dollar, we have imposed the Buy American policy which means now that our losses because of economic aid abroad, our general program which amounts to about four billion dollars, is now down as far as our dollar loss to five hundred million dollars, and we are hopeful that we can squeeze it even down further. We have also substituted local currency expenditures for dollar expenditures to cover local costs wherever possible; and sought to discourage (by a change in the customs law) heavy expenditures abroad by tourists to supplement restrictions already placed on military families. I will say I was alarmed to hear the other day of a study in the Defense Department of this question of dependents abroad, which indicated that those who had no dependents abroad spent more money abroad than those with dependents, so it indicates that for every solution there are additional problems.

Third, to encourage a greater movement of funds in this direction, and to discourage transfers in these other directions, we have set up a new program to attract foreign visitors; secured passage of a tax exemption encouraging foreign central banks to invest their capital in U.S. securities; kept our own short-term interest rates high enough to avoid unnecessary outflows; and urged our Allies to free their own private capital for investment here. At the same time, we have directed the Treasury, for the first time in a generation, to buy and sell foreign currencies in the international exchange markets so as to strengthen its ability to offset unfavorable developments affecting the value of the dollar.

Fourth, we have asked the Congress—and this is a matter which is controversial and to which this group has taken exception—we have asked the Congress to remove the artificial tax preference for American investment in highly developed countries with no capital shortage, and the unjustifiable tax avoidance loopholes available to those Americans investing in so-called "tax haven" nations. We do not seek to penalize those who wish to invest their capital abroad. We are committed to the free flow of capital, but we also want to make sure that our tax laws do not encourage the outward movement of capital in a way which does not serve our national purpose.

I am aware that many of you will argue that the investment abroad of these funds will mean that ultimately and in the long run these moneys will be coming back. But how long a run? And how long can we afford, without taking every responsible step, to try to bring this in balance in the short run? We can't wait till 1970, if we're losing two or three billion dollars a year. And we're now, for the first time, down to about sixteen billion, nine hundred million dollars in gold in the United States.

So that I want to emphasize that however unsatisfactory you may feel it is, it is not being done to harass business, but only because it represents one additional effort to try to bring the dollar into balance. And if we can increase our trade so that our surplus in trade is sufficient to make up these figures, then this kind of tax would be unnecessary.

Or, if this organization has some other plan or program—which does not affect our national security—which is more equitable, we'll be glad to listen to that. But we are concerned that while capital moves freely, the tax policies do not stimulate it.

And I emphasize this in saying again that I do not believe that exchange controls, based on the experience of the British and others, and our unique role as the banker of the world, would be either workable or helpful. But the recent flow of our capital to nations already fully developed has been a serious drain—in the shortrun—on our current balance of payments position. The eventual return from that capital is no help to us today. And at a time when we're hard-pressed to pay for the maintenance of our forces in Europe without unreasonably increasing our payments deficit and our gold outflow, I am sure you must realize that it makes no sense to be encouraging an exodus of capital through tax laws that were more appropriate at a time when Europe was deficient in capital. You probably are familiar with these figures: in 1960, the long-term outward flow of capital funds was a billion, seven hundred million dollars. The return was two billion, three hundred million dollars, and therefore you might argue that we're getting more back than we're sending out. But when those figures are broken down, we see that the outward investment into the developed countries, such as Western Europe, was a billion, five hundred million dollars, and the return was only one billion dollars, a loss therefore in dollars and potentially in gold of a half a billion dollars to these countries, while in the underdeveloped countries where we would like to see American capital be invested, we took in one billion, three hundred million and invested two hundred million dollars.

So that I would say, gentlemen, that all of the proposals which we will have to put forward in the coming months and years to try to bring this into balance—and I will say

that we are going to reduce without weakening our defenses our expenditures for military purposes from three billion dollars to two billion dollars, we do have to use every available means that we have. And if this organization has suggestions as to how it may be done, we want to hear them. The best way, of course, is by increasing our exports.

Fifth, and most important of all, we are seeking to increase our exports—and thus our surplus of exports over imports. I shall discuss our opportunities, but it is worth while recounting now that we have embarked on a stepped-up campaign of export promotion and trade fair exhibits—increased our agricultural exports—and to indicate the kind of problems that we're going to have, we send to Western Europe in agricultural exports nearly two billion dollars, which is one of our great dollar earners. We take in, in agricultural exports from Europe, only about 80 million dollars, a balance of trade for us of nearly a billion, 920 million dollars. And yet, as the Common Market begins to get more and more developed, with all of these countries beginning to face surplus problems, there isn't any doubt that one of our most important problems in maintaining this kind of dollar flow would be to maintain the free flow of our agricultural commodities into the Common Market. There's going to be no more difficult task than that, and therefore we have to recognize that this, too, may affect our balance of payments.

We have broadened the Export-Import Bank's loan guarantee system—created a new program of export credit insurance—and in a variety of ways sought to help you to keep American prices competitive. This requires—if we are to avoid the inflation that will price our goods out of the world markets—price and wage restraint by both industry and labor, and responsible budget policies by the government. It requires—if we are to offer modern products efficiently produced at a low cost—a higher rate of investment in new equipment, encouraged by the fullest use of existing capacity in a strong recovery, by the investment tax credit now pending before the House Ways and Means Committee, and by the depreciation reform now under study and already put into effect on textile machinery.

This organization has taken a position against our tax credit, and the reason is that you do not feel it is sufficient and you support a much more general overhaul of our depreciation. I support that, too, but our tax credit will cost a billion, 800 million in our revenue. We have suggested—and I know this has been unpopular—certain taxes to make up that revenue, because quite obviously we cannot carry out a tax reduction, in these critical times, without budget problems as difficult as they are. Therefore, while we would like, under ideal conditions, and had hoped, for example, to have a surplus this year before our additional expenditures for defense in July, it is very difficult for us to send up a broad tax depreciation scheme which might cost three billion dollars, with the expectation that other tax reductions would be added to it, at a time when we balance our budget with the greatest difficulty.

So that we're not unsympathetic, and I can think of very few tax changes that would be more useful to the country in stimulating employment and keeping us competitive, particularly with Western Europe. And the only reason we have not gone further in it, and the only reason we have limited ourselves to the proposal which is now before the House Ways and Means Committee, is because we do not have the available revenue to provide for a tax reduction this year.

So that I'm hopeful, in making your position known to the Congress this year, that while you will continue to commit yourselves to depreciation changes—and as I say, we have made some progress in textiles—you will also recognize what our budgetary problems are, and work with us in attempting to get the best arrangements we can at this time, and plan for more satisfactory arrangements in the future.

In short, achieving a healthy equilibrium in our international accounts depends in part upon the cooperation of our Allies—in part upon action by the Congress—in part upon the self-discipline exercised by this Administration in its executive and budgetary policies (and here I repeat my intention to submit a balanced budget in January)—and in part upon you and other members of the business community. (Labor, too, has its responsibility for price stability, and I shall stress this tomorrow in addressing the AFL–CIO.) I recognize that your efforts will be governed in part by the kind of atmosphere the government can help to create. That is why we intend to submit our balanced budget. The government must not be demanding more from the savings of the country, nor draining more from the available supplies of credit, when the national interest demands a priority for productive, creative investment—not only to spur our growth at home but to make sure that we can sell, and sell effectively, in markets abroad.

But your own responsibility is great—and there are three things in particular that you can do: *be competitive,* through lower costs and prices and better products and productivity. *Be export-minded.* In a very real sense, the British used to say they exported or died. We are going to meet our commitments. We've got to export. And we have to increase our exports, and however impressive it has been in the past, it must be better in the future for the security of this country.

And finally, *be calm,* in the sense of refraining from talk which really does not represent the facts, and which causes a concern about where we are going abroad. It is my hope that when we submit our balanced budget in January, that those who look at our fiscal situation from abroad and make their judgment, will recognize that we are in control, that we are moving ahead, and that the United States is a good bet.

All of us must share in this effort—for this in part, as I have said, is a part of the national security. And I don't want the United States pulling troops home because we're unable to meet our problems in other ways.

But we can be calm because our basic international position is strong—this year's deficit will be lower than last year's—our gold stores are large and the outflow is easing—we are going to make progress next year in diminishing it still further—we will submit a balanced budget—we are not undergoing a damaging inflation. We can, over the next few years, offset with the help of our Allies a billion dollars, as I have said, of our $3 billion overseas defense outlays; reduce, with the help of the Congress, the money which goes because of tax advantages; cut back still further that portion of our foreign aid procurement which is not already spent here; and take the other steps I have mentioned, including an increase in our exports, for which all the additional tools we need are well within our reach.

II. OUR BALANCE OF TRADE

One of those tools—one which we urgently need for our own well-being—is a new trade and tariff policy. The Reciprocal

Trade Agreements Act expires in June of next year. It must not simply be renewed—it must be replaced. If the West is to take the initiative in the economic arena—if the United States is to keep pace with the revolutionary changes which are taking place throughout the world—if our exports are to retain and expand their position in the world market—then we need a new and bold instrument of American trade policy.

For the world of trade is no longer the same. Some 90% of the Free World's industrial production may soon be concentrated in two great markets—the United States of America and an expanded European Common Market. Our own example—of 50 States without a trade barrier behind a common external tariff—helped to inspire the Common Market. Our support—ever since the close of World War II—has been thrown behind greater European unity. For we recognized long ago that such unity would produce a Europe in which the ancient rivalries which resulted in two world wars, for us as well as for them, could rest in peace—a Europe in which the strength and the destiny of Germany would be inextricably tied with the West—and a Europe no longer dependent upon us, but on the contrary, strong enough to share in full partnership with us the responsibilities and initiatives of the Free World.

Now this new "house of Europe" that we sought so long, under different Administrations, is actually rising, and it means vast new changes in our outlook as well. With the accession of the United Kingdom and other European nations to the Common Market, they will have almost twice as many people as we do—it will cover nations whose economies have been growing twice as fast as ours—and it will represent an area with a purchasing power which some day will rival our own. It could be—it should be—our most reliable and profitable customer. Its consumer demands are growing—particularly for the type of goods that we produce best, for American goods not previously sold and sometimes not even known in European markets today. It is an historic meeting of need and opportunity; at the very time that we urgently need to increase our exports, to protect our balance of payments and to pay for our troops abroad, a vast new market is rising across the Atlantic.

If, however, the United States is to enjoy this opportunity, it must have the means to persuade the Common Market to reduce external tariffs to a level which permits our products to enter on a truly competitive basis.

That is why a trade policy adequate to deal with a large number of small states is no longer adequate. For almost thirty years, the Reciprocal Trade Agreements Act has strengthened our foreign trade policy. But today the approaches and procedures provided for in that Act are totally irrelevant to the problems and opportunities that we confront. Its vitality is gone—a fresh approach is essential—and the longer we postpone its replacement, the more painful that step will be when it finally happens.

For this is no longer a matter of local economic interest but of high national policy. We can no longer haggle over item-by-item reductions with our principal trading partners, but must adjust our trading tools to keep pace with world trading patterns—and the EEC cannot bargain effectively on an item-by-item basis.

I am proposing, in short, a new American trade initiative which will make it possible for the economic potential of these two great markets to be harnessed together in a team capable of pulling the full weight of our common military, economic and political

aspirations. And I do not underrate at all the difficulties that we will have in developing this initiative. I am *not* proposing—nor is it either necessary or desirable—that we join the Common Market, alter our concepts of political sovereignty, establish a "rich man's" trading community, abandon our traditional most-favored-nations policy, create an Atlantic free trade area, or impair in any way our close economic ties with Canada, Japan and the rest of the Free World. And this, of course, is a problem of the greatest importance to us also. We do not want Japan left out of this great market, or Latin America which has depended so much on the European markets. It may find it now increasingly difficult because of competition from Africa to sell in Europe which could mean serious trouble for them and therefore for us in the long run both political as well as economic.

I am *not* proposing—nor is it either necessary or desirable—that in setting new policies on imports we do away altogether with our traditional safeguards and institutions. I believe we can provide more meaningful concepts of injury and relief, and far speedier proceedings. We can use tariffs to cushion adjustment instead of using them only to shut off competition. And the Federal government can aid that process of adjustment, through a program I shall discuss further tomorrow—not a welfare program, or a permanent subsidy, but a means of permitting the traditional American forces of adaptability and initiative to substitute progress for injury.

For obviously our imports will also increase—not as much as our exports, but they will increase. And we need those imports if other nations are to have the money to buy our exports and the incentive to lower their own tariff barriers. Because nobody is going to lower their barriers unless the United States makes a bargain with them which they feel to be in their own economic interest. We need those imports to give our consumers a wide choice of goods at competitive prices. We need those imports to give our industries and defense establishments the raw materials they require at prices they can afford—and to keep a healthy pressure on our own producers and workers to improve efficiency, develop better products, and avoid the inflation that could price us out of markets vital to our own prosperity.

Finally, let me make it clear that I am *not* proposing a unilateral lowering of our trade barriers. What I am proposing is a joint step on both sides of the Atlantic, aimed at benefiting not only the exporters of the countries concerned but the economies of all of the countries of the Free World. Led by the two great Common Markets of the Atlantic, trade barriers in all the industrial nations must be brought down. Surely it will be said that the bold vision which produced the EEC will fall short if it merely transfers European protectionism from the national to the continental level.

But if we can obtain from the Congress, and successfully use in negotiations, sufficient bargaining power to lower Common Market restrictions against our goods, every segment of the American economy will benefit. There are relatively few members of the business community who do not or could not transport, distribute or process either exports or imports. There are millions of American workers whose jobs depend on the sale of our goods abroad—making industrial sewing machines, or trucks, or aircraft parts, or chemicals, or equipment for oil fields or mining or construction. They may produce lubricants or resin; they may dig coal or plant cotton. In fact, the average American

farmer today depends on foreign markets to sell the crops grown on one out of every six acres he plants—in wheat, cotton, rice and tobacco, to name but a few examples. Our consumers, as mentioned, will benefit most of all.

But if American industry cannot increase its sales to the Common Market, and increase this nation's surplus of exports over imports, our international payments position and our commitments to the defense of freedom will be endangered.

If American businessmen cannot increase or even maintain their exports to the Common Market, they will surely step up their investment in new American-owned plants behind those tariff walls so they can compete on an equal basis—thereby taking capital away from us, as well as jobs from our own shores, and worsening still further our balance of payments position.

If American industry cannot increase its outlets in the Common Market, our own expansion will be stifled—the growth target of 50% in the sixties, adopted last month by the 20 nations of OECD for their combined gross national product, will not be reached—and our business community will lack the incentives to lower prices and improve technology which greater competition would otherwise inspire. The industries which would benefit the most from increased trade are our most efficient—even though in many cases they pay our highest wages, their goods can compete with the goods of any other nation. Those who would benefit the least, and are unwilling to adjust to competition, are standing in the way, as the NAM Economic Advisory Committee pointed out last year, of greater growth and a higher standard of living. They are endangering the profits and jobs of others, our efforts against inflation, our balance of payments position, and in the long run their own economic well-being because they will suffer from competition in the U.S. inevitably, if not from abroad—for, in order to avoid exertion, they accept paralysis.

Finally, let me add, if we cannot increase our sales abroad, we will diminish our stature in the Free World. Economic isolation and political leadership are wholly incompatible. The United Kingdom, faced with even more serious problems in her efforts to achieve both higher growth and reasonable balance of payments, is moving with boldness, welcoming, in the Prime Minister's words, "the brisk shower of competition." We cannot do less. For if the nations of the West can weld together on these problems a common program of action as extraordinary in economic history as NATO was unprecedented in military history, the long-range Communist aim of dividing and encircling us all is doomed to failure.

In every sense of the word, therefore, Capitalism is on trial as we debate these issues.

For many years in many lands, we have boasted of the virtues of the marketplace under free competitive enterprise, of America's ability to compete and sell, of the vitality of our system in keeping abreast with the times. Now the world will see whether we mean it or not—whether America will remain the foremost economic power in the world—or whether we will evacuate the field of power before a shot is fired, or go forth to meet new risks and tests of our ability.

The hour of decision has arrived. We cannot afford to "wait and see what happens," while the tide of events sweeps over and beyond us. We must use time as a tool, not as a couch. We must carve out our own destiny. This is what Americans have always done—and this, I have every confidence, is what we will continue to do in each new trial and opportunity that lies ahead.

NOTE: The President spoke at the Waldorf-Astoria Hotel in New York City. His opening words "Mr. President" referred to John A. McGovern, President of the Association.

498 Remarks in Miami at the Young Democrats Convention. *December 7, 1961*

Mr. Chairman, Mr. Mayor, Members of Congress, Young Democrats and others, ladies and gentlemen:

For all I've been reading in the last 3, 4, or 5 months about the great conservative revival that's sweeping the United States, I thought that perhaps no one was going to show up today. But I'm proud to be here today, and proud to be among those of you who not only in the future but today helped make the program of the Democratic Party.

Artemus Ward once said, about 50 years ago, "I am not a politician and my other habits are good, also." We are politicians,

and we believe, in this sense, that we recognize that a political party is not an end in itself but is a means of making progress for the American people.

Woodrow Wilson said, in 1913, "What use is a political party unless it serves the interests of the people?" What use is either one of the two great political parties if they really represent, to those who are active in them, only a means of expression and exercise? They are important. They are functional. They will endure only as they contribute to the well-being of the people of this country.

And although I read a good deal—as do you—about all the slogans for the solution of our problems that sweep across the United States—and slogans are important particularly if they tell something about what is behind them—but what I think we must hear from the political leaders of our two parties is not slogans attempting to invoke old memories of self-reliance and all the rest; what we really want to know is, how can the United States maintain its strength, maintain the peace, maintain full employment, improve the life of our people, spread its influence around the world, strengthen the cause of freedom, survive, endure, and prevail?

And it is to these great questions which are today far more complicated than they were in the days, even, of Franklin Roosevelt or Woodrow Wilson that we as Democrats, and those of us who are active in our Party and in our country, must address ourselves. Not merely to mouth the old slogans and the old programs.

How can the United States maintain full employment in a free economy and in a free society? A recession in 1958, a recession in 1960, a recession in 1954, a recession in 1949. Is this recovery now—which in the last 6 or 7 months has seen the economy move forward by over 10 percent—is this economy going to run out of gas again, at the end of 1962 or 1963 or 1964?

How can we find jobs for the hundreds and thousands of young people under 20 who today come into the labor market, many of whom drop out of school and can't find work? Twenty-five percent of all young Americans in their teens looking for jobs are unemployed. How can we attempt to make it possible in the next 10 years for the seven million young boys and girls—men and women—who want to find admission to our colleges when our colleges today are strained finding a place for three and a half million? How can the United States get richer and more powerful and still prevail and survive, when so much of the world is not getting richer but poorer?

How can we in this Hemisphere, north and south, hold the imagination of the people in this continent and make them feel that political freedom and economic abundance go hand in hand?

I think the problems pour upon us, and these are problems that can be met. But I think they can only be met by those who are willing to do the hard work and come up with hard solutions. And I believe that it is incumbent upon all of us who are interested in our country, all of us who are active in political life, to attempt to come forward—and most of all, you who will be the leaders of this country, who have the longest to look forward to, who will be active over the next 40 years and who therefore must live with the results of all the judgments that we make today.

What is this country and the world going to be like in 1970, 1980, and 1990 when we see atomic weapons proliferate around the world, missiles and all the rest? You are going to be living in the most hazardous period, of course, of the human race. Can the peace be maintained? Can our strength be increased? Can the chances of freedom prosper?

So I come here today, not merely to make an old-time political speech, but I come here because I believe the opportunity and the obligation upon you is great.

The Democratic Party is the oldest political party in the world, and the reason it is old is because from the time of Jefferson to the present day the Democratic Party has been realistic enough to recognize the kind of problems which are coming over the horizon in the years ahead, and has had programs and policies to meet them. The day that we have not, the day that the Democratic Party is not prepared to come forward with those programs and policies, regardless of our old memories and our old leaders, we will fade as the Whig Party faded and made way for the Republican Party.

A political party is like anything else in life; it is the survival of the fittest, and the fittest in American life today are those who look realistically at the challenges and attempt to move this country forward.

We can keep going by not merely invoking the past, but by using the past as a stimulus to the future, and all of the great leaders of the Democratic Party—Wilson's New Freedom, Roosevelt's New Deal, Truman's Fair Deal, and our New Frontier—are attempts to pick the United States up and move it.

So I come here today asking your help, not for the election of 1962, though I will then, and 1964, but in the coming months, so that this session of Congress will be fruitful, so that our country can use the coming months as the leader of the Free World to demonstrate that it is the leader in fact as well as in name, and that here in the United States there is not only a country dedicated to progress but there is a political party stretching back through the long years of our history, which in the coming days of this decade will give this country new leadership.

Thank you.

NOTE: The President spoke at the Deauville Hotel in Miami, Fla. His opening words "Mr. Chairman, Mr. Mayor" referred to John M. Bailey, Chairman of the National Democratic Committee; and Robert King High, Mayor of Miami.

499 Address in Miami at the Opening of the AFL–CIO Convention. *December 7, 1961*

Mr. Meany, Reverend Clergy, Governor Bryant, gentlemen, ladies:

It's warmer here today than it was yesterday!

I want to express my pleasure at this invitation. As one whose work and continuity of employment has depended in part upon the union movement, I want to say that I have been on the job, training for about 11 months, and feel that I have some seniority rights in the matter.

I'm delighted to be here with you and with Secretary of Labor Arthur Goldberg. I was up in New York stressing physical fitness, and in line with that Arthur went over with a group to Switzerland to climb some of the mountains there. They all got up about 5 and he was in bed—got up to join

them later—and when they all came back at 4 o'clock in the afternoon, he didn't come back with them. They sent out search parties and there was no sign of him that afternoon or night. Next day the Red Cross went out and they went around calling "Goldberg—Goldberg—it's the Red Cross." And this voice came down the mountain, "I gave at the office."

Those are the liberties you can take with members of the Cabinet. But I want to say it's a pleasure to be here. This is an important anniversary for all of us, the 20th anniversary of Pearl Harbor.

I suppose, really, the only two dates that most people remember where they were, were Pearl Harbor and the death of President Franklin Roosevelt. We face entirely different challenges on this Pearl Harbor. In many ways the challenges are more serious, and in a sense long-reaching, because I don't think that any of us had any doubt in those days that the United States would survive and prevail and our strength increase.

Now we are face to face in a most critical time with challenges all around the world, and you in the labor movement bear a heavy responsibility. Occasionally I read articles by those who say that the labor movement has fallen into dark days. I don't believe that, and I would be very distressed if it were true.

One of the great qualities about the United States which I don't think people realize who are not in the labor movement, is what a great asset for freedom the American labor movement represents, not only here but all around the world. It's no accident that Communists concentrate their attention on the trade union movement. They know that people—the working people—are frequently left out, that in many areas of the world they have no one to speak for them, and the Communists mislead them and say that they will protect their rights. So many go along.

But in the United States, because we have had a strong, free labor movement, the working people of this country have not felt that they were left out. And as long as the labor movement is strong and as long as it is committed to freedom, then I think that freedom in this country is strengthened. So I would hope that every American, whether he was on one side of the bargaining table or the other, or whether he was in a wholly different sphere of life, would recognize that the strength of a free American labor movement is vital to the maintenance of freedom in this country and all around the world.

And I am delighted that there are here today, I understand, nearly 150 trade union leaders from nearly 32 countries around the world. I believe—and I say this as President—that one of the great assets that this country has is the influence which this labor movement can promote around the world in demonstrating what a free trade union can do.

I hope that they will go back from this meeting recognizing that in the long run a strong labor movement is essential to the maintenance of democracy in their country. It's no accident that there has not been a strike in the Soviet Union for 30, or 35, or 40 years. The Communists who in Latin America, or Africa, or Asia say that they represent the people, cannot possibly—under any rule of reason or debate—say that a labor movement is free when it is not able to express its rights, not only in relationship to the employer but also to speak out and recognize the limitations of governmental power. We are not omniscient—we are not all-powerful—this is a free society, and management and labor, and the farmer and the citizen have their rights. We did not give them their rights in government. And I hope that those who go from this hall to Latin America, to Europe, to Africa, will recognize that we believe in freedom and in progress in this country, that we believe that freedom is not an end in itself, but we believe that freedom can bring material abundance and prosperity. And I want you to know that I consider this meeting and the house of labor vital to the interests of this country and the cause of freedom in the coming days.

What unites labor, what unites this country, is far more important than those things on which we may disagree. So, gentlemen and ladies, you are not only leaders of your unions but you occupy a position of responsibility as citizens of the United States; and therefore I felt it most appropriate to come here today and talk with you.

First, I want to express my appreciation to you for several things. For example, I appreciate the effort that those of you who represent the interests of the men and women who work at our missile plants have made. The fact that you have given and that the men and women who work there have lived up to the no-strike pledge at our missile and space sites has made an appreciable difference in the progress that we are making in these areas—and the country appreciates the effort you are making.

Secondly, we have for the first time a Presidential Advisory Committee on Labor-Management Policy which for once did not break up on the passage of the Wagner Act in 1935, but instead meets month by month in an attempt to work out and develop economic policies which will permit this country to go forward under conditions of full employment. And I want to thank you for the participation you have given that.

Third, as I said, I want to thank the labor movement for what it is doing abroad in strengthening the free labor movement, and I urge you to redouble your efforts. The hope, as I have said, of freedom in these countries rests in many parts with the labor movement. We do not want to leave the people of some countries a choice between placing their destiny in the hands of a few who hold in their hands most of the property and on the other side the Communist movement. We do not give them that choice. We want them to have the instruments of freedom to protect themselves and provide for progress in their country, and a strong, free labor movement can do it—and I hope you will concentrate your attention in the next 12 months in that area—in Latin America and all around the world.

The fact is that the head of the Congo—Adoula—who has been a strong figure for freedom, came out of the labor movement. And that's happening in country after country. And this is a great opportunity and responsibility for all of us to continue to work together.

And finally, I want to take this opportunity to express my thanks to the AFL-CIO for the support that it gave in the passage of our legislative program in the long session of the Congress. We did not always agree on every tactic. We may not have achieved every goal, but we can take some satisfaction in the fact that we did make progress toward a $1.25 minimum wage, that we did expand the coverage for the first time in 20 years; that we did pass the best housing act since 1949; that we did, finally, after two Presidential vetoes in the last 4 years, pass a bill providing assistance to those areas suffering from chronic unemployment; that we did pass a long-range water pollution bill; that we did pass increased Social Security benefits, a lowering of the retirement age in Social Security from 65 to 62 for men, temporary unemployment compensation, and aid to dependent children.

And we are coming back in January and we are going to start again.

The Gross National Product has climbed since January from $500 billion to an estimated $540 billion in the last quarter, and it's a pleasure for me to say that the November employment figures received this morning show not only two million more people than were working in February, but we have now an all-time high for November, 67,349,000 people working. But, more importantly, unlike the usual seasonal run in November, which ordinarily provides for an increase in unemployment of about a half a million, we have now brought the figure for the first time below the 7 percent where it's hovered down to 6.1 percent, and we're going to have to get it lower.

I would not claim we've achieved full recovery or the permanently high growth rate of which we are capable. Since the recession of '58, from which we only partially recovered, and going into the recession of 1960, too many men and women have been idle for too long a time and our first concern must still be with those unable to get work. Unemployment compensation must be placed on a permanent, rational basis of nationwide standards, and even more importantly those who are older and retired must be permitted under a system of Social Security to get assistance and relief from the staggering cost of their medical bills.

The time has come in the next session of the Congress to face the fact that our elder citizens do need these benefits, that their needs cannot be adequately met in any other way, and that every Member of the Congress should have the opportunity to go on the record, up or down, on this question— and I believe when it comes to the floor—as I believe it must—they are going to vote it up and through before they adjourn in July or August.

Now there are six areas that I believe that we need to give our attention to if the manpower budget is to be balanced. First, we must give special attention to the problems of our younger people. Dr. Conant's recent book only highlighted a fact which all of you are familiar with, and that is the problem of those who drop out of school before they have finished, because of hardships in their home, inadequate motivation or counseling or whatever it may be, and then drift without being able to find a decent job.

And this falls particularly heavily upon the young men and women who are in our minority groups. In addition to that, 26

million young people will be crowding into the labor market in the next 10 years. This can be a tremendous asset because we have many tasks that require their talent. But today there are one million young Americans under the age of 25 who are out of school and out of work. Millions of others leave school early, destined to fall for life into a pattern of being untrained, unskilled, and frequently unemployed.

It's for this reason that I have asked the Congress to pass a Youth Employment Opportunities Act to guide these hands so that they can make a life for themselves. Equally important, if our young people are to be well trained and skilled labor is going to be needed in the next years, and if they are to be inspired to finish their studies, the Federal Government must meet its responsibility in the field of education. I'm not satisfied if my particular community has a good school. I want to make sure that every child in this country has an adequate opportunity for a good education.

Thomas Jefferson once said, "If you expect a country to be ignorant and free, you expect what never was and never will be." It's not enough that our own home town has a good school, we want the United States as a country to be among the best educated in the world. And I believe that we must invest in our youth.

Secondly, we need a program of retraining our unemployed workers. All of you who live so close to this problem know what happens when technology changes and industries move out and men are left. And I've seen it in my own State of Massachusetts where textile workers were unemployed, unable to find work even with new electronic plants going up all around them. We want to make sure that our workers are able to take advantage of the new jobs that must inevitably come as technology changes in the

1960's. And I believe, therefore, that retraining deserves the attention of this Congress in the coming days.

And the third group requiring our attention consists of our minority citizens. All
of you know the statistics of those who are
first discharged and the last to be rehired too
often are among those who are members of
our minority groups. We want everyone to
have a chance, regardless of their race or
color, to have an opportunity to make a life
for themselves and their families, to get a
decent education so they have a fair chance
to compete, and then be judged on what's
in here and not on what's on the outside.
And the American labor movement has been
identified with this cause, and I know that
you will be in the future.

And we are making a great effort to make
sure that all those who secure Federal contracts—and there are billions of dollars spent
each year by the Federal Government—will
give fair opportunity to all of our citizens to
participate in that work.

Fourth, we want to provide opportunities
for plant re-investment. One of the matters
which is of concern in maintaining our economy now is the fact that we do not have as
much re-investment in our plants as we did,
for example, in 1955, '56 and '57. And we
want this economy and this rise to be continuous. And I believe we have to give as
much incentive as is possible to provide re-
investment in plants which makes work and
will keep our economy moving ahead.

And therefore I have suggested a tax
credit, which I'm hopeful the American
labor movement has not placed on its list of
those matters yet that it has not supported,
but it will consider this proposal as a method
of stimulating the economy so that this recovery does not run out of gas in 12 months
or 18 months from now, as the 1958–59 re-

covery, after the recession of 1958, ran out in
'60.

Fifth, to add to our arsenals of built-in
stabilizers so we can keep our economy moving ahead, it's my intention to ask the Congress at its next session for stand-by authority
somewhat along the lines of the bill introduced by Senator Clark of Pennsylvania, to
make grants-in-aid to communities for
needed public works when our unemployment begins to mount and our economy to
slow down.

Sixth and finally, we must expand our
job opportunities by stimulating our trade
abroad. I know that this is a matter to
which the labor movement has given a good
deal of attention. Mr. Meany made an outstanding speech on this matter several weeks
ago, and it's a matter which is of concern
to this administration. I'm sure you wonder,
perhaps, why we're placing so much emphasis on it, and I would like to say why we
are, very briefly.

The first is, this country must maintain
a favorable balance of trade or suffer severely
from the point of view of our national security. We sell abroad now nearly $5
billion more than we import. But unfortunately that $5 billion goes abroad in order to
maintain the national security requirements
of the United States.

We spend $3 billion of that in order to
keep our troops overseas. It costs us nearly
$700 to $800 million to keep our divisions in
Western Germany, and $300 million to keep
our troop establishments in France. And
what is true in France and Germany, which
are outposts of our commitments, is true in
other areas.

So that if we're not able to maintain a
favorable balance of trade, then of course
we will have to do as the British have had
to do, which is begin to bring our troops

back and lay the way open for other actions. So that this is a matter which involves very greatly our security, and unless you believe that the United States should retreat to our own hemisphere and forget our commitments abroad, then you can share with me my concern about what will happen if that balance of trade begins to drop.

Now the problems that we face have been intensified by the development of the Common Market. This is our best market for manufactured products. What I am concerned about is that we shall be able to keep moving our trade into those areas; otherwise what we will find is that American capital which cannot place its goods in that market will decide, as they are doing now, to build their plants in Western Europe, and then they hire Western European workers—and you suffer, and the country suffers, and the balance of payments suffers.

So this is a matter of the greatest importance to you—in fact, to all Americans. It is, for example, of the greatest importance to American farmers. They sell $2 billion of agricultural commodities to Western Europe. We bring in $80 million of agricultural commodities from Western Europe. In other words, we make almost $2 billion of our foreign exchange from that sale of agricultural commodities, and yet Western Europe has great agricultural resources which are increasing, and we are going to find it increasingly difficult unless we are able to negotiate from a position of strength with them. So this matter is important.

The purpose of this discussion is to increase employment. The purpose of this discussion is to strengthen the United States, and it is a matter which deserves our most profound attention.

Are we going to export our goods and our crops or, are we going to export our capital?

That's the question that we're now facing.

And I know that those of you who have been concerned about this know this to be a major problem. Last year, 1960, we invested abroad $1,700 million and we took in from our investments abroad $2,300 million—which sounded like it was a pretty good exchange. But if you analyze these figures you will see that we took in, from the underdeveloped world, which needs capital, we took in $1,300 million and we sent out in capital for investment $200 million. And yet this is the area that needs our investment. While in Western Europe we sent out $1,500 million and took in $1 billion. So that if this trend should continue and more and more Western Europe became the object of American investment, it affects us all and affects the people who work with you.

We are attempting to repeal those tax privileges which make it particularly attractive for American capital to invest in Western Europe. We passed laws in the days of the Marshall Plan when we wanted American capital over there, and as the result of that, there are provisions on the tax book which make it good business to go over there.

Now we want it all to be fair, and we have stated we are not putting in exchange controls, which we will not. But we recommended in January the passage of a bill which would lessen the tax privileges of investing in Western Europe and which would have given us $250 million in revenue and in balance of payments.

The tax privileges or the attractions should be in the underdeveloped world, where we have been taking capital out rather than putting it in, and not in Western Europe where the capital is sufficient and which does not serve that great national purpose. So this is a matter of concern for all of us and it is a matter which we must consider in the coming months.

The Common Market is a tremendous market. It has more people than we do. Its rate of growth is twice ours. Its income is about three-fifths of ours, and may some day be equal to ours. This can be a great asset not only to them but to us—a great strength tying Western Europe, the United States, and Latin America and Japan together as a great area of freedom. And I think that it represents one of the most hopeful signs since 1945. It is one place where the Free World can be on the offensive. And I'm anxious that the United States play its proper role to protect the interests of our people and to advance the cause of freedom. And I ask the careful consideration of the American labor movement in this area.

One of the problems which we have is to recognize that those who have been affected by imports have received no protection at all for a number of years from the United States Government. When I was a Senator in 1954, I introduced legislation to provide assistance to those industries which are hard-hit by imports. I am going to recommend in January a program which I hope the Congress will pass, which will provide a recognition of the national responsibility in the period of transition for those industries and people who may be adversely affected.

I am optimistic about the future of this country. This is a great country, with an energetic people, and I believe over the long period the people of this country and of the world really want freedom and wish to solve their own lives and their own destiny. I'm hopeful that we can be associated with that movement. I'm hopeful that you will continue to meet your responsibilities to your people as well as to the country. I hope that we can maintain a viable economy here with full employment. I'm hopeful we can be

competitive here and around the world. I'm hopeful that management and labor will recognize their responsibility to permit us to compete, that those of you who are in the area of wage negotiations will recognize the desirability of us maintaining as stable prices as possible, and that the area of productivity and stable prices—that your negotiations will take adequate calculation and account of this need for us to maintain a balance of trade in our favor. In the long run it's in the interests of your own workers.

Let me repeat: If we cannot maintain the balance of trade in our favor, which it now is, of $5 billion, and indeed increase it, then this country is going to face most serious problems. In the last 3 years, even though the balance of trade in our favor has been $5 billion, we have lost $5 billion in gold; and if this trend should go on year after year then the United States, as I have said, would have to make adjustments which would be extremely adverse to the cause of freedom around the world.

The solution rests with increasing our export trade, with remaining competitive, with our businesses selling abroad, finding new markets, and keeping our people working at home and around the world.

And it is a fact that the six countries of the Common Market who faced the problems that we now face, have had in the last 4 years full employment and an economic growth twice ours. Even a country which faced staggering economic problems a decade ago—Italy—has been steadily building its gold balance, cutting down its unemployment and moving ahead twice what we have over the last 4 years.

So what I am talking about is an opportunity, not a burden. This is a chance to move the United States forward in the 1960's, not only in the economic sphere but also to make a contribution to the cause of freedom.

And I come to Miami today and ask your help, as on other occasions other Presidents of the United States, stretching back to the time of Woodrow Wilson and Roosevelt and Truman, have come to the AF of L and the CIO—and each time this organization has said yes.

Thank you.

NOTE: The President spoke at the Americana Hotel in Miami. In his opening words he referred to George Meany, President of the AFL–CIO, and Farris Bryant, Governor of Florida.

In delivering the address the President virtually discarded the prepared text, portions of which were released by the White House, as follows:

Excerpts of Remarks by the President at the Fourth Convention of the AFL–CIO, Miami Beach, Florida, December 7, 1961

. . . Today is the twentieth anniversary of Pearl Harbor. The memory of that day is so immediate to so many that it is hard to realize that today's college freshmen were not even born on that day of shock and infamy.

It is a memory that should serve us well, not to renew old rancor, but to reaffirm our more ancient conviction that history belongs to the free, and the free must ever be vigilant. We cannot turn back to the days before Pearl Harbor when we believed our destiny was in our own hands, without regard to the fate and the ambitions of others. We cannot turn back to the days when a surprise attack was only the prelude to a long struggle—when there was always time to rearm, time to retool our industry, and time to gear up our economy, protected by two oceans.

America's Role.—The world is very different now, and so is America's role.

We are committed to supporting freedom of choice in any nation that wants it. We are committed to assisting the new and developing nations to stand straight and sturdy in the family of nations. And we are committed to providing the great bulwark of freedom's defenses, here and around the world.

At the same time, we are required to show by example that freedom and economic growth go hand in hand, to show by our achievements—including those of science, space, and industry—that this Nation is a leader, a teacher, and a doer of unsurpassable deeds.

All this requires more than arms and know-how. It requires an economic system strong enough to underwrite each of the goals we seek—competitive enough to hold its own in every world market—and dynamic enough to make the fullest use of every able hand and mind, of every willing citizen.

Labor's Role.—In these endeavors, the efforts and cooperation of organized labor have been essential. Permit me to cite a few examples:

(1) First, I can unequivocally state that all phases of our missile program are now on or ahead of schedule as a result of your unprecedented cooperation in giving me a voluntary "no-strike" pledge at our missile and space sites. Had the number of man days lost because of work stoppages at these sites continued at their previous rate, this Nation could not face the future with such confidence in its own strength. On behalf of all Americans, I thank you and congratulate you.

(2) Secondly, we have for the first time a Presidential Advisory Committee on Labor-Management Policy which—instead of breaking up in bitterness and frustration—has recognized the responsibilities which all of us have for achieving a higher growth rate, a competitive posture in world markets, and increased price stability and human well-being. I am not looking for a pale unanimity of view from this important committee, but I am looking for their constructive advice and counsel. If each segment of our society were to pursue only its own goals, we would soon have no society at all. But with responsibility comes progress—as your own history so dramatically shows.

(3) Third, the AFL–CIO has strengthened the cause of freedom around the world by strengthening the free union movements of other countries. It is not surprising that so many of the new political leaders in Asia, Africa, and Latin America began their careers as labor leaders. It is not surprising that in many of these countries the single most dynamic and democratic force for change has been the forces of organized labor.

And it is not surprising to find that so many of these organizations have been nurtured and encouraged by material and moral support from the greatest free labor movement in the world.

(4) Finally, I want to take this opportunity to express my personal thanks to the AFL–CIO for its tireless support of my legislative program in this last long session of the Congress. We may not have agreed on every tactic. We may not have achieved every goal. But we can take some satisfaction in the passage of the $1.25 minimum wage, with the first expanded coverage in history—from the passage of the Area Redevelopment Bill to help those long-neglected communities with chronic unemployment—from the passage of a water pollution bill and an unprecedented housing bill, both of them far stronger than those which had previously been vetoed—and from the passage of numerous other bills, improving Social Security, temporary unemployment compensation, aid to the dependent

children of the unemployed, and meeting other essential needs.

Economic Progress.—Those of us who fought for many years to secure this legislation—to get this country moving again—can take some satisfaction from the progress we are making. The American economy has begun to move, and move strongly, out of the lassitudes of recession. The gross national product climbed from 500 billion in January to an estimated 540 billion in this last quarter. Industrial production increased more than 10 percent. The number of substantial unemployment areas has fallen from 101 to 60. Average earnings and real earnings are both at an all-time high. And finally, I am able to announce with great pleasure that the November employment figures received this morning not only show a new high of 67,349,000 jobs—an all-time high for the month of November—but, more importantly, show that the rate of unemployment has fallen below the 6.8 percent level for the first time in a year to 6.1 percent.

I would not claim that the recovery measures of this Administration were solely responsible for these improvements. Our task was to give stimulation and confidence to an economy inherently strong by virtue of the breadth of its purchasing power, the wide variety of its enterprise and the skill of its labor force. But neither would I claim that we have achieved either the full recovery or the permanently high growth rate of which we are capable. Since the recession of 1958—from which we only partially recovered before sliding back into the recession of 1960—too many men and women have been standing idle in the shadow of unused plants at the very time our national goals are unfulfilled.

Our first concern must still be with those unable to work. Unemployment compensation must be placed on a permanent, rational basis of nationwide standards. And, even more important, those who are "too old to work and too young to die" must be protected through Social Security system against the staggering costs of medical care. The time has come, in this next session of the Congress, to face the fact that our elder citizens need these benefits—that their needs cannot be met in any other way—and that every member of the Congress should have an opportunity to vote this bill up, or vote it down and tell the people why.

The Manpower Budget.—But it is not enough to help those who are not working. Our success as a nation depends upon our ability to make sure that more men and women are working. I have pledged a balanced Federal budget for the coming fiscal year. But equally important is a balanced manpower budget. Four million unemployed men and women is as deplorable a deficit as any deficit of dollars. And there is only one place to balance the manpower budget—at full employment. For men hard at work are taxpayers—men out of work are tax users. And the best way to balance the national dollar budget is to balance the manpower budget at full employment.

I want to stress briefly six areas that need our attention if the manpower budget is to be balanced:

(1) First, we must give special attention to the employment outlook for young people. Twenty-six million will be crowding into the labor market in the next ten years. This ought to be a tremendous asset—for we have many tasks that require many talents.

But today there are already one million young Americans under the age of 25 who are both out of school and out of work. Millions of others are leaving school before completing their educations, destined to fall into the same harsh patterns of the untrained, the unskilled, and eventually the unemployed. It is for these reasons that I have asked the Congress to pass a new Youth Employment Opportunities Act—to guide these youthful hands toward constructive work instead of idle habits or mischief. It is equally important, if our young people are to be well-trained, and if they are to be inspired to finish their studies, that the Congress enact Federal aid for public school construction and teachers salaries. To handicap our Nation's youth is to handicap our Nation's future. Let us instead invest in our youth—and see that investment pay off in the future.

(2) Secondly, we need a program to train and retrain unemployed or under-employed workers in new skills and in new positions. I have seen unemployed textile workers in Massachusetts standing idle on the streets while great new electronics companies were advertising for men. I have seen the waste of able-bodied men in West Virginia who have dug coal all their lives, and who can only sit and wait and hope for the mines to some day re-open. We can use these men—they want to work—and the least we can do is show them how and where to work.

(3) The third group requiring attention, if we are to balance our manpower budget, consists of our minority citizens. Too often they are the last to be hired and the first to be fired. Too often they lack the equal education or the equal opportunity to do the kind of job they could otherwise do. This kind of discrimination makes no sense at all.

It is a blot on our democracy and a drag on our economy. The policies of this administration are now fully on the side of righting this wrong. And as we move forward in the realm of public policy, it is essential that the private policies of management and labor meet this common obligation to human dignity.

(4) Fourth, to provide new job opportunities in more modern and competitive industries, I am renewing my recommendation to the Congress for tax incentives to encourage capital plant expansion and improvement.

I know this proposal has not thus far enjoyed your support. But I want you to know that I am deeply convinced that this proposal is as essential as the other tax reforms submitted with it—that we must be able to produce more goods more efficiently if we are to achieve a full and lasting recovery.

(5) Fifth, to add to our arsenal of built-in stabilizers in the event of a recession, it is my intention to ask the Congress in its next session for standby authority, somewhat along the lines of the bill introduced by Senator Clark, to make grant-in-aid to communities for needed public works. We do not intend to go back to the days of leaf raking—but neither do we intend to go back to the days of bread lines. There is no need for this Nation to go through another recession with large pools of manpower in need of work standing around in large numbers of communities in need of public improvements.

(6) Sixth and finally, we must expand our job opportunities at home by expanding our trade with the world.

If we cannot obtain new bargaining power to open up overseas markets, our export industries will wither—and American labor will lose jobs. If American businessmen cannot compete from here for the growing purchasing power of the European Common Market, many more will build their plants over there—and American labor will lose jobs. If we cannot find expanding outlets for the goods of an expanding economy, this Nation's growth will be stifled—and American labor will lose jobs.

In short, we are confronted with a very basic decision: are we going to export our goods and crops—or are we going to export our capital and our job opportunities? Are we going to be the free world's greatest merchant trader—or merely its temporarily wealthiest banker?

This is no time for timid answers or tired solutions. The European Economic Community is closing the history books on 2,000 years of divisive and self-centered trading philosophies. The new, once underdeveloped nations are seeking new outlets for their raw materials and new manufactures.

No part of the world market is any longer ours by default. The competition grows keener. Our need to cover military and other expenditures abroad through greater dollar sales grows increasingly urgent. And the Soviet Union's economic and trade offensive grows greater every year.

This is the challenge which confronts our Nation in the markets of the world. America must rise to this challenge. Wherever our goods are offered in competition with the goods of other nations— whether at home or overseas—our goods must be offered at competitive prices.

This means that management must intensify its efforts to increase efficiency and thus stabilize or reduce unit costs and prices. This means that labor must demonstrate its responsibility in helping to keep overall wage movements in line with increases in productivity. And this means that the Federal Government must launch a new effort to scale down the barriers to our selling abroad.

When the current Reciprocal Trade Agreements Act expires in June, it must be replaced by a wholly new and bold approach, as revolutionary as the changes now going on in European commerce, as broad as our economic potential demands and deserves, and as challenging as the crisis and opportunity now facing American business and labor.

Import Competition.—There will be those who will oppose our new trade legislation and urge American labor to oppose it. Either they will not recognize, or they will not want you to recognize, five basic facts about import competition:

(1) The fact that we sell $5 billion more than we buy from the nations of the world—with favorable trade balances in Japan and every other major country—and that we need this new legislative authority to keep this balance in our favor, to help pay, among other obligations, for our forces stationed overseas;

(2) The fact that, once needless restraints are removed, the great bulk of American goods, produced by American know-how and with American efficiency, can compete with any goods and any prices anywhere in the world;

(3) The fact that about 70 percent of the goods we import are not produced at all in our own country, or not produced in sufficient quantity to affect many jobs, but must be imported to keep our own industrial wheels turning and our own stores and households supplied;

(4) The fact that those imports which do compete with our own products now represent only 1 percent of our total national production; and

(5) The fact, finally, that as our exports increase along with our imports, many more jobs will be created than lost. For if we cannot secure easy access to the Common Market for our exports, some portions of American industry may choose instead to build plants abroad rather than at home, with an added loss of jobs for American workers. We have no intention, may I add, of imposing controls on the export of our capital; but we have asked the Congress to remove needless tax concessions to investment in industrialized countries which

encourage American companies to build their plants abroad and then compete with our own goods both in our own markets and all over the world.

Trade Adjustment Assistance.—Nevertheless it is a fact that what is true for the Nation as a whole may not be true for particular companies, for individual workers. There will be cases in which some communities, some businesses, and some workers will not be able to maintain their footing against increased competition. I do not intend to see them made victims for the national welfare. I do not intend to give them a medal and an empty grocery bag.

Just as our Government helped in the readjustment of men from military to civilian life—just as it helped in the reconversion of our economy from wartime to a peacetime basis—so, too, does it have an obligation to help those who must adjust to a national trade policy adopted for the national good.

We could, of course, give those who claim injury what they mistakenly believe to be more absolute protection—raising our tariffs, driving potential trading partners into the arms of the Soviets, denying competitive prices to our consumers and industry, and shutting off the export markets abroad on which our own job and growth opportunities depend. That is one alternative—and in the long run, it only postpones or prolongs the agony of those who seek it.

But there is another alternative, I first proposed it in 1954 and I shall propose it to the Congress again next year. And that is to include in our trade proposals a program for adjustment assistance—a program to help those few communities, industries and workers who may actually be injured by increased import competition.

Such a program will supplement and coordinate, not duplicate, what we are already doing or proposing to do for depressed areas, for small business, for investment incentives, and for the retraining and compensation of our unemployed workers.

This cannot be and will not be a program of permanent Government paternalism. It is instead a program to afford time for American initiative, American adaptability, and American resiliency to assert themselves. Temporary tariff relief may be a part of the prescription in individual cases.

Whatever is required, we will make certain that no community suffers unduly from trade. For, on the contrary, America must trade—or suffer.

These are all, to be sure, new and untried concepts—but our challenges are new as well. America did not reach its present greatness by standing still, by refusing to try, to dare, to move ahead across uncharted seas. Now we must dare and do and move again—for the gain of the free spirit and for the profit of our souls.

500 Message to the Government and People of Tanganyika on the Occasion of Their Independence. *December 8, 1961*

ON BEHALF of the people of the United States of America, I extend the heartiest congratulations to the government and people of Tanganyika on the occasion of their independence.

Tanganyika's leaders, above all Prime Minister Julius Nyerere, and its people have brought their land to Freedom and equality among nations in a manner that has won the admiration of all Americans. For Americans also cherish individual liberty and national independence, and they share with Tanganyikans the knowledge that these goals are achieved and maintained only at the cost of unremitting labor and sacrifice.

Americans also share with the people of Tanganyika a profound respect for the prin-

ciples of the United Nations Charter. Tanganyika has passed to independence through a period of United Nations trusteeship under British administration. It is gratifying that this period ends with continuing cooperation between these two sovereign friends of the United States. Gratifying also is this new nation's example in the exercise of human rights in which Tanganyikans of different racial origins band as one to the task of economic and social progress. This new nation brings to world councils a welcome sense of responsibility and a staunch independence.

The people of the United States of America shall work to multiply and strengthen bonds of friendship with the government and people of Tanganyika. We look forward to working together with Tanganyikans in the cause of freedom, dignity and peace.

NOTE: The message was delivered to Prime Minister Julius Nyerere at Dar-es-Salaam on December 9 by Franklin D. Roosevelt, Jr., the President's personal representative at the Tanganyika independence celebration.

The message was released at Palm Beach, Fla.

501   Remarks to a Delegation of Women Assigned to Missions of the United Nations. *December* 11, 1961

LADIES, I want to express my great satisfaction in welcoming you to the White House. And also as a citizen not merely of the United States but also as an inhabitant of the globe in difficult times I want to express my appreciation to you and the appreciation of the people of this country for your efforts in the United Nations.

I was present in 1945 at San Francisco, as a member of the press, at the time that the United Nations was born. I know that at different times in the last 15 or 16 years this organization has come under criticism in many countries—I am sure all of yours, and my own here in the United States.

But recalling what Robert Frost, one of our poets, once said, "Don't take down the fence until you know why it was put up," I have a strong conviction that we should seek to strengthen the United Nations and make it the kind of instrument which all of us hope it will be.

I don't think, really, in any sense, the United Nations has failed as a concept. I think occasionally we fail it. And the more that we can do to strengthen the idea of a community of the world, to seek to develop manners by which the tensions of the world and the problems of the world can be solved in an orderly and peaceful way, I think that's in the common interest of all.

The United Nations has survived 16 difficult years. Countries once unknown have come into existence and are playing important parts in the United Nations. It has come to the present day and plays a most important part in the lives of all of us.

So I congratulate you for the work that you have done. We want you to know that you are very welcome to this country. We are glad that you are seeing something—however much we all admire New York, we are glad you are seeing something of the United States besides New York. And we hope that while you are visiting here you will come not only to Washington and New York, which in a sense are rather special parts of this country, but also go perhaps even to Boston and even further West.

I want to thank you very much indeed.

[*The U.N. delegate from Burma responded to the President's welcome. In her remarks she stated that when a woman was elected President, she was sure that the President would invite the men delegates to the White House. The President then resumed speaking.*]

I want to say that I had not expected that the standard of revolt would be raised in the royal pavilion here, but I'm always rather nervous about how you talk about women who are active in politics, whether they want to be talked about as women or as politicians, but I want you to know that we are grateful to have you as both today. Thank you very much.

NOTE: The President spoke in the Rose Garden at the White House.

502   Remarks at the Swearing In of Chester Bowles as the President's Special Representative and Adviser on African, Asian, and Latin American Affairs. *December 12, 1961*

I WANT to state what a pleasure it is to have Mr. Bowles accept this position of responsibility. As has already been announced, he's going to bear special burdens in the areas of Latin America, Africa, the Middle East, and Asia, that very vital section of our globe upon which so many pressures and forces now press and beat and move.

He is going to accompany me on our trip this weekend to Puerto Rico, Venezuela, and Colombia in his first days in this office, and then on other occasions will be traveling himself, and with me, and with others of the administration who have special competence in these vital matters.

So I want to say, Ambassador, you've had a long career of public service, but I can think of no job that you've had which carries with it so many responsibilities and burdens. And I think that the members of the Department of State and the members of the White House—and certainly Mr. Rusk, and speaking for myself personally, will count very heavily upon your counsel and experience in the coming days.

So we're glad to have you here.

NOTE: The ceremonies were held in the Fish Room at the White House.

503   Letter to Governor Rockefeller on Civil Defense. *December 14, 1961*

[Released December 14, 1961. Dated December 13, 1961]

Dear Governor Rockefeller:

I wish to express my personal thanks for the advice and assistance you have given in shaping the program on civil defense which I shall present to the Congress next year. Through your participation in the Civil Defense Committee of the Governors Conference you have helped the Department of Defense, to whom I have given the responsibility for our fallout shelter program, reach the indispensable understanding of problems at the state and local levels which any successful program must plan to meet.

I have assigned responsibility for the shelter program to the Department of Defense to underline the fact that a civil defense effort must be kept in proper perspective in relation to our other defense efforts, as well as because of the organizational and technical capabilities which that Department possesses.

I appreciate your taking the time from your busy schedule to help us in this way.

Sincerely,

JOHN F. KENNEDY

[The Honorable Nelson Rockefeller, Governor of the State of New York, Albany, New York]

504 Statement by the President on the Establishment of the
President's Commission on the Status of Women.
December 14, 1961

FORTY-ONE years have passed since the first national election in which women were permitted to vote.

As was foreseen by the early leaders, women have brought into public affairs great sensitivity to human need and opposition to selfish and corrupt purposes. These political contributions and the manifold activities of women in American communities are the outgrowth of a long tradition of pioneering by American women. They stand as an encouraging example to countries in which women are only now achieving equal political and social status.

Yet we do well not to be complacent about past progress. Undoubtedly the ever-advancing frontier in our country helped to break down attitudes carried over from feudal days. But we have by no means done enough to strengthen family life and at the same time encourage women to make their full contribution as citizens.

If our Nation is to be successful in the critical period ahead, we must rely upon the skills and devotion of all our people. In every time of crisis, women have served our country in difficult and hazardous ways. They will do so now, in the home and at work. We naturally deplore those economic conditions which require women to work unless they desire to do so, and the programs of our Administration are designed to improve family incomes so that women can make their own decisions in this area. Women should not be considered a marginal group to be employed periodically only to be denied opportunity to satisfy their needs and aspirations when unemployment rises or a war ends.

Women have basic rights which should be respected and fostered as part of our Nation's commitment to human dignity, freedom, and democracy.

It is appropriate at this time, when we are observing Human Rights Week, to set forth before the world the story of women's progress in a free, democratic society, to review recent accomplishments, and to acknowledge frankly the further steps that must be taken.

This is a task for the entire Nation.

To help with specific analysis and recommendations, I am today, upon the recommendation of the Secretary of Labor, establishing The President's Commission on the Status of Women. I am directing appropriate Federal departments and agencies to cooperate with the Commission in developing plans for advancing the full partnership of men and women in our national life.

The Commission is to complete its work and publish a report by October 1, 1963. I am asking that it consider the following broad range of topics, making recommendations on those where constructive action is needed:

1. Employment policies and practices of the Federal Government.

2. Employment policies and practices, including those on wages, under Federal contracts.

3. Effects of Federal social insurance programs and tax laws on the net earnings and other income of women.

4. Appraisal of Federal and State labor laws dealing with such matters as hours, night work, and wages, to determine whether they are accomplishing the purposes

799

for which they were established and whether they need to be adapted to changing technological, economic, and social conditions.

5. Differences in legal treatment of men and women in regard to political and civil rights, property rights, and family relations.

6. New and expanded services that may be required for women as wives, mothers, and workers, including education, counseling, training, home services, and arrangements for care of children during the working day.

In addition to its own small staff, the Commission will be assisted by the U.S. Department of Labor, the Civil Service Commission, and other appropriate Federal agencies. It will seek the cooperation of a wide variety of individuals and civic groups, especially national organizations which have already done so much to advance women's welfare; it will request information from the States on their laws and experience; it will utilize subcommittees to develop proposals in specialized fields.

It is my hope that the Commission's Report will indicate what remains to be done to demolish prejudices and outmoded customs which act as barriers to the full partnership of women in our democracy. The Commission will welcome recommendations from all groups on this crucial matter. Progress will require the cooperation of the whole community.

Many of the old legal disabilities have been swept away. Some still remain. But more than their removal is required. Attention must be given to opening up greater employment opportunities for women as well as removing remaining discriminations against them.

The great majority of women now seek gainful employment at some period of their lives. The community should make it possible for them to make the best use of their talents and to function constructively, both through legislation and through necessary supportive services by private or public agencies.

Women are entitled to equality of opportunity for employment in government and in industry. But a mere statement supporting equality of opportunity must be implemented by affirmative steps to see that the doors are really open for training, selection, advancement, and equal pay.

I believe that Federal employment practices should be a showcase of the feasibility and value of combining genuine equality of opportunity on the basis of merit with efficient service to the public.

It is my firm intent that the Federal career service be maintained in every respect without discrimination and with equal opportunity for employment and advancement. I have, therefore, requested the Chairman of the Civil Service Commission to review pertinent personnel policies and practices affecting the employment of women and to work with the various departments and agencies to assure that selection for any career position is hereafter made solely on the basis of individual merit and fitness, without regard to sex.

NOTE: Executive Order 10980 "Establishing the President's Commission on the Status of Women" was issued by the President on December 14, 1961 (26 F.R. 12059).

The release lists 26 members appointed to the Commission, including Mrs. Eleanor Roosevelt as chairman, Dr. Richard A. Lester, Professor of Economics, Princeton University, as vice chairman, and Mrs. Esther Peterson, Assistant Secretary of Labor, as executive vice chairman.

505   Exchange of Messages With the President of the Republic of Viet-Nam.   *December* 15, 1961

Dear Mr. President:

I have received your recent letter in which you described so cogently the dangerous condition caused by North Viet-Nam's efforts to take over your country. The situation in your embattled country is well known to me and to the American people. We have been deeply disturbed by the assault on your country. Our indignation has mounted as the deliberate savagery of the Communist program of assassination, kidnapping and wanton violence became clear.

Your letter underlines what our own information has convincingly shown—that the campaign of force and terror now being waged against your people and your Government is supported and directed from the outside by the authorities at Hanoi. They have thus violated the provisions of the Geneva Accords designed to ensure peace in Viet-Nam and to which they bound themselves in 1954.

At that time, the United States, although not a party to the Accords, declared that it "would view any renewal of the aggression in violation of the agreements with grave concern and as seriously threatening international peace and security." We continue to maintain that view.

In accordance with that declaration, and in response to your request, we are prepared to help the Republic of Viet-Nam to protect its people and to preserve its independence. We shall promptly increase our assistance to your defense effort as well as help relieve the destruction of the floods which you describe. I have already given the orders to get these programs underway.

The United States, like the Republic of Viet-Nam, remains devoted to the cause of peace and our primary purpose is to help your people maintain their independence. If the Communist authorities in North Viet-Nam will stop their campaign to destroy the Republic of Viet-Nam, the measures we are taking to assist your defense efforts will no longer be necessary. We shall seek to persuade the Communists to give up their attempts of force and subversion. In any case, we are confident that the Vietnamese people will preserve their independence and gain the peace and prosperity for which they have sought so hard and so long.

JOHN F. KENNEDY

NOTE: President Diem's letter, released with the President's reply, follows:

Dear Mr. President:

Since its birth, more than six years ago, the Republic of Viet-Nam has enjoyed the close friendship and cooperation of the United States of America.

Like the United States, the Republic of Viet-Nam has always been devoted to the preservation of peace. My people know only too well the sorrows of war. We have honored the 1954 Geneva Agreements even though they resulted in the partition of our country and the enslavement of more than half of our people by Communist tyranny. We have never considered the reunification of our nation by force. On the contrary, we have publicly pledged that we will not violate the demarcation line and the demilitarized zone set up by the agreements. We have always been prepared and have on many occasions stated our willingness to reunify Viet-Nam on the basis of democratic and truly free elections.

The record of the Communist authorities in the northern part of our country is quite otherwise. They not only consented to the division of Viet-Nam, but were eager for it. They pledged themselves to observe the Geneva Agreements and during the seven years since have never ceased to violate them. They call for free elections but are ignorant of the very meaning of the words. They talk of "peaceful reunification" and wage war against us.

From the beginning, the Communists resorted to terror in their efforts to subvert our people, destroy our government, and impose a Communist regime upon us. They have attacked defenseless teachers, closed schools, killed members of our anti-malarial program and looted hospitals. This is coldly calculated to destroy our government's humanitarian efforts to serve our people.

We have long sought to check the Communist attack from the North on our people by appeals to the International Control Commission. Over the years, we have repeatedly published to the world the evidence of the Communist plot to overthrow our government and seize control of all of Viet-Nam by illegal intrusions from outside our country. The evidence has mounted until now it is hardly necessary to rehearse it. Most recently, the kidnapping and brutal murder of our Chief Liaison Officer to the International Control Commission, Colonel Noang Thuy Nam, compelled us to speak out once more. In our October 24, 1961, letter to the ICC, we called attention again to the publicly stated determination of the Communist authorities in Hanoi to "liberate the South" by the overthrow of my government and the imposition of a Communist regime on our people. We cited the proof of massive infiltration of Communist agents and military elements into our country. We outlined the Communist strategy, which is simply the ruthless use of terror against the whole population, women and children included.

In the course of the last few months, the Communist assault on my people has achieved high ferocity. In October they caused more than 1,800 incidents of violence and more than 2,000 casualties. They have struck occasionally in battalion strength, and they are continually augmenting their forces by infiltration from the North. The level of their attacks is already such that our forces are stretched to the utmost. We are forced to defend every village, every hamlet, indeed every home against a foe whose tactic is always to strike at the defenseless.

A disastrous flood was recently added to the misfortunes of the Vietnamese people. The greater part of three provinces was inundated, with a great loss of property. We are now engaged in a nationwide effort to reconstruct and rehabilitate this area. The Communists are, of course, making this task doubly difficult, for they have seized upon the disruption of normal administration and communications as an opportunity to sow more destruction in the stricken area.

In short, the Vietnamese nation now faces what is perhaps the gravest crisis in its long history. For more than 2,000 years my people have lived and built, fought and died in this land. We have not always been free. Indeed, much of our history and many of its proudest moments have arisen from conquest by foreign powers and our struggle against great odds to regain or defend our precious independence. But it is not only our freedom which is at stake today, it is our national identity. For, if we lose this war, our people will be swallowed by the Communist Bloc, all our proud heritage will be blotted out by the "Socialist society" and Viet-Nam will leave the pages of history. We will lose our national soul.

Mr. President, my people and I are mindful of the great assistance which the United States has given us. Your help has not been lightly received, for the Vietnamese are proud people, and we are determined to do our part in the defense of the free world. It is clear to all of us that the defeat of the Viet Cong demands the total mobilization of our government and our people, and you may be sure that we will devote all of our resources of money, minds, and men to this great task.

But Viet-Nam is not a great power and the forces of International Communism now arrayed against us are more than we can meet with the resources at hand. We must have further assistance from the United States if we are to win the war now being waged against us.

We can certainly assure mankind that our action is purely defensive. Much as we regret the subjugation of more than half our people in North Viet-Nam, we have no intention, and indeed no means, to free them by use of force.

I have said that Viet-Nam is at war. War means many things, but most of all it means the death of brave people for a cause they believe in. Viet-Nam has suffered many wars, and through the centuries we have always had patriots and heroes who were willing to shed their blood for Viet-Nam. We will keep faith with them.

When Communism has long ebbed away into the past, my people will still be here, a free united nation growing from the deep roots of our Vietnamese heritage. They will remember your help in our time of need. This struggle will then be a part of our common history. And your help, your friendship, and the strong bonds between our two peoples will be a part of Viet-Nam, then as now.

NGO DINH DIEM

506 Remarks Upon Arrival at International Airport, San Juan, Puerto Rico. *December 15, 1961*

Governor:

It is a great experience to fly many hundreds of miles over the Atlantic Ocean to come to an island and be greeted in Spanish, to come to an island which has an entirely different tradition and history, which is made up of people of an entirely different cultural origin than on the mainland of the United States, and still be able to feel that I am in my country, here in this city and island, as I was in my country in Washington this morning.

And I'm particularly appreciative and glad that I've been welcomed by you, Governor. What you and your devoted associates and the people of this island have been able to do in the last decade, to build a better life, to tackle the difficult problems of education, and housing, and employment, and all the rest, has given us inspiration to feel that we can carry on a great cooperative effort throughout the entire hemisphere. And I think it most appropriate that the man who served under you in this great enterprise, Ambassador Ted Moscoso, who was our Ambassador to Venezuela, should now be the Director of the Alliance for Progress and be able to hold up encouragement to people everywhere in this hemisphere by pointing to what has been done on this island. And

also, another devoted public servant from this island, Arturo Morales-Carrion, who is now our Deputy Assistant Secretary of State for Latin America.

Puerto Rico serves as an admirable bridge between Latin America and North America. You have, I think, served to make it easier for us to understand each other, and therefore it is most important and appropriate that we should start this journey to two great countries, Venezuela and Colombia, that we should come here first.

I want to express the thanks of all of us to you—you welcomed our Peace Corps representatives and gave them training which I think has contributed to their success.

We come here today and I will value your counsel, and I'm sure as a result of our stay here that our journeys tomorrow and Sunday will be more fruitful.

Governor, I'm grateful to you, and I am grateful to your people. We have many of them on the mainland, and they are among our best citizens—and I'm glad to be in America this afternoon.

NOTE: The President's opening remark "Governor" referred to Luis Muñoz Marin, Governor of Puerto Rico.

Another text of these remarks was released by the White House prior to the actual delivery.

507 Remarks Upon Arrival at Maiquetia Airport, Caracas, Venezuela. *December 16, 1961*

Mr. President:

I'm more than happy to come to your country on my first visit as President of the United States, to one of our sister Republics in this hemisphere. And I am also proud

to be the first President of the United States to visit this country.

But in a very real sense I follow in the footsteps of my distinguished predecessor, President Franklin Roosevelt, who devoted so much of his efforts, so much of his talents to binding together the countries of this hemisphere, who are united by nature and united in their common aspirations.

We are, in my country, committed in the 1960's to seeing the work which was so effectively begun in the 1930's in the Good Neighbor policy—to see it come to fruition in a whole series of free societies stretching from the north to the south, free and sovereign and independent countries, inhabited by free people who are gradually increasing their standard of living, educating their children, housing their families, finding work for their people and security for their old age.

This is what we want for the people of my country—and this is what we want for the people of this hemisphere.

And I am proud to come here to this country where your distinguished President has for many months committed himself—long before the phrase was begun—committed himself to the principles of the Alianza para el Progreso. He has shown in this country what can be done, and therefore I am proud to come here, and I hope in the time that we are here that I will benefit from his counsel and advice.

Mr. President, Mrs. Kennedy and I are delighted to be your guests and we are proud to be here among your people.

Thank you very much.

NOTE: The President's opening words "Mr. President" referred to Romulo Betancourt, President of Venezuela.

Another text of these remarks was released by the White House prior to the actual delivery.

508   Remarks to the Staff at the American Embassy in Caracas. *December 16, 1961*

Ambassador, Mr. Stewart:

I want to express my thanks to you all, and to tell you that my wife and I have been most appreciative of the generous welcome which we've received from the people of this country.

I'm sure you realize how vital is the post to which you have been sent, and how important your work is to the United States. The first real effort which our country ever made in the field of international affairs involved our relations with this hemisphere and our sister Republics to the south. And a great stream, really, running through our national life in the United States has been our desire to establish closer and more intimate bonds.

This is particularly true in the 1960's, and we have, since our inception in January,

made this really great concentrated effort. The fact that we asked our Ambassador here to come home from this vital post to take over the leadership of the Alliance for Progress, I think this indicates how important we feel it is, before this decade is out, that the United States and Venezuela and other countries of the hemisphere are bound together in an effort to improve the life of all of our people.

Unless the United States is able to identify itself with this cause successfully, then all of our great efforts for freedom are going to be of no avail. This is a vital cause, and I am sure that in all your work here in this country, I hope that you emphasize how strongly we feel in our desire to join with them in an effort to raise the standard of living of the people of the entire hemisphere, through a system of freedom.

I consider this the most vital responsibility that any citizen of the United States stationed in this hemisphere can have. And I'm confident that you emphasize this daily in your work.

I want the United States to be identified with progress and with the welfare of the people, not as a distant great power which is uninterested in this hemisphere except in times of crisis. We want them to feel that day by day we are joined with them as partners—not only as neighbors but as partners and friends, in this common effort.

And therefore, I am very proud to be the first President of the United States to visit this country and I'm also very proud that I came here to begin this journey, and then to Colombia, because of the great efforts that the people of this country are making to improve their own lives.

I can't tell the difference between the natives of Venezuela and the Americans—maybe you could hold up your hands, all of you who work here, who happen to be citizens of this country. We want you to know how much we appreciate your service, and I hope you realize that in working for the United States, I think in the best sense you also are serving your country. We're grateful to all of you, and I am very grateful to those of you who are my fellow countrymen, and also to those who are fortunate enough to grow up and be able to speak Spanish, and serve as a bridge between the United States and this country in the coming years.

Thank you very much.

NOTE: In his opening words the President referred to Teodoro Moscoso, Former Ambassador to Venezuela, and C. Allan Stewart, Charge d'Affaires at the American Embassy in Caracas.

509   Remarks at the La Morita Resettlement Project Near Caracas. *December 16, 1961*

President Betancourt, Governor, ladies and gentlemen:

I want to express to you our warm appreciation and thanks for the generous welcome which you have given to Mrs. Kennedy and myself, and I know that in welcoming us you extend the hand of friendship to the people of my country who are so vitally interested and concerned with the common destiny of our hemisphere. And for this welcome we both thank you.

Tomorrow is the 131st anniversary of the birth of the great liberator of this country, who not only had the satisfaction and pride in liberating this country but also in a feat almost unprecedented in history, provided for the freedom and liberation of five countries—and I refer of course to Simon Bolivar.

I come here today in a tradition originated by him who saw and predicted that some day this hemisphere would be bound together by the closest of fraternal ties. And I come in the footsteps of a distinguished predecessor, Franklin Roosevelt, who in his own time and generation attempted to bring to fruition the work which Simon Bolivar had so well begun.

We today share the realization which President Roosevelt expressed in 1944, when he said that "true individual freedom cannot exist without economic security and independence."

With a system of national independence originated over a hundred years ago, with a policy of friendship and good neighborliness which was developed in the administration of President Roosevelt, now today in 1961 it is our obligation to move ahead and to bring to fruition the concept that along with national independence and individual liberty goes the well-being of the people themselves.

We do not merely talk of slogans, of democracy and freedom. It is our function here in this hemisphere in 1961 to make it possible for all the people not only to be free but to have a home and educate their children, and have a job for themselves and in security. And that is what we're determined to do.

Economic security, the bringing of a better life to all of our people must now be, in the sixties, the principal object and goal of the Inter-American system. And what is happening here today at La Morita, in pursuit of that goal, symbolizes the gigantic new steps that are now being taken.

From this day forward the Inter-American system represents not merely the unity of the governments that are involved, but the unity of peoples; not only a common goal of political alignment, but a common vow by all of our governments and all of our people to improve man's economic, social, and political well-being; not just an alliance for the protection of our countries, but an alliance of progress for our people. We will be, in the 1960's, more than good neighbors. We will be partners in building a better life for our people.

And here in Venezuela the meaning of the new Alianza para el Progreso is being demonstrated, for you have made a tradition and transition from a repressive dictatorship to a free life for the people of this country, to progressive democratic rule under one of the great democratic statesmen of the Western Hemisphere, your distinguished President Romulo Betancourt. And one of the first goals of the new spirit of this hemi-

sphere must be the elimination of tyranny from the north to the south, until this is a hemisphere, as Simon Bolivar once predicted, of free men and free countries, living under a system of liberty.

Mr. President, the achievement of these two freedoms, freedom from dictatorship and freedom from the bonds of economic and social injustice, must be the contribution of our generation in this decade.

It is in pursuit of these goals that I have come with you to La Morita. It is a long way from the noisy streets of Washington, D.C., to this field—but it is in this field and in fields and cities across our hemisphere that this battle must be fought—not in speeches by Presidents, or exchanges of diplomats, or studies by experts—though all those are important; but the work must be done here, here today, and tomorrow, all through this hemisphere, until our people live the kind of life, Mr. President, for which you have dedicated your life and to which the people of my country are committed.

Today, 86 families will receive titles to their own homes under a program which is already settled—38,000 families on 3,800,000 acres of land. This is your program, the program of your progressive, far-seeing government, and the people of my country will share in this program by making available more loans to build rural homes and more credits to finance your crops.

This program is at the heart of the Alianza para el Progreso, for no real progress is possible unless the benefits of increased prosperity are shared by the people themselves.

I do not hold the view, which some now preach, that the only way we can make economic progress is through dictatorship. I believe the reverse. I believe that the experiences of Eastern Europe, the wall in Berlin, the famine in China, the hardships in our own hemisphere, show that liberty and economic progress go hand in hand, provided the people and the government together are committed to progress for the people.

Ladies and gentlemen, I shall return to Washington on Monday and tell the people of my country that you and they are bound together in one of the great adventures of human experience, to make of our hemisphere a bright and shining light for all the world.

The United States and Venezuela are bound together and in the 1960's I believe that we can demonstrate so that all the world will want to follow our example—that free-

dom and prosperity can move hand in hand, and I am proud today to stand on this platform with your distinguished President, who has been working in this field for so many years, and who now is showing the people of this country and hemisphere what real progress for the people can mean.

I express our thanks to you, and I can tell you that the people of my country—in good times and bad—are committed to the progress of your people and this hemisphere.

Thank you very much.

NOTE: In his opening words the President referred to Romulo Betancourt, President of Venezuela, and J. M. Perez, Governor of the State of Aragua.

510 Joint Statement Following Discussions With the President of Venezuela. *December* 17, 1961

DURING their meeting in Caracas on December 16, 1961, the Presidents of the United States of America and of the Republic of Venezuela, John F. Kennedy and Romulo Betancourt, agreed to make the following declaration:

1. They reaffirm the irrevocable friendship of the two peoples and governments.

2. They confirm their adherence to the principles and standards of the United Nations and the Organization of American States which are dedicated to respect for human rights—to the effective practice of representative Democracy, with equal opportunity for all—to free self-determination by the people and to non-intervention.

3. They have confidence that freedom will prevail in all American countries and that the problems troubling America and the world will be solved peacefully.

4. The two Presidents expressed their determination to achieve the objectives of the Alianza para el Progreso in accord with the principles of the act of Bogota and Punta

del Este charter, and they discussed mutual Venezuelan and United States actions which are necessary for this purpose. Venezuela's achievement in formulating and implementing a realistic long-range plan for economic and social development, especially in the fields of industrial and agricultural development, land reform, education, housing and water supply, were reviewed in connection with the need to mobilize additional domestic and external resources. Substantial new loans, in addition to those already provided, are under consideration by the Inter-American Development Bank.

5. Both Presidents agreed that a special effort is necessary in 1962 to assure large-scale development of industry and commerce, both to reinforce the present pattern of recovery from Venezuela's 1960–1961 recession and to achieve sustained levels of economic growth with rapid improvements in living standards of underprivileged groups not yet reached by the development process.

6. Both Presidents expressed their con-

viction that far-reaching efforts in the social field in accordance with the spirit of the Alliance for Progress should go hand in hand with economic development programs. The prices of basic commodities and commercial practices of importing countries must give effective recognition to Latin America's dependence on exports. Such recognition is a vital factor in carrying out the spirit and letter of the charter of Punta del Este.

7. The Presidents discussed the great importance to the Venezuelan people of the large Guri Hydro-electric Dam as the base for intensive development of the Guayana Region. Special consideration was given to Venezuelan programs for slum clearance, low-cost housing and municipal and community development. The Presidents believe also that this stimulating approach should have wide applicability in accelerating local development, in solving the most important local problems and, equally important, in taking advantage of local eco-

nomic opportunities through community initiative.

8. During the next few months Venezuelan and United States officials will discuss in detail development loans and technical assistance to be provided by the United States Agency for International Development and other measures to support the Venezuelan Development Program and strengthen United States-Venezuelan economic relations. President Kennedy pledged all possible United States support and assistance to enable Venezuela to implement its development program on schedule, complementing Venezuelan efforts to this end.

9. President Kennedy and President Betancourt joined in expressing their hope that this statement made today in the birth place of Simon Bolivar will be received by the peoples of this continent as a message of faith and optimism.

NOTE: The joint statement was issued at Miraflores Palace in Caracas.

511 Remarks at Maiquetia Airport Upon Leaving for Colombia. *December 17, 1961*

Mr. President:

I want to express, on behalf of Mrs. Kennedy and myself, our great appreciation to you, sir, and Madame Betancourt, and also to the people of Venezuela and especially to the people of this city, who have made us most welcome.

I think this visit—I hope—has pleased our friends—confounded our enemies; and I think that it has brought our two countries,

whose fate has been so interwoven from our earliest days, closer together.

So, Mr. President, I don't think that we will travel any place where our welcome will be more heart-warming, and where we will leave with greater appreciation. And I hope in this way to give some slight indication of how grateful I am to all of you for making us feel so much at home.

512   Remarks Upon Arrival at El Dorado Airport, Bogotá, Colombia. *December 17, 1961*

Mr. President:

I want to express my great appreciation to you and to the people of this country for their generous welcome to my wife and to myself.

The relations which have existed between the United States and Colombia stretch back to the earliest days of both of our nations, and it is a source of pride to me, and I'm sure it is to you, that this country was the first of all of the countries of Latin America that broke relations with the Axis at the beginning of World War II, and was the only country during the difficult and dark days of the Korean War that sent a detachment to fight with great distinction.

Of the one thousand men in that detachment, over two-thirds of them were casualties, and of the 29 soldiers of this country who were taken prisoner, not one displayed anything but the strongest resistance and the strongest courage.

So I come here today to express our warm feeling of friendship, with great sincerity, to the people of this country.

We believe in freedom—in the United States and in Colombia. We are opposed to tyranny of any kind. We are for the social justice for our people, because we recognize that we cannot have freedom unless all of our people have an equal opportunity to the advantages of a productive life—homes—education—work.

These are the things to which the Alliance for Progress—the Alianza para el Progreso—is committed. And therefore, Mr. President, it is particularly appropriate that I should come to this country where you have taken so many steps to put into actual implementation the ideals and the practices to which we are committed.

It is a great pleasure and a source of pride and satisfaction to come here as President of the United States, and to extend once again our hand of friendship to you, and to accept the hand of friendship which you have so generously shown us today.

NOTE: The President's opening words "Mr. President" referred to Alberto Lleras Camargo, President of Colombia.

Another text of these remarks was released by the White House prior to the actual delivery.

513   Remarks at the Techo Housing Project in Bogotá. *December 17, 1961*

Mr. President:

I have come here today to reply to a speech which your distinguished President gave more than a year ago in Washington: "I do hope," Lleras Camargo said in Washington, "that as we come to understand our reciprocal problems better, by virtue of our same faith in our democratic system and in the creative power of liberty . . . we shall go on shaping in this part of the world a better dwelling place for men."

We have come to this open field today to join in making this a better dwelling place for men. And it is, I know, a source of pride to my people, as I'm sure it is to yours, to see this great effort to provide better housing for our people in this hemisphere.

We all of us believe in freedom. The great fight over the past decade in this hemisphere has been the fight against tyranny and dictatorship in countries which have been part of our sister Republics.

The great fight in the next 10 years, now that we have seen a whole system of new, progressive democracies established—the great fight in the next 10 years will be to make it possible for people to live a productive and fruitful life under a system of freedom. Those of us who love freedom realize that a man is not really free if he doesn't have a roof over his head, or if he cannot educate his children, or if he cannot find work, or if he cannot find security in his old age.

It is our responsibility, in this decade of the sixties, to provide the kind of life for our people that will permit freedom not only to survive but prevail—here and around the world, in every part of our hemisphere, in every part of the globe.

The Alianza para el Progreso is a phrase, but I think its real significance is here in this field. This is a battlefield, and I am glad that the Colombian Government under the leadership of your President and all of the people of this country—joining their efforts with the Inter-American Bank and the United States AID program—are going to see filling this field in the next months and years, home after home for people who desperately need it, schools for people who need to be educated, and a steadily rising standard of living for all of our people.

I therefore want to express my appreciation to all of you for your generosity in permitting us to be here today in Techo. There are other communities such as this across this country and across this hemisphere. And we are going to continue our efforts until in every part of our hemisphere the whole concept of progress and freedom is general.

We wish you success, and we are joined with you in this effort in the future, as we have on so many occasions in the past. We wish you well, and we want you to know that in my country we are committed to this effort, and we shall not desist from it until it has been completed.

Thank you.

NOTE: The President's opening words "Mr. President" referred to Alberto Lleras Camargo, President of Colombia.

514   Remarks at the San Carlos Palace to the American Embassy Staff in Bogotá. *December* 17, 1961

I WANT to express our thanks to you for being kind enough to come in from the embassy because we had planned to come out there but we were delayed.

I know that all of us as Americans are most appreciative of the generous reception which the people of this city and country have given us—and given us, really, in the name of the United States. And I know that their friendship for the United States is due in good part to your work here.

What we are anxious for is that the name of the United States and our reputation be identified as much as possible with the progressive interests of all the people. I hope that in all your work, and wherever you go, in all your contacts, that you will try as much as possible to associate yourselves with the well-being of all the people of Colombia, and to emphasize how concerned we are in the United States with the welfare of the people here—and throughout the entire hemisphere.

If we can do that, if the name of the United States can be identified with this great cause in the 1960's, then I think the interests of our country and the interests of freedom and the interests of this country are well served.

So I want to congratulate you on what you have done, and also to hope that in the future, as in the past, you will—on every day—attempt to, as much as possible, establish a most intimate relationship with the people of this country, holding out the hand of friendship to them.

You are, in addition to our distinguished Ambassador here, you are all ambassadors. When they see you they see the United States. Therefore, every one of you symbolizes our country, and that is a great re-sponsibility, far greater than it has ever been in the past.

So I am confident that those of you in the military, those of you in the AID program, the Information Service, and in the Foreign Service—those of you who may be secretaries in the embassies, all of you carry with you not only the prestige of the United States but also the reputation of the United States.

So we want to express our thanks to you for being kind enough to come to see us. We are indebted to you. And as I have said, I think the welcome we got today is in good part due to your efforts—and I know that you will continue them.

Thank you.

NOTE: The President spoke in the Cristo Salon at the San Carlos Palace. During his remarks he referred to Fulton Freeman, U.S. Ambassador to Colombia.

515   Address at a Dinner at the San Carlos Palace in Bogotá. *December* 17, 1961

Mr. President:

I want to express our great appreciation to the President for his generous words tonight, and also to the people of this city and to this country for their heart-warming welcome to Mrs. Kennedy and myself. I must say, that though we are far from home, you made us feel at home, so we want to express our thanks to you, and all of the citizens of your city and country.

In 1934, one of the greatest of my predecessors, President Franklin Roosevelt, was the first President of the United States to visit this country. He came in pursuit of a new policy—the policy of the Good Neighbor. This policy—based on the ideas of Bolivar and San Martin and Santander—recognized the common interests of the American states—denied that any nation in this hemisphere had the right to impose its will on any other nation—and called for a great cooperative effort to strengthen the spirit of human liberty here in the Americas.

I am here today—the second American President to visit Colombia—in that same spirit. For our generation also has a new policy—la Alianza para el Progreso. Today again, that policy calls for a joint effort to protect and extend the values of our civilization—going beyond the Good Neighbor policy to a great unified attack on the problems of our age. Today again, we deny the right of any state to impose its will upon any other. And today again, these new policies are based upon the vision and the imagination of the great statesmen of Latin America.

In 1960, your distinguished President, Dr. Lleras Camargo, addressed the United States Congress of which I was a Member. He spoke of the need for the American states to work together to conquer the evils of poverty and injustice. He called for participation by the United States. And, later in the same visit, he said, and I quote him, that "it is necessary to make a supreme effort in each country, with the cooperation of all the others, to prevent Western civilization from being threatened within the very stronghold that has defended it."

Those warnings of your President have been heard. The cooperative effort of our great free nations has begun. Help has already begun. And the stronghold of our civilization, the individual dignity of the individual, free man—has begun to strengthen the bulwarks of freedom.

No American has contributed more to this progress than your President who is universally admired as one of the great statesmen of this hemisphere. As a principal architect of the Rio Treaty and as Director General of the Organization of American States, he has striven to perfect the Inter-American system which was the dream of the man who once lived in this house— Simon Bolivar. And, recently, his bold initiative has strengthened the OAS against those extra-continental forces which seek to impose a new tyranny upon the Americas. As your President he has restored democratic government, strengthened your economy, and worked, within the free institutions, to improve the welfare of all Colombians. His concept of progressive, democratic government is at the heart of la Alianza para el Progreso. And I leave this country tonight

strengthened in purpose and understanding by his wise counsels.

But I know that Dr. Lleras Camargo would be the first to agree that even these impressive accomplishments of the past are inadequate in the face of the immense and urgent problems which now confront us.

Bolivar, in a letter written when he was in exile, and the cause of liberty seemed dim, wrote: "The veil has been torn asunder. We have already seen the light and it is not our desire to be thrust back into the darkness." In our time the veil again has been torn asunder. The millions of our people who have lived in hopeless poverty—patiently suffering hunger, social injustice, and ignorance—have now glimpsed the hope of a better and more abundant life for themselves and their children. And they do not intend to be thrust back into darkness.

La Alianza para el Progreso is designed to transform this hope into a reality. It calls for a vast and immediate effort on the part of all the Americas to satisfy the basic needs of our people for work and land, and homes and schools. It expects within the next ten years—the Decade of Development—to be well on the way toward satisfying these basic needs.

Much has already been done since la Alianza para el Progreso was announced on March 13. And today at Techo I saw some of the results of this effort.

There President Lleras and I—in the presence of the families of hundreds of workers—dedicated a housing project in which more than eighty thousand people will, for the first time, know what it will be like to live in a home in which they would want to raise their children. We also dedicated one of 18 schools—in which 30,000 children, the most valuable asset of this hemisphere—will be given their opportunity to study and to learn, and to build their lives.

And along with the social progress symbolized by the Techo project will also come an intensive effort to develop and industrialize the economies of Latin America—reducing dependence on raw materials and steadily narrowing the relative gap between the wealthy industrialized countries and the Republics of Latin America.

Thus la Alianza para el Progreso is a program which is revolutionary in its dimensions. It calls for staggering efforts by us all and unprecedented changes by us all. It raises far-reaching aspirations and demands difficult sacrifices. And although we have already done much in a short time, we must do much more and act much more swiftly in the months to come. For on the success of the Alliance—on our success in this hemisphere—depends the future of that human dignity and national independence for which our forebears in every country of the hemisphere struggled.

After the American wars of independence, the President of Colombia, Santander, said: "Arms have given us independence; laws will give us freedom." These prophetic words I think indicate the history of our hemisphere. For our real progress has not come about through violence or tyranny, but under the guidance of democratic leaders who realized the great capacity of free society for peaceful change—men such as Franklin Roosevelt in my own country and your distinguished President in your country.

It is this knowledge and experience which is the great contribution of our nations to the other nations of the world. There are those who tell us that the only road to economic progress is by violent Communist revolution, followed by the complete subjection of man to the will of the state.

They come with banners proclaiming that they have new doctrines; that history is on their side. But, in reality, they bring a doctrine which is as old as the Pharaohs of Egypt, and like the Pharaohs of Egypt, doomed by history.

They promise free elections, and free speech, and freedom of religion. But once power is achieved, elections are eliminated, speech is stifled, and the worship of God is prohibited.

They pledge economic progress and increased human welfare. But they have been unable to fulfill these pledges and their failure is etched in the dramatic contrast between a free and powerful and prosperous Western Europe and the grim, drab poverty of Communist Eastern Europe, or the hunger of China, or the wall which separates West Berlin from East Berlin. The fact is that the wall and the rifle squads of the last twelve months have shown us again—if we did not need to be shown—that when such doctrines have had to face the united will of free men, they have been defeated.

We are a young and strong people. Our doctrines—the doctrines lit by the leaders of your country and mine—now burn brightly in Africa and Asia and wherever men struggle to be free. And here in our own hemisphere we have successfully resisted efforts to impose the despotisms of the Old World on the nations of the New.

Today we face the greatest challenge to the vitality of our American revolution. Millions of our people—scattered across a vast and rich continent—endure lives of misery. We must prove to them that free institutions can best answer their implacable demand for social justice, for food, for material welfare and above all, for a new hope—for themselves and for their children. And in so proving the blessings of freedom in Latin America, we will be teaching the same lesson to a watchful and impatient world.

We in the United States have made many mistakes in our relations with Latin America. We have not always understood the magnitude of your problems, or accepted our share of responsibility for the welfare of the hemisphere. But we are committed in the United States—our will and our energy—to an untiring pursuit of that welfare and I have come to this country to reaffirm that dedication.

The leaders of Latin America, the industrialists and the landowners are, I am sure, also ready to admit past mistakes and accept new responsibilities. For unless all of us are willing to contribute our resources to national development, unless all of us are prepared not merely to accept, but initiate, basic land and tax reforms, unless all of us take the lead in improving the welfare of our people; then that leadership will be taken from us and the heritage of centuries of Western civilization will be consumed in a few months of violence.

This is the message I bring to those of us who are here tonight—and I am grateful that I have had an opportunity to be with you.

But I also want to talk to those beyond this dinner table, and beyond this room, and this old house. And that message is for the millions of people in a thousand cities and villages throughout the mountains and lands of our hemisphere. To all of them— to the workers, to the *campesinos* on the farms, to the women who toil each day for the welfare of their children—to all we bring a message of hope. Every day, every hour, in my country and in this country, and in all the countries of this hemisphere dedicated men and women are struggling to bring nearer the day when all have more to eat, and a decent roof over their heads, and schools for their children—when all will have a better and more abundant life to accompany that human dignity to which all men are entitled, and that love of freedom to which all of us are committed by our inheritance and our desire.

And tonight, here in this old city, I pledge to you the commitment of the United States of America, to that great cause.

Thank you.

NOTE: The President spoke at 10:10 p.m. at the San Carlos Palace. His opening words "Mr. President" referred to Alberto Lleras Camargo, President of Colombia.

Another text of this address was released by the White House prior to its actual delivery.

516   Remarks at the El Dorado Airport Upon Leaving for the United States. *December 17, 1961*

Mr. President:

I want to, on behalf of my wife and myself, express our most sincere thanks to you, and to your wife, for your greeting which you have given us today—and also for the opportunity that you have given to us and to all of our countrymen to see your city and

country, and to realize how close are the links which bind Colombia and the United States.

Perhaps the most encouraging event of most recent years in the world of freedom has been the closer links which have been bound together and tied together in Western

Europe, and which are now being molded in the same effective way here in this hemisphere.

It is, it seems to me, obligatory upon all those of us who believe in freedom to work together to make freedom, as you have said, Mr. President, not merely an abstraction or a phrase, but to demonstrate that under a system of freedom people can live the kind of dignified, productive life to which they all aspire.

I said this morning at Techo that the great fight of the last decade in this hemisphere was against tyranny and dictatorships. The great fight in the next decade— the decade in which we are now upon—is to prove that freedom and abundance go hand in hand.

I return tonight to the United States, and I do not want to leave without saying to the people of Colombia that my wife and I have received the most heart-warming welcome that we have ever received.

Their words to us this morning, and again at midnight as we left this ancient city, I think will be the greatest source of encouragement to the people of the United States, to realize that we are together in a great enterprise which is worthy of our effort.

So I thank you, Mr. President, and I thank all your countrymen.

And now *hasta luego*. Thank you.

NOTE: The President's opening words "Mr. President" referred to Alberto Lleras Camargo, President of Colombia.

517 Statement by the President on the Situation in the Dominican Republic. *December 20, 1961*

I WANT to make special note of the most encouraging developments in the Dominican Republic. The solution to the political difficulties in that country, the principal feature of which is the immediate creation of a council of state, was announced by President Balaguer on December 17 and has now been accepted by the principal elements of the democratic opposition. It represents, in my judgment, an impressive demonstration of statesmanship and responsibility by all concerned. This accomplishment by the democratic opposition and the Dominican government is all the more remarkable when it is recalled that only recently the Dominican Republic emerged from three decades of a harshly repressive regime which dedicated itself to stifling every democratic Dominican voice. This victory of the Dominican people

and its leaders is a striking demonstration of the fact that dictatorship can suppress but cannot destroy the aspirations of a people to live in freedom, dignity and peace.

The Dominican people still face long and difficult efforts to transform their aspirations into an effective, soundly-based democratic system. In this struggle, they have the assurance of our sympathetic and tangible support. I understand that the Organization of American States is now considering the lifting of the sanctions imposed upon the Dominican Republic by collective action in August 1960 and January 1961. If the Council of the OAS takes such action—and our representatives are supporting that step— we will resume diplomatic relations with the Dominican Republic promptly. When this takes place the Department of Agriculture will authorize purchases under the Dominican allocation of non-quota sugar for the first six months of 1962.

In addition, I propose to send, upon the installation of the new council of state, a United States Economic Assistance Mission, headed by Ambassador Teodoro Moscoso of AID and including Deputy Assistant Secretary of State Milton Barall, to visit the Dominican Republic. Its purpose will be to explore emergency requirements and the possibilities for longer-range cooperative programs under the Alliance for Progress, which can be of direct benefit to the Dominican people. I expect that this mission will arrive in the Dominican Republic late this month or very early in January.

I understand that Mr. Felipe Herrera, President of the Inter-American Development Bank, will head a high-level mission to the Dominican Republic in the near future to begin discussions and inquire into economic and social development projects.

These actions are intended to assist the new Dominican government and people in developing a sound economic and social structure, which is indispensable to an enduring democratic political system.

The Dominican people and their leaders confront a great and seldom given opportunity: the construction of a democratic society on the ruins of tyranny. It is a noble task, but it is not an easy one. We wish them well, and we assure them of our desire to assist them in their efforts.

NOTE: The statement was released at Palm Beach, Fla.

---

518 Remarks Upon Arrival at the Air Terminal in Hamilton, Bermuda. *December* 21, 1961

Your Excellency, Prime Minister:

I want to express my great pleasure at having an opportunity to talk to you again, and to visit you on your territory which has been the scene on other occasions of most important meetings beneficial to both our countries.

We have had, since I assumed the responsibility of the Presidency, meetings in Washington and in Florida and in London, and I think it most appropriate at this particular time in the affairs of the world that the United States and Great Britain should once again meet, and that we should have a chance to exchange our views and coordinate our policies.

So I am delighted to be here, Prime Minister, and I am most grateful to the Governor General for his warm welcome.

NOTE: Prime Minister Macmillan responded as follows:

"Mr. President, it is a very great pleasure to welcome you here on British soil where, as you say, other meetings have taken place between Presidents and Prime Ministers engaged in the task which occupies us—the strengthening of our friendship to preserve the peace of the world.

"That is what we are for—that is what we are trying to do.

"We are particularly grateful to you, Mr. President, for coming at a time of great personal anxiety and sorrow to you. We appreciate that. You have all our good wishes, and on speaking today I know that I speak not only for all those here assembled in this lovely island of Bermuda, but for all British people all over the world, wherever they may be.

"I thank you."

The President's opening words "Your Excellency" referred to Maj. Gen. Sir Julian Gascoigne, Governor of Bermuda.

519   Joint Statement Following Discussions in Bermuda With Prime Minister Macmillan.   *December 22, 1961*

THE PRESIDENT and the Prime Minister have had two days of valuable discussions surveying the world situation. Their discussions centered mainly on the question of Berlin, on nuclear problems and on the situation in the Congo. Their talks will form the basis of continued United States-United Kingdom cooperation during the coming months on a great variety of questions.

The President and the Prime Minister examined the situation concerning Berlin in the light of the decisions taken at the meetings of the Foreign Ministers of the Four Powers and of the NATO Council in Paris. In particular they discussed the steps to be taken in regard to the renewal of diplomatic contacts with the Soviet Union. The President has agreed as a consequence of the Paris meeting that the initial contact would be made by the U.S. Ambassador in Moscow and the Prime Minister has indicated that the British Ambassador would be available to play whatever part might be found helpful. The President and the Prime Minister agreed that the purpose should be to ascertain whether a reasonable basis for negotiation can be found. The other governments directly concerned will of course be fully consulted throughout. Consultations with the other governments concerned are continuing.

The President and the Prime Minister considered the problems of the nuclear arms race. They took note of the new situation created by the massive series of atmospheric tests conducted in recent months by the Soviet Government after long secret preparations. They agreed that it is now neces-sary, as a matter of prudent planning for the future, that pending the final decision preparations should be made for atmospheric testing to maintain the effectiveness of the deterrent.

Meanwhile, they continue to believe that no task is more urgent than the search for paths toward effective disarmament, and they pledge themselves to intensive and continued efforts in this direction.

Serious progress toward disarmament is the only way of breaking out of the dangerous contest so sharply renewed by the Soviet Union. The President and the Prime Minister believe that the plans for disarmament put forward by the United States in the current session of the United Nations General Assembly offer a basis for such progress, along with the treaty for ending nuclear tests which the two nations have so carefully prepared and so earnestly urged upon the Soviet Government.

The President and the Prime Minister reviewed recent developments in the Congo. They noted with satisfaction that, as an encouraging step toward understanding, a useful meeting had been held at Kitona between Mr. Adoula and Mr. Tshombe. They expressed their strong hope that further progress would be made through the efforts of both parties. It seemed to them of first importance that the present discussions should be actively continued in appropriate ways. They agreed on the importance of avoiding any renewal of armed action while genuine efforts at consultation are going forward.

In a general discussion of the economic

situation the President and the Prime Minister took note of progress in the negotiations between the United Kingdom and the European Economic Community and ex-

pressed the hope that these would be brought to a successful conclusion.

NOTE: The President and the Prime Minister met at Government House in Hamilton, where the statement was released.

520   Statement by the President on the Birthday of Woodrow Wilson. *December 28, 1961*

TODAY marks the birth of Woodrow Wilson, shaper of the first working plan for international cooperation among all peoples of the world. "What we seek," he said, "is the reign of law, based on the consent of the governed and sustained by the organized opinion of mankind." Every subsequent effort to create a stable world order has gone back for inspiration to his efforts and has owed much to his vision.

The papers of Woodrow Wilson are now being collected and edited under the auspices of the Woodrow Wilson Foundation. This

definitive edition will stand beside the papers of the great men of the formative period of our history—those of Adams and Franklin, Jefferson and Hamilton: a reminder that the twentieth century has not been lacking in the highest quality of leadership. This vitally important project has my heartiest endorsement and should have the support of every American who is devoted to what is best and most enduring in the American heritage.

NOTE: The statement was released at Palm Beach, Fla.

521   Message to Members of the Armed Forces Serving Overseas. *December 31, 1961*

[Broadcast over Armed Forces radio networks]

I EXTEND to each of you my thanks for your past year of service to our Nation and my best wishes for your continued efforts during 1962.

Spending long periods away from home in foreign lands entails—in many cases— personal sacrifice. But over the years, the defense of freedom has never been easy—and in today's world it is not apt to be easier.

Our foreign policy is based on goals of freedom and justice. It is in the interest of these goals that we ask you to serve your

country overseas. Your Nation depends on you and your colleagues, not just for the execution of American foreign policy, but for the embodiment of the spirit and ideals of our country.

Let this then be the New Year's resolution of Americans serving our country overseas: To show dedication to our highest national ideals by living and working in ways which will best illustrate these ideals to others.

NOTE: The message was released at Palm Beach, Fla.

522   Exchange of New Year Greetings Between the United States and the Soviet Union.   *December 31, 1961*

Nikita Khrushchev
   Chairman, Council of Ministers, U.S.S.R.
Leonid Brezhnev
   Chairman, Presidium of the Supreme Soviet, U.S.S.R.

As the year 1961 approaches its close I wish to extend to the people of the Soviet Union and to you and your families my most sincere wishes and those of the American people for a peaceful and prosperous New Year. The year which is ending has been a troubled one. It is my earnest hope that the coming year will strengthen the foundations of world peace and will bring an improvement in the relations between our countries, upon which so much depends. It is our grave responsibility to fulfill that hope. As President of the United States, I can state on behalf of the government and the American people that we will do our best to do so.

JOHN F. KENNEDY

NOTE: The Soviet leaders' message, dated December 29, 1961, follows:

Dear Mr. President:

In these few last hours of the expiring 1961 we are sending to the people of the United States the sincerest wishes for peace and happiness in the New Year and likewise our best wishes of personal happiness to you and to your entire family. Right now on the doorstep of the New Year the nations live with new hope that the coming year will be such a threshold in the development of events when there will be undertaken efficient steps in the cause of liquidation of centers of military danger. There is no doubt that on the state of affairs in Soviet-American relations depends very much whether humanity will go towards peace or war. At the meeting in Vienna the President of the United States and Chairman of Ministers of the USSR agreed that history imposed a great responsibility on our peoples for the destinies of the world. The Soviet people regard the future optimistically. They express hopes that in the coming year our countries will be able to find ways towards closer cooperation, will be able to find a basis for concerted actions and efforts for the good of all humanity.

On the part of the Soviet Union, as before, there will be no lack of resolution to do everything in its power in order to ensure durable and lasting peace on our planet.

N. KHRUSHCHEV
L. BREZHNEV

Appendix A—White House Press Releases, 1961

NOTE: Includes releases covering matters with which the President was closely concerned, except announcements of Presidential personnel appointments and approvals of legislation with which there was no accompanying statement.

Releases relating to Proclamations and Executive orders have not been included. These documents are separately listed in Appendix B.

For list of Press and Radio Conferences, see subject index under "News conferences."

January

20 Inaugural address

20 Dedication prepared by Robert Frost for the Inaugural ceremonies

21 White House announcement of major appointments in the Department of Agriculture and of the President's decision to expand the National Agricultural Advisory Commission

21 Exchange of greetings with leaders of the Soviet Union

21 Remarks at a meeting of the Democratic National Committee

21 Remarks at the swearing-in ceremonies of the members of the Cabinet

22 White House announcement of appointment of a special panel of advisers on conflict of interest and ethics in government

22 White House statement concerning the appointment of Hickman Price, Jr., and Rowland Burnstan as Assistant Secretaries of Commerce

23 Statement by the President concerning the appointment of Frank B. Ellis as Director, Office of Civil and Defense Mobilization

24 White House statement making public the report of the Food-for-Peace Task Force

24 Memorandum to Federal agencies and Executive order on the duties of the Director of the Food-for-Peace Program

25 White House announcement of the President's meeting with a special committee on economic conditions and the balance-of-payments problem

25 Letter to the President of the Senate and to the Speaker of the House urging enactment of a distressed area redevelopment bill

25 White House announcement of appointment of a panel of experts to review data relating to agreement on discontinuance of nuclear weapons tests

25 White House announcement of an emergency food program for the Congo

27 Letter to Secretary Ribicoff requesting him to undertake direction of Cuban refugee activities

January

27 Letter accepting resignation of Tracy S. Voorhees and thanking him for his efforts on behalf of Cuban refugees

28 Exchange of greetings with President Sukarno of Indonesia

29 Remarks at a swearing-in ceremony and reception for Presidential appointees

30 Annual message to the Congress on the State of the Union

31 Interview with Dave Garroway recorded for the 150th anniversary of the founding of Massachusetts General Hospital

31 Message greeting President Quadros of Brazil on the occasion of his inauguration

31 Message to President Kubitschek of Brazil

February

2 Letter to the Secretary of the Navy and statement by the President on the launching of the U.S.S. *Sam Houston*

2 Special message to the Congress: Program for Economic Recovery and Growth

2 Remarks on greeting representatives of the Baptist World Alliance at the White House

3 Statement by the President following a conference with Secretary Ribicoff on Cuban refugee problems

3 Telegram to the mayors of U.S. cities urging increased urban renewal activity

4 Exchange of greetings with Dr. Walter Hallstein, President of the European Economic Community

6 White House announcement of the acceptance of resignations of nine U.S. ambassadors

6 Letter to the President of the Senate and to the Speaker of the House transmitting bills extending unemployment benefits and providing aid to needy children

6 Special message to the Congress on gold and the balance of payments deficit

7 White House announcement concerning the tariff on imports of hard fiber cords and twines

Appendix A

Appendix A

Appendix A

824

Appendix A

825

Appendix A

827

Appendix A

May

31 White House announcement of the forthcoming visit of President Youlou of the Republic of the Congo

31 Remarks upon arrival at Orly Airport in Paris

31 Toasts of the President and President de Gaulle at the formal dinner in the Elysée Palace

June

1 Remarks to the staff of the U.S. Embassy in Paris

1 Remarks in Paris before the Assembly of the North Atlantic Treaty Organization

1 Remarks at a civic reception for President Kennedy at the Hôtel de Ville

1 Remarks at the Hôtel de Ville in Paris

2 Remarks at SHAPE Headquarters in Paris

2 Remarks at the Press luncheon at the Palais Chaillot in Paris

2 Joint statement following discussions with President de Gaulle

3 White House announcement of Cabinet members and Government officials participating in the 17th annual Washington Conference of the Advertising Council

3 Remarks upon arrival at the Schwechat Airport in Vienna

4 Joint statement following discussions with Premier Khrushchev in Vienna

4 Remarks at the Airport in Vienna upon leaving for London

4 Remarks upon arrival at the London Airport

5 Remarks to the staff of the U.S. Embassy in London

5 Transcript of interview by a correspondent of the British Broadcasting Company

5 Joint statement following discussion with Prime Minister Macmillan

6 Radio and television report to the American people on returning from Europe

7 Remarks at Annapolis to the graduating class of the United States Naval Academy

7 Letter to the President of the Senate and to the Speaker of the House on youth employment opportunities and training

7 Remarks at a dinner of the Big Brothers of America

8 Remarks of welcome to President Youlou of the Republic of Congo at the Washington National Airport

8 Joint statement following discussions with President Youlou

10 White House announcement of appointment of Dr. Allan Nevins as the President's Personal Representative at the José Rizal Centennial celebrations in the Philippines

June

10 White House announcement concerning the appointment of James W. Riddleberger as chairman of the Development Assistance Group

12 Special message to the Congress transmitting Reorganization Plan 6 of 1961

12 Special message to the Congress transmitting Reorganization Plan 7 of 1961

12 Toasts of the President and Prime Minister Fanfani of Italy

12 White House announcement of Public Health Service grant to Pan American Sanitary Bureau for inter-American medical research projects

13 Statement by the President on the appointment of Mayor Morrison as U.S. Ambassador to the Organization of American States

13 Letter to the President of the Senate and to the Speaker of the House transmitting bill on unemployment compensation

13 Joint statement following discussions with Prime Minister Fanfani of Italy

15 Remarks upon presenting the Collier Trophy to Adm. William F. Raborn, Jr.

16 White House announcement concerning the Water Pollution Control Advisory Board

16 Remarks at the National Conference on International Economic and Social Development

18 U.S. note to the Soviet Ministry of Foreign Affairs concerning the Geneva nuclear test ban negotiations

19 Remarks to the members of the Commission on Money and Credit

19 Letter to the Speaker of the House of Representatives on Federal assistance for urban transportation planning

21 Statement by the President on the Garrison diversion irrigation development in the Upper Missouri River Basin

21 Remarks upon activating by remote control the saline water conversion plant at Freeport, Tex.

21 Toasts of the President and Prime Minister Ikeda of Japan

22 Memorandum on employee-management relations in the Federal service

22 Memorandum on minimum wage rates of Government employees

22 Joint statement following discussions with Prime Minister Ikeda of Japan

23 Statement by the President upon the entry into force of the Antarctic Treaty

24 Letter to the Vice President on the need for developing operational communications satellites

26 Message to the members of the National Education Association meeting in Atlantic City

829

Appendix A

830

Appendix A

831

Appendix A

Appendix A

833

Appendix A

October

24 Remarks to an international group attending the Inter-American Archival Seminar

- 24 Message to Walter P. Marshall on the occasion of the transcontinental telegraph centennial

25 White House announcement concerning a study of international aviation problems

25 White House announcement concerning Project Gnome for the development of peaceful uses of nuclear explosives

26 Letter to Henry B. Gonzalez in support of his candidacy in Texas

26 White House announcement concerning a new Internal Revenue Service Center in Austin, Tex.

26 Letter to President Ngo Dinh Diem on the sixth anniversary of the Republic of Viet-Nam

26 Statement by the President to Cabinet officers and agency heads on the 1962 and 1963 budget outlook

27 Statement by the President concerning export credit facilities

28 White House announcement of additional participants in the White House Regional Conferences

29 White House announcement concerning additional members of Panel on Mental Retardation

29 Message to President Gursel following his election under the new Turkish constitution

29 Remarks at the airport at Fort Smith, Ark.

29 Remarks at Big Cedar, Okla., on the opening of the North-South Highway

30 White House statement announcing the explosion by the U.S.S.R. of a 50-megaton bomb

30 Message to a meeting on the Foreign Student in the United States

November

1 Letter to Prime Minister Ikeda of Japan suggesting an exchange of information on the problem of mental retardation

1 White House announcement of additional participants in the White House Regional Conferences

2 Remarks at the signing of the Delaware River Basin Compact

2 Statement by the President concerning the development and testing of nuclear weapons

2 Statement by the President in support of the reelection of Robert F. Wagner as mayor of New York City

2 Remarks at a political rally in Trenton, N.J.

3 Message to Adlai Stevenson following the election of U Thant by the United Nations

November

3 White House announcement concerning the White House Regional Conferences at Detroit and Chicago

3 Remarks of welcome to President Senghor of Senegal at the Washington National Airport

6 Message to President Kekkonen of Finland on his departure from the United States

6 Statement by the President upon announcing the appointment of Teodoro Moscoso as coordinator of Alliance for Progress programs

6 Remarks of welcome to Prime Minister Nehru of India at Andrews Air Force Base

7 Telegram to Chairman Brezhnev on the anniversary of the November Revolution in Russia

7 Remarks by telephone to the first White House Regional Conference meeting in Chicago

7 Letters concerning allocation of disaster-aid funds in Idaho

9 Joint statement following discussions with Prime Minister Nehru

9 Letter from Prime Minister Ikeda of Japan

9 White House statement following appointment of Henry Cabot Lodge as Director General of the Atlantic Institute

9 White House announcement concerning the President's meeting with members of the Commission on Campaign Costs

10 Telegram to Constantine Caramanlis following his reappointment as Prime Minister of Greece

10 Letter from Secretary Goldberg proposing a review of employment statistics

10 Statement by the President upon announcing the appointment of a panel to review employment statistics

10 White House announcement of the President's intention to review Pacific Fleet naval maneuvers on November 18

10 White House statement concerning plans for the establishment of a Presidential library and museum at Cambridge

10 Remarks upon presenting the Merchant Marine Achievement Award to Solon B. Turman

11 Statement by the President concerning an educational consortium to aid in developing a technical institute in India

11 Remarks at the Veterans Day Ceremony at Arlington National Cemetery

12 Message recorded for the centennial convocation of the Association of Land Grant Colleges and State Universities

13 Remarks to the trustees of the Union of American Hebrew Congregations

13 Remarks of welcome at the White House concert by Pablo Casals

Appendix A

Appendix B—Presidential Documents Published in the Federal Register, 1961

PROCLAMATIONS

Appendix B

EXECUTIVE ORDERS

Appendix B

Appendix B

PRESIDENTIAL DOCUMENTS OTHER THAN PROCLAMATIONS AND EXECUTIVE ORDERS

Appendix C—Presidential Reports to the Congress, 1961

Subject	Published	Sent to the Congress	Date of White House release
Commodity Credit Corporation	. . . . . .	Jan. 31	. . . .
Commission on International Rules of Judicial Procedure, 2d Annual	. . . . . .	Feb. 16	. . . .
Railroad Retirement Board	H. Doc. 27	Feb. 29	. . . .
Health Research Facilities Program	H. Doc. 110	Mar. 16	. . . .
Federal Assistance for Disaster Relief	H. Doc. 111	Mar. 16	Mar. 16
Public Law 480 (83d Congress):			
Thirteenth Semiannual	H. Doc. 131	Apr. 10	Apr. 10
Fourteenth Semiannual	H. Doc. 223	Aug. 14	Aug. 14
St. Lawrence Seaway Development Corporation	H. Doc. 153	May 3	. . . .
National Capital Housing Authority	. . . . . .	May 22	. . . .
Weather Modification	H. Doc. 213	July 18	. . . .
International Cultural Exchange and Trade Fair Participation Act	. . . . . .	July 18	. . . .
Office of Alien Property	. . . . . .	Aug. 7	. . . .
International Atomic Energy Agency	H. Doc. 233	Sept. 1	. . . .
Trade Agreements Program	H. Doc. 234	Sept. 1	. . . .
Lend Lease Operations	H. Doc. 205	Oct. 16 (S) Oct. 16(H)	. . . .
Housing and Home Finance Agency	. . . . . .	Dec. 13(H)	. . . .

844

Appendix D—Rules Governing This Publication

[Reprinted from the Federal Register, vol. 24, p. 2354, dated March 26, 1959]

TITLE 1—GENERAL PROVISIONS

Chapter I—Administrative Committee of the Federal Register

PART 32—PUBLIC PAPERS OF THE PRESI-
DENTS OF THE UNITED STATES

Sec.
32.1   Publication required.
32.2   Coverage of prior years.
32.3   Format, indexes, ancillaries.

SCOPE

32.10   Basic criteria.
32.11   Sources.

FREE DISTRIBUTION

32.15   Members of Congress.
32.16   The Supreme Court.
32.17   Executive agencies.

PAID DISTRIBUTION

32.20   Agency requisitions.
32.21   Extra copies.
32.22   Sale to public.

AUTHORITY: §§ 32.1 to 32.22 issued under sec. 6, 49 Stat. 501, as amended; 44 U. S. C. 306.

PUBLICATION AND FORMAT

§ 32.1 *Publication required.* There shall be published forthwith at the end of each calendar year, beginning with the year 1957, a special edition of the FEDERAL REGISTER designated "Public Papers of the Presidents of the United States." Each volume shall cover one calendar year and shall be identified further by the name of the President and the year covered.

§ 32.2 *Coverage of prior years.* After conferring with the National Historical Publications Commis-

sion with respect to the need therefor, the Administrative Committee may from time to time authorize the publication of similar volumes covering specified calendar years prior to 1957.

§ 32.3 *Format, indexes, ancillaries.* Each annual volume, divided into books whenever appropriate, shall be separately published in the binding and style deemed by the Administrative Committee to be suitable to the dignity of the office of President of the United States. Each volume shall be appropriately indexed and shall contain appropriate ancillary information respecting significant Presidential documents not published in full text.

SCOPE

§ 32.10 *Basic criteria.* The basic text of the volumes shall consist of oral utterances by the President or of writings subscribed by him. All materials selected for inclusion under these criteria must also be in the public domain by virtue of White House press release or otherwise.

§ 32.11 *Sources.* (a) The basic text of the volumes shall be selected from the official text of: (1) Communications to the Congress, (2) public addresses, (3) transcripts of press conferences, (4) public letters, (5) messages to heads of state, (6) statements released on miscellaneous subjects, and (7) formal executive documents promulgated in accordance with law.

(b) Ancillary text, notes, and tables shall be derived from official sources only.

FREE DISTRIBUTION

§ 32.15 *Members of Congress.* Each Member of Congress, during his term of office, shall be entitled to one copy of each annual volume published during such term; *Provided,* That authorization for furnishing such copies shall be submitted in writing to the Director and signed by the authorizing Member. [As amended effective Dec. 30, 1960, 25 F.R. 14009]

845

Appendix D

§ 32.16 *The Supreme Court.* The Supreme Court of the United States shall be entitled to twelve copies of the annual volumes.

§ 32.17 *Executive agencies.* The head of each department and the head of each independent agency in the executive branch of the Government shall be entitled to one copy of each annual volume upon application therefor in writing to the Director.

PAID DISTRIBUTION

§ 32.20 *Agency requisitions.* Each Federal agency shall be entitled to obtain at cost copies of the annual volumes for official use upon the timely submission to the Government Printing Office of a printing and binding requisition (Standard Form No. 1).

§ 32.21 *Extra copies.* All requests for extra copies of the annual volumes shall be addressed to the Superintendent of Documents, Government Printing Office, Washington 25, D.C. Extra copies shall be paid for by the agency or official requesting them.

§ 32.22 *Sale to public.* The annual volumes shall be placed on sale to the public by the Superintendent of Documents at prices determined by him under the general direction of the Administrative Committee.

*   *   *   *   *

ADMINISTRATIVE COMMITTEE OF
THE FEDERAL REGISTER,

WAYNE C. GROVER,
*Archivist of the United States,
Chairman.*

RAYMOND BLATTENBERGER,
*The Public Printer,
Member.*

WILLIAM O. BURTNER,
*Representative of the
Attorney General, Member.*

Approved March 20, 1959.

WILLIAM P. ROGERS,
Attorney General.

FRANKLIN FLOETE,
Administrator of General Services.

[F.R. Doc. 59–2517; Filed Mar. 25, 1959; 8:45 a.m.]

INDEX

[Main references are to items except as otherwise indicated]

847

Index

[Main references are to items except as otherwise indicated]

Index

[Main references are to items except as otherwise indicated]

Index

Index

Index

Index

[Main references are to items except as otherwise indicated]

Index

[Main references are to items except as otherwise indicated]

Index

[Main references are to items except as otherwise indicated]

Index

Index

[Main references are to items except as otherwise indicated]

861

Index

Index

[Main references are to items except as otherwise indicated]

Index

Index

Index

Index

Index

Index

[Main references are to items except as otherwise indicated]

Index

[Main references are to items except as otherwise indicated]

Housing—Continued
Older persons, 76, 448, 477
Public, 17, 76
Racial discrimination ban, 62 [10], 92 [12]
Veterans, 76, 94
Housing Act of 1961, 264
Housing and Home Finance Administrator (Robert C. Weaver), 31, 58, 70, 264, 371
Housing and Home Finance Agency, 15 [5], 17, 20, 49, 76, 96
Housing and Urban Affairs Department, 11, 76, 130
Houston, Sam, 16
Hoyt, Palmer, 153 n.
Hruska, Sen. Roman L., 476 n.
Huff, Sam, 496
Hughes, Richard J., 448, 455 [5]
Human Rights Week, 504
Humphrey, Don, 119 [2]
Humphrey, Sen. Hubert H., 8 [25], 63, 244, 388
Hungary, 138
Hunting stamps, 49
Hyannis, Mass., releases from, 266, 267, 269, 270, 271, 286, 311, 313, 314, 343–348, 367, 384, 386
Hyannis Port, Mass., 268 n., 298 n., 397, 483 n.
Hydroelectric power projects, 17, 49, 121, 445, 474
See also Power projects
Hydrogen bomb
Soviet explosion, 426, 442, 446
See also Atomic bomb; Nuclear weapons; Nuclear weapons tests

IA–ECOSOC. *See* Inter-American Economic and Social Council
Iakovos, Archbishop, 1 n.
ICA. *See* International Cooperation Administration
ICBM (intercontinental ballistic missile), 99, 222
Ice Patrol, International, 100
Idaho, floods, 83 [2]
Ikeda, Hayato, 444
Visit of, 249, 252

Illinois
Food distribution, 15 [3], 17
Gov. Otto Kerner, 155, 244, 454
Unemployment, 83 [18]
Immigration laws, 318 [21]
Immigration and Naturalization Service, Commissioner (Gen. J. M. Swing), 312
Imports, 8 [18], 11, 23, 488 [17, 18, 19], 497, 499
Cotton, 258 [10], 478, 488 [19]
Crabmeat, 483
Economic boycotts of, 71 [20]
From Cuba, 35 [8]
Residual fuel oil, 62 [13]
Inaugural address, 1
Comments on, 8 [28], 463
Income taxes, 15 [10], 17, 136
Foreign central banks, 23, 54
Independence, Mo., 448
India, 11, 26, 244, 387
Institute of Technology, U.S. participation in development, 460
Nehru, Jawaharlal, 11, 35 [1], 452, 455 [14], 456, 460
News conference remarks, 35 [1], 171 [14], 455 [14]
U.S. Ambassador Ellsworth Bunker, 244
Indian Affairs, Bureau of, 71 [5]
Indian Ocean expedition, 100
Indians
Cherokee and Creek, 16
First public housing loan, 371
Schools for children, 71 [5], 94
Seneca Nation, opposition to Kinzua Dam project, 71 [15], 320
Treaties with U.S., 71 [15]
Indochina, Geneva conference (1954), 92 [1]
Indonesia
Assistance and development, 146
Dispute with Netherlands, 119 [21]
Sukarno, Achmed, 119 [21], 143, 146, 359, 364, 365
U.S. Ambassador Howard P. Jones, 146
Industrial capacity, U.S., 11, 15 [23], 17, 33, 90
Industrial Conference Board, National, remarks, 33
Industrial plant and equipment, modernization, 33, 136

875

Index

Index

[Main references are to items except as otherwise indicated]

Index

Index

Index

Index

[Main references are to items except as otherwise indicated]

Index

Index

Index

Index

[Main references are to items except as otherwise indicated]

[Main references are to items except as otherwise indicated]

Index

[Main references are to items except as otherwise indicated]

Index

[Main references are to items except as otherwise indicated]

Index

Index

[Main references are to items except as otherwise indicated]

Index

[Main references are to items except as otherwise indicated]

Index

Index

Index

Index

Index

Index

[Main references are to items except as otherwise indicated]

Index